AESTHETICS
A CRITICAL ANTHOLOGY

PHOTO CREDITS

Frontispiece: *Half*, 1959 by Kenneth Noland. By permission of The Museum of Fine Arts, Houston. Museum purchase.

Anthony Caro, *Night Road*, 1972. By permission of The Museum of Fine Arts, Houston. Museum purchase.

Marcel Duchamp, *In Advance of the Broken Arm*. Yale University Art Gallery. Gift of Collection Société Anonyme.

Le Corbusier, Chapel of *Our Lady of the Heights*, Ronchamp, France, 1950–1955. Photographed from the east by R. J. Sclafani.

Barnett Newman, *Broken Obelisk*, 1967. By permission of the Rothko Chapel, Houston, Texas.

Claes Oldenburg, *Two Cheeseburgers, with Everything*, 1962. Collection, The Museum of Modern Art, New York. Philip Johnson Fund.

Jackson Pollock, *No. 6*, 1949. By permission of The Museum of Fine Arts, Houston. Gift of D. and J. de Menil.

Mark Rothko, *Untitled* (*No. 10*), 1957. Private Collection, U.S.A.

Frank Stella, *Moultonville I*, 1966. By permission of The Museum of Fine Arts, Houston. Anonymous gift.

Andy Warhol, *Campbell Soup Can–Tomato (green & purple version)*, 1965. Private Collection, U.S.A.

Library of Congress Catalog Card Number: 76-28127
Copyright © 1977 by St. Martin's Press, Inc.
All Rights Reserved.
Manufactured in the United States of America.
54
fe
For information, write: St. Martin's Press, Inc.,
175 Fifth Avenue, New York. N.Y. 10010

Cover design by Rick Fiala

ISBN: 0-321-00910-0

AESTHETICS

A CRITICAL ANTHOLOGY

George Dickie

R. J. Sclafani

EDITORS

ST. MARTIN'S PRESS *New York*

PREFACE

Twenty-five years ago aesthetics was considered the ugly duckling among the philosophical disciplines. Today, it occupies a respectable place in almost every philosophy curriculum. Two things account for this change: recent scholarship has re-established the historical importance of the subject; and, contemporary philosophers of considerable talent have been directing their efforts toward in-depth analyses of the concepts of art and the aesthetic.

Aesthetics: A Critical Anthology is the first text in the field which combines historical materials, works of recent scholarship, and contemporary critical analyses in an effort to present a comprehensive account of the field of aesthetics as it is currently understood in the Anglo-American world.

Any new text must be justified by what it offers that is new and different. Beyond its uniquely broad scope, *Aesthetics: A Critical Anthology* is distinguished by several new essays written especially for this volume. These include Stanley Bates on Tolstoy, Monroe Beardsley on the philosophy of literature, Peter Kivy on the logic of taste, Richard Schacht on Nietzsche, David Carrier on formalism and philosophy, and Robert Burch on Kant's aesthetics. In most cases these essays were written to fill gaps in the literature, as we explain in the introductions to the various parts of the book in which they appear. J. O. Urmson's essay, "Literature," while not written specifically for this book, is being published for the first time here.

Part Five explores a topic not previously examined in general aesthetics texts. The question of the Death of Art is hotly debated among artists, critics, and philosophers. The readings we have selected acquaint the student with both the historical origins and the contemporary flavor of this debate.

In presenting historical materials, we have been governed by two policies. First, in no case have we presented snippets from philosophical works of historical significance. The selections are always substantial; in fact, David Hume's *On The Standard of Taste* is presented in its entirety, and Aristotle's *Poetics* is complete except for a few passages concerning technicalities of the Greek language, omitted for the sake of readability. Second, in almost every case a historical selection is followed by a contemporary discussion of that selection. In some instances the discussion is a direct philosophical critique of the historical thesis; in other instances the discussion is of a more expository or scholarly nature. In either case, the discussions are critical and are intended to stimulate further thought.

Whenever a departure from this format occurs it is noted in the appropriate part introduction.

Many of the contemporary philosophers included here refer explicity to one another's views. In the part introductions the reader is alerted both to these explicit cross-references as well as to other less obvious relationships. It was part of our purpose in making the selections to give the reader a sense not only of the continuities in aesthetics but of the liveliness of contemporary dialogue and debate in the field.

Several photographs have been included; they are intended to illustrate and complement various selections. Each has been captioned with a quotation from, and a citation to, the relevant selection.

Finally, this text includes the most substantial bibliography available in a collection of this kind. At the end of each part, or subpart, selected subject bibliographies have been included. Complete references for all titles are given in the general bibliography at the end of the book.

For his invaluable help in researching the bibliographies and biographical notes, as well as for his efforts in other aspects of this project too numerous to mention, we wish to thank Robert Esenwein.

CONTENTS

GENERAL INTRODUCTION   1

PART ONE   Traditional Theories of Art and Contemporary
Critiques of these Theories   5

PLATO   Art as Imitation: from *The Republic*   9
ARTHUR DANTO   The Artistic Enfranchisement of Real
Objects: The Artworld   22
CLIVE BELL   Art as Significant Form: The Aesthetic
Hypothesis   36
BERYL LAKE STEELE   A Critique of Bell: from "A Study of
the Irrefutability of Two Aesthetic
Theories"   49
LEO TOLSTOY   Art as the Communication of Feeling: from
What is Art?   53
STANLEY BATES   Tolstoy Evaluated: Tolstoy's Theory of Art   83
R. G. COLLINGWOOD   Art as Imaginative Expression: from
The Principles of Art   94
RICHARD WOLLHEIM   A Critique of Collingwood and the
Ideal Theory of Art   124
Select Bibliography, Books, Articles   140

PART TWO   Contemporary Theories of Art and Contemporary
Critiques of these Theories   143

SUSANNE LANGER   Art as Symbolic Expression: from *Feeling
and Form*   146
SAMUEL BUFFORD   Langer Evaluated: Susanne Langer's Two
Philosophies of Art   166
TED COHEN   A Critique of the Institutional Theory of Art:
The Possibility of Art   183
GEORGE DICKIE   A Response to Cohen: The Actuality of Art   196
Select Bibliography, Books, Articles   200

PART THREE   Theories of Individual Arts, Traditional and
Contemporary   203

The Theory of Drama: Imitation and Reality   205

ARISTOTLE   Dramatic Imitation: The *Poetics*   207

G. M. A. Grube   A Commentary on Aristotle's Theory   232
Friedrich Nietzsche   Dramatic Reality: from *The Birth of
                           Tragedy*   239
Richard Schacht   Nietzsche on Art in *The Birth of Tragedy*   269
Select Bibliography, Books, Articles   312

The Theory of Literature: Words and Identity   315

Monroe C. Beardsley   The Philosophy of Literature   317
J. O. Urmson   Literature   334
Select Bibliography, Books, Articles   341

The Theory of Film: Metaphysical Roots   343

Sergie Eisenstein   The Cinema as an Outgrowth of Theater:
                           Through Theater to Cinema   345
Erwin Panofsky   Style and Medium in the Moving Pictures   351
Stanley Cavell   The World Viewed: Sights and Sounds   366
Select Bibliography, Books, Articles   383

The Theory of Music: Sound and Meaning   385

Richard Wagner   Music and the Amalgamated Arts: from
                           The Artwork of the Future   387
Eduard Hanslick   A Formalist Theory of Sound in Motion:
                           from *The Beautiful in Music*   407
Select Bibliography, Books, Articles   422

Formalism, Philosophy, and Contemporary Plastic Arts   423

Clement Greenberg   After Abstract Expressionism   425
Michael Fried   Art and Objecthood   438
David Carrier   Greenberg, Fried, and Philosophy:
                           American-Type Formalism   461
Select Bibliography, Books, Articles   469

PART FOUR   The Theory of Art Theory   471

Morris Weitz   Wittgenstein's Aesthetics   474
Marshall Cohen   Aesthetic Essence   485
Maurice Mandelbaum   Family Resemblances and
                           Generalization Concerning the Arts   500
Select Bibliography, Books, Articles   515

PART FIVE   The Death of Art   517

Georg Friedrich Wilhelm Hegel   The Evolution and
                                       Completion of Art
                                       History   522

MARCEL DUCHAMP   Art as Non-Aesthetic: I Like Breathing
                  Better than Working   540
DONALD KARSHAN   A Manifesto—The Seventies: Post-object
                  Art   548
ARTHUR DANTO   The Last Work of Art: Artworks and Real
                  Things   551
Select Bibliography, Books, Articles   563

PART SIX   Traditional Theories of the Aesthetic and
             Contemporary Discussions of These Theories   565
FRANCIS HUTCHESON   An Initial Theory of Taste   569
DAVID HUME   Of the Standard of Taste   592
JEROME STOLNITZ   On the Origins of "Aesthetic
                  Disinterestedness"   607
PETER KIVY   Recent Scholarship and the British Tradition:
             A Logic of Taste—The First Fifty Years   626
IMMANUEL KANT   A Theory of Aesthetic Judgment: from
                  The Critique of Judgement   643
ROBERT BURCH   Kant's Theory of Beauty as Ideal Art   688
ARTHUR SCHOPENHAUER   The World as Will and Idea   704
FREDERICK COPLESTON   Art as Escape: The Partial Escape—
                  Art   739
Select Bibliography, Books, Articles   753

PART SEVEN   Contemporary Theories of the Aesthetic and
               Contemporary Critiques of These Theories   755

EDWARD BULLOUGH   "Psychical Distance" as a Factor in Art
                  and an Aesthetic Principle   758
ALLAN CASEBIER   The Concept of Aesthetic Distance   783
GEORGE DICKIE   All Aesthetic Attitude Theories Fail: The
                  Myth of the Aesthetic Attitude   800
FRANK N. SIBLEY   A Contemporary Theory of Aesthetic
                  Qualities: Aesthetic Concepts   815
TED COHEN   Aesthetic/Non-aesthetic and the Concept of
                  Taste: A Critique of Sibley's Position   838
Select Bibliography, Books, Articles   866

LIST OF JOURNAL ABBREVIATIONS   870

BIBLIOGRAPHY   871

INDEX   889

AESTHETICS
A CRITICAL ANTHOLOGY

General Introduction

"Aesthetics" is a term commonly used to designate such diverse things as theories of beauty and the elegance of a logician's axiomatic system. Philosophically, the term has a far more precise designation. Today, those philosophers called aestheticians are concerned with two general enterprises—the theory of art and the theory of the aesthetic which emerged in the eighteenth and nineteenth centuries from the theory of beauty. In this volume the division of selections into theories of art (parts one to four) and theories of the aesthetic (parts six and seven) is one of two large-scale organizational features. The other organizational feature of the book is the practice, when possible, of presenting a selection followed by a critique of it. The two philosophical theories—the theory of art and the theory of the aesthetic—upon which the two-fold structure of the first organizational feature depends has its origins, as does so much in philosophy, in the thought of Plato. Accordingly, the first selection in part one is from Plato.

The history of the theory of art can be divided into three phases of vastly different lengths of time. The first phase begins with Plato's imitation theory of art in ancient Greece and ends in the twentieth century with Susanne Langer's theory of art as symbolic forms. The central feature of these theories of art has been an attempt to capture the *essence* of art in a definition or theory. In one form or another, Plato's view of art as imitation remained unchallenged until the late nineteenth century, when various competing theories began to be presented. They are represented in part one of this volume by Clive Bell's theory of art as significant form and by Tolstoy's and R. G. Collingwood's expressionist theories of art; in part two they are represented by Susanne Langer's theory of art as symbolic forms. The second phase in the history of art theory is really an antitheory movement. In the early 1950s a series of articles by various philosophers were published which contended that "art" could not be defined in the manner that the earlier theorists had assumed. Morris Weitz, whose recent article "Wittgenstein's Aesthetics" appears in part

four, was one of the most influential antitheorists. Maurice Mandelbaum
(part four) opened the third phase of the history of art theory by arguing
against Weitz and others that it may be possible to define "art" after all.
Arthur Danto's "The Artworld" (part one) also belongs to the beginning
of this third phase, as it argues that works of art exist within a complex
matrix he calls "the artworld." Drawing on both Mandelbaum and Danto,
George Dickie (part two) attempts to formulate what he calls an institutional definition of "art." Thus, the third phase has in common with
the first the view that "art" can be defined, but the manner of definition is
a very different sort.

The topic of part five suggests a fourth phase for art theory—its death.
Although the topic of that part is the death of art, if art were to die, so in
a sense would its theory. But what does it mean to speak of the death of
art? The nineteenth-century German philosopher Hegel first predicted
that art would die. For Hegel the death of art is part of a grand philosophy
of history involving an evolutionary development of the world as spirit,
or mind. The work of Marcel Duchamp, other so-called antiartists of the
early twentieth century, and some present-day antiartists suggests that art
might die in a more mundane way than Hegel had considered. Arthur
Danto in his "Artworks and Real Things" suggests that art has ceased to
be art by turning itself into philosophy—a fate, perhaps, worse than death.

Thus far this introduction has been concerned with art in general. Much
of the writing about art, however, has taken the form of treatises on the
particular arts. Part three consists of essays devoted to the theories of
literature, film, drama, music, and contemporary plastic art. These essays
reflect the great variety of arts as well as significant differences among
them. On some occasions, however, they reveal important insights about
art in general.

Parts one through five provide sufficient material for a course on the
philosophy of art.

The reader may have been surprised when at the beginning of this introduction it was asserted that the theory of the aesthetic originated in the
philosophy of Plato, since the notion of the aesthetic as it is currently
understood came into use during the nineteenth century. What was
meant by that assertion was that Plato was the first to develop a theory of
beauty, which during the eighteenth and nineteenth centuries was transformed into the theory of the aesthetic. Until the beginning of the eighteenth century, the theory of beauty along with the theory of art continued
to be the twin concerns of those philosophers who today would be called
aestheticians.

At that time such philosophers as Francis Hutcheson began developing
philosophies of *taste*. The theorists of taste continued to employ the
notion of beauty, but for them beauty was not an objective property of
things as it was for Plato; rather it was a complicated matter involving the
reaction of subjects (persons). Hence, the theory of taste subjectivized
the concept of beauty. In addition, these philosophers introduced addi-

tional concepts of appreciation—the sublime, the picturesque, and others—within the theory of taste. Beauty as well as these other concepts were subjectivized, and beauty became just one among a host of other concepts. *Taste* had replaced beauty as the central organizing concept of the theory of the appreciation of art and nature. From the beginning to the end of the eighteenth century, theories of taste were offered one after another. Eventually that manner of philosophizing ended.

During the nineteenth century, theories of aesthetic attitude replaced theories of taste as the dominant method of philosophizing about the appreciation of art and nature. Arthur Schopenhauer, the German philosopher, is perhaps the nineteenth century's most notable example of an aesthetic-attitude theorist. In this fashion the notion of the aesthetic replaced the notion of taste which had earlier displaced the concept of beauty. It is through this complicated route that the theory of the aesthetic can be traced to the philosophy of Plato.

Theories of aesthetic attitude continued to enjoy great popularity into the twentieth century and still do today. Recently some doubts have been raised about the adequacy of the aesthetic-attitude theory. Part six deals with the eighteenth-century theories of taste and the nineteenth-century theory of the aesthetic attitude. Part seven deals with twentieth-century versions of the aesthetic-attitude theory, as well as with a recent attempt of a somewhat different kind to characterize the aesthetic, as in Frank Sibley's seminal article "Aesthetic Concepts." Sibley attempts to distinguish between the aesthetic and the nonaesthetic qualities of things, and he tries to investigate the relation between these two different kinds of qualities. Whether Sibley's account of aesthetic qualities is related to, or derived from, theories of the aesthetic attitude is difficult to ascertain. Sibley makes use of the notion of the exercise of *taste* as the means of distinguishing aesthetic from nonaesthetic qualities, and this distinction suggests that his account owes more to the eighteenth- than to the nineteenth-century theory of the appreciation of art and nature. Thus, the debate over the theory of the aesthetic, like that over the philosophy of art, continues.

PART ONE

—◆◦•◦◆—

Traditional Theories of Art and Contemporary Critiques of these Theories

In the general introduction we outlined the two basic features of this book: (1) the division of our subject into theories of art and theories of the aesthetic and (2) the critical format around which our selections are structured. In part one we begin by presenting a number of prominent traditional theories of art, each followed by a contemporary critique. The traditional theories that were chosen are those of Plato, Bell, Tolstoy, and Collingwood. They have been selected both for their inherent philosophical interest and for their historical value. In some cases, Bell and Tolstoy, for example, the historical value of the theories probably outweighs their philosophical merit; all of these theories, however, are undeniably of major significance to the theory of art, historically and philosophically. Moreover, these theories generally received the most attention from philosophers during the last quarter century, and as we have stated, this collection aims at reflecting and crystalizing the current state of the discipline.

Selecting these theories of art from among the many existing ones requires further explanation. We ask the reader to keep in mind two important considerations. First, a number of traditional theorists who do not appear in this part of the book appear under different topic headings in later parts. Because their major works on art were concerned more directly with an analysis of drama as opposed to art per se, Aristotle and Nietzsche, both of monumental importance to the theory of art, are presented as theorists of drama in the section Theories of the Individual Arts. Similarly, Hanslick and Wagner, whose writings convey important insights about art

in general, are presented as theorists of music. And we have chosen to
present Hegel in part five, The Death of Art, for thematic reasons which
will be discussed in the introduction to that section. Our list of traditional
art theorists, then, is considerably lengthened when materials from other
sections are taken into account. The other consideration we ask the reader
to bear in mind is that several other traditional theorists who might once
have been loosely called art theorists are presented, under the more philosophically precise division of this collection, as theorists of the aesthetic.
Of course the theories of Hutcheson, Hume, Kant, and Schopenhauer are
crucial to our subject, and we have included them in this collection. As we
have suggested, however, they are best understood as theorists of the
aesthetic, not theorists of art.

Art and Ontology

It is not an understatement to say that Plato's theory of art as imitation
set the stage for practically all discussions of the nature of Western art for
the next two thousand years. Briefly stated, Plato argued that works of art
are imitations or representations of objects and situations in the physical
world. Since, however, these objects and situations are themselves imitations of ideal forms which transcend the world that we see and hear about
us, works of art turn out to be imitations of imitations. It would be pointless to attempt anything approaching a full explication of Plato's theory
in these introductory remarks. Scores of lengthy treatises have failed to
accomplish such a task. In general, we prefer the selections to speak for
themselves, and we prefer that readers make up their own mind concerning
the nature and merit of particular views. In keeping with this aim, we have
avoided capsule summaries of philosophers' views wherever possible emphasizing instead the rationale underlying our selections.

We simply note that Plato was principally concerned with the status
that works of art occupy in the realm of existing things. He often compared paintings, for example, to mirror images and illusions, making his
theory "ontological" in nature. Plato believed that because they were
imitations of imitations, works of art were inferior entities with respect
to other existing things. According to Plato, works of art are, then, ontologically inferior. In "The Artworld" Arthur Danto, a contemporary
American philosopher, argues that Plato's conception of the ontological
status of works of art is far too narrow and that it generates paradoxes
which Platonic philosophy could never resolve. Relying heavily on developments in twentieth-century art (Post-Impressionism, Abstract Expressionism, and Pop Art in particular), Danto argues that there are ontological
possibilities which the Imitation Theory of art never envisaged, possibilities
which have been successfully realized in twentieth-century art. Thus,
Danto's essay provides a powerful critique not just of Plato's theory, but
of all imitation theories of art. Moreover, Danto begins to develop a
theory of his own in this essay which he further elaborates in another essay,
"Artworks and Real Things" (see part five, The Death of Art). These two

essays can be read as companion pieces formulating a new contemporary theory of art not specifically delineated in part two, Contemporary Theories of Art. This is another example of the need, in collections such as this, to use materials in certain sections which could be used equally well in other sections. Whenever we use selections in this way we will specify doing so in our introductions (as here), and we will suggest alternate ways in which the reader might approach these selections.

Art, Intuition, and Significant Form

Clive Bell, a twentieth-century writer closely associated with the famous art critic Roger Fry, argued that "significant form" defines the nature of art. In so arguing, Bell stressed the importance of purely formal non-representational elements of works of art (visual art in particular). Bell helped pave the way in the English-speaking world for the acceptance of Post-Impressionist works as fully legitimate works of art. Beryl Steele argues that Bell's theory is a philosophical fabrication generated by a certain artistic prejudice. Steel claims that Bell's theory cannot claim to be "true" or "correct," because it has been constructed in such a way as to be immune to counterexamples. Steele is as much if not more concerned with Bell's method of theorizing as with the specific content of Bell's theory. Because of this, Steele's remarks can be read in conjunction with part four, The Theory of Art Theory.

Art, Feeling, and Experience

Tolstoy is justifiably famous as perhaps the greatest novelist in the history of Western literature. This is a principal reason, no doubt, why his theory of art continues to receive the attention it does, for few philosophers believe there is great philosophical merit to Tolstoy's theoretical writings on art. Tolstoy is usually considered to hold a naive and confused view of art as the communication of feeling through some sensuous medium. As Stanley Bates points out about Tolstoy's book *What Is Art?*, "It sometimes seems as though the chief function of this work for later aesthetic theory has been to provide a rich storehouse of examples of aesthetic fallacies." Nevertheless, Bates argues that Tolstoy's theory cannot be dismissed, and not simply because Tolstoy was a great novelist—he has valuable philosophical insights to offer as well. Bates gives us an illuminating exposition of Tolstoy's theory of art, distinguishing several questions Tolstoy was concerned to answer, questions which many philosophers have overlooked. Bates shows us that Tolstoy's theory is more complex than philosophers have hitherto thought it to be; he shows us that certain criticisms which philosophers have accepted as conclusive refutations of Tolstoy fail to address a number of crucial considerations of Tolstoy's theory. Bates does, however, go on to state what he takes to be the "deepest failure" of Tolstoy's theory: "That he does not recognize a potential tension, or, even incompatibility, between the artist's sincerity and the infectiousness of the work of art."

Art and Expression

Collingwood's theory of art as the expression of emotion is the most sophisticated theory of art produced in the twentieth century. Collingwood's distinction between art and craft and his critique of what he calls the "technical theory" of art have become commonplace in aesthetic thought since the publication of *The Principles of Art* in 1938. Unfortunately, Collingwood's philosophical style is somewhat alien to contemporary philosophers, for his is the language of nineteenth-century Romanticism, the language of Wordsworth and Coleridge. Because of his style Collingwood's theory is frequently misunderstood, and he is often thought to be simply reiterating the views of Benedetto Croce, whom Collingwood acknowledged as his single most influential intellectual progenitor on aesthetic matters.

Richard Wollheim believes that Collingwood and Croce basically share the same view of art. He also believes that Collingwood and Croce are fundamentally wrong because for both of these philosophers, works of art primarily exist in the heads of artists and only accidentally as objects in the real world. Wollheim relies heavily on the later philosophy of Ludwig Wittgenstein in formulating his critique of Collingwood and Croce. The importance of Wittgenstein's work to post–World War II aesthetics is discussed in detail by Morris Weitz in part four, The Theory of Art Theory. For this reason we will not discuss Wittgenstein at any length here. Wittgenstein had an enormous influence on twentieth-century philosophy, and his later work, from 1930 until his death in 1951, influenced aesthetic thought particularly in fundamental ways. Wollheim's critique of the so-called Croce–Collingwood theory of art provides an excellent case study of this influence.

Plato

ART AS IMITATION:
FROM *THE REPUBLIC*

Book X

Of the many excellences which I perceive in the order of our State, there is none which upon reflection pleases me better than the rule about poetry.*

What rule?

The rule about rejecting imitative poetry, which certainly ought not to be received; as I see far more clearly now that the parts of the soul have been distinguished.

What do you mean?

Speaking in confidence, for I should not like to have my words repeated to the tragedians and the rest of the imitative tribe—but I do not mind saying to you, that all poetical imitations are ruinous to the understanding of the hearers, and that the knowledge of what they are is the only antidote to them.

Explain the purport of your remark.

Well, I will tell you: although I have always from my earliest youth had an awe and love of Homer, which even now makes the words falter on my lips, for he is the great captain and teacher of the whole of that charming tragic company; but a man is not to be reverenced before the truth, and therefore I will speak out.

Very good, he said.

Listen to me then, or rather, answer me.

Put your question.

Can you tell me what imitation is? for I really do not know.

A likely thing, then, that I should know.

Plato (427/8 b.c.–348/7 b.c.). *Plato's* philosophical writings are of perennial interest. The issues he raised and the solutions he proposed are as central today as they were to him and his fellow Athenians.

Translated by Benjamin Jowett (3rd ed., London: Oxford University Press, 1892), Book X.

* This conversation takes place between Socrates and Glaucon.

Why not? for the duller eye may often see a thing sooner than the keener.

Very true, he said; but in your presence I could not muster courage to say even what I might have to say. Will you enquire yourself?

Well then, shall we begin as usual by assuming that whenever a number of individuals have a common name, they have also a corresponding idea or form:—do you understand me?

I do.

Let us take any instance; there are beds and tables in the world and many of them, are there not?

Yes.

But there are only two ideas or forms of them—one the idea of a bed, the other of a table.

True.

And the maker of either of them makes a bed or he makes a table for our use, in accordance with the idea—that is our way of speaking in this and similar instances—but no artificer makes the ideas themselves.

Certainly not.

And there is another artist,—I should like to know what you would say of him.

Who is he?

One who is the maker of all the works of all other workmen.

What an extraordinary man!

Wait a little, and there will be more reason for your saying so. For this is he who makes not only vessels of every kind, but plants and animals, himself and all other things—the earth and heaven, and the things which are in heaven or under the earth; he makes the gods also.

He must be a rare master of his art.

Oh! you are unbelieving, are you? Do you mean that there is no such maker or creator, or that in one sense there might be a maker of all these things but not in another? Do you not see that there is a way in which you could make them yourself?

What way?

An easy way enough; or rather, there are many ways in which the feat might be accomplished, none quicker than that of turning a mirror round and round—you would soon make the sun and the heavens, and the earth and yourself, and other animals and plants, and all the other creations of art as well as nature in the mirror.

Yes, he said; but that is an appearance only.

Very good, I said, you are coming to the point now; and the painter, as I conceive, is just a creator of this sort, is he not?

Of course.

But then I suppose you will say that what he creates is untrue. And yet there is a sense in which the painter also creates a bed?

Yes, he said, but not a real bed.

And what of the maker of the bed? did you not say that he does not make the idea which, according to our view, is the essence of the bed, but only a particular bed?

Yes, I did.

Then if he does not make that which exists he cannot make true existence, but only some semblance of existence; and if any one were to say that the work of the maker of the bed, or of any other workman, has real existence, he could hardly be supposed to be speaking the truth.

At any rate, he replied, philosophers would say that he was not speaking the truth.

No wonder, then, that his work too is an indistinct expression of truth.

No wonder.

Suppose that we enquire into the character of this imitator as illustrated by what has now been said?

If you please.

Well then, here are three beds; one existing in nature, which, as I think that we may say, is made by God,—no one else can be the maker?

No.

There is another which is the work of the carpenter?

Yes.

And the work of the painter is a third?

Yes.

Beds, then, are of three kinds, and there are three artists who superintend them: God, the maker of the bed, and the painter?

Yes, there are three of them.

God, whether from choice or from necessity, made one bed in nature and one only; two or more such ideal beds neither ever have been or ever will be made by God.

Why is that?

Because even if he had made but two, a third would still appear behind them which both of them would have for their idea, and that would be the ideal bed and not the two others.

Very true, he said.

God knew this, and He desired to be the real maker of a real bed, not a particular maker of a particular bed, and therefore He created a bed which by nature is one only.

So we believe.

Shall we, then, speak of Him as the natural author or maker of the bed?

Yes, he replied; inasmuch as by the natural process of creation He is the author of this and of all other things.

And what shall we say of the carpenter—is not he also the maker of the bed?

Yes.

But would you call the painter a creator and maker?

Certainly not.

Yet if he is not the maker what is he in relation to the bed?

I think, he said, that we may fairly designate him as the imitator of that which the others make.

Good, I said; then you call him who is third in the descent from nature an imitator?

Certainly, he said.

And the tragic poet is an imitator, and therefore, like all other imitators, he is thrice removed from the king and from the truth?

That appears to be the case.

Then about the imitator we are agreed. And now about the painter, I would like to know whether he imitates that which originally exists in nature, or only the creations of artists?

The latter.

As they are or as they appear? you have still to determine this.

What do you mean?

I mean, that you may look at a bed from different points of view, obliquely or directly or from any other point of view, and the bed will appear different, but there is no difference in reality. And the same of all things.

Yes, he said, the difference is only apparent.

Now let me ask you another question: Which is the art of painting—an imitation of things as they are, or as they appear—of appearance or of reality?

Of appearance.

Then the imitator, I said, is a long way off the truth, and can do all things because he lightly touches on a small part of them, and that part an image. For example: a painter will paint a cobbler, carpenter, or any other artist, though he knows nothing of their arts; and, if he is a good artist, he may deceive children or simple persons, when he shows them his picture of a carpenter from a distance, and they will fancy that they are looking at a real carpenter.

Certainly.

And whenever any one informs us that he has found a man who knows all the arts, and all things else that everybody knows, and every single thing, with a higher degree of accuracy than any other man—whoever tells us this, I think that we can only imagine him to be a simple creature who is likely to have been deceived by some wizard or actor whom he met, and whom he thought all-knowing, because he himself was unable to analyse the nature of knowledge and ignorance and imitation.

Most true.

And so, when we hear persons saying that the tragedians, and Homer, who is at their head, know all the arts and all things human, virtue as well as vice, and divine things too, for that the good poet must know what he is talking about, and that he who has not this knowledge can never be a poet, we ought to consider whether here also there is not a similar illusion. Perhaps they may have been deceived by imitators, and may never have remembered when they saw their works that these were but imitations thrice removed from the truth, and could easily be made without any knowledge of the truth, because they are appearances only and not real substances? Or, after all, they may be in the right, and poets do really know the things about which they seem to the many to speak well?

Yes, he said, by all means let the question be considered.

Now do you suppose that if a person were able to make the original as well as the image, he would devote himself to the image-making branch? Would he allow imitation to be the ruling principle of his life, as though he could do nothing better?

I should say not.

The real artist, who knew what he was imitating, would be interested in realities and not in imitations; and would desire to leave as memorials of himself works many and fair; and, instead of being the author of encomiums, he would prefer to be the theme of them.

Yes, he said, that would bring him much greater honour and profit.

Then I think that we must put a question to Homer; not about medicine, or any of the arts to which his poems only incidentally refer: we are not going to ask him, or any other poet, whether he has cured patients like Asclepius, or left behind him a school of medicine such as the Asclepiads were, or whether he only talks about medicine and other arts at second-hand; but we have a right to know respecting military tactics, politics, education, which are the chiefest and noblest subjects of his poems, and we may fairly ask him about them. 'Friend Homer,' then we say, 'if you are only in the second remove from truth in what you say of virtue, and not in the third—not an image maker or imitator—and if you are able to discern what pursuits make men better or worse in private or public life, tell us what State was ever better governed by your help? The good order of Lacedaemon is due to Lycurgus, and many other cities great and small have been similarly benefited by others; but who says that you have been a good legislator to them and have done them any good? Italy and Sicily can tell of Charondas, and there is Solon who is renowned among us; but what city has anything to say about you?' Is there any city which he might name?

I think not, said Glaucon; not even the Homeridae themselves pretend that he was a legislator.

Well, but is there any war on record which was carried on successfully by him, or aided by his counsels, when he was alive?

There is not.

Or is there any invention[1] of his applicable to the arts, or to human life, such as Thales the Milesian or Anacharsis the Scythian, and other ingenious men have made, which is attributed to him?

There is nothing at all of the kind.

But, if Homer never did any public service, was he privately a guide or teacher of any? Had he in his lifetime friends and associates who loved him, and handed down to posterity an Homeric way of life, as Pythagoras was beloved, and his successors, who at this day call their way of life by his name, do appear to have a certain distinction above other men?

---

[1] Omitting εἰς.

Nothing of the kind is recorded of him. For surely, Socrates, Creophylus, the companion of Homer, that child of flesh, whose name always makes us laugh, might be more justly ridiculed for his want of education, if, as is said, Homer was greatly neglected by him and others in his own day when he was alive?

Yes, I replied, that is the tradition. But can you imagine, Glaucon, that if Homer had really been able to educate and improve mankind, if he had possessed knowledge and not been a mere imitator—can you imagine, I say, that he would not have had many followers, and been honoured and loved by them? Protagoras of Abdera, and Prodicus of Ceos, and a host of others, have only to suggest to their contemporaries that they will never be able to manage either their own house or their State unless they are made by them presidents of education; and for this wisdom of theirs they are so much beloved that their companions all but carry them about on their heads. And are we to believe that the contemporaries of Homer, or again of Hesiod, would have allowed either of them to beg their way as rhapsodists, if they had really been able to improve mankind? Would they not have been as unwilling to part with them as with gold, and have compelled them to stay at home with them? Or, if the master would not stay, then the disciples would have followed him about everywhere, until they had got education enough?

Yes, Socrates, that, I think, is quite true.

Then must we not infer that all the poets, beginning with Homer, are only imitators; they copy images of virtue and the like, but the truth they never reach? The poet is like a painter who, as has already been observed, will make a likeness of a cobbler though he understands nothing of cobbling; and his picture is good enough for those who know no more than he does, and judge only by colours and figures. And so the poet lays over his words and expressions certain colours taken from the several arts, himself understanding their nature only enough to imitate them; and other people, who are as ignorant as he is, and judge only from his words, imagine that if he speaks of cobbling, or of military tactics, or of anything else in metre and harmony and rhythm, he speaks very well—such is the sweet influence which melody and rhythm by nature have. And I think that you must know, for you have often seen what a poor appearance the tales of poets make when stripped of the colours which music puts upon them, and recited in prose?

Yes, he said.

They are like faces which were never really beautiful, but only blooming; and now the bloom of youth has passed away from them?

Exactly.

Here is another point: The imitator or maker of the image knows nothing of true existence; he knows appearances only. Am I not right?

Yes.

Then let us have a clear understanding, and not be satisfied with half an explanation.

Proceed.

Of the painter we say that he will paint reins, and he will paint a bridle?

Yes.

And the worker in leather and brass will make them?

Certainly.

But does the painter know the right form of the bridle and reins? Nay, hardly even the maker; only the horseman who knows how to use them— he knows their right form.

Most true.

And may we not say the same of all things?

What?

That there are three arts which are concerned with all things: one which uses, another which makes, a third which imitates them?

Yes.

And the excellence or beauty or truth of every structure, animate or inanimate, and of every action of man, is relative to the use for which nature or the artist has intended them.

True.

Then the user of them must have the greatest experience of them, and he must indicate to the maker the good or bad qualities which develop themselves in use; for example, the flute-player will tell the flute-maker which of his flutes answer in playing; he will tell him how he ought to make them, and the other will attend to him?

Of course.

The one knows and therefore speaks about the goodness and badness of flutes, and the other believes and obeys him?

True.

The instrument is the same, but about the excellence or badness of it the maker will only attain belief; and this he will gain from him who knows, by talking to him and being compelled to hear what he has to say, whereas the user will have knowledge?

True.

But will the imitator have either? Will he know from use whether or no his drawing is correct or beautiful? or will he have right opinion from being compelled to associate with another who knows and gives him instructions?

Neither.

Then he will no more have true opinion than he will have knowledge about the goodness or badness of his imitations?

I suppose not.

The imitative artist will be in a brilliant state of intelligence about his own creations?

Nay, rather the reverse.

And yet he will go on imitating without knowing what makes a thing good or bad, but he will imitate that which appears to be good to the ignorant and to the vulgar?

Just so.

Thus far then we are pretty well agreed that the imitator has no knowledge worth mentioning. Imitation is only a kind of play or sport, and the tragic and epic poets are imitators in the highest degree?

Very true.

And now tell me, I beseech you, has not imitation been shown by us to be concerned with that which is thrice removed from the truth?

Certainly.

And what is the faculty in man to which imitation is addressed?

What do you mean?

I will explain: The body which is large when seen near, appears small when seen at a distance?

True.

And the same objects appear straight when looked at out of the water, and crooked when in the water; and the concave becomes convex, owing to the illusion about colours to which the sight is liable. An utter confusion thus arises in the mind; and there is a similar deception about painting in light and shade, and juggling, and other ingenious devices, which impose upon our weakness with all the arts of magic.

True.

And the arts of measuring and numbering and weighing come to the rescue of the human understanding—there is the beauty of them—and the apparent greater or less, or more or heavier, no longer reign in us, but give way before calculation and measure and weight?

Most true.

And this, surely, must be the work of the calculating and rational principle in the soul?

To be sure.

And when this principle measures and certifies that some things are equal, or that some are greater or less than others, there occurs an apparent contradiction?

True.

But were we not saying that such a contradiction is impossible—the same cannot have contrary opinions at the same time about the same?

Very true.

Then that part of the soul which has an opinion contrary to measure is not the same with that which has an opinion in accordance with measure?

True.

But the best part of the soul is that which trusts to measure and calculation?

Certainly.

And that which is opposed to them is one of the inferior principles of the soul?

No doubt.

That was the conclusion at which I wanted to arrive when I said that painting or drawing and imitation in general are engaged in a work which is remote from truth, and the companion and friend and associate of a principle which is remote from reason, and has no true or healthy aim.

Exactly.

The imitative art is an inferior who marries an inferior, and has inferior offspring.

Very true.

And is this confined to the sight only, or applicable to the hearing also, in reference to what is termed poetry?

Probably the same holds of poetry.

Do not rely, I said, on the analogy of painting; but let us examine further and see whether the faculty with which poetical imitation is concerned is good or bad.

By all means.

Let us state the question:—Imitation imitates the actions of men, whether voluntary or involuntary, on which a good or bad event has ensued, and they rejoice or sorrow accordingly. Is there anything more?

No, there is nothing else.

But in all this variety of circumstances is the man at unity with himself —or rather, as in the instance of sight there was confusion and opposition, so here also is there not strife and inconsistency in his life? Though I need hardly raise the question again, for, if I remember rightly, all this has been already admitted; and the soul has been acknowledged by us to be full of these and ten thousand similar oppositions occurring at the same moment?

And we were right, he said.

Yes, I said, thus far we were right; but there was an omission which must now be supplied.

What was the omission?

Were we not saying that a good man, when he loses his son or anything else which is most dear to him, will bear the loss with more equanimity than another?

Yes.

But will he have no sorrow, or shall we say that although he cannot help sorrowing, he will moderate his sorrow?

Yes, he said, the latter is the truer statement.

Tell me: will he be more likely to struggle and hold out against his sorrow when he is seen by his equals, or when he is by himself alone?

He will be more likely to hold out when he is in company.

But when he is left alone he will not mind saying or doing many things which he would be ashamed of any one hearing or seeing?

True.

There is a principle of law and reason in him which bids him resist, while passion is urging him to indulge his sorrow?

True.

But when a man is drawn in two opposite directions, to and from the same object, this, as we affirm, necessarily implies two distinct principles in him?

Certainly.

One of them is obedient to the law?

How do you mean?

The law would say that to be patient under suffering is best, and that we should not give way to impatience, as there is no knowing whether such things are good or evil; and nothing is gained by impatience; also, because no human thing is of serious importance, and grief stands in the way of that which at the moment is most required.

What is most required? he asked.

That we should take counsel about the past, and when the dice have been thrown order our affairs accordingly by the advice of reason; not, like children who have had a fall, keeping hold of the part struck and wasting time in setting up a howl, but accustoming the soul forthwith to apply a remedy, raising up that which is sickly and fallen, banishing the cry of sorrow by a real cure.

Yes, he said, there is no better way of meeting the attacks of fortune.

Yes, I said; and the higher principle is ready to follow this suggestion of reason?

Clearly.

And the other principle which inclines us to recollect of our troubles and to lamentation, and can never have enough of them, we may call irrational, indolent, and cowardly?

Indeed, we may.

And does not the latter—I mean the rebellious principle—furnish a great variety of materials for imitation? Whereas the wise and calm temperament, being always nearly equable, is not easy to imitate or to appreciate when imitated, especially at a theatre in which all sorts of men are gathered together. For the feeling represented is one to which they are strangers.

Certainly.

Then the imitative poet is not by nature made, nor his art intended, to affect or please the rational principle in the soul, that is if he aims at being popular; but he will prefer the passionate and fitful temper, which is easily imitated?

Clearly.

And now we may fairly take him and set him by the side of the painter, for he is like him in two ways: first, inasmuch as his creations have an inferior degree of truth—in this, I say, he is like him; and he is also like him in being concerned with an inferior part of the soul; and therefore we shall be right in not receiving him in a well-ordered State, because he awakens and nourishes and strengthens the feelings and impairs the reason. As in a city we cannot allow the evil to have authority and the good to be put out of the way, even so in the city which is within us we refuse to allow the imitative poet to create an evil constitution indulging the

irrational nature which has no discernment of greater and less, and thinks the same thing at one time great and at another small; and is a manufacturer of images very far removed from the truth.[2]

Very true.

But we have not yet brought forward the heaviest count in our accusation:—the power which poetry has of harming even the good (and there are very few who are not harmed), is surely an awful thing?

Yes, certainly, if the effect is what you say.

Hear and judge: The best of us, as I conceive, when we listen to a passage of Homer, or one of the tragedians in which he represents some pitiful hero who is drawling out his sorrows in a long oration, or possibly singing, and smiting his breast—the best of us, you know, delight in giving way to sympathy, and are in raptures at the excellence of the poet who stirs our feelings most.

Yes, of course I know.

But when any sorrow happens to ourselves, then you may observe that we pride ourselves on the opposite quality of quietness and endurance; this is the manly part, and that which delighted us when recited is now deemed to be the part of a woman.

I know, he said.

Now can we be right in praising that in another which a man would abominate and be ashamed of in his own person?

No, he said, that is certainly not reasonable.

Nay, I said, quite reasonable from one point of view.

What point of view?

If you consider, I said, that when we are in misfortune there is in us a natural hunger after sorrow and weeping, and that this feeling which is tamed and kept under control in our own calamities, is satisfied and delighted by the poets;—the better nature in each of us, not having been sufficiently trained by reason or habit, is then taken unawares because the sorrow is another's; and the spectator fancies that there can be no disgrace to himself in praising and pitying any one who comes telling him what a good man he is, and making unseasonable lamentations; he thinks that the pleasure is a gain, and why should he be supercilious and lose this and the poem too? For the reflection is not often made that from the evil of others the fruit of evil is reaped by ourselves, or that the feeling of pity which has gathered strength at the sight of the misfortunes of others, will not be repressed in our own misfortunes.

A very just remark.

And does not the same hold also of the ridiculous? There are jests which you would be ashamed to make yourself, and yet on the comic stage, or again in private, when you hear them, you are greatly amused by them, instead of being disgusted at their unseemliness;—the case of compassion recurs;—there is a principle within which is disposed to raise a laugh, and this was once kept in order by you because you were afraid

[2] Reading αφεστωτι.

of being thought a buffoon, but is now let out again and inspired by the theatre, and you are apt to be betrayed unconsciously to yourself into playing the comic poet in your own person.

Quite true, he said.

And the same may be said of lust and anger and all the other affections, of desire and pain and pleasure which are held to be inseparable from every action—in all of them poetry feeds and waters the passions instead of drying them up; she lets them rule instead of ruling them as they ought to be ruled, with a view to the happiness and virtue of mankind.

I cannot deny it.

Therefore, Glaucon, I said, whenever you meet with any of the eulogists of Homer declaring that he has been the educator of Hellas, and that he is profitable for the management and administration of human things, and that you should take him up and get to know him and regulate your whole life according to him, we may love and honour the intentions of these excellent people, as far as their lights extend; and we are ready to acknowledge that Homer is the greatest of poets and first of tragedy writers; but we must remain firm in our conviction that hymns to the gods and praises of famous men are the only poetry which ought to be admitted into our State. For if you go beyond this and allow the honeyed muse to enter, either in epic or lyric verse, not law and the reason of mankind, which by common consent has ever been deemed best, but pleasure and pain will be the rulers in our State.

That is most true, he said.

Let this then be our excuse for expelling poetry, that the argument constrained us; but let us also make an apology to her, lest she impute to us any harshness or want of politeness. We will tell her that there is an ancient quarrel between philosophy and poetry; of which there are many proofs, such as the saying of 'the yelping hound howling at her lord,' or of one 'mighty in the vain talk of fools,' and 'the mob of sages circumventing Zeus,' and the 'subtle thinkers who are beggars after all'; and there are ten thousand other signs of ancient enmity between them. Notwithstanding this, let us assure our sweet friend and the sister arts of imitation, that if she will only prove her title to existence in a well-ordered State we shall be delighted to receive her, knowing that we ourselves are very susceptible of her charms; but we may not on that account betray the truth. I dare say, Glaucon, that you are as much charmed by her as I am, especially when you see her in the garb of Homer?

Yes, indeed, I am greatly charmed.

Shall I propose, then, that she be allowed to return from exile, on this condition—that she is to make a defence of herself in lyrical or some other metre?

Certainly.

And to those of her defenders who are lovers of poetry and yet not poets, I think that we may grant a further privilege—they shall be allowed to speak in prose on her behalf: let them show not only that she is pleasant but also useful to States and to human life and we will gladly listen, for if this can be proved we shall surely be the gainers, I mean, if there is a use in poetry as well as a delight?

Certainly, he said, we shall be the gainers.

Arthur Danto

THE ARTISTIC ENFRANCHISEMENT OF REAL OBJECTS: THE ARTWORLD

Hamlet:
  Do you see nothing there?
The Queen:
  Nothing at all; yet all that is I see.

Shakespeare: Hamlet, Act III, Scene IV

Hamlet and Socrates, though in praise and deprecation respectively, spoke of art as a mirror held up to nature.* As with many disagreements in attitude, this one has a factual basis. Socrates saw mirrors as but reflecting what we can already see; so art, insofar as mirrorlike, yields idle accurate duplications of the appearances of things, and is of no cognitive benefit whatever. Hamlet, more acutely, recognized a remarkable feature of reflecting surfaces, namely that they show us what we could not otherwise perceive—our own face and form—and so art, insofar as it is mirrorlike, reveals us to ourselves, and is, even by socratic criteria, of some cognitive utility after all. As a philosopher, however, I find Socrates' discussion defective on other, perhaps less profound grounds than these. If a mirror-image of o is indeed an imitation of o, then, if art is imitation, mirror-images are art. But in fact mirroring objects no more is art than returning weapons to a madman is justice; and reference to mirrorings would be just the sly sort of counterinstance we would expect Socrates to bring forward in rebuttal of the theory he instead uses them to illustrate. If that theory requires us to class *these* as art, it thereby shows its inadequacy: »is an imitation« will not do as a sufficient condition for »is art«. Yet, perhaps because artists *were* engaged in imitation, in Socrates' time and after, the

Arthur Danto is Professor of Philosophy at Columbia University. He has published widely in all areas of philosophy including important works in the analytical tradition as well as works on Nietzsche and Sartre. Danto was also a member of the abstract expressionistic school of painting in New York in the 1950s.
* *Journal of Philosophy* (1964): 571–584. Reprinted by permission of the *Journal of Philosophy*.

insufficiency of the theory was not noticed until the invention of photography. Once rejected as a sufficient condition, mimesis was quickly discarded as even a necessary one; and since the achievement of Kandinsky, mimetic features have been relegated to the periphery of critical concern, so much so that some works survive in spite of possessing those virtues, excellence in which was once celebrated as the essence of art, narrowly escaping demotion to mere illustrations.

It is, of course, indispensable in socratic discussion that all participants be masters of the concept up for analysis, since the aim is to match a real defining expression to a term in active use, and the test for adequacy presumably consists in showing that the former analyzes and applies to all and only those things of which the latter is true. The popular disclaimer notwithstanding, then, Socrates' auditors purportedly knew what art was as well as what they liked; and a theory of art, regarded here as a real definition of 'Art', is accordingly not to be of great use in helping men to recognize instances of its application. Their antecedent ability to do this is precisely what the adequacy of the theory is to be tested against, the problem being only to make explicit what they already know. It is *our* use of the term that the theory allegedly means to capture, but we are supposed able, in the words of a recent writer, »to separate those objects which are works of art from those which are not, because . . . we know how correctly to use the word 'art' and to apply the phrase 'work of art'.« Theories, on this account, are somewhat like mirrorimages on Socrates' account, showing forth what we already know, wordy reflections of the actual linguistic practice we are masters in.

But telling artworks from other things is not so simple a matter, even for native speakers, and these days one might not be aware he was on artistic terrain without an artistic theory to tell him so. And part of the reason for this lies in the fact that terrain is constituted artistic in virtue of artistic theories, so that one use of theories, in addition to helping us discriminate art from the rest, consists in making art possible. Glaucon and the others could hardly have known what was art and what not: otherwise they would never have been taken in by mirror-images.

I. Suppose one thinks of the discovery of a whole new class of artworks as something analogous to the discovery of a whole new class of facts anywhere, viz., as something for theoreticians to explain. In science, as elsewhere, we often accommodate new facts to old theories via auxiliary hypotheses, a pardonable enough conservatism when the theory in question is deemed too valuable to be jettisoned all at once. Now the Imitation Theory of Art (IT) is, if one but thinks it through, an exceedingly powerful theory, explaining a great many phenomena connected with the causation and evaluation of artworks, bringing a surprising unity into a complex domain. Moreover, it is a simple matter to shore it up against many purported counterinstances by such auxiliary hypotheses as that the artist who deviates from mimeticity is perverse, inept, or mad. Ineptitude, chicanery, or folly are, in fact, testable predications. Suppose, then, tests reveal that these hypotheses fail to hold, that the theory, now beyond repair, must be replaced. And a new theory is worked out, capturing what it can of the old theory's competence, together with the heretofore recalcitrant facts. One might, thinking along these lines, represent certain episodes in the history of art as not dissimilar to certain episodes in the history of science, where a conceptual revolution is being effected and where refusal to countenance certain facts, while in part due to prejudice, inertia, and self-interest, is due also to the fact that a well-established, or at least widely credited theory is being threatened in such a way that all coherence goes.

Some such episode transpired with the advent of post-impressionist paintings. In terms of the prevailing artistic theory (IT), it was impossible to accept these as art unless inept art: otherwise they could be discounted as hoaxes, self-advertisements, or the visual counterparts of madmen's ravings. So to get them accepted *as* art, on a footing with the *Transfiguration* (not to speak of a Landseer stag), required not so much a revolution in taste as a theoretical revision of rather considerable proportions, involving not only the artistic enfranchisement of these objects, but an emphasis upon newly significant features of accepted artworks, so that quite different accounts of their status as artworks would now have to be given. As a result of the new theory's acceptance, not only were post-impressionist paintings taken up as art, but numbers of objects (masks, weapons, etc.) were transferred from anthropological museums (and heterogeneous other places) to *musées des beaux arts*, though, as we would expect from the fact that a criterion for the acceptance of a new theory is that it account for whatever the older one did, nothing had to be transferred out of the *musée des beaux arts*—even if there were internal rearrangements as between storage rooms and exhibition space. Countless native speakers hung upon suburban mantelpieces innumerable replicas of paradigm cases for teaching the expression 'work of art' that would have sent their Edwardian forebears into linguistic apoplexy.

To be sure, I distort by speaking of a theory: historically, there were several, all, interestingly enough, more or less defined in terms of the IT. Art-historical complexities must yield before the exigencies of logical exposition, and I shall speak as though there were one replacing theory, partially compensating for historical falsity by choosing one which was actually enunciated. According to it, the artists in question were to be understood not as unsuccessfully imitating real forms but as successfully creating new ones, quite as real as the forms which the older art had been thought, in its best examples, to be creditably imitating. Art, after all, had long since been thought of as creative (Vasari says that God was the first artist), and the post-impressionists were to be explained as genuinely creative, aiming, in Roger Fry's words, »not at illusion but reality.« This theory (RT) furnished a whole new mode of looking at painting, old and new. Indeed, one might almost interpret the crude drawing in Van Gogh and Cézanne, the dislocation of form from contour in Rouault and Dufy,

the arbitrary use of color planes in Gauguin and the Fauves, as so many ways of drawing attention to the fact that these were *non-imitations*, specifically intended not to deceive. Logically, this would be roughly like printing »Not Legal Tender« across a brilliantly counterfeited dollar bill, the resulting object (counterfeit *cum* inscription) rendered incapable of deceiving anyone. It is not an illusory dollar bill, but then, just because it is non-illusory it does not automatically become a real dollar bill either. It rather occupies a freshly opened area between real objects and real facsimiles of real objects: it is non-facsimile, if one requires a word, and a new contribution to the world. Thus, Van Gogh's *Potato Eaters*, as a consequence of certain unmistakable distortions, turns out to be a non-facsimile of real life potato eaters; and inasmuch as these are not facsimiles of potato eaters Van Gogh's picture, as a non-imitation, had as much right to be called a real object as did its putative subjects. By means of this theory (RT), artworks re-entered the thick of things from which socratic theory (IT) had sought to evict them: if no *more* real than what carpenters wrought, they were at least no *less* real. The Post-Impressionist won a victory in ontology.

It is in terms of RT that we must understand the artworks around us today. Thus Roy Lichtenstein paints comic-strip panels, though ten or twelve feet high. These are reasonably faithful projections onto a gigantesque scale of the homely frames from the daily tabloid, but it is precisely the scale that counts. A skilled engraver might incise *The Virgin and the Chancellor Rollin* on a pinhead, and it would be recognizable as such to the keen of sight, but an engraving of a Barnett Newman on a similar scale would be a blob, disappearing in the reduction. A *photograph* of a Lichtenstein is indiscernible from a photograph of a counterpart panel from *Steve Canyon*; but the photograph fails to capture the scale, and hence is as inaccurate a reproduction as a black-and-white engraving of Botticelli, scale being essential here as color there. Lichtensteins, then, are not imitations but *new entities*, as giant whelks would be. Jasper Johns, by contrast, paints objects with respect to which questions of scale are irrelevant. Yet his objects cannot be imitations, for they have the remarkable property that any intended copy of a member of this class of objects is automatically a member of the class itself, so that these objects are logically inimitable. Thus, a copy of a numeral just *is* that numeral: a painting of 3 is a 3 made of paint. Johns, in addition, paints targets, flags, and maps. Finally, in what I hope are not unwitting footnotes to Plato, two of our pioneers—Robert Rauschenberg and Claes Oldenburg—have made genuine beds.

Rauschenberg's bed hangs on a wall, and is streaked with some desultory housepaint. Oldenburg's bed is a rhomboid, narrower at one end than the other, with what one might speak of as a built-in perspective: ideal for small bedrooms. As beds, these sell at singularly inflated prices, but one *could* sleep in either of them: Rauschenberg has expressed the fear that someone might just climb into his bed and fall asleep. Imagine, now, a certain Testadura—a plain speaker and noted philistine—who is not aware that these are art, and who takes them to be reality simple and pure. He attributes the paintstreaks on Rauschenberg's bed to the slovenliness of the owner, and the bias in the Oldenburg bed to the ineptitude of the builder or the whimsy, perhaps, of whoever had it »custom-made.« These would be mistakes, but mistakes of rather an odd kind, and not terribly different from that made by the stunned birds who pecked the sham grapes of Zeuxis. They mistook art for reality, and so has Testadura. But it was meant to *be* reality, according to RT. Can one have mistaken reality for reality? How shall we describe Testadura's error? What, after all, prevents Oldenburg's creation from being a misshapen bed? This is equivalent to asking what makes it art, and with this query we enter a domain of conceptual inquiry where native speakers are poor guides: *they* are lost themselves.

II. To mistake an artwork for a real object is no great feat when an artwork is the real object one mistakes it for. The problem is how to avoid such errors, or to remove them once they are made. The artwork is a bed, and not a bed-illusion; so there is nothing like the traumatic encounter against a flat surface that brought it home to the birds of Zeuxis that they had been duped. Except for the guard cautioning Testadura not to sleep on the artworks, he might never have discovered that this was an artwork and not a bed; and since, after all, one cannot discover that a bed is not a bed, how is Testadura to realize that he has made an error? A certain sort of explanation is required, for the error here is a curiously philosophical one, rather like, if we may assume as correct some well-known views of P. F. Strawson, mistaking a person for a material body when the truth is that a person *is* a material body in the sense that a whole class of predicates, sensibly applicable to material bodies, are sensibly, and by appeal to no different criteria, applicable to persons. So you cannot *discover* that a person is not a material body.

We begin by explaining, perhaps, that the paintstreaks are not to be explained away, that they are *part* of the object, so the object is not a mere bed with—as it happens—streaks of paint spilled over it, but a complex object fabricated out of a bed and some painstreaks: a paint-bed. Similarly, a person is not a material body with—as it happens—some thoughts superadded, but is a complex entity made up of a body and some conscious states: a conscious-body. Persons, like artworks, must then be taken as irreducible to *parts* of themselves, and are in that sense primitive. Or, more accurately, the paintstreaks are not part of the real object—the bed—which happens to be part of the artwork, but are *like* the bed, part of the artwork as such. And this might be generalized into a rough characterization of artworks that happen to contain real objects as parts of themselves: not every part of an artwork A is part of a real object R when R is part of A and can, moreover, be detached from A and seen *merely* as R. The mistake thus far will have been to mistake A for *part* of itself, namely

R, even though it would not be incorrect to say that A is R, that the art-work is a bed. It is the 'is' which requires clarification here.

There is an *is* that figures prominently in statements concerning art-works which is not the *is* of either identity or predication; nor is it the *is* of existence, of identification, or some special *is* made up to serve a philo-sophic end. Nevertheless, it is in common usage, and is readily mastered by children. It is the sense of *is* in accordance with which a child, shown a circle and a triangle and asked which is him and which his sister, will point to the triangle saying »That is me«; or, in response to my question, the person next to me points to the man in purple and says »That one is Lear«; or in the gallery I point, for my companion's benefit, to a spot in the painting before us and say »That white dab is Icarus.« We do not mean, in these instances, that whatever is pointed to stands for, or repre-sents, what it is said to be, for the *word* 'Icarus' stands for or represents Icarus: yet I would not in the same sense of *is* point to the word and say »That is Icarus.« The sentence »That *a* is *b*« is perfectly compatible with »That *a* is not *b*« when the first employs this sense of *is* and the second employs some other, though *a* and *b* are used nonambiguously throughout. Often, indeed, the truth of the first *requires* the truth of the second. The first, in fact, is incompatible with »That *a* is not *b*« only when the *is* is used nonambiguously throughout. For want of a word I shall designate this the *is of artistic identification*; in each case in which it is used, the *a* stands for some specific physical property of, or physical part of, an object; and, finally, it is a necessary condition for something to be an artwork that some part or property of it be designable by the subject of a sentence that employs this special *is*. It is an *is*, incidentally, which has near-relatives in marginal and mythical pronouncements. (Thus, one *is* Quetzalcoatl; those *are* the Pillars of Hercules.)

Let me illustrate. Two painters are asked to decorate the east and west walls of a science library with frescoes to be respectively called *Newton's First Law* and *Newton's Third Law*. These paintings, when finally un-veiled, look, scale apart, as follows:

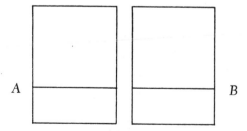

As objects I shall suppose the works to be indiscernible: a black horizontal line on a white ground, equally large in each dimension and element. B explains his work as follows: a mass, pressing downward, is met by a mass pressing upward: the lower mass reacts equally and oppositely to the upper one. A explains his work as follows: the line through the space is the path of an isolated particle. The path goes from edge to edge, to give the sense of its *going beyond*. If it ended or began within the space, the line would be curved: and it is parallel to the top and bottom edges, for if it were closer to one than to another, there would have to be a force accounting for it, and this is inconsistent with its being the path of an *isolated* particle.

Much follows from these artistic identifications. To regard the middle line as an edge (mass meeting mass) imposes the need to identify the top and bottom half of the picture as rectangles, and as two distinct parts (not necessarily as two masses, for the line could be the edge of *one* mass jutting up–or down–into empty space). If it is an edge, we cannot thus take the entire area of the painting as a single space: it is rather composed of two forms, or one form and a non-form. We could take the entire area as a single space only by taking the middle horizontal as a *line* which is not an edge. But this almost requires a three-dimensional identification of the whole picture: the area can be a flat surface which the line is *above* (*Jet-flight*), or *below* (*Submarine-path*), or *on* (*Line*), or *in* (*Fissure*), or *through* (*Newton's First Law*)— though in this last case the area is not a flat surface but a transparent cross section of absolute space. We could make all these prepositional qualifications clear by imagining perpendicular cross sections to the picture plane. Then, depending upon the applicable prepositional clause, the area is (artistically) interrupted or not by the horizontal element. If we take the line as *through* space, the edges of the picture are not really the edges of the space: the space goes beyond the picture if the line itself does; and we are in the same space as the line is. As B, the edges of the picture can be *part* of the picture in case the masses go right to the edges, so that the edges of the picture are *their* edges. In that case, the vertices of the picture would be the vertices of the masses, except that the masses have four vertices more than the picture itself does: here four vertices would be part of the art work which were not part of the real object. Again, the faces of the masses could be the face of the picture, and in looking at the picture, we are looking at these faces: but *space* has no face, and on the reading of A the work has to be read as faceless, and the face of the physical object would not be part of the artwork. Notice here how one artistic identification engenders another artistic identification and how, consistently with a given identification, we are *required* to give others and *precluded* from still others: indeed, a given identification determines how many elements the work is to contain. These different identifications are incompatible with one another, or generally so, and each might be said to make a different artwork, even though each artwork contains the identical real object as part of itself—or at least parts of the identical real object as parts of itself. There are, of course, senseless identifications: no one could, I think, sensibly read the middle horizontal as *Love's Labour's Lost* or *The Ascendency of St. Erasmus*. Finally, notice how acceptance of one identification rather than another is in effect to exchange one *world* for another. We could, indeed, enter a quiet poetic world by identifying the upper area with a clear and cloudless sky, reflected in the still surface of the water below, whiteness kept from whiteness only by the unreal boundary of the horizon.

And now Testadura, having hovered in the wings throughout this discussion, protests that *all he sees is paint*: a white painted oblong with a black line painted across it. And how right he really is: that is all he sees or that anybody can, we aesthetes included. So, if he asks us to show him what there is further to see, to demonstrate through pointing that this is an artwork (*Sea and Sky*), we cannot comply, for he has overlooked nothing (and it would be absurd to suppose he had, that there was something tiny we could point to and he, peering closely, say »So it is! A work of art after all!«). We cannot help him until he has mastered the *is of artistic identification* and so *constitutes* it a work of art. If he cannot achieve this, he will never look upon artworks: he will be like a child who sees sticks as sticks.

But what about pure abstractions, say something that looks just like A but is entitled No. 7? The 10th Street abstractionist blankly insists that there is nothing here but white paint and black, and none of our literary identifications need apply. What then distinguishes him from Testadura, whose philistine utterances are indiscernible from his? And how can it be an artwork for him and not for Testadura, when they agree that there is nothing that does not meet the eye? The answer, unpopular as it is likely to be to purists of every variety, lies in the fact that this artist has returned to the physicality of paint through an atmosphere compounded of artistic theories and the history of recent and remote painting, elements of which he is trying to refine out of his own work; and as a consequence of this his work belongs in this atmosphere and is part of this history. He has achieved abstraction through rejection of artistic identifications, returning to the real world from which such identifications remove us (he thinks), somewhat in the mode of Ch'ing Yuan, who wrote:

> Before I had studied Zen for thirty years, I saw mountains as mountains and waters as waters. When I arrived at a more intimate knowledge, I came to the point where I saw that mountains are not mountains, and waters are not waters. But now that I have got the very substance I am at rest. For it is just that I see mountains once again as mountains, and waters once again as waters.

His identification of what he has made is logically dependent upon the theories and history he rejects. The difference between his utterance and Testadura's »This is black paint and white paint and nothing more« lies in the fact that he is still using the *is* of artistic identification, so that his use of »That black paint is black paint« is not a tautology. Testadura is not at that stage. To see something as art requires something the eye cannot decry—an atmosphere of artistic theory, a knowledge of the history of art: an artworld.

III. Mr. Andy Warhol, the Pop artist, displays facsimiles of Brillo cartons, piled high, in neat stacks, as in the stockroom of the supermarket. They happen to be of wood, painted to look like cardboard, and why not? To paraphrase the critic of the *Times*, if one may make the facsimile of a human being out of bronze, why not the facsimile of a Brillo carton out of plywood? The cost of these boxes happens to be $2x10^3$ that of their homely counterparts in real life—a differential hardly ascribable to their advantage in durability. In fact the Brillo people might, at some slight increase in cost, make their boxes out of plywood without these becoming artworks, and Warhol might make *his* out of cardboard without their ceasing to be art. So we may forget questions of intrinsic value, and ask why the Brillo people cannot manufacture art and why Warhol cannot *but* make artworks. Well, his are made by hand, to be sure. Which is like an insane reversal of Picasso's strategy in pasting the label from a bottle of Suze onto a drawing, saying as it were that the academic artist, concerned with exact imitation, must always fall short of the real thing: so why not just *use* the real thing? The Pop artist laboriously reproduces machine-made objects by hand, e.g., painting the labels on coffee cans (one can hear the familiar commendation »Entirely made by hand« falling painfully out of the guide's vocabulary when confronted by these objects). But the difference cannot consist in craft: a man who carved pebbles out of stones and carefully constructed a work called *Gravel Pile* might invoke the labor theory of value to account for the price he demands; but the question is, What makes it art? And why need Warhol *make* these things anyway? Why not just scrawl his signature across one? Or crush one up and display it as *Crushed Brillo Box* (»A protest against mechanization . . . «) or simply display a Brillo carton as *Uncrushed Brillo Box* (»A bold affirmation of the plastic authenticity of industrial . . . «)? Is this man a kind of Midas, turning whatever he touches into the gold of pure art? And the whole world consisting of latent artworks waiting, like the bread and wine of reality, to be transfigured, through some dark mystery, into the indiscernible flesh and blood of the sacrament? Never mind that the Brillo box may not be good, much less great art. The impressive thing is that it is art at all. But if it is, why are not the indiscernible Brillo boxes that are in the stockroom? Or *has* the whole distinction between art and reality broken down.

Suppose a man collects objects (ready-mades), including a Brillo carton; we praise the exhibit for variety, ingenuity, what you will. Next he exhibits nothing but Brillo cartons, and we criticize it as dull, repetitive, self-plagiarizing—or (more profoundly) claim that he is obsessed by regularity and repetition, as in *Marienbad*. Or he piles them high, leaving a narrow path; we tread our way through the smooth opaque stacks and find it an unsettling experience, and write it up as the closing in of consumer products, confining us as prisoners: or we say he is a modern pyramid builder. True, we don't say these things about the stockboy. But then a stockroom is not an art gallery, and we cannot readily separate the Brillo cartons from the gallery they are in, any more than we can separate the Rauschenberg bed

"Is this man a kind of Midas, turning whatever he touches into the gold of pure art?" Arthur Danto in "The Artworld," p. 30.

"*The world has to be ready for certain things, the artworld no less than the real one.*" Arthur Danto in "The Artworld," *p. 33.*

from the paint upon it. Outside the gallery, they are pasteboard cartons. But then, scoured clean of paint, Rauschenberg's bed is a bed, just what it was before it was transformed into art. But then if we think this matter through, we discover that the artist has failed, really and of necessity, to produce a mere real object. He has produced an artwork, his use of real Brillo cartons being but an expansion of the resources available to artists, a contribution to *artists' materials*, as oil paint was, or *tuche*.

What in the end makes the difference between a Brillo box and a work of art consisting of a Brillo Box is a certain theory of art. It is the theory that takes it up into the world of art, and keeps it from collapsing into the real object which it is (in a sense of *is* other than that of artistic identifica- tion). Of course, without the theory, one is unlikely to see it as art, and in order to see it as part of the artworld, one must have mastered a good deal of artistic theory as well as a considerable amount of the history of recent New York painting. It could not have been art fifty years ago. But then there could not have been, everything being equal, flight insurance in the Middle Ages, or Etruscan typewriter erasers. The world has to be ready for certain things, the artworld no less than the real one. It is the role of artistic theories, these days as always, to make the artworld, and art, possible. It would, I should think, never have occurred to the painters of Lascaux that they were producing *art* on those walls. Not unless there were neolithic aestheticians.

IV. The artworld stands to the real world in something like the relation- ship in which the City of God stands to the Earthly City. Certain objects, like certain individuals, enjoy a double citizenship, but there remains, the RT notwithstanding, a fundamental contrast between artworks and real objects. Perhaps this was already dimly sensed by the early framers of the IT who, inchoately realizing the nonreality of art, were perhaps limited only in supposing that the sole way objects had of being other than real is to be sham, so that artworks necessarily had to be imitations of real objects. This was too narrow. So Yeats saw in writing »Once out of nature I shall never take/My bodily form from any natural thing.« It is but a matter of choice: and the Brillo box of the artworld may be just the Brillo box of the real one, separated and united by the *is* of artistic identification. But I should like to say some final words about the theories that make artworks possible, and their relationship to one another. In so doing, I shall beg some of the hardest philosophical questions I know.

I shall now think of pairs of predicates related to each other as »oppo- sites,« conceding straight off the vagueness of this *demodé* term. Contra- dictory predicates are not opposites, since one of each of them must apply to every object in the universe, and neither of a pair of opposites need apply to some objects in the universe. An object must first be of a certain kind before either of a pair of opposites applies to it, and then at most and at least one of the opposites must apply to it. So opposites are not contraries, for contraries may both be false of some objects in the universe, but opposites cannot both be false; for of some objects, neither of a pair of opposites *sensibly* applies, unless the object is of the right sort. Then, if the object is of the required kind, the opposites behave as contradictories. If F and non-F are opposites, an object o must be of a certain kind K before either of these sensibly applies; but if o is a member of K, then o either is F or non-F to the exclusion of the other. The class of pairs of opposites that sensibly apply to the $(ó)$ Ko I shall designate as the class of *K-relevant predicates*. And a necessary condition for an object to be of a kind K is that at least one pair of K-relevant opposites be sensibly applicable to it. But, in fact, if an object is of kind K, at least and at most one of each K-relevant pair of opposites applies to it.

I am now interested in the K-relevant predicates for the class K of artworks. And let F and non-F be an opposite pair of such predicates. Now it might happen that, throughout an entire period of time, every artwork is non-F. But since nothing thus far is both an artwork and F, it might never occur to anyone that non-F is an artistically relevant predicate. The non-F-ness of artworks goes unmarked. By contrast, all works up to a given time might be G, it never occurring to anyone until that time that something might both be an artwork and non-G; indeed, it might have been thought that G was a *defining trait* of artworks when in fact something might first have to be an artwork before G is sensibly predicable of it—in which case non-G might also be predicable of artworks, and G itself then could not have been a defining trait of this class.

Let G be 'is representational' and let F be 'is expressionist'. At a given time, these and their opposites are perhaps the only artrelevant predicates in critical use. Now letting '+' stand for a given predicate P and '−' for its opposite non-P, we may construct a style matrix more or less as follows:

F	G
+	+
+	−
−	+
−	−

The rows determine available styles, given the active critical vocabulary: representational expressionistic (e.g., Fauvism); representational nonexpressionistic (Ingres); nonrepresentational expressionistic (Abstract Expressionism); nonrepresentational nonexpressionist (hard-edge abstraction). Plainly, as we add artrelevant predicates, we increase the number of available styles at the rate of 2^n. It is, of course, not easy to see in advance which predicates are going to be added or replaced by their opposites, but suppose an artist determines that H shall henceforth be artistically relevant for his paintings. Then, in fact, both H and non-H become artistically relevant for *all* painting, and if his is the first and only painting that is H, every other painting in existence becomes non-H, and the entire community of paintings is enriched, together with a doubling of the available style opportunities. It is this retroactive enrichment of the entities in the artworld that makes it possible to discuss Raphael and De Kooning together, or Lichtenstein and Michelangelo. The greater the variety of artistically relevant predicates, the more complex the individual members of the artworld become; and the more one knows of the entire population of the artworld, the richer one's experience with any of its members.

In this regard, notice that, if there are m artistically relevant predicates, there is always a bottom row with m minuses. This row is apt to be occupied by purists. Having scoured their canvasses clear of what they regard as inessential, they credit themselves with having distilled out the essence of art. But this is just their fallacy: exactly as many artistically relevant predicates stand true of their square monochromes as stand true of any member of the Artworld, and they can *exist* as artworks only insofar as »impure« paintings exist. Strictly speaking, a black square by Reinhardt is artistically as rich as Titian's *Sacred and Profane Love*. This explains how less is more.

Fashion, as it happens, favors certain rows of the style matrix: museums, connoisseurs, and others are makeweights in the Artworld. To insist, or seek to, that all artists become representational, perhaps to gain entry into a specially prestigious exhibition, cuts the available style matrix in half: there are then $2^n/2$ ways of satisfying the requirement, and museums then can exhibit all these »approaches« to the topic they have set. But this is a matter of almost purely sociological interest: one row in the matrix is as legitimate as another. An artistic breakthrough consists, I suppose, in adding the possibility of a column to the matrix. Artists then, with greater or less alacrity, occupy the positions thus opened up: this is a remarkable feature of contemporary art, and for those unfamiliar with the matrix, it is hard, and perhaps impossible, to recognize certain positions as occupied by artworks. Nor would these things be artworks without the theories and the histories of the Artworld.

Brillo boxes enter the artworld with that same tonic incongruity the *commedia dell'arte* characters bring into *Ariadne auf Naxos*. Whatever is the artistically relevant predicate in virtue of which they gain their entry, the rest of the Artworld becomes that much the richer in having the opposite predicate available and applicable to its members. And, to return to the views of Hamlet with which we began this discussion, Brillo boxes may reveal us to ourselves as well as anything might: as a mirror held up to nature, they might serve to catch the conscience of our kings.

Clive Bell

ART AS SIGNIFICANT FORM:
THE AESTHETIC HYPOTHESIS

It is improbable that more nonsense has been written about aesthetics than about anything else: the literature of the subject is not large enough for that.* It is certain, however, that about no subject with which I am acquainted has so little been said that is at all to the purpose. The explanation is discoverable. He who would elaborate a plausible theory of aesthetics must possess two qualities—artistic sensibility and a turn for clear thinking. Without sensibility a man can have no aesthetic experience, and, obviously, theories not based on broad and deep aesthetic experience are worthless. Only those for whom art is a constant source of passionate emotion can possess the data from which profitable theories may be deduced; but to deduce profitable theories even from accurate data involves a certain amount of brain-work, and, unfortunately, robust intellects and delicate sensibilities are not inseparable. As often as not, the hardest thinkers have had no aesthetic experience whatever. I have a friend blessed with an intellect as keen as a drill, who, though he takes an interest in aesthetics, has never during a life of almost forty years been guilty of an aesthetic emotion. So, having no faculty for distinguishing a work of art from a handsaw, he is apt to rear up a pyramid of irrefragable argument on the hypothesis that a handsaw is a work of art. This defect robs his perspicuous and subtle reasoning of much of its value; for it has ever been a maxim that faultless logic can win but little credit for conclusions that are based on premises notoriously false. Every cloud, however, has its silver lining, and this insensibility, though unlucky in that it makes my friend incapable of choosing a sound basis for his argument, mercifully blinds him to the absurdity of his conclusions while leaving him in full enjoyment of his masterly dialectic. People who set out from the hypothesis that Sir Edwin Landseer was the finest painter that ever lived will feel no uneasiness about

Clive Bell (1881–1964). Bell was a highly influential critic who was a member of the famous Bloomsbury group which included such figures as Virginia Woolf, John Maynard Keynes, and G. E. Moore.
  * Selections from *Art* (London, 1914), pp. 3–37. Reprinted by permission of Chatto & Windus.

an aesthetic which proves that Giotto was the worst. So, my friend, when he arrives very logically at the conclusion that a work of art should be small or round or smooth, or that to appreciate fully a picture you should pace smartly before it or set it spinning like a top, cannot guess why I ask him whether he has lately been to Cambridge, a place he sometimes visits.

On the other hand, people who respond immediately and surely to works of art, though, in my judgment, more enviable than men of massive intellect but slight sensibility, are often quite as incapable of talking sense about aesthetics. Their heads are not always very clear. They possess the data on which any system must be based; but, generally, they want the power that draws correct inferences from true data. Having received aesthetic emotions from works of art, they are in a position to seek out the quality common to all that have moved them, but, in fact, they do nothing of the sort. I do not blame them. Why should they bother to examine their feelings when for them to feel is enough? Why should they stop to think when they are not very good at thinking? Why should they hunt for a common quality in all objects that move them in a particular way when they can linger over the many delicious and peculiar charms of each as it comes? So, if they write criticism and call it aesthetics, if they imagine that they are talking about Art when they are talking about particular works of art or even about the technique of painting, if, loving particular works they find tedious the consideration of art in general, perhaps they have chosen the better part. If they are not curious about the nature of their emotion, nor about the quality common to all objects that provoke it, they have my sympathy, and, as what they say is often charming and suggestive, my admiration too. Only let no one suppose that what they write and talk is aesthetics; it is criticism, or just "shop."

The starting-point for all systems of aesthetics must be the personal experience of a peculiar emotion. The objects that provoke this emotion we call works of art. All sensitive people agree that there is a peculiar emotion provoked by works of art. I do not mean, of course, that all works provoke the same emotion. On the contrary, every work produces a different emotion. But all these emotions are recognisably the same in kind; so far, at any rate, the best opinion is on my side. That there is a particular kind of emotion provoked by works of visual art, and that this emotion is provoked by every kind of visual art, by pictures, sculptures, buildings, pots, carvings, textiles, &c., &c., is not disputed, I think, by anyone capable of feeling it. This emotion is called the aesthetic emotion; and if we can discover some quality common and peculiar to all the objects that provoke it, we shall have solved what I take to be the central problem of aesthetics. We shall have discovered the essential quality in a work of art, the quality that distinguishes works of art from all other classes of objects.

For either all works of visual art have some common quality, or when we speak of "works of art" we gibber. Everyone speaks of "art," making a mental classification by which he distinguishes the class "works of art" from all other classes. What is the justification of this classification? What is the quality common and peculiar to all members of this class? Whatever it be, no doubt it is often found in company with other qualities; but they are adventitious—it is essential. There must be some one quality without which a work of art cannot exist; possessing which, in the least degree, no work is altogether worthless. What is this quality? What quality is shared by all objects that provoke our aesthetic emotions? What quality is common to Sta. Sophia and the windows at Chartres, Mexican sculpture, a Persian bowl, Chinese carpets, Giotto's frescoes at Padua, and the masterpieces of Poussin, Piero della Francesca, and Cézanne? Only one answer seems possible—significant form. In each, lines and colours combined in a particular way, certain forms and relations of forms, stir our aesthetic emotions. These relations and combinations of lines and colours, these aesthetically moving forms, I call "Significant Form"; and "Significant Form" is the one quality common to all works of visual art.

At this point it may be objected that I am making aesthetics a purely subjective business, since my only data are personal experiences of a particular emotion. It will be said that the objects that provoke this emotion vary with each individual, and that therefore a system of aesthetics can have no objective validity. It must be replied that any system of aesthetics which pretends to be based on some objective truth is so palpably ridiculous as not to be worth discussing. We have no other means of recognising a work of art than our feeling for it. The objects that provoke aesthetic emotion vary with each individual. Aesthetic judgments are, as the saying goes, matters of taste; and about tastes, as everyone is proud to admit, there is no disputing. A good critic may be able to make me see in a picture that had left me cold things that I had overlooked, till at last, receiving the aesthetic emotion, I recognise it as a work of art. To be continually pointing out those parts, the sum, or rather the combination, of which unite to produce significant form, is the function of criticism. But it is useless for a critic to tell me that something is a work of art; he must make me feel it for myself. This he can do only by making me see; he must get at my emotions through my eyes. Unless he can make me see something that moves me, he cannot force my emotions. I have no right to consider anything a work of art to which I cannot react emotionally; and I have no right to look for the essential quality in anything that I have not *felt* to be a work of art. The critic can affect my aesthetic theories only by affecting my aesthetic experience. All systems of aesthetics must be based on personal experience—that is to say, they must be subjective.

Yet, though all aesthetic theories must be based on aesthetic judgments, and ultimately all aesthetic judgments must be matters of personal taste, it would be rash to assert that no theory of aesthetics can have general validity. For, though A, B, C, D are the works that move me, and A, D, E, F the works that move you, it may well be that x is the only quality believed by either of us to be common to all the works in his list. We may all agree about aesthetics, and yet differ about particular works of art. We may differ as to the presence or absence of the quality x. My immediate object will be to show that significant form is the only quality common and peculiar to all the works of visual art that move me; and I will ask those whose aesthetic experience does not tally with mine to see whether this quality is not also, in their judgment, common to all works that move them, and whether they can discover any other quality of which the same can be said.

Also at this point a query arises, irrelevant indeed, but hardly to be suppressed: "Why are we so profoundly moved by forms related in a particular way?" The question is extremely interesting, but irrelevant to aesthetics. In pure aesthetics we have only to consider our emotion and its object: for the purposes of aesthetics we have no right, neither is there any necessity, to pry behind the object into the state of mind of him who made it. Later, I shall attempt to answer the question; for by so doing I may be able to develop my theory of the relation of art to life. I shall not, however, be under the delusion that I am rounding off my theory of aesthetics. For a discussion of aesthetics, it need be agreed only that forms arranged and combined according to certain unknown and mysterious laws do move us in a particular way, and that it is the business of an artist so to combine and arrange them that they shall move us. These moving combinations and arrangements I have called, for the sake of convenience and for a reason that will appear later, "Significant Form."

A third interruption has to be met.

"Are you forgetting about colour?" someone inquires. Certainly not; my term "significant form" included combinations of lines and of colours. The distinction between form and colour is an unreal one; you cannot conceive a colourless line or a colourless space; neither can you conceive a formless relation of colours. In a black and white drawing the spaces are all white and all are bounded by black lines; in most oil paintings the spaces are multi-coloured and so are the boundaries; you cannot imagine a boundary line without any content, or a content without a boundary line. Therefore, when I speak of significant form, I mean a combination of lines and colours (counting white and black as colours) that moves me aesthetically.

Some people may be surprised at my not having called this "beauty." Of course, to those who define beauty as "combinations of lines and colours that provoke aesthetic emotion," I willingly concede the right of substituting their word for mine. But most of us, however strict we may be, are apt to apply the epithet "beautiful" to objects that do not provoke that peculiar emotion produced by works of art. Everyone, I suspect, has called a butterfly or a flower beautiful. Does anyone feel the same kind of emotion for a butterfly or a flower that he feels for a cathedral or a picture? Surely, it is not what I call an aesthetic emotion that most of us feel, generally, for natural beauty. I shall suggest, later, that some people may, occasionally, see in nature what we see in art, and feel for her an aesthetic emotion; but I am satisfied that, as a rule, most people feel a very different kind of emotion for birds and flowers and the wings of butterflies from that which they feel for pictures, pots, temples and statues.

Why these beautiful things do not move us as works of art move is another, and not an aesthetic, question. For our immediate purpose we have to discover only what quality is common to objects that do move us as works of art. In the last part of this chapter, when I try to answer the question—"Why are we so profoundly moved by some combinations of lines and colours?" I shall hope to offer an acceptable explanation of why we are less profoundly moved by others.

Since we call a quality that does not raise the characteristic aesthetic emotion "Beauty," it would be misleading to call by the same name the quality that does. To make "beauty" the object of the aesthetic emotion, we must give to the word an over-strict and unfamiliar definition. Everyone sometimes uses "beauty" in an unaesthetic sense; most people habitually do so. To everyone, except perhaps here and there an occasional aesthete, the commonest sense of the word is unaesthetic. Of its grosser abuse, patent in our chatter about "beautiful huntin' " and "beautiful shootin'," I need not take account; it would be open to the precious to reply that they never do so abuse it. Besides, here there is no danger of confusion between the aesthetic and the non-aesthetic use; but when we speak of a beautiful woman there is. When an ordinary man speaks of a beautiful woman he certainly does not mean only that she moves him aesthetically; but when an artist calls a withered old hag beautiful he may sometimes mean what he means when he calls a battered torso beautiful. The ordinary man, if he be also a man of taste, will call the battered torso beautiful, but he will not call a withered hag beautiful because, in the matter of women, it is not to the aesthetic quality that the hag may possess, but to some other quality that he assigns the epithet. Indeed, most of us never dream of going for aesthetic emotions to human beings, from whom we ask something very different. This "something," when we find it in a young woman, we are apt to call "beauty." We live in a nice age. With the man-in-the-street "beautiful" is more often than not synonymous with "desirable"; the word does not necessarily connote any aesthetic reaction whatever, and I am tempted to believe that in the minds of many the sexual flavour of the word is stronger than the aesthetic. I have noticed a consistency in those to whom the most beautiful thing in the world is a beautiful woman, and the next most beautiful thing a picture of one. The confusion between aesthetic and sensual beauty is not in their case so great as might be supposed. Perhaps there is none; for perhaps they have never had an aesthetic emotion to confuse with their other emotions. The art that they call "beautiful" is generally closely related to the women. A beautiful picture is a photograph of a pretty girl; beautiful music, the music that provokes emotions similar to those provoked by young ladies in musical farces; and beautiful poetry, the poetry that recalls the same emotions felt, twenty years earlier, for the rector's daughter. Clearly the word "beauty" is used to connote the objects of quite distinguishable emotions, and that is a reason for not employing a term which would land me inevitably in confusions and misunderstandings with my readers.

On the other hand, with those who judge it more exact to call these combinations and arrangements of form that provoke our aesthetic emotions, not "significant form," but "significant relations of form," and then try to make the best of two worlds, the aesthetic and the metaphysical, by calling these relations "rhythm," I have no quarrel whatever. Having made it clear that by "significant form" I mean arrangements and combinations that move us in a particular way, I willingly join hands with those who prefer to give a different name to the same thing.

The hypothesis that significant form is the essential quality in a work of art has at least one merit denied to many more famous and more striking —it does help to explain things. We are all familiar with pictures that interest us and excite our admiration, but do not move us as works of art. To this class belongs what I call "Descriptive Painting"—that is, painting in which forms are used not as objects of emotion, but as means of suggesting emotion or conveying information. Portraits of psychological and historical value, topographical works, pictures that tell stories and suggest situations, illustrations of all sorts, belong to this class. That we all recognise the distinction is clear, for who has not said that such and such a drawing was excellent as illustration, but as a work of art worthless? Of course many descriptive pictures possess, amongst other qualities, formal significance, and are therefore works of art: but many more do not. They interest us; they may move us too in a hundred different ways, but they do not move us aesthetically. According to my hypothesis they are not works of art. They leave untouched our aesthetic emotions because it is not their forms but the ideas or information suggested or conveyed by their forms that affect us.

Few pictures are better known or liked than Frith's "Paddington Station"; certainly I should be the last to grudge it its popularity. Many a weary forty minutes have I whiled away disentangling its fascinating incidents and forging for each an imaginary past and an improbable future. But certain though it is that Frith's masterpiece, or engravings of it, have provided thousands with half-hours of curious and fanciful pleasure, it is not less certain that no one has experienced before it one half-second of aesthetic rapture—and this although the picture contains several pretty passages of colour, and is by no means badly painted. "Paddington Station" is not a work of art; it is an interesting and amusing document. In it line and colour are used to recount anecdotes, suggest ideas, and indicate the manners and customs of an age: they are not used to provoke aesthetic emotion. Forms and the relations of forms were for Frith not objects of emotion, but means of suggesting emotion and conveying ideas.

The ideas and information conveyed by "Paddington Station" are so amusing and so well presented that the picture has considerable value and is well worth preserving. But, with the perfection of photographic processes and of the cinematograph, pictures of this sort are becoming otiose. Who doubts that one of those *Daily Mirror* photographers in collaboration with a *Daily Mail* reporter can tell us far more about "London day by day" than any Royal Academician? For an account of manners and fashions we shall go, in future, to photographs, supported by a little bright journalism, rather than to descriptive painting. Had the imperial academicians of Nero, instead of manufacturing incredibly loathsome imitations of the antique, recorded in fresco and mosaic the manners and fashions of their day, their stuff, though artistic rubbish, would now be an historical goldmine. If only they had been Friths instead of being Alma Tademas! But photography has made impossible any such transmutation of modern rubbish. Therefore it must be confessed that pictures in the Frith tradition are grown superfluous; they merely waste the hours of able men who might be more profitably employed in works of a wider beneficence. Still, they are not unpleasant, which is more than can be said for that kind of descriptive painting of which "The Doctor" is the most flagrant example. Of course "The Doctor" is not a work of art. In it form is not used as an object of emotion, but as a means of suggesting emotions. This alone suffices to make it nugatory; it is worse than nugatory because the emotion it suggests is false. What it suggests is not pity and admiration but a sense of complacency in our own pitifulness and generosity. It is sentimental. Art is above morals, or, rather, all art is moral because, as I hope to show presently, works of art are immediate means to good. Once we have judged a thing a work of art, we have judged it ethically of the first importance and put it beyond the reach of the moralist. But descriptive pictures which are not works of art, and, therefore, are not necessarily means to good states of mind, are proper objects of the ethical philosopher's attention. Not being a work of art, "The Doctor" has none of the immense ethical value possessed by all objects that provoke aesthetic ecstasy; and the state of mind to which it is a means, as illustration, appears to me undesirable.

The works of those enterprising young men, the Italian Futurists, are notable examples of descriptive painting. Like the Royal Academicians, they use form, not to provoke aesthetic emotions, but to convey information and ideas. Indeed, the published theories of the Futurists prove that their pictures ought to have nothing whatever to do with art. Their social and political theories are respectable, but I would suggest to young Italian painters that it is possible to become a Futurist in thought and action and yet remain an artist, if one has the luck to be born one. To associate art with politics is always a mistake. Futurist pictures are descriptive because they aim at presenting in line and colour the chaos of the mind at a particular moment; their forms are not intended to promote aesthetic emotion but to convey information. These forms, by the way, whatever may be the nature of the ideas they suggest, are themselves anything but revolutionary. In such Futurist pictures as I have seen—perhaps I should except some by Severini—the drawing, whenever it becomes representative as it frequently does, is found to be in that soft and common convention brought into fashion by Besnard some thirty years ago, and much affected by Beaux-Art students ever since. As works of art, the Futurist pictures are negligible; but they are not to be judged as works of art. A good Futurist picture would succeed as a good piece of psychology succeeds; it would reveal, through line and colour, the complexities of an interesting state of mind. If Futurist pictures seem to fail, we must seek an explanation, not in a lack of artistic qualities that they never were intended to possess, but rather in the minds the states of which they are intended to reveal.

Most people who care much about art find that of the work that moves them most the greater part is what scholars call "Primitive." Of course there are bad primitives. For instance, I remember going, full of enthusiasm, to see one of the earliest Romanesque churches in Poitiers (Notre-Dame-la-Grande), and finding it as ill-proportioned, over-decorated, coarse, fat and heavy as any better class building by one of those highly civilised architects who flourished a thousand years earlier or eight hundred later. But such exceptions are rare. As a rule primitive art is good—and here again my hypothesis is helpful—for, as a rule, it is also free from descriptive qualities. In primitive art you will find no accurate representation; you will find only significant form. Yet no other art moves us so profoundly. Whether we consider Sumerian sculpture or pre-dynastic Egyptian art, or archaic Greek, or the Wei and T'ang masterpieces, or those early Japanese works of which I had the luck to see a few superb examples (especially two wooden Bodhisattvas) at the Shepherd's Bush Exhibition in 1910, or whether, coming nearer home, we consider the primitive Byzantine art of the sixth century and its primitive developments amongst the Western barbarians, or, turning far afield, we consider that mysterious and majestic art that flourished in Central and South America before the coming of the white men, in every case we observe three common characteristics—absence of representation, absence of technical swagger, sublimely impressive form. Nor is it hard to discover the connection between these three. Formal significance loses itself in preoccupation with exact representation and ostentatious cunning.

Naturally, it is said that if there is little representation and less saltimbancery in primitive art, that is because the primitives were unable to catch a likeness or cut intellectual capers. The contention is beside the point. There is truth in it, no doubt, though, were I a critic whose reputation depended on a power of impressing the public with a semblance of knowledge, I should be more cautious about urging it than such people generally are. For to suppose that the Byzantine masters wanted skill, or could not have created an illusion had they wished to do so, seems to imply ignorance of the amazingly dexterous realism of the notoriously bad works of that age. Very often, I fear, the misrepresentation of the primitives must be attributed to what the critics call, "wilful distortion." Be that as it may, the point is that, either from want of skill or want of will, primitives neither create illusions, nor make display of extravagant accomplishment, but concentrate their energies on the one thing needful—the creation of form. Thus have they created the finest works of art that we possess.

Let no one imagine that representation is bad in itself; a realistic form may be as significant, in its place as part of the design, as an abstract. But if a representative form has value, it is as form, not as representation. The representative element in a work of art may or may not be harmful; always it is irrelevant. For, to appreciate a work of art we need bring with us nothing fom life, no knowledge of its ideas and affairs, no familiarity with its emotions. Art transports us from the world of man's activity to a world of aesthetic exaltation. For a moment we are shut off from human interests; our anticipations and memories are arrested; we are lifted above the stream of life. The pure mathematician rapt in his studies knows a state of mind which I take to be similar, if not identical. He feels an emotion for his speculations which arises from no perceived relation between them and the lives of men, but springs, inhuman or super-human, from the heart of an abstract science. I wonder, sometimes, whether the appreciators of art and of mathematical solutions are not even more closely allied. Before we feel an aesthetic emotion for a combination of forms, do we not perceive intellectually the rightness and necessity of the combination? If we do, it would explain the fact that passing rapidly through a room we recognise a picture to be good, although we cannot say that it has provoked much emotion. We seem to have recognised intellectually the rightness of its forms without staying to fix our attention, and collect, as it were, their emotional significance. If this were so, it would be permissible to inquire whether it was the forms themselves or our perception of their rightness and necessity that caused aesthetic emotion. But I do not think I need linger to discuss the matter here. I have been inquiring why certan combinations of forms move us; I should not have travelled by other roads had I enquired, instead, why certain combinations are perceived to be right and necessary, and why our perception of their rightness and necessity is moving. What I have to say is this: the rapt philosopher, and he who contemplates a work of art, inhabit a world with an intense and peculiar significance of its own; that significance is unrelated to the significance of life. In this world the emotions of life find no place. It is a world with emotions of its own.

To appreciate a work of art we need bring with us nothing but a sense of form and colour and a knowledge of three-dimensional space. That bit of knowledge, I admit, is essential to the appreciation of many great works, since many of the most moving forms ever created are in three dimensions. To see a cube or a rhomboid as a flat pattern is to lower its significance, and a sense of three-dimensional space is essential to the full appreciation of most architectural forms. Pictures which would be insignificant if we saw them as flat patterns are profoundly moving because, in fact, we see them as related planes. If the representation of three-dimensional space is to be called "representation," then I agree that there is one kind of representation which is not irrelevant. Also, I agree that along with our feeling for line and colour we must bring with us our knowledge of space if we are to make the most of every kind of form. Nevertheless, there are magnificent designs to an appreciation of which this knowledge is not necessary: so, though it is not irrelevant to the appreciation of some works of art it is not essential to the appreciation of all. What we must say is that the representation of three-dimensional space is neither irrelevant nor essential to all art, and that every other sort of representation is irrelevant.

That there is an irrelevant representative or descriptive element in many great works of art is not in the least surprising. Why it is not surprising I shall try to show elsewhere. Representation is not of necessity baneful, and highly realistic forms may be extremely significant. Very often, however, representation is a sign of weakness in an artist. A painter too feeble to create forms that provoke more than a little aesthetic emotion will try to eke that little out by suggesting the emotions of life. To evoke the emotions of life he must use representation. Thus a man will paint an execution, and, fearing to miss with his first barrel of significant form, will try to hit with his second by raising an emotion of fear or pity. But if in the artist an inclination to play upon the emotions of life is often the sign of a flickering inspiration, in the spectator a tendency to seek, behind form, the emotions of life is a sign of defective sensibility always. It means that his aesthetic emotions are weak or, at any rate, imperfect. Before a work of art people who feel little or no emotion for pure form find themselves at a loss. They are deaf men at a concert. They know that they are in the presence of something great, but they lack the power of apprehending it. They know that they ought to feel for it a tremendous emotion, but it happens that the particular kind of emotion it can raise is one that they can feel hardly or not at all. And so they read into the forms of the work those facts and ideas for which they are capable of feeling emotion, and feel for them the emotions that they can feel—the ordinary emotions of life. When confronted by a picture, instinctively they refer back its forms to the world from which they came. They treat created form as though it were imitated form, a picture as though it were a photograph. Instead of going out on the stream of art into a new world of aesthetic experience, they turn a sharp corner and come straight home to the world of human interests. For them the significance of a work of art depends on what they bring to it; no new thing is added to their lives, only the old material is stirred. A good work of visual art carries a person who is capable of appreciating it out of life into ecstasy: to use art as a means to the emotions of life is to use a telescope for reading the news. You will notice that people who cannot feel pure aesthetic emotions remember pictures by their subjects; whereas people who can, as often as not, have no idea what the subject of a picture is. They have never noticed the representative element, and so when they discuss pictures they talk about the shapes of forms and the relations and quantities of colours. Often they can tell by the quality of a single line whether or no a man is a good artist. They are concerned only with lines and colours, their relations and quantities and qualities; but from these they win an emotion more profound and far more sublime than any that can be given by the description of facts and ideas.

This last sentence has a very confident ring—over-confident, some may think. Perhaps I shall be able to justify it, and make my meaning clearer too, if I give an account of my own feelings about music. I am not really musical. I do not understand music well. I find musical form exceedingly difficult to apprehend, and I am sure that the profounder subtleties of harmony and rhythm more often than not escape me. The form of a musical composition must be simple indeed if I am to grasp it honestly. My opinion about music is not worth having. Yet, sometimes, at a concert, though my appreciation of the music is limited and humble, it is pure. Sometimes, though I have poor understanding, I have a clean palate. Consequently, when I am feeling bright and clear and intent, at the beginning of a concert for instance, when something that I can grasp is being played, I get from music that pure aesthetic emotion that I get from visual art. It is less intense, and the rapture is evanescent; I understand music too ill for music to transport me far into the world of pure aesthetic ecstasy. But at moments I do appreciate music as pure musical form, as sounds combined according to the laws of a mysterious necessity, as pure art with a tremendous significance of its own and no relation whatever to the significance of life; and in those moments I lose myself in that infinitely sublime state of mind to which pure visual form transports me. How inferior is my normal state of mind at a concert. Tired or perplexed, I let slip my sense of form, my aesthetic emotion collapses, and I begin weaving into the harmonies, that I cannot grasp, the ideas of life. Incapable of feeling the austere emotions of art, I begin to read into the musical forms human emotions of terror and mystery, love and hate, and spend the minutes, pleasantly enough, in a world of turbid and inferior feeling. At such times, were the grossest pieces of onomatopoeic representation—the song of a bird, the galloping of horses, the cries of children, or the laughing of demons—to be introduced into the symphony, I should not be offended. Very likely I should be pleased; they would afford new points of departure for new trains of romantic feeling or heroic thought. I know very well what has happened. I have been using art as a means to the emotions of life and reading into it the ideas of life. I have been cutting blocks with a razor. I have tumbled from the superb peaks of aesthetic exaltation to the snug foothills of warm humanity. It is a jolly country. No one need be ashamed of enjoying himself there. Only no one who has ever been on the heights can help feeling a little crestfallen in the cosy valleys. And let no one imagine, because he has made merry in the warm tilth and quaint nooks of romance, that he can even guess at the austere and thrilling raptures of those who have climbed the cold, white peaks of art.

About music most people are as willing to be humble as I am. If they cannot grasp musical form and win from it a pure aesthetic emotion, they confess that they understand music imperfectly or not at all. They recognise quite clearly that there is a difference between the feeling of the musician for pure music and that of the cheerful concert-goer for what music suggests. The latter enjoys his own emotions, as he has every right to do, and recognises their inferiority. Unfortunately, people are apt to be less modest about their powers of appreciating visual art. Everyone is inclined to believe that out of pictures, at any rate, he can get all that there is to be got; everyone is ready to cry "humbug" and "impostor" at those who say that more can be had. The good faith of people who feel pure aesthetic emotions is called in question by those who have never felt anything of the sort. It is the prevalence of the representative element, I suppose, that makes the man in the street so sure that he knows a good picture when he sees one. For I have noticed that in matters of architecture, pottery, textiles, &c., ignorance and ineptitude are more willing to defer to the opinions of those who have been blest with peculiar sensibility. It is a pity that cultivated and intelligent men and women cannot be induced to believe that a great gift of aesthetic appreciation is at least as rare in visual as in musical art. A comparison of my own experience in both has enabled me to discriminate very clearly between pure and impure appreciation. Is it too much to ask that others should be as honest about their feelings for pictures as I have been about mine for music? For I am certain that most of those who visit galleries do feel very much what I feel at concerts. They have their moments of pure ecstasy; but the moments are short and unsure. Soon they fall back into the world of human interests and feel emotions, good no doubt, but inferior. I do not dream of saying that what they get from art is bad or nugatory; I say that they do not get the best that art can give. I do not say that they cannot understand art; rather I say that they cannot understand the state of mind of those who understand it best. I do not say that art means nothing or little to them; I say they miss its full significance. I do not suggest for one moment that their appreciation of art is a thing to be ashamed of; the majority of the charming and intelligent people with whom I am acquainted appreciate visual art impurely; and, by the way, the appreciation of almost all great writers has been impure. But provided that there be some fraction of pure aesthetic emotion, even a mixed and minor appreciation of art is, I am sure, one of the most valuable things in the world—so valuable, indeed, that in my giddier moments I have been tempted to believe that art might prove the world's salvation.

Yet, though the echoes and shadows of art enrich the life of the plains, her spirit dwells on the mountains. To him who woos, but woos impurely, she returns enriched what is brought. Like the sun, she warms the good seed in good soil and causes it to bring forth good fruit. But only to the perfect lover does she give a new strange gift—a gift beyond all price. Imperfect lovers bring to art and take away the ideas and emotions of their own age and civilisation. In twelfth-century Europe a man might have been greatly moved by a Romanesque church and found nothing in a T'ang picture. To a man of a later age, Greek sculpture meant much and

Mexican nothing, for only to the former could he bring a crowd of associated ideas to be the objects of familiar emotions. But the perfect lover, he who can feel the profound significance of form, is raised above the accidents of time and place. To him the problems of archaeology, history, and hagiography are impertinent. If the forms of a work are significant its provenance is irrelevant. Before the grandeur of those Sumerian figures in the Louvre he is carried on the same flood of emotion to the same aesthetic ecstasy as, more than four thousand years ago, the Chaldean lover was carried. It is the mark of great art that its appeal is universal and eternal. Significant form stands charged with the power to provoke aesthetic emotion in anyone capable of feeling it. The ideas of men go buzz and die like gnats; men change their institutions and their customs as they change their coats; the intellectual triumphs of one age are the follies of another; only great art remains stable and unobscure. Great art remains stable and unobscure because the feelings that it awakens are independent of time and place, because its kingdom is not of this world. To those who have and hold a sense of the significance of form what does it matter whether the forms that move them were created in Paris the day before yesterday or in Babylon fifty centuries ago? The forms of art are inexhaustible; but all lead by the same road of aesthetic emotion to the same world of aesthetic ecstasy.

Beryl Lake Steele

A CRITIQUE OF BELL: FROM "A STUDY OF THE IRREFUTABILITY OF TWO AESTHETIC THEORIES"

Clive Bell is his own best brief expositor:*

> The starting point for all systems of aesthetics must be the personal experience of a peculiar emotion. The objects which provoke this emotion we call works of art.[1]
> This emotion is called the aesthetic emotion; and if we can discover some quality peculiar to all the objects that provoke it, we shall have solved what I take to be the central problem of aesthetics. We shall have discovered the essential quality in a work of art. . . .[2]

This essential quality of works of art, Bell decides, is 'significant form.' Certain relations between forms, forms themselves, lines and colours are what stir our aesthetic emotions. If we ask which relations, etc., do this, the answer is, the significant ones. And if we ask, 'Significant of what?' the answer is given by Bell's 'metaphysical hypothesis,' that they are significant ultimately of the reality of things, of 'that which gives to all things their individual significance, the thing in itself, the ultimate reality.'[3]

The claim is first made that there exist aesthetic emotions which are only aroused by works of art. Then it is claimed that what is common to all works of art, or objects which arouse aesthetic emotions, is 'significant form.'

Beryl Lake Steele is a member of the faculty at the University of Surrey, England. In addition to her interest in aesthetics, Mrs. Steele has spent several years as an educator in African universities.

* Selections from "A Study of the Irrefutability of Two Aesthetic Theories," in *Aesthetics and Language*, ed. William Elton (Oxford, 1954), pp. 100–113. Reprinted by permission of the author and Basil Blackwell.

[1] Clive Bell, *Art* (London 1927), p. 6.
[2] *Ibid.*, p. 7.
[3] *Ibid.*, pp. 69–70.

The assertion that sensitive people have aesthetic emotions is surely empirical. We should confirm or falsify this by asking those who are acknowledged to be sensitive people whether they experience an emotion which is unique to situations in which they are appraising works of art. We are not concerned here with the truth of this claim, but simply with its semantic type, *i.e.* its empirical or *a priori* character. And it certainly seems to be empirical. Many people would be prepared to admit that there is an aesthetic emotion, although some may wish to say that natural objects as well as works of art arouse it. We can believe that if Clive Bell had been confronted with constant denials of the existence of the aesthetic emotion he could still sincerely claim that he frequently experienced it. His experience at least would back his claim that such experiences do exist, and as a matter of fact many others admit having emotions of this sort. Yet we believe that Bell would say that if he had never had such an experience, his aesthetic theory would not have arisen; he insists that this personal emotion is the starting point. Bell's theory, then, seems to have what we might call empirical feet on the ground. But from there it soars into what we might call metaphysical heights, and the same suspicion assails us as in the case of Croce's view.

What is common to all the works of art, or objects which arouse the aesthetic emotion, is significant form. Bell never explains clearly what significant form is; the 'metaphysical hypothesis' suggests that it is not merely a certain (unspecified) combination of lines and colours. (Bell concerns himself, as is evident, primarily with painting.) Roger Fry, who shared Bell's view, commented that significant form is more than pleasing patterns and so on, but that an attempt at full explanation would land him 'in the depths of mysticism': 'On the edge of that gulf I stop.'[4] As Wittgenstein's famous comment advises, 'Whereof one cannot speak, thereof one must be silent.'[5]

Whatever significant form is, the questions here are 'What are we to make of the view that it is the common denominator of works of art?' 'In what position would a person be if he denied it?'

This is a way of asking if the view is empirical. How could someone convince Clive Bell that works of art (supposing, for the sake of argument, they have a common feature) do not have significant form as an essential feature, or never have significant form at all. Someone might say that Frith's 'Paddington Station' is a work of art which, because it is purely descriptive of reality, has no significant form, and therefore Bell's view is false. But we know what Bell's answer would be; he gives it himself. 'Paddington Station' is *not* a work of art precisely because it does not have significant form, precisely because it is merely descriptive painting.[6] His critical judgments and his aesthetic theory seem to be in line. Apropos of the frequent praise he bestows on Cézanne in his critical works, he writes:

[4] Roger Fry, *Vision and Design* (London 1920), p. 302.
[5] Ludwig Wittgenstein, *Tractatus Logico-Philosophicus* (London 1947), p. 189.
[6] Bell, *op. cit.*, pp. 17–18.

Leo Tolstoy

ART AS THE COMMUNICATION
OF FEELING:
FROM *WHAT IS ART?*

Take up any one of our ordinary newspapers and you will find a part devoted to the theater and music.* In almost every number you will find a
description of some art exhibition, or of some particular picture, and you
will always find reviews of new works of art that have appeared, of volumes of poems, of short stories, or of novels.

Promptly, and in detail, as soon as it has occurred, an account is published of how such and such an actress or actor played this or that role
in such and such a drama, comedy, or opera, and of the merits of the performance, as well as of the contents of the new drama, comedy, or opera,
with its defects and merits. With as much care and detail, or even more,
we are told how such and such an artist has sung a certain piece, or has
played it on the piano or violin, and what were the merits and defects of
the piece and of the performance. In every large town there is sure to be
at least one, if not more than one, exhibition of new pictures, the merits
and defects of which are discussed in the utmost detail by critics and
connoisseurs.

New novels and poems, in separate volumes or in the magazines, appear almost every day, and the newspapers consider it their duty to give
their readers detailed accounts of these artistic productions.

For the support of art in Russia (where for the education of the people only a hundredth part is spent of what would be required to give every
one the opportunity of instruction), the government grants millions of
rubles in subsidies to academies, conservatories, and theaters. In France
twenty million francs are assigned for art, and similar grants are made in
Germany and England.

Count Leo Nikolaevich Tolstoy (1828–1910). Tolstoy's importance as a novelist is
well known. In *What Is Art?* he investigates the moral, social, and religious significance
of art.

* Selections from Chapters 1, 2, 4, 5, 6, 15 and 16 of *What is Art?*, translated by
Aylmer Maude (Indianapolis, 1960). Reprinted by permission of the Bobbs-Merrill
Company, Inc.

In every large town enormous buildings are erected for museums, academies, conservatories, dramatic schools, and for performances and concerts. Hundreds of thousands of workmen—carpenters, masons, painters, joiners, paperhangers, tailors, hairdressers, jewelers, molders, typesetters—spend their whole lives in hard labor to satisfy the demands of art, so that hardly any other department of human activity, except the military, consumes so much energy as this.

Not only is enormous labor spent on this activity, but in it, as in war, the very lives of men are sacrificed. Hundreds of thousands of people devote their lives from childhood to learning to twirl their legs rapidly (dancers), or to touch notes and strings very rapidly (musicians), or to draw with paint and represent what they see (artists), or to turn every phrase inside out and find a rhyme to every word. And these people, often very kind and clever, and capable of all sorts of useful labor, grow savage over their specialized and stupefying occupations, and become one-sided and self-complacent specialists, dull to all the serious phenomena of life and skillful only at rapidly twisting their legs, their tongues, or their fingers.

But even this stunting of human life is not the worst. I remember being once at the rehearsal of one of the most ordinary of the new operas which are produced at all the opera houses of Europe and America.

I arrived when the first act had already begun. To reach the auditorium I had to pass through the stage entrance. By dark entrances and passages I was led through the vaults of an enormous building, past immense machines for changing the scenery and for lighting, and there in the gloom and dust I saw workmen busily engaged. One of these men, pale, haggard, in a dirty blouse, with dirty, work-worn hands and cramped fingers, evidently tired and out of humor, went past me, angrily scolding another man. Ascending by a dark stair, I came out on the boards behind the scenes. Amid various poles and rings and scattered scenery, decorations, and curtains, stood and moved dozens, if not hundreds, of painted and dressed-up men, in costumes fitting tight to their thighs and calves, and also women, as usual, as nearly nude as might be. These were all singers, or members of the chorus, or ballet dancers, waiting their turns. My guide led me across the stage and, by means of a bridge of boards across the orchestra (in which perhaps a hundred musicians of all kinds, from kettledrum to flute and harp, were seated), to the dark pit-stalls.

On an elevation, between two lamps with reflectors, and in an armchair placed before a music stand, sat the director of the musical part, baton in hand, managing the orchestra and singers, and, in general, the production of the whole opera.

The performance had already begun, and on the stage a procession of Indians who had brought home a bride was being presented. Besides men and women in costume, two other men in ordinary clothes bustled and ran about on the stage; one was the director of the dramatic part, and the other, who stepped about in soft shoes and ran from place to place with 'significant form' is not an ordinary expression. There is reason for supposing that aestheticians have, in one sense, a special language adapted to the purposes of their own theories. Bell, for example, coined this phrase to establish his point that there is something which is very important to him about works of art. But he goes on to make it impossible to give an instance of even a purely imaginary thing which is both a work of art and lacks significant form.

Cézanne carried me off my feet before I ever noticed that his strongest characteristic was an insistence on the supremacy of significant form. When I noticed this, my admiration for Cézanne and some of his followers confirmed me in my aesthetic theories.[7]

Bell is impressed with the formal qualities of paintings. He says:

The pure mathematician rapt in his studies knows a state of mind which I take to be similar, if not identical . . . [with the aesthetic emotion aroused by significant form.][8]

Any painting, then, which someone might try to point out as an example of art which does not have significant form, would be denied to be a work of 'art for this very reason. No instance could possibly be produced of a work of art which did not have significant form, for anything which did not have significant form would not be counted as a work of art. 'Paddington Station' has not significant form; therefore, in spite of popular belief to the contrary, 'Paddington Station' is not a work of art. Likewise, since 'Paddington Station,' Bell judges, is not worthy of the title 'work of art,' it cannot have significant form. The upshot of the theory is that nothing can count as a work of art unless it has significant form. It begins to look as if 'Works of art have significant form' is like 'Squares have four sides.' 'Is a work of art' and 'has significant form' seem to mean the same, so that the latter does not say what anything must answer to in order to count as a work of art, except that it must be a work of art.

Certainly someone who wishes to deny that all works of art have significant form would not be able to produce any evidence to convince Bell. He might point to a Hogarth and say that it lacked significant form but was a work of art, but Bell would reply that either it has significant form or it is not a work of art. He might point to a Ben Nicholson and say that it had significant form but was not a work of art, or, for that matter, to a tree. But Bell is committed to the view that if something has significant form it is a work of art, and if something is a work of art, it has significant form. No exceptions are theoretically possible once his view is adopted. This is not the characteristic of an empirical view.

We can imagine water running uphill, but we cannot begin to imagine, according to Bell, a work of art which has no significant form. Adopting his view clearly amounts to deciding not to call anything which we do not also call 'significant form,' 'work of art.' We are reminded of the way in which we refuse to call anything 'square' which we do not also call 'four-sided.' It looks as if 'only those paintings, etc., are works of art which have significant form' is irrefutable, therefore non-empirical, and therefore in some sense a priori.

Of course, such sentences as 'Works of art have significant form' do not in ordinary language express a priori propositions. But then the expression

---

[7] Ibid., pp. 40–1.
[8] Ibid., p. 25.

So one is quite at a loss as to whom these things are done for. The man of culture is heartily sick of them, while to a real workingman they are utterly incomprehensible. If anyone can be pleased by these things (which is doubtful), it can only be some young footman or depraved artisan who has contracted the spirit of the upper classes but is not yet satiated with their amusement and wishes to show his breeding.

And all this nasty folly is prepared, not simply, nor with kindly merriment, but with anger and brutal cruelty.

It is said that it is all done for the sake of art, and that art is a very important thing. But is it true that art is so important that such sacrifices should be made for its sake? This question is especially urgent because art, for the sake of which the labor of millions, the lives of men, and, above all, love between man and man, are being sacrificed—this very art is becoming something more and more vague and uncertain to human perception.

Criticism, in which the lovers of art used to find support for their opinions, has latterly become so self-contradictory that, if we exclude from the domain of art all that to which the critics of various schools themselves deny the title, there is scarcely any art left.

The artists of various sects, like the theologians of the various sects, mutually exclude and destroy themselves. Listen to the artists of the schools of our times, and you will find, in all branches, each set of artists disowning others. In poetry the old Romanticists deny the Parnassiens and the Decadents; the Parnassiens disown the Romanticists and the Decadents; the Decadents disown all their predecessors and the Symbolists; the Symbolists disown all their predecessors and *les mages;* and *les mages* disown all, all their predecessors. Among novelists we have naturalists, psychologists, and "nature-ists," all rejecting each other. And it is the same in dramatic art, in painting, and in music. So art, which demands such tremendous labor sacrifices from the people, which stunts human lives and transgresses against human love, is not only *not* a thing clearly and firmly defined, but is understood in such contradictory ways by its own devotees that it is difficult to say what is meant by art, and especially what is good, useful art—art for the sake of which we might condone such sacrifices as are being offered at its shrine.

For the production of every ballet, circus, opera, operetta, exhibition, picture, concert, or printed book, the intense and unwilling labor of thousands of people is needed at what is often harmful and humiliating work. It were well if artists made all they require for themselves, but, as it is, they all need the help of workmen, not only to produce art, but also for their own usually luxurious maintenance. And, one way or other, they get it, either through payments from rich people or through subsidies given by government (in Russia, for instance, in grants of millions of rubles to theaters, conservatories, and academies). This money is collected from the people, some of whom have to sell their only cow to pay the tax and who never get those aesthetic pleasures which art gives.

It was all very well for a Greek or Roman artist, or even for a Russian artist of the first half of our century (when there were still slaves and it was considered right that there should be), with a quiet mind to make people serve him and his art; but in our day, when in all men there is at least some dim perception of the equal rights of all, it is impossible to constrain people to labor unwillingly for art without first deciding the question whether it is true that art is so good and so important an affair as to redeem this evil.

If not, we have the terrible probability to consider that while fearful sacrifices of the labor and lives of men, and of morality itself, are being made to art, that same art may be not only useless but even harmful.

And therefore it is necessary for a society in which works of art arise and are supported, to find out whether all that professes to be art is really art, whether (as is presupposed in our society) all that which is art is good, and whether it is important and worth those sacrifices which it necessitates. It is still more necessary for every conscientious artist to know this, that he may be sure that all he does has a valid meaning; that it is not merely an infatuation of the small circle of people among whom he lives which excites in him the false assurance that he is doing a good work; and that what he takes from others for the support of his often very luxurious life will be compensated for by those productions at which he works. And that is why answers to the above questions are especially important in our time.

What is this art which is considered so important and necessary for humanity that for its sake these sacrifices of labor, of human life, and even of goodness may be made?

"What is art? What a question! Art is architecture, sculpture, painting, music, and poetry in all its forms," usually replies the ordinary man, the are amateur, or even the artist himself, imagining the matter about which he is talking to be perfectly clear and uniformly understood by everybody. But in architecture, one inquires further, are there not simple buildings which are not objects of art, and buildings with artistic pretensions which are unsuccessful and ugly and therefore cannot be considered as works of art? Wherein lies the characteristic sign of a work of art?

It is the same in sculpture, in music, and in poetry. Art, in all its forms, is bounded on one side by the practically useful, and on the other by unsuccessful attempts at art. How is art to be marked off from each of these? The ordinary educated man of our circle, and even the artist who has not occupied himself especially with aesthetics, will not hesitate at this question either. He thinks the solution has been found long ago and is well known to everyone.

"Art is such activity as produces beauty," says such a man.

If art consists in that, then is a ballet or an operetta art? you inquire.

"Yes," says the ordinary man, though with some hesitation, "a good ballet or a graceful operetta is also art in so far as it manifests beauty."

But without even asking the ordinary man what differentiates the "good" ballet and the "graceful" operetta from their opposites (a question he would have much difficulty in answering), if you ask him whether the activity of costumers and hairdressers, who ornament the figures and faces of the women for the ballet and the operetta, is art, or the activity of Worth, the dressmaker, or of scent-makers and men cooks—then he will, in most cases, deny that their activity belongs to the sphere of art. But in this the ordinary man makes a mistake just because he is an ordinary man and not a specialist, and because he has not occupied himself with aesthetic questions. Had he looked into these matters, he would have seen in the great Renan's book, *Marc Aurele*, a dissertation showing that the tailor's work is art, and that those who do not see in the adornment of woman an affair of the highest art are very small-minded and dull. "C'est le grand art," says Renan. Moreover, he would have known that in many aesthetic systems—for instance, in the aesthetics of the learned Professor Kralik, *Weltschönheit, Versuch einer allgemeinen Aesthetik, von Richard Kralik,* and in *Les Problèmes de l'esthétique contemporaine* by Guyau— the arts of costume, of taste, and of touch are included.

. . .

To what do these definitions of beauty amount? Not reckoning the thoroughly inaccurate definitions of beauty which fail to cover the conception of art, and which suppose beauty to consist either in utility or in adjustment to a purpose, or in symmetry, or in order, or in proportion, or in smoothness, or in harmony of the parts, or in unity amid variety, or in various combinations of these—not reckoning these unsatisfactory attempts at objective definition, all the aesthetic definitions of beauty lead to two fundamental conceptions. The first is that beauty is something having an independent existence (existing in itself), that it is one of the manifestations of the absolutely Perfect, of the Idea, of the Spirit, of Will, or of God; the other is that beauty is a kind of pleasure we receive which does not have personal advantage for its object.

The first of these definitions was accepted by Fichte, Schelling, Hegel, Schopenhauer, and the philosophizing Frenchmen Cousin, Jouffroy, Ravaisson, and others, not to enumerate the second-rate aesthetic philosophers. And this same objective-mystical definition of beauty is held by a majority of the educated people of our day. It is a conception very widely spread, especially among the elder generation.

The second view, that beauty is a certain kind of pleasure we receive which does not have personal advantage for its aim, finds favor chiefly among the English aesthetic writers and is shared by the other part of our society, principally by the younger generation.

So there are (and it could not be otherwise) only two definitions of beauty: the one objective, mystical, merging this conception into that of the highest perfection, God—a fantastic definition, founded on nothing; the other, on the contrary, a very simple and intelligible subjective one, which considers beauty to be that which pleases (I do not add to the word "pleases" the words "without the aim of advantage," because "pleases" naturally presupposes the absence of the idea of profit).

On the one hand, beauty is viewed as something mystical and very elevated, but unfortunately at the same time very indefinite and, consequently, embracing philosophy, religion, and life itself (as in the theories of Schelling and Hegel and their German and French followers); or, on the other hand (as necessarily follows from the definition of Kant and his adherents), beauty is simply a certain kind of disinterested pleasure received by us. And this conception of beauty, although it seems very clear, is, unfortunately, again inexact, for it widens out on the other side; i.e., it includes the pleasure derived from drink, from food, from touching a delicate skin, etc., as is acknowledged by Guyau, Kralik, and others.

It is true that, following the development of the aesthetic doctrines on beauty, we may notice that, though at first (in the times when the foundations of the science of aesthetics were being laid) the metaphysical definition of beauty prevailed, yet the nearer we get to our own times, the more does an experimental definition (recently assuming a physiological form) come to the front, so that at last we even meet with such aestheticians as Véron and Sully who try to escape entirely from the conception of beauty. But such aestheticians have very little success, and with the majority of the public, as well as of artists and the learned, a conception of beauty is firmly held which agrees with the definitions contained in most of the aesthetic treatises, i.e., which regards beauty either as something mystical or metaphysical or as a special kind of enjoyment.

What, then, is this conception of beauty so stubbornly held to by people of our circle and day as furnishing a definition of art?

In the subjective aspect, we call beauty that which supplies us with a particular kind of pleasure.

In the objective aspect, we call beauty something absolutely perfect, and we acknowledge it to be so only because we receive, from the manifestation of this absolute perfection, a certain kind of pleasure; so this objective definition is nothing but the subjective conception differently expressed. In reality both conceptions of beauty amount to one and the same thing—namely, the reception by us of a certain kind of pleasure; i.e., we call "beauty" that which pleases us without evoking in us desire.

Such being the position of affairs, it would seem only natural that the science of art should decline to content itself with a definition of art based on beauty (i.e., on that which pleases), and seek a general definition which should apply to all artistic productions, and by reference to which we might decide whether a certain article belonged to the realm of art or not. But no such definition is supplied, as the reader may see from those summaries of the aesthetic theories which I have given, and as he may discover even more clearly from the original aesthetic works if he will be at the pains to read them. All attempts to define absolute beauty in itself—whether as an imitation of nature, or as suitability to its object, or as a correspondence of parts, or as symmetry, or as harmony, or as unity in variety, etc.—either define nothing at all or define only some traits of some artistic productions and are far from including all that everybody has always held, and still holds, to be art.

There is no objective definition of beauty. The existing definitions (both the metaphysical and the experimental) amount only to one and the same subjective definition, which (strange as it seems to say so) is that art is that which makes beauty manifest, and beauty is that which pleases (without exciting desire). Many aestheticians have felt the insufficiency and instability of such a definition, and, in order to give it a firm basis, have asked themselves why a thing pleases. And they have converted the discussion on beauty into a question concerning taste, as did Hutcheson, Voltaire, Diderot, and others. But all attempts to define what taste is must lead to nothing, as the reader may see both from the history of aesthetics and experimentally. There is and can be no explanation of why one thing pleases one man and displeases another, or vice versa. So that the whole existing science of aesthetics fails to do what we might expect from it, being a mental activity calling itself a science; namely, it does not define the qualities and laws of art or of the beautiful (if that be the content of art), or the nature of taste (if taste decides the question of art and its merit), and then, on the basis of such definitions, acknowledge as art those productions which correspond to these laws and reject those which do not come under them. But this science of aesthetics consists in first acknowledging a certain set of productions to be art (because they please us), and then framing such a theory of art that all those productions which please a certain circle of people should fit into it. There exists an art canon according to which certain productions favored by our circle are acknowledged as being art—Phidias, Sophocles, Homer, Titian, Raphael, Bach, Beethoven, Dante, Shakespeare, Goethe, and others—and the aesthetic laws must be such as to embrace all these productions. In aesthetic literature you will incessantly meet with opinions on the merit and importance of art, founded not on any certain laws by which this or that is held to be good or bad, but merely on the consideration whether this art tallies with the art canon we have drawn up.

The other day I was reading a far from ill-written book by Folgeldt. Discussing the demand for morality in works of art, the author plainly says that we must not demand morality in art. And in proof of this he advances the fact that if we admit such a demand, Shakespeare's *Romeo and Juliet* and Goethe's *Wilhelm Meister* would not fit into the definition of good art; but since both these books are included in our canon of art, he concludes that the demand is unjust. And therefore it is necessary to find a definition of art which shall fit the works; and instead of a demand for morality, Folgeldt postulates as the basis of art a demand for the important (*das Bedeutungsvolle*).

All the existing aesthetic standards are built on this plan. Instead of giving a definition of true art and then deciding what is and what is not good art by judging whether a work conforms or does not conform to the definition, a certain class of works which for some reason please a certain circle of people is accepted as being art, and a definition of art is then devised to cover all these productions. I recently came upon a remarkable instance of this method in a very good German work, *The History of Art in the Nineteenth Century*, by Muther. Describing the pre-Raphaelites, the Decadents and the Symbolists (who are already included in the canon of art), he not only does not venture to blame their tendency, but earnestly endeavors to widen his standard so that it may include them all, they appearing to him to represent a legitimate reaction from the excesses of realism. No matter what insanities appear in art, when once they find acceptance among the upper classes of our society a theory is quickly invented to explain and sanction them, just as if there had never been periods in history when certain special circles of people recognized and approved false, deformed, and insensate art which subsequently left no trace and has been utterly forgotten. And to what lengths the insanity and deformity of art may go, especially when, as in our days, it knows that it is considered infallible, may be seen by what is being done in the art of our circle today.

So the theory of art founded on beauty, expounded by aesthetics, and in dim outline professed by the public, is nothing but the setting up as good of that which has pleased and pleases us, i.e., pleases a certain class of people.

In order to define any human activity it is necessary to understand its sense and importance. And in order to do that it is primarily necessary to examine that activity in itself, in its dependence on its causes and in connection with its effects, and not merely in relation to the pleasure we can get from it.

If we say that the aim of any activity is merely our pleasure, and define it solely by that pleasure, our definition will evidently be a false one. But this is precisely what has occurred in the efforts to define art. Now, if we consider the food question it will not occur to anyone to affirm that the importance of food consists in the pleasure we receive when eating it. Everyone understands that the satisfaction of our taste cannot serve as a basis for our definition of the merits of food, and that we have therefore no right to presuppose that the dinners with cayenne pepper, Limburg cheese, alcohol, etc., to which we are accustomed and which please us, form the very best human food.

And in the same way, beauty, or that which pleases us, can in no sense serve as the basis for the definition of art; nor can a series of objects which afford us pleasure serve as the model of what art should be.

To see the aim and purpose of art in the pleasure we get from it is like assuming (as is done by people of the lowest moral development, e.g., by savages) that the purpose and aim of food is the pleasure derived when consuming it.

Just as people who conceive the aim and purpose of food to be pleasure cannot recognize the real meaning of eating, so people who consider the aim of art to be pleasure cannot realize its true meaning and purpose because they attribute to an activity the meaning of which lies in its connection with other phenomena of life, the false and exceptional aim of pleasure. People come to understand that the meaning of eating lies in the nourishment of the body only when they cease to consider that the object of that activity is pleasure. And it is the same with regard to art. People will come to understand the meaning of art only when they cease to consider that the aim of that activity is beauty, i.e., pleasure. The acknowledgment of beauty (i.e., of a certain kind of pleasure received from art) as being the aim of art not only fails to assist us in finding a definition of what art is, but, on the contrary, by transferring the question into a region quite foreign to art (into metaphysical, psychological, physio-logical, and even historical discussions as to why such a production pleases one person, and such another displeases or pleases someone else), it ren-ders such definition impossible. And since discussions as to why one man likes pears and another prefers meat do not help toward finding a defini-tion of what is essential in nourishment, so the solution of questions of taste in art (to which the discussions on art involuntarily come) not only does not help to make clear in what this particular human activity which we call art really consists, but renders such elucidation quite impossible until we rid ourselves of a conception which justifies every kind of art at the cost of confusing the whole matter.

To the question, what is this art to which is offered up the labor of millions, the very lives of men, and even morality itself? we have extracted replies from the existing aesthetics, which all amount to this: that the aim of art is beauty, that beauty is recognized by the enjoyment it gives, and that artistic enjoyment is a good and important thing because it *is* enjoyment. In a word, enjoyment is good because it is enjoyment. Thus what is considered the definition of art is no definition at all, but only a shuffle to justify existing art. Therefore, however strange it may seem to say so, in spite of the mountains of books written about art no exact definition of art has been constructed. And the reason for this is that the conception of art has been based on the conception of beauty.

What is art—if we put aside the conception of beauty, which confuses the whole matter? The latest and most comprehensible definitions of art, apart from the conception of beauty, are the following: (1) Art is an activity arising even in the animal kingdom, *a*, springing from sexual desire and the propensity to play (Schiller, Darwin, Spencer), and *b*, accom-panied by a pleasurable excitement of the nervous system (Grant Allen). This is the physiological-evolutionary definition. (2) Art is the external manifestation by means of lines, colors, movements, sounds, or words, of emotions felt by man (Véron). This is the experimental definition. Ac-cording to the very latest definition, (3) Art is "the production of some permanent object or passing action, which is fitted, not only to supply an active enjoyment to the producer, but to convey a pleasurable impression to a number of spectators or listeners, quite apart from any personal ad-vantage to be derived from it" (Sully).

Notwithstanding the superiority of these definitions to the metaphysical definitions which depended on the conception of beauty, they are yet far from exact. The first, the physiological-evolutionary definition (1*a*), is inexact because, instead of speaking about the artistic activity itself, which is the real matter in hand, it treats of the derivation of art. The modification of it (1*b*), based on the physiological effects on the human organism, is inexact because within the limits of such definition many other human activities can be included, as has occurred in the neo-aesthetic theories, which reckon as art the preparation of handsome clothes, pleasant scents, and even victuals.

The experimental definition (2), which makes art consist in the expression of emotions, is inexact because a man may express his emotions by means of lines, colors, sounds, or words, and yet may not act on others by such expression, and then the manifestation of his emotions is not art.

The third definition (that of Sully) is inexact because in the production of objects or actions affording pleasure to the producer and a pleasant emotion to the spectators or hearers, apart from personal advantage, may be included the showing of conjuring tricks or gymnastic exercises and other activities which are not art. And further, many things, the production of which does not afford pleasure to the producer and the sensation received from which is unpleasant, such as gloomy, heartrending scenes in a poetic description or a play, may nevertheless be undoubted works of art.

The inaccuracy of all these definitions arises from the fact that in them all (as also in the metaphysical definitions) the object considered is the pleasure art may give, and not the purpose it may serve in the life of man and of humanity.

In order correctly to define art, it is necessary, first of all, to cease to consider it as a means to pleasure and to consider it as one of the conditions of human life. Viewing it in this way we cannot fail to observe that art is one of the means of intercourse between man and man.

Every work of art causes the receiver to enter into a certain kind of relationship both with him who produced, or is producing, the art, and with all those who, simultaneously, previously, or subsequently, receive the same artistic impression.

Speech, transmitting the thoughts and experiences of men, serves as a means of union among them, and art acts in a similar manner. The peculiarity of this latter means of intercourse, distinguishing if from intercourse by means of words, consists in this, that whereas by words a man transmits his thoughts to another, by means of art he transmits his feelings.

The activity of art is based on the fact that a man, receiving through his sense of hearing or sight another man's expression of feeling, is capable of experiencing the emotion which moved the man who expressed it. To take the simplest example: one man laughs, and another who hears becomes merry; or a man weeps, and another who hears feels sorrow. A man is excited or irritated, and another man seeing him comes to a similar state of mind. By his movements or by the sounds of his voice, a man expresses courage and determination or sadness and calmness, and this state of mind passes on to others. A man suffers, expressing his sufferings by groans and spasms, and this suffering transmits itself to other people; a man expresses his feeling of admiration, devotion, fear, respect, or love to certain objects, persons, or phenomena, and others are infected by the same feelings of admiration, devotion, fear, respect, or love to the same objects, persons, and phenomena.

And it is upon this capacity of man to receive another man's expression of feeling and experience those feelings himself, that the activity of art is based.

If a man infects another or others directly, immediately, by his appearance or by the sounds he gives vent to at the very time he experiences the feeling; if he causes another man to yawn when he himself cannot help yawning, or to laugh or cry when he himself is obliged to laugh or cry, or to suffer when he himself is suffering—that does not amount to art.

Art begins when one person, with the object of joining another or others to himself in one and the same feeling, expresses that feeling by certain external indications. To take the simplest example: a boy, having experienced, let us say, fear on encountering a wolf, relates that encounter; and, in order to evoke in others the feeling he has experienced, describes himself, his condition before the encounter, the surroundings, the wood, his own lightheartedness, and then the wolf's appearance, its movements, the distance between himself and the wolf, etc. All this, if only the boy, when telling the story, again experiences the feelings he had lived through and infects the hearers and compels them to feel what the narrator had experienced, is art. If even the boy had not seen a wolf but had frequently been afraid of one, and if, wishing to evoke in others the fear he had felt, he invented an encounter with a wolf and recounted it so as to make his hearers share the feelings he experienced when he feared the wolf, that also would be art. And just in the same way it is art if a man, having experienced either the fear of suffering or the attraction of enjoyment (whether in reality or in imagination), expresses these feelings on canvas or in marble so that others are infected by them. And it is also art if a man feels or imagines to himself feelings of delight, gladness, sorrow, despair, courage, or despondency and the transition from one to another of these feelings, and expresses these feelings by sounds so that the hearers are infected by them and experience them as they were experienced by the composer.

The feelings with which the artist infects others may be most various— very strong or very weak, very important or very insignificant, very bad or very good: feelings of love for one's own country, self-devotion and submission to fate or to God expressed in a drama, raptures of lovers described in a novel, feelings of voluptuousness expressed in a picture, courage expressed in a triumphal march, merriment evoked by a dance, humor evoked by a funny story, the feeling of quietness transmitted by an evening landscape or by a lullaby, or the feeling of admiration evoked by a beautiful arabesque—it is all art.

If only the spectators or auditors are infected by the feelings which the author has felt, it is art.

To evoke in oneself a feeling one has once experienced, and having evoked it in oneself, then, by means of movements, lines, colors, sounds, or forms expressed in words, so to transmit that feeling that others may experience the same feeling—this is the activity of art.

Art is a human activity consisting in this, that one man consciously, by means of certain external signs, hands on to others feelings he has lived through, and that other people are infected by these feelings and also experience them.

Art is not, as the metaphysicians say, the manifestation of some mysterious Idea of beauty or God; it is not, as the aesthetical physiologists say, a game in which man lets off his excess of stored-up energy; it is not the expression of man's emotions by external signs; it is not the production of pleasing objects; and, above all, it is not pleasure; but it is a means of union among men, joining them together in the same feelings, and indispensable for the life and progress toward well-being of individuals and of humanity.

As, thanks to man's capacity to express thoughts by words, every man may know all that has been done for him in the realms of thought by all humanity before his day, and can in the present, thanks to this capacity to understand the thoughts of others, become a sharer in their activity and can himself hand on to his contemporaries and descendants the thoughts he has assimilated from others, as well as those which have arisen within himself; so, thanks to man's capacity to be infected with the feelings of others by means of art, all that is being lived through by his contemporaries is accessible to him, as well as the feelings experienced by men thousands of years ago, and he has also the possibility of transmitting his own feelings to others.

If people lacked this capacity to receive the thoughts conceived by the men who preceded them and to pass on to others their own thoughts, men would be like wild beasts, or like Kaspar Hauser.[1]

And if men lacked this other capacity of being infected by art, people might be almost more savage still, and, above all, more separated from, and more hostile to, one another.

And therefore the activity of art is a most important one, as important as the activity of speech itself and as generally diffused.

We are accustomed to understand art to be only what we hear and see in theaters, concerts, and exhibitions, together with buildings, statues, poems, novels. . . . But all this is but the smallest part of the art by which we communicate with each other in life. All human life is filled with works of art of every kind—from cradlesong, jest, mimicry, the ornamentation of houses, dress, and utensils, up to church services, buildings, monuments, and triumphal processions. It is all artistic activity. So that by art, in the limited sense of the word, we do not mean all human activity

---

[1] "The foundling of Nuremberg," found in the market place of that town on May 26, 1828, apparently some sixteen years old. He spoke little and was almost totally ignorant even of common objects. He subsequently explained that he had been brought up in confinement underground and visited by only one man, whom he seldom saw.—Tr.

transmitting feelings, but only that part which we for some reason select from it and to which we attach special importance.

This special importance has always been given by all men to that part of this activity which transmits feelings flowing from their religious perception, and this small part of art they have specifically called art, attaching to it the full meaning of the word.

That was how men of old—Socrates, Plato, and Aristotle—looked on art. Thus did the Hebrew prophets and the ancient Christians regard art; thus it was, and still is, understood by the Mohammedans, and thus it still is understood by religious folk among our own peasantry.

Some teachers of mankind—as Plato in his *Republic* and people such as the primitive Christians, the strict Mohammedans, and the Buddhists—have gone so far as to repudiate all art.

People viewing art in this way (in contradiction to the prevalent view of today which regards any art as good if only it affords pleasure) considered, and consider, that art (as contrasted with speech, which need not be listened to) is so highly dangerous in its power to infect people against their wills that mankind will lose far less by banishing all art than by tolerating each and every art.

Evidently such people were wrong in repudiating all art, for they denied that which cannot be denied—one of the indispensable means of communication, without which mankind could not exist. But not less wrong are the people of civilized European society of our class and day in favoring any art if it but serves beauty, i.e., gives people pleasure.

Formerly people feared lest among the works of art there might chance to be some causing corruption, and they prohibited art altogether. Now they only fear lest they should be deprived of any enjoyment art can afford, and patronize any art. And I think the last error is much grosser than the first and that its consequences are far more harmful.

But how could it happen that that very art, which in ancient times was merely tolerated (if tolerated at all), should have come in our times to be invariably considered a good thing if only it affords pleasure?

It has resulted from the following causes. The estimation of the value of art (i.e., of the feelings it transmits) depends on men's perception of the meaning of life, depends on what they consider to be the good and the evil of life. And what is good and what is evil is defined by what are termed religions.

Humanity unceasingly moves forward from a lower, more partial and obscure understanding of life to one more general and more lucid. And in this, as in every movement, there are leaders—those who have understood the meaning of life more clearly than others—and of these advanced men there is always one who has in his words and by his life expressed this meaning more clearly, accessibly, and strongly than others. This man's expression of the meaning of life, together with those superstitions, traditions, and ceremonies which usually form themselves round the memory of such a man, is what is called a religion. Religions are the exponents of the highest comprehension of life accessible to the best and foremost men at a given time in a given society—a comprehension toward which, inevitably and irresistibly, all the rest of that society must advance. And therefore only religions have always served, and still serve, as bases for the valuation of human sentiments. If feelings bring men nearer the ideal their religion indicates, if they are in harmony with it and do not contradict it, they are good; if they estrange men from it and oppose it, they are bad.

If the religion places the meaning of life in worshiping one God and fulfilling what is regarded as His will, as was the case among the Jews, then the feelings flowing from love to that God and to His law successfully transmitted through the art of poetry by the prophets, by the psalms, or by the epic of the book of Genesis, is good, high art. All opposing that, as for instance the transmission of feelings of devotion to strange gods or of feelings incompatible with the law of God, would be considered bad art. Or if, as was the case among the Greeks, the religion places the meaning of life in earthly happiness, in beauty and in strength, then art successfully transmitting the joy and energy of life would be considered good art, but art which transmitted feelings of effeminacy or despondency would be bad art. If the meaning of life is seen in the well-being of one's nation or in honoring one's ancestors and continuing the mode of life led by them, as was the case among the Romans and the Chinese respectively, then art transmitting feelings of joy at sacrificing one's personal well-being for the common weal, or at exalting one's ancestors and maintaining their traditions, would be considered good art, but art expressing feelings contrary to this would be regarded as bad. If the meaning of life is seen in freeing oneself from the yoke of animalism, as is the case among the Buddhists, then art successfully transmitting feelings that elevate the soul and humble the flesh will be good art, and all that transmits feelings strengthening the bodily passions will be bad art.

In every age and in every human society there exists a religious sense, common to that whole society, of what is good and what is bad, and it is this religious conception that decides the value of the feelings transmitted by art. And therefore, among all nations art which transmitted feelings considered to be good by this general religious sense was recognized as being good and was encouraged, but art which transmitted feelings considered to be bad by this general religious conception was recognized as being bad, and was rejected. All the rest of the immense field of art by means of which people communicate one with another was not esteemed at all, and was only noticed when it ran counter to the religious conception of its age, and then merely to be repudiated. Thus it was among all nations—Greeks, Jews, Indians, Egyptians, and Chinese—and so it was when Christianity appeared.

Art, in our society, has been so perverted that not only has bad art come to be considered good, but even the very perception of what art really is has been lost. In order to be able to speak about the art of our society, it is, therefore, first of all necessary to distinguish art from counterfeit art.

There is one indubitable indication distinguishing real art from its counterfeit, namely, the infectiousness of art. If a man, without exercising effort and without altering his standpoint on reading, hearing, or seeing another man's work, experiences a mental condition which unites him with that man and with other people who also partake of that work of art, then the object evoking that condition is a work of art. And however poetical, realistic, effectful, or interesting a work may be, it is not a work of art if it does not evoke that feeling (quite distinct from all other feelings) of joy and of spiritual union with another (the author) and with others (those who are also infected by it).

It is true that this indication is an *internal* one, and that there are people who have forgotten what the action of real art is, who expect something else from art (in our society the great majority are in this state), and that therefore such people may mistake for this aesthetic feeling the feeling of diversion and a certain excitement which they receive from counterfeits of art. But though it is impossible to undeceive these people, just as it is impossible to convince a man suffering from "Daltonism"[2] that green is not red, yet, for all that, this indication remains perfectly definite to those whose feeling for art is neither perverted nor atrophied, and it clearly distinguishes the feeling produced by art from all other feelings.

The chief peculiarity of this feeling is that the receiver of a true artistic impression is so united to the artist that he feels as if the work were his own and not someone else's—as if what it expresses were just what he had long been wishing to express. A real work of art destroys, in the consciousness of the receiver, the separation between himself and the artist—not that alone, but also between himself and all whose minds receive this work of art. In this freeing of our personality from its separation and isolation, in this uniting of it with others, lies the chief characteristic and the great attractive force of art.

If a man is infected by the author's condition of soul, if he feels this emotion and this union with others, then the object which has effected this is art; but if there be no such infection, if there be not this union with the author and with others who are moved by the same work—then it is not art. And not only is infection a sure sign of art, but the degree of infectiousness is also the sole measure of excellence in art.

The stronger the infection, the better is the art as art, speaking now apart from its subject matter, i.e., not considering the quality of the feelings it transmits.

And the degree of the infectiousness of art depends on three conditions:

1. On the greater or lesser individuality of the feeling transmitted;
2. on the greater or lesser clearness with which the feeling is transmitted;
3. on the sincerity of the artist, i.e., on the greater or lesser force with which the artist himself feels the emotion he transmits.

[2] [A kind of color blindness discovered by John Dalton.—Ed.]

The more individual the feeling transmitted the more strongly does it act on the receiver; the more individual the state of soul into which he is transferred, the more pleasure does the receiver obtain, and therefore the more readily and strongly does he join in it.

The clearness of expression assists infection because the receiver, who mingles in consciousness with the author, is the better satisfied the more clearly the feeling is transmitted, which, as it seems to him, he has long known and felt, and for which he has only now found expression.

But most of all is the degree of infectiousness of art increased by the degree of sincerity in the artist. As soon as the spectator, hearer, or reader feels that the artist is infected by his own production, and writes, sings, or plays for himself, and not merely to act on others, this mental condition of the artist infects the receiver; and contrariwise, as soon as the spectator, reader, or hearer feels that the author is not writing, singing, or playing for his own satisfaction—does not himself feel what he wishes to express—but is doing it for him, the receiver, a resistance immediately springs up, and the most individual and the newest feelings and the cleverest technique not only fail to produce any infection but actually repel.

I have mentioned three conditions of contagiousness in art, but they may be all summed up into one, the last, sincerity, i.e., that the artist should be impelled by an inner need to express his feeling. That condition includes the first; for if the artist is sincere he will express the feeling as he experienced it. And as each man is different from everyone else, his feeling will be individual for everyone else; and the more individual it is— the more the artist has drawn it from the depths of his nature—the more sympathetic and sincere will it be. And this same sincerity will impel the artist to find a clear expression of the feeling which he wishes to transmit.

Therefore this third condition—sincerity—is the most important of the three. It is always complied with in peasant art, and this explains why such art always acts so powerfully; but it is a condition almost entirely absent from our upper-class art, which is continually produced by artists actuated by personal aims of covetousness or vanity.

Such are the three conditions which divide art from its counterfeits, and which also decide the quality of every work of art apart from its subject matter.

The absence of any one of these conditions excludes a work from the category of art and relegates it to that of art's counterfeits. If the work does not transmit the artist's peculiarity of feeling and is therefore not individual, if it is unintelligibly expressed, or if it has not proceeded from the author's inner need for expression—it is not a work of art. If all these conditions are present, even in the smallest degree, then the work, even if a weak one, is yet a work of art.

The presence in various degrees of these three conditions—individuality, clearness, and sincerity—decides the merit of a work of art as art, apart from subject matter. All works of art take rank of merit according to the degree in which they fulfil the first, the second, and the third of these conditions. In one the individuality of the feeling transmitted may predominate; in another, clearness of expression; in a third, sincerity; while a fourth may have sincerity and individuality but be deficient in clearness; a fifth, individuality and clearness but less sincerity; and so forth, in all possible degrees and combinations.

Thus is art divided from that which is not art, and thus is the quality of art as art decided, independently of its subject matter, i.e., apart from whether the feelings it transmits are good or bad.

But how are we to define good and bad art with reference to its subject matter?

How are we to decide what is good or bad in the subject matter of art?

Art, like speech, is a means of communication, and therefore of progress, i.e., of the movement of humanity forward toward perfection. Speech renders accessible to men of the latest generations all the knowledge discovered by the experience and reflection, both of preceding generations and of the best and foremost men of their own times; art renders accessible to men of the latest generations all the feelings experienced by their predecessors, and those also which are being felt by their best and foremost contemporaries. And as the evolution of knowledge proceeds by truer and more necessary knowledge, dislodging and replacing what is mistaken and unnecessary, so the evolution of feeling proceeds through art—feelings less kind and less needful for the well-being of mankind are replaced by others kinder and more needful for that end. That is the purpose of art. And, speaking now of its subject matter, the more art fulfills that purpose the better the art, and the less it fulfils it, the worse the art.

And the appraisement of feelings (i.e., the acknowledgment of these or those feelings as being more or less good, more or less necessary for the well-being of mankind) is made by the religious perception of the age.

In every period of history, and in every human society, there exists an understanding of the meaning of life which represents the highest level to which men of that society have attained, an understanding defining the highest good at which that society aims. And this understanding is the religious perception of the given time and society. And this religious perception is always clearly expressed by some advanced men, and more or less vividly perceived by all the members of the society. Such a religious perception and its corresponding expression exists always in every society. If it appears to us that in our society there is no religious perception, this is not because there really is none, but only because we do not want to see it. And we often wish not to see it because it exposes the fact that our life is inconsistent with that religious perception.

Religious perception in a society is like the direction of a flowing river. If the river flows at all, it must have a direction. If a society lives, there must be a religious perception indicating the direction in which, more or less consciously, all its members tend.

And so there always has been, and there is, a religious perception in every society. And it is by the standard of this religious perception that the feelings transmitted by art have always been estimated. Only on the basis of this religious perception of their age have men always chosen from the endlessly varied spheres of art that art which transmitted feelings making religious perception operative in actual life. And such art has always been highly valued and encouraged, while art transmitting feelings already outlived, flowing from the antiquated religious perceptions of a former age, has always been condemned and despised. All the rest of art, transmitting those most diverse feelings by means of which people commune together, was not condemned, and was tolerated, if only it did not transmit feelings contrary to religious perception. Thus, for instance, among the Greeks art transmitting the feeling of beauty, strength, and courage (Hesiod, Homer, Phidias) was chosen, approved, and encouraged, while art transmitting feelings of rude sensuality, despondency, and effeminacy was condemned and despised. Among the Jews, art transmitting feelings of devotion and submission to the God of the Hebrews and to His will (the epic of Genesis, the prophets, the Psalms) was chosen and encouraged, while art transmitting feelings of idolatry (the golden calf) was condemned and despised. All the rest of art—stories, songs, dances, ornamentation of houses, of utensils, and of clothes—which was not contrary to religious perception was neither distinguished nor discussed. Thus, in regard to its subject matter, has art been appraised always and everywhere, and thus it should be appraised; for this attitude toward art proceeds from the fundamental characteristics of human nature, and those characteristics do not change.

I know that according to an opinion current in our times religion is a superstition which humanity has outgrown, and that it is therefore assumed that no such thing exists as a religious perception, common to us all, by which art, in our time, can be evaluated. I know that this is the opinion current in the pseudo-cultured circles of today. People who do not acknowledge Christianity in its true meaning because it undermines all their social privileges, and who, therefore, invent all kinds of philosophic and aesthetic theories to hide from themselves the meaninglessness and wrongness of their lives, cannot think otherwise. These people intentionally, or sometimes unintentionally, confusing the conception of a religious cult with the conception of religious perception think that by denying the cult they get rid of religious perception. But even the very attacks on religion and the attempts to establish a life-conception contrary to the religious perception of our times most clearly demonstrate the existence of a religious perception condemning the lives that are not in harmony with it.

If humanity progresses, i.e., moves forward, there must inevitably be a guide to the direction of that movement. And religions have always furnished that guide. All history shows that the progress of humanity is accomplished not otherwise than under the guidance of religion. But if the race cannot progress without the guidance of religion—and progress is always going on, and consequently also in our own times—then there must be a religion of our times. So that, whether it pleases or displeases the so-called cultured people of today, they must admit the existence of religion—not of a religious cult, Catholic, Protestant, or another, but of a religious perception—which, even in our times, is the guide always present where there is any progress. And if a religious perception exists among us, then our art should be appraised on the basis of that religious perception; and, as has always and everywhere been the case, art transmitting feelings flowing from the religious perception of our time should be chosen from all the indifferent art, should be acknowledged, highly esteemed, and encouraged, while art running counter to that perception should be condemned and despised, and all the remaining indifferent art should neither be distinguished nor encouraged.

The religious perception of our time, in its widest and most practical application, is the consciousness that our well-being, both material and spiritual, individual and collective, temporal and eternal, lies in the growth of brotherhood among all men—in their loving harmony with one another. This perception is not only expressed by Christ and all the best men of past ages, it is not only repeated in the most varied forms and from most diverse sides by the best men of our own times, but it already serves as a clue to all the complex labor of humanity, consisting as this labor does, on the one hand, in the destruction of physical and moral obstacles to the union of men, and, on the other hand, in establishing the principles common to all men which can and should unite them into one universal brotherhood. And it is on the basis of this perception that we should appraise all the phenomena of our life, and, among the rest, our art also; choosing from all its realms whatever transmits feelings flowing from this religious perception, highly prizing and encouraging such art, rejecting whatever is contrary to this perception, and not attributing to the rest of art an importance not properly pertaining to it.

The chief mistake made by people of the upper classes of the time of the so-called Renaissance—a mistake which we still perpetuate—was not that they ceased to value and to attach importance to religious art (people of that period could not attach importance to it, because, like our own upper classes, they could not believe in what the majority considered to be religion), but their mistake was that they set up in place of religious art, which was lacking, an insignificant art which aimed only at giving pleasure, i.e., they began to choose, to value, and to encourage in place of religious art something which in any case did not deserve such esteem and encouragement.

One of the Fathers of the Church said that the great evil is not that men do not know God, but that they have set up, instead of God, that which is not God. So also with art. The great misfortune of the people of the upper classes of our time is not so much that they are without a religious art as such; instead of a supreme religious art, chosen from all the rest as being specially important and valuable, they have chosen a most insignificant and, usually, harmful art which aims at pleasing certain people and which, therefore, if only by its exclusive nature, stands in contradiction to that Christian principle of universal union which forms the religious perception of our time. Instead of religious art, an empty and often vicious art is set up, and this hides from men's notice the need of that true religious art which should be present in order to improve life.

It is true that art which satisfies the demands of the religious perception of our time is quite unlike former art, but, notwithstanding this dissimilarity, to a man who does not intentionally hide the truth from himself, it is very clear and definite what does form the religious art of our age. In former times, when the highest religious perception united only some people (who, even if they formed a large society, were yet but one society surrounded by others—Jews, or Athenian, or Roman citizens), the feelings transmitted by the art of that time flowed from a desire for the might, greatness, glory, and prosperity of that society, and the heroes of art might be people who contributed to that prosperity by strength, by craft, by fraud, or by cruelty (Ulysses, Jacob, David, Samson, Hercules, and all the heroes). But the religious perception of our times does not select any one society of men; on the contrary, it demands the union of all—absolutely of all people without exception—and above every other virtue it sets brotherly love to all men. And therefore, the feelings transmitted by the art of our time not only cannot coincide with the feelings transmitted by former art, but must run counter to them.

Christian, truly Christian, art has been so long in establishing itself, and has not yet established itself, just because the Christian religious perception was not one of those small steps by which humanity advances regularly, but was an enormous revolution, which, if it has not already altered, must inevitably alter the entire life-conception of mankind, and, consequently, the whole internal organization of their life. It is true that the life of humanity, like that of an individual, moves regularly; but in that regular movement come, as it were, turning points which sharply divide the preceding from the subsequent life. Christianity was such a turning point; such, at least, it must appear to us who live by the Christian perception of life. Christian perception gave another, a new, direction to all human feelings, and therefore completely altered both the contents and the significance of art. The Greeks could make use of Persian art and the Romans could use Greek art, or, similarly, the Jews could use Egyptian art—the fundamental ideas were one and the same. Now the ideal was the greatness and prosperity of the Persians, now the greatness and prosperity of the Greeks, now that of the Romans. The same art was transferred into other conditions and served new nations. But the Christian ideal changed and reversed everything, so that, as the gospel puts it, "That which was exalted among men has become an abomination in the sight of God." The ideal is no longer the greatness of Pharaoh or of a Roman emperor, not the beauty of a Greek nor the wealth of Phoenicia, but humility, purity, compassion, love. The hero is no longer Dives,[3] but Lazarus the beggar; not Mary Magdalene in the day of her beauty, but in the day of her repentance; not those who acquire wealth, but those who

---

[3] [Reference is to the parable of the rich man and Lazarus (Luke 16:19–31). Although the parable does not name him, the rich man is commonly called "Dives," which is Latin for "rich man."— ED.]

have abandoned it; not those who dwell in palaces, but those who dwell in catacombs and huts; not those who rule over others, but those who acknowledge no authority but God's. And the greatest work of art is no longer a cathedral of victory[4] with statues of conquerors, but the representation of a human soul so transformed by love that a man who is tormented and murdered yet pities and loves his persecutors.

And the change is so great that men of the Christian world find it difficult to resist the inertia of the heathen art to which they have been accustomed all their lives. The subject matter of Christian religious art is so new to them, so unlike the subject matter of former art, that it seems to them as though Christian art were a denial of art, and they cling desperately to the old art. But this old art, having no longer in our day any source in religious perception, has lost its meaning and we shall have to abandon it whether we wish to or not.

The essence of the Christian perception consists in the recognition by every man of his sonship to God and of the consequent union of men with God and with one another, as is said in the gospel (John xvii. 21[5]). Therefore the subject matter of Christian art is such feeling as can unite men with God and with one another.

The expression *unite men with God and with one another* may seem obscure to people accustomed to the misuse of these words which is so customary, but the words have a perfectly clear meaning, nevertheless. They indicate that the Christian union of man (in contradiction to the partial, exclusive union of only some men) is that which unites all without exception.

Art, all art, has this characteristic, that it unites people. Every art causes those to whom the artist's feeling is transmitted to unite in soul with the artist, and also with all who receive the same impression. But non-Christian art, while uniting some people together, makes that very union a cause of separation between these united people and others; so that union of this kind is often a source, not only of division, but even of enmity toward others. Such is all patriotic art, with its anthems, poems, and monuments; such is all Church art, i.e., the art of certain cults, with their images, statues, processions, and other local ceremonies. Such art is belated and non-Christian art, uniting the people of one cult only to separate them yet more sharply from the members of other cults, and even to place them in relations of hostility to each other. Christian art is only such as tends to unite all without exception, either by evoking in them the perception that each man and all men stand in like relation toward God and toward their neighbor, or by evoking in them identical feelings which may even be the very simplest, provided only that they are not repugnant to Christianity and are natural to everyone without exception.

Good Christian art of our time may be unintelligible to people because

[4] There is in Moscow a magnificent "Cathedral of our Saviour," erected to commemorate the defeat of the French in the war of 1812.—TR.
[5] "That they all may be one; as thou, Father, art in me, and I in thee, that they also may be one in us."

of imperfections in its form or because men are inattentive to it, but it must be such that all men can experience the feelings it transmits. It must be the art, not of some one group of people, nor of one class, nor of one nationality, nor of one religious cult; that is, it must not transmit feelings which are accessible only to a man educated in a certain way, or only to an aristocrat, or a merchant, or only to a Russian, or a native of Japan, or a Roman Catholic, or a Buddhist, etc., but it must transmit feelings accessible to everyone. Only art of this kind can be acknowledged in our time to be good art, worthy of being chosen out from all the rest of art and encouraged.

Christian art, i.e., the art of our time, should be catholic in the original meaning of the word, i.e., universal, and therefore it should unite all men. And only two kinds of feeling do unite all men: first, feelings flowing from the perception of our sonship to God and of the brotherhood of man; and next, the simple feelings of common life, accessible to every one without exception—such as the feeling of merriment, of pity, of cheerfulness, of tranquillity, etc. Only these two kinds of feelings can now supply material for art good in its subject matter.

And the action of these two kinds of art, apparently so dissimilar, is one and the same. The feelings flowing from perception of our sonship to God and of the brotherhood of man—such as a feeling of sureness in truth, devotion to the will of God, self-sacrifice, respect for and love of man— evoked by Christian religious perception; and the simplest feelings—such as a softened or a merry mood caused by a song or an amusing jest intelligible to everyone, or by a touching story, or a drawing, or a little doll: both alike produce one and the same effect, the loving union of man with man. Sometimes people who are together are, if not hostile to one another, at least estranged in mood and feeling till perchance a story, a performance, a picture, or even a building, but most often of all music, unites them all as by an electric flash, and in place of their former isolation or even enmity they are all conscious of union and mutual love. Each is glad that another feels what he feels; glad of the communion established, not only between him and all present, but also with all now living who will yet share the same impression; and more than that, he feels the mysterious gladness of a communion which, reaching beyond the grave, unites us with all men of the past who have been moved by the same feelings, and with all men of the future who will yet be touched by them. And this effect is produced both by the religious art which transmits feelings of love to God and one's neighbor and by universal art transmitting the very simplest feelings common to all men.

The art of our time should be appraised differently from former art chiefly in this, that the art of our time, i.e., Christian art (basing itself on a religious perception which demands the union of man), excludes from the domain of art good in subject matter everything transmitting exclusive feelings which do not unite, but divide, men. It relegates such work to the category of art bad in its subject matter, while, on the other hand, it includes in the category of art good in subject matter a section not formerly admitted to deserve to be chosen out and respected, namely, universal art, transmitting even the most trifling and simple feelings if only they are accessible to all men without exception and therefore unite them. Such art cannot in our time but be esteemed good, for it attains the end which the religious perception of our time, i.e., Christianity, sets before humanity.

Christian art either evokes in men those feelings which, through love of God and of one's neighbor, draw them to greater and ever greater union and make them ready for and capable of such union, or evokes in them those feelings which show them that they are already united in the joys and sorrows of life. And therefore the Christian art of our time can be and is of two kinds: (1) art transmitting feelings flowing from a religious perception of man's position in the world in relation to God and to his neighbor—religious art in the limited meaning of the term; and (2) art transmitting the simplest feelings of common life, but such, always, as are accessible to all men in the whole world: the art of common life—the art of a people—universal art. Only these two kinds of art can be considered good art in our time.

The first, religious art—transmitting both positive feelings of love of God and one's neighbor, and negative feelings of indignation and horror at the violation of love—manifests itself chiefly in the form of words and to some extent also in painting and sculpture; the second kind (universal art), transmitting feelings accessible to all, manifests itself in words, in painting, in sculpture, in dances, in architecture, and, most of all, in music.

If I were asked to give modern examples of each of these kinds of art, then, as examples of the highest art flowing from love of God and man (both of the higher, positive, and of the lower, negative kind), in literature I should name *The Robbers* by Schiller; Victor Hugo's *Les Pauvres Gens* and *Les Misérables*; the novels and stories of Dickens, *The Tale of Two Cities, The Christmas Carol, The Chimes*, and others; *Uncle Tom's Cabin*; Dostoevsky's works, especially his *Memoirs from the House of Death*; and *Adam Bede* by George Eliot.

In modern painting, strange to say, works of this kind directly transmitting the Christian feeling of love of God and of one's neighbor are hardly to be found, especially among the works of the celebrated painters. There are plenty of pictures treating of the gospel stories; they, however, depict historical events with great wealth of detail, but do not, and cannot, transmit religious feeling not possessed by their painters. There are many pictures treating of the personal feelings of various people, but of pictures representing great deeds of self-sacrifice and of Christian love there are very few, and what there are, are principally by artists who are not celebrated and are for the most part not pictures, but merely sketches. Such, for instance, is the drawing by Kramskoy (worth many of his finished pictures), showing a drawing room with a balcony, past which troops are marching in triumph on their return from the war. On the balcony stands a wet nurse holding a baby and a boy. They are admiring the procession of the troops, but the mother, covering her face with a handkerchief, has fallen back on the sofa, sobbing. Such also is the picture by Walter Langley, to which I have already referred, and such again is a picture by the French artist Morlon, depicting a lifeboat hastening in a heavy storm to the relief of a steamer that is being wrecked. Approaching these in kind are pictures which represent the hard-working peasant with respect and love. Such are the pictures by Millet, and particularly his drawing, "The Man with the Hoe"; also pictures in this style by Jules Breton, Lhermitte, Defregger, and others. As examples of pictures evoking indignation and horror at the violation of love of God and man, Gay's picture, "Judgment," may serve, and also Leizen-Mayer's, "Signing the Death Warrant." But there are also very few of this kind. Anxiety about the technique and the beauty of the picture for the most part obscures the feeling. For instance, Gérôme's "Pollice Verso" expresses not so much horror at what is being perpetrated as attraction by the beauty of the spectacle.[6]

To give examples from the modern art of our upper classes of art of the second kind, good universal art or even of the art of a whole people, is yet more difficult, especially in literary art and music. If there are some works which by their inner contents might be assigned to this class (such as *Don Quixote*, Molière's comedies, *David Copperfield* and *The Pickwick Papers* by Dickens, Gogol's and Pushkin's tales, and some things of Maupassant's), these works are for the most part—from the exceptional nature of the feelings they transmit, the superfluity of special details of time and locality, and, above all, on account of the poverty of their subject matter in comparison with examples of universal ancient art (such, for instance, as the story of Joseph)—comprehensible only to people of their own circle. That Joseph's brethren, being jealous of his father's affection, sell him to the merchants; that Potiphar's wife wishes to tempt the youth; that having attained the highest station he takes pity on his brothers, including Benjamin, the favorite—these and all the rest are feelings accessible alike to a Russian peasant, a Chinese, an African, a child, or an old man, educated or uneducated; and it is all written with such restraint, is so free from any superfluous detail, that the story may be told to any circle and will be equally comprehensible and touching to everyone. But not such are the feelings of Don Quixote or of Molière's heroes (though Molière is perhaps the most universal and therefore the most excellent artist of modern times), nor of Pickwick and his friends. These feelings are not common to all men, but very exceptional; and therefore, to make them infectious, the authors have surrounded them with abundant details of time and place. And this abundance of detail makes the stories difficult of comprehension to all people not living within reach of the conditions described by the author.

The author of the novel of Joseph did not need to describe in detail, as would be done nowadays, the blood-stained coat of Joseph, the dwelling

---

[6] In this picture the spectators in the Roman Amphitheater are turning down their thumbs to show that they wish the vanquished gladiator to be killed.—Tr.

and dress of Jacob, the pose and attire of Potiphar's wife, and how, adjusting the bracelet on her left arm, she said, "Come to me," and so on, because the subject matter of feelings in this novel is so strong that all details except the most essential—such as that Joseph went out into another room to weep—are superfluous and would only hinder the transmission of feelings. And therefore this novel is accessible to all men, touches people of all nations and classes, young and old, and has lasted to our times, and will yet last for thousands of years to come. But strip the best novels of our times of their details and what will remain?

It is therefore impossible in modern literature to indicate works fully satisfying the demands of universality. Such works as exist are to a great extent spoiled by what is usually called "realism," but would be better termed "provincialism," in art.

In music the same occurs as in verbal art, and for similar reasons. In consequence of the poorness of the feeling they contain, the melodies of the modern composers are amazingly empty and insignificant. And to strengthen the impression produced by these empty melodies, the new musicians pile complex modulations onto each trivial melody, not only in their own national manner but also in the way characteristic of their own exclusive circle and particular musical school. Melody—every melody—is free and may be understood by all men; but as soon as it is bound up with a particular harmony, it ceases to be accessible except to people trained to such harmony, and it becomes strange, not only to common men of another nationality, but to all who do not belong to the circle whose members have accustomed themselves to certain forms of harmonization. So music, like poetry, travels in a vicious circle. Trivial and exclusive melodies, in order to make them attractive, are laden with harmonic, rhythmic, and orchestral complications, and thus become yet more exclusive; and, far from being universal, are not even national, i.e., they are not comprehensible to the whole people but only to some people.

In music, besides marches and dances by various composers which satisfy the demands of universal art, one can indicate very few works of this class: Bach's famous violin aria, Chopin's nocturne in E-flat major, and perhaps a dozen bits (not whole pieces, but parts) selected from the works of Haydn, Mozart, Schubert, Beethoven, and Chopin.[7]

Although in painting the same thing is repeated as in poetry and music—namely, that in order to make them more interesting, works weak in con-

---

[7] While offering as examples of art those that seem to me the best, I attach no special importance to my selections; for, besides being insufficiently informed in all branches of art, I belong to the class of people whose taste has, by false training, been perverted. And therefore my old, inured habits may cause me to err, and I may mistake for absolute merit the impression a work produced on me in my youth. My only purpose in mentioning examples of works of this or that class is to make my meaning clearer, and to show how, with my present views, I understand excellence in art in relation to its subject matter. I must, moreover, mention that I consign my own artistic productions to the category of bad art, excepting the story "God sees the Truth," which seeks a place in the first class, and "The Prisoner of the Caucasus," which belongs to the second.

ception are surrounded by minutely studied accessories of time and place
which give them a temporary and local interest but make them less universal—still, in painting, more than in the other spheres of art, may be
found works satisfying the demands of universal Christian art; that is to
say, there are more works expressing feelings in which all men may participate.

In the arts of painting and sculpture all pictures and statues in so-called
genre style, depictions of animals, landscapes and caricatures with subjects
comprehensible to everyone, and also all kinds of ornaments, are universal
in subject matter. Such productions in painting and sculpture are very
numerous (e.g., china dolls), but for the most part such objects (for instance, ornaments of all kinds) are either not considered to be art or are
considered to be art of a low quality. In reality all such objects, if only
they transmit a true feeling experienced by the artist and comprehensible
to everyone (however insignificant it may seem to us to be), are works of
really good Christian art.

I fear it will here be urged against me that, having denied that the
conception of beauty can supply a standard for works of art, I contradict
myself by acknowledging ornaments to be works of good art. The reproach
is unjust, for the subject matter of all kinds of ornamentation consists not
in the beauty but in the feeling (of admiration of, and delight in, the
combination of lines and colors) which the artist has experienced and
with which he infects the spectator. Art remains what it was and what it
must be: nothing but the infection by one man of another, or of others,
with the feelings experienced by the infector. Among those feelings is the
feeling of delight at what pleases the sight. Objects pleasing the sight may
be such as please a small or a large number of people, or such as please
all men. Ornaments for the most part are of the latter kind. A landscape
representing a very unusual view, or a genre picture of a special subject,
may not please everyone, but ornaments, from Yakutsk to the Greek, are
intelligible to everyone and evoke a similar feeling of admiration in all,
and therefore this despised kind of art should in Christian society be
esteemed far above exceptional, pretentious pictures and sculptures.

So there are only two kinds of good Christian art; all the rest of art
not comprised in these two divisions should be acknowledged to be bad
art, deserving not to be encouraged but to be driven out, denied, and despised as being art which does not unite, but divides, people. Such, in
literary art, are all novels and poems which transmit Church or patriotic
feelings, and also exclusive feelings pertaining only to the class of the
idle rich such as aristocratic honor, satiety, spleen, pessimism, and refined
and vicious feelings flowing from sex-love—quite incomprehensible to the
great majority of mankind.

In painting we must similarly place in the class of bad art all the
Church, patriotic, and exclusive pictures; all the pictures representing the
amusements and allurements of a rich and idle life; all the so-called symbolic pictures, in which the very meaning of the symbol is comprehensible
only to the people of a certain circle; and, above all, pictures with volup-

tuous subjects—all that odious female nudity which fills all the exhibitions and galleries. And to this class belongs almost all the chamber and opera music of our times, beginning especially from Beethoven (Schumann, Berlioz, Liszt, Wagner), by its subject matter devoted to the expression of feelings accessible only to people who have developed in themselves an unhealthy, nervous irritation evoked by this exclusive, artificial, and complex music.

"What! the *Ninth Symphony* not a good work of art!" I hear exclaimed by indignant voices.

And I reply, Most certainly it is not. All that I have written I have written with the sole purpose of finding a clear and reasonable criterion by which to judge the merits of works of art. And this criterion, coinciding with the indications of plain and sane sense, indubitably shows me that that symphony by Beethoven is not a good work of art. Of course, to people educated in the adoration of certain productions and of their authors, to people whose taste has been perverted just by being educated in such adoration, the acknowledgment that such a celebrated work is bad is amazing and strange. But how are we to escape the indications of reason and of common sense?

Beethoven's *Ninth Symphony* is considered a great work of art. To verify its claim to be such, I must first ask myself whether this work transmits the highest religious feeling. I reply in the negative, for music in itself cannot transmit those feelings; and therefore I ask myself next, Since this work does not belong to the highest kind of religious art, has it the other characteristic of the good art of our time—the quality of uniting all men in one common feeling: does it rank as Christian universal art? And again I have no option but to reply in the negative; for not only do I not see how the feelings transmitted by this work could unite people not specially trained to submit themselves to its complex hypnotism, but I am unable to imagine to myself a crowd of normal people who could understand anything of this long, confused, and artificial production, except short snatches which are lost in a sea of what is incomprehensible. And therefore, whether I like it or not, I am compelled to conclude that this work belongs to the rank of bad art. It is curious to note in this connection that attached to the end of this very symphony is a poem of Schiller's which (though somewhat obscurely) expresses this very thought, namely, that feeling (Schiller speaks only of the feeling of gladness) unites people and evokes love in them. But though this poem is sung at the end of the symphony, the music does not accord with the thought expressed in the verses; for the music is exclusive and does not unite all men, but unites only a few, dividing them off from the rest of mankind.

And just in this same way, in all branches of art, many and many works considered great by the upper classes of our society will have to be judged. By this one sure criterion we shall have to judge the celebrated *Divine Comedy* and *Jerusalem Delivered*, and a great part of Shakespeare's and Goethe's works, and in painting every representation of miracles, including Raphael's "Transfiguration," etc.

Whatever the work may be and however it may have been extolled, we have first to ask whether this work is one of real art or a counterfeit. Having acknowledged, on the basis of the indication of its infectiousness even to a small class of people, that a certain production belongs to the realm of art, it is necessary, on the basis of the indication of its accessibility, to decide the next question, Does this work belong to the category of bad, exclusive art, opposed to religious perception, or to Christian art uniting people? And having acknowledged an article to belong to real Christian art, we must then, according to whether it transmits the feelings flowing from love to God and man, or merely the simple feelings uniting all men, assign it a place in the ranks of religious art or in those of universal art.

Only on the basis of such verification shall we find it possible to select from the whole mass of what in our society claims to be art those works which form real, important, necessary spiritual food, and to separate them from all the harmful and useless art and from the counterfeits of art which surround us. Only on the basis of such verification shall we be able to rid ourselves of the pernicious results of harmful art and to avail ourselves of that beneficent action which is the purpose of true and good art and which is indispensable for the spiritual life of man and of humanity.

Stanley Bates

TOLSTOY EVALUATED:
TOLSTOY'S THEORY OF ART

Tolstoy's *What Is Art?* has provoked controversy from the time of its original publication.* It is a work which cannot be ignored because of the gigantic stature of its author. Even those who would dismiss it as the product of the troubled religious conscience of its author's old age must recognize that Tolstoy was rational when he wrote it, and that he regarded it as his definitive statement on aesthetics. Any work on aesthetics written by a man generally regarded as one of world literature's supreme artists has a *prima facie* claim to our attention. (Ironically, such aesthetic canonization is one of Tolstoy's targets of attack in the book.) And yet—it is rare for a reader of this work not to feel outraged by its theory, and dumbfounded by its critical judgments. Indeed, it sometimes seems as though the chief function of this work for later aesthetic theory has been to provide a rich storehouse of examples of aesthetic fallacies. (Mill's *Utilitarianism*, for a very long time, played a similar role for ethical theorists.) In this essay, I would like to separate out a number of different aspects of Tolstoy's thoughts on art in order to be able to say clearly why I think that *What Is Art?* is still a work worth encountering.

Tolstoy published *What Is Art?* at a critical point in the history of art. (Incidentally, I shall use "art" here to cover all of the fine arts as Tolstoy does. He draws his examples chiefly from literature, drama, opera, painting, and concert and chamber music. This may unjustly presuppose a unity in the different arts which they do not, in fact, possess. However, the presupposition is Tolstoy's, and it is not only his. Anyone who supposes that there is some single answer to Tolstoy's title question seems to share this presupposition.) The various movements in the arts that are subsumed under the rubric of modernism were either gathering force or well on their way to establishing a position which would dominate subsequent critical discussion, and dominate the practice of subsequent "advanced" artists. Tolstoy was uniformly hostile to the "advanced" art of his day in *What Is Art?* as we shall see. He did not base his hostility, however, on the fact

Stanley Bates is Chairman of the Department of Philosophy at Middlebury College, Vermont. He writes in ethics and other areas as well as aesthetics.
* This essay was written for this collection and is being published for the first time.

that this art deviated from the standards of "high" art as laid down over
the previous centuries. This kind of reaction, of course, did occur during
this period; it finds its most characteristic expression in the hostility of
official art schools to the new art, and in the outrage of some audiences
when exposed to new music. Tolstoy rather was moved from his rejection
of much of the art of his own time, to deal with a problem which Stanley
Cavell calls, " 'the threat of fraudulence', something I take to be endemic
to modern art."[1] There was a great deal of what purported to be art, that
Tolstoy wanted to reject as art at all.

> Both Tolstoy's *What Is Art?* and Nietzsche's *Birth of Tragedy* begin from
> an experience of the fraudulence of the art of their time. However obscure
> Nietzsche's invocation of Apollo and Dionysus and however simplistic
> Tolstoy's appeal to the artist's sincerity and the audience's 'infection' their
> use of these concepts is to specify the genuine in art in opposition to specific
> modes of fraudulence and their meaning is a function of that opposition.[2]

Tolstoy finds that he cannot deal with the art of his time without at the
same time raising the same questions about the traditions of high art and
the works canonized as masterpieces within those traditions.

Let me now turn to an account of Tolstoy's theory of art. It would be
useful to begin by separating a number of different questions to which
he addresses himself in *What Is Art?* Having done this we can then consider Tolstoy's answers to these questions and try to say what issues these
answers raise for us.

1. What is art as opposed to non-art? What is the criterion for something's
   being a work of art? Tolstoy claims that previous theories in the history
   of aesthetics have been hopelessly confused in their answers to this
   question.
2. What is good art as opposed to bad art? He makes an effort (not always
   successful) to keep this question separate from the question above.
3. What are the highest feelings of humanity? Tolstoy is led to this question
   by (2) above. It is here that he introduces his own religious views.
4. Which works are examples of good art, bad art, and non-art? It is here
   that Tolstoy makes his critical judgment on works of art or pseudo-works
   of art.

These seem to be the crucial questions dealt with in the book, though,
of course, Tolstoy touches on many other topics.

The answer to the first question is somewhat complicated. Tolstoy begins by rejecting all accounts which try somehow to base the criterion for
work of art on the concept of beauty. Though beauty may be important
in our judgment of works of art, it cannot by itself, according to Tolstoy,
provide the defining characteristic of art. A reason why this must be so
can be seen immediately if we simply recall to ourselves that other things

1. Stanley Cavell, *Must We Mean What We Say?* (New York: Charles Scribner's
   Sons, 1969), p. 176.
2. Ibid., p. 189.

than works of art (for example, natural phenomena: sunsets, animals, human beings, mountains) can be beautiful. It might be possible to define beauty by, in some way, relating it to human pleasure, but this will fail to distinguish art from non-art. Tolstoy says, "The inaccuracy of all these definitions arises from the fact that in them all . . . the object considered is the pleasure art may give, and not the purpose it may serve in the life of man and humanity . . . [Art is] one of the conditions of human life. Viewing it in this way we cannot fail to observe that art is one of the means of intercourse between man and man."[3] This is, of course, not yet a definition, but it does begin to point to that of which a definition of art must take account.

What specifically is the purpose which art serves? What kind of intercourse is it? Tolstoy here introduces, and depends on, a distinction between thoughts and feelings. Speech is the medium of the communication of thoughts; art is the means of communicating feelings. However, and this must be emphasized very strongly for Tolstoy has been misunderstood on this point, not all communication of feeling is art. Art is based on the human capacity to share the feelings of a fellow human being. (This is the capacity called sympathy by David Hume.) However, this capacity extends far beyond artistic activity. The critical paragraphs in Tolstoy's exposition, which he italicized himself and which constitutes his definition of art are:

> To evoke in oneself a feeling one has once experienced and having evoked it in oneself then by means of movements, lines, colours, sounds, or forms expressed in words, so to transmit that feeling that others experience the same feeling—this is the activity of art.
>
> Art is a human activity consisting in this, that one man consciously by means of certain external signs, hands on to others feelings he has lived through, and that others are infected by these feelings and also experience them.[4]

I have a number of observations to make on this definition. First, it requires the audience to receive the *same* feeling that the artist has felt. Here is the point at which the human capacity to receive the feelings of others is brought into play. Also it leads immediately to the conclusion that all genuine art requires *sincerity* on the part of the artist—a conclusion which Tolstoy shortly makes explicit. Second, a part of Tolstoy's definition which has been less often noted is that he includes a reference to the media of the various arts ("movements, line, colors, sounds, or forms expressed in words.") Tolstoy is often criticized for neglecting certain formal aspects of art, but he does include this reference in his basic definition. Third, Tolstoy requires a *conscious* manipulation of the medium by the artist. These second and third features of Tolstoy's definition are the specific features of art which enable Tolstoy to distinguish it

3. Leo Tolstoy, *What Is Art? and Essays on Art*, translated by Aylmer Maude (London: Oxford University Press, 1930), p. 120.
4. Ibid., p. 123.

from the human communication of feeling in general. Of course, this conscious manipulation of the medium does not need to include the intention to create a work of art; it only needs to include the conscious aim to communicate to another the feeling which the artist has had. Hence, in addition to feeling or emotion we require something like the Wordsworthian addition "recollected in tranquility." I say "something like" because Tolstoy may not require tranquility, but he does require more than the natural overt, expression of emotion, which some critics charge he makes equivalent to artistic activity.

It should also be noted, though, that this definition does cover more activity than is traditionally considered a part of the "fine arts." Tolstoy's own example of artistic activity is of a boy recounting his encounter with a wolf and trying to evoke in his audience the feelings that he experienced. This feature of his theory does not trouble the author, who decries the assumption that only the fine arts are art, and who denounces the claim that artistic activity is the exclusive province of the professional artist.

Finally, I shall simply point to the fact that Tolstoy relies on a largely uncriticized conception of feeling, and a distinction between feeling and thought, which would require very careful investigation before we could be in a position to judge his definition. Tolstoy does not have a philosophical account of feeling to offer, but in order to respond critically to his definition we would need such an account.

The second question I isolated above was: What is good art as opposed to bad art? Here we bring to bear standards of value on the products of artistic activity which have been identified in terms of his criterion of art. The activity of art involves the "infection" of an audience with a feeling experienced by the artist and re-presented by him or her. It would be very natural to suppose that the value of such a re-presentation would be determined by the value of the feeling or feelings which are communicated by it. Such, indeed, is the position which Tolstoy adopts. Hence, we move immediately to a broader conception of value than "aesthetic" value—and it is in terms of this broader conception that aesthetic value is to be determined. This seems to imply a complete subjection of art to nonartistic evaluation, and this seeming implication is, of course, what many of Tolstoy's critics find most objectionable about his entire theory of art as we shall see below. What does Tolstoy propose as the standard? "In every age and in every human society there exists a religious sense of what is good and what is bad common to that whole society, and it is this religious conception that decides the value of the feelings transmitted by art."[5] Here we seem not only to have a subjection of art to morality, but also a subjection of morality to religion. I have used the word "seems" here because I believe Tolstoy's position is somewhat more complex than it first appears, though these "seeming" characterizations have a great deal of truth in them. One indication that Tolstoy does not have a simple equation of

5. Ibid., p. 128ff.

artistically good to morally good is given when he writes, "If a work is a good work of art, then the feeling expressed by the artist—be it moral or immoral—transmits itself to other people."[6] This suggests that it is possible for there to be an immoral, good work of art and that this possibility would have been foreclosed by the equation. If we look more closely at Tolstoy's statement that it is "this religious conception that decides the value of the feelings transmitted by art," we shall see that it is the "feelings transmitted" rather than the work of art whose evaluation is being discussed. Tolstoy himself separates two aspects of evaluation in a later part of *What Is Art?* He writes of (1) the quality of art (which depends on its form) considered apart from its subject matter[7] and (2) the quality of the feelings which form the subject matter of these works.[8] It is the latter which is determined, according to him, by the religious conception; the former depends upon how well a particular work of art fulfills what has been determined by Tolstoy to be the necessary function of all works of art, that is, the infection of an audience with the author's "condition of soul" or feeling. "And not only is infection a sure sign of art, but the degree of infectiousness is also the sole measure of excellence in art."[9] He goes on to add, *"The stronger the infection the better is the art,* as art, speaking of it now apart from its subject-matter—that is, not considering the value of the feelings it transmits." It may seem strange to us to see this being advanced as Tolstoy's candidate for what is being judged when we talk about the *form* of a work of art. Many might consider this to be totally irrelevant to the consideration of the work of art "in itself." I would suggest that this indicates that we shall need to undertake an investigation of such a phrase as "the work of art in itself." Certainly Tolstoy's conception of it is broad enough to embrace those aspects which he includes under the concept of infection. Tolstoy goes further and gives three conditions which, he says, determine the degree of infectiousness. They are (1) the individuality of the feeling transmitted, (2) the clarity with which the feeling is transmitted, and (3) the sincerity of the artist. We are probably accustomed to thinking in such a way that only the second of these conditions seems relevant to the formal properties of the work of art. Part of the investigation into the concept of "the work of art in itself" would involve showing why we have become thus accustomed. For Tolstoy, the most important of these conditions is the sincerity of the artist, and he even claims that it—sincerity—includes the first two, for if the artist is sincere, he will express his own feeling in all its individuality, and he will be impelled to clarity in expressing his feelings.

I would argue that the two aspects of evaluation which Tolstoy separates are, ultimately, inextricably connected for him. (Again, this should not surprise us since most of us now probably assume that a form/subject-matter distinction is ultimately artificial.) We can see why this is so by

6. Ibid., p. 194.
7. Ibid., p. 227.
8. Ibid., p. 231.
9. Ibid., p. 228.

turning to what he has to say about the religious conception in terms of which we are to evaluate the feelings communicated. At this point, we are led to Tolstoy's answer to the third of the questions I distinguished: What are the highest feelings of humanity? One of the briefest statements of his answer to this question is the following:

> The religious perception of our time in its widest and most practical application is the consciousness that our well-being, both material and spiritual, individual and collective, temporal and eternal, lies in the growth of brotherhood among men—in their loving harmony with one another . . . And it is on the basis of this perception that we should appraise all the phenomena of our life and among the rest our art also . . .[10]

Now, I shall not undertake a critical examination of Tolstoy's religious belief here. What is crucial for us is to realize that he does have a definite view of what the religious truth is and that this is what allows him to evaluate human feelings. The standard is not a relativistic one, nor is it set by any standardized body of opinion. Those feelings which are valuable because they contribute to the growth of the brotherhood among men are the ones which are good. So far it seems as though we have two separate standards which may not be in agreement. One standard evaluates how infectious a work of art is; the other evaluates what is communicated by the work of art. However, I believe that these two standards must, in a certain way, come together. This is because Tolstoy has a normative view of sincerity. By this I mean that Tolstoy holds that his religious perception is based on the way the world is—that all men *are* brothers (and, presumably, that all men and women *are* brothers and sisters). Hence, someone whose feelings are not in accordance with this perception is wrong—Tolstoy's word is "perverted." Now it is clear that ultimately the "sincere" expression of "perverted" feelings cannot be rated as highly as the sincere expression of correct feelings. Hence, though there is a limited sense in which you can have an immoral, good work of art, in a broader sense this is not possible. Tolstoy is inclined to call the moral, good work of art "true" art or real art. Hence, ultimately the two different standards of evaluation come together through the concept of sincerity and the religious perception of life.

Now we come to Tolstoy's judgments of particular works of art. Tolstoy complained at the beginning of *What Is Art?* about the procedure of aesthetic theorists who assumed that they had a canon of works of art (or, of great art) and then tailored their theories to fit this canon. Since he refuses to do this it should not surprise or shock us that his judgments about the value of particular works of art are radically at variance with the usual judgments about our high culture. As I said at the beginning, this is probably the aspect of *What Is Art?* that produces the strongest immediate resistance on the part of the reader. Surely no theory which culminates in the outrageous claims that Tolstoy makes can be, in any

10. Ibid., p. 234ff.

way, acceptable. Let me give a list of some of the artists whose work Tolstoy condemns as pseudo-art or bad art: Aeschylus, Sophocles, Euripides, Aristophanes, Dante, Tasso, Shakespeare, Milton, Goethe, Baudelaire, Mallarme, Maeterlinck, Ibsen, Hauptmann, Michaelangelo, Raphael, Manet, Monet, Renoir, Pissaro, Sisley, most of Bach, late Beethoven, Liszt, Berlioz, Wagner, Brahms, Zola, Kipling, and almost all of the literary works of Leo Tolstoy (including *Anna Karenina* and *War and Peace.*) Though there have been and continue to be critical disputes over the relative merits of particular works of these artists, or over their claims to be considered as great artists, I can think of no one else beside Tolstoy who would reject so much of what has been thought to be the great art of the past. What this amounts to, as Tolstoy realizes, is a wholesale repudiation of the tradition of high art. Indeed, it is a rejection of most of western and Russian cultural history for centuries and centuries. I am not going to defend these judgments of Tolstoy's. I only want to make two points about them.

First, although Tolstoy does indulge in this mass condemnation, he also gives examples of works of art that satisfy his criteria of arthood and value. These include primarily folk art and religious literature of great antiquity (e.g., Genesis, the *Iliad*, some vedic hymns) as well as such works as *Les Miserables*, a number of works by Dickens, the works of Dostoyevsky, George Eliot's *Adam Bede*, *Don Quixote*, Moliere's comedies, and stories by Pushkin, Gogol, and Maupassant. Tolstoy used the "religious perception of our time" to judge these works and finds them good. Hence, his rejection of "high" art is not complete.

My second point is of more theoretical importance. If we resist Tolstoy's judgment, then we should be prepared to say why we value those works which he rejects. Most of us, most of the time, may be willing to accept the canonization of these masterpieces just *because* they play no important role in our lives. The only response in defense of these works, from us, that Tolstoy will accept, is one which links our experience of the work of these artists to our fundamental ethical, social, and religious concerns as human beings. Even if we reject his theory, we need our *own* experiences of art as data and some account of them in order to have responded to Tolstoy's challenge. Stanley Cavell writes:

> The list of figures whose art Tolstoy dismisses as fraudulent or irrelevant or bad, is, of course, unacceptably crazy . . . But the sanity of his procedure is this: it confronts the fact that we often do not find, and have never found, works we would include in a canon of works of art to be of importance or relevance to us. And the implication is that apart from this, we cannot know that they are art, or what makes them art.[11]

This seems to me Tolstoy's deepest relevance for us in thinking about art.

There are many questions that can be raised, and criticisms that can be

11. Cavell, *Must We Mean What We Say?* p. 193.

made, of Tolstoy's theorizing. Indeed, we may feel as Turgenev did when he wrote, "It is a great misfortune when a self-educated man of Tolstoy's type sets out to philosophize. He invariably climbs onto any old broomstick [and] invents some universal system that seems to provide a solution to every problem in three easy steps. . . ."[12] Many would object to the Platonizing assumption of the question, "What is art?" Tolstoy's account of history is impressionistic. His statement of his own religious views is as dogmatic as any made by a member of the churches which he attacks. He relies, as I have said earlier, at the critical point of his theory on a conception of feeling which needs considerable elucidation. However, I would like to concentrate on what seems to me to be the two most commonly made complaints about Tolstoy's theory, which are connected to each other.

First, it seems that, by invoking such concepts as "sincerity" and "infection" as both defining and evaluative standards of art, we deflect our attention from "the work of art itself" to its aesthetically irrelevant accompaniments. Various forms that this objection to Tolstoy might take would include charging him with committing some among the various aesthetic "fallacies" which critics and philosophers have attacked—for example, the "intentional fallacy," the "affective fallacy," the "pathetic fallacy."

The second commonly encountered charge against Tolstoy is that he introduces a moral criterion into the evaluation of art. There is, of course, a long tradition in philosophy extending from Plato through Rousseau to Sartre which does exactly this, but many people think that an important modern discovery is of the autonomy of art, and that moral criticism of art deflects us from the "work of art itself" as art. This second criticism, thus stated, can be seen as a special case of the first. The concept of the "work of art itself" is employed in each of these charges to help establish what is relevant and what is irrelevant for aesthetic judgment.

Obviously, I cannot even attempt to settle any of these issues here, but I do believe it is worth attempting to understand why someone could think that "sincerity," "infection," and moral criticism are irrelevant to aesthetics.

Suppose that we think of the relationship of the artist/work of art/ audience as correctly modeled on the relationship of craftsman (say, shoemaker)/product (say, shoes)/customer (shoe buyer and user). The artist makes something; the "something" is more or less like a physical object (a painting, a statue, a poem, a symphony); the something is then encountered by someone who apprehends it through his senses. (The last clause doesn't seem, even initially, to work very well for literary works of art, but we shall ignore that for the moment.) The relationship of the maker to the made, in this schematized account is that of cause to effect. The relationship of the thing made to the person who encounters it is

---

12. Quoted in Henri Troyat, *Tolstoy* (Garden City: Doubleday, 1967), p. 300.

that of causing some effect in the spectator. If we add to this account a Humian assumption about the nature of the causality—namely, that all cause/effect relationships are contingent and that it must be possible to identify (and, perhaps, to understand) each of the elements in these relationships independently of the other in order to assure this contingency —then we can better understand how one might come to think that the relationship of the artist to what he or she produces and the relationship of the work of art to its audience are irrelevant. Let me give one example of this sort of criticism of Tolstoy. Monroe Beardsley remarks, "Tolstoy's criteria of genuineness fail for well-known reasons—most decisively because the sincerity of the artist is seldom verifiable."[13] Cavell suggests that the "well-known" reason Beardsley has in mind are those advanced by him and W. K. Wimsatt in their celebrated article, "The Intentional Fallacy," wherein they claim to establish the irrelevance of an artist's intentions for understanding or evaluating a work of art. Cavell's response is, "It is still worth saying about such remarks that they appeal to a concept of intention as relevant to art which does not exist elsewhere. . . ."[14] This, I believe, is correct. Certainly, Tolstoy, in his account of art as a means of human intercourse and a condition of human life, rejects the schematized account I gave above.

I do not insist that simply because someone held something like the schematized account he would then be led to reject Tolstoy's theory because it commits the "intentional fallacy," and that those who do make this objection to Tolstoy do hold the schematized account. *That* would be to commit a real fallacy, the fallacy of affirming the consequent. However, I must say that this is the only plausible reason that presents itself to me, to account for a remark like Beardsley's.

If we wish to reject Tolstoy's theory of art, we should look closely and see the point at which we wish to demur. Perhaps, we would wish to say against him that *King Lear* or Beethoven's Ninth Symphony is a supreme work of art. But, if we feel that it is a supreme work of art precisely because it does convey to us the artist's own feeling of unity with all of humanity, then we are rejecting a particular judgment of Tolstoy's and not his theory. Perhaps we wish to disagree with him about what the religious perception of our time is—perhaps, we may even think our time has no religious perception and this is what makes it unique. But, if we think that *this* condition of our time (i.e., that it has no religious perception) is crucially relevant to its supreme works of art, we may still be accepting a considerable part of Tolstoy's theory. Only now, in order to argue with him, we shall have to articulate our own vision of history, society, and religion.

My own judgment of the deepest failure of Tolstoy's account is that he does not recognize a potential tension, or even incompatibility, between the artist's sincerity and the infectiousness of the work of art. Tolstoy's

13. Quoted in Cavell, *Must We Mean What We Say?* p. 226.
14. Ibid., p. 226.

theory rests on the assumption that the real artist could never find himself in a position in which it is really true that the times are out of joint and that the audience for genuine art may be missing. This, I suppose, is a function of his religious views. It relates to the relative neglect of formal considerations in his aesthetic theory.

Theorists like Tolstoy may show us why an "art for art's sake" theory is ultimately untenable. However, his explanations of the untenability of such a view tend to make it incomprehensible as to how this kind of "aesthetism" could have ever arisen. (It is important to remember that this claim about the autonomy of art and of the work of art is not just a view of philosophers and critics but that it has characteristically been a view of modernist artists.) Surely, the historical attraction of aestheticism requires explanation. John Dewey, for example, does attempt such an explanation by reference to such phenomena of modern times as nationalism, imperialism, capitalism, and the use of the museum system. Certainly, these phenomena have a role in our ultimate understanding of the history of the arts and of aesthetic theory. However, they belong to what I should call the external history of the arts.

To draw a very crude distinction, all of the arts have both an external and an internal history. (The ultimate point of drawing the distinction is to show how intimately these two histories may be related to each other.) The external history includes such factors as the system of patronage, the political restrictions placed on the arts, the movement of ideas in other areas, the historical position of the artist. The internal history of the art includes the evolution of the solutions to problems of form which are presented by artists in succeeding generations as they attempt to continue to write, to paint, to compose. One of the characteristic features of modernism in all of the arts is not just the coming to self-consciousness of the formal problems of the particular art but the acknowledgment of that self-consciousness in the work of art. Moreover, the formal problems are often no longer particular problems to be solved within the limits of acknowledged conventions, but fundamental problems about the possibility of any conventions at all through which serious conviction can be conveyed. Thus, it seems that an artist might be forced to choose between sincerity in how he can continue to write, to paint, to compose (what forms he can believe are available to him in those arts) and infecting an audience. (The dilemma is falsely posed because even in the sincere expression the concept of communicating to an audience is needed. But the artist may realize that the audience is not there, but has to be created —perhaps, in part, by his art.)

This is what Stanley Cavell is writing of when he says:

> Tolstoy called for sincerity from the artist and infection from his audience; he despised taste just because it revealed, and concealed, the loss of our *appetite* for life and consequently for art that matters. But he would not face the possible cost of the artist's radical, unconventionalized sincerity—that his work may become uninfectious and even (and even deliberately) unappetiz-

ing, forced to defeat the commonality which was to be art's high function, in order to remain art at all (art in exactly the sense Tolstoy meant, directed from and to genuine need).[15]

Cavell's own writing is the best on the philosophy of art that I know which deals with just this situation of the artist.

15. Cavell, *Must We Mean What We Say?* p. 206.

R. G. Collingwood

ART AS IMAGINATIVE EXPRESSION: FROM *THE PRINCIPLES OF ART*

Thirteen years ago I wrote, at the request of the Clarendon Press, a small book called *Outlines of a Philosophy of Art.** When that book went out of print early in the present year, I was asked either to revise it for a new edition or to replace it with another. I chose the latter course, not only because I have changed my mind on some things in the meantime, but also because the situation both of art and of aesthetic theory in this country has changed as well. There has been at any rate the beginning of what may prove an important revival in the arts themselves. Fashions which before the War seemed firmly entrenched, in spite of their obvious bankruptcy, and which even in 1924 were only moth-eaten, and hardly yet even beginning to be replaced by others, have begun to disappear, and new ones are growing up instead.

We have in this way a new drama, taking the place of the old 'slice of life' entertainment, in which the author's chief business was to represent everyday doings of ordinary people as the audience believed them to behave, and the actor's chief function to take a cigarette from his case, tap it, and put it between his lips. We have a new poetry, and we have a new way of painting. We have some very interesting experiments in a new way of writing prose. These things are gradually establishing themselves; but they are much hampered by rags and tatters of moribund theory which still encumber and intimidate the minds of people who ought to be welcoming the new developments.

At the same time, we have a new and very lively, if somewhat chaotic, growth of aesthetic theory and criticism, written mostly not by academic philosophers or amateurs of art, but by poets, dramatists, painters, and sculptors themselves. This is the reason for the appearance of the present book. As long as the theory of art was chiefly pursued in this country

R. G. Collingwood (1889–1943). Collingwood was Waynflete Professor of Metaphysics at Oxford University, England. He published extensively in philosophy as well as history. In addition to *The Principles of Art*, Collingwood also wrote *Speculum Mentis, An Essay on Philosophical Method, An Autobiography, An Essay on Metaphysics, The New Leviathan, The Idea of Nature*, and *The Idea of History*.
* Selections from *The Principles of Art* (Oxford, 1935), Books I, II, and III. Reprinted by permission of Oxford University Press.

by academic philosophers, I should not have thought it worth my time or my publisher's money to write upon it at such length as I have written here. But the recent development of literature on the subject shows that artists themselves are now interested in it (a thing which in England has not happened for over a century); and it is to contribute in my own way to this development, and thus indirectly to the new movement in the arts themselves, that I publish this work.

For I do not think of aesthetic theory as an attempt to investigate and expound eternal verities concerning the nature of an eternal object called Art, but as an attempt to reach, by thinking, the solution of certain problems arising out of the situation in which artists find themselves here and now. Everything written in this book has been written in the belief that it has a practical bearing, direct or indirect, upon the condition of art in England in 1937, and in the hope that artists primarily, and secondarily persons whose interest in art is lively and sympathetic, will find it of some use to them. Hardly any space is devoted to criticizing other people's aesthetic doctrines; not because I have not studied them, nor because I have dismissed them as not worth considering, but because I have something of my own to say, and think the best service I can do to a reader is to say it as clearly as I can.

Of the three parts into which it is divided, Book I is chiefly concerned to say things which any one tolerably acquainted with artistic work knows already; the purpose of this being to clear up our minds as to the distinction between art proper, which is what aesthetic is about, and certain other things which are different from it but are often called by the same name. Many false aesthetic theories are fairly accurate accounts of these other things, and much bad artistic practice comes from confusing them with art proper. These errors in theory and practice should disappear when the distinctions in question are properly apprehended.

In this way a preliminary account of art is reached; but a second difficulty is now encountered. This preliminary account, according to the schools of philosophy now most fashionable in our own country, cannot be true; for it traverses certain doctrines taught in those schools and therefore, according to them, is not so much false as nonsensical. Book II is therefore devoted to a philosophical exposition of the terms used in this preliminary account of art, and an attempt to show that the conceptions they express are justified in spite of the current prejudice against them; are indeed logically implied even in the philosophies that repudiate them.

The preliminary account of art has by now been converted into a philosophy of art. But a third question remains. Is this so-called philosophy of art a mere intellectual exercise, or has it practical consequences bearing on the way in which we ought to approach the practice of art (whether as artists or as audience) and hence, because a philosophy of art is a theory as to the place of art in life as a whole, the practice of life? As I have already indicated, the alternative I accept is the second one. In Book III, therefore, I have tried to point out some of these practical consequences by suggesting what kinds of obligation the acceptance of this aesthetic theory would impose upon artists and audiences, and in what kinds of way they could be met.

. . .

1. THE TWO CONDITIONS OF AN AESTHETIC THEORY

The business of this book is to answer the question: What is art?

A question of this kind has to be answered in two stages. First, we must make sure that the key word (in this case 'art') is a word which we know how to apply where it ought to be applied and refuse where it ought to be refused. It would not be much use beginning to argue about the correct definition of a general term whose instances we could not recognize when we saw them. Our first business, then, is to bring ourselves into a position in which we can say with confidence 'this and this and this are art; that and that and that are not art'.

This would be hardly worth insisting upon, but for two facts: that the word 'art' is a word in common use, and that it is used equivocally. If it had not been a word in common use, we could have decided for ourselves when to apply it and when to refuse it. But the problem we are concerned with is not one that can be approached in that way. It is one of those problems where what we want to do is to clarify and systematize ideas we already possess; consequently there is no point in using words according to a private rule of our own, we must use them in a way which fits on to common usage. This again would have been easy, but for the fact that common usage is ambiguous. The word 'art' means several different things; and we have to decide which of these usages is the one that interests us. Moreover, the other usages must not be simply jettisoned as irrelevant. They are very important for our inquiry; partly because false theories are generated by failure to distinguish them, so that in expounding one usage we must give a certain attention to others; partly because confusion be-tween the various senses of the word may produce bad practice as well as bad theory. We must therefore review the improper senses of the word 'art' in a careful and systematic way; so that at the end of it we can say not only 'that and that and that are not art', but 'that is not art because it is pseudo-art of kind A; that, because it is pseudo-art of kind B; and that, because it is pseudo-art of kind C'.

Secondly, we must proceed to a definition of the term 'art'. This comes second, and not first, because no one can even try to define a term until he has settled in his own mind a definite usage of it: no one can define a term in common use until he has satisfied himself that his personal usage of it harmonizes with the common usage. Definition necessarily means defining one thing in terms of something else; therefore, in order to define any given thing, one must have in one's head not only a clear idea of the thing to be defined, but an equally clear idea of all the other things by reference to which one defines it. People often go wrong over this. They think that in order to construct a definition or (what is the same thing) a 'theory' of something, it is enough to have a clear idea of that one thing. That is absurd. Having a clear idea of the thing enables them to recognize it when they see it, just as having a clear idea of a certain house enables them to recognize it when they are there; but defining the thing is like explaining where the house is or pointing out its position on the map; you must know its relations to other things as well, and if your ideas of these other things are vague, your definition will be worthless.

2. ARTIST-AESTHETICIANS AND PHILOSOPHER-AESTHETICIANS

Since any answer to the question 'What is art?' must divide itself into two stages, there are two ways in which it is liable to go wrong. It may settle the problem of usage satisfactorily but break down over the problem of definition; or it may deal competently with the problem of definition but fail over the problem of usage. These two kinds of failure may be described respectively as knowing what you are talking about, but talking nonsense; and talking sense but not knowing what you are talking about. The first kind gives us a treatment which is well informed and to the point, but messy and confused; the second, one which is neat and tidy, but irrelevant.

People who interest themselves in the philosophy of art fall roughly into two classes: artists with a leaning towards philosophy and philosophers with a taste for art. The artist-aesthetician knows what he is talking about. He can discriminate things that are art from things that are pseudo-art, and can say what these other things are: what it is that prevents them from being art, and what it is that deceives people into thinking that they are art. This is art-criticism, which is not identical with the philosophy of art, but only with the first of the two stages that go to make it up. It is a perfectly valid and valuable activity in itself; but the people who are good at it are not by any means necessarily able to achieve the second stage and offer a definition of art. All they can do is to recognize it. This is because they are content with too vague an idea of the relations in which art stands to things that are not art: I do not mean the various kinds of pseudo-art, but things like science, philosophy, and so forth. They are content to think of these relations are mere differences. To frame a definition of art, it is necessary to think wherein precisely these differences consist.

Philosopher-aestheticians are trained to do well just the thing that artist-aestheticians do badly. They are admirably protected against talking nonsense: but there is no security that they will know what they are talking about. Hence their theorizing, however competent in itself, is apt to be vitiated by weakness in its foundation of fact. They are tempted to evade this difficulty by saying: 'I do not profess to be a critic; I am not equal to adjudging the merits of Mr. Joyce, Mr. Eliot, Miss Sitwell, or Miss Stein; so I will stick to Shakespeare and Michelangelo and Beethoven. There is plenty to say about art if one bases it only on the acknowledged classics.'

This would be all right for a critic; but for a philosopher it will not do. Usage is particular, but theory is universal, and the truth at which it aims is *index sui et falsi*. The aesthetician who claims to know what it is that makes Shakespeare a poet is tacitly claiming to know whether Miss Stein is a poet, and if not, why not. The philosopher-aesthetician who sticks to classical artists is pretty sure to locate the essence of art not in what makes them artists but in what makes them classical, that is, acceptable to the academic mind.

Philosophers' aesthetic, not having a material criterion for the truth of theories in their relation to the facts, can only apply a formal criterion. It can detect logical flaws in a theory and therefore dismiss it as false; but it can never acclaim or propound any theory as true. It is wholly unconstructive; *tamquam virgo Deo consecrata, nihil parit*. Yet the fugitive and cloistered virtue of academic aesthetic is not without its uses, negative though they are. Its dialectic is a school in which the artist-aesthetician or critic can learn the lessons that will show him how to advance from art-criticism to aesthetic theory.

3. THE PRESENT SITUATION

The division between artist-aestheticians and philosopher-aestheticians corresponds fairly well with the facts as they stood half a century ago, but not with the facts of to-day. In the last generation, and increasingly in the last twenty years, the gulf between these two classes has been bridged by the appearance of a third class of aesthetic theorists: poets and painters and sculptors who have taken the trouble to train themselves in philosophy or psychology or both, and write not with the airs and graces of an essayist or the condescension of a hierophant, but with the modesty and seriousness of a man contributing to a discussion in which others beside himself are speaking, and out of which he hopes that truths not yet known even to himself will emerge.

This is one aspect of a profound change in the way in which artists think of themselves and their relation to other people. In the later nineteenth century the artist walked among us as a superior being, marked off even by his dress from common mortals; too high and ethereal to be questioned by others, too sure of his superiority to question himself, and resenting the suggestion that the mysteries of his craft should be analysed and theorized about by philosophers and other profane persons. To-day, instead of forming a mutual admiration society whose serene climate was broken from time to time by unedifying storms of jealousy, and whose aloofness from worldly concerns was marred now and then by scandalous contact with the law, artists go about like other men, pursuing a business in which they take no more than a decent pride, and criticizing each other publicly as to their ways of doing it. In this new soil a new growth of aesthetic theory has sprung up; rich in quantity and on the whole high in quality. It is too soon to write the history of this movement, but not too late to contribute to it; and it is only because such a movement is going on that a book like this can be published with some hope of its being read in the spirit in which it is written.

4. HISTORY OF THE WORD 'ART'

In order to clear up the ambiguities attaching to the word 'art', we must look to its history. The aesthetic sense of the word, the sense which here concerns us, is very recent in origin. *Ars* in ancient Latin, like τέχνη in Greek, means something quite different. It means a craft or specialized form of skill, like carpentry or smithying or surgery. The Greeks and Romans had no conception of what we call art as something different from craft; what we call art they regarded merely as a group of crafts, such as the craft of poetry (ποιητική τέχνη, *ars poetica*), which they conceived, sometimes no doubt with misgivings, as in principle just like carpentry and the rest, and differing from any one of these only in the sort of way in which any one of them differs from any other.

It is difficult for us to realize this fact, and still more so to realize its implications. If people have no word for a certain kind of thing, it is because they are not aware of it as a distinct kind. Admiring as we do the art of the ancient Greeks, we naturally suppose that they admired it in the same kind of spirit as ourselves. But we admire it as a kind of art, where the word 'art' carries with it all the subtle and elaborate implications of the modern European aesthetic consciousness. We can be perfectly certain that the Greeks did not admire it in any such way. They approached it from a different point of view. What this was, we can perhaps discover by reading what people like Plato wrote about it; but not without great pains, because the first thing every modern reader does, when he reads what Plato has to say about poetry, is to assume that Plato is describing an aesthetic experience similar to our own. The second thing he does is to lose his temper because Plato describes it so badly. With most readers there is no third stage.

Ars in medieval Latin, like 'art' in the early modern English which borrowed both word and sense, meant any special form of book-learning, such as grammar or logic, magic or astrology. That is still its meaning in the time of Shakespeare: 'lie there, my art', says Prospero, putting off his magic gown. But the Renaissance, first in Italy and then elsewhere, re-established the old meaning; and the Renaissance artists, like those of the ancient world, did actually think of themselves as craftsmen. It was not until the seventeenth century that the problems and conceptions of aesthetic began to be disentangled from those of technic or the philosophy of craft. In the late eighteenth century the disentanglement had gone so far as to establish a distinction between the fine arts and the useful arts; where 'fine' arts meant, not delicate or highly skilled arts, but 'beautiful' arts (*les beaux arts, le belle arti, die schöne Kunst*). In the nineteenth century this phrase, abbreviated by leaving out the epithet and generalized by substituting the singular for the distributive plural, became 'art'.

At this point the disentanglement of art from craft is theoretically complete. But only theoretically. The new use of the word 'art' is a flag placed on a hill-top by the first assailants; it does not prove that the hill-top is effectively occupied.

5. SYSTEMATIC AMBIGUITY

To make the occupation effective, the ambiguities attaching to the word must be cleared away and its proper meaning brought to light. The proper meaning of a word (I speak not of technical terms, which kindly god-parents furnish soon after birth with neat and tidy definitions, but of words in a living language) is never something upon which the word sits perched like a gull on a stone; it is something over which the word hovers like a gull over a ship's stern. Trying to fix the proper meaning in our minds is like coaxing the gull to settle in the rigging, with the rule that the gull must be alive when it settles: one must not shoot it and tie it there. The way to discover the proper meaning is to ask not, 'What do we mean?' but, 'What are we trying to mean?' And this involves the question 'What is preventing us from meaning what we are trying to mean?'

These impediments, the improper meanings which distract our minds from the proper one, are of three kinds. I shall call them obsolete meanings, analogical meanings, and courtesy meanings.

The obsolete meanings which every word with a history is bound to possess are the meanings it once had, and retains by force of habit. They form a trail behind the word like that of a shooting star, and divide themselves according to their distance from it into more and less obsolete. The very obsolete are not a danger to the present use of the word; they are dead and buried, and only the antiquary wishes to disinter them. But the less obsolete are a very grave danger. They cling to our minds like drowning men, and so jostle the present meaning that we can only distinguish it from them by the most careful analysis.

The analogical meanings arise from the fact that when we want to discuss the experience of other people we can only do so in our own language. Our own language has been invented for the purpose of expressing our own experience. When we use it for discussing other people's we assimilate their experience to our own. We cannot talk in English about the way in which a negro tribe thinks and feels without making them appear to think and feel like Englishmen; we cannot explain to our negro friends in their own language how Englishmen think and feel without making it appear to them that we think and feel like themselves.[1] Or rather, the assimilation of one kind of experience to another goes smoothly for a time, but sooner or later a break comes, as when we try to represent one kind of curve by means of another. When that happens, the person whose language is being used thinks that the other has gone more or less mad. Thus

---

[1] 'Let the reader consider any argument that would utterly demolish all Zande claims for the power of the oracle. If it were translated into Zande modes of thought [which is the same thing as saying, if it were translated into the Zande language] it would serve to support their entire structure of belief.' Evans-Pritchard, *Witchcraft, Oracles and Magic among the Azande* (1937), pp. 319–20.

in studying ancient history we use the word 'state' without scruple as a translation of πόλις. But the word 'state', which comes to us from the Italian Renaissance, was invented to express the new secularized political consciousness of the modern world. The Greeks had no such experience; their political consciousness was religious and political in one; so that what they meant by πόλις was something which looks to us like a confusion of Church and State. We have no words for such a thing, because we do not possess the thing. When we use for it words like 'state', 'political', and so forth, we are using them not in their proper sense, but in an analogical sense.

Courtesy meanings arise from the fact that the things we give names to are the things we regard as important. Whatever may be true of scientific technicalities, words in a living language are never used without some practical and emotional colouring, which sometimes takes precedence of its descriptive function. People claim or disclaim such titles as gentleman, or Christian, or communist, either descriptively, because they think they have or have not the qualities these titles connote; or emotionally, because they wish to possess or not to possess these qualities, and that irrespectively of whether they know what they are. The two alternatives are very far from being mutually exclusive. But when the descriptive motive is overshadowed by the emotional one, the word becomes a courtesy title or discourtesy title as the case may be.

Applying this to the word 'art', we find its proper meaning hedged about with well-established obsolete, analogical, and courtesy meanings. The only obsolete meaning of any importance is that which identifies art with craft. When this meaning gets tangled up with the proper one, the result is that special error which I call the technical theory of art; the theory that art is some kind of craft. The question then, of course, arises: What kind of craft is it? and here is vast scope for controversy between rival views as to its differentia. To that controversy this book will contribute nothing. The question is not whether art is this or that kind of craft, but whether it is any kind at all. And I do not propose even to refute the theory that it is some kind of craft. It is not a matter that stands in need of demonstration. We all know perfectly well that art is not craft; and all I wish to do is to remind the reader of the familiar differences which separate the two things.

Analogically, we use the word 'art' of many things which in certain ways (important ways, no doubt) resemble what we call art in our own modern European world, but in other ways are unlike it. The example which I shall consider is magical art. I will pause to explain what this means.

When the naturalistic animal-paintings and sculptures of the upper palaeolithic age were discovered in the last century, they were hailed as representing a newly found school of art. Before long, it was realized that this description implied a certain misunderstanding. To call them art implied the assumption that they were designed and executed with the same purpose as the modern works from which the name was extended to them; and it was found that this assumption was false. When Mr. John Skeaping, whose manner is obviously indebted to these palaeolithic predecessors, makes one of his beautiful animal-drawings, he frames it under glass, exhibits it in a place of public resort, expects people to go and look at it, and hopes that somebody will buy it, take it home, and hang it up to be contemplated and enjoyed by himself and his friends. All modern theories of art insist that what a work of art is for is to be thus contemplated. But when an Aurignacian or Magdalenian painter made such a drawing he put it where nobody lived, and often where people could never get near it at all without great trouble, and on some special occasion; and it appears that what he expected them to do was to stab it with spears or shoot arrows at it, after which, when it was defaced, he was ready to paint another on the top of it.

If Mr. Skeaping hid his drawings in a coal-cellar and expected anybody who found them to shoot them full of bullet-holes, aesthetic theorists would say that he was no artist, because he intended his drawings for consumption, as targets, and not for contemplation, as works of art. By the same argument, the palaeolithic paintings are not works of art, however much they may resemble them: the resemblance is superficial; what matters is the purpose, and the purpose is different. I need not here go into the reasons which have led archaeologists to decide that the purpose was magical, and that these paintings were accessories in some kind of ritual whereby hunters prefigured and so ensured the death or capture of the animals depicted.[2]

A similar magical or religious function is recognizable elsewhere. The portraits of ancient Egyptian sculpture were not designed for exhibition and contemplation; they were hidden away in the darkness of the tomb, unvisited, where no spectator could see them, but where they could do their magical work, whatever precisely that was, uninterrupted. Roman portraiture was derived from the images of ancestors which, keeping watch over the domestic life of their posterity, had a magical or religious purpose to which their artistic qualities were subservient. Greek drama and Greek sculpture began as accessories of religious cult. And the entire body of medieval Christian art shows the same purpose.

The terms 'art', 'artist', 'artistic', and so forth are much used as courtesy titles. When we consider in bulk the things which claim them, but, on the whole, claim them without real justification, it becomes apparent that the thing which most constantly demands and receives the courtesy title of art is the thing whose real name is amusement or entertainment. The vast majority of our literature in prose and verse, our painting and drawing and sculpture, our music, our dancing and acting, and so forth, is quite plainly and often quite explicitly designed to amuse, but is called art. Yet we know that there is a distinction. The gramophone trade, a recent one which has the outspokenness of an *enfant terrible*, actually states the

---

[2] English readers who want to go into the question may consult Count Bégouen, 'The Magical Origin of Prehistoric Art,' in *Antiquity*, iii (1929), pp. 5–19, and Baldwin Brown, *The Art of the Cave-Dweller* (1928).

distinction, or tries to, in its catalogues. Nearly all its records are issued frankly as amusement music; the small remainder is marked off as 'connoisseur's records' or the like. Painters and novelists make the same distinction, but not so publicly.

This is a fact of great interest for the aesthetic theorist, because, unless he grasps it, it may debauch his conception of art itself by causing him to identify art proper with amusement; and of equal interest to the historian of art, or rather of civilization as a whole, because it concerns him to understand the place which amusement occupies in relation to art and to civilization in general.

Our first business, then, is to investigate these three kinds of art falsely so called. When that has been done, we must see what there is left to be said about art proper.

Art and Craft

1. THE MEANING OF CRAFT

The first sense of the word 'art' to be distinguished from art proper is the obsolete sense in which it means what in this book I shall call craft. This is what *ars* means in ancient Latin, and what τεχνη means in Greek: the power to produce a preconceived result by means of consciously controlled and directed action. In order to take the first step towards a sound aesthetic, it is necessary to disentangle the notion of craft from that of art proper. In order to do this, again, we must first enumerate the chief characteristics of craft.

(1) Craft always involves a distinction between means and end, each clearly conceived as something distinct from the other but related to it. The term 'means' is loosely applied to things that are used in order to reach the end, such as tools, machines, or fuel. Strictly, it applies not to the things but to the actions concerned with them: manipulating the tools, tending the machines, or burning the fuel. These actions (as implied by the literal sense of the word means) are passed through or traversed in order to reach the end, and are left behind when the end is reached. This may serve to distinguish the idea of means from two other ideas with which it is sometimes confused: that of part, and that of material. The relation of part to whole is like that of means to end, in that the part is indispensable to the whole, is what it is because of its relation to the whole, and may exist by itself before the whole comes into existence; but when the whole exists the part exists too, whereas, when the end exists, the means have ceased to exist. As for the idea of material, we shall return to that in (4) below.

(2) It involves a distinction between planning and execution. The result to be obtained is preconceived or thought out before being arrived at. The craftsman knows what he wants to make before he makes it. This foreknowledge is absolutely indispensable to craft: if something, for example

stainless steel, is made without such foreknowledge, the making of it is not a case of craft but an accident. Moreover, this foreknowledge is not vague but precise. If a person sets out to make a table, but conceives the table only vaguely, as somewhere between two by four feet and three by six, and between two and three feet high, and so forth, he is no craftsman.

(3) Means and end are related in one way in the process of planning; in the opposite way in the process of execution. In planning the end is prior to the means. The end is thought out first, and afterwards the means are thought out. In execution the means come first, and the end is reached through them.

(4) There is a distinction between raw material and finished product or artifact. A craft is always exercised upon something, and aims at the transformation of this into something different. That upon which it works begins as raw material and ends as finished product. The raw material is found ready made before the special work of the craft begins.

(5) There is a distinction between form and matter. The matter is what is identical in the raw material and the finished product; the form is what is different, what the exercise of the craft changes. To describe the raw material as raw is not to imply that it is formless, but only that it has not yet the form which it is to acquire through 'transformation' into finished product.

(6) There is a hierarchical relation between various crafts, one supplying what another needs, one using what another provides. There are three kinds of hierarchy: of materials, of means, and of parts. (*a*) The raw material of one craft is the finished product of another. Thus the silviculturist propagates trees and looks after them as they grow, in order to provide raw material for the felling-men who transform them into logs; these are raw material for the saw-mill which transforms them into planks; and these, after a further process of selection and seasoning, become raw material for a joiner. (*b*) In the hierarchy of means, one craft supplies another with tools. Thus the timber-merchant supplies pit-props to the miner; the miner supplies coal to the blacksmith; the blacksmith supplies horseshoes to the farmer; and so on. (*c*) In the hierarchy of parts, a complex operation like the manufacture of a motor-car is parcelled out among a number of trades: one firm makes the engine, another the gears, another the chassis, another the tyres, another the electrical equipment, and so on; the final assembling is not strictly the manufacture of the car but only the bringing together of these parts. In one or more of these ways every craft has a hierarchical character; either as hierarchically related to other crafts, or as itself consisting of various heterogeneous operations hierarchically related among themselves.

Without claiming that these features together exhaust the notion of craft, or that each of them separately is peculiar to it, we may claim with tolerable confidence that where most of them are absent from a certain activity that activity is not a craft, and, if it is called by that name, is so called either by mistake or in a vague and inaccurate way.

2. TECHNICAL THEORY OF ART

It was the Greek philosophers who worked out the idea of craft, and it is in their writings that the above distinctions have been expounded once for all. The philosophy of craft, in fact, was one of the greatest and most solid achievements of the Greek mind, or at any rate of that school, from Socrates to Aristotle, whose work happens to have been most completely preserved.

Great discoveries seem to their makers even greater than they are. A person who has solved one problem is inevitably led to apply that solution to others. Once the Socratic school had laid down the main lines of a theory of craft, they were bound to look for instances of craft in all sorts of likely and unlikely places. To show how they met this temptation, here yielding to it and there resisting it, or first yielding to it and then laboriously correcting their error, would need a long essay. Two brilliant cases of successful resistance may, however, be mentioned: Plato's demonstration (*Republic*, 330 D–336 A) that justice is not a craft, with the pendant (336 E–354 A) that injustice is not one either; and Aristotle's rejection (*Metaphysics*, Λ) of the view stated in Plato's *Timaeus*, that the relation between God and the world is a case of the relations between craftsman and artifact.

When they came to deal with aesthetic problems, however, both Plato and Aristotle yielded to the temptation. They took it for granted that poetry, the only art which they discussed in detail, was a kind of craft, and spoke of this craft as ποιητικὴ τέχνη, poet-craft. What kind of craft was this?

There are some crafts, like cobbling, carpentering, or weaving, whose end is to produce a certain type of artifact; others, like agriculture or stock-breeding or horse-breaking, whose end is to produce or improve certain non-human types of organism; others again, like medicine or education or warfare, whose end is to bring certain human beings into certain states of body or mind. But we need not ask which of these is the genus of which poet-craft is a species, because they are not mutually exclusive. The cobbler or carpenter or weaver is not simply trying to produce shoes or carts or cloth. He produces these because there is a demand for them; that is, they are not ends to him, but means to the end of satisfying a specific demand. What he is really aiming at is the production of a certain state of mind in his customers, the state of having these demands satisfied. The same analysis applies to the second group. Thus in the end these three kinds of craft reduce to one. They are all ways of bringing human beings into certain desired conditions.

The same description is true of poet-craft. The poet is a kind of skilled producer; he produces for consumers; and the effect of his skill is to bring about in them certain states of mind, which are conceived in advance as desirable states. The poet, like any other kind of craftsman, must know what effect he is aiming at, and must learn by experience and precept, which is only the imparted experience of others, how to produce it. This is poet-craft, as conceived by Plato and Aristotle and, following them, such writers as Horace in his *Ars Poetica*. There will be analogous crafts of painting, sculpture, and so forth; music, at least for Plato, is not a separate art but is a constituent part of poetry.

I have gone back to the ancients, because their thought, in this matter as in so many others, has left permanent traces on our own, both for good and for ill. There are suggestions in some of them, especially in Plato, of a quite different view; but this is the one which they have made familiar, and upon which both the theory and the practice of the arts has for the most part rested down to the present time. Present-day fashions of thought have in some ways even tended to reinforce it. We are apt nowadays to think about most problems, including those of art, in terms either of economics or of psychology; and both ways of thinking tend to subsume the philosophy of art under the philosophy of craft. To the economist, art presents the appearance of a specialized group of industries; the artist is a producer, his audience consumers who pay him for benefits ultimately definable in terms of the states of mind which his productivity enables them to enjoy. To the psychologist, the audience consists of persons reacting in certain ways to stimuli provided by the artist; and the artist's business is to know what reactions are desired or desirable, and to provide the stimuli which will elicit them.

The technical theory of art is thus by no means a matter of merely antiquarian interest. It is actually the way in which most people nowadays think of art; and especially economists and psychologists, the people to whom we look (sometimes in vain) for special guidance in the problems of modern life.

But this theory is simply a vulgar error, as anybody can see who looks at it with a critical eye. It does not matter what kind of craft in particular is identified with art. It does not matter what the benefits are which the artist is regarded as conferring on his audience, or what the reactions are which he is supposed to elicit. Irrespectively of such details, our question is whether art is any kind of craft at all. It is easily answered by keeping in mind the half-dozen characteristics of craft enumerated in the preceding section, and asking whether they fit the case of art. And there must be no chopping of toes or squeezing of heels; the fit must be immediate and convincing. It is better to have no theory of art at all, than to have one which irks us from the first.

3. BREAK-DOWN OF THE THEORY

(1) The first characteristic of craft is the distinction between means and end. Is this present in works of art? According to the technical theory, yes. A poem is means to the production of a certain state of mind in the audience, as a horseshoe is means to the production of a certain state of mind in the man whose horse is shod. And the poem in its turn will be an

end to which other things are means. In the case of the horseshoe, this stage of the analysis is easy: we can enumerate lighting the forge, cutting a piece of iron off a bar, heating it, and so on. What is there analogous to these processes in the case of a poem? The poet may get paper and pen, fill the pen, sit down and square his elbows; but these actions are preparatory not to composition (which may go on in the poet's head) but to writing. Suppose the poem is a short one and composed without the use of any writing materials; what are the means by which the poet composes it? I can think of no answer, unless comic answers are wanted, such as 'using a rhyming dictionary', 'pounding his foot on the floor or wagging his head or hand to mark the metre', or 'getting drunk'. If one looks at the matter seriously, one sees that the only factors in the situation are the poet, the poetic labour of his mind, and the poem. And if any supporter of the technical theory says 'Right: then the poetic labour is the means, the poem the end', we shall ask him to find a blacksmith who can make a horseshoe by sheer labour, without forge, anvil, hammer, or tongs. It is because nothing corresponding to these exists in the case of the poem that the poem is not an end to which there are means.

Conversely, is a poem means to the production of a certain state of mind in an audience? Suppose a poet had read his verses to an audience, hoping that they would produce a certain result; and suppose the result were different; would that in itself prove the poem a bad one? It is a difficult question; some would say yes, others no. But if poetry were obviously a craft, the answer would be a prompt and unhesitating yes. The advocate of the technical theory must do a good deal of toe-chopping before he can get his facts to fit his theory at this point.

So far, the prospects of the technical theory are not too bright. Let us proceed.

(2) The distinction between planning and executing certainly exists in some works of art, namely those which are also works of craft or artifacts; for there is, of course, an overlap between these two things, as may be seen by the example of a building or a jar, which is made to order for the satisfaction of a specific demand, to serve a useful purpose, but may none the less be a work of art. But suppose a poet were making up verses as he walked; suddenly finding a line in his head, and then another, and then dissatisfied with them and altering them until he had got them to his liking: what is the plan which he is executing? He may have had a vague idea that if he went for a walk he would be able to compose poetry; but what were, so to speak, the measurements and specifications of the poem he planned to compose? He may, no doubt, have been hoping to compose a sonnet on a particular subject specified by the editor of a review; but the point is that he may not, and that he is none the less a poet for composing without having any definite plan in his head. Or suppose a sculptor were not making a Madonna and child, three feet high, in Hoptonwood stone, guaranteed to placate the chancellor of the diocese and obtain a faculty for placing it in the vacant niche over a certain church door; but were simply playing about with clay, and found the clay under his fingers

turning into a little dancing man: is this not a work of art because it was done without being planned in advance?

All this is very familiar. There would be no need to insist upon it, but that the technical theory of art relies on our forgetting it. While we are thinking of it, let us note the importance of not over-emphasizing it. Art as such does not imply the distinction between planning and execution. But (*a*) this is a merely negative characteristic, not a positive one. We must not erect the absence of plan into a positive force and call it inspiration, or the unconscious, or the like. (*b*) It is a permissible characteristic of art, not a compulsory one. If unplanned works of art are possible, it does not follow that no planned work is a work of art. That is the logical fallacy that underlies one, or some, of the various things called romanticism. It may very well be true that the only works of art which can be made altogether without a plan are trifling ones, and that the greatest and most serious ones always contain an element of planning and therefore an element of craft. But that would not justify the technical theory of art.

. . .

Art as Magic

1. WHAT MAGIC IS NOT: (I) PSEUDO-SCIENCE

Representation, we have seen, is always means to an end. The end is the re-evocation of certain emotions. According as these are evoked for their practical value or for their own sake, it is called magic or amusement.

My use of the term 'magic' in this connexion is certain to cause difficulty; but I cannot avoid it, for reasons which I hope will become clear. I must therefore see to it that the difficulty does not amount to misunderstanding, at any rate in the case of readers who wish to understand.

The word 'magic' as a rule carries no definite significance at all. It is used to denote certain practices current in 'savage' societies, and recognizable here and there in the less 'civilized' and less 'educated' strata of our own society, but it is used without any definite conception of what it connotes; and therefore, if some one asserts that, for example, the ceremonies of our own church are magical, neither he nor any one else can say what the assertion means, except that it is evidently intended to be abusive; it cannot be described as true or false. What I am here trying to do is to rescue the word 'magic' from this condition in which it is a meaningless term of abuse, and use it as a term with a definite meaning.

Its degradation into a term of abuse was the work of a school of anthropologists whose prestige has been deservedly great. Two generations ago, anthropologists set themselves the task of scientifically studying the civilizations different from our own which had been lumped together under the unintelligently depreciatory (or, at times, unintelligently laudatory) name of savage. Prominent among the customs of these civilizations they found practices of the kind which by common consent were called magical. As scientific students, it was their business to discover the motive of these practices. What, they asked themselves, is magic for?

The direction in which they looked for an answer to this question was determined by the prevailing influence of a positivistic philosophy which ignored man's emotional nature and reduced everything in human experience to terms of intellect, and further ignored every kind of intellectual activity except those which, according to the same philosophy, went to the making of natural science. This prejudice led them to compare the magical practices of the 'savage' (civilized men, they rashly assumed, had none, except for certain anomalous things which these anthropologists called survivals) with the practices of civilized man when he uses his scientific knowledge in order to control nature. The magician and the scientist, they concluded, belong to the same genus. Each is a person who attempts to control nature by the practical application of scientific knowledge. The difference is that the scientist actually possesses scientific knowledge, and consequently his attempts to control nature are successful: the magician possesses none, and therefore his attempts fail. For example, irrigating crops really makes them grow; but the savage, not knowing this, dances at them in the false belief that his example will encourage in the crops a spirit of emulation, and induce them to grow as high as he jumps. Thus, they concluded, magic is at bottom simply a special kind of error: it is erroneous natural science.

. . .

3. WHAT MAGIC IS

The only profitable way of theorizing about magic is to approach it from the side of art. The similarities between magic and applied science, on which the Tylor–Frazer theory rests, are very slight, and the dissimilarities are great. The magician as such is not a scientist; and if we admit this, and call him a bad scientist, we are merely finding a term of abuse for the characteristics that differentiate him from a scientist, without troubling to analyse those characteristics. The similarities between magic and neurosis, on which the Freudian theory rests, are just as strong or as weak as one pleases; for neurosis is a negative term, covering many different kinds of departure from our rough-and-ready standard of mental health; and there is no reason why one item in the list of qualifications demanded by a standard of mental health should not be a disbelief in magic. But the similarities between magic and art are both strong and intimate. Magical practices invariably contain, not as peripheral elements but as central elements, artistic activities like dances, songs, drawing, or modelling. Moreover, these elements have a function which in two ways resembles the function of amusement. (i) They are means to a preconceived end, and are therefore not art proper but craft. (ii) This end is the arousing of emotion.

. . .

4. MAGICAL ART

A magical art is an art which is representative and therefore evocative of emotion, and evokes of set purpose some emotions rather than others in order to discharge them into the affairs of practical life. Such an art may be good or bad when judged by aesthetic standards, but that kind of goodness or badness has little, if any, connexion with its efficacy in its own proper work. The brilliant naturalism of the admittedly magical palaeolithic animal paintings cannot be explained by their magical function. Any kind of scrawl or smudge would have served the purpose, if the neophyte on approaching it had been solemnly told that it 'was' a bison. When magical art reaches a high aesthetic level, this is because the society to which it belongs (not the artists alone, but artists and audience alike) demands of it an aesthetic excellence quite other than the very modest degree of competence which would enable it to fulfil its magical function. Such an art has a double motive. It remains at a high level only so long as the two motives are felt as absolutely coincident. As soon as a sculptor thinks to himself 'surely it is a waste of labour to finish this portrait with such care, when it is going to be shut up in a tomb as soon as it leaves my hand', the two motives have come apart in his mind. He has conceived the idea that something short of his best work, in the aesthetic sense of that phrase, would satisfy the needs of magic; and decadence at once begins. Indeed, it has begun already; for ideas of that kind only come up into consciousness long after they have begun to influence conduct.

Art as Amusement

1. AMUSEMENT ART

If an artifact is designed to stimulate a certain emotion, and if this emotion is intended not for discharge into the occupations of ordinary life, but for enjoyment as something of value in itself, the function of the artifact is to amuse or entertain. Magic is useful, in the sense that the emotions it excites have a practical function in the affairs of every day; amusement is not useful but only enjoyable, because there is a watertight bulkhead between its world and the world of common affairs. The emotions generated by amusement run their course within this watertight compartment.

Every emotion, dynamically considered, has two phases in its existence: charge or excitation, and discharge. The discharge of an emotion is some act done at the prompting of that emotion, by doing which we work the emotion off and relieve ourselves of the tension which, until thus discharged, it imposes upon us. The emotions generated by an amusement must be discharged, like any others; but they are discharged within the amusement itself. This is in fact the peculiarity of amusement. An amusement is a device for the discharge of emotions in such a way that they shall not interfere with the concerns of practical life. But since practical life is only definable as that part of life which is not amusement, this statement, if meant for a definition, would be circular. We must therefore say: to establish a distinction between amusement and practical life[3] is to divide experience into two parts, so related that the emotions generated in the one are not allowed to discharge themselves in the other. In the one, emotions are treated as ends in themselves; in the other, as forces whose operation achieves certain ends beyond them. The first part is now called amusement, the second part practical life.

.   .   .

4. REPRESENTATION AND THE CRITIC

The question may here be raised, how the practice of art-criticism is affected by identifying art with representation in either of its two forms. The critic's business, as we have already seen, is to establish a consistent usage of terms: to settle the nomenclature of the various things which come before him competing for a given name, saying, 'this is art, that is not art', and, being an expert in this business, performing it with authority. A person qualified so to perform it is called a judge; and judgement means verdict, the authoritative announcement that, for example, a man is innocent or guilty. Now, the business of art-criticism has been going on ever since at least the seventeenth century; but it has always been beset with difficulties. The critic knows, and always has known, that in theory he is concerned with something objective. In principle, the question whether this piece of verse is a poem or a sham poem is a question of fact, on which every one who is properly qualified to judge ought to agree. But what he finds, and always has found, is that in the first place the critics as a rule do not agree; in the second place, their verdict is as a rule reversed by posterity; and in the third place it is hardly ever welcomed and accepted as useful either by the artists or by the general public.

When the disagreements of critics are closely studied, it becomes evident that there is much more behind them than mere human liability to form different opinions about the same thing. The verdict of a jury in court, as judges are never tired of telling them, is a matter of opinion; and hence they sometimes disagree. But if they disagreed in the kind of way in which art-critics disagree, trial by jury would have been experimented with only once, if that, before being abolished for ever. The two kinds of disagreement differ in that the juror, if the case is being handled by a competent judge, has only one point at which he can go wrong. He has to give a verdict, and the judge tells him what the principles are upon which he must give it. The art-critic also has to give a verdict; but there is no agreement between him and his colleagues as to the principles on which it must be given.

.   .   .

---

[3] Aestheticians who discuss the relation between two mutually exclusive things called 'Art' and 'Life' are really discussing this distinction.

Art Proper: (1) as Expression

1. THE NEW PROBLEM

We have finished at last with the technical theory of art, and with the various kinds of art falsely so called to which it correctly applies. We shall return to it in the future only so far as it forces itself upon our notice and threatens to impede the development of our subject.

That subject is art proper. It is true that we have already been much concerned with this; but only in a negative way. We have been looking at it so far as was necessary in order to exclude from it the various things which falsely claimed inclusion in it. We must now turn to the positive side of this same business, and ask what kinds of things they are to which the name rightly belongs.

In doing this we are still dealing with what are called questions of fact, or what in the first chapter were called questions of usage, not with questions of theory. We shall not be trying to build up an argument which the reader is asked to examine and criticize, and accept if he finds no fatal flaw in it. We shall not be offering him information which he is asked to accept on the authority of witnesses. We shall be trying as best we can to remind ourselves of facts well known to us all: such facts as this, that on occasions of a certain kind we actually do use the word art or some kindred word to designate certain kinds of thing, and in the sense which we have now isolated as the proper sense of the word. Our business is to concentrate our attention on these usages until we can see them as consistent and systematic. This will be our work throughout this chapter and the next. The task of defining the usages thus systematized, and so constructing a theory of art proper, will come later.

. . .

This method will now be applied to the technical theory of art. The formula for the distortion is known from our analysis of the notion of craft in Chapter II, § 1. Because the inventors of the theory were prejudiced in favour of that notion, they forced their own ideas about art into conformity with it. The central and primary characteristic of craft is the distinction it involves between means and end. If art is to be conceived as craft, it must likewise be divisible into means and end. We have seen that actually it is not so divisible; but we have now to ask why anybody ever thought it was. What is there in the case of art which these people misunderstood by assimilating it to the well-known distinction of means and end? If there is nothing, the technical theory of art was a gratuitous and baseless invention; those who have stated and accepted it have been and are nothing but a pack of fools; and we have been wasting our time thinking about it. These are hypotheses I do not propose to adopt.

(1) This, then, is the first point we have learnt from our criticism: that there is in art proper a distinction resembling that between means and end, but not identical with it.

(2) The element which the technical theory calls the end is defined by it as the arousing of emotion. The idea of arousing (i.e. of bringing into existence, by determinate means, something whose existence is conceived in advance as possible and desirable) belongs to the philosophy of craft, and is obviously borrowed thence. But the same is not true of emotion. This, then, is our second point. Art has something to do with emotion; what it does with it has a certain resemblance to arousing it, but is not arousing it.

(3) What the technical theory calls the means is defined by it as the making of an artifact called a work of art. The making of this artifact is described according to the terms of the philosophy of craft: i.e. as the transformation of a given raw material by imposing on it a form preconceived as a plan in the maker's mind. To get the distortion out of this we must remove all these characteristics of craft, and thus we reach the third point. Art has something to do with making things, but these things are not material things, made by imposing form on matter, and they are not made by skill. They are things of some other kind, and made in some other way.

We now have three riddles to answer. For the present, no attempt will be made to answer the first: we shall treat it merely as a hint that the second and third should be treated separately. In this chapter, accordingly, we shall inquire into the relation between art and emotion; in the next, the relation between art and making.

2. EXPRESSING EMOTION AND AROUSING EMOTION

Our first question is this. Since the artist proper has something to do with emotion, and what he does with it is not to arouse it, what is it that he does? It will be remembered that the kind of answer we expect to this question is an answer derived from what we all know and all habitually say; nothing original or recondite, but something entirely commonplace.

Nothing could be more entirely commonplace than to say he expresses them. The idea is familiar to every artist, and to every one else who has any acquaintance with the arts. To state it is not to state a philosophical theory or definition of art; it is to state a fact or supposed fact about which, when we have sufficiently identified it, we shall have later to theorize philosophically. For the present it does not matter whether the fact that is alleged, when it is said that the artist expresses emotion, is really a fact or only supposed to be one. Whichever it is, we have to identify it, that is, to decide what it is that people are saying when they use the phrase. Later on, we shall have to see whether it will fit into a coherent theory.

They are referring to a situation, real or supposed, of a definite kind. When a man is said to express emotion, what is being said about him comes to this. At first, he is conscious of having an emotion, but not conscious of what this emotion is. All he is conscious of is a perturbation or excitement, which he feels going on within him, but of whose nature he is ignorant. While in this state, all he can say about his emotion is:

'I feel . . . I don't know what I feel.' From this helpless and oppressed
condition he extricates himself by doing something which we call expressing himself. This is an activity which has something to do with the thing
we call language: he expresses himself by speaking. It has also something
to do with consciousness: the emotion expressed is an emotion of whose
nature the person who feels it is no longer unconscious. It has also something to do with the way in which he feels the emotion. As unexpressed,
he feels it in what we have called a helpless and oppressed way; as expressed, he feels it in a way from which this sense of oppression has van-
ished. His mind is somehow lightened and eased.

This lightening of emotions which is somehow connected with the
expression of them has a certain resemblance to the 'catharsis' by which
emotions are earthed through being discharged into a make-believe situation; but the two things are not the same. Suppose the emotion is one
of anger. If it is effectively earthed, for example by fancying oneself kicking
some one down stairs, it is thereafter no longer present in the mind as
anger at all: we have worked it off and are rid of it. If it is expressed, for
example by putting it into the hot and bitter words, it does not disappear
from the mind; we remain angry; but instead of the sense of oppression
which accompanies an emotion of anger not yet recognized as such, we
have that sense of alleviation which comes when we are conscious of our
own emotion as anger, instead of being conscious of it only as an uniden-
tified pertubation. This is what we refer to when we say that it 'does us
good' to express our emotions.

The expression of an emotion by speech may be addressed to some one;
but if so it is not done with the intention of arousing a like emotion in
him. If there is any effect which we wish to produce in the hearer, it is
only the effect which we call making him understand how we feel. But,
as we have already seen, this is just the effect which expressing our emotions has on ourselves. It makes us, as well as the people to whom we talk,
understand how we feel. A person arousing emotion sets out to affect his
audience in a way in which he himself is not necessarily affected. He and
his audience stand in quite different relations to the act, very much as
physician and patient stand in quite different relations towards a drug
administered by the one and taken by the other. A person expressing emotion, on the contrary, is treating himself and his audience in the same kind
of way; he is making his emotions clear to his audience, and that is what
he is doing to himself.

It follows from this that the expression of emotion, simply as expression,
is not addressed to any particular audience. It is addressed primarily to the
speaker himself, and secondarily to any one who can understand. Here
again, the speaker's attitude towards his audience is quite unlike that of a
person desiring to arouse in his audience a certain emotion. If that is
what he wishes to do, he must know the audience he is addressing. He
must know what type of stimulus will produce the desired kind of reaction
in people of that particular sort; and he must adapt his language to his
audience in the sense of making sure that it contains stimuli appropriate

to their peculiarities. If what he wishes to do is to express his emotions intelligibly, he has to express them in such a way as to be intelligible to himself; his audience is then in the position of persons who overhear[4] him doing this. Thus the stimulus-and-reaction terminology has no applicability to the situation.

The means-and-end, or technique, terminology too is inapplicable. Until a man has expressed his emotion, he does not yet know what emotion it is. The act of expressing it is therefore an exploration of his own emotions. He is trying to find out what these emotions are. There is certainly here a directed process: an effort, that is, directed upon a certain end; but the end is not something foreseen and preconceived, to which appropriate means can be thought out in the light of our knowledge of its special character. Expression is an activity of which there can be no technique.

3. EXPRESSION AND INDIVIDUALIZATION

Expressing an emotion is not the same thing as describing it. To say 'I am angry' is to describe one's emotion, not to express it. The words in which it is expressed need not contain any reference to anger as such at all. Indeed, so far as they simply and solely express it, they cannot contain any such reference. The curse of Ernulphus, as invoked by Dr. Slop on the unknown person who tied certain knots, is a classical and supreme expression of anger; but it does not contain a single word descriptive of the emotion it expresses.

This is why, as literary critics well know, the use of epithets in poetry, or even in prose where expressiveness is aimed at, is a danger. If you want to express the terror which something causes, you must not give it an epithet like 'dreadful.' For that describes the emotion instead of expressing it, and your language becomes frigid, that is inexpressive, at once. A genuine poet, in his moments of genuine poetry, never mentions by name the emotions he is expressing.

Some people have thought that a poet who wishes to express a great variety of subtly differentiated emotions might be hampered by the lack of a vocabularly rich in words referring to the distinctions between them; and that psychology, by working out such a vocabulary, might render a valuable service to poetry. This is the opposite of the truth. The poet needs no such words at all; the existence or non-existence of a scientific terminology describing the emotions he wishes to express is to him a matter of perfect indifference. If such a terminology, where it exists, is allowed to affect his own use of language, it affects it for the worse.

The reason why description, so far from helping expression, actually damages it, is that description generalizes. To describe a thing is to call it a thing of such and such a kind: to bring it under a conception, to classify it. Expression, on the contrary, individualizes. The anger which I feel here and now, with a certain person, for a certain cause, is no doubt

---

[4] Further development of the ideas expressed here will make it necessary to qualify this word and assert a much more intimate relation between artist and audience.

an instance of anger, and in describing it as anger one is telling truth about it; but it is much more than mere anger: it is a peculiar anger, not quite like any anger that I ever felt before, and probably not quite like any anger I shall ever feel again. To become fully conscious of it means becoming conscious of it not merely as an instance of anger, but as this quite peculiar anger. Expressing it, we saw, has something to do with becoming conscious of it; therefore, if being fully conscious of it means being conscious of all its peculiarities, fully expressing it means expressing all its peculiarities. The poet, therefore, in proportion as he understands his business, gets as far away as possible from merely labelling his emotions as instances of this or that general kind, and takes enormous pains to individualize them by expressing them in terms which reveal their difference from any other emotion of the same sort.

This is a point in which art proper, as the expression of emotion, differs sharply and obviously from any craft whose aim it is to arouse emotion. The end which a craft sets out to realize is always conceived in general terms, never individualized. However accurately defined it may be, it is always defined as the production of a thing having characteristics that could be shared by other things. A joiner, making a table out of these pieces of wood and no others, makes it to measurements and specifications which, even if actually shared by no other table, might in principle be shared by other tables. A physician treating a patient for a certain complaint is trying to produce in him a condition which might be, and probably has been, often produced in others, namely, the condition of recovering from the complaint. So an 'artist' setting out to produce a certain emotion in his audience is setting out to produce not an individual emotion, but an emotion of a certain kind. It follows that the means appropriate to its production will be not individual means but means of a certain kind: that is to say, means which are always in principle replaceable by other similar means. As every good craftsman insists, there is always a 'right way' of performing any operation. A 'way' of acting is a general pattern to which various individual actions may conform. In order that the 'work of art' should produce its intended psychological effect, therefore, whether this effect be magical or merely amusing, what is necessary is that it should satisfy certain conditions, possess certain characteristics: in other words be, not this work and no other, but a work of this kind and of no other.

This explains the meaning of the generalization which Aristotle and others have ascribed to art. We have already seen that Aristotle's *Poetics* is concerned not with art proper but with representative art, and representative art of one definite kind. He is not analysing the religious drama of a hundred years before, he is analysing the amusement literature of the fourth century, and giving rules for its composition. The end being not individual but general (the production of an emotion of a certain kind) the means too are general (the portrayal, not of this individual act, but of an act of this sort; not, as he himself puts it, what Alcibiades did, but what anybody of a certain kind would do). Sir Joshua Reynolds's idea of generalization is in principle the same; he expounds it in connexion with what he calls 'the grand style', which means a style intended to produce emotions of a certain type. He is quite right; if you want to produce a typical case of a certain emotion, the way to do it is to put before your audience a representation of the typical features belonging to the kind of thing that produces it: make your kings very royal, your soldiers very soldierly, your women very feminine, your cottages very cottagesque, your oak-trees very oakish, and so on.

Art proper, as expression of emotion, has nothing to do with all this. The artist proper is a person who, grappling with the problem of expressing a certain emotion, says, 'I want to get this clear.' It is no use to him to get something else clear, however like it this other thing may be. Nothing will serve as a substitute. He does not want a thing of a certain kind, he wants a certain thing. This is why the kind of person who takes his literature as psychology, saying 'How admirably this writer depicts the feelings of women, or busdrivers, or homosexuals . . .', necessarily misunderstands every real work of art with which he comes into contact, and takes for good art, with infallible precision, what is not art at all.

4. SELECTION AND AESTHETIC EMOTION

It has sometimes been asked whether emotions can be divided into those suitable for expression by artists and those unsuitable. If by art one means art proper, and identifies this with expression, the only possible answer is that there can be no such distinction. Whatever is expressible is expressible. There may be ulterior motives in special cases which make it desirable to express some emotions and not others; but only if by 'express' one means express publicly, that is, allow people to overhear one expressing oneself. This is because one cannot possibly decide that a certain emotion is one which for some reason it would be undesirable to express thus publicly, unless one first becomes conscious of it; and doing this, as we saw, is somehow bound up with expressing it. If art means the expression of emotion, the artist as such must be absolutely candid; his speech must be absolutely free. This is not a precept, it is a statement. It does not mean that the artist ought to be candid, it means that he is an artist only in so far as he is candid. Any kind of selection, any decision to express this emotion and not that, is inartistic not in the sense that it damages the perfect sincerity which distinguishes good art from bad, but in the sense that it represents a further process of a non-artistic kind, carried out when the work of expression proper is already complete. For until that work is complete one does not know what emotions one feels; and is therefore not in a position to pick and choose, and give one of them preferential treatment.

From these considerations a certain corollary follows about the division of art into distinct arts. Two such divisions are current: one according to the medium in which the artist works, into painting, poetry, music, and the like; the other according to the kind of emotion he expresses, into tragic, comic, and so forth. We are concerned with the second. If the

difference between tragedy and comedy is a difference between the emotions they express, it is not a difference that can be present to the artist's
mind when he is beginning his work; if it were, he would know what
emotion he was going to express before he had expressed it. No artist,
therefore, so far as he is an artist proper, can set out to write a comedy, a
tragedy, an elegy, or the like. So far as he is an artist proper, he is just as
likely to write any one of these as any other; which is the truth that
Socrates was heard expounding towards the dawn, among the sleeping
figures in Agathon's dining-room.[5] These distinctions, therefore, have only
a very limited value. They can be properly used in two ways. (1) When a
work of art is complete, it can be labelled *ex post facto* as tragic, comic, or
the like, according to the character of the emotions chiefly expressed in it.
But understood in that sense the distinction is of no real importance. (2)
If we are talking about representational art, the case is very different. Here
the so-called artist knows in advance what kind of emotion he wishes to
excite, and will construct works of different kinds according to the different kinds of effect they are to produce. In the case of representational art,
therefore, distinctions of this kind are not only admissible as an *ex post
facto* classification of things to which in their origin it is alien; they are
present from the beginning as a determining factor in the so-called artist's
plan of work.

The same considerations provide an answer to the question whether
there is such a thing as a specific 'aesthetic emotion'. If it is said that there
is such an emotion independently of its expression in art, and that the
business of artists is to express it, we must answer that such a view is
nonsense. It implies, first, that artists have emotions of various kinds,
among which is this peculiar aesthetic emotion; secondly, that they select
this aesthetic emotion for expression. If the first proposition were true,
the second would have to be false. If artists only find out what their emotions are in the course of finding out how to express them, they cannot begin the work of expression by deciding what emotion to express.

In a different sense, however, it is true that there is a specific aesthetic
emotion. As we have seen, an unexpressed emotion is accompanied by a
feeling of oppression; when it is expressed and thus comes into consciousness the same emotion is accompanied by a new feeling of alleviation or
easement, the sense that this oppression is removed. It resembles the
feeling of relief that comes when a burdensome intellectual or moral problem has been solved. We may call it, if we like, the specific feeling of having successfully expressed ourselves; and there is no reason why it should not
be called a specific aesthetic emotion. But it is not a specific kind of emo-

---

[5] Plato, *Symposium*, 223. D. But if Aristodemus heard him correctly, Socrates was saying the right thing for the wrong reason. He is reported as arguing, not that a tragic
writer as such is also a comic one, but that ὁ τεχνῃ τραγωλοποιος is also a comic
writer. Emphasis on the word τεχνη is obviously implied; and this, with a reference
to the doctrine (*Republic*, 333 E–334 A) that craft is what Aristotle was to call a
potentiality of opposites, i.e. enables its possessor to do not one kind of thing only,
but that kind and the opposite kind too, shows that what Socrates was doing was to
assume the technical theory of art and draw from it the above conclusion.

tion pre-existing to the expression of it, and having the peculiarity that when it comes to be expressed it is expressed artistically. It is an emotional colouring which attends the expression of any emotion whatever.

· · ·

7. EXPRESSING EMOTION AND BETRAYING EMOTION

Finally, the expressing of emotion must not be confused with what may be called the betraying of it, that is, exhibiting symptoms of it. When it is said that the artist in the proper sense of that word is a person who expresses his emotions, this does not mean that if he is afraid he turns pale and stammers; if he is angry he turns red and bellows; and so forth. These things are no doubt called expressions; but just as we distinguish proper and improper senses of the word 'art', so we must distinguish proper and improper senses of the word 'expression', and in the context of a discussion about art this sense of expression is an improper sense. The characteristic mark of expression proper is lucidity or intelligibility; a person who expresses something thereby becomes conscious of what it is that he is expressing, and enables others to become conscious of it in himself and in them. Turning pale and stammering is a natural accompaniment of fear, but a person who in addition to being afraid also turns pale and stammers does not thereby become conscious of the precise quality of his emotion. About that he is as much in the dark as he would be if (were that possible) he could feel fear without also exhibiting these symptoms of it.

Confusion between these two senses of the word 'expression' may easily lead to false critical estimates, and so to false aesthetic theory. It is sometimes thought a merit in an actress that when she is acting a pathetic scene she can work herself up to such an extent as to weep real tears. There may be some ground for that opinion if acting is not an art but a craft, and if the actress's object in that scene is to produce grief in her audience; and even then the conclusion would follow only if it were true that grief cannot be produced in the audience unless symptoms of grief are exhibited by the performer. And no doubt this is how most people think of the actor's work. But if his business is not amusement but art, the object at which he is aiming is not to produce a preconceived emotional effect on his audience but by means of a system of expressions, or language, composed partly of speech and partly of gesture, to explore his own emotions: to discover emotions in himself of which he was unaware, and, by permitting the audience to witness the discovery, enable them to make a similar discovery about themselves. In that case it is not her ability to weep real tears that would mark out a good actress; it is her ability to make it clear to herself and her audience what the tears are about.

This applies to every kind of art. The artist never rants. A person who writes or paints or the like in order to blow off steam, using the traditional materials of art as means for exhibiting the symptoms of emotion, may deserve praise as an exhibitionist, but loses for the moment all claim to the title of artist. Exhibitionists have their uses; they may serve as an amusement, or they may be doing magic. The second category will contain, for example, those young men who, learning in the torment of their own bodies and minds what war is like, have stammered their indignation in verses, and published them in the hope of infecting others and causing them to abolish it. But these verses have nothing to do with poetry.

Thomas Hardy, at the end of a fine and tragic novel in which he has magnificently expressed his sorrow and indignation for the suffering inflicted by callous sentimentalism on trusting innocence, spoils everything by a last paragraph fastening his accusation upon 'the president of the immortals'. The note rings false, not because it is blasphemous (it offends no piety worthy of the name), but because it is rant. The case against God, so far as it exists, is complete already. The concluding paragraph adds nothing to it. All it does is to spoil the effect of the indictment by betraying a symptom of the emotion which the whole book has already expressed; as if a prosecuting counsel, at the end of his speech, spat in the prisoner's face.

The same fault is especially common in Beethoven. He was confirmed in it, no doubt, by his deafness; but the cause of it was not his deafness but a temperamental inclination to rant. It shows itself in the way his music screams and mutters instead of speaking, as in the soprano part of the Mass in D, or the layout of the opening page in the *Hammerklavier* Sonata. He must have known his failing and tried to overcome it, or he would never have spent so many of his ripest years among string quartets, where screaming and muttering are almost, one might say, physically impossible. Yet even there, the old Adam struts out in certain passages of the *Grosse Fuge*.

It does not, of course, follow that a dramatic writer may not rant in character. The tremendous rant at the end of *The Ascent of F6*, like the Shakespearian[6] ranting on which it is modelled, is done with tongue in cheek. It is not the author who is ranting, but the unbalanced character he depicts; the emotion the author is expressing is the emotion with which he contemplates that character; or rather, the emotion he has towards that secret and disowned part of himself for which the character stands.

· · ·

Art Proper: (2) As Imagination

1. THE PROBLEM DEFINED

The next question in the programme laid down at the beginning of the preceding chapter was put in this way: What is a work of art, granted that there is something in art proper (not only in art falsely so called) to which that name is applied, and that, since art is not craft, this thing is not an artifact? It is something made by the artist, but not made by trans-

---

[6] Shakespeare's characters rant (1) when they are characters in which he takes no interest at all, but which he uses simply as pegs on which to hang what the public wants, like Henry V; (2) when they are meant to be despicable, like Pistol; or (3) when they have lost their heads, like Hamlet in the graveyard.

forming a given raw material, nor by carrying out a preconceived plan, nor by way of realizing the means to a preconceived end. What is this kind of making?

. . .

5. THE WORK OF ART AS IMAGINARY OBJECT

If the making of a tune is an instance of imaginative creation, a tune is an imaginary thing. And the same applies to a poem or a painting or any other work of art. This seems paradoxical; we are apt to think that a tune is not an imaginary thing but a real thing, a real collection of noises; that a painting is a real piece of canvas covered with real colours; and so on. I hope to show, if the reader will have patience, that there is no paradox here; that both these propositions express what we do as a matter of fact say about works of art; and that they do not contradict one another, because they are concerned with different things.

When, speaking of a work of art (tune, picture, &c.), we mean by art a specific craft, intended as a stimulus for producing specific emotional effects in an audience, we certainly mean to designate by the term 'work of art' something that we should call real. The artist as magician or purveyor of amusement is necessarily a craftsman making real things, and making them out of some material according to some plan. His works are as real as the works of an engineer, and for the same reason.

But it does not at all follow that the same is true of an artist proper. His business is not to produce an emotional effect in an audience, but, for example, to make a tune. This tune is already complete and perfect when it exists merely as a tune in his head, that is, an imaginary tune. Next, he may arrange for the tune to be played before an audience. Now there comes into existence a real tune, a collection of noises. But which of these two things is the work of art? Which of them is the music? The answer is implied in what we have already said: the music, the work of art, is not the collection of noises, it is the tune in the composer's head. The noises made by the performers, and heard by the audience, are not the music at all; they are only means by which the audience, if they listen intelligently (not otherwise), can reconstruct for themselves the imaginary tune that existed in the composer's head.

This is not a paradox. It is not something παρα λοξαν, contrary to what we ordinarily believe and express in our ordinary speech. We all know perfectly well, and remind each other often enough, that a person who hears the noises the instruments make is not thereby possessing himself of the music. Perhaps no one can do that unless he does hear the noises; but there is something else which he must do as well. Our ordinary word for this other thing is listening; and the listening which we have to do when we hear the noises made by musicians is in a way rather like the thinking we have to do when we hear the noises made, for example, by a person lecturing on a scientific subject. We hear the sound of his voice; but what he is doing is not simply to make noises, but to develop a scientific thesis. The noises are meant to assist us in achieving what he assumes to be our purpose in coming to hear him lecture, that is, thinking this same scientific thesis for ourselves. The lecture, therefore, is not a collection of noises made by the lecturer with his organs of speech; it is a collection of scientific thoughts related to those noises in such a way that a person who not only hears but thinks as well becomes able to think thought by means of speech, if we like; but if we do, we must think of communication not as an 'imparting' of thought by the speaker to the hearer, the speaker somehow planting his thought in the hearer's receptive mind, but as a 'reproduction' of the speaker's thought by the hearer, in virtue of his own active thinking.

.   .   .

Art is not a luxury, and bad art not a thing we can afford to tolerate. To know ourselves is the foundation of all life that develops beyond the merely psychical level of experience. Unless consciousness does its work successfully, the facts which it offers to intellect, the only things upon which intellect can build its fabric of thought, are false from the beginning. A truthful consciousness gives intellect a firm foundation upon which to build; a corrupt consciousness forces intellect to build on a quicksand. The falsehoods which an untruthful consciousness imposes on the intellect are falsehoods which intellect can never correct for itself. In so far as consciousness is corrupted, the very wells of truth are poisoned. Intellect can build nothing firm. Moral ideals are castles in the air. Political and economic systems are mere cobwebs. Even common sanity and bodily health are no longer secure. But corruption of consciousness is the same thing as bad art.

I do not speak of these grave issues in order to magnify the office of any small section in our communities which arrogates to itself the name of artists. That would be absurd. Just as the life of a community depends for its very existence on honest dealing between man and man, the guardianship of this honesty being vested not in any one class or section, but in all and sundry, so the effort towards expression of emotions, the effort to overcome corruption of consciousness, is an effort that has to be made not by specialists only but by every one who uses language, whenever he uses it. Every utterance and every gesture that each one of us makes is a work of art. It is important to each one of us that in making them, however much he deceives others, he should not deceive himself. If he deceives himself in this matter, he has sown in himself a seed which, unless he roots it up again, may grow into any kind of wickedness, any kind of mental disease, any kind of stupidity and folly and insanity. Bad art, the corrupt consciousness, is the true *radix malorum*.

.   .   .

The artist must prophesy not in the sense that he foretells things to come, but in the sense that he tells his audience, at risk of their displeasure, the secrets of their own hearts. His business as an artist is to speak out, to make a clean breast. But what he has to utter is not, as the individualistic theory of art would have us think, his own secrets. As spokesman of his community, the secrets he must utter are theirs. The reason why they need him is that no community altogether knows its own heart; and by failing in this knowledge a community deceives itself on the one subject concerning which ignorance means death. For the evils which come from that ignorance the poet as prophet suggests no remedy, because he has already given one. The remedy is the poem itself. Art is the community's medicine for the worst disease of mind, the corruption of consciousness.

Richard Wollheim

A CRITIQUE OF COLLINGWOOD AND
THE IDEAL THEORY OF ART

Let us begin with the Ideal theory.* It is usual nowadays to think of this as the Croce-Collingwood theory, and to consider it in the extended form that it has been given by these two philosophers, who, moreover, differ only in points of detail or emphasis. I shall follow this practice, though (as elsewhere) recasting the original arguments where the requirements of this essay necessitate.

The Ideal theory can be stated in three propositions. First, that the work of art consists in an inner state or condition of the artist, called an intuition or an expression: secondly, that this state is not immediate or given, but is the product of a process, which is peculiar to the artist, and which involves articulation, organization, and unification: thirdly, that the intuition so developed may be externalized in a public form, in which case we have the artifact which is often but wrongly taken to be the work of art, but equally it need not be.

The origin of this theory, which we should understand before embarking upon criticism, lies in taking seriously the question, What is distinctive—or perhaps better, What is distinctively "art"—in a work of art?, and giving it an answer that has both a positive and a negative aspect.

In his *Encyclopaedia Britannica* article on "Aesthetics," Croce asks us to consider, as an example of both familiar and high art, the description given by Vergil of Aeneas' meeting with Andromache by the waters of the river Simois (*Aeneid*, iii, lines 294 seq.). The poetry here, he suggests, cannot consist in any of the details that the passage contains—the woes and shame of Andromache, the overcoming of misfortune, the many sad aftermaths of war and defeat—for these things could equally occur in works of history or criticism, and therefore must be in themselves "non-poetic": what we must do is to look beyond them to that which makes poetry out of them, and so we are led of necessity to a human experience.

Richard Wollheim is Grote Professor of Philosophy of Mind and Logic at The University of London. He is a philosopher of particular note who has published in all areas of the subject.

* Selection from *Art and Its Objects* (New York, 1968), Sections 22, 23, 45–52. Reprinted by permission of the author and Harper & Row Publishers, Inc.

And what is true of poetry is true of all the other arts. In order to reach the distinctively aesthetic, we must ignore the surface elements, which can equally be found in nonartistic or practical contexts, and go straight to the mind, which organizes them. Having in this way identified the work of art with an inner process, can we say anything more about this process?

It is at this point that the negative aspect of the theory takes over. What the artist characteristically does is best understood by contrast with—and this is perhaps Collingwood more than Croce—what the craftsman characteristically does. Since what is characteristic of the craftsman is the making of an artifact, or "fabrication," we can be certain that the artist's form of making, or "creation," is not this kind of thing at all.

The contrast between art and craft, which is central to Collingwood's *Principles of Art*, would appear to rest upon three distinctive characteristics of craft. First, every craft involves the notion of a means and an end, each distinctly conceived, the end being definitive of the particular craft, and the means whatever is employed to reach that end; secondly, every craft involves the distinction between planning and execution, where planning consists in foreknowledge of the desired result and calculation as to how best to achieve this, and the execution is the carrying out of this plan; finally, every craft presupposes a material upon which it is exercised and which it thereby transforms into something different. None of these characteristics, the theory argues, pertains to art.

That art does not have an end is established, it might seem, rather speciously by rebutting those theories which propose for art some obviously extrinsic aim like the arousing of emotion, or the stimulation of the intellect, or the encouragement of some practical activity: for these aims give rise to amusement, magic, propaganda, etc. But, it might be urged, why should not the end of Art be, say, just the production of an expressive object? To this one reply would be that this would not be, in the appropriate sense, a case of means and end, since the two would not be conceived separately. Another and more damaging reply would be that this would involve an assimilation of art to craft in its second characteristic. The artist is now thought of as working to a preconceived plan, or as having foreknowledge of what he intends to produce; and this is impossible.

The trouble with this argument—like the more general epistemological argument, of which it can be regarded as a special instance, i.e., that present knowledge of future happenings *tout court* is impossible—is that it acquires plausibility just because we don't know what degree of specificity is supposed to be attributed to what is said to be impossible. If a very high degree of specificity is intended, the argument is obviously cogent. The artist could not know to the minutest detail what he will do. However, if we lower the degree of specificity, the artist surely can have foreknowledge. It is, for instance, neither false nor derogatory to say that there were many occasions on which Verdi knew that he was going to compose an opera, or Bonnard to make a picture of his model. And, after all, the craftsman's foreknowledge will often be no fuller.

That every craft has its raw material and art doesn't—the third criterion of the distinction—is argued for by showing that there is no uniform sense in which we can attribute to the arts a material upon which the artist works. There is nothing out of which the poet can be said to make his poem in the sense in which the sculptor can be said (though falsely, according to the theory) to make his sculpture out of stone or steel.

I now wish to turn to criticism of the Ideal theory. For it must be understood that nothing that has so far been produced has had the character of an argument against the theory. At most we have had arguments against arguments historically advanced in support of it.

There are two arguments that are widely advanced against the Ideal theory.

The first is that by making the work of art something inner or mental, the link between artist and audience has been severed. There is now no object to which both can have access, for no one but the artist can ever know what he has produced.

Against this it might be retorted that this extreme sceptical or solipsistic conclusion would follow only if it was maintained that works of art could never be externalized: whereas all the Ideal theory asserts is that they need not be. A parallel exists in the way in which we can know what a man is thinking, even though his thoughts are something private, for he might disclose his thoughts to us. This retort, it might be felt, while avoiding scepticism, still leaves us too close to it for comfort. Even Collingwood, for instance, who was anxious to avoid the sceptical consequences of his theory, had to concede that on it the spectator can have only an "empirical" or "relative" assurance about the artist's imaginative experience, which, of course, just is, for Collingwood, the work of art. This seems quite at variance with our ordinary—and equally, as I hope to show, with our reflective—views about the public character of art.

The second argument is that the Ideal theory totally ignores the significance of the medium: it is a characteristic fact about works of art that they are in a medium, whereas the entities posited by the Ideal theory are free or unmediated. A first reaction to this argument might be to say that it is an exaggeration. At the lowest we need to make a distinction within the arts. In literature and music we can surely suppose a work of art to be complete before it is externalized without this having any negative implications for the medium. A poem or an aria could exist in the artist's head before it is written down: and although difficulties may exist in the case of a novel or an opera, we can conceive adjustments of mere detail in the theory that would accommodate them. But does this preserve the theory, even in this area? For, if the occurrence of certain experiences (say, the saying of words to oneself) justifies us in postulating the existence of a certain poem, this is not to say that the poem is those experiences. A fairer (though certainly not a clear) way of putting the matter would be to say that it is the object of those experiences. And the object of an experience need not be anything inner or mental.

Anyhow these cases should not preoccupy us. For (to return to the starting point of this whole discussion) it is not works of art of these kinds that provide crucial tests for the Ideal theory. What that theory has primarily to account for are those works of art which are particulars. The question therefore arises, If we are asked to think of, say, paintings and sculptures as intuitions existing in the artist's mind, which are only contingently externalized, is this compatible with the fact that such works are intrinsically in a medium?

An attempt has been made to defend the theory at this stage by appeal to a distinction between the "physical medium" and the "conceived medium": the physical medium being the stuff in the world, the conceived medium being the thought of this in the mind. The defence now consists in saying that the whole process of inner elaboration, on which the theory lays such weight and which Croce explicitly identifies with expression (*l'identità di intuizione ed espressione*), goes on in a medium in that it goes on in the conceived medium. So, for instance, when Leonardo scandalised the prior of S. Maria delle Grazie by standing for days on end in front of the wall he was to paint, without touching it with his brush—an incident Croce quotes as evidence of this "inner" process of expression—we may suppose that the thoughts that occupied his mind were of painted surface, were perhaps images of ever-developing articulation of what he was to set down. Thus a work of art was created that was both in an artist's mind and in a medium.

However, two difficulties still arise. The first concerns the nature of mental images. For it is hard to believe that mental images could be so articulated as in all respects to anticipate the physical pictures to be realised on wall or canvas. For this would involve not merely foreseeing, but also solving, all the problems that will arise, either necessarily or accidentally, in the working of the medium: and not merely is this implausible, but it is even arguable that the accreditation of certain material processes as the media of art is bound up with their inherent unpredictability: it is just because these materials present difficulties that can be dealt with only in the actual working of them that they are so suitable as expressive processes. Again—to borrow an argument from the philosophy of mind—is it even so clear what meaning we are to attach to the supposition that the image totally anticipates the picture? For unless the picture is one of minimal articulation, in which case we could have an image of the whole of it simultaneously, we will have to attribute to the image properties beyond those of which we are aware. But this, except in marginal cases, is objectionable: for by what right do we determine what these extra properties are? (Sartre has made this point by talking of the image's "essential poverty.")

A second difficulty is this: that if we do allow that the inner process is in a conceived medium, this seems to challenge the alleged primacy of the mental experience over the physical artifact, on which the Ideal theory is so insistent. For now the experience seems to derive its content from the nature of the artifact: it is because the artifact is of such and such a material that the image is in such and such a conceived medium. The problem why certain apparently arbitrarily identified stuffs or processes should be the vehicles of art—what I shall call the *bricoleur* problem, from the striking comparison made by Lévi-Strauss of human culture to a *bricoleur* or handiman, who improvises only partly useful objects out of old junk— is a very real one: but the answer to it cannot be that these are just the stuffs or processes that artists happen to think about or conceive in the mind. It is more plausible to believe that the painter thinks in images of paint or the sculptor in images of metal just because these, independently, are the media of art: his thinking presupposes that certain activities in the external world such as charging canvas with paint or welding have already become the accredited processes of art. In other words, there could not be Crocean "intuitions" unless there were, first, physical works of art.

.   .   .

In the mature expression of Wittgenstein's philosophy, the phrase "form of life" (*Lebensform*) makes a frequent appearance. Art is, in Wittgenstein's sense, a form of life.

The phrase appears as descriptive or invocatory of the total context within which alone language can exist: the complex of habits, experiences, skills, with which language interlocks in that it could not be operated without them and, equally, they cannot be identified without reference to it. In particular Wittgenstein set himself against two false views of language. According to the first view, language consists essentially in names: names are connected unambiguously with objects, which they denote: and it is in virtue of this denoting relation that the words that we utter, whether to ourselves or out loud, are about things, that our speech and thought are "of" the world. According to the second view, language in itself is a set of inert marks: in order to acquire a reference to things, what is needed are certain characteristic experiences on the part of the potential language-users, notably the experiences of meaning and (to a lesser degree) of understanding: it is in virtue of these experiences that what we utter, aloud or to ourselves, is about the world. There are obviously considerable differences between these two views. In a way they are diametrically opposite, in that one regards language as totally adherent for its distinctive character on certain experiences, the other regards it as altogether complete prior to them. Nevertheless, the two views also have something in common. For both presuppose that these experiences exist, and can be identified, quite separately from language; that is, both from language as a whole, and also from that piece of language which directly refers to them. (This last distinction is useful, but it would be wrong to press it too hard.) The characterization of language (alternatively, of this or that sublanguage) as "a form of life" is intended to dispute the separation on either level.

The characterization of art too as a form of life has certain parallel implications.

The first implication would be that we should not think that there is something which we call the artistic impulse or intention, and which can be identified quite independently of and prior to the institutions of art.

An attempt is sometimes made to explain artistic creativity (and, therefore, ultimately art itself) in terms of an artistic instinct, conceived, presumably, on the analogy of the sexual instinct or hunger. But if we pursue the analogy, it fails us. For there is no way in which we can ascribe manifestations to this artistic instinct until there are already established in society certain practices recognised as artistic: the sexual instinct, on the other hand, manifests itself in certain activities, whether or not society recognises them as sexual—indeed, in many cases, society actively denies their true character. To put the matter the other way round: If the sexual instincts are indulged, then certain sexual activities follow; we cannot, however, regard the arts as though we were observing in them the consequences that follow when the artistic instinct is indulged. Either way round the point is the same: in the case of sexuality, the connection between the instinct and its satisfaction in the world is immediate, in the case of art it is mediated by a practice or institution. (If it is not always true that the sexual instinct manifests itself directly, at least the mediation is through privately determined thoughts or phantasies, not through a public institution: the parallel in the sexual sphere to talking of an artistic instinct would be to postulate a "matrimonial" instinct.)

Nor does the more fashionable kind of analogy between the artistic instinct and disordered mental functioning, e.g. an obsession, fare any better. For, once again, there is an immediate connection between the obsession and the compulsive behaviour in which it is discharged, to which we find no parallel in art. There may, of course, be an obsessional element in much artistic activity, but the choice by the artist of certain activities, which in point of fact happen to be artistic activities, need not be obsessional. To put it in a way that may seem paradoxical, the kind of activity in which the artist engages need not be for him, as the compulsive behavior is of necessity for the obsessional, "meaningful": for on one level at any rate, the obsessional wants to do what he does, and in consequence the analysis of his obsession consists in tracing this wish to another and earlier wish, of which it is a symptom. It was just to distinguish art from this kind of case that Freud classed it as sublimation, where "sublimation" means the discharge of energy in socially acceptable channels.

Of course, this is not to deny that art is connected with instinctual movements, or that it could exist away from their vicissitudes. There are, indeed, certain psychic forces, such as the reparative drive or the desire to establish whole objects, without which the general forms that art takes, as well as its value, would be barely comprehensible. In much the same way, religious belief would be barely comprehensible without an understanding of early attitudes to parents: but it would miss the distinctive character of such beliefs to analyze them without remainder, in the case of each individual, into the personal motivation that leads him to embrace them.

The error against which this section has been directed is that of thinking that there is an artistic impulse that can be identified independently of the institutions of art. It does not follow that there is no such thing as an artistic impulse. On the contrary, there is, where this means the impulse to produce something as a work of art: an impulse which, as we have seen, constitutes, on the artist's side, the match to the aesthetic attitude, where this means the attitude of seeing something as a work of art. Indeed, reference to this impulse is necessary in order to escape from an error implicit in the very first section of this essay: that of seeing art as an unordered set of disjointed activities or products. For what gives art its unity is that the objects that centrally belong to it have been produced under the concept of art.

. . .

. . . If it is true that artistic creativity can occur only in so far as certain processes or stuffs are already accredited as the vehicles of art, then it becomes important to know how and why these accreditations are made. More specifically, are these accreditations entirely arbitrary: in the sense, for instance, in which it is arbitrary that, out of the whole stock of articulated sounds, some and not others, have been appropriated by the various natural languages as their phonetic representations? Furthermore, if they are arbitrary, does this mean that the artist is dominated by whoever is responsible for the accreditations—let us for the moment identify him with the spectator—and that the picture we have of the artist as a free agent is erroneous?

I shall begin with the second question: I shall concede that there is a way in which the spectator is supreme over the artist: and I shall then try to take away the air of paradox that attaches to this truth. In the first place, we are wrong to contrast the artist and the spectator as though we were dealing here with different classes of people. For in reality what we have are two different roles, which can be filled by the same person. Indeed, it seems a necessary fact that, though not all spectators are also artists, all artists are spectators. We have already touched upon his truth in considering expression, but it has many applications, not the least of which relates to the present problem of the social determination of art forms or art vehicles. Secondly, it is unnecessarily dramatic to speak here of "domination": even if we do think that the accreditation of art forms is arbitrary. For we might go back for a moment to the example by reference to which I introduced the notion of arbitrariness: I did so by reference to language. Now, do we think that the native speaker of a language is "dominated" in what he says by his predecessors and his contemporaries, in whose mouths his language has evolved to become what it now is?

We may now take up the first question and ask, Is it in fact arbitrary that certain processes and stuffs, and not others, have been accredited as the vehicles of art? It is obvious that we can make any single artistic process e.g. placing pigment on canvas, *seem* arbitrary by stripping away from it, in our minds, anything that gives it any air of familiarity or naturalness. But all that this shows is that, when we raise questions about the arbitrariness or otherwise of a certain process, we need to specify the context in relation to which they are asked. If we indicate—as we did just now in asking about painting—a quite "open," or zero-, context, the accreditation will clearly seem arbitrary. But it does not follow from this that it will seem arbitrary for all contexts or even for a large range of contexts.

Perhaps we can see this more clearly by going back, once again, to the phonetic problem. If we take a natural language in the abstract, it is obviously arbitrary that certain articulated sounds, not others, were chosen to be its phonemes: where this means little more than that there are others that could have been chosen. If we fill in the historical background, including the development of language, the arbitrariness diminishes. If we complete the context and include such facts as that native speakers of one language will barely be able to form the phonemes of another, any suggestion of arbitrariness that a particular man living in a particular society might think attaches to the sounds that he employs quite vanishes. In such a situation a man can scarcely think of his language other than as, in Hamann's phrase, "his wedded wife."

In the case of art a natural context in which to determine the arbitrariness or otherwise of the vehicles of art is provided by certain very general principles which have historically been advanced concerning the essential characteristics of a work of art. Examples would be: that the object must be enduring, or at least that it must survive (not be consumed in) appreciation; that it must be apprehended by the "theoretical" senses of sight and hearing; that it must exhibit internal differentiation, or be capable of being ordered; that it must not be inherently valuable, etc. Each of these principles can, of course, be questioned, and certainly as they stand none seems irreproachable. But that is not the point here: for I have introduced these principles solely to show the kind of context in which alone we can ask whether it is arbitrary that a certain stuff or process has become an accredited vehicle of art.

A second implication of the point that art is a form of life would be that we do wrong to postulate, of each work of art, a particular aesthetic intention or impulse which both accounts for that work and can be identified independently of it. For though there could be such a thing, there need not be.

. . . I invoked a distinction of Wittgenstein's between two senses of "peculiar" and "particular": there to make the point that if it is characteristic of works of art that we adopt a particular attitude towards them, i.e. the aesthetic, this attitude is particular in the intransitive sense. The same distinction can be used now, this time to make a point in reference not to art in general but to individual works of art; and that is that, if we say that a work of art expresses a particular state of mind, or even if we say of it that it expresses a particular state of mind with great intensity or poignancy, once again the word "particular" is used in its intransitive sense.

And once again this use brings with it its own dangers of misunderstanding. For if what a work of art expresses is only a particular state in an intransitive sense; or (to put it another way) if the phrase "what the work of art expresses" is only a reflexive construction; then (it might seem) works of art do not really express anything at all. If we cannot identify the state except through the work, then we have at best poor or highly generalised expression: alternatively, we have no expression at all. This is, for instance, how Hanslick would appear to have argued, when he concluded from the fact that music doesn't express definite feelings like piety, love, joy, or sadness, that it isn't an art of expression.

But the argument is misguided. For it must be emphasized that the difference between the two usages of "This expresses a particular state" does not correspond to any difference in the expressive function of the work, in the sense either of what is expressed or of how it is expressed. The difference lies simply in the way in which we refer to the inner state: whether we describe it, or whether we simply draw attention to or gesture towards it.

When we say *L'Embarquement pour l'Ile de Cythère*, or the second section of *En Blanc et Noir*, expresses a particular feeling, and we mean this intransitively, we are misunderstood if we are then asked "What feeling?" Nevertheless, if someone tells us that to him the painting or the piece of music means nothing, there are many resources we have at our disposal for trying to get him to see what is expressed. In the case of the music, we could play it in a certain way, we could compare it with other music, we could appeal to the desolate circumstances of its composition, we could ask him to think why he should be blind to this specific piece: in the case of the painting, we could read to him *A Prince of Court Painters*, pausing, say, on the sentence "The evening will be a wet one," we could show him other paintings by Watteau, we could point to the fragility of many of the resolutions in the picture. It almost looks as though in such cases we can compensate for how little we are able to say by how much we are able to do. Art rests on the fact that deep feelings pattern themselves in a coherent way all over our life and behaviour.

The appeal of the view that a work of art expresses nothing unless what it expresses can be put into (other) words, can be effectively reduced by setting beside it another view, no less well entrenched in the theory of art, to the effect that a work of art has no value if what it expresses, or more generally says, can be put into (other) words.

Now, if this view had been advanced solely with reference to the non-verbal arts, it would have been of dubious significance. Or it might have been countered that the reason why a work of art not in words should not be expressible in words is just that it was not originally in words i.e. the view reflects on the media of art, not on art itself. However, it is a significant fact that the view has been canvassed most heavily precisely in that area of art where its cutting-edge is sharpest: in literature. For if the literature is in a language rich enough to exhibit synonymy, the view would seem to assert something about art.

Within the so-called "New Criticism" it has been a characteristic tenet that there is a "heresy of paraphrase." It is, of course, conceded that we can try to formulate what a poem says. But what we produce can never be more than approximate; moreover, it does not lead us to the poem itself. For "the paraphrase is not the real core of meaning which constitutes the essence of the poem" (Cleanth Brooks).

This view would appear to have a number of different sources. One, which is of little aesthetic interest, is that sometimes in poetry language of such simplicity or directness is used (e.g. the Lucy poems, *Romances sans Paroles*) that it is hard to see where we would start if we tried to say the same thing in other words. But not all poetry employs such language: nor, moreover, is the employment of such language peculiar to poetry. In consequence, the heresy of paraphrase, in so far as it bases itself on this consideration, is an instance of faulty generalization. Another source is that even when the poetry is in a kind of language that admits of paraphrase—metaphor would be the supreme example here—any elucidation of what the poem says would have to contain, in addition to a paraphrase of the metaphors, an account of why these particular metaphors were used. A third source is that often in poetry there is such a high degree of concentration or superimposition of content that it is not reasonable to expect that we could separate out the various thoughts and feelings ("meanings," as they are sometimes called by critics) that are afforded expression in the work.

It is impossible in this essay to pursue these last two points, though they relate to very general and important features of art which cannot be ignored in a full understanding of the subject. One is the importance of the mode of presentation in art: a phrase which naturally changes its application somewhat as we move from medium to medium but includes very different things like brushwork, choice of imagery, interrelation of plot and subplots, etc. The other is the condensation characteristic of art. Both these points will be touched on later, and an attempt made to weave them into the emerging pattern of art.

In the light of the preceding discussion we might now turn back to the Croce-Collingwood theory of art and of the artistic process. For we are now in a position to see rather more sharply the error involved in that account. We can see it, that is, as an instance of a more general error.

For the equation, central to that theory, first of the work of art with an internally elaborated image or "intuition," and then of the artistic gift with the capacity to elaborate and refine images in this way, is just another attempt, though perhaps a peculiarly plausible one, to conceive of art in a way that makes no allusion to a form of life. For on this theory, not only can the artist create a particular work of art without in point of fact ever externalising it, but his capacity in general to create works of art, or his attainment as an artist (as we might put it), may flourish quite independently of there being in existence any means of externalization. The artist is an artist solely in virtue of his inner life: where "inner life," it will be appreciated, is understood narrowly so as not to include any thoughts or feelings that contain an explicit reference to art.

The analogy with language, which the phrase "form of life" suggests, should help us to see what is wrong here. For parallel to the conception of the artist as the man whose head is crammed with intuitions though he may know of no medium in which to externalise them, would be the conception of the thinker as a man with his head full of ideas though he possesses no language in which to express them. The second conception is evidently absurd. And if we do not always recognize the absurdity of the first conception too, this is because we do not allow the parallel. For we might rather think that the true parallel to the Crocean artist is, in the domain of language, the man who thinks to himself. But this would be wrong: for three reasons.

In the first place, the man who thinks to himself has already acquired a medium, or language. The peculiarity is in the way he employs it: that is, always internally. Secondly, it is a distinctive characteristic of language, to which there is no analogue in art (with the possible exception of the literary arts), that it has this internal employment. We can talk to ourselves, but we cannot (with the exception just noted) make works of art to ourselves. Thirdly, we must appreciate that it is an essential feature of the Croce-Collingwood thesis that not only can the artist make works of art to himself, but he may be in the situation in which he can only make works of art to himself: in other words, it is possible that he could have the intuitions and there be no way in the society of externalising them. But there is no parallel to this in the case of thought. For if we have language which we employ internally, then we always can, physical defects apart, also employ it externally: though in point of fact we may never do so. There could not be a language that it was impossible for someone who knew it to speak. Accordingly, the proper analogue to the artist, conceived according to the Croce-Collingwood theory, is not the thinker who has a medium of thought which he uses only to himself but the thinker who has no medium of thought, which, I have maintained, is an absurdity.

Freud, in several places, tried to approach the problem of the artistic personality by means of a comparison he proposed between the artist and the neurotic. For both the artist and the neurotic are people who, under the pressure of certain clamorous instincts, turn away from reality and lead a large part of their lives in the world of phantasy. But the artist differs from the neurotic in that he succeeds in finding "a path back to reality." Freud's thinking at this point is highly condensed. He would appear to have had a number of ideas in mind in using this phrase. But one of the ideas, perhaps the central one, is that the artist refuses to remain in that hallucinated condition to which the neurotic regresses, where the wish and the fulfilment of the wish are one. For the artist, unlike the neurotic, the phantasy is a starting point, not the culmination, of his activity. The energies which have initially driven him away from reality, he manages to harness to the process of making, out of the material of his wishes, an object that can then become a source of shared pleasure and consolation. For it is distinctive of the work of art, in contrast, that is, to the daydream, that it is free of the excessively personal or the utterly alien element that at once disfigure and impoverish the life of phantasy. By means of his achievement the artist can open to others unconscious sources of pleasure which hitherto they had been denied: and so, as Freud sanguinely puts it, the artist wins through his phantasy what the neurotic can win only in his phantasy: honour, power, and the love of women.

It will be apparent that on this account all art involves renunciation: renunciation, that is, of the immediate gratifications of phantasy. This feature is not peculiar to art, though it may be peculiarly powerful in art: it is shared with any activity in which there is a systematic abandonment of the pleasure principle in favour of the testing of wish and thought in reality. In the case of art this testing occurs twice over: first, in the confrontation of the artist and his medium, and then again in the confrontation of the artist and his society. On both occasions it is characteristic that the artist surrenders something that he cherishes in response to the stringencies of something that he recognizes as external to, and hence independent of, himself.

Now it is precisely this feature of art, art as renunciation—a feature. which accounts in some measure for the pathos of art, certainly of all great art, for the sense of loss so precariously balanced against the riches and grandeur of achievement—that the theory we have been considering totally denies. The Croce-Collingwood theory of the artist is, it might be said, a testimony to the omnipotent thinking from which, in point of fact, it is the mission of art to release us.

Hitherto in presenting art as a form of life, I have discussed it from the artist's point of view, not the spectator's: though, of course, the two discussions overlap, as do (as I have argued) the points of view themselves. Indeed, that they do is largely what warrants the phrase "form of life." However, within the form of life there is a distinctive function that accrues to the spectator: I now turn to it.

For guidance we must once again appeal to the analogy with language. What distinguishes the hearer of a language who knows it from one who doesn't is not that he reacts to it, whereas the other doesn't: for the other could, just as, say, a dog responds to his master's call. The difference is that the man who knows the language replaces an associative link, which might or might not be conditioned, with understanding. The man who does not know the language might associate to the words—or rather noises as they will be for him. . . . In this way he might even come to know as much about the speaker as the man who shares a language with him: but the distinctive feature is that his coming to know about the speaker and the speaker's revealing it will be two independent events, whereas the man who knows the language can't but find out what he is told.

However, how are we to use the analogy? Are we to say bluntly that it is distinctive of the spectator versed in art that he understands the work of art? Or are we to use the analogy more tentatively and say of the spectator that he characteristically replaces mere association to the work with a response that stands to art as understanding does to language?

Around the answer to this question whole theories of art (e.g. cognitive, subjective, contemplative) have been constructed. Their internecine conflict, which constitutes a large part of aesthetics, is sufficiently barren as to suggest that something has gone wrong in their initial formation. What appears to happen in most cases is this: Something is found in our characteristic reactions to art that corresponds to *a* use of a particular word: this word is then adopted as *the* word for the spectator's attitude: but when this happens, it is the whole of the use of the word, or its use in all contexts, that is collected: and the spectator's attitude is then pronounced to be all those things which are covered by this word. A theory is established, and an insight obscured. An example is provided by Tolstoy's theory of Art. Tolstoy, recognizing that there is an element of communication in all art, or that all art is, in *some* sense of the word, communication, then said that art *was* communication, then turned his back on the original recognition by insisting that art was, or was properly, communication in some further sense of the word than that in which it had originally forced itself upon him.

What I shall do is to retain the word "understand" to characterize the spectator's attitude, try not to import alien associations, and see what can be said about what is characteristically involved in this kind of understanding.

There are two points of a general character that it will be profitable to bear in mind throughout any such examination. I mention them here, though I shall not be able to elaborate more than a fraction of what they suggest.

The first is this: that for it to be in any way in order to talk of understanding apropos of art, there must be some kind of match or correspondence between the artist's activity and the spectator's reaction. Enough has already been said in connection with interpretation to make it clear that in the domain of art the match will never be complete. The spectator will always understand more than the artist intended, and the artist will always have intended more than any single spectator understands—to put it paradoxically. Nor, moreover, is it clear whether the match must be with what the artist actually did on the specific occasion of producing this particular work, or whether it has only to be with, say, the kind of thing that the artist does. Is the spectator's understanding to be directed upon the historical intention of the artist, or upon something more general or idealized? And if this element of uncertainty seems to put the understanding of art in jeopardy, we should appreciate that this is not a situation altogether peculiar to art. It is present in many cases where (as we say) we understand fully, or only too well, what someone really did or said.

Secondly, I suggest that, when we look round for examples on which to test any hypotheses that we might form about the spectator's attitude, it would be instructive to take cases where there is something which is a work of art which is habitually not regarded as one, and which we then at a certain moment come to see as one. Works of architecture that we pass daily in city streets unthinkingly are likely to provide fruitful instances. And it is significant what a very different view we are likely to get of the spectator's attitude from considering *these* cases rather than those which we are conventionally invited to consider in aesthetics, . . . i.e. cases where there is something that is not a work of art, which is habitually not regarded as one, and which we then at a certain point in time come to see as if it were one.

. . . I referred to a certain traditional view by saying that art in its expressive function possessed a kind of translucency: to put it another way, that if expression is not natural, but works through signs, as we may have to concede it does, then at least we may insist that these signs are iconic. We might think that we now have an elucidation of this rather cryptic view in the idea that it is characteristic of the spectator's attitude to art that he replaces association by understanding. For, it might be argued, the difference between iconic and non-iconic signs, which is generally treated as though it were a difference in the relations in which the signs stand to the referent, is really a difference in the relations in which we stand to the sign: to call a sign iconic is just to say of it that it is part of a well-entrenched or familiar language. The naturalness of a sign is a function of how natural we are with it. Now, to talk of replacing association by understanding is just to talk of a greater familiarity with the signs we use. Therefore, if we understand a sign, we can regard it as iconic, and in this way we have an over-all explanation of the iconic character of signs in art.

It would certainly seem to be true that we distinguish the cases where we "read off" certain information from a diagram from the cases where we just see it, largely on considerations of how entrenched the medium of communication is in our life and habits. We read off the colored picture from the black-and-white diagram, we read off the profile of the hill from the contour lines, just because these methods are so tangential to the processes by which we ordinarily acquire and distribute knowledge. However, we cannot conclude from this that any sign language that we regularly operate is for us iconic. Familiarity may be a necessary, but it is not a sufficient, condition of being iconic: otherwise we should have to regard any language of which we are native speakers as *eo ipso* iconic.

If, therefore, the suggestion before us has some plausibility, this is only because, in the original argument, at least one distinction too few was made. For the implication was that the distinction between cases where we "read off" information and cases where the information is conveyed iconically is exhaustive. But this is absurd. For instance, we do not *read off* something when we *read* it.

However, even if we cannot account for the distinction between iconic and noniconic signs entirely in terms of a particular relation in which we stand to the signs, i.e. our familiarity in handling them, some advantage can be obtained from looking at it in this way: if only because it attenuates the distinction. Intervening cases suggest themselves, and the peculiarity of an iconic sign is thus reduced.

Furthermore, even if we cannot analyze the distinction entirely in terms of this *one* attitude of ours toward signs, there may be *another* attitude of ours in terms of which the analysis can be completed: and in this way the original character, if not the detail, of the analysis may be preserved. Let us say that every (token) sign that we use has a cluster of properties. Ordinarily the degree of our attention to these properties varies greatly over their range: with spoken words, for instance, we pay great attention to the pitch, little to the speed. Now it may happen that, for some reason or other, we extend, or increase the scope of, our attention either intensively or extensively: we consider more properties, or the same properties more carefully. Now, my suggestion is that it is as, and when, signs become for us in this way "fuller" objects that we may also come to feel that they have a greater appropriateness to their referent. (As a deep explanation we might want to correlate the seeing of a sign as iconic with a regression to the "concrete thinking" of earliest infancy.) Of course, the adoption of this attitude on our part will not automatically bring it about that we see the sign as iconic, for the properties of the sign may themselves be recalcitrant: but it can be contributory towards it. However, once we have seen the sign as iconic through an increasing sensitivity to its many properties, we then tend to disguise this by talking as though there were just one very special property of the sign, that of being iconic, of which we had now become aware. We think that the sign is tied to its referent by one special link, whereas in point of fact there are merely many associations.

(I have, it will be observed, followed the convention whereby an iconic sign is thought of as matching, or resembling, or being congruent with, its *referent*: but why referent or reference, rather than *sense*, is left unexamined—as, for reasons of space, it will be here.)

I want to complete the present discussion by suggesting that it is part of the spectator's attitude to art that he should adopt *this* attitude towards the work: that he should make it the object of an ever-increasing or deepening attention. Here we have the mediating link between art and the iconicity of signs. More significantly, we have here further confirmation for the view, already insisted upon, . . . that the properties of a work of art cannot be demarcated: for, as our attention spreads over the object, more and more of its properties may become incorporated into its aesthetic nature. It was some such thought as this that we may believe Walter Pater to have intended when he appropriated the famous phrase that all art "aspires to the condition of music."

For the Ideal theory, see Benedetto Croce, *Aesthetic*, 2nd ed., Douglas Ainslie, trans. (London, 1922); and R. G. Collingwood, *The Principles of Art* (London, 1938). In his later writings Croce considerably diverged from the theory here attributed to him.

For criticism of the theory, see W. B. Gallie, "The Function of Philosophical Aesthetics," *Mind*, Vol. LVII (1948), pp. 302–321, reprinted in Elton.

On the importance of the medium, see Samuel Alexander, *Art and the Material* (Manchester, 1925), reprinted in his *Philosophical and Literary Pieces* (London, 1939); John Dewey, *Art as Experience* (New York, 1934);

Edward Bullough, *Aesthetics*, Elizabeth M. Wilkinson, ed. (Stanford, 1957); and Stuart Hampshire, *Feeling and Expression* (London, 1960).

The defence of the Ideal theory in terms of "conceived" versus "physical" medium is to be found in John Hospers, "The Croce-Collingwood Theory of Art," *Philosophy*, Vol. XXXI (October, 1956), pp. 291–308.

On images, see Alain, *Système des Beaux-Arts* (Paris, 1926), Livre I; J-P Sartre, *The Psychology of the Imagination*, trans. anon. (New York, 1948); and Hideko Ishiguro, "Imagination," *British Analytical Philosophy*, Alan Montefiore and Bernard Williams, eds. (London, 1966).

For the notion of form of life, see Ludwig Wittgenstein, *Philosophical Investigations* (New York, 1953).

For the analogy between art and language, see John Dewey, *Art as Experience* (New York, 1934); André Malraux, *The Voices of Silence*, Stuart Gilbert, trans. (New York, 1954); E. H. Gombrich, *Art and Illusion* (New York, 1960); and Maurice Merleau-Ponty, "Indirect Language and the Voices of Silence" in his *Signs*, Richard C. McCleary, trans. (Evanston, Ill., 1964).

For the reciprocity between artist and spectator, which is the theme of much of this essay, see Alain, *Système des Beaux-Arts* (Paris, 1926); John Dewey, *Art as Experience* (New York, 1934); also (surprisingly enough) R. G. Collingwood, *The Principles of Art* (London, 1938); and Mikel Dufrenne, *Phénomenologie de l'Expérience Esthétique* (Paris, 1953). Many of the crucial insights are to be found in G. W. F. Hegel, *Philosophy of Fine Art: Introduction*, Bernard Bosanquet, trans. (London, 1886).

For the idea of an artistic impulse, see e.g. Samuel Alexander, *Art and Instinct* (Oxford, 1927), reprinted in his *Philosophical and Literary Pieces* (London, 1939); and Étienne Souriau, *L'Avenir de l'Esthétique* (Paris, 1929).

A 19th century version of this approach took the form of tracing art to a play-impulse. This approach, which derives rather tenuously from Friedrich Schiller, *Letters on the Aesthetic Education of Man*, Reginald Snell, trans. (New Haven, 1954), is to be found in Herbert Spencer, *Essays* (London, 1858–1874); Konrad Lange, *Das Wesen der Kunst* (Berlin, 1901); and Karl Groos, *The Play of Man*, Elizabeth L. Baldwin, trans. (New York, 1901).

Another version of this approach in terms of a specific *Kunstwollen* or artistic volition is to be found in Alois Riegl, *Stilfragen* (Berlin, 1893); and Wilhelm Worringer, *Abstraction and Empathy*, Michael Bullock, trans. (London, 1953).

For criticism of the whole approach, see Mikel Dufrenne, *Phénomenologie de l'Expérience Esthétique* (Paris, 1953).

There are scattered implicit references to the *bricoleur* problem in Immanuel Kant, *Critique of Judgment*, J. C. Meredith, trans. (New York, 1928); G. W. F. Hegel, *Philosophy of Fine Art: Introduction*, Bernard Bosanquet, trans. (London, 1886); John Dewey, *Art as Experience* (New York, 1934). See also D. W. Prall, *Aesthetic Judgment* (New York, 1929); T. M. Greene, *The Arts and the Art of Criticism* (Princeton, 1940); Thomas Munro, *The Arts and their Interrelations* (New York, 1940).

For the argument that, if a work of art expresses anything, it must express something otherwise identifiable, see Eduard Hanslick, *The Beautiful in Music*, Gustav Cohen, trans. (New York, 1957). Hanslick's assumptions are criticised, somewhat perfunctorily, in Carroll C. Pratt, *The Meaning of Music* (New York, 1931), and Leonard B. Meyer, *Emotion and Meaning in Music* (Chicago, 1956). A view diametrically opposed to Hanslick is to be found in J. W. N. Sullivan, *Beethoven: His Spiritual Development* (New York, 1927).

See also Ludwig Wittgenstein, *Philosophical Investigations*, G. E. M. Anscombe, ed. (New York, 1953), *I* paras. 519–546, *II* vi, ix, and *The Blue and Brown Books* (New York, 1958), pp. 177–185, and *Letters and Conversations on Aesthetics*, etc. Cyril Barrett, ed. (New York, 1966), pp. 28–40.

The argument against paraphrasability is to be found in Cleanth Brooks and Robert Penn Warren, *Understanding Fiction* (New York, 1943), and Cleanth Brooks, *The Well-Wrought Urn* (New York, 1947).

The position is criticised in Yvor Winters, *In Defence of Reason* (Denver, 1947).

See also Stanley Cavell, "Aesthetic Problems of Modern Philosophy" in *Philosophy in America*, Max Black, ed. (New York, 1965).

For a criticism of the identification of the artist's achievement with the having of images, see Alain, *Système des Beaux-Arts* (Paris, 1926), Livre I; J-P Sartre, *The Psychology of the Imagination*, trans. anon., (New York, 1948); Henri Foçillon, *Life of Forms in Art*, Charles Beecher Hogan, trans. (New York, 1948).

For the distinction between the artist and the neurotic, see Sigmund Freud, *Introductory Lectures in Psycho-Analysis*, Joan Rivière, trans. (London, 1929), Lecture 23, and "Formulations concerning the two Principles in Mental Functioning" and "The Relation of the Poet to Day Dreaming" in *Collected Papers*, Ernest Jones, ed. (London, 1949), Vol. IV.

See also Marion Milner, *On Not Being Able to Paint*, 2nd ed. (London, 1957); and Hanna Segal, "A Psycho-Analytic Approach to Aesthetics," and Adrian Stokes, "Form in Art," both in *New Directions in Psycho-Analysis*, Melanie Klein *et al.*, eds. (London, 1955).

For the notion of understanding in connection with art, see e.g. Susanne Langer, *Philosophy in a New Key* (Cambridge, Mass., 1942); C. I. Lewis, *An Analysis of Knowledge and Valuation* (La Salle, Ill., 1946); Richard Rudner, "On Semiotic Aesthetics," *J.A.A.C.*, Vol. X (Sept., 1951), pp. 67–77, reprinted in Beardsley, and "Some Problems of Nonsemiotic Aesthetics," *J.A.A.C.*, Vol. XV (March, 1957), pp. 298–310; Rudolf Wittkower, "Interpretation of Visual Symbols in the Arts," in A. J. Ayer *et al.*, *Studies in Communication* (London, 1955); *Language, Thought and Culture*, P. Henlé, ed. (Ann Arbor, 1958), Chap. 9; John Hospers, *Meaning and Truth in the Arts* (Hamden, Conn., 1964).

See also Ludwig Wittgenstein, *Lectures and Conversations on Aesthetics*, etc., Cyril Barrett, ed. (New York, 1966).

Select Bibliography for Part One

Books

Leon Battista Alberti, *On Painting*; Samuel Alexander, *Beauty and Other Forms of Value*; Thomas Aquinas, *Basic Writings of St. Thomas Aquinas*; Karl Aschenbrenner and William B. Holther (trans.), *Reflections on Poetry: Alexander Gottlieb Baumgarten's Meditationes Philisophicae*; Erich Auerbach,

Mimesis; St. Augustine, *Confessions*; St. Augustine, *De Immortalitate Animae*; Monroe C. Beardsley, *Aesthetics: From Classical Greece to the Present*; Clive Bell, *Art*; Nicholas Boileau, *The Art of Poetry*; Bernard Bosanquet, *Three Lectures on Aesthetic*; Merle E. Brown, *Neo-Idealistic Aesthetics: Croce, Gentile, Collingwood*; Edmund Burke, *A Philosophical Enquiry into the Origin of our Ideas of the Sublime and Beautiful*; R. G. Collingwood, *Essays in the Philosophy of Art*; Benedetto Croce, *Aesthetic as Science of Expression and General Linguistic*; Benedetto Croce, *The Breviary of Aesthetic*; J. M. Crombie, *An Examination of Plato's Doctrines*; Raphael Demos, *The Philosophy of Plato*; John Dewey, *Art as Experience*; Denis Diderot, *The Beautiful*; Alan Donagan, *The Later Philosophy of R. G. Collingwood*; C. J. Ducasse, *The Philosophy of Art*; Marsilio Ficino, *Commentary on Plato's "Symposium"*; Roger Fry, *Vision and Design*; H. W. Garrod, *Tolstoi's Theory of Art*; Giovanni Gentile, *The Philosophy of Art*; Katherine Gilbert and Helmut Kuhn, *A History of Aesthetics*; Theodore M. Green, *The Arts and the Art of Criticism*; William Hogarth, *The Analysis of Beauty*; Leonardo da Vinci, *Treatise on Painting*; Gotthold Ephraim Lessing, *Laocoon: An Essay on the Limits of Painting and Poetry*; Rupert C. Lodge, *Plato's Theory of Art*; Longinus, *On the Sublime*; G. E. Moore, *Principia Ethica*; DeWitt H. Parker, *The Principles of Aesthetics*; Plato, *Collected Works*; Plotinus, *The Enneads*; Thomas Reid, *Essays on the Intellectual Powers of Man*; Sir Joshua Reynolds, *Discourses on Art*; George Santayana, *Reason in Art*; George Santayana, *The Sense of Beauty: Being the Outline of Aesthetic Theory*; Friedrich Schelling, *System of Transcendental Idealism*; Friedrich Schiller (Letters) *On the Aesthetic Education of Man*; Adam Smith, *Of the Nature of that Imitation Which Takes Place In What Are Called the Imitative Arts*; Goran Sorbom, *Mimesis and Art. Studies in the Origin and Early Development of an Aesthetic Vocabulary*; Heinrich Wolfflin, *Principles of Art History*; William Wordsworth, *Observations Prefixed to Lyrical Ballads*.

Articles

Henry Aiken, "Art as Expression and Surface"; Rudolf Arnheim, "Gestalt and Art"; Rudolf Arnheim, "The Gestalt Theory of Expression"; Rudolf Arnheim, "The Priority of Expression"; Jay E. Bachrach, "Richard Wollheim and the Work of Art"; Jay E. Bachrach, "Type and Token and the Identification of the Work of Art"; John Benson, "Emotion and Expression"; R. B. Braithwaite, Gilbert Ryle, and G. E. Moore, "Imaginary Objects" (Symposium); S. Buettner, "John Dewey and the Visual Arts in America"; Peter A. Carmichael, "Collingwood and Art Media"; Edward S. Casey, "Expression and Communication in Art"; Anthony J. Close, "Philosophical Theories of Art and Nature in Classical Antiquity"; Benedetto Croce, "On the Aesthetics of Dewey"; C. Daniels, "Tolstoy and Corrupt Art"; Arthur Danto, "Artworks and Real Things"; Arthur Danto, "The Transfiguration of the Commonplace"; John Dewey, "A Comment on the Foregoing Criticism"; Kenneth Dorter, "The Ion: Plato's Characterization of Art"; George H. Douglas, "A Reconsideration of the Dewey-Croce Exchange"; Louis Fraiberg, "Freud's Writings on Art"; L. Golden, "Plato's Concept of Memesis"; D. W. Gotshalk, "Aesthetic Expression"; John Hospers, "The Concept of Artistic Expression"; John Hospers, "Collingwood and Art Media: A Reply"; John Hospers, "The Croce-Collingwood Theory of Art"; Donald P. Kuspit, "Dewey's Critique of Art for Art's Sake"; Beryl Lake, "A Study of the Irrefutability of Two Aesthetic Theories"; DeWitt H. Parker, "The Nature of Art"; Richard Sclafani, "Art Works, Art Theory, and the Artworld"; Richard Sclafani, "Wollheim on Collingwood"; Eliseo Vivas, "Animadversions on Imitation and Expression."

PART TWO

Contemporary
Theories of Art and
Contemporary Critiques
of these Theories

The expounding and defending of philosophies of art has not been a popular activity since the late 1940s. In fact, only Susanne Langer in the 1940s and 1950s produced a philosophy of art. More recently, Arthur Danto and George Dickie have attempted to theorize about the essential nature of art. There seem to have been two factors which have discouraged attempts at philosophizing about the theory of art: (1) the proliferation of unsuccessful theories of art in the nineteenth and early twentieth century, and (2) the influence of a series of articles in the early 1950s inspired by the philosophy of Wittgenstein which argued persuasively that *art* is a concept that does not have necessary and sufficient conditions and, hence, cannot be captured by a definition or theory. Langer's philosophy of art predates this second influence, and, in fact, her theory continues in the tradition of the earlier theories of art. Danto's and Dickie's philosophizing about art comes after the Wittgensteinian influence and attempts to take it into account. No selection from Danto's work is included in this section, but his "Artworld" is included in part one as a commentary on Plato's philosophy of art and his "Artworks and Real Things" is the concluding essay of part five, which is concerned with the death of art.

The heart of Langer's philosophy of art is her definition: "Art is the creation of forms symbolic of human feeling." The most serious problem this definition faces is the meaning of the term "symbolic." A number of philosophers have adversely criticized her use of this term, noting that her use lacks the conventionality involved in the notion of symbolizing.

Langer has acknowledged the difficulty but persists in using the term "symbolic." Another question of importance is whether all art "symbolizes" (that is, represents or resembles) aspects of human feeling.

Samuel Bufford argues that Langer has two philosophies of art, the one just referred to and another which claims "it is the task of works of art to make perceivable or more perceivable to us aspects of our own experience or of the world around us." It would perhaps be better to say that Langer has *one* philosophy of art (forms symbolic of human feeling) which attempts to define the essential nature of art and a view about how art functions. Nevertheless, Bufford is correct in saying that Langer has two different things to say about art, and he is concerned with the relation or lack of relation between the two things she says.

Ted Cohen's attack and Dickie's reply, which ends this section, involves a controversy over some of the central points of Dickie's institutional theory of art. Cohen's essay refers to and discusses only Dickie's earliest, rather brief statement of the institutional theory, but the two essays taken together provide a fairly adequate picture of the theory. In order, however, to keep the reader from having a sense of entering in the middle of a conversation between two antagonists, a brief sketch of the institutional theory of art is included in this introduction.

Traditional theories of art, such as Langer's, tend to concentrate attention on the exhibited properties of art, that is, properties which can be observed in the works—for example, forms symbolic of human feeling. (Admittedly, however, artifactuality which is entailed by Langer's "Art is the *creation* of forms . . ." is not an exhibited property.) The institutional theory defines "art" entirely in terms of nonexhibited properties, a work of art in the classificatory sense is (1) an artifact (2) upon which some person or persons acting on behalf of a certain social institution (the artworld) has conferred the status of candidate for appreciation. (Cohen's essay quotes an earlier version of the definition which differs somewhat and uses the term "descriptive" rather than "classificatory.") The artworld referred to in the definition is the informal, social or cultural institution (practice) within which works of art are created, presented, appreciated, and talked about. The core personnel of the artworld are the artists (the creators), the presenters (museum and gallery directors, theater producers and directors, and the like), and the appreciators (museum-goers, theater-goers, and so on). The artworld contains peripheral personnel such as critics, theorists of various kinds, and philosophers of art. One may compare and contrast the institution of the artworld and its informal organization with a formal institution such as the state, which has rigorously defined laws and procedures. According to the institutional theory, works of art come into being by a person's acting on behalf of the artworld. In the case of ordinary art (paintings and the like), a person (artist) creates an artifact and by virtue of his knowledge of and engagement in the artworld confers on it the status of candidate for appreciation. In the case of extraordinary art such as Duchamp's dadaist *Fountain*, the artist took an already manufactured article (a urinal) and conferred on it the status of candidate for appreciation. The institutional theory can thus account for traditional art, dadaist art, and such modern developments as Warhol's *Brillo Carton* and Rauschenberg's *Bed*. The fullest account of the institutional theory is chapter one of Dickie's *Art and the Aesthetic*.

Susanne Langer

ART AS SYMBOLIC EXPRESSION: FROM *FEELING AND FORM*

In the book to which the present one is a sequel* there is a chapter entitled "On Significance in Music." The theory of significance there developed is a special theory, which does not pretend to any further application than the one made of it in that original realm, namely music. Yet, the more one reflects on the significance of art generally, the more the music theory appears as a lead. And the hypothesis certainly suggests itself that the oft-asserted fundamental unity of the arts lies not so much in parallels between their respective elements or analogies among their techniques, as in the singleness of their characteristic import, the meaning of "significance" with respect to any and each of them. "Significant Form" (which really has significance) is the essence of every art; it is what we mean by calling anything "artistic."

If the proposed lead will not betray us, we have here a principle of analysis that may be applied within each separate art gender in explaining its peculiar choice and use of materials; a criterion of what is or is not relevant in judging works of art in any realm; a direct exhibition of the unity of all the arts (without necessitating a resort to "origins" in fragmentary, doubtful history, and still more questionable prehistory); and the making of a truly general theory of art as such, wherein the several arts may be distinguished as well as connected, and almost any philosophical problems they present—problems of their relative values, their special powers or limitations, their social function, their connection with dream and fantasy or with actuality, etc., etc.—may be tackled with some hope of decision. The proper way to construct a general theory is by generalization of a special one; and I believe the analysis of musical significance in *Philosophy in a New Key* is capable of such generalization, and of furnishing a valid theory of significance for the whole Parnassus.

Susanne Langer is one of the most influential present day theorists of art. Her theory of art is elaborately set forth in *Philosophy in a New Key* (1942), *Feeling and Form* (1953), and *Problems of Art* (1957). She taught at Connecticut College where she is Professor Emeritus of Philosophy.

* Selection from *Feeling and Form* (New York, 1953). Reprinted by permission of Charles Scribner's Sons.

The study of musical significance grew out of a prior philosophical reflection on the meaning of the very popular term "expression." In the literature of aesthetics this word holds a prominent place; or rather, it holds prominent places, for it is employed in more than one sense and consequently changes its meaning from one book to another, and sometimes even from passage to passage in a single work. Sometimes writers who are actually in close agreement use it in incompatible ways, and literally contradict each other's statements, yet actually do not become aware of this fact, because each will read the word as the other intended it, not as he really used it where it happens to occur. Thus Roger Fry tried to elucidate Clive Bell's famous but cryptic phrase, "Significant Form," by identifying it with Flaubert's "expression of the Idea"; and Bell probably subscribes fully to Fry's exegesis, as far as it goes (which, as Fry remarks, is unfortunately not very far, since the "Idea" is the next hurdle). Yet Bell himself, trying to explain his meaning, says: "It is useless to go to a picture gallery in search of expression; you must go in search of Significant Form." Of course Bell is thinking here of "expression" in an entirely different sense. Perhaps he means that you should not look for the artist's *self*-expression, i.e., for a record of his emotions. Yet this reading is doubtful, for elsewhere in the same book he says: "It seems to me possible, though by no means certain, that created form moves us so profoundly because it expresses the emotion of its creator." Now, is the emotion of the creator the "Idea" in Flaubert's sense, or is it not? Or does the same work have, perhaps, two different expressive functions? And what about the kind we must *not* look for in a picture gallery?

We may, of course, look for any kind of expression we like, and there is even a fair chance that, whatever it be, we shall find it. A work of art is often a spontaneous expression of feeling, i.e., a symptom of the artist's state of mind. If it represents human beings it is probably also a rendering of some sort of facial expression which suggests the feelings those beings are supposed to have. Moreover, it may be said to "express," in another sense, the life of the society from which it stems, namely to *indicate* customs, dress, behavior, and to reflect confusion or decorum, violence or peace. And besides all these things it is sure to express the unconscious wishes and nightmares of its author. All these things may be found in museums and galleries if we choose to note them.

But they may also be found in wastebaskets and in the margins of schoolbooks. This does not mean that someone has discarded a work of art, or produced one when he was bored with long division. It merely means that all drawings, utterances, gestures, or personal records of any sort express feelings, beliefs, social conditions, and interesting neuroses; "expression" in any of these senses is not peculiar to art, and consequently is not what makes for artistic values.

Artistic significance, or "expression of the Idea," is "expression" in still a different sense and, indeed, a radically different one. In all the contexts mentioned above, the art work or other object functioned as a *sign* that pointed to some matter of fact—how someone felt, what he believed, when and where he lived, or what bedeviled his dreams. But *expression of an idea*, even in ordinary usage, where the "idea" has no capital *I*, does not refer to the signific function, i.e. the indication of a fact by some natural symptom or invented signal. It usually refers to the prime purpose of language, which is discourse, the presentation of mere ideas. When we say that something is well expressed, we do not necessarily believe the expressed idea to refer to our present situation, or even to be true, but only to be given clearly and objectively for contemplation. Such "expression" is the function of symbols: articulation and presentation of *concepts*. Herein symbols differ radically from signals.[1] A signal is comprehended if it serves to make us notice the object or situation it bespeaks. A symbol is understood when we conceive the idea it presents.

The logical difference between signals and symbols is sufficiently explained, I think, in *Philosophy in a New Key* to require no repetition here, although much more could be said about it than that rather general little treatise undertook to say. Here, as there, I shall go on to a consequent of the logical studies, a theory of significance that points the contrast between the functions of art and of discourse, respectively; but this time with reference to all the arts, not only the non-verbal and essentially non-representative art of music.

The theory of music, however, is our point of departure, wherefore it may be briefly recapitulated here as it finally stood in the earlier book:

The tonal structures we call "music" bear a close logical similarity to the forms of human feeling—forms of growth and of attenuation, flowing and stowing, conflict and resolution, speed, arrest, terrific excitement, calm, or subtle activation and dreamy lapses—not joy and sorrow perhaps, but the poignancy of either and both—the greatness and brevity and eternal passing of everything vitally felt. Such is the pattern, or logical form, of sentience; and the pattern of music is that same form worked out in pure, measured sound and silence. Music is a tonal analogue of emotive life.

Such formal analogy, or congruence of logical structures, is the prime requisite for the relation between a symbol and whatever it is to mean. The symbol and the object symbolized must have some common logical form.

But purely on the basis of formal analogy, there would be no telling which of two congruent structures was the symbol and which the meaning, since the relation of congruence, or formal likeness, is symmetrical, i.e. it works both ways. (If John looks so much like James that you can't tell him from James, then you can't tell James from John, either.) There must be

---

[1] In *Philosophy in a New Key* (cited hereafter as *New Key*) the major distinction was drawn .between "signs" and "symbols"; Charles W. Morris, in *Signs, Language and Behavior*, distinguishes between "signals" and "symbols." This seems to me a better use of words, since it leaves "sign" to cover both "signal" and "symbol," whereas my former usage left me without any generic term. I have, therefore, adopted his practice, despite the fact that it makes for a discrepancy in the terminology of two books that really belong together.

a motive for choosing, as between two entities or two systems, one to be the symbol of the other. Usually the decisive reason is that one is easier to perceive and handle than the other. Now sounds are much easier to produce, combine, perceive, and identify, than feelings. Forms of sentience occur only in the course of nature, but musical forms may be invented and intoned at will. Their general pattern may be reincarnated again and again by repeated performance. The effect is actually never quite the same even though the physical repetition may be exact, as in recorded music, because the exact degree of one's familiarity with a passage affects the experience of it, and this factor can never be made permanent. Yet within a fairly wide range such variations are, happily, unimportant. To some musical forms even much less subtle changes are not really disturbing, for instance certain differences of instrumentation and even, within limits, of pitch or tempo. To others, they are fatal. But in the main, sound is a negotiable medium, capable of voluntary composition and repetition, whereas feeling is not; this trait recommends tonal structures for symbolic purposes.

Furthermore, a symbol is used to articulate ideas of something we wish to think about, and until we have a fairly adequate symbolism we cannot think about it. So *interest* always plays a major part in making one thing, or realm of things, the meaning of something else, the symbol or system of symbols.

Sound, as a sheer sensory factor in experience, may be soothing or exciting, pleasing or torturing; but so are the factors of taste, smell, and touch. Selecting and exploiting such somatic influences is self-indulgence, a very different thing from art. An enlightened society usually has some means, public or private, to support its artists, because their work is regarded as a spiritual triumph and a claim to greatness for the whole tribe. But mere epicures would hardly achieve such fame. Even chefs, perfumers, and upholsterers, who produce the means of sensory pleasure for others, are not rated as the torchbearers of culture and inspired creators. Only their own advertisements bestow such titles on them. If music, patterned sound, had no other office than to stimulate and soothe our nerves, pleasing our ears as well-combined foods please our palates, it might be highly popular, but never culturally important. Its historic development would be too trivial a subject to engage many people in its lifelong study, though a few desperate Ph.D. theses might be wrung from its anecdotal past under the rubric of "social history." And music conservatories would be properly rated exactly like cooking schools.

Our interest in music arises from its intimate relation to the all-important life of feeling, whatever that relation may be. After much debate on current theories, the conclusion reached in *Philosophy in a New Key* is that the function of music is not stimulation of feeling, but expression of it; and furthermore, not the symptomatic expression of feelings that beset the composer but a symbolic expression of the forms of sentience as he understands them. It bespeaks his imagination of feelings rather than his own emotional state, and expresses what he *knows about* the so-called "inner life"; and this may exceed his personal case, because music is a symbolic form to him through which he may learn as well as utter ideas of human sensibility.

There are many difficulties involved in the assumption that music is a symbol, because we are so deeply impressed with the paragon of symbolic form, namely language, that we naturally carry its characteristics over into our conceptions and expectations of any other mode. Yet music is not a kind of language. Its significance is really something different from what is traditionally and properly called "meaning." Perhaps the logicians and positivistic philosophers who have objected to the term "implicit meaning," on the ground that "meaning" properly so-called is always explicable, definable, and translatable, are prompted by a perfectly rational desire to keep so difficult a term free from any further entanglements and sources of confusion; and if this can be done without barring the concept itself which I have designated as "implicit meaning," it certainly seems the part of wisdom to accept their strictures.

Probably the readiest way to understand the precise nature of musical symbolization is to consider the characteristics of language and then, by comparison and contrast, note the different structure of music, and the consequent differences and similarities between the respective functions of those two logical forms. Because the prime purpose of language is discourse, the conceptual framework that has developed under its influence is known as "discursive reason." Usually, when one speaks of "reason" at all, one tacitly assumes its discursive pattern. But in a broader sense any appreciation of form, any awareness of patterns in experience, is "reason"; and discourse with all its refinements (e.g. mathematical symbolism, which is an extension of language) is only one possible pattern. For practical communication, scientific knowledge, and philosophical thought it is the only instrument we have. But on just that account there are whole domains of experience that philosophers deem "ineffable." If those domains appear to anyone the most important, that person is naturally inclined to condemn philosophy and science as barren and false. To such an evaluation one is entitled; not, however, to the claim of a better way to philosophical truth through instinct, intuition, feeling, or what have you. Intuition is the basic process of all understanding, just as operative in discursive thought as in clear sense perception and immediate judgment; there will be more to say about that presently. But it is no substitute for discursive logic in the making of any theory, contingent or transcendental.

The difference between discursive and non-discursive logical forms, their respective advantages and limitations, and their consequent symbolic uses have already been discussed in the previous book, but because the theory, there developed, of music as a symbolic form is our starting point here for a whole philosophy of art, the underlying semantic principles should perhaps be explicitly recalled first.

In language, which is the most amazing symbolic system humanity has invented, separate words are assigned to separately conceived items in experience on a basis of simple, one-to-one correlation. A word that is not composite (made of two or more independently meaningful vocables, such as "omni-potent," "com-posite") may be assigned to mean any object *taken as one*. We may even, by fiat, take a word like "omnipotent," and regarding it as one, assign it a connotation that is not composite, for instance by naming a race horse "Omnipotent." Thus Praisegod Barbon ("Barebones") was an indivisible being although his name is a composite word. He had a brother called "If-Christ-had-not-come-into-the-world-thou-wouldst-have-been-damned." The simple correlation between a name and its bearer held here between a whole sentence taken as one word and an object to which it was arbitrarily assigned. Any symbol that names something is "taken as one"; so is the object. A "crowd" is a lot of people, but *taken as a lot,* i.e. as one crowd.

So long as we correlate symbols and concepts in this simple fashion we are free to pair them as we like. A word or mark used arbitrarily to denote or connote something may be called an associative symbol, for its meaning depends entirely on association. As soon, however, as words taken to denote different things are used in combination, something is expressed by the way they are combined. The whole complex is a symbol, because the combination of words brings their connotations irresistibly together in a complex, too, and this complex of ideas is analogous to the word-complex. To anyone who knows the meanings of all the constituent words in the name of Praisegod's brother, the name is likely to sound absurd, because it is a sentence. The concepts associated with the words form a complex concept, the parts of which are related in a pattern analogous to the word-pattern. Word-meanings and grammatical forms, or rules for word-using, may be freely assigned; but once they are accepted, propositions emerge automatically as the meanings of sentences. One may say that the elements of propositions are *named* by words, but propositions themselves are *articulated* by sentences.

A complex symbol such as a sentence, or a map (whose outlines correspond formally to the vastly greater outlines of a country), or a graph (analogous, perhaps, to invisible conditions, the rise and fall of prices, the progress of an epidemic) is an *articulate form*. Its characteristic symbolic function is what I call *logical expression*. It expresses relations; and it may "mean"—connote or denote—any complex of elements that is of the same articulate form as the symbol, the form which the symbol "expresses."

Music, like language, is an articulate form. Its parts not only fuse together to yield a greater entity, but in so doing they maintain some degree of separate existence, and the sensuous character of each element is affected by its function in the complex whole. This means that the greater entity we call a composition is not merely produced by mixture, like a new color made by mixing paints, but is *articulated,* i.e. its internal structure is given to our perception.

Why, then, is it not a *language* of feeling, as it has often been called? Because its elements are not words—independent associative symbols with a reference fixed by convention. Only as an articulate form is it found to fit anything; and since there is no meaning assigned to any of its parts, it lacks one of the basic characteristics of language—fixed association, and therewith a single, unequivocal reference. We are always free to fill its subtle articulate forms with any meaning that fits them; that is, it may convey an idea of anything conceivable in its logical image. So, although we do receive it as a significant form, and comprehend the processes of life and sentience through its audible, dynamic pattern, it is not a language, because it has no vocabulary.

Perhaps, in the same spirit of strict nomenclature, one really should not refer to its content as "meaning," either. Just as music is only loosely and inexactly called a language, so its symbolic function is only loosely called meaning, because the factor of conventional reference is missing from it. In *Philosophy in a New Key* music was called an "unconsummated" symbol.[2] But meaning, in the usual sense recognized in semantics, includes the condition of conventional reference, or consummation of the symbolic relationship. Music has *import* and this import is the pattern of sentience—the pattern of life itself, as it is felt and directly known. Let us therefore call the significance of music its "vital import" instead of "meaning," using "vital" not as a vague laudatory term, but as a qualifying adjective restricting the relevance of "import" to the dynamism of subjective experience.

So much, then, for the theory of music; music is "significant form," and its significance is that of a symbol, a highly articulated sensuous object, which by virtue of its dynamic structure can express the forms of vital experience which language is peculiarly unfit to convey. Feeling, life, motion and emotion constitute its import.

Here, in rough outline, is the special theory of music which may, I believe, be generalized to yield a theory of art as such. The basic concept is the articulate but non-discursive form having import without conventional reference, and therefore presenting itself not as a symbol in the ordinary sense, but as a "significant form," in which the factor of significance is not logically discriminated, but is felt as a quality rather than recognized as a function. If this basic concept be applicable to all products of what we call "the arts," i.e. if all works of art may be regarded as significant forms in exactly the same sense as musical works, then all the essential propositions in the theory of music may be extended to the other arts, for they all define or elucidate the nature of the symbol and its import.

That crucial generalization is already given by sheer circumstance: for the very term "significant form" was originally introduced in connection with other arts than music, in the development of another special theory; all that has so far been written about it was supposed to apply primarily, if not solely, to visual arts. Clive Bell, who coined the phrase, is an art critic, and (by his own testimony) not a musician. His own introduction of the term is given in the following words:

---

[2] Harvard University Press edition, p. 240; New American Library (Mentor) edition, p. 195.

"Every one speaks of 'art,' making a mental classification by which he distinguishes the class 'works of art' from all other classes. What is the justification of this classification? . . . There must be some one quality without which a work of art cannot exist; possessing which, in the least degree, no work is altogether worthless. What is this quality? What quality is shared by all objects that provoke our aesthetic emotions? What quality is common to Santa Sophia and the Windows at Chartres, Mexican sculpture, a Persian bowl, Chinese carpets, Giotto's frescoes at Padua, and the masterpieces of Poussin, Piero della Francesca, and Cézanne? Only one answer seems possible—significant form. In each, lines and colours combined in a particular way, certain forms and relations of forms, stir our aesthetic emotions. These relations and combinations of lines and colours, these aesthetically moving forms, I call 'Significant Form'; and 'Significant Form' is the one quality common to all works of visual art."[3]

Bell is convinced that the business of aesthetics is to contemplate the aesthetic emotion and its object, the work of art, and that the reason why certain objects move us as they do lies beyond the confines of aesthetics.[4] If that were so, there would be little of interest to contemplate. It seems to me that the *reason* for our immediate recognition of "significant form" is the heart of the aesthetical problem; and Bell himself has given several hints of a solution, although his perfectly justified dread of heuristic theories of art kept him from following out his own observations. But, in the light of the music theory that culminates in the concept of "significant form," perhaps the hints in his art theory are enough.

"Before we feel an aesthetic emotion for a combination of forms," he says (only to withdraw hastily, even before the end of the paragraph, from any philosophical commitment) "do we not perceive intellectually the rightness and necessity of the combination? If we do, it would explain the fact that passing rapidly through a room we recognize a picture to be good, although we cannot say that it has provoked much emotion. We seem to have recognized intellectually the rightness of its forms without staying to fix our attention, and collect, as it were, their emotional significance. If this were so, it would be permissible to inquire whether it was the forms themselves or our perception of their rightness and necessity that caused aesthetic emotion."[5]

Certainly "rightness and necessity" are properties with philosophical implications, and the perception of them a more telling incident than an inexplicable emotion. To recognize that something is right and necessary is a rational act, no matter how spontaneous and immediate the recognition may be; it points to an intellectual principle in artistic judgment, and a rational basis for the feeling Bell calls "the aesthetic emotion." This emotion is, I think, a result of artistic perception, as he suggested in the passage quoted above; it is a personal reaction to the discovery of "rightness and

[3] *Ibid.,* p. 8.
[4] *Ibid.,* p. 10.
[5] *Ibid.,* p. 26.

necessity" in the sensuous forms that evoke it. Whenever we experience it we are in the presence of Art, i.e. of "significant form." He himself has identified it as the same experience in art appreciation and in pure musical hearing, although he says he has rarely achieved it musically. But if it is common to visual and tonal arts, and if indeed it bespeaks the artistic value of its object, it offers another point of support for the theory that significant form is the essence of all art.

That, however, is about all that it offers. Bell's assertion that every theory of art must begin with the contemplation of "the aesthetic emotion," and that, indeed, nothing else is really the business of aesthetics,[6] seems to me entirely wrong. To dwell on one's state of mind in the presence of a work does not further one's understanding of the work and its value. The question of what gives one the emotion is exactly the question of what makes the object artistic; and that, to my mind, is where philosophical art theory begins.

The same criticism applies to all theories that begin with an analysis of the "aesthetic attitude": they do not get beyond it. Schopenhauer, who is chiefly responsible for the notion of a completely desireless state of pure, sensuous discrimination as the proper attitude toward works of art, did not make it the starting point of his system, but a consequence. Why, then, has it been so insistently employed, especially of late, as the chief datum in artistic experience?

Probably under pressure of the psychologistic currents that have tended, for the last fifty years at least, to force all philosophical problems of art into the confines of behaviorism and pragmatism, where they find neither development nor solution, but are assigned to vague realms of "value" and "interest," in which nothing of great value or interest has yet been done. The existence of art is accounted for, its value admitted, and there's an end of it. But the issues that really challenge the aesthetician—e.g., the exact nature and degree of interrelation among the arts, the meaning of "essential" and "unessential," the problem of translatability, or transposability, of artistic ideas—either cannot arise in a psychologistic context, or are answered, without real investigation, on the strength of some general premise that seems to cover them. The whole tenor of modern philosophy, especially in America, is uncongenial to serious speculation on the meaning and difficulty and seriousness of art works. Yet the pragmatic outlook, linked as it is with natural science, holds such sway over us that no academic discussion can resist its magnetic, orienting concepts; its basic psychologism underlies every doctrine that really looks respectable.

Now, the watchword of this established doctrine is "experience." If the leading philosophers publish assorted essays under such titles as *Freedom and Experience*,[7] or center their systematic discourse around *Experience and Nature*,[8] so that in their aesthetics, too, we are presented with *The*

[6] *Ibid.*, p. 10.
[7] *Essays in Honor of Horace M. Kallen* (1947).
[8] John Dewey (1925).

Aesthetic Experience[9] and *Art as Experience*,[10] it is natural enough that artists, who are amateurs in philosophy, try to treat their subject in the same vein, and write: *Experiencing American Pictures*,[11] or: *Dance—A Creative Art Experience*.[12] As far as possible, these writers who grope more or less for principles of intellectual analysis adopt the current terminology, and therewith they are committed to the prevailing fashion of thought.

Since this fashion has grown up under the mentorship of natural science, it brings with it not only the great ideals of empiricism, namely observation, analysis and verification, but also certain cherished hypotheses, primarily from the least perfect and successful of the sciences, psychology and sociology. The chief assumption that determines the entire procedure of pragmatic philosophy is that all human interests are direct or oblique manifestations of "drives" motivated by animal needs. This premise limits the class of admitted human interests to such as can, by one device or another, be interpreted in terms of animal psychology. An astonishingly great part of human behavior really does bear such interpretation without strain; and pragmatists, so far, do not admit that there is any point where the principle definitely fails, and its use falsifies our empirical findings.

The effect of the genetic premise on art theory is that aesthetic values must be treated either as direct satisfactions, i.e. pleasures, or as instrumental values, that is to say, means to fulfillment of biological needs. It is either a leisure interest, like sports and hobbies, or it is valuable for getting on with the world's work—strengthening morale, integrating social groups, or venting dangerous repressed feelings in a harmless emotional catharsis. But in either case, artistic experience is not essentially different from ordinary physical, practical, and social experience.[13]

The true connoisseurs of art, however, feel at once that to treat great art as a source of experiences not essentially different from the experiences of daily life—a stimulus to one's active feelings, and perhaps a means of communication between persons or groups, promoting mutual appreciation—is to miss the very essence of it, the thing that makes art as impor-

---

[9] Laurence Buermeyer (1924).
[10] John Dewey (1934).
[11] Ralph M. Pearson (1943).
[12] Margaret H'Doubler (1940).
[13] Cf. John Dewey, *Art as Experience*, p. 10: ". . . the forces that create the gulf between producer and consumer in modern society operate to create also a chasm between ordinary and esthetic experience. Finally we have, as a record of this chasm, accepted as if it were normal, the philosophies of art that locate it in a region inhabited by no other creature, and that emphasize beyond all reason the merely contemplative character of the esthetic."

Also I. A. Richards, *Principles of Literary Criticism*, pp. 16–17: "When we look at a picture, read a poem, or listen to music, we are not doing something quite unlike what we were doing on our way to the Gallery or when we dressed in the morning. The fashion in which the experience is caused in us is different, and as a rule the experience is more complex and, if we are successful, more unified. But our activity is not of a fundamentally different type."

Laurence Buermeyer, in *The Aesthetic Experience*, p. 79, follows his account of artistic expression with the statement: "This does not mean, once more, that what the artist has to say is different in kind from what is to be said in actual life, or that the realm of art is in any essential respect divorced from the realm of reality."

tant as science or even religion, yet sets it apart as an autonomous, creative function of a typically human mind. If, then, they feel constrained by the prevailing academic tradition to analyze their experience, attitude, response, or enjoyment, they can only begin by saying that aesthetic experience is different from any other, the attitude toward works of art is a highly special one, the characteristic response is an entirely separate emotion, something more than common enjoyment—not related to the pleasures or displeasures furnished by one's actual surroundings, and therefore disturbed by them rather than integrated with the contemporary scene.

This conviction does not spring from a sentimental concern for the glamor and dignity of the arts, as Mr. Dewey suggests;[14] it arises from the fact that when people in whom appreciation for some art—be it painting, music, drama, or what not—is spontaneous and pronounced, are induced by a psychologistic fashion to reflect on their attitude toward the works they appreciate, they find it not at all comparable with the attitude they have toward a new automobile, a beloved creature, or a glorious morning. They feel a different emotion, and in a different way. Since art is viewed as a special kind of "experience," inaccessible to those who cannot enter into the proper spirit, a veritable cult of the "aesthetic attitude" has grown up among patrons of the art gallery and the concert hall.

But the aesthetic attitude, which is supposed to beget the art experience in the presence of suitable objects (what makes them suitable seems to be a minor question, relegated to a time when "science" shall be ready to answer it), is hard to achieve, harder to maintain, and rarely complete. H. S. Langfeld, who wrote a whole book about it, described it as an attitude "that for most individuals has to be cultivated if it is to exist at all in midst of the opposing and therefore disturbing influences which are always present."[15] And David Prall, in his excellent *Aesthetic Analysis*, observes: "Even a young musical fanatic at a concert of his favorite music has some slight attention left for the comfort of his body and his posture, some vague sense of the direction of exists, a degree of attention most easily raised into prominence by any interference with his comfort by his neighbor's movements, or accidental noises coming from elsewhere, whether these indicate the danger of fire or some milder reason for taking action. Complete aesthetic absorption, strictly relevant to one object, is at least rare; the world as exclusively aesthetic surface is seldom if ever the sole object of our attention."[16]

Few listeners or spectators, in fact, ever quite attain the state which Roger Fry described, in *Vision and Design*, as "disinterested intensity of contemplation"[17]—the only state in which one may really perceive a

---

[14] Speaking of the separation of art from life "that many theorists and critics pride themselves upon holding and even elaborating," he attributes it to the desire to keep art "spiritual," and says in explanation: "For many persons an aura of mingled awe and unreality encompasses the 'spiritual' and the 'ideal' while 'matter' has become . . . something to be explained away or apologized for." John Dewey, *op. cit.*, p. 6.

[15] *The Aesthetic Attitude*, p. 65.

[16] *Aesthetic Analysis*, pp. 7–8.

[17] *Vision and Design*, p. 29.

work of art, and experience the aesthetic emotion. Most people are too busy or too lazy to uncouple their minds from all their usual interests before looking at a picture or a vase. That explains, presumably, what he remarked somewhat earlier in the same essay: "In proportion as art becomes purer the number of people to whom it appeals gets less. It cuts out all the romantic overtones which are the usual bait by which men are induced to accept a work of art. It appeals only to the aesthetic sensibility, and that in most men is comparatively weak."[18]

If the groundwork of all genuine art experience is really such a sophisticated, rare, and artificial attitude, it is something of a miracle that the world recognizes works of art as public treasures at all. And that primitive peoples, from the cave dwellers of Altamira to the early Greeks, should quite unmistakably have known what was beautiful, becomes a sheer absurdity.

There is that, at least, to be said for the pragmatists: they recognize the art interest as something natural and robust, not a precarious hot-house flower reserved for the very cultured and initiate. But the small compass of possible human interests permitted by their biological premises blinds them to the fact that a very spontaneous, even primitive activity may none the less be peculiarly human, and may require long study in its own terms before its relations to the rest of our behavior become clear. To say, as I. A. Richards does, that if we knew more about the nervous system and its responses to "certain stimuli" (note that "certain," when applied to hypothetical data, means "uncertain," since the data cannot be exactly designated) we would find that "the unpredictable and miraculous differences . . . in the total responses which slight changes in the arrangement of stimuli produce, can be fully accounted for in terms of the sensitiveness of the nervous system; and the mysteries of 'forms' are merely a consequence of our present ignorance of the detail of its action,"[19] is not only an absurd pretension (for how do we know what facts we would find and what their implications would prove to be, before we have found them?), but an empty hypothesis, because there is no elementary success that indicates the direction in which neurological aesthetics could develop. If a theoretical beginning existed, one could imagine an extension of the same procedure to describe artistic experience in terms of conditioned reflexes, rudimentary impulses, or perhaps cerebral vibrations; but so far the data furnished by galvanometers and encephalographs have not borne on artistic problems, even to the extent of explaining the simple, obvious difference of effect between a major scale and its parallel minor. The proposition that if we knew the facts we would find them to be thus and thus is merely an article of innocent, pseudo-scientific faith.

The psychological approach, dictated by the general empiricist trend in philosophy, has not brought us within range of any genuine problems of art. So, instead of studying the "slight changes of stimuli" which cause

[18] *Ibid.*, p. 15.
[19] *Op. cit.*, p. 172.

"unpredictable and miraculous changes" in our nervous responses, we might do better to look upon the art object as something in its own right, with properties independent of our prepared reactions—properties which command our reactions, and make art the autonomous and essential factor that it is in every human culture.

The concept of significant form as an articulate expression of feeling, reflecting the verbally ineffable and therefore unknown forms of sentience, offers at least a starting point for such inquiries. All articulation is difficult, exacting, and ingenious; the making of a symbol requires craftsmanship as truly as the making of a convenient bowl or an efficient paddle, and the techniques of expression are even more important social traditions than the skills of self-preservation, which an intelligent being can evolve by himself, at least in rudimentary ways, to meet a given situation. The fundamental technique of expression—language—is something we all have to learn by example and practice, i.e. by conscious or unconscious training.[20] People whose speech training has been very casual are less sensitive to what is exact and fitting for the expression of an idea than those of cultivated habit; not only with regard to arbitrary rules of usage, but in respect of logical *rightness and necessity* of expression, i.e. saying what they mean and not something else. Similarly, I believe, all making of expressive form is a craft. Therefore the normal evolution of art is in close association with practical skills—building, ceramics, weaving, carving, and magical practices of which the average civilized person no longer knows the importance;[21] and therefore, also, sensitivity to the rightness and necessity of visual or musical forms is apt to be more pronounced and sure in persons of some artistic training than in those who have only a bowing acquaintance with the arts. Technique is the means to the creation of expressive form, the symbol of sentience; the art process is the application of some human skill to this essential purpose.

At this point I will make bold to offer a definition of art, which serves to distinguish a "work of art" from anything else in the world, and at the same time to show why, and how, a utilitarian object may be *also* a work of art; and how a work of so-called "pure" art may fail of its purpose and be simply bad, just as a shoe that cannot be worn is simply bad by failing of its purpose. It serves, moreover, to establish the relation of art to physical skill, or making, on the one hand, and to feeling and expression on the other. Here is the tentative definition, on which the following chapters are built: Art is the creation of forms symbolic of human feeling.

The word "creation" is introduced here with full awareness of its problematical character. There is a definite reason to say a craftsman *produces* goods, but *creates* a thing of beauty; a builder *erects* a house, but *creates* an edifice if the house is a real work of architecture, however modest. An artifact as such is merely a combination of material parts, or a modification

---

[20] Cf. *New Key*, Chap. v, "Language."

[21] Yet a pervasive magical interest has probably been the natural tie between practical fitness and expressiveness in primitive artifacts. See *New Key*, chap. ix, "The Genesis of Artistic Import."

of a natural object to suit human purposes. It is not a creation, but an arrangement of given factors. A work of art, on the other hand, is more than an "arrangement" of given things—even qualitative things. Something emerges from the arrangement of tones or colors, which was not there before, and this, rather than the arranged material, is the symbol of sentience.

The making of this expressive form is the creative process that enlists a man's utmost technical skill in the service of his utmost conceptual power, imagination. Not the invention of new original turns, nor the adoption of novel themes, merits the word "creative," but the making of any work symbolic of feeling, even in the most canonical context and manner. A thousand people may have used every device and convention of it before. A Greek vase was almost always a creation, although its form was traditional and its decoration deviated but little from that of its numberless forerunners. The creative principle, nonetheless, was probably active in it from the first throw of the clay.

To expound that principle, and develop it in each autonomous realm of art, is the only way to justify the definition, which really is a philosophical theory of art in miniature.

Semblance

It is a curious fact that people who spend their lives in closest contact with the arts—artists, to whom the appreciation of beauty is certainly a continual and "immediate" experience—do not assume and cultivate the "aesthetic attitude." To them, the artistic value of a work is its most obvious property. They see it naturally and constantly; they do not have to make themselves, first, unaware of the rest of the world. Practical awareness may be there, in a secondary position, as it is for anyone who is engrossed in interesting talk or happenings; if it becomes too insistent to be ignored, they may become quite furious. But normally, the lure of the object is greater than the distractions that compete with it. It is not the percipient who discounts the surroundings, but the work of art which, if it is successful, detaches itself from the rest of the world; he merely sees it as it is presented to him.

Every real work of art has a tendency to appear thus dissociated from its mundane environment. The most immediate impression it creates is one of "otherness" from reality—the impression of an illusion enfolding the thing, action, statement, or flow of sound that constitutes the work. Even where the element of representation is absent, where nothing is imitated or feigned—in a lovely textile, a pot, a building, a sonata—this air of illusion, of being a sheer image, exists as forcibly as in the most deceptive picture or the most plausible narrative. Where an expert in the particular art in question perceives immediately a "rightness and necessity" of forms, the unversed but sensitive spectator perceives only a peculiar air of "otherness," which has been variously described as "strangeness," "semblance," "illusion," "transparency," "autonomy," or "self-sufficiency."

This detachment from actuality, the "otherness" that gives even a bona fide product like a building or a vase some aura of illusion, is a crucial factor, indicative of the very nature of art. It is neither chance nor caprice that has led aestheticians again and again to take account of it (and in a period dominated by a psychologistic outlook, to seek the explanation in a state of mind). In the element of "unreality," which has alternately troubled and delighted them, lies the clue to a very deep and essential problem: the problem of creativity.

What is "created" in a work of art? More than people generally realize when they speak of "being creative," or refer to the characters in a novel as the author's "creations." More than a delightful combination of sensory elements; far more than any reflection or "interpretation" of objects, people, events—the figments that artists *use* in their demiurgic work, and that have made some aestheticians refer to such work as "re-creation" rather than genuine creation. But an object that already exists—a vase of flowers, a living person—cannot be re-created. It would have to be destroyed to be recreated. Besides, a picture is neither a person nor a vase of flowers. It is an image, created for the first time out of things that are not imaginal, but quite realistic—canvas or paper, and paints or carbon or ink.

It is natural enough, perhaps, for naive reflection to center first of all round the relationship between an image and its object; and equally natural to treat a picture, statue, or a graphic description as an imitation of reality. The surprising thing is that long after art theory had passed the naive stage, and every serious thinker realized that imitation was neither the aim nor the measure of artistic creation, the traffic of the image with its model kept its central place among philosophical problems of art. It has figured as the question of form and content, of interpretation, of idealization, of belief and make-believe, and of impression and expression. Yet the idea of copying nature is not even applicable to all the arts. What does a building copy? On what given object does one model a melody?

A problem that will not die after philosophers have condemned it as irrelevant has still a gadfly mission in the intellectual world. Its significance merely is bigger, in fact, than any of its formulations. So here: the philosophical issue that is usually conceived in terms of image and object is really concerned with the nature of images as such and their essential difference from actualities. The difference is functional; consequently real objects, functioning in a way that is normal for images, may assume a purely imaginal status. That is why the character of an illusion may cling to works of art that do not represent anything. Imitation of other things is not the essential power of images, though it is a very important one by virtue of which the whole problem of fact and fiction originally came into the compass of our philosophical thought. But the true power of the image lies in the fact that it is an abstraction, a symbol, the bearer of an idea.

How can a work of art that does not represent anything—a building, a pot, a patterned textile—be called an image? It becomes an image when it presents itself purely to our vision, i.e. as a sheer visual form instead of a locally and practically related object. If we receive it as a completely visual thing, we abstract its appearance from its material existence. What we see in this way becomes simply a thing of vision—a form, an image. It detaches itself from its actual setting and acquires a different context.

An image in this sense, something that exists only for perception, abstracted from the physical and causal order, is the artist's creation. The image presented on a canvas is not a new "thing" among the things in the studio. The canvas was there, the paints were there; the painter has not added to them. Some excellent critics, and painters too, speak of his "arranging" forms and colors, and regard the resultant work primarily as an "arrangement." Whistler seems to have thought in these terms about his paintings. But even the forms are not phenomena in the order of actual things, as spots on a tablecloth are; the forms in a design—no matter how abstract—have a *life* that does not belong to mere spots. Something arises from the process of arranging colors on a surface, something that is created, not just gathered and set in a new order: that is the image. It emerges suddenly from the disposition of the pigments, and with its advent the very existence of the canvas and of the paint "arranged" on it seems to be abrogated; those actual objects become difficult to perceive in their own right. A new appearance has superseded their natural aspect.

An image is, indeed, a purely virtual "object." Its importance lies in the fact that we do not use it to guide us to something tangible and practical, but treat it as a complete entity with only visual attributes and relations. It has no others; its visible character is its entire being.

The most striking virtual objects in the natural world are optical—perfectly definite visible "things" that prove to be intangible, such as rainbows and mirages. Many people, therefore, regard an image or illusion as necessarily something visual. This conceptual limitation has even led some literary critics, who recognize the essentially imaginal character of poetry, to suppose that poets must be visual-minded people, and to judge that figures of speech which do not conjure up visual imagery are not truly poetic.[22] F. C. Prescott, with consistency that borders on the heroic, regards "The quality of mercy is not strained" as unpoetic because it suggests nothing visible.[23] But the poetic image is, in fact, not a painter's image at all. The exact difference, which is great and far-reaching, will be discussed in the following chapters; what concerns us right here is the broader meaning of "image" that accounts for the genuinely artistic character of non-visual arts without any reference to word painting, or other substitute for spreading pigments on a surface to make people see pictures.

[22] See, for example, Remy de Gourmont, *Le problème du style*, especially p. 47, where the author declares that the only people who can "write" are visual-minded people.
[23] *The Poetic Mind*, p. 49.

The word "image" is almost inseparably wedded to the sense of sight because our stock example of it is the looking-glass world that gives us a visible copy of the things opposite the mirror without a tactual or other sensory replica of them. But some of the alternative words that have been used to denote the virtual character of so-called "aesthetic objects" escape this association. Carl Gustav Jung, for instance, speaks of it as "semblance." His exemplary case of illusion is not the reflected image, but the dream; and in a dream there are sounds, smells, feelings, happenings, intentions, dangers—all sorts of invisible elements—as well as sights, and all are equally unreal by the measures of public fact. Dreams do not consist entirely of images, but everything in them is imaginary. The music heard in a dream comes from a virtual piano under the hands of an apparent musician; the whole experience is a semblance of events. It may be as vivid as any reality, yet it is what Schiller called "Schein."

Schiller was the first thinker who saw what really makes "Schein," or semblance, important for art: the fact that it liberates perception—and with it, the power of conception—from all practical purposes, and lets the mind dwell on the sheer appearance of things. The function of artistic illusion is not "make-believe," as many philosophers and psychologists assume, but the very opposite, disengagement from belief—the contemplation of sensory qualities without their usual meanings of "Here's that chair," "That's my telephone," "These figures ought to add up to the bank's statement," etc. The knowledge that what is before us has no practical significance in the world is what enables us to give attention to its appearance as such.

Everything has an aspect of appearance as well as a causal importance. Even so non-sensuous a thing as a fact or a possibility *appears* this way to one person and that way to another. That is its "semblance," whereby it may "resemble" other things, and—where the semblance is used to mislead judgment about its causal properties—is said to "dissemble" its nature. Where we know that an "object" consists entirely in its semblance, that apart from its appearance it has no cohesion and unity—like a rainbow, or a shadow—we call it a merely virtual object, or an illusion. In this literal sense a picture is an illusion; we see a face, a flower, a vista of sea or land, etc., and know that if we stretched out our hand to it we would touch a surface smeared with paint.

The object seen is given only to the sense of sight. That is the chief purpose of "imitation," or "objective" painting. To present things to sight which are known to be illusion is a ready (though by no means necessary) way to *abstract* visible forms from their usual context.

Normally, of course, semblance is not misleading; a thing is what it seems. But even where there is no deception, it may happen that an object—a vase, for instance, or a building—arrests one sense so exclusively that it seems to be given to that sense alone, and all its other properties become irrelevant. It is quite honestly there, but is *important* only for (say) its visual character. Then we are prone to accept it as a vision; there is such a concentration on appearance that one has a sense of seeing sheer appearances—that is, a sense of illusion.

Herein lies the "unreality" of art that tinges even perfectly real objects like pots, textiles, and temples. Whether we deal with actual illusions or with such quasi-illusions made by artistic emphasis, what is presented is, in either case, just what Schiller called "Schein"; and a pure semblance, or "Schein," among the husky substantial realities of the natural world, is a strange guest. Strangeness, separateness, otherness—call it what you will— is its obvious lot.

The semblance of a thing, thus thrown into relief, is its direct aesthetic quality. According to several eminent critics, this is what the artist tries to reveal for its own sake. But the emphasis on quality, or essence, is really only a stage in artistic conception. It is the making of a rarified element that serves, in its turn, for the making of something else—the imaginal art work itself. And this form is the non-discursive but articulate symbol of feeling.

Here is, I believe, the clear statement of what Clive Bell dealt with rather confusedly in a passage that identified "significant form" (not, however, significant of anything) with "aesthetic quality." The setting forth of pure quality, or semblance, creates a new dimension, apart from the familiar world. That is its office. In this dimension, all artistic forms are conceived and presented. Since their substance is illusion or "Schein" they are, from the standpoint of practical reality, *mere* forms; they exist only for the sense or the imagination that perceives them—like the fata morgana, or the elaborate, improbable structure of events in our dreams. The function of "semblance" is to give forms a new embodiment in purely qualitative, unreal instances, setting them free from their normal embodiment in real things so that they may be recognized in their own right, and freely conceived and composed in the interest of the artist's ultimate aim—significance, or logical expression.

All forms in art, then, are abstracted forms; their content is only a semblance, a pure appearance, whose function is to make them, too, apparent—more freely and wholly apparent than they could be if they were exemplified in a context of real circumstance and anxious interest. It is in this elementary sense that all art is abstract. Its very substance, quality without practical significance, is an abstraction from material existence; and exemplification in this illusory or quasi-illusory medium makes the forms of things (not only shapes, but logical forms,[24] e.g. proportions among degrees of importance in events, or among different speeds in motions) present themselves *in abstracto*. This fundamental abstractness belongs just as forcibly to the most illustrative murals and most realistic plays, provided they are good after their kind, as to the deliberate

[24] Mr. I. A. Richards, in his *Principles of Literary Criticism*, declares that when people speak of "logical form," they do not know just what they mean. Perhaps he does not know, but I do; and if he really cares to know, he will find an elementary but systematic explanation in chapter I of my *Introduction to Symbolic Logic*.

abstractions that are remote representations or entirely non-representative designs.

But abstract form as such is not an artistic ideal. To carry abstraction as far as possible, and achieve pure form in only the barest conceptual medium, is a logician's business, not a painter's or poet's. In art forms are abstracted only to be made clearly apparent, and are freed from their common uses only to be put to new uses: to act as symbols, to become expressive of human feeling.

An artistic symbol is a much more intricate thing than what we usually think of as a form, because it involves *all* the relationships of its elements to one another, all similarities and differences of quality, not only geometric or other familiar relations. That is why qualities enter directly into the form itself, not as its contents, but as constitutive elements in it. Our scientific convention of abstracting mathematical forms, which do not involve quality, and fitting them to experience, always makes qualitative factors "content"; and as scientific conventions rule our academic thinking, it has usually been taken for granted that in understanding art, too, one should think of form as opposed to qualitative "content." But on this uncritical assumption the whole conception of form and content comes to grief, and analysis ends in the confused assertion that art is "formed content," form and content are one.[25] The solution of that paradox is, that a work of art is a structure whose interrelated elements are often qualities, or properties of qualities such as their degrees of intensity; that qualities enter into the form and in this way are as much one with it as the relations which they, and they only, have; and that to speak of them as "content," from which the form could be abstracted logically, is nonsense. The form is built up out of relations peculiar to them; they are formal elements in the structure, not contents.

Yet forms are either empty abstractions, or they do have a content; and artistic forms have a very special one, namely their *import*. They are logically expressive, or significant, forms. They are symbols for the articulation of feeling, and convey the elusive and yet familiar pattern of sentience. And as essentially symbolic forms they lie in a different dimension from physical objects as such. They belong to the same category as language, though their logical form is a different one, and as myth and dream, though their function is not the same.

Herein lies the "strangeness" or "otherness" that characterizes an artistic object. The form is immediately given to perception, and yet it reaches beyond itself; it is semblance, but seems to be charged with reality. Like speech, that is physically nothing but little buzzing sounds, it is filled with its meaning, and its meaning is a reality. In an articulate symbol the symbolic import permeates the whole structure, because every articulation of that structure is an articulation of the idea it conveys; the mean-

---

[25] Morris Weitz, in his *Philosophy of the Arts*, offers an exhaustive analysis of the form-and-content problem, which shows up the conceptual muddles on which it rests. See Chap. 3, pp. 35–41.

ing (or, to speak accurately of a nondiscursive symbol, the vital import) is the content of the symbolic form, given with it, as it were, to perception.[26]

[26] In the case of language this pregnance of the physically trivial form with a conceptual import verges on the miraculous. As Bernard Bosanquet said, "Language is so transparent that it disappears, so to speak, into its own meaning, and we are left with no characteristic medium at all." (*Three Lectures on Aesthetics*, p. 64.)

Samuel Bufford

LANGER EVALUATED: SUSANNE LANGER'S TWO PHILOSOPHIES OF ART

In the writings of Susanne K. Langer* are two different and distinct philosophies of art.[1] The claim that works of art are expressions of human feeling in a sensuous form that presents them for our perception and contemplation is the one that virtually all of her commentators have concentrated on because it is the only one originally presented in *Philosophy in a New Key*, and because it is quite like theories presented by Croce, Collingwood, Dewey, Ducasse, and others. There is another part to what Langer presents, quite different and almost completely overlooked, and I shall argue that it constitutes by itself a different theory of art. This theory claims that it is the task of works of art to make perceivable or more perceivable to us aspects of our own experience or of the world around us. It appears first in Langer's article, "The Primary Illusions and the Great Orders of Art," and in subsequent writings the two theories are intertwined. I here undertake to unravel them.

I

Before describing the theory overlooked by Langer's commentators, which I shall call her "perceivability theory," I shall summarize the expression theory for which she is well known. Langer holds that works of art express emotions by standing for them, or representing them: a work of art is

Samuel Bufford teaches law at The Ohio State University, Columbus, Ohio.
* *The Journal of Aesthetics and Art Criticism*, Fall 1972, pp. 9–20. Reprinted by permission of *The Journal of Aesthetics and Art Criticism*.

[1] I will cite Langer's writings as follows: FF, *Feeling and Form* (New York: Charles Scribner's Sons, 1953); M, *Mind: An Essay in Human Feeling*, vol. 1 (Johns Hopkins Press, 1967); PA, *Problems of Art* (New York: Charles Scribner's Sons, 1957); PCA, "The Principles of Creation in Art," *The Hudson Review*, 2 (1950): 515–34; PIGOA, "The Primary Illusions and the Great Orders of Art," *The Hudson Review*, 3 (1950): 219–33; PNK, *Philosophy in a New Key* (Harvard University Press, 1942); PS, *Philosophical Sketches* (Johns Hopkins Press, 1962).

created to express its creator's ideas of immediate, felt, emotive life, to set forth directly what feeling is like (PA, p. 8). It is a composition of tensions and resolutions, balance and imbalance, and rhythmic coherence, corresponding to similar elements in living processes. Works of art express vital import, or what life feels like (PA, p. 60).[2] They present feeling for our contemplation by presenting, not actual feeling but *ideas* of feeling (FF, p. 59; PNK, p. 218). The feeling expressed is not simply what was felt on a particular occasion: it is influenced by the artist's background of emotional conception, his individual sensitivity, and his ways of articulating and projecting feeling (M, p. 112). He may express feeling that he has never felt; he expresses what he *knows* about human feeling, and this can be enlarged from two sources: works of art created by other artists, and suggestions for further development arising in the process of creating a particular work of art.

Feeling, in the broad sense Langer uses it, is the generic basis of all mental experience: sensation, emotion, imagination, memory, and reasoning (PS, p. 8). Felt experience is elaborated in the course of high organic development, intellectualized as brain functions are corticalized, and socialized with the evolution of speech and the growth of its communicative functions. The mechanisms of felt activity are heightened forms of unfelt vital rhythms, responses, and interactions. Langer holds that the entire psychological field—including human conception, responsible action, rationality, knowledge—is a vast and branching development of feeling, and any portion of it may be embodied in a work of art (M, p. 23). In general terms, the forms of human feeling include forms of growth and attenuation, flowing and stowing, conflict and resolution, speed, arrest, terrific excitement, calm, or subtle activation and dreamy lapses, the poignancy of joy or sorrow, the greatness and brevity and eternal passing of everything vitally felt (FF, p. 27). Non-poetic language is ill-suited to express this, she holds, but the great virtue of works of art is that they capture and freeze a feeling, so that we can study it (M, p. 67). In art, feeling is expressed symbolically, according to Langer. (By *symbol* she means any device that is used to abstract and conceptualize something [FF, p. xi; PNK, p. 60]). Works of art are symbols because they have the same kinds of elements and relations, or the same forms, as the processes of feeling. Works of art are not exactly like other symbols (Langer calls them "unconsummated symbols"): articulation is their function, or formulation, and not assertion (PNK, p. 240). Under the prompting of such semanticists as Ernest Nagel, she sometimes changes her language to say that works of art have import, and the import is the feeling that they express: to say that a work of art has import is to say that it seems to be imbued with feeling or emotion or mood, or that it is in some other way

---

[2] For a somewhat similar view in regard to music, see Roger Sessions, *The Musical Experience of Composer, Performer, Listener* (New York: Atheneum, 1965). Unlike Langer, he holds that the motion of the music is the vehicle of expression of feeling, and not tensions and resolutions. This would be inadequate for Langer because it would be inapplicable to non-temporal works of art.

more than what meets the eye or ear (PA, pp. 129, 134). Its import is imaginable feeling and emotion, imaginable subjective existence (PA, p. 113; FF, p. 52).

Langer contrasts the kind of form of works of art with the kind of form in language used in discourse, which she calls "discursive form" (PA, p. 164). While it has its root in discourse, discursive form is also used in systematic thinking, writing, and all other nonartistic uses of language. There is a considerable amount of experience, she claims, that cannot be presented in discursive form: the subjective aspects of experience—what it is like to be waking and moving, to be drowsy, slowing down, or to be sociable, or to feel self-sufficient but alone, what it feels like to pursue an elusive thought or to have a big idea—defy discursive formulation, and are essentially beyond expression in (non-poetic) language, but they are formulable in presentational form—the kind of form we find in works of art (PA, p. 22).

II

Langer's second theory of art holds that works of art abstract aspects of the world around us or our own experience to enable us to perceive these aspects more clearly. The point of creating a work of art is to abstract sounds, shapes, or movements to draw our attention to them (PA, p. 31). Aside from such abstractions, we tend to be unaware of the sounds, shapes, and movements in the world around us. We observe the objects we need to carry out the practical activities of our lives, which usually demand only that we notice generic features: we normally only read the labels, as it were, on the objects around us and trouble no further (FF, p. 58).[3] But works of art make us stop and take notice—notice how space looks, how time appears, what living is like. Each of the arts focuses on some aspect of the world or our experience.[4]

The perceivability theory arises in response to the question, what does an artist create? what is a work of art?[5] In this respect it is no different

---

[3] Langer follows the change rather consistently in her writings after FF. (In FF her usage is not consistent). Nagel argues that "symbol" has an established use in semantics, and Langer's usage of the term does not fit this use. He takes it to mean, "any occurrence (or type of occurrence), usually linguistic in status, which is taken to signify something else by way of tacit or explicit conventions or rules of language." "Symbolism and Science," *Symbols and Values: An Initial Study*, Thirteenth Symposium on Science, Philosophy and Religion (New York, 1954); as quoted in PA, p. 130. See also Nagel's review of PNK (*Journal of Philosophy*, 40 (1943): 323–29).

[4] For a similar theory, see Iredell Jenkins, *Art and the Human Enterprise* (Harvard Univ. Press, 1958). He contends that the function of artistic creation is "to articulate man's vague apprehensions of the particularity of things, and to embody and present these with great clarity and persuasion" (p. 116). "Art fills in the gaps and repairs the fractures that yawn so largely in our ordinary experience of particular things. The artist sharpens the contours of things, and brings us to a fuller and more acute discovery of what they offer to experience. By his treatment of the various elements and aspects of things, he gives these a prominence that we have to notice" (p. 158 f.).

[5] Langer says this explicitly only with regard to the dance and poetry in special lectures on them, PA, pp. 10, 143.

from the expression theory. How is it, then, that Langer comes up with a very different theory? She thinks it important to account for not only how the arts are alike, which her first theory has done, but also how they differ. The second theory explains what is distinctive about each realm of art.

There are two parts to this theory. The first is the contention that works of art are not like other things in the world around us. The second is a presentation of the aspect of experience that each of them makes "more perceivable." The two parts need not go together; the first might have been presented as an addition to the expression theory (I shall argue its separation below). The second part is thus the heart of the theory, and I shall argue that it is different from the expression theory, and that neither implies or requires the other.

Langer begins her discussion of the difference between works of art and other objects by pointing out the difference between aesthetic and non-aesthetic properties of works of art: for people with training in the arts, works of art detach themselves from the rest of the world and create the impression of "otherness" from reality (FF, p. 45). She says this because she thinks that "reality" consists of such things as amoebae, pectorals, and phonograph needles. Anything that is rather different from them is consequently "unreal." It follows that works of art are "unreal" and this unreality is obvious, at least to artists. It seems that this difference is obvious to most other people as well, even to those who do not think that works of art are consequently "unreal."

A second way Langer thinks works of art are different is they do not have material existence, while other things do (FF, p. 47). We abstract the appearances of such things as buildings and pots from their material existence to consider them as works of art. She says each appearance then becomes a vision, a form, or an image. Abstracted from its actual context, it acquires a different context; a picture is made with pigments on a piece of canvas, but the painting that emerges does not consist of pigment-on-canvas: it is a structure of space created by the painter (PA, p. 28). The pigments and canvas are not in the pictorial space; they are in the space of the room in which the picture hangs. The picture creating the pictorial space and the objects in it are an apparition: "It is there for our eyes but not for our hands, nor does its visible space, however great, have any normal acoustical properties for our ears." There are similar merely apparent objects in nature, such as rainbows, mirages, and simple reflections (PA, p. 29). But the most common is the mirror image, which has forced physicists to take account of this sort of space, which they call *virtual* space. From this technical usage in physics Langer derives her use of "virtual." Painting, then, presents virtual space, music virtual time, and literature virtual life. It is important that we consider works of art as appearances, or illusions, because this liberates perception, and with it the power of conception, from practical purposes, and lets us concentrate on the appearance of things (FF, p. 49). By this means we abstract visible forms from their usual contexts.

The virtual, according to Langer, is what distinguishes the real of art from the world of practical affairs. It is necessary that we recognize works of art to be virtual so that we do not respond to them in the wrong way. It is entirely inappropriate to jump up on stage to save the young lady from the villain, or to condemn a poem as obscene. It is Langer's explanation of what Edward Bullough tries to explain with this conception of "psychical distance," and what others have discussed with the conception of "aesthetic attitude" (*FF*, p. 318). The difficulty with these conceptions, Langer holds, is that they suggest that a person *does* something to put a work of art out of gear with his practical interests. Langer holds that perceiving works of art does not require a special activity on the part of the perceiver, such as "adopting an aesthetic attitude" or "establishing psychical distance": the work of art itself establishes this special relationship.[6]

Not only are works of art unreal; their particular way of being unreal is that they are illusions.[7] The purpose of illusion in art is to abstract the element of sensory appearance from the fabric of actual life and its complex interests, creating a sheer vision, a datum that is nothing but appearance and is clearly an object only for sight (*PA*, p. 31). Normal seeing is seeing material objects, and since paintings as works of art are not material objects, seeing them is seeing abnormally. The artist forces us to do this by creating a sensory illusion (*PA*, p. 34). Illusion in art cancels the usual process of factual judgment which carries us beyond what is presented to our senses, Langer says, and it is established by stylistic devices, such as meter in poetry.

Works of art, in addition to being illusions, are "images." Langer introduces this term as a synonym for *illusion*: ". . . this air of illusion, of being a sheer image, exists as forcibly in the most deceptive picture or the most plausible narrative" (*FF*, p. 45). A painting is an image created of canvas or paper and paints or carbon or ink, which are real things; even works of art that do not represent anything, such as buildings and pots, become images when they present themselves purely to our vision as sheer visual forms (*FF*, p. 46). In doing this, their appearances are abstracted from them as locally and practically related objects, which Langer says they are otherwise. Non-artistic objects, then, are objects that are related to others around them, and are used in one way or another. Images are the stuff of which imagination is made. While we often think of imagination and images in terms of visual models, Langer holds that imagination is not so limited: images of sound, bodily movement, and purposeful

[6] George Dickie has defended this viewpoint recently in "The Myth of the Aesthetic Attitude," *American Philosophical Quarterly*, 1 (1964): 56–65. See also Virgil Aldrich's criticism of Dickie, "Back to Aesthetic Experience," *JAAC* 24 (1966): 365–71, and Dickie's reply, "Attitude and Object," *JAAC* 25 (1966): 89–91.
[7] Langer gives no justification for saying that they are illusions, rather than hallucinations, mirages, toys, fakes, or something else that things may be when they are not what they appear. In fact, in calling them illusions she intends to assert that they *are* what they appear to be. If works of art are what they appear to be, if they do not hide something, it seems at least misleading to call them illusions. More of this later. For a discussion of how things can be unreal, see J. L. Austin, *Sense and Sensibility* (Oxford Univ. Press, 1964), chap. 7.

action also arise spontaneously in our minds—a tune "running through one's head" is an auditory image (M, p. 103).

Everything has an appearance, Langer says, and she calls this its "semblance." When an object consists entirely in its semblance, we call it "a merely virtual object, or an illusion." A virtual object, or illusion, then, hides nothing; it is what it appears to be, such as rainbows and shadows.

While it is true that rainbows and shadows are what they seem to be, we do not ordinarily call them "virtual objects." The only application of this term, aside from the writings of Langer and those influenced by her, is in optics. An object within the focal length of a lens will appear much larger when viewed through the lens, and the image thus seen is called a virtual image. But an object at the focal length or farther will make a real image on the opposite side of the lens, and this image is what it appears to be just as much as the virtual image. Neither do we call rainbows and shadows illusions. Illusions occur when things are *not* what they seem to be. An optical illusion occurs when a straight stick is partially immersed in water, and it appears bent. When on a clear day a distant mountain appears close, the apparent closeness is illusory. When things are what they seem, there is no possibility of having an illusion, as we normally use the term. Similarly, a person or an object or a state of affairs has a semblance only when it is not what it appears to be. If there is a semblance of order in the state, disorder threatens to erupt. If not, there is simply order, not a semblance thereof: if a state is orderly and peaceful, and it appears that way, then it is what it appears to be, and it has no semblance. Thus Langer's use of the terms "semblance" and "illusion" differs from what we usually mean by them. And her use of "virtual object" is at best an extension of the normal use. But once we understand how she is using these terms, they need give us no further difficulty: we shall resolve, whenever we encounter "virtual object" or "illusion," to substitute the phrase, "something that is what it appears to be"; similarly, "semblance" shall be "what a thing appears to be."

Every realm of art has a single primary illusion, Langer says. It is created when the artist first begins to work by the first stroke of a brush or pencil, by the first note on the page (FF, p. 84). There is an immediate mental shift from the "real" world to the world of illusion. The primacy of the primary illusion lies in the fact that this illusion is always created whenever any such work of art is made. Langer gives no account of what can be a realm of primary illusion and what cannot. Space and time become primary illusions, as do memory, history, and dreams. But imagination is left out (although Langer finds place for it in other parts of her theory) and action and making decisions and knowing are not included.

Each art has only one primary illusion, according to Langer. Every work of art in the field creates this primary illusion. Thus the differences among the arts can be explained by characterizing the different primary illusions that they create (PA, p. 82).

The interrelations of the arts are accounted for because the primary illusion of one art form may become the secondary illusion of another,

Langer says. A secondary illusion is a transient and incomplete appearance of an illusion that belongs to another field of art (M, p. 230). In contrast with the primary illusion, which is steady, complete, and ubiquitous in a work of art, secondary illusions never present completely developed realms of virtual time, space, etc. (M, p. 206). We find secondary illusions playing over primary illusions in all advanced artistic creations, she says.[8] A secondary illusion is used sometimes to express transient elementary feeling (M, p. 230). Some very prominent secondary illusions are "harmonic space" in music, movement in plastic art, and eloquence in the lines of a statue.

In addition to secondary illusions, a work of art may exhibit different modes of the same primary illusion (PA, p. 238). Thus while painting, sculpture, and architecture all create the primary illusion of space, a piece of sculpture may be picturesque or a building such as a Greek temple may be sculptile.

What can become a secondary illusion and what cannot? The only hint that Langer gives is to say that the primary illusion of one art may become the secondary illusion of another (FF, p. 117; PA, p. 83). While space may appear in music, this is not an incursion of painting into music. Space in music is harmonic space, and it is not at all the visual space in the plastic arts. What, then, does it mean to say that the primary illusion of one realm of art can become the secondary illusion of another? If space in music is not the same as space in painting, how are they related? If volume in music is different from volume in sculpture, how does the primary illusion of sculpture become a secondary illusion in music?[9] Langer seems not to have investigated beyond observing that the words used to describe the primary illusions are also used to describe secondary illusions, and that those used to describe the secondary illusions in one field of art are different from those used to describe the primary illusion for that art.

Secondary illusions become part of primary illusions through the process of assimilation, Langer says. Elements from other realms of art are swallowed up or assimilated in an art genre. In the dance, for example, space and time disappear almost entirely (FF, p. 204). Music must be swallowed by movement, and color, pictorial composition, and decor become the frame and foil of gesture. Similarly, in music the words of vocal music are no longer prose or poetry; they become elements of the music itself; the impurities lamented by the advocates of "pure" music become transformed when they are incorporated into music, and become part of music (FF, pp. 150, 152). The only way that the poetry of a song enters into the song is through the inspiration it gives to the composer (PA, p. 84). After that, the poem as a work of art is broken up and its words, sounds, and

---

[8] "Advanced artistic creations" presumably means works of art that are both complex and good.

[9] For a discussion of volume in music, see Hans Heinz Draeger, "The Concept of 'Tonal Body'," *Reflections on Art*, ed. Susanne K. Langer (Johns Hopkins Press, 1958).

images become musical material: the text of the song is swallowed, hide and hair.

III

We come now to the heart of Langer's perceivability theory of art. Since it first appears in Langer's discussion of the various arts, I shall discuss it in its application to each of them. For some of the arts, this theory is explicitly stated; for others, we shall have to draw it out from suggestions in the texts. I shall first consider the arts in which the theory is clear.

All of the plastic arts create virtual space, Langer says, and they make space visible in the various modes in which we instinctively conceive and negotiate it (*FF*, p. 104). The space in which we live and act is not what is treated in the plastic arts at all. The space in which we live is known by sight and touch, by free motion and restraint, by sounds far and near, by voices lost or re-echoed (*FF*, p. 72). The space of the plastic arts, on the other hand, is a purely visual space, limited by the frame, or by surrounding blanks, or by incongruous other things that cut it off, and it does not even share limits with the space around us: it is entirely self-contained and independent. There are different modes of virtual space, Langer says, and these distinguish the plastic arts. Painting creates virtual scene; sculpture, virtual kinetic volume; and architecture, virtual ethnic domain.

The purpose of painting is to make space visible and its continuity sensible (*FF*, p. 77). Everything that is pictured serves to define and to organize this space (*PA*, p. 143). In it we find background and foreground, highlights, empty air, motion, accent, intensity of color, depth of darkness, objects in relation to each other.

Sculpture is the creation of virtual kinetic volume, or virtual living three-dimensional form (*FF*, p. 90). We normally perceive volume through the sense of touch, but virtual volume in sculpture we perceive visually, she says. Nevertheless, it is tactual space that is seen in a piece of sculpture, and thus tactual space must be made visible. A sculpture presents us an image of the space surrounding our physical bodies (*FF*, p. 92). We are surrounded by an environment, a space in which we are at the center: the range of free motion in it, the breathing space, and the reach of our extremities define it and provide the point of orientation from which we plot the world of tangible reality—objects, distances, motions, shape and size and mass (*FF*, p. 90). We see a piece of sculpture as a center of a space of its own, much like the space that we are aware of through our senses.

Architecture is a total environment made visible, an ethnic domain made visible and tangible (*FF*, pp. 95, 98). A culture as such, Langer says, is made up of the activities of human beings, and is a continuous functional pattern of interlocking and intersecting actions (*FF*, p. 96). As such, it is intangible and invisible. A piece of architecture, on the other hand, is a physically present object that expresses the characteristic rhythmic functional patterns which constitute the culture.[10] Tribal culture is made visible in the temple, the tomb, the fortress, the hall, and the theater: Stonehenge, for instance, unified for the Druids earth and heaven, men and gods; the great tombs are the image of the underworld; by their windowless walls they create a womb of earth, and they are intended for silence and the reign of death; in a secular society, such as that of the Goths, the hall is the symbol of the human world (*FF*, p. 97). All of these, Langer says, are ways of making the environment or culture visible and tangible to the people who lived in and among the edifices.

Music makes time audible, and its form and continuity sensible (*FF*, p. 110). It spreads time out for our direct and complete apprehension by letting our hearing organize, fill, and shape it. It creates an image of time measured by the motion of forms of sound. Music moves in a realm of pure duration, radically different from the time in which our public and practical life proceeds, which is measured by a clock (*FF*, p. 109). Practical time is one-dimensional, much like the simple one-dimensional trickle of successive moments which constitute the conception of time in the conceptual framework of classical physics (*PA*, p. 37). Subjective time exists for us because we undergo tensions and their resolutions; their building-up, their ways of breaking or diminishing or merging into longer and greater tensions make a vast variety of temporal form (*FF*, p. 112). Felt time has a sort of voluminousness and complexity and variability that makes it utterly unlike metric time. Lived time is measurable only in terms of tensions and their resolutions—somatic, emotional, and mental tensions, which have a characteristic pattern. They pile one on top of another, and form a dense fabric of overlaying vital processes (*PA*, p. 35). Subjective time seems to have density and volume, Langer says, because living beings are indescribably complex; the tensions that compose the vital processes are not simply successive, but they have multiple, often incommensurable relations. Life is a dense fabric of tensions, and since each of them is a measure of time, the measurements do not coincide. Music presents to us an auditory apparition of this time (*FF*, p. 107; *PA*, p. 144). Rather than vaguely sense its passage, as we do through our ordinary life processes, we hear its passage. Like "felt time," what passes in music is not a one-dimensional time such as that measured by the clock. And because music is an image of this time, because music makes this time audible, it likewise has voluminousness, complexity, and variability.

The dance, Langer says, should be conceived as a play of vital forces

---

[10] There appears to be a conceptual muddle here, but not an important one. If a culture is made up of the activities of human beings, these activities, and consequently the culture, are certainly visible and tangible. We see activities and we can participate in them. Langer could still hold, however, that these actions are evanescent; they come and go, they are often inaccessible to us, they sometimes pass unnoticed, and it takes a complex and extended pattern of such actions to constitute a culture. On the other hand, in a work of architecture, we have a lasting and unchanging image of these various and fleeting activities. As such, Langer could hold that it is an image of our culture.

made visible (*FF*, p. 193). Not only is it the image of forces but it also provides men with their first conception of the powers which surround them (*FF*, p. 190). It makes visible to us the powers of darkness, military power, the realm of demons, spirits and gods, important social activities, such as birth, marriage, death, planting and harvesting, hunting, and puberty. The substance of dance is the same power that enchanted ancient caves and forests (*FF*, p. 206). The forces presented in a dance may be physical, psychical, mythical, or magical (PIGOA, p. 226). They are not the actual forces that move the dancers, she says, but lures and excitements, prescribed paths, engulfing rhythms, personal will, orgiastic, mystic, and musical causes. "In watching a ballet one is not aware of people running around, but of the dance *driving* this way, *drawn* that way, *gathering* here, *spreading* there" (PIGOA, pp. 226 f., italics in text; cf. *PA*. p. 5). The evolution of the dance as a developed art occurred in prehistory because primitive men lived in a world of demonic powers: subhuman or superhuman, gods or spooks or impersonal magic forces, good and bad luck (*PA*, p. 11; *FF*, p. 190). Dance was the primitive way of conceiving these powers, so that they could be invoked, adjured, challenged, or placated.

For the literary arts (poetry, novel, drama) Langer does not explicitly state the perceivability theory, but it is easily drawn out from what she does say.[11]

Literature creates the illusion of life in the mode of virtual past (*FF*, pp. 253, 266). A piece of literature uses structure, diction, images, names, and allusions to make an image of life (*FF*, p. 281). Our actual thoughts chase each other in haphazard fashion, and their complete form rarely develops. We think and act without paying particular attention to the thoughts and fantasies that lie behind our thought and action. Our past history is consequently only half perceived and half intellectually constructed (PIGOA, p. 229). Literary art, on the other hand, creates a complete "lived" piece of experience, where a thought is really seen in its passage, followed through from its whimsical rise to its final close; the idea is entertained fully because other thoughts do not interfere with it.

Many people have taken poetry to be a type of discourse, because it is composed of words. But this is the wrong way to understand it, she argues. Poetry does not assert anything; it does not inform us of anything. It presents us with a single image, and not the many images that recent theorists have suggested. The words used and the connotations they suggest contribute to this image, but they do not present separable images from which the poem is then constructed. The poetic use of language is essentially formulative, Langer says, in contrast with the common communicative functions of language. It is not a beautified discourse, a particularly effective way of telling things: it is not discourse, or a way of telling things at all. And since it need not be an experience that the artist

[11] Langer groups poetry, novel, and drama into one basic art field, which she calls "poesis," and indiscriminately calls a poet any writer in any of these fields. When she talks about what a poet does, it becomes difficult to determine whether she is talking about a writer of poetry or about a literary artist of some other kind.

(or anyone else) has had, it is a creation of imagined experience. Langer distinguishes two kinds of poetry, lyric and narrative. Lyric poetry, always in the present tense, creates an awareness of a subjective experience in a timeless present, since subjectivity is timeless to us (*FF*, p. 268). Narrative poetry creates the illusion of things past, the semblance of events lived and felt, like an abstracted and completed memory (*FF*, p. 269). The modern novel portrays to us the contemporary scene by taking our most pervasive interest in contemporary life as its theme—the evaluation and the hazards of personality (*FF*, p. 286).

Langer devotes considerable attention to explaining how destiny is presented in drama. The action in a drama builds up a tension between past and future (*FF*, p. 308). In drama a virtual human destiny is presented from the very beginning, which unfolds in the process of the play (*FF*, p. 310). The significance of stage actions is more apparent to us, because they do not include crosscurrents of other actions and divided interests that are irrelevant to the play, such as we find in our own world. Characters on stage have no unknown complexities. Every word and action, and even the dress and staging, give us distinctive information about a character. Because in the theater a virtual future unfolds before us, the import of every little act is heightened, and even the smallest act is oriented toward the future (*FF*, p. 324). Consequently, we do not see behavior, but the self-realization of people in action and passion. Comedy presents destiny in the guise of fortune, Langer says, the upset and recovery of equilibrium of the protagonist, his contest with the world and his triumph over it (*FF*, p. 331). Tragedy presents destiny as fate, life in its fulfillment and finality (*FF*, p. 333). Unlike fortune, which is capricious, fate is shaped essentially in advance.

It is a small step from the position that the literary arts function to make life imaginable to us to the view that this is its purpose. To the extent that functions are consciously intended, and they are not byproducts of other purposes, they are purposes pursued. Thus the perceivability theory is implied in what Langer says of the literary arts.

In summary, the perceivability theory centers on the contention that works of art make more perceivable to us aspects of either the world around us or our own experience. For the non-literary arts it is aspects of the world around us that are made more perceivable: visual space in the plastic arts, felt time in music, and the realm of powers in the dance. Human experience is made perceivable or imaginable in the literary arts: the present or the past in poetry, the contemporary society in the novel, and destiny in drama. The illusion doctrine tells us how works of art are different from other things in the world around us.

IV

Let us look more closely at the illusion doctrine now. It is not found in *Philosophy in a New Key*, just as the perceivability theory is not found there; it is first presented in an article which otherwise adheres to the expression theory (PCA). That it is developed at the same time in Langer's intellectual career as the perceivability theory, though, is attested by the appearance of the perceivability theory in a sequel article a few months later (PIGOA). Thereafter the illusion doctrine always appears where the perceivability theory is elaborated.

What does Langer mean by this term? An "illusion" is "something that is what it appears to be." The contrast, presumably, is with something that is not what it appears to be in the sense that it hides something from view or consideration. Is this a part of the expression theory? To express feeling an object does not have to be entirely exposed, hiding nothing from view or consideration. Why should expressions of feelings make them *wholly* perceivable, and not hide somewhat their structure? Is it not natural for our feelings to hide some of their aspects from us, just as do things in the world around us? We repress feelings when we are afraid of showing them or admitting them to ourselves. Langer might reject this argument, however, on the ground that the complete feeling need not be conscious: only the consciousness does the repressing—and the feeling remains as it was. But if this is the case, then still the feeling is hidden to others and to ourselves. Even if we say, as Langer does in *Mind: An Essay in Human Feeling*, that feelings are manifestations of organic tensions, this will not avoid the issue because organic tensions can be hidden from investigation or even from our own knowledge. There appears to be no reason to suppose that the forms of feeling are entirely what they appear to be, and consequently no reason to think that works of art need to have this characteristic in order to have the forms of feeling.

I have pointed out above that Langer introduces the illusion doctrine to account for the differences between works of art and other things, the phenomena that Edward Bullough tries to explain with his conception of "psychical distance." Can this be explained by the expression theory in some other way? In *Philosophy in a New Key* Langer says that psychical distance disappears when a symbol (a work of art), whose purpose is to let us *conceive* something, is confused with a sign, which causes us to deal with what it means (PNK, p. 223). If we take it as a sign, she says, we respond emotionally to it. On the other hand, if we take it as a symbol, then it gives us insight: " 'Psychical Distance' is simply the experience of apprehending through a symbol what was not articulated before." This is not a particularly good explanation but neither is the doctrine of illusion. It follows, then, that Langer's doctrine of illusion need not be connected to her expression theory. Let us examine to what extent it belongs to the perceivability theory.

Langer tells us that in most respects the space in paintings is not like the space in the world around us: it is not known by sight and touch, by free motion and restraint, far and near sounds, voices lost or re-echoed; it is an entirely visual space, which we can only see, just as we can only see the space in a mirror image (FF, p. 72). But by cutting off these other aspects of space as we experience it, painting is able to focus our attention

on precisely its visual character and thereby to make space visible to us.[12]
This argument can be generalized and applied to all the arts: by creating
an illusion a work of art abstracts from the world around us to present a
portion of it completely separated from the rest so that it concentrates our
attention on it. In daily life our attention is usually drawn to practical
consequences of actions and the world around us is generally viewed as a
collection of tools to be used in the various goals we pursue. Many different interests vie for our attention, and we are rarely able to concentrate
completely on one thing at a time. We rarely stop and notice, because of
the press of other obligations, how space looks or how time appears. By
abstracting an element of this experience, a work of art concentrates our
attention on it. The artist wrenches objects or experiences from their practical contexts, and forces us to concentrate on them by themselves, on
their appearances. A river becomes something to be looked at in a painting, with a character of its own wholly presented in the painting, and not
something to be bridged or used for water supply or for waste disposal. A
dramatic conflict is cut off from distracting influences that normally draw
our attention away from the drama in our own lives, sometimes hiding it
from us altogether. Thus the illusion doctrine belongs to the perceivability
theory of art, and not to the expression theory.[13]

V

I must now demonstrate the crucial point in the argument: that the two
theories are indeed distinct and not simply connected parts of one unifying
philosophy by arguing that the expression theory does not entail the perceivability theory, and vice versa. It would be useful to argue that either
theory can be consistently held without the other, but this is not possible,
since Langer's commentators have persuasively argued that the expression
theory cannot be consistently held at all, and I shall argue in a sequel that
the perceivability theory must be changed considerably, at least in its
details, to be acceptable. I shall argue, however, that the grounds for the
two theories are different, and they lead us to emphasize different aspects
of a given work of art.

Prima facie these two theories are different. The expression theory says
that a work of art is an expression of the artist's knowledge of feeling, that
this knowledge is projected in the work of art, and that the work of art is
a symbol of this feeling, or the feeling is its import. This appears very
different from the contention that works of art make perceptible to us
aspects of the world around us. It must be argued, however, that these are
not complementary aspects of a single theory. One might contend, in sup-

---

[12] Jenkins (p. 153) argues precisely this position, generalizing it to provide an explanation
of abstraction in art.
[13] The examples used here do not fit the perceivability theory as Langer presents it; in at
least some cases it should be reformulated to fit the examples presented here.

port of Langer, that it is precisely by making time audible, space visible, and life imaginable that one expresses feelings.

Although largely limited in application to music, the expression theory is first presented in *Philosophy in a New Key*, and here there is no mention of any aspect of the perceivability theory. Furthermore, the perceivability theory first appears in "The Primary Illusions and the Great Orders of Art," and in this article there is only passing mention of the expression theory.[14] The two theories get along quite well in these writings without each other, and the suggestions for development lead in different directions.

Let us consider the matter more closely. Suppose Langer were to argue that *Philosophy in a New Key* presents a germinal theory, which, when worked out in the later writings, entails what we have called the perceivability theory. The theory presented in *Philosophy in a New Key* is limited to music and, in generalizing it and applying it to the other arts, certainly developments will occur.

There are two developments in the expression theory after *Philosophy in a New Key*. One is the contention that non-temporal works of art (paintings, sculpture, architecture) can present forms of feelings, even though feelings are essentially dynamic, occurring over a period of time. In *Philosophy in a New Key*, Langer says that paintings can represent only momentary states (p. 73). By developing the conception of "dynamic image," that is, a static image of a dynamic process (e.g., river beds, waterfalls, dust screws), she is able to apply to the non-temporal arts her contention that art presents images; paintings are static images of dynamic processes, while musical works are dynamic images of dynamic processes.

Does the conception of dynamic image provide a connection between the expression theory and the perceivability theory? One might argue that a static image makes a dynamic process more perceptible. Most river beds do not make rivers more perceivable, because the river is there for all to see. But if the river has dried up or substantially receded, then the river bed presents us a static image of the river that flowed there in the past. But the wind bloweth where it listeth, and we usually only hear the sound thereof unless we see such occurrences as dust screws and tornado funnels. Sand dunes and the shapes of trees sometimes show us where the wind has been. But they, like the dry river bed, show us only what has occurred

---

[14] The two articles, PCA and PIGOA, appeared within a few months of each other in *The Hudson Review*. Aside from the first presentation of the illusion doctrine, "The Principles of Creation in Art" is devoted entirely (excepting one line, which is undeveloped) to the expression theory of art. "The Primary Illusions and the Great Orders of Art," on the other hand, is devoted entirely to the perceivability theory. Here we find Langer's thought at a turning point: either the two concerns presented in the two articles must be acknowledged to lead to different theories and thus commit Langer to two theories of art, or they must be brought under one roof and somehow reconciled. The latter, clearly the more desirable for a systematic philosopher such as Langer, is the one she chooses. I submit, however, that although she does put them both in one house (they appear together in all her later writing), they never live harmoniously together, and they are better separated.

in the past. Only dynamic images can make present events visible to us. Dust screws and tornado funnels show us forces that are acting at the moment: we do see whence the wind cometh and whither it goeth. Similarly, many other static images make dynamic processes visible to us. Nontemporal works of art, Langer holds, are such images.

But to argue thus is to present the perceivability theory, not the expression theory. The expression theory analyzes a dynamic image by showing the tensions and resolutions it presents. These tensions and resolutions, it then says, are like the tensions and resolutions of feelings, but in the case of feelings they occur over a period of time. In the perceivability theory it is the dynamic process (and only this) that is made perceivable; in the expression theory it is forms of feeling that are made perceivable. Thus the conception of a static image of a dynamic process may be used by either theory, but each theory uses it differently, and it does not connect the two theories.

A second development in the expression theory after *Philosophy in a New Key* is the conception of "intuition." But intuition does not belong exclusively to either theory, either. Since Langer holds that all perception is intuition of forms, this contention holds for both theories, and it does not provide a connection between them. The perceivability theory separates from the expression theory in the analysis of how what we perceive as a work of art is related to other aspects of our experience. What Langer says about intuition is epistemologically antecedent to this distinction. The perceivability theory holds that the forms we perceive make more perceivable aspects of the world around us or of our own life. The expression theory holds that the forms we perceive in works of art are projections of forms of feeling. Thus the conception of intuition does not belong to either theory, and it does not provide a bridge between them.

Does making space visible help the artist create a form which is iconic with a form of feeling? The elements of a painting, Langer tells us, are tensions and resolutions. What have these to do with space, visible or invisible? Arnheim argues that we do see tensions in the world around us, specifically in tree branches and arms and legs.[15] But it is *things* in the world around us that he argues have tensions, or present movement, and not the space in which they exist. He does not argue that these tensions make anything visible. If they do make anything visible, it is the objects which seem to move and the movement they present. Langer tells us that the space in painting, sculpture, and architecture is not like the space in the world around us in precisely this way: the space in the world around us does not have tensions and resolutions, and it is not shaped as space is in these works of art (*FF*, p. 72). Consequently, making visible the space in which we live is a very different task from creating something that has the form of a feeling.

If one holds that the nature of feeling is the interaction of psychic forces, for the dance, as Freudian psychologists have suggested, then a presenta-

---

[15] *Art and Visual Perception* (Univ. of California Press, 1954), p. 403.

tion of these forces will be useful to express human feelings. A presentation of forces in the dance will perhaps enable an arrangement of these forces to express the relationship of forces in the human psyche, and dance may thereby become an expression of these psychic forces. But these are not the forces that Langer contends are made visible by the dance: the forces it makes visible, she says, are forces in the world around us, the powers of darkness, military power, the realm of gods and demons, social activities such as birth, marriage, and death. So while this argument may be a good one, it does not fit Langer's analysis of the dance, and consequently is not a link between her two theories. Analogous arguments can be made for each of the other arts.

A further difference between the two theories arises because the expression theory is semiotic or cognitive, and the perceivability theory is non-semiotic or non-cognitive. The expression theory claims that works of art give us knowledge, although of a peculiar sort. Langer accepts the positivist dualism of knowledge and feeling, but she contends that works of art extend our realm of knowledge further into the realm of feeling than the positivists had supposed. The perceivability theory, on the other hand, does not claim to give us knowledge of any sort: it claims to heighten our awareness, to increase our perceptive sensitivity to the world around us and to our own experience. To support the contention that the arts give us knowledge, one must analyze what sort of knowledge it gives, characterize a distinction between truth and falsehood, and show that people who are acquainted with the arts indeed do have this knowledge. This analysis will be very different from that given to support a theory that contends that the arts provide us a heightened awareness of what we are ordinarily only dimly aware of. The latter will have to point out an increased awareness on the part of those who are acquainted with the arts, but it need not claim that they have access to a body of knowledge closed to other people. Thus the elaboration and the grounds of plausibility for these two theories are quite different.

These two theories of art lead us to concentrate our attention on different aspects of works of art, and thus to perceive them differently. The expression theory emphasizes the form of the work, in the special sense that Langer understands "form": tensions and interactions between shapes in paintings, between characters in drama, between dancers in the dance. The work of art becomes nothing but its form. The form is important for the expression theory because it is form that is a form of feeling, or a projection thereof. The perceivability theory, on the other hand, does not emphasize so strongly the form of the work of art. The whole art work, it holds, makes perceivable for us our experience or the world around us. Form is significant only insofar as it is important in the work of art itself. This importance varies from one work of art to another.

There is a more striking difference between the two theories when it comes to interpreting a work of art. For the expression theory, if we are to get at the heart of a work of art, we must discover the feeling-structure that it exhibits. For the perceivability theory, we must discover what it makes more perceivable or understandable for us. If it were feeling that the perceivability theory held is made more perceivable, then we would have only one theory here. But since feeling is not a possible value of the variable what is made perceivable in Langer's perceivability theory, these are two theories. Trying to discover the feeling-structure expressed in a work of art leads us to think about it and consequently to perceive it in one way; trying to discover which particular aspect of experience is made perceivable by it leads us to think about it and perceive it in a different way. A Gothic cathedral, for instance, according to the perceivability theory, makes perceivable to us the belief in God and the religious customs of the late medieval Christian era. Its spires tower above the rest of the town, casting the shadow of God over the town, its inhabitants, and their activities. The carving on the exterior tells not only the story of Christianity but also the history of the town and the activities of its people. Its floor plan makes perceivable the worship services and other religious (and sometimes secular) activities common to the people of that time. According to the expression theory, on the other hand, the formal relations between the elemens of the church architecture correspond to the formal elements of feelings. The vertical rising up of the spires symbolizes the feeling-structure of rising exhilaration, perhaps, or the feeling-structure of reaching upward toward God (and also that our reach is never sufficient: it always stops in the air). Perhaps it expresses majesty, evoking a feeling of awe in response (just as we should feel in the presence of God for whom the cathedral stands).

These interpretations are not exclusive; one might argue that the Gothic cathedral does all of these. I suggest only that the perceivability theory emphasizes the relationship between God (represented by the church) and the community, while the expression theory emphasizes individual feeling toward God. As a consequence, a viewer presupposing one theory will see the cathedral differently from the viewer presupposing the other.

The expression theory and the perceivability theory, then, are indeed two different theories of art. Where each appears first in Langer's writings it is separate from the other. Langer's attempts to connect them together as aspects of a single theory are unsuccessful. The reasons for accepting one theory are very different from those for accepting the other. One leads us to perceive works of art differently from the way we perceive them when guided by the other.

Ted Cohen

A CRITIQUE OF
THE INSTITUTIONAL THEORY OF ART:
THE POSSIBILITY OF ART

Among recent efforts to say what art is,* one of the most salubrious is
George Dickie's "Defining Art."[1] Like much of Dickie's best work, this
essay is brief, direct, and convincing in the way it uncomplicates what
philosophers have made murky. This time, however, I think he has tried to
make things more simple and ingenuous than they can be. The definition
Dickie presents and argues for is this:

> A work of art in the descriptive sense is (1) an artifact (2) upon which some
> society or some sub-group of a society has conferred the status of candidate
> for appreciation [p. 254b].

This definition is introduced early in Dickie's essay, and the rest of the
essay is given to elucidating and defending it. Instead of summarizing
here all Dickie has to say, I will quote relevant passages in the course of
my criticism. At the beginning, however, it may be helpful to note three
special features of Dickie's thesis.

(1) The somewhat checkered history of attempts to define art is usually
seen as a series of specifications of art-making properties. These properties,
though subtle and sometimes relational, have been understood to be
properties the eye can descry. The definitions which require these properties of artworks are widely thought to have been discredited, if not by
earlier examples, by the onslaught of problematic cases and counterexamples supplied by twentieth-century art. Each definition (for example,
"Art is imitation, or expression, or significant form, or symbolic feeling")
seems either to founder straightway, since many obvious artworks do not

Ted Cohen is Chairman of the Department of Philosophy at The University of
Chicago. In addition to his work in aesthetics, Cohen has also done extensive work on
Kant and J. L. Austin.
* "The Possibility of Art: Remarks on a Proposal by Dickie," *Philosophical Review*,
January 1973, pp. 69–82. Reprinted by permission of the *Philosophical Review*.

[1] George Dickie, "Defining Art," *American Philosophical Quarterly*, 6 (1969), 253–
256. All references to Dickie are to this essay and I will give page numbers paren-
thetically in the body of the text, using '*a*' and '*b*' to refer to the left and right columns of the pages.

display the allegedly necessary property, or to retreat into insignificance, since the property it cites cannot be seen and is presumed to be present only because the objects are artworks. Dickie aims from the outset to specify a property which cannot be found merely by inspecting a putative artwork. He says:

> What the eye cannot descry is a complicated non-exhibited characteristic of the artifacts in question [p. 254a].

The idea is that the property required by the second condition of the definition is to be, as Dickie calls it, a social property, a non-exhibited status obtained within an institution.

(2) Since the eighteenth century there have been a number of definitions of art in terms of something like appreciation. Conceptions of appreciation have varied and so has the strategy of the definition. Usually some minimal requirement is given—for instance, that a thing be an artifact—and then it is held that appreciation of the thing is a necessary or sufficient condition of its being an artwork. The principal refinements have consisted in making the condition more subtle—requiring that a thing be likely to be appreciated, or that it be intended to be appreciated, or that it should be appreciated. Dickie's second condition is subtle enough to transform the character of this kind of definition. All questions of actual appreciation are waived. What is required is that a thing be a candidate for appreciation, and actually being appreciated is neither necessary nor sufficient for that.

(3) Dickie agrees with Morris Weitz in distinguishing two senses—or uses, as he sometimes says—of the term 'work of art,' an evaluative sense and a descriptive sense. Thus the initial qualification in the definition. Dickie is interested in the expression 'work of art' only in its descriptive sense, and he has little to say about its evaluative sense. He does invoke the evaluative sense as an explanation of the propriety of remarks like "This driftwood is a work of art" which precludes their being counterexamples to the requirement that works of art be artifacts. Dickie holds that the descriptive and evaluative senses are distinct at least to this extent, that both artifacts and nonartifacts can be works of art in the descriptive sense. Furthermore, works of art in the descriptive sense need not be works of art in the evaluative sense. So being a work of art in one sense is neither necessary nor sufficient for being so in the other sense.

The third feature of the definition is less novel than the others. I mention it because I will claim, toward the end of my criticism, that Dickie's determination to keep out of the definition everything he takes to be a matter of merit has left his conception of art too spare.

The definition falls short, so to speak, both formally and materially, and it is the second condition which is defective. Despite the careful reference to candidacy for appreciation, and not to appreciation itself, we must be told something about appreciation—enough at least to give content to the notion of candidacy. Materially, what Dickie says about appreciation is too strong, even though very general; formally, it lacks a dimension without which it is not acute enough to discriminate art from other things.

What Appreciation Is

Dickie first says:

> The kind of appreciation I have in mind is simply the kind characteristic of our experiences of paintings, novels, and the like [p. 255*a*].

One may wonder whether there is such a kind of appreciation, and I believe there is not. It seems to me it is already too much to suppose that there is a kind of appreciation characteristic of our experiences of, say, Rembrandt, Cézanne, Pollock, Olitski, "and the like." But Dickie thinks this can be overcome.

> Indeed, if we mean by "appreciation" something like "in experiencing the qualities of a thing one finds them worthy or valuable," then there is no problem about the similarity of the various appreciations [p. 255*a*].

This suggestion fails to meet the one case Dickie speaks much about, that of Duchamp. Dickie calls Duchamp's "Fountain" a work of art with no hesitation, and I think he believes it a substantial achievement of his definition that it easily accommodates things like the works of Dada. But does it? I agree that whatever Dada's practitioners thought, their accomplishment was not simply the creation of Un-art. It was, however, the creation of something *different*. In understanding this I am inclined to follow Michael Fried, who has said this:

> the situation has been complicated still further by the calling into question, first by Dada and within the past decade by Neo-Dada figures such as Cage, Johns and Rauschenberg, of the already somewhat dubious concept of a "work of art." . . . It would, however, be mistaken to think of Dada—the most precious of movements—as opposed to art. Rather, Dada stands opposed to the notion of *value* or *quality* in art, and in that sense represents a reaction against the unprecedented demands modernist painting makes of its practitioners. (It is, I think, significant that Duchamp was a failed modernist—more exactly, a failed Cubist—before he turned his hand to the amusing inventions by which he is best known.) But there is a superficial similarity between modernist painting and Dada in one important respect: namely, that just as modernist painting has enabled one to see a blank canvas, a sequence of random spatters or a length of colored fabric as a picture, Dada and Neo-Dada have equipped one to treat virtually any object as a work of art—though it is far from clear exactly what this means.[2]

Whether or not one agrees with Fried, it seems clear that the "appreciation" of Dada was and is novel. If Fried is right, then to speak of Dada in terms of experiencing qualities one finds worthy or valuable is exactly

[2] Michael Fried, the catalogue essay for *Three American Painters*, an exhibition of Noland, Olitski, and Stella, Fogg Art Museum, Harvard University, 1965, p. 47.

wrong. Even if Fried is wrong, surely the one obvious point about Dada is that it is not the occasion for appreciation of the "kind characteristic of our experiences of paintings, novels, and the like." Of course Dickie has not said that Dada is, or is to be, appreciated in this way, but that it has acquired the status of being a candidate for such appreciation. But Dada in general, and certainly Duchamp's urinal, is virtually accompanied by an announcement that traditional appreciation (if there is such a thing) cannot occur. This suggests two things: (1) that being a candidate for appreciation in any but the emptiest sense of 'appreciation' (where it signifies any kind of apprehension appropriate to anything which is an art-work) is not part of what it is to be an artwork, at least not for some works, and (2) that possibilities concerning what *can* be appreciated have some bearing on what can be made a candidate for appreciation. The second point is not considered by Dickie, and this is responsible for what I think of as a formal gap in his definition.

What Can Be a Work of Art

The second condition Dickie calls a "social property" of art (p. 253*b*). This idea, that part of what makes a thing a work of art is, so to speak, an institutionalized property, is the genuinely novel feature of Dickie's definition. The idea is present in recent works by Danto and Wollheim,[3] but I find it clearest in Dickie's essay and I shall confine myself to his definition. There are two broad areas for questions about how a thing acquires the social property which makes it art: in what circumstances and by whom can this property be bestowed, and what qualifies a thing to receive this bestowal. In the first area I have some more or less standard questions which are not altogether rhetorical for I, at least, do not see how to answer them on the basis of Dickie's remarks. The second area is more important since there I think Dickie does not see any questions to be answered.

If part of what makes a thing a work of art issues from an "institution" or "social practice," then we need to be told something of the details of the institution. There is merit enough in articulating the claim that artness is partly an institutional property—if that is true, and I do not mean to badger Dickie about the details. As he says,

> lines of authority in the politico-legal world are by and large explicitly defined and incorporated into law, while lines of authority (or something like authority) in the artworld are nowhere codified. The artworld carries on its business at the level of customary practice [p. 255*a*].

What Dickie says about this customary practice, however, leaves things more confusing than they might have been if he had simply referred such a prac-

---

[3] Arthur Danto, "The Artworld," *Journal of Philosophy*, 61 (1964), 571–584; Richard Wollheim, *Art and Its Objects* (New York, 1968), esp. sec. 46, and "Minimal Art," *Arts Magazine*, 39 (1965), 26–32. Dickie cites Danto's paper as a stimulus to his own view.

tice and left it at that. Dickie sees a difference between a plumbing equipment salesman displaying his wares and Duchamp exhibiting his urinal, which he elucidates in this way:

> The difference is analogous to the difference between my uttering "I declare this man to be a candidate for alderman" and the head of the election board uttering the same sentence while acting in his official capacity [p. 255a].

But there is an ambiguity here: whose enfranchisement are we concerned with, some museum director's or Duchamp's? That Dickie means the former, or at least that he does not mean Duchamp, is suggested by this—

> The point is that Duchamp's act took place within a certain institutional setting and that makes all the difference. Our salesman of plumbing supplies could do what Duchamp did [p. 255b]—

and by his remark concerning a different case, "It all depends on the institutional setting" (p. 256a).

If Dickie is read this way, then his analogy is strikingly inept, for it is precisely not the case that our Dickie could do what the head of the election board did (make someone an aldermanic candidate). What the analogy suggests is that to make something art, one first must be an art-maker. I suspect that the analogy appeals to Dickie because it sets making-a-candidate-for-election beside making-a-candidate-for-appreciation. But it is clear that one needs status to bestow status in the political case. What about the case of art? What about the interchangeability of Duchamp and the plumbing supplier? What if a urinal merchant or a junk collector had attempted to carry out Duchamp's act, say with the very object Duchamp used, and had been turned away by the organizers of the show? Is that all there is to it: the urinal did not become art because it did not receive the requisite social property, though it received it later when Duchamp brought it around; and the only way in which Duchamp's being Duchamp figures is contingently (since the organizers knew him, they accepted his urinal)? Well, then what if Duchamp had been rejected as well? If he had then just sulked, that might be an end to it. But what if he displayed the rejected urinal in his own flat, set it out on a roped-off rug in the living room? Does that turn the trick? Then could the merchant do the same?

These are bewildering questions, and they become more annoying if we switch Duchamp and the salesman in the other direction. Suppose it is Duchamp who comes to your home, where perhaps you are in need of plumbing fixtures, and sets before you a number of objects, including the urinal. Now what? Dickie's account of appreciation does not help. Dickie notes (p. 255a) that the ordinary salesman is presenting his wares for appreciation, but insists that he is not conferring on them the status of candidate for appreciation. But he *could* be doing both things, couldn't he? Couldn't Duchamp? Suppose that Picasso came to your house hawking his paintings, and didn't care what you did with them. Or better, since you may believe that Picasso's paintings were already art before he got to your house, suppose that he came and was commissioned by you to do a sketch directly on the wall in order to disguise some cracks in the plaster.

That would be art, wouldn't it? And if it is when Picasso does it, why not when the neighborhood painter and plasterer do it? And if Duchamp's urinal is art just as readily for having been brought to your house as for having gotten into the show, why not the salesman's?

Before his discussion of Duchamp and the salesman, Dickie offers an adroit remark to help in accepting the notion of a "conferral of status" when it is clear that for much art this cannot be said to occur overtly (some artists never exhibit).

> What I want to suggest is that, just as two persons can acquire the status of common-law marriage within a legal system, an artifact can acquire the status of a candidate for appreciation within the system which Danto has called "the artworld" [p. 254*b*].

Then how is it that Picasso's merest scribble and, perhaps, Duchamp's urinal have a status not possessed by just anyone's mere scribble or spare urinal? Perhaps it is like this: one of the ways the "artworld" breeds Art is by way of enfranchising Artmakers. Anyone who did "Nude Descending a Staircase" and the rest would be an Artmaker (however good), but only an Artmaker could make that urinal Art (if it is art). It is because he did "Nude" that Duchamp is an artist; it is because he is Duchamp that "Fountain" is not just a misplaced urinal.[4]

This idea suggests that art and its institutions are inbred and self-justifying in ways that are hard to untangle, and I think that is plausible though I will not argue for it. It seems clear that Dickie does not agree with this. He says, after all, that the salesman could do what Duchamp did, and there is no suggestion that to do this the salesman must first acquire a power Duchamp already has. And, as noted, on this count the creation of an aldermanic candidate is a poor analogue (even Mayor Daley cannot make a man a candidate for alderman: he must make the election board make the man a candidate). The creation of a political candidate, like the act of christening, which Dickie refers to and which I will discuss later, seems an apt analogue of artmaking only so long as only one aspect is considered. In both artmaking and candidate-making there exist constraints in terms of the objects. The head of the election board cannot make just anyone a candidate. Typically there will be a minimum age, a residence requirement, a stipulation that there be no criminal record, a requirement that there be nominating petitions signed by some number of registered voters, and so on. Perhaps Dickie supposes his account of artmaking supplies an analogue for all this in the first condition, that the object be an artifact. But something is missing. There is nothing to match the connection between the qualifications imposed on a would-be alderman and the point in making someone a candidate for alderman. The qualifications, which the election board is bound to impose, derive from

---

[4] This suggestion, I suspect, would be much more agreeable to Danto than to Dickie. I say this only on the basis of some remembered remarks of Danto's made during discussions at the University of Illinois at Chicago Circle Aesthetics Institute, May, 1971. Despite Dickie's accurate recognition in Danto of a view broadly similar to his own in the matter of saying what art is, there are acute differences.

considerations of what aldermen do or are supposed to do. There is no doubt a blending together of considerations of what aldermen do and what they do well, but that need not be gone into. What connection of any kind is there between being an artifact and being appreciated? Why is it that only artifacts can be made candidates for appreciation, and, more important, why suppose that every artifact can be made such a candidate? This problem, and the failure of analogy in Dickie's failure to say anything about constraints in terms of the artmaker (about who can make something art as only a deputized official can make someone a political candidate), lead me to abandon Dickie's own analogy. If we are to get to the subtleties implicit in Dickie's suggestion, we need a different analogue for the act of making something art, one in which a distinction appears, not between having a power and not having it (as the head of the election board has a power not possessed by others), but between exercising a power we all have and not exercising it (like Duchamp's act which Dickie thinks anyone could have carried out). I believe that Dickie thinks we are all, or nearly all, in the artworld and that in the artworld everyone is empowered to make art. A suitable analogue may illuminate what limits the exercise of this power.

I take the act of conferring the status of candidate for appreciation to be (or to be like) what Austin called an illocution, or what he earlier might have called a performative.[5] The analogue chosen by Dickie, declaring someone a candidate in the uttering of certain words, is an illocution. To improve on it, we need a different illocution. I will use the act of promising, though it too is an imprecise analogue in some respects. There are a number of obscurities in our understanding of the mechanics of promising, but that is a help here, for it exposes the complexities that arise when we move from formalized rituals and ceremonial acts like christening and political licensing to less canonical ones like promising and, as Dickie thinks, making things art. Before getting back to the definition of art, I need to use promising to illustrate a point about illocutions which is not reflected in Dickie's conception of what is required to make art.

The act of promising accomplished in the saying of "I promise . . ." in appropriate circumstances is an illocution. Characteristically, this illocution precipitates various effects and consequences Austin calls perlocutions. Among possible perlocutions are, for instance, the recipient's feeling gratified in some way, his attributing to the speaker an intention to do what is promised, his acting in ways commensurate with or dependent on the speaker's doing what is promised. Though it oversimplifies things, I ask you to think of all these consequences or effects as one perlocution, a kind of generic response I will call "accepting" a promise. Promising is an illocution; having a promise accepted is a perlocution. In the case of promising

[5] The outlines of Austin's conceptions of illocutions and perlocutions are, I hope, familiar enough not to need rehearsing here, and it is only a general account that I am concerned with. For Austin's detailed account see his William James Lectures, published as *How to Do Things with Words* (Cambridge, Mass., 1962), esp. pp. 98 ff.

and securing acceptance, the illocution and the perlocution are associated, I think, on two levels: as a relation between promising and acceptance in general, and as a constraint on promising in particular instances.

In general, the perlocution is something like the rationale, or part of the rationale, for the illocution. It constitutes a general reason, a reason *überhaupt*, for performing the illocution—it gives the act a point. As Kant noted, if there is no acceptance of promises, then the act of promising becomes not merely a vain effort, but it ceases to be that kind of act—it ceases to be promising. This is not to say that there must be acceptance in every case, that there is no such thing as an unaccepted promise. The perlocution is detachable from the illocution in particular cases. But something does follow with regard to individual cases.

In any particular case it must be possible, or at least appear to those concerned to be possible, that the perlocution transpire. It is, so to speak, in the nature of the illocution to effect the perlocution, and if it is obvious to those involved that this effect cannot occur, then the illocution is in some way and to some degree abortive. That is why I cannot promise you something we both know, and know one another knows that I cannot deliver. There may be *some* point in my giving my word knowing you know that I cannot keep it, but it cannot be a point usual in cases of giving one's word, and so I am not simply "giving my word—period."[6]

Sometimes I cannot do an illocution because the illocutionary act is not open to do. I cannot christen a ship I have already christened nor marry you if you are already my wife. The illocution has been pre-empted. The pre-empting need not have been done by me: I cannot hire you if my partner has already signed you on, or arrest you if the sheriff has just booked you. But sometimes the illocution is no longer open because the associated perlocution has already been effected, whether or not by means of an illocution. For instance, I cannot argue the point with you if you are already persuaded, or warn you of a danger to which you are already alerted, or point out something you already see. Whether I can do these things is, perhaps, problematic if I am ignorant of what has already happened, but it seems clear that I cannot do them if I know that you are already persuaded, alert, or aware.

I take it as a kind of rule of thumb that the availability of at least some illocutions requires the openness of their associated perlocutions. The perlocution must be neither known to be already effected nor known to be clearly out of the question.

---

[6] I leave some principal questions concerning the relations between illocutions and perlocutions untreated here, trusting that I have said enough to clarify the point I will make about Dickie's definition. These questions—for instance, why we ought not simply to separate promises from non-promises, warnings from non-warnings, etc. without reference to perlocutions, whether every illocution is associated with some perlocution in the way promising is associated with securing acceptance, whether Austin was sufficiently acute in distinguishing illocutions from perlocutions by declaring only the former to be "conventional"—are taken up in my "Illocutions and Perlocutions," forthcoming in *Foundations of Language*.

Let me import these points about perlocutions into Dickie's definition. I construe the act of conferring the status of a candidate for appreciation to be like an illocution, and I take the actual appreciation of a thing with this status to be like an associated perlocution. Being appreciated is neither a necessary nor a sufficient condition for something's being a candidate for appreciation, just as having what I say (about what I will do) accepted is neither necessary nor sufficient for its being a promise. But if what I say is a promise, then it must seem possible that it be accepted. And (supposing Dickie's definition correct), if I am to succeed in conferring the status of art on an object, it must seem possible that it be appreciated. My utterance is not a promise just because I say so, just because it has the form 'I promise. . . .' (I cannot promise that I was on time yesterday, or that it will rain tomorrow.) And neither, I think, is x a work of art just because I say so. There are substantive constraints on what I can promise (however difficult it may be to formulate them), and there must be constraints on what I can make art. But what are they? Dickie names one—x must be an artifact.[7] But this is not enough. What of an artifact which clearly cannot be appreciated (in Dickie's sense)? I say that there are such things—for instance, ordinary thumbtacks, cheap white envelopes, the plastic forks given at some drive-in restaurants—and that if Dickie's definition were correct then these things could not be artworks because they could not receive the requisite status. Duchamp's urinal is like that. Things like that cannot acquire the status required by Dickie's second condition because it would be pointless or bizarre to give it to them.

Dickie's concrete mistake has been to suppose that Duchamp's "Fountain" has anything whatever to do with what Dickie calls appreciation. If such eccentric works are art, then if that requires that they have something in common with traditional art, it is not a candidacy for what they were designed to forestall and disdain. This material error is a symptom of a more formal, conceptual gap—namely, supposing that making something a candidate for appreciation can be altogether unilateral, so that any thing whatever could become a candidate upon someone's say-so. In fact, the untoward consequence of Dickie's suggestion is that it will rule out the very items Dickie is eager to accommodate. But then what about "Fountain"? Is Duchamp's "Fountain" a work of art, and Dickie's definition wrong because it misses this work, or is Dickie right and so "Fountain" not art? Neither of these choices is a healthy one. I am not clear about whether "Fountain" is a work of art, just like that. I am not as confident as either Dickie or Fried about this. If Fried is right, in the aftermath of Dada we are able to count nearly anything a work of art—but, he says, this leaves it unclear what it means to count something as a work of art. What is wrong with Dickie's definition, I think, is that as Dickie takes it, it is

---

[7] I have completely recast Dickie's formulation, so that it calls for an illocution to be done and imposes one constraint on the circumstances appropriate to that kind of illocution. I should point out that Dickie has a different model in mind. He takes himself to be giving a definition by genus (artifactuality) and differentia (candidacy for appreciation).

clear and it clearly applies to "Fountain." No definition should fit "Fountain" so comfortably. Why not takes some explaining.

To say that an illocution must be "pointless" if its associated perlocution is not open is not quite right. There can be a *point* in saying "I promise to love you forever" or "I promise never to feel anger again." Indeed, saying these things can be splendid ways, perhaps the only ways, of saying and doing some things. But that does not make these sayings promises (I think they cannot be promises because these things cannot be promised). Similarly, there can be a point, I suppose, in invoking a formula for bestowing the status of candidate for appreciation on a thing which cannot be an object of appreciation. But that will not give these things that status. In both kinds of cases, as with "pointless" illocutions in general, the effect is to draw attention from the thing said (or the putative object of appreciation) to the act of saying it (or the act of exhibiting it). If Austin is right, we cannot entirely separate the saying and the said without distortion, but we can identify, so to speak, the locus of significance and import: if the situation is normal and altogether unproblematic, the thing uttered (or the object of appreciation) engages us; if the situation is in certain ways remarkable, then however canonical the thing uttered seems, we will pass behind it to its genesis. What significance we can find in "Fountain" we find not in the urinal but in Duchamp's gesture. It is not that "Fountain" is simply a candidate for appreciation which cannot be appreciated (nor is "I promise to love you forever" simply a promise which cannot be accepted); its transparent resistance to appreciation is the sign that it is not simply a candidate for appreciation (as the fact that love cannot be promised is the sign that this utterance is not simply a promise).

It is not only the questionable conception of appreciation which undermines Dickie's definition. Let us ignore that for a while. At the end of his essay Dickie says:

> Now what I have been saying may sound like saying, "a work of art is an object of which someone has said, 'I christen this object a work of art.'"
> And I think it is rather like that. So one *can* make a work of art out a sow's ear, but of course that does not mean that it is a silk purse [p. 256b].

What I have been arguing is that it cannot be this simple: even if in the end it is successful christening which makes an object art, not every effort at christening is successful. There are bound to be conditions to be met both by the namer and the thing to be named, and if they are completely unsatisfied, then saying "I christen . . ." will not be to christen. If making a thing art is like an ordinary illocution, then there are prior constraints.[8]

---

[8] In Danto's "The Artworld" (*op. cit.*) I find a suggestion of a way to treat artmaking as an extraordinary illocution, one whose constraints are always emendable. In the last section of the essay, Danto ventures some remarks which, in rough summary, are to this effect: there is a set of pairs of artwork-relevant predicates. Each pair consists of two "opposite" predicates (e.g., "representational"/"nonrepresentational," "expressionist"/"nonexpressionist"). Opposites, unlike contradictories as usually construed, do not sensibly apply to all objects; but with regard to any artwork they behave as contradictories. (It is not true that anything is either representational or nonrepresen-

Austin's characteristic way of describing a kind of act or thing was to catalogue the dimensions in which it can be irregular. Thus a promise might be untoward, gauche, imprudent, impractical, ineffective, or unaccepted. As we move through various departures from the normal, pedestrian cases, passing through all the gross irregularities Austin called "infelicities," we come eventually to cases which are no longer promises. The boundary between non-promises and more or less failed promises is hard to locate, but (1) it exists, and (2) it is not identical with the boundary between utterances of the form "I promise . . ." and those without it, for this form is neither necessary nor sufficient. If artmaking is like an illocution, then a similar catalogue is in order, an account of the ways in which artmaking can be irregular. I do not blame Dickie for not yet supplying such a catalogue. I complain that he has not noted the importance of such a catalogue, for if artmaking is simply a matter of informal illocutions, then the catalogue may be the only substantial definition we can get or need. There must be a boundary, however hard to chart, between making art, and trying but failing to make art. Dickie cannot account for this, because the difference is not simply the difference between objects which have been called art (or candidates for appreciation) and those which have not.

Duchamp's "Fountain" is a difficult case. It is difficult in the adjustment it demands of us, but neither of the two adjustments likely to be suggested is in order. One is to give up defining art, pointing to "Fountain" as an illustration of the inevitable failure of any definition. The other is to formulate a definition which covers "Fountain" as neatly as "Nude." Perhaps the most helpful part of Dickie's view is the implicit suggestion of a way to avoid this choice. Instead of either of these responses, I think we must give up the compulsion to *decide* about "Fountain," to rule it in or out; and I think we can do this by taking seriously the suggestion that

---

tational; it is true that any artwork is either representational or nonrepresentational.) A necessary condition for an object to be an artwork is that at least one pair of artwork-relevant predicates be sensibly applicable to it. Danto remarks that an artistic breakthrough may consist in adding a pair of artwork-relevant predicates.

Then we might try to think of artmaking in this way: the constraints on what can be christened art are given by the condition that some artwork-relevant predicate pair be sensibly applicable to the object. But it is possible to make art of an unqualified object not by altering the object but by adding to the set of predicate pairs a pair already sensibly applicable to the object.

In order to work out the details of this suggestion, one will have to say something about how a predicate pair can be made a member of the set. The project is complicated by Danto's ingenious observation that once an object is an artwork all artwork-relevant predicate pairs apply. This means that after the fact, the new pair will be as definitive as the older ones of earlier artworks, and the older pairs will sensibly apply to the new work.

I should make clear that Danto's remarks are made in an altogether different context, and their adaptability to a discussion of the illocutionary act of making art is my own tentative suggestion. In any case, the suggestion is of no use to Dickie, who seems to conceive the act as an ordinary illocution. Indeed, whereas Danto's idea might at last give content to Morris Weitz's somewhat dogmatic claim that the conditions for a thing to be art are indefinitely corrigible ("The Role of Theory in Aesthetics," *Journal of Aesthetics and Art Criticism*, 15 [1956], 27–35), Dickie's essay is offered as an explicit refutation of Weitz.

whether "Fountain" is art depends upon whether and how a certain kind of act was performed.

Succeeding in getting "Fountain" under, or out from under, the term "art" is a delusive achievement: for the sake of a kind of ontological tidiness, most of what is interesting and instructive about "Fountain" is ignored. What we need to discuss are the ways in which "Fountain" is very much like normal art and the ways in which it is altogether unlike normal art, and then how this bears on the character of Duchamp's act of putting it forward and having it called art. When that discussion is done, nothing may be left to do. So it is with promising. Some cases are clearly promises, some clearly are not. Some are unclear. The unclear cases illuminate the clear ones as they bring out parts of the conception according to which the clear cases are clear. "I promise to wring your neck." Not a promise: I cannot promise what you do not want, knowing you do not want it. "I promise to keep all cigarettes out of your reach." This is not clear. Can I promise you something we agree you need even if we both know you do not want it? The hard thing to do is to hold on to the conviction that we know what art and promises are while refusing to suppose that we always can decide or need to decide.

Dickie and others have criticized earlier theories for having lost the good art/bad art distinction, often, as with Collingwood, willfully absorbing it into the very distinction between art and non-art. Ironically, Dickie has effectively reversed this: he has provided for room on the bad art side of the good art/bad art distinction for much of what is normally taken to be non-art. He says:

> Please remember that when I say "Fountain" is a work of art, I am not saying it is a good one. And in making this last remark I am not insinuating that it is a bad one either [p. 255*b*].

This is the view Dickie proposes to take of any object whatever. From this view the real difficulty, the philosophical anguish, will arise after the question of art has been settled, and that question is never more than a nominal problem encountered occasionally because "lines of authority (or something like authority) in the artworld are nowhere codified" (p. 255*a*) and so it may be hard to discover whether the thing has been christened. This view obscures too much. The works of the painters Fried discusses (Stella, Noland, Olitski) are clearly works of art, and the serious questions about them concern what kinds of paintings they are, and whether and why they are good. But there are very few such questions about "Fountain," most Dada works, and many contemporary works. The questions about them concern exactly whether and why they are art, and how they became anything like art. To make these questions easy is both to mistake the nature of these objects and to refuse to take seriously the question of the possibility of the creation of art.

". . . questions about [Dada works] concern exactly whether and why they are art . . ." Ted Cohen in "The Possibility of Art," p. 194.

George Dickie

A RESPONSE TO COHEN:
THE ACTUALITY OF ART

Recently* Ted Cohen[1] raised some criticisms of my views on the defini-tion of art.[2] His criticisms are made in the following way: (1) Cohen de-nies one thing I am assuming to be true, (2) argues that an analogy I use is misleading and suggests another analogy, and (3) raises a substantive objection to the definition.

1. The assumption he denies is my taking for granted that Duchamp's *Fountain* and other Dadaist works are works of art.
2. He impugns the adequacy of the political analogy I used in stating my view, arguing that it misleads and fails to specify clearly what empowers someone to confer the status in question. He states that the act of promising is a better analogy for the act of creating art.
3. The substantive objection is his argument that *Fountain*, and Dadaist works in general, fail to satisfy my definition of "art" because it is not possible to appreciate them. On this count, Cohen charges me with having failed to note that there are constraints which prevent the status of candidate for appreciation from being conferred on some things.

Before proceeding further, let me state the definition of "art" which Cohen is criticizing and then state a somewhat modified version of it pub-lished later.

A work of art in the descriptive sense is (1) an artifact (2) upon which some society or some sub-group of a society has conferred the status of candidate for appreciation.[3]

A work of art in the classificatory sense is (1) an artifact (2) upon which

George Dickie is Professor of Philosophy at The University of Illinois, Chicago Circle Campus. His work in aesthetics over the last 15 years was recently culminated with the publication of his book *Art and The Aesthetic: An Institutional Analysis* (1974).

* To be published in *The Personalist*. Printed here by permission of *The Personalist*.

[1] Ted Cohen, "The Possibility of Art: Remarks on a Proposal by Dickie," *The Philosophical Review*, 82 (1973), 69–82.
[2] Ted Cohen, "Defining Art," *American Philosophical Quarterly*, 6 (1969), 253–256.
[3] Ibid., 254.

some person or persons acting on behalf of a certain social institution (the artworld) has conferred the status of candidate for appreciation.[4]

I

First, I shall discuss Cohen's questioning of my assumption that *Fountain* is a work of art. At the beginning of his article, Cohen suggests that *Fountain* is not a work of art because, he says, it cannot be appreciated, but later he says, "I think we must give up the compulsion to *decide* about *Fountain*, to rule it in or out. . . ."[5] My basic reason for considering *Fountain* a work of art is the fact that it seems to occupy a position within our artworld similar to the *Mona Lisa*, *Nude Descending a Staircase*, and the like. It is written about in art history books; it is displayed in art galleries. When I saw it in a show about 1964, *Fountain* occupied the central location in the large hall devoted to the display of Duchamp's works. The Duchamp paintings in the show were hung on a wall to the side. It seems to me that there is nothing for us *to decide* about *Fountain* one way or the other; it is a work of art and an important one.

Whether *Fountain* is a work of art or not does not, as Cohen clearly sees, really bear on my main philosophical concern, which is to give a definition of "art." The definition I have given does not depend upon *Fountain*'s being captured or not. The reason that *Fountain* and similar works have played such a big role in my discussions is my contention that in such cases the conferring of status is most transparent. In the case of more ordinary art it is less easy to notice the *status* of the works as art because we are so used to experiencing such works and because their non-status features seize our attention. But, even if Cohen were right in saying that *Fountain* is not a work of art, my point about the conferring of status can still be made, and *Fountain*, taking this view, would just be a burlesque of the conferring of status.

II

Cohen finds my description of the conferring of the status of candidacy for appreciation confusing. Specifically, he finds my use of a political analogy misleading and my discussion of Duchamp and a hypothetical plumbing salesman puzzling. In trying to convey what I had in mind by the conferring of the status of candidacy for appreciation, I made use of a political analogy; namely, I likened the conferring of the status of candidate for appreciation to the conferring of the status of candidate for

[4] Ted Cohen, *Aesthetics: An Introduction* (New York, Pegasus, 1971), p. 101. See, also, my "Defining Art II" in Matthew Lipman, ed., *Contemporary Aesthetics* (Boston, Mass., 1973), pp. 118–131 and Chapter I of my book, *Art and the Aesthetic: An Institutional Analysis* (Ithaca, N.Y.: 1974).
[5] Cohen, "The Possibility of Art," p. 81.

alderman on a person by the head of the election board. Cohen takes this analogy to mean a person conferring the status of candidate for appreciation must himself antecedently have a status which enables him to do the conferring just as the head of the election board has.

I did not intend for every feature of my political analogy to be transferred to the artworld, although perhaps I was not very clear about this. Specifically, I did not intend to suggest that the ability to confer the status of candidate for appreciation is acquired in a formal, procedural way in the way in which the ability of an election board head to declare someone a candidate for office is acquired. My concern was simply to give an example of the conferring of status. I contrasted Duchamp's conferring of the status of candidate for appreciation on the urinal which became *Fountain* to a hypothetical plumbing salesman's displaying his wares for our appreciation, stating that the first case resulted in a work of art whereas the second would not. Cohen quotes my remark, "The point is that Duchamp's act took place within a certain institutional setting and that makes all the difference. Our salesman of plumbing supplies could do what Duchamp did. . . ."[6] Cohen took the reference to an "institutional setting" to mean that Duchamp had a status like the head of an election board which the salesman did not. He was then puzzled as to why I said the salesman could do what Duchamp did—what he called "the interchangeability of Duchamp and the plumbing supplier"—since it was clear that the salesman did not have a status analogous to that of an election board head.

But the interchangeability of Duchamp and the salesman actually rules out any implication that a formal status is required to confer the status of candidate for appreciation. My nonanalogous statements qualify my analogy; they make explicit which implications the analogy has in this particular discourse. The interchangeability, by the way, results from the fact that the plumbing supplier could have conferred the relevant status *if* he were able to see himself in relation to and as an agent of the artworld and wanted to create a work of art. I did remark that the plumbing salesman probably would not do so, and the reason I had in mind, but which I did not articulate, was that a plumbing salesman probably would not see himself in the necessary relationship to the artworld and probably would not have the same kind of desires that Duchamp had.

Cohen's misconstruing the intention of my political analogy and my use of the expression "institutional setting" leads him to raise the question of whether *Fountain* would have become a work of art if the organizers of the show had refused to allow it to enter. But, in speaking of an institutional setting, I was not talking about a thing's being in a museum or some similar physical institutional location; rather, I was referring to a social way of thinking about and regarding things—a social practice. Thus, although Duchamp's urinal probably would not have become a "famous" work of art if it had been refused a place in the show, it would have and

[6] Cohen, "Defining Art," p. 255.

$$G_w(X) \supset F_D(X) \quad \text{necessary}$$

$$F_H(X) \supset G_w(X) \quad \text{sufficient}$$

did become a work of art when Duchamp—aware of the nature of the artworld—began to treat it as a candidate for appreciation.

Unfortunately, my first formulation of the definition did lend itself to making Cohen's question somewhat plausible because it reads, ". . . upon which society or some sub-society of a society has conferred the status of candidate for appreciation." This seems to leave open the possibility that the concurrence of a large group is required in the making of a work of art. A few lines later, however, I remarked, "The status, therefore, must be conferrable by a single person's treating an artifact as a candidate for appreciation. . . ."[7] This remark, I think, forestalls Cohen's question of whether or not I thought Duchamp required the concurrence of the judges of the famous show in creating *Fountain*. The modified version of the definition quoted at the beginning more or less incorporates this consideration into the definition itself.

Cohen finds my analogy wanting because he thinks it implies that an unusual power similar to that of the head of an election board is required to confer the relevant status and because he is also quite certain that my view does not entail that such a power is required. He then suggests an analogy between the making of promises and the making of art, because, as he says promise making is a power that we may all exercise just as art making is a power that we may all exercise. He recognizes that promise making ". . . too is an imprecise analogue in some respects."[8] I do not want to argue about what is the best analogue of art making, but I do want to insist that my analogy be understood as it was qualified by my explicit remarks.

III

I will next deal with Cohen's contention that *Fountain* and Dadaist works generally cannot be appreciated and, hence, cannot satisfy the candidacy for appreciation part of my definition.[9] Cohen is clear that the definition does not require actual appreciation, but he claims that, just as it must be possible for a promise to be accepted in order to be a promise, it must be possible for a work of art to be appreciated for it to be a work of art. And, he claims, it is not possible to appreciate *Fountain* and other things such as "ordinary thumbtacks, cheap white envelopes, plastic forks given at some drive-in restaurants."[10] Cohen says that it is Duchamp's gesture which can be appreciated, not *Fountain* itself.

Fountain does have the gesture significance that Cohen attributes to it, specifically, it was a protest of a kind. But *Fountain* has many qualities which can be appreciated—its gleaming white surface, for example. In fact, it has several qualities which resemble whose of works of Brancusi

---

[7] Ibid., 254.
[8] Cohen, "The Possibility of Art," p. 76.
[9] This point is also discussed in Dickie, *Art and the Aesthetic*, pp. 41–42.
[10] Cohen, "The Possibility of Art," p. 78.

and Moore. Also, the very things which Cohen cites as paradigms of things which cannot be appreciated—ordinary thumbtacks, cheap white envelopes, and plastic forks—have appreciatable qualities which can be noted if one focuses attention on them. Photographs frequently bring out these qualities of quite ordinary things by focusing narrowly on them. It seems very likely that the constraint of appreciatability which Cohen wishes to place on my definition is vacuous, since it is unlikely that any object would lack some quality which is apreciatable.

In arguing that appreciatability of an object is required for its becoming a work of art, Cohen is proposing a second constraint besides artifactuality upon objects which may achieve the status of candidate for appreciation. But, even if he were wrong about appreciatability, he is right in that there may be constraints other than artifactuality. For example, a copy of an original painting which is attributed to the creator of the original is not a work of art because originality of the kind the copy lacks is required of a work of art. A copy of the *Mona Lisa* which is attributed to Da Vinci is not a work of art, but *L.H.O.O.Q.*—*Mona Lisa* with mustache and beard added in pencil—attributed to Duchamp is.[11] There well may be other constraints on objects which can be works of art. Nevertheless, from the great variety of things which are works of art, it is clear that the constraints (whatever they might be) are not very limiting, so that it is virtually the case that anything can become a work of art.

Finally, there is a minor puzzle at the end of Cohen's discussion. He quotes my remark:

> Please remember that when I say *Fountain* is a work of art, I am not saying it is a good one. And in making this last remark I am not insinuating that it is a bad one either.[12]

He comments on this passage saying that I have thus ". . . provided for room on the bad art side of the good art/bad art distinction for much of what is normally taken to be non-art."[13] But clearly my remark does not provide room for *Fountain* on the bad art side any more than it does on the good art side. The remark flatly states that I am not committing myself as to whether *Fountain* is good or bad art.

Select Bibliography for Part Two

Books

Virgil Aldrich, *Philosophy of Art*; George Dickie, *Art and the Aesthetic: An Institutional Analysis*; George Dickie, *Aesthetics*; Nelson Goodman, *Languages*

[11] For a brief discussion of this point, see Dickie, *Art and the Aesthetic*, pp. 46–48; see also Arthur Danto, "Art Works and Real Things," *Theoria*, Parts 1–3, 1973, 1–17.
[12] Cohen, "Defining Art," p. 255.
[13] Cohen, "The Possibility of Art," p. 81.

of Art; Martin Heidegger, *The Origin of the Work of Art*; Susanne K. Langer, *Philosophy in a New Key*; Susanne K. Langer, *Problems of Art*; Ruth Saw, *Aesthetics*; Francis E. Sparshott, *The Structure of Aesthetics*; Alan Tormey, *The Concept of Expression, A Study in Philosophical Psychology and Aesthetics*; William K. Wimsatt, Jr., *The Verbal Icon*; Ludwig Wittgenstein, *Lectures and Conversations on Aesthetics, Psychology, and Religious Belief*.

Articles

Arthur Berndtson, "Semblance, Symbol, and Expression in the Aesthetics of Susanne Langer"; Timothy Binkley, "Langer's Logical and Ontological Modes"; Curtis L. Carter, "Langer and Hofstadter on Painting and Language: A Critique"; Arthur Danto, "Artworks and Real Things"; Arthur Danto, "The Artworld"; Arthur Danto, "The Transfiguration of the Commonplace"; George Dickie, "Defining Art"; Marcia Eaton, "Art, Artifacts and Intentions"; Forest Hansen, "Langer's Expressive Form—An Interpretation"; Donald F. Henze, "The Work of Art"; Joseph Margolis, "The Identity of a Work of Art"; Joseph Margolis, "Mode of Existence of a Work of Art"; M. H. Mitias, "Art as a Social Institution"; Daniel Nathan, "Categories and Intentions"; James W. Newcomb, "Eisenstein's Aesthetics"; Stephen C. Pepper, "Autobiography of an Aesthetic"; Stephen C. Pepper, "Further Considerations on the Aesthetic Work of Art"; Melvin Rader, "Dickie and Socrates on Definition"; Ruth Saw, "What Is a 'Work of Art'?"; Richard Sclafani, "Art and Artifactuality"; Richard Sclafani, "Art as a Social Institution: Dickie's New Definition"; Richard Sclafani, "Art Works, Art Theory, and the Artworld"; Richard Sclafani, "The Logical Primitiveness of the Concept of a Work of Art"; Anita Silvers, "The Artworld Discarded"; Kendall L. Walton, "Categories of Art"; Kendall L. Walton, "Languages of Art: An Emendation"; Morris Weitz, "Professor Goodman on the Aesthetic"; Paul Ziff, "Goodman's Languages of Art."

PART THREE

---

*Theories
of Individual Arts,
Traditional and
Contemporary*

Parts one and two deal with art as it is generically understood. Although
various theorists in these sections emphasize different arts in their discussions (for example, Bell emphasizes painting, Tolstoy literature, Danto
the plastic arts, etc.), the primary aim of these theories is to provide an
analysis of art in general, putting aside whatever differences there may be
among the various arts. This is not to say that these theorists are unaware
of important differences among the literary arts, the plastic arts, the performing arts, and those arts which seem to cut across categories (film,
for example). It is to say only that their main concern is what sets art
apart from other things, and not what sets one art apart from another.

Clearly there are enormous differences among the arts. The most casual
observer could hardly fail to note that what makes literature literature
differs vastly from what makes painting painting. While differences among
the arts may not always be so great (between music and poetry for example), generally speaking there is much to be gained by treating individual arts individually. In part three we present a variety of theories
of the various individual arts. Since it would be impossible to survey all
the arts, we have chosen three areas with which theorists have been traditionally concerned, and two areas of special importance to contemporary
art and philosophy. The three traditional arts are literature, drama, and
music; the two areas of special contemporary importance are film and
recent work in the plastic arts. We believe that these selections adequately
represent the kind of endeavor that theorizing about the individual arts can

be. To facilitate the study of these multiple selections, we have provided a brief introduction for each section of this part.

We noted in the introduction to part one that in writing about the individual arts, theorists are sometimes developing indirectly a general theory of art. This is centainly true of the theories of drama of Aristotle and Nietzsche presented in this part. To a lesser extent, it is true of Hanslick and Wagner's theories of music as well. Cavell's essay on film is as much a general analysis of an art medium as it is of film per se. When reading a theory about an individual art, it is often helpful to keep in mind the implications of the theory for art in general.

THE THEORY OF DRAMA:
IMITATION AND REALITY

Aristotle's *Poetics* is probably the most famous work in the history of art theory. Aristotle's definition of tragedy as the dramatic imitation of a serious action which brings about a catharsis of pity and fear has had a tremendous impact on literature and criticism from the Renaissance to this day. The notion of catharsis in particular has been the source of centuries-old debates among philosophers, critics, and playwrights. In the twentieth century, Bertold Brecht went so far as to write a specifically non-Aristotelian drama.

The *Poetics* does not exhibit the tightness of structure, the rigor of argument, and the systematic exposition of typically Aristotelian works. This condition is probably due to the fact that the manuscript from which the *Poetics* was passed down to us was a series of lecture notes from which Aristotle intended to write a complete treatise. Thus, the *Poetics* contains flashes of brilliance, but at times it is repetitive and seemingly contradictory. Nevertheless, the *Poetics* is still the first work in the history of the subject to treat, in one form or another, virtually every problem with which the theory of art has subsequently been concerned.

Although the *Poetics* is un-Aristotelian in some ways, it is still a highly formal work in which Aristotle searches for first principles and a complete definition of his subject. In this case, his subject is the art of poetry in general, and the art of tragedy in particular. For Aristotle, a complete definition of any subject proceeds according to genus and species. First, Aristotle determines to which general category, or genus, a subject belongs. He then isolates his specific subject within that genus. For Aristotle, the genus of the art of tragedy is imitation; the species of the art is dramatic imitation (as opposed to painting and sculpture, which, for example, imitate by means of color and shape). Because tragedy is a species of imitation, Aristotle finds it necessary to compare and contrast tragedy with other forms of imitation throughout his *Poetics*. This procedure provides a way of determining the general theory of art which underlies his treatment of the poetic art.

What does Aristotle actually mean by "imitation"? And what does he have in mind when he says, for example, that plot is the principal element in the six-part definition of tragedy formulated by him? Commentators have argued questions such as these for centuries. To convey an idea of the scope and complexity of these arguments, we have selected an introductory commentary in the *Poetics* by G. M. A. Grube. Grube surveys a number of central concepts in the *Poetics*. In clear and straightforward language Grube expresses some of his own views about the *Poetics*; he indicates where and how there can be philological, historical, and philosophical controversy in interpreting this rich, seemingly inexhaustible, work.

While reading Aristotle one should don a philosophical thinking cap. For reading Nietzsche one must draw deeply from the well of human experience. Nietzsche's *The Birth of Tragedy* is a passionate work wherein he sought to reach to the very depths of artistic creativity, revealing simultaneously the terrible absurdity of existence and the power that art has in transfiguring this terror. The Apollinian and the Dionysian, the dream state and the state of intoxication, intellectual vision and orgiastic ecstasy—all of these Nietzschean notions are by now commonplace in our thinking about tragedy and art. If Aristotle demonstrates the value of art in imitation, Nietzsche reveals the power of art in reality: "Art is not merely the imitation of the reality of nature but rather a metaphysical supplement of the reality of nature. The tragic myth . . . participates freely in this metaphysical intention of art to transfigure. But what does it transfigure? . . . 'Look there!' 'Look closely!' This is your life, this is the hand on the clock of your existence."

The power of Nietzsche's prose, the deep sense of existential urgency he conveys, the brilliant insights of his impassioned mind—all of these combine to sustain the impression of the great work which *The Birth of Tragedy* undoubtedly is. Few philosophers, however, are willing to take on the task of explaining just what Nietzsche is saying when he claims that existence is absurd, that the metaphysical purpose of art is transfiguration, and so on. Is existence absurd? Does art transfigure one metaphysically? Must we simply sense the force of these observations without being able to explicate them in any detailed way? To date, there has been little written on Nietzsche which attempts to deal, in intelligible English, with questions such as these. Richard Schacht takes on this task. In "Nietzsche on Art in The Birth of Tragedy" Schacht presents us with an in-depth discussion, in understandable terms, of the central concepts in Nietzsche's theory of art and tragedy, and he critically evaluates Nietzsche's theory in doing so. Schacht's essay makes Nietzsche accessible, in English, in a way hitherto unavailable.

The Birth of Tragedy is a work of Nietzsche's youth. Later in his life he refined and corrected various ideas presented there in light of subsequent developments in his philosophical career. We added Nietzsche's "An Attempt At Self-Criticism" to supplement his ideas in *The Birth of Tragedy* and to present his work in its full maturity.

Aristotle

DRAMATIC IMITATION: FROM THE *POETICS*

1 Our subject being Poetry,* I propose to speak not only of the art in general but also of its species and their respective capacities; of the structure of plot required for a good poem; of the number and nature of the constituent parts of a poem; and likewise of any other matters in the same line of inquiry. Let us follow the natural order and begin with the primary facts.

Epic poetry and Tragedy, as also Comedy, Dithyrambic poetry, and most flute-playing and lyre-playing, are all, viewed as a whole, modes of imitation. But at the same time they differ from one another in three ways, either by a difference of kind in their means, or by differences in the objects, or in the manner of their imitations.

I. Just as colour and form are used as means by some, who (whether by art or constant practice) imitate and portray many things by their aid, and the voice is used by others; so also in the above-mentioned group of arts, the means with them as a whole are rhythm, language, and harmony —used, however, either singly or in certain combinations. A combination of harmony and rhythm alone is the means in flute-playing and lyre-playing, and any other arts there may be of the same description, e.g. imitative piping. Rhythm alone, without harmony, is the means in the dancer's imitations; for even he, by the rhythms of his attitudes, may represent men's characters, as well as what they do and suffer. There is further an art which imitates by language alone, without harmony, in prose or in verse, and if in verse, either in some one or in a plurality of metres. This form of imitation is to this day without a name. We have no common name for a mime of Sophron or Xenarchus and a Socratic Conversation; and we should still be without one even if the imitation in the two instances were in trimeters or elegiacs or some other kind of verse—though it is the way with people to take on 'poet' to the name of a metre, and talk of elegiac-poets and epic-poets, thinking that they call them poets not

Aristotle (384–322 B.C.). Aristotle ranks with Plato as one of the most important thinkers in Western Civilization.

* Translated by Ingram Bywater (1920). Reprinted by permission of the Oxford University Press.

by reason of the imitative nature of their work, but indiscriminately by reason of the metre they write in. Even if a theory of medicine or physical philosophy be put forth in a metrical form, it is usual to describe the writer in this way; Homer and Empedocles, however, have really nothing in common apart from their metre; so that, if the one is to be called a poet, the other should be termed a physicist rather than a poet. We should be in the same position also, if the imitation in these instances were in all the metres, like the *Centaur* (a rhapsody in a medley of all metres) of Chaeremon; and Chaeremon one has to recognize as a poet. So much, then, as to these arts. There are, lastly, certain other arts, which combine all the means enumerated, rhythm, melody, and verse, e.g. Dithyrambic and Nomic poetry, Tragedy and Comedy; with this difference, however, that the three kinds of means are in some of them employed together, and in others brought in separately, one after the other. These elements of difference in the above arts I term the means of their imitation.

2   II. The objects the imitator represents are actions, with agents who are necessarily either good men or bad—the diversities of human character being nearly always derivative from this primary distinction, since the line between virtue and vice is one dividing the whole of mankind. It follows, therefore, that the agents represented must be either above our own level of goodness, or beneath it, or just such as we are; in the same way as, with the painters, the personages of Polygnotus are better than we are, those of Pauson worse, and those of Dionysius just like ourselves. It is clear that each of the above-mentioned arts will admit of these differences, and that it will become a separate art by representing objects with this point of difference. Even in dancing, flute-playing, and lyre-playing such diversities are possible; and they are also possible in the nameless art that uses language, prose or verse without harmony, as its means; Homer's personages, for instance, are better than we are; Cleophon's are on our own level; and those of Hegemon of Thasos, the first writer of parodies, and Nicochares, the author of the *Diliad*, are beneath it. The same is true of the Dithyramb and the Nome: the personages may be presented in them with the difference exemplified in the . . . of . . . and Argas, and in the Cyclopses of Timotheus and Philoxenus. This difference it is that distinguishes Tragedy and Comedy also; the one would make its personages worse, and the other better, than the men of the present day.

3   III. A third difference in these arts is in the manner in which each kind of object is represented. Given both the same means and the same kind of object for imitation, one may either (1) speak at one moment in narrative and at another in an assumed character, as Homer does; or (2) one may remain the same throughout, without any such change; or (3) the imitators may represent the whole story dramatically, as though they were actually doing the things described.

As we said at the beginning, therefore, the differences in the imitation of these arts come under three heads, their means, their objects, and their manner.

So that as an imitator Sophocles will be on one side akin to Homer, both portraying good men; and on another to Aristophanes, since both present their personages as acting and doing. This in fact, according to some, is the reason for plays being termed dramas, because in a play the personages act the story. Hence too both Tragedy and Comedy are claimed by the Dorians as their discoveries; Comedy by the Megarians—by those in Greece as having arisen when Megara became a democracy, and by the Sicilian Megarians on the ground that the poet Epicharmus was of their country, and a good deal earlier than Chionides and Magnes; even Tragedy also is claimed by certain of the Peloponnesian Dorians. In support of this claim they point to the words 'comedy' and 'drama'. Their word for the out-lying hamlets, they say, is *comae*, whereas Athenians call them *demes*—thus assuming that comedians got the name not from their *comoe* or revels, but from their strolling from hamlet to hamlet, lack of appreciation keep-ing them out of the city. Their word also for 'to act', they say, is *dran*, whereas Athenians use *prattein*.

So much, then, as to the number and nature of the points of difference in the imitation of these arts.

4   It is clear that the general origin of poetry was due to two causes, each of them part of human nature. Imitation is natural to man from child-hood, one of his advantages over the lower animals being this, that he is the most imitative creature in the world, and learns at first by imitation. And it is also natural for all to delight in works of imitation. The truth of this second point is shown by experience: though the objects themselves may be painful to see, we delight to view the most realistic representations of them in art, the forms for example of the lowest animals and of dead bodies. The explanation is to be found in a further fact: to be learning something is the greatest of pleasures not only to the philosopher but also to the rest of mankind, however small their capacity for it; the reason of the delight in seeing the picture is that one is at the same time learning—gathering the meaning of things, e.g. that the man there is so-and-so; for if one has not seen the thing before, one's pleasure will not be in the pic-ture as an imitation of it, but will be due to the execution or colouring or some similar cause. Imitation, then, being natural to us—as also the sense of harmony and rhythm, the metres being obviously species of rhythms—it was through their original aptitude, and by a series of improvements for the most part gradual on their first efforts, that they created poetry out of their improvisations.

Poetry, however, soon broke up into two kinds according to the differ-ences of character in the individual poets; for the graver among them would represent noble actions, and those of noble personages; and the meaner sort the actions of the ignoble. The latter class produced invectives at first, just as others did hymns and panegyrics. We know of no such poem by any of the pre-Homeric poets, though there were probably many such writers among them; instances, however, may be found from Homer downwards, e.g. his *Margites,* and the similar poems of others. In this poetry of invective its natural fitness brought an iambic metre into use; hence our present term 'iambic', because it was the metre of their 'iambs' or invectives against one another. The result was that the old poets became some of them writers of heroic and others of iambic verse. Homer's position, however, is peculiar: just as he was in the serious style the poet of poets, standing alone not only through the literary excellence, but also through the dramatic character of his imitations, so too he was the first to outline for us the general forms of Comedy by producing not a dramatic invective, but a dramatic picture of the Ridiculous; his *Margites* in fact stands in the same relation to our comedies as the *Iliad* and *Odyssey* to our tragedies. As soon, however, as Tragedy and Comedy appeared in the field, those naturally drawn to the one line of poetry became writers of comedies instead of iambs, and those naturally drawn to the other, writers of tragedies instead of epics, because these new modes of art were grander and of more esteem than the old.

If it be asked whether Tragedy is now all that it need be in its formative elements, to consider that, and decide it theoretically and in relation to the theatres, is a matter for another inquiry.

It certainly began in improvisations—as did also Comedy; the one originating with the authors of the Dithyramb, the other with those of the phallic songs, which still survive as institutions in many of our cities. And its advance after that was little by little, through their improving on whatever they had before them at each stage. It was in fact only after a long series of changes that the movement of Tragedy stopped on its attaining to its natural form. (1) The number of actors was first increased to two by Aeschylus, who curtailed the business of the Chorus, and made the dialogue, or spoken portion, take the leading part in the play. (2) A third actor and scenery were due to Sophocles. (3) Tragedy acquired also its magnitude. Discarding short stories and a ludicrous diction through its passing out of its satyric stage, it assumed, though only at a late point in its progress, a tone of dignity; and its metre changed then from trochaic to iambic. The reason for their original use of the trochaic tetrameter was that their poetry was satyric and more connected with dancing than it now is. As soon, however, as a spoken part came in, nature herself found the appropriate metre. The iambic, we know, is the most speakable of metres, as is shown by the fact that we very often fall into it in conversation, whereas we rarely talk hexameters, and only when we depart from the speaking tone of voice. (4) Another change was a plurality of episodes or acts. As for the remaining matters, the superadded embellishments and the account of their introduction, these must be taken as said, as it would probably be a long piece of work to go through the details.

5 As for Comedy, it is (as has been observed an imitation of men worse than the average; worse, however, not as regards any and every sort of fault, but only as regards one particular kind, the Ridiculous, which is a species of the Ugly. The Ridiculous may be defined as a mistake or deformity not productive of pain or harm to others; the mask, for instance,

that excites laughter, is something ugly and distorted without causing pain.

Though the successive changes in Tragedy and their authors are not unknown, we cannot say the same of Comedy; its early stages passed unnoticed, because it was not as yet taken up in a serious way. It was only at a late point in its progress that a chorus of comedians was officially granted by the archon; they used to be mere volunteers. It had also already certain definite forms at the time when the record of those termed comic poets begins. Who it was who supplied it with masks, or prologues, or a plurality of actors and the like, has remained unknown. The invented Fable, or Plot, however, originated in Sicily with Epicharmus and Phormis; of Athenian poets Crates was the first to drop the Comedy of invective and frame stories of a general and non-personal nature, in other words, Fables or Plots.

Epic poetry, then, has been seen to agree with Tragedy to this extent, that of being an imitation of serious subjects in a grand kind of verse. It differs from it, however, (1) in that it is in one kind of verse and in narrative form; and (2) in its length—which is due to its action having no fixed limit of time, whereas Tragedy endeavours to keep as far as possible within a single circuit of the sun, or something near that. This, I say, is another point of difference between them, though at first the practice in this respect was just the same in tragedies as in epic poems. They differ also (3) in their constituents, some being common to both and others peculiar to Tragedy—hence a judge of good and bad in Tragedy is a judge of that in epic poetry also. All the parts of an epic are included in Tragedy; but those of Tragedy are not all of them to be found in the Epic.

6   Reserving hexameter poetry and Comedy for consideration hereafter, let us proceed now to the discussion of Tragedy; before doing so, however, we must gather up the definition resulting from what has been said. A tragedy, then, is the imitation of an action that is serious and also, as having magnitude, complete in itself; in language with pleasurable accessories, each kind brought in separately in the parts of the work; in a dramatic, not in a narrative form; with incidents arousing pity and fear, wherewith to accomplish its catharsis of such emotions. Here by 'language with pleasurable accessories' I mean that with rhythm and harmony or song superadded; and by 'the kinds separately' I mean that some portions are worked out with verse only, and others in turn with song.

I. As they act the stories, it follows that in the first place the Spectacle (or stage-appearance of the actors) must be some part of the whole; and in the second Melody and Diction, these two being the means of their imitation. Here by 'Diction' I mean merely this, the composition of the verses; and by 'Melody,' what is too completely understood to require explanation. But further: the subject represented also is an action; and the action involves agents, who must necessarily have their distinctive qualities both of character and thought, since it is from these that we ascribe certain qualities to their actions. There are in the natural order of things, therefore, two causes, Thought and Character, of their actions, and consequently of their success or failure in their lives. Now the action (that which was done) is represented in the play by the Fable or Plot. The Fable, in our present sense of the term, is simply this, the combination of the incidents, or things done in the story; whereas Character is what makes us ascribe certain moral qualities to the agents; and Thought is shown in all they say when proving a particular point or, it may be, enunciating a general truth. There are six parts consequently of every tragedy, as a whole (that is) of such or such quality, viz. a Fable or Plot, Characters, Diction, Thought, Spectacle, and Melody; two of them arising from the means, one from the manner, and three from the objects of the dramatic imitation; and there is nothing else besides these six. Of these, its formative elements, then, not a few of the dramatists have made due use, as every play, one may say, admits of Spectacle, Character, Fable, Diction, Melody and Thought.

II. The most important of the six is the combination of the incidents of the story. Tragedy is essentially an imitation not of persons but of action and life, of happiness and misery. All human happiness or misery takes the form of action; the end for which we live is a certain kind of activity, not a quality. Character gives us qualities, but it is in our actions —what we do—that we are happy or the reverse. In a play accordingly they do not act in order to portray the Characters; they include the Characters for the sake of the action. So that it is the action in it, i.e. its Fable or Plot, that is the end and purpose of the tragedy; and the end is everywhere the chief thing. Besides this, a tragedy is impossible without action, but there may be one without Character. The tragedies of most of the moderns are characterless—a defect common among poets of all kinds, and with its counterpart in painting in Zeuxis as compared with Polygnotus; for whereas the latter is strong in character, the work of Zeuxis is devoid of it. And again: one may string together a series of characteristic speeches of the utmost finish as regards Diction and Thought, and yet fail to produce the true tragic effect; but one will have much better success with a tragedy which, however inferior in these respects, has a Plot, a combination of incidents, in it. And again: the most powerful elements of attraction in Tragedy, the Peripeties and Discoveries, are parts of the Plot. A further proof is in the fact that beginners succeed earlier with the Diction and Characters than with the construction of a story; and the same may be said of nearly all the early dramatists. We maintain, therefore, that the first essential, the life and soul, so to speak, of Tragedy is the Plot; and that the Characters come second—compare the parallel in painting, where the most beautiful colours laid on without order will not give one the same pleasure as a simple black-and-white sketch of a portrait. We maintain that Tragedy is primarily an imitation of action, and that it is mainly for the sake of the action that it imitates the personal agents. Third comes the element of Thought, i.e. the power of saying whatever can be said, or what is appropriate to the occasion. This is what, in the speeches in Tragedy, falls under the arts of Politics and Rhetoric; for the older poets make their personages discourse like statesmen, and the modern like rhetoricians. One must not confuse it with Character. Character in a play is that which reveals the moral purpose of the agents, i.e. the sort of thing they seek or avoid, where that is not obvious—hence there is no room for Character in a speech on a purely indifferent subject. Thought, on the other hand, is shown in all they say when proving or disproving some particular point, or enunciating some universal proposition. Fourth among the literary elements is the Diction of the personages, i.e., as before explained, the expression of their thoughts in words, which is practically the same thing with verse as with prose. As for the two remaining parts, the Melody is the greatest of the pleasurable accessories of Tragedy. The Spectacle, though an attraction, is the least artistic of all the parts, and has least to do with the art of poetry. The tragic effect is quite possible without a public performance and actors; and besides, the getting-up of the Spectacle is more a matter for the costumier than the poet.

7   Having thus distinguished the parts, let us now consider the proper construction of the Fable or Plot, as that is at once the first and the most important thing in Tragedy. We have laid it down that a tragedy is an imitation of an action that is complete in itself, as a whole of some magnitude; for a whole may be of no magnitude to speak of. Now a whole is that which has beginning, middle, and end. A beginning is that which is not itself necessarily after anything else, and which has naturally something else after it; an end is that which is naturally after something itself, either as its necessary or usual consequent, and with nothing else after it; and a middle, that which is by nature after one thing and has also another after it. A well-constructed Plot, therefore, cannot either begin or end at any point one likes; beginning and end in it must be of the forms just described. Again: to be beautiful, a living creature, and every whole made up of parts, must not only present a certain order in its arrangement of parts, but also be of a certain definite magnitude. Beauty is a matter of size and order, and therefore impossible either (1) in a very minute creature, since our perception becomes indistinct as it approaches instantaneity; or (2) in a creature of vast size—one, say, 1,000 miles long— as in that case, instead of the object being seen all at once, the unity and wholeness of it is lost to the beholder. Just in the same way, then, as a beautiful whole made up of parts, or a beautiful living creature, must be of some size, but a size to be taken in by the eye, so a story or Plot must be of some length, but of a length to be taken in by the memory. As for the limit of its length, so far as that is relative to public performances and spectators, it does not fall within the theory of poetry. If they had to perform a hundred tragedies, they would be timed by water-clocks, as they are said to have been at one period. The limit, however, set by the actual nature of the thing is this: the longer the story, consistently with its being comprehensible as a whole, the finer it is by reason of its magnitude. As a rough general formula, 'a length which allows of the hero passing by a

series of probable or necessary stages from misfortune to happiness, or form happiness to misfortune,' may suffice as a limit for the magnitude of the story.

8   The Unity of a Plot does not consist, as some suppose, in its having one man as its subject. An infinity of things befall that one man, some of which it is impossible to reduce to unity; and in like manner there are many actions of one man which cannot be made to form one action. One sees, therefore, the mistake of all the poets who have written a *Heracleid*, a *Theseid*, or similar poems; they suppose that, because Heracles was one man, the story also of Heracles must be one story. Homer, however, evidently understood this point quite well, whether by art or instinct, just in the same way as he excels the rest in every other respect. In writing an *Odyssey*, he did not make the poem cover all that ever befell his hero—it befell him, for instance, to get wounded on Parnassus and also to feign madness at the time of the call to arms, but the two incidents had no necessary or probable connexion with one another—instead of doing that, he took as the subject of the *Odyssey*, as also of the *Iliad*, an action with a Unity of the kind we are describing. The truth is that, just as in the other imitative arts one imitation is always of one thing, so in poetry the story, as an imitation of action, must represent one action, a complete whole, with its several incidents so closely connected that the transposal or withdrawal of any one of them will disjoin and dislocate the whole. For that which makes no perceptible difference by its presence or absence is no real part of the whole.

9   From what we have said it will be seen that the poet's function is to describe, not the thing that has happened, but a kind of thing that might happen, i.e. what is possible as being probable or necessary. The distinction between historian and poet is not in the one writing prose and the other verse—you might put the work of Herodotus into verse, and it would still be a species of history; it consists really in this, that the one describes the thing that has been, and the other a kind of thing that might be. Hence poetry is something more philosophic and of graver import than history, since its statements are of the nature rather of universals, whereas those of history are singulars. By a universal statement I mean one as to what such or such a kind of man will probably or necessarily say or do—which is the aim of poetry, though it affixes proper names to the characters; by a singular statement, one as to what, say, Alcibiades did or had done to him. In Comedy this has become clear by this time; it is only when their plot is already made up of probable incidents that they give it a basis of proper names, choosing for the purpose any names that may occur to them, instead of writing like the old iambic poets about particular persons. In Tragedy, however, they still adhere to the historic names; and for this reason: what convinces is the possible; now whereas we are not yet sure as to the possibility of that which has not happened, that which has happened is manifestly possible, else it would not have come to pass.

Nevertheless even in Tragedy there are some plays with but one or two known names in them, the rest being inventions; and there are some without a single known name, e.g. Agathon's *Antheus*, in which both incidents and names are of the poet's invention; and it is no less delightful on that account. So that one must not aim at a rigid adherence to the traditional stories on which tragedies are based. It would be absurd, in fact, to do so, as even the known stories are only known to a few, though they are a delight none the less to all.

It is evident from the above that the poet must be more the poet of his stories or Plots than of his verses, inasmuch as he is a poet by virtue of the imitative element in his work, and it is actions that he imitates. And if he should come to take a subject from actual history, he is none the less a poet for that; since some historic occurrences may very well be in the probable and possible order of things; and it is in that aspect of them that he is their poet.

Of simple Plots and actions the episodic are the worst. I call a Plot episodic when there is neither probability nor necessity in the sequence of its episodes. Actions of this sort bad poets construct through their own fault, and good ones on account of the players. His work being for public performance, a good poet often stretches out a Plot beyond its capabilities, and is thus obliged to twist the sequence of incident.

Tragedy, however, is an imitation not only of a complete action, but also of incidents arousing pity and fear. Such incidents have the very greatest effect on the mind when they occur unexpectedly and at the same time in consequence of one another; there is more of the marvellous in them then than if they happened of themselves or by mere chance. Even matters of chance seem most marvellous if there is an appearance of design as it were in them; as for instance the statue of Mitys at Argos killed the author of Mitys' death by falling down on him when a looker-on at a public spectacle; for incidents like that we think to be not without a meaning. A Plot therefore, of this sort is necessarily finer than others.

10   Plots are either simple or complex, since the actions they represent are naturally of this twofold description. The action, proceeding in the way defined, as one continuous whole, I call simple, when the change in the hero's fortunes takes place without Peripety or Discovery; and complex, when it involves one or the other, or both. These should each of them arise out of the structure of the Plot itself, so as to be the consequence, necessary or probable, of the antecedents. There is a great difference between a thing happening *propter hoc* and *post hoc*.

11   A Peripety is the change of the kind described from one state of things within the play to its opposite, and that too in the way we are saying, in the probable or necessary sequence of events; as it is for instance in *Oedipus*: here the opposite state of things is produced by the Messenger, who, coming to gladden Oedipus and to remove his fears as to his mother, reveals the secret of his birth. And in *Lynceus*: just as he is being led off

for execution, with Danaus at his side to put him to death, the incidents preceding this bring it about that he is saved and Danaus put to death. A Discovery is, as the very word implies, a change from ignorance to knowledge, and thus to either love or hate, in the personages marked for good or evil fortune. The finest form of Discovery is one attended by Peripeties, like that which goes with the Discovery in *Oedipus*. There are no doubt other forms of it; what we have said may happen in a way in reference to inanimate things, even things of a very casual kind; and it is also possible to discover whether some one has done or not done something. But the form most directly connected with the Plot and the action of the piece is the first-mentioned. This, with a Peripety, will arouse either pity or fear—actions of that nature being what Tragedy is assumed to represent; and it will also serve to bring about the happy or unhappy ending. The Discovery, then, being of persons, it may be that of one party only to the other, the latter being already known; or both the parties may have to discover themselves. Iphigenia, for instance, was discovered to Orestes by sending the letter;[6] and another Discovery was required to reveal him to Iphigenia.

Two parts of the Plot, then, Peripety and Discovery, are on matters of this sort. A third part is Suffering; which we may define as an action of a destructive or painful nature, such as murders on the stage, tortures, woundings, and the like. The other two have been already explained.

12 The parts of Tragedy to be treated as formative elements in the whole were mentioned in a previous Chapter. From the point of view, however, of its quantity, i.e. the separate sections into which it is divided, a tragedy has the following parts: Prologue, Episode, Exode, and a choral portion, distinguished into Parode and Stasimon; these two are common to all tragedies, whereas songs from the stage and *Commoe* are only found in some. The Prologue is all that precedes the Parode of the chorus; an Episode all that comes in between two whole choral songs; the Exode all that follows after the last choral song. In the choral portion the Parode is the whole first statement of the chorus; a Stasimon, a song of the chorus without anapaests or trochees; a *Commos*, a lamentation sung by chorus and actor in concert. The parts of Tragedy to be used as formative elements in the whole we have already mentioned; the above are its parts from the point of view of its quantity, or the separate sections into which it is divided.

13 The next points after what we have said above will be these: (1) What is the poet to aim at, and what is he to avoid, in constructing his Plots? and (2) What are the conditions on which the tragic effect depends?

We assume that, for the finest form of Tragedy, the Plot must be not simple but complex; and further, that it must imitate actions arousing fear and pity, since that is the distinctive function of this kind of imitation. It follows, therefore, that there are three forms of Plot to be avoided.

(1) A good man must not be seen passing from happiness to misery, or (2) a bad man from misery to happiness. The first situation is not fear-inspiring or piteous, but simply odious to us. The second is the most untragic that can be; it has no one of the requisites of Tragedy; it does not appeal either to the human feeling in us, or to our pity, or to our fears. Nor, on the other hand, should (3) an extremely bad man be seen falling from happiness into misery. Such a story may arouse the human feeling in us, but it will not move us to either pity or fear; pity is occasioned by un-deserved misfortune, and fear by that of one like ourselves; so that there will be nothing either piteous or fear-inspiring in the situation. There re-mains, then, the intermediate kind of personage, a man not pre-eminently virtuous and just, whose misfortune, however, is brought upon him not by vice and depravity but by some error of judgement, of the number of those in the enjoyment of great reputation and prosperity; e.g. Oedipus, Thyestes, and the men of note of similar families. The perfect Plot, accord-ingly, must have a single, and not (as some tell us) a double issue; the change in the hero's fortunes must be not from misery to happiness, but on the contrary from happiness to misery; and the cause of it must lie not in any depravity, but in some great error on his part; the man himself being either such as we have described, or better, not worse, than that. Fact also confirms our theory. Though the poets began by accepting any tragic story that came to hand, in these days the finest tragedies are always on the story of some few houses, on that of Alcmeon, Oedipus, Orestes, Meleager, Thyestes, Telephus, or any others that may have been involved, as either agents or sufferers, in some deed of horror. The theoretically best tragedy, then, has a Plot of this description. The critics, therefore, are wrong who blame Euripides for taking this line in his tragedies, and giving many of them an unhappy ending. It is, as we have said, the right line to take. The best proof is this: on the stage, and in the public performances, such plays, properly worked out, are seen to be the most truly tragic; and Euripides, even if his execution be faulty in every other point, is seen to be nevertheless the most tragic certainly of the dramatists. After this comes the construction of Plot with some rank first, one with a double story (like the *Odyssey*) and an opposite issue for the good and the bad personages. It is ranked as first only through the weakness of the audiences; the poets merely follow their public, writing as its wishes dictate. But the pleasure here is not that of Tragedy. It belongs rather to Comedy, where the bitterest enemies in the piece (e.g. Orestes and Aegisthus) walk off good friends at the end, with no slaying of any one by any one.

14 The tragic fear and pity may be aroused by the Spectacle; but they may also be aroused by the very structure and incidents of the play—which is the better way and shows the better poet. The Plot in fact should be so framed that, even without seeing the things take place, he who simply hears the account of them shall be filled with horror and pity at the inci-dents; which is just the effect that the mere recital of the story in *Oedipus* would have on one. To produce this same effect by means of the Spectacle

is less artistic, and requires extraneous aid. Those, however, who make use of the Spectacle to put before us that which is merely monstrous and not productive of fear, are wholly out of touch with Tragedy; not every kind of pleasure should be required of a tragedy, but only its own proper pleasure.

The tragic pleasure is that of pity and fear, and the poet has to produce it by a work of imitation; it is clear, therefore, that the causes should be included in the incidents of his story. Let us see, then, what kinds of incident strike one as horrible, or rather as piteous. In a deed of this description the parties must necessarily be either friends, or enemies, or indifferent to one another. Now when enemy does it on enemy, there is nothing to move us to pity either in his doing or in his meditating the deed, except so far as the actual pain of the sufferer is concerned; and the same is true when the parties are indifferent to one another. Whenever the tragic deed, however, is done within the family—when murder or the like is done or mediated by brother on brother, by son on father, by mother on son, or son on mother—these are the situations the poet should seek after. The traditional stories, accordingly, must be kept as they are, e.g. the murder of Clytaemnestra by Orestes and of Eriphyle by Alcmeon. At the same time even with these there is something left to the poet himself; it is for him to devise the right way of treating them. Let us explain more clearly what we mean by 'the right way'. The deed of horror may be done by the doer knowingly and consciously, as in the old poets, and in Medea's murder of her children in Euripides. Or he may do it, but in ignorance of his relationship, and discover that afterwards, as does the Oedipus in Sophocles. Here the deed is outside the play; but it may be within it, like the act of the Alcmeon in Astydamas, or that of the Telegonus in *Ulysses Wounded*. A third possibility is for one meditating some deadly injury to another, in ignorance of his relationship, to make the discovery in time to draw back. These exhaust the possibilities, since the deed must necessarily be either done or not done, and either knowingly or unknowingly.

The worst situation is when the personage is with full knowledge on the point of doing the deed, and leaves it undone. It is odious and also (through the absence of suffering) untragic; hence it is that no one is made to act thus except in some few instances, e.g. Haemon and Creon in *Antigone*. Next after this comes the actual perpetration of the deed mediated. A better situation than that, however, is for the deed to be done in ignorance, and the relationship discovered afterwards, since there is nothing odious in it, and the Discovery will serve to astound us. But the best of all is the last; what we have in *Cresphontes*, for example, where Merope, on the point of slaying her son, recognizes him in time; in *Iphigenia*, where sister and brother are in a like position; and in *Helle*, where the son recognizes his mother, when on the point of giving her up to her enemy.

This will explain why our tragedies are restricted (as we said just now) to such a small number of families. It was accident rather than art that

led the poets in quest of subjects to embody this kind of incident in their
Plots. They are still obliged, accordingly, to have recourse to the families
in which such horrors have occurred.

On the construction of the Plot, and the kind of Plot required for
Tragedy, enough has now been said.

15 In the Characters there are four points to aim at. First and foremost,
that they shall be good. There will be an element of character in the play,
if (as has been observed) what a personage says or does reveals a certain
moral purpose; and a good element of character, if the purpose so revealed
is good. Such goodness is possible in every type of personage, even in a
woman or a slave, though the one is perhaps an inferior, and the other
a wholly worthless being. The second point is to make them appropriate.
The Character before us may be, say, manly; but it is not appropriate in a
female Character to be manly, or clever. The third is to make them like
the reality, which is not the same as their being good and appropriate, in
our sense of the term. The fourth is to make them consistent and the
same throughout; even if inconsistency be part of the man before one for
imitation as presenting that form of character, he should still be consistently inconsistent. We have an instance of baseness of character, not
required for the story, in the Menelaus in *Orestes*; of the incongruous and
unbefitting in the lamentation of Ulysses in *Scylla*, and in the (clever)
speech of Melanippe; and of inconsistency in *Iphigenia at Aulis*, where
Iphigenia the suppliant is utterly unlike the later Iphigenia. The right
thing, however, is in the Characters just as in the incidents of the play to
endeavour always after the necessary or the probable; so that whenever
such-and-such a personage says or does such-and-such a thing, it shall be
the necessary or probable outcome of his character; and whenever this
incident follows on that, it shall be either the necessary or the probable
consequence of it. From this one sees (to digress for a moment) that the
Dénouement also should arise out of the plot itself, and not depend on a
stage-artifice, as in *Medea*, or in the story of the (arrested) departure of
the Greeks in the *Iliad*. The artifice must be reserved for matters outside
the play—for past events beyond human knowledge, or events yet to come,
which require to be foretold or announced; since it is the privilege of the
Gods to know everything. There should be nothing improbable among
the actual incidents. If it be unavoidable, however, it should be outside
the tragedy, like the improbability in the *Oedipus* of Sophocles. But to
return to the Characters. As Tragedy is an imitation of personages better
than the ordinary man, we in our way should follow the example of good
portrait-painters, who reproduce the distinctive features of a man, and at
the same time, without losing the likeness, make him handsomer than he
is. The poet in like manner, in portraying men quick or slow to anger, or
with similar infirmities of character, must know how to represent them
as such, and at the same time as good men, as Agathon and Homer have
represented Achilles.

All these rules one must keep in mind throughout, and, further, those also for such points of stage-effect as directly depend on the art of the poet, since in these too one may often make mistakes. Enough, however, has been said on the subject in one of our published writings.

16 Discovery in general has been explained already. As for the species of Discovery, the first to be noted is (1) the least artistic form of it, of which the poets make most use through mere lack of invention, Discovery by signs or marks. Of these signs some are congenital, like the 'lance-head which the Earth-born have on them', or 'stars', such as Carcinus brings in his *Thyestes*; others acquired after birth—these latter being either marks on the body, e.g. scars, or external tokens, like necklaces, or (to take another sort of instance) the ark in the Discovery in *Tyro*. Even these, however, admit of two uses, a better and a worse; the scar of Ulysses is an instance; the Discovery of him through it is made in one way by the nurse and in another by the swineherds. A Discovery using signs as a means of assurance is less artistic, as indeed are all such as imply reflection; whereas one bringing them in all of a sudden, as in the *Bath-story*, is of a better order. Next after these are (2) Discoveries made directly by the poet; which are inartistic for that very reason; e.g. Orestes' Discovery of himself in *Iphigenia*: whereas his sister reveals who she is by the letter, Orestes is made to say himself what the poet rather than the story demands. This, therefore, is not far removed from the first-mentioned fault, since he might have presented certain tokens as well. Another instance is the 'shuttle's voice' in the *Tereus* of Sophocles. (3) A third species is Discovery through memory, from a man's consciousness being awakened by something seen. Thus in *The Cyprioe* of Dicaeogenes, the sight of the picture makes the man burst into tears; and in the *Tale of Alcinous*, hearing the harper Ulysses is reminded of the past and weeps; the Discovery of them being the result. (4) A fourth kind is Discovery through reasoning; e.g. in *The Choephoroe*; 'One like me is here; there is no one like me but Orestes; he, therefore, must be here.' Or that which Polyidus the Sophist suggested for *Iphigenia*; since it was natural for Orestes to reflect: 'My sister was sacrificed, and I am to be sacrificed like her.' Or that in the *Tydeus* of Theodectes: 'I came to find a son, and am to die myself.' Or that in *The Phinidae*: on seeing the place the women inferred their fate, that they were to die there, since they had also been exposed there. (5) There is, too, a composite Discovery arising from bad reasoning on the side of the other party. An instance of it is in *Ulysses the False Messenger*: he said he should know the bow—which he had not seen; but to suppose from that that he would know it again (as though he had once seen it) was bad reasoning. (6) The best of all Discoveries, however, is that arising from the incidents themselves, when the great surprise comes about through a probable incident, like that in the *Oedipus* of Sophocles; and also in *Iphigenia*; for it was not improbable that she should wish to have a letter taken home. These last are the only Discoveries independent of the artifice of signs and necklaces. Next after them come Discoveries through reasoning.

17 At the time when he is constructing his Plots, and engaged on the Diction in which they are worked out, the poet should remember (1) to put the actual scenes as far as possible before his eyes. In this way, seeing everything with the vividness of an eye-witness as it were, he will devise what is appropriate, and be least likely to overlook incongruities. This is shown by what was censured in Carcinus, the return of Amphiaraus from the sanctuary; it would have passed unnoticed, if it had not been actually seen by the audience; but on the stage his play failed, the incongruity of the incident offending the spectators. (2) As far as may be, too, the poet should even act his story with the very gestures of his personages. Given the same natural qualifications, he who feels the emotions to be described will be the most convincing; distress and anger, for instance, are portrayed most truthfully by one who is feeling them at the moment. Hence it is that poetry demands a man with a special gift for it, or else one with a touch of madness in him; the former can easily assume the required mood, and the latter may be actually beside himself with emotion. (3) His story, again, whether already made or of his own making, he should first simplify and reduce to a universal form, before proceeding to lengthen it out by the insertion of episodes. The following will show how the universal element in *Iphigenia*, for instance, may be viewed: A certain maiden having been offered in sacrifice, and spirited away from her sacrifices into another land, where the custom was to sacrifice all strangers to the Goddess, she was made there the priestess of this rite. Long after that the brother of the priestess happened to come; the fact, however, of the oracle having for a certain reason bidden him go thither, and his object in going, are outside the Plot of the play. On his coming he was arrested, and about to be sacrificed, when he revealed who he was—either as Euripides puts it, or (as suggested by Polyidus) by the not improbable exclamation, 'So I too am doomed to be sacrificed, as my sister was'; and the disclosure led to his salvation. This done, the next thing, after the proper names have been fixed as a basis for the story, is to work in episodes or accessory incidents. One must mind, however, that the episodes are appropriate, like the fit of madness in Orestes, which led to his arrest, and the purifying, which brought about his salvation. In plays, then, the episodes are short; in epic poetry they serve to lengthen out the poem. The argument of the *Odyssey* is not a long one. A certain man has been abroad many years; Poseidon is ever on the watch for him, and he is all alone. Matters at home too have come to this, that his substance is being wasted and his son's death plotted by suitors to his wife. Then he arrives there himself after his grievous sufferings; reveals himself, and falls on his enemies; and the end is his salvation and their death. This being all that is proper to the *Odyssey*, everything else in it is episode.

18 (4) There is a further point to be borne in mind. Every tragedy is in

part Complication and in part Dénouement; the incidents before the
opening scene, and often certain also of those within the play, forming
the Complication; and the rest the Dénouement. By Complication I mean
all from the beginning of the story to the point just before the change
in the hero's fortunes; by Dénouement, all from the beginning of the
change to the end. In the *Lynceus* of Theodectes, for instance, the Complication includes, together with the presupposed incidents, the seizure
of the child and that in turn of the parents; and the Dénouement all from
the indictment for the murder to the end. Now it is right, when one
speaks of a tragedy as the same or not the same as another, to do so on
the ground before all else of their Plot, i.e. as having the same or not the
same Complication and Dénouement. Yet there are many dramatists who,
after a good Complication, fail in the Dénouement. But it is necessary for
both points of construction to be always duly mastered. (5) There are
four distinct species of Tragedy—that being the number of the constituents
also that have been mentioned: first, the complex Tragedy, which is all
Peripety and Discovery; second, the Tragedy of suffering, e.g. the *Ajaxes*
and *Ixions*; third, the Tragedy of character, e.g. *The Phthiotides* and
Peleus. The fourth constituent is that of 'Spectacle', exemplified in *The
Phorcides*, in *Prometheus*, and in all plays with the scene laid in the nether
world. The poet's aim, then, should be to combine every element of interest, if possible, or else the more important and the major part of them.
This is now especially necessary owing to the unfair criticism to which the
poet is subjected in these days. Just because there have been poets before
him strong in the several species of tragedy, the critics now expect the one
man to surpass that which was the strong point of each one of his predecessors. (6) One should also remember what has been said more than once,
and not write a tragedy on an epic body of incident (i.e. one with a plurality of stories in it), by attempting to dramatize, for instance, the entire
story of the *Iliad*. In the epic owing to its scale every part is treated at
proper length; with a drama, however, on the same story the result is very
disappointing. This is shown by the fact that all who have dramatized the
fall of Illium in its entirety, and not part by part, like Euripides, of the
whole of the Niobe story, instead of a portion, like Aeschylus, either fail
utterly or have but ill success on the stage; for that and that alone was
enough to ruin even a play by Agathon. Yet in their Peripeties, as also in
their simple plots, the poets I mean show wonderful skill in aiming at the
kind of effect they desire—a tragic situation that arouses the human feeling in one, like the clever villain (e.g. Sisyphus) deceived, or the brave
wrongdoer worsted. This is probable, however, only in Agathon's sense,
when he speaks of the probability of even improbabilities coming to pass.
(7) The Chorus too should be regarded as one of the actors; it should be
an integral part of the whole, and take a share in the action—that which it
has in Sophocles, rather than in Euripides. With the later poets, however,
the songs in a play of theirs have no more to do with the Plot of that than
of any other tragedy. Hence it is that they are now singing intercalary

pieces, a practice first introduced by Agathon. And yet what real difference is there between singing such intercalary pieces, and attempting to fit in a speech, or even a whole act, from one play into another?

19 The Plot and Characters having been discussed, it remains to consider the Diction and Thought. As for the Thought, we may assume what is said of it in our Art of Rhetoric, as it belongs more properly to that department of inquiry. The Thought of the personages is shown in everything to be effected by their language—in every effort to prove or disprove, to arouse emotion (pity, fear, anger, and the like), or to maximize or minimize things. It is clear, also, that their mental procedure must be on the same lines n their actions likewise, whenever they wish them to arouse pity or horror, or to have a look of importance or probability. The only difference is that with the act the impression has to be made without explanation; whereas with the spoken word it has to be produced by the speaker, and result from his language. What, indeed, would be the good of the speaker, if things appeared in the required light even apart from anything he says.

As regards the Diction, one subject for inquiry under this head is the turns given to the language when spoken; e.g. the difference between command and prayer, simple statement and threat, question and answer, and so forth. The theory of such matters, however, belongs to Elocution and the professors of that art. Whether the poet knows these things or not, his art as a poet is never seriously criticized on that account. What fault can one see in Homer's 'Sing of the wrath, Goddess'?—which Protagoras has criticized as being a command where a prayer was meant, since to bid one do or not do, he tells us, is a command. Let us pass over this, then, as appertaining to another art, and not to that of poetry.

20 The Diction viewed as a whole is made up of the following parts: the Letter (or ultimate element), the Syllable, the Conjunction, the Article, the Noun, the Verb, the Case, and the Speech. (1) The Letter is an indivisible sound of a particular kind, one that may become a factor in an intelligible sound. Indivisible sounds are uttered by the brutes also, but no one of these is a Letter in our sense of the term. These elementary sounds are either vowels, semi-vowels, or mutes. A vowel is a Letter having an audible sound without the addition of another Letter. A semi-vowel, one having an audible sound by the addition of another Letter; e.g. S and R. A mute, one having no sound at all by itself, but becoming audible by an addition, that of one of the Letters which have a sound of some sort of their own; e.g. G and D. The Letters differ in various ways: as produced by different conformations or in different regions of the mouth; as aspirated, not aspirated, or sometimes one and sometimes the other; as long, short, or of variable quantity; and further as having an acute, grave, or intermediate accent. The details of these matters we must leave to the metricians. (2) A Syllable is a non-significant composite sound, made up of a mute and a Letter having a sound (a vowel or semi-vowel); for GR,

without an A, is just as much a Syllable as GRA, with an A. The various forms of the Syllable also belong to the theory of metre. (3) A Conjunction is (*a*) a non-significant sound which, when one significant sound is formable out of several, neither hinders nor aids the union, and which, if the Speech thus formed stands by itself (apart from other Speeches), must not be inserted at the beginning of it. . . . Or (*b*) a non-significant sound capable of combining two or more significant sounds into one. . . . (4) An Article is a non-significant sound marking the beginning, end, or dividing-point of a Speech, its natural place being either at the extremities or in the middle. (5) A Noun or name is a composite significant sound not involving the idea of time, with parts which have no significance by themselves in it. It is to be remembered that in a compound we do not think of the parts as having a significance also by themselves; in the name 'Theodorus', for instance. . . . (6) A Verb is a composite significant sound involving the idea of time, with parts which (just as in the Noun) have no significance by themselves in it. Whereas the word 'man' or 'white' does not imply *when*, 'walks' and 'has walked,' involve in addition to the idea of walking that of time present or time past. (7) A Case of a Noun or Verb is when the word means 'of' or 'to' a thing, and so forth, or for one or many (e.g. 'man' and 'men'); or it may consist merely in the mode of utterance, e.g. in question, command, &c. 'Walked?' and 'Walk!' are Cases of the verb 'to walk' of this last kind. (8) A Speech is a composite significant sound, some of the parts of which have a certain significance by themselves. It may be observed that a Speech is not always made up of Noun and Verb; it may be without a Verb, like the definition of man; but it will always have some part with a certain significance by itself. In the Speech 'Cleon walks', 'Cleon' is an instance of such a part. A Speech is said to be one in two ways, either as signifying one thing, or as a union of several Speeches made into one by conjunction. Thus the *Iliad* is one Speech by conjunction of several; and the definition of man is one through its signifying one thing.

21 Nouns are of two kinds, either (1) simple, i.e. made up of non-significant parts or (2) double; in the latter case the word may be made up either of a significant and a non-significant part (a distinction which disappears in the compound), or of two significant parts. It is possible also to have triple, quadruple, or higher compounds, like most of our amplified names; e.g. 'Hermocaïcoxanthus' and the like.

Whatever its structure, a Noun must always be either (1) the ordinary word for the thing, or (2) a strange word, or (3) a metaphor, or (4) an ornamental word, or (5) a coined word, or (6) a word lengthened out, or (7) curtailed, or (8) altered in form. By the ordinary word I mean that in general use in a country; and by a strange word, one in use elsewhere. So that the same word may obviously be at once strange and ordinary, though not in reference to the same people; . . . Metaphor consists in giving the thing a name that belongs to something else; the transference being either from genus to species, or from species to genus, or from species to species, or on grounds of analogy. That from genus to species is exemplified in 'Here stands my ship'; for lying at anchor is the 'standing' of a particular kind of thing. That from species to genus in 'Truly ten thousand good deeds has Ulysses wrought', where 'ten thousand', which is a particular large number, is put in place of the generic 'a large number'. That from species to species in 'Drawing the life with the bronze', and in 'Severing with the enduring bronze'; where the poet uses 'draw' in the sense of 'sever' and 'sever' in that of 'draw', both words meaning to 'take away' something. That from analogy is possible whenever there are four terms so related that the second (B) is to the first (A), as the fourth (D) to the third (C); for one may then metaphorically put D in lieu of B, and B in lieu of D. Now and then, too, they qualify the metaphor by adding on to it that to which the word it supplants is relative. Thus a cup (B) is in relation to Dionysus (A) what a shield (D) is to Ares (C). The cup accordingly will be metaphorically described as the 'shield of *Dionysus*' (D + A), and the shield as the 'cup *of Ares*' (B + C). Or to take another instance: As old age (D) is to life (C), so is evening (B) to day (A). One will accordingly describe evening (B) as the 'old age *of the day*' (D + A)—or by the Empedoclean equivalent; and old age (D) as the 'evening' or 'sunset *of life*' (B + C). It may be that some of the terms thus related have no special name of their own, but for all that they will be metaphorically decribed in just the same way. Thus a cast forth seed-corn is called 'sowing'; but to cast forth its flame, as said of the sun, has no special name. This nameless act (B), however, stands in just the same relation to its object, sunlight (A), as sowing (D) to the seed-corn (C). Hence the expression in the poet, 'sowing around a god-created *flame*' (D + A). There is also another form of qualified metaphor. Having given the thing the alien name, one may by a negative addition deny of it one of the attributes naturally associated with its new name. An instance of this would be to call the shield not the 'cup *of Ares*', as in the former case, but a 'cup *that holds no wine*'. . . . . A coined word is a name which, being quite unknown among a people, is given the poet himself. . . . . A word is said to be lengthened out, when it has a short vowel made long, or an extra syllable inserted. . . . It is said to be curtailed, when it has lost a part. . . . It is an altered word, when part is left as it was and part is of the poet's making.

                                   .   .   .

The Nouns themselves (to whatever class they may belong) are either masculines, feminines, or intermediates (neuter). All ending in N, P, Σ, or in the two compounds of this last, Ψ and Ξ, are masculines. All ending in the invariably long vowels, H and Ω, and in A among the vowels that may be long, are feminines. So that there is an equal number of masculine and feminine terminations, as Ψ and Ξ are the same as Σ, and need not be counted. There is no Noun, however, ending in a mute or in either of the two short vowels, E and O. Only three . . . end in I and five in Y. The intermediates, or neuters, end in the variable vowels or in N, P, Σ.

22 The perfection of Diction is for it to be at once clear and not mean. The clearest indeed is that made up of the ordinary words for things, but it is mean, as is shown by the poetry of Cleophon and Sthenelus. On the other hand the Diction becomes distinguished and non-prosaic by the use of unfamiliar terms, i.e. strange words, metaphors, lengthened forms, and everything that deviates from the ordinary modes of speech.—But a whole statement in such terms will be either a riddle or a barbarism, a riddle, if made up of metaphors, a barbarism, if made up of strange words. The very nature indeed of a riddle is this, to describe a fact in an impossible combination of words (which cannot be done with the real names for things, but can be with their metaphorical substitutes); e.g. 'I saw a man glue brass on another with fire', and the like. The corresponding use of strange words results in a barbarism.—A certain admixture, accordingly, of unfamiliar terms is necessary. These, the strange word, the metaphor, the ornamental equivalent, &c., will save the language from seeming mean and prosaic, while the ordinary words in it will secure the requisite clearness. What helps most, however, to render the Diction at once clear and non-prosaic is the use of the lengthened, curtailed, and altered forms of words. Their deviation from the ordinary words will, by making the language unlike that in general use, give it a non-prosaic appearance; and their having much in common with the words in general use will give it the quality of clearness. It is not right, then, to condemn these modes of speech, and ridicule the poet for using them, as some have done; e.g. the elder Euclid, who said it was easy to make poetry if one were to be allowed to lengthen the words in the statement itself as much as one likes. . . . A too apparent use of these licences has certainly a ludicrous effect, but they are not alone in that; the rule of moderation applies to all the constituents of the poetic vocabulary; even with metaphors, strange words, and the rest, the effect will be the same, if one uses them improperly and with a view to provoking laughter. The proper use of them is a very different thing. To realize the difference one should take an epic verse and see how it reads when the normal words are introduced. The same should be done too with the strange word, the metaphor, and the rest; for one has only to put the ordinary words in their place to see the truth of what we are saying. The same iambic, for instance, is found in Aeschylus and Euripides, and as it stands in the former it is a poor line; whereas Euripides, by the change of a single word, the substitution of a strange for what is by usage the ordinary word, has made it seem a fine one.

. . .

It is a great thing, indeed, to make a proper use of these poetical forms, as also of compounds and strange words. But the greatest thing by far is to be a master of metaphor. It is the one thing that cannot be learnt from others; and it is also a sign of genius, since a good metaphor implies an intuitive perception of the similarity in dissimilars.

Of the kinds of words we have enumerated it may be observed that compounds are most in place in the dithyramb, strange words in heroic, and metaphors in iambic poetry. Heroic poetry, indeed, may avail itself of them all. But in iambic verse, which models itself as far as possible on the spoken language, only those kinds of words are in place which are allowable also in an oration, i.e. the ordinary word, the metaphor, and the ornamental equivalent.

Let this, then, suffice as an account of Tragedy, the art imitating by means of action on the stage.

23 As for the poetry which merely narrates, or imitates by means of versified language (without action), it is evident that it has several points in common with Tragedy.

I. The construction of its stories should clearly be like that in a drama; they should be based on a single action, one that is a complete whole in itself, with a beginning, middle, and end, so as to enable the work to produce its own proper pleasure with all the organic unity of a living. Nor should one suppose that there is anything like them in our usual histories. A history has to deal not with one action, but with one period and all that happened in that to one or more persons, however disconnected the several events may have been. Just as two events may take place at the same time, e.g. the sea-fight off Salamis and the battle with the Carthaginians in Sicily, without converging to the same end, so too of two consecutive events one may sometimes come after the other with no one end as their common issue. Nevertheless most of our epic poets, one may say, ignore the distinction.

Herein, then, to repeat what we have said before, we have a further proof of Homer's marvellous superiority to the rest. He did not attempt to deal even with the Trojan war in its entirety, though it was a whole with a definite beginning and end—through a feeling apparently that it was too long a story to be taken in in one view, or if not that, too complicated from the variety of incident in it. As it is, he has singled out one section of the whole; many of the other incidents, however, he brings in as episodes, using the Catalogue of the Ships, for instance, and other episodes to relieve the uniformity of his narrative. As for the other epic poets, they treat of one man, or one period; or else of an action which, although one, has a multiplicity of parts in it. This last is what the authors of the *Cypria* and *Little Iliad* have done. And the result is that, whereas the *Iliad* or *Odyssey* supplies materials for only one, or at most two tragedies, the *Cypria* does that for several and the *Little Iliad* for more than eight: for an *Adjudgment of Arms*, a *Philoctetes*, a *Neoptolemus*, a *Eurypylus*, a *Ulysses as Beggar*, a *Laconian Women*, a *Fall of Ilium*, and a *Departure of the Fleet*; as also a *Sinon*, and a *Women of Troy*.

24 II. Besides this, Epic poetry must divide into the same species as Tragedy; it must be either simple or complex, a story of character or one of suffering. Its parts, too, with the exception of Song and Spectacle, must be the same, as it requires Peripeties, Discoveries, and scenes of suffering just like Tragedy. Lastly, the Thought and Diction in it must be good in

their way. All these elements appear in Homer first; and he has made due use of them. His two poems are each examples of construction, the *Iliad* simple and a story of suffering, the *Odyssey* complex (there is Discovery throughout it) and a story of character. And they are more than this, since in Diction and Thought too they surpass all other poems.

There is, however, a difference in the Epic as compared with Tragedy, (1) in its length, and (2) in its metre. (1) As to its length, the limit already suggested will suffice: it must be possible for the beginning and end of the work to be taken in in one view—a condition which will be fulfilled if the poem be shorter than the old epics, and about as long as the series of tragedies offered for one hearing. For the extension of its length epic poetry has a special advantage, of which it makes large use. In a play one cannot represent an action with a number of parts going on simultaneously; one is limited to the part on the stage and connected with the actors. Whereas in epic poetry the narrative form makes it possible for one to describe a number of simultaneous incidents; and these, if germane to the subject, increase the body of the poem. This then is a gain to the Epic, tending to give it grandeur, and also variety of interest and room for episodes of diverse kinds. Uniformity of incident by the satiety it soon creates is apt to ruin tragedies on the stage. (2) As for its metre, the heroic has been assigned it from experience; were any one to attempt a narrative poem in some one, or in several, of the other metres, the incongruity of the thing would be apparent. The heroic in fact is the gravest and weightiest of metres—which is what makes it more tolerant than the rest of strange words and metaphors, that also being a point in which the narrative form of poetry goes beyond all others. The iambic and trochaic, on the other hand, are metres of movement, the one representing that of life and action, the other that of the dance. Still more unnatural would it appear, if one were to write an epic in a medley of metres, as Chaeremon did. Hence it is that no one has ever written a long story in any but heroic verse; nature herself, as we have said, teaches us to select the metre appropriate to such a story.

Homer, admirable as he is in every other respect, is especially so in this, that he alone among epic poets is not unaware of the part to be played by the poet himself in the poem. The poet should say very little *in propria persona*, as he is no imitator when doing that. Whereas the other poets are perpetually coming forward in person, and say but little, and that only here and there, as imitators, Homer after a brief preface brings in forthwith a man, a woman, or some other Character—no one of them characterless, but each with distinctive characteristics.

The marvellous is certainly required in Tragedy. The Epic, however, affords more opening for the improbable, the chief factor in the marvellous, because in it the agents are not visibly before one. The scene of the pursuit of Hector would be ridiculous on the stage—the Greeks halting instead of pursuing him, and Achilles shaking his head to stop them; but in the poem the absurdity is overlooked. The marvellous, however, is a cause of pleasure, as is shown by the fact that we all tell a story with additions, in the belief that we are doing our hearers a pleasure.

Homer more than any other has taught the rest of us the art of framing lies in the right way. I mean the use of paralogism. Whenever, if A is or happens, a consequent, B, is or happens, men's notion is that, if the B is, the A also is—but that is a false conclusion. Accordingly, if A is untrue, but there is something else, B, that on the assumption of its truth follows as its consequent, the right thing then is to add on the B. Just because we know the truth of the consequent, we are in our minds led on to the erroneous inference of the truth of the antecedent. Here is an instance, from the *Bath-story* in the *Odyssey*.

A likely impossibility is always preferable to an unconvincing possibility. The story should never be made up of improbable incidents; there should be nothing of the sort in it. If, however, such incidents are unavoidable, they should be outside the piece, like the hero's ignorance in *Oedipus* of the circumstances of Laius' death; not within it, like the report of the Pythian games in *Electra*, or the man's having come to Mysia from Tegea without uttering a word on the way, in *The Mysians*. So that it is ridiculous to say that one's Plot would have been spoilt without them, since it is fundamentally wrong to make up such Plots. If the poet has taken such a Plot, however, and one sees that he might have put it in a more probable form, he is guilty of absurdity as well as a fault of art. Even in the *Odyssey* the improbabilities in the setting-ashore of Ulysses would be clearly intolerable in the hands of an inferior poet. As it is, the poet conceals them, his other excellences veiling their absurdity. Elaborate Diction, however, is required only in places where there is no action, and no Character or Thought to be revealed. Where there is Character or Thought, on the other hand, an over-ornate Diction tends to obscure them.

25 As regards Problems and their Solutions, one may see the number and nature of the assumptions on which they proceed by viewing the matter in the following way. (1) The poet being an imitator just like the painter or other maker of likenesses, he must necessarily in all instances represent things in one or other of three aspects, either as they were or are, or as they are said or thought to be or to have been, or as they ought to be. (2) All this he does in language, with an admixture, it may be, of strange words and metaphors, as also of the various modified forms of words, since the use of these is conceded in poetry. (3) It is to be remembered, too, that there is not the same kind of correctness in poetry as in politics, or indeed any other art. There is, however, within the limits of poetry itself a possibility of two kinds of error, the one directly, the other only accidentally connected with the art. If the poet meant to describe the thing correctly, and failed through lack of power of expression, his art itself is at fault. But if it was through his having meant to describe it in some incorrect way (e.g. to make the horse in movement have both right legs thrown forward) that the technical error (one in a matter of, say, medicine or some other special science), or impossibilities of whatever kind they may be, have got into his description, his error in that case is not in the essentials of the poetic art. These, therefore, must be the premisses of the Solutions in answer to criticisms involved in the Problems.

I. As to the criticisms relating to the poet's art itself. Any impossibilities there may be in his descriptions of things are faults. But from another point of view they are justifiable, if they serve the end of poetry itself—if (to assume what we have said of that end) they make the effect of either that very portion of the work or some other portion more astounding. The Pursuit of Hector is an instance in point, If, however, the poetic end might have been as well or better attained without sacrifice of technical correctness in such matters, the impossibility is not to be justified, since the description should be, if it can, entirely free from error. One may ask, too, whether the error is in a matter directly or only accidentally connected with the poetic art; since it is a lesser error in an artist not to know, for instance, that the hind has no horns, than to produce an unrecognizable picture of one.

II. If the poet's description be criticized as not true to fact, one may urge perhaps that the object ought to be as described—an answer like that of Sophocles, who said that he drew men as they ought to be, and Euripides as they were. If the description, however, be neither true nor of the thing as it ought to be, the answer must be then, that it is in accordance with opinion. The tales about Gods, for instance, may be as wrong as Xenophanes thinks, neither true nor the better thing to say; but they are certainly in accordance with opinion. Of other statements in poetry one may perhaps say, not that they are better than the truth, but that the fact was so at the time; e.g. the description of the arms: 'their spears stood upright, butt-end upon the ground'; for that was the usual way of fixing them then, as it is still with the Illyrians. As for the question whether something said or done in a poem is morally right or not, in dealing with that one should consider not only the intrinsic quality of the actual word or deed, but also the person who says or does it, the person to whom he says or does it, the time, the means, and the motive of the agent—whether he does it to attain a greater good, or to avoid a greater evil.

· · ·

26 The question may be raised whether the epic or the tragic is the higher form of imitation. It may be argued that, if the less vulgar is the higher, and the less vulgar is always that which addresses the better public, an art addressing any and every one is of a very vulgar order. It is a belief that their public cannot see the meaning, unless they add something themselves, that causes the perpetual movements of the performers—bad flute-players, for instance, rolling about, if quoit-throwing is to be represented, and pulling at the conductor, if Scylla is the subject of the piece. Tragedy, then, is said to be an art of this order—to be in fact just what the later actors were in the eyes of their predecessors; for Mynniscus used to call Callippides 'the ape', because he thought he so overacted his parts; and a similar view was taken of Pindarus also. All Tragedy, however, is said to

stand to the Epic as the newer to the older school of actors. The one, accordingly, is said to address a cultivated audience, which does not need the accompaniment of gesture; the other, an uncultivated one. If, therefore, Tragedy is a vulgar art, it must clearly be lower than the Epic.

The answer to this is twofold. In the first place, one may urge (1) that the censure does not touch the art of the dramatic poet, but only that of his interpreter; for it is quite possible to overdo the gesturing even in an epic recital, as did Sosistratus, and in a singing contest, as did Mnasitheus of Opus. (2) That one should not condemn all movement, unless one means to condemn even the dance, but only that of ignoble people— which is the point of the criticism passed on Callippides and in the present day on others, that their women are not like gentlewomen. (3) That Tragedy may produce its effect even without movement or action in just the same way as Epic poetry; for from the mere reading of a play its quality may be seen. So that, if it be superior in all other respects, this element of inferiority is no necessary part of it.

In the second place, one must remember (1) that Tragedy has everything that the Epic has (even the epic metre being admissible), together with a not inconsiderable addition in the shape of the Music (a very real factor in the pleasure of the drama) and the Spectacle. (2) That its reality of presentation is felt in the play as read, as well as in the play as acted. (3) That the tragic imitation requires less space for the attainment of its end; which is a great advantage, since the more concentrated effect is more pleasurable than one with a large admixture of time to dilute it— consider the *Oedipus* of Sophocles, for instance, and the effect of expanding it into the number of lines of the *Iliad*. (4) That there is less unity in the imitation of the epic poets, as is proved by the fact that any one work of theirs supplies matter for several tragedies; the result being that, if they take what is really a single story, it seems curt when briefly told, and thin and waterish when on the scale of length usual with their verse. In saying that there is less unity in an epic, I mean an epic made up of a plurality of actions, in the same way as the *Iliad* and *Odyssey* have many such parts, each one of them in itself of some magnitude; yet the structure of the two Homeric poems is as perfect as can be, and the action in them is as nearly as possible one action. If, then, Tragedy is superior in these respects, and also, besides these, in its poetic effect (since the two forms of poetry should give us, not any or every pleasure, but the very special kind we have mentioned), it is clear that, as attaining the poetic effect better than the Epic, it will be the higher form of art.

So much for Tragedy and Epic poetry—for these two arts in general and their species; the number and nature of their constituent parts; the causes of success and failure in them; the Objections of the critics, and the Solutions in answer to them.

G. M. A. Grube

A COMMENTARY ON
ARISTOTLE'S THEORY

The question is sometimes raised whether we should look upon the *Poetics* as a handbook of rules telling tragic poets how they should proceed in order to write good tragedies, or whether it is rather a collection of musings, often extraordinarily illuminating, by a great thinker on the subject of tragedy.* It may, in part at least, have been intended to be the former; but there can be no doubt that its greatness is due to its being, in fact, the latter. The style is very uneven. Some parts are written with reasonable care, but other parts are abrupt, ill-constructed, repetitive, contradictory, even ungrammatical. More clearly than any other work of Aristotle, the *Poetics* can only have been a set of lecture notes with later additions and interpolations by the lecturer himself.[1] We may well envy the original audience who had the opportunity of asking a few questions for purposes of clarification!

Here we will briefly discuss some of the more important and controversial points. We will try to establish what Aristotle meant, not what he should have meant to satisfy our modern minds, nor what he should have said to avoid the ambiguity he so rightly deplored in others.

Art as Imitation

When Aristotle says that poetry is imitation he is following Plato, and he clarifies this rather ambiguous conception. In the third book of the *Republic* Plato used *mimêsis* in the sense, mainly, of impersonation;[2] in the

G. M. A. *Grube* is Professor of Classics, Trinity College, The University of Toronto. He is well-known for his work on Aristotle as well as other Classical subjects.

* Selections from Professor Grube's Introduction to his translation of *The Poetics* (Indianapolis, 1958). Reprinted by permission of the Bobbs-Merrill Company, Inc.

[1] It is fascinating to try to isolate such additions. The reader will find a thorough study of the *Poetics* from this point of view in D. De Montmollin, *La Poétique d'Aristote* (Neuchâtel, 1951), and Else's commentary.
[2] *Republic* 3. 392d and ff. See also 10. 595a–608d; especially 598b for the metaphysical sense, and 604e–605c for the psychological effect of *mimêsis*. Aristotle also uses the word once in the *Poetics* in the restricted sense of impersonation, where he says that, when speaking in his own person, a poet is not "imitating." See ch. 24, note 5 below.

tenth book he used it in a wider sense to mean emotional identification or *sympatheia* where he discusses the psychological effects of poetry, and also in the more natural sense of imitation when he argues that the poet who imitates sensual life (itself an imitation of the Ideal) is at two removes from the truth. In the *Laws*, however, Plato mentions the theory that art is imitation as an obvious truth accepted by poet, actor, and audience alike.[3] The same idea of art as "imitation" is found in Xenophon, and in Aristophanes as well.[4] This famous theory of imitation is, in fact, not a Platonic theory so much as a generally accepted view which Plato uses in differing senses for his own purposes in his attacks on the poets. Aristotle mentions it at the beginning of the *Poetics*, not as a view that has to be argued, but as one that can be taken for granted and made the basis for his argument that the different genres of poetry should be differentiated by the nature of their imitation, i.e., by differences in the objects, means, and manner of their imitation.

And indeed it *is* almost a truism (or at least it was until quite recently) that art must be true to life. This does not mean a photographic copy, although Plato deliberately reduces it almost to that meaning when he is arguing *ad poetam*. It means that the situations, characters, emotions portrayed or evoked (for to both Plato and Aristotle music is "imitative") must strike us as true, so that this recognition of the model in the imitation gives us the pleasure described in the fourth chapter of the *Poetics*. And Aristotle expresses all this by explaining that, if accused of untruth, the poet may reply that he is imitating things as they are, as they were, as they ought to be, or as men thought they were, i.e., that he is representing the present, the past, the ideal,[5] or men's beliefs about them. But the converse of this is that he *must* represent one of these or else the critic is right. Aristotle does not allow mere fancy on the stage. *Mimêsis* has often been translated as "representation" and "to represent," but that misses the peculiar flavor of the Greek word, which *is* more restrictive. It also sidesteps an age-long controversy.

Evil on the Stage

Here again Aristotle is improving on Plato, who refused to allow any evil deed or person on the stage, all because of his fear of emotional identifica-

---

[3] *Laws* 2. 668b–c: "Everybody would surely agree to this much about *mousikê*, that all its compositions are imitation and representation. Would not all men agree to this, the poets and the audience and the actors?"

[4] In Xenophon, *Memorabilia* 3. 10. 1–8, Socrates is proving to a painter that he can imitate or represent (εκμιμεισθαι) not only the physical, but the qualities of the soul as well. In Aristophanes, *Thesmaphoriazusae* 156, we find the notion of *mimêsis* used humorously where Agathon is dressed as a woman to compose an ode for women.

[5] *Poetics* ch. 25. Not too much should be made of this "imitation of the ideal" as a new and peculiarly Aristotelian change in the theory of *mimêsis*. It is found in Plato, *Republic* 5. 472d: "Do you think a man is any the less a good painter if he paints a model such as the most beautiful man would be, and, having made everything fit in this picture, then cannot prove that such a man can exist?"

tion on the part of the audience. Aristotle realizes that this in effect means no drama but at best a series of epic-like recitations with the occasional enactment of the "nicer" scenes. He accepts the ultimate moral purpose of tragedy when he states baldly that his characters must be "good," but he immediately qualifies this Platonic position when he gives as an example to be condemned the Menelaus in Euripides' *Orestes* because he is "*unnecessarily* evil."[6] In a later passage he states that, in judging whether a particular deed or speech is "good," we should look beyond the particular incident and relate it to the character, the circumstances, indeed the whole play. Looked at in this way, the particular evil deed or speech may be found "to secure a greater good or avoid a greater evil," i.e., it may serve the moral purpose of the drama as a whole. There is no evidence to support the contention that Aristotle's ultimate judgment on a drama as a whole is purely aesthetic—no Greek writer's appraisal ever was; such a divorce between the good and the beautiful is quite un-Greek—but he certainly takes a much more sensible and acceptable view of the matter than Plato did.

A Good Action?

The same question of Aristotle's moral view of drama arises in connection with the first clause of his definition of tragedy: "an imitation of an action which is *good*." Here the word is *sudaios*, and those who want to empty it of moral implication translate "a serious action" or "an action of high importance." The action here is, of course, that of the whole play, not a particular incident. It is the commentators who create the problem by here again introducing the distinction between a moral and an aesthetic judgment which is foreign to Aristotle. He tells us himself a few lines later that an "action" derives its quality from the character and mind of the doer.

When the same word *spoudaios* is applied to a character, it is always in a context which we would call moral. However, Aristotle must use a fairly mild word, for characters who are completely virtuous or vicious are not, to him, fit subjects of tragedy (or comedy either). It does not help us to speak of men "of a higher type," or "of a lower type" (*phauloteros*), for it would have sorely puzzled Aristotle, I believe, how a man could be of a higher type without being a better man, or of a lower type without being a worse one, and the nature of the action is tied to the nature of the man who performs it. To Aristotle, the *êthos* of a man included his mind as well as his morals, in fact his whole personality. Our word "character" has a much more restricted sense.

---

[6] In ch. 15. The later passage is in ch. 25. The use of καλως is here clearly moral (as so often), at least in part. The context makes this quite clear. It corresponds to Plato's use of ευ in *Laws* 2. 669a–b.

The definition of comedy provides an enlightening parallel. "Comedy is
. . . an imitation of men who are 'inferior' but not altogether vicious. . . ."[7]
There is no possible doubt of the moral significance of the word "vice"
(*kakia*), and the inferior men have less of the same thing. This obviously
carries over to the statement which follows a few lines later where tragedy
is said to be the "imitation of *spoudaioteroi*." We may translate this as
"superior" or as "men of a higher type," but obviously to Aristotle (and
I should have thought to any man of sense) a higher type of man is a
"better" type of man! The same is true of the passage in the second chapter where Homer and Sophocles are contrasted with Aristophanes because they imitate "superior" men. Again (ch. 2): "Since those who make
imitations represent men in action, these men must be either 'superior or
inferior,' either 'better' (*beltious*) than we know them in life, or worse, or
of the same kind. For character derives, one might say, from these qualities,
and all men's characters differ in virtue (*aretê*) or vice (*kakia*)." The
words in question are here so completely identified with words of clear
moral significance that they simply cannot be emptied of moral implications when they are applied to characters, or to action (which derives its
qualities from characters) anywhere in the *Poetics* in order to make
Aristotle conform to the canons of judgment of modern commentators.

Aristotle fully realized that an art must be judged on its own premises
("correctness for a poet is not the same as for a politician"), but that
these premises were, in the case of tragedy, purely aesthetic, and therefore amoral, is a thought that simply could not have occurred to him, and
there are other passages of the *Poetics* to prove it.[8]

---

[7] At the beginning of ch. 5. Not only does Aristotle refer to the *Poetics* for a further
explanation of catharsis (see above) but he also, in *Rhetoric* 1. 11. 29 (1372a 2),
says that "the ridiculous has been sufficiently defined in the *Poetics*"; a similar passage,
Rhetoric 3. 18 (1419b 6), states that the different types of jokes were also discussed
in our treatise. It is supposed that a second book has been lost. Professor Lane-Cooper,
in *An Aristotelian Theory of Comedy* (New York, 1922) has ingeniously reconstructed
it. The evidence for a second book is carefully reviewed by A. P. McMahon in "A Lost
Book of the Poetics," *Harvard Studies in Classical Philology*, 28 (1917), pp. 1–46.
McMahon does not believe a second book was ever written.

[8] Other relevant passages are as follows:

In ch. 4 we are told that poetry developed in two directions *"according to men's
character*. The more noble-minded imitated the noble (καλας) deeds of noble men,
the more common those of inferior men. . . ." This is, of course, the customary use
of καλος in a moral at least as much as an aesthetic sense, and we are therefore not
surprised to find the first type of literature imitating τα σπονδαια. In this context the
word cannot be emptied of moral implications, however we translate it.

When we are told that poetry is σπονδαιοτερον than history (ch. 9), we may translate this "a higher thing" or a more "serious pursuit" than history, but even here
Aristotle means it is a *better* thing. It will be more beneficial in its result, make men
better (morally and in every other way).

The word is also used in the passage discussed above (ch. 25), where Aristotle is
correcting Plato's extreme rejection of evil on the stage: "We must not only look to
see if the particular words or actions are good or bad (σπουδαιον η φαυλον)" but keep
in view the circumstances, the character, etc. Here, as far as I can see, *all translators
take the words in the sense of morally good or bad, for nothing else makes sense.*

The Tragic Hero

Aristotle's remarks on the character of the tragic hero are among the most illuminating and suggestive in the book. They are extremely brief: he has just told us that the downfall of the virtuous man is not tragic; and neither is that of a complete scoundrel (ch. 13):

> We are left with a character in between the other two: a man who is not outstanding in righteousness, or in wickedness and vice, and he should fall into misfortune through some *hamartia*. He should also be famous, or prosperous, like Oedipus, Thyestes, and the noted men of such families.

And a few lines further, the best kind of plot requires an unhappy ending which must come about, not through wickedness, but "through a great *hamartia* in such a character as we have mentioned or one better rather than worse."

The requirement that the character be like ourselves makes possible the *sympatheia*, the emotional identification which is necessary if we are to feel pity or fear, for pity is defined in the *Rhetoric* (2. 8.) as:

> the kind of pain we feel at the sight of a fatal or painful evil which happens to one *who does not deserve it, an evil which we might expect to befall ourselves or one of those close to us* and when it seems near. Clearly, to feel pity a *person must think that he himself, or someone belonging to him, is liable to suffer. . . .*

Aristotle, with typical Greek realism, recognizes that tragic pity can never be completely disinterested, and it seems reasonable that we should be able to identify ourselves more closely with a character who is neither hero nor villain.

There is an apparent contradiction, however, with the earlier statement (ch. 2) that the tragic character must be better than life (this was arrived at on other grounds, namely, that tragedy was "better" than comedy), and Aristotle seems conscious of this when he adds, a few lines later in ch. 13, "a character such as we have described or better rather than worse"; and again in the passage where he says the poet must imitate the portrait painter who draws a good likeness and yet makes it "more beautiful than life" (ch. 15). At any rate it must be sufficiently like life (i.e., like ourselves) for us to feel closely akin. Nor need we be disturbed by the next requirement, that the tragic heroes must be the great ones of the earth. Aristotle is no doubt thinking of the impressiveness of the tragic stage, and until very recent times the world's dramatists have largely followed his advice. In any case, the spectator will not find this "greatness" much of an obstacle to emotional identification in the dreamland of the theater.

Hamartia

The real problem in Aristole's description of the tragic hero is the nature of *hamartia*. The word can mean mistake, error, flaw, wrongdoing, and it has been variously interpreted as "a moral flaw," "an error of judgment," or a mere "misstep."

Let us be clear, first, that Aristotle is describing the tragic character, and that the *hamartia* is in that character, not external to it, for then his actions would cease to be "probable or inevitable." It is quite possible for a man to be in such a situation that he is inevitably led into error through no fault of his own (Oedipus is a perfect example), where he is a victim of circumstances, but this merely begs the question, for it will still be the nature of his response to the circumstances that will both show his character and affect his tragedy. Aristotle does not say anywhere that the misfortune is his hero's fault, he only says that it comes about, in the play, through a *hamartia* in his character.

Granted then that the *hamartia* is in the character, is it a moral weakness or an error of judgment? Those who hold the first view believe that the hero is morally responsible for his tragedy; those who hold the second view seem to think that he is not. But are we not, here again, forcing upon Aristotle a choice between clear alternatives that are ours, not his? He does not say the hero is responsible for his tragedy or that it is his fault. All he says is that there is some flaw or weakness in the personality of the hero which brings about his tragedy. Indeed, this follows logically from his previous statement, for if the hero were flawless he would be quite perfect and no tragic hero. I do not believe that Aristotle here makes any distinction between a moral flaw and a flaw in mental judgment. Each is a flaw or weakness in the personality of the hero, either may bring about the tragedy or bring it about at that particular time; neither makes him deserve it, but either again may make it seem natural that it should come about and is therefore dramatically satisfying. Besides, if pity is to be aroused, the misfortune must be undeserved in any case. Aristotle is not concerned to fix any responsibility or blame but to see that the tragedy should seem "probable or inevitable."

This, I believe, is a good example of a seminal idea imperfectly realized and imperfectly expressed, but opening the way to such kindred notions as conflict within the personality, which is one possible kind of flaw—a lack of *sophrosyne* in the Platonic sense of integration and harmony.

Reversal and Recognition

Peripeteia or reversal (ch. 11) is a *reversal of direction or intent, not of fortune.* What is developing, or intended to develop, in one direction suddenly takes an unexpected and unintended turn. This implies many things, more than Aristotle could possibly realize; but to translate *peripeteia* by "the irony of Fate" or "the irony of events" is to falsify the thought and to destroy the simplicity of expression, the pointing straight to the root of things, which is one of the charms of the *Poetics*. True, it is often difficult to fit the simpler thought into our more complicated, and much vaguer, pattern of ideas.

So, too, with recognition. Here again Aristotle caught a glimpse of much more than he was able to formulate. It should be perfectly clear that he is thinking of recognition between persons, and all his examples are of that kind. This is completely obscured if we translate *anagnôrisis* by "discovery" or "disclosure." It is true that Aristotle himself realized that his idea was capable of much wider application when he added, almost as an afterthought: "There are, to be sure, other forms of recognition: the knowledge acquired may be of inanimate objects, indeed of anything; one may recognize that someone has, or has not, done something." But even this does not go far enough, and he immediately returns to the recognition of persons. The modern meaning of discovery is much wider, and if Aristotle had realized the implications of his own idea he would never have said that there is no recognition in the *Iliad* but that there is "throughout the *Odyssey*" (ch. 24). Every reader of the *Iliad* knows that the tragedy of Achilles comes when he "recognizes," after the death of Patroclus, that there are things in life more important than honor and personal revenge. It is a perfect example of discovery in the wider sense, but that wider sense cannot be found in Aristotle.

There are many other suggestive and illuminating ideas to be found in the *Poetics*: the overriding importance of the plot, the different types of tragedy, its six elements, the need for the poet to feel the emotions he tries to communicate, the right and wrong critical attitudes, the essential and incidental flaws, and so on. We may disagree with him, but he will often start a fruitful train of thought or a profitable discussion. His meaning, however, is in most cases clear.

phenomena present a contrast analogous to that existing between the Apollinian and the Dionysian. It was in dreams, says Lucretius, that the glorious divine figures first appeared to the souls of men; in dreams the great shaper beheld the splendid bodies of superhuman beings; and the Hellenic poet, if questioned about the mysteries of poetic inspiration, would likewise have suggested dreams and he might have given an explanation like that of Hans Sachs in the *Meistersinger:*

> The poet's task is this, my friend,
> to read his dreams and comprehend.
> The truest human fancy seems
> to be revealed to us in dreams:
> all poems and versification
> are but true dreams' interpretation.[3]

The beautiful illusion[4] of the dream worlds, in the creation of which every man is truly an artist, is the prerequisite of all plastic art, and, as we shall see, of an important part of poetry also. In our dreams we delight in the immediate understanding of figures; all forms speak to us; there is nothing unimportant or superfluous. But even when this dream reality it most intense, we still have, glimmering through it, the sensation that it is *mere appearance:* at least this is my experience, and for its frequency—indeed, normality—I could adduce many proofs, including the saying of the poets.

Philosophical men even have a presentiment that the reality in which we live and have our being is also mere appearance, and that another, quite different reality lies beneath it. Schopenhauer actually indicates as the criterion of philosophical ability the occasional ability to view men and things as mere phantoms or dream images. Thus the aesthetically sensitive man stands in the same relation to the reality of dreams as the philosopher does to the reality of existence; he is a close and willing observer, for these images afford him an interpretation of life, and by reflecting on these processes he trains himself for life.

It is not only the agreeable and friendly images that he experiences as something universally intelligible: the serious, the troubled, the sad, the gloomy, the sudden restraints, the tricks of accident, anxious expectations, in short, the whole divine comedy of life, including the inferno, also pass before him, not like mere shadows on a wall—for he lives and suffers with these scenes—and yet not without that fleeting sensation of illusion. And perhaps many will, like myself, recall how amid the dangers and terrors of dreams they have occasionally said to themselves in self-encouragement,

---

[3] Wagner's original text reads:
> Mein Freund, das grad' ist Dichters Werk,
> dass er sein Träumen deut' und merk'.
> Glaubt mir, des Menschen wahrster Wahn
> wird ihm im Traume aufgethan:
> all' Dichtkunst und Poëterei
> ist nichts als Wahrtraum-Deuterei.

[4] *Schein* has been rendered in these pages sometimes as "illusion" and sometimes as "mere appearance."

Friedrich Nietzsche

DRAMATIC REALITY:
FROM *THE BIRTH OF TRAGEDY*

We shall have gained much for the science of aesthetics, once we perceive not merely by logical inference, but with the immediate certainty of vision, that the continuous development of art is bound up with the *Apollinian* and *Dionysian* duality—just as procreation depends on the duality of the sexes, involving perpetual strife with only periodically intervening reconciliations.* The terms Dionysian and Appollinian we borrow from the Greeks, who disclose to the discerning mind the profound mysteries of their view of art, not, to be sure, in concepts, but in the intensely clear figures of their gods. Through Apollo and Dionysus, the two art deities of the Greeks, we come to recognize that in the Greek world there existed a tremendous opposition, in origin and aims,[1] between the Apollinian art of sculpture, and the nonimagistic, Dionysian art of music. These two different tendencies run parallel to each other, for the most part openly at variance; and they continually incite each other to new and more powerful births, which perpetuate an antagonism, only superficially reconciled by the common term "art"; till eventually,[2] by a metaphysical miracle of the Hellenic "will," they appear coupled with each other, and through this coupling ultimately generate an equally Dionysian and Appollinian form of art—Attic tragedy.

In order to grasp these two tendencies, let us first conceive of them as the separate art words of *dreams* and *intoxication*. These physiological

Friedrich Nietzsche (1844–1900). The noted German Philosopher is often called a Nihilist, and often called an Existentialist. His tempestuous life and works have long been subject to misunderstanding. *The Birth of Tragedy* (1872) and *The Will To Power* (1901) contain Nietzsche's thoughts on art.

* Selections from *The Birth of Tragedy*, translated by Walter Kaufmann (New York, 1967), including an "Atttempt at Self-Criticism." Reprinted by permission of Random House, Inc.

[1] In the first edition: ". . . an opposition of style: two different tendencies run parallel in it, for the most part in conflict; and they . . ." Most of the changes in the revision of 1874 are as slight as this (compare the next footnote) and therefore not indicated in the following pages. This translation, like the standard German editions, follows Nietzsche's revision.

[2] First edition: "till eventually, at the moment of the flowering of the Hellenic 'will,' they appear fused to generate together the art form of Attic tragedy."

and not without success: "It is a dream! I will dream on!" I have likewise heard of people who were able to continue one and the same dream for three and even more successive nights—facts which indicate clearly how our innermost being, our common ground, experiences dreams with profound delight and a joyous necessity.

This joyous necessity of the dream experience has been embodied by the Greeks in their Apollo: Apollo, the god of all plastic energies, is at the same time the soothsaying god. He, who (as the etymology of the name indicates) is the "shining one,"[5] the deity of light, is also ruler over the beautiful illusion of the inner world of fantasy. The higher truth, the perfection of these states in contrast to the incompletely intelligible everyday world, this deep consciousness of nature, healing and helping in sleep and dreams, is at the same time the symbolical analogue of the soothsaying faculty and of the arts generally, which make life possible and worth living. But we must also include in our image of Apollo that delicate boundary which the dream image must not overstep lest it have a pathological effect (in which case mere appearance would deceive us as if it were crude reality). We must keep in mind that measured restraint, that freedom from the wilder emotions, that calm of the sculptor god. His eye must be "sunlike," as befits his origin; even when it is angry and distempered it is still hallowed by beautiful illusion. And so, in one sense, we might apply to Apollo the words of Schopenhauer when he speaks of the man wrapped in the veil of *māyā*[6] (*Welt als Wille und Vorstellung*, I, p. 416[7]): "Just as in a stormy sea that, unbounded in all directions, raises and drops mountainous waves, howling, a sailor sits in a boat and trusts in his frail bark: so in the midst of a world of torments the individual human being sits quietly, supported by and trusting in the *principium individuationis*."[8] In fact, we might say of Apollo that in him the unshaken faith in this *principium* and the calm repose of the man wrapped up in it receive their most sublime expression; and we might call Appollo himself the glorious divine image of the *principium individuationis*, through whose gestures and eyes all the joy and wisdom of "illusion," together with its beauty, speak to us.

In the same work Schopenhauer has depicted for us the tremendous *terror* which seizes man when he is suddenly dumfounded by the cognitive form of phenomena because the principle of sufficient reason, in some one of its manifestations, seems to suffer an exception. If we add to this terror the blissful ecstasy that wells from the innermost depths of man, indeed

[5] *Der "Scheinende."* The German words for illusion and appearance are *Schein* and *Erscheinung.*

[6] A Sanskrit word usually translated as illusion. For detailed discussions see, e.g., *A Source Book of Indian Philosophy*, ed. S. Radhakrishnan and Charles Moore (Princeton, N.J., Princeton University Press, 1957); Heinrich Zimmer, *Philosophies of India*, ed. Joseph Campbell (New York, Meridian Books, 1956); and Helmuth von Glasenapp, *Die Philosophie der Inder* (Stuttgart, Kröner, 1949), consulting the indices.

[7] This reference, like subsequent references to the same work, is Nietzsche's own and refers to the edition of 1873 edited by Julius Frauenstädt—still one of the standard editions of Schopenhauer's works.

[8] Principle of individuation.

of nature, at this collapse of the *principium individuationis*, we steal a
glimpse into the nature of the *Dionysian*, which is brought home to us
most intimately by the analogy of intoxication.

Either under the influence of the narcotic draught, of which the songs
of all primitive men and peoples speak, or with the potent coming of
spring that penetrates all nature with joy, these Dionysian emotions awake,
and as they grow in intensity everything subjective vanishes into complete
self-forgetfulness. In the German Middle Ages, too, singing and dancing
crowds, ever increasing in number, whirled themselves from place to place
under this same Dionysian impulse. In these dancers of St. John and St.
Vitus, we rediscover the Bacchic choruses of the Greeks, with their prehistory in Asia Minor, as far back as Babylon and the orgiastic Sacaea.[9]
There are some who, from obtuseness or lack of experience, turn away
from such phenomena as from "folk-diseases," with contempt or pity born
of the consciousness of their own "healthy-mindedness." But of course
such poor wretches have no idea how corpselike and ghostly their so-called
"healthy-mindedness" looks when the glowing life of the Dionysian revelers
roars past them.

Under the charm of the Dionysian not only is the union between man
and man reaffirmed, but nature which has become alienated, hostile, or
subjugated, celebrates once more her reconciliation with her lost son,[10]
man. Freely, earth proffers her gifts, and peacefully the beasts of prey of
the rocks and desert approach. The chariot of Dionysus is covered with
flowers and garlands; panthers and tigers walk under its yoke. Transform
Beethoven's "Hymn to Joy" into a painting; let your imagination conceive
the multitudes bowing to the dust, awestruck—then you will approach the
Dionysian. Now the slave is a free man; now all the rigid, hostile barriers
that necessity, caprice, or "impudent convention"[11] have fixed between
man and man are broken. Now, with the gospel of universal harmony,
each one feels himself not only united, reconciled, and fused with his
neighbor, but as one with him, as if the veil of *māyā* had been torn aside
and were now merely fluttering in tatters before the mysterious primordial
unity.

In song and in dance man expresses himself as a member of a higher
community; he has forgotten how to walk and speak and is on the way
toward flying into the air, dancing. His very gestures express enchantment.
Just as the animals now talk, and the earth yields milk and honey, supernatural sounds emanate from him, too: he feels himself a god, he himself
now walks about enchanted, in ecstasy, like the gods he saw walking in
his dreams. He is no longer an artist, he has become a work of art: in these
paroxysms of intoxication the artistic power of all nature reveals itself to

---

[9] A Babylonian festival that lasted five days and was marked by general license. During
this time slaves are said to have ruled their masters, and a criminal was given all royal
rights before he was put to death at the end of the festival. For references, see, e.g.,
The Oxford Classical Dictionary.

[10] In German, "the prodigal son" is *der verlorene Sohn* (the lost son).

[11] An allusion to Friedrich Schiller's hymn *An die Freude* (to joy), used by Beethoven
in the final movement of his Ninth Symphony.

the highest gratification of the primordial unity. The noblest clay, the most costly marble, man, is here kneaded and cut, and to the sound of the chisel strokes of the Dionysian world-artist rings out the cry of the Eleusinian mysteries: "Do you prostrate yourselves, millions? Do you sense your Maker, world?"[12]

Thus far we have considered the Apollinian and its opposite, the Dionysian, as artistic energies which burst forth from nature herself, *without the mediation of the human artist*—energies in which nature's art impulses are satisfied in the most immediate and direct way—first in the image world of dreams, whose completeness is not dependent upon the intellectual attitude or the artistic culture of any single being; and then as intoxicated reality, which likewise does not heed the single unit, but even seeks to destroy the individual and redeem him by a mystic feeling of oneness. With reference to these immediate art-states of nature, every artist is an "imitator," that is to say, either an Apollinian artist in dreams, or a Dionysian artist in ecstasies, or finally—as for example in Greek tragedy—at once artist in both dreams and ecstasies; so we may perhaps picture him sinking down in his Dionysian intoxication and mystical self-abnegation, alone and apart from the singing revelers, and we may imagine how, through Apollinian dream-inspiration, his own state, i.e., his oneness with the inmost ground of the world, is revealed to him in a *symbolical dream image.*

So much for these general premises and contrasts. Let us now approach the *Greeks* in order to learn how highly these *art impulses of nature* were developed in them. Thus we shall be in a position to understand and appreciate more deeply that relation of the Greek artist to his archetypes which is, according to the Aristotelian expression, "the imitation of nature." In spite of all the dream literature and the numerous dream anecdotes of the Greeks, we can speak of their *dreams* only conjecturally, though with reasonable assurance. If we consider the incredibly precise and unerring plastic power of their eyes, together with their vivid, frank delight in colors, we can hardly refrain from assuming even for their dreams (to the shame of all those born later) a certain logic of line and contour, colors and groups, a certain pictorial sequence reminding us of their finest bas-reliefs whose perfection would certainly justify us, if a comparison were possible, in designating the dreaming Greeks as Homers and Homer as a dreaming Greek—in a deeper sense than that in which modern man, speaking of his dreams, ventures to compare himself with Shakespeare.

On the other hand, we need not conjecture regarding the immense gap which separates the *Dionysian Greek* from the Dionysian barbarian. From all quarters of the ancient world—to say nothing here of the modern—from Rome to Babylon, we can point to the existence of Dionysian festivals, types which bear, at best, the same relation to the Greek festivals which the bearded satyr, who borrowed his name and attributes from the goat,

---

[12] Quotation from Schiller's hymn.

bears to Dionysus himself. In nearly every case these festivals centered in extravagant sexual licentiousness, whose waves overwhelmed all family life and its venerable traditions; the most savage natural instincts were unleashed, including even that horrible mixture of sensuality and cruelty which has always seemed to me to be the real "witches' brew." For some time, however, the Greeks were apparently perfectly insulated and guarded against the feverish excitements of these festivals, though knowledge of them must have come to Greece on all the routes of land and sea; for the figure of Apollo, rising full of pride, held out the Gorgon's head to this grotesquely uncouth Dionysian power—and really could not have countered any more dangerous force. It is in Doric art that this majestically rejecting attitude of Apollo is immortalized.

The opposition between Apollo and Dionysus became more hazardous and even impossible, when similar impulses finally burst forth from the deepest roots of the Hellenic nature and made a path for themselves: the Delphic god, by a seasonably effected reconciliation, now contented himself with taking the destructive weapons from the hands of his powerful antagonist. This reconciliation is the most important moment in the history of the Greek cult: wherever we turn we note the revolutions resulting from this event. The two antagonists were reconciled; the boundary lines to be observed henceforth by each were sharply defined, and there was to be a periodical exchange of gifts of esteem. At bottom, however, the chasm was not bridged over. But if we observe how, under the pressure of this treaty of peace, the Dionysian power revealed itself, we shall now recognize in the Dionysian orgies of the Greeks, as compared with the Babylonian Sacaea with their reversion of man to the tiger and the ape, the significance of festivals of world redemption and days of transfiguration. It is with them that nature for the first time attains her artistic jubilee; it is with them that the destruction of the *principium individuationis* for the first time becomes an artistic phenomenon.

The horrible "witches' brew" of sensuality and cruelty becomes ineffective; only the curious blending and duality in the emotions of the Dionysian revelers remind us—as medicines remind us of deadly poisons—of the phenomenon that pain begets joy, that ecstasy may wring sounds of agony from us. At the very climax of joy there sounds a cry of horror or a yearning lamentation for an irretrievable loss. In these Greek festivals, nature seems to reveal a sentimental[13] trait; it is as if she were heaving a sigh at her dismemberment into individuals. The song and pantomime of such dually-minded revelers was something new and unheard-of in the Homeric-Greek world; and the Dionysian *music* in particular excited awe and terror. If music, as it would seem, had been known previously as an Apollinian art, it was so, strictly speaking, only as the wave beat of rhythm, whose formative power was developed for the representation of Appollian states. The music of Apollo was Doric architectonics in tones, but in tones that were merely suggestive, such as those of the cithara. The very element which

---

[13] *Sentimentalisch* (not *sentimental*): an allusion to Schiller's influential contrast of *naïve* (Goethean) poetry with his own *sentimentalische Dichtung*.

forms the essence of Dionysian music (and hence of music in general) is carefully excluded as un-Apollinian—namely, the emotional power of the tone, the uniform flow of the melody, and the utterly incomparable world of harmony. In the Dionysian dithyramb man is incited to the greatest exaltation of all his symbolic faculties; something never before experienced struggles for utterance—the annihilation of the viel of *māyā*, oneness as the soul of the race and of nature iself. The essence of nature is now to be expressed symbolically; we need a new world of symbols; and the entire symbolism of the body is called into play, not the mere symbolism of the lips, face, and speech but the whole pantomine of dancing, forcing every member into rhythmic movement. Then the other symbolic powers suddenly press forward, particularly those of music, in rhythmics, dynamics, and harmony. To grasp this collective release of all the symbolic powers, man must have already attained that height of self-abnegation which seeks to express itself symbolically through all these powers—and so the dithyrambic votary of Dionysus is understood only by his peers. With what astonishment must the Apollinian Greek have beheld him! With an astonishment that was all the greater the more it was mingled with the shuddering suspicion that all this was actually not so very alien to him after all, in fact, that it was only his Apollinian consciousness which, like a veil, hid this Dionysian world from his vision.

To understand this, it becomes necessary to level the artistic structure of the *Apollinian culture*, as it were, stone by stone, till the foundations on which it rests become visible. First of all we see the glorious *Olympian* figures of the gods, standing on the gables of this structure. Their deeds, pictured in brilliant reliefs, adorn its friezes. We must not be misled by the fact that Apollo stands side by side with the others as an individual deity, without any claim to priority of rank. For the same impulse that embodied itself in Apollo gave birth to this entire Olympian world, and in this sense Apollo is its father. What terrific need was it that could produce such an illustrious company of Olympian beings?

Whoever approaches these Olympians with another religion in his heart, searching among them for moral elevation, even for sanctity, for disincarnate spirituality, for charity and benevolence, will soon be forced to turn his back on them, discouraged and disappointed. For there is nothing here that suggests asceticism, spirituality, or duty. We hear nothing but the accents of an exuberant, triumphant life in which all things, whether good or evil, are deified.[14] And so the spectator may stand quite bewildered before this fantastic excess of life, asking himself by virtue of what magic potion these high-spirited men could have found life so enjoyable that, wherever they turned, their eyes beheld the smile of Helen, the ideal picture of their own existence, "floating in sweet sensuality." But to this spectator, who has already turned his back, we must say: "Do not go away,

[14] This presage of the later coinage "beyond good and evil" is lost when *böse* is mistranslated as "bad" instead of "evil."

but stay and hear what Greek folk wisdom has to say of this very life, which with such inexplicable gaiety unfolds itself before your eyes.

"There is an ancient story that King Midas hunted in the forest a long time for the wise Silenus, the companion of Dionysus, without capturing him. When Silenus at last fell into his hands, the king asked what was the best and most desirable of all things for man. Fixed and immovable, the demigod said not a word, till at last, urged by the king, he gave a shrill laugh and broke out into these words: 'Oh, wretched ephemeral race, children of chance and misery, why do you compel me to tell you what it would be most expedient for you not to hear? What is best of all is utterly beyond your reach: not to be born, not to *be*, to be *nothing*. But the second best for you is—to die soon.' "[15]

How is the world of the Olympian gods related to this folk wisdom? Even as the rapturous vision of the tortured martyr to his suffering.

Now it is as if the Olympian magic mountain[16] had opened before us and revealed its roots to us. The Greek knew and felt the terror and horror of existence. That he might endure this terror at all, he had to interpose between himself and life the radiant dream-birth of the Olympians. That overwhelming dismay in the face of the titanic powers of nature, the Moira[17] enthroned inexorably over all knowledge, the vulture of the great lover of mankind, Prometheus, the terrible fate of the wise Oedipus, the family curse of the Atridae which drove Orestes to matricide: in short, that entire philosophy of the sylvan god, with its mythical exemplars, which caused the downfall of the melancholy Etruscans—all this was again and again overcome by the Greeks with the aid of the Olympian *middle world* of art; or at any rate it was veiled and withdrawn from sight. It was in order to be able to live that the Greeks had to create these gods from a most profound need. Perhaps we may picture the process to ourselves somewhat as follows: out of the original Titanic divine order of terror, the Olympian divine order of joy gradually evolved through the Apollinian impulse toward beauty, just as roses burst from thorny bushes. How else could this people, so sensitive, so vehement in its desires, so singularly capable of *suffering*, have endured existence, if it had not been revealed to them in their gods, surrounded with a higher glory?

The same impulse which calls art into being, as the complement and consummation of existence, seducing one to a continuation of life, was also the cause of the Olympian world which the Hellenic "will" made use of as a transfiguring mirror. Thus do the gods justify the life of man: they themselves live it—the only satisfactory theodicy! Existence under the bright sunshine of such gods is regarded as desirable in itself, and the real pain of Homeric men is caused by parting from it, especially by early parting: so that now, reversing the wisdom of Silenus, we might say of the Greeks that "to die soon is worst of all for them, the next worst—to die at all." Once heard, it will ring out again; do not forget the lament of

---

[15] Cf. Sophocles, *Oedipus at Colonus*, lines 1224ff.
[16] *Zauberberg*, as in the title of Thomas Mann's novel.
[17] Fate.

the short-lived Achilles, mourning the leaflike change and vicissitudes of the race of men and the decline of the heroic age. It is not unworthy of the greatest hero to long for a continuation of life, even though he live as a day laborer.[18] At the Apollinian stage of development, the "will" longs so vehemently for this existence, the Homeric man feels himself so completely at one with it, that lamentation itself becomes a song of praise.

Here we should note that this harmony which is contemplated with such longing by modern man, in fact, this oneness of man with nature (for which Schiller introduced the technical term "naïve"), is by no means a simple condition that comes into being naturally and as if inevitably. It is not a condition that, like a terrestrial paradise, *must* necessarily be found at the gate of every culture. Only a romantic age could believe this, an age which conceived of the artist in terms of Rousseau's *Emile* and imagined that in Homer it had found such an artist Emile, reared at the bosom of nature. Where we encounter the "naïve" in art, we should recognize the highest effect of Apollinian culture—which always must first overthrow an empire of Titans and slay monsters, and which must have triumphed over an abysmal and terrifying view of the world and the keenest susceptibility to suffering through recourse to the most forceful and pleasurable illusions. But how rarely is the naïve attained—that consummate immersion in the beauty of mere appearance! How unutterably sublime is *Homer* therefore, who, as an individual being, bears the same relation to this Apollinian folk culture as the individual dream artist does to the dream faculty of the people and of nature in general.

The Homeric "naïveté" can be understood only as the complete victory of Apollinian illusion: this is one of those illusions which nature so frequently employs to achieve her own ends. The true goal is veiled by a phantasm: and while we stretch out our hands for the latter, nature attains the former by means of our hands for the latter, nature attains the former by means of our illusion. In the Greeks the "will" wished to contemplate itself in the transfiguration of genius and the world of art; in order to glorify themselves, its creatures had to feel themselves worthy of glory; they had to behold themselves again in a higher sphere, without this perfect world of contemplation acting as a command or a reproach. This is the sphere of beauty, in which they saw their mirror images, the Olympians. With this mirroring of beauty the Hellenic will combated its artistically correlative talent for suffering and for the wisdom of suffering—and, as a monument of its victory, we have Homer, the naïve artist.

Now the dream analogy may throw some light on the naïve artist. Let us imagine the dreamer: in the midst of the illusion of the dream world and without disturbing it, he calls out to himself: "It is a dream, I will dream on." What must we infer? That he experiences a deep inner joy in dream contemplation; on the other hand, to be at all able to dream with this inner joy in contemplation, he must have completely lost sight of the

[18] An allusion to Homer's *Odyssey*, XI, lines 489ff.

waking reality and its ominous obtrusiveness. Guided by the dream-reading Apollo, we may interpret all these phenomena in roughly this way.

Though it is certain that of the two halves of our existence, the waking and the dreaming states, the former appeals to us as infinitely preferable, more important, excellent, and worthy of being lived, indeed, as that which alone is lived—yet in relation to that mysterious ground of our being of which we are the phenomena, I should, paradoxical as it may seem, maintain the very opposite estimate of the value of dreams. For the more clearly I perceive in nature those omnipotent art impulses, and in them an ardent longing for illusion, for redemption through illusion, the more I feel myself impelled to the metaphysical assumption that the truly existent primal unity, eternally suffering and contradictory, also needs the rapturous vision, the pleasurable illusion, for its continuous redemption. And we, completely wrapped up in this illusion and composed of it, are compelled to consider this illusion as the truly nonexistent—i.e., as a perpetual becoming in time, space, and causality—in other words, as empirical reality. If, for the moment, we do not consider the question of our own "reality," if we conceive of our empirical existence, and of that of the world in general, as a continuously manifested representation of the primal unity, we shall then have to look upon the dream as a *mere appearance of mere appearance*, hence as a still higher appeasement of the primordial desire for mere appearance. And that is why the innermost heart of nature feels that ineffable joy in the naïve artist and the naïve work of art, which is likewise only "mere appearance of mere appearance."

In a symbolic painting, *Raphael*, himself one of these immortal "naïve" ones, has represented for us this demotion of appearance to the level of mere appearance, the primitive process of the naïve artist and of Apollinian culture. In his *Transfiguration*, the lower half of the picture, with the possessed boy, the despairing bearers, the bewildered, terrified disciples, shows us the reflection of suffering, primal and eternal, the sole ground of the world: the "mere appearance" here is the reflection of eternal contradiction, the father of things. From this mere appearance arises, like ambrosial vapor, a new visionary world of mere appearances, invisible to those wrapped in the first appearance—a radiant floating in purest bliss, a serene contemplation beaming from wide-open eyes. Here we have presented, in the most sublime artistic symbolism, that Apollinian world of beauty and its substratum, the terrible wisdom of Silenus; and intuitively we comprehend their necessary interdependence. Apollo, however, again appears to us the apotheosis of the *principium individuationis*, in which alone is consummated the perpetually attained goal of the primal unity, its redemption through mere appearance. With his sublime gestures, he shows us how necessary is the entire world of suffering, that by means of it the individual may be impelled to realize the redeeming vision, and then, sunk in contemplation of it, sit quietly in his tossing bark, amid the waves.

If we conceive of it all as imperative and mandatory, this apotheosis of individuation knows but one law—the individual, i.e., the delimiting of the boundaries of the individual, *measure* in the Helenic sense. Apollo, as ethical deity, exacts measure of his disciples, and, to be able to maintain it, he requires self-knowledge. And so, side by side with the aesthetic necessity for beauty, there occur the demands "know theyself" and "nothing in excess"; consequently overweening pride and excess are regarded as the truly hostile demons of the non-Apollinian sphere, hence as characteristics of the pre-Apollinian age—that of the Titans; and of the extra-Apollinian world—that of the barbarians. Because of his titanic love for man, Prometheus must be torn to pieces by vultures; because of his excessive wisdom, which could solve the riddle of the Sphinx, Oedipus must be plunged into a bewildering vortex of crime. Thus did the Delphic god interpret the Greek past.

The effects wrought by the *Dionysian* also seemed "titanic" and "barbaric" to the Apollinian Greek; while at the same time he could not conceal from himself that he, too, was inwardly related to these overthrown Titans and heroes. Indeed, he had to recognize even more than this: despite all its beauty and moderation, his entire existence rested on a hidden substratum of suffering and of knowledge, revealed to him by the Dionysian. And behold: Apollo could not live without Dionysus! The "titanic" and the "barbaric" were in the last analysis as necessary as the Apollinian.

And now let us imagine how into this world, built on mere appearance and moderation and artificially dammed up, there penetrated, in tones ever more bewitching and alluring, the ecstatic sound of the Dionysian festival; how in these strains all of nature's *excess* in pleasure, grief, and knowledge became audible, even in piercing shrieks; and let us ask ourselves what the psalmodizing artist of Apollo, with his phantom harp-sound, could mean in the face of this demonic folk-song! The muses of the arts of "illusion" paled before an art that, in its intoxication, spoke the truth. The wisdom of Silenus cried "Woe! woe!" to the serene Olympians. The indiviual, with all his restraint and proportion, succumbed to the self-oblivion of the Dionysian states, forgetting the precepts of Apollo. *Excess* revealed itself as truth. Contradiction, the bliss born of pain, spoke out from the very heart of nature. And so, wherever the Dionysian prevailed, the Apollinian was checked and destroyed. But, on the other hand, it is equally certain that, wherever the first Dionysian onslaught was successfully withstood, the authority and majesty of the Delphic god exhibited itself as more rigid and menacing than ever. For to me the *Doric* state[19] and Doric art are explicable only as a permanent military encampment of the Apollinian. Only incessant resistance to the titanic-barbaric nature of the Dionysian could account for the long survival of an art so defiantly prim and so encompassed with bulwarks, a training so warlike and rigorous, and a political structure so cruel and relentless.

Up to this point we have simply enlarged upon the observation made at the beginning of this essay: that the Dionysian and the Apollinian, in new

[19] Sparta.

births ever following and mutually augmenting one another, controlled the Hellenic genius; that out of the age of "bronze," with its wars of the Titans and its rigorous folk philosophy, the Homeric world developed under the sway of the Apollinian impulse to beauty; that this "naïve" splendor was again overwhelmed by the influx of the Dionysian; and that against this new power the Apollinian rose to the austere majesty of Doric art and the Doric view of the world. If amid the strife to these two hostile principles, the older Hellenic history thus falls into four great periods of art, we are now impelled to inquire after the final goal of these developments and processes, lest perchance we should regard the last-attained period, the period of Doric art, as the climax and aim of these artistic impulses. And here the sublime and celebrated art of *Attic tragedy* and the dramatic dithyramb presents itself as the common goal of both these tendencies whose mysterious union, after many and long precursory struggles, found glorious consummation in this child—at once Antigone and Cassandra.[20]

We must now avail ourselves of all the principles of art considered so far, in order to find our way through the labyrinth, as we must call it, of *the origin of Greek tragedy*. I do not think I am unreasonable in saying that the problem of this origin has as yet not even been seriously posed, to say nothing of solved, however often the ragged tatters of ancient tradition have been sewn together in various combinations and torn apart again. This tradition tells us quite unequivocally *that tragedy arose from the tragic chorus*, and was originally only chorus and nothing but chorus. Hence we consider it our duty to look into the heart of this tragic chorus as the real proto-drama, without resting satisfied with such arty clichés as that the chorus is the "ideal spectator" or that it represents the people in contrast to the aristocratic region of the scene.

. . .

It is indeed an "ideal" domain, as Schiller correctly perceived, in which the Greek satyr chorus, the chorus of primitive tragedy, was wont to dwell. It is a domain raised high above the actual paths of mortals. For this chorus the Greek built up the scaffolding of a fictitious *natural state* and on it placed fictitious *natural beings*. On this foundation tragedy developed and so, of course, it could dispense from the beginning with a painstaking portrayal of reality. Yet it is no arbitrary world placed by whim between heaven and earth; rather it is a world with the same reality and credibility that Olympus with its inhabitants possessed for the believing Hellene. The satyr, as the Dionysian chorist, lives in a religiously acknowledged reality under the sanction of myth and cult. That tragedy should begin with him, that he should be the voice of the Dionysian wisdom of tragedy, is just

---

[20] In footnote 32 of his first polemic (1872) Wilamowitz said: "Whoever explains these last words, to which Mephistopheles' remark about the witch's arithmetic [Goethe's *Faust*, lines 2565–66] applies, receives a suitable reward from me." It would seem that Sophocles' Antigone is here seen as representative of the Apollinian, while Aeschylus' Cassandra (in *Agamemnon*) is associated with the Dionysian.

as strange a phenomenon for us as the general derivation of tragedy form the chorus.

Perhaps we shall have a point of departure for our inquiry if I put forward the proposition that the satyr, the fictitious natural being, bears the same relation to the man of culture that Dionysian music bears to civilization. Concerning the latter, Richard Wagner says that it is nullified[21] by music just as lamplight is nullified by the light of day. Similarly, I believe, the Greek man of culture felt himself nullified in the presence of the satyric chorus; and this is the most immediate effect of the Dionysian tragedy, that the state and society and, quite generally, the gulfs between man and man give way to an overwhelming feeling of unity leading back to the very heart of nature. The metaphysical comfort—with which, I am suggesting even now, every true tragedy leaves us—that life is at the bottom of things, despite all the changes of appearances, indestructibly powerful and pleasurable—this comfort appears in incarnate clarity in the chorus of satyrs, a chorus of natural beings who live ineradicably, as it were, behind all civilization and remain eternally the same, despite the changes of generations and of the history of nations.

With this chorus the profound Hellene, uniquely susceptible to the tenderest and deepest suffering, comforts himself, having looked boldly right into the terrible destructiveness of so-called world history as well as the cruelty of nature, and being in danger of longing for a Buddhistic negation of the will.[22] Art saves him, and through art—life.

For the rapture of the Dionysian state with its annihilation of the ordinary bounds and limits of existence contains, while it lasts, a *lethargic* element in which all personal experiences of the past become immersed. This chasm of oblivion separates the worlds of everyday reality and of Dionysian reality. But as soon as this everyday reality re-enters consciousness, it is experienced as such, with nausea: an ascetic, will-negating mood is the fruit of these states.

In this sense the Dionysian man resembles Hamlet: both have once looked truly into the essence of things, they have *gained knowledge,* and nausea inhibits action; for their action could not change anything in the eternal nature of things; they feel it to be ridiculous or humiliating that they should be asked to set right a world that is out of joint. Knowledge kills action; action requires the veils of illusion: that is the doctrine of Hamlet, not that cheap wisdom of Jack the Dreamer who reflects too much and, as it were, from an excess of possibilities does not get around to action. Not reflection, no—true knowledge, an insight into the horrible truth, outweighs any motive for action, both in Hamlet and in the Dionysian man.

---

[21] *Aufgehoben:* one of Hegel's favorite words, which can also mean lifted up or preserved.

[22] Here Nietzsche's emancipation from Schopenhauer becomes evident, and their difference from each other concerns the central subject of the whole book: the significance of tragedy. Nietzsche writes about tragedy as the great life-affirming alternative to Schopenhauer's negation of the will. One can be as honest and free of optimistic illusions as Schopenhauer was, and still celebrate life as fundamentally powerful and pleasurable as the Greeks did.

Now no comfort avails any more; longing transcends a world after death, even the gods; existence is negated along with its glittering reflection in the gods or in an immortal beyond. Conscious of the truth he has once seen, man now sees everywhere only the horror or absurdity of existence; now he understands what is symbolic in Ophelia's fate; now he understands the wisdom of the sylvan god, Silenus: he is nauseated.

Here, when the danger to his will is greatest, *art* approaches as a saving sorceress, expert at healing. She alone knows how to turn these nauseous thoughts about the horror or absurdity of existence into notions with which one can live: these are the *sublime* as the artistic taming of the horrible, and the *comic* as the artistic discharge of the nausea of absurdity. The satyr chorus of the dithyramb is the saving deed of Greek art; faced with the intermediary world of these Dionysian companions, the feelings described here exhausted themselves.[23]

The satyr, like the idyllic shepherd of more recent times, is the offspring of a longing for the primitive and the natural; but how firmly and fearlessly the Greek embraced the man of the woods, and how timorously and mawkishly modern man dallied with the flattering image of a sentimental, flute-playing, tender shepherd! Nature, as yet unchanged by knowledge, with the bolts of culture still unbroken—that is what the Greek saw in his satyr who nevertheless was not a mere ape. On the contrary, the satyr was the archetype of man, the embodiment of his highest and most intense emotions, the ecstatic reveler enraptured by the proximity of his god, the sympathetic companion in whom the suffering of the god is repeated, one who proclaims wisdom from the very heart of nature, a symbol of the sexual omnipotence of nature which the Greeks used to contemplate with reverent wonder.

The satyr was something sublime and divine: thus he had to appear to the painfully broken vision of Dionysian man. The contrived shepherd in his dress-ups would have offended him: on the unconcealed and vigorously magnificent characters of nature, his eye rested with sublime satisfaction; here the true human being was disclosed, the bearded satyr jubilating to his god. Confronted with him, the man of culture shriveled into a mendacious caricature.

Schiller is right about these origins of tragic art, too: the chorus is a living wall against the assaults of reality because it—the satyr chorus—represents existence more truthfully, really, and completely than the man of culture does who ordinarily considers himself as the only reality. The sphere of poetry does not lie outside the world as a fantastic impossibility spawned by a poet's brain: it desires to be just the opposite, the unvar-

---

[23] Having finally broken loose from Schopenhauer, Nietzsche for the first time shows the brilliancy of his own genius. It is doubtful whether anyone before him had illuminated *Hamlet* so extensively in so few words: the passage invites comparison with Freuds great footnote on *Hamlet* in the first edition of *Die Traumdeutung* (interpretation of dreams), 1900. Even more obviously, the last three paragraphs invite comparison with existentialist literature, notably, but by no means only, Sartre's *La Nausée* (1938).

nished expression of the truth, and must precisely for that reason discard the mendacious finery of that alleged reality of the man of culture.

The contrast between this real truth of nature and the lie of culture that poses as if it were the only reality is similar to that between the eternal core of things, the thing-in-itself, and the whole world of appearances:[24] just as tragedy, with its metaphysical comfort, points to the eternal life of this core of existence which abides through the perpetual destruction of appearances, the symbolism of the satyr chorus proclaims this primordial relationship between the thing-in-itself and appearance.[25] The idyllic shepherd of modern man is merely a counterfeit of the sum of cultural illusions that are allegedly nature; the Dionysian Greek wants truth and nature in their most forceful form—and sees himself changed, as by magic, into a satyr.

· · ·

Such magic transformation is the presupposition of all dramatic art. In this magic transformation the Dionysian reveler sees himself as a satyr, *and as a satyr, in turn, he sees the god*, which means that in his metamorphosis he beholds another vision outside himself, as the Apollinian complement of his own state. With this new vision the drama is complete.

In the light of this insight we must understand Greek tragedy as the Dionysian chorus which ever anew discharges itself in an Apollinian world of images. Thus the choral parts with which tragedy is interlaced are, as it were, the womb that gave birth to the whole of the so-called dialogue, that is, the entire world of the stage, the real drama. In several successive discharges this primal ground of tragedy radiates this vision of the drama which is by all means a dream apparition and to that extent epic in nature; but on the other hand, being the objectification of a Dionysian state, it represents not Apollinian redemption through mere appearance but, on the contrary, the shattering of the individual and his fusion with primal being. Thus the drama is the Dionysian embodiment of Dionysian insights and effects and thereby separated, as by a tremendous chasm, from the epic.

· · ·

The tradition is undisputed that Greek tragedy in its earliest form had for its sole theme the sufferings of Dionysus and that for a long time the only stage hero was Dionysus himself. But it may be claimed with equal confidence that until Euripides, Dionysus never ceased to be the tragic hero; that all the celebrated figures of the Greek stage—Prometheus, Oedipus, etc.—are mere masks of this original hero, Dionysus. That behind all these masks there is a deity, that is one essential reason for the typical "ideality" of these famous figures which has caused so much astonishment. Somebody, I do not know who, has claimed that all individuals, taken as individuals, are comic and hence untragic—from which it would follow that the Greeks simply *could* not suffer individuals on the tragic stage. In fact, this is what they seem to have felt; and the Platonic distinction and

---

[24] The word translated as "appearances" in this passage is *Erscheinungen*.
[25] Here Nietzsche returns to Schopenhauer's perspective.

evaluation of the "idea" and the "idol," the mere image, is very deeply rooted in the Hellenic character.

Using Plato's terms we should have to speak of the tragic figures of the Hellenic stage somewhat as follows: the one truly real Dionysus appears in a variety of forms, in the mask of a fighting hero, and entangled, as it were, in the net of the individual will. The god who appears talks and acts so as to resemble an erring, striving, suffering individual. That he *appears* at all with such epic precision and clarity is the work of the dream-interpreter, Apollo, who through this symbolic appearance interprets to the chorus its Dionysian state. In truth, however, the hero is the suffering Dionysus of the Mysteries, the god experiencing in himself the agonies of individuation, of whom wonderful myths tell that as a boy he was torn to pieces by the Titans and now is worshiped in this state as Zagreus. Thus it is intimated that this dismemberment, the properly Dionysian *suffering*, is like a transformation into air, water, earth, and fire, that we are therefore to regard the state of individuation as the origin and primal cause of all suffering, as something objectionable in itself. From the smile of this Dionysus sprang the Olympian gods, from his tears sprang man. In this existence as a dismembered god, Dionysus possesses the dual nature of a cruel, barbarized demon and a mild, gentle ruler. But the hope of the epopts[26] looked toward a rebirth of Dionysus, which we must now dimly conceive as the end of individuation. It was for this coming third Dionysus that the epopts' roaring hymns of joy resounded. And it is this hope alone that casts a gleam of joy upon the features of a world torn asunder and shattered into individuals; this is symbolized in the myth of Demeter, sunk in eternal sorrow, who *rejoices* again for the first time when told that she may *once more* give birth to Dionysus. This view of things already provides us with all the elements of a profound and pessimistic view of the world, together with the *mystery doctrine of tragedy*: the fundamental knowledge of the oneness of everything existent, the conception of individuation as the primal cause of evil, and of art as the joyous hope that the spell of individuation may be broken in augury of a restored oneness.

We have already suggested that the Homeric epos is the poem of Olympian culture, in which this culture has sung its own song of victory over the terrors of the war of the Titans. Under the predominating influence of tragic poetry, these Homeric myths are now born anew; and this metempsychosis reveals that in the meantime the Olympian culture also has been conquered by a still more profound view of the world. The defiant Titan Prometheus has announced to his Olympian tormentor that some day the greatest danger will menace his rule, unless Zeus should enter into an alliance with him in time. In Aeschylus we recognize how the terrified Zeus, fearful of his end, allies himself with the Titan. Thus the former age of the Titans is once more recovered from Tartarus and brought to the light.

The philosophy of wild and naked nature beholds with the frank, un-

---

[26] Those initiated into the mysteries.

dissembling gaze of truth the myths of the Homeric world as they dance past: they turn pale, they tremble under the piercing glance of this goddess[27]—till the powerful fist of the Dionysian artist forces them into the service of the new deity. Dionysian truth takes over the entire domain of myth as the symbolism of *its* knowledge which it makes known partly in the public cult of tragedy and partly in the secret celebrations of dramatic mysteries, but always in the old mythical garb.

.   .   .

Let us array ourselves in the armor of the insights we have acquired. In contrast to all those who are intent on deriving the arts from one exclusive principle, as the necessary vital source of every work of art, I shall keep my eyes fixed on the two artistic deities of the Greeks, Apollo and Dionysus, and recognize in them the living and conspicuous representatives of *two* worlds of art differing in their intrinsic essence and in their highest aims. I see Apollo as the transfiguring genius of the *principium individuationis* through which alone the redemption in illusion is truly to be obtained; while by the mystical triumphant cry of Dionysus the spell of individuation is broken, and the way lies open to the Mothers of Being,[28] to the innermost heart of things. This extraordinary contrast, which stretches like a yawning gulf between plastic art as the Apollinian, and music as the Dionysian art,[29] has revealed itself to only one of the great thinkers, to such an extent that, even without this clue to the symbolism of the Hellenic divinities, he conceded to music a character and an origin different from all the other arts, because, unlike them, it is not a copy of the phenomenon, but an immediate copy of the will itself, and therefore complements *everything physical in the world* and every phenomenon by representing *what is metaphysical*, the thing in itself. (Schopenhauer, *Welt als Wille und Vorstellung*, I, p. 310.)

To this most important insight of aesthetics (with which, in the most serious sense, aesthetics properly begins), Richard Wagner, by way of confirmation of its eternal truth, affixed his seal, when he asserted in his *Beethoven* that music must be evaluated according to aesthetic principles quite different from those which apply to all plastic arts, and not, in general, according to the category of beauty; although an erroneous aesthetics,

[27] Truth.
[28] An allusion to Goethe's *Faust*, lines 6216ff.
[29] Nietzsche clearly did not mean to imply that all music is "Dionysian." Yet it did not occur to him at this time to consider Mozart's music as an alternative to Wagner's. Mozart is not mentioned in *The Birth of Tragedy*. He is mentioned elsewhere by the young Nietzsche, and all references express love and admiration. But it was only in 1880, in *The Wanderer and His Shadow* (section 165), after his break with Wagner, that Nietzsche offered a contrast of Wagner and Mozart in one of his books—without mentioning Wagner by name. Eventually, he included this passage and some comparable ones from *Beyond Good and Evil* (1886) in *Nietzsche contra Wagner*. When it occurred to Nietzsche that Mozart's music was not Dionysian, he also realized that Wagner's music was not really "Dionysian" either, but rather "romantic" and "decadent." See *Nietzsche contra Wagner* (in *The Portable Nietzsche*, especially pp. 667ff.) and section 370 of *The Gay Science* (in Kaufmann, *Nietzsche*, Chapter 12, section V).

inspired by a mistaken and degenerate art,[30] has, by virtue of the concept of beauty obtaining in the plastic domain, accustomed itself to demand of music an effect similar to that produced by works of plastic art, namely, the arousing of *delight in beautiful forms*. Having recognized this extraordinary contrast, I felt a strong need to approach the essence of Greek tragedy and, with it, the profoundest revelation of the Hellenic genius; for I at last thought that I possessed a charm to enable me—far beyond the phraseology of our usual aesthetics—to represent vividly to my mind the fundamental problem of tragedy; whereby I was granted such a surprising and unusual insight into the Hellenic character that it necessarily seemed to me as if our classical-Hellenic science that bears itself so proudly had thus far contrived to subsist mainly on shadow plays and externals.

· · ·

According to the doctrine of Schopenhauer, therefore, we understand music as the immediate language of the will, and we feel our fancy stimulated to give form to this invisible and yet so actively stirred spirt-world which speaks to us, and we feel prompted to embody it in an analogous example. On the other hand, image and concept, under the influence of a truly corresponding music, acquire a higher significance. Dionysian art therefore is wont to exercise two kinds of influences on the Apollinian art faculty: music incites to the *symbolic intuition* of Dionysian universality, and music allows the symbolic image to emerge *in its highest significance*. From these facts, intelligible in themselves and not inaccessible to a more penetrating examination, I infer the capacity of music to give birth to *myth* (the most significant example), and particularly the *tragic* myth: the myth which expresses Dionysian knowledge in symbols. In the phenomenon of the lyrist, I have shown how music strives to express its nature in Apollinian images. If now we reflect that music at its highest stage must seek to attain also to its highest objectification in images, we must deem it possible that it also knows how to find the symbolic expression for its unique Dionysian wisdom; and where shall we seek for this expression if not in tragedy and, in general, in the conception of the tragic?

From the nature of art as it is usually conceived according to the single category of appearance and beauty, the tragic cannot honestly be deduced at all; it is only through the spirit of music that we can understand the joy involved in the annihilation of the individual. For it is only in particular examples of such annihilation that we see clearly the eternal phenomenon of Dionysian art, which gives expression to the will in its omnipotence, as it were, behind the *principium individuationis*, the eternal life beyond all phenomena, and despite all annhilation. The metaphysical joy in the tragic is a translation of the instinctive unconscious Dionysian wisdom into the language of images: the hero, the highest manifestation of the will, is negated for our pleasure, because he is only phenomenon, and because the

---

[30] *Entartete Kunst:* the term was made infamous by the Nazis when they subsumed under it a great deal of modern art which was officially proscribed. But the Nazis wanted "beautiful forms" and raged against art which did not aim at "beauty," while Nietzsche criticizes the assumption that all art must aim at "beautiful forms."

eternal life of the will is not affected by his annihilation. "We believe in eternal life," exclaims tragedy; while music is the immediate idea of this life. Plastic art has an altogether different aim: here Apollo overcomes the suffering of the individual by the radiant glorification of the *eternity of the phenomenon:* here beauty triumphs over the suffering inherent in life; pain is obliterated by lies from the features of nature. In Dionysian art and its tragic symbolism the same nature cries to us with its true, undissembled voice: "Be as I am! Amid the ceaseless flux of phenomena I am the eternally creative primordial mother, eternally impelling to existence, eternally finding satisfaction in this change of phenomena!"

Dionysian art, too, wishes to convince us of the eternal joy of existence: only we are to seek this joy not in phenomena, but behind them. We are to recognize that all that comes into being must be ready for a sorrowful end; we are forced to look into the terrors of the individual existence—yet we are not to become rigid with fear: a metaphysical comfort tears us momentarily from the bustle of the changing figures. We are really for a brief moment primordial being itself, feeling its raging desire for existence and joy in existence; the struggle, the pain, the destruction of phenomena, now appear necessary to us, in view of the excess of countless forms of existence which force and push one another into life, in view of the exuberant fertility of the universal will. We are pierced by the maddening sting of these pains just when we have become, as it were, one with the infinite primordial joy in existence, and when we anticipate, in Dionysian ecstasy, the indestructibility and eternity of this joy. In spite of fear and pity, we are the happy living beings, not as individuals, but as the *one* living being, with whose creative joy we are united.

The history of the rise of Greek tragedy now tells us with luminous precision how the tragic art of the Greeks was really born of the spirit of music. With this conception we believe we have done justice for the first time to the primitive and astonishing significance of the chorus. At the same time, however, we must admit that the meaning of tragic myth set forth above never became clear in transparent concepts to the Greek poets, not to speak of the Greek philosophers: their heroes speak, as it were, more superficially than they act; the myth does not at all obtain adequate objectification in the spoken word. The structure of the scenes and the visual images reveal a deeper wisdom than the poet himself can put into words and concepts: the same is also observable in Shakespeare, whose Hamlet, for instance, similarly, talks more superficially than he acts, so that the previously mentioned lesson of Hamlet is to be deduced, not from his words, but from a profound contemplation and survey of the whole.

.   .   .

It is an eternal phenomenon: the insatiable will always find a way to detain its creatures in life and compel them to live on, by means of an illusion spread over things. One is chained by the Socratic love of knowledge and the delusion of being able thereby to heal the eternal wound of existence; another is ensnared by art's seductive veil of beauty fluttering before his eyes; still another by the metaphysical comfort that beneath the whirl of phenomena eternal life flows on indestructibly—to say nothing of the more vulgar and almost more powerful illusions which the will always has at hand. These three stages of illusion are actually designed only for the more nobly formed natures, who actually feel profoundly the weight and burden of existence, and must be deluded by exquisite stimulants into forgetfulness of their displeasure. All that we call culture is made up of these stimulants; and, according to the proportion of the ingredients, we have either a dominantly *Socratic* or *artistic* or *tragic* culture; or, if historical exemplifications are permitted, there is either an Alexandrian or a Hellenic or a Buddhistic culture.[31]

. . .

But let us ask by means of what remedy it was possible for the Greeks during their great period, in spite of the extraordinary strength of their Dionysian and political instincts, not to exhaust themselves either in ecstatic brooding or in a consuming chase after worldly power and worldly honor, but rather to attain that splendid mixture which resembles a noble wine in making one feel fiery and contemplative at the same time. Here we must clearly think of the tremendous power that stimulated, purified, and discharged the whole life of the people: *tragedy*. We cannot begin to sense its highest value until it confronts us, as it did the Greeks, as the quintessence of all prophylactic powers of healing, as the mediator that worked among the strongest and in themselves most fatal qualities of the people.

Tragedy absorbs the highest ecstasies of music, so that it truly brings music, both among the Greeks and among us, to its perfection; but then it places the tragic myth and the tragic hero next to it, and he, like a powerful Titan, takes the whole Dionysian world upon his back and thus relieves us of this burden. On the other hand, by means of the same tragic myth, in the person of the tragic hero, it knows how to redeem us from the greedy thirst for this existence, and with an admonishing gesture it reminds us of another existence and a higher pleasure for which the struggling hero prepares himself by means of his destruction, not by means of his triumphs. Between the universal validity of its music and the listener, receptive in his Dionysian state, tragedy places a sublime parable, the myth, and deceives the listener into feeling that the music is merely the highest means to bring life into the vivid world of myth. Relying on this noble deception, it may now move its limbs in dithyrambic dances and yield unhesitatingly to an ecstatic feeling of freedom in which it could not

---

[31] All editions published by Nietzsche himself contains these words, and Wilamowitz cited this passage both in 1872 (p. 6) and in 1873 (p. 6). The standard editions of Nietzsche's collected works substitute "an Indian (Brahmanic) culture" for "Buddhistic culture." According to volume I (p. 599) of the so-called Grossoktav edition of Nietzsche's *Werke* (1905), this change is based on "a penciled correction in Nietzsche's own hand in his copy of the *second* version." It would seem that both "Buddhistic" and "Brahmanic" depend on some misconception; neither seems to make much sense.

dare to wallow as pure music without this deception. The myth protects us against the music, while on the other hand it alone gives music the highest freedom. In return, music imparts to the tragic myth an intense and convincing metaphysical significance that word and image without this singular help could never have attained. And above all, it is through music that the tragic spectator is overcome by an assured premonition of a highest pleasure[32] attained through destruction and negation, so he feels as if the innermost abyss of things spoke to him perceptibly.

If these last sentences have perhaps managed to give only a preliminary expression to these difficult ideas and are immediately intelligible only to few, I nevertheless may not desist at this point from trying to stimulate my friends to further efforts and must ask them to use a single example of our common experience in order to prepare themselves for a general insight. In giving this example, I must not appeal to those who use the images of what happens on the stage, the words and emotions of the acting persons, in order to approach with their help the musical feeling; for these people do not speak music as their mother tongue and, in spite of this help, never get beyond the entrance halls of musical perception, without ever being able to as much as touch the inner sanctum. Some of them, like Gervinus,[33] do not even reach the entrance halls. I must appeal only to those who, immediately related to music, have in it, as it were, their motherly womb, and are related to things almost exclusively through unconscious musical relations. To these genuine musicians I direct the question whether they can imagine a human being who would be able to perceive the third act of *Tristan and Isolde*, without any aid of word and image, purely as a tremendous symphonic movement, without expiring in a spasmodic unharnessing of all the wings of the soul?

Suppose a human being has thus put his ear, as it were, to the heart chamber of the world will and felt the roaring desire for existence pouring from there into all the veins of the world, as a thundering current or as the gentlest brook, dissolving into a mist—how could he fail to break suddenly? How could he endure to perceive the echo of innumerable shouts of pleasure and woe in the "wide space of the world night," enclosed in the wretched glass capsule of the human individual, without inexorably fleeing toward his primordial home, as he hears this shepherd's dance of metaphysics? But if such a work could nevertheless be perceived as a whole, without denial of individual existence; if such a creation could be created without smashing its creator—whence do we take the solution of such a contradiction?

Here the tragic myth and the tragic hero intervene between our highest musical emotion and this music—at bottom only as symbols of the most universal facts, of which only music can speak so directly. But if our feelings were those of entirely Dionysian beings, myths as a symbol would

---

[32] An allusion to Faust's last words in lines 11,585f. of Goethe's play.
[33] G. G. Gervinus, author of *Shakespeare*, 2 vols., Leipzig, 1850, 3rd ed., 1862; English tr., *Shakespeare, Commentaries*, 1863.

remain totally ineffective and unnoticed, and would never for a moment keep us from listening to the re-echo of the *universalia ante rem*.[34] Yet here the *Apollinian* power erupts to restore the almost shattered individual with the healing balm of blissful illusion; suddenly we imagine we see only Tristan, motionless, asking himself dully: "The old tune, why does it wake me?" And what once seemed to us like a hollow sigh from the core of being now merely wants to tell us how "desolate and empty the sea."[35] And where, breathless, we once thought we were being extinguished in a convulsive distention of all our feelings, and little remained to tie us to our present existence, we now hear and see only the hero wounded to death, yet not dying, with his despairing cry: "Longing! Longing! In death still longing! for very longing not dying!" And where, formerly after such an excess and superabundance of consuming agonies, the jubilation of the horn cut through our hearts almost like the ultimate agony, the rejoicing Kurwenal now stands between us and this "jubilation in itself," his face turned toward the ship which carries Isolde. However powerfully pity affects us, it nevertheless saves us in a way from the primordial suffering of the world, just as the symbolic image of the myth saves us from the immediate perception of the highest world-idea, just as thought and word save us from the uninhibited effusion of the unconscious will. The glorious Apollinian illusion makes it appear as if even the tone world confronted us as a sculpted world, as if the fate of Tristan and Isolde had been formed and molded in it, too, as in an exceedingly tender and expressive material.

Thus the Apollinian tears us out of the Dionysian universality and lets us find delight in individuals; it attaches our pity to them, and by means of them it satisfies our sense of beauty which longs for great and sublime forms; it presents images of life to us, and incites us to comprehend in thought the core of life they contain. With the immense impact of the image, the concept, the ethical teaching, and the sympathetic emotion, the Apollinian tears man from his orgiastic self-annihilation and blinds him to the universality of the Dionysian process, deluding him into the belief that he is seeing a single image of the world (*Tristan and Isolde*, for instance), and that, *through music*, he is merely supposed to *see* it still better and more profoundly. What can the healing magic of Apollo not accomplish when it can even create the illusion that the Dionysian is really in the service of the Apollinian and capable of enhancing its effects —as if music were essentially the art of presenting an Apollinian content?

By means of the pre-established harmony between perfect drama and its music, the drama attains a superlative vividness unattainable in mere spoken drama. In the independently moving lines of the melody all the living figures of the scene simplify themselves before us to the distinctness of curved lines, and the harmonies of these lines sympathize in a most delicate manner with the events on the stage. These harmonies make the relations of things immediately perceptible to us in a sensuous, by no

---

[34] The universals before (antedating) the thing.
[35] Wie "*öd und leer das Meer*," also quoted from *Tristan und Isolde* by T. S. Eliot in *The Waste Land* (1922), line 42.

means abstract manner, and thus we perceive that it is only in these relations that the essence of a character and of a melodic line is revealed
clearly. And while music thus compels us to see more and more profoundly than usual, and we see the action on the stage as a delicate web,
the world of the stage is expanded infinitely and illuminated for our spiri-
tualized eye. How could a word-poet furnish anything analogous, when
he strives to attain this internal expansion and illumination of the visible
stage-world by means of a much more imperfect mechanism, indirectly,
proceeding from word and concept? Although musical tragedy also avails
itself of the word, it can at the same time place beside it the basis and
origin of the word, making the development of the word clear to us, from
the inside.

Concerning the process just described, however, we may still say with
equal assurance that it is merely a glorious appearance, namely, the aforementioned Apollinian *illusion* whose influence aims to deliver us from
the Dionysian flood and excess. For, at bottom, the relation of music to
drama is precisely the reverse: music is the real idea of the world, drama
is but the reflection of this idea, a single silhouette of it. The identity between the melody and the living figure, between the harmony and the
character relations of that figure, is true in a sense opposite to what one
would suppose on the contemplation of musical tragedy. Even if we agi-
tate and enliven the figure in the most visible manner, and illuminate it
from within, it still remains merely a phenomenon from which no bridge
leads us to true reality, into the heart of the world. But music speaks out
of this heart; and though countless phenomena of the kind were to accompany this music, they could never exhaust its essence, but would always
be nothing more than its externalized copies.

As for the intricate relationship of music and drama, nothing can be
explained, while everything may be confused, by the popular and thoroughly false contrast of soul and body; but the unphilosophical crudeness
of this contrast seems to have become—who knows for what reasons—a
readily accepted article of faith among our aestheticians, while they have
learned nothing of the contrast of the phenomenon and the thing-in-itself
—or, for equally unknown reasons, have not cared to learn anything
about it.

Should our analysis have established that the Apollinian element in
tragedy has by means of its illusion gained a complete victory over the
primoridal Dionysian element of music, making music subservient to its
aims, namely, to make the drama as vivid as possible—it would certainly be
necessary to add a very important qualification: at the most essential point
this Apollinian illusion is broken and annihilated. The drama that, with
the aid of music, unfolds itself before us with such inwardly illumined distinctness in all its movements and figures, as if we saw the texture coming
into being on the loom as the shuttle flies to and fro—attains as a whole
an effect that transcends *all Apollinian artistic effects*. In the total effect
of tragedy, the Dionysian predominates once again. Tragedy closes with a
sound which could never come from the realm of Apollinian art. And thus

the Apollinian illusion reveals itself as what it really is—the veiling during the performance of the tragedy of the real Dionysian effect; but the latter is so powerful that it ends by forcing the Apollinian drama itself into a sphere where it begins to speak with Dionysian wisdom and even denies itself and its Apollinian visibility. Thus the intricate relation of the Apollinian and the Dionysian in tragedy may really be symbolized by a fraternal union of the two deities: Dionysus speaks the language of Apollo; and Apollo, finally the language of Dionysus; and so the highest goal of tragedy and of all art is attained.

. . .

Among the peculiar art effects of musical tragedy we had to emphasize an Apollinian *illusion* by means of which we were supposed to be saved from the immediate unity with Dionysian music, while our musical excitement could discharge itself in an Apollinian field and in relation to a visible intermediary world that had been interposed. At the same time we thought that we had observed how precisely through this discharge the intermediary world of the action on the stage, and the drama in general, had been made visible and intelligible from the inside to a degree that in all other Apollinian art remains unattained. Where the Apollinian receives wings from the spirit of music and soars, we thus found the highest intensification of its powers, and in this fraternal union of Apollo and Dionysus we had to recognize the apex of the Apollinian as well as the Dionysian aims of art.

To be sure, the Apollinian projection that is thus illuminated from inside by music does not achieve the peculiar effect of the weaker degrees of Apollinian art. What the epic or the animated stone can do, compelling the contemplative eye to find calm delight in the world of individuation, that could not be attained here, in spite of a higher animation and clarity. We looked at the drama and with penetrating eye reached its inner world of motives—and yet we felt as if only a parable passed us by, whose most profound meaning we almost thought we could guess and that we wished to draw away like a curtain in order to behold the primordial image behind it. The brightest clarity of the image did not suffice us, for this seemed to wish just as much to reveal something as to conceal something. Its revelation, being like a parable, seemed to summon us to tear the veil and to uncover the mysterious background; but at the same time this all-illuminated total visibility cast a spell over the eyes and prevented them from penetrating deeper.

Those who have never had the experience of having to see at the same time that they also longed to transcend all seeing will scarcely be able to imagine how definitely and clearly these two processes coexist and are felt at the same time, as one contemplates the tragic myth. But all truly aesthetic spectators will confirm that among the peculiar effects of tragedy this coexistence is the most remarkable. Now transfer this phenomenon of the aesthetic spectator into an analogous process in the tragic artist, and you will have understood the genesis of the *tragic myth*. With the Apollinian art sphere he shares the complete pleasure in mere appearance and in seeing, yet at the same time he negates this pleasure and finds a still higher satisfaction in the destruction of the visible world of mere appearance.

The content of the tragic myth is, first of all, an epic event and the glorification of the fighting hero. But what is the origin of this enigmatic trait that the suffering and the fate of the hero, the most painful triumphs, the most agonizing oppositions of motives, in short, the exemplification of this wisdom of Silenus, or, to put it aesthetically, that which is ugly and disharmonic, is represented ever anew in such countless forms and with such a distinct preference—and precisely in the most fruitful and youthful period of a people? Surely a higher pleasure must be perceived in all this.

That life is really so tragic would least of all exlain the origin of an art form—assuming that art is not merely imitation of the reality of nature but rather a metaphysical supplement of the reality of nature, placed beside it for its overcoming. The tragic myth, too, insofar as it belongs to art at all, participates fully in this metaphysical intention of art to transfigure. But what does it transfigure when it presents the world of appearance in the image of the suffering hero? Least of all the "reality" of this world of appearance, for it says to us: "Look there! Look closely! This is your life, this is the hand on the clock of your existence."

And the myth should show us this life in order to thus transfigure it for us? But if not, in what then lies the aesthetic pleasure with which we let these images, too, pass before us? I ask about the aesthetic pleasure, though I know full well that many of these images also produce at times a moral delight, for example, under that form of pity or moral triumph. But those who would derive the effect of the tragic solely from these moral sources —which, to be sure, has been the custom in aesthetics all too long—should least of all believe that they have thus accomplished something for art, which above all must demand purity in its sphere. If you would explain the tragic myth, the first requirement is to seek the pleasure that is peculiar to it in the purely aesthetic sphere, without transgressing into the region of pity, fear, or the morally sublime. How can the ugly and the disharmonic, the content of the tragic myth, stimulate aesthetic pleasure?

Here it becomes necessary to take a bold running start and leap into a metaphysics of art, by repeating the sentence written above, that existence and the world seem justified only as an aesthetic phenomenon. In this sense, it is precisely the tragic myth that has to convince us that even the ugly and disharmonic are part of an artistic game that the will in the eternal amplitude of its pleasure plays with itself. But this primordial phenomenon of Dionysian art is difficult to grasp, and there is only one direct way to make it intelligible and grasp it immediately: through the wonderful significance of *musical dissonance*. Quite generally, only music, placed beside the world, can give us an idea of what is meant by the justification of the world as an aesthetic phenomenon. The joy aroused by the tragic myth has the same origin as the joyous sensation of dissonance in music. The Dionysian, with its primordial joy experienced even in pain, is the common source of music and tragic myth.

Is it not possible that by calling to our aid the musical relation of dissonance we may meanwhile have made the difficult problem of the tragic effect much easier? For we now understand what it means to wish to see tragedy and at the same time to long to get beyond all seeing: referring to the artistically employed dissonances, we should have to characterize the corresponding state by saying that we desire to hear and at the same time long to get beyond all hearing. That striving for the infinite, the wing-beat of longing that accompanies the highest delight in clearly perceived reality, reminds us that in both states we must recognize a Dionysian phenomenon: again and again it reveals to us the playful construction and destruction of the individual world as the overflow of a primordial delight. Thus the dark Heraclitus compares the world-building force to a playing child that places stones here and there and builds sand hills only to overthrow them again.

· · ·

Music and tragic myth are equally expressions of the Dionysian capacity of a people, and they are inseparable.[36] Both derive from a sphere of art that lies beyond the Apollinian; both transfigure a region in whose joyous chords dissonance as well as the terrible image of the world fade away charmingly; both play with the sting of displeasure, trusting in their exceedingly powerful magic arts; and by means of this play both justify the existence of even the "worst world." Thus the Dionysian is seen to be, compared to the Apollinian, the eternal and original artistic power that first calls the whole world of phenomena into existence—and it is only in the midst of this world that a new transfiguring illusion[37] becomes necessary in order to keep the animated world of individuation alive.

If we could imagine dissonance become man—and what else is man? —this dissonance, to be able to live, would need a splendid illusion[38] that would cover dissonance with a veil of beauty. This is the true artistic aim of Apollo in whose name we comprehend all those countless illusions of the beauty of mere appearance[39] that at every moment make life worth living at all and prompt the desire to live on in order to experience the next moment.

Of this foundation of all existence—the Dionysian basic ground of the world—not one whit more may enter the consciousness of the human individual than can be overcome again by this Apollinian power of transfiguration. Thus these two art drives must unfold their powers in a strict proportion, according to the law of eternal justice. Where the Dionysian powers rise up as impetuously as we experience them now, Apollo, too,

---

[36] The rhapsody on Wagner continues, heedless of Mozart and Beethoven, Handel and Haydn, and scores of others.

[37] *Verklärungsschein* could also mean a transfiguring halo.

[38] *Illusion.*

[39] *Illusionen des schönen Scheins.*

must already have descended among us, wrapped in a cloud; and the next generation will probably behold his most ample beautiful effects.

.   .   .

Attempt at a Self-Criticism

Whatever may be at the bottom of this questionable book, it must have been an exceptionally significant and fascinating question, and deeply personal at that: the time in which it was written, in *spite* of which it was written, bears witness to that—the exciting time of the Franco-Prussian War of 1870/71. As the thunder of the battle of Wörth was rolling over Europe, the muser and riddle-friend who was to be the father of this book sat somewhere in an Apline nook, very bemused and beriddled, hence very concerned and yet unconcerned, and wrote down his thoughts about the Greeks—the core of the strange and almost inaccessible book to which this belated preface (or postscript) shall now be added. A few weeks later— and he himself was to be found under the walls of Metz, still wedded to the question marks that he had placed after the alleged "cheerfulness" of the Greeks and of Greek art. Eventually, in that month of profoundest suspense when the peace treaty was being debated at Versailles, he, too, attained peace with himself and, slowly convalescing from an illness con- tracted at the front, completed the final draft of *The birth of Tragedy out of the Spirit of Music.*—Out of music? Music and tragedy? Greeks and the music of tragedy? Greeks and the art form of pessimism? The best turned out, most beautiful, most envied type of humanity to date, those most apt to seduce us to life, the Greeks—how now? They of all people should have *needed* tragedy? Even more—art? For what—Greek art?

You will guess where the big question mark concerning the value of existence had thus been raised. Is pessimism *necessarily* a sign of decline, decay, degeneration, weary and weak instincts—as it once was in India and now is, to all appearances, among us, "modern" men and Europeans? Is there a pessimism of *strength*? An intellectual predilection for the hard, gruesome, evil, problematic aspect of existence, prompted by well-being, by overflowing health, by the *fullness* of existence? It is perhaps possible to suffer precisely from overfullness? The sharp-eyed courage that tempts and attempts, that *craves* the frightful as the enemy, the worthy enemy, against whom one can test one's strength? From whom one can learn what it means "to be frightened"? What is the significance of the *tragic* myth among the Greeks of the best, the strongest, the most courageous period? And the tremendous phenomenon of the Dionysian—and, born from it, tragedy—what might they signify?—And again: that of which tragedy died, the Socratism of morality, the dialectics, frugality, and cheerfulness of the theoretical man—how now? might not this very Socratism be a sign of decline, of weariness, of infection, of the anarchical dissolution of the instincts? And the "Greek cheerfulness" of the later Greeks—merely the afterglow of the sunset? The Epicureans' resolve *against* pessimism—a mere precaution of the afflicted? And science itself, our science—indeed, what is the significance of all science, viewed as a symptom of life? For what—worse yet, *whence*—all science? How now? Is the resolve to be so scientific about everything perhaps a kind of fear of, an escape from, pessimism? A subtle last resort against—*truth*? And, morally speaking, a sort of cowardice and falseness? Amorally speaking a ruse? O Socrates, Socrates, was that perhaps *your* secret? O enigmatic ironist, was that perhaps your—irony?

What I then got hold of, something frightful and dangerous, a problem with horns but not necessarily a bull, in any case a *new* problem—today I should say that it was *the problem of science itself*, science considered for the first time as problematic, as questionable. But the book in which my youthful courage and suspicion found an outlet—what an *impossible* book had to result from a task so uncongenial to youth! Constructed from a lot of immature, overgreen personal experiences, all of them close to the limits of communication, presented in the context of *art*—for the problem of science cannot be recognized in the context of science—a book perhaps for artists who also have an analytic and retrospective penchant (in other words, an exceptional type of artist for whom one might have to look far and wide and really would not care to look); a book full of psychological innovations and artists' secrets, with an artists' metaphysics in the background; a youthful work full of the intrepid mood of youth, the moodiness of youth, independent, defiantly self-reliant even when it seems to bow before an authority and personal reverence; in sum, a first book, also in every bad sense of that label. In spite of the problem which seems congenial to old age, the book is marked by every defect of youth, with its "length in excess" and its "storm and stress." On the other hand, considering its success (especially with the great artist to whom it addressed itself as in a dialogue, Richard Wagner), it is a *proven* book, I mean one that in any case satisfied "the best minds of the time."[40] In view of that, it really ought to be treated with some consideration and taciturnity. Still, I do not want to suppress entirely how disagreeable it now seems to me, how strange it appears now, after sixteen years—before a much older, a hundred times more demanding, but by no means colder eye which has not become a stranger to the task which this audacious book dared to tackle for the first time: *to look at science in the perspective of the artist, but at art in that of life.*

To say it once more: today I find it an impossible book: I consider it badly written, ponderous, embarrassing, image-mad and image-confused, sentimental, in places saccharine to the point of effeminacy, uneven in tempo, without the will to logical cleanliness, very convinced and therefore disdainful of proof, mistrustful even of the *propriety* of proof, a book for initiates, "music" for those dedicated to music, those who are closely

---

[40] An allusion to Schiller's lines in *Wallensteins Lager*: "He that has satisfied the best minds of the times has lived for all times."

related to begin with on the basis of common and rare aesthetic experiences, "music" meant as a sign of recognition for close relatives *in artibus*[41]—an arrogant and rhapsodic book that sought to exclude right from the beginning the *profanum vulgus*[42] of "the educated" even more than "the mass" or "folk." Still, the effect of the book proved and proves that it had a knack for seeking out fellow-rhapsodizers and for luring them on to new secret paths and dancing places. What found expression here was anyway—this was admitted with as much curiosity as antipathy—a *strange* voice, the disciple of a still "unknown God," one who concealed himself for the time being under the scholar's hood, under the gravity and dialectical ill humor of the German, even under the bad manners of the Wagnerian. Here was a spirit with strange, still nameless needs, a memory bursting with questions, experiences, concealed things after which the name of Dionysus was added as one more question mark. What spoke here—as was admitted, not without suspicion—was something like a mystical, almost maenadic soul that stammered with difficulty, a feat of the will, as in a strange tongue, almost undecided whether it should communicate or conceal itself. It should have *sung*, this "new soul"—and not spoken![43] What I had to say then—too bad that I did not dare say it as a poet: perhaps I had the ability. Or at least as a philologist: after all, even today practically everything in this field remains to be discovered and dug up by philologists! Above all, the problem that there *is* a problem here—and that the Greeks, as long as we lack an answer to the question "what is Dionysian?" remain as totally uncomprehended and unimaginable as ever.[44]

Indeed, what is Dionysian?—This book contains an answer: one "who knows" is talking, the initiate and disciple of his god. *Now* I should perhaps speak more cautiously and less eloquently about such a difficult psychological question as that concerning the origin of tragedy among the Greeks. The question of the Greek's relation to pain, his degree of sensitivity, is basic: did this relation remain constant? Or did it change radically? The question is whether his ever stronger *craving for beauty*, for festivals, pleasures, new cults was rooted in some deficiency, privation, melancholy, pain? Supposing that this were true—and Pericles (or Thu-

---

[41] In the arts.

[42] The profane crowd.

[43] When Nietzsche died in 1900, Stefan George, the most remarkable German poet of his generation, after Rilke, wrote a poem on "Nietzsche" that ends: "it should have sung, not spoken, this new soul." For George's whole poem, see *Twenty German Poets: A Bilingual Collection* (New York, The Modern Library, 1963).

[44] The conception of the Dionysian in *The Birth* differs from Nietzsche's later conception of the Dionysian. He originally introduced the term to symbolize the tendencies that found expression in the festivals of Dionysus, and contrasted the Dionysian with the Apollinian; but in his later thought the Dionysian stands for the creative employment of the passions and the affirmation of life in spite of suffering—as it were, for the synthesis of the Dionysian, as originally conceived, with the Apollinian—and it is contrasted with the Christian negaton of life and extirpation of the passions. In the *Twilight of the Idols*, written in 1888, the outlook of the old Goethe can thus be called Dionysian (section 49).

ides) suggests as much in the great funeral oration—how should we
n have to explain the origin of the opposite craving, which developed
ier in time, the *craving for the ugly*; the good, severe will of the older
eks to pessimism, to the tragic myth, to the image of everything underlying existence that is frightful, evil, a riddle, destructive, fatal? What,
then, would be the origin of tragedy? Perhaps *joy*, strength, overflowing
health, overgreat fullness? And what, then, is the significance, physiologically speaking, of that madness out of which tragic and comic art developed—the Dionysian madness? How now? Is madness perhaps not
necessarily the symptom of degeneration, decline, and the final stage of
culture? Are there perhaps—a question for psychiatrists—neuroses of
health? of the youth and youthfulness of a people? Where does that synthesis of god and billy goat in the satyr point? What experience of himself, what urge compelled the Greek to conceive the Dionysian enthusiast
and primeval man as a satyr? And regarding the origin of the tragic
chorus: did those centuries when the Greek body flourished and the Greek
soul foamed over with health perhaps know endemic ecstasies? Visions and
hallucinations shared by entire communities or assemblies at a cult? How
now? Should the Greeks, precisely in the abundance of their youth, have
had the will to the tragic and have been pessimists? Should it have been
madness, to use one of Plato's phrases, that brought the greatest blessings
upon Greece? On the other hand, conversely, could it be that the Greeks
became more and more optimistic, superficial, and histrionic precisely in
the period of dissolution and weakness—more and more ardent for logic
and logicizing the world and thus more "cheerful" and "scientific"? How
now? Could it be possible that, in spite of all "modern ideas" and the
prejudices of a democratic taste, the triumph of *optimism*, the gradual
prevalence of *rationality*, practical and theoretical *utilitarianism*, no less
than democracy itself which developed at the same time, might all have
been symptoms of a decline of strength, of impending old age, and of
physiological weariness? These, and not pessimism? Was Epicure an op-
timist—precisely because he was *afflicted?*

It is apparent that it was a whole cluster of grave questions with which
this book burdened itself. Let us add the gravest question of all. What,
seen in the perspective of *life*, is the significance of morality?

Richard Schacht

NIETZSCHE ON ART IN
THE BIRTH OF TRAGEDY

I

No higher significance could be assigned to art than that which Nietzsche assigns to it in the opening section of *The Birth of Tragedy** (hereafter BT): "The arts generally" are said to "make life possible and worth living" (p. 35).[1] Art is never far from Nietzsche's mind, even when he is dealing with matters seemingly far removed from it. Thus, for example, he some years later characterized his "view of the world" as "anti-metaphysical" to be sure, "but an artistic one"; and he even went so far on another subsequent occasion as to speak of "the world as a work of art which gives birth to itself."[2] He also includes a number of artists among the "higher men" whom he takes to stand out from the greater part of mankind hitherto and likens to artists both the "philosophers of the future" he envisages and the "overman" he declares to be "the meaning of the earth." Indeed, he even aspired to art himself, investing much effort and a good deal of himself in poetic and musical composition.

His views with respect to art and artists underwent a number of changes in the course of his productive life; but he by no means abandoned either his early concern with it nor the whole of his initial understanding and estimation of it in his later years. It would be an error to take the position set forth in BT to be "Nietzsche's philosophy of art"; but it is with this book (purporting in the very first sentence to make a major contribution to "the science of aesthetics") that his efforts along these lines began. It amply warrants extended discussion on a number of counts; for, while it constitutes his first word about art rather than his last, it is

Richard Schacht is Associate Professor of Philosophy at The University of Illinois, Champaign-Urbana. He is known for his work on German Philosophy of the nineteenth century.

* This essay was written for this collection and is published here for the first time.

[1] All page references and quotations, unless otherwise indicated, are to and from Walter Kaufmann's translation of BT (New York: Random House/Vintage, 1967).

[2] In notes published in *The Will to Power*, Walter Kaufmann, ed., translated by Walter Kaufmann and R. J. Hollingdale (New York: Random House/Vintage, 1967), numbered 1048 and 796.

not only of intellectual-biographical significance but also of considerable interest in its own right and has long been recognized as a classic contribution to the philosophical literature on art. I therefore shall devote the whole of this essay to it, postponing consideration of his subsequent modifications of his views relating to art for another occasion.

II

In a later preface to BT entitled "Attempt at a Self-Criticism," written some fourteen years after its publication, Nietzsche shows himself to be his own best critic—both severe and insightful. He readily acknowledges that "this questionable book" has many faults, not the least of which is that it is so obviously "a first book." It would be hard to imagine any fair-minded reviewer speaking more harshly of it than he does, when he writes

> . . . today I find it an impossible book: I consider it badly written, ponderous, embarrassing, image-mad and image-confused, sentimental, in places saccharine . . . , uneven in tempo, without the will to logical cleanliness, very convinced and therefore disdainful of proof (p. 19). . . .

He recognizes the seriousness of the defects resulting from his having been under both the spell of Wagner and the sway of Schopenhauer; he scornfully brands the book's author a romantic, a pessimist and an "art-deifier"; and he emphatically repudiates his suggestion of the desirability of "a new art, the *art of metaphysical comfort*," urging instead that one "learn the art of *this-worldly* comfort" rather than allow this dangerous temptation to seduce one (pp. 25–26).

Yet he also observes that the book poses a number of questions of the utmost importance and moves at least some distance toward a proper treatment of them. "The problem of science," "the significance of morality," and indeed "the value of existence" are among the "whole cluster of grave questions with which the book burdened itself" (p. 22). But the question in the foreground of this cluster, which guides and structures his treatment of these others, concerns the nature of art and its significance in human life—Greek art in particular, but by no means exclusively. Thus he refers to "the task which this audacious book dared to tackle for the first time: *to look at science in the perspective of the artist, but at art in that of life*" (p. 19).

Nietzsche's interest in art was by no means either exclusively academic or merely personal; and the urgency he felt with respect to the task to which he refers was not at all simply a function of his belief that Greek art and art generally had not previously been adequately understood by his fellow classical philologists and aestheticians. In his original preface to the book, he speaks disparagingly of readers who may "find it offensive that an aesthetic problem should be taken so seriously," and who are unable to consider art more than a "pleasant sideline, a readily dispensable tinkling of bells that accompanies the 'seriousness of life'. . . ." Against them, he advances the startling contention that "art represents the highest task and the truly metaphysical activity of this life" (pp. 31–32). And it has been observed, he goes on to maintain, that "the arts generally" serve to "make life possible and worth living" (p. 35).

It remains to be seen what he has in mind in speaking of art making life "possible" and, further, "worth living," as well as in terming art "the truly metaphysical activity of this life." But these passages provide an ample indication of the centrality of art both in the cluster of issues he deals with in BT and also in his thinking about them. And it is well worth nothing that, while "tragedy" is singled out from among the other arts in the title of the book (with music also receiving special mention), it is art generally with which he is actually concerned. To be sure, Nietzsche insists upon the necessity of distinguishing and differently analyzing various art forms and attaches special significance to tragic art (and Greek tragedy in particular, though not exclusively) among them. And it remains to be considered whether he regards "art" as anything more than a mere "common term" (p. 33) for a number of entirely different things. But it is "the arts" with which he deals, not tragic art alone, and it is with his treatment of this larger subject that I shall be concerned in this essay.

Nietzsche makes no attempt to conceal the influence of Schopenhauer on both his conception of reality and his thinking about the arts. This influence is so considerable that some preliminary remarks about it are a virtual necessity here, particularly in view of the fact that Nietzsche makes little independent effort to justify those aspects of his thinking deriving from this remarkable predecessor. And the influence of Schopenhauer is much more germaine to the content of Nietzsche's interpretation of the arts than is the impact of Wagner upon him during this period; for, while the latter obviously (and lamentably) affects considerable portions of the book, the ways in which it manifests itself are largely external and incidental to the main elements of the discussion of the nature and significance of art. For this reason I shall confine these preliminary remarks largely to Schopenhauer.

III

Schopenhauer may fairly be said to have been Nietzsche's primary philosophical inspiration, in a twofold way. On the one hand, Nietzsche was initially convinced of the soundness of much of what Schopenhauer had to say about the world, life, and the arts; of this, more in a moment. But, on the other hand, he was deeply unsettled by Schopenhauer's dark conclusions with respect to "the value of existence" and the worth of living. Most of his contemporaries tended to dismiss Schopenhauer as a morbidly pessimistic crank even while being appreciative of his stylistic brilliance. But Nietzsche saw that he had raised profoundly serious questions about life, which could no longer be answered as theologians and philosophers traditionally had answered them, and to which new answers had to be found if those given by Schopenhauer himself were not to prevail. Schopenhauer had concluded that existence is utterly unjustifiable and valueless, except in the negative sense that the inevitable preponderance of suffering endows it with an actual disvalue; and that, for anyone who considered the matter soberly and clearsightedly, oblivion had to be acknowledged to be preferable to life.

Nietzsche felt obliged to grant that Schopenhauer had a *prima facie* case and had placed the burden of proof upon anyone who would hold otherwise. He accepted the challenge Schopenhauer had thus posed; and much of his own thought may be regarded as an attempt to meet this challenge and to establish a viable alternative verdict even while acknowledging that Schopenhauer had been basically right in his perception of the conditions and character of life in this world. And both in BT and subsequently, art figures centrally in his efforts to accomplish this task. Thus it is one of his central contentions in BT that "it is only as an *aesthetic phenomenon* that existence and the world are eternally justified" (p. 52). And it is to art that he refers, in discussing the comparably dangerous predicament of "the profound Hellene" upon "having looked boldly right into the terrible destructiveness of so-called world history as well as the cruelty of nature," saying, "Art saves him, and through art—life" (p. 59). The complex relation between "art" and "life" is one of the basic problems with which Nietzsche is concerned; and his thinking with respect to it can best be understood in the light of a brief further consideration of certain of Schopenhauer's views.

Schopenhaurer was one of the most important forerunners of the movement later known as *Lebensphilosophie* (and in the emergence of which Nietzsche played a crucial role). A disciple of Kant's, he accepted the Kantian distinction between "phenomena" and "things in themselves"; but he reinterpreted both this distinction and its member terms (and also Kant's conception of the nature of the mind and its crucial role in the generation of the phenomenal world of experience). And the perspective from which he effected this reinterpretation, while encumbered with the language of introspective-psychological description, was fundamentally that of *life*. Man's nature and existence—and therewith the human mind and human experience—were regarded by him as but one of a great many variations on a theme played throughout the world of nature, rather than as distinct from and transcending it; and the whole of nature—rather than so-called "organic nature" alone—was supposed to have the same fundamental character.

The world "in itself" for Schopenhauer, while not in principle unknowable, was not identical with phenomena as we experience them; and it neither contained nor consisted in matter in motion, irreducible mental substances, or fundamental rational structures. Rather, it had the character of a vast, formless, aimless, turbulent principle operating along lines suggested by the idea of "willing," and which Schopenhauer elected to call "will."[3] The world was conceived as a profusion of processes, in which this single basic principle manifested itself in many different ways and of which the phenomena of nature as we experience them are appearances of certain instances of it. Each form of existence (such as man) was held to be one possible *type* (or "grade") of manifestation of this dynamic principle, analogous to a Platonic "Idea"—a notion taken over by Schopenhauer and employed in this connection, to designate the blueprints (as it were) followed by his demiurgic "will" in its concrete articulation.[4]

Schopenhauer conceived the plastic arts as having to do essentially with the discernment and representation of these Ideas, while music for him had the essentially different function of reflecting the nature of the underlying "will" itself.[5] To tragedy, on the other hand, he attributed yet another kind of function—to reveal the fate inexorably awaiting all specific manifestations of this will and the hopelessness of the plight of even the greatest in this essentially irrational world of ceaseless strife and destruction. This recognition was for him the deepest wisdom that either art or philosophy can yield, rendering insignificant not only the concerns with which we ordinarily are preoccupied, but also all knowledge—whether consisting in the cognition of relations among phenomena attainable through scientific investigation, or in the relatively higher-order discernment of the ideas to which all existence conforms, or in the still higher knowledge of the nature of the world will, attainable through the arts and philosophical thought.

Schopenhauer's reason for taking this darkly pessimistic position was, briefly put, that in his view existence in general and life in particular are characterized by ceaseless struggle and striving, inevitably resulting in destruction and (among sentient forms of life) involving incessant suffering of one sort or another. The whole affair, as he saw it, is quite pointless, since nothing of any value is thereby attained (the perpetuation of life merely continuing the striving and suffering). No transcendent purposes are thereby served; no pleasures, enjoyments, or satisfactions attainable can suffice to overbalance the sufferings life involves, thus excluding a hedonic justification of living; and so life stands condemned at the bar of evaluative judgment. It is, in a word, absurd. Ceaseless striving, inescapable suffering, inevitable destruction—all pointless, with no meaning and no justification, no redemption or after worldly restitution, and with the only deliverance being that of death and oblivion:[6] this is Schopenhauer's world as *Wille und Vorstellung*—the pre-Christian apprehension of life attributed by Nietzsche in BT to the Greeks, recurring again in the modern world as Christianity enters its death throes.

Nietzsche does not question the soundness of this picture in BT; and, even though he later rejected the Schopenhauerian metaphysics, which he

---

[3] Arthur Schopenhauer, *The World as Will and Idea*, translated by R. B. Haldane and J. Kemp (London: Routledge & Kegan Paul, 1964), Second Book; see § 19.
[4] Ibid.; cf. § 26.
[5] Ibid., Third Book.
[6] Ibid., Fourth Book; see, for example, § 71.

here accepts, he continued to concur with this general account of the circumstances attending life in the world. To live is to struggle, suffer, and die; and, while there is more to living than that, no amount of "progress" in any field of human enterprise can succeed in altering these basic parameters of individual human existence. Even more significantly, for Nietzsche as well as for Schopenhauer and Nietzsche's Greeks, it is not possible to discern any teleological *justification* of what the individual is thus fated to undergo, either historically or supernaturally. We can look neither to a future utopia nor to a life hereafter that might serve to render endurable and meaningful "the terror and horror of existence."

IV

How can one manage to endure life in a world of the sort described by Schopenhauer, once one recognizes it for what it is—endure it, and beyond that *affirm* it as desirable and worth living despite the "terrors and horrors" that are inseparable from it? "Suppose a human being has thus put his ear, as it were, to the heart chamber of the world will," Nietzsche writes, "how could he fail to *break?*" (p. 127). He terms this general recognition of the world's nature and of the fate of the individual within it "Dionysian wisdom"; and he compares the situation of the Greek who attained it to that of Hamlet—and implicity to that of modern man (with a Schopenhauerian-existentialist world view) as well:

> In this sense the Dionysian man resembles Hamlet: both have once looked truly into the essence of things, they have *gained knowledge*, and nausea inhibits action; for their action could not change anything in the external nature of things. . . .
>
> Now no comfort avails any more. . . . Conscious of the truth he has once seen, man now sees everywhere only the horror or absurdity of existence . . . . : he is nauseated (p. 60).

Nietzsche desperately wanted to find some sort of solution to this predicament—though he cloaked his longing in the guise of a more detached interest in the question of how it has been possible for "life" to manage to "detain its creatures in existence" even when the erroneous beliefs which commonly shield them are no longer in operation. For this reason his attention was drawn to a people who were already very much on his mind owing to his professional concerns and who constituted a perfect subject for a case study along these lines: the early Greeks. There were no brute savages, mindlessly and insensitively propelled through life by blind instinctive urges; rather, they were highly intelligent, sensitive, and cognizant of the ways of the world. And what is more, they were sustained neither by anything like Judeo-Christian religious belief nor by any myth of historical progress and human perfectibility. Yet they did not succumb to Schopenhauerian pessimism; on the contrary, they were perhaps the most vigorous, creative, life-affirming people the world has known. And thus Nietzsche was drawn irresistibly to them, asking of them, How did they do it? What was the secret of their liberation from the action- and affirmation-inhibiting nausea which seemingly ought to have been the result of their own Dionysian wisdom?

The answer, he believed, lay in that which was the most striking and glorious achievement of their culture: their art. Thus the passage cited continues,

> Here, where the danger to [the] will is greatest, *art* approaches as a saving sorceress, expert at healing. She alone knows how to turn these nauseous thoughts about the horror or absurdity of existence into notions with which one can live (p. 60).

This is the guiding idea of Nietzsche's whole treatment of art in general, as well as tragedy in particular, in BT. The main themes of this work are summarized in the following lines from its concluding section, which expand upon this idea by making reference to the key concepts of the "Dionysian" and "Apollinian" and bring to the fore the most central and crucial notions in Nietzsche's entire philosophy of art—the notions of *overcoming* and *transfiguration:*

> Thus the Dionysian is seen to be, compared to the Apollinian, the eternal and original artistic power that first calls the whole world of phenomena into existence—and it is only in the midst of this world that a new transfiguring illusion becomes necessary in order to keep the animated world of individuation alive.
>
> If we could imagine dissonance became man—and what else is man—this dissonance, to be able to live, would need a splendid illusion that would cover dissonance with a veil of beauty. This is the true artistic aim of Apollo in whose name we comprehend all those countless illusions of the beauty of mere appearance that at every moment make life worth living at all and prompt the desire to live on in order to experience the next moment.
>
> Of this foundation of all existence—the Dionysian basic ground of the world—not one whit more may enter the consciousness of the human individual than can be overcome again by this Apollinian power of transfiguration (p. 143).

V

Before turning to a closer consideration of these conceptions, a fundamental ambivalence in Nietzsche's thinking about the relation between art and life in BT must be noted. And in this connection I shall refer briefly to Nietzsche's thinking about art after as well as in BT.

From first to last, he was deeply convinced that art requires to be understood not as a self-contained and self-enclosed sphere of activity and experience detached from the rest of life, but rather as intimately bound up with life and as having the greatest significance in and for it. This is reflected in his later observation (in his "Self-Criticism") that art in BT is viewed "in the perspective of life"—a circumstance he regards as one of the signal merits of the work, its many inadequacies not withstanding. And it is one of the most decisive and distinctive features of his general philosophical position that its development is characterized by a kind of dialectic between his understanding of life and the world and his understanding of art—each affecting the other and bringing about changes in the other as the other worked changes upon it.

The underlying unity of the nations of art and life in Nietzsche's thinking is to be seen in BT in his treatment of the basic impulses operative in art—the Dionysian and the Apollinian—as identical with basic tendencies discernable in man and nature alike. And the consequences of his conviction of the existence of this unity are apparent in the subsequent development of the two notions which gradually move to the center of his discussions of man, life and the world in his later writings: the "overman" and the "will to power." For I would suggest that the latter is to be understood as an outgrowth of the dual notions of the Dionysian and Apollinian "art impulses of nature," in which they are *aufgehoben* in the threefold Hegelian sense of this term (in a manner lending itself to a further union with Nietzsche's successor conception to Schopenhauer's world will, his world of "energy-quanta"). And I would also suggest that the "overman" is to be construed as a symbol of human life raised to the level of art, in which crude self-assertive struggle is sublimated into creativity that is no longer subject to the demands and limitations associated with the "human, all-too-human."

The overcoming of the initial meaningless and repugnant character of existence, through the creative transformation of the existing, cardinally characterizes both art and life as Nietzsche ultimately comes to understand them. And this means for him both that life is essentially artistic and that art is an expression of the fundamental nature of life. "Will to power" is properly understood only if it is conceived as a disposition to effect such creatively transformative overcoming, in nature, human life generally, and art alike. And the overman is the apotheosis of this fundamental disposition, the ultimate incarnation of the basic character of reality generally to which all existence, life, and art are owing.

In BT, of course, neither "will to power" nor "overman" makes an appearance, and the relation between art and life is discussed in other terms. One of the most notable features of the discussion, however, is Nietzsche's readiness to employ the term "art" not only to refer in a conventional manner to sculpture, music, and the other standard "art forms" (kinds of work of art, their production, and their experience), but also in a broader, extended sense. For example, Nietzsche suggests that "every man is truly an artist" to the extent that it is part of the experience of everyone to engage in the "creation" of "the beautiful illusion" of "dream worlds" (p. 34), even though no "works of art" in the usual sense are thereby produced. Furthermore, turning his attention from such (Apollinian) "dreaming" to the experience of what he calls "Dionysian ecstasies," Nietzsche speaks of the Dionysian throng as *being* "works of art" themselves: here "man . . . is no longer an artist, he has become a work of art . . . . The noblest clay, the costliest marble, man, is here kneaded and cut . . ." (p. 37).

Most strikingly of all, however, Nietzsche refers constantly to "nature" herself as "artistic" and terms both the Apollinian and the Dionysian tendencies "art-impulses" *of nature.* Thus he initially presents them "as artistic energies which burst forth from nature herself, without the mediation of the human artist," and goes on to say, "With reference to these immediate art-states of nature every artist is an 'imitator'" (p. 38). And he is not merely suggesting that nature is thus "artistic" as well as man, albeit in different ways; for he contends that these two "art-states of nature" are "the only two art impulses" (p. 83), and he even goes so far as to attribute the true authorship of *all* art to "nature" rather than to human agency considered in its own right. "One thing above all must be clear to us. The entire comedy of art is neither performed for our betterment or education, nor are we the true authors of this art world." The human artist is said to be merely "the medium through which the one truly existent subject celebrates his release in appearance." Artists and the rest of us alike are "merely images and artistic projections for the true author," which is the fundamental principle of reality—the world will—itself; and we "have our highest dignity in our significance as works of art," as creations of this ultimate "artist," rather than as producers and appreciators of art objects (p. 52).

Yet Nietzsche also speaks of art very differently, and in a way that suggests a much less direct and even contrasting relation between it and the world. Thus, for example, he writes that "the highest, and indeed the truly serious task of art" is "to save the eye from grazing into the horrors of night and to deliver the subject by the healing balm of illusion from the spasms of the agitations of the will" (p. 118).

Again and again, he asserts that art in all of its forms deals in "illusion" and even "lies." Art spreads a "veil of beauty" over a harsh reality—and, when Nietzsche speaks of it as a "transfiguring mirror" (p. 43), the emphasis belongs not on the latter term but rather on the former, which does away with any accurate reflection. Thus he writes that "art is not merely imitation of the reality of nature but rather a metaphysical supplement of the reality of nature, placed beside it for its overcoming" (p. 140). And here the concluding passage of the entire work, cited earlier, should be recalled, in which Nietzsche returns to this theme of the necessity of overcoming whatever consciousness of the world's nature is attained by means of an art of "transfiguration" capable of covering over what has been glimpsed with a "splendid illusion" (p. 143). It was the "terror and horror of existence" from which the Greeks needed to be saved; and "it was in order to be able to live" that they developed their art: "all this was again and again overcome by the Greeks with the aid of the Olympian *middle world* of art; or at any rate it was veiled and withdrawn from sight" (p. 42). Nor does this apply only to nontragic art forms; for Nietzsche asserts that "the tragic myth too, insofar as it belongs to art at all, participates fully in this metaphysical intention of art to transfigure" (p. 140).

Even while thinking along these lines, however, Nietzsche envisages a fundamental link between "art" and "life," in that the latter is held to have been the source of the Greek's salvation from the desperate situation in which it also placed him: "Art saves him, and through art—life" (p. 59). Life thus is cast in a dual role, with the consequence that the relation of art to it is also a dual one.

Can the world of art in the narrower sense be thought of as a world "supplementing the reality of nature, placed beside it for its overcoming," and therefore distinct from it and contrasting to it—and at the same time as the creation of this very nature itself, expressing its own basic "artistic impulses," and therefore fundamentally homogeneous and identical to it? In BT, Nietzsche tries to have it both ways, but it is far from clear that it is possible to do so.

VI

In any event, it should be clear by now that Nietzsche thinks of what art *is* in terms of *what art does* and *how art does it*; and that for him the answers to these two questions are to be given in terms of the notions of *overcoming* (*Überwinding*) and *transfiguration* (*Verklärung*). These two notions recur repeatedly throughout BT and figure centrally in most of his major pronouncements about art—regardless of what art forms he may be considering and notwithstanding any basic differences between them.

It should further be evident that the former is to be understood in relation to certain human needs which Nietzsche regards as fundamental and profoundly compelling, thereby endowing art with an extraordinary importance transcending that of mere enjoyment or satisfaction derived from self-expression. And his interpretation of art in terms of the latter notion also clearly involves him in a fundamental break with Schopenhaeur and all other cognitivist philosophers of art; for, if art is essentially a matter of transfiguration, its ministrations to our needs will necessarily proceed otherwise than by heightening our powers of insight and understanding.

Nietzsche's frequent references to "illusions" in a number of contexts make this obvious, but the point applies even where this latter notion does not (notably, in the case of music). Otherwise put, even where some sort of "truth" about reality is purported to come through in art, Nietzsche takes it to be essential to the artistic character of the expression that a transfiguration of the "true" content has occurred in its artistic treatment —and its artistic character and quality attaches entirely to the element of transfiguration, rather than to this content and its transmission. On this point, however, more shall be said later.

It is important to bear in mind the general applicability of the notions of overcoming and transfiguration when turning to Nietzsche's discussion of the art impulses and art forms he is intent upon distinguishing, both to properly interpret what he says about them individually and to avoid the error of supposing that he takes them to be entirely different phenomena united by nothing more than a shared name. For, while he begins by speaking of "the science of aesthetics" and of "the continuous development of art," thereby implying some degree of unity of both the discipline and its subject, he immediately introduces the notion of "the *Apollinian* and *Dionysian* duality," asserts that "art" is but a "common term" until the two are "coupled with each other" (p. 33), and goes on to analyze them along very different lines—even to the point of maintaining that these notions represent "*two* worlds of art differing in their intrinsic essence and in their highest aims" (p. 99). These "art impulses" and "worlds of art," however, while very different indeed for Nietzsche, are nonetheless both "*art* impulses" and "worlds *of art.*" That they have more than merely this same "art" denomination in common is testified to by the fact that their "coupling" had a fruitful artistic issue (tragedy) itself suggests.

Indeed, it would seem that the categorization of the various specific art forms in terms of this "duality" is distinctly awkward, if not totally artificial, as soon as one looks past the Greeks. The distinction he proposes may indeed be a useful one, but "pure' instances of each are few and far between even when one considers particular works of art, not to mention entire art forms as we know them. It would thus seem unwise to attribute any great significance to the fundamental bifurcation of the world of art suggested by some of Nietzsche's remarks and to impute to him the thesis that all assertions about "art" generally (as opposed to Apollinian art and Dionysian art, plus tragic art) are illegitimate in principle. And the same applies with respect to his assertion that "every artist is . . . either an Apollinian artist in dreams, or a Dionysian artist in ecstasies, or finally—as for example in Greek tragedy—at once an artist in both dreams and ecstasies" (p. 38). One can appreciate the distinctions to which he is seeking to draw attention without insisting upon the logical implications for the notion of art which the rigidity of his language invites one to draw.

VII

The important point of Nietzsche's discussion of the Apollinian-Dionysian duality is that it is a mistake, in his view, to conceive of the arts as though they reflect the uniform operation of but a single sort of impulse and, further, that any analysis of them is superficial if it does not take account of the deep-seated character of the several impulses from which they do arise in human nature (and indeed in nature more generally).

Schopenhauer had suggested that music required to be understood in terms fundamentally different from those appropriate to the plastic arts—the latter being concerned with the representation of the ideas to which the manifestations of the will in the realm of appearances conform, and the former mirroring the underlying essential nature of this Will itself.

Nietzsche believed that Schopenhauer had put his finger on an important basic difference here. And he further accepted the suggestion that the distinction between these art forms was linked to the distinction between the world will in itself and the world of appearances, even to the point of concurring with the view that music constitutes a kind of "copy" of the former. But he by no means simply took over Schopenhauer's views along these lines, merely introducing the labels Apollinian and Dionysian in the course of restating them. He qualifies his endorsement of the idea that music "copies" the world will even as he gives it. For he holds that in music the nature of this ultimate reality is expressed *symbolically*, with the consequence that music is neither will nor a true copy of it, and that it is the symbolic character rather than the expressive or representative function of music that endows it with the status of art. Even here, he contends, transfiguration occurs, and it is upon the nature of this transfiguration, rather than upon the "mirroring" relation as such, that Nietzsche focuses his attention.

Even more radical is his departure from Schopenhauer with respect to the plastic arts. Gone is all reference to anything metaphysically comparable to the latter's ideas and, with it, any suggestion that here too a kind of cognitive function is performed.

Schopenhauer had linked the plastic arts to philosophical contemplation of the essential natures of different kinds of phenomenal manifestations of the will; Nietzsche, on the other hand, associates them with *dreaming*, and with that creative imagining which is a kind of waking dream. The forms fashioned by the plastic artist are construed not as representations of types to which existing particulars do and must more or less adequately conform, but rather as *idealizing transfigurations* of experienced phenomena—"beautiful illusions" making up a "dream world" that departs radically from the "real world" of ordinary experience "placed alongside it for its overcoming" (p. 140).

Thus, according to Nietzsche, neither in Apollinian nor in Dionysian art do we encounter unvarnished representations of the world, as it is in itself, as it presents itself to us in experience, or as it might be conceived by a thinker concerned with the natures of the types to which all existing things belong. The impulses to the creation of art for him are not cognitive impulses of any sort; rather, if they stand in any relation at all to knowledge, he holds that this relation may best be conceived as an *antidotal* one. And it is undoubtedly in part to stress the extent of his departure from any cognitively oriented interpretation of art that Nietzsche introduces his discussion of the Apollinian and the Dionysian by dwelling upon their connection with the phenomena of dreaming and intoxication. Each of these phenomena, he maintains, manifests a deeply rooted and profoundly important aspect of man's nature, and each answers to a powerful need. And the strength of the hold art exerts upon us can be understood only if it is recognized that the different art forms have their origins in these basic impulses and emerge in answer to these strong needs.

VIII

Nietzsche's discussion of Apollinian and Dionysian duality in BT is intended to bring out both the radical difference between what he thus takes to be the two basic life-serving and art-generating impulses these names designate as well as the possibility of their interpenetration and, further, the great importance (for "life" and art alike) of the results when this occurs. In this connection, it is of some interest to observe that Nietzsche was not the first to make such a suggestion. Indeed, what he has to say along these lines is strikingly reminiscent of certain ideas of a writer who receives considerable discussion in BT in a number of other contexts: Friedrich Schiller.

In a published series of "letters" dealing with "the aesthetic education of man,"[7] Schiller had advanced the idea that art is the product of the interplay of two fundamental "impulses" associated with what he took to be the two basic aspects of man's constitution: man's "natural" side and his "rational" side. Schiller had called these impulses man's "sensuous impulse" and man's "form impulse" and had spoken of a "play impulse" as the result of their union. He moreover had analyzed aesthetic experience in terms of "delight in appearances" and art as the creation of such delightful appearances in response to the human need for such an alternative to the normal one-sided preoccupations of our lives. Indeed, he had even gone so far as to proclaim the domain of art and aesthetic experience to be that in which alone man's full humanity is attained and in which the human spirit finds its deepest and highest imperative satisfied.

The similarities between Schiller and Nietzsche in BT thus are rather extensive, even though Nietzsche must be credited with considerable originality in transforming the rather commonplace "nature/reason" dichotomy underlying Schiller's duality of "sensuous" and "form" impulses into his Dionysian-Apollinian duality associated with two less superficially conceived fundamental dispositions of human and organic nature. Schiller's eighteenth century understanding of sensuous nature seems quaintly naive next to Nietzsche's conception of the Dionysian, to say the least; the latter bears an awesome aspect that is at once terrifying and exhilarating. Beside it the former pales, as does a shower in relation to a storm, or a brook to a high sea. But the two are undeniably related—and so also are Nietzsche's conception of the Apollinian and Schiller's notion of an impulse to "form." For the Apollinian tendency is just such an impulse, even though Nietzsche does not derive it from "reason" but, rather, maintains that reason ultimately originates precisely in it. And Nietzsche is echoing Schiller's celebration of the ideal of a perfect integration of his two impulses when he asserts that in tragic art "Dionysus speaks the language of Apollo; and Apollo finally the language of Dionysus; and so the highest goal of tragedy and of all art is attained" (p. 130). And again:

---

[7] Friedrich Schiller, *On the Aesthetic Education of Man, In a Series of Letters*, translated by Reginald Snell (New York: Frederich Ungar, 1965).

Where the Apollinian receives wings from the spirit of music and soars, we [find] the highest intensification of its powers, and in this fraternal union of Apollo and Dionysus we . . . recognize the apex of the Apollinian as well as the Dionysian forms of art (p. 139).

IX

Before turning to the details of Nietzsche's account of tragic art in which union is held to be effected on the highest level attainable, however, it is necessary to consider more closely what he means by the terms Dionysian and Apollinian and by the different types of art forms he distinguishes and characterizes by reference to them. At the outset of his discussion of the Apollinian and Dionysian duality, Nietzsche singles out two artforms as paradigms of each—"the Apollinian art of sculpture and the nonimagistic, Dionysian art of music" (p. 33)—but then moves immediately to a consideration of the more fundamental experimental "states" (also termed Apollinian and Dionysian) to which he takes all such art forms to be related: dreaming and intoxication.

He contends that human beings are so constituted as to be impelled to each by deeply rooted dispositions and to respond to each with powerful but differing positive feelings. Thus he suggests that there is something in "our innermost being" which "experiences dreams with profound delight and joyous necessity" (p. 35), while it is likewise the case that "paroxysms of intoxication" are accompanied by a "blissful ecstasy that wells up from the innermost depths of man, indeed of nature . . ." (p. 36).

It is these feelings of "profound delight" on the one hand and of "blissful ecstasy" on the other which are held to characterize the experience of the respective Apollinian and Dionysian art forms. These forms touch the same deep chords in our nature and so produce the same sort of response. And this is taken to be the key to understanding how it is that they are able to perform their life-sustaining functions (to the extent that they manage to do so). Thus Nietzsche explains his use of the name of Apollo in terms of its association with "all those countless illusions of the beauty of mere appearances that at every moment make life worth living at all and prompt the desire to live or in order to experience the next moment" (p. 143)—whether in "dreams" or in the "imagistic" art which is a refinement and elevation to a higher plane of development of the "creation" of the "beautiful illusion of the dream worlds" (p. 34). And he can likewise suggest that "Dionysian art, too, wishes to convince us of the eternal joy of existence: only we are to seek this joy not in phenomena, but behind them," through being ecstatically transported into a state of momentary identification with "primordial being itself, feeling its raging desire for existence and joy in existence; the struggle, the pain, the destruction of phenomena now appear necessary for us." Here "we are the happy living beings, not as individuals, but as the *one* living being, with whose creative joy we are united" (p. 104–05).

As Nietzsche views them, dreaming and intoxication are not merely analogs to art, or pre-forms of art, or even experiential sources of artistic activity. Rather, there is an important sense in which they themselves *are* artistic phenomena—only the "artist" in these cases is no human being but, rather, "nature," working in the medium of human life. In this context, the Dionysian and Apollinian require to be conceived "as artistic energies which burst forth from nature herself, without the mediation of the human artist—energies in which nature's art impulses are satisfied in the most immediate and direct way" (p. 38). Nietzsche does not mean this to be construed merely metaphorically; for it is his contention that human artistic activities are to be regarded as of a piece with these more basic life processes—developments of them, to be sure, but outgrowths sufficiently similar to them fundamentally to warrant regarding "every artist as an 'imitator' " in relation to "these immediate art-states of nature." Thus he also contends that "only insofar as the genius in the act of artistic creation coalesces with this primordial artist of the world, does he learn anything of the eternal essence of art . . ." (p. 52).

It may be noted in this connection that for Nietzsche it is in this respect —and only in this respect—that art may properly be conceived as involving "the imitation of nature." That is, art imitates nature in that the same sort of thing goes on in the former instance as goes on (among other things) in the latter. But, precisely because creative transformation is involved in the former no less than in the latter (as part of the very "imitation" in question), true art no more involves the attempt exactly to represent nature as it confronts us than dreaming and intoxication faithfully record it—nor yet again does true art merely give expression to the contents of experiences had while in these states.

This last point is of particular importance. It is true that for Nietzsche these states are the point of departure and inspiration for artistic creation, and he does consider it appropriate to speak of "every artist" as "either an Apollinian artist in dreams, or a Dionysian artist in ecstasies," or both at once (p. 38). But here the terms "dreams" and "ecstasies" *are* being used metaphorically; for it is no less central to Nietzsche's analysis of both types of (human) art that they involve the *further* transfiguration of what is experienced in these "art-states of nature." To fail to perceive the relation between the arts and these states results in one sort of interpretive inadequacy. But to fail to perceive that there is also a difference between them results in another. Nietzsche wishes to show a close connection between the two, but he does not wish to collapse the distinction between the members of each pair.

X

Having said this, it must immediately be granted that Nietzsche does employ the language of "representation" in speaking of the relation between both Apollinian and Dionysian art forms and the content of what might be termed the "visions" associated with both Apollinian and Dionysian experiential states more broadly and fundamentally conceived. It has already been noted that he is willing to speak with Schopenhaeur of (Dionysian) music as a "copy" of the "primal unity" underlying all appearances (p. 49). It has also been observed that he conceives of Dionysian art as effecting a kind of identification of the individual with this underlying reality through a captivating revelation of its nature as conveyed by "the Dionysian artist" who has glimpsed it and "identified himself with" it (p. 49). To this it must be added that he also speaks of the employment of "the best of rhythm" and tonal architectonics in Apollinian music "for the representation of Apollinian states" (p. 40). And, while it is "mere appearances" rather than the reality underlying them with which all such states are held to be concerned, the "beautiful illusions" of Apollinian plastic art are suggested to be, if not such appearances themselves, at any rate "appearances of" *those* appearances (p. 45).

In short, Nietzsche holds that there is at least a kind of "mirroring" relation between what is discerned in Dionysian states and what one finds in Dionysian art, and also between what is envisaged in Apollinian states and what one finds in Apollinian art. Indeed, it can even be said that for Nietzsche the efforts of artists of both sorts serve at once to share and to heighten experiences centering upon the contents of the respective sorts of vision. Were this not so, the "joy in existence" deriving from the "blissful ecstasy" generated by the one and the "profound delight" arising from the other (through the generation and intensification of which these types of art are held to perform their life-sustaining function) could not be stimulated by art.

The solution to this difficulty is to be found in the fact that for Nietzsche art transforms even as it thus "represents," that it is no simple faithful mirror of the contents of these states but, rather, "a transfiguring mirror" (p. 43). And it is one of the central points of his discussion of these two types of art that they not only transfigure even as they mirror but, moreover, that they transfigure the already dissimilar contents of the visions associated with the two kinds of state in quite different ways. In view of this double difference, it is perhaps understandable that Nietzsche could have been moved to speak of "two worlds of art differing in their intrinsic essence" (p. 99).

The basic contrast he is concerned with establishing here may be expressed in terms of the distinction between *images* and *symbols,* and the double difference just mentioned bears importantly upon it. In the case of what Nietzsche calls Apollinian art, the chaotic play of crude and ephemeral appearances associated with such basic Apollinian experiential states as dreaming and imagination undergoes a transformative process, issuing in the creation of enduring, idealized images—"beautiful illusions," as Nietzsche often terms them, illusory because nothing either in the flux of appearance or beyond it corresponds to them, and of greater beauty than the haphazardly constituted contents of this flux. They are transfigurations of appearances, images akin to the stuff of dreams but also contrasting markedly to them.

In the case of Dionysian art, on the other hand, the transformation from which it issues is of the experience of the inexhaustible, dynamic "primal unity" that is "beyond all phenomena and despite all annihilation" associated with such basic Dionysian states as intoxication and orgiastic revelry. What *this* transformation gives rise to is "a new world of symbols," in which "the essence of nature is now . . . expressed symbolically" (p. 40); and it is the resulting *symbolic forms* in which Dionysian art consists. These symbolic forms are transfigurations of ecstatic states —expressions akin to immediate Dionysian ecstasy but, again, differing markedly from it, no less than from the underlying reality glimpsed in it. Thus Nietzsche holds that "Dionysian art . . . gives expression to the will in its omnipotence, at it were, behind the *principium individuationis*" (p. 104)—and yet insists that even so paradigmatic a case of such art as music is not to be thought of as identical with this will: "music, according to its essence, cannot possibly be will. To be will it would have to be wholly banished from the realm of art" (p. 55). For were it the same as will, it would lack the transfigured character definitive of all art.

In short, it would be an error to infer from such passages as the following that transfiguration exclusively characterizes Apollinian—as opposed to Dionysian—art:

> I see Apollo as the transfiguring genius of the *principium individuationis* through which alone the redemption in illusion is truly to be obtained; while by the mystical triumphant cry of Dionysus the spell of individuation is broken, and the way lies open to . . . the innermost heart of things (pp. 99–100).

Dionysian art does not involve the kind of transfiguration that is encountered in the case of Apollinian art—but it does involve transfiguration nonetheless. It is in terms of the difference between the kinds of transfiguration involved, rather than in terms of a division of the various art forms into the "plastic arts" on the one hand and the "musical arts" on the other, that Nietzsche's "Apollinian-Dionysian dualty" in art is to be understood. And, so understood, this contrast may be seen not to be rigidly tied to the conventional (and also rather artificial) division of art forms just mentioned but, rather, to cut across this division, in fact as well as in principle. (Thus, for example, we find Nietzsche distinguishing between different types of music, one Dionysian and one Apollinian.)

In short, it is Nietzsche's contention that there is one sort of art in which the works produced have a symbolically expressive character and another sort in which the works produced do not, having instead the character of idealized images or "beautiful illusions." And it is one of the seemingly curious but important points of his analysis that the kinds of art generally regarded as most clearly "representational" fall largely into the latter category, while those generally thought of as primarily "nonpresentational" belong in the former. The idealized images of Apollinian art are not to be thought of as having the function either of faithfully representing or of symbolically expressing anything at all. They are rather to be thought of as beautiful illusions to be contemplated simply for what they are in themselves and to be enjoyed solely on account of their intrinsic beauty. They are, as Nietzsche says, a "supplement of the reality of nature, placed beside it for its overcoming" (p. 140). And, if there is any significant relation between them and this "reality," it does not consist in their genetic link to the experiential phenomena of which they are transfigurations but, rather, in their ability to lead us to think better of the world of ordinary experience by regarding it in the "transfiguring mirror" they constitute, "surrounded with a higher glory" (p. 43). Through Apollinian art, the world of ordinary experience is not actually transformed and its harshness eliminated. But, to the extent that the idealized images created through the transformative activity of the Apollinian artist admit to association with that which we encounter in this world, our attitude toward the latter benefits from this association, as our delight in these images carries over into our general disposition toward anything resembling them.

Once again, however, it is not knowledge that we thereby attain but, rather, only an altered state of mind, brought about by "recourse to the most forceful and pleasurable illusions" and "seducing one to a continuation of life" (p. 43). One may have reservations about the psychological validity of these latter contentions, or about the effectiveness of the process indicated (as indeed Nietzsche himself has and sets forth later in his analysis). These reservations do not touch Nietzsche's main point here, however, concerning the status of those works of art he terms Apollinian. They are beautiful illusions, idealized images which neither represent nor symbolize but, rather, delight precisely by virtue of the beauty they possess as a result of the creative transfiguration accomplished in their production.

XI

In the case of Dionysian art, matters stand quite differently. The Dionysian artist too is creative, and not merely someone with insight and the ability to communicate it—notwithstanding Nietzsche's assertion that, in the paradigm case of such art, "he produces [a] copy of [the] primal unity as music" (p. 49). It may be that there is a kind of "re-echoing" of the nature of this fundamental reality in instances of Dionysian art, as Nietzsche goes on alternately to put the point (p. 50). In terms of this metaphor, however, such art is no less a "transfiguring echo-chamber" than Apollinian art is a "transfiguring mirror," for the artistic "re-echoing" does not stand in the same near-immediate relation of identity to this "primal unity" as does them more basic Dionysian phenomenon of intoxication but, rather, comes back in an altered form, the creative production of which involves "the greatest exaltation of all [man's] symbolic faculties."

Thus, Nietzsche goes on to say, "the essence of nature is now to be expressed symbolically; we need a new world of symbols" (p. 40)—and it is this "new world of symbols" which constitutes both the language and the substance of Dionysian art. The issue is somewhat confused by Nietzsche's use of the term Dionysian to refer to the "primal unity" itself ("the Dionysian basic ground of the world," etc.) and also to insight into its nature and the plight of the individual in such a world ("Dionysian wisdom"), as well as to such art, which draws upon man's "symbolic powers" and thereby transfigures even while giving expression to the former. But, once again, it must be borne in mind that for Nietzsche, like other art forms, "it belongs to art at all" only insofar as it "participates fully in this metaphysical intention of art to transfigure" (p. 140).

The symbolism of which Nietzsche is speaking here, however, is of a rather special sort. At least in its origins, it is neither conventional nor intentional and is far removed from the use of words to formulate and express thoughts. Thus, in discussion the "Dionysian dithyramb" (which he takes to be the proto-form of Dionysian art), he writes that in order to develop the "new world of symbols" needed to be able to express "the essense of nature" symbolically,

> . . . the entire symbolism of the body is called into play . . . , the whole pantomine of dancing, forcing every member into rhythmic movement. Then the other symbolic powers suddenly press forward, particularly those of music, in rhythmics, dynamics, and harmony (p. 50).

Nietzsche appears to conceive of the symbolic powers involved in such music and dancing as sublimations of deeper and darker natural impulses and of the symbolism in which they give rise as *natural* in a significant sense, even if also as more than "merely" natural. The first point is important: we have to do here with no "reversion of man to the tiger and the ape" but, rather, with a transformation of the merely natural in which "nature for the first time attains her artistic jubilee," and "days of transfiguration" supplant the nights of the "horrible 'witches' brew' of sensuality and cruelty" of pre-Dionysian savagery (p. 40). But the second point is no less important: the expressions in which such music and dancing consist, while symbolic, have a natural affinity with the reality they symbolize. And this reality is deeper than that of all individual thought, all social conventions, and all "appearance," for its expression involves "the destruction of the *principium individuationis*" (p. 40) and the "height of self-abnegation" on the part of those through whom this expression is achieved. The Dionysian artist does not employ symbols to express some specific thought or emotion he happens to have had, or some particular feature of the cultural life and experience he shares with other members of his society; "he has identified himself with the primal unity," in all its "pain and contradiction" and also its inexhaustible and indestructible vitality (p. 49)—and, thus "released from his individual will," he gives symbolic expression to the nature of the fundamental reality with which he identifies (p. 52).

XII

The development of Dionysian art is thus a matter of the refinement and elaboration of those symbolic forms answering to the "symbolic powers" and resources available to the human artist and serving to give expression to the nature of the reality encountered when one penetrates beyond and beneath all individuated appearances and all perceptible images, idealized or "real." And, to avoid misunderstanding Nietzsche's meaning in speaking of symbolization here, it is important to see that he takes these art forms to express "the essence of nature" symbolically, not on the level of any specific "content" that may be discerned in cases of various instances of them but, rather, on the deeper level of the general character of these art forms. Some sorts and even some instances of (Dionysian) music and dance may be superior to others in terms of the adequacy with which they perform this expressive function, but it is essentially the character of these art forms as such that accounts for their symbolic significance and their ability to perform this function.

The symbolic expression of "the essence of nature" is to be confused neither with conceptualization nor with representation. That music and dance do not present us with concepts purporting to describe this reality will be obvious, but it is no less important to recognize that they do not confront us with pictures of reality either. This is in part because, for Nietzsche, it cannot in principle be pictured, but it is also because we are not dealing here with images that could conceivably perform a picturing function. Dancing might seem to be an exception, but Nietzsche considers it clearly to belong with music rather than sculpture as an art form, the essential character of which is a matter of "rhythmics, dynamics and harmony" rather than the fashioning of idealized images. What matters is what is conveyed through the movements made, not what poses are struck. And, as in the case of music, the former is understood to pertain to the character of that reality of which all perceptible phenomena are merely appearances. Dancing is "pantomime" (p. 40), symbolically expressive of something no image or series of images can capture and represent.

Because the movements of dancing and the sounds of music differ in character from the reality whose nature they symbolically express, however, these symbolic forms too may be said to constitute a world of beautiful illusions, albeit of a sort different from that encountered in the case of Apollinian art. And their attraction for us is not merely a matter of the function of symbolic expression they perform. They may *mediate* our own attainment of (temporary) identification with the reality they smbolically express (a point to which I shall shortly turn), rather as the gestures, facial expressions, and sounds made by someone feeling some emotion may mediate our coming to empathize with them. But the relation between the two is no more one of identity or epistemic correspondence in the former case than in the latter. Symbolic expressions do not stand in a truth relationship to that which they express, even though they may be more or less apt and effective, and symbolic forms have experiential features of their own which are not to be found in that which may be expressed by means of them. That which they express is transfigured in its expression, and this transformation yields a new domain of experiential phenomena with qualities admitting of extensive development and refinement in their own right.

Thus music is both more and less than that which Nietzsche takes it to express; it is sound, while the "primal unity" is not, and the "art world" of musical sounds is in a significant sense other than "the essence of nature." And it is no mere transparent medium through which the latter is brought before us distinctly and unadorned; while not opaqe, as Apollinian art may be said to be in this context, it is at most only translucent. Neither the fact of its mere translucency, however, nor the fact of the transformation it involves is considered by Nietzsche to be detrimental to its mediating function. On the contrary, he takes them actually to enhance it. For he believes that we could not endure the full glare of an unmediated encounter with the world's essential nature and that it is only *as transfigured* through its expression in the entrancing symbolic forms of the Dionysian arts that a nondestructive identification with it is possible.

In short, in these arts the world's nature is expressed in a form that attracts rather than repels us—a symbolic form, the attractiveness of which is bound up with the transfiguration involved in this symbolization and made possible by the character of the "new world of symbols" under consideration. Dionysian art does not have the character of a "veil of illusion" radically different from the reality of nature and "placed alongside it for its overcoming," as does Apollinian art for Nietzsche. Yet it does have a somewhat analogous character and function in that it expresses the reality of nature in a manner enabling us to overcome our abhorence of it and derive "joy in existence" from identification with it, by means of a quasi-"illusory" *medium* of transfiguring symbolic forms.

XIII

Before proceeding further, I wish to pause briefly to make several comments relating to the interpretation and evaluation of Nietzsche's thinking along the lines I have been developing. In particular, I would urge that its interest ought not be taken to depend upon the tenability of Nietzsche's talk of "the essence of nature" and of his understanding of it in BT. He continued to avail himself of the notions of the Apollinian and the Dionysian long after he changed his views on these matters. And the basic outlines of his conception of two types of art along the lines under consideration do not stand or fall with them.

The most fundamental and crucial ideas he seeks to advance in this connection are that art is essentially not representational (or imitative) with respect to the world either as we perceive it or as it is apprehended in cognition but, rather, that it is transfigurative; that, on the other hand, the transfigurations it involves are more than mere pleasing expressions of emotions or fancies in sensuous form; and that they are not all of the same kind. One does not have to subscribe to the version of the appearance/reality distinction which he accepts here (but later rejects), or to his contention that art is the "highest task and truly metaphysical activity of this life," or to his conviction that it has the purpose of performing the kind of "overcoming" function he describes in relation to the "terror and horror of existence" to follow him this far—and farther still.

Thus, for example, when one turns one's attention to the task of giving a positive account of the character of these transfigurations, it seems quite reasonable to suggest that a fundamental distinction is to be noted between cases of works of art in which some larger meaning is conveyed and others in which interest centers entirely upon the qualities of the works themselves. With regard to the latter, one ought not allow one's understanding of what Nietzsche is getting at to be governed by an overly narrow and rigid construal of either member term of such expressions as beautiful illusions and idealized images. And, with regard to the former, it is possible (and, I would urge, desirable) to generalize what Nietzsche is saying in such a way that the notion of symbolic expression—of features of reality transcending both the works themselves and the inner life and specific intentions of the artist—is retained but liberated from the confines of the metaphysics to which he here links it.

XIV

Returning to Nietzsche's discussion itself, it is next to be observed that he does not take the notions of transfiguration and illusion to apply only to works of Apollinian and Dionysian art conceived as objects of aesthetic experience but, rather, also to the subjects of such experience insofar as they become absorbed in them. This point is of great importance in connection with his treatment of tragic art, as well as in his analysis of these two art forms. And for this reason it warrants close attention. The entire significance of art is missed, for Nietzsche, if one does not recognize that the consciousness of those experiencing these art forms undergoes a transformation analogous to that occurring in their creation—and that, with this transformation, the experiencing subject's very psychological identity is in a sense transfigured, even if only temporarily and in a way that does not alter the basic reality of his human nature and of his existence in the world. The latter circumstance is what renders it appropriate to speak of illusion here—though Nietzsche is no less concerned to indicate the value of such illusion "for life" than he is to point out its illusory character.

The subjective transformation associated with the objective one involved in the creation of the work of art, however, has a very different character in the two general sorts of cases under consideration. Thus Nietzsche contends that they constitute two fundamentally distinct stratagems by means of which "the insatiable will" at the heart of nature conspires to "detain its creatures in life and compel them to live on" (p. 109). He discusses them in terms of what occurs in the case of the Dionysian man and in the case of the Apollinian man, and for the sake of convenience I shall follow him in this—with the understanding, however, that these expressions refer to contrasting types of psychological states rather than to distinct groups of human beings.

That an inward transformation occurs in the course of the kind of experience appropriate to Dionysian art has already been intimated in Nietzsche's observation that one in the grip of the "paroxysms of intoxication" in which the Dionysian impulse primordially manifests itself "has become a work of art" (p. 37). It has also been suggested that he takes Dionysian art to mediate an identification of the individual with the reality underlying the appearances whose nature is expressed symbolically in it. It is a common observation that art has the remarkable power to *transport* us, not only into the domain established through artistic creation, but also out of our ordinary selves and everyday lives. Nietzsche seizes upon this idea and elaborates it—in a manner, it may be remarked, influenced significantly by Schopenhauer. Schopenhauer had contrasted our normal condition as creatures and captives of will, absorbed in the constant struggle for existence characterizing all life in the world, with a radically different condition purported to be temporarily attainable through aesthetic experience; "he who is sunk in this perception is no longer individual," Schopenhauer had written, but rather "is pure, will-less, painless, timeless subject of knowledge."[8]

Nietzsche modifies this suggestion and expands it so that it applies both to the contemplation of idealized images that elevates one above the world of ordinary experience and action and to the experience of enrapturing symbolic expressions of the reality underlying this phenomenal world that carries one beyond it. Yet in either event he agrees with Schopenhauer that one so affected is "no longer individual" or at any rate ceases for the moment to have the psychological identity associated with his ordinary individual existence. The transformation undergone by the Apollinian man (which is most akin to that indicated by Schopenhauer) will be considered shortly. That transformation undergone by the Dionysian man was not envisioned by Schopenhauer, at least in connection with art, for it involves not the attainment of contemplative will-lessness but, rather, the effecting of a far deeper psychological union with the world will than that which is merely a matter of our being its creatures and having to live under the conditions it imposes upon all its particular instances.

The Dionysian man does not exchange his physiological and sociocultural identity and situation in the world for another or escape them altogether in the course of the "destruction of the *principium individuationis*" of which Nietzsche speaks. As an experiental phenomenon, however, this destruction is very real: the Dionysian man is psychologically transformed into one for whom the only reality of which he is aware—and

[8] Schopenhauer, *The World as Will and Idea*, § 34.

therefore that with which he himself identifies—is that which is expressed in the movements, tonalities, or other symbolic forms in which he is immersed. Thus Nietzsche contends that, through the experience of Dionysian are, "we are really for a brief moment primordial being itself, feeling its raging desire for existence and joy in existence; the struggle, the pain, the destruction of phenomena, now appear necessary for us . . ." (p. 104). As one in a state of intoxication may be said (quite appropriately, even if only psychologically) not to "be himself," one immersed in the surge and flow of an instance of this type of aesthetic experience "loses himself" in it. His consciousness is caught up in it and his self-consciousness is altered accordingly, whether this transformation manifests itself behaviorally in an enraptured cessation of ordinary activity, in outward inaction making inward tumult, or in entrance into overt participation in the event as well. Such experience is of being blissful, but also in the original and literal sense of the term *ekstasis*, which denotes a standing out from, beside, beyond (oneself).

To the extent that one's own existence may be conceived as being actually a moment of the reality expressed in Dionysian art and with which one thus comes to feel at one through its mediation, this transformation may be said to have the significance of a dispelling of the illusion involved in one's ordinary consciousness of oneself as something distinct from it and to be characterized in other terms. But, to the extent that such experience leads one to identify oneself so completely with this reality that one feels oneself to enjoy even those of its features that actually characterize it only as a whole, with which one is not truly identical, this transformation may also be said to have the significance of the fostering of another, different illusion. Thus Nietzsche suggests that, here no less than in the case of Apollinian art, we are dealing with a way in which, "by means of an illusion," life conspires "to detain its creatures in existence" despite the harshness of the conditions it imposes upon them—in this instance, through "the metaphysical comfort that beneath the whirl of phenomena eternal life flows on indestructibly" (pp. 109–10).

The illusion in question is not that "life flows on indestructibly" despite the ephemerality of phenomena—for it does. We may be "comforted" (and more) through the transformation of our psychological identity enabling us to achieve a sense of unity with this indestructible and inexhaustible underlying reality, of which we are truly manifestations. But, while such comfort may be termed metaphysical, this transfiguration is not, for it leaves our actual status in the world unchanged and the basic conditions of our human existence unaltered—as we discover that when the moment passes the Dionysian aesthetic experience comes to an end, and we "return to ourselves," our psychological identities transformed back again into their original non-Dionysian state. The only enduring comfort is the recollection of the rapture of the Dionysian experience and the knowledge that it remains available to us. But a profound danger attends this kind of "overcoming," of which Nietzsche is acutely aware: the letdown may be great, the disparity between Dionysian states and ordinary life distressing, the illusion discerned, and its recognition found disconcerting—and thus the long-term effect of such experience may be detrimental rather than conducive to life (pp. 59–60). It is for this reason, more than any other, that Nietzsche has reservations about Dionysian art and experience generally, despite the evident fascination they have for him.

These reservations would appear to be well founded. And as Nietzsche also observes, in connection with the historical supersession of Dionysianism by other cultural forms, Dionysian art may no longer perform the larger function in human life which he takes to have called it into existence. Yet it by no means follows that it constitutes a closed chapter in the development of art. Its capacity to move us, enrapture us, transport us, and transform our sense of identity is in Nietzsche's view ensured by very basic features of our human nature, and it does not succumb to the passing of the ability of a people to live under its immediate spell. The psychological transfiguration Nietzsche describes is one which he takes to occur not merely in those who meet this description but, rather, in all of us when we open ourselves to the experience of Dionysian art. To the extent that we do so, when we do, we approach the condition of Nietzsche's Dionysian man; indeed, we are changed and *become* as Dionysian man, if only in these moments.

XV

Nietzsche's Apollinian man constitutes a very different case, being the product of quite another kind of psychological transformation. As has already been observed, Nietzsche conceives of it in terms rather similar to those employed by Schopenhauer. The latter, it will be recalled, had maintained that the plastic arts are to be understood as seeking to represent the Platonic ideas associated with the different grades of objectifications of will and that one absorbed in the contemplation of these ideas —either as such or through their artistic representation—is elevated from the status of a mere particular living and striving individual to that of "pure, will-less timeless subject of knowledge." For Nietzsche, one cannot appropriately speak here of knowledge, since that with which we are confronted in the images of Apollinian art are not representations of anything of the kind but, rather, beautiful illusions. He does, however, conceive of the subject of Apollinian aesthetic experience as transformed, through the contemplation of these idealized images, from an individual caught in the web of the world into something like Schopenhauer's pure subject of knowledge transcending time and will—and with them, his own particular individuality and circumstances. As in the previous case, this transcendence is held to be not only merely temporary but also fundamentally illusory, and the resulting transformation only psychological rather than genuinely ontological. Here, too, Nietzsche sees the cunning hand of nature at work, in this instance "detaining its creatures in life" through rendering the Apollinian man "ensnared by art's seductive veil of beauty fluttering before his eyes" (p. 109).

The realm of Apollinian art is a kind of "dream world, an Olympian *middle world* of art" (p. 43) that is neither the everyday world nor the underlying world of will but, rather, a created world by means of which the latter is "veiled and withdrawn from sight" and the former is supplanted as the focus of concern. And entrance into this world is possible, Nietzsche holds, only for a kind of dreamer, or Olympian spectator, detached from the kinds of involvements and concerns that both characterize the everyday world and endow us with our ordinary psychological identities. Indeed, it requires that one *become* such a "pure spectator"— or, rather, that the images presented are such that they induce a kind of contemplative consciousness through which one's psychological identity is transformed into that of such a subject. They stand outside of time and change, need and strife, and to become absorbed in them is for Nietzsche to have one's consciousness comparably transformed. If, in the experience of Dionysian art, one is enraptured, one may be said here to be entranced. And, in a state of such entrancement, it is as if one had become a part of this world of images—not as one of them, but as a placeless, disembodied center of awareness, a subject fit for such objects and answering to their nature.

Schopenhauer had spoken of the occurrence of a significant release and liberation from the "world of will," however temporary and incomplete, in aesthetic experience of this sort, as a result of which one effectively ceases to be a creature and captive of this will for its duration. And for Nietzsche too, while Apollinian art involves "the arousing of delight in beautiful forms" (p. 100), this is not to be construed merely in the sense of providing us with pleasure but, rather, in terms of an overcoming of the distress associated with our human condition through what is felt to be a kind of redemption from it. "Here Apollo overcomes the suffering of the individual by the radiant glorification of the *eternity of the Phenomenon*; here beauty triumphs over the suffering inherent in life" (p. 104), for the Apollinian man "is absorbed in the pure contemplation of images" (p. 50), the beauty of which strongly attracts us and brings us under their spell, causing us to banish all else from our minds and seemingly to become nothing but the delighted awareness of them. Our delight is genuine, and our psychological transformation real—even though on a more fundamental level both the objects of such consciousness and this self-consciousness are merely two aspects of the Apollinian illusion, which is but "one of those illusions which nature so frequently employs to achieve her own ends" (p. 44).

This illusion, however, is by no means as insubstantial as the term might seem to suggest. One indication of this, on Nietzsche's account, is the very fact that it is powerful enough to enable "nature" to achieve her end of "seducing one to a continuation of life" by means of it (p. 43). And if it is the case, as Nietzsche claims in this same sentence, that Apollinian art is thus "called into being, as the complement and consummation of existence," it follows that it is no *mere* illusion which leaves the reality of human life unaffected. It may not alter the human condition. But, if it is in some significant sense the "consummation of existence," it may be truly said to effect a significant transformation of "existence," or at least that portion of it which is the reality of human life. Art may be created by man, but man is also recreated or transfigured by art.

The kind of experience and spirituality which become attainable in relation to the idealized images of Apollinian art may not constitute an elevation of those who attain to them entirely beyond the reach of the entanglements of ordinary life and the deeper harsh realities of existence in this world. Yet they do render the existence of those attaining to them qualitatively different from that of those who remain entirely immersed in the former or who further succeed only in finding occasional respite through Dionysian experience. It is Nietzsche's appreciation of the magnitude of this qualitative difference that accounts for his celebration of the achievement of the archaic Greeks in their creation of Apollinian art, both plastic and epic.

Life cannot in the end be lived merely on the plane of Apollinian aesthetic experience, or even simply in the radiation of the reflected glory with which Apollinian art is capable of lighting the world of ordinary experience. The human condition is too recalcitrant, and the undercurrent of the "Dionysian ground of existence" too strong, for the psychological transformation involved in the ascent into the realm of Apollinian art prevails indefinitely. Absorbing and delightful as this kind of experience is, it suffers from the fatal weakness of failing to come to terms with basic aspects of human life in the world that do not disappear when veiled, despite "recourse to the most forceful and pleasurable illusions" (p. 43). Yet Nietzsche is by no means disposed to conclude that what might be termed "the Apollinian experiment" is to be regarded as a mere blind alley, to be abandoned in favor of the Dionysian alternative. For these two alternatives to life lived solely on the plane of dull immersion in the affairs of everyday existence, and also to reversion "to the tiger and the ape" and Schopenhauerian ascetic withdrawal, are not the only ones. There remains at least one other, which Nietzsche associates with the phenomenon of tragic art. And in this connection his suggestion should be kept in mind that the "Apollinian illusion" is a development in which there is to be found the "consummation of existence," for, "illusion" though it may be, the kind of transfiguration it involves—both of the objects and the subjects of experience—is of the utmost importance in the emergence alike of tragic art and the more viable form of human existence he associates with it.

XVI

Thus, BT's full original title (*The Birth of Tragedy, Out of the Spirit of Music*) notwithstanding, Nietzsche conceives tragic art to be no less Apollinian than Dionysian in origin and nature. At the very outset of the book, he advances this contention with respect to the archetype of it, asserting that "by a metaphysical miracle of the Hellenic 'will,' " the "tendencies" associated with each "appear coupled with each other, and through this coupling ultimately generate an equally Dionysian and Apollinian form of art—Attic tragedy" (p. 33). The burden of his entire discussion of it is that its emergence presupposed not only the prior development of the art of Dionysian transfiguration, but also the *retransfiguration* of the latter under the influence of the likewise previously developed art of Apollinian transfiguration.

The birth of tragedy for Nietzsche was an event of the greatest actual and possible future significance, for it did not merely involve the appearance of a qualitatively new art form, thus opening another chapter in the development of art. It also made possible a further qualitative transformation of human life, which he conceives to have been and to be of far greater moment than is generally recognized. "Tragic art" and "Attic tragedy" are by no means synonymous for him; the later is without question a paradigm case of the former, and there may be no better way to approach the former than by the course Nietzsche follows in BT, of investigating the latter. But the possibility of tragic art did not end with the expiration of Attic tragedy and is not wedded to the dramatic form of the works produced by the classical tragedians. Nor is Nietzsche here thinking in addition merely of Elizabethan tragic drama, together with the tragic opera of his own time, but rather of what he characterizes more generally as *tragic myth*.

Moreover, and even more importantly, he does not conceive of tragic art as a phenomenon the significance of which is confined to but a single sphere of human experience and cultural life. Rather, he views it as the potential foundation and guiding force of an entire form of culture and human existence, which alone is capable of filling the void left by the collapse of "optimistic" life-sustaining myths (both religious and philosophical-scientific). And he looks to it to assume anew the function of "making life possible and worth living," which neither Apollinian nor Dionysian art as such is capable any longer of performing. The former may continue to entrance and delight us, and the latter to enrapture and excite us, and both may continue to transport and transform us in their respective fashions, but the power of the illusions they involve to sustain us has been lost.

Schopenhauer himself had borne witness to this, having concluded that nontragic art could not suffice to render life worth affirming, suggesting that the only genuine redemption possible for man is an ascetic rather than an aesthetic one. In this connection, he had also taken the position that tragic art serves merely to underscore this view. Here, however, Nietzsche parts company with him, and on no uncertain terms, for he takes Schopenhauer both to have construed the character of tragic art very superficially and inadequately and to have failed completely to appreciate its potentially powerful positive psychological impact.

This last point warrants brief elaboration before turning to a consideration of Nietzsche's interpretation of this art form. In the light of some of his remarks, one could be forgiven for supposing that his understanding of the psychological effect of tragedy is not very different from Aristotle's. Aristotle had maintained that this effect is basically one of catharsis; the tragedian constructs a dramatic means of enabling us to be purged of the feelings of fear and pity arising in connection with our recognition of our own plight in this world and threatening to paralyze us, by arousing such feelings directed toward a tragic figure and discharging them upon this figure. In this way, our capacity to feel them for ourselves is held to be diminshed (at least for a time), thus enabling us to return to the world of action temporarily unimpaired by them.

Nietzsche says something of a similar nature, in connection with comedy as well as tragedy. One who "sees everywhere only the horror or absurdity of existence" may be beyond the reach of the consolations of lesser art forms, but even here, "when the danger to his will is greatest," art still has the capacity to save him, for it—and it alone—is able to "turn these nauseous thoughts . . . into notions with which one can live: These are the *sublime* as the artistic taming of the horrible, and the *comic* as the artistic discharge of absurdity." The details of his account differ from those of Aristotle's, but Nietzsche is close to him when he concludes that the effect of this "saving deed of Greek art" upon the Greeks who were thus endangered was that "the feelings described here exhausted themselves" (p. 60).

However, to say this much is by no means to say enough, for, if one confines one's attention to this aspect of the experience of tragic art alone, one misses something of even greater significance than the discharge or exhaustion of such negative feelings—namely, the powerful *positive* feelings generated at the same time, which are akin to those associated with Dionysian aesthetic experience.

In a word, what is absent from the above account is reference to the tremendous *exhilaration* that tragic art serves to inspire, notwithstanding the distressing fate of the central tragic figures. This exhilaration is much more than a mere feeling of relief from the torment occasioned by the negative feelings of which one is purged. And it is also different in both magnitude and kind from the delight associated with Apollinian aesthetic experience, even though certain aspects of works of tragic art may occasion such delight, or at least admit of being experienced in an Apollinian manner. Thus Nietzsche contends that "the drama . . . attains as a whole an effect that transcends *all Apollinian* effects" (p. 130).

There may be those whom tragedy does not affect in this way (Schopenhauer would appear to have been one), but that, for Nietzsche, says something about *them* rather than about the nature of tragic art. Exhilaration is, in his view, an essential feature of the proper effect such art should have, and this phenomenon both renders comprehensible why he attaches such great significance to tragic art and guides his interpretation of it it—for it is his conviction that it holds the key to the understanding of the nature of this art form and that no analysis of tragic art can be considered sound or adequate that does not do justice to it.

XVII

In tragedy, according to Nietzsche, we find elements of both Apollinian and Dionysian art—not, however, merely externally combined but, rather, employed in a subtle interplay and, indeed, played off against each other as well as utilized to enhance each other. But, even more importantly, these elements do not retain their entire original character, taking on instead certain aspects of the other and losing certain of their own. Thus he contends that here "Dionysus speaks the language of Apollo; and Apollo, finally, the language of Dionysus" (p. 130). To be sure, this role reversal of the two "languages" is by no means complete, but the point is an important one and warrants careful attention. Again, speaking metaphorically, Nietzsche contends that "in this fraternal union of Apollo and Dionysus," we find that "an Appollinian *illusion*" is employed to admit the Dionysian "spirit of music" into our experience, while at the same time protecting against an "immediate unity with Dionysian music" by requiring it to be expressed "in an Apollinian field." And we also find that "the Apollinian receives wings from the spirit and soars," surpassing all "weaker degrees of Apollinian art" by being "illuminated from the inside by music" to an extent that "in all other Apollinian art remain unattained" (p. 139).

Nietzsche's specific meaning here may be far from immediately apparent. Yet these remarks should make it quite clear that he is not saying simply that tragic art is a kind of hybrid of Apollinian idealized images and Dionysian symbolically expressive forms, in which these are conjoined in such a way as to draw upon the artistic natures of each and establish experiential middle ground between the entrancement of the former and rapture the latter. And in this connection it is both crucial and illuminating to bear in mind the passage cited earlier from the last section of the book, in which he contends—clearly with tragic art specifically in mind—that, with respect to the underlying nature and character of the world and existence in it, "not one whit more may enter the consciousness of the human individual than can be overcome again by [the] Apollinian power of transfiguration" (p. 143). To be able to endure the consciousness of them of which we are capable and which cannot in the long run be prevented from emerging, and to be able further to embrace and affirm life despite the attainment of such an awareness, a transformation of this consciousness is necessary. In its starkest, simplest and most vivid form, according to Nietzsche, it would be overwhelmingly horrible, "nauseating," paralyzing and unendurable, save in temporary transports of Dionysian ecstatic self-trancendence which cannot be sustained and so constitute no adequate long-term recourse.

For Nietzsche, tragic art alone, is truly equal to this task, and thus the problem before us is to determine how his conception of its nature enables him to so regard it. As has been seen, he holds that it enables us to experience the terrible not as merely terrible but, rather, as sublime and that it achieves something akin to a Dionysian effect upon us, which however is not identical with it—for it does not take the kind of life-endangering toll that Dionysian intoxication does, inducing an experiential state that differs as significantly from such intoxication as it does from Apollinian dreaming. In the long run it has the character of a tonic rather than a depressant; its aftermath is held to be exhilaration, rather than either the overall exhaustion which follows upon Dionysian excitement or the exasperation which Apollinian exaltation leaves in its train. And, considered more immediately, it might be said to enthrall, rather than to entrance *or* enrapture. So to describe what tragic art does is not to give an analysis of it, though Nietzsche's conception of its nature requires to be comprehended in the light of this understanding of its effects.

XVIII

Tragic art too, for Nietzsche, may be said to constitute a kind of "transfiguring mirror." It is a mirror, however, in which we see reflected neither "appearances" idealizingly transfigured nor the character of the reality underlying them symbolically expressed. We are confronted instead with "images of life"—reflections of the human (and our) condition, highlighting both the individuation it involves and the fate bound up with the latter in a world in which all individual existence is ephemeral, harsh, and ridden with strife and suffering. What we encounter, however, is not a stark and brutally "realistic" portrayal of this condition as such. We see it in transfigured form—even though this transfiguration of it does not consist in its radical transmutation into a merely imaginary, idealized condition *contrasting* to the actual human condition on these counts. And it likewise does not involve the effective obliteration of the salient features of human life through the diversion of attention from the entire domain of individuation to the collective, the impersonal, the merely vital and the enduring aspects of life underlying it. Rather, the kind of transfiguration occurring here is one which pertains to our perception of individual human existence—*as* existence that is individual rather than merely a part of an inexhaustible and indestructible flow of life and that is human rather than above and beyond the conditions to which man is subject.

This transfiguration pertains first to the character of the dramatic figures with which we are confronted—or, rather, it comes about first in the context of our confrontation with them, but it does not remain confined to this encounter, serving rather to alter our apprehension of the human condition more generally. It is in this sense above all that tragic art may be said to serve as a transfiguring mirror: it works a transformation upon our consciousness of the human reality that is also our own, at the same time as it reflects that reality for us to behold. The fate of the tragic figure takes on the aspect of something sublime rather than merely horrible, and thus, without being denied or glossed over, it ceases to inspire mere "nausea," moving us instead to fascination and awe. The life of the tragic figure is endowed with a significance that entirely alters its aspect, and what might seem from a simple recitation of the brute facts of the matter to be a merely wretched and distressing tale emerges as an enthralling and moving spectacle.

Tragic art presents us neither with an ideal to be admired and emulated nor with an avenue by means of which to escape all thought of the hard realities of life. The latter are very much in evidence, and the tragic figure caught up in them is one with whom, as an individual, we emphasize but with whom, as a character, we do not identify. Yet the manner of presentation of such figures, which renders them tragic and not merely pathetic, does much more than merely purge us of our self-directed feelings of fear and pity through an empathic discharge. It can have a powerful positive impact upon the way in which we perceive our human condition and experience the reality of our own lives, by revealing them to us in a very different light from that in which we would otherwise tend to view them. The point might be put by saying that the tragic artist, not through the persona of the tragic figure per se but in the larger structure of the tragic drama, interposes a medium between us and the reality of human existence which does more than simply give expression to the *latter*, for the medium further shapes and colors our consciousness of reality and is able to help us attain an affirmative attitude toward it precisely by virtue of doing so.

In short, tragic art provides us with a way of apprehending this reality that enables us to come to terms with it—and not only to endure but also to affirm what we thereby see, as we thereby learn to see it. In this way it resembles Dionysian art. And for Nietzsche this similarity of tragic art to the Dionysian arts is by no means merely fortuitous. In tragic myth, as in music and dance, something transcending mere appearances is symbolically expressed—and in being so expressed is transformed for our consciousness. Here, however, the symbolic forms employed are not primarily those characteristic of these Dionysian art forms but, rather, are drawn from the initially nonsymbolic domain of Apollinian art. This is a point to which I shall turn shortly.

XIX

First, however, another point relative to the foregoing observation needs to be made. In tragic art attention is focused upon individual figures whose stature is Apollinian in that they are not only individual but also idealized "images of life"—no mere ordinary human beings but "great and sublime forms." By means of them, the tragic art "satisfies our sense of beauty," which delights in such idealized images, and also "incites us to comprehend in thought the core of life they contain" (p. 178). To the extent that tragedy does the former, it has an "Apollinian artistic effect"; yet its effect is by no means simply Apollinian, as is already indicated simply by the fact that it also does the latter. To the extent that tragedy does this, these images do not function merely as idealizations whose contemplation as such delights us; they also have the significance of *symbols*, whose interest for us is also a matter of what they convey about the "life" they symbolize, the life in which both they and we participate.

Beyond this fact, however, it is a basic feature of tragic art, according to Nietzsche, that "at the most essential point this Apollinian illusion is broken and annihilated" (p. 130). While that on which the tragic figures stand as symbols is not thereby shown to be merely illusory, the figures themselves are destroyed, succumbing to forces which shatter their individual existence and give the lie to the appearance of self-contained and impervious reality of these "great and sublime forms." And yet the impact of tragic art upon us is by no means merely that of depression and despair, as one would expect if not merely our immediate attention but moreover our entire awareness were attuned entirely to these "glorious appearances." On a deeper level of apprehension, according to Nietzsche, we respond to the dramatic expression (in classical tragedy, through the chorus) of the inexhaustible and indestructible power of the forces of life in relation to which all individual existence is merely ephemeral. What Nietzsche calls "the spirit of music" speaks above the relation of what befalls the tragic figures, with the result that "in the total effect of the tragedy, the Dionysian predominates once again" (p. 130), and we are exhilarated rather than merely mortified.

This "total effect," however, is not purely Dionysian, and the difference is crucial both with respect to the understanding of tragic art as well as to its "value for life." A discernment of and identification with the larger and deeper reality transcending the existence of the tragic figures and all individuals is attained—but not through an enraptured ascent into a state of consciousness in which the former alone absorbs us. Rather, this occurs in a manner which at the same time not only leaves us very much aware of individuals and the conditions of their existence but, moreover, actually heightens this awareness. And the attendant exhilaration, while akin to Dionysian excitement, neither depends upon the attainment of such Dionysian transport nor endures for only so long as our consciousness remains thus transformed. On the contrary, it is wedded to a vivid recognition of the plight of particular individuals, and it carries over after the event when our own lives once again come to the fore.

Thus on Nietzsche's account of the experience of tragic art, we identify completely neither with the tragic figures nor with the chorus (or its counterparts in nonclassical tragic art forms). And, while he holds that it is through a partial identification with the latter that a modified kind of "Dionysian effect" occurs, this identification is more subliminal than direct and is tempered by the focus of our immediate attention upon the tragic figures and what transpires as their individual lives unfold. Tragic art differs from Dionysian art in character and impact, just as Dionysian art is not tragic. And Nietzsche's contention that "the Dionysian predominates" in the total effect of tragic art should not be construed too simplistically. A fundamentally Dionysian chord is sounded, and our responsiveness to it is tapped, but this is done to achieve an importantly

different effect. For what occurs, on Nietzsche's analysis, is not a transformation of our consciousness along lines rendering us oblivious to our
individual existence but, rather, a transfiguration of the character of our
consciousness with respect to such existence.

To be sure, we do also achieve what Nietzche terms the "metaphysical
comfort," initially connected with Dionysian art, that "beneath the whirl
of phenomena eternal life flows on indestructibly" (pp. 109–10). But this
is not all. While sensing this, we lose sight of and forget neither the "greta
and sublime forms" and their fate nor ourselves and the conditions of our
existence. The latter recognition does not detract from our exhilaration;
our exhilaration is not merely a reflection of the aforementioned comfort,
and the positive transfiguration of our consciousness with respect to the
latter is not simply the consequence of an affect-transfer occasioned by
its conjunction with this Dionysian identification.

XX

Nietzsche does go on, in this connection, to speak of tragic art working
to bring it about so that "the more nobly formed" individuals who "feel
profoundly the weight and burden of existence" are "deluded by exquisite
stimulants into forgetfulness of their displeasure" with respect to their
lot (p. 110). But "forgetfulness of their displeasure" here is neither tantamount to a Dionysian forgetting of themselves nor achieved at the cost
of such forgetting. And, while Nietzsche does consider it appropriate to
say that this involves their being "deluded by exquisite stimulants," both
the "stimulants" and the "delusion" here differ significantly from those
associated with the refined intoxication of Dionysian rapture—for that
which acts as a stimulant is not only the dramatic expression of "eternal
life flowing on indestructibly" despite the destruction of the tragic figures, but also the manner of representation of these figures and of their
confrontation with their fate. And it is not only a sense of identification
with the former in its inexhaustible vitality and indestructibility that constitutes the operative delusion here. For this also and even more importantly pertains to the altered consciousness of one's own individual
existence and lot which is derived from its reflection in the transfiguring
mirror of this representation.

Life regarded as tragic is no longer life seen as merely wretched and
pathetic; and the "displeasure" associated with "the weight and burden of
existence" is overshadowed and forgotten when the latter takes on the
aspect of tragic fate rather than mere senseless suffering and annihilation.
The fate of the tragic figure, when nobly met rather than basely suffered,
enhances rather than detracts from his stature, and the figure serves as a
symbolic medium through which individual existence more generally is
enhanced for us. It is in these terms that the exquisite stimulant distinctively characteristic of tragic art is to be conceived, even though it is
strongly supplemented by the presence of that which is characteristic of
Dionysian art as well.

It is only because of the presence of the former as well as the latter that tragic art is not simply exciting and then debilitating but, rather, more enduringly exhilarating. The idea that exhilaration thus attends the attainment of a tragic sense of life may at first seem rather odd. Its apparent oddity disappears, however, once it is recognized that this view of life is not a grim pessimism to which one is driven once the untenability of all forms of religions and secular "optimism" is discerned. It is no mere stark and unavoidable conclusion but, rather, a signal accomplishment, and Nietzsche takes it to contrast in an incomparably more appealing and satisfying way to the much starker, utterly bleak conception of individual existence as the unmitigated and unadorned tale of mere ceaseless striving, senseless suffering, and inevitable destruction it was proclaimed to be by Schopenhauer and ancient wisdom alike.

As has been noted, Nietzsche contends that tragic art "participates fully in [the] metaphysical intention of art to transfigure." He further maintains, however, that it does so differently from both Apollinian and Dionysian art. Thus he writes, "But what does it transfigure when it presents the world of appearance in the image of the suffering hero? Least of all the 'reality' of this world of appearance . . ." (p. 140). Apollinian art transfigures appearances as such and, at the same time, our consciousness of ourselves in relation to them. Dionysian art does likewise with respect to the nature of the world beyond and beneath all such appearances. Tragic art, on the other hand, is concerned neither with appearances as such nor with the underlying world will itself. It has to do with human existence in this world, which is a matter neither of a mere array of the former nor of the ceaseless surge of the latter.

In the tragic figure we encounter a personified transfiguration of human existence, in which such existence is neither transmuted into idealized imagery purged of all conflict, pain, blemish, and vulnerability nor reduced to the status of anonymous and individually insignificant instantiations of life. In contrast to what occurs in both of these cases, it is here ennobled within the very conditions imposed upon it. And it is by means of this transfiguration that tragic art works its distinctive transformation of our consciousness of ourselves. Thus Nietzsche goes on to contend that "it is precisely the tragic myth that has to convince us that even the ugly and disharmonic are part of an artistic game that the will in the eternal amplitude of its pleasure plays with itself" (p. 141).

The unique achievement of tragic art is thus held to be that it fundamentally alters our apprehension of human existence and the circumstances associated with it, which result in the suffering and destruction of even such extraordinary figures as the central characters of tragic drama and myth. Through it, these circumstances cease to stand as *objections* to human life and its worth and emerge instead as features of it which—as part of the larger whole human lives are and can be—actually contribute to its overall significance and attractiveness. And thus, Nietzsche suggests, it serves to bring it about that existence can "seem justified" *aesthetically* "only as an aesthetic phenomenon." (p. 141) Nietzsche's use of the term "only" here is highly important, for his general point is that it is *only* in this way, in the last analysis, that it is possible for us to find human life and our own existence endurable and worthwhile without recourse to illusions which radically misrepresent the actual nature of our human reality and the world more generally.

XXI

It has been observed, however, that for Nietzsche this transfiguration of our consciousness of ourselves itself involves a delusion. Thus Nietzsche considers it appropriate to refer to it and the tragic art which brings it about as one of "the stages of illusion"—albeit one "designed . . . for the more nobly formed natures." And, given that this is so, one might well wonder why he considers it to be either superior to "the more vulgar and almost more powerful illusions which the will always has at hand" (p. 110), and how he can suppose it to be any less subject in the long run than they are to the disillusionment which eventually undermines the latter and renders them ineffective.

This problem is indeed a serious one and may at least in part account for Nietzsche's subsequent revision of his thinking with respect to the significance of both this art form and art generally. In BT, however, he would appear to consider the kind of illusion involved here to constitute a special case, even though he also is concerned to draw attention to the way in which, in the instance of Greek tragedy, it could be and was subverted—together with the tragic sense of life with which it was associated—through the rise of a new (and more dangerously illusory) form of "optimism" personified by Socrates.

This illusion relates to the treatment of the central figures in tragic art and the corresponding transformation of our self-consciousness. It does not, however, consist simply in the employment in tragic art of an Apollinian illusion, even though it is a part of the nature of this art to make use of such an element. With respect to the latter, Nietzsche speaks of the presence of an "Apollinian *illusion* whose influence aims to deliver us from the Dionysian flood and excess," in that it "tears us out of the Dionysian universality and lets us find delight in individuals . . ." (pp. 128–29). But a further sort of illusion is created at the same time, for which this "deliverance" is necessary but of which it is not strictly constitutive. It clearly differs from the former, for it is not dispelled and shattered when "this Apollinian illusion is broken and annihilated," and is revealed as "merely a glorious appearance" (pp. 129–30). Were it thus also destroyed, we then would either be drawn back into the "universality" of the "Dionysian flood and excess" or else returned bereft of both illusion and joy to ordinary life, albeit perhaps temporarily relieved through catharsis of fear and pity.

According to Nietzsche, however, neither of these is the sequel to this collapse of the Apollinian illusion in the case of genuine tragic art. A further "illusion" remains, which is in a sense the issue of both this illusion now dispelled and its likewise supplanted Dionysian counterpart. Although this new illusion also centers upon the tragic figure, this figure

now no longer simply has the status of an idealized Apollinian image satisfying our sense of beauty, for in tragic art this figure is no mere glorious
appearance of interest simply as such and in itself; it is made to take on a
Dionysian expressive function by being transformed into a symbol. An
Apollinian image is endowed with a Dionysian significance, and the result
is something neither exclusively Apollinian nor purely Dionysian, but par-
taking to a significant extent of both the ideality of the former and the
vitality of the latter.

Thus Nietzsche suggests that in Greek tragedy a Dionysian impulse
"discharges itself in an Apollinian world of images" (pp. 64-65), in a
manner which leaves neither unchanged. He characterizes the result genet-
ically as a *symbolical dream image,* born through the union in the tragic
artist of "Dionysian intoxication" and "Apollinian dream inspiration" (p.
38). Its genesis notwithstanding, however, this result does not merely
express the same thing Dionysian music does, only in a different symbolic
medium. And its import is not simply that the individuality associated
with Apollinian imagery is assimilated to and submerged in Dionysian
universality any more than it is that Dionysian reality is overcome and
transmuted into pure Apollinian ideality. In the tragic figure a double
effect is achieved: Dionysian reality is sublimated and Apollinian ideality
is brought down to earth. Both meet on the plane of individual human
existence and yield a transfigured representation of it in which the conditions of human existence are at once preserved and transformed.

The symbolic significance of the tragic figure survives the destruction
of this figure as a particular character, the recognition that his great and
sublime form is merely a glorious appearance and the breaking and annihilation of the Apollinian illusion involved in our initial apprehension
of him along Apollinian lines. But this is because the tragic figure is *not
intended* merely to satisfy our sense of beauty. It is made to do so initially
to engage our interest in this figure as an individual, who is not to be
lost sight of—for here we are by no means to be rendered oblivious to
all individual human existence, as we are in the case of Dionysian art. As
the tragedy unfolds, however, our attention is increasingly drawn to something in the tragic figure that transcends his glorious appearance as such.
And it is to this that Nietzsche is referring when he contends that tragic
art "presents images of life to us, and incites us to comprehend in thought
the core of life they contain" (p. 128).

It is in these terms that an essential part of the symbolic significance of
the tragic figure is to be conceived, and what is thus symbolically signified
is not annihilated and obliterated when the Apollinian illusion is shattered
and swept aside. It is something having to do with "life"—*human* life—
and the reality of human existence. It is not, however, mere undifferentiated Dionysian universality, even though the fundamentally Dionysian
character of "the core of life" is not passed over but, rather, is incorporated into the image. In this connection, it should be recalled that for
Nietzsche "it is precisely the tragic myth that has to convince us that
even the ugly and the disharmonic are part of an artistic game" (p. 141) in

terms of which reality in general is to be conceived, and human life along with it.

Dionysian art is held to convey to us a sense that things of this sort do not fatally flaw this macrocosmic "game" as a whole but, rather, contribute to its fundamentally positive "artistic" character. But here it is suggested that tragic art goes a step further, persuading us that they likewise may be accepted and affirmed as features of our own human lives, which even on the microcosmic scale of individual existence can thus be experienced as having an "aesthetic" justification. And, very importantly for Nietzsche, this alteration of their aspect is achieved not by means of a resort to religious or metaphysical fictions, thereby either assimilating them to larger designs of supernatural powers or relegating them to the status of mere appearance. It is instead accomplished through their artistic incorporation into an aesthetically appealing and satisfying vision of life. If this involves no resort to any such fiction, however, wherein lies the illusion?

XXII

As has been observed in connection with Apollinian and Dionysian art, there is for Nietzsche a significant sense in which all images, like appearances more generally, are to be considered illusory. And so, for that matter, are all symbols, for neither may be supposed to correspond even approximately, let alone exactly, to the actual nature of reality. No relation of resemblance obtains between these sorts of experiential phenomena and the constitution of this underlying reality itself; the difference is qualitative, and profound. But it is by no means only in this very basic (and relatively uninteresting) respect that Nietzsche takes tragic art too to involve the generation of illusion.

He further is not thinking here of the obvious circumstance that tragic myth differs from historical fact and that tragic figures are generally fictitious characters. No illusions are created with respect to either of these points. Nor does he have in mind what he calls "the metaphysical comfort" with which "every true tragedy leaves us," that "life is at the bottom of all things, despite all changes of appearances, indestructibly powerful and pleasurable" (p. 59). This Dionysian (and not distinctively tragic) insight, he holds, is entirely sound. And there is likewise nothing illusory for him in the conviction he takes tragic art to seek to impart to us that "even the ugly and the disharmonic are part of an artistic game" played by "the will" in its "eternal amplitude" (p. 141), on both the macrocosmic scale and in the microcosm of human life, for this too he holds actually to be the case. The principal kind of illusion he discerns in tragic art and takes to be distinctively and crucially characteristic of it is not a matter of any of these things as such.

It has already been observed that this illusion centers on the "image of life" with which we are confronted in the tragic figure. While such figures are not simply "realistically" drawn, or fictitious but true-to-life individuals, or representatives of the elemental characteristics of "Dionysian universality" (as is the chorus), they are not mere Apollinian beautiful illusions either. Like Apollinian idealized images, however, they constitute something on the order of a "supplement of the reality of nature," and of that of ordinary human existence along with it, "placed beside it for its overcoming" (p. 140). The "core of life they contain" is the same as our own, but this core is artistically transformed into images of life expressing possibilities which are more human than mere glorious appearances, and yet which differ markedly from the commonplace, in ways moreover answering to no predetermined human essence or foreordained human ideal. They thus can in no sense be said to confront us with the "truth" of human existence. And, since what they confront us with is something other than truth, they may be said to present us with a kind of illusion. It is in this sense that Nietzsche remarks to this effect are to be understood.

Yet this illusion is no *mere* illusion, and the transformed consciousness of ourselves which emerges when we view our own lives in the light of the manner of those of these tragic figures is not *merely* illusory, for the creations in which they consist are not distorted or erroneous representations of something that has a fixed and immutable character and cannot be otherwise. And they also are not simply imaginary substitutes temporarily usurping a position in our consciousness that is normally and more properly occupied by our ordinary conception of our own mundane reality. Rather, they are symbols of *human* possibility. And as such they serve to carry us beyond the mere acknowledgment of intractable aspects of the human condition, enabling us to discern ways in which the latter may be confronted and transformed into occasions for the endowment of life with grandeur and dignity.

By means of these symbols, human life thus may come to take on an aesthetic significance sufficing to overcome the distressing character of its harsh basic features. It stands revealed as a potentially aesthetic phenomenon, "justifiable" accordingly in our estimation even in the face of its hardest circumstances. And of paramount importance for Nietzsche is the fact that tragic art works this feat in a non-Apollinian way; it does not confine this perception to the tragic figure themselves, while precluding its application to our lives. These figures stand as symbols serving to facilitate our apprehension of the possibilities they express, together with "the core of life they contain," as our own—and so to alter the aspect of our own lives.

To say that this is all illusion, as Nietzsche does, is neither to deny the reality of this alteration nor to downplay its significance. Rather, it is to make the point that our lives thus acquire an experimential character which is no part of their fundamental objective nature and that this occurs through the transforming mediation of created images enabling us to discern aesthetic significance in human existence, notwithstanding that its basic circumstances warrant the attribution to it of no significance whatsoever.

XXIII

The principal feature of tragic art thus is not the chorus (or its counterparts in instances of it other than Greek tragedy), through which "Dionysian wisdom" is given expression, considered simply as such. Neither is it the tragic figure regarded apart from this Dionysian background, in all his "epic clearness and beauty" or as a glorious appearance fated for annihilation. To be sure, both are essential elements of tragic art, and it is further the case for Nietzsche that *"tragic myth* is to be understood only as a symbolization of Dionysian wisdom through Apollinian artifices" (p. 131). But even this characterization of the relation effected between these two elements does not adequately convey the nature of the result. Nietzsche does contend that "the highest goal of tragedy and of all art is attained" when it thus comes about that "Dionysus speaks the language of Apollo; and Apollo, finally, the language of Dionysus" (p. 130). Yet it would be an error to suppose that this goal consists merely in the supersession of Apollinian and ordinary forms of consciousness alike by a triumphantly reascendant Dionysianism.

This point can hardly be overemphasized, for it is of the greatest importance. What is at issue here, once again, is the "aesthetic justification" not simply of the world generally, but also of human existence, as we do and must live it—and this is something that presupposes the supersession of Dionysian as well as Apollinian (and also ordinary) consciousness. Tragic art is held to be capable of accomplishing this result only by virtue of the "fraternal union of Apollo and Dionysus" occurring in it, not by a victory of the latter over the former. The quasi-Apollinian tragic figure may be "annihilated," but the entire Apollinian element is not. And, while "the Dionysian predominates" in "the total effect of the tragedy" (p. 130), it does not emerge in sole possession of the field. If human existence is to be "justified" *despite* its inescapable harsh conditions and fate, it cannot be exhibited in such a way that only the suffering and destruction it involves are made to stand as its final truth, with all aesthetically justifying characteristics being reserved to the "primordial unity" that flows on beneath the surface of individuation and appearance.

In tragic art the Apollinian is neither merely assimilated into the Dionysian, nor is it the fundamental import of tragedy that the true status and meaning of human existence is to be conceived exclusively in terms of the nature of Dionysian reality, which gives the lie to all Apollinian transfiguration. The Apollinian is transformed through being brought into relation with the Dionysian, but not shattered and bannished or deprived of all significance. On the contrary, Nietzsche contends that it thereby "receives wings from the spirit of music and soars" (p. 139) more powerfully than it ever can otherwise—and leaves its mark on the Dionysian, which is likewise transformed in this "union." To be sure, the underlying character of the world itself and of the human condition is not thereby altered, but the aspect of human existence is, even while it is apprehended against the background of this Dionysian reality.

The consciousness of human existence and of ourselves which Nietzsche terms "tragic" is neither purely Apollinian nor merely Dionysian, for the tragic myth in accordance with which it is shaped places this existence we share in a new and different light. A new way of seeing it becomes possible, in that our relation to the reality that is at once the ground and the abyss of our existence comes to be regarded as amenable to Apollinian transformation. Here our own existence as individuals is not something to which it is necessary to be oblivious to experience aesthetic enjoyment, as in the cases of Apollinian delight and Dionysian rapture in their separate and more basic aesthetic forms. Rather, human life itself becomes the focus of a kind of aesthetic satisfaction identical with neither but related to both through its treatment in a way that brings our capacity for responses of both sorts into play in relation to it.

While the last word in tragedy might seem to belong to Dionysian reality and Dionysian wisdom, therefore, it in fact does not—even if it does not belong to Apollinian ideality and optimism either. The former is as hopelessly pessimistic with respect to human existence as it actually can and must be lived as the latter is naive and unrealistic—whereas tragedy is neither but, rather, is fundamentally and strongly affirmative in relation to it. In the attainment of a tragic sense of life, the "terror and horror of existence" are surmounted through the remarkable alchemy of tragic art which transmutes the terrible and horrible into the sublime and magnificent. And the key to this transmutation is not the quickening of that sense of "metaphysical comfort" that "beneath the whirl of phenomena eternal life flows an indestructibility"—though this too occurs. It is rather the "Apollinian power of transfiguration," which alone enables us to endure and affirm the existence that is ours as parts of this "whirl," not only in moments of Dionysian rapture, self-abnegation and obliviousness to the human condition, but also when we acknowledge our individuality and confront the circumstances of human life.

XXIV

Nietzsche may often seem to be more concerned with what might be termed the ecstatic component of the experience of tragic art than with this companion feature of it. Yet it is the latter which he finally stresses, when he concludes his discussion by emphasizing that "of this foundation of all existence—the Dionysian basic ground of the world—not one whit more may enter the consciousness of the human individual than can be overcome again by this Apollinian power of transfiguration" (p. 143). This power must be brought to bear upon our consciousness of our existence as human individuals, not merely upon our awareness of "the Dionysian basic ground of the world" as such, if we are to be able to find our lives endurable and worth living. It would avail us little to regard the world generally as justified if no comparable justification were discernable when we turned to a consideration of our own existence.

In both Apollinian and Dionysian art, the kinds of experience involved focus upon something transcending our existence. Moreover, they serve to sustain us only to the extent that the satisfactions attained during episodes in which we are transported beyond ourselves are strong enough to compensate for the dissatisfactions we experience in the intervals upon which they have no significant direct and positive impact. Each has definite shortcomings in this connection, however, and, for Nietzsche in BT, it is only tragic myth which affords the possibility of overcoming them, by contributing to the establishment of an ability to derive aesthetic satisfaction along lines connecting much more directly with our own lives. It transforms what might otherwise be taken to be life at its worst into life at its best, endowing even suffering and destruction with aesthetic quality—not as such, to be sure, but as central elements of an aesthetically charged whole in which are interwoven the tragic figure's life, circumstances, flaws, strivings, sufferings, and destruction.

In a sense, tragic art may thus be said to accomplish the Apollinianization of the Dionysian, in our consciousness of the latter if not also in its actual nature. But it may perhaps more appropriately be said to accomplish a complex and radical transformation of something else, in a less one-sided manner: the aspect of our human existence, at once along partly Apollinian and partly Dionysian lines. What is thus transformed is not tragedy, for the accomplishment of tragic art is not the transformation of tragedy into something else. Tragedy, rather, is the *issue* of this artistic transformation, through which existence comes to be experienced as tragic. This is indeed an artistic accomplishment, since tragedy no less than beauty may be said to exist only in the eye of the beholder, whose sensibility has been formed and cultivated by art. It is no brute fact of human existence but, rather, an acquired aspect it may come to bear through the transfiguring agency of the tragic artist.

There is illusion in the apprehension of existence as bearing the aspect of tragedy, since its tragic character is a matter of the imposition of significant form upon its given sundry features, rather than of the intrinsic nature of any or all of the latter. And there is a further illusion involved in what Nietzsche terms the noble deception generated to the effect that something more than this is encountered here, for tragic art does not merely transform our manner of regarding existence by means of its elaboration of "a sublime parable, the myth." It also "deceives the listener into feeling that the music"—that is, the symbolic expression of the undercurrent of life that is manifested both in the tragic figure and in the forces to which this figure succumbs—"is merely the highest means to bring life into the vivid world of myth" (p. 126).

It is in this way that the tragic myth comes to be endowed with what Nietzsche terms its "intense and convincing metaphysical significance" (p. 126)—and also its most profoundly illusory character, for it leads us to feel something to be the deepest and highest "truth" of human existence —the tragic character it is capable of coming to bear, with all the sublimity and majesty devolving upon it therefrom—which is no part of either its fundamental nature or any intrinsic essence legitimately attributable to it. Yet according to Nietzsche, tragic art requires ultimately to be conceived as working in the service of life. Here too, what we are said to be dealing with is simply another means, even if also the most exalted one, through which "the insatiable will" manages to "detain its creatures in life and compel them to live on" (p. 109)—in this case by employing tragic myth to lend human existence an aspect endowing it with an aesthetic justifiability. But it does this in such a way that we are led to view life as through it were a means to the end of actualizing the aesthetic values associated with human existence as it is revealed in the transfiguring mirror of tragic myth.

<h1 style="text-align:center">XXV</h1>

In BT, Nietzsche places his hope for a revitalization of Western civilization, in the face of the collapse of both other worldly religiousness and rationalistic-scientific optimism, in a re-emergence of a tragic sense of life. But, as he readily acknowledges, such a view of life cannot be sustained in the absence of tragic myth and an acceptance of the understanding of human existence associated with some instance of it. It is for this reason that he devotes so much discussion in this work to the importance of myth and to the need for a new and compelling form of tragic myth in the modern Western world. He ventures to hope that the ground for a "rebirth of tragedy" and a new "tragic culture" is being prepared by science itself, as it "speeds irresistibly toward its limits where its optimism, concealed in the essence of logic, suffers shipwreck" (p. 97). As this point is reached, he suggests, a "new form of insight breaks through, *tragic insight* which, merely to be endured, needs art as a protection and remedy" (p. 98). But he recognizes that the "shipwreck" of which he speaks, consisting in the collapse of the belief that scientific or other rational modes of inquiry will lead to the discovery of truths establishing the meaning and justifiability of existence, is only a negative condition of such a rebirth and renewal and by no means suffices to accomplish it. Tragic myth alone is held to be capable of doing this, by means of tragic art. For this reason he speaks of art as "even a necessary correlative, of and supplement for science" (p. 93).

Nietzsche obviously thought, when he wrote BT, that Wagner was well on the way to accomplishing the task he thus envisaged. The details of his discussion of this and related matters, however, are of relatively little intrinsic interest—especially since he soon after lost his enthusiasm for Wagner and abandoned his commitment to the ultimacy and indispensibility of that form of art he associates here with tragic myth. He further seems to have become convinced that art generally has a significance in relation to life and that it also has a variety of features to which his analysis of it in BT does not do justice. In any event, he subsequently approached the arts somewhat differently, placing less emphasis upon differences between the various art forms and the kinds of experience associated with them and concerning himself more with the phenomenon of artistic creativity generally.

While many of his later observations about art are unquestionably of considerable interest, and while there are a number of respects in which his later thinking concerning it is clearly superior to his treatment of it in BT (most notably as a result of his self-emancipation from Schopenhauer and Wagner and of his stylistic and philosophical maturation), several points reflecting favorably upon this work are to be noted.

First, although he devoted at least some (and often considerable) attention to art in nearly all of his later writings, he never again subjected it to a comparably comprehensive, intensive, and sustained analysis or treated it with a similar breadth of vision. Second, although he subsequently deepened and modified his understanding of art in certain important ways and recast his views with respect to it in the light of basic alterations in his understanding of the natures of man, life, and reality, he retained most of the fundamental notions in terms of which he interprets it in BT, in one form or another, and continued to give them central roles in his subsequent discussions of it. Finally, it should be clear that, however unsatisfactory, questionable, and excessive some of what he says in BT may be, he is to be credited in this early effort with a number of extremely valuable insights concerning such things as the relation between art and life, the transfigurative character of art, the nature of artistic creation, the distinction between imagistic and symbolically expressive art forms, and the distinctive character and impact of tragic art.

It may be that few classics in the literature of the philosophy of art are as flawed in as many particular respects as is BT, but it is also the case that few so richly reward patience with their flaws and close attention to their substance.

Select Bibliography for Part Three

THE THEORY OF DRAMA

Books

Erich Auerbach, *Mimesis*; A. C. Bradley, *Oxford Lectures on Poetry*; A. C. Bradley, *Shakesperean Tragedy*; S. H. Butcher, *Aristotle's Theory of Poetry and Fine Art*; Arthur Danto, *Nietzsche as Philosopher*; G. F. Else, *Aristotle's Poetics: The Argument*; Ernest Jones, *Hamlet and Oedipus*; Walter A. Kaufmann, *Nietzsche*; Walter A. Kaufmann, *Tragedy and Philosophy*; A. H. J. Knight, *Some Aspects of the Life and Works of Nietzsche*; Frank Alfred Lea, *The Tragic Philosopher*; Friedrich Nietzsche, *The Will to Power*; Whitney J. Oates, *Aristotle and the Problem of Value*; Friedrich Schlegel, *Lectures on the*

History of Literature, Ancient and Modern; Goran Sorbom, *Mimesis and Art. Studies in the Origin and Early Development of an Aesthetic Vocabulary.*

Articles

Stanley Hyman, "Freud and the Climate of Tragedy"; Catherine Lord, "Tragedy Without Character: Poetics VI. 1450a24"; James Richard McNally, "Characteristics of Art in the Text of Aristotle"; Ruby Meager, "Tragedy"; A. M. Quinton and Ruby Meager, "Tragedy" (Symposium); Marvin Rosenberg, "Drama Is Arousal"; Leon Rosenstein, "Metaphysical Foundations of the Theories of Tragedy in Hegel and Nietzsche"; Jerome Stolnitz, "Notes on Comedy and Tragedy."

THE THEORY OF LITERATURE:
WORDS AND IDENTITY

In the film *Farenheit 451* a futuristic society is portrayed where the state attempts to destroy all books. A group of revolutionaries subverts the state's efforts by committing entire works to memory, passing them down to future generations as oral tradition. Thus, an old man who is known as *Pride and Prejudice* teaches Jane Austen's novel to a child before he dies. The child then becomes known as *Pride and Prejudice*. In this manner, novels, philosophical treatises, and nonfiction works are kept in existence.

This futuristic society is a product of the imagination, of course, but the situation portrayed does raise some important questions about the identity of literary works. Suppose one has a copy of *Pride and Prejudice* on the bookshelf. Of what, exactly, is it a copy? It is clear that no particular copy of the book is identical with the work itself. It is also clear that not even the original manuscript of the book is identical with the work itself. If I destroyed my copy of the book, or if the original manuscript were destroyed, the work itself need not be destroyed. As the film's example shows, if no copies of the book existed at all it would still be possible to keep the work in existence through oral tradition. Austen could have composed it orally, as *The Iliad* was composed. If it is neither my copy, nor anyone else's copy, nor the original manuscript, what then is *Pride and Prejudice*?

This is one of the central questions within the philosophy of literature which Beardsley and Urmson attempt to answer in the essays presented here. Their respective answers diverge considerably. Beardsley is inclined to answer the question primarily in terms of the innumerable conventions involved in assigning literary status. In fact, his primary concern is to distinguish among different kinds of texts. He acknowledges that these conventions are far from adequately understood. His own essay is an attempt to map the terrain that must be covered in order to produce an adequate theory of the status of literary works. This makes Beardsley's essay especially valuable, for in mapping his terrain he not only surveys major topics within the philosophy of literature; he also suggests a broad-based account of the philosophy of literature itself.

In his clear and nontechnical essay, Urmson argues that literary works are best understood as analogous to musical, balletic, and theatrical works. In itself, this is not an original suggestion. Aristotle divided the arts in a similar manner (into the plastic arts on the one hand and the literary-musical arts on the other). What is novel about Urmson's account is his treatment of literary works within the category of the literary-musical arts. Urmson suggests that the best account of what the literary artist does is to provide a set of instructions or a recipe which, if executed, results in the performance of a work. This may seem clear enough for theatrical works, but what about novels and short stories? Who executes the instructions when one is sitting at home reading a novel? Urmson argues that reading a novel is analogous to reading a play, or to reading a balletic or a musical score. This makes all literary works performative in nature. Whatever conventions may be involved in assigning literary status, Urmson believes that it is crucial to bear in mind that, first and foremost, literary works are performances, and that the status of a literary work as a performance must be accounted for independently of any particular literary conventions.

Monroe C. Beardsley

THE PHILOSOPHY
OF LITERATURE

We might be amused at a brash barroom philosopher who announced that he could philosophize about anything—and we might even start trying to think of examples that would puncture the boast.* On second thought, though, why not? Sermons in stones, they say—and, according to Walt Whitman, "a mouse is miracle enough to stagger sextillions of infidels." Perhaps a sufficiently deep or determined thinker could manage to extract some philosophical juice from even the humblest object or event. Still, on third thought—if we get that far—we had better pause to consider what actually is being claimed. What is philosophizing? The relevance of this question is pointed up by a conversation David Hume once had.

> "I am surprised, Mr. Hume," said Thomas White, a decent rich merchant of London, "that a man of your good sense should think of being a philosopher. Why, I now took it into my head to be a philosopher for some time, but tired of it most confoundedly, and very soon gave it up."
> "Pray, sir," said Mr. Hume, "in what branch of philosophy did you employ your researches? What books did you read?"
> "Books?" said Mr. White; "nay, sir, I read no books, but I used to sit you whole forenoons a-yawning and poking the fire."[1]

Before we could say with assurance whether there could be a philosophy of ————, we would want to know what a "philosophy of" something is to consist in, and what sort of word may legitimately replace that blank.

In seeking to understand what kind of inquiry philosophy of literature is, or ought to be, I know no better guide than a recent book on the philosophy of education by James McClellan—even if we can't follow his trail exactly. What properly fits into the blank in "philosophy of ————" is always (according to McClellan) the name of a practice, which is a form

Monroe C. Beardsley is Professor of Philosophy at Temple University. He is one of the best known writers in aesthetics in the Anglo-American world. His major work *Aesthetics: Problems in the Philosophy of Criticism* was published in 1958 and has had an enormous influence on the subject.

* This essay was written for this collection and is published here for the first time.

[1] From Ernest Campbell Mossner, *The Forgotten Hume* (New York: Columbia Univ. Press, 1943), p. xii.

of activity defined by a system of rules or canons governing the actions of those engaged in the practice. The philosophy of a practice has as its purpose "to discover the distinctive form which human reason assumes in that practice."[2] In its "revelatory" aspect, this inquiry aims to make explicit "some general features(s) of human reason as exemplified in the practice."

> It doesn't require philosophy to point out that each of us can follow a story, a proof, and a lawyer's advice. We are engaged in philosophy of history, mathematics, and law from their revelatory aspects when we (try to) uncover the presupposed canons of reason which make "following" in each case a rational activity.

In its "critical" aspect, the philosophy of a practice examines those canons against "the most general principles of rationality we can discern"—those of logic and ethics.

When we try to fit the philosophy of literature into this pattern, some genuine difficulties arise at once; and the two most fundamental ones deserve some preliminary discussion. They center on the concepts of *practice* and *reason*.

I

A practice is an activity governed by a system of rules: "in those terms," McClellan remarks,

> law is clearly a practice, so are engineering, medicine, mathematics. . . . Neither art nor the criticism of art is clearly a practice. . . . Love is unequivocally *not* a practice, though it is often perverted into a facsimile of one or more practices.[3]

Literature can certainly be thought of as an activity. It probably comes more naturally to most of us to think of literature as a collection of objects, of books and magazines and so on stacked in libraries or homes—though if pressed we would also be willing to add stories told in various cultures but not written down or printed and tape-recordings of old radio shows never yet transcribed. All these are literary *products*, and they enter into processes of production and consumption. So—staying with our own culture for the most part—we have two basic literary activities: that of composing a literary work deliberately and that of reading it understandingly. Around these, of course, cluster other familiar activities that may justify our calling literature a social institution: those of publishers, printers, librarians, book sellers, book collectors, book reviewers, and such. But authoring (i.e., composing a literary work) and literating (i.e., reading a literary work) are central, and reciprocal.

In literature we find, apparently, a distinguishable form of activity, but is it a practice? For our present purposes we need not develop the lurking

[2] James E. McClellan, *The Philosophy of Education*, Foundations of Philosophy Series (Englewood Cliffs, N.J.: Prentice-Hall, 1976), p. 2.
[3] Ibid., pp. 1–2.

complexities of this question, but some of them may be noted for future reflection. Consider authoring, the making of literary works. It is an activity that certainly includes rule following (at least in the usual case): rules of English grammar, for example, and sometimes more contingent ones (if the short story is for a particular magazine, it may not be over 6,000 words long).

It was once thought by respected literary critics that every literary work must belong to a certain fixed type, or genre, and must follow the rules of that genre (as that a satire is to be in heroic couplets); but hardly anyone would agree with such a view now. The rules of grammar, though they impose restrictions on most authors, don't really define the activity of authoring, since, just because a paragraph is grammatical, it doesn't follow that it is a literary work. Textbooks that purport to teach people how to write fiction or poetry do often contain a lot of general advice, like "Make your characters three dimensional" or "Avoid metaphors that are clichés ('the moon looked down')." But these are not the kind of rule that defines a practice; they are (supposed to be) aids in *improving* practice. Note how in any game there are rules that define or constitute the game—rules you have to follow in order to play the game at all—and practical "rules of thumb" that experienced players bear in mind in order to play the game *well*.

So perhaps we can't really call authoring a practice. What about literating? Again, you can't read a novel in English without knowing the rules of English syntax and the semantical rules governing the words. But these rules apply to *all* reading; they are not distinctive of literating (a word I made up for this occasion). Of course, again, there are various principles, of varying degrees of usefulness, which it might in general be well to follow if we wish to read literature with the greatest possible understanding and enjoyment. But these don't make literating a practice. It has been suggested that our encounters with literary works have some features of a game; for example, in detective stories both sides must play fair in that the author is bound by the rule that all essential clues are to be provided for the reader and the reader is bound by the rule that he is not to look at the last chapter until he gets to it. No doubt the detective story genre has a touch of game-like quality (though whether or not it is literature might be debated).

On a more sophisticated level, a view has developed (out of the contemporary movement known as "structuralism") that the literator follows certain broad "codes" or "conventions" in interpreting a literary work—and even that there is a sort of implicit "narrative contract" between author and literator, licensing certain expectations from the latter.[4] These ideas are important; I shall return to them later. If they should become confirmed, they would go far toward demonstrating that authoring-literating is a (dual) practice. In the meantime, however, we may be content to soften

---

[4] For an excellent discussion, see Jonathan Culler, *Structuralist Poetics: Structuralism, Linguistics, and the Study of Literature* (Ithaca, N.Y.: Cornell University Press, 1975), chapters 6–9.

McClellan's requirement that the only thing we can have a philosophy of is a practice. Let us say that any distinctive form of activity (A) can be the occasion of a philosophy of A.

But this decision now raises questions about the other part of McClellan's formula: that to philosophize about A is to study "human reason as exemplified in" A. It is easy to see human reason as exemplified in a system of rules—partly because we may think (what may not be true) that the rules were deliberately devised, and that therefore there must be some reason for having them, and partly because we know (a little about) how to argue for and against rules—whether there should, or should not, for example, be a rule that all controversial articles in the high school newspaper are to be approved by the principal before publication.

Now it may be quite true that, in general, practices will provide more to philosophize about than other activities, just because they are constituted by rules. Still, an activity—if it has a distinctive form and is widely carried on—may be more or less reasonable too. It may involve, and on analysis exhibit, distinctive modes of thinking (as legal reasoning differs from that typical of experimental psychology). It may have its own special purposes and be more or less rationally ordered for the successful fulfillment of those purposes. It may presuppose the truth of important general assumptions about human nature, or knowledge, or reality; and these would be subject to philosophical scrutiny.

Still, some uneasiness may linger. What, you may wonder, does reason have to do with literature at all? Why should we expect there to be any "distinctive form that reason assumes" in authoring and literating? Recall, for example, McClellan's reference to following a story—after which it turned out that he was thinking of historical narrative, which, naturally, we can philosophize about because history purports to be a branch of human knowledge obtained by characteristic methods and tested against recognized canons of historical inquiry. But when we read *Pinocchio* or *The Forsyte Saga* we are following a story too; only here the story is about events that never happened to people who never were. We have fiction. No question, it seems, of claims to knowledge about the real world, methods of investigation, or standards of truth or probability. So where does reason come into the picture, to give the would-be philosopher something to get hold of?

We must look more closely to see it—but looking closely is, after all, no novelty to the philosopher. First, in fiction writing (including tale telling) we have a very widespread form of activity, which suggests that it is not without a point. Reason appears in the tendency of this activity (if we discover that it *has* a tendency) to satisfy rather basic and pervasive human needs or to afford significant satisfactions. Second, if stories may be told well or poorly, and differences in quality can be discerned, then reason appears in whatever skills and aptitudes are required (a) to tell stories well rather than poorly and (b) to judge correctly that a particular telling is good or poor. Third, if understanding a story, in the fullest degree, is something that one person may be better at than another person, then reason appears in learning and teaching how to follow stories most under-standingly.

In short, experience suggests (1) that it is possible for a justification, or adequate reason, to be given for engaging in such an activity as authoring-literating, (2) that it is possible for reasons to be given for telling a story in one way rather than another, or for telling one story rather than an-other, and (3) that it is possible for reasons to be given for understanding a literary work in one way rather than in another. How much of a philos-ophy of literature it is possible to have—how extensive, how systematic, how significant it can be—depends on the extent to which these possibili-ties turn out, on investigation, to be actualities.

To touch on just one of the questions I have raised, if *The Forsyte Saga* is superior as a literary work to *Pinocchio* (not better to read to children, but just better literature), then there must be some reason *why* it is better; something about it must make it better, or explain why it is better. One of the special forms reason assumes in literating (and indirectly in author-ing, since the writer, as he writes, must constantly criticize his own work) is that of making reasonable judgments about the comparative literary value of novels, short stories, poems, and the like. I don't mean to imply that the literator must always be a kind of critic, only that it is natural for his interest in literature to generate questions about comparative liter-ary value. Such questions call for reasoned answers. The sort of reasoning typically involved has its distinctive form—it is not like the reasoning in law or in experimental psychology. Thus it presents an opportunity for—it invites—philosophical reflection.

II

To fill out the foregoing rather abstract account of the philosophy of litera-ture, we must look at some of the central and basic problems that this branch of philosophy encounters and aims to solve. Let us begin with authoring.

"Authoring" has been defined here; but the illumination provided by any definition depends on the terms it uses, and in the present case the key term is "literary work." One of the earliest questions to arise in the philos-ophy of literature is bound to be, What is a literary work? Until we can answer this question, we do not fully understand what authoring is.

Someone sits down, pen, pencil, or typewriter in hand (or you can supply a tape-recorder if you prefer), and writes

a shopping list
a note to be left on the refrigerator door for Johnny
a letter to Senator S about taxes
a children's story about a pair of mischievous twin wombats
a report on some laboratory experiments designed to develop featherless chickens

There is a handy term for what is produced in all these cases: "text." Now a text is not the same thing as the particular physical object which is an instance of it. When you write down a shopping list, you are making marks on paper; the marked paper is a new object in the world. If your list is different from any previous one, you have also produced a new text. If you copy someone else's shopping list, you have produced a new instance of the same text. All copies of *The Three Musketeers* (at least, those with no really puzzling typographical errors) are examples of the same text, though there are thousands of copies. So it is useful to have two terms: "text-token" for the particular volume your presented to your nephew, "text-type" for the sequence of words common to all volumes containing *The Three Musketeers*. When I write "text" I always mean "text-type."

By the definition I have proposed, writing a shopping list is not authoring, since a shopping list is not a literary work. Or could it be? (Of course it could be a *part* of a literary work—of a short story about a compulsive shopper or of a poem about the materialistic values of contemporary America.) Here's the problem: How are we to distinguish the literary texts from all the rest?

There are various ways of trying to make such a distinction: (1) We might look for objective features of the texts themselves that are present in literary texts but not in others. For example, we might note that some texts are in meter and also rhyme (they are verse), and we might propose that any such text is a literary text. This would not cover all literary texts, but it would be a start—if we really think it reasonable to classify, say, "Thirty days hath September" as a literary work. (2) We might look for defining features in the process of creation itself, in the writer's intention. (3) We might look for distinctive effects of the text on people who read it. (4) We might look for some other more complicated relationship between the text and certain social institutions (e.g., literature is what has been given that name by reputable critics). Or (5) We might try some combination of these.

I want to give some sense of the potential complications of this apparently simple question, "What is a literary text?" even though we won't be able to pursue them very far here. Probably the most useful thing to do is to propose an answer and discuss some of its strengths and weaknesses briefly, then leave it to you to consider other strengths and (especially) weaknesses that I have overlooked. If you end up by rejecting my answer, you will at least be in a better position to suggest your own alternative.

My proposal is to approach the task of carving out the class of literary texts in two stages. Stage 1 makes use of the concept of *fictional text*—and right away another important problem in the philosophy of literature turns up. For there are a number of subtleties in this concept, which only careful analysis can cope with. The main distinction is apparent enough. The shopping list you might find crumpled on the floor near the supermarket check-out counter is a *real* text: In composing it, someone was actually recording a resolution to buy those items and, presumably, carried it out. The shopping list you might find in a short story about a compulsive shopper was never actually drawn up or used by any real person (since the character in the story doesn't exist): It is a make-believe shopping list. Again: Let's say the letter to the Senator alluded to above begins with these words:

> Dear Senator S:
>   I think it is a crying shame that the legislature is once again considering the imposition of a state income tax on us hardworking citizens who are already groaning under the burden of countless oppressive taxes. . . .

You don't have to read more than a line or two to see that here someone really is complaining about the situation. Suppose the story about the mischievous twin wombats begins:

> Willie and Wanda, the wombat twins, rubbed their eyes as they awoke one spring and dashed out of their homey cave with cries of joy. . . .

You don't have to read more than a line or two to see that no one is really claiming that such a thing ever happened—in no way could this be taken for biography, zoology, or mammalian ethology.

A real text, then, is (roughly) one used to perform an action involving an attempt to communicate, in a broad sense: it is used to deplore, to describe, to plead, to threaten, to express affection, or whatever. A fictional text is one that has the general form of a communication, but in fact is not one: no such action is being performed. It is a kind of play-acting on paper. This definition is highly simplified, but it will have to serve for the present.[5] My proposal as stage 1, then, is that all fictional texts are literary works. They are not all *good* or *great* literary works—you see that children's stories, nursery rhymes, pornographic novels, and Polish jokes are swept into my broad category. But it is a significant category, since the distinction between fictional and nonfictional texts cuts rather deep across the entire range of texts and since the appropriate response to a fictional text obviously differs so greatly from that to a nonfictional text. There are complexities here, which we must not deny, even if we set them aside. For example, a short story about a rape is fictional, a newspaper account is nonfictional; yet you might well have some of the same emotions in reading them. Still, in important respects your reactions must differ: for example, the actual rape may move you to write a letter to the newspaper blaming the police for inadequate patrolling, but you can't blame the police for fictional rapes.

Ordinarily, normally, the texts we encounter and expect to encounter are (in the sense used above) real. The fictional twist is special and more sophisticated. Thus for a text to be fictional, it is not enough for the *author* to know it is not real or for him not to care whether it is or not;

---

[5] For further discussion, see "The Concept of Literature," in Frank Brady, John Palmer, and Martin Price, eds., *Literary Theory and Structure* (New Haven, Conn.: Yale Univ. Press, 1973) and references given there.

he must signal to the reader, or potential reader, that his text is not real. A simple and common way of doing this is to attach a label: "A Novel," "A Romance," "A Fantasy," whatever. Then the librarians know which shelf to place the text-tokens on, and the reader is in no danger of mistaking fiction for fact.

But one of the ways of expanding the boundaries of literature, and one of the great opportunities for literary invention, especially in our time, is the possibility of making the text itself declare its fictionality. The wombat story is an obvious case of this: we doubt that wombats can utter "cries of joy," and this anthropomorphizing of the creatures is a cue to fictionality. More subtle devices are needed in highly realistic novels, which carefully build up an imaginary world that could easily be a real one. In an interesting and perceptive essay, Philip Stevick has discussed an apparent tendency in some contemporary fictionalists to reject the idea of building an imaginary world, and to attain a special tone of mocking, a kind of put-on.[6] He quotes from Woody Allen's account of Lord Sandwich's efforts to invent the sandwich:

> 1745: After four years of frenzied labor, he is convinced he is on the threshold of success. He exhibits before his peers two slices of turkey with a slice of bread in the middle. His work is rejected by all but David Hume, who senses the imminence of something great and encourages him. Heartened by the philosopher's friendship, he returns to work with renewed vigor.[7]

How do we know that this is, as we say, "meant to be funny"—or, more precisely, that it is humorous fiction rather than a wildly misinformed attempt at culinary history? It is, of course, no part of our present task to answer such questions—they are for the critic and literary theorist. What is to be noted here, however, is that the very status of a text as a literary work, in virtue of its fictionality, may depend on the author's ability to plant the proper cues, which can be correctly read by the literator in order to recognize the text as fictional and, thus, as literature. Here is one place where reason assumes a characteristic form in authoring, for the construction of systems of signs, and the invention and establishment of new signs, are rational activities, and traffic with signs of fictional status are inherently involved in the activity of authoring.

It must be acknowledged that the nature of fictionality, and of the innumerable conventions involved in assigning fictional status, is still far from fully understood. This is one of the items of unfinished business in the philosophy of literature. It is obvious that the absurdity (but by what standards?) of supposing that a great philosopher like David Hume, amiable though he was, would be impressed by such paltry fruit of "four years of frenzied labor" serves as a signal that the ostensible speaker in this passage does not literally believe what he is saying. But can we general-

[6] See "Lies, Fictions, and Mock-Facts," *The Western Humanities Review*, 30 (1976), 1–12.
[7] *Getting Even* (New York: Warner Paperback Library, 1972), p. 34.

ize from this? Are there underlying principles? How, for example, do we know when a text is ironic?[8]

(The difficulty and subtlety of the task I have described has just been pointed up for me by a packet of mustard received—along with an imitation of the celebrated Earl's invention—on an airplane trip. It is inscribed:

MADE WITH WHITE WINE. Grey Poupon. Daring French mustard pioneer. Lived in 1777. Added white wine to mustard, creating smooth aristocratic taste. A truly great man who lent his name to a truly great mustard. Grey Poupon.

How many cues help us to take this passage straight—on the assumption that it was *not* written by Woody Allen?)

But of course the making and planting of fictional cues is by no means the only point at which we can discern reason in authoring. It is by thinking, often hard and complicated thinking, that the author shapes his plot, regulates the rhythmic variations in pace as he tells his story, selects from among the thoughts that come to him those words and actions that will most sharply reveal key traits of his characters and, sometimes, provides us with profound visions of human life and of the universe that we are left to reflect upon. I do not mean to suggest that the process of writing a novel or a poem is purely a matter of cold calculation or of puzzle-solving; no more—and indeed much less—than most human activities is it free of sudden inspirations, feelings, and emotion of all sorts. But whatever else it also is, authoring is a mode of thinking. And wherever thinking appears, we may, as philosophers, ask how well it is done—as judged against the basic canons of logical reasoning.

III

My propopsal was to define "literary work" in two stages, by marking out the two subclasses of literary texts. One subclass consists of all fictional texts: in them, however serious may be their ultimate import, we find a peculiar play with language, an imaginative invention, that justifies our considering them as works of literary art. The other subclass consists, to put it very concisely at first, of those texts in which we can discern an *artistic intention*.

What makes a text real, in the sense here assigned to this term, is that it does in fact enter into a process of linguistic interaction connected, at least indirectly, with other actual or potential behavior. Pope's *Essay on Man* expounds a philosophy and argues for it. Winston Churchill's famous radio speech after the retreat from Dunkirk summoned the people of Great Britain to rise above their crushing defeat and stand firm against

[8] For an interesting recent discussion of the problem of signaling and recognizing irony, see Göran Hermerén, "Intention and Interpretation in Literary Criticism," *New Literary History*, 7 (1975–76), 71–74.

Hitlerism. John Lothrop Motley's *Rise of the Dutch Republic* describes, explains, and interprets numerous historical events in the long struggle of the Low Countries to free themselves from Spain. But these are more than real texts: Pope's poem has a great deal of cleverness and wit, sharpened by the heroic couplets; Churchill's speech has powerful language and rises to a magnificent climax; Motley shapes his story artfully and exhibits a strong feeling of moral indignation through his supple and eloquent style. It is such features that (by stage 2) enable us to classify these works as literature. Even the report on a laboratory experiment designed to produce featherless chickens might conceivably rise to literature in a similar way—though the odds are against it.

The immediate problem, of course, is to clarify the key term I have introduced: "artistic intention." The problem is, indeed, so large that we cannot hope to resolve it here, but we can get some sense of its dimensions and ramifications. To begin with, we may try expanding our stage 2 proposal in somewhat different terms:

> X is a literary work if a substantial role in X's creation was played by the intention to make it capable of satisfying an aesthetic interest.

So—you may say—we understand that an artistic intention is an intention to satisfy an aesthetic interest, but that only pushes the problem back one step: What is an aesthetic interest?

Before returning to this question, we should note some other problematic features of this proposal. First, can we tolerate the rather vague term "substantial role"? I suspect that we must. On the one hand, we wouldn't want to count the shopping list or refrigerator note to Johnny as literary texts, I should think: they are about as purely utilitarian as anything can be. On the other hand, we must make room within the class of literary texts for Pope, Churchill, and Motley, who clearly made a conscious effort to produce something more than plain philosophy, oration, and history. But it is a matter of degree how much concern the writer has with these aesthetic aspects of his work, and so the line between literary real texts and nonliterary real texts is bound to be fuzzy. Still, as long as there are many clear-cut examples on both sides, the distinction is useful: the fuzziness merely reminds us to avoid future arguments about the admittedly borderline cases (for example, some essays by Freud or some letters of William James).

Second, you may question the introduction of intention in this context: does this not risk running afoul of the so-called "intentional fallacy"? I think not. I agree fully with what is said by Maurice Mandelbaum in a fine essay that is in fact highly relevant to the problems we are now considering.

> The phrase "the intentional fallacy" originally referred to a particular method of criticism, that is, to a method of interpreting and evaluating given works of art; it was not the aim of Wimsatt and Beardsley to distinguish between art and nonart. These two problems are, I believe, fundamentally

different in character. However, I do not feel sure that Professor Beardsley has noted this fact. . . .[9]

The fact is duly noted. In distinguishing between art and nonart in the particular case of literature (that is, between literary works of art and other texts), we have to appeal at some point to an artistic intention.

There are problems, however, about our knowledge of this intention. In some few cases we may have external evidence that the historian wished his narrative to have dramatic form, as well as faithfulness to fact, and may have wished his style to be not only accurate but subtle and expressive. Even if he failed to fulfill these intentions, we may charitably classify his work as literature, while rating it rather low. Mostly, of course, we discern the artistic intention in the work itself. The narrative is in fact dramatically shaped, the characters are three-dimensional and live, the style carries heavy overtones, now ironic, now compassionate, now angry, now judicious. Such works, one may say, proclaim that they are literature by being quite good literature. Since it is highly probable that the writer knew what he had done and wanted it that way, we can legitimately infer the intention from the deed. In cases like this, it may seem that we can for all practical purposes dispense with the appeal to intention; yet I think the literary merits betoken literary status only via the inference to artistic intention. And this is shown by the fact that some texts with (perhaps modest) literary merits are still never thought of as literature, because the intention is so concentrated on biology, social psychology, astronomy, or political propaganda.

Third, then, we return to the concept of producing a text capable of satisfying an aesthetic interest. And the effort to clarify this concept plunges us at once into one of the deepest and most controversial problems in the philosophy of literature. Consider fictional texts for the moment; they toil not, neither do they spin. They don't help us buy groceries, fight wars, stop littering the streets, learn the ways of God to man, or understand the rise of the Dutch Republic. Yet if the activity of producing them is rationally justifiable, it must have some point. A person can cut words out of the newspaper, toss them in a hat, draw them out at random, and paste them up. And there is no law against his claiming to have produced a poem. But this claim is purely verbal, and wholly empty, unless he has a concept of what a literary work is and of what value a literary work may have. His activity is simply pointless. But we do not believe it was pointless of Jane Austen to write *Persuasion* or of Keats to write his "Ode on a Grecian Urn."

Since fictional texts are good for nothing in the usual ways of being good, they must be good for something else: for satisfying an aesthetic interest. If we can come to understand what this means, we can also understand how real texts sometimes rise to literature in that they offer (or at least

---

[9] "Family Resemblances and Generalization Concerning the Arts," *American Philosophical Quarterly*, 2 (1965), 5n.

purport to offer) a similar satisfaction, over and above their usefulness in the context of human life.

One way to start an inquiry into the nature of aesthetic interests (or interest, if there is only one) would be to look for some very plain, simple, and uncontroversial examples. Thus consider someone who likes (or buys, or keeps, or looks at) a vase because of its delicate colors and graceful shape: no one (I suppose) will be unwilling to call his interest in the vase aesthetic. And if he is interested in the shape of a novel's plot—in the neat way the complications are developed and worked out to a dramatic climax, with a final tying up of all the threads (as in *Tom Jones*)—that interest, too, is evidently aesthetic. This is fairly easy to agree on, and we may even risk the generalization that any interest in form or quality for its own sake is an aesthetic interest. (But that begins to raise problems.) Now suppose he is interested in the philosophy of a literary work—say, Tolstoy's philosophy of history, in *War and Peace*. Then we may want to suggest a distinction: if what interests him is the truth of that philosophy or its logical consistency or its historical antecedents and influence, then his interest in the novel is not aesthetic; but if what interests him is the character of that philosophy (its bold sweep, say) or its organic relationship to the structure and recurrent themes of the novel, then his interest *is* aesthetic—indeed, it is an interest in form and quality.

How far this suggestion can be carried is a matter of some importance, ultimately, in the philosophy of literature; it is also highly debatable. Not that we must insist on a sharp line between aesthetic and other interests, of course; vagueness may be inescapable and acceptable here, too. But it seems that some line must be drawn if we are to find a point in authoring, whether of fictional texts or of nonfictional texts that aspire to literary status.

The line of thought just sketched (all too thinly) moves toward what some would call a "formalist" conception of aesthetic interest, and it has long been recognized that, of all the arts, literature is least likely, on the face of it, to take kindly to such a treatment. It may well seem to you—as you think of other features of other literary works to test the proposed analysis—that formalism is bound to leave out too much. What! Are aesthetic interests limited to form and quality alone? Even granted that this includes a lot of things—wit, humor, tragic power, dramatic intensity, style, and more—it may not include everything that you would want to say we can take an aesthetic interest in.

Therefore it may be well, in lieu of a thorough discussion of this most basic problem, to set forth (though with equal sketchiness) an alternative kind of view. Let's call it "cognitivism," since its central emphasis is on knowledge. What we ask from literature, on this theory, and what we get a good deal of from the best literature, is knowledge—more particularly, understanding of human beings, ourselves and others. The point of authoring (and of literature) is ultimately to promote this human understanding. How does this point differ from that of psychology and social science? Only in that literary works consitute a fundamentally different kind of symbol system from the texts of psychology, sociology, anthropology, and the like.

There are various ways of trying to make this distinction, and all of them have difficulties that have not yet been cleared up (more unfinished business for the philosophy of literature). For example, we might argue that psychology (taking that as a paradigm science of human behavior and human action) has its characteristic methods, involving induction, generalization, classification, and so on. But in literature persons and events and situations are given a symbolic form that enables us to obtain insights into new possibilities of human character and human life, personal and social. Stated so badly, such a view may strike you as more problematical than plausible, and it may not even be very intelligible. My purpose is merely to point out that here is a possible way of answering our pending question: it is to say (roughly) that to take an aesthetic interest in literature is to take an interest in the understanding of human nature and the human condition that it provides, *not* in the form of general statements, but in the form of the symbolic meaning of characters and events. If it should turn out that the point of authoring is to cater to aesthetic interests, so conceived, then, very clearly indeed, we could discern in authoring a special form of reason, which it would be the task of philosophy to articulate, to explain, and to assess.

IV

Because of the reciprocal relationship between authoring and literating, much of what we have said about forms of reason in the activity of authoring has also had implications for the activity of literating. Yet to round out this very preliminary and very general attempt to characterize the philosophy of literature, we may turn to literating for a closer view, asking in what ways it, too, is rational—that is, involves thinking, makes use of principles that are subject to philosophical examination.

Literating, we said, is reading, but not all reading is literating. Like all reading, literating is made possible by the possession of a particular sort of learned skill, which is now often called "linguistic competence." Competence in reading (English) is the ability to interpret and construct texts by using the rules of (English) syntax and semantics. If the word "rules" troubles you here, we can fall back on a looser term, "convention," without, however, attempting to define this adequately. It is a syntactical convention in English that, in a simple sentence with a transitive verb, that which is denoted by the noun that follows the verb is that which undergoes the action denoted by the verb: given "The dog bit the man," we can also write "The man was bitten by the dog." It is a semantic convention in English that dogs are animals, that nothing can be a dog that is not an animal. The kind of thing that is involved in reading competence, then, is being able to apply conventions of these sorts in understanding (or in composing) texts—even if one cannot explicitly formulate the conventions.

The theory that I now plan to introduce and briefly discuss would be called a "structuralist" theory of literature, though the name is not apt. I am not concerned to represent the views of any particular school, or even person, though I borrow heavily from a literary theorist cited earlier, Jonathan Culler. My purpose is not to advance the theory for prompt acceptance, but to raise some rather basic questions about the nature of literature and of literating—questions which, even if the structuralists have gone some way toward answering them, still are due much further reflection and investigation.

In recognizing a distinction between literary texts and other texts, we implicitly acknowledge that there is more to literating than to reading. It evidently requires a higher order of talent—perhaps talent of a quite different kind—to read literature than to read practical messages. This talent may be called a specifically *literary competence*, if we can explain it in terms of its own conventions, which the author uses and the literator is guided by. There would then be two kinds of conventions involved in literating. If, then, we can make a case for literating as essentially a process of using conventions to understand texts (but conventions of a higher order than the syntactical and semantical ones), it would follow that literating, whatever else it is (and of course it is more than that), is an activity involving signs and sign systems and, hence, is a rational activity.

The concept of literary competence rests on the concept of specifically literary conventions. Can there be such things? Now, in one sense of the term, we are familiar with such conventions. A very clear case is the so-called "fourth wall" convention of the proscenium arch stage. Perhaps somewhat roughly, we may formulate this convention as a rule for the spectator: the vertical plane at the front of the stage is to be thought of as an invisible fourth wall of the room that is represented on the stage. It is fair, I think, to say that we learn this convention in our early play-going experiences and that anyone (say, from a different culture) who has not yet caught on to it must be inadequately oriented toward events on a stage. Of course there are other modes of staging that do not use this convention, but the spectator has to know how to tell when it is in effect.

To see how a theory of literary competence might be developed, let us consider some suggestions by Culler. He proposes a convention that might be stated as a slogan: in reading a poem, coherence is to be maximized. In a notable passage, William Empson commented on two lines from the translation of a Chinese fragment:

> Swiftly the years, beyond recall.
> Silent the stillness of this spring morning.

Culler Comments:

> In this case the most obvious feature of literary competence is the intent at totality of the interpretive process: poems are supposed to cohere, and one must therefore discover a semantic level at which the two lines can be

related to one another. An obvious point of contact is the contrast between "swiftly" and "stillness," and there is thus a primary condition on "invention": any interpretation should succeed in making thematic capital out of this opposition. . . .[10]

He notes also that "years" in the first line and "this . . . morning" in the second introduce a "dimension of time" and "provide another opposition and point of contact."

This "convention of thematic unity"[11] is, evidently, extremely general, but there is some initial plausibility in claiming that learning to literate (if we choose to put it that way) is in part learning to follow this convention, though in particular cases perhaps without deliberate reflection.

However, some questions arise. First, there is the matter of scope. Some theorists of avant-garde literature might question whether the convention is universal: perhaps in reading a modern work like John Barth's *Lost in the Funhouse*, the correct convention is not to seek to make it cohere but to keep it jumbled (as, for example, in the title piece's insertions of textbook material on fictional plots into the story). Perhaps, on the other hand, what makes literature avant-garde is just that the literator has to work harder to make connections, though it is still true that what makes literature (or at least good literature) is that connections can be made and, at some level, coherence attained. In any case, this question is one for the literary theorist; there could be literary conventions of various degrees of generality.

Second, there is the question of justification: why should we follow the convention at all? This leads, somewhat circuitously, back into basic questions about the point of authoring-literating. One might argue that seeking coherence, or supplying the most probable coherence, is just part of the literating game, as trying to take tricks is part of contract bridge. But there would still be the nagging philosophical question: why should we play this game? And that, in the end, depends, I suppose, on deciding what is the function of literature and then showing that this function can only, or best, be realized by the sort of literating that uses the coherence convention.

Third, is there really a convention of coherence? Do we need to think of literating in these terms? That coherence is to be looked for may be a useful prescription for the literator, but maybe it is a rule for *good* literating, rather than a rule that defines or partially constitutes the very process itself. It doesn't look much like the fourth wall convention, which is a principle for understanding part of what is signified by a particular mode of staging. Why don't we just say, instead, that poems *are* more or less coherent, depending on whether their parts have more or less intimate connections? It is a semantic fact about the Chinese fragment that periods of time are referred to in each line; that is a connection and helps to

---

[10] Culler, *Structuralist Poetics: Structuralism, Linguistics, and the Study of Literature*, p. 126.
[11] Ibid., p. 116.

bring the lines together. So it is with other, including subtler, relationships. And we might as well say: read the poem trying to find whatever there is in it. But that's a queer sort of "convention."

Culler might well reply that coherence, in the end, is not a quality of the text, but something the reader has to make out of it and that literary competence consists partly in knowing how to do this properly. This is certainly arguable. It is also arguable that the emphasis on literary competence tempts us to find more arbitrariness in criticism than is really there. For example:

> Rather than say, for example, that literary texts are fictional, we might cite this as a convention of literary interpretation and say that to read a text as literature is to read it is fiction. Such a reversal may, at first sight, seem trivial, but to restate propositions about poetic or novelistic discourse as procedures of reading is a crucial reorientation for a number of reasons, wherein lie the revitalizing powers of a structuralist poetics.[12]

"Trivial" is not the word that occurs to me. Fictionality cannot, I think, plausibly be regarded as something we can confer on a text at will; even if it depends on special signaling conventions, it is a function of the text's own features (and sometimes circumstances of production). Moreover, I do not think that "to read . . . as literature" one of Martin Luther King, Jr.'s speeches or a scientific essay by T. H. Huxley requires us to forget that these are real texts.

According to Culler:

> The primary convention is what might be called the rule of significance: read the poem as expressing a significant attitude to some problem concerning man and/or his relation to the universe.[13]

So stated, this might seem a rather ambitious prescription. As applied by Culler to Blake's little poem on the sunflower, it leads us to read the sunflower's turning toward the sun as a symbol of certain human aspirations. I don't object. But it might be hazardous to insist that we impose comparable profundities on all the poems we read. Perhaps the idea is just that we should keep on the lookout for such extended meanings. But granted that all poems offer symbolic objects and events, I wonder if we shouldn't watch for some warrants in the poem for making quite so much of them. In short, this convention of significance needs elaboration and clarification—and perhaps also philosophical defense. Once more:

> The convention that poems may be read as statements about poetry is extremely powerful. If a poem seems utterly banal it is possible to take banality of statement as a statement about banality and hence to derive a suggestion that poetry can go no further than language, which is inevitably distinct from immediate experience, or, alternatively, that poetry should celebrate the objects of the world by simply naming them.[14]

[12] Ibid., p. 128.
[13] Ibid., p. 115.
[14] Ibid., p. 177.

Here is a formula for injecting whole new realms of significance into the dullest passages of Walt Whitman—or even "Thirty days hath September." There is no doubt that various contemporary critics have played this game and commended it to others. But is that sufficient reason for supposing that any such convention exists, or is in force, at least at this high level of generality? Are we at liberty to take (are we even *required* to take) the sunflower's seeking the sun as a figure for the poet's seeking of beauty or truth?

If literary competence consists in the mastery of a set of special literary conventions, perhaps they will turn out to be of a lower order of generality than those just discussed—though still quite general, and functional. I have not meant to disparage Jonathan Culler's extremely penetrating and challenging discussion of these problems, but only to set forth some of the issues raised by this most interesting way of analyzing the process of literating. The view clearly would call for philosophical investigation: the construction of a general theory of literating, perhaps some codification or at least classification of the types of convention involved, and an examination of the rationale for adopting, or for acknowledging, such conventions. In that way, we would move toward a truly philosophic understanding of what literature, considered as a process or activity, is all about: why it ought to exist and flourish and how it necessarily engages and rewards human reason in one of its most complex and subtle forms.

J. O. Urmson

LITERATURE

I wish, in this essay, to raise and suggest answers to two questions about literature.* First is the question of the ontological status of a literary work— the question what sort of thing is a poem, a novel, a history. Second is whether or not, when we read a literary work, it is analogous to anything that anybody does in relation to other major arts forms. To pursue these questions I must first make some remarks about these other major art forms, excluding literature, for, since my problem is about what seems, at first sight, to be anomalous features of literature, I must indicate what I take to be normality.

Leaving literature, for the present then, I think that most of the major art forms, in their most common manifestations in Western culture, can be divided into two groups. The reader is asked to note that this is a historical generalization, not a statement of logical or conceptual necessities. First there is the group, which includes painting and sculpture, where the creative artist himself normally fashions the object which is the work of art. We are all, no doubt, aware of imaginative fantasies to the contrary, such as Collingwood's view that all art works are in some way mental, but I assume in this paper that such an art work as a painting or a sculpture is a physical object which can be stolen, on defaced, or stored in a bank and can need to be preserved and restored. This is the common sense view which can be rejected only at the expense of conceptual innovation. Thus it is the work of art as both conceived and made by its creator that spectators typically contemplate in the case of such arts as painting and sculpture. This is no doubt an oversimplified story. There may, for example, be foundry workers involved in the production of a bronze statue, but rightly or wrongly we think of them as living tools of the sculptor, with whom, from beginning to end, all artistic decisions rest.

Then a second group of arts exists, including music, theater, ballet, and opera in their standard forms, in which the audience or spectators do not witness, without any intermediaries, the work made by the creative artist. There is a need for executant artists, with a serious aesthetic role as inter-

J. O. Urmson is a Fellow of Corpus Christi College, Oxford University, where he tutors in philosophy. He is one of the best known writers on analytical philosophy. His *Philosophical Analysis* is a classic on the subject, and his many other writing and editing projects in philosophy have been of central interest for many years.

* This essay is being published for the first time in this collection.

preters. We see and listen to dancers, instrumentalists, and actors, not to choreographers, composers, and playwrights. That the creative artist may from time to time be his own interpreter in performance does not in any way invalidate this distinction.

Now it is only in the case of the performing arts that serious doubts about the identity of the work of art arises, at least at the common sense level. It requires philosophical sophistication even to understand the suggestion that the *Mona Lisa* is not something that usually can be found hanging on a wall of the Louvre. But the case is quite different with regard to the performing arts. It is plain common sense to see that a symphony, a ballet, or a play cannot be simply identified with any physical object, such as a book or manuscript, or with any event, such as a performance. We can, indeed, speak of hearing Beethoven's Fifth Symphony, as we can speak of seeing Michaelangelo's *David*, but, if we hear the Fifth Symphony, it is equally correct to say that we hear a performance of it, whereas there is nothing even analogous to a performance of the *David* that we could witness.

I have argued in a paper entitled "The Performing Arts" (in *Contemporary British Philosophy*, 4) that the best account to give of the contribution of the creative artist in the case of those arts, or works of art, which require also a performer or executant is that he provides a recipe or set of performing instructions for the executant-artist. A similar opinion has, of course, been put forward by others. Thus, when Beethoven composed the Fifth Symphony, he thought out and wrote down a set of instructions for an orchestra. Similarly, the playwright provides a set of instructions for the actors and the creator of a ballet a set of instructions for the dancers. This view seems more plausible than others that are current. Thus, to say that a musical work is a class of performances requires one to say that the composer created such a class—a view which becomes especially uncomfortable if we consider an unperformed work. The suggestion of Wollheim and others that the creative artist creates a type, and Stevenson's view that he creates a megatype, also cause discomfort. It is hard to see how there can be a type or a megatype before there are any tokens.

What may be called a set of performing instructions in the case of temporal arts such as music and ballet, where what the audience witnesses is a set of events that take time, is more naturally called a recipe in the case of such nontemporal arts as require an executant artist. Such nontemporal arts as painting and sculpture, which typically require no artist beyond the creator, comprise works which, as we have seen, are physical objects. Such art works take time to make, and we may spend time contemplating them, but they do not themselves take time. But, if we may consider cooking as an art, it is one which requires an executant artist, the cook, who may be, but need not be, the creator of the recipe he follows. The pecan pie or the hamburger has a status problematic in the same way as that of a symphony or ballet. In my view, to create *the* pecan pie is to provide a recipe which, if followed by the executant cook, will result in *a* pecan pie.

So I say that a creative artist may do one of two things. He may himself produce the work of art which the spectator witnesses and which will be a physical object, or he may produce a set of instructions for execution by others. It is rather obvious why, if one wishes to have permanent works of art in the temporal arts, such as music, the creative artist should produce only a set of instructions. There do not have to be permanent works of music; one could have a music which consisted entirely of free improvisation and in which there were no permanent works. It would also be theoretically possible to devise a painting notation so that a creative artist could give a set of instructions for executant painters to follow and produce a set of equally valid interpretations of the painting, analogous to musical performances. It is not difficult to see why we in fact do not do this, except in the case of some rudimentary children's painting games. I have neither claimed that any art form must include performing artists as well as creators nor claimed that any art form cannot do so. I merely observe that the standard classics of painting and sculpture conform to one type and that the standard classics of music, theater, and ballet to the other, and I note that one can see good practical reasons why, with traditional techniques, highly organized art works do fall into these two categories. One would not wish to hear a group improvisation of an opera.

Not all arts fit readily into this twofold classification, more particularly not all applied arts, as is clear from the case of architecture. It is quite interesting to consider such cases, though I do not think that they raise very serious philosophical problems. I think it is largely a matter of loose fit to accounts produced for the paradigm cases. There are also novel variations within the arts discussed: What, for example, are we to say of musical composition directly onto tape in an electronic laboratory, and will the account of live theater readily cover the cinematograph? Still, it is not our present task to examine these problems, but to ask whether or not we can give an adequate account of literature in the light of the characterization of the other arts put forward in this paper.

We have distinguished two categories of works of art. First, there are those directly created by the creative artist when there is no executant artist and the identity of the work is unproblematic; second, there are those where the creative artist produces a recipe or set of instructions for performing or for executant artists and where the identity of the work of art is problematic. Now literature appears, at least at first sight, to be anomalous with respect to this classification. On the one hand, there seem to be no executant artists or performers here: who could such artist be? When one, say, reads a novel to oneself, there seems to be only oneself and the novelist involved. Is the reader in fact the executant artist with himself as audience as the pianist who can play to himself as audience and the dancer who can dance for his own satisfaction? But I do not seem to myself to be exhibiting any technical or interpretative skills when I read to myself, and there are other grave objections to this suggestion which we must notice later. Yet, if there is no performing or executant artist, how can I myself be the audience or spectator?

On the other hand, we cannot readily assimilate literature to sculpture and painting. For one thing, the identity of the novel or other literary work seems to be problematic in the same way as that of the musical balletic or theatrical work. In the case of these other arts, we have attempted to explain their problematic status in terms of a recipe or set of instructions for executant artists. But, how can the literary work be a set of instructions for executant artists if there are none such?

So literature seems to be a counterexample to my theory, for, if the theory will not work when applied to literature, that certainly casts doubt upon its acceptability. We surely need a theory which will account equally for all cases in which the identity of the work of art is problematic, for it would be an act of desperation to claim that the status of, say, *Pride and Prejudice* was radically different from that of the *Sleeping Beauty* ballet or Beethoven's Fifth Symphony.

That then is my problem. For those who find my view of the other arts unacceptable, in any case the problem does not exist in the specific form in which I see it, but there will still be the old traditional problem of the identity of a literary work.

Now I am not sure how this problem is to be answered, but I am going to suggest an answer in accordance with my general theory. I am going to suggest that, contrary to first appearances, literature is in principle a performing art.

If we are to make this claim, the most natural thing is first to revive the view that, in reading a literary work to oneself, one is simultaneously performer and audience, just as when one plays a piece of music to oneself. I have already raised the objection to this view that one does not seem to to oneself, when so reading, to be utilizing any technical or interpretative skills, but this appeal to subjective feelings is, no doubt, of little weight, so we must notice a more serious objection to it.

If we consider a musical score as a set of instructions to the performer, then, for example, the musical notation of the first bar of the first violin's line in the score of Beethoven's Fifth Symphony must be regarded as a shorthand instruction to the players to play three consecutive G naturals, each a quarter of the total time of a bar, the total duration of which is indicated by the metronome mark at the top of the page. Similarly, if in his script an actor reads

Tom (*looking out of the window*): It is beginning to rain.

He will, if he is playing the part of Tom, take it as an instruction to look out of the window of the stage set and say "It is beginning to rain." Thus we can distinguish quite clearly the performer's reading of the instructions from his action in accordance with them, and it is in his act of complying with the instructions, not the reading of them, that he shows his technical and interpretative skill. That I can read and understand the instruction to the violinist just as well as he can gives me neither his skill nor his interpretative insight.

But, in the case of the solitary novel reader, the situation is not similar.

Not only do we have to make him simultaneously performer and audience, we have to collapse into one act his reading of the instructions and his compliance with them. This explains one's initial uneasiness at the suggestion and is surely too implausible in itself. This horse will not run.

If we are to separate the reading of instructions from the act of complying with them, we must claim, I think, that literature is essentially an oral act. Moreover, this move is not made simply in an attempt to save a theory, for with regard to some literature it has an immediate plausibility. If we consider such a work as the *Iliad*, there is good reason to believe that before writing was known to the Greeks there were bards who had learned the poem by heart and who went around giving performances of it, or of excerpts from it. They, the performers, were taught it orally, that is, by example, just as performers in other arts may still be taught their parts other than by studying the score. It is not implausible to think of the *Iliad* as having been written down, probably in the seventh century B.C., as a set of instructions, as a score, for bards. It is fairly certain that Herodotus wrote his *Histories* as a score and that people first got to know them by hearing public performances. No doubt the first performances, *epideixis*, as the Greeks called them, were given by Herodotus himself, but the distinction of creator and performer is not obliterated by the same man's undertaking both roles. Further, in cultures less generously supplied with printing presses than we are, the tradition of purely oral poetry still survives.

It is clear also that even in Western civilization many poets today think of poetry as essentially an oral art; poetry for them is essentially something to be listened to, and so a performer is required. If you now read it aloud to yourself, attempting to equal the skills of the professional poetry reader, this, rather than silent novel reading, would be like playing the piano to oneself as a performance. Also, we must not forget that he gave readings from his novels in public and that reading aloud within the family group is an activity once common and not yet dead.

But this account will certainly not cover the bulk of modern literature. If much ancient and some modern literature was designed by its creators primarily to be heard, the written word being primarily a score for the performer, this is certainly not true of the great bulk of modern literature. While much of the best literature of all ages can with advantage be read aloud, it is more than doubtful that Dickens's novels, let alone *The Decline and Fall of the Roman Empire*, were ever intended primarily for oral performance.

Faced with this difficulty, let us go back to the case of music. Music is essentially sound; the performer produces sounds in accordance with the instructions of the composer. But there is such a thing as the skill of silent score reading, a skill which some very proficient performers have only to a slight extent. But a reasonably musical person can, after instruction and practice, look at a simple melodic line in a score and recognize what it would sound like if it were performed; he knows what musical sounds would be heard if the instructions were obeyed. Very gifted musicians, after elaborate training, can acquire the same facility in reading complex scores with transposed parts, unusual clefs, and the like. Musical score reading of this kind is neither original creation nor performance, the two factors we originally considered, nor even the sort of reading required of the performer. It is the reading of a recipe or set of instructions with the ability to recognize what would result from following them. I am reliably informed that experienced cooks may acquire the same skill; they may be able to read the recipe and recognize what the confection would taste like.

It would be implausible to say that musical score readers are giving a performance to themselves or that readers of cookery recipes are preparing a private and immaterial feast. Apart from the fact that they need hear no sound (they may or may not hum to themselves), considered, absurdly, as performances, what the best score readers normally do would be intolerably bad. They habitually read through the slower bits far faster than they perfectly well know that the music should go, and, for many reasons, nobody can read a fast complex piece at a speed that he recognizes to be that of the music. Score reading is something quite distinct from composition or performance. The music critic, Ernest Newman, who went blind in old age, expressed the wish that he had become deaf instead, since he preferred to read a score and imagine an ideal performance than to hear what he usually heard. And some music is probably intended primarily for score readers. Some of the puzzle canons at the beginning of Bach's *Musical Offering* were surely intended primarily for the score reader, and it has been known for composers to attempt to make the notes they wrote visual representations of the cross of some other symbol.

Now I suggest that learning to read an ordinary language is like learning to read a score silently to oneself. It is probably easier, and more of us get a thorough training in it and, consequently, mastery of it. There is therefore a large potential market of verbal score readers.

My claim is that the vast literature primarily intended for private reading in silence should be regarded as analogous to a set of musical scores intended primarily for score reading rather than for performance. So reading *Hamlet* to oneself will not be so unlike reading *War and Peace*. But, whereas the text of *Hamlet* was certainly primarily a score or set of instructions for actors and, thus, like a normal musical score, *War and Peace*, like some vast poetic dramas, is left to the score reader. Reading the text of *Hamlet* is surely not a performance, yet it is equally surely not very unlike reading the text of *War and Peace*.

So my claim is that literature is in logical character a performing art, but one in which in practice we frequently, though far from invariably, confine ourselves to score reading. We read to find out how the performance will go and are then content. This view is, I believe, somewhat confirmed by some of the critical remarks we make about literary style. Even in the case of works which would not normally be read aloud it is a commonplace to speak of assonance, dissonance, sonority, rhythm; we reject as unstylish conjunctions of consonants which would be awkward to say aloud, though we easily read them. We criticize the writing in terms of how it would sound, if it were spoken. Contrast the case of logical notation which is not literature and for which we have only a makeshift oral rendering: who would think of criticizing a piece of writing in formal logic as unstylish because our conventional oral reading of it was awkward in sound?

It is certainly not the case that all literature can be covered without remainder by this account. Sometimes its character as written is important, and not merely in the way that we prefer elegantly printed literature as we like elegantly printed musical scores. The poems of E. E. Cummings are a very clear case. Again, it is essential that Lewis Carroll's mouse's tale should be printed in the shape of a mouse's tail in the way it regularly is unless we are to miss a pun which could not be brought out orally. At a level of, no doubt, very lightweight literary art, but still literary art, we have such poems as

> While cycling downhill Lord Fermanagh
> Broke his bike, and he hadn't a spanagh,
> But the pieces Lord Crichton
> Was able to tichton
> In quite a professional managh.

Whatever interest this jingle has, the aberrational spelling no doubt is an important part of it.

I cannot account for these cases within my theory, but I do not think they need disturb me, any more than that the notation of Schumann's music is full of cryptograms that need to be accounted for in a general discussion of music and its notation. I think that the simple fact is that the notation of a piece of music may also be a code, that a jingle with audible rhyme may be written in a way which is a jest about English spelling, and that, in the case of E. E. Cummings, typography may be used, rather like dynamic marks in a musical score, as a hint to a correct reading.

So I can now formally give answers to the two questions with which I started. I resolve the problem of the ontological status of a literary work by saying that for a literary work to exist it is a necessary and sufficient condition that a set of instructions should exist such that any oral performance which complies with that set of instructions is a performance of the work in question. I resolve the problem of the relation of reading a literary work to what we find in other art forms by saying that is analogous to reading the score of a musical work, of a play, or of a ballet. In each of these cases we neither create the work nor perform the work when we read the score, but we become aware of what we would witness if we were to witness a performance.

That there are other questions about literature than those I have attempted to answer is obvious. That one can find problems about my answers is also obvious. It is possible to write at length about the notion of compliance with a set of instructions of which I have made unelucidated use. But one thing at a time is usually enough, so attempting even a sketch of answers to two questions is, for me, sufficiently ambitious.

Select Bibliography for Part Three

THE THEORY OF LITERATURE

Books

Monroe C. Beardsley, *The Possibility of Criticism*; Jean-Paul Sartre, *What Is Literature?*; William K. Wimsatt, Jr., *The Verbal Icon*; William K. Wimsatt, Jr., and Cleanth Brooks, *Literary Criticism: A Short History*.

Articles

Henry Aiken, "The Aesthetic Relevance of Artists' Intentions"; Henry Aiken, "The Aesthetic Relevance of Belief"; Henry Aiken, "The Concept of Relevance in Aesthetics"; Karl Aschenbrenner, "Critical Reasoning"; Monroe C. Beardsley, "Modes of Interpretation"; Monroe C. Beardsley, "On the Generality of Critical Reasons"; Clive Bell, "The 'Difference' of Literature"; Douglas Berggren, "The Use and Abuse of Metaphor"; Arnold Berleant, "The Verbal Presence: An Aesthetics of Literary Performance"; M. Black, "Metaphor"; Kenneth Burke, "Semantic and Poetic Meaning"; W. Charlton, "Living and Dead Metaphors"; Ted Cohen, "Notes on Metaphor"; T. J. Diffey, "Morality and Literary Criticism"; T. S. Eliot, "The Frontiers of Criticism"; Northrop Frye, "The Archetypes of Literature"; Richard M. Gale, "The Fictive Use of Language"; Eric Gilman, "The Use of Moral Concepts in Literary Criticism"; John Hospers, "Implied Truths in Literature"; Isabel C. Hungerland, "The Concept of Intention in Art Criticism"; Isabel C. Hungerland, "Contextual Implication"; Lawrence W. Hyman, "Literature and Morality in Contemporary Criticism"; A. Kazin, "Psychoanalysis and Literary Culture Today"; Richard C. Kuhns, "Criticism and the Problem of Intention"; Berel Lang, "The Intentional Fallacy Revisited"; Earl R. MacCormac, "Metaphor Revisited"; Margaret MacDonald and Michael Scriven, "The Language of Fiction" (Symposium); A. Mackie "The Structure of Aesthetically Interesting Metaphors"; Joseph Margolis, "Critics and Literature"; Peter Mew, "Metaphor and Truth"; David Pole, "Morality and the Assessment of Literature"; Warren A. Shibles, "Metaphor: An Annotated Bibliography and History"; Charles L. Stevenson, "On 'What is a Poem?'"; Eliseo Vivas, "What is a Poem?"; William K. Wamsatt, Jr., and Monroe C. Beardsley, "The Affective Fallacy"; William K. Wimsatt, Jr., and Monroe C. Beardsley, "The Intentional Fallacy."

THE THEORY OF FILM:
METAPHYSICAL ROOTS

In many ways film is unique among the arts. Writing in the 1930s, the great art historian Erwin Panofsky noted, "Film art is the only art the development of which men now living have witnessed from the very beginnings." Panofsky and subsequent writers on film have taken advantage of this fact, investigating both historically and philosophically the idea of artistic origins. These investigations have produced some of the most stimulating work in the theory of art in recent years.

The theories of film we have selected for this text—by Eisenstein, Panofsky, and Cavell—represent three stages in the development of a classic conception of the subject. The conception of film to which these theorists subscribe can be characterized by two statements made by Panofsky in the essay presented here: "The medium of the movies is physical reality as such . . . Its [the moving picture] substance remains a series of visual sequences held together by an uninterrupted flow of movement in space . . ." Sergei Eisenstein was the first theorist to articulate carefully this conception. "Primo: photo-fragments of nature are recorded; secondo: these fragments are combined in various ways. Thus, the shot (frame), and thus montage." Panofsky developed this idea in what can be thought of as its middle period. Cavell represents the culmination of this tradition, giving us a philosophically sophisticated orchestration of this classic theme: "The material basis of the media of movies . . . is a succession of automatic world projections." Other prominent figures who subscribe to this conception of film are Federico Fellini, Michelangelo Antonioni, Charles Chaplin, François Truffaut, and André Bazin, to mention just a few.

Film can be thought of as the product of two things: motion picture photography and theater. Eisenstein gives us a perspicuous account of the natural relation of film to theater in the early days of the cinema. Like the contemporary filmmaker Ingmar Bergman, Eisenstein was first a playwright and director before he turned to cinema. From the start, however, Eisenstein realized that the possibilities specific to cinema were quite different from those of theater. Panofsky attempts a full-scale theoretical account of these differences, and in so doing he argues that film has unique possibilities which define a distinct artistic medium. Panofsky calls these possibilities the dynamization of space and the spatialization of time. It is clear from what Cavell says about Panofsky that these possibilities are as much metaphysical as artistic. Cavell believes that Panofsky is insufficiently aware of the philosophical difficulties which arise when one attempts an ontological or metaphysical characterization of a medium. His own theory aims at avoiding the pitfalls of metaphysical theorizing about film while at the same time capturing what is ontologically unique about the medium. Cavell relies heavily on the tradition to which Eisenstein, Panofsky, Bazin, and others belong, but his is the most sophisticated statement within that tradition.

Sergei Eisenstein

THE CINEMA AS AN OUTGROWTH
OF THEATER: THROUGH
THEATER TO CINEMA

It is interesting to retrace the different paths of today's cinema workers to their creative beginnings, which together compose the multi-colored background of the Soviet cinema.* In the early 1920s we all came to the Soviet cinema as something not yet existent. We came upon no ready-built city; there were no squares, no streets laid out; not even little crooked lanes and blind alleys, such as we may find in the cinemetropolis of our day. We came like bedouins or goldseekers to a place with unimaginably great possibilities, only a small section of which has even now been developed.

We pitched our tents and dragged into camp our experiences in varied fields. Private activities, accidental past professions, unguessed crafts, unsuspected eruditions—all were pooled and went into the building of something that had, as yet, no written traditions, no exact stylistic requirements, nor even formulated demands.

Without going too far into the theoretical debris of the specifics of cinema, I want here to discuss two of its features. These are features of other arts as well, but the film is particularly accountable to them. *Primo:* photo-fragments of nature are recorded; *secundo:* these fragments are combined in various ways. Thus, the shot (or frame), and thus, montage.

Photography is a system of reproduction to fix real events and elements of actuality. These reproductions, or photo-reflections, may be combined in various ways. Both as reflections and in the manner of their combination, they permit any degree of distortion—either technically unavoidable or deliberately calculated. The results fluctuate from exact naturalistic combinations of visual, interrelated experiences to complete alterations,

Sergei M. Eisenstein (1898–1948). Eisenstein is undoubtedly the greatest Soviet film-maker and film theoretician of the twentieth century. In addition to his two great theoretical works on film, *Film Form* and *Film Sense*, Eisenstein made the following film classics: *Strike* (1924), *The Battleship Potemkin* (1925), *October* (1927), *The General Line* (1929), *Que Viva Mexico!* (1931 unfinished), *Alexander Nevsky* (1938), and *Ivan The Terrible* Parts I & II (1945–1946).

* From *Film Form: Essays in Film Theory* by Sergei Eisenstein. Edited and translated by Jay Leyda. Copyright 1949 by Harcourt Brace Jovanovich, Inc. and reprinted with their permission.

arrangements unforeseen by nature, and even to abstract formalism, with remnants of reality.

The apparent arbitrariness of matter, in its relation to the *status quo* of nature, is much less arbitrary than it seems. The final order is inevitably determined, consciously or unconsciously, by the social premises of the maker of the film-composition. His class-determined tendency is the basis of what seems to be an arbitrary cinematographic relation to the object placed, or found, before the camera.

We should like to find in this two-fold process (the fragment and its relationships) a hint as to the specifics of cinema, but we cannot deny that this process is to be found in other art mediums, whether close to cinema or not (and which art is not close to cinema?). Nevertheless, it is possible to insist that these features are specific to the film because film-specifics lie not in the process itself but in the degree to which these features are intensified.

The musician uses a scale of sounds; the painter, a scale of tones; the writer, a row of sounds and words—and these are all taken to an equal degree from nature. But the immutable fragment of actual reality in these cases is narrower and more neutral in meaning, and therefore more flexible in combination, so that when they are put together they lose all visible signs of being combined, appearing as one organic unit. A chord, or even three successive notes, seems to be an organic unit. Why should the combination of three pieces of film in montage be considered as a three-fold collision, as impulses of three successive images?

A blue tone is mixed with a red tone and the result is thought of as violet, and not as a "double exposure" of red and blue. The same unity of word fragments makes all sorts of expressive variations possible. How easily three shades of meaning can be distinguished in language—for example: "a window without light," "a dark window," and "an unlit window."

Now try to express these various nuances in the composition of the frame. Is it at all possible?

If it is, then what complicated context will be needed in order to string the film-pieces onto the film-thread so that the black shape on the wall will begin to show either as a "dark" or as an "unlit" window? How much wit and ingenuity will be expended in order to reach an effect that words achieve so simply?

The frame is much less independently workable than the word or the sound. Therefore the mutual work of frame and montage is really an enlargement in scale of a process microscopically inherent in all arts. However, in the film this process is raised to such a degree that it seems to acquire a new quality.

The shot, considered as material for the purpose of composition, is more resistant than granite. This resistance is specific to it. The shot's tendency toward complete factual immutability is rooted in its nature. This resistance has largely determined the richness and variety of montage forms and styles—for montage becomes the mightiest means for a really important creative remolding of nature.

Thus the cinema is able, more than any other art, to disclose the process that goes on microscopically in all other arts.

The minimum "distortable" fragment of nature is the shot; ingenuity in its combinations is montage.

Analysis of this problem received the closest attention during the second half-decade of Soviet cinema (1925–1930), an attention often carried to excess. Any infinitesimal alteration of a fact or event before the camera grew, beyond all lawful limit, into whole theories of documentalism. The lawful necessity of combining these fragments of reality grew into montage conceptions which presumed to supplant all other elements of film-expression.

Within normal limits these features enter, as elements, into any style of cinematography. But they are not opposed to nor can they replace other problems—for instance the problem of *story*.

To return to the double process indicated at the beginning of these notes: if this process is characteristic of cinema, finding its fullest expression during the second stage of Soviet cinema, it will be rewarding to investigate the creative biographies of film-workers of that period, seeing how these features emerged, how they developed in pre-cinema work. All the roads of that period led towards one Rome. I shall try to describe the path that carried me to cinema principles.

Usually my film career is said to have begun with my production of Ostrovsky's play, *Enough Simplicity in Every Sage*, at the Proletcult Theatre (Moscow, March 1923). This is both true and untrue. It is not true if it is based solely on the fact that this production contained a short comic film made especially for it (not separate, but included in the montage plan of the spectacle). It is more nearly true if it is based on the character of the production, for even then the elements of the specifics mentioned above could be detected.

We have agreed that the first sign of a cinema tendency is one showing events with the least distortion, aiming at the factual reality of the fragments.

A search in this direction shows my film tendencies beginning three years earlier, in the production of *The Mexican* (from Jack London's story). Here, my participation brought into the theater "events" themselves—a purely cinematographic element, as distinguished from "reactions to events"—which is a purely theatrical element.

This is the plot: A Mexican revolutionary group needs money for its activities. A boy, a Mexican, offers to find the money. He trains for boxing, and contracts to let the champion beat him for a fraction of the prize. Instead he beats up the champion, winning the entire prize. Now that I am better acquainted with the specifics of the Mexican revolutionary struggle, not to mention the technique of boxing, I would not think of interpreting this material as we did in 1920, let alone using so unconvincing a plot.

The play's climax is the prize-fight. In accordance with the most hallowed Art Theatre traditions, this was to take place backstage (like the bull-fight in *Carmen*), while the actors on stage were to show excitement in the fight only they can see, as well as to portray the various emotions of the persons concerned in the outcome.

My first move (trespassing upon the director's job, since I was there in the official capacity of designer only) was to propose that the fight be brought into view. Moreover I suggested that the scene be staged in the center of the auditorium to re-create the same circumstances under which a real boxing match takes place. Thus we dared the concreteness of factual events. The fight was to be carefully planned in advance but was to be utterly realistic.

The playing of our young worker-actors in the fight scene differed radically from their acting elsewhere in the production. In every other scene, one emotion gave rise to a further emotion (they were working in the Stanislavsky system), which in turn was used as a means to affect the audience; but in the fight scene the audience was excited directly.

While the other scenes influenced the audience through intonation, gestures, and mimicry, our scene employed realistic, even textural means— real fighting, bodies crashing to the ring floor, panting, the shine of sweat on torsos, and finally, the unforgettable smacking of gloves against taut skin and strained muscles. Illusionary scenery gave way to a realistic ring (though not in the center of the hall, thanks to that plague of every theatrical enterprise, the fireman) and extras closed the circle around the ring.

Thus my realization that I had struck new ore, an actualmaterialistic element in theater. In *The Sage*, this element appeared on a new and clearer level. The eccentricity of the production exposed this same line, through fantastic contrasts. The tendency developed not only from illusionary acting movement, but from the physical fact of acrobatics. A gesture expands into gymnastics, rage is expressed through a somersault, exaltation through a *salto-mortale*, lyricism on "the mast of death." The grotesque of this style permitted leaps from one type of expression to another, as well as unexpected intertwinings of the two expressions. In a later production, *Listen, Moscow* (summer 1923), these two separate lines of "real doing" and "pictorial imagination" went through a synthesis expressed in a specific technique of acting.

These two principles appeared again in Tretiakov's *Gas Masks* (1923–24), with still sharper irreconcilability, broken so noticeably that had this been a film it would have remained, as we say, "on the shelf."

What was the matter? The conflict between materialpractical and fictitious-descriptive principles was somehow patched up in the melodrama, but here they broke up and we failed completely. The cart dropped to pieces, and its driver dropped into the cinema.

This all happened because one day the director had the marvelous idea of producing this play about a gas factory—in a real gas factory.

As we realized later, the real interiors of the factory had nothing to do with our theatrical fiction. At the same time the plastic charm of reality in the factory became so strong that the element of actuality rose with fresh strength—took things into its own hands—and finally had to leave an art where it could not command.

Thereby bringing us to the brink of cinema.

But this is not the end of our adventures with theater work. Having come to the screen, this other tendency flourished, and became known as "typage." This "typage" is just as typical a feature of this cinema period as "montage." And be it known that I do not want to limit the concept of "typage" or "montage" to my own works.

I want to point out that "typage" must be understood as broader than merely a face without make-up, or a substitution of "naturally expressive" types for actors. In my opinion, "typage" included a specific approach to the events embraced by the content of the film. Here again was the method of least interference with the natural course and combinations of events. In concept, from beginning to end, *October* is pure "typage."

A typage tendency may be rooted in theater; growing out of the theater into film, it presents possibilities for excellent stylistic growth, in a broad sense—as an indicator of definite affinities to real life through the camera.[1]

And now let us examine the second feature of film-specifics, the principles of montage. How was this expressed and shaped in my work before joining the cinema?

In the midst of the flood of eccentricity in *The Sage*, including a short film comedy, we can find the first hints of a sharply expressed montage.

The action moves through an elaborate tissue of intrigue. Mamayev sends his nephew, Glumov, to his wife as guardian. Glumov takes liberties beyond his uncle's instructions and his aunt takes the courtship seriously. At the same time Glumov begins to negotiate for a marriage with Mamayev's niece, Turussina, but conceals these intentions from the aunt, Mamayeva. Courting the aunt, Glumov deceives the uncle; flattering the uncle, Glumov arranges with him the deception of the aunt.

Glumov, on a comic plane, echoes the situations, the overwhelming passions, the thunder of finance, that his French prototype, Balzac's Rastignac, experiences. Rastignac's type in Russia was still in the cradle. Money-making was still a sort of child's game between uncles and nephews, aunts and their gallants. It remains in the family, and remains trivial. Hence, the comedy. But the intrigue and entanglements are already present, playing on two fronts at the same time—with both hands—with dual characters . . . and we showed all this with an intertwined montage of two different scenes (of Mamayev giving his instructions, and of Glumov putting them into execution). The surprising intersections of the

---

[1] Eisenstein has said that one might define typage as a modern development of the *Commedia dell'arte*—with its seven stock figures multiplied into infinity. The relationship lies not in numbers, but in audience conditioning. Upon entrance of Pantalone or the Captain, his mask tells the audience immediately what to expect of this figure. Modern film typage is based on the need for presenting each new figure in our first glimpse of him so sharply and completely that further use of this figure may be as a known element. Thus new, immediate conventions are created. An amplification of this approach is given in the author's comments on Lavater.—EDITOR.

two dialogues sharpen the characters and the play, quicken the tempo, and multiply the comic possibilities.

For the production of *The Sage* the stage was shaped like a circus arena, edged with a red barrier, and three-quarters surrounded by the audience. The other quarter was hung with a striped curtain, in front of which stood a small raised platform, several steps high. The scene with Mamayev (Shtraukh) took place downstage while the Mamayeva (Yanukova) fragments occurred on the platform. Instead of changing scenes, Glumov (Yezikanov) ran from one scene to the other and back—taking a fragment of dialogue from one scene, interrupting it with a fragment from the other scene—the dialogue thus colliding, creating new meanings and sometimes word-plays. Glumov's leaps acted as *caesurae* between the dialogue fragments.

And the "cutting" increased in tempo. What was most interesting was that the extreme sharpness of the eccentricity was not torn from the context of this part of the play; it never became comical just for comedy's sake, but stuck to its theme, sharpened by its scenic embodiment.

Another distinct film feature at work here was the new meaning acquired by common phrases in a new environment.

Everyone who has had in his hands a piece of film to be edited knows by experience how neutral it remains, even though a part of a planned sequence, until it is joined with another piece, when it suddenly acquires and conveys a sharper and quite different meaning than that planned for it at the time of filming.

This was the foundation of that wise and wicked art of reediting the work of others, the most profound examples of which can be found during the dawn of our cinematography, when all the master film-editors—Esther Schub, the Vassiliyev brothers, Benjamin Boitler, and Birrois—were engaged in reworking ingeniously the film imported after the revolution.

I cannot resist the pleasure of citing here one montage *tour de force* of this sort, executed by Boitler. One film bought from Germany was *Danton*, with Emil Jannings. As released on our screens, this scene was shown: Camille Desmoulins is condemned to the guillotine. Greatly agitated, Danton rushes to Robespierre, who turns aside and slowly wipes away a tear. The sub-title said, approximately, "In the name of freedom I had to sacrifice a friend. . . ." Fine.

But who could have guessed that in the German original, Danton, represented as an idler, a petticoat-chaser, a splendid chap and the only positive figure in the midst of evil characters, that this Danton ran to the evil Robespierre and . . . spat in his face? And that it was this spit that Robespierre wiped from his face with a handkerchief? And that the title indicated Robespierre's hatred of Danton, a hate that in the end of the film motivates the condemnation of Jannings-Danton to the guillotine?!

Two tiny cuts reversed the entire significance of this scene!

. . .

Erwin Panofsky

STYLE AND MEDIUM IN
THE MOVING PICTURES

Film art is the only art the development of which men now living, have witnessed from the very beginnings; and this development is all the more interesting as it took place under conditions contrary to precedent.* It was not an artistic urge that gave rise to the discovery and gradual perfection of a new technique; it was a technical invention that gave rise to the discovery and gradual perfection of a new art.

From this we understand two fundamental facts. First, that the primordial basis of the enjoyment of moving pictures was not an objective interest in a specific subject matter, much less an aesthetic interest in the formal presentation of subject matter, but the sheer delight in the fact that things seemed to move, no matter what things they were. Second, that films—first exhibited in "kinetoscopes," viz., cinematographic peepshows, but projectable to a screen since as early as 1894—are, originally, a product of genuine folk art (whereas, as a rule, folk art derives from what is known as "higher art"). At the very beginning of things we find the simple recording of movements: galloping horses, railroad trains, fire engines, sporting events, street scenes. And when it had come to the making of narrative films these were produced by photographers who were anything but "producers" or "directors," performed by people who were anything but actors, and enjoyed by people who would have been much offended had anyone called them "art lovers."

The casts of these archaic films were usually collected in a "café" where unemployed supers or ordinary citizens possessed of a suitable exterior were wont to assemble at a given hour. An enterprising photographer would walk in, hire four or five convenient characters and make the picture while carefully instructing them what to do: "Now, you pretend to hit this lady over the head"; and (to the lady): "And you pretend to fall down in

Erwin Panofsky is one of the great art historians of this or any century. His important list of works includes *Studies in Iconology* and *Meaning in the Visual Arts*. Panofsky prepared "Style and Medium in the Moving Pictures" to enlist support for the new film library of the Museum of Modern Art which had begun in 1934. This essay remains the best single piece of film aesthetics to date.

* Reprinted by permission of the Department of Art and Archaeology, Princeton University. Originally published in 1934.

a heap." Productions like these were shown, together with those purely factual recordings of "movement for movement's sake," in a few small and dingy cinemas most frequented by the "lower classes" and a sprinkling of youngsters in quest of adventure (about 1905, I happen to remember there was only one obscure and faintly disreputable *kino* in the whole city of Berlin, bearing, for some unfathomable reason, the English name of "The Meeting Room"). Small wonder that the "better classes," when they slowly began to venture into these early picture theaters, did so, not by way of seeking normal and possibly serious entertainment, but with that characteristic sensation of selfconscious condescension with which we may plunge, in gay company, into the folkloristic depths of Coney Island or a European Kermis; even a few years ago it was the regulation attitude of the socially or intellectually prominent that one could confess to enjoying such austerely educational films as "The Sex Life of the Starfish" or films with "beautiful scenery," but never to a serious liking for narratives.

Today there is no denying that narrative films are not only "art"—not often good art, to be sure, but this applies to other media as well—but also, besides architecture, cartooning, and "commercial design," the only visual art entirely alive. The "movies" have re-established that dynamic contact between art production and art consumption which, for reasons too complex to be considered here, is sorely attentuated, if not entirely interrupted, in many other fields of artistic endeavor. Whether we like it or not, it is the movies that mold, more than any other single force, the opinions, the taste, the language, the dress, the behavior, and even the physical appearance of a public comprising more than 60% of the population of the earth. If all the serious lyrical poets, composers, painters and sculptors were forced by law to stop their activities, a rather small fraction of the general public would become aware of the fact and a still smaller fraction would seriously regret it. If the same thing were to happen with the movies the social consequences would be catastrophic.

· · ·

In the beginning, then, there were the straight recordings of movement no matter what moved, viz., the prehistoric ancestors of our "documentaries"; and, soon after, the early narratives, viz., the prehistoric ancestors of our "feature films." The craving for a narrative element could be satisfied only by borrowing from older arts, and one should expect that the natural thing would have been to borrow from the theater, a theater play being apparently the *genus proximum* to a narrative film in that it consists of a narrative enacted by persons that move. But in reality the imitation of stage performances was a comparatively late and thoroughly frustrated development. What happened at the start was a very different thing: instead of imitating a theatrical performance already endowed with a certain amount of motion, the earliest films added movement to works of art originally stationary, so that the dazzling technical invention might achieve a triumph of its own without intruding upon the sphere of higher culture. The living language, which is always right, has endorsed this sensible choice when it still speaks of a "moving picture" or, simply, a "picture," instead of accepting the pretentious and fundamentally erroneous "screen play."

The stationary works enlivened in the earliest movies were indeed pictures: bad nineteenth-century paintings and postcards (or wax works *à la* Madame Tussaud's), supplemented by the comic strips—a most important root of cinematic art—and the subject matter of popular songs, pulp magazines and dime novels; and the films descending from this ancestry appealed directly and very intensly to a folk art mentality. They gratified—often simultaneously—first: a primitive sense of justice and decorum when virtue and industry were rewarded while vice and laziness were punished; second, plain sentimentality when "the thin trickle of a fictive love interest" took its course "through somewhat serpentine channels," or when, father, dear father, returned from the saloon to find his child dying of diphtheria; third, a primordial instinct for bloodshed and cruelty when Andreas Hofer faced the firing squad, or when (in a film of 1893/94) the head of Mary Queen of Scots actually came off; fourth, a taste for mild pornography (I remember with great pleasure a French film of *ca.* 1900 wherein a seemingly but not really well-rounded lady as well as a seemingly but not really slender one were shown changing to bathing suits—an honest, straightforward *porcheria* much less objectionable than the now extinct Betty Boop films and, I am sorry to say, some of the more recent Walt Disney production); and, finally, that crude sense of humor, graphically described as "slap-stick," which feeds upon the sadistic and the pornographic instinct, either singly or in combination.

Not until as late as *ca.* 1905 was a film adaptation of "Faust" ventured upon (cast still "unknown," characteristically enough), and not until 1911 did Sarah Bernhardt lend her prestige to an unbelievably funny film tragedy *Queen Elizabeth of England*. These films represent the first conscious attempt at transplanting the movies from the folk art level to that of "real art"; but they also bear witness to the fact that this commendable goal could not be reached in so simple a manner. It was soon realized that the imitation of a theater performance with a set stage, fixed entries and exits, and distinctly literary ambitions is the one thing the film must avoid.

The legitimate paths of evolution were opened, not by running away from the folk art character of the primitive film but by developing it within the limits of its own possibilities. Those primordial archetypes of film productions on the folk art level—success or retribution, sentiment, sensation, pornography, and crude humor—could blossom forth into genuine history, tragedy and romance, crime and adventure, and comedy, as soon as it was realized that they could be transfigured: not by an artificial injection of literary values but by the exploitation of the unique and specific possibilities of the new medium. Significantly, the beginnings of this legitimate development antedate the attempts at endowing the film with higher values of a foreign order (the crucial period being the years from 1902 to *ca.* 1905), and the decisive steps were taken by people who were laymen or outsiders from the view-point of the serious stage.

. . .

These unique and specific possibilities can be defined as *dynamization of space* and, accordingly, *spatialization of time*. This statement is self-evident to the point of triviality but it belongs to that kind of truths which, just because of their triviality, are easily forgotten or neglected: all that which exists in space, even the walls of a room or the Rock of Gibraltar, can and should be invested with a semblance of movement, while all that which happens in time, even the thoughts and feelings in the souls of men, can and should be made visible.

In a theater, space is static, that is, the space represented on the stage, as well as the spatial relation of the beholder to the spectacle, are unalterably fixed. The spectator cannot leave his seat, and the setting of the stage cannot change, during one act (except for such incidentals as rising moons or gathering clouds and such illegitimate re-borrowings from the film as turning wings or gliding backdrops). But, in return for this restriction, the theater has the advantage that time, the medium of emotion and thought conveyable by speech, is free and independent of anything that may happen in visible space. Hamlet may deliver his famous monologue lying on a couch in the middle distance, doing nothing and only dimly discernible to the spectator and listener, and yet by his mere words enthrall him with a feeling of intensest emotional action.

With the movies the situation is reversed. Here, too, the spectator occupies a fixed seat, but only physically, not as the subject of an aesthetic experience. Aesthetically, he is in permanent motion as his eye identifies itself with the lens of the camera which permanently shifts in distance and direction. And as movable as the spectator is, as movable is, for the same reason, the space presented to him. Not only bodies move in space, but space itself does, approaching, receding, turning, dissolving and recrystallizing as it appears through the controlled locomotion and focusing of the camera and through the cutting and editing of the various shots—not to mention such special effects as visions, transformations, disappearances, slow-motion and fast-motion shots, reversals and trick films. This opens up a world of possibilities of which the stage can never dream. Quite apart from such photographic tricks as the participation of disembodied spirits in the action of the *Topper* series, or the more effective wonders wrought by Roland Young in *The Man Who Could Work Miracles*, there is, on the purely factual level, an untold wealth of themes as inaccessible to the "legitimate" stage as a fog or a snowstorm is to the sculptor; all sorts of violent elemental phenomena and, conversely, events too microscopic to be visible under normal conditions (such as the life-saving injection with the serum flown in at the very last moment, or the fatal bite of the yellow fever mosquito); full-scale battle scenes: all kinds of operations, not only in the surgical sense but also in the sense of any actual construction, destruction or experimentation, as is *Louis Pasteur* or *Madame Curie*; a really grand party, moving through many rooms of a mansion or palace. Features like these, even the mere shifting of the scene from one place to another by means of a car perilously negotiating heavy traffic or a motor-boat steered through a nocturnal harbour, will not only always retain their primitive cinematic appeal but also remain enormously effective as a means of stirring the emotions and creating suspense. In addition, the movies have the power, entirely denied to the theater, to convey psychological experiences by directly projecting their content to the screen, substituting, as it were, the eye of the beholder for the consciousness of the character (as when the imaginings and hallucinations of the drunkard in the otherwise overrated *Lost Weekend* appear as stark realities instead of being described by mere words. But any attempt to convey thought and feelings exclusively, or even primarily, by speech leaves us with a feeling of embarrassment, boredom, or both.

What I mean by thoughts and feelings "conveyed exclusively, or even primarily, by speech" is simply this: contrary to naïve expectation, the invention of the sound track in 1928 has been unable to change the basic fact that a moving picture, even when it has learned to talk, remains a picture that moves, and does not convert itself into a piece of writing that is enacted. Its substance remains a series of visual sequences held together by an uninterrupted flow of movement in space (except, of course, for such checks and pauses as have the same compositional value as a rest in music), and not a sustained study in human character and destiny transmitted by effective, let alone "beautiful," diction. I cannot remember a more misleading statement about the movies than Mr. Eric Bentley's in *The Playwright as Thinker*, p. 289: "[The potentialities of the talking screen] differ from those of the silent screen in adding the dimension of dialogue—which, potentially, is poetry." I would suggest: "The potentialities of the talking screen differ from those of the silent screen in integrating visible movement with dialogue which therefore, had better not be poetry."

All of us, if we are old enough to remember the period prior to 1928, recall the old-time pianist who, with his eyes glued on the screen, would accompany the events with music adapted to their mood and rhythm; and we also recall the weird and spectral feeling overtaking us when this pianist left his post for a few minutes and the film was allowed to run by itself, the darkness haunted by the monotonous rattle of the machinery. Even the silent film, then, was never mute. The visible spectacle always required, and received, an audible accompaniment which, from the very beginning, distinguished the film from simple pantomime and rather classed it— *mutatis mutandis*—with the ballet. The advent of the talkie meant, not so much an "addition" as a transformation: the transformation of musical sound into articulate speech and, therefore, of quasipantomime into an entirely new species of spectacle which differs from the ballet, and agrees with the stage play, in that its acoustic component consists of intelligible words, but differs from the stage play and agrees with the ballet in that this acoustic component is not detachable from the visual. In a film, that which we hear remains, for good or worse, inextricably fused with that which we see; the sound, articulate or not, cannot express any more than is expressed, at the same time, by visible movement; and in a good film it does not even attempt to do so. To put it briefly: the play—or, as it is very properly called, the "script"—of a moving picture is subject to what might be termed the *principle of coexpressibility*.

Empirical proof of this principle is furnished by the fact that, wherever the dialogical or monological element gains temporary prominence there appears, with the inevitability of a natural law, the "close-up." What does the close-up achieve? In showing us, in magnification, either the face of the speaker or the face of the listeners or both in alternation, the camera transforms the human physiognomy into a huge field of action where—given the qualification of the performers—every subtle movement of the features, almost imperceptible from a natural distance, becomes an expressive event in visible space and thereby completely integrates itself with the expressive content of the spoken word; whereas on the stage, the spoken word makes a stronger rather than a weaker impression if we are not permitted to count the hairs in Romeo's mustache.

This does not mean that the scenario is a negligible factor in the making of a moving picture. It only means that its artistic intention differs in kind from that of a stage play, and much more from that of a novel or a piece of poetry. As the success of a Gothic jamb figure depends, not only upon its quality as a piece of sculpture but also, or even more so, upon its integrability with the architecture of the portal, so does the success of a movie script—not unlike that of an opera libretto—depend, not only upon its quality as a piece of literature but also, or even more so, upon its integrability with the events on the screen.

As a result—another empirical proof of the coexpressibility principle— good movie scripts are unlikely to make good reading and have seldom been published in book form: whereas, conversely, good stage plays have to be severely altered, cut, and, on the other hand, enriched by interpolations to make good movie scripts. In Shaw's *Pygmalion*, for instance, the actual process of Eliza's phonetic education and, still more important, her final triumph at the grand party, are wisely omitted; we see—or, rather, hear—some samples of her gradual linguistic improvement and finally encounter her, upon her return from the reception, victorious and splendidly arrayed but deeply hurt for want of recognition and sympathy. In the film adaptation, precisely these two scenes are not only supplied but also strongly emphasized; we witness the fascinating activities in the laboratory with its array of spinning disks and mirrors, organ pipes and dancing flames, and we participate in the ambassadorial party, with many moments of impending catastrophe and a little counter-intrigue thrown in for suspense. Unquestionably these two scenes, entirely absent from the play, and indeed unachievable upon the stage, were the highlights of the film; whereas the Shavian dialogue, however severely cut, turned out to fall a little flat in certain moments. And wherever, as in so many other films, a poetic emotion, a musical outburst, or a literary conceit (even, I am grieved to say, some of the wisecracks of Groucho Marx) entirely lose contact with visible movement, they strike the sensitive spectators as, literally, out of place. It is certainly terrible when a soft-boiled He-Man, after the suicide of his mistress, casts a twelve-foot glance upon her photograph and says something less-than-coexpressible to the effect that he would never foregt her. But when he recites, instead, a piece of poetry as sublimely more-than-coexpressible as Romeo's monologue at the bier of Juliet, it is still worse. Reinhardt's *Midsummer Night's Dream* is probably the most unfortunate major film ever produced; and Olivier's *Henry V* owes its comparative success, apart from the all but providential adaptability of this particular play, to so many *tours de force* that it will remain, God willing, an exception rather than set a pattern. It combines "judicious pruning" with the interpolation of pageantry, non-verbal comedy and melodrama; it uses a device perhaps best designated as "oblique close-up" (Mr. Olivier's beautiful face inwardly listening to but not pronouncing the great soliloquy); and, most notably, it shifts between three levels of archaeological reality: a reconstruction of Elizabethan London, a reconstruction of the events of 1415 as laid down in Shakespeare's play, and the reconstruction of a performance of this play on Shakespeare's own stage. All this is perfectly legitimate; but, even so, the highest praise of the film will always come from those who, like the critics of the *New Yorker*, are not quite in sympathy with either the movies *au naturel* or Shakespeare *au naturel*.

.   .   .

As the writings of Conan Doyle potentially contain all modern mystery stories (except for the tough specimens of the Dashiell Hammett school), so do the films produced between 1900 and 1910 pre-establish the subject matter and methods of the moving picture as we know it. This period produced the incunabula of the Western and the crime film (Edwin S. Porter's amazing *Great Train Robbery* of 1903) from which developed the modern Gangster, Adventure, and Mystery pictures (the latter, if well done, is still one of the most honest and genuine forms of film entertainment, space being doubly charged with time as the beholder asks himself, not only "what is going to happen?" but also "what has happened before?"). The same period saw the emergence of the fantastically imaginative film (Méliès) which was to lead to the expressionist and surrealist experiments (*The Cabinet of Dr. Caligari, Sang d'un Poète,* etc.), on the one hand, and to the more superficial and spectator fairy tales *à la* Arabian Nights, on the other. Comedy, late to triumph in Charlie Chaplin, the still insufficiently appreciated Buster Keaton, the Marx Brothers, and the pre-Hollywood creations of René Clair, reached a respectable level in Max Linder and others. In historical and melodramatic films the foundations were laid for movie iconography and movie symbolism, and in the early work of D. W. Griffith we find, not only remarkable attempts at psychological analysis (*Edgar Allen Poe*) and social criticism (*A Corner in Wheat*) but also such basic technical innovations as the long-shot, the flash-back and the close-up. And modest trick-films and cartoons paved the way to Felix the Cat, Pop-Eye the Sailor, and Felix's prodigious offspring, Mickey Mouse.

Within their self-imposed limitations the earlier Disney films, and certain sequences in the later ones,[1] represent, as it were, a chemically pure distillation of cinematic possibilities. They retain the most important folk-loristic elements—sadism, pornography, the humor engendered by both, and moral justice—almost without dilution and often fuse these elements into a variation on the primitive and inexhaustible David-and-Goliath motif, the triumph of the seemingly weak over the seemingly strong; and their fantastic independence of the natural laws gives them the power to integrate space with time to such perfection that the spatial and temporal experiences of sight and hearing come to be almost interconvertible. A series of soap bubbles, successively punctured, emits a series of sounds exactly corresponding in pitch and volume to the size of the bubbles; the three uvulae of Willie the Whale—small, large and medium—vibrate in consonance with tenor, bass and baritone notes; and the very concept of stationary existence is completely abolished. No object in creation, whether it be a house, a piano, a tree, or an alarm clock, lacks the faculties of organic, in fact anthropomorphic, movement, facial expression and phonetic articulation. Incidentally, even in normal, "realistic" films the inanimate object, provides that it is dynamizable, can play the role of a leading character as do the ancient railroad engines in Buster Keaton's *General* and *Niagara Falls*. How the earlier Russian films exploited the possibility of heroizing all sorts of machinery lives in everybody's memory; and it is perhaps more than an accident that the two films which will go down in history as the great comical and the great serious masterpiece of the silent period bear the names and immortalize the personalities of two big ships: Keaton's *Navigator* (1924) and Eisenstein's *Potemkin* (1925).

. . .

---

[1] I make this distinction because it was, in my opinion, a fall from grace when *Snow-White* introduced the human figure and when *Fantasia* attempted to picturalize The World's Great Music. The very virtue of the animated cartoon is to animate, that is to say, endow lifeless things with life, or living things with a different kind of life. It effects a metamorphosis, and such a metamorphosis is wonderfully present in Disney's animals, plants, thunderclouds and railroad trains. Whereas his dwarfs, glamorized princesses, hillbillies, baseball players, rouged centaurs and *amigos* from South America are not transformations but caricatures at best, and fakes or vulgarities at worst. Concerning music, however, it should be borne in mind that its cinematic use is no less predicated upon the principle of co-expressibility than is the cinematic use of the spoken word. There is music permitting or even requiring the accompaniment of visible action (such as dances, ballet music and any kind of operatic compositions) and music of which the opposite is true; and this is, again, not a question of quality (most of us rightly prefer a waltz by Johann Strauss to a symphony by Sibelius) but one of intention. In *Fantasia* the hippopotamus ballet was wonderful, and the Pastoral Symphony and Ave Maria sequences were deplorable, not because the cartooning in the first case was infinitely better than in the two others (*cf. above*), and certainly not because Beethoven and Schubert are too sacred for picturalization, but simply because Ponchielli's Dance of the Hours is coexpressible while the Pastoral Symphony and the Ave Maria are not. In cases like these even the best imaginable music and the best imaginable cartoon will impair rather than enhance each other's effectiveness.

Experimental proof of all this was furnished by Disney's more recent *Make Mine Music* where The World's Great Music was fortunately restricted to Prokofieff. Even among the other sequences the most successful ones were those in which the human element was either absent or reduced to a minimum; Willie the Whale, the Ballad of Johnny Fedora and Alice Blue-Bonnet, and, above all, the truly magnificent Goodman Quartet.

The evolution from the jerky beginnings to this grand climax offers the fascinating spectacle of a new artistic medium gradually becoming conscious of its legitimate, that is, exclusive, possibilities and limitations—a spectacle not unlike the development of the mosaic, which started out with transposing illusionistic genre pictures into a more durable material and culminated in the hieratic supernaturalism of Ravenna; or the development of line engraving, which started out as a cheap and handy substitute for book illumination and culminated in the purely "graphic" style of Dürer.

Just so the silent movies developed a definite style of their own, adapted to the specific conditions of the medium. A hitherto unknown language was forced upon a public not yet capable of reading it, and the more proficient the public became the more refinement could develop in the language. For a Saxon peasant of around 800 it was not easy to understand the meaning of a picture showing a man as he pours water over the head of another man, and even later many people found it difficult to grasp the significance of two ladies standing behind the throne of an emperor. For the public of around 1910 it was no less difficult to understand the meaning of the speechless action in a moving picture, and the producers employed means of clarification similar to those we find in medieval art. One of these were printed titles or letters, striking equivalents of the medieval *tituli* and scrolls (at a still earlier date there even used to be explainers who would say, *viva voce*: "Now he thinks his wife is dead but she isn't" or: "I don't wish to offend the ladies in the audience but I doubt that any of them would have done that much for her child"). Another, less obtrusive method of explanation was the introduction of a fixed iconography which from the outset informed the spectator about the basic facts and characters, much as the two ladies behind the emperor, when carrying a sword and a cross, respectively, were uniquely determined as Fortitude and Faith. There arose, identifiable by standardized appearance, behavior, and attributes, the wellremembered types of the Vamp and the Straight Girl (perhaps the most convincing modern equivalents of the medieval personifications of the Vices and Virtues), the Family Man, and the Villain, the latter marked by a black mustache and walking stick. Nocturnal scenes were printed on blue or green film. A checkered table cloth meant, once for all, a "poor but honest" milieu; a happy marriage, soon to be endangered by the shadows from the past, was symbolized by the young wife's pouring the breakfast coffee for her husband; the first kiss was invariably announced by the lady's gently playing with her partner's necktie and was invariably accompanied by her kicking out with her left foot. The conduct of the characters was predetermined accordingly. The poor but honest laborer who, after leaving his little house with the checkered table cloth, came upon an abandoned baby could not but take it to his home and bring it up as best he could; the Family Man could not but yield, however temporarily, to the temptations of the Vamp. As a result these early melodramas had a highly gratifying and soothing quality in that events took shape, without the complications of individual psychology, according to a pure Aristotelian logic so badly missed in real life.

Devices like these became gradually less necessary as the public grew accustomed to interpret the action by itself and were virtually abolished by the invention of the talking film. But even now there survive—quite legitimately, I think—the remnants of a "fixed attitude and attribute" principle and, more basic, a primitive or folkloristic concept of plot construction. Even today we take it for granted that the diphtheria of a baby tends to occur when the parents are out, and, having occurred, solves all their matrimonial problems. Even today we demand of a decent mystery film that the butler, though he may be anything from an agent of the British Secret Service to the real father of the daughter of the house, must not turn out to be the murderer. Even today we love to see Pasteur, Zola, or Ehrlich win out against stupidity and wickedness, with their respective wives trusting and trusting all the time. Even today we much prefer a happy finale to a gloomy one, and insist, at the very least, on the observance of the Aristotelian rule that the story have a beginning, a middle, and an ending—a rule the abrogation of which has done so much to estrange the general public from the more elevated spheres of modern writing. Primitive symbolism, too, survives in such amusing details as the last sequence of *Casablanca* where the delightfully crooked and right-minded *Préfet de Police* casts an empty bottle of Vichy water into the wastepaper basket; and in such telling symbols of the supernatural as Sir Cedric Hardwicke's Death in the guise of a "gentleman in a dustcoat trying" (*On Borrowed Time*) or Claude Rains' Hermes Psychopompos in the striped trousers of an airline manager (*Here Comes Mister Jordan*).

The most conspicuous advances were made in directing, lighting, camera work, cutting, and acting proper. But while in most of these fields the evolution proceeded continuously—though, of course, not without detours, breakdowns and archaic relapses—the development of acting suffered a sudden interruption by the invention of the talking film; so that the style of acting in the silents can already be evaluated in retrospect, as a lost art not unlike the painting technique of Jan van Eyck or, to take up our previous simile, the burin technique of Dürer. It was soon realized that acting in a silent film neither meant a pantomimic exaggeration of stage acting (as was generally and erroneously assumed by professional stage actors who more and more frequently condescended to perform in the movies), nor could dispense with stylization altogether; a man photographed while walking down a gangway in ordinary, every-day-life fashion looked like anything but a man walking down a gangway when the result appeared on the screen. If the picture was to look both natural and meaningful the acting had to be done in a manner equally different from the style of the stage and the reality of ordinary life; speech had to be made dispensable by establishing an organic relation between the acting and the technical procedure of cinephotography—much as in Dürer's prints color had been made dispensable by establishing an organic relation between the design and the technical procedure of line engraving.

This was precisely what the great actors of the silent period accomplished, and it is a significant fact that the best of them did not come from the stage, whose crystallized tradition prevented Duse's only film, *Cenere*, from being more than a priceless record of Duse. They came instead from the circus or the variety, as was the case of Chaplin, Keaton and Will Rogers; from nothing in particular, as was the case of Theda Bara, of her greater European parallel, the Danish actress Asta Nielsen, and of Garbo; or from everything under the sun, as was the case of Douglas Fairbanks. The style of these "old masters" was indeed comparable to the style of line engraving in that it was, and had to be, exaggerated in comparison with stage acting (just as the sharply incised and vigorously curved *tailles* of the burin are exaggerated in comparison with pencil strokes or brushwork), but richer, subtler and infinitely more precise. The advent of the talkies, reducing if not abolishing this difference between movie acting and stage acting, thus confronted the actors and actresses of the silent screen with a serious problem. Buster Keaton yielded to temptation and fell. Chaplin first tried to stand his ground and to remain an exquisite archaist but finally gave in, with only moderate success (*The Dictator*). Only the glorious Harpo has thus far successfully refused to utter a single articulate sound; and only Greta Garbo succeeded, in a measure, in transforming her style in principle. But even in her case one cannot help feeling that her first talking picture, *Anna Christie*, where she could ensconce herself, most of the time, in mute or monosyllabic sullenness, was better than her later performances; and in the second, talking version of *Anna Karenina*, the weakest moment is certainly when she delivers a big Ibsenian speech to her husband, and the strongest when she silently moves along the platform of the railroad station while her despair takes shape in the consonance of her movement (and expression) with the movement of the nocturnal space around her, filled with the real noises of the trains and the imaginary sound of the "little men with the iron hammers" that drives her, relentlessly and almost without her realizing it, under the wheels.

Small wonder that there is sometimes felt a kind of nostalgia for the silent period and that devices have been worked out to combine the virtues of sound and speech with those of silent acting, such as the "oblique close-up" already mentioned in connection with *Henry* V; the dance behind glass doors in *Sous les Toits de Paris*; or, in the *Histoire d'un Tricheur*, Sacha Guitry's recital of the events of his youth while the events themselves are "silently" enacted on the screen. However, this nostalgic feeling is no argument against the talkies as such. Their evolution has shown that, in art, every gain entails a certain loss on the other side of the ledger; but that the gain remains a gain, provided that the basic nature of the medium is realized and respected. One can imagine that, when the cave-men of Altamira began to paint their buffaloes in natural colors instead of merely incising the contours, the more conservative cave-men foretold the end of palaeolithic art. But palaeolithic art went on, and so will the movies. New technical inventions always tend to dwarf the values already attained, especially in a medium that owes its very existence to technical experimentation. The earliest talkies were infinitely inferior to the then mature silents, and most of the present technicolor films are still inferior to the now mature talkies in black and white. But even if Aldous Huxley's nightmare should come true and the experiences of taste, smell and touch should be added to those of sight and hearing, even then we may say with the Apostle, as we have said when first confronted with the sound track and the technicolor film: "We are troubled on every side, yet not distressed; we are perplexed, but not in despair."

.   .   .

From the law of time-charged space and space-bound time, there follows the fact that the "*screen play*," in contrast to the theater play, *has no aesthetic existence independent of its performance, and that its characters have no aesthetic existence outside the actors.*

The playwright writes in the fond hope that his work will be an imperishable jewel in the treasure house of civilization and will be presented in hundreds of performances that are but transient variations on a "work" that is constant. The script writer, on the other hand, writes for one producer, one director and one cast. Their work achieves the same degree of permanence as does his; and should the same or a similar scenario ever be filmed by a different director and a different cast there will result an altogether different "play."

Othello and Nora are definite, substantial figures created by the playwright. They can be played well or badly, and they can be "interpreted" in one way or another; but they most definitely exist, no matter who plays them or even whether they are played at all. The character in a film, however, lives and dies with the actor. It is not the entity "Othello" interpreted by Robeson or the entity "Nora" interpreted by Duse; it is the entity "Greta Garbo" incarnate in a figure called Anna Christie or the entity "Robert Montgomery" incarnate in a murderer who, for all we know or care to know, may forever remain anonymous but will never cease to haunt our memories. Even when the names of the characters happen to be Henry VIII or Anna Karenina, the King who ruled England from 1509 to 1547 and the woman created by Tolstoi do not exist outside the being of Garbo and Laughton. They are but empty and incorporeal outlines like the shadows in Homer's Hades, assuming the character of reality only when filled with the life blood of an actor. Conversely, if a movie role is badly played there remains literally nothing of it, no matter how interesting the character's psychology or how elaborate the words.

What applies to the actor applies, *mutatis mutandis*, to most of the other artists, or artisans, who contribute to the making of a film: the director, the sound man, the enormously important camera man, even the make-up man. A sage production is rehearsed until everything is ready, and then it is repeatedly performed in three consecutive hours. At each performance everybody has to be on hand and does his work; and afterwards he goes home and to bed. The work of the stage actor may thus be likened to that of a musician, and that of the stage director to that of a conductor. Like these, they have a certain répertoire which they have studied and present in a number of complete but transitory performances, be it "Hamlet" today and "Ghosts" tomorrow, or "Life with Father" *per saecula saeculorum*. The activities of the film actor and the film director, however, are comparable, respectively, to those of the plastic artist and the architect, rather than to those of the musician and conductor. Stage work is continuous but transitory; film work is discontinuous but permanent. Individual sequences are done piecemeal and out of order according to the most efficient use of sets and personnel. Each bit is done over and over again until it stands; and when the whole has been cut and composed everyone is through with it forever. Needless to say that this very procedure cannot but emphasize the curious consubstantiality that exists between the person of the movie actor and his role. Coming into existence piece by piece, regardless of the natural sequence of events, the "character" can grow into a unified whole only if the actor manages to be, not merely to play, Henry VIII or Anna Karenina throughout the entire wearisome period of shooting. I have it on the best of authorities that Laughton was really difficult to live with in the particular six or eight weeks during which he was doing —or rather being—Captain Bligh.

It might be said that a film, called into being by a cooperative effort in which all contributions have the same degree of performance, is the nearest modern equivalent of a medieval cathedral; the role of the producer corresponding, more or less, to that of the bishop or archbishop; that of the director to that of the architect-in-chief; that of the scenario writers to that of the scholastic advisers, establishing the iconographical program; and that of the actors, camera men, cutters, sound men, make-up men and the divers technicians to that of those whose work provided the physical entity of the finished product, from the sculptors, glass painters, bronze casters, carpenters and skilled masons down to the quarry men and woodsmen. And if you speak to any one of these collaborators he will tell you, with perfect *bona fides*, that his is really the most important job—which is quite true to the extent that it is indispensable.

This comparison may seem sacrilegious, not only because there are, proportionally, fewer good films than there are good cathedrals, but also because the movies are commercial. However, if commercial art be defined as all art not primarily produced in order to gratify the creative urge of its maker but primarily intended to meet the requirements of a patron or a buying public, it must be said that non-commercial art is the exception rather than the rule, and a fairly recent and not always felicitous exception at that. While it is true that commercial art is always in danger of ending up as a prostitute, it is equally true that non-commercial art is always in danger of ending up as an old maid. Non-commercial art has given us Seurat's *Grande Jatte* and Shakespeare's Sonnets, but also much that is esoteric to the point of incommunicability. Conversely, commercial art has given us much that is vulgar or snobbish (two aspects of the same thing) to the point of loathsomeness, but also Dürer's prints and Shakespeare's plays. For, we must not forget that Dürer's prints were partly made on commission and partly intended to be sold in the open market; and that Shakespeare's plays—in contrast to the earlier masques and *intermezzi* which were produced at court by aristocratic amateurs and could afford to be so incomprehensible that even those who described them in printed monographs occasionally failed to grasp their intended significance—were meant to appeal, and did appeal, not only to the select few but also to everyone who was prepared to pay a shilling for admission.

It is this requirement of communicability that makes commercial art more vital than non-commercial, and therefore potentially much more effective for better or for worse. The commercial producer can both educate and pervert the general public, and can allow the general public—or rather his idea of the general public—both to educate and to pervert himself. As is demonstrated by a number of excellent films that proved to be great box office successes, the public does not refuse to accept good products if it gets them. That it does not get them very often is caused, not so much by commercialism as such as by too little discernment and, paradoxical though it may seem, too much timidity in its application. Hollywood believes that it must produce "what the public wants" while the public would take whatever Hollywood produces. If Hollywood were to decide for itself what it wants it would get away with it—even if it should decide to "depart from evil and do good." For, to revert to whence we started: in modern life the movies are what most other forms of art have ceased to be, not an adornment but a necessity.

That this should be so is understandable, not only from a sociological but also from an art-historical point of view. The processes of all the earlier representational arts conform, in a higher or lesser degree, to an idealistic conception of the world. These arts operate from top to bottom, so to speak, and not from bottom to top; they start with an idea to be projected into shapeless matter and not with the objects that constitute the physical world. The painter works on a blank wall or canvas which he organizes into a likeness of things and persons according to his idea (however much this idea may have been nourished by reality); he does not work with the things and persons themselves even if he works "from the model." The same is true of the sculptor with his shapeless mass of clay or his untooled block of stone or wood; of the writer with his sheet of paper or his dictaphone; and even of the stage designer with his empty and sorely limited section of space. It is the movies, and only the movies, that do justice to that materialistic interpretation of the universe which, whether we like it or not, pervades contemporary civilization. Excepting the very special case of the animated cartoon, the movies organize material things and persons, not a neutral medium, into a composition that receives its style, and may even become fantastic or pretervoluntarily symbolic,[2] not so

---

[2] I cannot help feeling that the final sequence of the Marx Brothers film *Night in Casablanca*—where Harpo unaccountably usurps the pilot's seat of a big airplane, causes incalculable havoc by flicking one tiny little control after another, and waxes the more insane with joy the greater the disproportion between the smallness of his effort and the magnitude of the disaster—is a magnificent and terrifying symbol of man's behavior in the "atomic age." No doubt the Marx Brothers would vigorously reject this interpretation; but so would Dürer have done had anyone told him that his Apocalypse foreshadowed the cataclysm of the Reformation.

much by an interpretation in the artist's mind as by the actual manipulation of physical objects and recording machinery. The medium of the movies is physical reality as such: the physical reality of eighteenth-century Versailles—no matter whether it be the original or a Hollywood facsimile indistinguishable therefrom for all aesthetic intents and purposes—or of a suburban home in Westchester; the physical reality of the Rue de Lappe in Paris or of the Gobi Desert, of Paul Ehrlich's apartment in Frankfurt or of the streets of New York in the rain; the physical reality of engines and animals, of Edward G. Robinson and Jimmy Cagney. All these objects and persons must be organized into a work of art. They can be arranged in all sorts of ways ("arrangement" comprising, of course, such things as make-up, lighting and camera work); but there is no running away from them. From this point of view it becomes evident that an attempt at subjecting the world to artistic pre-stylization, as in the expressionist settings of *The Cabinet of Doctor Caligari* (1919), could be no more than an exciting experiment that could exert but little influence upon the general course of events. To pre-stylize reality prior to tackling it amounts to dodging the problem. The problem is to manipulate and shoot unstylized reality in such a way that the result has style. This is a proposition no less legitimate and no less difficult than any proposition in the older arts.

Stanley Cavell

SIGHTS AND SOUNDS:
FROM *THE WORLD VIEWED*

. . . What is film?
The beginning of an answer is given by the two continuously intelligent, interesting, and to me useful theorists I have read on the subject.* Erwin Panofsky puts it this way: "The medium of the movies is physical reality as such."[1] André Bazin emphasizes essentially this idea many times and many ways: at one point he says, "Cinema is committed to communicate only by way of what is real"; and then, "The Cinema [is] of its essence a dramaturgy of Nature."[2] "Physical reality as such," taken literally, is not correct: that phrase better fits the specialized pleasures of *tableaux vivants*, or formal gardens, or Minimal Art. What Panofsky and Bazin have in mind is that the basis of the medium of movies is photographic, and that a photograph is *of* reality or nature. If to this we add that the medium is one in which the photographic image is projected and gathered on a screen, our question becomes: What happens to reality when it is projected and screened?

That it is reality that we have to deal with, or some mode of depicting it, finds surprising confirmation in the way movies are remembered, and misremembered. It is tempting to suppose that movies are hard to remember the way dreams are, and that is not a bad analogy. As with dreams, you do sometimes *find* yourself remembering moments in a film, and a procedure in *trying* to remember is to find your way back to a characteristic mood the thing has left you with. But, unlike dreams, other people can help you remember, indeed are often indispensable to the enterprise of remembering. Movies are hard to remember, the way the actual events of

Stanley Cavell is Walter M. Cabot Professor of Aesthetics and General Theory of Value at Harvard University. He has published a number of highly influential essays in several areas of philosophy some of which are collected under the title, *Must We Mean What We Say?*

* Selections from *The World Viewed: Reflections on the Ontology of Film* (New York, 1971), chapters 2, 3, 4, 5, and 6. By permission of the author.

[1] (p. 16). Erwin Panofsky, "Style and Medium in the Moving Pictures," in Daniel Talbot, ed., *Film* (New York: Simon and Schuster, 1959), p. 31.
[2] (p. 16). André Bazin, *What Is Cinema?*, trans. Hugh Gray (Berkeley: University of California Press, 1967), p. 110.

yesterday are. And yet, again like dreams, certain moments from films viewed decades ago will nag as vividly as moments of childhood. It is as if you had to remember what happened *before* you slept. Which suggests that film awakens as much as it enfolds you.

It may seem that this starting point—the projection of reality—begs the question of the medium of film, because movies, and writing about movies, have from their beginnings also recognized that film can depict the fantastic as readily as the natural.[3] What is true about that idea is not denied in speaking of movies as "communicating by way of what is real": the displacement of objects and persons from their natural sequences and locales is itself an acknowledgment of the physicality of their existence. It is as if, for all their insistence on the newness of the medium, the anti-realist theorists could not shake the idea that it was essentially a form of painting, for it was painting which had visually repudiated—anyway, forgone—the representation of reality. This would have helped them neglect the differences between representation and projection. But an immediate fact about the medium of the photograph (still or in motion) is that it is not painting. (An immediate fact about the *history* of photography is that this was not at first obvious.)

What does this mean—not painting? A photograph does not present us with "likenesses" of things; it presents us, we want to say with the things themselves. But wanting to say that may well make us ontologically restless. "Photographs present us with things themselves" sounds, and ought to sound, false or paradoxical. Obviously a photograph of an earthquake, or of Garbo, is not an earthkquake happening (fortunately), or Garbo in the flesh (unfortunately). But this is not very informative. And, moreover, it is no less paradoxical or false to hold up a photograph of Garbo and say, "That is not Garbo," if all you mean is that the object you are holding up is not a human creature. Such troubles in notating so obvious a fact suggest that we do not know what a photograph is; we do not know how to place it ontologically. We might say that we don't know how to thing of the *connection* between a photograph and what it is a photograph of. The image is not a likeness; it is not exactly a replica, or a relic, or a shadow, or an apparition either, though all of these natural candidates share a striking feature with photographs—an aura or history of magic surrounding them.

One might wonder that similar questions do not arise about recordings of sound. I mean, on the whole we would be hard put to find it false or paradoxical to say, listening to a record, "That's an English horn"; there is no trace of temptation to add (as it were, to oneself), "But I know it's really only a recording." Why? A child might be very puzzled by the remark, said in the presence of a phonograph. "That's an English horn," if

[3] (p. 17). Certainly I am not concerned to deny that there may be, through film, what Paul Rotha in his *The Film Till Now* (first published in 1930) refers to as "possibilities . . . open for the great sound and visual [i.e., non-dialogue sound, and perhaps non-photographically visual] cinema of the future." But in the meantime the movies have been what they have been.

something else had already been pointed out to him as an English horn. Similarly, he might be very puzzled by the remark, said of a photograph, "That's your grandmother." Very early, children are *no longer* puzzled by such remarks, luckily. But that doesn't mean we know why they were puzzled, or why they no longer are. And I am suggesting that we don't know either of these things about ourselves.

Is the difference between auditory and visual transcription a function of the fact that we are fully accustomed to hearing things that are invisible, not present to us, not present with us? We would be in trouble if we weren't so accustomed, because it is the nature of hearing that what is heard comes *from* someplace, whereas what you can see you can look *at*. It is why sounds are warnings, or calls; it is way our access to another world is normally through voices from it; and why a man can be spoken to by God and survive, but not if he sees God, in which case he is no longer in *this* world. Whereas we are not accustomed to seeing things that are invisible, or not present to us, not present with us; or we are not accustomed to acknowledging that we do (except for dreams). Yet this seems, ontologically, to be what is happening when we look at a photograph: we see things that are not present.

Someone will object: "That is playing with words. We're not seeing something not present; we are looking at something perfectly present, namely, a *photograph*." But that is affirming something I have not denied. On the contrary, I am precisely describing, or wishing to describe, what it means to say that there is this photograph here. It may be felt that I make too great a mystery of these objects. My feeling is rather that we have forgotten how mysterious these things are, and in general how *different* things are from one another, as though we had forgotten how to value them. This is in fact something movies teach us.

Suppose one tried accounting for the familiarity of recordings by saying, "When I say, listening to a record, 'That's an English horn,' what I really mean is, 'That's the *sound* of an English horn'; moreover, when I am in the presence of an English horn playing, I still don't literally hear the horn, I hear the sound of the horn. So I don't worry about hearing a horn when the horn is not present, because *what* I hear is exactly the same the same (ontologically the same, and if my equipment is good enough, empirically the same) whether the thing is present or not." What this rigmarole calls attention to is that sounds can be perfectly copied, and that we have various interests in copying them. (For example, if they couldn't be copied, people would never learn to talk.) It is interesting that there is no comparable rigmarole about visual transcriptions. The problem is not that photographs are not visual copies of objects, or that objects can't be visually copied. The problem is that even if a photograph were a copy of an object, so to speak, it would not bear the relation to its object that a recording bears to the sound it copies. We said that the record reproduces its sound, but we cannot say that a photograph reproduces a sight (or a look, or an appearance). It can seem that language is missing a word at this place. Well, you can always invent a word. But one doesn't know what a pin the word *on* here. It isn't that there aren't sights to see, nor even that a sight has by definition to be especially *worth* seeing (hence could not be the sort of thing we are *always* seeing), whereas sounds are being thought of here, not unplausibly, as what we always hear. A sight *is* an object (usually a very large object, like the Grand Canyon or Versailles, although small southern children are frequently held, by the person in charge of them, to be sights) or an extraordinary happening, like the aurora borealis; and what you see, when you sight something, is an object —anyway, not the sight of an object. Nor will the epistemologist's "sense-data" or "surfaces" provide correct descriptions here. For we are not going to say that photographs provide us with the sense-data of the objects they contain, because if the sense-data of photographs were the same as the sense-data of the objects they contain, we couldn't tell a photograph of an object from the object itself. To say that a photograph is of the surfaces of objects suggests that it emphasizes texture. What is missing is not a word, but, so to speak, something in nature—the fact that objects don't *make* sights, or *have* sights. I feel like saying: Objects are too *close* to their sights to give them up for reproducing; in order to reproduce the sights they (as it were) make, you have to reproduce *them*—make a mold, or take an impression. Is that what a photograph does? We might, as Bazin does on occasion, try thinking of a photograph as a visual mold or a visual impression. My dissatisfaction with that idea is, I think, that physical molds and impressions and imprints have clear procedures for getting *rid* of their originals, whereas in a photograph, the original is still as present as it ever was. Not present as it once was to the camera; but that is only a mold-machine, not the mold itself.

Photographs are not *hand*-made; they are manufactured. And what is manufactured is an image of the world. The inescapable fact of mechanism or automatism in the making of these images is the feature Bazin points to as "[satisfying], once and for all and in its very essence, our obsession with realism."[4]

It is essential to get to the right depth of this fact of automatism. It is, for example, misleading to say, as Bazin does, that "photography has freed the plastic arts from their obsession with likeness,"[5] for this makes it seem (and it does often look) as if photography and painting were in competition, or that painting had wanted something that photography broke in and satisfied. So far as photography satisfied a wish, it satisfied a wish not confined to painters, but the human wish, intensifying in the West since the Reformation, to escape subjectivity and metaphysical isolation—a wish for the power to reach this world, having for so long tried, at last hopelessly, to manifest fidelity to another. And painting was not "freed" —and not by photography—from its obsession with likeness. Painting in Manet, was *forced* to forgo likeness exactly because of its own obsession with reality, because the illusions it had learned to create did not provide

[4] (p. 20). Bazin, *op. cit.*, p. 12.
[5] (p. 21). *Loc. cit.*

the conviction in reality, the connection with reality, that it craved.[6] One might even say that in withdrawing from likeness, painting freed photography to be invented.⌉

And if what is meant is that photography freed painting from the idea that a painting had to be a picture (that is, *of* or *about* something else), that is also not true. Painting did not free itself, did not force itself to maintain itself apart, from *all* objective reference until long after the establishment of photography; and then not because it finally dawned on painters that painting were not pictures, but because that was the way to maintain connection with (the history of) the art of painting, to maintain conviction in its power to create paintings, meaningful objects in paint.

And are we sure that the final denial of objective reference amounts to a complete yielding of connection with reality—once, that is, we have given up the idea that "connection with reality" is to be understood as "provision of likeness"? We can be sure that the view of painting as dead without reality, and the view of painting as dead with it, are both in need of development in the views each takes of reality and of painting. We can say, painting and reality no longer *assure* one another.

It could be said further that what painting wanted, in wanting connection with reality, was a sense of *presentness*[7]—not exactly a conviction of the world's presence to us, but of our presence to it. At some point the unhinging of our consciousness from he world interposed our subjectivity between us and our presentness to the world. Then our subjectivity became what is present to us, individuality became isolation. The route to conviction in reality was through the acknowledgment of that endless presence of self. What is called expressionism is one possibility of representing this acknowledgment. But it would, I think, be truer to think of expressionism as a representation of our *response* to this new fact of our condition—our terror of ourselves in isolation—rather than as a representation of the world from within the condition of isolation itself. It would, to that extent, not be a new mastery of fate by creating selfhood against no matter what odds; it would be the sealing of the self's fate by theatricalizing it. Apart from the wish for selfhood (hence the always simultaneous granting of otherness as well), I do not understand the value of art. Apart from this wish and its achievement, art is exhibition.

To speak of our subjectivity as the route back to our conviction in reality is to speak of romanticism. Perhaps romanticism can be understood as the natural struggle between the representation and the acknowledgment of our subjectivity (between the acting out and the facing off of ourselves, as psychoanalysts would more or less say). Hence, Kant, and Hegel; hence Blake secreting the world he believes in; hence Wordsworth competing with the history of poetry by writing out himself, writing him-

---

[6] (p. 21). See Michael Fried, *Three American Painters* (Cambridge, Mass.: Fogg Art Museum, Harvard University, 1965), n. 3; and "Manet's Sources," *Artforum*, March 1969, pp. 28–79.
[7] (p. 22). See Michael Fried, "Art and Objecthood," *Artforum*, June 1967; reprinted in Gregory Battrock, ed., *Minimal Art* (New York: E. P. Dutton, 1968), pp. 116–47.

self back into the world. A century later Heidegger is investigating Being by investigating *Dasein* (because it is in *Dasein* that Being shows up best, namely as questionable), and Wittgenstein investigates the world ("the possibilities of phenomena") by investigating what we say, what we are inclined to say, what our pictures of phenomena are, in order to wrest the world from our possessions so that we may possess it again. Then the recent major painting which Fried describes as objects of *presentness* would be painting's latest effort to maintain its conviction in its own power to establish connection with reality—by permitting us presentness to ourselves, apart from which there is no hope for a world.

Photography overcame subjectivity in a way undreamed of by painting, a way that could not satisfy painting, one which does not so much defect the act of painting as escape it altogether: by *automatism*, by removing the human agent from task of reproduction.

One could accordingly say that photography was never in competition with painting. What happened was that at some point the quest for visual reality, or the "memory of the present" (as Baudelaire put it), split apart. To maintain conviction in our connection with reality, to maintain our presentness, painting accepts the recession of the world. Photography maintains the presentness of the world by accepting our absence from it. The reality in a photograph is present to me while I am not present to it; and a world I know, and see, but to which I am nevertheless not present (through no fault of my subjectivity), is a world past.

Photograph and Screen

Let us notice the specific sense in which photographs are of the world, of reality as a whole. You can always ask, pointing to an object in a photograph—a building, say—what lies behind it, totally obscured by it. This only accidentally makes sense when asked of an object in a painting. You can always ask, of an area photographed, what lies adjacent to that area, beyond the frame. This generally makes no sense asked of a painting. You can ask these questions of objects in photographs because they have answers in reality. The world of a painting is not continuous with the world of its frame; at its frame, a world finds its limits. We might say: A painting *is* a world; a photograph is *of* the world. What happens in a photograph is that *it* comes to an end. A photograph is cropped, not necessarily by a paper cutter or by masking but by the camera itself. The camera crops it by predetermining the amount of view it will accept; cutting, masking, enlarging, predetermine the amount after the fact. (Something like this phenomenon shows up in recent painting. In this respect, these paintings have found, at the extremest negation of the photographic, media that achieve the condition of photographs.) The camera, being finite, crops a portion from an indefinitely larger field; continuous portions of that field could be included in the photograph in fact taken; in prin-

ciple, it could all be taken. Hence objects in photographs that run past
the edge do not feel cut; they are aimed at, shot, stopped live. When a
photograph is cropped, the rest of the world is cut *out*. The implied presence of the rest of the world, and its explicit rejection, are as essential in
the experience of a photograph as what it explicitly presents. A camera is
an opening in a box: that is the best emblem of the fact that a camera
holding on an object is holding the rest of the world away. The camera
has been praised for extending the senses; it may, as the world goes, deserve more praise for confining them, leaving room for thought.

The world of a moving picture is screened. The screen is not a support,
not like a canvas; there is nothing to support, that way. It holds a projection, as light as light. A screen is a barrier. What does the silver screen
screen? It screens me from the world it holds—that is, makes me invisible.
And it screens that world from me—that is, screens its existence from me.
That the projected world does not exist (now) is its only difference from
reality. (There is no feature, or set of features, in which it differs. Existence is not a predicate.) Because it is the field of a photograph, the
screen has no frame; that is to say, no border. Its limits are not so much
the edges of a given shape as they are the limitations, or capacity, of a
container. The screen *is* a frame; the frame is the whole field of the screen
—as a frame of film is the whole field of a photograph, like the frame of a
loom or a house. In this sense, the screen-frame is a mold, or form.[8]

[8] (p. 25). When painting found out how to acknowledge the fact that paintings had
shapes, shapes became forms, not in the sense of patterns, but in the sense of con-
tainers. A form then could *give* its shape to what it contained. And content could
transfer its significance as painting to what contains it. Then shape *pervades*, like
gravity, or energy, or air. (See Michael Fried, "Shape as Form," *Artforum*, November
1966; reprinted in Henry Geldzahler's catalogue, *New York Painting and Sculpture:
1940–1970* [New York: E. P. Dutton, 1969].)
   This is not, as far as we yet know, a possibility of the film or screen frame—which
only repeats the fact that a film is not a painting. The most important feature of the
screen format remains what it was from the beginning of movies—its scale, its absolute largeness. Variation of format—e.g., CinemaScope—is a matter determined, so
far as I can tell, by questions of convenience and inconvenience, and by fashion.
Though perhaps, as in painting, the declaration of color as such required or benefited
from the even greater expanses of wider screens.
   The idea may seen obviously false or foolish that the essential ontological difference
between the world as it is and as it is screened is that the screened world does not
exist; because this overlooks—or perhaps obscurely states—a fully obvious difference
between them, viz., that the screened world is two-dimensional. I do not deny the
obscurity, but better a real obscurity than a false clarity. For *what* is two-dimensional?
The world which is screened is not; its objects and motions are as three-dimensional
as ours. The screen itself, then? Or the images on it? We seem to understand what it
means to say that a painting is two-dimensional. But that depends on our understanding that the support on which paint is laid is a three-dimensional object, and that
the description of *that* object will not (except in an exceptional or vacuous sense) be the
description of a painting. More significantly, it depends on our understanding of the
support as *limiting* the extent of the painting in two dimensions. This is not the relation between the screen and the images projected across it. It seems all right to say
that the screen is two-dimensional, but it would not follow that what you see there
has the same dimensionality—any more than in the case of paint, its support, and the
painting. Shadows are two-dimensional, but they are cast by three-dimensional objects
—tracings of opacity, not gradations of it. This suggests that phenomenologically the
idea of two-dimensionality is an idea of either transparency or outline. Projected
images are not shadows; rather, one might say, they are shades.

The fact that in a moving picture successive film frames are fit flush into the fixed screen frame results in a phenomenological frame that is indefinitely extendible and contractible, limited in the smallness of the object it can grasp only by the state of its technology, and in largeness only by the span of the world. Drawing the camera back, and panning it, are two ways of extending the frame; a close-up is of a part of the body, or of one object or small set of objects, supported by and reverberating the whole frame of nature. The altering frame is the image of perfect attention. Early in its history the cinema discovered the possibility of *calling* attention to persons and parts of persons and objects; but it is equally a possibility of the medium not to call attention to them but, rather, to let the world happen, to let its parts draw attention to themselves according to their natural weight. This possibility is less explored than its opposite. Dreyer, Flaherty, Vigo, Renior, and Antonioni are masters of it.

Audience, Actor, and Star

The depth of the automatism of photography is to be read not alone in its mechanical production of an image of reality, but in its mechanical defeat of our presense to that reality. The audience in a theater can be defined as those to whom the actors are present while they are not present to the actors.[9] But movies allow the audience to be mechanically absent. The fact that I am invisible and inaudible to the actors, and fixed in position, no longer needs accounting for; it is not part of a convention I have to comply with; the proceedings do not have to make good the fact that I do nothing in the face of tragedy, or that I laugh at the follies of others. In viewing a movie my helplessness is mechanically assured: I am present not at something happening, which I must confirm, but at something that has happened, which I absorb (like a memory). In this, movies resemble novels, a fact mirrored in the sound of narration itself, whose tense is the past.

It might be said: "But surely there is the obvious difference between a movie house and a theater that is not recorded by what has so far been said and that outweighs all this fiddle of differences. The obvious difference is that in a theater we are in the presence of an actor, in a movie house we are not. You have said that in both places the actor is in our presence and in neither are we in his, the difference lying in the mode of our absence. But there is also the plain fact that in a theater a real man is *there*, and in a movie no real man is there. That is obviously essential to the differences between our responses to a play and to a film." What that means must not be denied; but the fact remains to be understood. Bazin meets it head on by simply denying that "the screen is incapable of putting us 'in the presence of' the actor"; it, so to speak, relays his presence to us,

---

[9] (p. 25). This idea is developed to some extent in my essays on *Endgame* and *King Lear* in *Must We Mean What We Say?* (New York: Scribner's, 1969).

as by mirrors.[10] Bazin's idea here really fits the facts of live television, in which the thing we are presented with is happening simultaneously with its presentation. But in live television, what is present to us while it is happening is not the world, but an event standing out from the world. Its point is not to reveal, but to cover (as with a gun), to keep something on view.

It is an incontestable fact that in a motion picture no live human being is up there. But a human *something* is, and something unlike anything else we know. We can stick to our plain description of that human something as "in our presence while we are not in his" (present *at* him, because looking at him, but not present *to* him) and still account for the difference between his live presence and his photographed presence to us. We need to consider what is present or, rather, since the topic is the human being, *who* is present.

One's first impulse may be to say that in a play the character is present, whereas in a film the actor is. That sounds phony or false: one wants to say that both are present in both. But there is more to it, ontologically more. Here I think of a fine passage of Panofsky's:

> Othello or Nora are definite, substantial figures created by the playwright. They can be played well or badly, and they can be "interpreted" in one way or another; but they most definitely exist, no matter who plays them or even whether they are played at all. The character in a film, however, lives and dies with the actor. It is not the entity "Othello" interpreted by Robeson or the entity "Nora" interpreted by Duse, it is the entity "Greta Garbo" incarnate in a figure called Anna Christie or the entity "Robert Montgomery" incarnate in a murderer who, for all we know or care to know, may forever remain anonymous but will never cease to haunt our memories.[11]

If the character lives and dies with the actor, that ought to mean that the actor lives and dies with the character. I think that is correct, but it needs clarification. Let us develop it slightly.

For the stage, an actor works himself into a role; for the screen, a performer takes the role onto himself. The stage actor explores his potentialities and the possibilities of his role simultaneously; in performance these meet at a point in spiritual space—the better the performance, the deeper the point. In this respect, a role in a play is like a position in a game, say, third base: various people can play it, but the great third baseman is a man who has accepted and trained his skills and instincts most perfectly and matches them most intimately with his discoveries of the possibilities and necessities of third base. The screen performer explores his role like an attic and takes stock of his physical and temperamental endowment; he lends his being to the role and accepts only what fits; the rest is nonexistent. On the stage there are two beings, and the being of the character assaults the being of the actor; the actor survives only by yielding. A screen performance requires not so much training as planning.

[10] (p. 26). Bazin, *op. cit.*, p. 97.
[11] (p. 27). Panofsky, *op. cit.*, p. 28.

Of course, both the actor and the performer require, and can make use of, experience. The actor's role is his subject for study, and there is no end to it. But the screen performer is essentially not an actor at all: he *is* the subject of study, and a study not his own. (That is what the content of a photograph is—its subject.) On a screen the study is projected; on a stage the actor is the projector. An exemplary stage performance is one which, for a time, most fully creates a character. After Paul Scofield's performance in *King Lear*, we know who King Lear is, we have seen him in flesh. An exemplary screen performance is one in which, at a time, a star is born. After *The Maltese Falcon* we know a new star, only distantly a person. "Bogart" *means* "the figure created in a given set of films." His presence in those films is who he is, not merely in the sense in which a photograph of an event is that event; but in the sense that if those films did not exist, Bogart would not exist, the name "Bogart" would not mean what it does. The figure it names is not only in our presence, we are in his, in the only sense we could ever be. That is all the "presence" he has.

But it is complicated. A full development of all this would require us to place such facts as these: Humphrey Bogart was a man, and he appeared in movies both before and after the ones that created "Bogart." Some of them did not create a new star (say, the stable groom in *Dark Victory*), some of them defined stars—anyway meteors—that may be incompatible with Bogart (e.g.. Duke Mantee and Fred C. Dobbs) but that are related to that figure and may enter into our later experience of it. And Humphrey Bogart was both an accomplished actor and a vivid subject for a camera. Some people are, just as some people are both good pitchers and good hitters; but there are so few that it is surprising that the word "actor" keeps on being used in place of the more beautiful and more accurate word "star"; the stars are only to gaze at, after the fact, and their actions divine our projects. Finally, we must note the sense in which the creation of a (screen) performer is also the creation of a character—not the kind of character an author creates, but the kind that certain real people are: a type.

Types; Cycles as Genres

Around this point our attention turns from the physical medium of cinema in general to the specific forms or genres the medium has taken in the course of its history.

Both Panofsky and Bazin begin at the beginning, noting and approving that early movies adapt popular or folk arts and themes and performers and characters: farce, melodrama, circus, music hall, romance, etc. And both are gratifyingly contemptuous of intellectuals who could not come to terms with those facts of life. (Such intellectuals are the alter egos of the film promoters they so heartily despise. Roxy once advertised a movie as "Art, in every sense of the word"; his better half declaims, "That is not art, in any sense of the word.") Our question is, why did such forms and themes and characters lend themselves to film? Bazin, in what I have read of him, is silent on the subject, except to express gratitude to film for reviving these ancient forms, and to justify in general the legitimacy of adaptation from one art to another. Arnold Hauser, if I understand him, suggests wrong answers, in a passage that includes the remark "Only a young art can be popular,"[12] a remark that not only is in itself baffling (did Verdi and Dickens and Chaplin and Frank Loesser work in young arts?) but suggests that it was ony natural for the movies to pick up the forms they did. It *was* natural—anyway it happened fast enough—but not because movies were destined to popularity (they were at first no more popular than other forms of entertainment). In any case, popular arts are likely to pick up the forms and themes of high art for their material— popular theater naturally *burlesques*. And it means next to nothing to say that movies are young, because we do not know what the normal life span of an art is supposed to be, nor what would count as a unit of measure. Panofsky raises the question of the appropriateness of these original forms, but his answer is misleading.

> The legitimate paths of evolution [for the film] were opened, not by running away from the folk art character of the primitive film but by developing it within the limits of its own possibilities. Those primordial archetypes of film productions on the folk art level—success or retribution, sentiment, sensation, pornography, and crude humor—could blossom forth into genuine history, tragedy and romance, crime and adventure, and comedy as soon as it was realized that they could be transfigured—not by an artificial injection of literary values but by the exploitation of the unique and specific possibilities of the new medium.[13]

The instinct here is sound, but the region is full of traps. What are "the unique and specific possibilities of the new medium"? Panofsky defines them as dynamization of space and spatialization of time—that is, in a movie things move, and you can be moved instantaneously from anywhere to anywhere, and you can witness successively events happening at the same time. He speaks of these properties as "self-evident to the point of triviality" and, because of that, "easily forgotten or neglected." One hardly disputes this, or its importance. But we still do not understand what makes these properties "the possibilities of the medium." I am not now asking how one would know that these are *the* unique and specific possibilities (though I will soon get back to that); I am asking what it means to call them possibilities at all.

Why, for example, didn't the medium begin and remain in the condition of home movies, one shot just physically tacked on to another, cut and edited simply according to subject? (Newsreels essentially did, and they are nevertheless valuable, enough so to have justified the invention of moving pictures.) The answer seems obvious: narrative movies emerged because someone "saw the possibilities" of the medium—cutting and

[12] (p. 30). "The Film Age," in Talbot, *op. cit.*, p. 74.
[13] (p. 30). Panofsky, *op. cit.*, p. 18.

editing and taking shots at different distances from the subject. But again, these are mere actualities of film mechanics: every home movie and newsreel contains them. We could say: To make them "possibilities of the medium" is to realize what will give them *significance*—for example, the narrative and physical rhythms of melodrama, farce, American comedy of the 1930s. It is not as if film-makers saw these possibilities and then looked for something to apply them to. It is truer to say that someone with the wish to make a movie saw that certain established forms would give point to certain properties of film.

This perhaps sounds like quibbling, but what it means is that the aesthetic possibilities of a medium are not givens. You can no more tell what will give significance to the unique and specific aesthetic possibilities of projecting photographic images by thinking about them or seeing some, than you can tell what will give significance to the possibilities of paint by thinking about paint or by looking some over. You have to think about painting, and paintings; you have to think about motion pictures. What does this "thinking about them" consist in? Whatever the useful criticism of an art consists in. (Painters before Jackson Pollock had dripped paint, even deliberately. Pollock made dripping into a medium of painting.) I feel like saying: The first successful movies—i.e., the first moving pictures accepted as motion pictures—were not applications of a medium that was defined by given possibilities, but the *creation of a medium* by their giving significance to specific possibilities. Only the art itself can discover its possibilities, and the discovery of a new possibility is the discovery of a new medium. A medium is something through which or by means of which something specific gets done or said in particular ways. It provides, one might say, particular ways to get through to someone, to make sense; in art, they are forms, like forms of speech. To discover ways of making sense is always a matter of the relation of an artist to his art, each discovering the other.

Panofsky uncharacteristically skips a step when he describes the early silent films as an "unknown language . . . forced upon a public not yet capable of reading it."[14] His notion is (with good reason, writing when he did) of a few industrialists forcing their productions upon an addicted multitude. But from the beginning the language was not "unknown"; it was known to its creators, those who found themselves speaking it; and in the beginning there was no "public" in question; there were just some curious people. There soon was a public, but that just proves how easy the thing was to know. If we are to say that there was an "unknown" something, it was less like a language than like a fact—in particular, the fact that something is intelligible. So while it may be true, as Panofsky says, that "for a Saxon peasant of around 800 it was not easy to understand the meaning of a picture showing a man as he pours water over the head of another man," this has nothing special to do with the problems of a moviegoer. The meaning of that act of pouring in certain communi-

---

[14] (p. 32). *Ibid.*, p. 24.

ties is still not easy to understand; it was and is impossible to understand for anyone to whom the practice of baptism is unknown. Why did Panofsky suppose that comparable understanding is essential, or uniquely important, to the reading of movies? Apparently he needed an explanation for the persistence in movies of "fixed iconography"—"the well-remembered types of the Vamp and the Straight Girl . . . the Family Man, and the Villain," characters whose conduct was "predetermined accordingly"—an explanation for the persistence of an obviously primitive or folkloristic element in a rapidly developing medium. For he goes on, otherwise inexplicably, to say that "devices like these became gradually less necessary as the public grew accustomed to interpret the action by itself and were virtually abolished by the invention of the talking film." In fact such devices persist as long as there are still Westerns and gangster films and comedies and musicals and romances. *Which* specific iconography the Villain is given will alter with the times, but that his iconography remains specific (i.e., operates according to a "fixed attitude and attribute" principle[15]) seems undeniable: if Jack Pallance in *Shane* is not a Villain, no honest home was ever in danger. Films have changed, but that is not because we don't need such explanations any longer; it is because we can't *accept* them.

[These facts are accounted for by the actualities of the film medium itself: types are exactly what carry the forms movies have relied upon. These media created new types, or combinations and ironic reversals of types; but there they were, and stayed. Does this mean that movies can never create individuals, only types? What it means is that this is the movies' way of creating individuals: they create *individualities*. For what makes someone a type is not his similarity with other members of that type but his striking separateness from other people.]

Until recently, types of black human beings were not created in film: black people were stereotypes—mammies, shiftless servants, loyal retainers, entertainers. We were not given, and were not in a position to be given, individualities that projected particular *ways* of inhabiting a social role; we recognized only the role. Occasionally the humanity behind the role would manifest itself; and the result was a revelation not of a human individuality, but of an entire realm of humanity becoming visible. When in *Gone With the Wind* Vivien Leigh, having counted on Butterfly McQueen's professed knowledge of midwifery, and finding her as ignorant as herself, slaps her in rage and terror, the movement can stun us with a question: What was the white girl assuming about blackness when she believed the casual claim of a black girl, younger and duller and more ignorant than herself, to know all about the mysteries of childbirth? The assumption, though apparently complimentary, is dehumanizing—with such creatures knowledge of the body comes from nowhere, and in general they are to be trusted absolutely or not at all, like lions in a cage, with whom you either do or do not know how to deal. After the slap, we are

---

[15] (p. 33). *Ibid.*, p. 25.

left with two young girls equally frightened in a humanly desperate situation, one limited by a distraction which expects and forgets that it is to be bullied, the other by an energetic resourcefulness which knows only how to bully. At the end of Michael Curtiz' *Breaking Point*, as the wounded John Garfield is carried from his boat to the dock, awaited by his wife and children and, just outside the circle, by the other woman in his life (Patricia Neal), the camera pulls away, holding on the still waiting child of his black partner, who only the unconscious Garfield knows has been killed. The poignance of the silent and unnoticed black child overwhelms the yarn we had been shown. Is he supposed to symbolize the fact of general human isolation and abandonment? Or the fact that every action has consequences for innocent bystanders? Or that children are the real sufferers from the entangled efforts of adults to straighten out their lives? The effect here is to rebuke Garfield for attaching so much importance to the loss of his arm, and generally to blot out attention to individual suffering by invoking a massive social evil about which this film has nothing to say.

The general difference between a film type and a stage type is that the individuality captured on film naturally takes precedence over the social role in which that individuality gets expressed. Because on film social role appears arbitrary or incidental, movies have an inherent tendency toward the democratic, or anyway the idea of human equality. (But because of film's equally natural attraction to crowds, it has opposite tendencies toward the fascistic or populistic.) This depends upon recognizing film types as inhabited by figures we have met or may well meet in other circumstances. The recognized recurrence of film performers will become a central idea as we proceed. At the moment I am emphasizing only that in the case of black performers there was until recently no other place for them to recur in, except just the role within which we have already met them. For example, we would not have expected to see them as parents or siblings. I cannot at the moment remember a black person in a film making an ordinary purchase—say of a newspaper, or a ticket to a movie or for a train, let alone writing a check. (*Pinky* and *A Raisin in the Sun* prove the rule: in the former, the making of a purchase is a climactic scene in the film; in the latter, it provides the whole subject and structure.)

One recalls the lists of stars of every magnitude who have provided the movie camera with human subjects—individuals capable of filling its need for individualities, whose individualities in turn, whose inflections of demeanor and disposition were given full play in its projection. They provided, and still provide, staples for impersonators: one gesture or syllable of mood, two strides, or a passing mannerism was enough to single them out from all other creatures. They realized the myth of singularity—that we can still be found, behind our disguises of bravado and cowardice, by someone, perhaps a god, capable of defeating our self-defeats. This was always more important than their distinction by beauty. Their singularity made them more like us—anyway, made their difference from us less a matter of metaphysics, to which we must accede, than a matter of responsibility, to which we must bend. But then that made them even more glamorous. That they should be able to stand upon their singularity! If one did that, one might be found, and called out, too soon, or at an inconvenient moment.

What was wrong with type-casting in films was not that it displaced some other, better principle of casting, but that factors irrelevant to filmmaking often influenced the particular figures chosen. Similarly, the familiar historical fact that there are movie cycles, taken by certain movie theorists as in itself a mark of unscrupulous commercialism, is a possibility internal to the medium; one could even say, it is the best emblem of the fact that a medium had been created. For a cycle is a genre (prison movies, Civil War movies, horror movies, etc.); and a genre is a medium.

As Hollywood developed, the original types ramified into individualities as various and subtle, as far-reaching in their capacities to inflect mood and release fantasy, as any set of characters who inhabited the great theaters of our world. We do not know them by such names as Pulcinella, Crispin, Harlequin, Pantaloon, the Doctor, the Captain, Columbine; we call them the Public Enemy, the Priest, James Cagney, Pat O'Brien, the Confederate Spy, the Army Scout, Randolph Scott, Gary Cooper, Gable, Paul Muni, the Reporter, the Sergeant, the Sheriff, the Deputy, the D.A., the Quack, the Shyster, the Other Woman, the Fallen Woman, the Moll, the Dance Hall Hostess. Hollywood was the theater in which they appeared, because the films of Hollywood constituted a world, with recurrent faces more familiar to me than the faces of the neighbors of all the places I have lived.

The great movie comedians—Chaplin, Keaton, W. C. Fields—form a set of types that could not have been adapted from any other medium. Its creation depended upon two conditions of the film medium mentioned earlier. These conditions seem to be necessities, not merely possibilities, so I will say that two necessities of the medium were discovered or expanded in the creation of these types. First, movie performers cannot project, but are projected. Second, photographs are of the world, in which human beings are not ontologically favored over the rest of nature, in which objects are not props but natural allies (or enemies) of the human character. The first necessity—projected visibility—permits the sublime comprehensibility of Chaplin's natural choreography; the second—ontological equality—permits his Proustian or Jamesian relationships with Murphy beds and flights of stairs and with vases on runners on tables on rollers: the heroism of momentary survival, Nietzsche's man as a tightrope across an abyss. These necessities permit not merely the locales of Keaton's extrications, but the philosophical mood of his countenance and the Olympic resourcefulness of his body; permit him to be perhaps the only constantly beautiful and continuously hilarious man ever seen, as though the ugliness in laughter should be redeemed. They permit Fields to mutter and suffer and curse obsessively, but heard and seen only by us; because his attributes are those of the gentleman (confident swagger and elegant manners, gloves, cane, outer heartiness), he can manifest continuously, with the remorselessness of nature, the psychic brutalities of bourgeois civilization.

Ideas of Origin

It is inevitable that in theorizing about film one at some point speculates about its origins, because despite its recentness, its origin remains obscure. The facts are well enough known about the invention and the inventors of the camera, and about improvements in fixing and then moving the image it captures. The problem is that the invention of the photographic picture is not the same thing as the creation of photography as a medium for making sense. The historical problem is like any other: a chronicle of the facts preceding the appearance of this technology does not explain why it happened when and as it did. Panofsky opens his study of film by remarking, "It was not an artistic urge that gave rise to the discovery and gradual perfection of a new technique; it was a technical invention that gave rise to the discovery and gradual perfection of a new art." We seem to understand this, but do we understand it? Panofsky assumes we know what it is that at any time has "given rise" to a "new art." He mentions an "artistic urge," but that is hardly a candidate to serve as an explanation; it would be about as useful as explaining the rise of modern science by appealing to "a scientific urge." There may be such urges, but they are themselves rather badly in need of explanation. Panofsky cites an artistic urge explicitly as the occasion for a new "technique." But the motion picture is not a new *technique*, any more than the airplane is. (What did we use to do that such a thing enables us to do better?) Yet some idea of flying, and an urge to do it, preceded the mechanical invention of the airplane. What is "given rise to" by such inventions as movable type or the microscope or the steam engine or the pianoforte?

It would be surprising if the history of the establishment of an artistic medium were less complex a problem for the historical understanding than (say) the rise of modern science. I take Bazin to be suggesting this when he reverses the apparent relation between the relevant technology and the idea of cinema, emphasizing that the idea preceded the technology, parts of it by centuries, and that parts of the technology preceded the invention of movies, some of it by centuries. So what has to be explained is not merely how the feat was technically accomplished but, for example, what stood in the way of its happening earlier. Surprisingly, Bazin, in the selection of essays I have read, does not include the contemporary condition of the related arts as a part of the ideological superstructure that elicited the new material basis of firm. But it is certainly relevant that the burning issue during the latter half of the nineteenth century, in painting and in the novel and in the theater, was realism. And unless film captured possibilities opened up by the arts themselves, it is hard to image that its possibilities as an artistic medium would have shown up as, and as suddenly as, they did.

The idea of and wish for the world re-created in its own image was satisfied *at last* by cinema. Brazin calls this the myth of total cinema. But it had always been one of the myths of art; each of the arts had satisfied it in its own way. The mirror was in various hands held up to nature. In some ways it was more fully satisfied in theater. (Since theater is on the whole not now a major art for us, it on the whole no longer makes contact with its historical and psychological sources; so we are rarely gripped by the trauma we must once have suffered when the leader of the chorus stopped contributing to a narrative or song and turned to face the others, suffering incarnation.)

What is cinema's way of satisfying the myth? Automatically, we said. But what does that mean—mean mythically, as it were? It means satisfying it without *my* having to do anything, satisfying it *by* wishing. In a word, *magically*. I have found myself asking: How could film be art, since all the major arts arise in some way out of religion? Now I can answer: Because movies arise out of magic; from *below* the world.

The better a film, the more it makes contact with this source of its inspiration; it never wholly loses touch with the magic lantern behind it. This suggests why movies of the fantastic (*The Cabinet of Dr. Caligari, Blood of a Poet*) and filmed scenes of magic (say, materialization and dematerialization), while they have provided moods and devices, have never established themselves as cinematic media, however strongly this "possibility" is suggested by the physical medium of film: they are technically and psychologically trivial compared with the medium of magic itself. It is otherwise if the presented magic is itself made technically or physically interesting (*The Invisible Man, Dr. Jeckyll and Mr. Hyde, Frankenstein, 2001: A Space Odyssey*), but then that becomes another way of confirming the physicality of our world. Science presents itself, in movies, as magic, which was indeed one source of science. In particular, projected science retains magic's mystery and forbiddenness. Science-fiction films exploit not merely certain obvious aspects of adventure, and of a physicality that special effects specialize in, but also the terrific mumbo-jumbo of hearsay science: "My God, the thing is impervious to the negative beta ray! We must reverse the atom recalcitration spatter, before it's too late!" The dialogue has the surface of those tinbox-and-lever contraptions that were sufficiently convincing in prime *Flash Gordon*. These films are carried by the immediacy of the fantasy that motivates them (say, destruction by lower or higher forms of life, as though the precariousness of human life is due to its biological stage of development); together with the myth of the one way and last change in which the (external) danger can be averted. And certainly the beauty of forms and motions in Frankenstein's laboratory is essential to the success of *Frankenstein*; computers seem primitive in comparison. It always made more sense to steal from God than to try to outwit him.

How do movies reproduce the world magically? Not by literally presenting us with the world, but by permitting us to view it unseen. This is not a wish for power over creation (as Pygmalion's was), but a wish not to need power, not to have to bear its burdens. It is, in this sense, the reverse of the myth of Faust. And the wish for invisibility is old enough. Gods have profited from it, and Plato tells it at the end of the *Republic* as the Myth of the Ring of Gyges. In viewing films, the sense of invisibility is an expression of modern privacy or anonymity. It is as though the world's projection explains our forms of unknownness and of our inability to know. The explanation is not so much that the world is passing us by, as that we are displaced from our natural habitation within it, placed at a distance from it. The screen overcomes our fixed distance; it makes displacement appear as our natural condition.[16]

Select Bibliography for Part Three

THE THEORY OF FILM

Books

Rudolph Arnheim, *Film*; Andre Bazin, *What Is Cinema?*; Stanley Cavell, *Must We Mean What We Say?*; Peter Cowie, *Antonioni, Bergman, Renais*; Jorn Donner, *The Personal Vision of Ingemar Bergman*; Sergei Eisenstein, *Film Form: Essays in Film Theory*; Penelope Houston, *The Contemporary Cinema*; Lewis Jacobs, *The Rise of the American Film*; Arthur Knight, *The Liveliest Art*; Siegfried Kracauer, *Theory of Film*; Ernest Lindgren, *The Art of Film*; H. P. Manoogian, *The Film-Maker's Art*; Gerald Mast and Marshall Cohen, *Film Theory and Criticism: Introductory Readings*; Erwin Panofsky, *Meaning in the Visual Arts*; V. I. Pudovkin, *Film Technique and Film Acting*; Karel Reisz, *The Technique of Film Editing*; Paul Rotha, *Documentary Film*; Daniel Talbot, *Film: An Anthology*.

Articles

Stanley Cavell, "More of the World Viewed"; William Earle, "Revolt Against Realism in the Films"; Douglas P. Lackey, "Reflections on Cavell's Ontology

---

[16] Within that condition, objects as such may seem displaced; any close-up of an object may render it *trouvé*. Dadaists and surrealists found in film a direct confirmation of their ideologies or sensibilities, particularly in film's massive capacities for nostalgia and free juxtaposition. This confirmation is, I gather, sometimes taken to mean that dadaist and surrealist films constitute the *avant-garde* of film-making. It might equally be taken to show why film made these movements obsolete, as the world has. One might say: Nothing is more surrealist than the ordinary events of the modern world; and nothing less reveals that fact than a surrealist attitude. This says nothing about the value of particular surrealist films, which must succeed or fail on the same terms as any others.

Ideas of displacement (or contrasted position), of privacy, and of the inability to know are linked in my study of the problem of other minds, "Knowing and Acknowledging," in *Must We Mean What We Say?*

of Film"; Paul D. McGlynn, "Point of View and the Craft of Cinema"; James W. Newcomb, "Eisenstein's Aesthetics"; Henry P. Raleigh, "Film: The Revival of Aesthetic Symbolism"; Alexander Sesonske, "Vision via Film Form"; Alexander Sesonske, "The World Viewed"; Francis E. Sparshott, "Basic Film Aesthetics."

THE THEORY OF MUSIC: SOUND AND MEANING

The nineteenth century witnessed a burst of activity not only in the musical arts but in debates among composers and critics concerning the nature of music. One of the greatest and most bitter of these debates took place between Richard Wagner, the famous German composer, and Eduard Hanslick, a prominent Viennese music critic. Only Nietzsche's diatribe against Wagner in the philosopher's later career rivals the Wagner-Hanslick conflict for personal invective and scorn. We present selections from two of the theoretical treatises upon which the Wagner-Hanslick debate was built—Wagner's *The Artwork of the Future* and Hanslick's *The Beautiful in Music*.

Does music have meaning? If so, what kind of meaning is it capable of bearing? Program notes might tell us that a certain passage represents a pastoral scene, that another passage portrays a storm, and so on. But, would we perceive any of these images without the program notes to guide us? Questions such as these set the stage for Wagner's famous *Gesamtkunstwerk* (collective-art) theory which he first presented in *The Artwork of the Future*. In that work Wagner called for a new form of art—an ideal synthesis of all the arts (poetry, music, drama, etc.) which might achieve the ultimate expression of the human spirit. Wagner was strongly influenced by Arthur Schopenhauer's philosophical treatise *The World as Will and Idea*. Wagner thought that the artwork of the future could express both of the central features of Schopenhauer's system: the *Idea*, which could be embodied in words, and the *Will*, which music and only music is capable of expressing. To appreciate the philosophical background of Wagner's position it is important to study Schopenhauer's aesthetic theory, presented in part six.

Hanslick's foremost concern was to establish the autonomy of music on a broad theoretical level. If he could do this, then Wagner's argument for artistic heteronomy would be dashed. Hanslick argues persuasively that music can neither arouse nor represent specific feelings; still less can it represent ideas. It is commonplace, Hanslick argues, that different people will say different things when asked what a given piece of music or a given passage is supposed to express or represent specifically. For Hanslick music is capable of expressing certain dynamic manifestations of emotions and ideas (e.g., the clamor associated with combat, the whispering associated with love); but it cannot represent combat or love themselves.

Hanslick's theory remains one of the most intelligent discussions of musical aesthetics to date. Wagner lives through his music, of course, but Hanslick seems to have won the theoretical debate.

Richard Wagner

MUSIC AND THE AMALGAMATED ARTS: FROM *THE ARTWORK OF THE FUTURE*

Artistic Man, and Art as Derived Directly from Him.

MAN AS HIS OWN ARTISTIC SUBJECT AND MATERIAL

Man's nature is twofold, an *outer* and an *inner*.* The senses to which he offers himself as a subject for Art, are those of *Vision* and of *Hearing*: to the eye appeals the outer man, the inner to the ear.

The eye apprehends the *bodily form of man,* compares it with surrounding objects, and discriminates between it and them. The corporeal man and the spontaneous expression of his sensations of physical anguish or physical well-being, called up by outward contact, appeal directly to the eye; while indirectly he imparts to it, by means of facial play and gesture, those emotions of the inner man which are not directly cognisable by the eye. Again, through the expression of the eye itself, which directly meets the eye of the beholder, man is able to impart to the latter not only the feelings of the heart, but even the characteristic activity of the brain; and the more distinctly can the outer man express the inner, the higher does he show his rank as an artistic being.

But the inner man can only find *direct* communication through the ear, and that by means of *his voice's* Tone. Tone is the immediate utterance of feeling and has its physical seat within the heart, whence start and whither flow the waves of life-blood. Through the sense of hearing, tone urges forth from the feeling of one heart to the feeling of its fellow: the grief and joy of the emotional-man impart themselves directly to his counterpart through the manifold expression of vocal tone; and where the outer corporeal-man finds his limits of expressing to the eye the qualities

Richard Wagner (1813–1883). Wagner is one of the greatest composers in the history of Western music. Like Nietzsche's, his life was tempestuous, giving rise to strong pro- and anti-Wagner movements. Wagner wrote extensively on the nature of his art.

* Selections from *The Artwork of the Future,* translated by William Ashton Ellis (London, 1892), vol. I of *Richard Wagner's Prose Works.*

of those inner feelings of the heart he fain would utter and convey, there steps in to his aid the sought-for envoy, and takes his message through the voice to hearing, through hearing to the feelings of the heart.

Yet where, again, the direct expression of vocal tone finds its limits of conveying the separate feelings of the heart in clear and sharply outlined definition to the sympathies of the recipient inner man, there enters on the scene, through the vehicle of vocal tone, the determinative utterance of *Speech*. *Speech* is the condensation of the element of Voice, and the Word is the crystallised measure of Tone. In Speech, feeling conveys itself by ear to feeling, but to that likewise to be condensed and crystallised feeling to which it seeks to bring itself in sure and unmistakable understanding. It is thus the organ of that special feeling which reasons with itself and yearns for others' understanding,—the Intellect.—For the more vague and general feeling the immediate attributes of Tone sufficed. This general feeling therefore abode by Tone, as its adequate and materially contenting utterance; in the *quantitative* value of its compass it found the means of, so to say, accenting its own peculiar *qualities* in their universal bearings. But the *definite* need which seeks by Speech to gain an understanding is more decided and more pressing; it abides not in contentment with its physical expression, for it has to differentiate its own subjective feeling from a general feeling, and therefore to depict and to describe what Tone gave forth directly as the expression of this general feeling. The speaker has therefore to take his images from correlative but diverse objects, and to weld them with each other. In this mediate and complex process he has to take a wider field; and, under pressure of his quest for comprehension, he accelerates this process by the utmost brevity of his lingering over Tone, and by complete abandonment of its general powers of expression. Through this enforced renunciation, through this giving up of all delight in the physical element of his own utterance—at least of that degree of pleasure which the corporeal and the emotional-man experience in their method of expression,—the intellectual-man attains the faculty of giving by means of his speech-organ that certain utterance in seeking which the former found their bounds, each in his own degree. His capability is unlimited: he collects and sifts the universal, parts and unites according to his need and pleasure the images which all his senses bear him from the outer world; he binds and looses the particular and general even as he judges best, in order to appease his own desire for a sure and intelligible utterance of his feelings, his reflections, or his will. Yet he finds once more his limit where, in the agitation of his feelings, in the living pulse of joy or the violence of grief,—there, where the particular and arbitrary draw back before the generality and spontaneity of the feeling that usurps his heart; where from out the egoism of his narrowed and conditioned personal sensations he finds himself again amid the wide communion of all-embracing world-emotions, a partaker in the unconditioned truth of universal feeling and emotion; where, finally, he has to subordinate his individual selfwill to the dictates of Necessity, be it of grief or joy, and to hearken in place of commanding,—he craves for the only adequate and direct expression of his endlessly enhanced emotion. Here must he reach back once more to the universal mode of utterance; and, in exact proportion as he has pressed forward to his special standpoint, has he now to retrace his steps and borrow from the emotional man the physical tones of feeling, from the corporeal man the physical gestures of the body. For where it is a question of giving utterance, immediate and yet most certain, to the highest and the truest that man can ever utter, there above all must man display himself in his entirety; and this whole man is the man of understanding united with the man of heart and man of body, —but neither of these parts for self alone.—

The progress of the man of understanding, from the bodily man and through the man of feeling, is that of an ever increasing accommodation, just as his organ of expression, Speech, is the most mediate and dependent; for all the attributes that lie beneath him must be normally developed, before the conditions of *his* normal attributes can be at hand. But the most conditioned faculty is at like time the most exalted; and the joy in his own self, engendered by the knowledge of his higher, unsurpassable attributes, betrays the intellectual-man into the arrogant imagining that he may use those attributes which are really his foundation-props as the handmaids of his own caprice. The sovereign might of physical sensation and heart-emotion, however, breaks down his pride of intellect, as soon as these proclaim their sway as one which all men must obey in common, as that of feelings and emotions of the race. The isolated feeling, the separate emotion, which show themselves in the individual, aroused by this or that particular phenomenon, he is able to suppress or subjugate in favour of a richer combination of manifold phenomena conceived by him; but the richest combination of all the phenomena that he can cognise leads him at last to *Man as a species and an integral factor in the totality of Nature*; and, in presence of this great, all-mastering phenomenon, his pride breaks down. He now can only will the universal, true, and unconditional; he yields himself, not to a love for this or that particular object, but to wide Love itself. Thus does the egoist become a communist, the unit all, the man God, the art-variety Art.

THE THREE VARIETIES OF HUMANISTIC ART, IN THEIR ORIGINAL UNION.

The three chief artistic faculties of the entire man have once, and of their own spontaneous impulse, evolved to a trinitarian utterance of human Art; and this was in the primal, earliest manifested art-work, the *Lyric*, and its later, more conscious, loftiest completion, the *Drama*.

The arts of *Dance*, of *Tone*, and *Poetry*: thus call themselves the three primeval sisters whom we see at once entwine their measures wherever the conditions necessary for artistic manifestment have arisen. By their nature they are inseparable without disbanding the stately minuet of Art; for in this dance, which is the very cadence of Art itself, they are so wondrous closely interlaced with one another, of fairest love and inclination, so mutually bound up in each other's life, of body and of spirit: that each of the three partners, unlinked from the united chain and bereft thus of her own life and motion, can only carry on an artificially in-breathed and borrowed life;—not giving forth her sacred ordinances, as in their trinity, but now receiving despotic rules for mechanical movement.

As we gaze on this entrancing measure of the truest and most high-born Muses of artistic man, we see the three first stepping forward, each with her loving arm entwined around her sister's neck; then, now this one and now that, as though to show the others her beauteous form in full and individual symmetry, loosing herself from their embrace, and merely brush-ing with her utmost finger-tips the others' hands. Again the one, rapt by the spectacle of the twin-beauty of her close-locked sisters, bending herself before them; next the two, transported by her unique charm, greeting the one with tender homage; until at last, all three, tight-clapsed, breast on breast, and limb to limb, melt with the fervour of love-kisses into one only, living shape of beauty.—Such is the love and life, the wooing and the winning of Art; its separate units, ever themselves and ever for each other, severing in richest contrast and re-uniting in most blissful harmony.

This is Art the free. The sweet and forceful impulse in that dance of sisters, in the *impulse of Freedom*; the love-kiss of their enlocked embraces, the *transport of a freedom won.*

The solitary unit is unfree, because confined and fettered in un-Love; the *associate is free,* because unfettered and unconfined through Love.—

In every creature that exists the mightiest impulse is that of its *Life*; this is the resistless force of the correlation of those conditions which have first called into being that which here exists,—thus, of those things or life-forces which, in that which has arisen through them, are *that* which they will to be—and, willing, can be—in this their point of common union. Man appeases his Life-need by *taking* from Nature: this is no theft, but a receiving, an adoptment, an absorption of that which, as a condition of man's life, wills to be adopted into and absorbed in him. For these condi-tions of man's Life, *themselves* his Life-needs, are not forsooth upheaved by birth,—rather do they endure and feed themselves within him and by him so long as e'er he lives; and the dissolution of their bond, itself is—Death.

But the Life-need of man's life-needs is the *need of Love*. As the condi-tions of natural human life are contained in the love-bond of subordinated nature-forces, which craved for their agreement, their redemption, their adoption into the higher principle, Man; so does man find his agreement, his redemption, his appeasement, likewise in something higher; and this higher thing is the *human race, the fellowship of man*, for there is but one thing higher than *man's* self, and that is—Men. But man can only gain the stilling of his life-need through Giving, through *Giving of himself* to other men, and in its highest climax, to *all the world of human beings.* The monstrous sin of the absolute egoist is that he sees in (fellow) Men also nothing but the natural conditionments of his own existence, and—albeit in a quite particular, barbaric-cultivated manner—*consumes* them like the fruits and beasts of nature; thus will not *give,* but only *take.*

Now as Man is not free except through Love, neither is anything that proceeds, or is derived, from him. Freedom is the satisfaction of an imperative Need, and the highest freedom is the satisfaction of the highest need: but the highest human need is *Love*.

No living thing can issue from the true and undistorted nature of mankind or be derived from it, unless it fully answers to the characteristic essence of that nature: but the most characteristic token of this essence is the need of Love.

Each separate faculty of man is limited by bounds; but his united, agreed, and reciprocally helping faculties—and thus his faculties in *mutual love* of one another—combine to form the self-completing, unbounded, universal faculty of men. Thus too has every *artistic* faculty of man its natural bounds, since man has not *one only* Sense but separate *Senses*; while every faculty springs from its special sense, and therefore each single faculty must find its bounds in the confines of its correlated sense. But the boundaries of the separate senses are also their joint meeting-points, those points at which they melt in one another and each agrees with each: and exactly so do the faculties that are derived from them touch one another and agree. Their confines, therefore, are removed by this agreement; but only those that love each other can agree, and 'to love' means: to acknowledge the other, and at like time to know one's self. Thus Knowledge through Love is Freedom; and the freedom of man's faculties is—*All-faculty*.

Only the Art which answers to this 'all-faculty' of man is, therefore, *free*; and not the Art-*variety*, which only issues from a single human faculty. The Arts of Dance, of Tone, of Poetry, are each confined within their several bounds; in contact with these bounds each feels herself unfree, be it not that, across their common boundary, she reaches out her hand to her neighbouring art in unrestrained acknowledgment of love. The very grasping of this hand lifts her above the barrier; her full embrace, her full absorption in her sister—*i.e.* her own complete ascension beyond the set-up barrier—casts down the fence itself. And when every barrier has thus fallen, then are there no more *arts* and no more boundaries, but only *Art*, the universal, undivided.

It is a sorry misconception of Freedom—that of the being who would fain be free in loneliness. The impulse to loose one's self from commonalty, to be free and independent for individual self alone, can only lead to the direct antithesis of the state so arbitrarily striven after: namely to utmost lack of self-dependence.—Nothing in Nature is self-dependent excepting that which has the conditionments of its self-standing not merely in itself, but also outside of itself: for the inner are first possible by virtue of the outer. That which would separate[1] itself must, necessarily, first have

---

[1] The verb "*unterscheiden*" is here used in so many different shades of its meaning that it is impossible to do justice in a translation to the philosophical play of words. Literally it means: "to cleave asunder," and hence, "to separate, to distinguish, to discern, to discriminate, to differentiate." There being no one English word that will embrace the varying sense in which the term is here employed, I have been forced to replace it by varying expressions.—Tr.

that from which to separate. He who would fain be nothing but himself, must first know what he is; but this he only learns by distinguishing from what he is not: were he able to lop off entirely that which differs from him, then were he himself no differentiated entity, and thus no longer cognisable by himself. In order to will to be the whole thing which of and in himself he is, the individual must learn to be absolutely not the thing he is not; but the thing that is absolutely what *he* is not, is that thing which lies apart from him; and only in the fullest of communion with that which is apart from him, in the completest absorption into the commonalty of those who differ from him, can he ever be completely *what* he is by nature, what he must be, and as a reasonable being, can but will to be. Thus only in Communism does Egoism find its perfect satisfaction.

That Egoism, however, which has brought such immeasurable woe into the world and so lamentable a mutilation and insincerity into Art, is of another breed to the natural and rational egoism which finds its perfect satisfaction in the community of all. In pious indignation it wards off the name of "Egoism" from it, and dubs itself "Brotherly-" and "Christian-" "Art-" and "Artist-Love"; founds temples to God and Art; builds hospitals, to make ailing old-age young and sound,—and schools to make youth old and ailing; establishes "faculties," courts of justice, governments, states, and what not else?—merely to prove that it is not Egoism. And this is just the most irredeemable feature of it, and that which makes it utterly pernicious both to itself and to the general commonalty. This is the isolation of the single, in which each severed nullity shall rank as somewhat, but the great commonalty as naught; in which each unit struts as something special and "original," while the whole, forsooth, can then be nothing in particular and for ever a mere imitation. This is the self-dependence order to be "free by help of God;" pretends to be what others *are*; and, briefly, follows the inversion of the teaching of Jesus Christ: "To *take* is more blessed than to give."

This is the genuine Egoism, in which each *isolated art-variety* would give itself the airs of universal Art; while, in truth, it only thereby loses its own peculiar attributes. Let us pry a little closer into what, under such conditions, has befallen those three most sweet Hellenic sisters!—

· · ·

THE ART OF TONE.

The ocean binds and separates the land: so does Music bind and separate the two opposite poles of human Art, the arts of Dance and Poetry.

She is the *heart* of man; the blood, which takes this heart for starting-point, gives to the outward-facing flesh its warm and lively tint,—while it feeds the inward-coursing brain-nerves with its welling pulse. Without the heart's activity, the action of the brain would be no more than of a mere automation; the action of the body's outer members, a mechanical and senseless motion. Through the heart the understanding feels itself allied with the whole body, and the man of mere 'five-senses' mounts upwards to the energy of Reason.

But the organ of the heart is *tone*; its conscious speech, the *art of Tone*. She is the full and flowing heart-love, that ennobles the material sense of pleasure, and humanises immaterial thought. Through Tone are Dance and Poetry brought to mutual understanding: in her are intercrossed in loving blend the laws by which they each proclaim their own true nature; in her, the wilfulness of each becomes instinctive 'Will' (*"Unwillkür-lichen"*), the Measure of Poetry and the Beat of Dance become the un-dictated Rhythm of the Heart-throb.

Does she receive from her sisters the conditions under which she mani-fests herself, so does she give them back to them in infinite embellishment, as the conditions of their own enunciation. If Dance conveys to Tone her own peculiar law of motion, so does Tone bring it back to her with soul and sense embodied in her Rhythm, for the measure of more noble, more intelligible motion. If Tone obtains from Poetry her pregnant coil of sharp-cut Words, entwined by meaning and by measure, and takes it as a solid mesh of thought wherewith to gird her boundless fluid mass of sound: so does she hand her sister back this ideal coil of yearning syllables, that indirectly shadow forth in images, but cannot yet express their thought with all the truth and cogence of necessity,—and hands it as the direct utterance of Feeling, the unerring vindicator and redeemer, *Melody*.

In *Rhythm* and in *Melody*, ensouled by Tone, both Dance and Poetry regain their own true essence, materialised and endlessly enhanced and beautified; and thus they learn to know and love themselves. But melody and rhythm are the *arms* of Tone, with which she locks her sisters in the close embrace of triple growth; they are the *shores* through which *the sea*, herself, unites two continents. If this sea draws backward from the shores, and broadens out the waste of an abyss between itself and each of them, then can no light-winged ship bear aught from either continent unto the other; forever must they rest dissundered,—until some outcome of ma-chinery, perchance a railroad, shall bridge the waste! Then men shall start therefrom, forsooth upon their steamboats, to cross the open sea; the breath of all-enlivening breezes replaced by sickening fumes from the machine. Blow the winds of heaven eastward: what matters it?—the ma-chine shall clatter westward, or wherever else men choose to go. Even as the dance-wright fetches from the continent of Poetry, across the steam-tamed ocean crests of Music, the programme for his novel ballet; while the play-concoctor imports from the far-off continent of Dance just so much leg-gymnastics as he deems expedient for filling up a halting situ-ation.—

Let us see, then, what has come to sister Tone, since the death of all-loving father, *Drama!*—

We cannot yet give up our simile of the *Ocean*, for picturing Tone's nature. If *Melody* and *Rhythm* are the shores through which the art of Tone lays fruitful hands upon twain continents of art, allied to her of yore: so is Sound itself her fluent, native element, and its immeasurable expanse of waters make out the sea of *Harmony*. The eye knows but the surface of this sea; its depth the depth of Heart alone can fathom. Upwards from its lightless bottom it expands into a sun-bright mirror; the ever-widening rings of Rhythm cross over on it from one shore; from the shady valleys of the other arise the yearning zephyrs that rouse this restful surface to the grace of swelling, sinking waves of Melody.

Man dives into this sea; only to give himself once more, refreshed and radiant, to the light of day. His heart feels widened wondrously, when he peers down into this depth, pregnant with unimaginable possibilities whose bottom his eye shall never plumb, whose seeming bottomlessness thus fills him with the sense of marvel and the presage of Infinity. It is the depth and infinity of Nature herself, who veils from the prying eye of Man the unfathomable womb of her eternal Seed-time, her Begetting, and her Yearning; even because man's eye can only grasp the already manifested, the Blossom, the Begotten, the Fulfilled. This Nature is, however, none other than *the nature of the human heart itself*, which holds within its shrine the feelings of desire and love in their most infinite capacity; which is *itself* Desire and Love, and—as in its insatiable longing it yet wills nothing but itself—can only grasp and comprehend itself.

If this sea stir up its waters of itself, if it beget the ground of its commotion from the depths of its own element: then is this agitation an endless one and never pacified; for ever returning on itself unstilled, and ever roused afresh by its eternal longing. But if the vast reach of this Desire be kindled by an outward object; if this measure-giving object step toward it from the sure and sharply outlined world of manifestment; if sun-girt, slender, blithely-moving Man incend the flame of this desire by the lightning of his glancing eye,—if he ruffle with his swelling breath the elastic crystal of the sea,—then let the fire crackle as it may, let the ocean's bosom heave with ne'er so violent a storm: yet the flame at last, when its wild glow has smouldered down, will shine with mild serenity of light,—the sea-rind, the last foam-wreath of its giant crests dissolved, will crisp itself at last to the soft play of rippling waves; and Man, rejoicing in the sweet harmony of his whole being, will entrust himself to the beloved element in some frail coracle, and steer his steadfast course towards the beacon of that kindly light.—

The *Greek*, when he took ship upon his sea, ne'er let the coast line fade from sight: for him it was the trusty stream that bore him from one haven to the next, the stream on which he passed between the friendly strands amidst the music of his rhythmic oars,—here lending glances to the wood-nymphs' dance, there bending ear to sacred hymns whose melodious string of meaning words was wafted by the breezes from the temple on the mountain-top. On the surface of the water were truly mirrored back to him the jutting coasts, with all their peaks and valleys, trees and flowers and men, deep-set within the æther's blue; and this undulating mirror-picture, softly swayed by the fresh fan of gentle gusts, he deemed was *Harmony*.—

The *Christian* left the shores of Life.—Farther afield, beyond all confines, he sought the sea,—to find himself at last upon the Ocean, twixt sea and heaven, boundlessly alone. The Word, the word of *Faith* was his only compass; and it pointed him unswervingly toward Heaven. This heaven brooded far above him, it sank down on every side in the horizon, and fenced his sea around. But the sailor never reached that confine; from century to century he floated on without redemption, towards this ever imminent, but never reached, new home; until he fell a-doubting of the virtue of his compass, and cast it, as the last remaining human bauble, grimly overboard. And now, denuded of all ties, he gave himself without a rudder to the never-ending turmoil of the waves' caprice. In unstilled, ireful love-rage, he stirred the waters of the sea against the unattainable and distant heaven: he urged the insatiate greed of that desire and love which, reft of an external object, must ever only crave and love itself,—that deepest, unredeemable hell of restless Egoism, which stretches out without an end, and wills and wishes, yet ever and forever can only wish and will itself,—he urged it 'gainst the abstract universalism of heaven's blue, that universal longing without the shadow of an 'object'—against the very vault of absolute un-objectivity. Bliss, unconditioned bliss,—to gain in widest, most unbounded measure the *height of bliss*, and yet to stay completely *wrapt in self*: this was the unallayable desire of Christian passion. So reared the sea from out its deepest depth to heaven, so sank it ever back again to its own depths; ever its unmixed self, and therefore ever unappeased,—like the all-usurping, measureless desire of the heart that ne'er will give itself and dare to be consumed in an external object, but damns itself to everlasting *selfish solitude*.

Yet in Nature each immensity strives after Measure; the unconfined draws bounds around itself; the elements condense at last to definite show; and even the boundless sea of Christian yearning found the new shore on which its turbid waves might break. Where on the farthest horizon we thought to find the ever made-for, never happed-on gateway into the realms of Heaven unlimited, there did the boldest of all seafarers discover *land* at last,—man-tenanted, real, and blissful land. Through his discovery the wide ocean is now only meted out, but made for men an inland sea, round which the coasts are merely broadened out in unimaginably ampler circle. Did Columbus teach us to take ship across the ocean, and thus to bind in one each continent of Earth; did his world-historical discovery convert the narrow-seeing national-man into a universal and all-seeing *Man*: so, by the hero who explored the broad and seeming shoreless sea of absolute Music unto its very bounds, are won the new and never dreamt-of coasts which this sea no longer now divorces from the old and primal continent of man, but *binds together* with it for the new-born, happy art-life of the Manhood of the Future. And this hero is none other than—*Beethoven*.—

When Tone unloosed her from the chain of sisters, she took as her unrelinquishable, her foremost life's-condition—just as light-minded sister Dance had filched from *her* her rhythmic measure—from thoughtful sister Poetry her Word; yet not the human-breathing spirit of the musing ("*dichtende*") word, but only its bare corporeal condensation ("*ver-*

dichtete") into tones. As she had abandoned her rhythmic beat to parting Dance's use and pleasure, she thenceforth built upon the Word alone; the word of Christian Creed, that toneless, fluid, scattering word which, un-withstanding and right gladly, soon gave to her complete dominion over it. But the more this word evaporated into the mere stammer of humility, the mere babbling of implicit, childlike love, so much the more imperatively did Tone see herself impelled to shape herself from out the exhaustless depths of her own liquid nature. The struggle for such shaping is the building up of *Harmony*.

Harmony grows from below upwards as a perpendicular pillar, by the joining-together and overlaying of correlated tone-stuffs. Unceasing alterna-tion of such columns, each freshly risen member taking rank beside its fellows, constitutes the only possibility of absolute harmonic movement 'in breadth.' The feeling of needful care for the beauty of this motion 'in breadth' is foreign to the nature of absolute Harmony; she knows but the beauty of her columns' changing play of colour, but not the grace of their marshalling in point of 'time,'—for that is the work of Rhythm. On the other hand, the inexhaustible variety of this play of colours is the ever-fruitful source on which she draws, with immoderate self-satisfaction, to show herself in constant change of garb; while the life-breath which en-souls and sets in motion this restless, capricious, and self-conditioning change, is the essence of elemental tone itself, the outbreathing of an un-fathomable, all-dominating heart's-desire. In the kingdom of Harmony there is therefore no beginning and no end; just as the objectless and self-devouring fervour of the soul, all ignorant of its source, is nothing but itself, nothing but longing, yearning, tossing, pining—and *dying out, i.e.* dying without having assuaged itself in any 'object'; thus dying without death, and therefore everlasting falling back upon itself.

So long as the Word was in power, it commanded both beginning and ending; but when it was engulfed in the bottomless depths of Harmony, when it became naught but "groanings and sighings of the soul,"—as on the ardent summit of the music of the Catholic Church,—then was the word capriciously hoisted to the capitals of those harmonic columns, of that unrhythmic melody, and cast as though from wave to wave; while the measureless harmonic possibilities must draw from out themselves the laws for their own finite manifestment. There is no other artistic faculty of man that answers to the character of Harmony: it cannot find its mirror in the physical precision of the movements of the body, nor in the logical induction of the thinking brain,—it cannot set up for itself its standard in the recognised necessity of the material world of show, like Thought, nor like corporeal Motion in the periodic calculation of its instinctive, physi-cally governed properties: it is like a nature-force which men perceive but cannot comprehend. Summoned by outer—not by inner—necessity to resolve on surer and more finite manifestment, Harmony must mould from out its own immensurate depths the laws for its own following. These laws of harmonic sequence, based on the nature of Affinity,—just as those harmonic columns, the chords, were formed by the affinity of tone-stuffs,—unite themselves into one standard, which sets up salutary bounds around the giant playground of capricious possibilities. They allow the most varied choice from amid the kingdom of harmonic families, and extend the possibility of union by elective-affinity ("*Wahlverwand-schaftliche Verbindungen*") with the members of neighbouring families, almost to free liking; they demand, however, before all a strict observance of the house-laws of affinity of the family once chosen, and a faithful tarry-ing with it, for sake of a happy end. But this end itself, and thus the measure of the composition's extension *in time*, the countless laws of harmonic decorum can neither give nor govern. As the scientifically teach-able or learnable department of the art of Tone, they can cleave the fluid tonal masses of Harmony asunder, and part them into fenced-off bodies; but they cannot assign the periodic measure of these fenced-off masses.

When the limit-setting might of Speech was swallowed up, and yet the art of Tone, now turned to Harmony, could never find her time-assigning law within herself: then was she forced to face towards the remnant of the rhythmic beat that Dance had left for her to garner. Rhythmic figures must now enliven harmony; their change, their recurrence, their parting and uniting, must condense the fluid breadths of Harmony—as Word had earlier done with Tone—and bring their periods to more sure conclusion. But no inner necessity, striving after purely human exposition, lay at the bottom of this rhythmic livening; not the feeling, thinking, will-ing Man, such as proclaims himself by speech and bodily motion, was its motive power; nothing but an *outer* necessity, which Harmony, in struggle for her selfish close, had taken up into herself. This rhythmic interchange and shaping, which moved not of its inner, own necessity, could therefore only borrow life from arbitrary laws and canons. These laws and canons are those of *Counterpoint*.

Counterpoint, with its multiple births and offshoots, is Art's artificial playing-with-itself, the mathematics of Feeling, the mechanical rhythm of egoistic Harmony. In its invention, abstract Tone indulged her whim to pass as the sole and only self-supporting Art;—as that art which owes its being, its absolute and godlike nature, to no human Need soever, but purely to *itself*. The wilful quite naturally believes itself the absolute and right monopolist; and it is certain that to her own caprice alone could Music thank her self-sufficient airs, for that mechanical, contrapunctal artifice was quite incapable of answering any *soul-need*. Music therefore, in her pride, had become her own direct antithesis: from a *heart's* concern, a matter of the *intellect*; from the utterance of unshackled Christian soul's-desire, the cashbook of a modern market-speculation.

The living breath of fair, immortal, nobly-feeling Human Voice, stream-ing ever fresh and young from the bosom of the Folk, blew this contra-punctal house of cards, too, of a heap. The *Folk-tune*, that had rested faithful to its own untarnished grace; the simple, surely outline. *Song*, close-woven with the poem, soared-up on its elastic pinions to the regions of the beauty-lacking, scientifically-musical artworld, with news of joyous ransom. This world was longing to paint *men* again, to set men to sing—

not pipes; so it seized the folk-tune for its purpose, and constructed out of it the *opera-air*. But just as Dance had seized the folk-dance, to freshen herself therewith when needed, and to convert it to an artificial compost according to the dictates of her modish taste,—so did this genteel Operatic tone-art behave to the folk-tune. She had not grasped the *entire* man, to show him in his whole artistic stature and nature-bidden necessity, but only the *singing* man; and in his song she had not seized the Ballad of the Folk, with all its innate generative force, but merely the melodic Tune, abstracted from the poem, to which she set conventional and purposely insipid sentences, according to her pleasure; it was not the beating heart of the nightingale, but only its warbling throat that men could fathom, and practised themselves to imitate. Just as the art-dancer had set his legs, with their manifold but still monotonous bendings, flingings, and gyrations, to *vary* the natural folk-dance which he could not of himself develop further,—so did the art-singer set his throat to paraphrase with countless ornaments, to alter by a host of flourishes, those tunes which he had stolen from the People's mouth, but whose nature he could never fertilise afresh; and thus another species of mechanical dexterity filled up the place which contrapunctal ingenuity had left forlorn. We need not further characterise the repugnant, ineffably repulsive disfigurement and rending of the folk-tune, such as cries out from the modern operatic *Aria* —for truly it is nothing but a mutilated folk-tune, and in no wise a specific fresh invention—such as, in entire contempt of Nature and all human feeling, and severed from all basis of poetic speech, now tickles the imbecile ears of our opera-frequenters with its lifeless, soul-less toy of fashion. We must content ourselves with candidly, though mournfully, avowing that our modern public sums up in *it* its whole idea of Music's essence.—

But apart from this public and its subservient fashion-mongers and mode-purveyors, the inmost individual essence of Tone was yet to soar up from its plumbless depths, in all the unlost plenitude of its unmeasured faculties, to redemption in the sunlight of the universal, *one* Art of the Future. And this spring it was to take from off *that* ground which is the ground of all sheer human art: the *plastic motion of the body*, portrayed in musical *Rhythm*.

Though in the Christian lisping of the stereotyped Word, eternally repeated until it lost itself in utter dearth of Thought, the human *voice* had shrunk at last to a mere physical and flexible implement of Tone: yet, by its side, those tone-implements which mechanism had devised for Dance's ample escort had been elaborated to ever more enhanced expressive faculty. As bearers of the dance-tune, the *rhythmic Melody* had been consigned to their exclusive care; and, by reason of the ease with which their blended forces took up the element of Christian Harmony, to them now fell the call for all further evolution of the art of Tone from out itself. *The harmonised dance* is the basis of the richest art-work of the modern *Symphony*.—Even this 'harmonised dance' fell as a savoury prey into the hands of counterpoint-concocting mechanism; which loosed it from obedient devotion to its mistress, body-swaying Dance, and made it now to take its turns and capers from *its* rules. Yet it needed but the warm lifebreath of the natural folk-tune to beat upon the leathern harness of this schooled and contrapunctal dance,—and lo! it stretched at once to the elastic flesh of fairest human artwork. This artwork, in its highest culmination, is *the Symphony of Haydn, of Mozart, and Beethoven.*

In the Symphony of Haydn the rhythmic dance-melody moves with all the blithesome freshness of youth: its entwinements, disseverings, and re-unitings, though carried out with highest contrapunctal ingenuity, yet hardly show a trace of the results of such ingenious treatment; but rather take the character peculiar to a dance ordained by laws of freest Phantasy, —so redolent are they of the warm and actual breath of joyous human Life. To the more tempered motion of the middle section of the symphony we see assigned by Haydn a broad expansion of the simple song-tune of the Folk; in this it spreads by laws of *melos* peculiar to the character of Song, through soaring graduations and 'repeats' enlivened by most manifold expression. This form of melody became the very element of the Symphony of song-abundant, and song-glad *Mozart.* He breathed into his instruments the passionate breath of *Human Voice,* that voice toward which his genius bent with overmastering love. He led the stanchless stream of teeming Harmony into the very heart of Melody; as though in restless care to give it, only mouthed by Instruments, in recompense the depth of feeling and of fervour that forms the exhaustless source of human utterance within the inmost chambers of the heart. Whilst, in his Symphonies, Mozart to some extent but made short work of everything that lay apart from this his individual impulse and, with all his remarkable dexterity in counterpoint, departed little from those traditional canons which he himself helped forward to stability: he lifted up the 'singing' power of instrumental music to such a height that it was now enabled, not only to embrace the mirth and inward still content which it had learnt from Haydn, but the whole depth of endless heart's-desire.

It was *Beethoven* who opened up the boundless faculty of Instrumental Music for expressing elemental storm and stress. His power it was, that took the basic essence of the Christian's Harmony, that bottomless sea of unhedged fulness and unceasing motion, and clove in twain the fetters of its freedom. *Harmonic Melody*—for so must we designate this melody divorced from speech, in distinction from the Rhythmic Melody of dance —was capable, though merely borne by instruments, of the most limitless expression together with the most unfettered treatment. In long, connected tracts of sound, as in larger, smaller, or even smallest fragments, it turned beneath the Master's poet hand to vowels, syllables, and words and phrases of a speech in which a message hitherto unheard, and never spoken yet, could promulgate itself. Each letter of this speech was an infinitely soul-full element; and the measure of the joinery of these elements was utmost free commensuration, such as could be exercised by none but a tone-poet who longed for the unmeasured utterance of this unfathomed yearning.

Glad in this unspeakably expressive language, but suffering beneath the weight of longing of his artist soul—a longing which, in its infinity, could only be an 'object to itself, not satisfy itself outside—the happy-wretched, see-glad and sea-weary mariner sought for a surer haven wherein to anchor from the blissful storms of passionate tumult. Was his faculty of speech unending—so also was the yearning which inspired that speech with its eternal breath. How then proclaim the end, the satisfaction, of this yearning, in the selfsame tongue that was naught but its expression? If the utterance of immeasurable heart-yearning be vented in this elemental speech of absolute tone, then the *endlessness* of such utterance, like that of the yearning itself, is its only true Necessity; the yearning cannot find contentment in any finite *slutting-off* of sound,—for that could only be Caprice. Now by the definite expression which it borrows from the rhythmic dance-melody, Instrumental Music may well portray and bring to close a placid and self-bounded mood; for reason that it takes its measure from an originally outward-lying object, namely the motion of the body. If a tone-piece yield itself *ab initio* to this expression, which must always be conceived as that of mirth, in greater or in less degree,—then, even mid the richest, most luxuriant unfolding of the faculty of tonal speech, it holds within itself the necessary grounds of every phase of 'satisfaction'; while equally inevitably must this 'satisfaction' be a matter of caprice, and therefore in truth unsatisfying, when that sure and sharp-cut mode of utterance endeavours merely *thus* to terminate the storms of endless yearning. The transition from the endless agitation of desire to a mood of joyous satisfaction, can necessarily take place no otherwise than by the ascension of desire into an *object*. But, in keeping with the character of infinite yearning, this 'object' can be none other than such an one as shows itself with finite, physical and ethical exactitude. Absolute Music, however, finds well-marked bounds dividing her from such an object; without indulging in the most arbitrary of assumptions, she can now and never, of her own unaided powers, bring the physical and ethical Man to distinct and plainly recognisable presentment. Even in her most infinite enhancement, she still is but *emotion*; she enters *in the train* of the ethical deed, but not as that *Deed itself*; she can set moods and feelings side by side, but not evolve one mood from out another by any dictate of her own Necessity;—she lacks the *Moral Will*.

What inimitable art did Beethoven employ in his "C-minor Symphony," in order to steer his ship from the ocean of infinite yearning to the haven of fulfilment! He was able to raise the utterance of his music *almost* to a moral resolve, but not to speak aloud that final word; and after every onset of the Will, without a moral handhold, we feel tormented by the equal possibility of falling back again to suffering, as of being led to lasting victory. Nay, this falling-back must almost seem to us more 'necessary' than the morally ungrounded triumph, which therefore—not being a necessary consummation, but a mere arbitrary gift of grace—has not the power to lift us up and yield to us that *ethical* satisfaction which we demand as outcome of the yearning of the heart.

Who felt more uncontented with this victory than Beethoven himself?

Was he lief to win a second of the sort? 'Twas well enough for the brain-less herd of imitators, who from glorious 'major'-jubilation, after van-quished 'minor'-tribulation, prepared themselves unceasing triumphs,—but not for the Master, who was called to write upon his works the *world-history of Music*.

With reverent awe, he shunned to cast himself afresh into that sea of boundless and insatiate yearning. He turned his steps towards the blithe-some, life-glad Men he spied encamped on breezy meads, along the out-skirt of some fragrant wood beneath the sunny heaven; kissing, dancing, frolicking. There in shadow of the trees, amid the rustling of the leaves, beside the tender gossip of the brook, he made a happy pact with Nature; there he felt that he was Man, felt all his yearning thrust back deep into his breast before the sovereignty of sweet and blissful *manifestment*. So thankful was he toward this manifestment that, faithfully and in frank humility, he superscribed the separate portions of the tone-work, which he built from this idyllic mood, with the names of those life-pictures whose contemplation had aroused it in him:—"Reminiscences of Country Life" he called the whole.

But in very deed they were only "Reminiscences"—pictures, and not the direct and physical actuality. Towards this actuality he was impelled with all the force of the artist's inexpugnable (*"nothwendig"*) yearning. To give his tone-shapes that same compactness, that directly cognisable and physi-cally sure stability, which he had witnessed with such blessed solace in Nature's own phenomena,—this was the soul of the joyous impulse which created for us that glorious work the "Symphony in A major." All tumult, all yearning and storming of the heart become here the blissful insolence of joy, which snatches us away with bacchanalian might and bears us through the roomy space of Nature, through all the streams and seas of Life, shouting in glad self-consciousness as we tread throughout the Uni-verse the daring measures of this human sphere-dance. This symphony is the *Apotheosis of Dance* herself: it is Dance in her highest aspect, as it were the loftiest Deed of bodily motion incorporated in an ideal mould of tone. Melody and Harmony unite around the sturdy bones of Rhythm to firm and fleshy human shapes, which now with giant limbs' agility, and now with soft, elastic pliance, *almost before our very eyes*, close up the supple, teeming ranks; the while now gently, now with daring, now serious,[2] now wanton, now pensive, and again exulting, the deathless strain sounds forth and forth; until, in the last whirl of delight, a kiss of triumph seals the last embrace.

---

[2] Amid the solemn-striding rhythm of the second section, a secondary theme uplifts its wailing, yearning song; to that rhythm, which shows its firm-set tread throughout the entire piece, without a pause, this longing melody clings like the ivy to the oak, which without its clasping of the mighty bole would trail its crumpled, straggling wreaths upon the soil, in forlorn rankness; but now, while weaving a rich trapping for the rough oak-rind, it gains for itself a sure and undishevelled outline from the stalwart figure of the tree. How brainlessly has this deeply significant device of Beethoven been ex-ploited by our modern instrumental-composers, with their eternal "subsidiary themes!" — R. WAGNER.

And yet these happy dancers were merely shadowed forth in tones, mere sounds that imitated men! Like a second Prometheus who fashioned men of clay ("*Thon*") Beethoven had sought to fashion them of *tone*. Yet not from 'Thon' or Tone, but from both substances together, must Man, the image of life-giving Zeus, be made. Were Prometheus' mouldings only offered to the *eye*, so were those of Beethoven only offered to the *ear*. But only *where eye and ear confirm each other's sentience of him, is the whole artistic Man at hand.*

But where could Beethoven find *those* men, to whom to stretch out hands across the element of his music? Those men with hearts so broad that he could pour into them the mighty torrent of his harmonic tones? With frames so stoutly fair that his melodic rhythms should *bear* them and not *crush* them?—Alas, from nowhere came to him the brotherly Prometheus who could show to him these men! He needs must gird his loins about, and start *to find out for himself the country of the Manhood of the Future.*

From the shore of Dance he cast himself once more upon that endless sea, from which he had erstwhile found a refuge on this shore; the sea of unallayable heart-yearning. But 'twas in a stoutly-built and giant-bolted ship that he embarked upon the stormy voyage; with firm-clenched fist he grasped the mighty helm: he *knew* the journey's goal, and was determined to attain it. No imaginary triumphs would he prepare himself, nor after boldly overcome privations tack back once more to the lazy haven of his home; for he desired to measure out the ocean's bounds, and find the land which needs must lie beyond the waste of waters.

Thus did the Master urge his course through unheard-of possibilities of absolute tone-speech—not by fleetly slipping past them, but by speaking out their utmost syllable from the deepest chambers of his heart—forward to where the mariner begins to sound the sea-depth with his plumb; where, above the broadly stretched-forth shingles of the new continent, he touches on the heightening crests of solid ground; where he has now to decide him whether he shall face about towards the bottomless ocean, or cast his anchor on the new-found shore. But it was no madcap love of sea-adventure, that had spurred the Master to so far a journey; with might and main he willed to land on this new world, for toward *it* alone had he set sail. Staunchly he threw his anchor out; and this anchor was *the Word*. Yet this Word was not that arbitrary and senseless cud which the modish singer chews from side to side, as the gristle of his vocal tone; but the necessary, all-powerful, and all-uniting word into which the full torrent of the heart's emotions may pour its stream; the steadfast haven for the restless wanderer; the light that lightens up the night of endless yearning: the word that the redeemed world-man cries out aloud from the fulness of the world-heart. This was the word which Beethoven set as crown upon the forehead of his tone-creation; and this word was:—"*Freude!*" ("Rejoice!") With this word he cries to men: "*Breast to breast, ye mortal millions! This one kiss to all the world!*"—And this *Word* will be the language of the *Art-work of the Future.*—

The Last Symphony of Beethoven is the redemption of Music from out her own peculiar element into the realm of *universal Art*. It is the human Evangel of the art of the Future. Beyond it no forward step is possible; for upon it the perfect Art-work of the Future alone can follow, the *universal Drama* to which Beethoven has forged for us the key.

Thus has Music of herself fulfilled what neither of the other severed arts had skill to do. Each of these arts but eked out her own self-centred emptiness by *taking*, and egoistic borrowing; neither, therefore, had the skill to *be herself*, and of herself to weave the girdle wherewith to the link the whole. But Tone, in that she *was herself* completely, and moved amid her own unsullied element, attained the force of the most heroic renouncing her own self, to reach out to her sisters the hand of rescue. She thus has kept herself as *heart* that binds both head and limbs in one; and it is not without significance, that it is precisely the art of Tone which has gained so wide extension through all the branches of our modern public life.

To get a clearer insight into the *contradictory* spirit of this public life, however, we must first bear in mind that it was *by no means a mutual coöperation between art-hood and publicity, nay, not even a mutual coöperation of tone-artists themselves*, that carried through the titanic process we have here reviewed: but *simply a richly-gifted individual*, who took up into his solitary self the spirit of community that was absent from our public life; nay, from the fulness of his being, united with the fulness of musical resource, evolved within himself this spirit of community which his artist soul had been the first to yearn for. We see this wonderful creative process, which breathes the fashioning breath of Life through all the symphonies of Beethoven, not only completed by the Master in the most secluded loneliness, but not so much as *comprehended* by his artistic fellows; the rather, shamefully *misunderstood* by them. The forms in which the Master brought to light his world-historical wrestling after Art, remained but *forms* in the eyes of contemporaneous and succeeding music-makers, and passed through Mannerism across to Mode; and despite the fact that no other instrumental composer could, even within these forms, divulge the smallest shred of original inventiveness, yet none lost courage to write symphonies and suchlike pieces by the ream, without a moment happening on the thought that the *last* symphony had *already been written.*[3] Thus have we lived to see Beethoven's great world-voyage

[3] Whosoever may undertake to write the special history of instrumental music since Beethoven, will undoubtedly have to take account of isolated phenomena which are of such a nature as to merit a particular and close attention. He who regards the history of Art, however, from so wide-reaching a point of view as here was necessary, can only keep to its decisive moments; he must leave unconsidered whatever lies aside from these 'moments,' or is merely their derivative. But the more undeniably is great ability evinced by such detached phenomena, so much the more strikingly do *they themselves* prove, by the barrenness of all their art-endeavour, that in their peculiar art-province somewhat may have yet been left to discover in respect of technical treatment, but nothing in respect of the living spirit, now that *that* has once been spoken which Beethoven spoke through Music. In the great universal Art-work of the Future there will ever be fresh regions to discover; but not in the separate branch of art, when once the latter—as Music, by Beethoven—has already been led to universalism but yet would linger in her solitary round.—R. WAGNER.

of discovery—that unique and thoroughly unrepeatable feat whose consummation we have witnessed in his *"Freude"*-symphony, as the last and boldest venture of his genius—once more superfluously attempted in foolishest simplicity, and happily got over without one hardship. A new *genre*, a "Symphony with Choruses"—was all the dullards saw therein! Why should not X or Y be also able to write a "Symphony with Choruses"? Why should not "God the Lord" be praised from swelling throat in the Finale, after three preceding instrumental sections had paved the way as featly as might be? Thus has Columbus only discovered America for the sugary hucksters of our time!

The ground of this repugnant phenomenon, however, lies deep within the very nature of our modern music. The art of Tone, set free from those of Dance and Poetry, is no longer an art instinctively necessary to man. It has been forced to construct itself by laws which, taken from its own peculiar nature, find no affinity and no elucidation in any purely human manifestment. Each of the other arts held fast by the measure of the outer human figure, of the outward human life, or of Nature itself,—howsoever capriciously it might disfigure this unconditional first principle. Tone,—which found alone in timid Hearing, susceptible to every cheat and fancy, her outward, human measure,—must frame herself more abstract laws, perforce, and bind these laws into a compact scientific system. This system has been the basis of all modern music: founded on this system, tower was heaped on tower; and the higher soared the edifice, the more inalienable grew the fixed foundation,—this founding which was nowise that of Nature. To the sculptor, the painter, and the poet, their laws of Art explain the course of *Nature*; without an inner understanding of Nature they can make no thing of beauty. To the musician are explained the laws of Harmony, of Counterpoint; his learning, without which he can build no musical structure, is an abstract, scientific system. By attained dexterity in its application, he becomes a craftsman; and from this craftsmanlike standpoint he looks out upon the outer world, which must needs appear to *him* a different thing from what it does to the unadmitted worldling,—the *layman*. The uninitiate layman thus stands abashed before this artificial product of art-music, and very rightly can grasp no whit of it but what appeals directly to the heart; from all the built-up prodigy, however, this only meets him in the unconditioned ear-delight of Melody. All else but leaves him cold, or baffles him with its disquiet; for the simple reason that he does not, and cannot, understand it. Our modern concert-public, which feigns a warmth and satisfaction in presence of the art-symphony, merely lies and plays the hypocrite; and the proof of this hypocrisy is evident enough so soon as, after such a symphony, a modern and melodious operatic 'number' is performed,—as often happens even in our most renowned concert-institutes,—when we may hear the genuine musical pulse of the audience beat high at once in unfeigned joy.

A vital coherence between our art-music and our public taste, must be emphatically denied: where it would fain proclaim its existence, it is affected and untrue; or, with a certain section of our Folk which may from

time to time be unaffectedly moved by the drastic power of a Beethove-
nian sypmphony, it is—to say the least—unclear, and the impression produced by these tone-works is at bottom but imperfect and fragmentary.
But where this coherence is not to hand, the guild-like federation of our
art-professors can only be an outward one; while the growth and fashioning of art from within outwards cannot depend upon a fellowship which is
nothing but an artificial system,—but only in the separate unit, from the
individuality of its specific nature, can a natural formative and evolutionary impulse take operation by its own instinctive inner laws. Only on
the fulness of the special gifts of an individual artist-nature, can that art-
creative impulse feed itself which nowhere finds its nourishment in outer
Nature; for this individuality alone can find in its particularity, in its
personal intuition, in its distinctive longing, craving, and willing, the stuff
wherewith to give the art-mass form, the stuff for which it looks in vain
in outer Nature. In the individuality of this one and separate human being does Music first become a purely human art; she devours up this individuality,—from the dissolution of its elements to gain her own condense-
ment, her own individualisation.

Thus we see in Music as in the other arts, though from totally different
causes, mannerisms and so-called 'schools' proceeding for the most part
from the individuality of a particular artist. These 'schools' were the guilds
that gathered—in imitation, nay in repetition—round some great master in
whom the soul of Music had individualised itself. So long as Music had
not fulfilled her world-historical task: so long might the widely spreading
branches of these schools grow up into fresh stems, under this or that congenial fertiliser. But so soon as that task had been accomplished by the
greatest of all musical individualities, so soon as Tone had used the force
of that individuality to clothe her deepest secrets with the broadest form
in which she still might stay an egoistic, self-sufficient art,—so soon, in
one word, as *Beethoven* had written his Last Symphony,—then all the
musical guilds might patch and cobble as they would, to bring an absolute
music-man to market: only a patched and cobbled harlequin, no sinewy,
robust son of Nature, could issue now from out their workshops. After
Haydn and Mozart, a Beethoven not only could, but *must* come; the
genie of Music claimed him of Necessity, and without a moment's lingering—he was there. Who now will be to Beethoven what *he* was to Mozart
and Haydn, in the realm of absolute music? The greatest genius would
not here avail, since the genie of Music no longer needs him.

Ye give yourselves a bootless labour, when, as an opiate for your egoistic
tingling for 'production', ye fain would deny the cataclysmic significance
of Beethoven's Last Symphony; and even your obtuseness will not save
you, by which ye make it possible not once to understand this work! Do
what ye will; look right away from Beethoven, fumble after Mozart, gird
you round with Sebastian Bach; write Symphonies with or without choruses, write Masses, Oratorios,—the sexless embryos of Opera!—make
songs without words, and operas without texts:—ye still bring naught to
light that has a breath of true life in it. For look ye,—ye lack *Belief!* the

great belief in the necessity of what ye do! Ye have but the belief of sim-
pletons, the false belief in the possible necessity of your own selfish
caprice!—

In grazing across the busy wilderness of our musical art-world; in witnessing the hopeless sterility of this art-chaos, for all its everlasting ogling;
in presence of this formless brew, whose lees are mouldering pedantic
shamelessness, and from which, with all its solemn arrogance of musical
'old-master'-hood, at last but dissolute Italian opera-airs or wanton French
cancan-tunes can rise as artificial distillate to the glare of modern public
life;—in short, in pondering on this utter creative incapacity, we look,
without an instant's blenching, towards the great catastrophe which shall
make an end of the whole unwieldy musical monstrosity, to clear free
space for the Art-work of the Future; in which true Music will truly have
no minor rôle to play, but to which both breath and breathing space are
utterly forbidden on such a musical soil as ours.

Eduard Hanslick

A FORMALIST THEORY
OF SOUND IN MOTION:
FROM *THE BEAUTIFUL IN MUSIC*

Does Music Represent Feelings?

The proposition that the feelings are the subject which music has to represent is due partly to the theory according to which the ultimate aim of music is to excite feelings and partly to an amended form of this theory.*

A philosophical disquisition into an art demands a clear definition of its subject matter. The diversity of the subject matter of the various arts and the fundamental difference in the mode of treatment are a natural sequence of the dissimilarity of the senses to which they severally appeal. Every art comprises a range of ideas which it expresses after its own fashion in sound, language, color, stone, etc. A work of art, therefore, endows a definite conception with a material form of beauty. This definite conception, its embodiment, and the union of both are the conditions of an aesthetic ideal with which a critical examination into every art is indissolubly connected.

The subject of a poem, a painting, or a statue may be expressed in words and reduced to ideas. We say, for instance, this picture represents a flower girl, this statue a gladiator, this poem one of Roland's exploits. Upon the more or less perfect embodiment of the particular subject in the artist's production depends our verdict respecting the beauty of the work of art.

The whole gamut of human feelings has with almost complete unanimity been proclaimed to be the subject of music, since the emotions were thought to be in antithesis to the definiteness of intellectual conceptions. This was supposed to be the feature by which the musical ideal is distinguished from the ideal of the other fine arts and poetry. According

Eduard Hanslick (1825–1904). Born in Prague, Hanslick later became Professor of Music at the University of Vienna and music critic for the famous journal *Weiner Zeitung*. Aesthetically, he championed Brahms and scorned Wagner. His influence among his contemporaries was as strong as a critic's influence has ever been.

* Selections from *The Beautiful in Music*, translated by Gustav Cohen (Indianapolis, 1957), chapter II. Reprinted by permission of the Bobbs-Merrill Company, Inc.

to this theory, therefore, sound and its ingenious combinations are but the material and the medium of expression by which the composer represents love, courage, piety, and delight. The innumerable varieties of emotion constitute the idea which, on being translated into sound, assumes the form of a musical composition. The beautiful melody and the skillful harmony as such do not charm us, but only what they imply: the whispering of love, or the clamor of ardent combatants.

In order to escape from such vague notions we must, first of all, sever from their habitual associations metaphors of the above description. The *whispering* may be expressed, true, but not the whispering of love; the *clamor* may be reproduced, undoubtedly, but not the clamor of ardent combatants. Music may reproduce phenomena such as whispering, storming, roaring, but the feelings of love or anger have only a subjective existence.

Definite feelings and emotions are unsusceptible of being embodied in music.

Our emotions have no isolated existence in the mind and cannot, therefore, be evoked by an art which is incapable of representing the remaining series of mental states. They are, on the contrary, dependent on physiological and pathological conditions, on notions and judgments—in fact, on all the processes of human reasoning which so many conceive as antithetical to the emotions.

What, then, transforms an indefinite feeling into a definite one—into the feeling of longing, hope, or love? Is it the mere degree of intensity, the fluctuating rate of inner motion? Assuredly not. The latter may be the same in the case of dissimilar feelings or may, in the case of the same feeling, vary with the time and the person. Only by virtue of ideas and judgments—unconscious though we may be of them when our feelings run high—can an indefinite state of mind pass into a definite feeling. The feeling of hope is inseparable from the conception of a happier state which is to come, and which we compare with the actual state. The feeling of sadness involves the notion of a past state of happiness. These are perfectly definite ideas or conceptions, and in default of them—the apparatus of thought, as it were—no feeling can be called "hope" or "sadness," for through them alone can a feeling assume a definite character. On excluding these conceptions from consciousness, nothing remains but a vague sense of motion which at best could not rise above a general feeling of satisfaction or discomfort. The feeling of love cannot be conceived apart from the image of the beloved being, or apart from the desire and the longing for the possession of the object of our affections. It is not the kind óf phychical activity but the intellectual substratum, the subject underlying it, which constitutes it love. Dynamically speaking love may be gentle or impetuous, buoyant or depressed, and yet it remains love. This reflection alone ought to make it clear that music can express only those qualifying adjectives, and not the substantive, love, itself. A determinate feeling (a passion, an emotion) as such never exists without a definable

meaning which can, of course, only be communicated through the medium of definite ideas. Now, since music as an "indefinite form of speech"
is admittedly incapable of expressing definite ideas, is it not a psychologically unavoidable conclusion that it is likewise incapable of expressing
definite emotions? For the definite character of an emotion rests entirely
on the meaning involved in it.

How it is that music may, nevertheless, awaken feelings (though not
necessarily so) such as sadness and joy we shall try to explain hereafter
when we come to examine music from a subjective point of view. At this
stage of our inquiry it is enough to determine whether music is capable of
representing any definite emotion whatever. To this question only a negative answer can be given, the definiteness of an emotion being inseparably
connected with concrete notions and conceptions, and to reduce these to
a material form is altogether beyond the power of music. A certain class
of ideas, however, is quite susceptible of being adequately expressed by
means which unquestionably belong to the sphere of music proper. This
class comprises all ideas which, consistently with the organ to which they
appeal, are associated with audible changes of strength, motion, and
ratio: the ideas of intensity waxing and diminishing; of motion hastening
and lingering; of ingeniously complex and simple progression, etc. The
aesthetic expression of music may be described by terms such as graceful,
gentle, violent, vigorous, elegant, fresh—all these ideas being expressible
by corresponding modifications of sound. We may, therefore, use those
adjectives as directly describing musical phenomena without thinking of
the ethical meanings attaching to them in a psychological sense, and
which, from the habit of associating ideas, we readily ascribe to the effect
of the music, or even mistake for purely musical properties.

The ideas which a composer expresses are mainly and primarily of a
purely musical nature. His imagination conceives a definite and graceful
melody aiming at nothing beyond itself. Every concrete phenomenon
suggests the class to which it belongs or some still wider conception in
which the latter is included, and by continuing this process the idea of
the absolute is reached at last. This is true also of musical phenomena.
This melodious adagio, for instance, softly dying away, suggests the ideas
of gentleness and concord in the abstract. Over imaginative faculty, ever
ready to establish relations between the conceptions of art and our sentiments, may construe these softly ebbing strains of music in a still loftier
sense, e.g., as the placid resignation of a mind at peace with itself; and
they may rouse even a vague sense of everlasting rest.

The primary aim of poetry, sculpture, and painting is likewise to produce some concrete image. Only by way of inference can the picture of a
flower girl call up the wider notion of maidenly content and modesty, the
picture of a snow-covered churchyard the transitoriness of earthly existence. In like manner, but far more vaguely and capriciously, may the
listener discover in a piece of music the idea of youthful contentedness or
that of transitoriness. These abstract notions, however, are by no means

the subject matter of the pictures or the musical compositions, and it is still more absurd to talk as if the feelings of "transitoriness" or of "youthful contentedness" could be represented by them.

There are ideas which, though not occurring as feelings, are yet capable of being fully expressed by music; and conversely, there are feelings which affect our minds but which are so constituted as to defy their adequate expression by any ideas which music can represent.

What part of the feelings, then, can music represent, if not the subject involved in them?

Only their dynamic properties. It may reproduce the motion accompanying phychical action, according to its momentum: speed, slowness, strength, weakness, increasing and decreasing intensity. But motion is only one of the concomitants of feeling, not the feeling itself. It is a popular fallacy to suppose that the descriptive power of music is sufficiently qualified by saying that, although incapable of representing the subject of a feeling, it may represent the feeling itself—not the object of love, but the feeling of love. In reality, however, music can do neither. It cannot reproduce the feeling of love but only the element of motion; and this may occur in any other feeling just as well as in love, and in no case is it the distinctive feature. The term "love" is as abstract as "virtue" or "immortality," and it is quite superfluous to assure us that music is unable to express abstract notions. No art can do this, for it is a matter of course that only definite and concrete ideas (those that have assumed a living form, as it were) can be incorporated by an art. But no instrumental composition can describe the ideas of love, wrath, or fear, since there is no causal nexus between these ideas and certain combinations of sound. Which of the elements inherent in these ideas, then, does music turn to account so effectually? Only the element of motion—in the wider sense, of course, according to which the increasing and decreasing force of a single note or chord is "motion" also. This is the element which music has in common with our emotions and which, with creative power, it contrives to exhibit in an endless variety of forms and contrasts.

Though the idea of motion appears to us a most far-reaching and important one, it has hitherto been conspicuously disregarded in all inquiries into the nature and action of music.

Whatever else there is in music that apparently pictures states of feeling is symbolical.

Sounds, like colors, are originally associated in our minds with certain symbolical meanings which produce their effects independently of and antecedently to any design of art. Every color has a character of its own; it is not a mere cipher into which the artist blows the breath of life, but a force. Between it and certain states of mind, Nature herself has established a sympathetic connection. Are we not all acquainted with the unsophisticated meanings of colors, so dear to the popular imagination, which cultured minds have exalted into poetic refinement? Green is associated with a feeling of hope, blue with fidelity. Rosenkranz recognizes "graceful dignity" in orange, "philistine politeness" in violet, etc. (*Psychologie*, 2nd ed., p. 102.)

In like manner, the first elements of music, such as the various keys, chords, and timbres, have severally a character of their own. There exists, in fact, a but-too-ready art of interpreting the meanings of musical elements. Schubart's symbolism of the keys in music forms a counterpart, as it were, to Goethe's interpretation of colors. Such elements (sounds, colors), however, when employed for the purposes of art, are subject to laws quite distinct from those upon which the effect of their isolated action depends. When looking at a historical painting we should never think of construing the red appearing in it as always meaning joy, or the white as always meaning innocence. Just as little in a symphony would the key of A flat major always awaken romantic feelings or the key of B minor always misanthropic ones, every triad a feeling of satisfaction and every diminished seventh a feeling of despair. Aesthetically speaking, such primordially distinctive traits are nonexistent when viewed in the light of those wider laws to which they are subordinate. The relation in question cannot for a moment be assumed to express or represent anything definite whatsoever. We called it "symbolical" because the subject is exhibited not directly but in a form essentially different from it. If yellow is the emblem of jealousy, the key of G major that of gaiety, the cypress that of mourning, such interpretations, and the definite character of our emotions, imply a psychophysiological relation. The color, the sound, or the plant as such are not related to our emotions, but only the meanings we ourselves attach to them. We cannot, therefore, speak of an isolated chord as representing a determinate feeling, and much less can we do so when it occurs in a connected piece of music.

Beyond the analogy of motion, and the symbolism of sounds, music possesses no means for fulfilling its alleged mission.

Seeing, then, how easy it is to deduce from the inherent nature of sound the inability of music to represent definite emotions, it seems almost incredible that our everyday experience should nevertheless have failed firmly to establish this fact. Let those who, when listening to some instrumental composition, imagine the strings to quiver with a profusion of feeling clearly show what feeling is the subject of the music. The experiment is indispensable. If, for instance, we were to listen to Beethoven's "Overture to Prometheus," an attentive and musical ear would successively discover more or less the following: the notes of the first bar, after a fall into the lower fourth, rise gently and in rapid succession, a movement repeated in the second bar. The third and fourth bars continue it in wider limits. The jet propelled by the fountain comes trickling down in drops, but rises once more, only to repeat in the following four bars the figure of the preceding four. The listener thus perceives that the first and second bars of the melody are symmetrical, that these two bars and the succeeding two are likewise so, and that the same is true of the wider arc of the first four bars and the corresponding arc of the following four. The bass which indicates the rhythm marks the beginning of each of the first three bars with one single beat, the fourth with two beats, while the same rotation is observed in the next four bars. The fourth bar, therefore, is different from the first three, and, this point of difference becoming symmetrical through being repeated in the following four bars, agreeably impresses the ear as an unexpected development within the former limits. The harmony of the theme exhibits the same correspondence of one large and two small arcs: the common chord of C of the first four bars corresponds to the chord of $\frac{6}{4}$ of the fifth and sixth, and to the chord of $\frac{6}{5}$ of the seventh and eighth bars. This systematic correspondence of melody, rhythm, and harmony results in a structure composed of parts at once symmetrical and dissimilar, into which further gradations of light and shade are introduced through the timbre peculiar to each instrument and the varying volume of sound:

Any subject other than the one alluded to we absolutely fail to find in the theme, and still less could we state what feeling it represents or necessarily arouses in the listener. An analysis of this kind, it is true, reduces to a skeleton a body glowing with life; it destroys the beauty, but at the same time it destroys all false constructions.

No other theme of instrumental music will fare any better than the one which we have selected at random. A numerous class of music lovers think that it is a characteristic feature only of the older "classical" music to disregard the representation of feelings, and it is readily admitted that no feeling can be shown to form the subject of the forty-eight preludes and fugues of J. S. Bach's *Well-Tempered Clavichord*. However glaringly unscientific and arbitrary such a distinction may be—a distinction, by the way, which has its explanation in the fact that the older music affords still more unmistakable proof that it aims at nothing beyond itself, and that interpretations of the kind mentioned would, in this case, present more obstacles than attractions—this alone is enough to prove that music need not necessarily awaken feelings, or that it must necessarily be the object of music to represent them. The whole domain of florid counterpoint would then have to be ignored. But if large departments of art, which can be defended both on historical and aesthetic grounds, have to be passed over for the sake of a theory, it may be concluded that such a theory is false. Though a single leak will sink a ship, those who are not content with that are at liberty to knock out the whole bottom. Let them play the theme of a symphony by Mozart or Haydn, an adagio by Beethoven, a scherzo by Mendelssohn, one of Schumann's or Chopin's compositions for the piano, anything, in short, from the stock of our standard music; or again, the most popular themes from overtures of Auber, Donizetti, and Flotow. Who would be bold enough to point out a definite feeling as the subject of any of these themes? One will say "love." He may be right. Another thinks it is "longing." Perhaps so. A third feels it to be "religious fervor." Who can contradict him? Now, how can we talk of a definite feeling being represented when nobody really knows what is represented? Probably all will agree about the beauty or beauties of the composition, whereas all will differ regarding its subject. To "represent" something is to exhibit it clearly, to set it before us distinctly. But how can we call that the subject represented by an art which is really its vaguest and most indefinite element, and which must, therefore, forever remain highly debatable ground?

We have intentionally selected examples from instrumental music, for only what is true of the latter is true also of music as such. If we wish to decide the question whether music possesses the character of definiteness, what its nature and properties are, and what its limits and tendencies, no other than instrumental music can be taken into consideration. What instrumental music is unable to achieve lies also beyond the pale of music proper, for it alone is pure and self-subsistent music. No matter whether we regard vocal music as superior to or more effective than instrumental music—an unscientific proceeding, by the way, which is generally the up-shot of one-sided dilettantism—we cannot help admitting that the term "music," in its true meaning, must exclude compositions in which words are set to music. In vocal or operatic music it is impossible to draw so nice a distinction between the effect of the music and that of the words that an exact definition of the share which each has had in the production of the whole becomes practicable. An inquiry into the subject of music must leave out even compositions with inscriptions, or so-called program music. Its union with poetry, though enhancing the power of the music, does not widen its limits.

Vocal music is an undecomposable compound, and it is impossible to gauge the relative importance of each of its constituents. In discussing the effect of poetry, nobody, surely, will cite the opera as an example. Now, it requires a greater effort, but no deeper insight, to follow the same line of thought when the fundamental principles of musical aesthetics are in question.

Vocal music colors, as it were, the poetic drawing. In the musical ele-ments we were able to discover the most brilliant and delicate hues and an abundance of symbolic meanings. Though by their aid it might be possible to transform a second-rate poem into a passionate effusion of the soul, it is not the music but the words which determine the subject of a vocal composition. Not the coloring but the drawing renders the repre-sented subject intelligible. We appeal to the listener's faculty of abstrac-tion, and beg him to think, in a purely musical sense, of some dramatically effective melody apart from the context. A melody, for instance, which impresses us as highly dramatic and which is intended to represent the feeling of rage can express this state of mind in no other way than by quick and impetuous motion. Words expressing passionate love, though diametrically opposed in meaning, might, therefore, be suitably rendered by the same melody.

At a time when thousands (among whom there were men like Jean Jacques Rousseau) were moved to tears by the air from *Orpheus:*

> J'ai perdu mon Eurydice
> Rien n'égale mon malheur,

Boyé, a contemporary of Gluck, observed that precisely the same melody would accord equally well, if not better, with words conveying exactly the reverse, thus:

> J'ai trouvé mon Eurydice,
> Rien n'égale mon bonheur.

The following is the beginning of the aria in question, which, for the sake of brevity, we give with piano accompaniment but in all other respects exactly as in the original Italian score:

Orfeo

Vivace

Che fa - rò sen -za Eu - ri - di - ce! do-ve an-

drò sen-za il mio ben! che fa - rò do-ve an-

drò; che fa - rò sen - za il mio

ben, do - ve an-drò sen -za il mio ben.

We, for our part, are not of opinion that in this case the composer is quite free from blame, inasmuch as music most assuredly possesses accents which more truly express a feeling of profound sorrow. If, however, from among innumerable instances we selected the one quoted, we have done so because, in the first place, it affects the composer who is credited with the greatest dramatic accuracy; and, secondly, because several generations have hailed this very melody as most correctly rendering the supreme grief which the words express.

But even far more definite and expressive passages from vocal music, when considered apart from the text, enable us at best to guess the feeling they are intended to convey. They resemble a silhouette, the original of which we recognize only after being told whose likeness it is.

What is true of isolated passages is true also in a wider application. There are many cases where an entirely new text has been employed for a complete musical work. If Meyerbeer's *Huguenots*, after changing the scene of action, the time, the characters, and the plot, were to be performed as "The Ghibellines of Pisa," though so clumsy an adaptation would undoubtedly produce a disagreeable impression, the purely musical part would in no way suffer. And yet the religious feeling and fanaticism which are entirely wanting in "The Ghibellines" are supposed to be the motive power in *The Huguenots*. Luther's hymn must not be cited as counter-evidence, as it is merely a quotation. From a musical point of view it is consistent with any profession of faith whatever. Has the reader ever heard the *allegro fugato* from the overture to *The Magic Flute* changed into a vocal quartet of quarreling Jewish peddlers? Mozart's music, though not altered in the smallest degree, fits the low text appallingly well, and the enjoyment we derive from the gravity of the music in the opera can be no heartier than our laugh at the farcical humor of the parody. We might quote numberless instances of the plastic character of every musical theme and every human emotion. The feeling of religious fervor is rightly considered to be the least liable to musical misconstruction. Yet there are countless village and country churches in Germany in which at Eucharist pieces like Proch's "Alpine Horn" or the finale from the *Sonnambula* (with the coquettish leap to the tenth) are performed on the organ. Foreigners who visit churches in Italy hear, to their amazement, the most popular themes from operas by Rossini, Bellini, Donizetti, and Verdi. Pieces like these and of a still more secular character, provided they do not altogether lose the quality of sobriety, are far from interfering with the devotions of the congregation, who, on the contrary, appear to be greatly edified. If music as such were capable of representing the feeling of piety, a *quid pro quo* of this kind would be as unlikely as the contingency of a preacher reciting from the pulpit a novel by Tieck or an act of Parliament. The greatest masters of sacred music afford abundant examples in proof of our proposition. Handel, in particular, set to work with the greatest nonchalance in this respect. Winterfeld has shown that many of the most celebrated airs from *The Messiah*, including those most of all admired as being especially suggestive of piety, were taken from secular duets (mostly erotic) composed in the years 1711–1712, when Handel set to music certain madrigals by Mauro Ortensio for the Electoral Princess Caroline of Hanover. The music of the second duet,

> No, di voi non vo' fidarmi,
> Cieco amor, crudel beltá;
> Troppo siete menzognere
> Lusinghiere deitá!

Handel employed unaltered both in key and melody for the chorus in the first part of *The Messiah*, "For unto us a Child is born." The third part of the same duet, *So per prova i vostri inganni*, contains the same themes which occur in the chorus of the second part of *The Messiah*, "All we like sheep." The music of the madrigal (No. 16, duet for soprano and alto) is essentially the same as the duet from the third part of *The Messiah*, "O Death, where is thy sting?" But the words of the madrigal are as follows:

> Se tu non lasci amore
> Mio cor, ti pentirai
> Lo so ben io!

There is a vast number of similar instances, but we need only refer here to the entire series of pastoral pieces from the "Christmas Oratorio" which, as is well known, were naïvely taken from secular cantatas composed for special occasions. And Gluck, whose music, we are taught, attained the sublime height of dramatic accuracy only by every note being scrupulously adapted to each special case, nay, by the melodies being extracted from the very rhythm of the syllables—Gluck has transferred to his *Armida* no fewer than five airs from his earlier Italian operas (compare with the author's *Die moderne Oper*, p. 16). It is obvious, therefore, that vocal music, which in theory can never determine the principles of music proper, is likewise, in practice, powerless to call in question the canons which experience has established for instrumental music.

The proposition which we are endeavoring to disprove has become, as it were, part and parcel of current musical aesthetics, so that all derivative and collateral theories enjoy the same reputation of invulnerability. To the latter belongs the theory that music is able to reproduce visual and auditory impressions of a nonmusical nature. Whenever the question of the representation of objects by musical means (*Tonmalerei*) is under debate we are, with an air of wisdom, assured over and over again that, though music is unable to portray phenomena which are foreign to its province, it nevertheless may picture the feelings which they excite. The very reverse is the case. Music can undertake to imitate objective phenomena only, and never the specific feeling they arouse. The falling of snow, the fluttering of birds, and the rising of the sun can be painted musically only by producing auditory impressions which are dynamically related to those phenomena. In point of strength, pitch, velocity, and rhythm, sounds present to the ear a figure bearing that degree of analogy to certain visual impressions which sensations of various kinds bear to one another. As there is, physiologically speaking, such a thing as a vicarious function (up to a certain point), so may sense impressions, aesthetically speaking, become vicarious also. There is a well-founded analogy between motion in space and motion in time; between the color, texture, and size of an object and the pitch, timbre, and strength of a tone; and it is for this reason quite practicable to paint an object musically. The pretension, however, to describe by musical means the "feeling" which the falling snow, the crowing cock, or a flash of lightning excites in us is simply ludicrous.

Although, as far as we remember, all musical theorists tacitly accept and base their arguments on the postulate that music has the power of representing definite emotions, yet their better judgment has kept them from openly avowing it. The conspicuous absence of definite ideas in music troubled their minds and induced them to lay down the somewhat modified principle that the object of music was to awaken and represent indefinite, emotions. Rationally understood, this can only mean that music ought to deal with the *motion* accompanying a feeling, regardless of its essential part, with what is felt; in other words, that its function is restricted to the reproduction of what we termed the dynamic element of an emotion, a function which we unhesitatingly conceded to music. But this property does not enable music to represent indefinite feelings, for to "represent" something "indefinite" is a contradiction in terms. Psychical motion, considered as motion apart from the state of mind it involves, can never become the object of an art, because without an answer to the query, What is moving, or what is being moved? an art has nothing tangible to work upon. That which is implied in the proposition—namely, that music is not intended to represent a definite feeling (which is undoubtedly true)—is only a negative aspect of the question. But what is the positive, the creative, factor in a musical composition? An indefinite feeling as such cannot supply a subject; to utilize it an art would, first of all, have to solve the problem: What *form* can be given to it? The function of art consists in *individualizing*, in evolving the definite out of the indefinite, the particular out of the general. The theory respecting "indefinite feelings" would reverse this process. It lands us in even greater difficulties than the theory that music represents something, though it is impossible to define what. This position is but a step removed from the clear recognition that music represents no feelings, either definite or indefinite. Yet where is the musician who would deprive his art of that domain which from time immemorial has been claimed as belonging to it?

This conclusion might give rise to the view that the representation of definite feelings by music, though impracticable, may yet be adopted as an ideal, never wholly realizable, but which it is possible, and even necessary, to approach more and more closely. The many high-sounding phrases respecting the tendency of music to cast off its vagueness and to become concrete speech, no less than the fulsome praises bestowed on compositions aiming—or supposed to be aiming—at this, are proof of the popularity of the theory in question.

Having absolutely denied the possibility of representing emotions by musical means, we must be still more emphatic in refuting the fallacy which considers this the aesthetic touchstone of music.

The beautiful in music would not depend on the accurate representation of feelings even if such a representation were possible. Let us, for argument's sake, assume the possibility and examine it from a practical point of view.

It is manifestly out of the question to test this fallacy with instrumental music, as the latter could be shown to represent definite feelings only by arguing in a circle. We must, therefore, make the experiment with vocal music as being that music whose office it is to emphasize clearly defined states of mind.

Here the words determine the subject to be described; music may give it life and breath, and impart to it a more or less distinct individuality. This is done by utilizing as far as possible the characteristics peculiar to motion and the symbols associated with sounds. If greater attention is bestowed on the words than on the production of purely musical beauty, a high degree of individuality may be secured—may, the delusion may even arise that the music alone expresses the emotion which, though susceptible of intensification, was already immutably contained in the words. Such a tendency is in its consequences on a par with the alleged practicability of representing a certain feeling as the subject of a given "piece of music." Suppose there did exist perfect congruity between the real and the assumed power of music, that it was possible to represent feelings by musical means, and that these feelings were the subject of musical compositions. If this assumption be granted, we should be logically compelled to call those compositions the best which perform the task in the most perfect manner. Yet do we not all know compositions of exquisite beauty without any definite subject? We need but instance Bach's preludes and fugues. On the other hand, there are vocal compositions which aim at the most accurate expression of certain emotions within the limits referred to, and in which the supreme goal is truthfulness in this descriptive process. On close examination we find that the rigor with which music is subordinated to words is generally in an inverse ratio to the independent beauty of the former; otherwise expressed, that rhetorico-dramatical precision and musical perfection go together but halfway, and then proceed in different directions.

The recitative affords a good illustration of this truth, since it is that form of music which best accommodates itself to rhetorical requirements down to the very accent of each individual word, never even attempting to be more than a faithful copy of rapidly changing states of mind. This, therefore, in strict accordance with theory before us, should be the highest and most perfect music. But in the recitative, music degenerates into a mere shadow and relinquishes its individual sphere of action altogether. Is not this proof that the representing of definite states of mind is contrary to the nature of music, and that in their ultimate bearings they are antagonistic to one another? Let anyone play a long recitative, leaving out the words, and inquire into its musical merit and subject. Any kind of music claiming to be the sole factor in producing a given effect should be able to stand this test.

This is by no means true of the recitative alone; the most elevated and excellent forms of music equally bear out the assertion that the beautiful tends to disappear in proportion as the expression of some specific feeling is aimed at; for the former can expand only if untrammeled by alien factors, whereas the latter relegates music to a subservient place.

We will now ascend from the declamatory principle in the recitative to the dramatic principle in the opera. In Mozart's operas there is perfect congruity between the music and the words. Even the most intricate parts, the finales, are beautiful if judged as a whole, quite apart from the words, although certain portions in the middle might become somewhat obscure without them. To do justice in a like degree both to the musical and the dramatic requirements is rightly considered to be the ideal of the opera. But that for this reason there should be perpetual warfare between the principles of dramatic nicety and musical beauty, entailing never-ending concessions on both sides, has, to my knowledge, never been conclusively demonstrated. The principle involved in the opera is not undermined or weakened by the fact that all the parts are sung—our imagination being easily reconciled to an illusion of this kind—but it is the constraint imposed alike upon music and words that leads to continual acts of trespass or concession, and reduces the opera, as it were, to a constitutional government whose very existence depends upon an incessant struggle between two parties equally entitled to power. It is from this conflict, in which the composer allows now one principle and now the other to prevail, that all the imperfections of the opera arise, and from which, at the same time, all rules important for operatic works are deduced. The principles in which music and the drama are grounded, if pushed to their logical consequences, are mutually destructive; but they point in so similar a direction that they appear almost parallel.

The dance is a similar case in point, of which any ballet is a proof. The more the graceful rhythm of the figures is sacrificed in the attempt to speak by gesture and dumb show, and to convey definite thoughts and emotions, the closer is the approximation to the low rank of mere pantomime. The prominence given to the dramatic principle in the dance proportionately lessens its rhythmical and plastic beauty. The opera can never be quite on a level with recited drama or with purely instrumental music. A good opera composer will, therefore, constantly endeavor to combine and reconcile the two factors instead of automatically emphasizing now one and now the other. When in doubt, however, he will always allow the claim of music to prevail, the chief element in the opera being not dramatic but musical beauty. This is evident from the different attitudes of mind in which we listen to a play or an opera in which the same subject is treated. The neglect of the musical part will always be far more keenly felt.

As regards the history of the art of music, it appears to us that the importance of the celebrated controversy between the disciples of Gluck and those of Piccinni lies in the fact that the question of the internal conflict in the opera caused by the incompatibility of the musical and the dramatic principles was then for the first time thoroughly discussed. The controversy, it is true, was carried on without a clear perception of the immense influence which the outcome would have on the whole mode of thinking, He who does not shrink from the labor—a very profitable labor, by the way—of tracing this musical controversy to its sources will notice in the vast range from adulation down to ill-breeding all the wit and cleverness of French polemics, but likewise so childish a treatment of the abstract side of the question, and such want of deeper knowledge, that the science of musical aesthetics could gain nothing from the endless disputation. The most gifted controversialists—Suard and the Abbé Arnaud on Gluck's side, and Marmontel and La Harpe of the opposite camp—though repeatedly going beyond the limits of Gluck's critique and into a more minute examination of the dramatic principle of the opera and its relation to music, treated this relation, nevertheless, as one of the many properties of the opera, but by no means as one of the most vital importance. It never struck them that the very life of the opera depended on the nature of this relationship. It is certainly remarkable how very near some of Gluck's opponents, in particular, were at times to the position from which the fallacy of the dramatic principle can be clearly seen and confuted. Thus La Harpe, in the *Journal de Politique et de Littérature* of October 5, 1777, says:

On objecte qu'il n'est pas naturel de chanter un air de cette nature dans une situation passionée, que c'est un moyen d'arrêter la scène et de nuir à l'effet. Je trouve ces objections absolument illusoires. D'abord, dès qu'on admet le chant, il faut l'admettre le plus beau possible et il n'est pas plus naturel de chanter mal, que de chanter bien. Tous les arts sont fondés sur des conventions, sur des données. Quand je viens à l'opéra, c'est pour entendre la musique. Je n'ignore pas, qu'Alceste ne faisait ses Adieux à Admète en chantant un air; mais comme Alceste est sur le Théatre pour chanter, si je retrouve sa douleur et son amour dans un air bien mélodieux, je jouirai de son chant en m'intéressant à son infortune.

Is it credible that La Harpe should have failed to recognize the security and unassailableness of his position? For, after a while, it occurs to him to object to the duet of Agamemnon and Achilles in *Iphigenia* because "it is inconsistent with the dignity of the two heroes to talk simultaneously." With this remark he quits the vantage ground of the principle of purely musical beauty and tacitly—nay, unconsciously—accepts the theory of his adversaries.

The more scrupulous we are in keeping pure the dramatic element of the opera by withholding from it the vivifying breath of musical beauty, the more quickly it faints away like a bird in the exhausted receiver of an air pump. We have, therefore, no course open but to fall back upon the pure, spoken drama which, at all events, is proof of the impossibility of the opera; unless, though fully aware of the unreality involved, we assign to the musical element the foremost rank. In the true exercise of the art, this fact has, indeed, never been questioned. Even Gluck, the most orthodox dramaturgist, although he originated the fallacy that opera music should be nothing but exalted declamation, did, in practice, often allow his musical genius to get the better of him, and this invariably to the great advantage of the work. The same holds good of Richard Wagner.

For the object of these pages, it is enough to denounce emphatically as false Wagner's principal theorem as stated in the first volume of *Oper und Drama:* "The misconception respecting the opera, viewed as a work of art, consists in the fact that the means (the music) is regarded as the end, and the end (the drama) as the means." An opera, however, in which the music is really and truly employed solely as a medium for dramatic expression is a musical monstrosity.

One of the inferences to be drawn from Wagner's proposition (respecting the means and the end) is that all composers who have set indifferent librettos to anything better than indifferent music were guilty of a great impropriety, as we ourselves are in admiring such music.

The connection of poetry with music and with the opera is a sort of morganatic union, and the more closely we examine this morganatic union of musical beauty and definite thoughts, the more skeptical do we become as regards its indissolubility.

How is it that in every song slight alterations may be introduced which, without in the least detracting from the accuracy of expression, immediately destroy the beauty of the theme? This would be impossible if the latter were inseparably connected with the former. Again, how is it that many a song, though adequately expressing the drift of the poem, is nevertheless quite intolerable? The theory that music is capable of expressing emotions furnishes us with no explanation.

Select Bibliography for Part Three

THE THEORY OF MUSIC

Books

Wilson Coker, *Music and Meaning: A Theoretical Introduction to Musical Aesthetics*; Joseph Goddard, *The Deeper Sources of the Beauty and Expression of Music*; Edmund Gurney, *The Power of Sound*; Glenn Haydon, *On the Meaning of Music*; F. Howes, *Music and Its Meanings*; Leonard B. Meyer, *Emotion and Meaning in Music*; Leonard B. Meyer, *Music, the Arts and Ideas*; Julius Portnoy, *The Philosopher and Music*; Carroll C. Pratt, *Meaning in Music*.

Articles

Robert Charles Clark, "Total Control and Change in Musics: A Philosophical Analysis"; Gordon K. Greene, "For Whom and Why Does a Composer Prepare a Score"; Ervin Laszlo, "Affect and Expression in Music"; Alan Tormey, "Indeterminacy and Identity in Art"; William E. Webster, "Music Is Not a 'Notational System'"; Sidney Zink, "Is the Music Really Sad?"

FORMALISM, PHILOSOPHY, AND CONTEMPORARY PLASTIC ARTS

Since the mid-1950s art criticism has become increasingly important to philosophy and to the arts themselves. This situation is due, in part, to the fact that in many ways the plastic arts are no longer self-sustaining. These days, artworks often require an elaborate philosophical and critical rationale in order to be understood as artworks. In "The Artworld" (part one) and "Artworks and Real Things" (part five), Arthur Danto demonstrates the relevance of philosophy to contemporary art. In this section Clement Greenberg and Michael Fried demonstrate the relevance of criticism.

In "After Abstract Expressionism" Greenberg says, "a stretched up canvas already exists as a picture—though not necessarily as a successful one." How is this possible? According to Greenberg, and to Fried, who follows him on this point, it is possible because such an object can have "presence." "Presence" is defined as a kind of formal objecthood which can be conferred by such things as size and scale as well as a specific look of nonart. But how are we to understand such notions as "nonart," "presence," and the like? According to Greenberg and Fried, we must understand "modernist" painting (i.e., painting since Manet, 1860s) and the recent history of painting and sculpture in order to see how these notions make sense. In the two essays presented here Greenberg and Fried guide us through the labyrinth of contemporary plastic art, helping us to make sense of a wide variety of recent works in terms of their formal properties.

What, exactly, is formalism? And what is the status of formalist criticism today? David Carrier discusses these questions in "American-Type Formalism." Carrier places the work of Greenberg and Fried in perspective, outlining the major features of their views, citing important contributions they have made, and considering criticisms of their general approach to art and art criticism. At the end of his essay Carrier suggests that formalist criticism seems to be on the wane. Whether this is due to the emergence of new, post formalist art or whether this is symptomatic of a stagnation or decline in the history of American art are questions Carrier leaves open. In fact, these questions are considered in part five, The Death of Art. Readers can make up their own mind on this matter after studying the selections presented there.

The work of Greenberg and Fried is related to a number of other selections in this book. Arthur Danto's essays have already been mentioned in this connection. The following essays should also be noted: Ted Cohen, "The Possibility of Art" and George Dickie, "The Actuality of Art" (both in part two); Stanley Cavell, *The World Viewed* (part three); and the essays of Duchamp and Karshan (part five). The work of Greenberg and Fried also relates in a more general way to the selections from Kant in part six.

Clement Greenberg

AFTER ABSTRACT EXPRESSIONISM

Twenty-odd years ago all the ambitious young painters I knew in New York saw abstract art as the only way out.* Rightly or wrongly, they could see no other way in which to go in order to say something personal, therefore new, therefore worth saying. Representational art confronted their ambition with too many occupied positions. But it was not so much representation survived in Picasso (as it does today in Dubuffet) and in Léger, Braque, Klee and Miró, but the art of these masters was felt as virtually abstract, and so even was some of Matisse's. It was from this art, in fact, along with Mondrian's, that the painters I am speaking of got their most important lessons in abstraction.

In those years serious abstract art seemed inseparable from the canons of Synthetic Cubism, which meant cleanly marked contours, closed and more or less regular shapes, and flat colour. It may not have been necessary to observe all these canons literally, but it was necessary to keep oriented to them. Because this orientation was accepted so implicitly, without idea of an alternative, it became by the end of the 1930's something cramping and constricting in its own right. Despite the appreciation of Klee (whose influence freed at least Tobey, Ralph Rosenborg, and even Loren MacIver), and though the early abstract pictures of Kandinsky were beginning to be admired in New York, most of the young artists I have in mind continued to believe that the only way to real style in abstract art lay through trued and faired, silhouetted and flattened forms. Any other way seemed an evasion or, at best, too idiosyncratic for more than one artist to take at a time.

This was pretty much the plight of abstract art in New York up into the early 1940's—and I say "plight" advisedly. Good abstract painting was produced in New York during that time: not only by Stuart Davis, but also by Bolotowsky, Cavallon, Diller, Ferren, Glarner, Balcomb and

Clement Greenberg is a highly influential contemporary critic who has written for most of the leading journals including *The Partisan Review, The Nation, Commentary, Arts, Art News, Art Forum, Studio International,* and several others.
* Published in *Art International*, vol. VI, no. 8, 1962. Reprinted by permission of the author and *Art International*.

Gertrude Greene, George L. K. Morris, and a few others, all of whom adhered to "closed" Cubism. Some of Gorky's work of that period looks more independent now than it used to, and de Kooning was then doing what I think remain his supreme paintings, unshown though they were. Nevertheless, the sense of how confining serious abstract art had become under the canons of closed Cubism betrayed itself in the feeling that Stuart Davis had to be overcome rather than emulated. This was unfair, but I can see in retrospect why it may have been necessary. As good as he was—and still is—Davis remained a provincial artist, and there was a dim, unspoken feeling in the air that provincialism was what had most to be overcome. Yet it seemed at the same time harder than ever before to paint ambitiously enough to break out of provincialism.

This helps explain why Baziotes' Surrealist-influenced pictures of 1942 came like a breath of fresh air. Daring to hint at illusionist space, they somehow (unlike Matta's paintings of that time) got away with it, and did not strike one as taking the easy way out—or at least not altogether. The real break-out came, however, with Pollock's and Hofmann's first one-man shows, in October 1943 and March 1944 respectively. There I saw abstract paintings that were painterly in what impressed me as being for the first time a full-blown way. The earlier Kandinsky looked clean-shaven by comparison, and Klee like a tidy miniaturist: neither had been quite so loose or open, much less so extravagant in his use of paint. The only precedent lay in representational painting, and that Pollock and Hofmann were not completely abstract in their first shows had its significance.

It was like a general thaw. In 1943 and 1944 Gorky, too, became much more painterly, under the influence of landscape and the early Kandinsky. Several students and former students of Hofmann began painting abstract pictures under Bonnard's or Rouault's influence. De Kooning, whose abandonment of closed, if not exactly Synthetic Cubism, dates from around 1946, was in another few years accepting the influence of Soutine. And even some of the old stand-bys of the American Abstract Artists group were starting to loosen up.

"Painterly" was not the word used, but it was what was really meant, as I see it, when Robert Coates called the new open abstract art in New York "Abstract Expressionism". It was, in effect, a painterly reaction against the tightness of Synthetic Cubism that at first used the vocabulary itself of Synthetic Cubism. Painterliness, combined with what remained an essentially Cubist feeling for design, was what artists as different as Gorky and Pollock had in common in the middle 1940's. If the label "Abstract Expressionism" means anything, it means painterliness: loose, rapid handling, or the look of it; masses that blotted and fused instead of shapes that stayed distinct; large and conspicuous rhythms; broken colour;

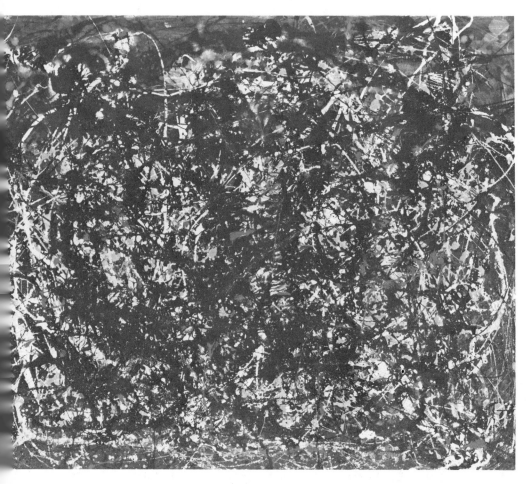

"If the label 'Abstract Expressionism' means anything, it means painter-liness: loose, rapid handling, or the look of it . . ." *Clement Greenberg in "After Abstract Expressionism," p. 426.*

uneven saturations or densities of paint, exhibited brush, knife, or finger marks—in short, a constellation of qualities like those defined by Woelfflin when he extracted his notion of the *Malerische* from Baroque art. As we can now see, the displacing of the quasi-geometrical as the dominant mode in New York abstract art after 1943 offers another instance of that cyclical alternation of painterly and non-painterly which has marked the evolution of Western art (at progressively shorter intervals after Manet) since the 16th century. Painterly abstraction tended to be less flat, or less taut in its flatness, than closed abstraction, and contained many more velleities towards illusion. The Kandinskys of 1910—1918, so like landscapes, had already revealed this, and Abstract Expressionism again revealed it, and continued to reveal it. This should not have been surprising. The painterly had started out as a means, first and foremost, to a heightened illusion of three-dimensional space, and in the course of painting and time uneven saturations of paint and colour, and broken or blurred outlines, came to evoke space in depth more immediately and automatically than perspective lines did. Whereas space in depth in the abstract or near-abstract art of the 1920's and 1930's had been a matter largely of "diagram" and association, in the painterly 1940's and 1950's it could not help becoming once again a matter more of *trompe-l'œil illusion*. Not that space in depth became deeper—not at all—but it did become more tangible, more a thing of immediate perception and less one of "reading". In June 1948, *Partisan Review* published a communication from George L. K. Morris in which he took me to task for, among other things, preferring what he called "behind-the-frame" painting. My rejoinder was that Mr. Morris had succumbed to the kind of dogmatism that held that one species of art must in a given period be better than any other species. Nevertheless, his dogmatism did not take away from the acuteness of his "behind-the-frame" characterization, especially in its implications, as I only later came to recognize. Hofmann's and Pollock's and Gorky's pictures did stay further behind their frames than Mondrian's or Picasso's post-1913 pictures did. This in itself said nothing about their relative esthetic value, and Mr. Morris was altogether wrong in inferring that it did, but he did have a real point in insinuating that painterly abstraction was headed backwards in terms of the evolution of style (even if going backwards in these terms was, at that time, almost the only way to go forward in terms of major quality).

Later, as the 1950's wore on, a good deal in Abstract Expressionist painting began fairly to cry out for a more coherent illusion of three-dimensional space, and to the extent that it did this it cried out for representation, since such coherence can be created only through the tangible representation of three-dimensional objects. It was most logical therefore that when painterly abstraction in New York finally crystallized into a set manner, it did so in a series of outspokenly representational works, namely de Kooning's "Women" pictures of 1952–1955. This manner, as returned to abstract art by de Kooning himself and the countless artists he has influenced, I call "homeless representation." I mean by this a plastic and descriptive painterliness that is applied to abstract ends, but which continues to suggest representational ones. In itself "homeless representation" is neither good nor bad, and maybe some of the best results of Abstract Expressionism in the past were got by flirting with representation. Badness becomes endemic to a manner only when it hardens into mannerism. This is just what happened to "homeless representation" in the mid-1950's, in de Kooning's art, in Guston's, in the post-1954 art of Kline, and in that of their many imitators. It is on the basis therefore of its actual results that I find fault with "homeless representation," not because of any *parti pris*; it's because what were merely its logical contradictions have turned into artistic ones too.

Something similar has happened to the two main tendencies of the European version of painterly abstraction, which likewise emerged during the war. In Europe too painterly abstraction presses towards the three-dimensional; but if one tendency leans, like our "homeless representation," towards the three-dimensionality of illusion, the other leans towards the literal three-dimensionality of piled-on paint, and for its part could be called "furtive bas-relief." Yet the latter tendency happens to be more closely affiliated with representation, even if only schematic representation, because it took its start from Dubuffet and Fautrier, and came to a head —though not to an extreme—in the representational works de Staël did in his last years. The former, the "homeless representation," tendency got its start, on the other hand, from the linear abstraction of Hartung, Wols, and Mathieu. I do not profess to be able to explain the logic at work in this situation, but I think that one clue to it lies in the extent to which the strongest exponents of "furtive bas-relief" rely on the non-painterly use of line, and at the same time on monochromatic effects that do not need the coherence achieved through tangible representation, because they have the coherence that belongs automatically to literally three-dimensional space. For the rest, painterly abstraction in Europe has likewise degenerated into an affair largely of mannerisms, whether those of "furtive bas-relief" or those of "homeless representation." And there too a vast quantity of abstract art that is bad because mannered is relieved, within the orbit of the mannerisms, only by felicitous minor art. For our Johns and Diebenkorn, Europe has its Tápies and Sugai to show. This comparison may be unfair to Diebenkorn, whose case is so exemplary that it is worth pausing over. His development so far is what one might say the development of Abstract Expressionism as a whole should have been. Earlier on he was the only *abstract* painter, as far as I know, to do something substantially independent with de Kooning's touch (and it makes no difference that he did it with the help of Rothko's design). More recently, he has let the logic of that touch carry him back (with Matisse's help) to representational art, and one might say that this consistency of logic is partly responsible for his becoming at least as good a representational as he was an abstract painter. That de Kooning's touch remains as unmistakable as before in his art does not diminish the success of his change. Uneven densities of paint, as produced by smearing, swiping, scrubbing, and scumbling, had in de Kooning's own hands created gradations of light and dark like those of conventional shading; though these were kept from actually modeling back into deep space by the declamatory abruptness with which they were juxtaposed, deep space is, nevertheless, increasingly suggested in almost everything de Kooning has done lately. By letting this suggestion become a forthright statement, Diebenkorn (along with another Californian, Elmer Bischoff) has, in effect, found a home for de Kooning's touch where it can fulfill itself more truthfully, though modestly, than it has been able to so far in de Kooning's own art. There are painters in New York too who have begun to put de Kooning's manner to the uses of outright representational art, but until now their success has been less consistent or less significant. Jasper Johns, however, should not be classed with them, even though, strictly speaking, he too is a representational artist. His case is another exemplary one, for he brings de Kooning's influence to a head by suspending it clearly, as if were, between abstraction and representation. The motifs of Johns' paintings, as William Rubin pointed out in these pages a few years ago, are always two-dimensional to start with, being taken from a repertory of man-made signs and images not too different from the one on which Picasso and Braque drew for the stenciled and affixed elements of their 1911–1913 Cubism. Unlike the two Cubist masters, Johns is interested in the literary irony that results from *representing* flat and artificial configurations which in actuality can only be *reproduced*; nonetheless, the abiding interest of his art, as distinguished from its journalistic one, lies largely in the area of the formal or plastic. Just as the vivid possibility of deep space in photographs of signs or housefronts or in Harnett's and Peto's paintings of pin-up boards, sets off the inherent flatness of the objects shown, so the painterly paintedness of a Johns picture sets off, and is set off by, the flatness of his number, letter, target, flag and map images.

By means of this "dialectic" the arrival of Abstract Expressionism at homeless representation is declared and spelled out. The original flatness of the canvas, with a few outlines stenciled on it, is shown as sufficing to represent adequately all that a picture by Johns really does represent. The paint surface itself, with it de Kooning-esque play of lights and darks, is shown, on the other hand, as being completely superfluous to this end. Everything that usually serves representation and illusion is left to serve nothing but itself, that is abstraction; while everything that usually serves the abstract or decorative—flatness, bare outlines, all-over or symmetrical design—is put to the service of representation. And the more explicit this contradiction is made, the more effective in every sense the picture tends to be. When the image is too obscured the paint surface is liable to become less pointedly superfluous; conversely, when the image is left too prominent it is liable to reduce the whole picture to a mere image (an image, that is, on the order of Johns' "sculptures," which, even when their bronze surfaces are left unpainted, amount to nothing more than what they really are: cast reproductions of man-made objects that, as far as three-dimensional art is concerned, could never be anything other than merely reproducible). The effect of a Johns picture is also weakened, often, when it is done in bright colours instead of neutral ones like black and gray, for these, being the shading hues *par excellence*, are just those that become the most exhibitedly and poignantly superfluous when applied to ineluctably flat images.

I do not mean to imply that the effectiveness of Johns' painting depends on a device. There is far more to it than that; otherwise I would not get the kind of pleasure from it that I do. But the fact that as much of his art can be explained as has been explained here without the exertion of any particular powers of insight would indicate a certain narrowness. Johns sings the swan-song of "homeless representation," and like most swan-songs, it carries only a limited distance.

Echoes of Analytical Cubism and of its transition of Synthetic Cubism are not found in Johns alone among the Abstract Expressionists, early and late—far from it. The whole evolution of Abstract Expressionism could, in fact, be described as a devolution from a Synthetic kind of abstract Cubism to an Analytical kind. By 1911, original Analytical Cubism itself had arrived at homeless representation: a way of depicting objects in planar segments kept parallel to the picture plane that ended up by effacing the objects themselves. In the all-over Pollock and in the de Kooning of the last seven or eight years, analogous planar segments are analogously deployed (smaller in Pollock, larger in de Kooning), with the principal difference being in their articulation or jointing, which is no longer governed by the model in nature. Yet, as I have tried to show, de Kooning's large facet-planes seem to grope for such a model; nor does the indeterminate space created by Pollock's webs and blotches always function as abstract space. Whereas Analytical Cubism had arrived at the brink of outright abstraction by pursuing both art and nature, Abstract Expressionism returned to the verge of nature by pursuing, apparently, art alone. In several of his black and white pictures of 1951 Pollock signalled this return; de Kooning, in his "Women" series of 1952–1955, which marked his real transition from Synthetic to Analytical Cubism, did more than signal it.

Meanwhile another return was being made, though not under the auspices of Abstract Expressionism proper. Analytical Cubism, besides being a case of homeless representation, had embodied a synthesis of the painterly and non-painterly. Synthetic Cubism and Mondrian had dissolved this synthesis in favor of the non-painterly, and Abstract Expressionism, as we have seen, reacted violently in the opposite direction. Just before 1950 something like a new synthesis of painterly and non-painterly began to emerge in New York abstract art, as if to complete its inverted recapitulation of the evolution of original Cubism.

Actually, most of the New York painters first called Abstract Expressionists have not been painterly in a consistent or committed way. This is true even of Hofmann; the best things he has done in recent years, and they are among the best he has ever done, move towards a synthesis of their own in which the painterly is fused with the linear at the same time that Fauvism is fused with Cubism. Kline turned painterly only after 1954, to the cost of his art, as is negatively confirmed by the improvement it showed whenever he reverted, as he frequently did in the last two years or so of his life, to his old sharp-edged manner. Motherwell has been painterly off and on, and several of his masterpieces of the late 1940's were quite so, but most of his successful pictures still tend towards the non-painterly. Gottlieb likewise wavers between the painterly and non-painterly, and though he has done some superb pictures in both manners, his wavering somehow has the effect of making him disloyal to his greatest gift, which is for colour. As regards that gift he would have done well, I feel, to take a hint from the example of three New York painters who stand somewhat apart from Abstract Expressionism. They are Newman, Rothko, and Still, who have renounced painterliness, or at least the painterliness associated with Abstract Expressionism, for the sake, precisely, of a vision keyed to the primacy of colour.

Like so much of painterly art before it, Abstract Expressionism has worked in the end to reduce the role of colour: unequal densities of paint become, as I have said, so many differences of light and dark, and these deprive colour of both its purity and its fullness. At the same time it has also worked against true openness, which is supposed to be another quintessentially painterly aim: the slapdash application of paint ends by crowding the picture plane into a compact jumble—a jumble that is another version, as we see it in de Kooning and his followers, of academically Cubist compactness. Still, Newman, and Rothko turn away from the painterliness of Abstract Expressionism as though to save the objects of painterliness—colour and openness—from painterliness itself. This is why their art could be called a synthesis of painterly and non-painterly or, better, a transcending of the differences between the two. Not a reconciling of these—that belonged to Analytical Cubism, and these three Americans happen to be the first serious abstract painters, the first abstract painters of *style*, really to break with Cubism.

Clyfford Still, who is one of the great innovators of modernist art, is the leader and pioneer here. Setting himself against the immemorial insistence on light and dark contrast, he asserted instead colour's capacity to act through the contrast of pure hues in relative independence of light and dark design. Late Impressionism was the precedent here, and as in the late Monet, the suppression of value contrasts created a new kind of openness. The picture no longer divided itself into shapes or even patches, but into zones and areas and fields of colour. This became essential, but it was left to Newman and Rothko to show how completely so. If Still's largest paintings, and especially his horizontal ones, fail so often to realize the monumental openness they promise, it is not only because he will choose a surface too large for what he has to say; it is also because too many of his smaller colour areas will fail really to function as areas and will remain simply patches—patches whose rustic-Gothic intricacies of outline halt the free flow of colour-space.

With Newman and Rothko, temperaments that might strike one as being natively far more painterly than Still's administer themselves copious antidotes in the form of the rectilinear. The rectilinear is kept ambiguous, however: Rothko fuzzes and melts all his dividing lines; Newman will insert an uneven edge as foil to his ruled ones. Like Still, they make a show of studiedness, as if to demonstrate their rejection of the mannerisms which have become inseparable by now from rapid brush or knife handling. Newman's occasional brushy edge, and the torn but exact one left by Still's knife, are there as if to advertise both their awareness and their repudiation of the easy effects of spontaneity.

Still continues to invest in surface textures, and there is no question but that the tactile irregularities of his surfaces, with their contrasts of matt and shiny, paint coat and priming, contribute to the intensity of his art. But by renouncing tactility, and detail in drawing, Newman and Rothko achieve what I find a more positive openness and colour. The rectilinear is open by definition: it calls the least attention to drawing and gets least in the way of colour-space. A thin paint surface likewise gets least in the way of colour-space, by excluding tactile associations. Here both Rothko and Newman take their lead from Milton Avery, who took his from Matisse. At the same time colour is given more autonomy by being relieved of its localizing and denotative function. It no longer fills in or specifies an area or even plane, but speaks for itself by dissolving all definiteness of shape and distance. To this end—as Still was the first to show—it has to be warm colour, or cool colour infused with warmth. It has also to be uniform in hue, with only the subtlest variations of value if any at all, and spread over an absolutely, not merely relatively, large area. Size guarantees the purity as well as the intensity needed to suggest indeterminate space: more blue simply being bluer than less blue. This too is why the picture has to be confined to so few colours. Here again, Still showed the way, the vision of the two- or three-colour picture, as E. C. Goossen calls it, being his in the first place (whatever help towards it he may have got from the Miró of 1924–1930).

"The rectilinear is kept ambiguous, however: Rothko fuzzes and melts all his dividing lines . . ." Clement Greenberg in "After Abstract Expressionism," p. 433.

But Newman and Rothko stand or fall by colour more obviously than Still does. (Where Newman often fails is in using natively warm colours like red and orange, Rothko in using pale ones, or else in trying to *draw*, as in his disastrous "Seagram" murals.) Yet the ultimate effect sought is one of more than chromatic intensity; it is rather one of an almost literal openness that embraces and absorbs colour in the act of being created by it. Openness, and not only in painting, is the quality that seems most to exhilarate the attuned eyes of our time. Facile explanations suggests themselves here which I leave the reader to explore for himself. Let it suffice to say that by the new openness they have attained Newman, Rothko, and Still point to what I would risk saying is the only way to high pictorial art in the near future. And they also point to that way by their repudiation of virtuosity of execution.

Elsewhere I have written of the kind of self-critical process which I think provides the infra-logic of modernist art ("Modernist Painting" in *Arts Yearbook 4*, 1961). The aim of the selfcriticism, which is entirely empirical and not at all an affair of theory, is to determine the irreducible working essence of art and the separate arts. Under the testing of modernism more and more of the conventions of the art of painting have shown themselves to be dispensable, unessential. By now it has been established, it would seem, that the irreducible essence of pictorial art consists in but two constitutive conventions or norms: flatness and the delimitation of flatness; and that the observance of merely these two norms is enough to create an object which can be experienced as a picture: thus a stretched or tacked-up canvas already exists as a picture—though not necessarily as a *successful* one. (The paradoxical outcome of this reduction has been not to contract, but actually to expand the possibilities of the pictorial: much more than before lends itself now to being experienced pictorially or in meaningful relation to the pictorial: all sorts of large and small items that used to belong entirely to the realm of the arbitrary and the visually meaningless.)

As it seems to me, Newman, Rothko, and Still have swung the self-criticism of modernist painting in a new direction simply by continuing it in its old one. The question now asked through their art is no longer what constitutes art, or the art of painting, as such, but what irreducibly constitutes *good* art as such. Or rather, what is the ultimate source of value or quality in art? And the worked-out answer appears to be: not skill, training, or anything else having to do with execution or performance, but conception alone. Culture or taste may be a necessary condition of conception, but conception is alone decisive. Conception can also be called invention, inspiration, or even intuition (in the usage of Croce, who did anticipate theoretically what practice has just now discovered and confirmed for itself). It is true that skill used to be a vessel of inspiration and do the office of conception, but that was when the best pictorial art was the most naturalistic pictorial art.

Inspiration alone belongs altogether to the individual; everything else, including skill, can now be acquired by any one. Inspiration remains the only factor in the creation of a successful work of art that cannot be copied or imitated. This has been left to artists like Newman and Mondrian to make explicit (and it is really the only thing Newman and Mondrian have in common). Newman's pictures look easy to copy, and maybe they really are. But they are far from easy to conceive, and their quality and meaning lies almost entirely in their conception. That, to me, is self-evident, but even if it were not, the frustrated efforts of Newman's imitators would reveal it. The onlooker who says his child could paint a Newman may be right, but Newman would have to be there to tell the child *exactly* what to do. The *exact* choices of colour, medium, size, shape, proportion—including the size and shape of the support—are what alone determine the quality of the result, and these choices depend solely on inspiration or conception. Like Rothko and Still, Newman happens to be a conventionally skilled artist—need I say it? But if he uses his skill, it is to suppress the evidence of it. And the suppression is part of the triumph of his art, next to which most other contemporary painting begins to look fussy.

It is because of this that the admiration of some of the strongest among the newer or younger American abstract artists goes out to Newman particularly. Newman's rejection of virtuosity confirms them in what they themselves renounce, and it also confirms them in what they dare. It confirms painters like Louis and Noland because, paradoxically enough, they have not been directly influenced by Newman—or, for that matter, by Still or Rothko either. They may pursue a related vision of colour and openness, but they do so all the more resolutely because it is not a derived one. Louis and Noland do not make two- or three-colour pictures, for one thing, and for another, they have been influenced in both vision and means by Pollock more than by any one else. Yet this takes nothing away from Newman, Rothko, or Still, and I stress the point only to clear up misconceptions circulated by journalists and curators. The fact that, so far, the direct influence of these three has been a crushing one, and that the only younger artist who has yet been able to assert himself under it is Sam Francis, may attest, indeed, to the very power of their art.

The crux of the matter of the aftermath of Abstract Expressionism has, in any case, little to do with influence in itself. Where artists divide in the last resort is where safe taste leaves off. And this is as true in what begins to look like the aftermath of Abstract Expressionism as it ever was. The painters who follow Newman, Rothko, or Still, individually or collectively, are as safe by now in their taste as they would be following de Kooning or Gorky or Kline. And I have the impression, anyhow, that some of those who have chosen to do the first, and not the second, have done so because they feel frustrated, *merely* frustrated, by the going versions of Abstract Expressionism in New York.

This applies even more, I feel, to those other artists in this country who have now gone in for "Neo-Dada" (I except Johns), or construction-collage, or ironic comments on the banalities of the industrial environment. Least of all have *they* broken with safe taste. Whatever novel objects they represent or insert in their works, not one of them has taken a chance with colour or design that the Cubists or Abstract Expressionists did not take before them (what happens when a real chance is taken with colour can be seen from the shocked distaste that the "pure" painting of Jules Olitski elicits among New York artists). Nor has any one of them, whether he harpoons stuffed whales to plane surfaces, or fills water-closet bowls with diamonds, yet dared to arrange these things ouside the directional lines of the "all-over" Cubist grid. The results have in every case a conventional and Cubist prettiness that hardly entitles them to be discussed under the heading "After Abstract Expressionism." Nor can those artists, either, be discussed under this heading whose contribution consists in depicting plucked chickens instead of dead pheasants, or coffee cans or pieces of pastry instead of flowers in vases. Not that I do not find the clear and straightforward academic handling of their pictures refreshing after the turgidities of Abstract Expressionism; yet the effect is only momentary, since novelty, as distinct from originality, has no staying power.

Michael Fried

ART AND
OBJECTHOOD

Edwards' journals frequently explored and tested a meditation he seldom
allowed to reach print; if all the world were annihilated, he wrote . . . and
a new world were freshly created, though it were to exist in every particular
in the same manner as this world, it would not be the same. Therefore,
because there is continuity, which is time, "it is certain with me that the
world exists anew every moment; that the existence of things every moment
ceases in is every moment renewed." The abiding assurance it that "we every
moment see the same proof of a God as we should have seen if we had seen
Him create the world at first."

—Perry Miller, Jonathan Edwards

I

The enterprise known variously as Minimal Art, ABC Art, Primary Structures and Specific Objects is largely ideological.* It seeks to declare and
occupy a position—one which can be formulated in words, and in fact
has been formulated by some of its leading practitioners. If this distinguishes it from modernist painting and sculpture on the one hand, it also
marks an important difference between Minimal Art—or, as I prefer to
call it, *literalist* art—and Pop or Op Art on the other. From its inception,
literalist art has amounted to something more than an episode in the
history of taste. It belongs rather to the history—almost the *natural* history
—of sensibility; and it is not an isolated episode but the expression of a
general and pervasive condition. Its seriousness is vouched for by the fact
that it is in relation both to modernist painting and modernist sculpture
that literalist art defines or locates the position it aspires to occupy. (This,
I suggest, is what makes what it declares something that deserves to be

Michael Fried is Professor of Art at Johns Hopkins University. His *Three American
Painters* and numerous critical essays have made him a leading contemporary critic. He
has had a strong influence on philosophical reflections on art in recent years.
* Published in *Art Forum*, June 1967. Reprinted by permission of *Art Forum*. Also
reprinted in *Minimal Art*, edited by Gregory Battcock (New York, 1968), pp. 116–
147.

called a *position*.) Specifically, literalist art conceives of itself as neither one nor the other; on the contrary, it is motivated by specific reservations, or worse, about both; and it aspires, perhaps not exactly, or not immediately, to displace them, but in any case to establish itself as an independent art on a footing with either.

The literalist case against painting rests mainly on two counts: the relational character of almost all painting; and the ubiquitousness, indeed the virtual inescapability, of pictorial illusion. In Donald Judd's view,

> when you start relating parts, in the first place, you're assuming you have a vague whole—the rectangle of the canvas—and definite parts, which is all screwed up, because you should have a definite *whole* and maybe no parts, or very few.[1]

The more the shape of the support is emphasized, as in recent modernist painting, the tighter the situation becomes:

> The elements inside the rectangle are broad and simple and correspond closely to the rectangle. The shapes and surface are only those which can occur plausibly within and on a rectangular plane. The parts are few and so subordinate to unity as not to be parts in an ordinary sense. A painting is nearly an entity, one thing, and not the indefinable sum of a group of entities and references. The one thing overpowers the earlier painting. It also establishes the rectangle as a definite form; it is no longer a fairly neutral limit. A form can be used only in so many ways. The rectangular plane is given a · life span. The simplicity required to emphasize the rectangle limits the arrangements possible within it.

Painting is here seen as an art on the verge of exhaustion, one in which the range of acceptable solutions to a basic problem—how to organize the surface of the picture—is severely restricted. The use of shaped rather than rectangular supports can, from the literalist point of view, merely prolong the agony. The obvious response is to give up working on a single plane in favor of three dimensions. That, moreover, automatically

> gets rid of the problem of illusionism and of literal space, space in and around marks and colors—which is riddance of one of the salient and most objectionable relics of European art. The several limits of painting are no longer present. A work can be as powerful as it can be thought to be. Actual space is intrinsically more powerful and specific than paint on a flat surface.

[1] This was said by Judd in an interview with Bruce Glaser, edited by Lucy R. Lippard and published as "Questions to Stella and Judd," *Art News*, Vol. LXV, No. 5, September 1966. The remarks attributed in the present essay to Judd and Morris have been taken from this interview, from Judd's essay "Specific Objects," *Arts Yearbook*, No. 8, 1965, or from Robert Morris's essays, "Notes on Sculpture" and "Notes on Sculpture, Part 2," published in ARTFORUM, Vol. IV, No. 6, February 1966, and Vol. V, No. 2, October 1966 respectively. (I have also taken one remark by Morris from the catalog to the exhibition "Eight Sculptors: the Ambiguous Image," held at the Walker Art Center, October–December 1966.) I should add that in laying out what seems to me the position Judd and Morris hold in common I have ignored various differences between them, and have used certain remarks in contexts for which they may not have been intended. Moreover, I have not always indicated which of them actually said or wrote a particular phrase; the alternative would have been to litter the text with footnotes.

The literalist attitude toward sculpture is more ambiguous. Judd, for example, seems to think of what he calls Specific Objects as something other than sculpture, while Robert Morris conceives of his own unmistakably literalist work as resuming the lapsed tradition of Constructivist sculpture established by Tatlin, Rodchenko, Gabo, Pevsner and Vantongerloo. But this and other disagreements are less important than the views Judd and Morris hold in common. Above all they are opposed to sculpture which, like most painting, is "made part by part, by addition, composed" and in which "specific elements . . . separate from the whole, thus setting up relationships within the work." (They would include the work of David Smith and Anthony Caro under this description.) It is worth remarking that the "part-by-part" and "relational" character of most sculpture is associated by Judd with what he calls *anthropomorphism:* "A beam thrusts; a piece of iron follows a gesture; together they form a naturalistic and anthropomorphic image. The space corresponds." Against such "multipart, inflected" sculpture Judd and Morris assert the values of wholeness, singleness and indivisibility—of a work's being, as nearly as possible, "one thing," a single "Specific Object." Morris devotes considerable attention to "the use of strong gestalt or of unitary-type forms to avoid divisiveness"; while Judd is chiefly interested in the kind of wholeness that can be achieved through the repetition of identical units. The order at work in his pieces, as he once remarked of that in Stella's stripe paintings, "is simply order, like that of continuity, one thing after another." For both Judd and Morris, however, the critical factor is *shape.* Morris's "unitary forms" are polyhedrons that resist being grasped other than as a single shape: the gestalt simply *is* the "constant, known shape." And shape itself is, in his system, "the most important sculptural value." Similarly, speaking of his own work, Judd has remarked that

> the big problem is that anything that is not absolutely plain begins to have parts in some way. The thing is to be able to work and do different things and yet not break up the wholeness that a piece has. To me the piece with the brass and the five verticals is above all *that shape.*

The shape *is* the object: at any rate what secures the wholeness of the object is the singleness of the shape. It is, I believe, this emphasis on shape that accounts for the impression, which numerous critics have mentioned, that Judd's and Morris's pieces are *hollow.*

II

Shape has also been central to the most important painting of the past several years. In several recent essays[2] I have tried to show how, in the

[2] "Shape as Form: Frank Stella's New Paintings," ARTFORUM, Vol. V, No. 3, November 1966; "Jules Olitski," the catalog introduction to the exhibition of his work currently at the Corcoran Gallery, Washington, D.C.; and "Ronald Davis: Surface and Illusion," ARTFORUM, Vol. V, No. 8, April 1967.

"*The shape is the object: at any rate what secures the wholeness of the object is the singleness of the shape.*" Michael Fried in "Art and Objecthood," p. 440.

work of Noland, Olitski and Stella, a conflict has gradually emerged between shape as a fundamental property of objects and shape as a medium of painting. Roughly, the success or failure of a given painting has come to depend on its ability to hold or stamp itself out or compel conviction as shape—that, or somehow to stave off or elude the question of whether or not it does so. Olitski's early spray paintings are the purest example of paintings that either hold or fail to hold as shapes; while in his more recent pictures, as well as in the best of Noland's and Stella's recent work, the demand that a given picture hold as shape is staved off or eluded in various ways. What is at stake in this is whether the paintings or objects in question are experienced as paintings or as objects: and what decides their identity as *painting* is their confronting of the demand that they hold as shapes. Otherwise they are experienced as nothing more than objects. This can be summed up in the assertion that modernist painting has come to find it imperative that it defeat or suspend its own objecthood, and that the crucial factor in this undertaking is shape, but shape which must belong to *painting*—it must be pictorial, not merely literal. Whereas literalist art stakes everything on shape as a given property of objects, if not, indeed, as a kind of object in its own right. It aspires, not to defeat or suspend its own objecthood, but on the contrary to discover and project objecthood as such.

In his essay *Recentness of Sculpture* Clement Greenberg discusses the effect of *presence* which, from the start, has been associated with literalist work.[3] This comes up in connection with the work of Anne Truitt, an artist Greenberg believes anticipated the literalists (he calls them Minimalists):

> Truitt's art did flirt with the look of non-art, and her 1963 show was the first in which I noticed how this look could confer an effect of *presence*. Truitt's art did flirt with the look of non-art, and her 1963 show was the first in which I noticed how this look could confer an effect of *presence*. That presence as achieved through size was esthetically extraneous, I already knew. That presence as achieved through the look of non-art was likewise esthetically extraneous, I did not yet know. Truitt's sculpture had this kind of presence but did not *hide* behind it. That sculpture could hide behind it—just as painting did—I found out only after repeated acquaintance with Minimal works of art: Judd's, Morris', Andre's, Steiner's, some but not all of Smithson's, some but not all of Lewitt's. Minimal art can also hide behind presence as size: I think of Balden (though I am not sure whether he is a certified Minimalist) as well as of some of the artists just mentioned.

Presence can be conferred by size or by the look of non-art. Furthermore, what non-art means today, and has meant for several years, is fairly specific. In *After Abstract Expressionism* Greenberg wrote that "a stretched

---

[3] Published in the catalog to the Los Angeles County Museum of Art's current exhibition, *American Sculpture of the Sixties*. The verb "project" as I have just used it is taken from Greenberg's statement, "The ostensible aim of the Minimalists is to 'project' objects and ensembles of objects that are just nudgeable into art."

"I have tried to show how, in the work of Noland, Olitski and Stella, a conflict has gradually emerged between shape as a fundamental property of objects and shape as a medium of painting." Michael Fried in "Art and Objecthood," p. 440.

or tacked-up canvas already exists as a picture—though not necessarily as a *successful* one."[4] For that reason, as he remarks in *Recentness of Sculpture*, the "look of non-art was no longer available to painting." Instead, "the borderline between art and non-art had to be sought in the three-dimensional, where sculpture was, and where everything material that was not art also was." Greenberg goes on to say:

> The look of machinery is shunned now because it does not go far enough toward the look of non-art, which is presumably an "inert" look that offers the eye a minimum of "interesting" incident—unlike the machine look,

---

[4] "After Abstract Expressionism," *Art International*, Vol. VI, No. 8, October 25, 1962, p. 30. The passage from which this has been taken reads as follows:

> Under the testing of modernism more and more of the conventions of the art of painting have shown themselves to be dispensable, unessential. By now it has been established, it would seem, that the irreducible essence of pictorial art consists in but two constitutive conventions or norms: flatness and the delimitation of flatness; and that the observance of merely these two norms is enough to create an object which can be experienced as a picture: thus a stretched or tacked-up canvas already exists as a picture—though not necessarily as a successful one.

In its broad outline this is undoubtedly correct. There are, however, certain qualifications that can be made.

To begin with, it is not quite enough to say that a bare canvas tacked to a wall is not "necessarily" a successful picture; it would, I think, be less of an exaggeration to say that it is not *conceivably* one. It may be countered that future circumstances might be such as to *make* it a successful painting; but I would argue that, for that to happen, the enterprise of painting would have to change so drastically that nothing more than the name would remain. (It would require a far greater change than that which painting has undergone from Manet to Noland, Olitski and Stella!) Moreover, seeing something as a painting in the sense that one sees the tacked-up canvas as a painting, and being convinced that a particular work can stand comparison with the painting of the past whose quality is not in doubt, are altogether different experiences: it is, I want to say, as though unless something compels conviction as to its quality it is no more than trivially or nominally a painting. This suggests that flatness and the delimitation of flatness ought not to be thought of as the "irreducible essence of pictorial art" but rather as something like the *minimal conditions for something's being seen as a painting*; and that the crucial question is not what these minimal and, so to speak, timeless conditions are, but rather what, at a given moment, is capable of compelling conviction, of succeeding as painting. This is not to say that painting *has no* essence; it *is* to claim that that essence—*i.e.*, that which inspires conviction—is largely determined by, and therefore changes continually in response to, the vital work of the recent past. The essence of painting is not something irreducible. Rather, the task of the modernist painter is to discover those conventions which, at a given moment, *alone* are capable of establishing his work's identity as painting.

Greenberg approaches this position when he adds, "As it seems to me, Newman, Rothko, and Still have swung the self-criticism of modernist painting in a new direction simply by continuing it in its old one. The question now asked through their art is no longer what constitutes art, or the art of painting, as such, but what irreducibly constitutes *good* art as such. Or rather, what is the ultimate source of value or quality in art?" But I would argue that what modernism has meant is that the two questions —What constitutes the art of painting? And what constitutes *good* painting?—are no longer separable; the first disappears into the second. (I am, of course, taking issue here with the version of modernism put forward in my *Three American Painters*.)

For more on the nature of essence and convention in the modernist arts see my essays on Stella and Olitski mentioned above, as well as Stanley Cavell, *Music Discomposed* and *Rejoinders* to critics of that essay, to be published as part of a symposium by the University of Pittsburgh Press in a volume entitled *Art, Mind and Religion*. Cavell's pieces will also appear in *Must We Mean What We Say?*, a book of his essays to be published in the spring of 1968 by Scribner's.

which is arty by comparison (and when I think of Tinguely I would agree with this). Still, no matter how simple the object may be, there remain the relations and interrelations of surface, contour and spatial interval. Minimal works are readable as art as almost anything is today—including a door, a table, or a blank sheet of paper . . . Yet it would seem that a kind of art nearer the condition of non-art could not be envisaged or ideated at this moment.

The meaning in this context of "the condition of non-art" is what I have been calling objecthood. It is as though objecthood alone can, in the present circumstances, secure something's identity, if not as non-art, at least as neither painting nor sculpture; or as though a work of art—more accurately, a work of modernist painting or sculpture—were in some essential respect *not an object*.

There is, in any case, a sharp contrast between the literalist espousal of objecthood—almost, it seems, as an art in its own right—and modernist painting's self-imposed imperative that it defeat or suspend its own objecthood through the medium of shape. In fact, from the perspective of recent modernist painting, the literalist position evinces a sensibility not simply alien but antithetical to its own: as though, from that perspective, the demands of art and the conditions of objecthood are in direct conflict.

Here the question arises: What is it about objecthood as projected and hypostatized by the literalists that makes it, if only from the perspective of recent modernist painting, antithetical to art?

III

The answer I want to propose is this: the literalist espousal of objecthood amounts to nothing other than a plea for a new genre of theater; and theater is now the negation of art.

Literalist sensibility is theatrical because, to begin with, it is concerned with the actual circumstances in which the beholder encounters literalist work. Morris makes this explicit. Whereas in previous art "what is to be had from the work is located strictly within [it]," the experience of literalist art is of an object *in a situation*—one which, virtually by definition, *includes the beholder:*

> The better new work takes relationships out of the work and makes them a function of space, light, and the viewer's field of vision. The object is but one of the terms in the newer esthetic. It is in some way more reflexive because one's awareness of oneself existing in the same space as the work is stronger than in previous work, with its many internal relationships. One is more aware than before that he himself is establishing relationships as he apprehends the object from various positions and under varying conditions of light and spatial context.

Morris believes that this awareness is heightened by "the strength of the

constant, known shape, the gestalt," against which the appearance of the
piece from different points of view is constantly being compared. It is
intensified also by the large scale of much literalist work:

> The awareness of scale is a function of the comparison made between that
> constant, one's body size, and the object. Space between the subject and
> the object is implied in such a comparison.

The larger the object the more we are forced to keep our distance from it:

> It is this necessary greater distance of the object in space from our bodies,
> in order that it be seen at all, that structures the non-personal or public
> mode [which Morris advocates]. However, it is just this distance between
> object and subject which creates a more extended situation, because physical
> participation becomes necessary.

The theatricality of Morris's notion of the "non-personal or public mode"
seems obvious: the largeness of the piece, in conjunction with its non-
relational, unitary character, *distances* the beholder—not just physically
but psychically. It is, one might say, precisely this distancing that *makes*
the beholder a subject and the piece in question . . . an object. But it
does not follow that the larger the piece the more securely its "public"
character is established; on the contrary "beyond a certain size the object
can overwhelm and the gigantic scale becomes the loaded term." Morris
wants to achieve presence through objecthood, which requires a certain
largeness of scale, rather than through size alone. But he is also aware that
this distinction is anything but hard and fast:

> For the space of the room itself is a structuring factor both in its cubic
> shape and in terms of the kind of compression different sized and propor-
> tioned rooms can effect upon the object-subject terms. That the space of the
> room becomes of such importance does not mean that an environmental
> situation is being established. The total space is hopefully altered in certain
> desired ways by the presence of the object. It is not controlled in the sense
> of being ordered by an aggregate of objects or by some shaping of the space
> surrounding the viewer.

The object, not the beholder, must remain the center or focus of the
situation; but the situation itself *belongs to* the beholder—it is *his* situation. Or as Morris has remarked, "I wish to emphasize that things are
in a space with oneself, rather than . . . [that] one is in a space surrounded by things." Again, there is no clear or hard distinction between
the two states of affairs: one is, after all, *always* surrounded by things. But
the things that are literalist works of art must somehow *confront* the
beholder—they must, one might almost say, be placed not just in his space
but in his way. None of this, Morris maintains,

> indicates a lack of interest in the object itself. But the concerns now are
> for more control of . . . the entire situation. Control is necessary if the
> variables of object, light, space, body, are to function. The object has not
> become less important. It has merely become less self-important.

It is, I think, worth remarking that "the entire situation" means exactly that: *all* of it—including, it seems, the beholder's *body*. There is nothing within his field of vision—nothing that he takes note of in any way—that, as it were, declares its irrelevance to the situation, and therefore to the experience, in question. On the contrary, for something to be perceived at all is for it to be perceived as part of that situation. Everything counts—not as part of the object, but as part of the situation in which its object-hood is established and on which that objecthood at least partly depends.

IV

Furthermore, the presence of literalist art, which Greenberg was the first to analyze, is basically a theatrical effect or quality—a kind of *stage* presence. It is a function, not just of the obtrusiveness and, often, even aggressiveness of literalist work, but of the special complicity which that work extorts from the beholder. Something is said to have presence when it demands that the beholder take it into account, that he take it *seriously* —and when the fulfillment of that demand consists simply in being *aware* of it and, so to speak, in acting accordingly. (Certain modes of seriousness are closed to him by the work itself, *i.e.*, those established by the finest painting and sculpture of the recent past. But, of course, *those* are hardly modes of seriousness in which most people feel at home, or even which they find tolerable.) Here again the experience of being distanced by the work in question seems crucial: the beholder knows himself to stand in an indeterminate, open-ended—and unexacting—relation *as subject* to the impassive object on the wall or floor. In fact, being distanced by such objects is not, I suggest, entirely unlike being distanced, or crowded, by the silent presence of another *person*; the experience of coming upon literalist objects unexpectedly—for example, in somewhat darkened rooms —can be strongly, if momentarily, disquieting in just this way.

There are three main reasons why this is so. First, the size of much literalist work, as Morris's remarks imply, compares fairly closely with that of the human body. In this context Tony Smith's replies to questions about his six-foot cube, *Die*, are highly suggestive:

Q: Why didn't you make it larger so that it would loom over the observer?
A: I was not making a monument.
Q: Then why didn't you make it smaller so that the observer could see over the top?
A: I was not making an object.[5]

One way of describing what Smith *was* making might be something like a surrogate person—that is, a kind of *statue*. (This reading finds support in the caption to a photograph of another of Smith's pieces, *The Black Box*, published in last December's ARTFORUM, in which Samuel Wag-staff, Jr., presumably with the artist's sanction, observed "One can see the

[5] Quoted by Morris as the epigraph to his "Notes on Sculpture, Part 2."

two-by-fours under the piece, which keep it from appearing like architecture or a monument, and set if off as sculpture." The two-by-fours are, in effect, a rudimentary *pedestal*, and thereby reinforce the statue-like quality of the piece.) Second, the entities or beings encountered in everyday experience in terms that most closely approach the literalist ideals of the non-relational, the unitary and the holistic are *other persons*. Similarly, the literalist predilection for symmetry, and in general for a kind of order that "is simply order . . . one thing after another," is rooted, not, as Judd seems to believe, in new philosophical and scientific principles, whatever he takes these to be, but in *nature*. And third, the apparent hollowness of most literalist work—the quality of having an *inside*—is almost blatantly anthropomorphic. It is, as numerous commentators have remarked approvingly, as though the work in question has an inner, even secret, life—an effect that is perhaps made most explicit in Morris's *Untitled* (1965–66), a large ring-like form in two halves, with fluorescent light glowing from within at the narrow gap between the two. In the same spirit Tony Smith has said, "I'm interested in the inscrutability and mysteriousness of the thing."[6] He has also been quoted as saying:

> More and more I've become interested in pneumatic structures. In these, all of the material is in tension. But it is the character of the form which appeals to me. The biomorphic forms which result from the construction have a dream-like quality for me, at least like what is said to be a fairly common type of American dream.

Smith's interest in pneumatic structures may seem surprising, but it is consistent both with his own work and with literalist sensibility generally. Pneumatic structures can be described as hollow with a vengeance—the fact that they are not "obdurate, solid masses" (Morris) being *insisted on* instead of taken for granted. That the forms which result are "biomorphic" reveals something, I think, about what hollowness means in literalist art.

V

I am suggesting, then, that a kind of latent or hidden naturalism, indeed anthropomorphism, lies at the core of literalist theory and practice. The concept of presence all but says as much, though rarely so nakedly as in Tony Smith's statement, "I didn't think of them [*i.e.*, the sculptures he "always" made] as sculptures but as presences of a sort." The latency or hiddenness of the anthropomorphism has been such that the literalists themselves have, as we have seen, felt free to characterize the modernist art they *oppose*, e.g., the sculpture of David Smith and Anthony Caro, as anthropomorphic—a characterization whose teeth, imaginary to begin

---

[6] Except for the Morris epigraph already quoted, all statements by Tony Smith have been taken from Samuel Wagstaff, Jr.'s, "Talking to Tony Smith," ARTFORUM, Vol. V, No. 4, December 1966.

with, have just been pulled. By the same token, however, what is wrong with literalist work is not that it is anthropomorphic but that the meaning and, equally, the hiddenness of its anthropomorphism are incurably theatrical. (Not all literalist art hides or masks its anthropomorphism; the work of lesser figures like Steiner wears it on its sleeve.) *The crucial distinction that I am proposing so far is between work that is fundamentally theatrical and work that is not.* It is theatricality which, whatever the differences between them, links artists like Bladen and Grosvenor,[7] both of whom have allowed "gigantic scale [to become] the loaded term" (Morris), with other, more restrained figures like Judd, Morris, Andre, McCracken, LeWitt and—despite the *size* of some of his pieces—Tony Smith.[8] And it is in the interest, though not explicitly in the *name*, of theater that literalist ideology rejects both modernist painting and, at least in the hands of its most distinguished recent practitioners, modernist sculpture.

In this connection Tony Smith's description of a car ride taken at night on the New Jersey Turnpike before it was finished makes compelling reading:

When I was teaching at Cooper Union in the first year or two of the fifties, someone told me how I could get on to the unfinished New Jersey Turnpike. I took three students and drove from somewhere in the Meadows to New Brunswick. It was a dark night and there were no lights or shoulder markers, lines, railings, or anything at all except the dark pavement moving through the landscape of the flats, rimmed by hills in the distance, but punctuated by stacks, towers, fumes, and colored lights. This drive was a revealing experience. The road and much of the landscape was artificial, and yet it couldn't be called a work of art. On the other hand, it did something for me that art had never done. At first I didn't know what it was, but its effect was to liberate me from many of the views I had had about art. It seemed that there had been a reality there which had not had any expression in art.

The experience on the road was something mapped out but not socially recognized. I thought to myself, it ought to be clear that's the end of art. Most painting looks pretty pictorial after that. There is no way you can frame it, you just have to experience it. Later I discovered some abandoned airstrips in Europe—abandoned works, Surrealist landscapes, something that had nothing to do with any function, created worlds without tradition. Artificial landscape without cultural precedent began to dawn on me. There is a drill ground in Nuremberg large enough to accommodate two million men. The entire field is enclosed with high embankments and towers. The concrete approach is three sixteen-inch steps, one above the other, stretching for a mile or so.

---

[7] In the catalog to last spring's *Primary Structures* exhibition at the Jewish Museum, Bladen wrote, "How do you make the inside the outside?", and Grosvenor, "I don't want my work to be thought of as 'large sculpture,' they are ideas which operate in the space between floor and ceiling." The relevance of these statements to what I have adduced as evidence for the theatricality of literalist theory and practice seems obvious.

[8] It is theatricality, too, that links all these artists to other figures as disparate as Kaprow, Cornell, Rauschenberg, Oldenburg, Kienholz, Segal, Samaras, Christo, Kusama . . . the list could go on indefinitely.

What seems to have been revealed to Smith that night was the pictorial nature of painting—even, one might say, the conventional nature of art. And *this* Smith seems to have understood, not as laying bare the essence of art, but as announcing its end. In comparison with the unmarked, unlit, all but unstructured turnpike—more precisely, with the turnpike as experienced from within the car, travelling on it—art appears to have struck Smith as almost absurdly small ("All art today is an art of postage stamps," he has said), circumscribed, conventional . . . There was, he seems to have felt, no way to "frame" his experience on the road, that is, no way to make sense of it in terms of art, to make *art* of it, at least as art then was. Rather, "you just have to experience it"—as it *happens,* as it merely *is.* (The experience *alone* is what matters.) There is no suggestion that this is problematic in any way. The experience is clearly regarded by Smith as wholly accessible to everyone, not just in principle but in fact, and the question of whether or not one has really *had* it does not arise. That this appeals to Smith can be seen from his praise of Corbusier as "more available" than Michelangelo: "The direct and primitive experience of the High Court Building at Chandigahr is like the Pueblos of the South-west under a fantastic overhanging cliff. It's something everyone can understand." It is, I think, hardly necessary to add that the availability of modernist art is not of this kind, and that the rightness or relevance of one's conviction about specific modernist works, a conviction that begins and ends in one's experience of the work itself, is always open to question.

But what *was* Smith's experience on the turnpike? Or to put the same question another way, if the turnpike, airstrips and drill ground are not works of art, what *are* they? What, indeed, if not empty, or "abandoned," *situations?* And what was Smith's experience if not the experience of what I have been calling *theater?* It is as though the turnpike, airstrips and drill ground reveal the theatrical character of literalist art, only without the object, that is, *without the art itself*—as though the object is needed only within a *room*[9] (or, perhaps, in any circumstances less extreme than these). In each of the above cases the object is, so to speak, *replaced* by something: for example, on the turnpike by the constant onrush of the road, the simultaneous recession of new reaches of dark pavement illumined by the onrushing headlights, the sense of the turnpike itself as something enormous, abandoned, derelict, existing for Smith alone and for those in the car with him . . . This last point is important. On the one hand, the turnpike, airstrips and drill ground belong to no one; on the other, the situation established by Smith's presence is in each case felt by him to be *his.* Moreover, in each case being able to go on and on indefinitely is of the essence. What replaces the object—what does the same job of distancing or isolating the beholder, of making him a subject, that the object did in the closed room—is above all the endlessness, or

---

[9] The concept of a room is, mostly clandestinely, important to literalist art and theory. In fact, it can often be substituted for the word "space" in the latter: something is in my space if it is in the same *room* with me (and if it is placed so that I can hardly fail to notice it).

objectlessness, of the approach or onrush or perspective. It is the explicitness, that is to say, the sheer persistence, with which the experience presents itself as directed at him from outside (on the turnpike from outside the *car*) that simultaneously makes him a subject—makes him subject—and establishes the experience itself as something like that of an object, or rather, of objecthood. No wonder Morris's speculations about how to put literalist work outdoors remain strangely inconclusive:

> Why not put the work outdoors and further change the terms? A real need exists to allow this next step to become practical. Architecturally designed sculpture courts are not the answer nor is the placement of work outside cubic architectural forms. Ideally, it is a space without architecture as background and reference, that would give different terms to work with.

Unless the pieces are set down in a wholly natural context, and Morris does not seem to be advocating this, some sort of artificial but not quite architectural setting must be constructed. What Smith's remarks seem to suggest is that the more effective—meaning effective as *theater*—the setting is made, the more superfluous the works themselves become.

VI

Smith's account of his experience on the turnpike bears witness to theater's profound hostility to the arts, and discloses, precisely in the absence of the object and in what takes its place, what might be called the theatricality of objecthood. By the same token, however, the imperative that modernist painting defeat or suspend its objecthood is at bottom the imperative that it *defeat or suspend theater*. And *this* means that there is a war going on between theater and modernist painting, between the theatrical and the pictorial—a war which, despite the literalists' explicit rejection of modernist painting and sculpture, is not basically a matter of program and ideology but of experience, conviction, sensibility. (For example, it was a particular experience that *engendered* Smith's conviction that painting—in fact, that the arts as such—were finished.)

The starkness and apparent irreconcilability of this conflict is something new. I remarked earlier that objecthood has become an issue for modernist painting only within the past several years. This, however, is not to say that *before* the present situation came into being, paintings, or sculptures for that matter, simply were *objects*. It would, I think, be closer to the truth to say that they *simply* were not.[10] The risk, even the possibility,

---

[10] Stanley Cavell has remarked in seminar that for Kant in the *Critique of Judgment* a work of art is not an object. I will take this opportunity to acknowledge the fact that without innumerable conversations with Cavell during the past few years, and without what I have learned from him in courses and seminars, the present essay—and not it alone—would have been inconceivable. I want also to express my gratitude and indebtedness to the composer John Harbison, who, together with his wife, the violinist Rosemary Harbison, have given me whatever initiation into modern music I have had, both for that initiation and for numerous insights bearing on the subject of this essay.

of seeing works of art as *nothing more* than objects did not exist. That this possibility began to present itself around 1960 was largely the result of developments within modernist painting. Roughly, the more nearly assimilable to objects certain advanced painting had come to seem, the more the entire history of painting since Manet could be understood— delusively, I believe—as consisting in the progressive (though ultimately inadequate) revelation of its essential objecthood,[11] and the more urgent became the need for modernist painting to make explicit its conventional —specifically, its *pictorial*—essence by defeating or suspending its own objecthood through the medium of shape. The view of modernist painting as tending toward objecthood is implict in Judd's remark, "The new [*i.e.,* literalist] work obviously resembles sculpture more than it does painting, but it is nearer to painting"; and it is in this view that literalist sensibility in general is grounded. Literalist sensibility is, therefore, a response to the *same* developments that have largely compelled modernist painting to undo its objecthood—more precisely, the same developments *seen differently,* that is, in theatrical terms, by a sensibility *already* theatrical, already (to say the worst) corrupted or perverted by theater. Similarly, what has compelled modernist painting to defeat or suspend its own objecthood is not just developments internal to itself, but the same general, enveloping, infectious theatricality that corrupted literalist sensibility in the first place and in the grip of which the developments in question—and modernist painting in general—are seen as nothing more than an uncompelling and presenceless kind of theater. It was the need to break the fingers of this grip that made objecthood an issue for modernist painting.

Objecthood has also become an issue for modernist sculpture. This is true despite the fact that sculpture, being three-dimensional, resembles both ordinary objects and literalist work in a way that painting does not. Almost ten years ago Clement Greenberg summed up what he saw as the emergence of a new sculptural "style," whose master is undoubtedly David Smith, in the following terms:

> To render substance entirely optical, and form, whether pictorial, sculptural or architectural, as an integral part of ambient space—this brings anti-illusionism full circle. Instead of the illusion of things, we are now offered the illusion of modalities: namely, that matter is incorporeal, weightless and exists only optically like a mirage.[12]

Since 1960 this development has been carried to a succession of climaxes by the English sculptor Anthony Caro, whose work is far more *specifically*

---

[11] One way of describing this view might be to say that it draws something like a false inference from the fact that the increasingly explicit acknowledgment of the literal character of the support has been central to the development of modernist painting: namely, that literalness *as such* is an artistic value of supreme importance. In "Shape as Form" I argued that this inference is blind to certain vital considerations; and implied that literalness—more precisely, the literalness of the support—is a value only *within* modernist painting, and then only because it has been *made* one by the history of that enterprise.

[12] "The New Sculpture," *Art and Culture*, Boston, 1961, p. 144.

resistant to being seen in terms of objecthood than that of David Smith. A characteristic sculpture by Caro consists, I want to say, in the mutual and naked *juxtaposition* of the I-beams, girders, cylinders, lengths of piping, sheet metal and grill which it comprises rather than in the compound *object* which they compose. The mutual inflection of one element by another, rather than the identity of each, is what is crucial—though of course altering the identity of any element would be at least as drastic as altering its placement. (The identity of each element matters is somewhat the same way as the fact that it is an *arm*, or *this* arm, that makes a particular gesture; or as the fact that it is *this* word or *this* note and not another that occurs in a particular place in a sentence or melody.) The individual elements bestow significance on one another precisely by virtue of their juxtaposition: it is in this sense, a sense inextricably involved with the concept of meaning, that everything in Caro's art that is worth looking at is in its syntax. Caro's concentration upon syntax amounts, in Greenberg's view, to "an emphasis on abstractness, on radical unlikeness to nature."[13] And Greenberg goes on to remark, "No other sculptor has gone as far from the structural logic of ordinary ponderable things." It is worth emphasizing, however, that this is a function of more than the lowness, openness, part-by-partness, absence of enclosing profiles and centers of interest, unperspicuousness, etc., etc., of Caro's sculptures. Rather they defeat, or allay, objecthood by imitating, not gestures exactly, but the *efficacy* of gesture; like certain music and poetry, they are possessed by the knowledge of the human body and how, in innumerable ways and moods, it makes meaning. It is as though Caro's sculptures essentialize meaningfulness *as such*—as though the possibility of meaning what we say and do *alone* makes his sculpture possible. All this, it is hardly necessary to add, makes Caro's art a fountainhead of anti-literalist and anti-theatrical sensibility.

There is another, more general respect in which objecthood has become an issue for the most ambitious recent modernist sculpture and that is in regard to *color*. This is a large and difficult subject which I cannot hope to do more than touch on here.[14] Briefly, however, color has become problematic for modernist sculpture, not because one senses that it has been *applied*, but because the color of a given sculpture, whether applied or the natural state of the material, is identical with its surface; and inasmuch as all objects have surface, awareness of the sculpture's surface implies its objecthood—thereby threatening to qualify or mitigate the

---

[13] This and the following remark are taken from Greenberg's essay, "Anthony Caro," *Arts Yearbook*, No. 8, 1965. Caro's first step in this direction, the elimination of the pedestal, seems in retrospect to have been motivated not by the desire to present his work without artificial aids so much as by the need to undermine its objecthood. His work has revealed the extent to which merely putting something on a pedestal *confirms* its objecthood; though merely removing the pedestal does not in itself undermine objecthood, as literalist work proves.

[14] See Greenberg's "Anthony Caro" and the last section of my "Shape as Form" for more, though not a great deal more, about color in sculpture.

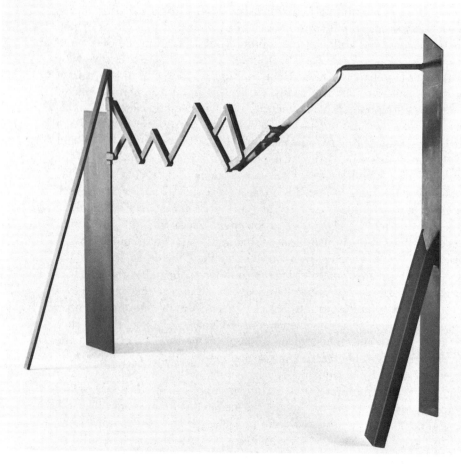

". . . everything in Caro's art that is worth looking at is in its syntax."
Michael Fried in "Art and Objecthood," p. 453.

undermining of objecthood achieved by opticality and, in Caro's pieces, by their syntax as well. It is in this connection, I believe, that a very recent sculpture, *Bunga*, by Jules Olitski ought to be seen. *Bunga* consists of between fifteen and twenty metal tubes, ten feet long and of various diameters, placed upright, riveted together and then sprayed with paint of different colors; the dominant hue is yellow and yellow-orange, but the top and "rear" of the piece are suffused with a deep rose, and close looking reveals as well flecks and even thin trickles of green and red. A rather wide red band has been painted around the top of the piece, while a much thinner band in two different blues (one at the "front" and another at the "rear") circumscribes the very bottom. Obviously, *Bunga* relates intimately to Olitski's spray paintings, especially those of the past year or so in which he has worked with paint and brush at or near the limits of the support. At the same time, it amounts to something far more than an attempt simply to make or "translate" his paintings into sculptures, namely, an attempt to establish surface—the surface, so to speak, of *painting*—as a medium of sculpture. The use of tubes, each of which one sees, incredibly, as *flat*—that is, flat but *rolled*—makes *Bunga's* surface more like that of a painting than like that of an object: like painting, and unlike both ordinary objects and other sculpture, *Bunga* is *all* surface. And of course what declares or establishes that surface is color, Olitski's sprayed color.

VII

At this point I want to make a claim which I cannot hope to prove or substantiate but which nevertheless I believe to be true: *viz.*, that theater and theatricality are at war today, not simply with modernist painting (or modernist painting and sculpture), but with art as such—and to the extent that the different arts can be described as modernist, with modernist sensibility as such. This claim can be broken down into three propositions or theses:

1. *The success, even the survival, of the arts has come increasingly to depend on their ability to defeat theater.* This is perhaps nowhere more evident than within theater itself, where the need to defeat what I have been calling theater has chiefly made itself felt as the need to establish a drastically different relation to its audience. (The relevant texts are, of course, Brecht and Artaud.)[15] For theater *has* an audience—it *exists* for

---

[15] The need to achieve a new relation to the spectator which Brecht felt and which he discussed time and again in his writings on theater was not simply the result of his Marxism. On the contrary, his discovery of Marx seems to have been in part the discovery of what this relation might be like, what it might mean: "When I read Marx's *Capital* I understood my plays. Naturally I want to see this book widely circulated. It wasn't of course that I found I had unconsciously written a whole pile of Marxist plays; but this man Marx was the only spectator for my plays I'd ever come across." (*Brecht on Theater*, edited and translated by John Willett, New York, 1964.) In this general connection see Stanley Cavell's essay on Beckett's *End-Game*, "Ending the Waiting Game," to be published in *Must We Mean What We Say?*

one—in a way the other arts do not; in fact, this more than anything else is what modernist sensibility finds intolerable in theater generally. Here it should be remarked that literalist art, too, possesses an audience, though a somewhat special one: that the beholder is confronted by literalist work within a situation which he experiences as *his* means that there is an important sense in which the work in question exists for him *alone*, even if he is not actually alone with the work at the time. It may seem paradoxical to claim both that literalist sensibility aspires to an ideal of "something everyone can understand" (Smith) *and* that literalist art addresses itself to the beholder alone, but the paradox is only apparent. Someone has merely to enter the room in which a literalist work has been placed to *become* that beholder, that audience of one—almost as though the work in question has been *waiting for* him. And inasmuch as literalist work *depends on* the beholder, is *incomplete* without him, it *has* been. And once he is in the room the work refuses, obstinately, to let him alone—which is to say, it refuses to stop confronting him, distancing him, isolating him. (Such isolation is not solitude any more than such confrontation is communion.)

It is the overcoming of theater which modernist sensibility finds most exalting and which it experiences as the hallmark of high art in our time. There is, however, one art which, by its very nature, *escapes* theater entirely—the movies.[16] This helps explain why movies in general, including frankly appalling ones, are acceptable to modernist sensibility whereas all but the most successful painting, sculpture, music and poetry is not. Because cinema escapes theater—automatically, as it were—it provides a welcome and absorbing refuge to sensibilities at war with theater and theatricality. At the same time, the automatic, guaranteed character of the refuge—more accurately, the fact that what is provided is a refuge from theater and not a triumph over it, absorption not conviction—means that the cinema, even at its most experimental, is not a *modernist* art.

2. *Art degenerates as it approaches the condition of theater.* Theater is the common denominator that binds a large and seemingly disparate variety of activities to one another, and which distinguishes those activities from the radically different enterprises of the modernist arts. Here as elsewhere the question of value or level is central. For example, a failure to register the enormous difference in quality between, say, the music of Carter and that of Cage or between the paintings of Louis and those of Rauschenberg means that the real distinctions—between music and theater in the first instance and between painting and theater in the

---

[16] Exactly how the movies escape theater is a beautiful question, and there is no doubt that a phenomenology of the cinema that concentrated on the similarities and differences between it and the theater—e.g., that in the movies the actors are not physically present, the film itself is projected away from us, the screen is not experienced as a kind of object existing, so to speak, in a specific physical relation to us, etc.—would be extremely rewarding. Cavell, again, has called attention, in conversation, to the sort of *remembering* that goes into giving an account of a movie, and more generally to the particular difficulties involved in giving such an account.

second—are displaced by the illusion that the barriers between the arts
are in the process of crumbling (Cage and Rauschenberg being seen, correctly, as similar) and that the arts themselves are at last sliding toward
some kind of final, implosive, hugely desirable synthesis.[17] Whereas in
fact the individual arts have never been more explicitly concerned with
the conventions that constitute their respective essences.

3. *The concepts of quality and value—and to the extent that these are
central to art, the concept of art itself—are meaningful, or wholly meaningful, only* within the *individual arts. What lies* between the *arts is theater.*
It is, I think, significant that in their various statements the literalists have
largely avoided the issue of value or quality at the same time as they have
shown considerable uncertainty as to whether or not what they are making
is art. To describe their enterprise as an attempt to establish a *new* art
does not remove the uncertainty; at most it points to its source. Judd himself has as much as acknowledged the problematic character of the literalist
enterprise by his claim, "A work needs only to be interesting." For Judd,
as for literalist sensibility generally, all that matters is whether or not
a given work is able to elicit and sustain (his) *interest.* Whereas within
the modernist arts nothing short of *conviction*—specifically, the conviction
that a particular painting or sculpture or poem or piece of music can or
cannot support comparison with past work within that art whose quality
is not in doubt—matters at all. (Literalist work is often condemned—when
it *is* condemned— for being boring. A tougher charge would be that it is
merely interesting.)

The interest of a given work resides, in Judd's view, both in its character
as a whole and in the sheer *specificity* of the materials of which it is made:

> Most of the work involves new materials, either recent inventions or things
> not used before in art . . . Materials vary greatly and are simply materials
> —formica, aluminum, cold-rolled steel, plexiglas, red and common brass, and
> so forth. They are specific. If they are used directly, they are more specific.
> Also, they are usually aggressive. There is an objectivity to the obdurate
> identity of a material.

[17] This is the view of Susan Sontag, whose various essays, collected in *Against Interpretation,* amount to perhaps the purest—certainly the most egregious—expression of
what I have been calling theatrical sensibility in recent criticism. In this sense they
are indeed the "case studies for an esthetic, a theory of my own sensibility" that she
takes them to be. In a characteristic passage Miss Sontag contends:

> Art today is a new kind of instrument, an instrument for modifying conscious-
> ness and organizing new modes of sensibility. And the means for practicing art
> have been radically extended . . . Painters no longer feel themselves confined
> to canvas and paint, but employ hair, photographs, wax, sand, bicycle tires, their
> own toothbrushes and socks . . . All kinds of conventionally accepted bound-
> aries have thereby been challenged: not just the one between the "scientific" and
> the "literary-artistic" cultures, or the one between "art" and "non-art"; but also
> many established distinctions within the world of culture itself—that between
> form and content, the frivolous and the serious, and (a favorite of literary in-
> tellectuals) "high" and "low" culture. (pp. 296–97).

The truth is that the distinction between the frivolous and the serious becomes more
urgent, even absolute, every day, and the enterprises of the modernist arts more
purely motivated by the felt need to perpetuate the standards and values of the high
art of the past.

Like the shape of the object, the materials do not represent, signify or allude to anything; they are what they are and nothing more. And what they are is not, strictly speaking, something that is grasped or intuited or recognized or even seen once and for all. Rather, the "obdurate identity" of a specific material, like the wholeness of the shape, is simply stated or given or established at the very outset, if not before the outset; accordingly, the experience of both is one of endlessness, of inexhaustibility, of being able to go on and on letting, for example, the material itself confront one in all its literalness, its "objectivity," its absence of anything beyond itself. In a similar vein Morris has written:

> Characteristic of a gestalt is that once it is established all the information about it, qua gestalt, is exhausted. (One does not, for example, seek the gestalt of a gestalt.) . . . One is then both free of the shape and bound to it. Free or released because of the exhaustion of information about it, as shape, and bound to it because it remains constant and indivisible.

The same note is struck by Tony Smith in a statement, the first sentence of which I quoted earlier:

> I'm interested in the inscrutability and mysteriousness of the thing. Something obvious on the face of it (like a washing machine or a pump), is of no further interest. A Bennington earthenware jar, for instance, has subtlety of color, largeness of form, a general suggestion of substance, generosity, is calm and reassuring—qualities which take it beyond pure utility. It continues to nourish us time and time again. We can't see it in a second, we continue to read it. There is something absurd in the fact that you can go back to a cube in the same way.

Like Judd's Specific Objects and Morris's gestalts or unitary forms, Smith's cube is *always* of further interest; one never feels that one has come to the end of it; it is inexhaustible. It is inexhaustible, however, not because of any fullness—*that* is the inexhaustibility of art—but because there is nothing there to exhaust. It is endless the way a road might be: if it were circular, for example.

Endlessness, being able to go on and on, even having to go on and on, is central both to the concept of interest and to that of objecthood. In fact, it seems to be the experience that most deeply excites literalist sensibility, and which literalist artists seek to objectify in their work. Smith's account of his experience on the unfinished turnpike is a case in point. Similarly, Morris's claim that in the best new work the beholder is made aware that "he himself is establishing relationships as he apprehends the object from various positions and under varying conditions of light and spatial context" amounts to the claim that the beholder is made aware of the endlessness and inexhaustibility if not of the object itself at any rate of his experience of it. This awareness is further exacerbated by what might be called the *inclusiveness* of his situation, that is, by the fact, remarked earlier, that everything he observes counts as part of the situation and hence is felt to bear in some way that remains undefined on his experience of the object.

Here finally I want to emphasize something that may already have become clear: the experience in question *persists in time*, and the presentment of endlessness which, I have been claiming, is central to literalist art and theory is essentially a presentment of endless, or indefinite, *duration*. Once again Smith's account of his night drive is relevant, as well as his remark, "We can't see it [*i.e.*, the jar and, by implication, the cube] in a second, we continue to read it." Morris, too, has stated explicitly "The experience of the work necessarily exists in time"—though it would make no difference if he had not. The literalist preoccupation with time—more precisely, with the *duration of the experience*—is, I suggest, paradigmatically theatrical: as though theater confronts the beholder, and thereby isolates him, with the endlessness not just of objecthood but of *time*; or as though the sense which, at bottom, theater addresses is a sense of temporality, of time both passing and to come, *simultaneously approaching and receding*, as if apprehended in an infinite perspective . . .[18] This preoccupation marks a profound difference between literalist work and modernist painting and sculpture. It is as though one's experience of the latter *has no* duration—not because one *in fact* experiences a picture by Noland or Olitski or a sculpture by David Smith or Caro in no time at all, but because *at every moment the work itself is wholly manifest*. (This is true of sculpture despite the obvious fact that, being three-dimensional, it can be seen from an infinite number of points of view. One's experience of a Caro is not incomplete, and one's conviction as to its quality is not suspended, simply because one has seen it only from where one is standing. Moreover, in the grip of his best work one's view of the sculpture is, so to speak, *eclipsed* by the sculpture itself—which it is plainly meaningless to speak of as only *partly* present.) It is this continuous and entire presentness, amounting, as it were, to the perpetual creation of itself, that one experiences as a kind of *instantaneousness*: as though if only one were infinitely more acute, a single infinitely brief instant would be long enough

---

[18] The connection between spatial recession and some such experience of temporality— almost as if the first were a kind of natural metaphor for the second—is present in much Surrealist painting (e.g., De Chirico, Dali, Tanguy, Magritte). Moreover, temporality—manifested, for example, as expectation, dread, anxiety, presentiment, memory, nostalgia, stasis—is often the explicit subject of their paintings. There is, in fact, a deep affinity between literalist and Surrealist sensibility (at any rate, as the latter makes itself felt in the work of the above painters) which ought to be noted. Both employ imagery which is at once holistic and, in a sense fragmentary, incomplete; both resort to a similar anthropormorphizing of objects or conglomerations of objects (in Surrealism the use of dolls and mannikins makes this explicit); both are capable of achieving remarkable effects of "presence"; and both tend to deploy, and isolate, objects and persons in *situations*—the closed room and the abandoned artificial landscape are as important to Surrealism as to literalism. (Tony Smith, it will be recalled, described the airstrips, etc., as "Surrealist landscapes.") This can be summed up by saying that Surrealist sensibility, as manifested in the work of certain artists, and literalist sensibility are both *theatrical*. I do not wish, however, to be understood as saying that because they are theatrical, all Surrealist works which share the above characteristics fail as art; a conspicuous example of major work that can be described in those terms is Giacometti's Surrealist sculptures. On the other hand, it is perhaps not without significance that Smith's supreme example of a Surrealist landscape was the parade ground at Nuremberg.

to see everything, to experinece the work in all its depth and fullness, to be forever convinced by it. (Here it is worth noting that the concept of interest implies temporality in the form of continuing attention directed at the object, whereas the concept of conviction does not.) I want to claim that it is by virtue of their presentness and instantaneousness that modernist painting and sculpture defeat theater. In fact, I am tempted far beyond my knowledge to suggest that, faced with the need to defeat theater, it is above all to the condition of painting and sculpture—the condition, that is, of existing in, indeed of secreting or constituting, a continuous and perpetual *present*—that the other contemporary modernist art, most notably poetry and music, aspire.[19]

VIII

This essay will be read as an attack on certain artists (and critics) and as a defense of others. And of course it is true that the desire to distinguish between what is to me the authentic art of our time and other work which, whatever the dedication, passion and intelligence of its creators, seems to me to share certain characteristics associated here with the concepts of literalism and theater, has specifically motivated what I have written. More generally, however, I have wanted to call attention to the utter pervasiveness—the virtual universality—of the sensibility or mode of being which I have characterized as corrupted or perverted by theater. We are all literalists most or all of our lives. Presentness is grace.

---

[19] What this means in each art will naturally be different. Music is in perhaps the most difficult situation, being compelled to engage with and, hopefully, to defeat theater on what has become theater's home grounds and almost exclusive property, *time*. Besides, the physical circumstances of a concert closely resemble those of a theatrial performance. It may have been the desire for something like presentness that, at least to some extent, led Brecht to advocate a non-illusionistic theater, in which the actors would not identify with the characters they play but rather would show them forth, and in which temporality itself would be presented in a new light:

> Just as the actor no longer has to persuade the audience that it is the author's character and not himself that is standing on the stage, so also he need not pretend that the events taking place on the stage have never been rehearsed, and are now happening for the first and only time. Schiller's distinction is no longer valid: that the rhapsodist has to treat his material as wholly in the past: the mime his, as wholly here and now. It should be apparent all through his performance that 'even at the start and in the middle he knows how it ends' and he must 'thus maintain a calm independence throughout.' He narrates the story of his character by vivid portrayal, always knowing more than it does and treating 'now' and 'here' not as a pretense made possible by the rules of the game but as something to be distinguished from yesterday and some other place, so as to make visible the knotting together of the events. (p. 194)

What remains unclear, however, is whether the handling of time Brecht calls for is tantamount to authentic presentness, or merely to what I have been calling presence —*i.e.*, to the presentment of time itself as though it were a kind of literalist object. In poetry the need for presentness manifests itself in the lyric poem; this is a subject which requires its own treatment.

For a disiussion of time in the theater see Stanley Cavell, "The Avoidance of Love: A Reading of King Lear," to be published in *Must We Mean What We Say?*

David Carrier

GREENBERG, FRIED, AND PHILOSOPHY: AMERICAN-TYPE FORMALISM

Clement Greenberg* has said, "I conceive of Kant as the first real modernist."[1] I believe that Greenberg had the following Kantian points in mind when he said (1) the aesthetic is a distinct sort of experience, based upon feeling, not taste as intellectual comprehension; (2) the aesthetic is an experience of formal values of the artwork; (3) these formal values suggest aesthetic ideas; and (4) the aesthetic experience is either of the beautiful or the sublime.[2] Both Greenberg and Michael Fried see their formalist aesthetics as deriving from Kant's philosophy. Within Kant's philosophy, however, little is said about how this theory could be used as an account of what happens when we see a painting, or how the theory might be used as a basis for art criticism. Greenberg and Fried develop Kant's theory in both of these directions. In this essay, my primary aim is to give an exposition of the Greenberg-Fried theory of the plastic arts. In the last section I consider certain criticisms of their formalist approach to art.

I

"The arts" could only "save themselves" from being "assimilated to entertainment . . . by showing that the kind of experience they provided was valuable in its own right and not to be obtained from any other kind of activity."[3] In this passage Greenberg not only endorses the general Kantian point about the distinctiveness of the aesthetic, he suggests a

David Carrier is Assistant Professor of Philosophy at Carnegie-Mellon University. Carrier researches in aesthetics and is particularly interested in recent movements in the arts and in art criticism.

* This essay was written for this collection and is published here for the first time.

[1] Greenberg, "Modernist Painting," *Arts Yearbook*, 4 (1961), 103.
[2] On Kant, I have found the following helpful: Donald W. Crawford, *Kant's Aesthetic Theory* (Madison, Wisc.: Univ. of Wisconsin, 1974); Michael Podro, *The Manifold in Perception* (Oxford: Clarendon, 1972); and Richard Kuhns, "That Kant Did Not Complete His Argument Concerning the Relation of Art to Morality and How It Might Be Completed," *Idealistic Studies*, 52 (1975), 190–206.
[3] Clement Greenberg, *Art and Culture* (Boston: Beacon, 1961), p. 133.

certain analysis of the evolution of "modernist" painting as well (by modernist painting, Greenberg has in mind painting since Manet). He applies this analysis to post-World War II visual art in particular.

Greenberg finds two sources for developments in American painting since 1945. First, Cezanne's concern to produce, in his reaction to impressionism, a picture space of solidly constructed forms, a world of forms as solidly holding as Poussin's.[4] Second, Monet's attempt, working out of a tradition going back to Turner, to use large color masses with relatively unemphasized value contrasts.[5] Both Cezanne and Monet aimed at depicting nature accurately. Ironically, the result of their efforts to be true to nature was to lead painting toward abstractness, for Cezanne's use of small color planes to suggest volume as well as Monet's large, barely differentiated masses of color drew attention to the surface of the canvas itself. Cezanne's work led "to the skeleton of traditional painting," whereas Monet's led to "the shadow of one."[6] Previously one looked through the painting's surface "into a stage. Modernism . . . rendered this stage shallower . . . until now its backdrop has become the same as its curtain, which has . . . become all the painter has left to work on."[7] The picture space has become so shallow as to not be able to "contain" any represented objects.

The cubists drew out the implications of Cezanne's work, and Matisse developed the implications of Monet's use of color. Greenbergs's essay, "Collage," describes how cubism moved toward abstraction by emphasizing Cezanne's planes of color more strongly. "The illusion of depth and relief became abstracted from specific three-dimensional entities and was rendered largely as the illusion of depth and relief *as such*. . . ."[8] Matisse moved toward abstractness in a different way, using "the extension of sheer surface" of areas of color to provide "an equivalent of the space" of the old masters.

American abstract expressionist painting of the 1940s and 1950s drew on both traditions. Of abstract expressionist painting Greenberg says, "the eye has trouble locating central emphases and is directly compelled to treat the whole of the surface as a single undifferentiated field of interest. . . ."[9] This "all overness" is just what the old masters avoided. Sir Joshua Reynolds, for example, developed rules to "prevent" the eye from being distracted and confused by a multiplicity of objects of equal magnitude. . . ."[10] Greenberg notes, "All overness" produces "an illusion of indeterminate but somehow definitely shallow depth."[11] Cubist planes of color have lost their explicit positioning relative to the picture frame. Now,

[4] Ibid., pp. 52, 98.
[5] Ibid., pp. 41–45, 222.
[6] Ibid., p. 44.
[7] Ibid., pp. 70–83.
[8] Greenberg, *Henri Matisse* (New York: Acquavella Galleries, 1973).
[9] Greenberg, *Art and Culture*, p. 137.
[10] Joshua Reynolds, *Discourses on Art* (New York: Collier Books, 1966), p. 139.
[11] Greenberg, *Art and Culture*, p. 218.

Greenberg says, the painter relies on composing with a field of color "so large that its enclosing edges would lay outside . . . of the artist's field of vision. . . ."[12] In the succeeding generation, that is, in the generation following abstract expressionism, there were further formal transformations. I turn now to the Greenberg-Fried discussion of that period.

Fried is primarily interested in four painters of this period: Louis, and, slightly after him, Noland, Stella, and Olitski. These artists use two structural principles: purely optical nontactile space and deductive structure. Greenberg described that optical space as follows: "The old masters created an illusion of space in depth that one could imagine oneself walking into, but the analogous illusion created by the modernist painter can only be . . . traveled through . . . with the eye."[13] Fried makes this point by noting that ordinarily what we see in the world is also what we can touch, but here we have the illusion of "a space addressed to eyesight alone."[14]

Louis's paintings present this kind of optical space by developing a principle latent in Pollock's work of the late 1940s, in which he dripped swirling lines of paint on canvases. Because those lines overlapped themselves in intricate fashion, it was impossible to see them as the edge of some shape. Louis discovered how to use not just line, but also color in this fashion. Fried says, "If *successive waves* of thinned pigment, each a different color, were stained into . . . a canvas, what was produced was a single . . . configuration within which the individual configurations left by each wave . . . were still visible."[15] The result is not a deep space built up from a mass of different color. Rather, we see floating, intermingled layers of color.

According to Fried, we can distinguish between literal shape, that is, the actual shape of a canvas, and depicted shape, namely, the shape as it appears to be.[16] With a rectangular canvas, for example, the literal shape (two parallel pairs of sides intersecting in right angles) coincides with the shape as it appears to be. But imagine seeing a triangle intersecting one corner of that rectangle. While the literal shape would be a complicated, irregular seven-sided polygon, we would actually appear to see a triangle penetrating a square. The kind of structure exhibited by paintings in which the internal relations of shapes are derived from the frame edge of the canvas is called a "deductive structure."

Fried regards Noland, whose paintings, like Louis's are based on color staining, as the first key figure in the development of deductive structure. In making paintings of concentric circular rings, or chevrons, however, Noland discovered that these shapes worked most effectively if constrained by the need to relate deductively to the canvas frame. Without such de-

---

[12] Ibid., p. 219.

[13] Greenberg, "Modernist Painting," p. 106.

[14] Michael Fried, *Three American Painters* (Cambridge, Mass: Fogg Art Museum, 1965), p. 22.

[15] Ibid., p. 14.

[16] Michael Fried, "Shape as Form: Frank Stella's New Painting," *Artforum*, 5 (1966), 18; my example is drawn from p. 23.

ductive structure Noland's paintings would have been merely decorative.

Noland's paintings are organized both in terms of an optical space and deductive structure. Stella and Olitski developed further these two structural principles. Fried finds Stella's early paintings "nothing but structure."[17] Here Stella used oddly shaped canvases, generating within a given canvas a series of stripes parallel to the stretcher edge. In later works he used frames that developed the contrast between literal and depicted shape. Olitski's paintings do not use deductive structure; they are made in self-conscious opposition to that structure. "They . . . acknowledge the existence of deductive structure as an achievement the ambitious . . . painter . . . cannot simply ignore."[18] Olitski's paintings, like Louis's, are based upon optical illusionism. But Louis worked before deductive structure was a key issue, and so could bypass that problem, whereas Olitski, working later, had to take account of deductive structure, even in his attempt to *exclude* it from his work. His paintings are composed of sprays of different colors merging together across the entire canvas. A relation to the frame edge is established from within these merging colors. According to Fried, his works "depend for their success upon the new and more acute awareness of the shape . . . of the support embodied for the first time in deductive structure . . . our conviction in front of his most successful paintings is that the framing-edge has been arrived at by the colors themselves. . . ."[19]

Nothing could look more different from a Raphael than these modernist paintings. Nevertheless, the aim of formalist criticism is to show the continuities in art history; to show how through a series of formal transformations one can move from Raphael to Olitski. Hence, Greenberg says, there is nothing in modernist painting "that cannot be shown to have evolved out of either Cubism or Impressionism . . . just as I cannot see anything essential in Cubism or Impressionism whose development cannot be traced back to the Renaissance."[20]

II

There is another tradition of modern art as well, one based loosely upon the notion of the sublime. This tradition of "theatrical art," to use Fried's phrase, denies all the values of modernism. Theatrical art is based upon the following suggestion: Why not carry the modernist preoccupation with the flat canvas surface to its ultimate conclusion? Why not give up the whole illusionist tradition? If, as Fried notes, "paintings are in no essential respect different from other classes of objects in the world,"[21] then why

[17] Fried, *Three American Painters*, p. 40.
[18] Fried, "Jules Olitski's New Paintings," *Artforum*, 24, (1965), 37.
[19] Ibid., p. 40.
[20] Greenberg, "How Art Writing Earns Its Bad Name," *Encounter*, 18 (1962), 70.
[21] Fried, *Three American Painters*, p. 43.

not find artistic merit in any object whatsoever. Greenberg echoes this sentiment: "No matter how simple [any] . . . object may be, . . . [it is as] readable as art, as almost anything is today."[22]

Such theatrical art takes various forms. Around 1915 Duchamp took various ordinary objects—such as a urinal or a hat rack—and introduced them into museums. These "ready mades" were already manufactured objects that, by choosing them, he made into artworks. Minimal art of the 1960s took different forms: symmetrical arrangements of boxes stretching across the gallery floor, regular patterns of blocks leaning against each other, tiles covering the floor, piles of logs, and other building materials. Theatrical art, like the sublime, is based upon an extremely diverse collection of objects. What defines the theatrical is the kind of relation all these objects have to the spectator.

Earlier formalists anticipated what Fried says about the theatrical. Writing on the baroque style of painting, the noted historian Heinrich Woelfflin said, "In principle [it] avoids making the picture look as if it were arranged for contemplation and could be ever exhausted in contemplation."[23] Rogey Fry said of Caravaggio's paintings, "What he aimed at was to produce the most vivid shock of surprised acquiescence."[24] Two key points about theatrical art emerge from these remarks: (1) it seems to be endless and inexhaustible, and (2) it must "play" to a spectator.

The compositional relations found by formalists in modernist painting are relations between the different parts of the artwork. Since modernist painting is complete without any audience, these relations are created by the artist alone (as Stanley Cavell, following Greenberg and Fried, believes).[25] Theatrical art does require an audience because it replaces these formal relations *within* the artwork with the artwork's relation to an audience.

Theatrical art denies that making art requires artists, persons with special skill and intelligence. Rather, any object can be made into an artwork. Duchamp's ready mades make this point. The only difference between a urinal in a plumbing shop and those particular objects presented in the museum is that when we contemplate the object only outside of the museum the objects serves a practical function. Since any object can be contemplated in this fashion, Fried believes that all the theatrical artist had done is call public attention to something that was art to begin with—and banal at that—which is made no more intrinsically interesting by being put into a recognized art context; that is, we can treat any object as an artwork by contemplating its texture and shape. But, since interest-

[22] Greenberg, "Recentness of Sculpture", reprinted in Battcock, ed., *Minimal Art* (New York: Dutton, 1968) p. 183.
[23] H. Woelfflin, *Principles of Art History* (New York: Dover, 1957), p. 196–7; the discussion of the baroque in Rudolf Wittkower, *Art and Architecture in Italy 1600–1750* (Harmondsworth: Penguin, 1973) is relevant to understanding Fried's account of the theatrical.
[24] Rober Fry, *Transformations* (London, 1922), p. 158.
[25] Stanley Cavell, *The World Viewed* (New York: Viking, 1971), p. 111.

ing art is not just appropriated in that fashion, minimal art is really simply minimally art.

The potential endlessness of our experience with theatrical art, Fried notes in section VII of "Art and Objecthood," arises not because the artist had done so much, but because the artist has done so little. The theatrical artist does not create formal relations within his artworks; he leaves it to the spectator to find those relations. Theatrical artworks seem formless because the spectator is left to find form in them. Studying the shadows on a roughly textured wall would be endless, for nothing could count as "finishing" such a task. By doing less than a modernist artist, the theatrical artist has not given the spectator the opportunity to do more.

For Greenberg and Fried modernist painting has its equivalents to the illusionism of the old masters. Through its use of an optical space and deductive structure modernism acknowledges the status of a painting as an object. Theatrical works, however, "cannot be said to acknowledge literalness; they simply *are literal*."[26] Theatrical artist make the error of seeing that people acknowledge frankness but concluding that what matters is only the frankness, not the acknowledgment of it.

By comparing their formal relations, we can find one of two paintings better than the other. But theatrical art, because it is formless, is beyond "good" and "bad," and it would be meaningless to compare two theatrical objects, which, by their denial of quality distinctions, seek to announce the end of art history. By abdicating the traditional task of "making" the artwork, the minimal artist himself is announcing that he is not an artist. Kant said, "A beauty of nature is a beautiful thing; beauty of art is a *beautiful representation* of a thing."[27] The theatrical artist wants to abolish art entirely in favor of "nature," and this is what makes theatrical art particularly alien to formalism.

Another way to make the distinction between modernist and theatrical art is by reference to Kant's notion of aesthetic ideas. Greenberg and Fried have frequently noted that the importance of modernist painting depends upon its expressive powers:

Greenberg on Louis: "if these paintings fail as vehicles and expressions of feeling, they fail entirely. . . ."[28]

Fried on Stella's works: "They demand to be experienced in their terrific immediacy and directness, as a gesture or cry. . . ."[29]

Fried on Noland's works: they possess "a richness and complexity of

---

[26] Fried, "Shape as Form: Frank Stella's New Paintings," p. 22; also, "Art and Objecthood," footnote 11.
[27] Immanuel Kant, *The Critique of Judgment*, translated by Meredith (Oxford: Oxford University Press, 1952), p. 172.
[28] Greenberg, quoted in Fried, *Morris Louis 1912–1962* (Boston: Museum of Fine Arts, 1967), p. 82.
[29] Fried, "Jules Olitski's New Paintings," p. 37.

human content . . . the central concept for understanding (them) . . . is that of personal identity, of the self. . . ."[30]

It would be a mistake to ask exactly what feelings these works express, as the expressive power of aesthetic ideas lies not in their identifying precisely particular feelings but, rather, in suggesting, through the artwork's formal qualities, a multitude of ideas too rich to be put into words.

Modernist paintings yield these expressive meanings because they are made by an artist. The expressive power of modernist art is based upon the ordering given them by the artist. Theatrical art lacks expressive power. Because of its formlessness, theatrical art is no more expressive than any object we might come across at random in our daily experience.

III

Thus far, I have considered neither alternatives to formalist criticism nor the objections to its basic posture. I shall briefly discuss both these considerations now.

Following the critical approach of Adrian Stokes, Andrew Forge emphasizes the "eternal values" of painting. We can distinguish between two responses to a painting "as representation and object . . . and as an item in a historical sequence. . . ."[31] In formalism, one always views paintings in historical terms, the value of a given work to be grasped only when its place within a historical sequence is clear. The Stokes-Forge theory argues against formalism on the grounds that it deals with an intellectual abstraction—the historical sequence. Formalism takes us away from our immediate sensory experiences of seeing before us these colors, these shapes, these textures.

A second alternative to formalism is sociological, whereby one views painting as arising within a particular historical-sociopolitical context. Greenberg, for example, sees abstract expressionism as extending the formal qualities of cubism. For Harold Rosenberg, however, no correct analysis of abstract expressionism could exclude the condition of the artist in American society in the late 1940s.

> Only the blank canvas . . . offered the opportunity for a doing that would not be seized upon in midmotion by the depersonalizing machine of capitalist society, or by the depersonalizing machine of the world-wide opposition to that society. The American painter discovered a new function for art as the action that belonged to himself.[32]

Here the objection to formalism is that it adopts too limited a historical perspective.

[30] Fried, *Anthony Caro* (London: Hayward Gallery, 1969), p. 7.
[31] Andrew Forge, "Painting and the Struggle for the Whole Self," *Artforum*, 14 (1975), 46; this general viewpoint comes from the art criticism of Adrian Stokes.
[32] Harold Rosenberg, *The Anxious Object* (New York: New American Library, 1969), p. 38.

These two criticisms of formalism tug in opposite directions. The first finds it too much concerned with art history, the second too little. Seeing how formalists respond to such critiques can give us a further perspective on their brand of art criticism.

Since so much has been said in this paper about formalist arguments, something now needs to be said about the limits of argument in art criticism. If someone does not agree with his tastes, Fried says, "no critical arguments can take the place of feeling it."[33] The formalist theory should only serve as a way of describing our sensory experience of art, not as an intellectual apparatus which would come between us and our aesthetic experience. Greenberg says, "aesthetic judgment is not voluntary."[34] Ultimately, then, there can be no debate about aesthetic judgments.

In one passage Fried expresses his exasperation at critics who claim to admire both theatrical and modernist works. "I'm tempted to contend that if one saw Noland's or Olitski's paintings . . . as they demand to be seen, one could not also admire certain other works."[35] Here, in saying both that aesthetic judgment is ultimately beyond debate and that certain aesthetic disagreements seem almost incomprehensible, formalism reflects a tension that is implicit in Kant's theory. Are aesthetic judgments about mental states and, hence, subjective? Or are they about physical objects and, hence, objective?

Formalists certainly do see art history in impersonal terms. "The logic of Impressionism," Greenberg says, "had to work itself out regardless of the volition of individuals."[36] Although Greenberg thinks this way perhaps because of his background in Marxism, he is appealing here to a fact about human action admitted not only by the Hegelian-Marxist tradition, but also by such recent analytic philosophers as Anscombe—namely, that we cannot know all the consequences of our actions and that the future effects of those actions may be unrecognizable to us. Cezanne might have had all sorts of reasons coming from his private emotional life or the condition of French society during his lifetime for painting as he did. But what makes his paintings important for art history is his formal innovations.

> The "all-over" may answer the feeling that all hierarchical distinctions have been . . . exhausted . . . that no area or order of experience is intrinsically superior to any other . . . to our increasing faith in and taste for the immediate, the concrete, the irreducible.[37]

But implicit in his account is the recognition that such sociological points are useful, if not made too specific or used as a basis for explaining stylistic changes. Otherwise, very difficult questions arise. Why, for ex-

---

[33] Fried, *Three American Painters*, p. 5.
[34] Greenberg, "Seminar One," *Arts Magazine*, November 1973, p. 45.
[35] Fried, untitled, in *Art Criticism in the Sixties* (New York: October House, 1967), no pagination.
[36] Greenberg, *Art and Culture*, p. 171.
[37] Greenberg, *Art and Culture*, pp. 157, 139.

ample, was the conspicuous American crisis of the 1960s not reflected in visual art?

For Fried, social concerns simply have no relevance to modernist paint-ing.[38] In the 1960s there were many attempts to politicize the artworld, and the formalist insistence on the aloofness of art from society was viewed suspiciously. Modernist painting had nothing to say about the war in Vietnam, or feminism, or the struggles of blacks. Whether the critics of formalism are right in thinking that painting can serve as an instrument to transform society, or whether the absurdity of such a demand is a clear reflection of the social impotence of artists, are questions that cannot be answered here.

From the perspective of 1977, formalist criticism seems to have lost some ground. Greenberg has some claim to being *the* critic of the 1940s and 1950s in a way that neither he nor Fried can claim to be the critics of the 1960s or 1970s. Greenberg has published relatively little on that more recent art. Fried's writing about that art, too, are academic in style in a way that Greenberg's writings never have been. Many of the important tastes of the artworld during the past decade—pop art, minimal art, con-ceptual art, feminist art—have been reacted to by these formalists in purely negative terms. Today, many people in the artworld would think the heroic days of American-style formalism to belong to the past—to roughly 1945–1965. Right now, formalist criticism of current art seems of relatively periph-eral interest. Whether this change in the status of formalism is due to the development of new postformalist types of art or merely a reflection of a period of relative stagnation or even decline in the history of American art is an immensely important question. But I shall say nothing about the answer to that question here.

Select Bibliography for Part Three

FORMALISM, PHILOSOPHY AND
CONTEMPORARY PLASTIC ARTS

Books

Michael Fried, *Three American Painters*; Dzahler Giel, *New York Painting and Sculpture: 1940–1970*; Clement Greenberg, *Art and Culture*; Hilaire Hiler, *Why Abstract?*; Renato Poggioli, *The Theory of the Avant-Garde*.

Articles

Marcel Brion, "Abstract Art"; Michael Fried, "Manet's Sources"; David F. Martin, "The Persistent Presence of Abstract Painting"; Herta Pauly, "Aes-thetic Decadence Today Viewed in Terms of Schiller's Three Impulses."

[38] Fried, *Three American Painters*, p. 7.

PART FOUR

The Theory
of Art Theory

As most of the traditional theories of art presented here demonstrate, it is generally assumed that the art theorist should provide a definition which enables us to distinguish art from non-art. Whether the definitions are simple, like Bell's, or complex, like Aristotle's, they propose the necessary and sufficient conditions for something to be a work of art. A necessary condition is simply a condition which *must* be met if an object is to qualify as a work of art (e.g., for Bell it must possess "significant form"). A sufficient condition is a condition which, if met, *guarantees* that the object is a work of art (e.g., for Collingwood any object which expresses emotion is guaranteed to be a work of art). It is clear, however, that the theorists of art encountered here differ radically on just what the necessary and sufficient conditions of art may be. As we shall see, this is true also of theorists who attempt to define "aesthetic" in similar manner. Given these radical disagreements, perhaps we should stop asking "What is the true definition of art?" and ask instead "Does it make sense to try to find a true definition of art?" For a quarter of a century after World War II philosophers in the English-speaking world concentrated on this latter question. In effect, the theory of art became the theory of art theory.

In the period 1945–1960, a score of important essays appeared challenging the assumption of traditional art theory that a correct definition of art could be formulated. Among the most important of these essays, all of which are cited in the bibliography of the collection, are the following: "The Function of Philosophical Aesthetics" and "Art as an Essentially Contested Concept" by W. B. Gallie; "The Task of Defining a Work of Art" by Paul Ziff; "Does Traditional Aesthetics Rest on a Mistake?" by William Kennick; and "The Role of Theory in Aesthetics" by Morris Weitz. We have not reprinted these essays in this collection for three reasons: (1) they are already widely anthologized, and thus widely available elsewhere;

(2) Maurice Mandelbaum in his essay in this part "Family-Resemblances and Generalizations Concerning the Arts" discusses several of these essays in detail, concentrating on the Ziff and Weitz essays in particular; and (3) these essays have been superseded by the two essays we have chosen, Weitz's "Wittgenstein's Aesthetics" and Marshall Cohen's "Aesthetic Essence."

In "Wittgenstein's Aesthetics," which appeared some fifteen years after the publication of "The Role of Theory in Aesthetics," Weitz puts in perspective the main ideas he developed in the earlier essay by (1) taking up the historical question of Wittgenstein's influence on aesthetics in the English-speaking world, and (2) considering a number of problems which arose in connection with the main thesis of his first essay. Ludwig Wittgenstein (1889–1951), a native of Vienna, spent most of his philosophical career in England. Although he wrote most of his works in the German language, his influence was felt most strongly in the English-speaking world (see Norman Malcolm's *Ludwig Wittgenstein: A Memoir*, with a biographical sketch of Wittgenstein by G. H. Von Wright for an excellent informal account of Wittgenstein's life and career). As Weitz points out, however, Wittgenstein never wrote anything concerning aesthetics per se that is of any major significance to the subject (some of his lectures transcribed by students were published under the title *Lectures and Conversations on Aesthetics, Religion, and Psychology*). Wittgenstein's considerable influence on the subject must be understood in terms of the application by other philosophers of certain ideas he developed in the major work of his later period, *Philosophical Investigations*. Weitz traces Wittgenstein's influence by concentrating on these ideas and their applications to aesthetics.

Weitz himself came under Wittgenstein's influence in the 1950s. This culminated in an essay, "The Role of Theory in Aesthetics," which was to dominate the theory of art for some time. Using as a model Wittgenstein's analysis of the concept of a game in the *Investigations*, and borrowing the expression "open-textured concept" from another philosopher who was deeply influenced by Wittgenstein, Fredrick Waismann, Weitz argued that "art" cannot be defined because it is an open-textured concept. An open-textured concept, as Weitz understood it in his first paper, is a concept which has no necessary and sufficient conditions for its application—a concept whose conditions of application are perennially changeable. Because the concept of "art" in general, and subconcepts of art such as "novel," "tragedy," "drama," and so on could be shown to be open-textured, Weitz argued that none of them could be defined in the traditional manner. Thus, in one fell swoop Weitz argued to put an end to the traditional search for true definitions of "art" and its subconcepts.

Although Weitz's view enjoyed widespread acceptance for quite some time, both he and other philosophers came to see that the "open-textured" position was not immune to criticism. Maurice Mandelbaum, in the essay reprinted here, argued that Weitz's analysis was inconclusive. Weitz himself had undertaken an extensive book, *Hamlet and the Philosophy of*

Literary Criticism, which yielded results not entirely compatible with the findings of his earlier paper. Weitz realized that his analysis of conceptual openness was incomplete, and that a number of distinctions between different kinds of open concepts was called for. In "Wittgenstein's Aesthetics," Weitz is still prepared to accept the main thesis of his earlier work, but he has modified his thesis in important ways, making it a more viable critique of traditional art theory.

Weitz's modifications notwithstanding, Mandelbaum believes that Weitz and other philosophers of his ilk simply do not prove their case. In fact, Mandelbaum argues against Wittgenstein himself, claiming that Wittgenstein failed to note important differences among different kinds of properties which games, art, and other things possess. When these distinctions are taken into account, Mandelbaum sees no reason why the traditional aims of art theory cannot be realized. The thrust of Mandelbaum's argument is to show that one cannot prove in advance that no definition of art could be correct (as Weitz had tried to do), and from the fact that no satisfactory definition of art has yet been found, it does not follow that it is logically impossible to find one. Mandelbaum's essay remains the most broad-based critique of Wittgenstein, Weitz, et al. to date.

Weitz's concern with the logical impossibility of art theory, and Mandelbaum's concern with the logical possibility of the enterprise, represent one side of the art theory coin. The other side is represented by philosophers who concentrate not so much on logical questions in general, but on specific theories in particular. These philosophers prefer to scrutinize the arts themselves to determine whether in fact various definitions apply. Marshall Cohen's "Aesthetic Essence" is perhaps the best essay of this type. Cohen's essay is a storehouse of counterexamples to a variety of attempts to define "art" and the "aesthetic." He considers such diverse artists as T. S. Eliot, Le Corbusier, James Joyce, Dostoyevsky, Rothko, and Antonioni, to mention a few, and he considers such diverse theorists as Dewey, Langer, Roger Fry, Bullough, J. O. Urmson, and many others. Cohen's technique of amassing scores of artists, artworks, and theories of art and the aesthetic is valuable not only because it provides a rich source of examples and critiques, but because it also provides a general perspective from which the practical problems of trying to define "art" and the "aesthetic" can be viewed.

It is primarily for this latter reason that Cohen's essay is included here in The Theory of Art Theory, rather than in part seven on contemporary theories of the aesthetic. There may be a number of affinities between Cohen's essay and, for example, Dickie's essay "The Myth of the Aesthetic Attitude" in part seven. Insofar as this is true, Cohen's essay could have been used there as well. It must be noted, however, that Cohen is a philosopher who is specifically aware of the way in which the concepts of art and the aesthetic tend to dovetail. Because of this, and because he deals with the interrelationships between these concepts, his essay is equally at home in this section.

Morris Weitz

WITTGENSTEIN'S
AESTHETICS

It is not impossible that it should fall to the lot of this work, in its poverty
and in the darkness of this time, to bring light into one brain or another—
but, of course, it is not likely.

Wittgenstein, *Philosophical Investigations*

We know more about Wittgenstein's artistic tastes than we do about
his aesthetics.* His various biographers have told us of his great and abiding interest in music and literature, and of his creative talents in architecture and sculpture. But I have found no mention of a passion for painting;
and even in literature his admiration for Dostoevsky and Tolstoy seems to
have been joined with an indifference to, among too many others, Proust.
This neglect, if it was a neglect, is a pity, since, as at least one Wittgensteinian—John Wisdom—has perceived, there is a striking affinity in
philosophical vision between the greatest novelist and the greatest philosopher of our age.

Wittgenstein, we learn from G. E. Moore and others, lectured on and
talked about aesthetics from time to time to his students at Cambridge.
Some of this material has been collected, edited, and published in a little
book, *Lectures & Conversations on Aesthetics, Psychology and Religious
Belief.*[1] In that book there are suggestive remarks, among other things,

Morris Weitz is Professor of Philosophy at Brandeis University. He has been a
leading figure in American aesthetics for many years. His essays and books, including
Hamlet and The Philosophy of Literary Criticism, have stimulated much discussion in
leading journals.

* This essay was originally published in *Language and Aesthetics* edited by Benjamin
R. Tilghman, University of Kansas Press, 1973. Reprinted by permission of the editor
and the University of Kansas Press.

[1] Ludwig Wittgenstein, *Lectures & Conversations on Aesthetics, Psychology and Religious Belief*, compiled from notes taken by Yorick Smythies, Rush Rhees, and James
Taylor and edited by Cyril Barrett (Berkeley, Calif.: University of California Press,
1967).

about the aesthetic predicates "beautiful" and "lovely," which Wittgenstein says function primarily as interjections but mostly in ordinary discourse, since they hardly appear in the language of professional criticism; about the need to elucidate talk about art in the larger context of its particular cultural milieu; and about explanation in criticism as the giving of reasons rather than of causes. In any case, it seems to me that there is nothing in that recorded text to warrant it as a great or even an important contribution to aesthetics.

We must therefore look elsewhere. Moore, in his report, records that Wittgenstein introduced his discussion of aesthetics with his later famous description of "game" as a family rather than essence concept.[2] "And he seemed to hold definitely that there is nothing in common in our different uses of the word 'beautiful,' saying that we use it 'in a hundred different games'—that, e.g. the beauty of a face is something different from the beauty of a chair or a flower or the binding of a book."[3]

As revolutionary as this idea becomes in the *Investigations* and as influential as it is today among philosophers, it is very curious that Wittgenstein introduces his unfortunately slight discussion of aesthetics in the *Investigations* with examples of "seeing what is in common" rather than with families in which their members have nothing in common. After enumerating a number of these examples, Wittgenstein writes:

> For imagine having to sketch a sharply defined picture "corresponding" to a blurred one. In the latter there is a blurred red rectangle: for it you put down a sharply defined one. Of course—several such sharply defined rectangles can be drawn to correspond to the indefinite one.—But if the colours in the original merge without a hint of any outline won't it become a hopeless task to draw a sharp picture corresponding to the blurred one? Won't you then have to say: "Here I might just as well draw a circle or heart as a rectangle, for all the colours merge." Anything—and nothing—is right.—And this is the position you are in if you look for definitions corresponding to our concepts in aesthetics and ethics.[4]

Wittgenstein immediately suggests that we can resolve this difficulty by reminding ourselves of the families of meanings of aesthetic and ethical words. But it is not at all clear that such a reminder does resolve the problem he poses. For in what he imagines in his blurred figure, it is the vagueness of the phenomenon and not any family resemblances that renders precision impossible. Thus, if we take his analogy seriously, putative definitions of aesthetic concepts become impossible attempts to make precise that which is inherently imprecise; they are not, as his "games" analogy suggests, misdescriptions of the logical grammar of aesthetic concepts, that is, statements of the necessary and sufficient criteria of concepts whose very employment rests on there not being such criteria.

[2] G. E. Moore, "Wittgenstein's Lectures in 1930–33," *Mind* 63, nos. 249, 251, and 253.
[3] Ibid., no. 253, p. 17.
[4] Ludwig Wittgenstein, *Philosophical Investigations*, trans. by G. E. M. Anscombe, 3d ed. (New York: Macmillan Co., 1958), §77.

Is it the inherent blur of artistic or aesthetic phenomena that forecloses on the possibility of definitions in aesthetics? Is art or the beautiful like a rectangle in which all its colors merge with no hint of outlines among them? T. S. Eliot comes close to an affirmative answer in "East Coker":*

> . . . And so each venture
> Is a new beginning, a raid on the inarticulate
> With shabby equipment always deteriorating
> In the general mess of imprecision of feeling,
> Undisciplined squads of emotion. . . .

But such a wholesale view of language in relation to the world, whether Eliot's or Wittgenstein's, grossly distorts the phenomena in question—not all of art and morals share this general mess of imprecision. More importantly, however, it violates the dictum that logical grammar is conceptual, not ontological. For Wittgenstein, it cannot be the nature of art but rather the uses of "art" that preclude any definition of the concept of art.

The *Lectures on Aesthetics* begins: "The subject (Aesthetics) is very big and entirely misunderstood as far as I can see." But it is the misconceptions, not the bigness, of aesthetics that allow us to return to Wittgenstein's discussion of "game" in the *Investigations* as the focal point of his contribution to aesthetics. To be sure, in so far as much of aesthetics has to do with problems of meaning, understanding, emotion, imagination, and intention, the whole of the *Investigations*, which is concerned with these problems, is of course relevant to aesthetics. Indeed, at least two of his concepts in the *Investigations*—"seeing as" and "forms of life"—have already become central in two important recent books—Virgil Aldrich's *Philosophy of Art*[5] and Richard Wollheim's *Art and Its Objects*.[6] Nevertheless, it seems to me that the treatment of "game" as an open rather than closed concept is central in his contribution to aesthetics. I will therefore restrict myself to it and its far-reaching implications in this paper.

What, now, is Wittgenstein's doctrine of open concepts that I claim is his basic contribution to aesthetics? Fundamentally, it is a rejection of the doctrine that all concepts are and must be governed by sets of necessary and sufficient conditions or criteria. This doctrine, Wittgenstein sees, pervades the history of philosophy and reaches a culmination in his *Tractatus Logico-Philosophicus*.

> Thought is surrounded by a halo.—Its essence, logic, presents an order, in fact the a priori order of the world: that is, the order of *possibilities*, which must be common to both world and thought. But this order, it seems, must be *utterly simple*. It is *prior* to all experience, must run through all experience; no empirical cloudiness or uncertainty can be allowed to affect it—It must

---

* T. S. Eliot, "East Coker," in *Four Quartets*, used by permission of Harcourt Brace Jovanovich, Inc.
[5] Virgil C. Aldrich, *Philosophy of Art* (Englewood Cliffs, N.J.: Prentice-Hall, 1963).
[6] Richard Wollheim, *Art and Its Objects: An Introduction to Aesthetics* (New York: Harper & Row, 1968).

rather be of the purest crystal. But this crystal does not appear as an abstraction; but as something concrete; indeed, as the most concrete, as it were the *hardest* thing there is (*Tractatus Logico-Philosophicus* No. 5.5563).

We are under the illusion that what is peculiar, profound, essential, in our investigation, resides in its trying to grasp the incomparable essence of language. That is, the order existing between the concepts of proposition, word, proof, truth, experience, and so on. This order is a *super*-order between —so to speak—*super*-concepts. Whereas, of course, if the words "language," "experience," "world," have a use, it must be as humble a one as that of the words "table," "lamp," "door."[7]

It is this illusion that philosophy is the attempt to grasp the essence of language that Wittgenstein dispels in his famous treatment of "games" and "family resemblances," by now the *locus classicus* of open concepts. Wittgenstein has been talking about and considering the implications of a number of primitive language-games. He then raises a crucial objection: I talk about language-games without saying what their essence is; what they have in common by virtue of which they are language-games or parts of language. Is this not the easy way out?

We need Wittgenstein's exact reply: "And this is true.—Instead of producing something common to all that we call language, I am saying that these phenomena have no one thing in common which makes us use the same word for all,—but that they are *related* to one another in many different ways. And it is because of this relationship, or these relationships, that we call them all 'language.' "[8]

Wittgenstein's question and answer, as it appears, are not ontological. For he neither asks whether there is an essence of language-games nor denies that there is. His question is rather one of logical grammar: whether the assumption that there is or must be an essence of language-games in order to be able to use the word "language-game" is true. His answer is that it is not true; instead, that our correct use of the word is founded on relationships, that is, family resemblances. So, in effect, he is asking whether, and denying that, it is a necessary condition of our correct, intelligible use of "language-game" that there is or must be a corresponding essence. We need not assume that the criteria for this word correspond to a set of necessary and sufficient properties which is shared by all language-games in order to explain what makes us use the same word for them.

Wittgenstein rejects the linguistic thesis of concepts—that they are or must be governed by necessary and sufficient criteria. His commitment to logical grammar precludes his rejection of the ontological thesis that concepts are or must be universals consisting of necessary and sufficient properties. However, because the ontological thesis entails the linguistic, his denial of the latter entails the denial of the former. To deny that "language-game" is or must be governed by necessary and sufficient criteria

[7] Wittgenstein, *Philosophical Investigations*, §97.
[8] Ibid., §65.

is to deny an implication of the doctrine that language-games have or must have a set of necessary and sufficient properties and, by *modus tollendo tollens*, to deny the doctrine itself.

What, now, are the criteria or conditions of the correct use of "language-game," according to Wittgenstein? Shifting from "language-game" to "game," Wittgenstein begins by reminding us of our ordinary, everyday use of the term to describe and to classify certain activities: ball-games, such as football and baseball; board-games, such as chess and checkers; card-games, such as poker and solitaire; and track and field games, subsumed under, say, Olympic games.

These are all paradigms of games. Yet they have nothing in common (no essence) by virtue of which they are called "games" or which makes us use the same word for all. At most they have certain features, such as amusement, winning and losing, competition, skill, luck, rules, and so forth; but none of these is necessary or sufficient. Instead these features constitute a family. It is this family—family resemblances—not some essence, that furnish the criteria of "games." "Game," therefore, can be said to be governed by a disjunctive set of criteria that corresponds to a disjunctive set of properties, where no one of these criteria or properties is necessary or sufficient. The concept of game, then, is open, not closed, for Wittgenstein, in the precise sense that it functions under a disjunctive set of criteria which corresponds to certain family resemblances, but that these criteria are neither necessary nor sufficient.

It is these criteria that make us use the same word for all games, that enable us to explain what a game is, and to justify our claim that we know what a game is without having to provide a definition of "game." The questions, "*What* is a game?" "*Is x* a game?" "*Why is x* a game?" require game-giving reasons; but these reasons fall back on undisputed examples and family resemblances, not on a disjunctive set of properties shared by all members of the class of games.

"Game," then, as open in Wittgenstein's sense, is a perennially flexible concept. That is, its historically assigned use must accommodate any new example of game, with its new property. The set of nonnecessary, nonsufficient criteria allow us to extend these criteria to cover a new case, $x+1$. We decide to call $x+1$ a game because it is sufficiently similar to the accepted examples to allow its dissimilarity to become a new criterion of "game." "$X+1$ is a game" expresses a decision to enlarge our criteria, not an inference from a true definition of "game."

Is "game" also perennially debatable? That is, is each of its criteria always open to question, challenge, rejection, and replacement by another criterion? Not for Wittgenstein. None of the criteria—"amusement," "skill," "competition," and so forth—is open to challenge or rejection. These criteria furnish good reasons for something being a game even though they are not necessary or sufficient. "X is a game because it involves competition" hardly invites the query, "But what has competition to do with it?"

In the *Investigations* all the open concepts are perennially flexible ones. None are perennially debatable. The main assault is on the traditional doctrine that they are or must be closed. But how extensive is Wittgenstein's use of open concepts? The openness of "game" serves as a model for "language-game," hence of "language" itself. Is "language" open, as Wittgenstein describes it? To be sure, he offers no set of definitive criteria; and he interprets it as marking out a family of cases, with their family resemblances. But does he also deny, as he does with "game," that the concept of language has some necessary conditions? Can there be a language without terms that serve to identify items in the world and that serve to reidentify these items—in short, without rules? Wittgenstein's powerful arguments against the possibility of a language that only one person could understand—what some call "a private language"—strongly suggest that "rules" is a necessary criterion of "language" in a way it is not of "game," and that consequently "language" is not open as "game" is, at least for Wittgenstein. "Language" is open only in the minimal sense that it has no set of necessary and sufficient criteria, although it has and must have some necessary ones.

Similar difficulties engulf one as one tries to locate other central concepts of the *Investigations* on Wittgenstein's logical map: pain, seeing, understanding, imaging, thinking, intending, willing, hoping, to mention some of them. Are all of them perennially flexible? Does any of them have necessary criteria, or are all of them governed by expandable sets of nonnecessary, non-sufficient criteria? There is an entire unwritten book here on the range of open concepts in the *Investigations*, scarcely begun, yet in my opinion absolutely crucial in the understanding of that work and especially, so far as our immediate purpose is concerned, of Wittgenstein's contribution to aesthetics. Only this much, I think, is clear and indisputable: that Wittgenstein offers no wholesale view of the logic of concepts, not even that his elucidation of "game" and his demolition of the traditional essence doctrine are to serve as a model for all games. For what may be true of the concept of game may not be true of the concept of a particular game. "Major-league baseball," for example, unlike "game," though fluid and flexible enough in its history, can perform its assigned role only under the overall condition that it is governed by a set of definitive criteria so fixed as to ensure that no unresolvable doubts and disputes can arise. So too with understanding. It is certainly a family of cases, with varying sets of properties. But one kind of understanding, namely, understanding a mathematical formula—as Wittgenstein is at great pains to point out—is necessarily a capacity to go on. Here, "being able to apply the formula" is a necessary criterion of the concept of understanding a mathematical formula. So in this case, the logic of the genus "understanding" differs from the logic of the species "understanding a mathematical formula."

Much of the *Investigations* revolves around the rejection of one purportedly necessary criterion for the correct use of mental concepts, namely, the criterion of an inner, private mental state. Wittgenstein does not so much deny that these states exist as he denies their status as a criterion for our mental concepts. His behaviorism is a logical behaviorism about the role and necessarily outward criteria of mental concepts, not a psychological behaviorism about mental states. His logical behaviorism repudiates *in toto* one kind of concept, that whose necessary and sufficient criteria are privately mental; it rejects as well one kind of necessary criterion, that of a private state. But it does not affirm only one kind of open concept, that which is governed by disjunctive sets of nonnecessary, nonsufficient criteria. Other kinds of concepts are acknowledged, especially those with some necessary albeit no definitive criteria, and those that allow for new members with their new properties of the set. What his logical behaviorism does not include but must allow for are the perennially debatable concepts. It is this omission that confers on the *Investigations* a surprising moderation about the conceptual life and which, I think, contrasts sharply with the more radical demands made on our understanding of concepts by aesthetics.

There are, it seems to me, at least three very important logical kinds of concepts in aesthetics: the perennially flexible, the perennially debatable, and the irreducibly vague. None is closed, that is, governed by sets of definitive criteria. All are therefore open in the sense that they function under nondefinitive sets of criteria. But each differs from the others, and only one is open in Wittgenstein's sense of family resemblances rather than a common denominator.

In aesthetics, there are certain genre concepts, such as "drama," "novel," perhaps "art" itself, that are perennially flexible. Other genre concepts, of which "tragedy" is the most revealing example, are also perennially debatable. Style concepts, such as "Baroque" or "Mannerism," are irreducibly vague.

In an early paper, "The Role of Theory in Aesthetics,"[9] inspired by both Wittgenstein and Waismann on open concepts, I argued that a number of genre concepts are open in contrast to the traditional assumption that all of them are and must be governed by definitive sets of criteria. Thus, "novel," "drama," "satire," "tragedy," and "art," I claimed, are open. But considering all of these together conflated two very different kinds of concepts, neither of which is governed by sets of necessary and sufficient criteria. "Drama," "novel," and "art"—as their uses reveal—have certain criteria that though neither necessary nor sufficient are undebatable, in a way that "tragedy" does not. For example, "X is a drama because it has plot" cannot be challenged in the way in which "X is a tragedy because it has *hamartia*" can. "Plot" is neither necessary nor sufficient for something being a drama, but neither can it be challenged, as *"hamartia"* or any other criterion of "tragedy" can. If we follow Wittgenstein's advice to look and see how the concept of tragedy functions, especially if we

---

[9] Morris Weitz, "The Role of Theory in Aesthetics," *Journal of Aesthetics and Art Criticism*, 1956.

survey the range of disagreement among philosophers about what tragedy is or the more revealing disagreements among critics as to why, for example, *Hamlet* is a tragedy or Hamlet is tragic, we shall find, as I did find in my *Hamlet and the Philosophy of Literary Criticism*, that every criterion of tragedy—every tragedy-giving reason—has been and remains perennially rejectable.[10] Wittgenstein's model of "game" as a family concept, in which every criterion, though not necessary or sufficient, is not rejectable either, illuminates some genre concepts, such as "drama," "novel," and "art," but it does not clarify the perennial debatability of other genre concepts, such as "tragedy." For these concepts we need a more radical theory of openness than family resemblances and flexibility.

Investigation of the concept of style and of particular style concepts produces another variant of openness, also unnoticed by Wittgenstein, indeed, so far as I can determine, overlooked by all logicians in their discussions of vagueness. Here again, if we turn from abstract theories of style by aestheticians and art historians to the style-giving reasons preferred by art historians for a particular work of art or artist being or not being of a particular style, we find in their range of disagreement concepts whose logic of criteria differs from that of genre concepts.

Consider, as an example of a style concept in art history, "Mannerism." Art historians use this concept to label, describe, interpret, and evaluate or reevaluate certain works of art with certain specified characteristics in a specified region of space and time, but primarily to Italian paintings of the sixteenth century. For one historian, Walter Friedlander,[11] "Mannerism" functions under what he calls the "decisive" criterion of subjective spirituality, which comprises an unnatural figure in unnatural space with its attendant expressive property of asymmetrical beauty: let us call these three criteria a, b, and c. For another great historian of Mannerism, Max Dvorak,[12] the term functions under similar criteria, a and b, but he interprets the expressive property as religious rather than as pictorial, so let us call it d. For a third historian of the movement, Lionello Venturi,[13] "Mannerism" functions under a cluster of "salient" criteria: Friedlander's a, b, and c, to which he adds an intense play of light and shadow, e, and a preoccupation with form for its own sake, f, thereby dismissing Dvorak's criterion of religious spirituality. No criterion, he claims, is necessary, no collection of them is sufficient, for the correct use of "Mannerism." For

---

[10] Morris Weitz, *Hamlet and the Philosophy of Literary Criticism* (Chicago: University of Chicago Press, 1964), especially chap. 17. See also Weitz, "Tragedy," *Encyclopedia of Philosophy* (New York: Macmillan Co. and Free Press, 1967).

[11] See Walter Friedlander, "The Rise of the Anti-Classical Style in Italian Painting in 1520," reprinted in Friedlander, *Mannerism and Anti-Mannerism in Italian Painting* (New York: Shocken Books, 1965).

[12] See Max Dvorak, "El Greco and Mannerism," first delivered as a lecture in 1920, published in his *Kunstgeschichte als Geistesgeschichte*, 1953. Translated in part in *Magazine of Art*, 1953.

[13] See Lionello Venturi, *The Sixteenth Century, From Leonardo to El Greco* (New York: Skira, 1956).

a fourth historian, Craig Smyth,[14] who completely rejects traditional theories and criteria, "Mannerism" functions under a general criterion, "*maniera*"—let us call it *m*—which in turn functions under the criterion of ideal uniformity of pose and gesture—*n*—and which he regards as definitive for both "Mannerism" and "*maniera*" in Italian painting of the sixteenth century. For a fifth historian, John Shearman,[15] "Mannerism" functions also under the same general criterion of "*maniera*." But he interprets "*maniera*" as refinement, artificiality, difficulty, and grace—*o*, *p*, *q*, and *r*—which he also claims are definitive for both "*maniera*" and "Mannerism." Finally, for a sixth historian, Sydney Freedberg[16]—who attempts to reconcile Friedlander with his recent opponents—"Mannerism" functions under two sets of criteria: "*maniera*," to which he adds the criterion of "the multiplicity and multivalence of meanings" in the paintings of the *maniera* artists—*s*—and the criterion of experimental and anticlassical expressionism —*t*—to cover the early mannerist painters.

Now, in every case we can ask whether these criteria are clear and are precisely applicable to the works specified as manneristic by the historians. If they are not clear or are questionable in their application, they are vague. But they are not vague in the way in which the individual sets of criteria—*a*, *b*, and *c*; *a*, *b*, and *d*; "*maniera*" (as *n*; as *o*, *p*, *q*, and *r*; as *s*); or *s* and *t*—are vague; or even as all these sets together are vague. For the vagueness of the sets, taken individually or collectively, is a vagueness of the incompleteness and incompletability of the set. Therefore the fundamental vagueness of "Mannerism" as a style concept consists in the perennial possibility of intelligibly enlarging or exchanging the criteria for its correct use. Unless we acknowledge this irreducible vagueness of the concept of Mannerism, we cannot make sense of the different moves that art historians have made and that future historians may make as they choose different criteria in order to present a new account of Mannerism.

What, now, is the relation between the openness of at least some genre concepts and the irreducible vagueness of at least one style concept? Is "Mannerism" like "tragedy," which is open in the sense of having no necessary or sufficient criteria and no undebatable ones; or like "drama," which is open in Wittgenstein's sense of having no necessary or sufficient criteria but at least some undebatable ones, such as "plot" or "characters"? "Mannerism," as its history reveals, has no necessary or sufficient criteria and no unchallengeable criteria, and thus is more like "tragedy" than like "drama." But it differs from these genre concepts in two important respects. First, its assigned role does not require that it accommodate new

---

[14] See C. H. Smyth, "Mannerism and *Maniera*," in Millard Miess, ed., *The Renaissance and Mannerism* (*Studies in Western Art: Acts of the Twentieth International Congress of the History of Art* [Princeton, N.J.: Princeton University Press, 1963]), 2:174–99.

[15] See John Shearman, *Mannerism* (Harmondsworth, Middlesex, England: Penguin Books, 1967).

[16] See S. J. Freedberg, "Observations on the Painting of the Maniera," *Art Bulletin*, June 1965.

cases with their new properties: its flexibility does not extend to future works of art in the way that these genre concepts do. Rather, its flexibility relates to past works of art that are historically bound by space and time. Second, the disagreements over the correct use of "Mannerism" converse more on the exchange of sets of criteria than on their enlargement to cover new cases or on the rejection of putatively necessary criteria. Because of these two differences I am inclined to regard "Mannerism" as distinct from genre concepts and perhaps akin to the explanatory concept of centrality in the criticism of works of art. For the debates and disagreements over what is central or most important in a particular work of art seem to have the same vast array of irreducible vagueness as what is to count as Mannerism.

Whether these differences mark a radical distinction between openness and irreducible vagueness, I do not know. But I am confident that all who render open concepts closed and vague concepts complete misunderstand these concepts as well as foreclose on their historically assigned roles. Wittgenstein's great contribution to aesthetics, in his explorations of the logical grammar of concepts, is that he has made such conceptual discoveries possible.

Marshall Cohen

AESTHETIC ESSENCE

One of the typical assumptions of traditional aesthetic theory has been that certain features must characterize all objects properly regarded as works of fine art.* And the further assumption that some of these features characterize only works (or only successful works) of fine art has occasioned both the search for a definition of art and the attempt to elicit an ultimate ground of critical judgement. It has long been apparent that the traditional theories have made inadequate suggestions as to what these features might in fact be. For most of the suggested properties do not seem even to constitute necessary conditions for the application of the notions of art or of successful art. This is true of beauty and of the expression of emotion; it is true of illusion and of *mimesis*. As Nietzsche has taught us that tragic art is characterized by terror rather than beauty, Eliot has revealed that poetry 'in the tradition' constitutes an escape from, not an expression of, emotion. Since Maurice Denis it has been understood that the canvas may be treated, not as a three-dimensional illusion, but as a two-dimensional reality. And if Le Corbusier has encouraged the doctrine of *mimesis* in designing the chapel at Ronchamp, he has rejected it firmly at the Villa Savoie. Furthermore, if some feature such as significant form, or organic unity, should ever be described with enough clarity to allow us to determine its presence or absence, it seems obvious that it would not be difficult to show that it is, even if a necessary, not a sufficient condition of art. These difficulties have long been apparent, and in recent years they have often been interpreted in the light of Wittgenstein's cautionary observation that the use of a general term need not be supported by the presence of a property common to the 'objects' to which it properly applies. (Like Wittgenstein I do not mean by 'properties' elaborate disjunctive ones.) As a consequence, many writers have begun to suggest that the difficulty in the philosophy of art is not that we have so far failed to dis-

Marshall Cohen is Professor of Philosophy at The City University of New York. He is a well-known critic who publishes regularly in journals such as the *Partisan Review* and *The New York Times Book Review*. Recently he has co-edited a collection on film entitled *Film Theory and Criticism: Introductory Readings*.

* Originally published in *Philosophy in America*, chapter IV, edited by Max Black (London, 1962). Reprinted by permission of Allen & Unwin Ltd. and Cornell University Press.

". . . Le Corbusier has encouraged the doctrine of mimesis in designing the chapel at Ronchamp . . ." Marshall Cohen in "Aesthetic Essence," p. 484.

cover the required property or properties, but that we have continued to assume without justification that there are such properties to seek.

In this essay I wish to indicate that analogous assumptions and difficulties pervade other areas of aesthetic investigation. For the notion lingers on (even among philosophers of a Wittgensteinian persuasion) that if there is no property common to all works of art there may yet be some property or properties common to our proper experience of these works of art, or to the preconditions of that experience, or to the criteria of our aesthetic judgements. Indeed, it is arguable that such assumptions are more typical of, and more central to, modern aesthetic thinking than the theory more regularly attacked. (Kant's doctrine of disinterestedness, Schiller's doctrine of play, and Coleridge's doctrine of the suspension of disbelief, are not, after all, primarily doctrines about the nature of works of art.) Certain forms of this doctrine of aesthetic essence, as we may call it, are logically independent of the doctrine of artistic essence and have been maintained by writers who explicitly rejected that doctrine. Edward Bullough was in fact driven to his doctrine that there is a feature common to 'all aesthetic impressions' precisely because he believed 'that the discovery in the objective world of Art of a common feature of sufficient concreteness to make it applicable both to all works and to each one separately cannot reasonably be hoped for'. It is because 'theoretical unification of the empirical facts on purely objective lines is either so vague or so artificial as to be practically valueless' that he thought one must turn to psychology and attempt to find some feature 'common to all aesthetic impressions' even if it must be derived from works that are highly 'divergent'. It is in 'aesthetic consciousness', not in artistic objects, that one is to discover the desired 'common meeting ground', the subject of 'the modern conception of aesthetics'.[1] A search for an aesthetic essence may well succeed the search for an artistic essence. And it may take the form either of a psychological search for features common to aesthetic experience, or its preconditions, or of a logical inquiry into the features common to the criteria of specifically aesthetic judgement. In the discussion that follows, I shall wish to show that there is no reason to believe that either the psychological or the logical form of this doctrine of aesthetic essence is true. There is no reason to believe any property essential to aesthetic experience or certainly, to believe that such a property distinguishes aesthetic from, say, 'practical,' or intellectual experience. And it is doubtful whether there is any feature essential to the criteria employed in aesthetic appraisal, not to speak of one that distinguishes them from the criteria employed in scientific or moral, economic or technical, appraisal. In addition to indicating the dubiousness of these doctrines I shall hope to show some of their unfortunate consequences. For their acceptance encourages unfortunate attitudes in artistic education and scholarship, and it may interfere with the enjoyment of art and with the full exercise of critical judgement. In some of its forms the

---

[1] Edward Bullough, *Aesthetics*, Stanford 1957, p. 57.

doctrine is incompatible, too, with what I take to be central features of the modern conception of art.

I

It is habitually assumed that there is an element common to our experiences of works of art (or to experiences called 'aesthetic'). Or if not, it is at least supposed that there are certain mental states necessary for the having of these experiences. I call the first assumption the doctrine of aesthetic experience and the second (in view of its most frequent form) the doctrine of an aesthetic attitude. A straightforward commitment to the doctrine of aesthetic experience may be illustrated by a passage from Roger Fry. He writes:

> If we compare in our minds responses experienced in turn in face of different works of art of the most diverse kinds—as, for instance, architectural, pictorial, musical or literary—we recognize that our state of mind in each case has been of a similar kind . . . and that (there is something) common to all these experiences (and) peculiar to them (which) . . . we might conveniently label . . . the specifically aesthetic state of mind.[2]

Fry tells us that there is some element common, and peculiar, to our experience of all works of art. But he does not mention any marks by which we can identify it. Other writers have been more specific. Thus, Bullough remarks in his classic discussion of the various ways, aesthetic and non-aesthetic, of regarding a fog at sea that so long as we regard it practically (or non-aesthetically) we shall experience anxiety, strain, and tension. But he holds that once we adopt the aesthetic attitude toward it we shall experience delight and pleasure.[3] This mode of distinguishing aesthetic from practical experience has a long history in hedonistic aesthetics (and Bullough's specific formulation is an obvious attempt to restate in empirical psychological terms Schopenhauer's conception of art as a release from the pressures of the Will), but it is unworkable. Santayana, the acutest of the hedonistic aestheticians, realized that pleasure characterizes not only aesthetic but also practical activity. He knew the doctrines of the *Nicomachean Ethics* and defined the experience of beauty as the experience of pleasure objectified, because he knew that it must be some very special kind of pleasure that could be peculiar to the aesthetic experience of beauty. But, as we may question whether beauty is, indeed, the essential property of art, we may question whether pleasure, which aestheticians have normally supposed to be characteristic of its apprehension is, truly, an essential feature of aesthetic experience. That beauty is the essence of art has been questioned by Nietzsche and Tolstoy, by Veron and Marinetti, by Eliot and Wittgenstein. And most of them would, I expect, deny that delight or pleasure constitutes the essence of aesthetic experi-

[2] Roger Fry, *Transformations*, Garden City 1956, pp. 1–2.
[3] Bullough, *op. cit.*, pp. 93–94.

ence. Surely, anxiety, tension, and stress, which Bullough takes to be incompatible with aesthetic experience, are in fact essential to the effects not
only of detective fiction (from Oedipus to the present) but (to suggest
only obvious sources) much metaphysical poetry, *Sturm und Drang* music,
and expressionist painting. The muzzles of the battleship *Potemkin*,
pointed at the audience, are positively menacing. The element of truth in
theories of psychical distance may be that there are limits to the degrees
of intensity that such states as anxiety, tension, and stress may attain and
yet remain compatible with aesthetic experience. But if this is true, it is
probably equally true of such states as those of pleasure and delight.

It does not seem possible to determine *a priori* the variety of sensations, feelings, and attitudes that works of art may engender, and empirical
investigation does not seem to have revealed any essential property of
those already acknowledged. I do not wish to deny, on the other hand,
that certain sensations, feelings, and attitudes may be incompatible with
the experience of anything we should conceivably regard as art. But it is
worth noting that whenever some actual limit has been proposed, in
theory or in practice, it has been characteristic of modern artists to attempt to demonstrate its arbitrariness. If there are no specific sensations,
feelings, or the like that are peculiarly aesthetic sensations or feelings, it
might, nevertheless, be maintained, as by Dewey, that there are certain
formal characteristics of experiences that are peculiarly aesthetic. But this
thesis, too, is difficult to maintain. It is virtually impossible decisively to
refute the various positive suggestions that have been made. For the terms
employed, or the uses made of them, are so vague as to defy a confident
presentation of counter-examples. Nevertheless, one may wonder whether
unity (even unity understood to require that the experience be pervaded
by a single individualizing quality)[4] will serve to distinguish aesthetic from
non-aesthetic experiences. Surely, the experience of riding a crowded sub-
way, or of being badly beaten, has at least as great a degree of unity as
(and is more surely pervaded by a single individualizing quality than) the
experience of hearing many a sonata or symphonic suite, or of reading
many a picaresque novel or chronicle play. And such supplementary characteristics—I choose the least vague—as consummatory quality,[5] or continuity,[6] do not seem any more persuasive. Consummatory quality is more
frequently associated with sexual than with aesthetic experience, and various artistic techniques (of which cinematic *montage* is perhaps the most
obvious) are often exploited to create just that gappy, 'breathless', or discontinuous quality that Dewey assigns to practical experience. It is true
that a writer such as Dewey would be perfectly content to allow that works
of art are not the exclusive sources of aesthetic experience. Yet even those
who regard this as a desirable theoretical development may hesitate to subscribe to a formal characterization of aesthetic experience that excludes

[4] John Dewey, *Art as Experience*, New York 1934, pp. 35 ff.
[5] *Ibid.*
[6] *Ibid.*

the experience of central works of art and is satisfied by the experience of brushing one's teeth, or still better, of having them pulled. We do not, and I expect that we cannot, possess a theory about the essential nature of aesthetic experience, if this theory is intended (as perhaps it is not) to encompass the experience of all examples and kinds of art. In what follows I shall, nevertheless, use the phrase 'aesthetic experience' to comprehend the experiences that do characteristically arise from the apprehension of works of art.

II

There are plainly certain capacities with which one must be endowed, certain accomplishments one must possess, certain attitudes one must be able to sustain, and certain activities one must be able to perform, if one is to respond adequately to a work of art. Some conditions are logically necessary for particular aesthetic experiences. Thus the man who is tone-deaf cannot enjoy music, and the man who is ignorant of the history of literature cannot apprehend Joyce's *Ulysses*. It is arguable that other conditions are causally necessary. Perhaps one must be capable of patience to enjoy Proust's novel or an Antonioni film, or of concentration to apprehend a complicated fugue. That some such conditions are required for particular aesthetic experiences no one will deny. But whether, as many aestheticians have suggested, there are certain activities or psychological states that are always and everywhere required for (and, even, that insure) the having of aesthetic experience may be questioned. It is important, not only for theoretical reasons, to question such theses. For, in so far as conditions that are not necessary are taken to be so, inappropriate training is proposed, and false instructions are offered, to those who wish to quicken their aesthetic responses. Quickening one's aesthetic responses is not a general problem, but a series of specific problems. In addition, in so far as insufficient conditions are taken to be sufficient, inadequate training and preparation are suggested. I am inclined to believe that there are, in particular, no special activities (such as contemplating) and no psychological states (such as maintaining 'psychical distance') that are required for having aesthetic experience. And as these are, perhaps, the most prestigious candidates I shall discuss them below. But if it is important to question whether any particular states are required, it is even more important to question whether we can know, in advance of the fact, what activities or states of mind will insure the proper apprehension of a work of art. And beyond activities and states of mind, what sensory capacities, what knowledge, courage, or imagination.

The choice of contemplation as the essential precondition (or, indeed, the essential element) of aesthetic experience is, doubtless, influenced by the traditional opposition of the *vita activa* to the *vita contemplativa*. In the modern version that concerns us, however, it is neither philosophical nor religious contemplation that is contrasted with the life of action, but aesthetic contemplation that is contrasted with physical activity, intellectual labour, and practical interest. (In a transitional figure, such as Schopenhauer, the distinction between philosophical or religious and aesthetic contemplation tends to fail.) This elaborate history has left us with a profoundly confused and (as Maritain suggests) perverted term. And this makes a discussion of aesthetic theories in which the concept of contemplation figures crucially exceptionally difficult. The term 'contemplation' is used in aesthetic contexts by many writers simply to comprehend whatever conditions they suppose necessary for obtaining aesthetic experience. But when the term is employed in this manner the question is effectively begged whether there is any feature common to the bewildering variety of psychological states, and even physical activities, that may be required for obtaining the varieties of aesthetic experience. So, too, is the question begged whether the term 'contemplation' can serve both this broad purpose and yet be understood to preclude (as it is normally understood by these same writers to preclude) various physical actions, intellectual operations, or moral interests. There is no point from which one can contemplate Wright's Guggenheim Museum or Le Corbusier's Carpenter Center (the aesthetic experience requires physical movement), no way of apropriating a novel of Broch's or Mann's without engaging in the meditation and cogitation that Richard of St Victor contrasts with contemplation, no way of feeling the excitement of Goya's *The Disasters of War* or Dostoyevsky's *The Possessed* without exercising those moral and political interests that are typically contrasted with aesthetic, ironic, or disinterested contemplation.

It would not do, however, to represent all theorists as presenting us with so unsatisfactory a situation. No contemporary aesthetician has, so far as I know, investigated the subject of contemplation with the kind of detail that can be found in Richard of St Victor, who in addition to distinguishing contemplation from meditation and cogitation noticed its six varieties. But the term 'contemplation' is at least employed with some sense of its non-technical use by an occasional writer on the visual arts. Thus, Pudovkin, who is interested in establishing that 'the camera compels the spectator to see as the director wishes' knows that the camera 'is charged with a conditional relation to the object shot. Now, urged by heightened interest, it delves into details; now it contemplates the general whole of the picture'.[7] Pudovkin observes the difference between delving into and contemplating a scene. And if the camera can force us to see in these different ways so, I think, can the painter. If one ought to contemplate a Redon or a Rothko, one ought to scrutinize the Westminster Psalter, survey a Tiepolo ceiling, regard a Watteau, and peer at a scene of

[7] V. I. Pudovkin, *Film Technique and Film Acting*, London 1958, pp. 154–155.

Breughel.[8] If we attend to these distinctions we shall be in a position to deny that we must contemplate these works to have a proper aesthetic experience of them. Nor is it the case, as might be suspected, that writers who observe these distinctions do so because they are innocent of philosophical plans for the concept of contemplation. Here we come upon an instance where a form of the doctrine of aesthetic essence is not independent of a theory about the nature of art.

From the Greeks onward it has been supposed that contemplation requires special kinds of objects, and sometimes that only contemplation is capable of discerning these objects. Modern aesthetics reflects this tradition. For the artistically embodied Ideas of Schopenhauer and the Significant Forms of Bell and Fry require contemplation. And it is assumed that in so far as other modes of vision are present they must be directed to non-aesthetic or aesthetically irrelevant aspects of the work of art. A hint of this may be found in Roger Fry's discussion of Breughel's 'Carrying of the Cross'. 'We are invited,' he writes, 'by the whole method of treatment, to come close and peer at each figure in turn and read from it those details which express its particular state of mind so that we may gradually, almost as we might in a novel, bring them together to build up a highly complex psychological structure.[9] Fry dislikes Breughel's kind of painting, and what he dislikes about it is what makes it proper to 'peer at it' and 'read it closely' (rather than 'contemplate' it as one would a Cezanne). For peering displays a psychological, rather than an aesthetic, interest, and Breughel is literary, even novelistic, rather than painterly and significantly formalistic. In a word, his painting is non-aesthetic in its appeal, and this is reflected in the fact that it is apprehended by the allegedly non-aesthetic activity of peering. We must, however, stand with Pudovkin and Breughel for the right to delve and peer. The notion that contemplation is the essential condition of aesthetic experience is often no more than a reflection of the theorist's negligent assumption that the rapt Oriental contemplating a Chinese vase is the paradigm of aesthetic experience. When it is not, it is likely to enshrine partisan tastes such as Fry's.

III

In addition to implying misleading accounts of the conditions of aesthetic experience, psychological versions of the theory of aesthetic essence have provided one of the main motivations for false conceptions of the nature and elements of art itself. The notion that some psychological state, such

[8] Cf. Paul Ziff, 'Reason in Art Criticism', reprinted in Joseph Margolis, ed., *Philosophy Looks at the Arts*, New York 1962, pp. 164 ff. I am grateful to Professor Ziff, as well as to Professors Rogers Albritton and Stanley Cavell, for reading and criticizing an earlier version of this manuscript.

[9] Fry, *op. cit.*, p. 19.

as Bullough's psychical distance, is the necessary (and, indeed, the sufficient) condition of aesthetic experience has led both Bullough and Mrs
Langer to attempt to explain its presence or absence by some doctrine
about the nature or elements of art. Mrs Langer, for instance, constructs
her doctrine that the work of art is an appearance or illusion in order to explain how art imposes an aesthetic 'attitude' and how, by its very nature,
it cannot sustain a practical interest.[10] (She falsely assimilates works of
art to shadows and rainbows, and forgets the practical uses of signs and
wonders.) Bullough's doctrine is less extreme, and despite some remarks
in the tradition of Schiller, he does not clearly commit himself to the view
of art as appearance or illusion. Nevertheless, it is his view that various
features of works of art either encourage, or discourage, the occurrence of
a state of mind that he calls 'psychical distance'. I wish to argue that there
is no need to assume the presence of such a state as a precondition or element of aesthetic experience. In addition, I shall argue that the interpretation of works of art on the assumption that the function of certain of
their stylistic traits is to induce this state leads to a misinterpretation of
them.

The psychological state supposed to be the necessary condition of aesthetic experience has been described by Prall as involving a loss of the
sense of one's body, by Schopenhauer as involving a loss of the sense of
one's self, and by Ethel Puffer as being akin to hypnosis. (Schopenhauer
discourages an appeal to spirituous drinks or opium to achieve this state,
and suggests, rather, a cold bath and a night's sleep.) Bullough's suggestion, if less patently false, is yet communicated in a metaphor susceptible
of many interpretations. The most typical interpretation is one under
which we may say that James or Brecht, or their readers, maintain their
distance from Verena Tarrant or from Galy Gay. However, in this sense,
we also say that distance is not maintained from Isabel Archer or Mother
Courage. But this cannot be the proper interpretation of Bullough's term,
for a lack of distance in this sense is fully compatible with aesthetic experience. (And we may contradict those critics who suppose that the maintenance of distance makes *The Bostonians* a greater novel than *The Portrait of a Lady*. I do not know whether anyone has made so bold a move
in the case of Brecht.) How, then, are we to interpret Bullough? While he
thinks of distance as a psychic state, we know that on occasion he relates
it in an exceptionally straightforward way to certain behavioural manifestations. When we suffer tension, stress, or anxiety we tend to react practically to the situation. It is his view that certain elements of works of art
arouse such feelings; in particular, those representing humanly compelling
situations. For this reason works of art also include other elements to at-

---

[10] Susanne Langer, *Feeling and Form*, New York 1953. See the discussion of Mrs.
Langer's views in Marshall Cohen, 'Appearance and the Aesthetic Attitude,' *The
Journal of Philosophy*, vol. 56 (November 5, 1959), pp. 921–24. The article is reprinted in Marvin Levich, ed., *Aesthetics and the Philosophy of Criticism*, New York
1963.

tenuate or 'distance' those feelings and to inhibit action. In the case of the theatre, for instance, these elements would include the raised stage and the use of costumes and verse. Now Bullough mentions as a clear case of the loss of distance the yokel who leaps upon the stage to save the hapless heroine.[11] Bullough would have us believe that the pressure of his feelings induces the yokel to gain the stage and that the operation of the distancing factors has kept the rest of the audience in their seats. But can we not imagine that the yokel has acted coolly out of an ignorant sense of honour while the carriage-trade has remained in its place seething with emotion? (I assume for the purposes of this discussion that their seething is compatible with the maintenance of sufficient psychical distance.) The operative factors here may not be feelings at all, but rather the presence and absence of knowledge of what a play is and of how one behaves in the theatre. If so, the satisfaction of at least this behavioural criterion of 'psychical' distance, namely, staying put, may be compatible with a wide range of feelings or with none at all. And, indeed, this assumption comports best with the introspective situation.

If knowledge of what a play is should be sufficient to keep the yokel seated, and if no particular feelings or emotions are required to keep the audience in its seats, it will be inappropriate to account for certain elements of a work of art by their tendency to enforce, and others by their tendency to undermine, such psychical states. If the yokel learns what it is to go to a play we shall be able to do the play in a field, without costumes, and in prose, and still expect him to react properly. Thus, the function of the raised stage, costumes, and verse need not be to keep him seated. Indeed, the very stylistic qualities that Bullough supposes to be distancing because of their anti-realistic nature may operate in precisely the opposite fashion. Let us take the theatrical case. The raised stage, appropriate for the performance of Ibsen's plays, tends to make the playgoer less conscious of the rest of the audience. And allowing him to peep into a realistic set peopled with literally costumed characters actually adds to the 'realism' of the play. (Hence the habitual failure of arena-stage productions of Ibsen.) Nor can it plausibly be maintained that the general function of verse is to attenuate responses to the represented events. This does not seem to have been the effect of Aeschylus' verse on the women who gave birth at his plays, or of Shakespeare's on Dr Johnson's reaction to the final scene of King Lear. Alternatively, O'Neill's prosy climaxes (Lavinia's 'O fiddlesticks!') hardly seem to increase the reality of these scenes.

If Bullough's suggestions are often misleading, they are even more often irrelevant. He supposes—it is only an extension of his treatment of the yokel —that anti-realistic (highly-distanced) styles are required mainly to inhibit and to render aesthetic the practical impulses of relatively primitive and unsophisticated peoples. But his hypothesis is quite irrelevant to the prob-

---

[11] Bullough, op. cit. p. 98. See the discussion of Bullough's views in George Dickie, 'Is Psychology Relevant to Aesthetics?' The Philosophical Review, vol. 71 (July 1962), pp. 297–300.

lem of the modern anti-realistic style that has occasioned the brilliant speculations of Ortega and Malraux. For this 'dehumanized' style is the expression, as Ortega indicates, not of the aesthetically unsophisticated masses, but, on the contrary, of an aesthetic elite.[12] And Malraux's argument is of a logical type that Bullough's mode of analysis does not even allow him. For where Bullough's method would lead him to find in the modern renewal of the anti-humanistic or 'transcendental' style a (psychological) purpose similar to that served by this style in the past, it is open to Malraux to suggest that this style has a (non-psychological) purpose exactly opposite to that which it previously served. (It is, he thinks, a 'photographic negative' of previous transcendental styles and serves to express a new humanism rather than to cancel a discredited one.)[13] The possibility of offering quite different accounts of the functions of similar stylistic elements on different occasions and of finding these explanations not in psychological factors but, perhaps, in considerations of history or of *Weltanschauung* seems all to the good. Bullough's attempt to relate such explanations to the fortunes of some otiose and unidentifiable psychological state cannot be regarded as useful procedure. Like Mrs Langer's theory that all works of art are appearances or illusions, Bullough's notion that stylistic elements should be understood as increasing or decreasing distance may be dismissed with its questionable motivation. There is no way of determining the precondition of all aesthetic experience just as there is no way of knowing what qualities such experience must bear.

IV

We have analysed the psychological version of the doctrine of aesthetic essence as it bears on aesthetic experience and its preconditions and on the nature and the analysis of art. It will be useful to conclude by examining the logical version of the doctrine in its relation to the problem of aesthetic judgement and the criticism of art. We are characteristically invited to make aesthetic judgements when making them would not be the obvious thing to do or when it is felt that, although this is the obvious thing to do, it has not been done. Thus, we may be asked to pass an aesthetic judgement on a car in a conversation in which we have all along been assessing its technical efficacy, or the economics of running it. Alternatively, and this is typical of critical contexts, we may insist that we have, in fact, made an aesthetic (or an artistic, or a literary) judgement. Our point will be to forestall the objection, or to reject the accusation, that we have in fact made a moral, or a technical, or an economic one. It has been suggested that these various kinds of judgement can be distinguished from one another by reference to the criteria that are relevant to making them. Thus,

---

[12] José Ortega y Gasset, *The Dehumanization of Art*, Garden City 1956.
[13] André Malraux, *The Voices of Silence*, Garden City 1953; Joseph Frank, 'Malraux's Metaphysics', *The Sewanee Review*, vol. 70 (Autumn 1962), p. 646.

there is a special set of aesthetic criteria, as distinguished from moral, and intellectual, and economic criteria, and it is on the basis of these aesthetic criteria that we make our aesthetic judgements. J. O. Urmson, for instance, regards it as the central task of the philosopher of aesthetics 'to clarify the principles on which we select the special set of criteria of value that are properly counted as relevant to aesthetic judgement.'[14] And, although he does not commit himself to the view that a single principle specifies this special set of 'criteria,' the very assumption that there is such a special set supplies a major source of encouragement for the view that some single property does characterize the criteria of aesthetic judgement. In fact, Urmson himself proposes that at least in the simplest cases (and it is not obvious how he would allow more complicated ones to alter his view) aesthetic judgements are judgements of how things look or smell or otherwise present themselves to the senses. It will not be our purpose in this section to propose any alternative analysis of the nature of aesthetic judgements or to suggest any peculiarity of the logic of aesthetic arguments. Our purpose will be to call into question the suggestion that the criteria of aesthetic judgement can be characterized by a feature such as the one Urmson suggests, or that these criteria from a set that characteristically excludes moral, scientific, or ideological criteria. Urmson writes that 'it would be a very odd person who denied that the sound of the words of a poem was one of the criteria of aesthetic judgement of a poem, or who maintained that being scientifically accurate and up to date was another.'[15] Urmson's notion that 'the sound of the words of a poem' is one of the criteria of the aesthetic judgement of poems is simply a manifestation of his more general principle that aesthetic criteria appear to be those concerned with 'the way the object in question looks or presents itself to the other senses.'[16] There is, of course, some plain confusion here. Urmson does not really propose a criterion. 'The sound of the words of a poem' does not constitute a criterion of evaluation. What is it about these sounds that is aesthetically meritorious? Even if we waive this objection, however, it is worth noting that critics as various as Bradley and Croce and I. A. Richards have denied that any feature of the sounds of the words of a poem constitutes an important source of poetic merit. As Eliot puts it 'the music of poetry is not something that exists apart from its meaning.'[17] It does not, of course, follow from what Eliot actually says that our judgements of poems might not be confined to some quality of their sounds. This might be the case even if this quality 'could not exist' outside meaningful contexts. But, as a matter of fact, we rarely, if ever, judge poems (even the poems of Verlaine, Swinburne, or Wallace Stevens) simply by their sounds (a doctrine with which Urmson appears to be flirt-

---

[14] J. O. Urmson, 'What Makes a Situation Aesthetic?' reprinted in Margolis, *op. cit.*, p. 20.
[15] *Ibid.*, p. 22.
[16] J. O. Urmson, 'What Makes a Situation Aesthetic?' reprinted in Margolis, *op. cit.*, p. 25.
[17] T. S. Eliot, 'The Music of Poetry,' *On Poetry and Poets*, New York 1961, p. 21.

ing) and often enough we do not judge them by their sounds at all. We may by-pass the question whether, in general, music may be said to have sounds or paintings looks. (To be sure, performed music occasionally has a muffled sound, and paintings often have a faded look. But even when they do have such properties, aesthetic judgements may be required positively to ignore them.) The fact is that even the narrowest conception of aesthetic judgement invokes criteria for assessing the formal structure of the work of art or, say, its success in exploiting the medium. It does not seem possible to extend Urmson's principle even to such indisputably aesthetic criteria, and no further principle suggests itself. But even if some feature could be discovered that might cover such aesthetic criteria it would be necessary to question whether those criteria typically classified as moral, scientific, and ideological are, in fact, as Urmson suggests, irrelevant to the making of aesthetic judgements. If they should, in fact, turn out to be relevant, this would not only be of the greatest interest in itself but it would incalculably increase the improbability of discovering some feature common to all the criteria, moral and scientific as well as aesthetic, relevant to aesthetic judgement. And it would indicate that any such property would have to characterize not only aesthetic criteria but certain moral and scientific criteria as well.

A more promising line of objection to the notion that only 'aesthetic' criteria are relevant to aesthetic judgement may seem to be provided by such characteristic critical remarks as that Mary McCarthy's novels are unsuccessful because she is incapable of loving her characters. This may look like a straightforward moral (or psychological) judgement of the novel. And, indeed, it is not impossible to take it that way. But neither is it necessary to take it that way. We may understand the critic to be saying (in an elliptical way that some find misleading) that the characters do not have all the dimensions of life. They lack all those characteristics that only the eye of love can discern. Interpreted in this way the objection may be regarded as an aesthetic judgement criticizing the novels for failing to achieve 'the illusion of life.' If so, it might be argued that Urmson is wrong and that here we have a case where a moral ground (the incapacity to love) is, indeed, 'relevant to' an aesthetic judgement (the novel's lack or verisimilitude). The difficulty with this kind of example is, however, that the 'moral' or psychological fact is relevant to an explanation of why Mary McCarthy cannot write successful 'realistic' novels. What is required is, however, that the fact be relevant to establishing the judgement that the novels do not in fact create 'the illusion of life.' And this it does not do. (Indeed, the psychological fact only becomes relevant to the explanation once the aesthetic fact to be explained has been established.) If the psychological or moral fact is not relevant to making the judgement, certainly it is not its ground. It is true that we say the novels fail to dramatize certain dimensions of reality because Mary McCarthy cannot love her characters. But to take this as establishing that the lack of love is a ground for our judgement is to confuse a causal with a criterial use of 'because.' What we are doing is offering an explanation of the aesthetic failure and not saying that it is in virtue of the fact that Mary McCarthy cannot love her characters that we judge the novels to be unconvincing. Mary McCarthy's alleged moral or psychological failing is not operating as a criterion of aesthetic judgement at all, so it cannot be an example of a moral criterion of such a judgement. A more pertinent example is required.

It will be remembered that Urmson chooses as his example of extreme oddity the person who maintained that being scientifically accurate and up to date was in fact a criterion of aesthetic judgement. (In fact, in one form or another, it is a far more usual criterion of aesthetic excellence than is the possession of some quality of sound.) It is, perhaps, unfair to remind Urmson that Pound was exhibiting one of the central motives of the modern aesthetic creed when he demanded that poets 'make it new.' (Unfair, because the newness he had in mind was a kind of newness impossible for science.) But it is surely fair to cite a judgement like the one Lionel Trilling passes on the recent American novel. 'It is questionable,' he writes, 'whether any American novel since *Babbitt* has told us a new thing about our social life. In psychology the novel relies either on a mechanical or classical use of psychiatry or on the insights that were established by the novelists of fifty years ago.'[18] Unless psychology and social science are ruled out as not really scientific we would appear to have a clear and typical counter-example to Urmson's observation (he rightly sets great store by field work among the critics) and a case of a scientific criterion employed in making an aesthetic judgement. For Trilling means to condemn the recent American novel as an artistic achievement.

It is open to writers of Urmson's persuasion either to deny that such judgements are indeed aesthetic judgements (a position I do not propose to consider here) or to argue that the ostensibly non-aesthetic criteria are in fact really aesthetic ones. Wellek and Warren,[19] for instance, feel that they would have to reject Eliot's dictum that the critic must consider whether a poem is 'coherent, mature, and founded on the facts of experience' unless they could show the criteria in question to be aesthetic ones. They observe, then, that coherence is not merely a logical but also an aesthetic criterion. It is not obvious whether they are saying that 'coherence' has two different senses, or whether they are saying that a criterion may fall into a number of different categories. The first, however, seems the more likely. For they go on to suggest that the other criteria, apparently psychological and epistemological, are to be understood as aesthetic. Thus, the psychological criterion of maturity is to be understood as a demand for complexity, and they find that the epistemological criterion of truth to experience 'registers itself in aesthetic terms of vividness, intensity, patterned contrast, width or depth, static or kinetic.' This will not do. Obviously, many works regarded as mature (either for their own qualities or because of their position in an *oeuvre*) are not remarkable for their com-

---

[18] Lionel Trilling, *The Liberal Imagination*, New York 1950, p. 263.
[19] René Wellek and Austin Warren, *Theory of Literature*, New York 1949, p. 257.

plexity. The maturity of *Oedipus at Colonus*, *The Tempest*, and *When We Dead Awaken*, is evidenced by the authority of their relative simplicity, and they are less complex than *Oedipus Rex*, *Troilus and Cressida*, and *Peer Gynt*. And, surely, the truth to experience Eliot has in mind displays itself in the calm of Dante (as narrator, not pilgrim) rather than in the intensity of Shelley, in the muted measure of *Four Quartets* rather than in the vividness of 'The Hippopotamus' or 'Mr. Apollinax.' It simply does not seem possible to reduce the criterion of maturity to that of complexity. And more importantly, it does not seem possible to reduce the criterion of truth, either as it is invoked by Trilling or by Eliot, to an aesthetic criterion. If that is so, it would appear to be the case that scientific—and, as it would be still simpler to show, moral—criteria are relevant to the making of aesthetic judgements. Urmson's assumption that the sub-set of such criteria will exclude moral, intellectual, and other criteria, is false. And the hope of discovering some property common to the criteria relevant to aesthetic judgement, in so far as it is based on the assumption that such criteria are, indeed, excluded, will lose its plausibility.

If the aesthetic purists cannot show that ostensibly non-aesthetic criteria are really aesthetic ones, they might try to avoid the conclusion we have reached by denying that they are criteria at all. Or, at least, that they are the real or ultimate criteria of aesthetic judgements. The purists might hold that whenever aesthetic judgements appear to rely on non-aesthetic criteria they can be shown actually or implicitly to invoke some further aesthetic criterion. And it will always be the case that the facts relevant to determining whether the non-aesthetic criteria have been satisfied will be relevant to deciding whether the further aesthetic criteria have been satisfied. If these relations did not obtain, it might be held, the judgement would not be accepted as an aesthetic one. Thus, Trilling may praise James' *The Princess Casamassima* for satisfying just those historical and epistemological criteria he regards the modern American novel as having failed to satisfy. But the aesthetic purists might argue that we accept the judgement as aesthetic only because we take an implicit criterion to be a genuinely aesthetic one. In this case, perhaps, that the demands of the genre are satisfied (and in the case of realistic fiction one of these demands is for genuine historical comprehension). Similarly, they might seek to show that often, at least, when we appear to be appealing to scientific, moral, intellectual, and even economic criteria, we are actually appealing to aesthetic ones. If we merely look at what he writes, we may suppose the critic to be praising Mann's *Dr Faustus* simply for the brilliance of his historical diagnosis, D. H. Lawrence's *Women in Love* for its moral profundity, Schoenberg's Opus 23 piano pieces for their intellectual audacity, and Fabergé jewellery or the Taj Mahal for their expensiveness. But it may be possible to argue that in each case the fundamental criterion of judgement is in fact aesthetic. We are really judging that Mann achieves his artistic intentions, that Lawrence has fully realized the potentialities of the novel, that Schoenberg has renewed an exhausted musical art, and that Fabergé has exploited his materials in the manner best calculated to reveal their peculiar virtue. Whether a position such as the one sketched here can be precisely stated (so that one knows, for instance, how the existence and identity of the implicit criterion is to be determined) and whether it can be defended in detail (some such theory is assumed by many to be *a priori* true) cannot be decided here. I am much inclined to doubt it. But I am still more inclined to doubt whether some property will be found that is essential even to the considerable variety of aesthetic criteria that are likely to be acknowledged if the thesis in question is to be defended at all. For aesthetic criteria are numerous and make reference not only to the sensory and formal features of objects and to expressive and technical qualities of media but also to the intentions of artists, the dialectical demands of particular arts, the expectations of aesthetic elites, and the impersonal progress of the institutions of art.

It is perhaps worth insisting that I do not suppose all judgements of works of art to be aesthetic judgements. And it is important to distinguish those judgements that we regard as aesthetic (even when they are based on moral criteria) from those we do not. For this is to distinguish D. H. Lawrence's judgement of Galsworthy's novels and Santayana's of Whitman's poetry from the Congressional hack's judgement of Martha Graham's dances or the Party hack's judgement of *Dr Zhivago*. But neither do I wish to suggest that we ought never to pass moral or political judgements on works of art. In the Republic it may be necessary to pass Plato's flattering judgement on poets. And in France, at least, it may already be necessary to demand that every writer of fiction ask what would happen if everyone read what he wrote. For the consequences of words are not merely aesthetic consequences. Sartre was, therefore, right to remind us of Mosca's observation beside the coach that carried Fabrice and Sanseverina away.[20] 'If the word Love comes up between them, I'm lost.'

[20] Jean-Paul Sartre, *What Is Literature?* New York 1949. Reprinted as *Existentialism and Literature*, New York 1962, pp. 23–24.

Maurice Mandelbaum

FAMILY RESEMBLANCES AND GENERALIZATION CONCERNING THE ARTS

In 1954 William Elton collected and published a group of essays under the title *Aesthetics and Language*.* As his introduction made clear, a common feature of these essays was the application to aesthetic problems of some of the doctrines characteristic of recent British linguistic philosophy.[1] While this mode of philosophizing has not had as pervasive an influence on aesthetics as it has had on most other branches of philosophy,[2] there have been a number of important articles which, in addition to those contained in the Elton volume, suggest the direction in which this influence runs. Among these articles one might mention "The Task of Defining a Work of Art" by Paul Ziff,[3] "The Role of Theory in Aesthetics" by Morris Weitz,[4] Charles L. Stevenson's "On 'What is a Poem' "[5] and W. E. Kennick's "Does Traditional Aesthetics Rest on a Mistake?"[6] In each of them one finds a conviction which was also present in most of the essays in the Elton volume: that it is a mistake to offer generalizations concerning the arts, or, to put the matter in a more provocative manner, that it is a mistake to attempt to discuss what art, or beauty, or the aesthetic, or a poem, *essentially* is. In partial support of this contention, some writers have made explicit use of Wittgenstein's doctrine of *family resemblances;*

Maurice Mandelbaum is Professor of Philosophy at Johns Hopkins University. He is a well-known philosophical figure in America who has long contributed books and essays to the subject.

* Originally published in *American Philosophical Quarterly*, vol. 2, no. 3, 1965. Reprinted by permission of *American Philosophical Quarterly*.

[1] See William Elton (ed.), *Aesthetics and Language* (Oxford, Basil Blackwell, 1954), p. 1, n. 1 and 2.
[2] A discussion of this fact is to be found in Jerome Stolnitz, "Notes on Analytic Philosophy and Aesthetics," *British Journal of Aesthetics*, vol. 3 (1961), pp. 210–222.
[3] *Philosophical Review*, vol. 62 (1953), pp. 58–78.
[4] *Journal of Aesthetics and Art Criticism*, vol. 15 (1956), pp. 27–35.
[5] *Philosophical Review*, vol. 66 (1957), pp. 329–362.
[6] *Mind*, vol. 67 (1958), pp. 317–334. In addition to the articles already referred to, I might mention "The Uses of Works of Art" by Teddy Brunius in *Journal of Aesthetics and Art Criticism*, vol. 22 (1963), pp. 123–133, which refers to both Weitz and Kennick, but raises other questions with which I am not here concerned.

Morris Weitz, for example, has placed it in the forefront of his discussion. However, in that influential and frequently anthologized article, Professor Weitz made no attempt to analyze, clarify, or defend the doctrine itself. Since its use with respect to aesthetics has provided the means by which others have sought to escape the need of generalizing concerning the arts, I shall begin my discussion with a consideration of it.

I

The *locus classicus* for Wittgenstein's doctrine of family resemblances is in Part I of *Philosophical Investigations*, sections 65–77.[7] In discussing what he refers to as language-games, Wittgenstein says:

> Instead of producing something common to all that we call language, I am saying that these phenomena have no one thing in common which makes us use the same word for all—but they are *related* to one another in many different ways. And it is because of this relationship, or these relationships, that we call them all "language." (§65)

He then illustrates his contention by citing a variety of *games*, such as board games, card games, ball games, etc., and concludes:

> We see a complicated network of similarities overlapping and criss-crossing: sometimes overall similarities of detail. (§66)
> I can think of no better expression to characterize these similarities than "family resemblances": for the various resemblances between members of a family: build, features, colour of eyes, gait, temperament, etc., etc. overlap and criss-cross in the same way.—And I shall say: "games" form a family. (§67)

In short, what Wittgenstein aims to establish is that one need not suppose that all instances of those entities to which we apply a common name do in fact possess any one feature in common. Instead, the use of a common name is grounded in the crisscrossing and overlapping of resembling features among otherwise heterogeneous objects and activities.

Wittgenstein's concrete illustrations of the diversity among various types of games may at first make his doctrine of family resemblances extremely plausible. For example, we do not hesitate to characterize tennis, chess, bridge, and solitaire as games, even though a comparison of them fails to reveal any specific feature which is the same in each of them. Nonetheless, I do not believe that his doctrine of family resemblances, as it stands, provides an adequate analysis of why a common name, such as "a game," is in all cases applied or withheld.

Consider first the following case. Let us assume that you know how to play that form of solitaire called "Canfield"; suppose also that you are

[7] Ludwig Wittgenstein, *Philosophical Investigations*, translated by G. E. M. Anscombe (New York, Macmillan, 1973), pp. 31–36. A parallel passage is to be found in "The Blue Book": see *Preliminary Studies for the "Philosophical Investigations," Generally Known as The Blue and Brown Books* (Oxford, Basil Blackwell, 1958), pp. 17–18.

acquainted with a number of other varieties of solitaire (Wittgenstein uses "patience," i.e., "solitaire," as one instance of a form of game). Were you to see me shuffling a pack of cards, arranging the cards in piles, some face up and some face down, turning cards over one-by-one, sometimes placing them in one pile, then another, shifting piles, etc., you might say: "I see you are playing cards. What game are you playing?" However, to this I might answer: "I am not playing a game; I am telling (or reading) fortunes." Will the resemblances between what you have seen me doing and the characteristics of card games with which you are familiar permit you to contradict me and say that I am indeed playing some sort of game? Ordinary usage would not, I believe, sanction our describing fortune-telling as an example of playing a game, no matter how striking may be the resemblances between the ways in which cards are handled in playing solitaire and in telling fortunes. Or, to choose another example, we may say that while certain forms of wrestling contests are sometimes character-ized as games (Wittgenstein mentions "*Kampfspiele*")[8] an angry struggle between two boys, each trying to make the other give in, is not to be char-acterized as a game. Yet one can find a great many resembling features between such a struggle and a wrestling match in a gymnasium. What would seem to be crucial in our designation of an activity as a game is, therefore, not merely a matter of noting a number of specific resemblances between it and other activities which we denote as games, but involves something further.

To suggest what sort of characteristic this "something further" might possibly be, it will be helpful to pay closer attention to the notion of what constitutes a family resemblance. Suppose that you are shown ten or a dozen photographs and you are then asked to decide which among them exhibit strong resemblances.[9] You might have no difficulty in selecting, say, three of the photographs in which the subjects were markedly round-headed, had a strongly prognathous profile, rather deep-set eyes, and dark curly hair.[10] In some extended, metaphorical sense you might say that the similarities in their features constituted a family resemblance among

---

[8] Ludwig Wittgenstein, *Philosophical Investigations*, §66, p. 31. For reasons which are obscure, Miss Anscombe translates "*Kampfspiele*" as "Olympic games."

[9] In an article which is closely related to my discussion, but which uses different argu-ments to support a similar point, Haig Khatchadourian has shown that Wittgenstein is less explicit than he should have been with respect to the levels of determinateness at which these resemblances are significant for our use of common names. See "Com-mon Names and 'Family Resemblances'," *Philosophy and Phenomenological Research*, vol. 18 (1957–58), pp. 341–358. (For a related, but less closely relevant article by Professor Khatchadourian see "Art-Names and Aesthetic Judgments," *Philosophy*, vol. 36 [1961], pp. 30–48.)

[10] It is to be noted that this constitutes a closer resemblance than that involved in what Wittgenstein calls "family resemblances," since in my illustration the specific similari-ties all pertain to a single set of features, with respect to each one of which all three of the subjects directly resemble one another. In Wittgenstein's use of the notion of family resemblances there is, however, no one set of resembling features common to each member of the "family"; there is merely a criss-crossing and overlapping among the elements which constitute the resemblances among the various persons. Thus, in order to conform to his usage, my illustration would have to be made more compli-cated, and the degree of resemblance would become more attenuated. For example,

them. The sense, however, would be metaphorical, since in the absence of a biological kinship of a certain degree of proximity we would be inclined to speak only of resemblances, and not of a *family* resemblance. What marks the difference between a literal and a metaphorical sense of the notion of "family resemblances" is, therefore, the existence of a genetic connection in the former case and not in the latter. Wittgenstein, however, failed to make explicit the fact that the literal, root notion of a family resemblance includes this genetic connection no less than it includes the existence of noticeable physiognomic resemblances.[11] Had the existence of such a *twofold* criterion been made explicit by him, he would have noted that there is in fact an attribute common to all who bear a family resemblance to each other: they are related through a common ancestry. Such a relationship is not, of course, one among the specific features of those who share a family resemblance; it nonetheless differentiates them from those who are not to be regarded as members of a single family.[12] If, then, it is possible that the analogy of family resemblances could

---

we would have to introduce the photographs of other subjects in which, for example, recessive chins would supplant prognathous profiles among those who shared the other characteristics; some would have blond instead of dark hair, and protruberant instead of deep-set eyes, but would in each case resemble the others in other respects, etc. However, if what I say concerning family resemblances holds of the stronger similarities present in my illustration, it should hold *a fortiori* of the weaker form of family resemblances to which Wittgenstein draws our attention.

[11] Although Wittgenstein failed to make explicit the fact that a genetic connection was involved in his notion of "family resemblances," I think that he did in fact presuppose such a connection. If I am not mistaken, the original German makes this clearer than does the Anscombe translation. The German text reads:

> Ich kann diese Ähnlichkeiten nicht besser charakterisieren, als durch das Wort "Familienähnlichkeiten"; denn so übergreifen und kreuzen sich die verschiedenen Ähnlichkeiten, die zwischen den Gliedern einer Familie bestehen: Wuchs, Gesichtszüge, Augenfarbe, Gang, Temperament, etc., etc. (§67).

Modifying Miss Anscombe's translation in as few respects as possible, I suggest that a translation of this passage might read:

> I can think of no better expression to characterize these similarities than "family resemblances," since various similarities which obtain among the members of a family—their build, features, color of eyes, gait, temperament, etc., etc.—overlap and criss-cross in the same way.

This translation differs from Miss Anscombe's (which has been quoted above) in that it makes more explicit the fact that the similarities are similarities among the members of a single family, and are not themselves definitive of what constitutes a *family* resemblance.

[12] Were this aspect of the twofold criterion to be abandoned, and were our use of common names to be solely determined by the existence of overlapping and criss-crossing relations, it is difficult to see how a halt would ever be called to the spread of such names. Robert J. Richman has called attention to the same problem in " 'Something Common'," *Journal of Philosophy*, vol. 59 (1962), pp. 821–830. He speaks of what he calls "the Problem of Wide-Open Texture," and says: "the notion of family resemblances may account for our extending the application of a given general term, but it does not seem to place any limit on this process" (p. 829).

In an article entitled "The Problem of the Model-Language Game in Wittgenstein's Later Philosophy," *Philosophy*, vol. 36 (1961), pp. 333–351, Helen Hervey also calls attention to the fact that "a family is so-called by virtue of its common ancestry" (p. 334). She also mentions (p. 335) what Richman referred to as the problem of "the wide-open texture."

tell us something about how games may be related to one another, one should explore the possibility that, in spite of their great dissimilarities, games may possess a common attribute which, like biological connection, is not itself one among their directly exhibited characteristics. Unfortunately, such a possibility was not explored by Wittgenstein.

To be sure, Wittgenstein does not explicitly state that the resemblances which are correlated with our use of common names must be of a sort that are directly exhibited. Nonetheless, all of his illustrations in the relevant passages involve aspects of games which would be included in a description of how a particular game is to be played; that is, when he commands us to "look and see" whether there is anything common to all games,[13] the "anything" is taken to represent precisely the sort of manifest feature that is described in rule-books, such as Hoyle. However, as we have seen in the case of family resemblances, what constitutes a *family* is not defined in terms of the manifest features of a random group of people; we must first characterize the *family* relationship in terms of genetic ties, and then observe to what extent those who are connected in this way *resemble* one another.[14] In the case of games, the analogue to genetic ties might be the purpose for the sake of which various games were formulated by those who invented or modified them, e.g., the potentiality of a game to be of absorbing non-practical interest to either participants or spectators. If there were any such common feature one would not expect it to be defined in a rule book, such as Hoyle, since rule books only attempt to tell us how to play a particular game: our interest in playing a game, and our understanding of what constitutes a game, is already presupposed by the authors of such books.

It is not my present concern to characterize any feature common to most or all of those activities which we call games, nor would I wish to argue on the analogy of family resemblances that there *must be* any such feature. If the question is to be decided, it must be decided by an attempt to "look and see." However, it is important that we look in the right place and in the right ways if we are looking for a common feature; we should not assume that any feature common to all games must be some manifest characteristic, such as whether they are to be played with a ball or with cards, or how many players there must be in order for the game to be played. If we were to rely exclusively on such features we should, as I have suggested, be apt to link solitaire with fortune-telling, and wrestling matches with fights, rather than (say) linking solitaire with cribbage and wrestling matches with weight-lifting. It is, then, my contention that Wittgenstein's emphasis on directly exhibited resemblances, and his failure to consider other possible similarities, led to a failure on his part to provide

---

[13] Ludwig Wittgenstein, *Philosophical Investigations*, §66, p. 31.
[14] Although I have only mentioned the existence of genetic connections among members of a family, I should of course not wish to exclude the effects of habitual association in giving rise to some of the resemblances which Wittgenstein mentions. I have stressed genetic connection only because it is the simplest and most obvious illustration of the point I have wished to make.

an adequate clue as to what—in some cases at least—governs our use of common names.[15]

If the foregoing remarks are correct, we are now in a position to see that the radical denigration of generalization concerning the arts, which has come to be almost a hallmark of the writings of those most influenced by recent British philosophy, may involve serious errors, and may not constitute a notable advance.

II

In turning from Wittgenstein's statements concerning family resemblances to the use to which his doctrine has been put by writers on aesthetics, we must first note what these writers are *not* attempting to do. In the first place, they are not seeking to clarify the relationships which exist among the many different senses in which the word "art" is used. Any dictionary offers a variety of such senses (e.g., the art of navigation, art as guile, art as the craft of the artist, etc.), and it is not difficult to find a pattern of family resemblances existing among many of them. However, an analysis of such resemblances, and of their differences, has not, as a matter of fact, been of interest to the writers of the articles with which we are here concerned. In the second place, these writers have not been primarily interested in analyzing how words such as "work of art" or "artist" or "art" are ordinarily used by those who are neither aestheticians nor art critics; their concern has been with the writing which make up the tradition of "aesthetic theory." In the third place, we must note that the concern of these writers has not been to show that family resemblances do in fact exist among the various arts, or among various works of art; on the contrary, they have used the doctrine of family resemblances in a *negative* fashion. In this, they have of course followed Wittgenstein's own example. The position which they have sought to establish is that traditional aesthetic theory has been mistaken in assuming that there is any essential property or defining characteristic of works of art (or any set of such properties or characteristics); as a consequence, they have contended that most of the questions which have been asked by those engaged in writing on aesthetics are mistaken sorts of questions.

However, as the preceding discussion of Wittgenstein should have served to make clear, one cannot assume that if there is any one characteristic common to all works of art it must consist in some specific, directly exhibited feature. Like the biological connections among those who are connected by family resemblances, or like the intentions on the basis of

---

[15] I do not deny that directly exhibited resemblances often play a part in our use of common names: this is a fact explicitly noted at least as long ago as by Locke. However, similarities in origin, similarities in use, and similarities in intention may also play significant roles. It is such factors that Wittgenstein overlooks in his specific discussions of family resemblances and of games.

which we distinguish between fortune-telling and card games, such a characteristic might be a relational attribute, rather than some characteristic at which one could directly point and say: "It is this particular feature of the object which leads me to designate it as a work of art." A relational attribute of the required sort might, for example, only be apprehended if one were to consider specific art objects as having been created by someone for some actual or possible audience.

The suggestion that the essential nature of art is to be found in such a relational attribute is surely not implausible when one recalls some of the many traditional theories of art. For example, art has sometimes been characterized as being one special form of communication or of expression, or as being a special form of wish-fulfillment, or as being a presentation of truth in sensuous form. Such theories do not assume that in each poem, painting, play, and sonata there is a specific ingredient which identifies it as a work of art; rather, that which is held to be common to these otherwise diverse objects is a relationship which is assumed to have existed, or is known to have existed, between certain of their characteristics and the activities and the intentions of those who made them.[16]

While we may acknowledge that it is difficult to find any set of attributes—whether relational or not—which can serve to characterize the nature of a work of art (and which will not be as vulnerable to criticism

---

[16] I know of no passage in which Wittgenstein takes such a possibility into account. In fact, if the passage from "The Blue Book" to which I have already alluded may be regarded as representative, we may say that Wittgenstein's view of traditional aesthetic theories was quite without foundation. In that passage he said:

> The idea of a general concept being a common property of its particular instances connects up with other primitive, too simple, ideas of the structure of language. It is comparable to the idea that *properties* are *ingredients* of the things which have the properties, e.g., that beauty is an ingredient of all beautiful things as alcohol is of beer and wine, and that we therefore could have pure beauty, unadulterated by anything that is beautiful (p. 17).

I fail to be able to identify any aesthetic theory of which such a statement would be true. It would not, for example, be true of Clive Bell's doctrine of "significant form," nor would it presumably be true of G. E. Moore's view of beauty, since both Bell and Moore hold that beauty depends upon the specific nature of the other qualities which characterize that which is beautiful.

However, it may be objected that when I suggest that what is common to works of art involves reference to "intentions," I overlook "the intentional fallacy" (see W. K. Wimsatt, Jr., and Monroe C. Beardsley, "The Intentional Fallacy," *Sewanee Review*, vol. 54 [1946], pp. 468–488). This is not the case. The phrase "the intentional fallacy" originally referred to a particular method of criticism, that is, to a method of interpreting and evaluating given works of art; it was not the aim of Wimsatt and Beardsley to distinguish between art and non-art. These two problems are, I believe, fundamentally different in character. However, I do not feel sure that Professor Beardsley has noted this fact, for in a recent article in which he set out to criticize those who have been influenced by the doctrine of family resemblances he apparently felt himself obliged to define art *solely* in terms of some characteristic in the object itself (see "The Definition of the Arts," *Journal of Aesthetics and Art Criticism*, vol. 20 [1961], pp. 175–187). Had he been willing to relate this characteristic to the activity and intention of those who make objects having such a characteristic, his discussion would not, I believe, have been susceptible to many of the criticisms leveled against it by Professor Douglas Morgan and Mary Mothersill (*ibid.*, pp. 187–198).

as many other such characterizations have been),[17] it is important to note that the difficulties inherent in this task are not really avoided by those who appeal to the notion of family resemblances. As soon as one attempts to elucidate how the term "art" is in fact used in the context of art criticism, most of the same problems which have arisen in the history of aesthetic theory will again make their appearance. In other words, linguistic analysis does not provide a means of escape from the issues which have been of major concern in traditional aesthetics. This fact may be illustrated through examining a portion of one of the articles to which I have already alluded, Paul Ziff's article entitled "The Task of Defining a Work of Art."

To explain how the term "a work of art" is used, and to show the difficulties one encounters if one seeks to generalize concerning the arts, Professor Ziff chooses as his starting point one clear-cut example of a work of art and sets out to describe it. The work he chooses is a painting by Poussin, and his description runs as follows:

> Suppose we point to Poussin's "The Rape of the Sabine Women" as our clearest available case of a work of art. We could describe it by saying, first, that it is a painting. Secondly, it was made, and what is more, made deliberately and self-consciously with obvious skill and care, by Nicolas Poussin. Thirdly, the painter intended it to be displayed in a place where it could be looked at and appreciated, where it could be contemplated and admired. . . . Fourthly, the painting is or was exhibited in a museum gallery where people do contemplate, study, observe, admire, criticize, and discuss it. What I wish to refer to here by speaking of contemplating, studying, and observing a painting, is simply what we may do when we are concerned with a painting like this. For example, when we look at this painting by Poussin, we may attend to its sensuous features, to its "look and feel." Thus we attend to the play of light and color, to dissonances, contrasts, and harmonies of hues, values, and intensities. We notice patterns and pigmentation, textures, decorations, and embellishments. We may also attend to the structure, design, composition, and organization of the work. Thus we look for unity, and we also look for variety, for balance and movement. We attend to the formal interrelations and cross connexions in the work, to its underlying structure. . . . Fifthly, this work is a representational painting with a definite subject matter; it depicts a certain mythological scene. Sixthly, the painting is an elaborate and certainly complex formal structure. Finally, the painting is a good painting. And this is to say simply that the Poussin painting is worth contemplating, studying, and observing in the way I have ever so roughly described.[18]

With reference to this description we must first note that it is clearly not meant to be anything like a complete description of the Poussin paint-

---

[17] I do not say "*all*" such definitions, for I think that one can find a number of convergent definitions of art, each of which has considerable merit, though each may differ slightly from the others in its emphasis.

[18] *Op. cit.*, pp. 60–61. It is an interesting problem, but not germane to our present concerns, to consider whether Poussin's painting should be classified as a "mythological" painting, as Professor Ziff describes it, or whether it should be regarded as an historical painting.

ing; it is at most a description of those aspects of that painting which are relevant to its being called a work of art. For example, neither the weight of the painting nor its insurable value is mentioned. Thus, whether because of his own preconceptions, or because of our ordinary assumptions concerning how the term "work of art" is to be used, Professor Ziff focuses attention on some aspects of the Poussin painting than upon others. In doing so, he is making an implicit appeal to what is at least a minimal aesthetic theory, that is, he is supposing that neither weight nor insurable value need be mentioned when we list the characteristics which lead us to say of a particular piece of painted canvas that it is a work of art. In the second place, we must note that of the seven characteristics which he mentions, not all are treated by Professor Ziff as being independent of one another; nor are all related to one another in identical ways. It will be instructive to note some of the differences among their relationships, since it is precisely here that many of the traditional problems of aesthetic theory once again take their rise.

For example, we are bound to note that Professor Ziff related the seventh characteristic of the Poussin painting to its fourth characteristic: the fact that it is a good painting is, he holds, related to the characteristics which we find that it possesses when we contemplate, observe, and study it. Its goodness, however, is not claimed to be related to its first, third, or fifth characteristics: in other words, Professor Ziff is apparently not claiming that the goodness of this particular work of art depends upon its being a painting rather than being some other sort of work of art which is capable of being contemplated, studied, etc.; nor is he claiming that its goodness is dependent upon the fact that it was intended to be hung in a place where it can be observed and studied; nor upon the fact that it is a representational painting which depicts a mythological scene. If we next turn to the question of how the goodness of this painting is related to the fact that it was "made deliberately and self-consciously, with obvious skill and care by Nicolas Poussin," Professor Ziff's position is somewhat less explicit, but what he would say is probably quite clear. Suppose that the phrase "obvious skill" were deleted from the description of this characteristic: would the fact that this painting had been deliberately and self-consciously made, and had been made with care (but perhaps not with skill), provide a sufficient basis for predicating goodness of it? I should doubt that Professor Ziff would hold that it would, since many bad paintings may be supposed to have been made deliberately, self-consciously, and with care. Yet, if this is so, how is the maker's skill related to the object's goodness? Perhaps the fact that "obvious skill" is attributed to Poussin is meant to suggest that Poussin intended that "The Rape of the Sabine Women" should possess those qualities which Professor Ziff notes that we find in it when we contemplate, study, and observe it in the way in which he suggests that it should be contemplated. If this is what is suggested by attributing skill to the artist, it is surely clear that Professor Ziff has without argument built an aesthetic theory into his description of the Poussin painting. That theory is implicit both in the characteristics which he chooses as being aesthetically relevant, and in the relations which he holds as obtaining among these characteristics.

If it be doubted that Professor Ziff's description contains at least an implicit aesthetic theory, consider the fact that in one of the passages in which he describes the Poussin painting (but which I did not include in my foreshortened quotation from that description), he speaks of the fact that in contemplating, studying, and observing this painting "we are concerned with both two-dimensional and three-dimensional movements, the balance and opposition, thrust and recoil, of spaces and volumes." Since the goodness of a painting has been said by him to depend upon the qualities which we find in it when we contemplate, study, and observe it, it follows that these features of the Poussin painting contribute to its goodness. And I should suppose that they are also included in what Professor Ziff calls the sixth characteristic of the Poussin painting, namely its "complex formal structure." Thus, presumably, the goodness of a painting does depend, in part at least, upon its formal structure. On the other hand, Professor Ziff never suggests that the goodness of the Poussin painting depends upon the fact that it is a representational painting, and that it has a mythological (or historical) subject matter, rather than some other sort of subject matter. In fact, when he discusses critics such as Kenyon Cox and Royal Cortissoz, Professor Ziff would apparently—and quite properly—wish to separate himself from them, rejecting the view that what makes a painting a good painting has any necessary relation to the fact that it is not a representational painting of a certain sort. Thus, Professor Ziff's account of the aesthetically relevant features of the Poussin painting, and his statements concerning the interrelationships among the various features of that painting, define a particular aesthetic position.

The position which I have been attributing to him is one with which I happen to agree. However, that fact is not of any importance in the present discussion. What is important to note is that Professor Ziff's characterization of the Poussin painting contains an implicit theory of the nature of a work of art. According to that theory, the goodness of a painting depends upon its possession of certain objective qualities, that these qualities are (in part at least) elements in its formal structure, and that the artist intended that we should perceive these qualities in contemplating and studying the painting. (Had he not had this intention, would we be able to say that he had made the object self-consciously, deliberately, *and* with skill?) Further, this implicit theory must be assumed to be a theory which is general in import, and not confined to how we should look at this one painting only. Were this not so, the sort of description of the Poussin painting which was given by Professor Ziff would not have helped to establish a clear-cut case of what is to be designated as a work of art. For example, were someone to describe the same painting in terms of its size, weight, and insurable value (as might be done were it to be moved from museum to museum), we would not thereby learn how the term "work of art" is to be used. In failing to note that his description of the Poussin painting actually did involve a theory of the nature of art, Professor Ziff proceeded to treat that description as if he had done nothing more than bring forward a list of seven independent characteristics of the painting he was examining. In so doing, he turned the question of whether there are any features common to all works of art into a question of whether one or more of these seven specific indices could be found in all objects to which the term "work of art" is applied. Inevitably, his conclusion was negative, and he therefore held that "no one of the characteristics listed is necessarily a characteristic of a work of art."[19]

However, as we have seen, Professor Ziff's description of the Poussin painting was not actually confined to noting the specific qualities which were characteristic of the pictorial surface of that painting; it included references to the relations between these qualities and the aim of Poussin, and references to the ways in which a painting having such qualities is to be contemplated by others. Had he turned his attention to examining these relationships between object, artist, and contemplator, it would assuredly have been more difficult for him to assert that "neither a poem, nor a novel, nor a musical composition can be said to be a work of art in the same sense of the phrase in which a painting or a statue or a vase can be said to be a work of art."[20] In fact, had he carefully traced the relationships which he assumed to exist among some of the characteristics of the Poussin painting, he might have found that, contrary to his inclinations, he was well advanced toward putting forward explicit generalizations concerning the arts.

III

While Professor Ziff's argument against generalization depends upon the fact that the various artistic media are significantly different from one another, the possibility of generalizing concerning the arts has also been challenged on historical grounds. It is to Morris Weitz's use of the latter argument that I shall now turn.

In "The Role of Theory in Aesthetics" Professor Weitz places his primary emphasis on the fact that art forms are not static. From this fact he argues that it is futile to attempt to state the conditions which are necessary and sufficient for an object to be a work of art. What he claims is that the concept "art" must be treated as an open concept, since new art forms have developed in the past, and since any art form (such as the novel) may

---

[19] *Ibid.*, p. 64.

[20] *Ibid.*, p. 66. For example, Ziff denies that a poem can be said to be "exhibited or displayed." Yet it is surely the case that in printing a poem or in presenting a reading of a poem, the relation between the work and its audience, and the relation between artist, work, and audience, is not wholly dissimilar to that which obtains when an artist exhibits a painting. If this be doubted, consider whether there is not a closer affinity between these two cases than there is between a painter *exhibiting* a painting and a manufacturer *exhibiting* a new line of fountain pens.

undergo radical transformations from generation to generation. One brief statement from Professor Weitz's article can serve to summarize this view:

> What I am arguing, then, is that the very expansive, adventurous character of art, its ever-present changes and novel creations, makes it logically impossible to ensure any set of defining properties. We can, of course, choose to close the concept. But to do this with "art' or "tragedy" or portraiture, etc. is ludicrous since it forecloses the very conditions of creativity in the arts.[21]

Unfortunately, Professor Weitz fails to offer any cogent argument in substantiation of this claim. The lacuna in his discussion is to be found in the fact that the question of whether a particular concept is open or closed (i.e., whether a set of necessary and sufficient conditions can be offered for its use) is not identical with the question of whether future instances to which the very same concept is applied may or may not possess genuinely novel properties. In other words, Professor Weitz has not shown that every novelty in the instances to which we apply a term involves a stretching of the term's connotation.

By way of illustration, consider the classificatory label "representational painting." One can assuredly define this particular form of art without defining it in such a way that it will include only those paintings which depict either a mythological event or a religious scene. Historical paintings, interiors, fête-champêtres, and still life can all count as "representational" according to any adequate definition of this mode of painting, and there is no reason why such a definition could not have been formulated prior to the emergence of any of these novel species of the representational mode. Thus, to define a particular form of art—and to define it truly and accurately—is not necessarily to set one's self in opposition to whatever new creations may arise within that particular form.[22] Consequently, it would be mistaken to suppose that all attempts to state the defining properties of various art forms are prescriptive in character and authoritarian in their effect.

This conclusion is not confined to cases in which an established form of art, such as representational painting, undergoes changes; it can also be shown to be compatible with the fact that radically new art forms arise. For example, if the concept "a work of art" had been carefully defined prior to the invention of cameras, is there any reason to suppose that such

---

[21] *Op. cit.*, p. 32.

[22] To be sure, if no continuing characteristic is to be found, the fact of change will demand that the concept be treated as having been an open one. This was precisely the position taken by Max Black in a discussion of the concept "science." (See "The Definition of Scientific Method," in *Science and Civilization*, edited by Robert C. Stauffer [Madison, Wisconsin, 1949].) Paul Ziff refers to the influence of Professor Black's discussion upon his own views, and the views of Morris Weitz are assuredly similar. However, even if Professor Black's view of the changes in the concept "science" is a correct one (as I should be prepared to think that it may be), it does not follow that the same argument applies in the case of art. Nor does the fact that the meaning of "science" has undergone profound changes in the past imply that further analogous changes will occur in the future.

a definition would have proved an obstacle to viewing photography or the movies as constituting new art forms? To be sure, one can imagine definitions which might have done so. However, it was not Professor Weitz's aim to show that one or another definition of art had been a poor definition; he wished to establish the general thesis that there was a necessary incompatability, which he denoted as a logical impossibility, between allowing for novelty and creativity in the arts and stating the defining properties of a work of art. He failed to establish this thesis since he offered no arguments to prove that new sorts of instantiation of a previously defined concept will necessarily involve us in changing the definition of that concept.

To be sure, if neither photography nor the movies had developed along lines which satisfied the same sorts of interest that the other arts satisfied, and if the kinds of standards which were applied in the other arts were not seen to be relevant when applied to photography and to the movies, then the antecedently formulated definition of art would have functioned as a closed concept, and it would have been used to exclude all photographers and all motion-picture makers from the class of those who were to be termed "artists." However, what would the defender of the openness of concepts hold that one should have done under these circumstances? Suppose, for example, that all photographers had in fact been the equivalent of passport photographers, and that they had been motivated by no other interests and controlled by no other standards than those which govern the making of photographs for passports and licenses: would the defender of open concepts be likely to have expanded the concept of what is to count as an art in order to have included photography? The present inclusion of photography among the arts is justified, I should hold, precisely because photography arises out of the same sorts of interest, and can satisfy the same sorts of interest, and our criticism of it employs the same sorts of standards, as is the case with respect to the other arts.

Bearing this in mind, we are in a position to see that still another article which has sometimes been cited by those who argue for the openness of the concept "a work of art" does not justify the conclusions which have been drawn from it. That article is Paul Oskar Kristeller's learned and informative study entitled "The Modern System of the Arts."[23] The way in which Professor Kristeller states the aim of his article suggests that he too would deny that traditional aesthetic theory is capable of formulating adequate generalizations concerning the arts. He states his aim in saying:

> The basic notion that the five "major arts" constitute an area all by themselves, clearly separated by common characteristics from the crafts, the sciences and other human activities has been taken for granted by most writers on aesthetics from Kant to the present day. . . .
>
> It is my purpose to show that this system of the five major arts, which underlies all modern aesthetics and is so familiar to us all, is of comparatively

---

[23] *Journal of the History of Ideas*, vol. 12 (1951), pp. 496–527, and vol. 13 (1952), pp. 17–46. This study has been cited by both Elton (*op. cit.*, p. 2) and Kennick (*op. cit.*, p. 320) in substantiation of their views.

recent origin and did not assume definite shape before the eighteenth century, although it had many ingredients which go back to classical, mediaeval, and Renaissance thought.[24]

However, the fact that *the classification of the arts* has undoubtedly changed during the history of Western thought, does not of itself suggest that *aesthetic theory* must undergo comparable changes. Should this be doubted, one may note that Professor Kristeller's article does not show in what specific ways attempts to classify or systematize the arts are integral to, or are presupposed by, or are consequences of, the formulation of an aesthetic theory. This is no minor cavil, for if one examines the writers on aesthetics who are currently attacked for their attempts to generalize concerning the nature of art, one finds that they are not (by and large) writers whose discussions are closely allied to the discussions of those with whom Kristeller's article was primarily concerned. Furthermore, it is to be noted that Kristeller did not carry his discussion beyond Kant. This terminal point was justified by him on the ground that the system of the arts has not substantially changed since Kant's time.[25] However, when one recalls that Kant's work is generally regarded as standing near the beginning of modern aesthetic theory—and surely not near its end—one has reason to suspect that questions concerning "the system of the arts" and questions concerning aesthetic theory constitute distinct, and probably separate sets of questions. A survey of recent aesthetic theory bears this out. Since the time of Hegel and of Schopenhauer there have been comparatively few influential aesthetic theories which have made the problem of the diversity of art forms, and the classification of these forms, central to their consideration of the nature of art.[26] For example, the aesthetic theories of Santayana, Croce, Alexander, Dewey, Prall, or Collingwood cannot be said to have been dependent upon any particular systematic classification of the arts. In so far as these theories may be taken as representative of attempts to generalize concerning the arts, it is strange that current attacks on traditional aesthetics should have supposed that any special measure of support was to be derived from Kristeller's article.

Should one wish to understand why current discussions have overlooked the gap between an article such as Kristeller's and the lessons ostensibly derived from it, an explanation might be found in the lack of concern evinced by contemporary analytic philosophers for the traditional problems of aesthetic theory. For example, one looks in vain in the Elton volume for a careful appraisal of the relations between aesthetic theory and art criticism, and how the functions of each might differ from the functions of the

---

[24] *Op. cit.*, vol. 12, p. 497.
[25] *Op. cit.*, vol. 13, p. 43; also, pp. 4 ff.
[26] One exception is to be found in T. M. Greene: *The Arts and the Art of Criticism* (Princeton, 1940). This work is cited by Kristeller, and is one of the only two which he cites in support of the view that the system of the arts has not changed since Kant's day (*op. cit.*, vol. 12, p. 497, n. 4). The other work cited by him is Paul Franke's *System der Kunstwissenschaft* (Brünn/Leipzig, 1938), which also offers a classification of the arts, but only within a framework of aesthetic theory which could easily embrace whatever historical changes the arts undergo.

other. A striking example of the failure to consider this sort of problem is also to be found in John Wisdom's often cited dicta concerning "the dullness" of aesthetic theory.[27] In examining his views one finds that the books on art which Wisdom finds *not* to be dull are books such as Edmund Wilson's *Axel's Castle*, in which a critic "brings out features of the art he writes about, or better, brings home the character of what he writes about."[28] In short, it is not theory—it is not aesthetic theory at all—that Wisdom is seeking: he happens to be interested in criticism.

I do not wish to be taken as denying the importance of criticism, nor as belittling the contribution which a thorough acquaintance with the practice of criticism in all of the arts may make to general aesthetic theory. However, it is important to note that the work of any critic presupposes at least an implicit aesthetic theory, which—as critic—it is not his aim to establish or, in general, to defend. This fact can only be overlooked by those who confine themselves to a narrow range of criticism: for example, to the criticism appearing in our own time in those journals which are read by those with whom we have intellectual, political, and social affinities. When we do not so confine ourselves, we rapidly discover that there is, and has been, an enormous variety in criticism, and that this variety represents (in part at least) the effect of differing aesthetic preconceptions. To evaluate criticism itself we must, then, sometimes undertake to evaluate these preconceptions. In short, we must do aesthetics ourselves.

However, for many of the critics of traditional aesthetics this is an option which does not appeal. If I am not mistaken, it is not difficult to see why this should have come to be so. In the first place, it has come to be one of the marks of contemporary analytic philosophy to hold that philosophic problems are problems which cannot be solved by appeals to matters of fact. Thus, to choose but a single instance, questions of the relations between aesthetic perception and other instances of perceiving— for example, questions concerning psychical distance, or empathic perception, or the role of form in aesthetic perception—are not considered to be questions with which a philosopher ought to try to deal. In the second place, the task of the philosopher has come to be seen as consisting largely of the unsnarling of tangles into which others have gotten themselves. As a consequence, the attempt to find a synoptic interpretation of some broad range of facts—an attempt which has in the past been regarded as one of the major tasks of a philosopher—has either been denigrated or totally overlooked.[29] Therefore, problems such as the claims of the arts to render

---

[27] See "Things and Persons," *Proceedings of the Aristotelian Society, Supplementary Volume XXII* (1948), pp. 207–210.

[28] *Ibid.*, p. 209.

[29] For example, W. B. Gallie's "The Function of Philosophical Aesthetics," in the Elton volume, argues for "a journeyman's aesthetics," which will take up individual problems, one by one, these problems being of the sort which arise when a critic or poet gets into a muddle about terms such as "abstraction" or "imagination." For this purpose the tools of the philosopher are taken to be the tools of logical analysis (*op. cit.*, p. 35); a concern with the history of the arts, with psychology, or a direct and wide-ranging experience of the arts seems not to be presupposed.

a true account of human character and destiny, or questions concerning the relations between aesthetic goodness and standards of greatness in art, or an estimate of the significance of variability in aesthetic judgments, are not presently fashionable. And it must be admitted that if philosophers wish not to have to face either factual problems or synoptic tasks, these are indeed questions which are more comfortably avoided than pursued.

Select Bibliography for Part Four

Books

Haig Khatchadourian, *The Concept of Art*; Peter Kivy, *Speaking of Art*; Joseph Margolis, *The Language of Art and Art Criticism*.

Articles

Henry Aiken, "Criteria for an Adequate Aesthetics"; V. C. Aldrich, "Pictures and Persons—An Analogy"; H. G. Alexander, "Art, Imagination, and Cultural Reality"; Van Meter Ames, "Is It Art?"; Karl Aschenbrenner, "Aesthetic Theory—Conflict and Conciliation"; Karl Aschenbrenner, "The Philosopher's Interest in Art"; Lee B. Brown, "Definitions and Art Theory"; Lee B. Brown, "Traditional Aesthetics Revisited"; F. Graeme Chalmers, "The Study of Art in a Cultural Context"; Margaret Chattersee, "Some Philosophical Problems Arising in the Arts"; Arthur Danto, "The Artworld"; Arthur Danto, "The Transfiguration of the Commonplace"; W. B. Gallic, "Art as an Essential Concept"; W. B. Gallie, "The Function of Philosophical Aesthetics"; William E. Kennick, "Does Traditional Aesthetics Rest on a Mistake?"; Haig Khatchadourian, "Family Resemblances and the Classification of Works of Art"; Haig Khatchadourian, "Is It Art? Is It Good Art?"; Beryl Lake, "A Study of the Irrefutability of Two Aesthetic Theories"; Anthony R. Manser, "Games and Family Resemblances"; Joseph Margolis, "The Identity of a Work of Art"; Joseph Margolis, "Mr. Weitz and the Definition of Art"; Joseph Margolis, "Recent Work in Aesthetics"; Thomas Munro, " 'The Afternoon of a Faun' and the Interrelation of the Arts"; J. A. Passmore, "The Dreariness of Aesthetics"; Max Rieser, "Problems of Artistic Form: The Concept of Art"; Mary Carman Rose, "Linguistic Analysis and Aesthetic Inquiry: A Critique"; Richard J. Sclafani, " 'Art,' Wittgenstein, and Open-Textured Concepts"; Richard J. Sclafani, "Art Works, Art Theory, and the Artworld"; Anita Silvers, "The Artworld Discarded"; B. R. Tilghman, "Wittgenstein, Games and Art"; Morris Weitz, "The Role of Theory in Aesthetics"; Lewis K. Zerby, "A Reconsideration of the Role of Theory in Aesthetics—A Reply to Morris Weitz"; Paul Ziff, "The Task of Defining a Work of Art."

A second example of the limitations imposed upon aesthetics by contemporary linguistic analysis is to be found in Professor Weitz's article. He states that "the root problem of philosophy itself is to explain the relation between the employment of certain kinds of concepts and the conditions under which they can be correctly applied" (*op. cit.*, p. 30).

PART FIVE

———◆•■•◆———

The Death
of Art

Early in this century, Marcel Duchamp tried to enter in an art show, a common urinal which he entitled "Fountain." Although he failed in his attempt, "Fountain" became a celebrated cause in the world of art and, eventually, acquired the status of a work of art. This seems to have opened the floodgates to almost every imaginable form of radicalism in the art-world.

Today we are confronted with "works" and the like, "happenings" sponsored by leading museums, galleries, patrons, and the like, that seem to be as outrageous as possible. In the early 1970s Piero Mangoni, for example, sent cans of his own excrement to his Milan gallery labeled "Mierda d'Artista." Chris Burden has recently had himself shot with a rifle, crucified on a Volkswagen, and nearly electrocuted. In 1969 Robert Barry closed an Amsterdam gallery for two weeks, claiming that to be his "show." All of these "works of art" have received a great deal of attention in newspapers, journals, and the broadcasting media. More conventionally, one supposes, Andy Warhol "made" Brillo boxes, Claes Oldenburg "made" giant hamburgers, and Dan Flavin "made" sculptures consisting of ordinary fluorescent lights. These are just a few among thousands of examples of recent "works of art." They are representative of what has been going on in the vanguard of art activity over the last twenty years. Although other far more conventional art activities are still practiced, one is tempted to ask, "If these aforementioned examples are typical of the new art movements, are we not forced to conclude that art has come, or is coming, to an end?"

However tempting it may be to answer this question affirmatively, we must be careful not to overlook a number of problems which arise when one tries seriously, and not, as is usually the case, frivolously, to argue that art is dead. The expression "antiart," for example, seems to be a highly appropriate designation of the kind of works mentioned above. Yet, what exactly is antiart? The best answer to this question seems to be that because the very possibility of antiart depends upon the framework of what Danto called "The Artworld" (part one), although admittedly it does nothing with this framework, antiart is really a peculiar kind of art. It is a kind of art which, if practiced by all artists, however, would be tantamount to the death of art, since its ultimate effect would be to abolish the very framework which makes art possible. Is this a theoretically sound possibility? In the early nineteenth century, Hegel prophesied that art would come to an end. Today, Arthur Danto thinks that it has ended. Thus, we begin this part with Hegel and end with Danto. The selections from Duchamp and Karshan provide substantive indications of some of the occurrences in art that might direct us toward the conclusion that Hegel's prophecy has been realized.

Hegel's views on art form part of an elaborate metaphysical system which has come to be called Absolute Idealism. Like Plato's theory, Hegel's metaphysical system is vast and complex and cannot be fully explained in this introduction. For our purposes it will be sufficient to sketch some of Hegel's central ideas about art and metaphysics. Hegel considered Mind or Spirit to encompass all of reality, and through the activity of thought Mind or Spirit ceaselessly unfolds itself. He held that this internal unfolding process constitutes the history of all that is, ever was, or ever will be. What he called the Absolute Mind or Spirit is the ultimate object of the highest knowledge—the ultimate truth. That which is "truth in itself and for itself" Hegel called the Absolute Idea.

Ultimately, Hegel argued that the Absolute Idea reveals itself in three forms: art, religion, and in its highest form, philosophy. For him, art reveals the Absolute Idea through sensuous or material configuration which he identifies with Beauty. Because the evolutionary unfolding of Mind points in the direction of ever greater spiritualization, the capacities of art to reveal the absolute become progressively limited. In fact, Hegel hints that with Romanticism, art may have reached the stage where it has done all it can to reveal the Absolute Idea. If this is true, the "evolution of centuries" he mentions at the end of his selection might be complete. We may now be witnessing the twilight of art history or even its aftermath, the death of art.

Throughout his career, Marcel Duchamp seemed to do everything possible—albeit inadvertently—to substantiate Hegel's prophecy. Duchamp was perhaps the greatest artistic iconoclast of this century. In "I Like Breathing Better Than Working," an interview with the critic Pierre Cabanne, Duchamp exhibits the wit, irony, and self-deprecation which characterized his entire career. "I've played my part as artistic clown," he says. Yet, as the Dickie-Cohen debate and numerous other discussions indicate, Duchamp's work has become controversial in important ways. Duchamp and his followers have made a concerted effort to "de-aestheticize" art, an effort which many writers have claimed has revolutionized art activity in the twentieth century.

It is partly in the spirit of Duchamp's work that we can come to grasp the Pop Art movement as embodied in the works of Andy Warhol and others, and the conceptual art movement which has recently come to the fore. The designation "Conceptual Art" is discussed by Donald Karshan in some detail in a short statement which can be taken as the manifesto of the conceptualist movement. According to Karshan, conceptual art is post-object art: "Post-Object Art is based on the premise that the idea of art has expanded beyond the object or visual experience to an area of serious art investigations." Karshan suggests that because the primary business of Conceptual Art is to investigate the concept of art itself, it really becomes a kind of second-order philosophical inquiry into the nature of art. This theme is explored further by Arthur Danto.

Beginning where he left off in "The Artworld," Danto opens his essay "Artworks and Real Things" with the startling suggestion that this very essay may be the final artwork in the history of art. Most of his essay is occupied with an extended discussion of the ontological questions Danto had already raised in "The Artworld." Danto argues here that the ontological paradoxes generated by the Imitation Theory of art can be resolved only by artists making "non-imitations which are radically distinct from all heretofore existing things." Rauschenberg's stuffed goat garlanded with a tire is an example of such an "unentrenched" object. But common objects in our everyday world, the products of industrial designers, such as beds and can openers, could be visually indiscernible from objects which are works of art consisting of beds and can openers. To escape the ontological dilemma once and for all, Danto claims that we must turn to the philosophy of art itself: "The relationship between art and reality has traditionally been the province of philosophy . . . By bringing within itself what it [sic] had been traditionally regarded as logically apart from art transforms itself into philosophy." Danto's conclusion may sound suspiciously Hegelian in tone. As it turns out, Danto acknowledges, explicitly, that it is. We have come full circle in this part when Danto says that art's becoming its own subject is "like the Absolute of Hegel, which finally achieved congruence with itself by becoming self-contemplative in the respect that what it contemplates is itself in contemplation."

Georg Friedrich Wilhelm Hegel

THE EVOLUTION AND
COMPLETION OF
ART HISTORY

V

1. After the above introductory observations* we may now pass on to the
consideration of our subject itself.† We are, however, still within the introduction; and being so I do not propose to attempt anything more than
indicate by way of sketch the main outlines of the general course of the
scientific inquiry which is to follow it. Inasmuch, however, as we have
referred to art as issuing from the absolute Idea itself, and, indeed, have
assigned as its end the sensuous presentation of the Absolute itself, it will
be incumbent on us to conduct this survey of the entire field in such a
way, as at least to disclose generally, how the particular parts originate
in the notional concept of the beauty of art. We must therefore attempt to
awaken some idea of this notion in its broadest significance.

It has already been stated that the content of art is the Idea, and the
form of its display the configuration of the sensuous or plastic image. It is
further the function of art to mediate these two aspects under the reconciled mode of free totality. The *first* determinant implied by this is the
demand that the content, which has to secure artistic representation, shall
disclose an essential capacity for such display. If this is not so all that we
possess is a defective combination. A content that, independently, is ill
adapted to plastic form and external presentment is compelled to accept
this form, or a matter that is of itself prosaic in its character is driven to
make the best it can of a mode of presentation which is antagonistic to its
nature.

The *second* requirement, which is deducible from the first, is the demand
that the content of art should be nothing essentially abstract. This does

Georg Friedrich Wilhelm Hegel (1770–1831). The famous German philosopher who
founded the school known as Absolute Idealism. Hegel wrote voluminously toward a
comprehensive systematic position on all philosophical topics.

* Selections from *The Philosophy of Fine Art*, chapter 5, translated by F. P. B.
Osmaston (London, 1920). Reprinted by permission of G. Bell and Sons, Ltd.

† This final section is called the Division of the Subject.

not mean, however, that it should be merely concrete in the sense that the sensuous object is such in its contrast to all that is spiritual and the content of thought, regarding these as the essentially simple and abstract. Everything that possesses truth for Spirit, no less than as part of Nature, is essentially concrete, and, despite its universality, possesses both ideality[1] and particularity essentially within it. When we state, for example, of God that he is simple One, the Supreme Being as such, we have thereby merely given utterance to a lifeless abstraction of the irrational understanding. Such a God, as He is thus not conceived in His concrete truth, can supply no content for art, least of all plastic art. Consequently neither the Jews nor the Turks have been able to represent their God, who is not even an abstraction of the understanding in the above sense, under the positive mode in which Christians have represented Him. For in Christianity God is conceived in His Truth, and as such essentially concrete, as personality,[2] as the subjective focus of conscious life, or, more accurately defined, as Spirit. And what He is as Spirit is made explicit to the religious apprehension as a trinity of persons, which at the same time are, in their independence, regarded as One. Here is essentiality, universality, and particularity, no less than their reconciled unity, and it is only a unity such as this which gives us the concrete. And inasmuch as a content, in order to unveil truth at all, must be of this concrete character, art makes the demand for a like concreteness, and, for this reason, that a purely abstract universal does not in itself possess the property to proceed to particularity and external manifestation, and to unity with itself therein.

If, then, a sensuous form and configuration is to be correspondent with a true and therefore concrete content, such must in the third place likewise be as clearly individual, entirely concrete and a self-enclosed unity. This character of concreteness, predictable of both aspects of art, the content no less than the representation, is just the point in which both coalesce and fall in with one another. The natural form of the human body is, for example, such a sensuous concrete capable of displaying Spirit in its essential concreteness and of adapting itself wholly to such a presentment. For which reason we must quit ourselves of the idea that it is a matter of mere accident that an actual phenomenon of the objective world is ac-

---

[1] *Subjektivität.* That is, the ideality of consciousness, or thought.
[2] Professor Bosanquet, in his note on this passage, expresses the opinion that Hegel when he writes thus is referring "To the self-consciousness of individual human beings as constituting, and reflecting on, an ideal unity between them." This no doubt, as he suggests, does put a somewhat unnatural meaning on the word "person" or "subjekt." No doubt there is a sense in which we can ascribe personality to a state, or nation, in the concrete unity of its life. But while admitting that unity such as this, which is not sensuous but ideal, can be "effective and actual," I find it difficult to conclude that Hegel did himself hold that the unity of the Divine Being was *merely* identical with the unity or totality of concrete human life as reflected upon by single individuals. How far is human life as a whole on this Earth a unity or totality at all? That question has been discussed by Professor Bradley and others with very different conclusions. Nay, how far does human existence itself exhaust the actually present realization or self-realization of self-conscious Spirit or Intelligence? Whatever may be the wisest answer to such and other questions I can hardly think that Hegel would have accepted Professor Bosanquet's interpretation as completely adequate.

cepted as the mode in which to embody such a form coalescent with truth. Art does not lay hold of this form either because it is simply there or because there is no other. The concrete content itself implies the presence of external and actual, we may even add the sensuous appearance. But to make this possible this sensuous concrete, which is essentially impressed with a content that is open to mind, is also essentially addressed to the inward conscious life, and the external mode of its configuration, whereby it is visible to perception and the world of idea, has for its aim the being there exclusively for the soul and mind of man. This is the sole reason that content and artistic conformation are dovetailed one into the other. The *purely* sensuous concrete, that is external Nature as such, does not exclusively originate in such an end. The variously coloured plumage of birds is resplendent unseen; the notes of this song are unheard. The Cereus,[3] which only blossoms for a night, withers away without any admiration from another in the wilderness of the southern forests; and these forests, receptacles themselves of the most beautiful and luxuriant vegetation, with the richest and most aromatic perfumes, perish and collapse in like manner unenjoyed. The work of art has no such naive and independent being. It is essentially a question, an address to the responding soul of man, an appeal to affections and intelligence.

Although the endowment by art of sensuous shape is not in this respect accidental, yet on the other hand it is not the highest mode of grasping the spiritually concrete. Thought is a higher mode of presentment than that of the sensuous concrete. Though abstract in a relative sense; yet it must not be one-sided, but concrete thinking, in order to be true and rational. The extent to which a definite content possesses for its appropriate form sensuous artistic representation, or essentially requires, in virtue of its nature, a higher and more spiritual embodiment is a question of difference exemplified at once if we compare the Greek gods with God as conceived under Christian ideas. The Greek god is not abstract, but individual, and is in close association with the natural human form. The Christian God is also, no doubt, a concrete personality, but under the mode of pure spiritual actuality, who is cognized as Spirit and in Spirit.[4] His medium of determinate existence is therefore essentially knowledge of the mind and not external natural shape, by means of which His representation can only be imperfect, and not in the entire depths of His idea or notional concept.

Inasmuch, however, as it is the function of art to represent the Idea to immediate vision in sensuous shape and not in the form of thought and pure spirituality in the strict sense, and inasmuch as the value and intrinsic worth of this presentment consists in the correspondence and unity of the two aspects, that is the Idea and its sensuous shape, the supreme level and excellence of art and the reality, which is truly consonant with its notion,

[3] *Fackeldistel*, "Torch thistle," a plant of the genus Cereus.
[4] Or, "as mind and in mind."

will depend upon the degree of intimacy and union with which idea and configuration appear together in elaborated fusion. The higher truth consequently is spiritual content which has received the shape adequate to the conception of its essence; and this it is which supplies the principle of division for the philosophy of art. For before the mind can attain to the true notion of its absolute essence, it is constrained to traverse a series of stages rooted in this very notional concept; and to this course of stages which it unfolds to itself, corresponds a coalescent series, immediately related therewith, of the plastic types of art, under the configuration whereof mind as art-spirit presents to itself the consciousness of itself.[5]

This evolution within the art-spirit has further itself two sides in virtue of its intrinsic nature. *First*, that is to say, the development is itself a spiritual and universal one; in other words there are the definite and comprehensive views of the world[6] in their series of gradations which give artistic embodiment to the specific but widely embracing consciousness of Nature, man, and God. *Secondly*, this ideal or *universal* art-development has to provide for itself immediate existence and sensuous configuration, and the definite modes of this art-actualization in the sensuous medium are themselves a totality of necessary distinctions in the realm of art—that is to say, they are the *particular types* of art. No doubt the types of artistic configuration on the one hand are, in respect to their spirituality, of a general character, and not restricted to any one material, and the sensuous existence is similarly itself of varied multiplicity of medium. Inasmuch, however, as this material potentially possesses, precisely as the mind or spirit does, the Idea for its inward soul or significance, it follows that a definite sensuous involves with itself a closer relation and secret bond of association with the spiritual distinctions and specific types of artistic embodiment.[7]

Relatively to these points of view our philosophy will be divided into three fundamental parts.

First, we have a *general* part. It has for its content and object the universal Idea of fine art, conceived here as the Ideal, together with the more elaborated relation under which it is placed respectively to Nature and human artistic production.

Secondly, we have evolved from the notional concept of the beauty of art a *particular* part, in so far as the essential distinctions, which this idea

---

[5] That is to say, presents to itself a conscious grasp of itself as such Art-spirit (*als künstlerischer*).

[6] The two evolutions here alluded to are (i) that of a particular way of regarding Nature, man, and God in a particular age and nation such as the Egyptian, Greek, and Christian viewed in express relation to art; (ii) The several arts—sculpture, music, poetry, etc., each on their own foundation and viewed relatively to the former evolution.

[7] The point, of course, is that the different media of the several arts are inherently, and in virtue of the fact that we have not here *mere* matter as opposed to that which is intellectual rather than sensuous, but matter in which the notional concept is already essentially present or pregnant (sound is, for instance, more ideal than the spatial matter of architecture), adapted to the particular arts in which they serve as the medium of expression.

contains in itself, are unfolded in a graduated series of *particular* modes of configuration.[8]

Thirdly, there results a *final* part which has to consider the particularized content of fine art itself. It consists in the advance of art to the sensuous realization of its shapes and its consummation in a system of the several arts and their genera and species.

2. In respect to the first and second of these divisions it is important to recollect, in order to make all that follows intelligible, that the Idea, viewed as the beautiful in art, is not the Idea in the strict sense, that is as a metaphysical Logic apprehends it as the Absolute. It is rather the Idea as carried into concrete form in the direction of express realization, and as having entered into immediate and adequate unity with such reality. For the *Idea as such*, although it is both potentially and explicitly true, is only truth in its universality and not as yet presented in objective embodiment. The Idea as fine art, however, is the Idea with the more specific property of being essentially individual reality, in other words, an individual configuration of reality whose express function it is to make manifest the Idea—in its appearance. This amounts to the demand that the Idea and its formative configuration as concrete realization must be brought together under a mode of complete adequacy. The Idea as so conceived, a reality, that is to say, moulded in conformity with the notional concept of the Idea, is the Ideal. The problem of such consonancy might, in the first instance, be understood in the wholly formal sense that the Idea might be any idea so long as the actual shape, it matters not what the shape might be, represented this particular Idea and no other. In that case, however, the required truth of the Ideal is a fact simply interchangeable with mere correctness, a correctness which consists in the expression of any significance in a manner adapted to it, provided that its meaning is thereby directly discoverable in the form. The Ideal, however, is not to be thus understood. According to the standard or test of its own nature any content whatever can receive adequate presentation, but it does not necessarily thereby possess a claim to be the fine art of the Ideal. Nay, more, in comparison with ideal beauty the presentation will even appear defective. And in this connection we may once for all observe—though actual proof is reserved to a later stage—that the defects of a work of art are not invariably to be attributed to defects of executive skill. *Defectiveness of form* arises also from *defectiveness of content*. The Chinese, Hindoos, and Egyptians, for example, in their artistic images, sculptured deities and idols, never passed beyond a formless condition, or a definition of

---

[8] Professor Bosanquet explains these "plastic forms" (*Gestaltungs formen*) as the various modifications of the subject-matter of art (Trans., p. 140 note). I am not quite sure of the meaning here intended. It would apparently identify the term with the *Gebilde* referred to in the third division. I should myself rather incline to think that Hegel had mainly in his mind the specific general types, that is, the three relations of the Idea itself to its external configuration, viewed as a historical evolution, which Hegel calls symbolic, classical, and romantic. Perhaps this is what Professor Bosanquet means. But in that case it does not appear to me so much the subject-matter as the generic forms in the shaping of that matter.

shape that was vicious and false, and were unable to master true beauty. And this was so for the reason that their mythological conceptions, the content and thought of their works of art, were still essentially indeterminate, or only determinate in a false sense, did not, in fact, attain to a content which was absolute in itself. Viewed in this sense the excellence of works of art is so much the greater in the degree that their content and thought is ideal and profound. And in affirming this we have not merely in our mind the degree of executive mastery displayed in the grasp and imitation of natural form as we find it in the objective world. For in certain stages of the artistic consciousness and its reproductive effects the desertion and distortion of the conformations of Nature is not so much due to unintentional technical inexperience or lack of ability, as it is to deliberate alteration, which originates in the mental content itself, and is demanded by the same. From this point of view there is therefore imperfect art, which, both in technical and other respects, may be quite consummate in its *own specific sphere*, yet if tested with the true notion of art and the Ideal can only appear as defective. Only in the highest art are the Idea and the artistic presentation truly consonant with one another in the sense that the objective embodiment of the Idea is in itself essentially and as realized the true configuration, because the content of the Idea thus expressed is itself in truth the genuine content. It is appertinent to this, as already noted, that the Idea must be defined in and through itself as concrete totality, thereby essentially possessing in itself the principle and standard of its particularization and definition as thus manifested objectively. For example, the Christian imagination will only be able to represent God in human form and with man's means of spiritual expression, because it is herein that God Himself is fully known in Himself as mind or Spirit. Determinacy is, as it were, the bridge to phenomenal presence. Where this determinacy is not totality derived from the Idea itself, where the Idea is not conceived as that which is self-definitive and self-differentiating, it remains abstract and possesses its definition, and with it the principle for the particular mode of embodiment adapted to itself not within itself but as something outside it. And owing to this the Idea is also still abstract and the configuration it assumes is not as yet posited by itself. The Idea, however, which is essentially concrete, carries the principle of its manifestation in itself, and is thereby the means of its own free manifestation. Thus it is only the truly concrete Idea that is able to evoke the true embodiment, and this appropriate coalescence of both is the Ideal.

3. But inasmuch as in this way the Idea is concrete unity, this unity can only enter the artistic consciousness by the expansion and further mediation of the particular aspects of the Idea; and it is through this evolution that the beauty of art receives a *totality of particular stages and forms*. Therefore, after we have considered fine art in its essence and on its own account, we must see how the beautiful in its entirety breaks up into its particular determinations. This gives, as our second part, the *doctrine of the types of art*. The origin of these types is to be found in the varied ways under which the Idea is conceived as the content of art; it is by this

means that a distinction in the mode of form under which it manifests itself is conditioned. These types are therefore simply the different modes of relation which obtain between the Idea and its configuration, relations which emanate from the Idea itself, and thereby present us with the general basis of division for this sphere. For the principle of division must always be found in the notional concept, the particularization and division of which it is.

We have here to consider *three* relations of the Idea to its external process of configuration.

(*a*) *First*, the origin of artistic creation proceeds from the Idea when, being itself still involved in defective definition and obscurity, or in vicious and untrue determinacy, it becomes embodied in the shapes of art. As indeterminate it does not as yet possess in itself that individuality which the Ideal demands. Its abstract character and one-sidedness leaves its objective presentment still defective and contingent. Consequently this first type of art is rather a mere search after plastic configuration than a power of genuine representation. The Idea has not as yet found the formative principle within itself, and therefore still continues to be the mere effort and strain to find it. We may in general terms describe this form as the *symbolic* type of art. The abstract Idea possesses in it its external shape outside itself in the purely material substance of Nature, from which the shaping process proceeds, and to which in its expression it is entirely yoked. Natural objects are thus in the first instance left just as they are, while, at the same time the substantive Idea is imposed upon them as their significance, so that their function is henceforth to express the same, and they claim to be interpreted, as though the Idea itself was present in them. A rationale of this is to be found in the fact that the external objects of reality do essentially possess an aspect in which they are qualified to express a universal import. But as a completely adequate coalescence is not yet possible, all that can be the outcome of such a relation is an *abstract attribute*, as when a lion is understood to symbolize strength.

On the other hand this abstractness of the relation makes present to consciousness no less markedly how the Idea stands relatively to natural phenomena as an alien; and albeit it expatiates in all these shapes, having no other means of expression among all that is real, and seeks after itself in their unrest and defects of genuine proportion, yet for all that it finds them inadequate to meet its needs. It consequently exaggerates natural shapes and the phenomena of Nature in every degree of indefinite and limitless extension; it flounders about in them like a drunkard, and seethes and ferments, doing violence to their truth with the distorted growth of unnatural shapes, and strives vainly by the contrast, hugeness, and splendour of the forms accepted to exalt the phenomena to the plane of the Idea. For the Idea is here still more or less indeterminate, and unadaptable, while the objects of Nature are wholly definite in their shape.

Hence, on account of the incompatibility of the two sides of ideality and objective form to one another, the relation of the Idea to the other becomes a *negative* one. The former, being in its nature ideal, is unsatisfied with such an embodiment, and posits itself as its inward or ideally universal substance under a relation of *sublimity* over and above all this inadequate superfluity of natural form. In virtue of this sublimity the natural phenomena, of course, and the human form and event are accepted and left simply as they are, but at the same time, recognized as unequal to their significance, which is exalted far above all earthly content.

These features constitute in general terms the character of the primitive artistic pantheism of the East, which, on the one hand, charges the meanest objects with the significance of the absolute Idea, or, on the other, compels natural form, by doing violence to its structure, to express its world-ideas. And, in consequence, it becomes bizarre, grotesque, and deficient in taste, or turns the infinite but abstract freedom of the substantive Idea contemptuously against all phenomenal existence as alike nugatory and evanescent. By such means the significance cannot be completely presented in the expression, and despite all straining and endeavour the final inadequacy of plastic configuration to Idea remains insuperable. Such may be accepted as the first type of art—symbolic art with its yearning, its fermentation, its mystery, and sublimity.

(*b*) In the *second* type of art, which we propose to call "*Classical*," the twofold defect of symbolic art is annulled. Now the symbolic configuration is imperfect, because, first, the Idea here only enters into consciousness in *abstract* determinacy or indeterminateness: and, secondly, by reason of the fact that the coalescence of import with embodiment can only throughout remain defective, and in its turn also wholly abstract. The classical art-type solves both these difficulties. It is, in fact, the free and adequate embodiment of the Idea in the shape which, according to its notional concept, is uniquely appropriate to the Idea itself. The Idea is consequently able to unite in free and completely assonant concord with it. For this reason the classical type of art is the first to present us with the creation and vision of the complete Ideal, and to establish the same as realized fact.

The conformability, however, of notion and reality in the classical type ought not to be taken in the purely *formal* sense of the coalescence of a content with its external form, any more than this was possible in the case of the Ideal. Otherwise every copy from Nature, and every kind of portrait, every landscape, flower, scene, and so forth, which form the aim of the presentment, would at once become classical in virtue of the fact of the agreement it offers between such content and form. In classical art, on the contrary, the characteristic feature of the content consists in this, that it is itself concrete Idea, and as such the concrete spiritual; for it is only that which pertains to Spirit which is veritable ideality.[9] To secure such a content we must find out that in Nature which on its own account is that which is essentially and explicitly appropriate to the spiritual. It must be the *original* notion itself,[10] which has invented the form for concrete

---

[9] *Das Wahrhaft Innere.* That is, the inward of the truth of conscious life.
[10] Means apparently the notion in its absolute sense.

spirituality, and now the *subjective* notion—in the present case the spirit of art—has merely *discovered* it, and made it, as an existence possessed of natural shape, concordant with free and individual spirituality. Such a configuration, which the Idea essentially possesses as spiritual, and indeed as individually determinate spirituality, when it must perforce appear as a temporal phenomenon, is the *human form*. Personification and anthropomorphism have frequently been abused as a degradation of the spiritual. But art, in so far as its function is to bring to vision the spiritual in sensuous guise, must advance to such anthropomorphism, inasmuch as Spirit is only adequately presented to perception in its bodily presence. The transmigration of souls in this respect an abstract conception,[11] and physiology ought to make it one of its fundamental principles, that life has necessarily, in the course of its evolution, to proceed to the human form, for the reason that it is alone the visible phenomenon adequate to the expression of intelligence.

The human bodily form, then, is employed in the classical type of art not as purely sensuous existence, but exclusively as the existence and natural shape appropriate to mind. It has therefore to be relieved of all the defective excrescences which adhere to it in its purely physical aspect, and from the contingent finiteness of its phenomenal appearance. The external shape must in this way be purified in order to express in itself the content adequate for such a purpose; and, furthermore, along with this, that the coalescence of import and embodiment may be complete, the spirituality which constitutes the content must be of such a character that it is completely able to express itself in the natural form of man, without projecting beyond the limits of such expression within the sensuous and purely physical sphere of existence. Under such a condition Spirit is at the same time defined as particular, the spirit or mind of man, not as simply absolute and eternal. In this latter case it is only capable of asserting and expressing itself as intellectual being.[12]

Out of this latter distinction arises, in its turn, the defect which brings about the dissolution of the classical type of art, and makes the demand for a third and higher form, namely the *romantic* type.

(c) The romantic type of art annuls the completed union of the Idea and its reality, and occurs, if on a higher plane, to the difference and opposition of both sides, which remained unovercome in symbolic art. The classical type of art no doubt attained the highest excellence of which the sensuous embodiment of art is capable. The defect, such as it is, is due to the defect which obtains in art itself throughout, the limitations of its entire province, that is to say. The limitation consists in this, that art in general and, agreeably to its fundamental idea, accepts for its object Spirit, the notion of which is infinite concrete universality, under the guise of sensuously concrete form. In the classical type it sets up the perfected

---

[11] Because it represents spirit as independent of an appropriate bodily form.
[12] What appears to be denoted by *Geistigkeit* is the generic term of intelligence—that activity of conscious life which does not necessarily make us think of a single individual—the common nature of all spirit.

coalescence of spiritual and sensuous existence as adequate conformation of both. As a matter of fact, however, in this fusion mind itself is not represented agreeably to its *true notional concept*. Mind is the infinite subjectivity of the Idea, which as absolute inwardness,[13] is not capable of freely expanding in its entire independence, so long as it remains within the mould of the bodily shape, fused therein as in the existence wholly congenial to it.

To escape from such a condition the romantic type of art once more cancels that inseparable unity of the classical type, by securing a content which passes beyond the classical stage and its mode of expression. This content, if we may recall familiar ideas—is coincident with what Christianity affirms to be true of God as Spirit, in contrast to the Greek faith in gods which forms the essential and most fitting content of classical art. In Greek art the concrete ideal substance is potentially, but not as fully realized, the unity of the human and divine nature; a unity which for the very reason that it is purely *immediate* and not wholly explicit, is manifested without defect under an immediate and *sensuous* mode. The Greek god is the object of naive intuition and sensuous imagination. His shape is therefore the bodily form of man. The sphere of his power and his being is individual and individually limited; and in his opposition to the individual person[14] is an essence and a power with whom the inward life of soul[15] is merely potentially in unity, but does not itself possess this unity as inward subjective knowledge. The higher stage is the *knowledge* of this *implied* unity, which in its latency the classical art-type receives as its content and is able to perfectly represent in bodily shape. This elevation of mere potentiality into self-conscious knowledge constitutes an enormous difference. It is nothing less than the infinite difference which, for example, separates man generally from the animal creation. Man is animal; but even in his animal functions he is not restricted within the potential sphere as the animal is, but becomes conscious of them, learns to understand them, and raises them—as, for instance, the process of digestion—into self-conscious science. By this means man dissolves the boundaries of his merely potential immediacy; in virtue of the very fact that he knows himself to be animal he ceases to be merely animal, and as mind is endowed with self-knowledge.

If, then, in this way the unity of the human and divine nature, which in the previous stage was potential, is raised out of this immediate into a self-conscious unit, it follows that the genuine medium for the reality of this content is no longer the sensuous and immediate existence of what is spiritual, that is, the physical body of man, but the *self-aware* inner life of *soul* itself. Now it is Christianity—for the reason that it presents to mind God as *Spirit*, and not as particular individual spirit, but as absolute in spirit and in truth—which steps back from the sensuousness of imagina-

---

[13] By *Innerlichkeit*, which might also be rendered as pure ideality, what is signified is that in a mental state there are no parts outside of each other.
[14] *Subjekt*, *i.e.*, the individual Ego of self-consciousness.
[15] *Das subjektive Innere*, lit., the subjective inner state.

tion into the inward life of reason, and makes *this* rather than *bodily* form the medium and determinate existence of its content. So also, the unity of the human and divine nature is a conscious unity exclusively capable of realization by means of *spiritual* knowledge, and in *Spirit*. The new content secured thereby is consequently not indefeasibly bound up with the sensuous presentation, as the mode completely adequate, but is rather delivered from this immediate existence, which has to be hypostatized as a negative factor, overcome and reflected back into the spiritual unity. In this way romantic art must be regarded as art transcending itself, albeit within the boundary of its own province, and in the form of art itself.

We may therefore briefly summarize our conclusion that in this third stage the object of art consists in the free and concrete presence of spiritual activity,[16] whose vocation it is to appear as such a presence or activity for the inner world of conscious intelligence. In consonance with such an object art cannot merely work for sensuous perception. It must deliver itself to the inward life, which coalesces with its object simply as though this were none other than itself,[17] in other words, to the intimacy of soul, to the heart, the emotional life, which as the medium of Spirit itself essentially strives after freedom, and seeks and possesses its reconciliation only in the inner chamber of spirit. It is this inward or ideal world which constitutes the content of the romantic sphere: it will therefore necessarily discover its representation as such inner idea or feeling, and in the show or appearance of the same. The world of the soul and intelligence celebrates its triumph over the external world, and, actually in the medium of that outer world, makes that victory to appear, by reason of which the sensuous appearance sinks into worthlessness.

On the other hand, this type of art, like every other, needs an external vehicle of expression. As already stated, the spiritual content has here withdrawn from the external world and its immediate unity into its own world. The sensuous externality of form is consequently accepted and represented, as in the symbolic type, as unessential and transient; furthermore the subjective finite spirit and volition is treated in a similar way; a treatment which even includes the idiosyncrasies or caprice of individuals, character, action, or the particular features of incident and plot. The aspect of external existence is committed to contingency and handed over to the adventurous action of imagination, whose caprice is just as able to reflect the facts given *as* they are,[18] as it can change the shapes of the external world into a medley of its own invention and distort them to mere caricature. For this external element has no longer its notion and significance in its own essential province, as in classical art. It is now discovered in the emotional realm, and this is manifested in the medium of that realm itself rather than in the external and *its* form of reality, and is able to secure or

---

[16] *Geistigkeit.* Professor Bosanquet translates it here "intellectual being."
[17] The distinction between a percipient and an external object falls away. The content displayed is part of the soul-life itself.
[18] Professor Bosanquet apparently assumes a negative has slipped out. But the text probably is correct in the rather awkward form in which it stands.

to recover again the condition of reconciliation with itself in every accident, in all the chance circumstance that falls into independent shape, in
all misfortune and sorrow, nay, in crime itself.

Hence it comes about that the characteristics of symbolic art, its indifference, incompatibility and severance of Idea from configurative expression, are here reproduced once more, if with essential difference. And this
difference consists in the fact that in romantic art the Idea, whose defectiveness, in the case of the symbol, brought with it the defect of external
form, has to display itself as Spirit and in the medium of soul-life as essentially self-complete. And it is to complete fundamentally this higher perfection that it withdraws itself from the external element. It can, in short,
seek and consummate its true reality and manifestation nowhere but in
its own domain.

This we may take to be in general terms the character of the symbolic,
romantic types of art, which in fact constitute the three relations of the
Idea to its embodiment in the realm of human art. They consist in the
aspiration after, the attainment and transcendency of the Ideal, viewed as
the true concrete notion of beauty.

4. In contrast to these two previous divisions of our subject the *third*
part presupposes the notional concept of the Ideal, and the universal art-
types. It in other words consists in their realization through specific sensuous media. We have consequently no longer to deal with the inner or
ideal evolution of the beauty of art in conformity with its widest and most
fundamental determinations. What we have now before us to consider is
how these ideal determinants pass into actual existence, how they are
distinguishable in their external aspect, and how they give an independent
and a realized shape to every element implied in the evolution of this Idea
of beauty as *a work of art*, and not merely as a *universal type*. Now it is
the peculiar differences immanent in the Idea of beauty which are carried
over by it into external existence. For this reason in this third fundamental
division these general art-types must themselves supply the basic principle
for the articulation and definition of the *particular arts*. Or, to put the
same thing another way, the several species of art possess in themselves the
same essential differences, which we have already become acquainted with
as the universal art-types. *External* objectivity, however, to which these
types are subjected in a sensuous and consequently *specific* material, necessitates the differentiation of these types into diverse and independent
modes of realization, in other words, those of particular arts. Each general
type discovers its determinate character in one determinate external
material or medium, in which its adequate presentation is secured under
the manner it prescribes. But, from another point of view, these types of
art, inasmuch as their definition is none the less consistent with the fact
of the *universality* of their typical import, break through the boundaries of
their *specific* realization in some definite art-species, and achieve an existence in other arts no less, although their position in such is of subordinate
importance. For this reason, albeit the particular arts belong specifically to
one of these general art-types respectively, the *adequate* external embodi-

ment whereof they severally constitute, yet this does not prevent them, each after its own mode of external configuration, from representing the totality of these art-types.[19] To summarize, then, in this third principal division we are dealing with the beauty of art, as it unveils itself in a world of realized beauty by means of the arts and their creations. The content of this world is the beautiful, and the true beautiful, as we have seen, is spiritual being in concrete form, the Ideal; or apprehended with still more intimacy it is the absolute mind and truth itself. This region of divine truth artistically presented to sensuous vision and emotion forms the centre of the entire world of art. It is the independent, free and divine Image,[20] which has completely appropriated the externality of form and medium, and now wears them simply as the means of its self-manifestation. Inasmuch, however, as the beautiful is unfolded here as *objective* reality, and in this process is differentiated into particular aspects and phases, this centre posits its extremes, as realized in their peculiar actuality, in antithetical relation to itself. Thus one of these extremes consists of an objectivity as yet devoid of mind, which we may call the natural environment of God. Here the external element, when it receives form, remains as it was, and does not possess its spiritual aim and content in itself, but in another.[21] The other extreme is the divine as inward, something known, as the manifold particularized *subjective* existence of Deity. It is the truth as operative and vital in sense, soul, and intelligence of particular persons, which does not persist as poured forth into its mould of external shape, but returns into the inward life of individuals. The Divine is under such a mode at once distinguishable from its pure manifestation as Godhead, and passes itself thereby into the variety of particularization which belongs to every kind of particular subjective knowledge, feeling, perception, and emotion. In the analogous province of religion with which art, at its highest elevation, is immediately connected, we conceive the same distinction as follows. First, we imagine the natural life on Earth in its finitude as standing on one side; but then, secondly, the human consciousness accepts God for its object, in which the distinction between objectivity and subjectivity falls away; then, finally, we advance from God as such to the devotion of the *community*, that is to God as He is alive and present in the subjective consciousness. These three fundamental modifications present themselves in the world of art in independent evolution.

(*a*) The *first* of the particular arts with which, according to their fundamental principle, we have to start is architecture considered as a fine art. Its function consists in so elaborating the external material of inorganic Nature that the same becomes intimately connected with Spirit as an artistic and external environment. Its medium is matter itself as an external

---

[19] Thus poetry is primarily a romantic art, but in the Epic it is affiliated with the objective character of classical art, or we may say that there is a romantic and classical type of architecture, though the art is primarily symbolic.

[20] *Gestalt*. Plastic power is perhaps a better translation.

[21] He means that in architecture the building is merely a shrine or environment of the image of the god.

object, a heavy mass that is subject to mechanical laws; and its forms persist as the forms of inorganic Nature coordinated with the relations of the abstract understanding such as symmetry and so forth. In this material and in these forms the Ideal is incapable of realization as concrete spirituality, and the reality thus presented remains confronting the Idea as an external fabric with which it enters into no fusion, or has only entered so far as to establish an abstract relation. And it is in consequence of this that the fundamental type of the art of building is that of *symbolism*. Architecture is in fact the first pioneer on the highway toward the adequate realization of Godhead. In this service it is put to severe labour with objective nature, that it may disengage it by its effort from the confused growth of finitude and the distortions of contingency. By this means it levels a space for the God, informs His external environment, and builds Him His temple, as a fit place for the concentration of Spirit, and its direction to the absolute objects of intelligent life. It raises an enclosure for the congregation of those assembled, as a defence against the threatening of the tempest, against rain, the hurricane, and savage animals. It in short reveals the will thus to assemble, and although under an external relation, yet in agreement with the principles of art. A significance such as this it can to a greater or less extent import into its material and its forms, in proportion as the determinate content of its fabric, which is the object of its operations and effort, is more or less significant, is more concrete or more abstract, more profound in penetrating its own essential depth, or more obscure and superficial. Indeed architecture may in this respect proceed so far in the execution of such a purpose as to create an adequate artistic existence for such an ideal content in its very forms and material. In doing so, however, it has already passed beyond its peculiar province and is diverted into the stage immediately above it of sculpture. For the boundary of sculpture lies precisely in this that it retains the spiritual as an inward being which persists in direct contrast to the external embodiment of architecture. It can consequently merely point to that which is absorbed in soul-life as to something external to itself.

(*b*) Nevertheless, as above explained, the external and inorganic world is purified by architecture, it is coordinated under symmetrical laws, and made cognate with mind, and as a result the temple of God, the house of his community, stands before us. Into this temple, in the *second* place, the God himself enters in the lightning-flash of individuality which smites its way into the inert mass, permeating the same with its presence. In other words the infinite[22] and no longer purely symmetrical form belonging to intelligence brings as it were to a focus and informs the shape in which it is most at home. This is the task of *sculpture*. In so far as in it the inward life of Spirit, to which the art of architecture can merely point away to, makes its dwelling within the sensuous shape and its external material, and to the extent that these two sides come into plastic communion with

[22] Infinite, of course, in the concrete sense of rounded in itself, as the circle, or, still more, the living organism.

one another in such a manner that neither is predominant, sculpture receives as its fundamental type the *classical* art-form.

For this reason the sensuous element on its own account admits of no expression here which is not affected by spiritual affinities,[23] just as, conversely, sculpture can reproduce with completeness no spiritual content, which does not maintain throughout adequate presentation to perception in bodily form. What sculpture, in short, has to do is to make the presence of Spirit stand before us in its bodily shape and in immediate union therewith at rest and in blessedness; and this form has to be made vital by means of the content of spiritual individuality. The external sensuous material is consequently no longer elaborated either in conformity with its mechanical quality alone, as a mass of weight, nor in shapes of the inorganic world simply, nor in entire indifference to colour, etc. It is carried into the ideal forms of the human figure, and, we may add, in the completeness of all three spatial dimensions. In other words and relatively to such a process we must maintain for sculpture that in it the inward or ideal content of Spirit are first revealed in their eternal repose and essential self-stability. To such repose and unity with itself there can only correspond that external shape which itself persists in such unity and repose. And this condition is satisfied by configuration viewed in its *abstract spatiality*.[24] The spirit which sculpture represents is that which is essentially sound, not broken up in the play of chance conceits and passions; and for this reason its external form also is not dissolved in the manifold variety of appearance, but exhibits itself under this one presentment only as the abstraction of space in the totality of its dimensions.

Assuming, then, that the art of architecture has executed its temple, and the hand of sculpture has placed therein the image of the god, we have in the *third* place to assume the *community* of the faithful as confronting the god thus presented to vision in the wide chambers of his dwelling-place. Now this community is the spiritual reflection into its own world of that sensuous presence, the subjective and inward animating life of soul, in its union with which, both for the artistic content and the external material which manifests it, the determining principle may be identified with particularization in varied shapes and qualities, individualization and the life of soul[25] which they imply. The downright and solid fact of unity the god possesses in sculpture breaks up into the multiplicity of a world of particular souls,[26] whose union is no longer sensuous but wholly ideal.

Here for the first time God Himself is revealed as veritably Spirit—viz., the Spirit revealed in His community. Here at last He is seen apprehended as this moving to-and-fro, as this alternation between His own essential unity and His realization in the knowledge of individual persons and that

---

[23] Lit., "which is not also that of the spiritual sphere."
[24] That is, an object limited only in space.
[25] *Subjecktivität*. The particularization in romantic art implies the presence of an ideal element imported by the soul of the artist, which appeals directly to the soul in its emotional life. Compare a picture by an Italian master with a Greek statue.
[26] Lit., "A multiplicity of isolated examples of inwardness."

separation which it involves, as also in the universal spiritual being[27] and union of the many. In such a community God is disengaged from the abstraction of His unfolded self-seclusion and self-identity, no less than from the immediate absorption in bodily shape, in which He is presented by sculpture. He is, in a word, lifted into the actual sphere of spiritual existence and knowledge, into the reflected appearance, whose manifestation is essentially inward and the life of heart and soul. Thereby the higher content is now the nature of Spirit, and that in its ultimate or absolute shape. But at the same time the separation to which we have alluded displays this as *particular* spiritual being, a specific emotional life. Moreover, for the reason that the main thing here is not the untroubled repose of the God in himself,[28] but his manifestation simply, the Being which is *for another*, self-revealment in fact, it follows that, on the plane we have now reached, all the varied content of human subjectivity in its vital movement and activity, whether viewed as passion, action, or event, or more generally the wide realm of human feeling, volition and its discontinuance, become one and all for their own sake objects of artistic representation.

Agreeably with such a content the sensuous element of art has likewise to show itself potentially adapted to such particularization and the display of such an inward content of heart and mind. Media of this description are supplied by colour, musical tones, and finally in sound as mere sign for ideal perceptions and conceptions; and we further obtain the means of realizing with the use of such media a content of this kind in the arts of painting, music, and poetry. Throughout this sphere the sensuous medium is found to be essentially disparate in itself and throughout posited[29] as ideal. In this way it responds in the highest degree to the fundamentally spiritual content of art, and the coalescence of spiritual significance and sensuous material attains a more intimate union than was possible either in architecture or sculpture. At the same time such a union is necessarily more near to soul-life, leaning exclusively to the subjective side of human experience; one which, in so far as form and content are thus constrained to particularization and to posit their result as ideal, can only be actually effected at the expense of the objective universality of the content as also of the fusion with the immediately sensuous medium.[30]

The arts, then, which are lifted into a higher strain of ideality, abandon-

---

[27] That is, in the life shared by all as one community actuated by a common purpose.

[28] As in sculpture.

[29] Professor Bosanquet's note is here (Trans., p. 166) "Posited or laid down to be ideal. This almost is equal to made *to be* in the sense of *not being*. In other words musical sound is "ideal" as existing, *quà* work of art, in memory only, the moment in which it is actually heard being fugitive. A picture is equally so in respect of the third dimension, which has to be read into it. Poetry is almost wholly ideal, *i.e.*, uses hardly any sensuous element, and appeals almost wholly to what exists in the *mind*."

[30] By particularization is meant the variety in the material of colours, musical tones, and ideas, which latter are really quite as much the medium of poetry as written language. The *sensuous* medium is here an abstract sign and, as Hegel would contend, nothing more than this.

ing as they do the symbolism of architecture and the classical Ideal of
sculpture, accept their predominant type from the *romantic* art-form; and
these are the arts most fitted to express its mode of configuration. They
are, however, a totality of arts, because the romantic type is itself essentially the most concrete.

(*c*) The articulation of this *third sphere* of the particular arts may be
fixed as follows:

(*α*) The *first* art which comes next to sculpture is that of painting. It
avails itself for a medium of its content and the plastic configuration of
the same of visibility as such, to the extent that it is differentiated in its
own nature, in other words is defined in the continuity of colour. No
doubt the material of architecture and sculpture is likewise both visible
and coloured. It is, however, not, as in painting, visibility in its pure
nature, not the essentially simple light, which by its differentiating of itself
in its opposition to darkness, and in association with that darkness gives
rise to colour.[31] This quality of visibility made essentially ideal[32] and
treated as such no longer either requires, as in architecture, the abstractly
mechanical qualities of mass as appropriate to materials of weight, nor,
as is the case with sculpture, the complete dimensuration of spatial condition, even when concentrated into organic forms. The visibility and the
making apparent, which belong to painting, possess differences of quality
under a more ideal mode—that is, in the specific varieties of colour—which
liberates art from the objective totality, of spatial condition, by being
limited to a plane surface.

On the other hand the content also attains the widest compass of particularity. Whatever can find a place in the human heart, as emotion, idea,
and purpose, whatever it is capable of actually shaping—all such diversity
may form part of the varied presentations of painting. The entire world
of particular existence, from the most exalted embodiment of mind to the
most insignificant natural fact, finds a place here. For it is possible even
for finite Nature, in its particular scenes and phenomena, to form part of
such artistic display, provided only that we have some reference to conscious life which makes it akin to human thought and emotion.[33]

(*β*) The *second* art which continues the further realization of the
romantic type and forms as distinct contrast to painting is that of *music*.
Its medium, albeit still sensuous, yet proceeds into still profounder subjectivity and particularization. We have here, too, the deliberate treatment
of the sensuous medium as ideal, and it consists in the negation and

---

[31] Reference, of course, to Hegel's unfortunate acceptance of Goethe's theory of colour.
[32] The colour of art is not merely ideal as applied to only two dimensions of space, but
also is "subjective" in the artistic treatment of it under a definite "scheme." It is not
clear whether Hegel alludes also to this; apparently not, though it is the most important feature. In fact, even assuming his theory of light to be correct, it is difficult
entirely to follow his distinction between the appearance of colour on a flat or a
round surface. As *natural* colour the one would be as ideal as the other. Only regarded
as a composition would painting present distinction.
[33] It is obvious that the reference here is mainly to an intentional appeal to the human
soul through the content of the composition. But the appeal may also be made through
the technique and artistic treatment of the medium itself.

idealization into the isolated unity of a single point,[34] the indifferent external collocation of space,[35] whose complete appearance is retained by painting and deliberately feigned in its completeness. This isolated point, viewed as this process of negation, is an essentially concrete and active process of cancellation within the determinate substance of the material medium, viewed, that is, as motion and vibration of the material object within itself and in its relation to itself. Such an inchoate ideality of matter, which no longer appears under the form of space, but as temporal idealty,[36] is sound or tone. We have here the sensuous set down as negated, and its abstract visibility converted into audibility. In other words sound liberates the ideal content from its fetters in the material substance. This earliest[37] secured inwardness of matter and impregnation of it with soul-life supplies the medium for the intimacy and soul of Spirit—itself as yet indefinite—permitting, as it does, the echo and reverberation of man's emotional world through its entire range of feelings and passions. In this way music forms the centre of the romantic arts, just as sculpture represents the midway point of arrest between architecture and the arts of the romantic subjectivity. Thus, too, it forms the point of transition between the abstract, spatial sensuousness of painting and the abstract spirituality of poetry. Music carries within itself, like architecture, and in contrast to the emotional world simply and its inward self-seclusion, a relation of quantity conformable to the principles of the understanding and their modes of co-ordinated configuration.[38]

(γ) We must look for our *third* and most spiritual type of artistic presentation among the romantic arts in that of *poetry*. The supreme characteristic of poetry consists in the power with which it brings into vassalage of the mind and its conceptions the sensuous element from which music and painting began to liberate art. For sound, the only remaining external material retained by poetry, is in it no longer the feeling of the sonorous itself, but is a mere sign without independent significance. And it is, moreover, a sign of idea which has become essentially concrete, and not merely[39] of indefinite feeling and its subtle modes and gradations. And this is how sound develops into the Word, as essentially articulate voice, whose intention it is to indicate ideas and thoughts. The purely negative moment to which music advanced now asserts itself

---

[34] The parts of a chord are not in space, but are ideally cognized. Hegel describes this by saying that music idealizes space and concentrates it to a point. It would perhaps be more intelligible to say that it transmutes the positive effects of a material substance in motion into the positive and more ideal condition of time. The point which is continually negated is at least quâ music the point, or rather, moment, of a temporal process.

[35] By the indifferent externality of space is signified the fact that the parts of space, though external to each other, are not qualitatively distinguishable.

[36] Succession in time is "more ideal" than coexistence in space because it exists only as continuity in a conscious subject.

[37] Painting no doubt introduces ideal elements into the artistic composition of colour, but the colour still remains the appearance of a material thing or superficies.

[38] That is to say, music or harmony is based on a solid conformity to law on the part of its tones in their conjunction and succession, their structure and resolution.

[39] As in painting.

as the wholly concrete point, the point which is mind itself, the self-conscious individual, which produces from itself the infinite expansion of its ideas and unites the same with the temporal condition of sound. Yet this sensuous element, which was still in music immediately united to emotion, is in poetry separated from the content of consciousness. Mind, in short, here determines this content for its own sake and apart from all else into the content of idea; to express such idea it no doubt avails itself of sound, but employs it merely as a sign without independent worth or substance. Thus viewed, the sound here may be just as well reproduced by the mere letter, for the audible, like the visible, is here reduced to a mere indication of mind.[40] For this reason, the true medium of poetical representation is the poetical imagination and the intellectual presentation itself; and inasmuch as this element is common to all types of art it follows that poetry is a common thread through them all, and is developed independently in each. Poetry is, in short, the universal art of the mind, which has become essentially free, and which is not fettered in its realization to an externally sensuous material, but which is creatively active in the space and time belonging to the inner world of ideas and emotion. Yet it is precisely in this its highest phase, that art terminates, by transcending itself; it is just here that it deserts the medium of a harmonious presentation of mind in sensuous shape and passes from the poetry of imaginative idea into the prose of thought.

Such we may accept as the articulate totality of the particular arts; they are the external art of architecture, the objective art of sculpture and the subjective arts of painting, music, and poetry. Many other classifications than these have been attempted, for a work of art presents such a wealth of aspects, that it is quite possible, as has frequently been the case, to make first one and then another the basis of division. For instance, you may take the sensuous medium simply. Architecture may then be viewed as a kind of crystallization; sculpture, as the organic configuration of material in its sensuous and spatial totality; painting as the coloured surface and line, while in music, space, as such, passes over into the point or moment of time replete with content in itself, until we come finally to poetry, where the external medium is wholly suppressed into insignificance.

---

[40] The views here propounded suggest considerable criticism. It appears to me that the stress here laid upon the intelligible content of poetry as contrasted with the sensuous qualities of its form as modulated speech is certainly untenable. What we call the music of verse may unquestionably be most intimately associated with the ideal content expressed; but apart from the artistic collocation of language as sound no less than symbol we certainly do not get the art of poetry. Even where Hegel deals directly with rhythm and rhyme in the body of the treatise I think it is clear he underrates all that is implied in the difference between the musical expression of poetry as contrasted even with the sonorous language of mere prose. A further question upon which more doubt is permissible in how far the actual script in written or printed letters is not entitled to be regarded as at least in part the sensuous medium. No doubt the poem is not dependent upon it as a painting is upon colour, or the canvas which supports it, for it may be recited. But at least it is practically dependent upon it for its preservation. The point may very possibly appear, however, as nugatory or entirely unimportant, beside the question whether the medium of the art is not really imaginative idea rather than articulate speech.

Or, again, these differences have been viewed with reference to their purely abstract conditions of space and time. Such abstract divisions of works of art may, as their medium also may be consequentially traced in their characteristic features. They cannot, however, be worked out as the final and fundamental principle, because such aspects themselves derive their origins from a higher principle, and must therefore fall into subordination thereto.

This higher principle we have discovered in the types of art—symbolic, classical, and romantic—which are the universal stages or phases of the Idea of beauty itself.

Their relation to the individual arts in their concrete manifestation as embodiment is of a kind that these arts constitute the real and positive existence of these general art-types. For *symbolic* art attains its most adequate realization and most pertinent application in *architecture*, in which it expatiates in the full import of its notion, and is not as yet depreciated, as it were, into the merely inorganic nature dealt with by some other art. The *classical* type of art finds its unfettered realization, on the other hand, in sculpture, treating architecture merely as the enclosure which surrounds it, and being unable to elaborate painting and music into the wholly adequate[41] forms of its content. Finally, the *romantic* art-type is supreme in the products of painting and music, and likewise in poetical composition, as their preeminent and unconditionally adequate modes of expression. Poetry is, however, conformable to all types of the beautiful, and its embrace reaches them all for the reason that the poetic imagination is its own proper medium, and imagination is essential to every creation of beauty, whatever its type may be.

To sum up, then, what the particular arts realize in particular works of art, are according to their fundamental conception, simply the universal types which constitute the self-unfolding Idea of beauty. It is as the external realization of this Idea that the wide Pantheon of art is being raised; and the architect and builder thereof is the spirit of beauty as it gradually comes to self-cognition, and to complete which the history of the world will require its evolution of centuries.

[41] *Absolute Formen*. Adequate in the sense of being unconditionally so.

Marcel Duchamp

ART AS NON-AESTHETIC:
I LIKE BREATHING
BETTER THAN WORKING

PIERRE CABANNE: You have said, "A painting that doesn't shock isn't worth painting."*

MARCEL DUCHAMP: That's a little rash, but fair enough. In the production of any genius, great painter or great artist, there are really only four or five things that really count in his life. The rest is just everyday filler. Generally, these four or five things shocked when they first appeared. Whether it's "Les Demoiselles d'Avignon," or "La Grande Jatte," they're always shocking works. In this sense, I do not feel like going to admire every Renoir, or even all of Seurat. . . . Still, I like Seurat a lot—that's another question. I dream of rarity, what otherwise could be known as a superior aesthetic. People like Rembrandt or Cimabue worked every day for forty or fifty years, and it is we, posterity, who have decided that this was very good because it was painted by Cimabue or Rembrandt. Any little bit of trash by Cimabue is still very much admired. It's a piece of trash next to three or four things he made which I don't know about anyway, but which exist. I apply this rule to all artists.

CABANNE: You have also said that the artist is unaware of the real significance of his work and that the spectator should always participate in supplementing the creation by interpreting it.

DUCHAMP: Exactly. Because I consider, in effect, that if someone, any genius, were living in the heart of Africa and doing extraordinary paintings every day, without anyone's seeing them, he wouldn't exist. To put it another way, the artist exists only if he is known. Consequently, one can envisage the existence of a hundred thousand geniuses who are suicides, who kill themselves, who disappear, because they didn't know

Marcel Duchamp was one of the founders of Dadaism. He is one of the great artistic iconoclasts of this century, often imitated, but never surpassed for wit and insight.

* Originally published in *The Documents of 20th Century Art: Dialogues with Marcel Duchamp* by Pierre Cabanne (London, 1958). Reprinted by permission of The Viking Press.

what to do to make themselves known, to push themselves, and to become famous.

I believe very strongly in the "medium" aspect of the artist.[1] The artist makes something, then one day, he is recognized by the intervention of the public, of the spectator; so later he goes on to posterity. You can't stop that, because, in brief, it's a product of two poles—there's the pole of the one who makes the work, and the pole of the one who looks at it. I give the latter as much importance as the one who makes it.

Naturally, no artist accepts this interpretation. But when you get right down to it, what is an artist? As much as the furniture maker, say Boulle, he's the man who owns a "Boulle." A work is also made of the admiration we bring to it.

African wooden spoons were nothing at the time when they were made, they were simply functional; later they became beautiful things, "works of art."

Don't you think the spectator's role is important?

CABANNE: Certainly, but I don't completely agree with you. Take, for example, "Les Demoiselles d'Avignon." The public didn't see it until twenty or thirty years after it was done, but still it was something very important for the few people Picasso showed it to.

DUCHAMP: Yes, but there are perhaps other works which were important at the beginning, and which have disappeared. I'm thinking of Girieud, whom I liked a lot.

CABANNE: Metzinger, too.

DUCHAMP: Yes. The pruning is done on a grand scale. In fifty years, well, well!

CABANNE: Are you thinking that a man like Girieud made an unknown masterpiece?

DUCHAMP: No. Not at all. Properly, any masterpiece is called that by the spectator as a last resort. It is the onlooker who makes the museum, who provides the elements of the museum. Is the museum the final form of comprehension, of judgment?

The word "judgment" is a terrible thing, too. It's so problematical, so weak. That a society decides to accept certain works, and out of them make a Louvre, which lasts a few centuries. But to talk about truth and real, absolute judgment—I don't believe in it at all.

CABANNE: Do you go to museums?

DUCHAMP: Almost never. I haven't been to the Louvre for twenty years. It doesn't interest me, because I have these doubts about the value of the judgments which decided that all these pictures should be presented to the Louvre, instead of others which weren't even considered, and which might have been there. So fundamentally we content ourselves with the opinion which says that there exists a fleeting infatuation, a style based on a momentary taste; this momentary taste disappears,

[1] I.e., the artist as a medium.

and, despite everything, certain things still remain. This is not a very good explanation, nor does it necessarily hold up.

CABANNE: Still, you accepted the idea that *your* entire work would be in a museum?

DUCHAMP: I accepted because there are practical things in life that one can't stop. I wasn't going to refuse. I could have torn them up or broken them; that would have been an idiotic gesture.

CABANNE: You could have asked that they be in a nonpublic place.

DUCHAMP: No. That would have been insanely pretentious.

CABANNE: Being protected yourself, you could have wanted to protect your work. . . .

DUCHAMP: Certainly. I'm slightly embarrassed by the publicity aspect which things take on, because of that society of onlookers who force them to re-enter a normal current, or, at least, what is called normal. The group of onlookers is a lot stronger than the group of painters. They oblige you to do specific things. To refuse would be ridiculous. To refuse the Nobel Prize is ridiculous.

CABANNE: Would you accept going into the Institute of Art?

DUCHAMP: No, my God, no! I couldn't! Besides, for a painter that doesn't mean much! Aren't they all literary people, I think, the members of the Institute?

CABANNE: No. There are painters too. Rather worldly ones.

DUCHAMP: The academic sort?

CABANNE: Yes.

DUCHAMP: No. I wouldn't sign a request to belong to the Institute. Anyway, it surely won't be proposed to me.

CABANNE: Who are the old masters you like?

DUCHAMP: I don't know them very well, really. I have appreciated Piero de Cosimo. . . .

CABANNE: You like the medieval primitives?

DUCHAMP: The primitives, yes. After that, there are some things I find hard to accept, like Raphael. Because one senses that they've been put there, and that classes of society have kept them there.

CABANNE: In 1924, you took part in a chess tournament in Nice. From there you went to Italy. Why did you go there?

DUCHAMP: To see a friend.

CABANNE: You didn't go for artistic reasons?

DUCHAMP: No. None at all. I spent a day in Florence. I didn't see anything. I also spent two or three weeks around Rome, in a district where there were several artists, but it wasn't at all to work or to look at pictures. No, I really haven't seen much of Italy. I went to Florence a little more seriously, I think, three years ago. I finally went to the Uffizi Gallery. Obviously, there's a lot there, but I really can't enjoy beginning an "artistic" education, in the old sense of the word? That doesn't interest me; I don't know why; I can't explain it.

CABANNE: When you were young, didn't you ever experience the desire to be artistically cultured?

DUCHAMP: Maybe, but it was a very mediocre desire. I would have wanted to work, but deep down I'm enormously lazy. I like living, breathing, better than working. I don't think that the work I've done can have any social importance whatsoever in the future. Therefore, if you wish, my art would be that of living: each second, each breath is a work which is inscribed nowhere, which is neither visual nor cerebral. It's a sort of constant euphoria.

CABANNE: That's what Roché said. Your best work has been the use of your time.

DUCHAMP: That's right. I really think that's right.

CABANNE: Toward 1924–25, you made some new projects for optical machines.

DUCHAMP: Yes. At that time, I felt a small attraction toward the optical. Without really ever calling it that. I made a little thing that turned, that visually gave a corkscrew effect, and this attracted me; it was amusing. At first I made it with spirals . . . not even spirals—they were off-center circles which, inscribed one inside the other, formed a spiral, but not in the geometric sense; rather in the visual effect. I was busy with that from 1921 to 1925.

Later, using the same procedure, I found a way of getting objects in relief.[2] Thanks to an offhand perspective, that is, as seen from below or from the ceiling, you got a thing which, in concentric circles, forms the image of a real object, like a soft-boiled egg, like a fish turning around in a fishbowl; you see the fishbowl in three dimensions. What interested me most was that it was a scientific phenomenon which existed in another way than when I had found it. I saw an optician at that time who told me, "That thing is used to restore sight to one-eyed people, or at least the impression of the third dimension." Because, it seems, they lose it.

At that moment my experiments interested a few specialists. Me, it amused me.

CABANNE: But it's very retinal!

DUCHAMP: Yes, but it's something you can't do for fifteen, or even ten years. After a while, it's finished.

CABANNE: You didn't do much with it.

DUCHAMP: No. Only in 1934. Then it was finished.

CABANNE: Some time before that, you had discovered a new activity. A rather unexpected one, moreover. Breaking your detachment, you began buying and selling paintings.

DUHAMP: That was with Picabia. We agreed that I would help him with his auction at the Hôtel Drouot. A fictitious auction, however, since the proceeds were for him. But obviously he didn't want to be mixed up in it, because he couldn't sell his paintings at the Salle Drouot under the title "Sale of Picabias by Picabia!" It was simply to avoid the bad effect that would have had. It was an amusing experience. It was all

---

[2] "Rotorelief."

very important for him, because, until then, no one had had the idea
of showing Picabias to the public, let alone selling them, giving them a
commercial value. . . .

I bought a few little things then. I don't remember what, any more.
. . .

CABANNE: You bought back your own works, for Arensberg.

DUCHAMP: There was the Quinn auction, in New York.[3] Quinn died in
1925, and his collection was auctioned off; that's where I bought the
Brancusis.

CABANNE: Then you organized a Brancusi show in New York.

DUCHAMP: To sell them again, at once. It was Brancusi who had asked us,
Roché and me, to buy back his works. He was afraid that if they were
put up for public sale, they would make only two or three hundred
dollars apiece, when he had already sold them for a lot more. We
arranged with Mrs. Rumsey, a great friend of Brancusi, to buy back
from the Brummer Gallery twenty-two Brancusis for eight thousand
dollars, which was very cheap, even at that time.

We split three ways. We reimbursed Mrs. Rumsey for what she had
put up, and then we—Roché and I—had about fifteen Brancusis, which
we divided. This commercial aspect of my life made me a living. When
I needed money, I'd go to Roché and say, "I have a small Brancusi for
sale; how much will you give me?" Because at that moment the price
was very low. That lasted for fifteen or twenty years.

CABANNE: The progressive rise of Brancusi prices helped you.

DUCHAMP: Yes, but at the time it wasn't at all foreseeable.

CABANNE: Wasn't your commercial activity in contradiction to your attitude?

DUCHAMP: No. One must live. It was simply because I didn't have enough
money. One must do something to eat. Eating, always eating, and
painting for the sake of painting, are two different things. Both can
certainly be done simultaneously, without one destroying the other.
And then, I didn't attach much importance to selling them. I bought
back one of my paintings, which was also in the Quinn sale, directly
from Brummer. Then I sold it, a year or two later, to a fellow from
Canada. This was amusing. It didn't require much work from me.

CABANNE: Because it was during this period that Arensberg decided to
gather your works together, and to give them to the Philadelphia
Museum. You helped him round them up.

DUCHAMP: Yes, that's right.

CABANNE: Fundamentally, was it a way of valorizing yourself?

DUCHAMP: No, no, absolutely not.

CABANNE: At least, you preferred that your works be assembled in a single
place where they could be seen.

DUCHAMP: That is true. I had a certain love for what I was making, and
this love was translated into that form.

[3] John Quinn, the great New York lawyer, had an important collection. He was one of
the first admirers of Brancusi.

CABANNE: Still your craftsman self.

DUCHAMP: I wanted the whole body of work to stay together. Moreover, I found that my works weren't numerous enough to make a profit painting after painting. And, above all, I wanted as much as possible not to make money. Generally the paintings I sold were my old ones. For instance, when I left for America there were a lot of paintings that stayed in France; I had them sent over and Arensberg bought them. There were also things that belonged to other people. My sister had a portrait of my father, which she wanted to keep. She had to be persuaded to sell it to Arensberg.

CABANNE: You've never dreamed of saving something for yourself?

DUCHAMP: Yes. An amusing thing. In New York, I had a "Glass" which I had given to Roché in 1915.[4] It was broken. I had put it between two other glass panes, in a wooden case, and Roché, then on his way back to France, took it with him.

Forty years later, my wife wanted to buy it. We had to pay through the nose to have it back! It's amusing. I wasn't at all mad at Roché, but the thing that I had given him he sold back to my wife at an astronomical price. Because it was she who bought it back, not me!

CABANNE: But wasn't Roché very rich?

DUCHAMP: He had made a fortune in paintings. Or from the commissions he got on the Brancusis. He was a charming man, who found it completely natural that one should pay. Whether it be me or someone else, it was all the same.

CABANNE: You, too, had a rather curious idea of how to make money. You made some insignias bearing the four letters D A D A, which you wanted to sell, I think, for a dollar.

DUCHAMP: It was amusing.

CABANNE: It was a sort of amulet, a fetish.

DUCHAMP: It wasn't to make money. It wasn't at all lucrative. Besides, I never made any of the insignia.

CABANNE: Never?

DUCHAMP: No.

CABANNE: You wrote to Tzara that the fact of buying it would "consecrate" the Dada buyer. It would also protect him from certain illnesses, certain vexations. Something like "the little pink pills for everything."

DUCHAMP: Yes. At a certain point, Breton had had the idea of opening up a Surrealist office, to give people advice. It's in the same spirit.

CABANNE: Nineteen twenty-six is the year that the "Large Glass" was cracked.

DUCHAMP: While I was gone, it was shown in an international exhibition at the Brooklyn Museum. The people who sent it back to Katherine Dreier, to whom it belonged, weren't professionals; they were careless. They put the two glasses one on top of the other, in a truck, flat in a box, but more or less well packed, without knowing if there were glass or

---

[4] The "Nine Malic Moulds."

marmalade inside. And after forty miles, it was marmalade. The only curious thing was that the two pieces were one on top of the other, and the cracks on each were in the same places.

CABANNE: The cracks follow the direction of the network of stoppages, it's astonishing all the same.

DUCHAMP: Exactly, and in the same sense. It constitutes a symmetry which seems voluntary; but that wasn't the case at all.

CABANNE: When one sees the "Large Glass," one doesn't imagine it intact at all.

DUCHAMP: No. It's a lot better with the breaks, a hundred times better. It's the destiny of things.

CABANNE: The intervention of chance that you count on so often.

DUCHAMP: I respect it; I have ended up loving it.[5]

. . .

CABANNE: In Houston, Texas, in 1957, you took part in a discussion on art at the University, with some very serious people.

DUCHAMP: Yes. I got in my two cents' worth, on the artist as a medium. I read a paper, and there was a discussion.

CABANNE: At the end of this discussion you said, "I've played my part as artistic clown." You have a funny opinion of yourself!

DUCHAMP: Naturally, because all these things I was doing were demanded, or requested. I had no reason to say, "But I'm above all that, I don't want to do it." It was amusing. In general, speaking in public is a part of an artist's life. But it's very hard to speak in public, unless you're a born orator. It was a game for me to see what I could do, to keep from being ridiculous. When you hear your own voice in front of five hundred people, it's very unpleasant, unless you're used to it and like it, like a politician. As far as I was concerned, it broadened my horizon a little. Later, I gave talks on myself, my work. It was always the same subject.

CABANNE: Did you take yourself seriously?

DUCHAMP: I wasn't taking myself seriously; I was making some money. That was the main reason. To make things easy and not be obliged to go into complicated theories, I always spoke on my own work. When I used a slide projector, I explained each picture, more or less. It was a very simple system, and it's done often in the United States, where artists are often invited to speak. To students, generally.

CABANNE: One has the impression that every time you commit yourself to a position, you attenuate it by irony or sarcasm.

DUCHAMP: I always do. Because I don't believe in positions.

CABANNE: But what do you believe in?

DUCHAMP: Nothing, of course! The word "belief" is another error. It's like the word "judgment," they're both horrible ideas, on which the world is based. I hope it won't be like that on the moon!

CABANNE: Nevertheless, you believe in yourself?

DUCHAMP: No.

[5] There is an etching by Duchamp showing the "Glass" unbroken, and another showing how it would have been, had he finished it.

CABANNE: Not even that.

DUCHAMP: I don't believe in the word "being." The idea of being is a human invention.

CABANNE: You like words so much?

DUCHAMP: Oh, yes, poetic words.

CABANNE: "Being" is very poetic.

DUCHAMP: No, not at all. It's an essential concept, which doesn't exist at all in reality, and which I don't believe in, though people in general have a cast-iron belief in it. No one ever thinks of not believing in "I am," no?

CABANNE: What is the most poetic word?

DUCHAMP: I have no idea. I don't have one handy. In any case, they would be words distorted by their sense.

CABANNE: Word games?

DUCHAMP: Yes, word games. Assonances, things like that, like the "delay" in the "Glass"; I like that very much. "Backward," that means something.

CABANNE: Even the word "Duchamp" is very poetic.

DUCHAMP: Yes. Nevertheless, Jacques Villon didn't waste any time changing names, not only "Duchamp" into "Villon," but also "Gaston" into "Jacques!" There are periods when words lose their salt.

CABANNE: You're the only brother to keep his name.

DUCHAMP: I was sort of obligated to. One of us had to!

Donald Karshan

A MANIFESTO—
THE SEVENTIES:
POST-OBJECT ART

One is always dubious about suggesting that a new artistic activity is "radical."* This is due, I suspect, to the situation which has occurred in the recent past where each slight change in artistic priorities has been heralded as a "breakthrough." Consequently I feel hesitant to make such a claim now, even though such a claim would be justified and supportable.

The "radical" art referred to here is currently described as "idea art," "analytic art," or "conceptual art." This last term, "conceptual art," has taken on a wider meaning in the past few months to occasionally include that which, in the scope of this exhibition, I would limit consideration of as work with a "conceptual aspect." The art chosen for this exhibition is work that, at its most materialistic extreme, is the most "conceptual aspect" of work often categorized as "anti-form," "earthworks," "art povera" and so on. On the other end of the spectrum is the "radical" art previously mentioned and, obviously, the area between the two extremes is filled as well.

That which separates the "radical" or, as I prefer to name it, the *"Post-Object Art,"* from the rest, is its *complete* break from formal esthetic considerations, while at the same time equally divorced from dada, gestural, or mystical and poetic activity or justification.

The earlier versions of a conceptual kind of art—such as Sol Lewitt's or Donald Judd's—was actually a nonexpressionistic system by which to build sculpture. And while this work is historically significant, and probably was necessary for the existence of the work under discussion, it should not be confused as being the same.

Certain aspects of Post-Object Art have their "roots" in mainstream Twentieth Century art, and indeed, it is a logical outgrowth of the accomplishments of the art of the modern period. If one considers painting and

Donald Karshan is a conceptual artist who was Director of The New York Cultural Center. He is currently living in Paris.

* Originally published in *Conceptual Art and Conceptual Aspects*, The New York Cultural Center, 1970. Reprinted by permission of the author.

sculpture the "language" of past art, it is easy to see that the art of the modern period, that is, the art since Manet, of a century ago, has changed its focus from the use of this language to convey a thought external to the work itself (portraiture, religious and historical scenes, etc.), to focusing on the "language" itself. And in this unique way, art became "art oriented."

From the beginning of the modern period, with the multiple movements in the School of Paris, through to the American abstract expressionists, and even up until the very recent past, artists felt compelled to analyze art only through the use of its traditional language, or in terms that could be equivocated with that language. Likewise, an illusion was perpetrated that the forms of art were timeless, and that any new reality could be ceaselessly paralleled using the omnipresent paint and canvas. The marriage of a 17th, 18th and 19th Century art form and the new consciousness of the Twentieth Century was a superficial and unharmonious one.

For those who have always associated art with the *objects* of painting and sculpture, this new work, not unlike all the new work to emerge in this century, will seem like a far cry indeed from the masterpieces of earlier cultures. Inevitably, however, it is the young artists, and the young artists alone, who define what art is, and will be. Because art is man-made, its existence and the nature of its existence is dependent on its capacity to be continually redefined and made "real" again and again by each generation.

In this end of the Twentieth Century we now know that art does indeed exist as an idea. And we know that quality exists in the thinking of the artist, not in the object he employs—if he employs an object at all. We begin to understand that painting and sculpture are simply unreal in the coming age of computers and instant travel.

Post-Object Art is based on the premise that the idea of art has expanded beyond the object or visual experience to an area of serious art "investigations." That is, to a philosophical-like inquiry into the nature of the concept "art" so that the working procedure of the artist not only encompasses the formulation of works, but also annexes the traditional one of the critic.

Joseph Kosuth, the American earliest to begin such work, has stated: ". . . conceptual art, then, is an inquiry by artists that understand that artistic activity is not solely limited to the framing of art propositions, but further the investigation of the function, meaning, and use of any and all (art) propositions, and their consideration within the concept of the general term "art." And as well, that an artist's dependence on the critic or writer to cultivate the conceptual implications of his art propositions, and argue their explication, is either intellectual irresponsibility or the naivest kind of mysticism."

In Europe, the work in England of Terry Atkinson and Michael Baldwin began this activity there, and it was they who later founded The Art & Language Press, the publisher of the journal *Art-Language*. There is also a New York-based group called The Society For Theoretical Art and

Analysis, comprised of the three artists Ian Burn, Mel Ramsden, and Roger Cutforth.

The nature of this artistic inquiry has enabled us to present in the catalogue, under "Information I," several text documents which clarify the nature of this work, and as well, eight text works—most of which are published there for the first time.

On Kawara, one of the first artists to begin working in this entire sphere of activity, began by employing as "meaningless" or flat subject matter, that which was the most direct and immediate—namely the man-made systems and structures that direct and measure his living time on earth. Kawara, a sort of artist's artist, has deliberately lived in relative obscurity until quite recently. The gallery devoted to his work in this exhibition is the first large installation of his work in the western hemisphere, and his first major public exposure in eleven years.

In the area I refer to as "conceptual aspects" many of the artists use the camera as an opinion-less copying device. The use of photography allows a "conceptual" kind of presentation—such as a photographic documentation of subject matter which is "frozen" into use by a system, and subsequently only exists as photographs; the subexperiential presentation of outdoor works, that exist no longer—or never did exist; and for various informational kinds of structure. One of the first to use the camera in such a way, Douglas Huebler, has said, "I use the camera as a 'dumb' copying device that only serves to document whatever phenomena appear before it through the conditions set by a system."

In this exhibition of twenty-nine artists from seven different countries, there are seventy-five works—nearly fifty of which are comprised of text only. This exhibition, we are pleased to point out, is the first exhibition of its kind devoted to this *specific* area of contemporary art on a museum level in the United States.

Arthur C. Danto

THE LAST WORK OF ART:
ARTWORKS AND REAL THINGS

The children imitating the cormorants,
Are more wonderful
Than the real cormorants.

Issa

Painting relates to both art and life . . .
(I try to work in that gap between the two.)

Rauschenberg

From philosophers bred to expect a certain stylistic austerity, I beg indulgence for what may strike them as an intolerable wildness in the following paper.* It is a philosophical reflection on New York painting from circa 1961 to circa 1969, and a certain wildness in the subject may explain the wildness I apologize for in its treatment. Explain but not excuse, I will be told: the properties of the subject treated of need never penetrate the treatment itself; Freud's papers on sexuality are exemplarily unarousing, papers in logic are not logical *merely* in consequence of their subject. But in a way the paper is part of its own subject, since it becomes an artwork at the end. Perhaps the final creation in the period it treats of. Perhaps the final artwork in the history of art!

I

Rauschenberg's self-consciously characterized activity exemplifies an ancient task imposed generically upon artists in consequence of an alienating

This paper was read in an earlier version at a conference on the philosophy of art at the University of Illinois at Chicago Circle. I am grateful to Professor George Dickie for having invited it. For prodromal reflections on much the same topic, see my paper "The Artworld," in *Journal of Philosophy*, vol. 61 (1964), pp. 571–584.

* Originally published in *Theoria*, XXXIX, 1973, pp. 1–17. Reprinted by permission of *Theoria*.

criticism by Plato of art as such. Art allegedly stands at a certain invidious remove from reality, so that in fabricating those entities whose production defines their essence, artists are contaminated at the outset with a kind of ontological inferiority. They bear, as well, the stigma of a moral reprobation, for with their productions they charm the souls of artlovers with shadows of shadows. Finally, speaking as a precocious therapist as well as a true philistine, Plato insinuates that art is a sort of perversion, a substitute, deflected, compensatory activity engaged in by those who are impotent to *be* what as a *pis-aller* they *imitate*. Stunned by this triple indictment into a quest for redemption, artists have sought a way towards ontological promotion, which means of course collapsing the space between reality and art. That there should, by Rauschenberg's testimony, still remain an insulating vacuity between the two which even *he* has failed to drain of emptiness, stimulates a question regarding the philosophical suitability of the task.

To treat as a defect exactly what makes a certain thing or activity possible and valuable is almost a formula for generating platonic philosophy, and in the case of art an argument may be mounted to show that its possibility and value is logically tied up with putting reality at a distance. It was, for example, an astonishing discovery that representations of barbaric rites need *themselves* no more be barbaric than representations of any x whatever need have the properties of x-hood. By *imitating* practices it was *horrifying* to engage in (Nietzsche), the Greeks spontaneously put such practices at a distance and invented civilization in the process; for civilization consists in the awareness of media as media and hence of reality as reality. So just those who gave birth to tragedy defeated an insupportable reality by putting between themselves and it a spiritualizing distance it is typical of Plato to find demeaning. It may be granted that this achievement creates the major problem of representational art, which is sufficiently to resemble the realities it denotes that identification of it as a representation of the latter is possible, while remaining sufficiently different that confusion of the two is difficult. Aristotle, who explains the pleasure men take in art through the pleasure they take in imitations, is clearly aware that the pleasure in question (which is intellectual) logically presupposes the knowledge that it *is* an imitation and not the real thing it resembles and denotes. We may take (a minor) pleasure in a man imitating a crow-call of a sort we do not commonly take in crow-calls themselves, but this pleasure is rooted in cognition: we must know enough of crow-calls to know that these are what the man is imitating (and not, say, giraffe-calls), and must know that he and not crows is the provenance of the caws. One further condition for pleasure is this, that the man *is* imitating and not just an unfortunate crowboy, afflicted from birth with a crowish pharynx. These crucial asymmetries need not be purchased at the price of decreased verisimilitude, and it is not unreasonable to insist upon a perfect acoustical indiscernibility between true and sham crow-calls, so that the uninformed in matters of art might—like an overhearing crow, in fact—be deluded and adopt attitudes appropriate to the reality of crows.

The knowledge upon which artistic pleasure (in contrast with *aesthetic* pleasure) depends is thus external to and at right angles to the sounds themselves, since they concern the causes and conditions of the sounds and their relation to the real world. So the option is always available to the mimetic artist to rub away all differences between artworks and real things providing he is assured that the audience has a clear grasp of the distances.

It was in the exercise of this option, for example, that Euripides undertook the abolition of the chorus, inasmuch as *real* confrontation, *real* frenzies of jealousy commonly transpire without benefit of the ubiquitous, nosy, and largely disapproving chorus inexplicably (*to him*) deemed necessary for the action to get on by his predecessors. And in a similar spirit of realism, the stony edifying heroes of the past are replaced by plain folks, and their cosmic suffering with the commonplace heartpains of such (for example) as us. So there *was* some basis for the wonder of his contemporary, Socrates (who may, considering his Egyptolatry in the *Laws*, have been disapproving not so much of art as of *realistic* art in the *Republic*), as to what the *point* of drama any longer could be: if we *have* the real thing, of what service is an idle iteration of it? And so he created a dilemma by looking inversely at the cognitive relations Aristotle subsequently rectified: either there is going to be a discrepancy, and mimesis fails, or art succeeds in erasing the discrepancy, in which case it just *is* reality, a roundabout way of getting what we already *have*. And, as one of his successors has elegantly phrased it: "one of the damned things is enough." Art fails if it is indiscernible from reality, and it equally if oppositely fails if it is not.

We are all familiar enough with one attempt to escape this dilemma, which consists in locating art in whatever makes for the discrepancies between reality and imitations of it. Euripides, it is argued, went in just the wrong direction. Let us instead make objects which are *insistently* art by virtue of the fact that no one can mistake them for reality. So the disfiguring conventions abolished in the name of reality become reintroduced in the name of art, and one settles for perhaps a self-conscious woodenness, a deliberate archaism, an operatic falseness so marked and underscored that it must be apparent to any audience that illusion could never have been our intent. *Non*-imitativeness becomes the criterion of art, the more artificial and the less imitative in consequence, the purer the art in question. But a fresh dilemma awaits at the other end of the inevitable route, namely that non-imitativeness is *also* the criterion of reality, so the more purely art things become, the closer they verge on reality, and *pure* art collapses into pure *reality*. Well, this may after all be the route to ontological promotion, but the other side of the dilemma asks what makes us want to call *art* what by common consent is reality? So in order to preserve a distinction, we reverse directions, hardly with a light heart since the same dilemma, we recall, awaits us at the other end. And there seems, on the face of it, only one available way to escape the unedifying shuttle from dilemma to dilemma, which is to make non-imitations which are radically distinct from all heretofore existing real things. Like Rauschenberg's stuffed goat garlanded with a tire! It is with such unentrenched objects, like combines and emerubies, that the abysses between life and art are to be filled!

There remains then only the nagging question of whether all unentrenched objects are to be reckoned artworks, e.g., consider the first can-opener. I know of an object indiscernible from what happen to be our routine can-openers, which *is* an artwork:

> The single starkness of its short, ugly, ominous blade-like extremity, embodying aggressiveness and masculinity, contrast formally as well as symbolically with the frivolous diminishing helix, which swings freely (but upon a fixed enslaving axis!) and is pure, helpless femininity. The two motifs are symbiotically sustained in a single, powerful composition, no less universal and hopeful for its miniature scale and commonplace material.[1]

As an artwork, of course, it has the elusive defining properties of artworks, significant form *compris*. In virtue of its indiscernibility from the domestic utensil, then, one might think it uncouth if not unintelligible to withhold predication of significant form to the latter, merely on grounds of conspicuous *Zuhandenheit* (one *could* open cans with the work the critic of the *Gazette* was so stirred by) or large numbers. For it would be startling that two things should have the same shape and yet one have and the other lack significant form. Or it would be were we to forget for an inadvertent moment the existence of a Polynesian language in which the sentence "Beans are high in protein," indiscernible acoustically from the English sentence "Beans are high in protein" actually means, in its own language, what "Motherhood is sacred" means in English. And it induces profound filial sentiments when audited by native speakers though hardly that with us. So perhaps significant form is supervenient upon a semantical reading, itself a weak function of language affiliation which mere inscriptional congruity happens to underdetermine? The question is suitably rhetorical at this point, for my concern is that the logical intersection of the non-imitative and the non-entrenched may as easily be peopled with artworks as by real things, and *may* in fact have pairs of indiscernible objects, one an artwork and one not. In view of this possibility, we must avert our eyes from the objects themselves in a counter-phenomenological turn—*Von den Sachen selbst!*—and see whatever it is, which clearly does *not* meet the eye, which keeps art and reality from leaking hopelessly into one another's territory. Only so can we escape the dilemma of Socrates, which has generated so much art-history through the misunderstandings it epitomizes and encourages.

II

Borges merits credit for, amongst other things, having discovered the Pierre Menard Phenomenon: two art-objects, in this instance two frag-

---

[1] *Gazette des beaux arts*, vol. 14, no. 6, pp. 430–431. My translation.

ments of the *Quixote*, which though verbally indiscriminable have radically non-overlapping and incompatible *artistic* properties. The art-works in question stand to their common physical embodiment in something like the relationship in which a set of isomers may stand to a common molecular formula, which then underdetermines and hence fails to explain the differences in their chemical reactions. The difference, of course, is given by the way the elements recorded in the formula are put together. Of the two *Quixotes*, for example, one is "more subtle" and the other "more clumsy" than its counterpart. That of Cervantes is the more coarse: it "opposes to the fiction of chivalry the tawdry provincial reality of his country." Menard's ("On the other hand . . ."!) selects for *its* reality "the land of Carmen during the century of Lepanto and Lope de Vega." Menard's work is an oblique condemnation of *Salammbô*, which Cervantes' could hardly have been. Though visibly identical, one is almost incomparably richer than the other and, Borges writes, "The contrast in style is also vivid. The archaic style of Menard—quite foreign, after all— suffers from a certain affectation. Not so that of his forerunner, who handles with ease the current Spanish of his time." Menard, were he to have *completed* his *Quixote*, would have had the task of creating at least one character in excess of Cervantes': the author of the (so-called in Menard's but *not* so-called in Cervantes') "Autobiographical Fragment." And so on. Menard's work was *his*, not a copy nor an accidentally congruent achievement of the sort involved in the discovery that the painters of Jupiter are making (there being no question here of cultural diffusion) flat works using the primary colors and staggeringly like Mondrians, but rather a fresh, in its own way remarkable creation. A mere copy would have no *literary* value at all, but would be merely an exercise in facsimilitation, and a *forgery* of so well known a work would be a fiasco. It is a precondition for the Menard phenomenon that author and audience alike know (not the original but) the *other* Quixote. But Menard's is not a quotation either, as it were, for quotations in this sense *merely* resemble the expressions they denote without having *any* of the artistically relevant properties of the latter: *quotations* cannot be scintillating, original, profound, searching, or whatever what is quoted may be. There are, indeed, theories of quotation according to which they lack *any* semantical structure, which their originals seldom lack. So a *quotation* of the Quixote (*either* Quixote) would be artistically null though quite superimposable upon its original. Quotations, in fact, are striking examples of objects indiscernible from originals which are not artworks though the latter are. Copies (in general) lack the properties of the originals they denote and resemble. A copy of a cow is not a cow, a copy of an artwork is not an artwork.

Quotations are entities difficult to locate ontologically, like reflections and shadows, being neither artworks nor real things, inasmuch as they are parasitic upon reality, and have in particular that degree of derivedness assigned by Plato to artworks as class. So though a copy—or quotation—of an artwork is logically excluded from the class of artworks, it raises too many special questions to be taken as our specific example of an entity indiscernible from an artwork though not one. But it is not difficult to generate less intricate examples. Consider, for the moment, *neckties*, which have begun to work their way into the artworld, e.g., Jim Dine's *Universal Tie*, John Duff's *Tie Piece*, etc. Suppose Picasso exhibits now a tie, painted uniform blue in order to reject any touch of *le peinture* as decisively as the Strozzi altarpiece rejects, as an act of artistic will, giottesque perspective. One says: my child could do *that*. Well, true enough, there is nothing beyond infantile capability here: so let a child, with his stilted deliberateness, color one of his father's ties an all over blue, no brush-strokes 'to make it nice.' I would hesitate to predict a magnificent future in art for this child on the basis of his having caused the existence of something indistinguishable from something created by the greatest master of modern times. I would go further, and say that he has not produced an artwork. For something prevents *his* object from entering the artworld, as it prevents from entering that world those confections by a would-be van Meegeren of Montmartre who sees at once the Picasso tie as a chance for clever forgery. Three such objects would give rise to one of those marvelous Shakespearean plots, of confused twins and mistaken identities, a possibility not a joking one for Kahnwieler (or was it Kootz?) who takes all the necessary precautions. *In spite of which*, let us suppose, the ties get mixed up, and the child's tie hangs to this very day in the Museum of the Municipality of Talloir. Picasso, of course, disputes its authenticity, and refuses to sign it (in fact he signs the forgery). The original was confiscated by the Ministry of Counterfacts. I look forward to the time when a doctoral candidate under Professor Theodore Reff straightens out the attributions by counting threads, though the status of a forgery with an authentic signature remains for philosohers of art to settle. Professor Goodman has an intriguing argument that sooner or later differences are bound to turn up, that what looks identically similar today will look artistically so diverse tomorrow that men will wonder how the case I have described would ever have arisen. Well, sufficient unto the day may be the similarities thereof: tomorrow's differentiations would appear *whichever* of the three ties were to hang in the museum, and I am inclined to feel that any seen differences will ultimately be used to reenforce the attribution, right or wrong, which is the accepted one. But that leaves still unsettled the ontological questions, besides generating a kind of absurdity of connoisseurship by bringing into the aesthetics of this order of object the refined peering appropriate, say, to Poussin or Morandi or Cézanne. None of whom, though clearly not for reasons of artistic ineptitude, would have been able to make an artwork out of a painted tie. So it isn't just that Picasso happens to be an *artist* that makes the difference in the cases at hand. But the further reasons are interesting.

For one thing, there would have been no room in the artworld of Cézanne's time for a painted necktie. Not everything can be an artwork at every time: the artworld must be ready for it. Much as not every line which is *witty* in a given context can be witty in all. Pliny tells of a contest between rival painters, the first drawing a straight line; the second drawing, in a different color, a line *within* that line; the first drawing an ultimately fine line within this. One does not ordinarily think of lines as having sides, but with each inscribed line, a space exists between its edges and the edges of the containing line, so that the result would be like five very thin strips of color. Nested lines, each making space where none was believed possible, shows remarkable steadiness of hand and eye, and bears witness to the singular prowess of Parahesios and his rival here. And the object was a wonder in its time. But not an artwork! No more than the famous free-hand circle of Giotto. But I could see exactly such an object turning up on Madison Avenue today, a synthesis, perhaps, of Barnett Newman and Frank Stella. Such an object in the time of Parahesios would have *merely* been a set-piece of draughtsmanly control. So it is not even as though, on the Berkeleyan assumption that only artworks can anticipate artworks, Parahesios were a predecessor of the contemporary painter of fine stripes. Parahesios could not have modified his perception of art, nor that of his times, to accommodate his *tour de main* as an artistic achievement. But Picasso's artworld was ready to receive, at Picasso's hand, a necktie: for he had made a chimpanzee out of a toy, a bull out of a bicycle seat, a goat out of a basket, a venus out of a gas-jet: so why not a *tie out of a tie?* It had room not only in the artworld, but in the corpus of the artist, in a way in which the identical object, from the hands of Cézanne, would have had room for neither. Cézanne could only have made a mountain out of paint, in the received and traditional manner of such transformations. He did not have the option even of making paint out of paint, in the later manner of the Abstract Expressionists.

But while these considerations serve to show that the identical object could, in one art-historical context be an artwork and in another one not, the problem remains of moving from *posse ad esse*. What, apart from the possibility, makes it actually a work of art in the context of late Picasso? And what makes then the differences between what Picasso did and his contemporaries, the child and the forger, did? Only when the world was ready for "Necktie" could the comedy of mistaken identities have transpired, and while it is easy to see how, given the sharp and exact resemblances, an artwork which was a necktie should have been confused with a necktie which was not an artwork, the task of explicating the differences remains.

One way to see the matter is this: Picasso *used* the necktie to *make a statement*, the forger employed the necktie to copy what Picasso made a statement with, but made *no* statement by means of his. And this would be true even were he inspired by van Meegeren to invent, say, a rose-colored necktie to fill a gap in Picasso's development. The child and Cézanne are simply making noise. Their objects have no location in the history of art. Part at least of what Picasso's statement is about is art, and art had not developed appropriately by the time of Cézanne for such a statement to have been intelligible, nor can the child in question have sufficiently internalized the history and theory of art to make a statement, much less *this* statement, by means of the painted necktie. At least the right relations hold between the four objects to enable a distinction structurally of a piece with that between statement, echo, and noise to be made. And though a real enough object—a hand-painted tie!—Picasso's work stands at just the right remove from reality for it to *be* a statement, indeed a statement in part about reality and art sufficiently penetrating to enable its own enfranchisement into the world of art. It enters at a phase of art-history when the consciousness of the difference between reality and art is part of what makes the difference between art and reality.

III

Testamorbida is a playwright who deals in Found Drama. Disgusted with theatricality, he has run through the tiresome post-Pirandello devices for washing the boundaries away between life and art, and has sickened of the contrived atmospheres of happenings. Nothing is going to be real enough save reality. So he declares his latest play to have been everything that happened in the life of a family in Astoria between last Saturday and tonight, the family in question having been picked by throwing a dart at the map of the town. How natural are the actors! They have no need to overcome the distance from their roles by stanislaviskyian exercise, since they *are* what they play. Or 'play.' The author 'ends' the play by fiat at eleven-ten (curtain), and has the after-theater party with friends at the West End Bar. No reviews, there was no audience, there was just one 'performance.' For all the 'actors' know, it was an ordinary evening, pizza and television, hair put up in rollers, a wrong number and a tooth-ache. All that makes this slice of life an artwork is the declaration that it is so, plus the meta-artistic vocabulary: 'actor,' 'dialogue,' 'natural,' 'begin-ning,' 'end.' And perhaps the title, which may be as descriptive as you please, viz., "What a Family in Astoria Did . . . ."

Titles are borne by artworks, interestingly enough, though not by things indiscernible from them which are *not* artworks, e.g., another period in the life of that or any family in Astoria or anywhere. Even 'Untitled' is a kind of title: non-artworks are not entitled even to be untitled. Cézanne's hand-painted necktie may bear a label, say at the Cézanne House, along with other memorabilia, but 'Cézanne's Necktie' is not its title (Cézanne's Necktie' could be the title of Picasso's tie if it were painted in just the color of the Louvre's *Vase Bleu*). Noblemen have titles too. 'Title' has the ring of status, of something which can be conferred. It has, indeed, enough of the ring of legality to suggest that 'artwork'—perhaps like 'person!'—is after all an ascriptive term rather than a descriptive—or exclusively descriptive—one.

Ascriptivity, as I understand it, is a property of predicates when they attach to objects in the light of certain conventions, and which apply less on the basis of certain necessary and sufficient conditions than of certain defeating conditions not holding. 'Person' is defeasible, for example, through such avenues as minority, subcompetence, disenfranchisement, financial responsibility and liability, and the like. A corporation can consist of a single person, who is not identical with the corporation in question, and the distinction between that person and the corporation he belongs to is perhaps enough like the distinction between an artwork and the physical object it consists in but is not identical with that we can think of artworks in terms of privileges, exemptions, rights, and the like. Thus artworks, which happen to contain neckties, are entitled to hang in museums, in a way in which neckties indiscernible from the former are not. They have, again, a certain peer-group which their indiscernible but plebeian counterparts do not. The blue necktie which is an artwork belongs with the Cowper-Niccolini Madonna and the Cathedral of Laon, while the necktie just like it which is not an artwork belongs just with the collars and cufflinks of banal haberdashery, somewhat abîmé by blue-paint. The blue necktie, indeed, is in the museum and in the collection, but its counterparts, though they can be geometrically in the museum, are there only in the way sofas and palm-trees typically are. There is, in fact, a kind of In-der-Pinakothek-sein not so awfully different from the In-der-Welt-sein which pertains to persons in contrast with things. A necktie which is an artwork differs from one which is not like a person differs from a body: metaphysically, it takes two sets of predicates amazingly similar to the P- and M-predicates which persons take on a well-known theory of P. F. Strawson's: no accident, perhaps, if 'person' too is an ascriptive predicate. The blue necktie, thus, which is an artwork, is by Picasso, whereas its counterpart is not by Cézanne even though he put the paint on it. And so forth. So let us try this out for a moment, stressing here the defeating conditions, less to strike a blow against Testamorbida than to see what kind of thing it is that can be subject to defeat of this order. I shall mention only two defeating conditions as enough for our purposes, though hardly exhausting the list. Indeed, were art to evolve, new defeating conditions would emerge.

(1) *Fakes*. If illusion were the aim after all of art, then there would be just exactly the same triumph in getting Stendhal to swoon at a fake Guido Reni as causing birds to peck at painted grapes. There is, I believe, no stigma attached to painting pictures of pictures: Burliuk once told me that, since artists paint the things they love and since *he* loved *pictures*, he saw no obstacle to painting pictures of pictures, viz., of Hogarth's *Shrimp Girl*. It *happens* that Burliuk remained himself, his picture of the *Shrimp Girl* deviating from the *Shrimp Girl* roughly as he differed from Hogarth. He was not, on the other hand, pretending the *Shrimp Girl* was *his* any more than he was pretending that Westhampton, which he also and in the same spirit painted pictures of, was *his*: what was *his* was the painting, a statement in paint which denoted the *Shrimp Girl* as his seascapes denoted glimpses of Westhampton: so we are distanced as much from the one motif as from the other, admiring in

both cases the vehicle. Well, a man might love his own paintings as much as he loves those of others, so what was to have prevented Burliuk from painting, say, his *Portrait of Leda?* This is not a case of *copying* the latter, so that we have two copies of the same painting: it is explicitly a painting *of* a painting, a different thing altogether, though it might exactly enough resemble a copy. A copy is defective, for example, insofar as it deviates from the original, but the question of deviation is simply irrelevant if it is a painting of a painting: much as we do not expect the artist to use chlorophyl in depicting trees. Now, if deviation is irrelevant, so is non-deviation. A copy is, indeed, just like a quotation, showing what we are to respond to rather than being what we are to respond to: whereas a painting of a painting is something *to* which we respond. Artists who repeat themselves, the Pierre Menard phenomenon notwithstanding, raise some remarkable questions. Schumann's last composition was based on a theme he claimed was dictated to him by angels in his sleep, but was *in fact* the slow movement of his own recently published Violin Concerto. (Is it an accident that Schumann was working on a book of quotations at the time of his *Zusammenbruch?*) Robert Desnos's *Dernier Poème à Youki* ("*J'ai tant rêvé de toi que tu perds ta réalité . . .*") is simply, according to Mary Ann Caws, "a retranslation into French of the rough and truncated translation into Czech" of his earlier and famous poem addressed to the actress Yvonne George: but was Desnos delirious when he addressed this poem, at his death, to Youki (or did he confuse Youki and Yvonne) or think it was a new poem or what? (I mention Schumann and Desnos in case someone thinks Goodman's distinction of one- and two-stage arts has any bearing). Repetitions are maddening.

A fake pretends to be a statement but is not one. It lacks the required relation to the artist. That we should mistake a fake for a real work (or *vice versa*) does not matter. Once we discover that it is a fake, it loses its stature as an artwork because it loses its structure as a statement. It at best retains a certain interest as a decorative object. Insofar as being a fake is a defeating condition, it is analytical to the concept of an artwork that it be "original." Which does not entail that it need or cannot be derivative, imitative, influenced, "in the manner of," or whatever. We are not required to invent a language in order to make a statement. Being an original means that the work must in a deep sense originate with the artist we believe to have done it.

(2) *Non-artistic provenance.* It is analytically true that artworks can only be *by* artists, so that an object, however much (or exactly) it may resemble an artwork is not *by* whoever is responsible for its existence, unless he is an artist. But "artist" is as ascriptive a term as "artwork," and in fact "by" is as ascriptive as either. Since, after all, not everything whose existence we owe to artists are *by* him. Consider the customs inspector who bears the stings of past and recent *gaffes* by his peers and decides to take no chances: a certain piece of polished brass—in fact the bushing for a submarine—is declared an artwork. But *his* so calling it that no more makes it an artwork than someone in the same métier calling an object

near of morphic kin to it *not* an artwork made the latter *not* be one. What injustice, then, if an artist decides to exhibit the bushing as a found object.

Douaniers, children, chimpanzees, counterfeiters: tracing an object to any of these defeats it as an artwork, demotes it to the status of a mere real object. Hence the logical irrelevance of the claim that a child, a chimpanzee, a forger or, *à la rigueur*, a customs inspector could *do* any of them. The mere object perhaps does not lie outside their powers. But as an artwork it does. Much in the way in which not everyone who can say the words "I pronounce you man and wife" can marry people, nor who can pronounce the words "Thirty days or thirty dollars" can *sentence* a man. So the question of whether an object is *by* someone, and how one is qualified to make artworks out of real things, are of a piece with the question of whether it is an artwork.

The moment something is considered an artwork, it becomes subject to an *interpretation*. It owes its existence as an artwork to this, and when its claim to art is defeated, it loses its interpretation and becomes a mere thing. The interpretation is in some measure a function of the artistic context of the work: it means something different depending upon its art-historical location, its antecedents, and the like. And as an artwork, finally, it acquires a structure which an object photographically similar to it is simply disqualified from sustaining if it is a real thing. Art exists in an atmosphere of interpretation and an artwork is thus a vehicle of interpretation. The space between art and reality is like the space between language and reality partly because art *is* a language of sorts, in the sense at least that an artwork says something, and so presupposes a body of sayers and interpreters who are in position, who define what being in position is, to interpret an object. There is no art without those who speak the language of the artworld, and who know enough of the difference between artworks and real things to recognize that calling an artwork a real thing *is* an interpretation of it, and one which depends for its point and appreciation on the contrast between the artworld and the real-world. And it is exactly with reference to this that the defeating conditions for ascription of "artwork" are to be understood. If this is so, then ontological promotion of art is hardly to be looked for. It is a logical impossibility. Or nearly so: for there is one further move to reckon with.

IV

Much as philosophy has come to be increasingly its own subject, has turned reflexively inward onto itself, so art has done, having become increasingly its own (and only) subject: like the Absolute of Hegel, which finally achieved congruence with itself by becoming self-contemplative in the respect that *what* it contemplates is itself in contemplation. Rosenberg thus reads the canvas as an arena in which a real action occurs when an artist (but *nota bene: only* when an *artist*) makes a wipe of paint upon it: a stroke. To appreciate that the boundaries have been crossed, we must read the stroke as saying, in effect, about itself, that it *is* a stroke and not a representation of anything. Which the indiscernible strokes made by housepainters cannot *begin* to say, though it is true that they are strokes and not representations. In perhaps the subtlest suite of paintings in our time, such strokes—fat, ropy, expressionist—have been read with a deadly literalness of their makers' or the latter's ideologues intention as (mere) real things, and made the subject of paintings as much as if they were apples, by Roy Lichtenstein. These are paintings *of* brush strokes. And Lichtenstein's paintings say, about themselves, at least this: that they *are* not but only represent brush strokes, and yet they are art. The boundaries between reality and art as much inform these works as they did the initial impulses of the Abstract Expressionists they impale. The boundaries between art and reality, indeed, become *internal* to art itself. And this is a revolution. For when one is able to bring within oneself what separates oneself from the world, viz., as when Berkeley brings the brain into the mind, the distinction between mind and brain now standing as a distinction within the mind itself, everything is profoundly altered. And in a curious way, the Platonic challenge has been met. Not by promoting art but by demoting reality, conquering it in the sense that when a line is engulfed, what lies on both sides of that line is engulfed as well. To incorporate one's own boundaries in an act of spiritual topology is to transcend those boundaries, like turning oneself inside out and taking one's external environment in as now part of oneself.

I would like briefly to note two consequences of this. The first is that it has been a profoundly disorienting maneuver, increasingly felt as the categories which pertain to art suddenly pertain to what we always believed contrasted essentially with art. Politics becomes a form of theater, clothing a kind of costume, human relations a kind of role, life a game. We interpret ourselves and our gestures as we once interpreted artworks. We look for meanings and unities, we become players in a play.

The other consequence is more interesting. The relationship between reality and art has traditionally been the province of philosophy, since the latter is analytically concerned with relations between the world and its representations, the space between representation and life. By bringing within itself what it had traditionally been regarded as logically apart from, art transforms itself into philosophy, in effect. The distinction between philosophy of art and art itself is no longer tenable, and by a curious, astounding magic we have been made over into contributors to a field we had always believed it our task merely to analyze from without.

Select Bibliography for Part Five

Books

G. W. F. Hegel, *The Introduction to Hegel's Theory of Fine Art*; Ursula Meyer, *Conceptual Art*; W. T. Stace, *The Philosophy of Hegel*.

Articles

Gene Blocker, "Hegel on Aesthetic Internalization"; George Boas, "Historical Periods"; Herta Pauly, "Aesthetic Decadence Today Viewed in Terms of Schiller's Three Impulses"; Leon Rosenstein, "Metaphysical Foundations of the Theories of Tragedy in Hegel and Nietzsche"; Richard Sclafani, "What Kind of Nonsense Is This?"

PART SIX

Traditional
Theories of the Aesthetic
and Contemporary Discussions
of these Theories

This part is concerned with two kinds of theory—eighteenth-century theory of taste and nineteenth-century aesthetic–attitude theory. Both kinds of theory are primarily concerned with giving an account of what is involved in the experience and appreciation of beauty in art and nature. By contrast with the earlier platonic conception of beauty as an objective property of things, both of these theories focus on the subject experiencing beauty. Thus, with the publication of these theories, the faculties and experiences of persons became the prime subject matter.

The theory of taste begins, at least in Great Britain, as pointed out by Peter Kivy, with the publication in 1712 of Joseph Addison's sketchy remarks on the subject. The two most important systematic developments in this area of thought were generated by Francis Hutcheson and David Hume. The general philosophical tradition within which their theories of taste developed was the empiricism of John Locke. The other important influence on these theorists was, as Jerome Stolnitz shows, the notion of disinterestedness introduced into the theory of the appreciation of beauty by the third Earl of Shaftesbury. Shaftesbury's view is also sometimes considered a theory of taste, but if it is so called it should be noted that it differs strikingly from those of other British thinkers who developed theories of taste. Whereas the others—Addison, Hutcheson, Hume, Edmund Burke, Alexander Gerard, and Archibald Alison—worked within the empiricist tradition of Locke, Shaftesbury was an antiempiricist who wrote of the appreciation of beauty in platonic or neoplatonic terms.

The theory of taste which developed from Addison in 1712 to Alison

in 1790 exhibits a constant five-part structure, although the various thinkers filled in particular parts of the structure in different ways. The first
structural part is *perception*, which for all the British theorists was simply
the mode whereby one knows the objects in the world and their characteristics. The second structural part is the *faculty of taste*. The theorists
differ as to the nature of this faculty. Addison rather vaguely spoke of
the imagination. Hutcheson wrote in considerable detail of the faculty
of taste as an internal sense of beauty. An internal sense contrasts with
the external senses, such as vision and hearing, which cognize the world;
an internal sense reacts to what the external senses apprehend. An internal
sense resembles an external sense in that the former works automatically
and cannot be influenced by interest. Burke rejected the notion of the
faculty of taste as a special sense and spoke simply in terms of the
propensity to experience pleasure and pain. Hume did not have much
to say about the nature of the faculty of taste but concentrated on other
aspects of the theory. The third structural part of the theory of taste is
the *mental product* which exists when the faculty of taste reacts. The
theorists generally understood this product to be pleasure. The fourth
structural part is the *kind of object* in the perceived world to which the
faculty of taste reacts. It is here that the theorists differ most. Hutcheson
said it is based on the perception of *uniformity in variety*. Burke, rather
than specifying a formula, gave a list of properties: smoothness, smallness,
and the like. Hume spoke vaguely of "certain qualities in objects." Alison
wrote of the perception of something which is a sign of, or is expressive
of, a quality of mind (nobility, for example). The fifth and final structural part is *judgments of taste*, for example, a judgment such as "This
painting is beautiful." Such a judgment means that a perceived object
(the painting) in virtue of some characteristic (say, uniformity in variety)
causes the faculty of taste to react and produce pleasure.

All theorists of taste make use of the notion of disinterestedness. For
Hutcheson, the alleged fact that the faculty of taste was a *sense* insured
disinterestedness because this meant that the faculty reacted automatically
and was indifferent to interest. Hutcheson was aware, of course, that the
faculty can be influenced by custom, training, and even the accidental
association of ideas. By contrast with Hutcheson, Alison, at the end of
the eighteenth century, rejected the notion of a special sense as the faculty
of taste and instead developed an elaborate account of what goes on in
the mind of a person who experiences beauty. Alison included disinterestedness in his approach by claiming that any practical interests held by
a person may interfere with, and be destructive of, the experience of
beauty. For Hutcheson, disinterestedness was insured by the nature of
the faculty of taste; for Alison disinterestedness was something to be
achieved by freeing oneself from practical interests which distract from
the experience of beauty.

We have presented a sketch of the philosophical background and
structure of the theories of taste offered by the eighteenth-century British
philosophers. These theories contrast markedly with the aesthetic–attitude

theories of certain nineteenth-century thinkers. The structure of the aesthetic–attitude theories is simpler than the structure of theories of taste. In attitude studies the faculty of perception assumes a central role. For the aesthetic–attitude theories there are two kinds of perception: ordinary and aesthetic.

Aesthetic–attitude theories have been presented in strong and weak versions. A strong version such as that offered by the German philosopher Arthur Schopenhauer maintains that whatever is viewed with aesthetic perception is thereby made beautiful (with a few restrictions, such as the obscene and the disgusting). A weak version of the theory, such as that offered by Edward Bullough in part seven, maintained that viewing with aesthetic perception is a necessary condition for experiencing the aesthetic properties of things—which they possess inherently and independently of aesthetic perception. The aesthetic–attitude theories dispense with the faculty of taste, with a specific kind of object (uniformity in variety, for example) which triggers the faculties of taste and pleasure. In dispensing with the need for a specific kind of object to trigger a faculty of taste, the aesthetic–attitude theories take a further step toward subjectivity. The strong version gives the subject (perceiver) almost complete control over what is experienced as beautiful, and the weak version gives the subject (perceiver) veto power over what can be experienced as beautiful.

The theories of taste, especially when viewed in contrast with platonic conceptions of beauty, were themselves steps in the direction of subjectivity because they centered theoretical considerations on the perceptions and reactions of subjects. The notion of disinterestedness is retained in aesthetic–attitude theories, but it is aesthetic perception that is supposed to be disinterested and, thereby, capable of determining its object to be beautiful or of making aesthetic qualities available to the perceiver. In this theoretical stance, judgments of taste have been replaced by aesthetic judgments, which refer to the objects of aesthetic perception.

F. J. Copleston, the noted historian of philosophy, gives a clear exposition of Schopenhauer's theory in the essay presented here. Although his primary aim is to explain the theory, Copleston develops some interesting criticisms of Schopenhauer as well. Copleston does not distinguish, explicitly, between strong and weak versions of aesthetic–attitude theories (this distinction was developed subsequent to Copleston's essay). It is clear, however, that Copleston's criticisms are most forceful when understood as criticisms of a strong version of theory.

Jerome Stolnitz's "On the Origins of 'Aesthetic Disinterestedness'" is a ground-breaking work demonstrating the role of disinterestedness in theories of taste from Shaftesbury (where it is first related to the appreciation of beauty) to Alison. Very skillfully, he details how disinterestedness was employed in the theories of Shaftesbury, Addison, Burke, Gerard, and Alison. It is debatable, however, whether Stolnitz was correct in claiming that the views of Addison and Alison involve the notion of aesthetic perception or aesthetic attention and are, therefore, early versions of aesthetic–attitude theory. But this controversial point is minor and Stolnitz's article has done a very great deal in helping us come to a better understanding of the eighteenth-century theories of taste.

The theory of taste of the German philosopher Immanuel Kant, published in 1890, falls both temporally and theoretically between the theories of the British philosophers of taste and the later aesthetic–attitude theorists. Kant's theory clearly retains the five-part structure of the earlier theories of taste. For Kant, the *faculty of taste* is the set of ordinary cognitive faculties (the understanding and the imagination) functioning in an unusual way. For him, the mental product of the faculty of taste's reaction is *pleasure*. Kant offers an account of *judgments of taste* similar to those of the earlier theorists, except that for reasons inherent in his theory he maintains that such judgments are always singular (about an individual object) and never universal (about a whole set of objects). The kind of perceived object which, according to Kant, triggers the faculty of taste is one which exhibits the *form of purpose*. Why purposiveness must be worked into the theory is difficult to explain, but it derives from a general feature of Kant's philosophy. This difficulty notwithstanding, not just any form will trigger the faculty of taste, only one which has the form of purpose. Robert Burch's essay presented here is primarily concerned with linking Kant's theory of taste (beauty) at this point (the form of purpose) to Kant's theory of art.

Kant's conception of *perception* clearly sets him apart from the British theorists of taste and makes possible the development of the later aesthetic–attitude theories. The British theorists, working in the tradition of Locke, assumed perception to be a *passive* function of the mind which simply reveals to us the nature of the perceived world. Before he began work on the theory of taste, Kant had developed a theory of the mind, according to which mind is an active force which to a large extent forms and constitutes the objects that we perceive. Kant's theory of taste was then worked out within this more general philosophical framework. One of the prime functions of the mind, according to Kant, is to give to experience the spatial and temporal *form* that it has. Thus, when Kant maintained that an object's *form* of purpose triggers the faculty of taste, he is saying that the faculty of taste is triggered by an object—having such aspect (its form) as a result of the activity of a subject's mind. Thus, Kant has made the aspect of the perceived world which triggers the faculty of taste to a degree subjective, that is, dependent upon the activity of a subject's mind. It was this development in Kant's general philosophy and in his theory of taste that made possible the development of the even more subjective aesthetic–attitude theories.

Francis Hutcheson

AN INITIAL THEORY
OF TASTE

The Preface

There is no part of philosophy of more importance than a just knowledge
of human nature and its various powers and dispositions.* Our late
inquiries have been very much employed about our understanding and
the several methods of obtaining truth. We generally acknowledge that
the importance of any truth is nothing else than its moment or its efficacy
to make men happy or to give them the greatest and most lasting pleasure;
and wisdom denotes only a capacity of pursuing this end by the best
means. It must surely then be of the greatest importance to have distinct
conceptions of this end itself, as well as of the means necessary to obtain
it, so that we may find out which are the greatest and most lasting
pleasures and, thus, not employ our reason, after all our laborious improvements of it, in trifling pursuits. Indeed, it is to be feared that without
this inquiry most of our studies will be of very little use to us, for they
seem to have scarcely any other tendency than to lead us into speculative
knowledge itself. Nor are we distinctly told how it is that knowledge, or
truth, is pleasant to us.

This consideration put the author of the following papers upon inquiring into the various pleasures which human nature is capable of receiving.
We shall generally find in our modern philosophic writings nothing
further on this head than some bare division of them into sensible, and
rational, and some trite commonplace arguments to prove the latter more
valuable than the former. Our sensible pleasures are slightly passed over
and explained only by some instances in tastes, smells, sounds, or such
like, which men of any tolerable reflection generally look upon as very
trifling satisfactions. Our rational pleasures have had much the same kind

Francis Hutcheson (1694–1746). One of the first British Empiricist philosophers
who wrote on Beauty and Morals. Hutcheson's work is currently undergoing a revival.
New editions of his works are appearing, and philosophers and scholars are once again
paying him notice.
* Selections from the original edition of *An Inquiry into the Original of our Ideas of
Beauty and Virtue* (London, 1725).

of treatment. We are seldom taught any other notion of rational pleasure than that which we have upon reflecting on our possession, or claim to those objects, which may be occasions of pleasure. Such objects we call advantageous. But advantage, or interest, cannot be distinctly conceived, till we know what those pleasures are which advantageous objects are apt to excite, and what senses or powers of perception we have with respect to such objects. We may perhaps find such an inquiry of more importance in morals, to prove what we call the reality of virtue, or that it is the surest happiness of the agent, than one would at first imagine.

In reflecting upon our external senses, we plainly see that our perceptions of pleasure, or pain, do not depend directly on our will. Objects do not please us, according as we incline they should. The presence of some objects necessarily pleases us, and the presence of others necessarily displeases us. Nor by our will, do we procure pleasure or avoid pain except by procuring the former kinds of objects and avoiding the latter. By the very frame of our nature, the one is made the occasion of delight, and the other of dissatisfaction.

The same observation will hold in all our other pleasures and pains. For there are many other sorts of objects which please, or displease, us as necessarily as material objects do when they operate upon our organs of sense. There is scarcely any object which our minds are employed about which is not thus constituted the necessary occasion of some pleasure or pain. Thus we find ourselves pleased with a regular form, a piece of architecture or painting, a composition of notes, a theorem, an action, an affection, a character. And we are conscious that this pleasure necessarily arises from the contemplation of the idea, which is then present in our minds with all its circumstances, even though some of these ideas have nothing of what we call sensible perception in them. And in those which have, the pleasure arises from some uniformity, order, arrangement, or imitation, not from the simple ideas of color, sound, or mode of extension separately considered.

These determinations to be pleased with any forms, or ideas which occur to our observation, are what the author chooses to call senses, distinguishing them from the powers which commonly go by that name, by calling our power of perceiving the beauty of regularity, order, harmony, an internal sense. And the determination to be pleased with the contemplation of those affections, actions, or characters of rational agents which we call virtuous is what he marks by the name of a moral sense.

His principal design is to show "That human nature was not left quite indifferent in the affair of virtue, to form to itself observations concerning the advantage, or disadvantage of actions, and accordingly to regulate its conduct." The weakness of our reason, and the avocations arising from the infirmity and necessities of our nature, are so great that very few men could ever have formed those long deductions of reason which show some actions to be in the whole advantageous to the agent, and their contraries pernicious. The author of nature has much better furnished us for a life of virtuous conduct than our moralists seem to imagine by almost as quick and powerful instructions as we have for the preservation of our bodies. He has made virtue a lovely form, to excite our pursuit of it, and has given us strong affections to be springs of each virtuous action.

This moral sense of beauty in actions and affections may appear strange at first view. Some of our moralists themselves are offended at it in my Lord Shaftesbury, so accustomed are they to deduce every approbation, or aversion, from rational views of interest (except it be merely in the simple ideas of the external senses) and have such a horror at innate ideas, which they imagine this borders upon. But this moral sense has no relation to innate ideas, as will appear in the second treatise. Our gentlemen of good taste can tell us of a great many senses, tastes, and relishes for beauty, harmony, imitation in painting and poetry. And may not we find too in mankind a relish for a beauty in characters, in manners? I doubt we have made philosophy, as well as religion, by our foolish management of it, so austere and ungainly a form that a gentleman cannot easily bring himself to like it, and those who are strangers to it can scarcely bear to hear our description of it. So much is it changed from what was once the delight of the finest gentlemen among the ancients and their recreation after the hurry of public affairs!

In the first treatise, the author has perhaps in some instances gone too far in supposing a greater agreement of mankind in their sense of beauty than experience will confirm, but all he is solicitous about is to show "That there is some sense of beauty natural to men; that we find as great an agreement of men in their relishes of forms, as in their external senses which all agree to be natural; and that pleasure or pain, delight or aversion, are naturally joined to their perceptions." If the reader is convinced of such determinations of the mind to be pleased with forms, proportions, resemblances, and theorems, it will be no difficult matter to apprehend another superior sense, natural also to men, determining them to be pleased with actions, characters, and affections. This is the moral sense, which makes the subject of the second treatise.

The proper occasions of perception by the external senses occur to us as soon as we come into the world, whence perhaps we easily look upon these senses to be natural, but the objects of the superior senses of beauty and virtue generally do not. It is probably some little time before children reflect, or at least let us know that they reflect, upon proportion and similitude, upon affections, characters, and tempers, or come to know the external actions which are evidences of them. Hence we imagine that their sense of beauty, and their moral sentiments of actions, must be entirely owing to instruction and education, whereas it is as easy to conceive how a character or a temper, as soon as it is observed, may be constituted by nature the necessary occasion of pleasure or an object of approbation, as a taste or a sound, though it be sometime before these objects present themselves to our observation.

Sect. I Concerning some Powers of Perception, Distinct from What Is Generally Understood by Sensation

To make the following observations understood, it may be necessary to introduce some definitions and observations, either universally acknowledged or sufficiently proved by many writers both ancient and modern, concerning our perceptions called sensations and the actions of the mind consequent upon them.

1. Those ideas which are raised in the mind upon the presence of external objects, and their acting upon our bodies, are called sensations. We find that the mind in such cases is passive and has not power directly to prevent the perception or idea or to vary it at its reception, as long as we continue our bodies in a state fit to be acted upon by the external object.

2. When two perceptions are entirely different from each other, or agree in nothing but the general idea of sensation, we call the powers of receiving those different perceptions different senses. Thus seeing and hearing denote the different powers of receiving the ideas of colors and sounds. And, although colors have vast differences among themselves, as also have sounds, there is a great agreement among the most opposite colors than between any color and a sound; hence, we call all colors perceptions of the same sense. All the several senses seem to have their distinct organs, except feeling, which is in some degree diffused over the whole body.

3. The mind has a power of compounding ideas which were received separately, of comparing their objects by means of the ideas, and of observing their relations and each of the simple ideas which might perhaps have been impressed jointly in the sensation. This last operation we commonly call abstraction.

4. The ideas of substances are compounded of the various simple ideas jointly impressed when they presented themselves to our senses. We define substances only by enumerating these sensible ideas. And such definitions may raise an idea clear enough of the substance in the mind of one who never immediately perceived the substance, provided he has separately received by his senses all the simple ideas which are in the composition of the complex one of the substance defined. But if there be any simple ideas which he has not received, or if he lacks any of the senses necessary for the perception of them, no definition can raise any simple idea which has not been before perceived by the senses.

5. Hence it follows "That, when instruction, education, or prejudice of any kind raise any desire or aversion toward an object, this desire or aversion must be founded upon an opinion of some perfection or of some

deficiency in those qualities for perception of which we have the proper senses." Thus if beauty be desired by one who has not the sense of sight, the desire must be raised by some apprehended regularity of figure, sweetness of voice, smoothness, softness, or some other quality perceivable by the other senses without relation to the ideas of color.

6. Many of our sensitive perceptions are pleasant, and many are painful, immediately, without any knowledge of the cause of this pleasure or pain, or the means by which the objects excite it or are the occasions of it, or our seeing to what further advantage or detriment the use of such objects might tend. And the most accurate knowledge of these things would vary neither the pleasure nor pain of the perception, however it might give a rational pleasure distinct from the sensible or might raise a distinct joy, from a prospect of further advantage in the object, or aversion, from an apprehension of evil.

7. The simple ideas raised in different persons by the same object are probably in some way different, when they disagree in their approbation or dislike, and in the same person, when his fancy at one time differs from what it was at another. This will appear from reflecting on those objects to which we have now an aversion though they were formerly agreeable. And we shall generally find that there is some accidental conjunction of a disagreeable idea which always recurs with the object, as in those wines to which men acquire an aversion after they have taken them in an emetic preparation. In this case we are conscious that the idea is altered from what it was when that wine was agreeable by the conjunction of the ideas of loathing and sickness of stomach. The like change of idea may be insensibly made by the change of our bodies as we advance in years, or when we are accustomed to any object which may occasion an indifference toward meats we were fond of in our childhood, and may make some objects cease to raise the disagreeable ideas which they excited upon our first use of them. Many of our simple perceptions are disagreeable only through the too great intenseness of the quality. Thus moderate light is agreeable, very strong light may be painful; moderate bitter may be pleasant, a higher degree may be offensive. A change in our organs will necessarily occasion a change in the intenseness of the perception at least and sometimes will even occasion a quite contrary perception. Thus a warm hand shall feel that water cold which a cold hand shall feel warm.

We shall not find it perhaps so easy to account for the diversity of fancy in more complex ideas of objects wherein we regard many ideas of different senses at once, as in some perceptions of those called primary qualities and some secondary, as explained by Mr. Locke—for instance, in the different fancies about architecture, gardening, dress. Of architecture and gardening, we shall offer something in Sect. VI; as to dress, we may generally account for the diversity of fancies from a like conjunction of ideas. Thus, if, either from anything in nature or from the opinion of our country or acquaintance, the fancying of glaring colors be looked upon as evidence of levity or of any other evil quality of mind, or if any color or fashion be commonly used by rustics or by men of any disagreeable profession, employment, or temper, these additional ideas may recur constantly with that of the color or fashion and cause a constant dislike to them in those who join the additional ideas, even though the color or form is in no way disagreeable to themselves and actually does please others who ascribe no such ideas to them. But there seems to be no ground for believing such a diversity in human minds, that is, that the same simple idea or perception should give pleasure to one and pain to another, or to the same person at different times, though this is not to say that it seems a contradiction or that the same simple idea should do so.

8. The only pleasure of sense which our philosophers seem to consider is that which accompanies the simple ideas of sensation. But there are vastly greater pleasures in those complex ideas of objects which obtain the names of beautiful, regular, harmonious. Thus everyone acknowledges he is more delighted with a fine face or a just picture than with the view of any one color, were it as strong and lively as possible, and more pleased with a prospect of the sun arising among settled clouds and coloring their edges than with a starry hemisphere, a fine landscape, a regular building than with a clear blue sky, a smooth sea, or a large open plain, not diversified by woods, hills, waters, buildings, and yet even these latter appearances are not quite simple. So, in music, the pleasure of fine composition is incomparably greater than that of any one note, however sweet, full, or swelling.

9. Let it be observed that, in the following papers, the word beauty is taken for the idea raised in us and a sense of beauty for our power of receiving this idea. Harmony also denotes our pleasant ideas arising from composition of sounds, a good ear (as it is generally taken) being the power of perceiving this pleasure. In the following sections, an attempt is made to discover "what is the immediate occasion of these pleasant ideas, or what real quality in the objects ordinarily excites them."

10. It is of no consequence whether we call these ideas of beauty and harmony perceptions of the external senses of seeing and hearing, or not. I should rather choose to call our power of perceiving these ideas an internal sense, were it only for the convenience of distinguishing them from other sensations of seeing and hearing which men may have without perception of beauty and harmony. It is plain from experience that many men have, in the common meaning, the senses of seeing and hearing perfect enough; they perceive all the simple ideas separately and have their pleasure. They distinguish them from each other, such as one color from another, either as quite different or as the stronger or fainter of the same color when they are placed beside each other, although they may often confound their names when they occur apart from each other, as some do the names of green and blue. They can tell, in separate notes, the higher, lower, sharper, or flatter when separately sounded. In figures, they discern the length, breadth, width of each line, surface, angle and may be as capable of hearing and seeing at great distances as any men whatsoever. And yet, perhaps, they shall find no pleasure in musical

compositions, in painting, architecture, natural landscape or, perhaps, but a very weak one in comparison with what others enjoy from the same objects. This greater capacity of receiving such pleasant ideas we commonly call a fine genius or taste. In music we seem universally to acknowledge something like a distinct sense from the external one of hearing and call it a good ear. And we should probably acknowledge the like distinction in other objects, had we the distinct names to denote these powers of perception.

11. There will appear another reason, perhaps afterwards, for calling this power of perceiving the ideas of beauty an internal sense, for it is from this, that in some other affairs where our external senses are not much concerned, we discern a sort of beauty very like, in many respects, to that observed in sensible objects and accompanied with like pleasure. Such is that beauty perceived in theorems or universal truths, in general causes, and in some extensive principles of action.

12. Let everyone here consider how different we must suppose the perception to be with which a poet is transported upon the prospect of any of those objects of natural beauty which ravish us even in his description, from that cold lifeless conception which we image in a dull critic, or one of the virtuosos, without what we call a fine taste. This latter class of men may have greater perfection in that knowledge which is derived from external sensation. They can tell all the specific differences of trees, herbs, minerals, metals; they know the form of every leaf, stalk, root, flower, and seed of all the species about which the poet is often very ignorant. And yet the poet shall have a vastly more delightful perception of the whole—and not only the poet, but any man of a fine taste. Our external senses may, by measuring, teach us all the proportions of architecture to the tenth of an inch and the situation of every muscle in the human body, and a good memory may retain these. And yet there is still something further necessary, not only to make a man a complete master in architecture, painting, or statuary, but even a tolerable judge in these works, or capable of receiving the highest pleasure in contemplating them. Since then there are such different powers of perception where what are commonly called the external senses are the same, since the most accurate knowledge of what the external senses discover often does not give the pleasure of beauty or harmony which yet one of a good taste will enjoy at once without much knowledge. We may justly use another name for these higher, and more delightful, perceptions of beauty and harmony and call the power of receiving such impressions an internal sense. The difference of the perceptions seems sufficient to vindicate the use of a different name, especially when we are told in what meaning the word is applied.

13. This superior power of perception is justly called a sense, because of its affinity to the other senses in that the pleasure neither arises from any knowledge of principles, proportions, causes, or of the usefulness of the object, but strikes us at first with the idea of beauty, nor does the

most accurate knowledge increase this pleasure of beauty, however it may add a distinct rational pleasure from prospects of advantage, or from the increase of knowledge.

14. And, further, the ideas of beauty and harmony, like other sensible ideas, are necessarily pleasant to us, as well as immediately so; neither can any resolution of our own, nor any prospect of advantage or disadvantage, vary the beauty or deformity of an object, for, as in the external sensations, no view of interest will make an object grateful, and no view of detriment, distinct from immediate pain in the perception, will make it disagreeable to the sense. So propose the whole world as a reward, or threaten the greatest evil, to make us approve a deformed object or disapprove a beautiful one; dissimulation may be procured by rewards or threatenings, or we may in external conduct abstain from any pursuit of the beautiful and pursue the deformed. But our sentiments of the forms and our perceptions would continue invariably the same.

15. Hence it plainly appears "that some objects are immediately the occasions of this pleasure of beauty, that we have senses fitted for perceiving it, and that it is distinct from that joy which arises from self-love upon prospect of advantage." Do not we often see convenience and use neglected to obtain beauty, without any other prospect of advantage in the beautiful form than the suggesting the pleasant ideas of beauty? Now this shows us that, however we may pursue beautiful objects from self-love, with a view to obtain the pleasures of beauty, as in architecture, gardening, and many other affairs, there must be a sense of beauty antecedent to prospects even of this advantage, without which sense these objects would not be thus advantageous or excite in us this pleasure which constitutes them advantageous. Our sense of beauty from objects by which they are constituted good to us is very distinct from our desire of them when they are thus constituted. Our desire of beauty may be counterbalanced by rewards or threats, but never our sense of it, even as fear of death, or love of life, may make us choose and desire a bitter portion, or neglect those meats which the sense of taste would recommend as pleasant. And yet no prospect of advantage, or fear of evil, can make that potion agreeable to the sense, or meat disagreeable to it, which was not so antecedently to this prospect. Just in the same manner as to the sense of beauty and harmony is it that the pursuit of such objects is frequently neglected, from prospects of advantage, aversion to labor, or any other motive of self-love, which does not prove that we have no sense of beauty, but only that our desire of it may be counterbalanced by a stronger desire. So gold outweighing silver is never adduced as a proof that the latter is void of gravity.

16. Had we no such sense of beauty and harmony, houses, gardens, dress, equipage might have been recommended to us as convenient, fruitful, warm, easy, but never as beautiful. And in faces I see nothing which could please us but liveliness of color and smoothness of surface. And yet nothing is more certain than the fact that all these objects are recommended under quite different views on many occasions and that no

custom, education, or example could ever give us perceptions distinct from those of the senses which we had the use of before, or recommend objects under another conception than our being grateful to have them. But the influence of custom, education, and example upon the sense of beauty shall be treated below.

17. Beauty is either original or comparative, or, if any like the terms better, absolute, or relative. Only let it be observed that by absolute or original beauty is not meant any quality supposed to be in the object which should of itself be beautiful without relation to any mind which perceives it, for beauty, like other names of sensible ideas, properly denotes the perception of some mind; so cold, hot, sweet, and bitter denote in our minds sensations to which perhaps there is no resemblance in the objects which excite these ideas in us, however we generally imagine that there is something in the object just like our perception. The ideas of beauty and harmony being excited upon our perception of some primary quality, and having relation to figure and time, may indeed have a nearer resemblance to objects than these sensations, which seem not so much any pictures of objects, as modifications of the perceiving mind. And yet were there no mind with a sense of beauty to contemplate objects, I see not how they could be called beautiful. We therefore by absolute beauty understand only that beauty, which we perceive in objects without comparison to anything external, of which the object is supposed an imitation or picture, such as that beauty perceived from the works of nature, artificial forms, figures, or theorems. Comparative or relative beauty is that which we perceive in objects commonly considered as imitations or resemblances of something else. These two kinds of beauty are the subject of the three following sections.

Sect. II Of Original or Absolute Beauty

1. Since it is certain that we have ideas of beauty and harmony, let us examine what quality in objects excites these ideas or is the occasion of them. And let it be here observed that our inquiry is only about the qualities which are beautiful to men, or about the foundation of their sense of beauty, for, as was above hinted, beauty has always relation to the sense of some mind, and when we afterwards show how generally the objects which occur to us are beautiful, we mean that such objects are agreeable to the sense of men. As there are not a few objects which seem no way beautiful to men, so we see a variety of other animals who seem delighted with them; they may have senses otherwise constituted than those of men and may have the ideas of beauty excited by objects of a quite different form. We see animals fitted for every place, and what to men appears rude and shapeless, or loathsome, may be to them a paradise.

2. That we may more distinctly discover the general foundation or occasion of the ideas of beauty among men, it will be necessary to consider it first in its simpler kinds, such as occurs to us in regular figures. And we

may perhaps find that the same foundation extends to all the more complex species of it.

3. The figures which excite in us the ideas of beauty seem to be those in which there is uniformity amidst variety. There are many conceptions of objects which are agreeable upon other accounts, such as grandeur, novelty, sanctity, and some others, which shall be mentioned hereafter. But what we call beautiful in objects, to speak in the mathematical style, seems to be in a compound ratio of uniformity and variety. Thus where the uniformity of bodies is equal, the beauty is as the variety, and where the variety is equal, the beauty is as the uniformity. This will be plain from examples.

First, the variety increases the beauty in equal uniformity. The beauty of an equilateral triangle is less than that of the square, which is less than that of a pentagon, and this again is surpassed by the hexagon. When indeed the number of sides is much increased, the proportion of them to the radius or to the diameter of the figure, or of the circle to which regular polygons have an obvious relation, is so much lost to our observation that the beauty does not always increase with the number of sides, and the want of parallelism in the sides of heptagons and other figures of odd numbers may also diminish their beauty. So, in solids, the eicosihedron surpasses the dodecahedron and thus the octahedron, which is still more beautiful than the cube, and this again surpasses the regular pyramid. The obvious ground of this is greater variety with equal uniformity.

The greater uniformity increases the beauty amidst equal variety in these instances: An equilateral triangle, or even an isosceles, surpasses the scalenum; a square surpasses the rhombus or lozenge, and this again the rhomboid, which is still more beautiful than the trapezium or any figure with irregular curved sides. So the regular solids vastly surpass all other solids of equal number of plain surfaces. And the same is observable not only in the five perfectly regular solids but in all those which have any considerable uniformity, such as cylinders, prisms, pyramids, and obelisks, which please every eye more than any rude figures, where there is no unity or resemblance among the parts.

Instances of the compound ratio we have in comparing circles or spheres with ellipses or spheroids and in comparing the compound solids, the exoctahedron, and eicosidodecahedron with the perfectly regular ones of which they are compounded are not very eccentric. And we shall find that the want of that most perfect uniformity observable in the latter is compensated by the greater variety in the others, so that the beauty is nearly equal.

4. These observations would probably hold true for the most part and might be confirmed by the judgment of children in the simpler figures, where the variety is not too great for their comprehension. And however uncertain some of the particular aforesaid instances may seem, it is perpetually to be observed that children are fond of all regular figures in their little diversions, even though they be no more convenient or useful to them than the figures of our common pebbles. We see how early they

discover a taste or sense of beauty in desiring to see buildings, regular gardens, or even representations of them in pictures of any kind.

5. It is the same foundation which we have for our sense of beauty in the works of nature. In every part of the world which we call beautiful, there is a vast uniformity amidst an almost infinite variety. Many parts of the universe seem not at all designed for the use of man; in fact, it is but a very small spot with which we have any acquaintance. The figures and motions of the great bodies are not obvious to our senses but are found out by reasoning and reflection upon many long observations. And yet as far as we can by sense discover or by reasoning enlarge our knowledge and extend our imagination, we generally find their structure, order, and motion agreeable to our sense of beauty. Every particular object in nature does not indeed appear beautiful to us, but there is a vast profusion of beauty over most of the objects which occur either to our senses or reasonings upon observation. That is, not to mention the apparent situation of the heavenly bodies in the circumference of a great sphere, which is wholly occasioned by the imperfection of our sight in discerning distances, the forms of all the great bodies in the universe are nearly spherical, the orbits of their revolutions generally elliptical and without great eccentricity, in those which continually occur to our observation. Now these are figures of great uniformity and therefore pleasing to us.

Further, to pass by the less obvious uniformity in the proportion of their quantities of matter, distances, and times of revolving to each other, what can exhibit a greater instance of uniformity amidst variety than the constant tenor of revolutions in nearly equal times of each planet around its axis and the central fire or sun through all the ages of which we have any records and in nearly the same orbit and, by which, after certain periods, all the same appearances are again renewed? The alternate successions of light and shade, or day and night, are constantly pursuing each other around each planet with an agreeable and regular diversity in the times they possess the several hemispheres in the summer, harvest, winter, and spring, and the various phases, aspects, and situations of the planets to each other, their conjunctions, and their oppositions in which they suddenly darken each other with their conic shades in eclipses are repeated to us at their fixed periods with invariable constancy. These are the beauties which charm the astronomer and make his tedious calculations pleasant.

6. Again, as to the dry part of the surface of our globe, a great part of which is covered with a very pleasant inoffensive color, how beautifully is it diversified with various degrees of light and shade according to the different situations of the parts of its surface, in mountains, valleys, hills, and open plains which are variously inclined toward the great luminary!

7. If we descend to the more minute works of nature, what vast uniformity there is among all the species of plants and vegetables in the manner of their growth and propagation! What exact resemblance there is among all the plants of the same species whose numbers surpass our imagination! And this uniformity is not only observable in the form in gross; rather, in this it is not so very exact in all instances but in the

structure of their minutest parts, which no eye unassisted with glasses can discern. In the almost infinite multitude of leaves, fruit, seed, or flowers of any one species, we often see an exact uniformity in the structure and situation of the smallest fibers. This is the beauty which charms an ingenious botanist.

.   .   .

14. But in all these instances of beauty let it be observed that the pleasure is communicated to those who never reflected on this general foundation and that all here alleged is this, "That the pleasant sensation arises only from objects in which there is uniformity amidst variety." We may have the sensation without knowing what is the occasion of it, as a man's taste may suggest ideas of sweets, acids, and bitters, though he be ignorant of the forms of the small bodies or their motions which excite these perceptions in him.

Sect. III Of the Beauty of Theorems

1. The beauty of theorems, or universal truths demonstrated, deserves a distinct consideration, being of a nature pretty different from the former kinds of beauty, and yet there is none in which we shall see such an amazing variety with uniformity. Hence what arises is a very great pleasure distinct from prospects of any further advantage.

2. In one theorem, for example, we may find included, with the most exact agreement, not an infinite multitude of particular truths, but often an infinity of infinities, so that, although the necessity of forming abstract ideas and universal theorems arises perhaps from the limitation of our minds which cannot admit an infinite multitude of singular ideas or judgments at once, this power gives us an evidence of the largeness of the human capacity above our imagination. Thus, for instance, the forty-seventh proposition of the first book of Euclid's *Elements* contains an infinite multitude of truths concerning the infinite possible sizes of right-angled triangles as you make the area greater or less, and in each of these sizes you may find an infinite multitude of dissimilar triangles as you vary the proportion of the base to the perpendicular, all which infinities of infinites agree in the general theorem. In algebraic and fluxional calculations, we shall still find a greater variety of particular truths included in general theorems, not only in general equations applicable to all kinds of quantity, but in more particular investigations of areas and tangents, in which one manner of operation shall discover theorems applicable to infinite orders or species of curves, to the infinite sizes of each species, and to the infinite points of the infinite individuals of each size.

3. That we may the better discern this agreement, or unity of an infinity of objects, in the general theorem to be the foundation of the beauty or pleasure attending their discovery, let us compare our satisfaction in such discoveries with the uneasy state of mind in which we are when we can only measure lines or surfaces by a scale or are making experiments which

we can reduce to no general canon but only heaping up a multitude of particular incoherent observations. Now each of these trials discovers a new truth, but with no pleasure or beauty, notwithstanding the variety, till we can discover some sort of unity or reduce them to some general canon.

4. Again, let us take a metaphysical axiom such as this that every whole is greater that its part, and we shall find no beauty in the contemplation, for, though this proposition contains many infinities of particular truths, the unity is inconsiderable, since they all agree only in a vague undetermined conception of whole and part and in an indefinite excess of the former above the latter, which is sometimes great and sometimes small. So, should we hear that the cylinder is greater than the inscribed sphere, and this again greater than the cone of the same altitude and diameter with the base, we shall find no pleasure in this knowledge of a general relation of greater and less without any precise difference or proportion. But, when we see the universal exact agreement of all possible sizes of such systems of solids that they preserve to each other the constant ratio of 3, 2, 1, how beautiful is the theorem, and how are we ravished with its first discovery!

We may likewise observe that easy or obvious propositions, even where the unity is sufficiently distinct and determinate, do not please us so much as those which being less obvious give us some surprise in the discovery. Thus we find little pleasure in discovering that a line bisecting the vertical angle of an isosceles triangle bisects the base, or the reverse, or, that equilateral triangles are equiangular. These truths we almost know intuitively without demonstration. They are like common goods or those which men have long possessed which do not give such sensible joys as much smaller new additions may give us. But let none hence imagine that the sole pleasure of theorems is from surprise, for the same novelty of a single experiment does not please us much. And we ought not to conclude from the greater pleasure accompanying a new or unexpected advantage that surprise or novelty is the only pleasure of life, or the only ground of delight in truth.

5. There is another beauty in propositions which cannot be omitted, namely, when one theorem contains a vast multitude of corollaries easily deducible from it. Thus that theorem which gives us the equation of a curve, whence perhaps most of its properties may be deduced, does in some way please and satisfy our mind above any other proposition. Such a theorem also is the thirty-fifth of the first book of Euclid, from which the whole art of measuring right-lined areas is deduced by resolution into triangles which are the halves of so many parallelograms, and these are each respectively equal to so many rectangles of the base into the perpendicular altitude. The forty-seventh, of the first book is another of like beauty, and so are many others.

In the search of nature there is like beauty in the knowledge of some great principles or universal forces from which innumerable effects do flow. Such is gravitation in Sir Isaac Newton's scheme; such also is the knowledge of the original of rights, perfect and imperfect and external, allienable and unalienable, with their manner of translations, from whence the greatest part of moral duties may be deduced in the various relations of human life.

. . .

8. As to the works of art, were we to run through the various artificial contrivances or structures, we should constantly find the foundation of the beauty which appears in them to be some kind of uniformity or unity of proportion among the parts, and of each part to the whole. As there is a vast diversity of proportions possible, and different kinds of uniformity, so there is room enough for that diversity of fancies observable in architecture, gardening, and such like arts in different nations. They all may have uniformity, though the parts in one may differ from those in another. The Chinese or Persian buildings are not like the Grecian and Roman, and yet the former has its uniformity of the various parts to each other and to the whole, as well as the latter.

Sect. IV   Of Relative or Comparative Beauty

1. If the preceding thoughts concerning the foundation of absolute beauty be just, we may easily understand wherein relative beauty consists. All beauty is relative to the sense of some mind perceiving it, but what we call relative is that which is apprehended in any object commonly considered as an imitation of some original. And this beauty is founded on a conformity or a kind of unity between the original and the copy. The original may be either some object in nature or some established idea, for, if there be any known ideas as a standard and rules to fix this image or idea by, we may make a beautiful imitation. Thus a sculptor, painter, or poet may please us with a Hercules, if his piece retains that grandeur and those marks of strength and courage which we imagine in that hero.

And farther, to obtain comparative beauty alone, it is not necessary that there be any beauty in the original. The imitation of absolute beauty may indeed in the whole make a more lovely piece, so that an exact imitation shall still be beautiful, though the original were entirely void of it. Thus the deformities of old age, or the rudest rocks or mountains in a landscape, in a picture, if well represented, shall have abundant beauty, though perhaps not so great as if the original were absolutely beautiful and as well represented.

2. The same observation holds true in the descriptions of the poets either of natural objects or persons, and this relative beauty is what they should principally endeavor to obtain as the peculiar beauty of their works. By the Moratæ Fabulæ we are not to understand virtuous manners in a moral sense, but a just representation of manners or characters as they are in nature, and the fact that the actions and sentiments must be suited to the characters of the persons to whom they are ascribed in epic and dramatic poetry. Perhaps very good reasons may be suggested from the

nature of our passions to prove that a poet should not draw his characters perfectly virtuous; these characters indeed abstractly considered might give more pleasure and have more beauty than the imperfect ones which occur in life with a mixture of good and evil. But it may suffice at present to suggest against this choice in that we have more lively ideas of imperfect men with all their passions than we do of morally perfect heroes, such as those that really never occur to our observation and of which consequently we cannot judge exactly as to their agreement with the copy. And, further, through consciousness of our own state, we are more nearly touched and affected by the imperfect characters, since in them we see represented in the persons of others the contrasts of inclinations and the struggles between the passions of self-love and those of honor and virtue which we often feel in our own breasts. This is the perfection of beauty for which Homer is justly admired, as well as for the variety of his characters.

3. Many other beauties of poetry may be reduced under this class of relative beauty. The probability is absolutely necessary to make us imagine resemblance, since it is by resemblance that the similitudes, metaphors, and allegories are made beautiful, whether the subject or the thing compared to it have beauty or not; the beauty indeed is greater when both have some original beauty or dignity as well as resemblance. And this is the foundation of the rule of studying decency in metaphors and similes as well as likeness. The measures and cadence are instances of harmony and come under the heading of absolute beauty.

4. We may here observe a strange proneness in our minds to make perpetual comparisons of all things which occur to our observation, even those which would seem very remote. There are certain resemblances in the motions of all animals upon like passions which easily found a comparison, but this does not serve to entertain our fancy. Inanimate objects often have positions that resemble those of the human body in various circumstances, and these airs or gestures of the body are indications of certain dispositions in the mind, so that our very passions and affections as well as other circumstances obtain a resemblance to natural inanimate objects. Thus a tempest at sea is often an emblem of wrath; a plant or tree drooping under the rain is an emblem of a person in sorrow; a poppy bending its stalk, or a flower withering when cut by the plow, resembles the death of a blooming hero; an aged oak in the mountains shall represent an old empire; a flame seizing a wood shall represent a war. In short, everything in nature, by our strange inclination to resemblance, shall be brought to represent other things, even the most remote, especially the passions and circumstances of human nature in which we are more nearly concerned. And to confirm this, and furnish instances of it, one need only look into Homer or Virgil. A fruitful fancy would find in a grove, or a wood, an emblem for every character in a commonwealth and every turn of temper or station in *life*.

.   .   .

Sect. VI Of the Universality of the Sense of Beauty among Men

1. We insinuated before "that all beauty has a relation to some perceiving power," and consequently that, since we know not how great a variety of senses there may be among animals, there is no form in nature concerning which we can pronounce "that it has no beauty," for it may still please some perceiving power. But our inquiry is confined to men, and before we examine the universality of this sense of beauty, or their agreement in approving uniformity, it may be proper to consider "whether, as the other senses which give us pleasure do also give us pain, so this sense of beauty does make some objects disagreeable to us, and the occasion of pain."

That many objects give no pleasure to our sense is obvious—many are certainly void of beauty. But then there is no form which seems necessarily disagreeable of itself when we dread no other evil from it and compare it with nothing better of the kind. Many objects are naturally displeasing and distasteful to our external senses just as others are pleasing and agreeable, as smells, tastes, and some separate sounds. But, as to our sense of beauty, no composition of objects which give not unpleasant simple ideas seems positively unpleasant or painful of itself had we never observed anything better of the kind. Deformity is only the absence of beauty, or deficiency in the beauty expected in any species. Thus bad music pleases rustics who never heard any better, and the finest ear is not offended by the tuning of instruments if it is not too tedious and when no harmony is expected, whereas a much smaller dissonance shall offend amidst the performance when harmony is expected. A rude heap of stones is no way offensive to one who shall be displeased with irregularity in architecture when beauty was expected. And had there been a species of that form which we call now ugly or deformed, and had we never seen or expected greater beauty, we should have received no disgust from it, even though the pleasure would not have been so great in this form as in those we now admire. Our sense of beauty seems designed to give us positive pleasure but not positive pain or disgust that is any greater than what arises from disappointment.

2. There are indeed many faces which at first view are apt to raise dislike, but this is generally not from any positive deformity which of itself is positively displeasing; rather, it is from want of expected beauty or much more from some natural indications of morally bad dispositions which we all acquire a faculty of discerning in countenances, airs, and gestures. That this is not occasioned by any form positively disgusting will appear from this if, upon long acquaintance, we are sure of finding sweetness of temper, humanity, and cheerfulness, and, even though the bodily form continues, it shall give us no disgust or displeasure, whereas, if anything was naturally disagreeable, or the occasion of pain, or positive distaste, it would always continue so, even though the aversion we might

have toward it were counterbalanced by other considerations. There are horrors raised by some objects which are only the effect of fear for ourselves or compassion toward others, when either reason or some foolish association of ideas makes us appehend danger and not the effect of anything in the form of itself, for we find that most of those objects which excite horror at first, such as ravenous beasts, a tempestuous sea, a craggy precipice, a dark shady valley, may become the occasions of pleasure when experience or reason has removed the fear.

3. We shall see hereafter "that associations of ideas make objects pleasant, and delightful, which are not naturally apt to give any such pleasures, and that, in the same way, the casual conjunctions of ideas may give a disgust where there is nothing disagreeable in the form itself." And this is the occasion of many fantastic aversions to figures of some animals and to some other forms. Thus swine, serpents of all kinds, and some insects really beautiful enough are beheld with aversion by many people who have got some accidental ideas associated to them. And, for distastes of this kind, no other account can be given.

4. But, as to the universal agreement of mankind in their sense of beauty from uniformity amidst variety, we must consult experience. And, as we allow all men reason, since all men are capable of understanding simple arguments, though few are capable of complex demonstrations, so in this case it must be sufficient to prove this sense of beauty universal, "if all men are better pleased with uniformity in the simpler instances than the contrary, even when there is no advantage observed attending it and, likewise, if all men, according as their capacity enlarges, so as to receive and compare more complex ideas, have a greater delight in uniformity and are pleased with its more complex kinds, both original and relative."

Now let us consider if ever any person was void of this sense in the simpler instances. Few trials have been made in the simplest instances of harmony, because as soon as we find an ear incapable of relishing complex compositions, such as our tunes are, no further pains are employed about such. But, in figures, did ever any man make choice of a trapezium or any irregular curve for the ichnography or plan of his house without necessity or some great motive of convenience, or to make the opposite walls not parallel or unequal in height? Were ever trapeziums, irregular polygons, or curves chosen for the forms of doors or windows, though these figures might have answered the uses as well and would have often saved a great part of the time, labor, and expense to workmen which is now employed in suiting the stones and timber to the regular forms? Among all the fantastic modes of dress, none was ever quite void of uniformity, if it were only the resemblance of two sides of the same robe and in some general aptitude to the human form. The representational painting had always relative beauty by its resemblance to other objects, and often those objects were originally beautiful. But never were any so extravagant as to affect such figures as are made by the casual spilling of liquid colors. Who was ever pleased with an inequality of heights in windows of the same range or dissimilar shapes of them, with unequal legs or arms, eyes or cheeks in a mistress? It must however be acknowledged "That interest may often counterbalance our sense of beauty in this affair as well as in others, and superior good qualities may make us overlook such imperfections."

5. Further, it may perhaps appear "That regularity and uniformity are so copiously diffused through the universe, and we are so readily determined to pursue this as the foundation of beauty in works of art, that there is scarcely anything ever fancied as beautiful where there is not really something of this uniformity and regularity." We are indeed often mistaken in imagining that there is the greatest possible beauty, where it is but very imperfect, but still it is some degree of beauty which pleases, even though there may be higher degrees which we do not observe, and our sense acts with full regularity when we are pleased, even though we are kept by a false prejudice from pursuing objects which would please us more.

A Goth, for instance, is mistaken, when from education he imagines the architecture of his country to be the most perfect. And a conjunction of some hostile ideas may make him adverse to Roman buildings and study to demolish them, as some of our reformers did papal buildings, not being able to separate the ideas of the superstitious worship from the forms of the buildings where it was practiced. And yet it is still real beauty which pleases the Goth, founded upon uniformity amidst variety. For the Gothic pillars are uniform to each other, not only in their sections, which are lozenge formed, but also in their heights and ornaments. Their arches are not one uniform curve, yet they are segments of similar curves and generally equal in the same ranges. Indian buildings have some kind of uniformity, and many of the Eastern nations, though they differ much from us, have great regularity in their manner as did the Romans in theirs. Our Indian screens, which wonderfully supply the regular imaginations of our ladies with ideas of deformity in which nature is very churlish and sparing, do indeed lack all the beauty arising from proportion of parts and conformity to nature; yet they cannot divest themselves of all beauty and uniformity in the separate parts. And this diversification of the human body into various contortions may give some wild pleasure from variety, since some uniformity to the human shape is still retained.

6. There is one sort of beauty which might perhaps have been better mentioned before but will not be impertinent here, because the taste or relish of it is universal in all nations and with the young as well as the old, and that is the beauty of history. Everyone knows how dull a study it is to read over a collection of newspapers which shall perhaps relate all the same events with history: The superior pleasure then of history must arise, like that of poetry, from manners just as when we see a character well drawn wherein we find the secret causes of a great diversity of seemingly inconsistent actions, or an interest of state laid open, or an artful view nicely unfolded, the execution of which influences very different and opposite actions as the circumstances may alter. Now this reduces the whole to a unity of design at least. And this may be observed in the very fables

which entertain children; otherwise, we cannot make them relish them.

7. What has been said will probably be assented to, if we always remember in our inquiries into the universality of the sense of beauty, "That there may be real beauty where there is not the greatest, and that there are an infinity of different forms which may all have some unity and yet differ from each other," so that men may have different fancies of beauty, but uniformity will be the universal foundation of our approbation of any form whatsoever as beautiful. And we shall find that it is so in the architecture, gardening, dress, equipage, and furniture of houses, even among the most uncultivated nations, where uniformity still pleases, without any other advantage than the pleasure of the contemplation of it.

8. On this subject, we should consider how, in like cases, we form very different judgments concerning the internal and external senses. Nothing is more ordinary among those who, after Mr. Locke, have shaken off the groundless opinions about innate ideas then allege "That all our relish for beauty and order is either from prospect of advantage, custom, or education," for no other reason but for the variety of fancies in the world. And from this they conclude "That our fancies do not arise from any natural power of perception or sense." Yet all allow that our external senses are natural and that the pleasures or pains of their sensations, however they may be increased or diminished by custom or education and counterbalanced by interest, really precede custom, habit, education, or prospect of interest. Now it is certain "That there is at least as great a variety of fancies about their objects, as the objects of beauty." But, in fact, it is much more difficult, and perhaps impossible, to bring the fancies or relishes of the external senses to any general foundation at all, or to find any rule for the agreeable or disagreeable, though we all allow "that these are natural powers of perception."

9. The reason for this different judgment can be no other than our having distinct names for the external senses and none, or very few, for the internal and, by this are led, as in many other cases, to look upon the former as more fixed, real, and natural than the latter. The sense of harmony has got its name, a good ear, and we are generally brought to acknowledge that this is a natural power of perception or a sense in some way distinct from hearing. Now it is certain "That there is, as necessary, a perception of beauty upon the presence of regular objects, just as there is of harmony upon hearing certain sounds."

10. But let it be observed here once and for all "That an internal sense no more presupposes an innate idea, or principle of knowledge, than the external." Both are natural powers of perception or determinations of the mind to receive necessarily certain ideas from the presence of objects. The internal sense is a passive power of receiving ideas of beauty from all objects in which there is uniformity amidst variety. And there seems to be nothing more difficult in this matter than that the mind should be always determined to receive the idea of sweet when particles of such a form enter the pores of the tongue, or to have the idea of sound upon any

quick undulation of the air. The one seems to have as little connection with its idea as the other. And the same power could with equal ease constitute the former's occasion of ideas as the latter.

11. The association of ideas hinted at above is one great cause of the apparent diversity of fancies in the sense of beauty as well as in the external senses, and it often makes men have an aversion to objects of beauty and a liking to others lacking it but under different conceptions than those of beauty or deformity. And here it may not be improper to give some instances of some of these associations. The beauty of trees, their cool shades, and their aptness to conceal from observation have made groves and woods the usual retreat to those who love solitude, especially to the religious, the pensive, the melancholy, and the amorous. And do not we find that we have so joined the ideas of these dispositions of mind with those external objects that they always recur to us along with them? The cunning of the heathen priests might make such obscure places the scene of the fictitious appearances of their deities, and hence we ascribe ideas of something divine to them. We know the like effect in the ideas of our churches from the perpetual use of them only in religious exercises. The faint light in Gothic buildings has had the same association of a very foreign idea, which our poet shows in his epithet,

A dim religious light.

In like manner it is known that often all the circumstances of actions, or places, or dresses of persons, or voice or song, which have occurred at any time together when we were strongly affected by any passion will be so connected that any one of these will make all the rest recur. And this is often the occasion both of great pleasure and pain, delight and aversion to many objects, which of themselves might have been perfectly indifferent to us. But these approbations, or distastes, are remote from the ideas of beauty, being plainly different ideas.

12. There is also another charm to various persons in music, which is distinct from the harmony and is occasioned by its raising of agreeable passions. The human voice is obviously varied by all the stronger passions. And, when our ear discerns any resemblance between the air of a tune, whether sung or played upon an instrument, in its time, or modulation, or any other circumstance, and the sound of the human voice in any passion, we shall be touched by it in a very sensible manner and have melancholy, joy, gravity, or thoughtfulness excited in us by a sort of sympathy or contagion. The same connection is observable between the very air of a tune and the words expressing any passion which we have heard it fitted to, so that they shall both recur to us together, though but one of them affects our senses.

Now in such a diversity of pleasing or displeasing ideas which may be joined with forms of bodies, or tunes, when men are of such different dispositions and prone to such a variety of passions, it is no wonder "that they should often disagree in their fancies of objects, even though their sense of beauty and harmony were perfectly uniform," because many other ideas may either please or displease, according to persons' tempers and past circumstances. We know how agreeable a very wild country may be to any person who has spent the cheerful days of his youth in it, and how disagreeable very beautiful places may be if they were the scenes of his misery. And this may help us in many cases to account for the diversities of fancy without denying the uniformity of our internal sense of beauty.

13. Grandeur and novelty are two ideas that differ from beauty but that often recommend objects to us. The reason for this is foreign to the present subject.

Sect. VII   Of the Power of Custom, Education, and Example as to Our Internal Senses

1. Custom, education, and example are so often alleged in this affair as the occasion of our relish for beautiful objects, and for our approbation of, or delight in, a certain conduct in life, in a moral sense, that it is necessary to examine these three particularly to make it appear "that there is a natural power of perception or sense of beauty in objects that precedes all custom, education, or example."

2. Custom, as distinct from the other two, operates in this manner. As to actions, it only enables the mind or body more easily to perform those actions which have been frequently repeated. It neither leads us to apprehend them under any other view than those under which we were capable of apprehending them at first, nor does it give us any new power of perception about them. We are naturally capable of sentiments of fear and dread of any powerful presence, and so custom may connect the ideas of religious horror to certain buildings. But custom could never have made a being naturally incapable of fear receive such ideas. So, had we no other power of perceiving or forming ideas of actions but as they were advantageous or disadvantageous, custom could only have made us more ready at perceiving the advantage or disadvantage of actions. But this is not to our present purpose.

As to our approbation of, or delight in, external objects, when the blood or spirits of which anatomists talk are roused, quickened, or fermented as they call it, in any agreeable manner by medicine or nutriment, or any glands frequently stimulated to secretion, it is certain that, to preserve the body's ease, we shall delight in objects of taste which in and of themselves are not immediately pleasant to it if they promote that agreeable state to which the body had been accustomed. Further, custom will so alter the state of the body that what at first raised uneasy sensations will cease to do so, or perhaps raise another agreeable idea of the same sense. But custom can never give us any idea of a sense different from those we had prior to it; it will never make those who have no sight approve objects as colored, or those who have no taste approve meats as delicious, however they might approve them as strengthening or exhilarating. When our glands and the parts about them were void of feeling, did we perceive no pleasure from certain brisker motions in the blood? Custom could never make stimulating or intoxicating fluids or medicines agreeable when they were not so to the taste. So, by like reasoning, had we no natural sense of beauty from uniformity, custom could never have made us imagine any beauty in objects; that is, if we had had no ear, custom could never have given us the pleasures of harmony. When we have these natural senses antecedently, custom may make us capable of extending our views further and of receiving more complex ideas of beauty in bodies, or harmony in sounds, by increasing our attention and quickness of perception. But however custom may increase our power of receiving or comparing complex ideas, it seems rather to weaken than to strengthen the ideas of beauty or the impressions of pleasure from regular objects; otherwise, how is it possible that any person could go into the open air on a sunny day, or clear evening, without the most extravagant raptures such as those Milton ascribes to our ancestor after his first creation? For such raptures any person should certainly fall into, when first viewing that kind of scene.

Custom in like manner may make it easier for any person to discern the use of a complex machine and approve it as advantageous, but he would never have imagined it beautiful had he no natural sense of beauty. Custom may make us quicker in apprehending the truth of complex theorems, but, although we all find the pleasure or beauty of theorems as strong at first as ever, custom makes us more capable of retaining and comparing complex ideas so as to discern more complicated uniformity which escapes the observation of novices in any art. However, all this presupposes a natural sense of beauty in uniformity, for, had there been nothing in forms which was constituted as the necessary occasion of pleasure to our senses, no repetition of indifferent ideas as to pleasure or pain, beauty or deformity, could ever have made them grow pleasing or displeasing.

3. The effect of education is this: that thereby we receive many speculative opinions, which are sometimes true and sometimes false, and are often led to believe that objects may be naturally apt to give pleasure or pain to our external senses, but which in reality have no such qualities. And further, by education, there are some strong associations of ideas without any reason, by mere accident sometimes, as well as by design, which it is very hard for us ever after to break asunder. Thus aversions are raised to darkness, and to many kinds of meat, and to certain innocent actions. Approbations without ground are raised in like manner. But in all these instances education never makes us apprehend any qualities in objects for which we do not naturally have senses capable of perceiving. We know what sickness of the stomach is and may without ground believe that very healthful meats will raise this, and, by our sight and smell, we receive disagreeable ideas of the food of swine, and their sties, and perhaps cannot prevent the recurrence of these ideas at table. But never were men naturally blindly prejudiced against objects, as of a disagreeable color, or in favor of others, as of a beautiful color; they perhaps hear men disparage

one color and may imagine this color to be some quite different sensible quality of the other senses, but that is all. And, in the same way, a man naturally void of taste could by no education receive the ideas of taste or be prejudiced in favor of meats as delicious. So, had we no natural sense of beauty and harmony, we could never be prejudiced in favor of objects or sounds as being beautiful or harmonious. Education may make an unattentive Goth imagine that his countrymen have attained the perfection of architecture and an aversion to his enemies, the Romans, may have created some disagreeable ideas about Roman buildings, even causing them to be demolished, but he would never have formed these prejudices had he been void of a sense of beauty. Did blind men debate ever whether purple or scarlet were the finer color? Or could any education prejudice them in favor of either as colors?

Thus education and custom may influence our internal senses, where they already exist, by enlarging the capacity of our minds to retain and compare the parts of complex compositions, and then, if the finest objects are presented to us, we grow conscious of a pleasure far superior to what common performances excite. But all this presupposes that our sense of beauty is natural. Instruction in anatomy and observation of nature and those airs of the countenance and attitudes of body which accompany any sentiment, action, or passion may enable us to know where there is a just imitation. But why should an exact imitation please upon observation, if we did not naturally have a sense of beauty in it, any more than observing the situation of fifty or a hundred pebbles thrown at random? And, should we observe them ever so often, we should never dream of their growing beautiful.

David Hume

OF THE STANDARD
OF TASTE

The great variety of Taste, as well as of opinion, which prevails in the world, is too obvious not to have fallen under every one's observation.* Men of the most confined knowledge are able to remark a difference of taste in the narrow circle of their acquaintance, even where the persons have been educated under the same government, and have early imbibed the same prejudices. But those, who can enlarge their view to contemplate distant nations and remote ages, are still more surprized at the great inconsistence and contrariety. We are apt to call *barbarous* whatever departs widely from our own taste and apprehension: But soon find the epithet of reproach retorted on us. And the highest arrogance and self-conceit is at last startled, on observing an equal assurance on all sides, and scruples, amidst such a contest of sentiment, to pronounce positively in its own favour.

As this variety of taste is obvious to the most careless enquirer; so will it be found, on examination, to be still greater in reality than in appearance. The sentiments of men often differ with regard to beauty and deformity of all kinds, even while their general discourse is the same. There are certain terms in every language, which import blame, and others praise; and all men, who use the same tongue, must agree in their application of them. Every voice is united in applauding elegance, propriety, simplicity, spirit in writing; and in blaming fustian, affectation, coldness, and a false brilliancy: But when critics come to particulars, this seeming unanimity vanishes; and it is found, that they had affixed a very different meaning to their expressions. In all matters of opinion and science, the case is opposite: The difference among men is there oftener found to lie in generals than in particulars; and to be less in reality than in appearance. An explanation of the terms commonly ends the controversy; and the disputants are sur-

David Hume (1711–1776). In the opinion of many, Hume is the greatest philosopher in the British tradition. His *A Treatise of Human Nature* and *Enquiries* are philosophical classics of grand proportions. "On The Standard of Taste" is a short essay which is still the primary source on the subject of taste.

* Hume's essay is reprinted here in its entirety. This essay first appeared in 1757 in Hume's *Four Dissertations*. It was later included in his *Essays and Treatises on Several Subjects*.

prized to find, that they had been quarrelling, while at bottom they agreed in their judgment.

Those who found morality on sentiment, more than on reason, are inclined to comprehend ethics under the former observation, and to maintain, that, in all questions, which regard conduct and manners, the difference among men is really greater than at first sight it appears. It is indeed obvious, that writers of all nations and all ages concur in applauding justice, humanity, magnanimity, prudence, veracity; and in blaming the opposite qualities. Even poets and other authors, whose compositions are chiefly calculated to please the imagination, are yet found, from Homer down to Fenelon, to inculcate the same moral precepts, and to bestow their applause and blame on the same virtues and vices. This great unanimity is usually ascribed to the influence of plain reason; which, in all these cases, maintains similar sentiments in all men, and prevents those controversies, to which the abstract sciences are so much exposed. So far as the unanimity is real, this account may be admitted as satisfactory: But we must also allow that some part of the seeming harmony in morals may be accounted for from the very nature of language. The word *virtue*, with its equivalent in every tongue, implies praise; as that of *vice* does blame: And no one, without the most obvious and grossest impropriety, could affix reproach to a term, which in general acceptation is understood in a good sense; or bestow applause, where the idiom requires disapprobation. Homer's general precepts, where he delivers any such, will never be controverted; but it is obvious, that, when he draws particular pictures of manners, and represents heroism in Achilles and prudence in Ulysses, he intermixes a much greater degree of ferocity in the former, and of cunning and fraud in the latter, than Fenelon would admit of. The sage Ulysses in the Greek poet seems to delight in lies and fictions, and often employs them without any necessity or even advantage: But his more scrupulous son, in the French epic writer, exposes himself to the most imminent perils, rather than depart from the most exact line of truth and veracity.

The admirers and followers of the Alcoran insist on the excellent moral precepts interspersed throughout that wild and absurd performance. But it is to be supposed, that the Arabic words, which correspond to the English, equity, justice, temperance, meekness, charity, were such as, from the constant use of that tongue, must always be taken in a good sense; and it would have argued the greatest ignorance, not of morals, but of language, to have mentioned them with any epithets, besides those of applause and approbation. But would we know, whether the pretended prophet had really attained a just sentiment of morals? Let us attend to his narration; and we shall soon find, that he bestows praise on such instances of treachery, inhumanity, cruelty, revenge, bigotry, as are utterly incompatible with civilized society. No steady rule of right seems there to be attended to; and every action is blamed or praised, so far only as it is beneficial or hurtful to the true believers.

The merit of delivering true general precepts in ethics is indeed very small. Whoever recommends any moral virtues, really does no more than is implied in the terms themselves. That people, who invented the word *charity*, and used it in a good sense, inculcated more clearly and much more efficaciously, the precept, *be charitable*, than any pretended legislator or prophet, who should insert such a *maxim* in his writings. Of all expressions, those, which, together with their other meaning, imply a degree either of blame or approbation, are the least liable to be perverted or mistaken.

It is natural for us to seek a *Standard of Taste*; a rule, by which the various sentiments of men may be reconciled; at least, a decision, afforded, confirming one sentiment, and condemning another.

There is a species of philosophy, which cuts off all hopes of success in such an attempt, and represents the impossibility of ever attaining any standard of taste. The difference, it is said, is very wide between judgment and sentiment. All sentiment is right; because sentiment has a reference to nothing beyond itself, and is always real, wherever a man is conscious of it. But all determinations of the understanding are not right; because they have a reference to something beyond themselves, to wit, real matter of fact; and are not always conformable to that standard. Among a thousand different opinions which different men may entertain of the same subject, there is one, and but one, that is just and true; and the only difficulty is to fix and ascertain it. On the contrary, a thousand different sentiments, excited by the same object, are all right: Because no sentiment represents what is really in the object. It only marks a certain conformity or relation between the object and the organs or faculties of the mind; and if that conformity did not really exist, the sentiment could never possibly have being. Beauty is no quality in things themselves: It exists merely in the mind which contemplates them; and each mind perceives a different beauty. One person may even perceive deformity, where another is sensible of beauty; and every individual ought to acquiesce in his own sentiment, without pretending to regulate those of others. To seek the real beauty, or real deformity, is as fruitless an enquiry, as to pretend to ascertain the real sweet or real bitter. According to the disposition of the organs, the same object may be both sweet and bitter; and the proverb has justly determined it to be fruitless to dispute concerning tastes. It is very natural, and even quite necessary, to extend this axiom to mental, as well as bodily taste; and thus common sense, which is so often at variance with philosophy, especially with the sceptical kind, is found, in one instance at least, to agree in pronouncing the same decision.

But though this axiom, by passing into a proverb, seems to have attained the sanction of common sense; there is certainly a species of common sense which opposes it, at least serves to modify and restrain it. Whoever would assert an equality of genius and elegance between Ogilby and Milton, or Bunyan and Addison, would be thought to defend no less an extravagance, than if he had maintained a mole-hill to be as high as Teneriffe, or a pond as extensive as the ocean. Though there may be found persons, who give the preference to the former authors; no one pays attention to such a taste; and we pronounce without scruple the sentiment of these pretended critics to be absurd and ridiculous. The principle of the natural equality of tastes is then totally forgot, and while we admit it on some occasions, where the objects seem near an equality, it appears an extravagant paradox, or rather a palpable absurdity, where objects so disproportioned are compared together.

It is evident that none of the rules of composition are fixed by reasonings *a priori,* or can be esteemed abstract conclusions of the understanding, from comparing those habitudes and relations of ideas, which are eternal and immutable. Their foundation is the same with that of all the practical sciences, experience; nor are they any thing but general observations, concerning what has been universally found to please in all countries and in all ages. Many of the beauties of poetry and even of eloquence are founded on falsehood and fiction, on hyperboles, metaphors, and an abuse or perversion of terms from their natural meaning. To check the sallies of the imagination, and to reduce every expression to geometrical truth and exactness, would be the most contrary to the laws of criticism; because it would produce a work, which, by universal experience, has been found the most insipid and disagreeable. But though poetry can never submit to exact truth, it must be confined by rules of art, discovered to the author either by genius or observation. If some negligent or irregular writers have pleased, they have not pleased by their transgressions of rule or order, but in spite of these transgressions: They have possessed other beauties, which were conformable to just criticism; and the force of these beauties has been able to overpower censure, and give the mind a satisfaction superior to the disgust arising from the blemishes. Ariosto pleases; but not by his monstrous and improbable fictions, by his bizarre mixture of the serious and comic styles, by the want of coherence in his stories, or by the continual interruptions of his narration. He charms by the force and clearness of his expression, by the readiness and variety of his inventions, and by his natural pictures of the passions, especially those of the gay and amorous kind: And however his faults may diminish our satisfaction, they are not able entirely to destroy it. Did our pleasure really arise from those parts of his poem, which we denominate faults, this would be no objection to criticism in general: It would only be an objection to those particular rules of criticism, which would establish such circumstances to be faults, and would represent them as universally blameable. If they are found to please, they cannot be faults; let the pleasure, which they produce, be ever so unexpected and unaccountable.

But though all the general rules of art are founded only on experience and on the observation of the common sentiments of human nature, we must not imagine, that, on every occasion, the feelings of men will be conformable to these rules. Those finer emotions of the mind are of a very tender and delicate nature, and require the concurrence of many favourable circumstances to make them play with facility and exactness, according to their general and established principles. The least exterior hindrance to such small springs, or the least internal disorder, disturbs their motion, and confounds the operation of the whole machine. When we would make an experiment of this nature, and would try the force of any beauty or deformity, we must choose with care a proper time and place, and bring the fancy to a suitable situation and disposition. A perfect serenity of mind, a recollection of thought, a due attention to the object; if any of these circumstances be wanting, our experiment will be fallacious, and we shall be unable to judge of the catholic and universal beauty. The relation, which nature has placed between the form and the sentiment, will at least be more obscure; and it will require greater accuracy to trace and discern it. We shall be able to ascertain its influence not so much from the operation of each particular beauty, as from the durable admiration, which attends those works, that have survived all the caprices of mode and fashion, all the mistakes of ignorance and envy.

The same Homer, who pleased at Athens and Rome two thousand years ago, is still admired at Paris and at London. All the changes of climate, government, religion, and language, have not been able to obscure his glory. Authority or prejudice may give a temporary vogue to a bad poet or orator; but his reputation will never be durable or general. When his compositions are examined by posterity or by foreigners, the enchantment is dissipated, and his faults appear in their true colours. On the contrary, a real genius, the longer his works endure, and the more wide they are spread, the more sincere is the admiration which he meets with. Envy and jealousy have too much place in a narrow circle; and even familiar acquaintance with his person may diminish the applause due to his performances: But when these obstructions are removed, the beauties, which are naturally fitted to excite agreeable sentiments, immediately display their energy; and while the world endures, they maintain their authority over the minds of men.

It appears then, that, amidst all the variety and caprice of taste, there are certain general principles of approbation or blame, whose influence a careful eye may trace in all operations of the mind. Some particular forms or qualities, from the original structure of the internal fabric, are calculated to please, and others to displease; and if they fail of their effect in any particular instance, it is from some apparent defect or imperfection in the organ. A man in a fever would not insist on his palate as able to decide concerning flavours; nor would one, affected with the jaundice, pretend to give a verdict with regard to colours. In each creature, there is a sound and a defective state; and the former alone can be supposed to afford us a true standard of taste and sentiment. If, in the sound state of the organ, there be an entire or a considerable uniformity of sentiment among men, we may thence derive an idea of the perfect beauty; in like manner as the appearance of objects in day-light, to the eye of a man in health, is denominated their true and real colour, even while colour is allowed to be merely a phantasm of the senses.

Many and frequent are the defects in the internal organs, which prevent or weaken the influence of those general principles, on which depends our sentiment of beauty or deformity. Though some objects, by the structure of the mind, be naturally calculated to give pleasure, it is not to be expected, that in every individual the pleasure will be equally felt. Particular incidents and situations occur, which either throw a false light on the objects, or hinder the true from conveying to the imagination the proper sentiment and perception.

One obvious cause, why many feel not the proper sentiment of beauty, is the want of that *delicacy* of imagination, which is requisite to convey a sensibility of those finer emotions. This delicacy every one pretends to: Every one talks of it; and would reduce every kind of taste or sentiment to its standard. But as our intention in this essay is to mingle some light of the understanding with the feelings of sentiment, it will be proper to give a more accurate definition of delicacy, than has hitherto been attempted. And not to draw our philosophy from too profound a source, we shall have recourse to a noted story in Don Quixote.

It is with good reason, says Sancho to the squire with the great nose, that I pretend to have a judgment in wine: This is a quality hereditary in our family. Two of my kinsmen were once called to give their opinion of a hogshead, which was supposed to be excellent, being old and of a good vintage. One of them tastes it; considers it; and after mature reflection pronounces the wine to be good, were it not for a small taste of leather, which he perceived in it. The other, after using the same precautions, gives also his verdict in favour of the wine; but with the reserve of a taste of iron, which he could easily distinguish. You cannot imagine how much they were both ridiculed for their judgment. But who laughed in the end? On emptying the hogshead, there was found at the bottom, an old key with a leathern thong tied to it.

The great resemblance between mental and bodily taste will easily teach us to apply this story. Though it be certain, that beauty and deformity, more than sweet and bitter, are not qualities in objects, but belong entirely to the sentiment, internal or external; it must be allowed, that there are certain qualities in objects, which are fitted by nature to produce those particular feelings. Now as these qualities may be found in a small degree, or may be mixed and confounded with each other, it often happens, that the taste is not affected with such minute qualities, or is not able to distinguish all the particular flavours, amidst the disorder, in which they are presented. Where the organs are so fine, as to allow nothing to escape them; and at the same time so exact as to perceive every ingredient in the composition: This we call delicacy of taste, whether we employ these terms in the literal or metaphorical sense. Here then the general rules of beauty are of use; being drawn from established models, and from the observation of what pleases or displeases, when presented singly and in a high degree: And if the same qualities, in a continued composition and in a smaller degree, affect not the organs with a sensible delight or uneasiness, we exclude the person from all pretensions to this delicacy. To produce these general rules or avowed patterns of composition is like finding the key with the leathern thong; which justified the verdict of Sancho's kinsmen, and confounded those pretended judges who had condemned them. Though the hogshead had never been emptied, the taste of the one was still equally delicate, and that of the other equally dull and languid: But it would have been more difficult to have proved the superiority of the former, to the conviction of every by-stander. In like manner, though the beauties of writing had never been methodized, or reduced to general principles; though no excellent models had ever been acknowledged; the different degrees of taste would still have subsisted, and the judgment of one man been preferable to that of another; but it would not have been so easy to silence the bad critic, who might always insist upon his particular sentiment, and refuse to submit to his antagonist. But when we show him an avowed principle of art; when we illustrate this principle by examples, whose operation, from his own particular taste, he acknowledges to be conformable to the principle; when we prove, that the same principle may be applied to the present case, where he did not perceive or feel its influence: He must conclude, upon the whole, that the fault lies in himself, and that he wants the delicacy, which is requisite to make him sensible of every beauty and every blemish, in any composition or discourse.

It is acknowledged to be the perfection of every sense or faculty, to perceive with exactness its most minute objects, and allow nothing to escape its notice and observation. The smaller the objects are, which become sensible to the eye, the finer is that organ, and the more elaborate its make and composition. A good palate is not tried by strong flavours; but by a mixture of small ingredients, where we are still sensible of each part, notwithstanding its minuteness and its confusion with the rest. In like manner, a quick and acute perception of beauty and deformity must be the perfection of our mental taste; nor can a man be satisfied with himself while he suspects, that any excellence or blemish in a discourse has passed him unobserved. In this case, the perfection of the man, and the perfection of the sense or feeling, are found to be united. A very delicate palate, on many occasions, may be a great inconvenience both to a man himself and to his friends: But a delicate taste of wit or beauty must always be a desirable quality; because it is the source of all the finest and most innocent enjoyments, of which human nature is susceptible. In this decision the sentiments of all mankind are agreed. Wherever you can ascertain a delicacy of taste, it is sure to meet with approbation; and the best way of ascertaining it is to appeal to those models and principles, which have been established by the uniform consent and experience of nations and ages.

But though there be naturally a wide difference in point of delicacy between one person and another, nothing tends further to encrease and improve this talent, than *practice* in a particular art, and the frequent survey or contemplation of a particular species of beauty. When objects of any kind are first presented to the eye or imagination, the sentiment, which attends them, is obscure and confused; and the mind is, in a great measure, incapable of pronouncing concerning their merits or defects. The taste cannot perceive the several excellences of the performance; much less distinguish the particular character of each excellency, and ascertain its quality and degree. If it pronounce the whole in general to be beautiful or deformed, it is the utmost that can be expected; and even this judgment, a person, so unpractised, will be apt to deliver with great hesitation and reserve. But allow him to acquire experience in those objects, his feeling becomes more exact and nice: He not only perceives the beauties and defects of each part, but marks the distinguishing species of each quality, and assigns it suitable praise or blame. A clear and distinct sentiment attends him through the whole survey of the objects; and he discerns that very degree and kind of approbation or displeasure, which each part is naturally fitted to produce. The mist dissipates, which seemed formerly to hang over the object: The organ acquires greater perfection in its operations; and can pronounce, without danger of mistake, concerning the merits of every performance. In a word, the same address and dexterity, which practice gives to the execution of any work, is also acquired by the same means, in the judging of it.

So advantageous is practice to the discernment of beauty, that, before we can give judgment on any work of importance, it will even be requisite, that that very individual performance be more than once perused by us, and be surveyed in different lights with attention and deliberation. There is a flutter or hurry of thought which attends the first perusal of any piece, and which confounds the genuine sentiment of beauty. The relation of the parts is not discerned: The true characters of style are little distinguished: The several perfections and defects seem wrapped up in a species of confusion, and present themselves indistinctly to the imagination. Not to mention, that there is a species of beauty, which, as it is florid and superficial, pleases at first; but being found incompatible with a just expression either of reason or passion, soon palls upon the taste, and is then rejected with disdain, at least rated at a much lower value.

It is impossible to continue in the practice of contemplating any order of beauty, without being frequently obliged to form *comparisons* between the several species and degrees of excellence, and estimating their proportion to each other. A man, who has had no opportunity of comparing the different kinds of beauty, is indeed totally unqualified to pronounce an opinion with regard to any object presented to him. By comparison alone we fix the epithets of praise or blame, and learn how to assign the due degree of each. The coarsest daubing contains a certain lustre of colours and exactness of imitation, which are so far beauties, and would affect the mind of a peasant or Indian with the highest admiration. The most vulgar ballads are not entirely destitute of harmony or nature; and none but a person, familiarized to superior beauties, would pronounce their numbers harsh, or narration uninteresting. A great inferiority of beauty gives pain to a person conversant in the highest excellence of the kind, and is for that reason pronounced a deformity: As the most finished object, with which we are acquainted, is naturally supposed to have reached the pinnacle of perfection, and to be entitled to the highest applause. One accustomed to see, and examine, and weigh the several performances, admired in different ages and nations, can only rate the merits of a work exhibited to his view, and assign its proper rank among the productions of genius.

But to enable a critic the more fully to execute this undertaking, he must preserve his mind free from all *prejudice*, and allow nothing to enter into his consideration, but the very object which is submitted to his examination. We may observe, that every work of art, in order to produce its due effect on the mind, must be surveyed in a certain point of view, and cannot be fully relished by persons, whose situation, real or imaginary, is not conformable to that which is required by the performance. An orator addresses himself to a particular audience, and must have a regard to their particular genius, interests, opinions, passions, and prejudices; otherwise he hopes in vain to govern their resolutions, and inflame their affections. Should they even have entertained some prepossessions against him, however unreasonable, he must not overlook this disadvantage; but, before he enters upon the subject, must endeavour to conciliate their affection, and acquire their good graces. A critic of a different age or nation, who should peruse this discourse, must have all these circumstances in his eye, and must place himself in the same situation as the audience, in order to form a true judgment of the oration. In like manner, when any work is addressed to the public, though I should have a friendship or enmity with the author, I must depart from this situation; and considering myself as a man in general, forget, if possible, my individual being and my peculiar circumstances. A person influenced by prejudice, complies not with this condition; but obstinately maintains his natural position, without placing himself in that point of view, which the performance supposes. If the work be addressed to persons of a different age or nation, he makes no allowance for their peculiar views and prejudices; but, full of the manners of his own age and country, rashly condemns what seemed admirable in the eyes of those for whom alone the discourse was calculated. If the work be executed for the public, he never sufficiently enlarges his comprehension, or forgets his interest as a friend or enemy, as a rival or commentator. By this means, his sentiments are perverted; nor have the same beauties and blemishes the same influence upon him, as if he had imposed a proper violence on his imagination, and had forgotten himself for a moment. So far his taste evidently departs from the true standard; and of consequence loses all credit and authority.

It is well known, that in all questions, submitted to the understanding, prejudice is destructive of sound judgment, and perverts all operations of the intellectual faculties: It is no less contrary to good taste; nor has it less influence to corrupt our sentiment of beauty. It belongs to *good sense* to check its influence in both cases; and in this respect, as well as in many others, reason, if not an essential part of taste, is at least requisite to the operations of this latter faculty. In all the nobler productions of genius, there is a mutual relation and correspondence of parts; nor can either the beauties or blemishes be perceived by him, whose thought is not capacious enough to comprehend all those parts, and compare them with each other, in order to perceive the consistence and uniformity of the whole. Every work of art has also a certain end or purpose, for which it is calculated; and is to be deemed more or less perfect, as it is more or less fitted to attain this end. The object of eloquence is to persuade, of history to instruct, of poetry to please by means of the passions and the imagination. These ends we must carry constantly in our view, when we peruse any performance; and we must be able to judge how far the means employed are adapted to their respective purposes. Besides, every kind of composition, even the most poetical, is nothing but a chain of propositions and reasonings; not always, indeed, the justest and most exact, but still plausible and specious, however disguised by the colouring of the imagination. The persons introduced in tragedy and epic poetry, must be represented as reasoning, and thinking, and concluding, and acting, suitably to their character and circumstances; and without judgment, as well as taste and invention, a poet can never hope to succeed in so delicate an undertaking. Not to mention, that the same excellence of faculties which contributes to the improvement of reason, the same clearness of conception, the same exactness of distinction, the same vivacity of apprehension, are essential to the operations of true taste, and are its infallible concomitants. It seldom, or never happens, that a man of sense, who has experience in any art, cannot judge of its beauty; and it is no less rare to meet with a man who has a just taste without a sound understanding.

Thus, though the principles of taste be universal, and, nearly, if not entirely the same in all men; yet few are qualified to give judgment on any work of art, or establish their own sentiment as the standard of beauty. The organs of internal sensation are seldom so perfect as to allow the general principles their full play, and produce a feeling correspondent to those principles. They either labour under some defect, or are vitiated by some disorder; and by that means, excite a sentiment, which may be pronounced erroneous. When the critic has no delicacy, he judges without any distinction, and is only affected by the grosser and more palpable qualities of the object: The finer touches pass unnoticed and disregarded. Where he is not aided by practice, his verdict is attended with confusion and hesitation. Where no comparison has been employed, the most frivolous beauties, such as rather merit the name of defects, are the object of his admiration. Where he lies under the influence of prejudice, all his natural sentiments are perverted. Where good sense is wanting, he is not qualified to discern the beauties of design and reasoning, which are the highest and most excellent. Under some or other of these imperfections, the generality of men labour; and hence a true judge in the finer arts is observed, even during the most polished ages, to be so rare a character: Strong sense, united to delicate sentiment, improved by practice, perfected by comparison, and cleared of all prejudice, can alone entitle critics to this valuable character; and the joint verdict of such, wherever they are to be found, is the true standard of taste and beauty.

But where are such critics to be found? By what marks are they to be known? How distinguish them from pretenders? These questions are embarrassing; and seem to throw us back into the same uncertainty, from which, during the course of this essay, we have endeavoured to extricate ourselves.

But if we consider the matter aright, these are questions of fact, not of sentiment. Whether any particular person be endowed with good sense and a delicate imagination, free from prejudice, may often be the subject of dispute, and be liable to great discussion and enquiry: But that such a character is valuable and estimable will be agreed in by all mankind. Where these doubts occur, men can do no more than in other disputable questions, which are submitted to the understanding: They must produce the best-arguments, that their invention suggests to them; they must acknowledge a true and decisive standard to exist somewhere, to wit, real existence and matter of fact; and they must have indulgence to such as differ from them in their appeals to this standard. It is sufficient for our present purpose, if we have proved, that the taste of all individuals is not upon an equal footing, and that some men in general, however difficult to be particularly pitched upon, will be acknowledged by universal senti-ment to have a preference above others.

But in reality the difficulty of finding, even in particulars, the standard of taste, is not so great as it is represented. Though in speculation, we may readily avow a certain criterion in science and deny it in sentiment, the matter is found in practice to be much more hard to ascertain in the former case than in the latter. Theories of abstract philosophy, systems of profound theology, have prevailed during one age: In a successive pe-riod, these have been universally exploded: Their absurdity has been detected: Other theories and systems have supplied their place, which again gave place to their successors: And nothing has been experienced more liable to the revolutions of chance and fashion than these pretended decisions of science. The case is not the same with the beauties of elo-quence and poetry. Just expressions of passion and nature are sure, after a little time, to gain public applause, which they maintain for ever. Aristotle, and Plato, and Epicurus, and Descartes, may successively yield to each other: But Terence and Virgil maintain an universal, undisputed empire over the minds of men. The abstract philosophy of Cicero has lost its credit: The vehemence of his oratory is still the object of our admiration.

Though men of delicate taste be rare, they are easily to be distinguished in society, by the soundness of their understanding and the superiority of their faculties above the rest of mankind. The ascendant, which they acquire, gives a prevalence to that lively approbation, with which they re-ceive any productions of genius, and renders it generally predominant. Many men, when left to themselves, have but a faint and dubious per-ception of beauty, who yet are capable of relishing any fine stroke, which is pointed out to them. Every convert to the admiration of the real poet or orator is the cause of some new conversion. And though prejudices may prevail for a time, they never unite in celebrating any rival to the true genius, but yield at last to the force of nature and just sentiment. Thus, though a civilized nation may easily be mistaken in the choice of their admired philosopher, they never have been found long to err, in their affection for a favorite epic or tragic author.

But notwithstanding all our endeavours to fix a standard of taste, and reconcile the discordant apprehensions of men, there still remain two sources of variation, which are not sufficient indeed to confound all the boundaries of beauty and deformity, but will often serve to produce a difference in the degrees of our approbation or blame. The one is the different humours of particular men; the other, the particular manners and opinions of our age and country. The general principles of taste are uniform in human nature: Where men vary in their judgments, some defect or perversion in the faculties may commonly be remarked; proceeding either from prejudice, from want of practice, or want of delicacy; and there is just reason for approving one taste, and condemning another. But where there is such a diversity in the internal frame or external situation as is entirely blameless on both sides, and leaves no room to give one the preference above the other; in that case a certain degree of diversity in judgment is unavoidable, and we seek in vain for a standard, by which we can reconcile the contrary sentiments.

A young man, whose passions are warm, will be more sensibly touched with amorous and tender images, than a man more advanced in years, who takes pleasure in wise, philosophical reflections concerning the conduct of life and moderation of the passions. At twenty, Ovid may be the favourite author; Horace at forty; and perhaps Tacitus at fifty. Vainly would we, in such cases, endeavour to enter into the sentiments of others, and divest ourselves of those propensities, which are natural to us. We choose our favourite author as we do our friend, from a conformity of humour and disposition. Mirth or passion, sentiment or reflection; whichever of these most predominates in our temper, it gives us a peculiar sympathy with the writer who resembles us.

One person is more pleased with the sublime; another with the tender; a third with raillery. One has a strong sensibility to blemishes, and is extremely studious of correctness: Another has a more lively feeling of beauties, and pardons twenty absurdities and defects for one elevated or pathetic stroke. The ear of this man is entirely turned towards conciseness and energy; that man is delighted with a copious, rich, and harmonious expression. Simplicity is affected by one; ornament by another. Comedy, tragedy, satire, odes, have each its partizans, who prefer that particular species of writing to all others. It is plainly an error in a critic, to confine his approbation to one species or style of writing, and condemn all the rest. But it is almost impossible not to feel a predilection for that which suits our particular turn and disposition. Such preferences are innocent and unavoidable, and can never reasonably be the object of dispute, because there is no standard, by which they can be decided.

For a like reason, we are more pleased, in the course of our reading, with pictures and characters, that resemble objects which are found in our own age or country, than with those which describe a different set of customs. It is not without some effort, that we reconcile ourselves to the simplicity of ancient manners, and behold princesses carrying water from the spring, and kings and heroes dressing their own victuals. We may allow in general, that the representation of such manners is no fault in the author, nor deformity in the piece; but we are not so sensibly touched with them. For this reason, comedy is not easily transferred from one age or nation to another. A Frenchman or Englishman is not pleased with the Andria of Terence, or Clitia of Machiavel; where the fine lady, upon whom all the play turns, never once appears to the spectators, but is always kept behind the scenes, suitably to the reserved humour of the ancient Greeks and modern Italians. A man of learning and reflection can make allowance for these peculiarities of manners; but a common audience can never divest themselves so far of their usual ideas and sentiments, as to relish pictures which in no wise resemble them.

But here there occurs a reflection, which may, perhaps, be useful in examining the celebrated controversy concerning ancient and modern learning; where we often find the one side excusing any seeming absurdity in the ancients from the manners of the age, and the other refusing to admit this excuse, or at least, admitting it only as an apology for the author, not for the performance. In my opinion, the proper boundaries in this subject have seldom been fixed between the contending parties. Where any innocent peculiarities of manners are represented, such as those above mentioned, they ought certainly to be admitted; and a man, who is shocked with them, gives an evident proof of false delicacy and refinement. The poet's *monument more durable than brass*, must fall to the ground like common brick or clay, were men to make no allowance for the continual revolutions of manners and customs, and would admit of nothing but what was suitable to the prevailing fashion. Must we throw aside the pictures of our ancestors, because of their ruffs and far-dingales? But where the ideas of morality and decency alter from one age to another, and where vicious manners are described, without being marked with the proper characters of blame and disapprobation; this must be allowed to disfigure the poem, and to be a real deformity. I cannot, nor is it proper I should, enter into such sentiments; and however I may excuse the poet, on account of the manners of his age, I never can relish the composition. The want of humanity and of decency, so conspicuous in the characters drawn by several of the ancient poets, even sometimes by Homer and the Greek tragedians, diminishes considerably the merit of their noble performances, and gives modern authors an advantage over them. We are not interested in the fortunes and sentiments of such rough heroes: We are displeased to find the limits of vice and virtue so much confounded: And whatever indulgence we may give to the writer on account of his prejudices, we cannot prevail on ourselves to enter into his sentiments, or bear an affection to characters, which we plainly discover to be blameable.

The case is not the same with moral principles, as with speculative opinions of any kind. These are in continual flux and revolution. The son embraces a different system from the father. Nay, there scarcely is any man, who can boast of great constancy and uniformity in this particular. Whatever speculative errors may be found in the polite writings of any age or country, they detract but little from the value of those compositions. There needs but a certain turn of thought or imagination to make us enter into all the opinions, which then prevailed, and relish the sentiments or conclusions derived from them. But a very violent effort is requisite to change our judgment of manners, and excite sentiments of approbation or blame, love or hatred, different from those to which the mind from long custom has been familiarized. And where a man is confident of the rectitude of that moral standard, by which he judges, he is justly jealous of it, and will not pervert the sentiments of his heart for a moment, in complaisance to any writer whatsoever.

Of all speculative errors, those, which regard religion, are the most excusable in compositions of genius; nor is it ever permitted to judge of the civility or wisdom of any people, or even of single persons, by the grossness or refinement of their theological principles. The same good sense, that directs men in the ordinary occurrences of life, is not hearkened to in religious matters, which are supposed to be placed altogether above the cognizance of human reason. On this account, all the absurdities of the pagan system of theology must be overlooked by every critic, who would pretend to form a just notion of ancient poetry; and our posterity, in their turn, must have the same indulgence to their forefathers. No religious principles can ever be imputed as a fault to any poet, while they remain merely principles, and take not such strong possession of his heart, as to lay him under the imputation of *bigotry* or *superstition*. Where that happens, they confound the sentiments of morality, and alter the natural boundaries of vice and virtue. They are therefore eternal blemishes, according to the principle above mentioned; nor are the prejudices and false opinions of the age sufficient to justify them.

It is essential to the Roman catholic religion to inspire a violent hatred of every other worship, and to represent all pagans, mahometans, and heretics as the objects of divine wrath and vengeance. Such sentiments, though they are in reality very blameable, are considered as virtues by the zealots of that communion, and are represented in their tragedies and epic poems as a kind of divine heroism. This bigotry has disfigured two very fine tragedies of the French theatre. Polieucte and Athalia; where an intemperate zeal for particular modes of worship is set off with all the pomp imaginable, and forms the predominant character of the heroes. 'What is this,' says the sublime Joad to Josabet, finding her in discourse with Mathan, the priest of Baal, 'Does the daughter of David speak to this traitor? Are you not afraid, lest the earth should open and pour forth flames to devour you both? Or lest these holy walls should fall and crush you together? What is his purpose? Why comes that enemy of God hither to poison the air, which we breathe, with his horrid presence?' Such sentiments are received with great applause on the theatre of Paris; but at London the spectators would be full as much pleased to hear Achilles tell Agamemnon, that he was a dog in his forehead, and a deer in his heart, or Jupiter threaten Juno with a sound drubbing, if she will not be quiet.

Religious principles are also a blemish in any polite composition, when they rise up to superstition, and intrude themselves into every sentiment, however remote from any connection with religion. It is no excuse for the poet, that the customs of his country had burthened life with so many religious ceremonies and observances, that no part of it was exempt from that yoke. It must for ever be ridiculous in Petrarch to compare his mistress Laura, to Jesus Christ. Nor is it less ridiculous in that agreeable libertine, Boccace, very seriously to give thanks to God Almighty and the ladies, for their assistance in defending him against his enemies.

Jerome Stolnitz

OF THE ORIGINS OF
"AESTHETIC DISINTERESTEDNESS"

We cannot understand modern aesthetic theory* unless we understand the concept of "disinterestedness." If any one belief is the common property of modern thought, it is that a certain mode of attention is indispensable to and distinctive of the perception of beautiful things. We meet it in Kant, Schopenhauer, Croce, Bergson, and also, what is almost more revealing, in those, such as the Marxists, whose desperate protest against it shows how well-entrenched the belief has become. And yet, as these things are measured, "disinterestedness" is a fairly recent idea. Either it does not occur at all in the thought of antiquity, the medieval period, and the Renaissance, or if it does, as in Thomas,[1] the allusion is cursory and undeveloped. By contrast, in Kant, who takes disinterestedness to be the "First Moment of the Judgment of Taste," from which the claim of the judgment to be universally valid, is "deducible,"[2] or in Schopenhauer, whose account of "pure, will-less contemplation" inaugurates his aesthetic and who defines "art" and "genius" and ranks the art-forms by reference to it, disinterestedness comes first, both in the order of exposition and of logic.

The significance of "disinterestedness" is not, however, confined to aesthetic theory proper. Filtered down into art criticism and the quotidian appreciation of art and nature, the idea has also transformed habits of seeing and judging. It is, in our own time, so much a commonplace that the work of art and the aesthetic object generally is "autonomous" and "self-contained," and must be apprehended as such, that we have to catch ourselves up. This has not always been a commonplace. Indeed, throughout most of the history of Western art, this notion would have seemed not so much false as incomprehensible. During these periods, the values

Jerome Stolnitz is Professor of Philosophy at Lehman College, City University of New York. He is well-known for his scholarly and philosophical work on aesthetics, especially for his work *Aesthetics and The Philosophy of Art Criticism*.

* This essay was originally published in *The Journal of Aesthetics and Art Criticism*, winter, 1961, pp. 131–143. Reprinted by permission of *The Journal of Aesthetics and Art Criticism*.

[1] Cf. *Summa Theologica*, Ia, 2ac, quaest. 27, art. 1.
[2] Immanuel Kant, *The Critique of Judgment*, trans. Meredith (Oxford, 1952), p. 50.

of art are iconic or otherwise cognitive, or moral, or social, with nothing
left over that art can call its own. To repudiate this conception of art is
"the most tremendous change . . . in the whole history of art."[3] Yet it
has not, even now, been properly appraised, except perhaps by Malraux.
Here I only venture the suggestion that "disinterestedness," more than
any other single idea, made this movement articulate and gave impetus
to it.

The present paper is concerned with aesthetic theory solely. I want to
trace the origins of "disinterestedness" and to show that they are to be
found where the origins of modern aesthetic theory are to be found, viz.,
in eighteenth-century British thought. The British did not invent and
never use the words "aesthetic" or "aesthetics," but it is simply frivolous to
allow this to decide who "created" aesthetic theory. The British were the
first to envision the possibility of a philosophical discipline, embracing the
study of all of the arts, one which would be, moreover, autonomous,
because its subject-matter is not explicable by any of the other disciplines.
And the British were the first to act upon and realize this program.

The argument of the paper is that the motive idea in their thinking
was "disinterestedness."

I

The concept comes into being slowly, even deviously. It has its roots,
indeed, in contemporary controversies in ethics and religion, and only
gradually does it take on the distinctively aesthetic meaning which we
attach to it today.

Lord Shaftesbury, writing in the opening decade of the eighteenth
century, is the first philosopher to call attention to disinterested perception.[4] "Interest" and "interestedness" were very much in the air at the
time. In ethics, Hobbes had by no means been commonly accepted, but he
could not be ignored. In religion, the cognate conception that prayer and
religious belief are devices of intelligent egoism, had become prevalent.
Shaftesbury, like the Cambridge Platonists before him,[5] thought these doctrines both false and wicked.

> There can . . . be little doubt that, like most of the other ethical writers of
> his time, he was mainly impelled to his task through the shock which had
> been given to the current moral sentiment by the paradoxes of Hobbes, and
> through the desire to arrest the progress of doctrines at which society was
> then seriously alarmed.[6]

"Interest" is an ethical or, we might now say, an axiological notion. For
Shaftesbury, as for his contemporaries, it designates the state of well-being

---

[3] Arnold Hauser, *The Social History of Art* (London, 1952), I, 91.
[4] A more extended analysis, along somewhat different lines, will be found in Jerome
  Stolnitz, "On the Significance of Lord Shaftesbury in Modern Aesthetic Theory,"
  Philosophical Quarterly, 11 (1961), 97–113.
[5] Cf. R. L. Brett, *The Third Earl of Shaftesbury* (London, 1951), p. 32.
[6] Thomas Fowler, *Shaftesbury and Hutcheson* (New York, 1883), pp. 99–100.

or the genuine and long-range good. It can be used in speaking either of an individual or of society.[7] Occasionally, however, Shaftesbury uses the term to refer, not to the good, but to the desire or motive to achieve the good. In these cases, it is always the "private" good, never the "common" good, which is intended. Thus Shaftesbury uses it interchangeably with "self-interest" (I, 77, 317). This connotation of egoism is preserved in "interested" and "interestedness." These terms designate actions which are motivated by regard for the well-being of the agent, rather than toward "the good and interest of his species and community" (I, 315), or to the propensity of character to perform such actions. So Shaftesbury speaks of "interestedness or self-love" (I, 317).

It might appear to follow that benevolent or altruistic actions, in one obvious respect the opposite of "interested" actions, are properly called "disinterested." Yet Shaftesbury rarely, if ever (I, 67), uses "disinterested" in this way. If he had, the term would not have found a place in aesthetics. Whatever it may mean to say that the aesthetic percipient is disinterested, the locution almost certainly does not mean that he is seeking to promote social well-being.

The opposite of "interestedness" begins to appear in Shaftesbury's polemic against egoism in ethics and instrumentalism in religion. What he wishes above all to insist is that hope of reward or fear of punishment is "fatal to virtue" (I, 275) and to piety as well. Those actions which are performed without such motives give the lie to any purely egoistic reading of human nature (I, 67, 68, 69). At this point, however, "disinterested" has only the negative or privative meaning, "not motivated by self-concern." Shaftesbury has still to present an alternative to Hobbes, by explaining the nature of true goodness and holiness.

A man cannot be virtuous if he "[aims] at it through love of the reward. But," Shaftesbury goes on to say, "as soon as he is come to have any affection towards what is morally good, and can like or affect such good for its own sake, as good and amiable in itself, then he is in some degree good and virtuous, and not till then" (I, 274). Similarly, Shaftesbury opposes "the disinterested love of God" to "[serving] God . . . for interest merely" (II, 55). When one loves God disinterestedly, one loves God simply for His own sake (II, 55), because of "the excellence of the object" (II, 56).

In these passages, Shaftesbury is rejecting "interestedness." But he is not urging concern for some desired consequence other than self-good. He is urging, rather, that genuine moral and religious concern are with what is intrinsic and that they are therefore terminal. They are not instrumental and therefore anticipatory. The whole selfishness-unselfishness controversy has now been transcended. Unlike his contemporary anti-Hobbesians, Shaftesbury does not identify moral rightness with benevolence.[8] Ethics is not a question of consequences.

---

[7] Anthony, Earl of Shaftesbury, *Characteristics*, ed. Robertson (London, 1900), I, 70, 87, 243, 252, 282, 315, 338.

[8] *Ibid.*, I, 253 ff; 286 ff. Shaftesbury is not consistent, however; cf. I, 266.

To many philosophers, this is an odd thing to say of ethics and, though perhaps somewhat less so, of religion as well. On the usual showing, morality is "practical" because it involves the choice of actions for the realization of certain ends. Whether it be odd or not, whether Shaftesbury's theory is a viable ethics or not (these are not our questions), Shaftesbury not only gives up consequences—he also gives up the traditional preoccupation with action generally.[9] On his account, the moral life is far less a matter of choosing and executing one's decision, than of "liking" or "loving" the "view or contemplation" (II, 176) of virtue. Indeed, for Shaftesbury, the virtuous man is like nothing so much as the art-lover, from whom he differs only in the objects which he apprehends:

> The case is the same in the mental or moral subjects as in the ordinary bodies or common objects of sense. The shapes, motions, colours, and proportions of these latter being presented to our eye, there necessarily results a beauty or deformity, according to the different measure, arrangement, and disposition of their several parts. So in behavior and actions. . . . [The mind] finds a foul and fair, a harmonious and a dissonant, as really and truly here as in any musical numbers or in the outward forms or representations of sensible things. (I, 251)

The capacity for such perception and for the feeling of approbation or disapprobation is virtue. For virtue "is itself," Shaftesbury says "no other than the love of order and beauty . . ." (I, 279).

Shaftesbury's ethical theory thus turns out to be very nearly indistinguishable from an aesthetic theory. It is usually thought that the aesthetic viewpoint lends itself more readily to manners than to morals, for "propriety" and "fittingness" are the salient notions in manners, and actions there do not have the import and are not hedged about with the sanctions of morality. So Shaftesbury speaks of the "decorum and grace" of "gentility or politeness" and of our "pleasure and enjoyment in the very survey and contemplation of this kind" (II, 267). He cannot, however, be justly charged with slipping over unthinkingly from manners into ethics. For he does it knowingly and deliberately. He says that his aim is "to recommend morals on the same foot with . . . manners" (II, 257). Crucial to both is the "grace" or "harmony" of action and, more important, character. That is why Shaftesbury will not identify virtue with benevolence. Immoderate benevolence is just as reprehensible as excessive self-interest, for it too destroys the harmony of character (I, 253, 286 ff.).

We have seen that the significance of "interestedness" is "practical," because it refers to actions directed toward an anticipated goal. When Shaftesbury uses "disinterested" privatively, to describe those who do not act morally or worship God with an eye to future reward, the reference of the term is still to actions and the motives to actions. When he describes morality and religion as the "love" of their respective objects "for its own sake," the term no longer has to do with choice and action but with a mode of attention and concern. A man is "disinterested" now, when

---

[9] Cf. Fowler, *op. cit.*, p. 72.

he takes no thought for any consequences whatever. When, furthermore, Shaftesbury goes on to describe the virtuous man as a spectator, devoted to "the very survey and contemplation" of beauty in manners and morals, the initial "practical" significance of "disinterested" is supplanted altogether by the perceptual. The term now denotes the state of "barely seeing and admiring" (II, 270 n.). Given the etymology of the word "aesthetic," it is, for the first time, appropriate to speak of "aesthetic disinterestedness."

Setting out the analysis in this way will be misleading, if it makes it sound as though Shaftesbury arrived at the concept by working backward from ethics. The historical occasion was, to be sure, the fight over egoism and the vocabulary was, necessarily, non-aesthetic. But the whole impulse and bent of Shaftesbury's thought, from the very beginning, was toward the aesthetic. The student of Plato and Plotinus, he had proclaimed, "Seek for the *kalon* in everything."[10] He applied his aesthetic insight to ethics, but not to ethics exclusively. Other objects besides moral "affections" and character can be looked at disinterestedly. Thus we find, suddenly obtruding itself into a discussion of benevolence, a passage in which Shaftesbury describes the enjoyment of mathematics. The perception of mathematical objects "relates not in the least to any private interest of the creature, nor has for its object any self-good or advantage of the private system" (I, 296). In such experience, "The admiration, joy, or love turns wholly upon what is exterior and foreign to ourselves" (I, 296). Shaftesbury goes on to give a terse and decisive reply to those who were later to protest against the notion of "aesthetic disinterestedness," "Oh, but don't you listen to the music for the sake of the pleasure you're going to get?":

. . . though the reflected joy or pleasure which arises from the notice of this pleasure once perceived, may be interpreted a self-passion or interested regard, yet the original satisfaction can be no other than what results from the love of truth, proportion, order and symmetry in the things without. (I, 296)

Shaftesbury's most extended description of aesthetic disinterestedness occurs in one of his last works. The passage adds little that is new substantively. Yet here the aesthetic comes into its own for the first time: aesthetic perception is no longer run together with moral and religious virtue, "disinterestedness" leaves behind its origins in the Hobbes controversy, which are still in evidence in the passage on mathematics, and instead of moral character or geometrical proof, Shaftesbury chooses a much more familiar kind of aesthetic object, viz., scenes in nature. What is new in the passage is that Shaftesbury opposes disinterestedness to the desire to possess or use the object. This way of putting it is widely adopted in later British thought and in modern aesthetics generally. It may therefore be worth pointing out that disregard for possession or use is only an inference from or a specification of the broader proposition that

[10] Quoted in Fowler, *op. cit.*, p. 44.

the aesthetic spectator does not relate the object to any purposes that outrun the act of perception itself.

> Imagine then . . . if being taken with the beauty of the ocean, which you see yonder at a distance, it should come into your head to seek how to command it, and, like some mighty admiral, ride master of the sea, would not the fancy be a little absurd? (II, 126)

The enjoyment which would arise from "possessing" the ocean is "very different from that which should naturally follow from the contemplation of the ocean's beauty" (II, 127). Shaftesbury cites other objects which arouse "eager desires, wishes and hopes" (II, 127)—land, the fruit of trees and "human forms." These do not "[satisfy] by mere view" (II, 128).

There is no need, at this point, to spend much time on the two theorists who (in both senses) followed Shaftesbury, viz., Addison and Hutcheson. The former will be treated at some length in the final section of this paper. Hutcheson's account of disinterestedness for the most part merely echoes Shaftesbury's. He excludes "feeling to what farther advantage or detriment the use of such objects might tend,"[11] and he singles out "the desire of possession or property."[12] Elsewhere Hutcheson says that there is "no uneasiness of appetite" (*PA*, p. 101) prior to aesthetic perception. He also re-states Shaftesbury's distinction between the enjoyment of beauty and the second-order awareness of such enjoyment, which is non-aesthetic (*PA*, p. 28). In only one respect is Hutcheson's analysis significantly different. He excludes from the aesthetic any concern for knowledge about the object. Such knowledge may be welcomed "from prospects of advantage" (*Inq.*, p. 11) and it may arouse intellectual or cognitive pleasure. Yet it is wholly different from the enjoyment of beauty and can have no effect upon this experience (*Inq.*, pp. 4, 11). This, again, is only a development of Shaftesbury's insights that the aesthetic interest is in perception alone and that it terminates upon the object itself. It would follow that the aesthetic interest is indifferent to the causal and other relationships which the object has to things beyond itself. Yet the inference which Hutcheson draws is worth remarking, because it becomes increasingly conspicuous in later aesthetic theory.[13]

Shaftesbury was one of the most widely-read authors of his time[14] and it was, doubtless, chiefly due to this fact that, by the middle of the century, "disinterestedness" had become a staple in British thought. This is shown, though in different ways, in the writings of Burke (1757) and Gerard (1759). In the latter, there is only one fleeting reference to the concept. Gerard is discussing sensibility, by which he means the capacity to respond to an aesthetic object. Among the forces which inhibit sen-

---

[11] [Francis Hutcheson], *An Inquiry into the Original of our Ideas of Beauty and Virtue*, 4th ed. (London, 1738), p. 4. This work will be designated *Inq*.

[12] [Francis Hutcheson], *An Essay on the Nature and Conduct of the Passions and Affections* (London, 1728), p. 102. This work will be designated *PA*.

[13] Cf., e.g., Schopenhauer, *The World as Will and Idea*, Bk. III, Second Aspect.

[14] Cf. Brett, *op. cit.*, pp. 56, 186.

sibility, are "gratification of appetite" and "the pursuits of gain."[15] Gerard says no more than this. He does not explain why these activities are inimical to aesthetic response. It is reasonable to suppose that he did not have to. Gerard could assume (the *Essay* was written for a philosophical competition) that even so elliptical a reference would be understood by those who were familiar with the works of the early-century philosophers.

Little more than Gerard does Burke treat of disinterestedness in its own right. What is, perhaps, even more instructive is that he *uses* the concept, to explicate other concepts and to meet the dialectical problems which they run into. These other concepts are "beauty" and "sublimity," to which, as its title indicates, Burke's *Enquiry* is chiefly addressed.

Burke begins his discussion of beauty by defining it as "that quality . . . in bodies by which they cause love. . . ."[16] He then goes on to say that by "love" "I mean that satisfaction which arises to the mind upon contemplating any thing beautiful. . . ." (p. 91). The definitions are circular but the fault might be mitigated if, so to speak, the circle were not quite so narrow. What is required is an elaboration of the meaning of "love." When Burke speaks, instead, of "affection and tenderness" (p. 51), little is accomplished, for these are, at best, only synonyms and they are about equally vague. Failing an analysis of the felt quality of the emotion itself, Burke, like other philosophers and psychologists in the same predicament, turns to the psychological states which accompany the emotion. It is at this point that "disinterestedness" goes to work for him. For Burke distinguishes love "from desire or lust, which is an energy of the mind, that hurries us on to the possession of certain objects" (p. 51). By implication, therefore, Burke describes the kind of interest which is taken in the object of love. Thus Burke is one of the many theorists who take the desire for possession to be paradigmatic of non-disinterested behavior.[17] We shall see in a moment that he does not simply identify the two. With this qualification, and noting the reference to "contemplation," in the sentence quoted above, we may take it that love is the pleasure or satisfaction which is felt in perceiving a beautiful object disinterestedly.

Disinterestedness is especially important in Burke's theory of beauty. He holds that things are beautiful when they are small, delicate, smooth, soft, curved (p. 124). Indeed they are probably best epitomized by the female body, to which Burke alludes continually and which he apostrophizes so eloquently. When he speaks of "the affection which possesses an ordinary man at the sight of a delicate smooth skin" (p. 108), or of "the deceitful maze . . . about the neck and breasts . . . through which the unsteady eye slides giddily" (p. 115), then it is important to be reminded

---

[15] Alexander Gerard, *An Essay on Taste*, 2nd ed. (Edinburgh, 1764), p. 99. Cf., also, p. 105.

[16] Edmund Burke, A *Philosophical Enquiry into the Origin of our Ideas of the Sublime and Beautiful*, ed. Boulton (London, 1958), p. 91.

[17] Cf. above, p. 135.

that a beautiful object can be perceived as such only if the sole interest of the perceiver is in perceiving.

The forces which threaten to subvert perception, in the case of the sublime, are very different. For beauty and sublimity, considered either as objective properties or as "ideas," are, Burke holds, "opposite and contradictory" (p. 125). Sublime things are large, rugged, massive, "dark and gloomy" (p. 124). Hence they do not arouse love or tenderness. "Indeed," Burke argues, "terror is in all cases whatsoever . . . the ruling principle of the sublime" (p. 58). A thing is terrible when it is "fitted in any sort to excite the ideas of pain, and danger" (p. 39). These passions "belong to self-preservation" (pp. 38 ff.). Thus a sublime object is one which is thought and felt to pose a threat to the spectator's well-being.[18] Now there is no question of an object being so attractive and alluring that one will "hurry on to possession," but just the opposite.

Burke was not the first to discern fearfulness in the sublime. John Dennis had spoken of the "horror" and "terror" which he felt upon seeing the Alps.[19] But Dennis nowhere differentiates such emotions from those of non-aesthetic experience.[20] By contrast, Burke preserves the phenomenological insight and sets it into aesthetic theory. He can do so because he, unlike Dennis, is aware of and employs the concept of disinterestedness.

We have seen that the concept comes into Burke's analysis of beauty only implicitly, by opposition to "desire or lust." So too in the present case. The corresponding distinction is now between the sublime and what is "simply terrible" (p. 40). The sublime, like the terrible, "is an idea belonging to self-preservation" (p. 86). Burke makes out the distinction in this way: "When danger or pain press too nearly, they are incapable of giving any delight . . . but at certain distances, and with certain modifications, they may be, and they are delightful . . ." (p. 40). The word "distances" reminds the modern reader of Bullough's "psychical distance." Burke does not describe "distancing" as a deliberate act of will, whereby the object is "put out of gear with our practical self."[21] Yet he seems to be working toward just such a notion as this. "Delight" is an aesthetic term, for he defines "the sublime" by reference to it (p. 51). The purport of the passage is, then, that the sublime can be experienced only when self-concern can be kept from becoming too great.

But this requires "certain modifications" in the situation of danger: ". . . if the pain and terror are so modified as not to be actually noxious; if the pain is not carried to violence, and the terror is not conversant about the present destruction of the person . . . these emotions . . . are capable of producing delight" (p. 136). Burke cannot mean by this that

---

[18] Cf., however, pp. 136 ff.
[19] Cf. Samuel II, Monk, *The Sublime: A Study of Critical Theories in XVIII-Century England* (New York, 1935), p. 207.
[20] *Ibid.*, p. 64.
[21] Edward Bullough, "Psychical Distance as a Factor in Art and an Aesthetic Principle," in Vivas and Krieger, eds., *The Problems of Aesthetics* (New York, 1953), p. 397.

the object presents *no* threat whatever. If this were the case, then, for one thing, the emotions of self-preservation would not be aroused and we would not feel what, according to Burke, we do in fact feel in the face of the sublime—"that state of the soul, in which all its motions are suspended, with some degree of horror" (p. 57). Moreover, Burke does not take the experience to be merely "fictitious" or "make-believe." He gives as instances of the sublime, "real-life" objects such as "serpents and poisonous animals" (p. 57), and the brunt of his powerful analysis of tragedy is to weaken the distinction between "fiction" and "reality" (pp. 47–48). Still we are left with the operative phrases, "actually noxious and destructive."

Prof. Monk offers a gloss upon "if the terror is not conversant about the present destruction of the person": "that is, if it can be regarded theoretically" (p. 97). I would hesitate to use the word "theoretically," if only because Burke specifically and vigorously denies that the experience is rational or intellectual (p. 57). Despite this objection, the gloss is suggestive. Prof. Monk is very likely using "theoretically" as the opposite of "practically," to mean "detached, not motivated to action" (pp. 161–162). Let us therefore say that a dangerous object can arouse delight only "if it can be regarded disinterestedly." Then the distinction between the sublime and the "simply terrible" is that, in the case of the former, the interest in perceiving is not usurped by the practical interest in preserving oneself.

This reading transfers the emphasis away from the objective features of the situation to the attitude of the percipient. Whether his experience is aesthetic depends not on how great he takes the threat of the object o be, but on whether he continues to contemplate it. Burke, in general, proceeds on the common-sense assumption that contemplation is possible only if the danger is not too immediate to be ignored. Therefore he attempts, not very successfully, to fix the appropriate degree of "distance" or "noxiousness." Elsewhere, however, Burke makes the issue turn solely on disinterestedness. He says that if we do not "shun" the object, but rather "approach" it and "dwell upon" it, we can feel delight (p. 45).

Taking the experience of sublimity to be disinterested, is all of a piece with Burke's account of the felt quality of the experience—"a sort of tranquillity tinged with terror" (p. 136). The self is and is known to be imperilled. Self-concern is therefore inescapable. Yet to be disinterested entails the inhibition of any action on behalf of the self. One is a spectator rather than an agent. One's involvement is controlled and tempered by the detachment of selflessness. Thus delight can be felt in perceiving an object which would otherwise arouse only "an apprehension of pain or death" (p. 131).

"Disinterestedness," once it had been defined by Shaftesbury, recurred throughout eighteenth-century British thought. It is an important, even strategic concept in all of the philosophers whom I have cited. And yet, there is this to see about it: none of these philosophers treats the concept in its own right. They use it, rather only in elucidating other concepts.

We have just found this in Burke, for whom disinterestedness sets off the emotions of love and delight from their non-aesthetic opposites. Hutcheson employs "disinterestedness" to describe the workings of the "internal sense" of beauty (*Inq.*, p. 11; *PA*, pp. 101–102) and thereby to differentiate this faculty of the mind from others. Disinterestedness is not, then, taken to be an isolable feature of the aesthetic experience. It is taken to characterize either the faculties of aesthetic awareness or the responses which are aroused in the course of the experience.

When we come to Archibald Alison, at the close of the century (1790), the contrast is striking. The very first question treated in the *Essays* is that of the "state of mind" which is required to appreciate beauty and sublimity.[22] Alison has, of course, his own theory of the faculties of aesthetic experience. They are, for him, imagination and emotion. But the whole point of his opening discussion is that they can function aesthetically only when the spectator has disposed himself in a certain way. Alison therefore isolates and holds up for scrutiny what we would now call "the aesthetic attitude." The governing idea remains, as it was in his predecessors, attending to an object with no interest other than that in perceiving itself. Yet Alison's way of going about it brings out what is only implicit in the earlier thinkers: "disinterested," in the first instance, denotes a way of organizing attention and only after this meaning has been established can it be used to qualify such notions as "internal sense" or Burke's "love." In dissociating the aesthetic attitude from the other elements of aesthetic experience, Alison points the way to later aesthetic theory. Indeed, he did the job so well that those who came after him borrowed his account of the aesthetic "state of mind" and ignored or rejected his associationist theories of imagination and "emotions of taste," to which it was intended as a prolegomenon.

In treating the aesthetic attitude in its own right, Alison brings a new subtlety and refinement into our understanding of disinterestedness. Lord Shaftesbury had pointed out that aesthetic perception is object-centered, that it "turns wholly upon what is exterior and foreign to ourselves."[23] Shaftesbury and his successors had therefore ruled out the self-concern of "interest." Alison, too, follows Shaftesbury in excluding from the aesthetic "the useful, the agreeable, the fitting, or the convenient in objects" (p. 19). All of these are involved in "the gratification of . . . appetite" (pp. 170–171). But Alison then proceeds to single out other, much less obvious threats to object-centered perception. It is not enough merely to have no self-seeking motives. We must "be in that temper of mind which suits with" (p. 217) the aesthetic object. "That state of mind . . . is most favorable to the emotions of taste . . in which the attention is so little occupied by any private or particular object of thought, as to leave us open to all the impressions, which the objects that are before us can produce. It is upon the vacant and unemployed, accordingly, that the

---

[22] Archibald Alison, *Essays on the Nature and Principles of Taste*, 4th ed. (Edinburgh, 1815), Essay I, chap. I, sect. II et seq. All page references are to Vol. I.
[23] Cf. above, p. 134.

objects of taste make the strongest impression" (pp. 10–11). Alison gives as examples of those who are oblivious to the beauty of nature, "the husbandman," "the man of business," and "the philosopher" (p. 95). The first two are obviously "interested." The philosopher, however, "who goes out . . . to reason or reflect" (p. 95), is not. The woodland is not, for him, something to be exploited or profit from. But again, the question has become, for Alison, not merely one of motive but of attention. The philosopher's reflection, since it keeps him from being "open to all the impressions" of the landscape, is anti-aesthetic. He must "withdraw . . . attention from the particular objects of [his] thought" and "abandon" (p. 95) himself to the scenery.

When Alison's predecessors wanted to illustrate the limits of aesthetic perception, they spoke of objects which, in some clear and obvious way, arouse self-concern. Thus, as we have seen, Shaftesbury enumerates objects which arouse "eager desires," whether economic or sensual,[24] and Burke treats of the "simply terrible."[25] Alison, however, in the very same connection, speaks of the Venus de Medici and the Apollo Belvedere. Earlier in the eighteenth century and prior to it, these would have been taken almost automatically to be what we should now call "aesthetic objects." Yet, for Alison, they are not "objects of taste" inherently and unconditionally. The whole century is a Copernican Revolution in aesthetics—whether an object is beautiful or sublime depends upon the experience of the spectator[26]—which here reaches its clearest expression. An object can be aesthetic only when certain conditions of attention and interest have been satisfied. And this true even of what had been thought to be the very type of a beautiful and aesthetic object, the classic Greek statue. A man "may observe their dimensions, he may study their proportions, he may attend to the particular state of their preservation, the history of their discovery, or even the nature of the marble of which they are made" (p. 98). But then the statues are not "objects of taste" or, alternatively, his experience is not aesthetic. If he is concerned with any of these, he will be unable to appreciate the "majesty" and "grace" (p. 98) of the statue.

Alison distinguishes the aesthetic percipient, not only from the art historian and scholar, but also from the critic. Indeed, he holds that criticism "never fails to destroy" (p. 100) appreciation. Disinterested attention is impossible because the critic considers the work of art either "in relation . . . to rules" (p. 100) or by comparing it to other works (p. 12). In either case, attention does not terminate upon the work itself.

The ideal state of mind, then, is to be "vacant and unemployed." Not that Alison takes this to be the same as apathy or vacuity. He says explicitly that appreciation is impossible "with minds fatigued," in "moments of listlessness and languor" (p. 96). The object is, precisely, at-

---

[24] Cf. above, p. 134.
[25] Cf. above, p. 136.
[26] This is shown at some length in Jerome Stolnitz, " 'Beauty': Some Stages in the History of an Idea," *Journal of the History of Ideas*, XXII (April–June, 1961), 185–204.

tended to. Then the aesthetic response, Alison says, takes place "spontaneously . . . in a kind of bewitching reverie" (p. 21). What emerges from Alison's account is the peculiar, perhaps paradoxical two-sidedness of the aesthetic experience: the governing attitude is vigilance and control, attention to the object which scrupulously shuts out whatever might diminish or subvert it; yet the total experience is one of ease, fluidity, and delight, what Alison's exact contemporaries in Germany called "freedom."

This is a phenomenology, or the beginnings of one, that can, I think, stand on its own merits. What is more important for our purposes, however, is that Alison has given new significance to "disinterestedness." In its origins, the term has to do with the notion of the self. As the opposite of "interestedness," it is equivalent in meaning to "non-selfishness."[27] When Shaftesbury used "disinterested" to denote perception of a thing "for its own sake," the salient antithesis became that between "object-centered" and "self-centered." Alison, undertaking to study "the state of mind most favorable to the emotions of taste," elucidates this distinction. Attention can be object-centered only when there are no thoughts or feelings to divert attention to the proprietary self. As Alison's examples of the philosopher and art historian make clear, this has nothing to do with "selfishness," in the traditional sense. "Impersonal" or "selfless" are now much closer to the mark than is "unselfish." To perceive disinterestedly is to make oneself a pure, unflawed mirror, prepared to receive without distortion "all the impressions, which the objects that are before us can produce."

When Shaftesbury formulated the concept of "disinterestedness," he took the first and crucial step toward setting off the aesthetic as a distinctive mode of experience. That there is such a mode of experience was a radically new idea in Western thought. It is not surprising, therefore, that in Shaftesbury and in his successors, such experience is defined chiefly by opposition to certain kinds of non-aesthetic behavior—moral, religious, instrumental, cognitive—whose existence and nature were already commonly recognized. Certain crucial features of the aesthetic are brought out in this way. Yet, in these thinkers, the analysis tends to center upon the gross and readily observable differences between aesthetic and non-aesthetic experience, e.g., the presence or absence of "appetite." By the time of Alison, after ninety years of prolific thought and writing by the British, "the aesthetic" has become a self-conscious and articulate idea. Alison need not, consequently, consider it merely by opposition to the non-aesthetic; he can examine the peculiarities of the aesthetic "state of mind" itself; and he can therefore bring out its less obvious features and make more subtle discriminations, e.g., between the aesthetic percipient and the critic, than his predecessors had discerned. Alison's phenomenology of the aesthetic attitude is, I believe, the most acute and revealing of any British theorist. Yet he was able to show *what* the aesthetic "state of mind" is like only after his countrymen had shown *that* such a "state of mind" exists.

---

[27] Cf. above, p. 132.

II

Like all seminal philosophical ideas, "disinterestedness" turns out to be important in ways that could hardly have been intended or even imagined at the time that it was brought to birth. "Disinterestedness" was not just one among other aesthetic concepts. It exercised, I now want to argue, a great, even a decisive influence upon the development of aesthetic theory as a whole in eighteenth-century Britain. Indeed, I want to show, "disinterestedness" is a major watershed in the history of aesthetics. For it transforms the conception of what aesthetic theory is and what it tries to do.

My argument will be based chiefly on an analysis of Addison's *Spectator* "Essays" (1712).

Addison, announcing his forthcoming papers on "The Pleasures of the Imagination," promises something "entirely new."[28] They were just that.

Whether we are going to say that there was any aesthetic theory at all prior to the eighteenth century is, as Prof. Kristeller reminds us, a question of what we mean by "aesthetics."[29] Suppose we say that there was (it seems very daring not to do so). Still we must recognize that either in respect of the scope of aesthetic theory, or of its central concepts, or of the problems to which it is mainly addressed, or all three of these, pre-eighteenth century aesthetics is a very different discipline. It would, of course, be a big job to demonstrate this. But though I must speak summarily, it is not, I think, inaccurate to say that the foundational concepts of traditional thought are those of beauty and/or of some particular art-form, e.g., painting or the visual arts, or *genre*, e.g., the epic. These concepts set limits to the field of study and they generate the major problems. "Beauty" being taken as synonymous with "aesthetic value," the task of the theorist is to determine which properties, e.g., harmony, constitute a thing beautiful and, often, as in Plato, Plotinus, Thomas, to make out the ontological status of beauty. The analyses of *genres*, so abundant in the Renaissance and neo-classical periods, set forth the potentialities and limitations inherent in the given *genre* and thereby the conditions under which a particular work is a good one of its kind or beautiful. Such treatises are often, however, little more than technical manuals. Moreover, they make little or no reference beyond the *genre* to some larger subject-matter, of art or the aesthetic in general.

The most obvious changes, when we come to Addison and the other Britishers, are the abandonment of the metaphysical approach *von Oben herab*[30] and the introduction of the psychological, introspective approach —"a diligent examination of our passions in our own breasts," as Burke put it (p. 1). Yet the decisive change, that which has been taken over

---

[28] *Spectator* no. 409, in *The Works of Joseph Addison*, ed. Greene (New York, 1856), VI, 321.
[29] Paul O. Kristeller, "The Modern System of the Arts: A Study in the History of Aesthetics," *Journal of the History of Ideas*, XII (1951), 500.
[30] Shaftesbury is the conspicuous exception. Cf. above, n. 4.

from the British by modern aesthetics generally, is not one of temper or method but of logic. It is to be found in the concepts which are employed for aesthetic inquiry and in the way in which they are related to each other.

That experiences are to be inventorized in terms of the faculties of awareness is, at the beginning of the eighteenth century, received doctrine, as is the distinction between the senses, imagination, and understanding. Of these, Addison takes imagination for his subject. Yet where we might therefore expect an explicit account of the nature and workings of this faculty, we find instead that in Addison, as in the later British aestheticians, "imagination" is a markedly "vague" concept.[31] Addison himself complains of its "loose and uncircumscribed sense" (no. 411, p. 323), but he does not live up to his promise to "fix and determine" (p. 323) the meaning. In the "Essay's" it "(designates) a conglomerate faculty."[32]

Let us revert briefly to *Spectator* no. 409, which just precedes the "Essays on the Imagination." These Addison defines "fine taste" as " 'that faculty of the soul, which discerns the beauties of an author with pleasure . . .' " (p. 316). The thing to see about this definition is that it can, without any change whatever, also serve as the definition of "imagination," as Addison uses this term in the "Essays." To cite just one example: in no. 412, the fancy, which is, for Addison, synonymous with imagination (no. 411, p. 323), is said to be "delighted" and "pleased" by the beauty which it finds in an object (p. 331). It seems almost to be indifferent to Addison which of these "faculty" words he uses. We might write this off on the grounds that Addison is much more the essayist than the philosopher, but then we find the same sort of thing in a far more careful thinker, his close contemporary Francis Hutcheson. The latter must also find a faculty for the "pleasant perceptions" of beauty; he assigns them to "an internal sense" (*PA*, p. 5). But he also says that "These we may call, after Mr. Addison, the pleasures of the imagination" (*PA*, p. 5). What is more, when the internal sense or imagination is developed, it can be called "taste" (*Inq.*, p. 9). And as if this were not enough, Hutcheson says breezily of "internal sense" that "Whoever dislikes this name may substitute another" (*PA*, p. 5).

The meaning of "imagination" is imprecise, but this appears not to matter. The meaning of a philosophical concept is often less important than its dialectical function. What work does "imagination" do in Addison's system? The answer is, I propose, that "imagination" or "taste" or "inner sense"—it now seems clear that it hardly matters which—does not so much designate an entity as it announces a fact. The fact is the disinterested perception of beauty. Addison, like every other major British aesthetician,[33] illustrates such perception by opposing it to the most

[31] W. J. Bate, *From Classic to Romantic: Premises of Taste in Eighteenth-Century England* (Harvard Univ. Press, 1946), p. 113.
[32] Walter John Hipple, Jr., *The Beautiful, The Sublime, and The Picturesque in Eighteenth-Century British Aesthetic Theory* (Southern Illinois U. P., 1957), p. 14.
[33] Cf. above, pp. 132, 135, 137, 139.

obvious sort of "interested" behavior: "A man of polite imagination . . . often feels a greater satisfaction in the prospect of fields and meadows, than another does in the possession" (no. 411, p. 325). The received psychology classifies experiences in terms of faculties. Addison can point to the experience of looking at "fields and meadows" disinterestedly only by assigning it to a faculty. The rubric "imagination" marks off this experience and names it. The "Essays" are devoted to "the Imagination" because imagination provides a habitat for disinterestedness.

Why does Addison single out the imagination? Less, I think, because of what it is—Addison's vagueness is symptomatic of this—than because of what it is not. The only remaining alternatives, among the "faculties of the soul," are sensation and understanding. And each of these is, in its very nature, incompatible with disinterested perception.

> [The pleasures of the imagination] do not require such a bent of thought as is necessary to our more serious employments, nor, at the same time, suffer the mind to sink into . . . sensual delights. (p. 325)

The "pleasures of sense," to consider them first, because they are "sensual," are "gross" (p. 324). Addison, in his essayist's fashion, says no more than this. But the purport becomes clear if, again, we turn to his immediate contemporaries, where the point is argued.

Addison, describing the experience of beauty, says that "We are struck, we know not how, with the symmetry of any thing we see, and immediately assent to the beauty of an object" (p. 324–325). So, too, Shaftesbury had written: "The shapes, motions, colours and proportions of these (objects) being presented to our eye, there necessarily results a beauty or deformity."[34] For both Addison and Shaftesbury, beauty impresses itself upon the percipient, coercively and directly. In this, beauty resembles all properties that are apprehended by sensation.[35] That is why Shaftesbury says that beauty "is immediately perceived by a plain internal sensation" (II, 63). And yet it is, precisely, *internal* sensation." For, Shaftesbury contends, gratification taken in "the objects of sense," as such, is wholly distinct from the enjoyment of beauty. Such gratification is like that "of the inferior creatures" (II, 128), when they seek food. It presupposes and cannot occur apart from "eager desires, wishes, and hopes," which are not "suitable" to the "refined contemplation of beauty" (II, 127–128). In a word, the pleasures of sense are always and necessarily "interested," for Shaftesbury.[36] Hence, he concludes, beauty is "never in body itself" (II, 132) and cannot be grasped by the bodily eye. Hutcheson, similarly, holds that all of the pleasures of "the external senses" arise from "desire" (PA, p. 7). They are therefore "sensual" (PA, pp. 5, 114) and "voluptuous" (PA, p. 114). The "pleasures of imagination" or, interchangeably, as we

---

[34] Cf. above, p. 133.

[35] Cf. John Locke, *Essay Concerning Human Understanding*, ed. Fraser (New York, 1959), I, 142.

[36] This argument is expounded in detail and criticized in the paper referred to above, n. 4.

have noted,[37] of the inner sense, involve "no uneasiness of appetite."[38]

It is this kind of argument, I suggest, that is implicit in Addison's summary exclusion of the "pleasures of sense." Yet if these pleasures are "gross," those of understanding are—Addison uses Shaftesbury's word—"refined" (p. 324). If the understanding is, in its turn, to be excluded, it will have to be on different grounds.

Here, Addison's argument is less terse but it is still too condensed. For he advances two different considerations. They are run together, in the passage quoted above, when Addison speaks of "such a bent of thought as is necessary to our more serious employments." The point of the latter phrase is that the understanding is, in its own way, "interested." Whether it deals with philosophy, history, or science (no. 420), the understanding is "serious" because it is devoted to the acquisition of knowledge (no. 411, p. 324). There is always a purpose for the sake of which it is exercised. The exercise of imagination is, by contrast, "innocent" (p. 325). Yet this seems not to be Addison's major argument. The pleasures of the imagination, he also says, do not "require a bent of thought." As we have just seen, Addison takes the experience of beauty to be perceptual. "It is but opening the eye, and the scene enters" (p. 324). The imagination finds satisfaction in dwelling upon the ideas of color, figure, etc. One's interest is in perceiving and in that alone. But such an interest cannot possibly be fulfilled in the understanding. Here the characteristic object is not "the prospect of fields and meadows," but rather "a demonstration" (p. 324), which must be "worked out by dint of thinking" (p. 326). Addison, accordingly, opposes the pleasures of the imagination to those of understanding when he insists that the former require "very little attention of thought or application of mind" (p. 324). It is only when the process of discursive reasoning gives rise to an image that beauty can be experienced: ". . . a truth in the understanding is as it were reflected by the imagination; we are able to see something like colour and shape in a notion" (no. 421, p. 370).

I want to pause here to open a parenthesis. My thesis has been that the animating idea in Addison is "disinterestedness" and that he devotes the "Essays" to the imagination because this faculty uniquely, so he holds, can be employed disinterestedly. Whether he is right in thinking this, let us remark that there is no *inherent* or necessary connection between the concepts of "disinterestedness" and "imagination." Addison has to use empirical arguments, drawing upon the specific workings of each of the three faculties, to make his case. More generally, there is nothing in the meaning of "disinterestedness" which entails that any specific faculty can alone be under the aegis of this attitude and serve this interest.

My parenthesis is to suggest that Addison's "Essays" are typical of a great deal of modern aesthetic theory. For much of the dialectic of modern theory has revolved around the issue: Given the meaning of "disinterested-

[37] Cf. above, p. 140.
[38] Cf. above, p. 137.

ness," which faculty or which contents of awareness or which objects can alone satisfy the conditions which it specifies?

If we confine ourselves to the first fifty years of eighteenth-century British aesthetics, we find Shaftesbury, Addison, and Burke in substantial agreement over disinterestedness. Yet Shaftesbury, for the reasons given a moment ago, contends that only reason, "the diviner part," can be the avenue of aesthetic perception (II, 144), Addison singles out imagination, and Burke, sensation (pp. 45, 91, 112). Analogues in our time would be Prall ("sensuous surface"), Ducasse (emotion), and Parker (imagination). The dialectic results from the apparent limitations of these and, perhaps, of any comparable theories. Indeed, the tensions which call out dialectic are discernible not only among but even within each of the eighteenth-century theories. Shaftesbury qualifies his position by granting beauty to sensory objects, though this order of beauty is, he would have it, less "real and essential" (II, 270–271). Burke is forced to give up his thoroughgoing sensationism when he admits association into the experience of the sublime (pp. 57 ff., 130). And if Addison sticks to imagination, it is only because its meaning is "loose and uncircumscribed."[39] Since his exposition is brief and undeveloped, the stresses and strains are not displayed so extensively as they are in Shaftesbury and Burke. Yet what does or can it mean, in the passage quoted above, to have an image of "something like colour and shape"? Again, what Addison calls the "secondary pleasures of the imagination" arise from the act of comparing two ideas (no. 416, p. 319). Is such comparison the work of the imagination? Addison likens it, rather, to cognitive activity (p. 349) and, not surprisingly, he is uncertain whether a "secondary pleasure" is to be assigned to the understanding or the imagination (no. 418, p. 358).

The question which is enjoined upon us, with which I close the parenthesis, is not, Which theory of this kind will be more viable than its predecessors?, but rather, Is it necessary to have any theory of this kind, to restrict disinterested perception to a single faculty or a specific class of objects?

If, for "the pleasures of the imagination," we read "the experience of disinterested perception," then it is fair to say that the aesthetic experience, in all but name, is Addison's subject. The first of the "Essays" (no. 411) distinguishes disinterested perception from sensation and understanding. The later essays are devoted to the objects of such perception, viz., the beautiful, the sublime, and the novel (no. 412), its kinds, viz., "primary" and "secondary" (no. 416), and the ways in which it functions in the enjoyment of the various arts and of nature (nos. 414–421).

The concepts of beauty or of some specific art-form are no longer, as in earlier aesthetics,[40] foundational. The concept which organizes the field of inquiry and by reference to which, as I shall show, all of the other major concepts are defined, is now "the aesthetic." Addison claimed that his was an "entirely new . . . undertaking" because it would examine aesthetic

[39] Cf. above, p. 139.
[40] Cf. above, p. 133.

experience "at large" (no. 409, p. 321). He made good his claim. With this conceptual reconstruction, aesthetic theory takes on a greater generality and unity than it had ever possessed before.

Addison does not use the locution "fine art," but he treats together all of the arts which are now classified in this way, i.e., literature, music, and painting, sculpture and architecture (no. 416, pp. 347–9). This is a staple of modern aesthetics but, in Addison, it occurs almost for the first time in Western thought.[41] A "stature, picture, description, or sound" (no. 416, p. 349) are brought together because they all have common effects upon the imagination. Therefore the modern notion that art is "fine" when it is addressed to aesthetic perception is also prefigured in Addison. (Among the later British aestheticians, Burke speaks of "the works of imagination and the elegant arts" (p. 13); Kames says that "The fine arts are intended to entertain us, by making pleasant impressions; and, by that circumstance, are distinguished from the useful arts";[42] and Alison says of "the Fine Arts" that "The object of these arts is to produce the emotions of taste" [I, 117].

But works of art, even though, now, of all the arts, are no longer the sole concern of the theorist. Aesthetic experience "at large" includes nature (no. 414) and the sciences (nos. 420–421), so far as they are objects of disinterested perception. By contrast to traditional theory, no object is admitted to or excluded from the realm of the aesthetic because of its inherent nature.[43] It is the attitude of the percipient that is decisive: "A man of polite imagination[44] [has] a kind of property in every thing he sees: . . . he looks upon the world, as it were in another light, and discovers in it a multitude of charms, that conceal themselves from the generality of mankind" (no. 411, p. 325). Hence "almost every thing about us" can arouse a pleasure of the imagination (no. 413, p. 334). At the same time, Addison holds that things can be valuable aesthetically in different ways. He breaks away from the traditional view that "beauty" is the primary or even the sole value-category by taking sublimity and novelty to be equally important (no. 412). Thus "beauty," like "art," is subordinated logically to the position of a subclass of the aesthetic.[45] Following Addison, Burke, as we have seen,[46] pushes back the boundaries of the aesthetic to include even what is terrible and painful. This catholicity in the denotation of "aesthetic object" is still another differentiating feature of modern aesthetics, and one of the most interesting, yet it has gone strangely unremarked.

Finally, like "fine art" and "beauty," "good taste" comes to be defined by reference to disinterestedness. The "man of polite imagination" is one

[41] Cf. Kristeller, *op. cit.* (1952), 17 ff.
[42] [Henry Home], *Elements of Criticism*, 7th ed. (Edinburgh, 1788), I, 13. Cf., also, II, 431.
[43] Cf. above, p. 139.
[44] Cf. above, p. 140.
[45] The history of the concept of beauty in eighteenth-century British thought is traced in some detail in the paper referred to above, n. 26.
[46] Cf. above, p. 135.

who can look upon things without any desire for possession.[47] But for "polite imagination" we can read "good taste" or "fine taste." We have seen that "imagination" and "taste" are, for Addison, very nearly inter-changeable[48] and the respective adjectives are apposite. Thus the attitude of aesthetic perception itself becomes a necessary condition of good taste, and this too is "entirely new" in aesthetic thought.

Prof. Carritt says of Addison: ". . . to him the succeeding critics of his century owed almost everything."[49] I would make a larger claim. In taking "aesthetic perception" to be foundational to aesthetic theory, and in the conceptual structure which they elaborate on the basis of it, the "Essays on the Pleasures of the Imagination" constitute the starting-point of modern aesthetics.

---

[47] Cf. above, p. 140.
[48] Cf. above, p. 140.
[49] E. F. Carritt, "Addison, Kant, and Wordsworth," in *Essays and Studies of the English Association*, XXII (Oxford, 1937), p. 27.

Peter Kivy

RECENT SCHOLARSHIP AND THE
BRITISH TRADITION:
A LOGIC OF TASTE
—THE FIRST FIFTY YEARS

". . . the logic of Taste, if I may be allowed the expression . . ."

Edmund Burke

(1) A Logic of Taste?

In an obviously uncomplimentary characterization* of what he described
a few years back as "the present trend" in philosophy of science, Paul K.
Feyerabend wrote, "Take a subject that is full of unsatisfactory features,
where pseudo explanations abound and non sequiturs are the rule, and
many philosophers will point out that the subject is not so bad after all,
that it possesses a 'logic of its own' and must be judged by the standards
of this logic."[1] Shorn of its exaggeration and innuendo, this is a fairly
accurate reflection not only of recent trends in philosophy of science but
in other branches of philosophy as well, for titles which begin "The Logic
of . . ." are as common these days in philosophical journals and publishers' lists as fleas on a dog.

It is of course clear that Professor Feyerabend's rather overdrawn caricature does contain a warning that must be heeded. To defend astrology or
entrail reading on the grounds that each has a "logic of its own" and

Peter Kivy is Chairman of the Department of Philosophy at Rutgers University, New-
ark Campus. He is a leading scholar in eighteenth-century aesthetics and also writes in
a contemporary vein. *Speaking About Art* is one of his recent works.

* This essay was written for this collection and is published here for the first time.

[1] Paul K. Feyerabend, "Comments on Baker's 'The Role of Simplicity in Explanation',"
*Current Issues in the Philosophy of Science: Proceedings of Section L of the American
Association for the Advancement of Science, 1959*, Herbert Feigl and Grover Maxwell,
eds. (New York: Holt, Rinehart and Winston, 1961), p. 279.

therefore should not be judged harshly because it violates our standards of good inductive inference is, doubtless, carrying the "Logic of . . ." movement to its logically absurd conclusion. But, whether we are committing this kind of logical howler when, for instance, we insist that there is a "logic of moral discourse" or that explanations in physics and psychology may be, in some deep sense, different in kind, is not all that obvious.

So it seems to me that the discovery of what might be called a "logic of aesthetic discourse"—in other words, a "logic of taste"—is not, at least on first reflection, a foredoomed and misguided endeavor. But my subject here is not what I have discovered the logic of taste to be; rather, it is some of the kinds of things it was thought to be during a crucial period in the history of modern aesthetic theory: from the publication of Joseph Addison's paper on taste and those *On the Pleasures of the Imagination*, in 1712, to Alexander Gerard's dissertation "Of the Standard of Taste," added to the third edition of his *Essay on Taste*, in 1780. I shall not, however, be a neutral observer of these proceedings, for, if I am not entirely clear about what the logic of taste is, I have a pretty good idea of some of the things it is not. And my examination of this seminal period in the history of aesthetics is motivated not merely by historical curiosity (which is a worthwhile enough motive) but by a desire to know the answer to the question that some of the most talented men of the British Enlightenment failed to answer. How they failed is as important to me as what they said in failing.

But why begin with Addison, and why in Britain?

Most philosophers who worry about such things seem to agree that the discipline of aesthetics, as practiced by professional philosophers today, came into being in Britain early in the eighteenth century and that Addison's *Spectator* papers *On the Pleasures of the Imagination* is the inaugural work, if any single work is.[2] So part of the answer to our question is: begin with Addison because he is the beginning of the discipline to which this study is intended to contribute.

But there is more to be said than that, and it involves asking ourselves why such a contemporary-sounding phrase as "the logic of taste" should ever have been coined in the eighteenth century at all. The answer, I would suggest, is that philosophers start trying to demonstrate the logic of this or that in response to philosophical skepticism. And it is only in the presence of aesthetic skepticism that the quest for an aesthetic logic will arise as such. At other times it is simply taken for granted. It was the climate of aesthetic skepticism at the beginning of the eighteenth century which gave rise to Burke's phrase and the philosophical inquiry which it (somewhat belatedly) baptized.

I think we can, now, frame a more satisfactory justification for beginning a study of the logic of aesthetic discourse with Addison. Part of the justification is, indeed, that Addison marks the beginning of modern

[2] Jerome Stolnitz, for example, calls Addison's *On the Pleasures of the Imagination* "the starting point of modern aesthetics," in "On the Origins of 'Aesthetic Disinterestedness'," *Journal of Aesthetics and Art Criticism*, XX (1961), 143.

aesthetics, if anyone does. But we can add that necessary for a philosophically interesting theory of the logic of taste is a climate of philosophical skepticism which casts serious doubt on its possibility. Such a climate existed in the early years of the eighteenth century as never before, except perhaps in the *Ion* and the skeptical Socrates. But Plato is a plausible starting place for *anything* in philosophy. And the reasons for not *always* starting with Plato are obvious enough to permit me to pass them over in silence.

(2) *Addison: Materials for a Theory*

What, then, is Addison's account of taste? And can it really be thought of as (in Burke's phrase), a "logic" of the thing?

In his paper on taste, Addison begins by defining taste as "that faculty of the soul, which discerns the beauties of an author with pleasure, and the imperfections with dislike."[3] Hutcheson and his followers would have read "sense" for "faculty" here. But there is no evidence that Addison meant anything more by "faculty" than "ability,"[4] or, rather, a combination of an ability and a propensity, for, while we *discern* beauty with our taste, and we *discern* imperfection with it, we also enjoy the former when we discern it, and dislike the latter. And, although it seems all right to call discernment an ability, it hardly seems appropriate to talk about an ability to like or dislike or enjoy. So we may conclude that for Addison, "taste" for the beautiful is an ability to discern and a propensity for enjoying it, and, conversely, an ability to discern its absence and a propensity for disliking this lack.

So much, then, for what taste is. How do I know if I possess it? Addison offers us three tests, but I shall pass over the third as it is not, I think, of any particular interest.[5] The first is the familiar "test of time":

> If a man would know whether he is possessed of this faculty, I would have him read over the celebrated works of antiquity, which have stood the test of so many different ages and countries, or those works among the moderns which have the sanction of the politer part of our contemporaries. If, upon perusal of such writings, he does not find himself delighted in an extraordinary manner, or if, upon reading the admired passages in such authors, he finds a coldness and indifference in his thoughts, he ought to conclude, not (as is too usual among tasteless readers) that the author wants those

---

[3] *The Spectator*, Alexander Chalmers, ed. (New York: D. Appleton, 1879), vol. V, p. 20 (Paper No. 409).

[4] Stolnitz ("On the Origins of 'Aesthetic Disinterestedness'," pp. 139–140), quite rightly, I think, argues that for Addison "taste" and "imagination" are names for the same faculty; and thus the pleasure of taste for the beautiful in Paper 409 is one of the pleasures of the imagination which give Papers 411–422 their name.

[5] The third test presupposes that a thought expressed by a great writer will have a different effect on the reader than the same thought expressed by "a person of ordinary genius" (Addison, *On the Pleasures of the Imagination*, p. 21); hence, if the thoughts of great writers have the appropriate effect on me, then I know that I have taste. But what the specific nature of this effect is Addison does not make clear.

perfections which have been admired in him, but that he himself wants the faculty of discovering them.[6]

One test, then, for the presence of taste is to see if you are delighted by those works whose excellence is generally agreed upon. It is, on first reflection, an egregious example of either the *vox populi* argument (if you emphasize the reference to "so many different ages and countries") or the argument from authority (if you fix your eye on "the politer part of our contemporaries"). But more of that in a moment.

The second taste test, a refinement, really, of the first, is to determine if you are pleased with the *proper* qualities of what you are perceiving. It is no good just to be pleased, say, by Bach; you must be pleased by what he is universally admired for. Thus, the taste tester must, Addison writes, "in the second place, be very careful to observe, whether he tastes the distinguishing perfections, or, if I may be allowed to call them so, the specific qualities of the author whom he peruses; whether he is particularly pleased with Livy for his manner of telling a story, with Sallust for his entering into those internal principles of action which arise from characters and manners of the persons he describes, or with Tacitus for his displaying those outward motives of safety and interest, which give birth to the whole series of transactions which he relates."[7] In other words, we are to render unto Caesar that which is Caesar's and unto Livy that which is Livy's.

Three questions may now occur to the thoughtful reader of Addison's essay on taste. First, How do I know when I am experiencing the pleasure of taste in the beautiful? I can, after all, be reading a beautiful book, be experiencing pleasure in the reading, and yet my pleasure may be sexual pleasure, because the book is sexually arousing, or ego satisfaction, if it is a book I have written, or any number of other things. Is there any particular "feel" that pleasure in the beautiful has, that other pleasures do not? Does it have some special *quale?*

Second, What is the "excellence" in books, and other beautiful objects, that occasions the pleasure? Addison promises at the close of the paper on taste to answer this question in the succeeding papers *On the Pleasures of the Imagination.*

Third, Is there any special state of mind which renders us particularly receptive to the beautiful? For, clearly, there are states of mind that would be completely inimical either to its perception or to its enjoyment. A cutpurse, about to be drawn and quartered, is not likely to perceive or enjoy the beauty of the Twenty-third Psalm, no matter how eloquently it is rendered by the *clergyman* in attendance.

To all of these questions we can detect at least the trace of an answer in *On the Pleasures of the Imagination.* And when, with the help of a little hindsight, we combine these with what we already have in the paper on taste, the bare bones of a "logic of taste" will begin to emerge.

---

[6] Addison, *On the Pleasures of the Imagination,* pp. 20–21.
[7] Ibid., p. 21.

First, then, What is the "phenomenology" of the feeling of beauty? It is, Addison says, "an inward joy, . . . a cheerfulness and delight. . . ."[8] Not much of a description, you will say, but I am not really concerned here with its adequacy—merely that a description is attempted at all, for it is the logical structure of Addison's theory that concerns me, not the details of its working out.

Second, What is it in objects that causes us to feel this "inward joy," this peculiar "cheerfulness and delight?" Here we must recognize a division of beauties into three kinds: (1) The beauty that creatures perceive in members of their own species, which is caused, Addison tells us, by "several modifications of matter which the mind, without any previous consideration, pronounces at first sight beautiful or deformed."[9] (2) The "beauty that we find in the several productions of art and nature," which "consists either in the gaiety or variety of colours, in the symmetry and proportion of parts, in the arrangement and disposition of bodies, or in a just mixture and concurrence of all together."[10] (3) The beauty of resemblance, which may be the result of a work of nature resembling a work of art, or a work of art resembling a work of nature, for "the productions of nature rise in value according as they more or less resemble those of art . . . ," and "artificial works receive a greater advantage from their resemblance of such as are natural. . . ."[11]

Third, What is the optimal state of the perceivers of beauty? What renders them most receptive? We enter dangerous territory here. But it is territory that has been explored carefully before, and I am not so much interested in a detailed map as merely the general lie of the land. Briefly, then, there is a doctrine, familiar to philosophers of art, called the doctrine of "aesthetic disinterestedness." It has existed in various forms, it is still alive (but not so well as it used to be), and it holds that there is a special attitude of disengagement from practical concerns, which has as its ultimate result the perception of aesthetic "qualities."[12]

There are at least two forms that the doctrine might take as regards what happens when we assume the aesthetic attitude of disinterestedness. It might be that in taking the attitude we make ourselves receptive to aesthetic qualities, or that in taking the attitude we (one way or another) "transform" the ordinary qualities of the world into aesthetic ones. I take it that Addison, and the others with whom we will be concerned here, held the former version of the doctrine, namely, that there is an attitude which

---

[8] Ibid., p. 36 (Paper No. 412).
[9] Ibid.
[10] Ibid., pp. 37–38.
[11] Ibid., p. 47 (Paper No. 414).
[12] If Professor Stolnitz is right, the doctrine originates in Shaftesbury. See his "On the Significance of Lord Shaftesbury in Modern Aesthetic Theory," *Philosophical Quarterly*, XI (1961). If George Dickie is right, the British version of the doctrine in the eighteenth century was more markedly different from the modern version than Professor Stolnitz makes out. See Professor Dickie's "Taste and attitude: the origin of the aesthetic," *Theoria*, XXXIX (1973). I have purposely kept my statement of the doctrine as vague as intelligibility permits in order to avoid a philosophical detour so extensive that we will never get back to the subject at hand.

renders us receptive to the perception of aesthetic qualities. In Addison's case it is an attitude in which the demands of the understanding are put aside so that the pleasures of taste, which are pleasures of perception, may be experienced unimpeded.[13] By such means "A man of polite imagination is let into a great many pleasures that the vulgar are not capable of receiving."[14] The pleasure of beauty is one of this number.

To put these pieces together into a "logic of taste" was not in Addison's nature to do, and to seek it in the *Spectator* would be like looking for a metaphysical treatise in "Talk of the Town."[15] But two thinkers more systematic than Addison, Francis Hutcheson and David Hume, did fashion a "logic" of aesthetic discourse, the materials of which, I would argue, were waiting to be synthesized in Addison's papers. We have these materials before us. Let us see how they can be manipulated.

Addison begins, as we have seen, with the "test of time": if we are pleased with what has pleased our ancestors, then our taste is sound. It is an obvious appeal to authority, for, clearly, when Addison talks about what has continued to please since antiquity, he is talking about what has pleased the people worth pleasing. And it takes no Doctor of Subtleties to see that such an argument is not going to satisfy the aesthetic skeptic. If you tell him that he proves his taste by comparing it with someone else's, he will surely want to know how *that* person's taste is to be proved, and we will clearly be in danger of either begging the question or being drawn into an infinite regress.

But with a little jostling, the appeal to authority can become something much more philosophically respectable: the appeal to some kind of ideal observer or normal perceiver. When the oculist tests your eyes, after all, he is proving them against what others have perceived in the past. But it is not an argument from authority: he is not committing an elementary logical fallacy.

Suppose, then, that there are seeds of an appeal to the normal or ideal aesthetic perceiver in Addison. What more is needed for us to have a reasonably complete perceptual model of aesthetic value judgment? And do we find it in Addison?

Well, besides our oculist having the notion of a normal or ideal perceiver, he has, of course, a rather sophisticated theory of what happens when, for example, his subject sees (or fails to see) the color red. Part of that theory is a specification of those properties that cause his subject to perceive colors. And Addison has, as we have seen, a theory about what causes us to feel the pleasure of beauty. Our oculist must also assume that his subject knows the sensation of redness when he has it, and Addison provides us with a description that enables us to identify the pleasure of beauty. (Of course the sensation of redness, unlike the feeling of beauty in Addison's papers, is simple, and hence no description of it is possible.) But even if there is a red object before my eyes, and I am a normal or

---

[13] Following Stolnitz, "On the Origins of 'Aesthetic Disinterestedness'," pp. 139–143.
[14] Addison, *On the Pleasures of the Imagination*, p. 31 (Paper No. 411).
[15] I am speaking of it as in the days of Ross. Today, likely as not, you *would* find one.

ideal perceiver, I may still fail to see the red; sufficient conditions for the perception of color must prevail. And here too we can find an analogue in Addison, in the notion of the aesthetic attitude. It can be seen as the condition under which the normal aesthetic perceiver will experience the pleasure of beauty when the proper object is being attended to.

So we have, in Addison's *On the Pleasures of the Imagination*, the building blocks for a logic of taste, using, as its model, the logic of perceptual judgments such as "X is red." What is required is the philosophical mortar to assemble them into a viable structure. That mortar was supplied by Hutcheson and Hume who, each in his own way, constructed a perceptual "logic of taste."

(3) Hutcheson and Hume:
Taste as Perception

If Addison's *On the Pleasures of the Imagination* marks the beginning of modern aesthetic theory, Francis Hutcheson's *Inquiry Concerning Beauty, Order, Harmony, Design* is the first milestone—the first systematic philosophical treatise.[16] That Hutcheson's logic of taste embodies a perceptual model hardly requires stating, for, although he did not coin the phrase "sense of beauty," and he was not the first to make philosophical use of it, he made it so much his own that his age and his century thought of him as the founder of the tradition which it named. But, whereas Hutcheson had the logic of sense perception in mind when he explicated the logic of taste, he by no means thought that "X is beautiful" could be analyzed point for point as (for example) "X is red" could.

To take the most obvious (but by no means trivial) difference, the oculist can examine my organs of sight for physical defects, but the critic cannot examine my sense of beauty in any closely analogous way. So to say that Hutcheson utilized a perceptual model for his analysis of aesthetic value judgments is to say that he thought of them as crucially similar to perceptual judgments, not that he was foolish enough to think them identical. Our task, then, is to extract Hutcheson's analysis of "X is beautiful," keeping in mind the rough outline of the perceptual model which we distilled from Addison, the main characteristics being (1) an identifiable sensation of the beautiful, (2) an identifiable cause of the sensation, (3) an ideal or normal perceiver of the sensation, and (4) the conditions under which the cause of the sensation produces it in the ideal or normal perceiver.

The crucial passage for any analysis of Hutcheson on aesthetic discourse

---

[16] This is the first of two treatises (the second being *An Inquiry Concerning Moral Good and Evil*) which Hutcheson published together under the title, *Inquiry into the Original of our Ideas of Beauty and Virtue*. It went through four editions during his lifetime, all under his supervision: 1725, 1726, 1729, 1738.

begins, "the word *beauty* is taken for *the idea raised in us.* . . ."[17] We can immediately conclude from this statement that when I assert that something is beautiful, I am, to begin with, either *describing* or *expressing* a feeling or idea of beauty. This part of the meaning of "X is beautiful" I call the "feeling moment," and it is this I first want to isolate.

The content of the feeling moment of "X is beautiful" may have reference either to the speaker's feeling or to the feeling of some other individual (the ideal observer) or group of individuals (the majority of normal observers). If it is the first, we would be giving a first person interpretation of the feeling moment; if the second, a third person interpretation. The first person interpretation can be understood in either a cognitive or a noncognitive way. In the cognitive interpretation, "X is beautiful" is thought to describe the state of mind of the speaker and, hence, is true or false, depending upon the accuracy or inaccuracy of the description. In the noncognitivist interpretation, however, "X is beautiful" is thought to express or evince and not describe the state of mind of the speaker and, hence, cannot be true or false.

Suppose now, for the sake of argument, that we opt for a first person interpretation. Are we to choose the cognitive or the noncognitive variety? I shall argue here for a cognitive analysis on the grounds that it is the only one Hutcheson's underlying commitments would allow. And, although this is not the place to raise the question, I think that similar considerations rule out recent attempts to prove that Hutcheson was an ethical noncognitivist.[18]

In a passage which closely parallels Locke's account of language in Book III of the *Essay Concerning Human Understanding*, Hutcheson pretty much closes the door on any noncognitive linguistic expressions. He writes

we know that by custom words or sounds are made signs of ideas and combinations of words signs of judgments. We know that men generally by words express their sentiments and profess to speak, as far as they know, according to what is matter of fact, so that their profession is to speak the truth.[19]

Bearing in mind that in this context to "express" one's "sentiments" means to express one's opinions, we can summarize Hutcheson's account of language as follows: (1) Words signify ideas. (2) Sentences (i.e., "combina-

---

[17] Francis Hutcheson, *Inquiry Concerning Beauty, Order, Harmony, Design*, Peter Kivy, ed. (The Hague: Martinus Nijhoff, 1973), p. 34. The text quoted in the present paper is always that of the first edition (1725). For a more detailed and comprehensive account of Hutcheson's views, along similar lines, see my *The Seventh Sense: A Study of Francis Hutcheson's Aesthetics, and its Influence in Eighteenth-Century Britain* (New York: Lenox Hill, forthcoming), Chapters II–IV.

[18] William Frankena, "Hutcheson's Moral Sense Theory," *Journal of the History of Ideas*, XVI (1955); William T. Blackstone, *Francis Hutcheson and Contemporary Ethical Theory* (Athens, Ga.: Univ. of Georgia Press, 1965); Bernard Peach, ed., *Francis Hutcheson: Illustrations on the Moral Sense* (Cambridge, Mass.: Harvard Univ. Press, 1971).

[19] *Letters Between the Late Mr. Gilbert Burnet and Mr. Hutcheson Concerning the True Foundation of Virtue or Moral Goodness* (1735), reprinted in Peach, Ibid., p. 212.

tions of words") signify judgments. (3) Judgments are made by men to convey matters of fact and, hence, are either true or false. There is, then, no room in Hutcheson's account of language for expressions of an non-cognitive kind. All linguistic utterances are utterances either of truth or falsity. And what *we* would construe as linguistic expressions of emotion could only be construed by Hutcheson as statements about emotions, true or false as the case might be. If this is a correct characterization of Hutcheson's linguistic views, a noncognitive interpretation of his aesthetics is simply out of the question.

If we opt for a first person analysis, then, we are committed to a cognitive analysis of the feeling moment of "X is beautiful," and the next order of business is to decide between a first person and a third person analysis. This decision is complicated additionally by a further distinction that we must make between the idea of beauty as "occurrent" or as "dispositional,"[20] for, when we ascribe the idea of beauty to ourselves or others in the statement "X is beautiful," we may mean that the idea is presently being experienced by ourselves or others, or that we or others have a disposition to experience it under appropriate conditions. I would interpret Hutcheson as giving a first person analysis since, unlike Hume, he does not suggest that beauty be defined in terms of a concensus of feelings. And I would further suggest that it is a dispositional account, thus allowing for the instances in which Hutcheson is clearly talking about objects being beautiful although unperceived.

The feeling moment of "X is beautiful" can be interpreted, then, as "I have the feeling of beauty whenever contemplating X." But now two further questions press themselves upon us: As in the case of Addison, we will want to know what it is that distinguishes the feeling of beauty from the other pleasurable feelings we might experience in the perception of X. And we will want to know, as well, what else there is to the assertion "X is beautiful" besides the feeling moment.

In answer to the first question, two responses seem plausible on first reflection: that the idea of beauty is identified by its cause, or by its peculiar subjective "feel."

Hutcheson, as is well known, believed that the idea of beauty is raised by a complex quality which he called *uniformity amidst variety*. Thus the possibility immediately suggests itself that I recognize the idea of beauty by identifying it as a pleasurable feeling caused by uniformity amidst variety. This does not, however, seem to be the answer Hutcheson intends, for we can know that X is beautiful, in Hutcheson's view, without first knowing that the cause of the feeling of beauty is uniformity amidst variety: "We may have the sensation without knowing what is the occasion of it," Hutcheson writes, "as a man's taste may suggest ideas of sweets, acids, bitters, though he be ignorant of the forms of the small bodies, or their motions, which excite these perceptions in him,"[21] the implication

---

[20] See C. D. Broad, "Some Reflections on Moral-Sense Theories in Ethics," *Proceedings of the Aristotelian Society*, XLV (1944–45).

[21] Hutcheson, *Inquiry Concerning Beauty*, p. 47.

being here, clearly, that we can identify the sensation of beauty without knowing that uniformity amidst variety is its cause.

What Hutcheson seems to be maintaining, rather, is that the sensation of beauty is identified by some felt quality of the sensation itself. Thus he writes on one occasion that "this pleasure of beauty . . . is distinct from that *joy* which arises upon prospect of advantage."[22] I would suggest the passage be understood in this way. The pleasure of beauty has a distinctly different feel—a different "taste," if you will—from another pleasure, "joy," which is experienced in perceiving objects from the practical point of view, rather than simply for their own sake. This attitude, which is, of course, Hutcheson's version of the attitude of "aesthetic disinterestedness," renders us susceptible of receiving a particular kind of pleasure, namely, the pleasure of beauty, upon perceiving objects with uniformity amidst variety —the latter being construed as the cause of the former.

Let us return now to the analysis of "X is beautiful," and to the problem of determining what further content besides the feeling moment it reveals. I do not believe it reveals anything further. It is Hutcheson's view that those objects giving rise to the idea of beauty are by and large those in which there is *uniformity amidst variety*, a conclusion, I presume, reached by inductive inference and stated as a causal law. However, this does not imply that when we assert that "X is beautiful," we are asserting anything about uniformity amidst variety. The connection between the idea of beauty and uniformity amidst variety is a contingent one. Just as I can know that fire engines are red without having a theory of perception, so too I can know that something is beautiful without knowing that the idea of beauty is caused by uniformity amidst variety. And the fact that I assert "X is beautiful" when X lacks uniformity amidst variety does not mean that I have made a mistake—only that I differ from the normal. There is, to be sure, an elaborate explanation, on Hutcheson's view, as to *why* such deviations occur, relying heavily on the principle of the association of ideas. But the details of this explanation cast no further light on Hutcheson's logic of taste.

The time perhaps is late for a refutation of Hutcheson's aesthetic sense doctrine, for, although individual insights of value may remain, no one, I expect, will be tempted to adopt Hutcheson's system as a plausible account of an aesthetic experience. Thus, extended criticism is scarcely needed here. But just as certain of Hutcheson's isolated remarks point in promising directions, so certain of his mistakes prove instructive; both serve as a warning to contemporary workers in the field, and in helping us understand the advance made by Hume in dealing with the problem of taste. Let me briefly touch on two such mistakes before leaving Hutcheson for his more illustrious contemporary. The two mistakes, as we shall see, are closely related.

Hutcheson's logic of taste, I have argued, is derived from a perceptual model. His emphasis lies heavily on the property which causes us to have

---

[22] Ibid., p. 37.

the sensation of beauty. And one element of the model, although available to Hutcheson in Addison's seminal reflections, is completely lacking, namely, the notion of an ideal or normal aesthetic perceiver.

The property itself, *uniformity amidst variety*, strikes us, on first reflection, as an entirely relevant one. But the way Hutcheson deals with it seems perverse. For we do not imagine ourselves, I would think, adducing the presence of *uniformity amidst variety* as part of a *causal explanation* of our aesthetic feelings. Rather, its presence is adduced as a *reason* for making a particular aesthetic judgment. When I say "It is beautiful because it has *uniformity amidst variety*," the "because" is not a causal one (as in "He died because his kidneys failed") but rather a justificatory one (as in "It is right because it will benefit mankind"). It is not a causal theory that is wanted here. And although Hutcheson has certainly provided us with *one* of the criteria for aesthetic merit, he has presented it in the completely unacceptable role of a causal property with which we (often unknowingly) interact, rather than an aesthetic feature which we perceive and adduce in defending our aesthetic judgments.

This leads us directly to the second of Hutcheson's mistakes, namely, the lack of a qualified aesthetic observer, for it is this concept that would, in the perceptual model, bear the weight of the standard of correctness and incorrectness that Hutcheson's theory essentially ignores. A causal theory such as Hutcheson is giving can provide criteria of taste only if there is some ideal or normal perceiver to serve as the standard against which our success or failure to causally interact with objects of aesthetic perception can be measured and evaluated. I do not think such a theory will work for aesthetics, even if this missing link is put in, but without it the theory is doomed from the start. In the absence of such a standard, our successes and failures can deviate from the normal but not from the correct.[23] It is this issue that Hume saw far more clearly than did Hutcheson, as is evidenced by the fact that his emphasis was in just the opposite direction: on the qualified observer and away from the possible cause of the sensation of beauty.

Hume, who, by his own admission, found close affinities with Hutcheson, produced in his essay "Of the Standard of Taste" the most mature aesthetic document to come out of the British Enlightenment, and one of the few real masterpieces of which the philosophy of art can boast. Beneath its mask of easy-going literary charm lies a solid philosophical core that can sustain close and critical scrutiny. The task Hume set himself was to steer a safe course between an out-and-out aesthetic relativism and a rigid aesthetic rationalism, neither of which he thought tenable. The problem is still with us, and Hume's answer still worth the trouble of considering.

It is clear from the way Hume introduces the problem of taste that he

---

[23] See Carolyn Wilker Korsmeyer, "Relativism and Hutcheson's Aesthetic Theory," *Journal of the History of Ideas*, XXXVI (1975). Ms. Korsmeyer's conclusions are marred, it seems to me, by the failure to distinguish, in her discussion of the standard of taste, between the "normal" and the "correct."

cannot accept a straightforward first person analysis of "X is beautiful." Although he recognizes its prima facie plausibility, as expressed in the old adage that there is no disputing about tastes, he recognizes too that there is a counterintuition which balks at the idea of indifference in the choice between pushpin and poetry or *King Lear* and breaking crockery. Thus, although it might seem on first reflection that "the proverb has justly determined it to be fruitless to dispute concerning tastes . . . ," Hume insists nevertheless that "there is a species of common sense, which opposes it, at least serves to modify and restrain it."[24] Hume was already committed in the *Treatise of Human Nature* to the view that matters of taste are determined by feelings of pleasure or, to use the more generic term, "sentiment." The problem he faced in the essay on taste was how to escape what appeared to be the inevitable but unpalatable conclusion of this view: *de gustibus non est disputandum.*

A classic interpretation of Hume's ethics infers that Hume is maintaining that there would be general agreement in matters of morals *if* there were agreement in the relevant matters of fact which attend moral decision making and that, since all matters of fact are, at least in principle, susceptible of a rational determination, all moral disagreements are also, in principle, resolvable by rational means. I believe that Hume is maintaining something like this with regard to aesthetic disputes. In questions concerning beauty and deformity, Hume is arguing, we can "translate" (so to speak) matters of sentiment into matters of fact.[25]

Now the difference between a judgment of sentiment and a "scientific" or "factual" judgment is, as Hume puts it, that in the latter "the mind does nothing but run over its objects, as they are supposed to stand in reality, without adding any thing to them, or diminishing any thing from them," whereas "In the former case, the mind is not content with merely surveying its objects, as they stand in themselves: it also feels a sentiment of delight or uneasiness, approbation or blame, consequent to that survey; and this sentiment determines it to affix the epithet *beautiful or deformed, desirable or odious.*"[26] But although a feeling of delight or uneasiness may of course arise in anyone, and perhaps license anyone, on this basis, to affirm that something *appears* to them beautiful (or deformed), it does not license them to affirm that it *is* so. For the standard of taste, according to which the reality is known from the appearance, is not established simply by anyone's feeling: as Hume remarks, "few are qualified to give judgment on any work of art, or establish their own sentiment as the standard of beauty."[27]

We may, then, analyze "X seems beautiful" in a straightforward subjectivist way as something like "I experience delight in contemplating X."

---

[24] David Hume, "Of the Standard of Taste," *Essays, Moral, Political and Literary* (Oxford Univ. Press, 1963), p. 235.

[25] I have presented a similar interpretation of Hume in a somewhat different way in "Hume's Standard of Taste: Breaking the Circle," *British Journal of Aesthetics,* VII (1967).

[26] Hume, "The Sceptic," *Essays,* pp. 166–167.

[27] Hume, "Of the Standard of Taste," *Essays,* pp. 246–247.

But when it comes to the assertion "X is beautiful," it is not my approval, or yours, but the qualified observer's that decides the case. The correct analysis of "X is beautiful" seems to be something along the lines of "X would give pleasure to the majority of qualified observers." And the question immediately arises as to how we are to determine who the qualified observers are. But as difficult as this question may be, it is, Hume claims, a more tractable one because it is a question "of fact, not sentiment." "It is sufficient for our present purpose," Hume argues, "if we have proved, that the taste of all individuals is not upon equal footing, and that some men in general, however difficult to be particularly pitched upon, will be acknowledged by universal sentiment [opinion] to have a preference above others."[28]

Whether the features that make a qualified aesthetic observer are as universally acknowledged and above controversy as Hume suggests is questionable. In any event, Hume isolates five such features as definitive of the guardians of taste: "*strong sense*, united to *delicate sentiment*, improved by *practice*, perfected by *comparison* [of one art work with another], and *cleared of all prejudice*, can alone entitle critics to this character; and the joint verdict of such, wherever they are to be found, is the true standard of taste and beauty."[29]

At this point in Hume's argument, the objection has frequently been made in the past that a vicious circle is being drawn whereby beauty is analyzed in terms of the qualified observer and the qualified observer in terms of the ability to recognize beauty. I shall not rehash this objection here[30] but, rather, press Hume on another point, namely, whether or not an attempt to establish a qualified observer is a plausible strategic move in the game Hume is playing.

If we recall once more the materials which Addison provided for a perceptual logic of taste—a means for identifying the sensation of beauty, a theory of what it is that causes the sensation, an account of what conditions are most favorable to the arousal of the sensation, and, finally, appeal to the normal or ideal perceiver—we are, I think, impressed not by how *many* of them Hume took up but, rather, how *few*. Of a "phenomenology" of the sentiment of beauty, there is not a trace, as far as I can make out, in Hume's writings. And although there are some half-hearted attempts, here and there, at isolating the quality (or qualities) in objects that give rise to the sentiment,[31] there is no real systematic effort, suggesting, I would think, Hume's low opinion of the problem's importance. The notion of "optimal conditions" does indeed play a part, but it has been conflated with the notion of the ideal or normal observer. So what becomes apparent is that Hume has put all of his aesthetic eggs in one

[28] Ibid., p. 248.
[29] Ibid., p. 247; italics mine.
[30] For a discussion of this objection, and a possible answer to it, see "Hume's Standard of Taste: Breaking the Circle," pp. 60–63.
[31] For a recent account of Hume's efforts in this direction, see William H. Halberstadt, "A Problem in Hume's Aesthetics," *Journal of Aesthetics and Art Criticism*, XXX (1971).

basket: the major operator, indeed almost the *only* operator, in Hume's philosophy of taste is the ideal aesthetic observer. The rest, he seems to be implying, does not belong in philosophy at all, and the details of its working out are irrelevant to the logical problem of the beautiful.

I think that Hume's instincts here are correct, for, as I argued previously, it is the ideal or normal observer that, in the perceptual model, transforms a causal theory of what properties generate what sensations into a *standard* which tells us what responses are correct and what ones mistaken. Having chosen the perceptual model in aesthetics, and realizing that the problem of taste was a problem of *justification,* not *explanation,* Hume had no other choice than to direct his full attention to the ideal or optimal aesthetic observer. And, if we can show that the notion of an ideal or normal aesthetic observer will not wash, we will, at a single stroke, have also shown that the logic of taste cannot be accommodated by a perceptual model.

Now I believe that there are many indications that the ideal or normal aesthetic observer cannot do for the judgment "X is beautiful" what its nonaesthetic prototype can do for "X is red." I shall confine myself here to one of these.

In a recent and influential paper called (appropriately enough) "The Logic of Aesthetic Concepts," Isabel C. Hungerland writes of the notion of the normal aesthetic observer,

> But a rebel from within, or a Philistine from without, may dispute my standards of [aesthetic] "normality." Time and again the rebel or the Philistine has partly or wholly prevailed. . . . In the end, Sensibility does not function like Sense![32]

What Mrs. Hungerland is driving at here, I think, is that there is, in aesthetic contexts, a kind of basic vulnerability about the (so-called) "normal" or "ideal" perceiver which his counterpart, say, in color perception does not have. We can reasonably dispute about whether an object is red, but not about whether a certain kind of perceiver should or should not count as normal. That is why appealing to the normal perceiver settles the question. But in the aesthetic case we are just as likely to be arguing about what kind of perceiver should be recommended or admired as what kind of object.

Should the ideal aesthetic observer be passionate or cold-blooded, emotional, or cerebral? Poet or peasant, of the elite or the masses? In the ivory tower, or in the ash can? Political or apolitical, moral or immoral? Sensitive to craftsmanship or aesthetic surface, technique or impression? Quick to judge or slow in judgment? All these are questions that have been part and parcel of the evolution of artistic and aesthetic movements and schools, just as much as have questions about the recommended aesthetic properties of works of art. We need not—and should not—conclude from this that there is no reason giving in criticism, but

[32] Isabel C. Hungerland, "The Logic of Aesthetic Concepts," *Proceedings and Addresses of the American Philosophical Association,* XXXVI (1962–63), p. 58.

what we must conclude is that the reason giving cannot consist in an appeal to a normal or ideal aesthetic perceiver. Hume was certainly right on the mark in seeing the question of taste as a question of reason giving. Where he erred was in his choice of a reason giving model. In this Mrs. Hungerland is correct. Sensibility does not function like "Sense."

(4) *Kames and Gerard: Taste as Science*

In 1759, Alexander Gerard published one of the more important and interesting aesthetic treatises of the British Enlightenment, *An Essay on Taste*. The third edition of the work (1780) contained an extended disquisition called, not very surprisingly, "Of the Standard of Taste."[33] As we have seen, Hutcheson and Hume, each in his own way, represents a development of the perceptual model of taste adumbrated by Addison. Gerard introduces a new model: the inductive one. But its seeds are already present in Addison, in his empirical predispositions; in Hutcheson and Hume, it exists as an implied part of the perceptual logic.

The pleasures of taste, according to Gerard, cannot be distinguished from one another subjectively; that is, we cannot tell simply by the felt quality of the pleasure whether it is, say, the pleasure of beauty or the pleasure of grandeur or whatever. "The gratifications of taste agree in this, that they are all pleasant; they are likewise analogous in other respects." But there are, he maintains, certain groups of qualities that produce pleasure, and an object, depending upon which group it might contain, is called "beautiful," or "grand," and so on.

> If the object which pleases us, possess uniformity, variety, and proportion, we are sure that it is beautiful. If it possess amplitude along with simplicity, we know that it is grand.[34]

Now we discover which groups of qualities please by induction: from our own experience and "from the general experience of mankind. . . ."[35] Thus,

> All objects which produce the same species of pleasure however different in other respects, have some qualities in common. It is by means of these qualities, that they produce this pleasure. It belongs to criticism to investigate and ascertain these qualities.[36]

---

[33] As the title of this paper indicates, I have wished to confine myself to the fifty-year period beginning in 1712 with Addison's *On the Pleasures of the Imagination*, which would put the 1780 edition of Gerard's work well out of range. But W. J. Hipple, who has a knack for knowing this kind of thing, assures us that the argument, and perhaps even the text itself of this edition to the original *Essay*, "had been worked out years before, at the time of discussions in the Aberdeen Philosophical Society." This could place Gerard's "Of the Standard of Taste" as early as 1758–1759, well within my purview. See Hipple's introduction to Alexander Gerard, *An Essay on Taste* (Gainsville, Fla.: Scholars' Facsimiles and Reprints, 1963), p. xxii.

[34] Gerard, *An Essay on Taste*, p. 255. The pagination of the edition cited corresponds to that of the third edition (1780).

[35] Ibid., p. 261.

[36] Ibid., p. 253.

And it is the discovery of these qualities that provides us with a standard of taste: "principles for deciding between discordant appreciations."

We can imagine the inductive process going something like this. Objects A, B, C, and D all cause Mr. Smith, Mr. Jones, Ms. Doe, and Ms. Roe to be pleased and to pronounce the objects beautiful. Objects E, F, G, and H all cause Mr. Smith, Mr. Jones, Ms. Doe, and Ms. Roe to be pleased and to pronounce the objects grand. We discover, on closer scrutiny, that objects A, B, C, and D have in common uniformity, variety, and proportion, and only those, and we find that objects E, F, G, and H have in common amplitude and simplicity, and only those. We conclude by the method of sameness that the conjunction of uniformity, variety, and proportion causes the pleasure of beauty and that the conjunction of amplitude and simplicity causes the pleasure of grandeur.[37]

It is possible at this point to enunciate two principles of taste in the form of hypothetical imperatives: (1) To cause the pleasure of beauty, make an object with uniformity, variety, and proportion. (2) To cause the pleasure of grandeur, make an object with amplitude and simplicity.

There are, to be sure, very obvious difficulties with these two induction-based imperatives. It is certain that they are not valid, and it is doubtful that any valid ones very much like them could ever be established. But let us put these scruples aside, accept the imperatives with all their crimes broad blown, and see what logical model they yield for judgments of taste.

Clearly, these practical imperatives are directed to the makers of art, not to the perceivers. And *if* such imperatives were possible, they would indeed provide a standard of "correct" and "incorrect" judgment for *them*. If, for example, the physician accepts the "end" of the hypothetical imperative, "To calm a hysteric, administer a tranquilizer," and adopts as his means the administering of caffeine, he has made a mistake. Likewise, given the validity of the practical imperative "To raise the pleasure of beauty, make objects with uniformity, variety, and proportion," I would be making a mistake if I accepted the end and adopted as my means the fashioning of objects with amplitude, and simplicity, but without uniformity, variety, and proportion.

But we are equally, if not *more* interested in the other party to taste: the perceiver of the object. And here our troubles really start. Suppose the physician administers Valium to the hysteric, and he fails to respond. Would we say that the hysteric has "made a mistake" by ignoring the valid practical imperative? No more, then, would we say that the Philistine has "made a mistake" by not responding with the pleasure of beauty when he is confronted with uniformity, variety, and proportion. If our induction is a good one, and the imperative valid, he has reacted *abnormally*— but not *incorrectly*. We believe, to be sure, that aesthetic reactions are more in our power to change than our reactions to drugs. And so we might say to the Philistine, "If you want to be *normal*, take steps to react the

---

[37] There is no reason why we cannot, in Gerard's view, use more complex inductive procedures. I choose the method of sameness, in its most primitive form, for simplicity of exposition only.

way we do to 'beautiful' objects." But the Philistine may not accept the end of normality as a particularly desirable one, and there our argument with him terminates. Normality, after all, is not, like health and happiness, an end we have a right to expect all of us share.

Lord Kames must have been well aware of this problem when he posed to himself the question, "doth it not seem whimsical, and perhaps absurd, to assert, that a man *ought not* be pleased when he is, or that he *ought* to be pleased when he is not?"[38] And as Lord Kames, by Gerard's own admission,[39] was espousing a view very similar to his own with regard to the logic of taste, it is not inappropriate to conclude these remarks on Gerard with Kames's strikingly Humean answer to his own question. (I say strikingly Humean because it is reminiscent of Hume's "retreat to psychology," best exemplified by the celebrated treatment of causality.)

Kames essentially admits that there is no rational justification for calling deviations from the normal aesthetic response "incorrect." It is indeed "whimsical" and "absurd" to do so. But we have a psychological compulsion to do so, nevertheless, just as, according to Hume, we have a psychological compulsion to expect events in the future to follow those they have followed in the past, even though there is no "rational" justification for it. So, says Kames, "my disgust is raised . . . by differing from what I judge to be the common standard [the normal]"[40]; that is, I am psychologically repelled by the abnormal, in myself as well as in anyone else: "Every remarkable deviation from the standard [the normal] is disagreeable, and raises in us a painful emotion: monstrous births, exciting the curiosity of a philosopher, fail not at the same time to excite a sort of horror."[41] And we are left, then, with a psychological explanation for why we condemn aberrant tastes as mistaken: it is to rid ourselves of a psychological irritant by negative reinforcement. But we remain without the sought-after rational justification for doing so. The inductive model, like the perceptual one, fails to reveal a proper "logic of taste" but leads, rather, to a Humean skepticism.

Where, then, do we go from here? We can, of course, accept the skeptical conclusion and give up the quest. Or we can, in the face of Feyerabend's warning, widen our notion of rationality to encompass other "logical" models. The latter alternative is today being vigorously exploited. Whether or not success lies in that direction is yet to be determined.[42]

---

[38] Henry Home, Lord Kames, *Elements of Criticism*, 6th ed. (Edinburgh, 1785), vol. II, p. 488. The first edition of Kames's influential book appeared in 1762.

[39] Gerard, *An Essay on Taste*, p. 247n.

[40] Kames (Home), *Elements of Criticism*, vol. II, p. 494.

[41] Ibid., vol. II, p. 492.

[42] An earlier version of the present paper was presented to the Columbia University Seminar on Eighteenth Century European Culture, 20 March, 1975. I am extremely grateful to all those in attendance, for a valuable and stimulating discussion, and, especially, to Professor John H. Middendorf for his encouragement. I also want to express my thanks to Professor Jack Glickman for reading and commenting on another early version of this paper.

Immanuel Kant

A THEORY OF AESTHETIC JUDG
FROM *THE CRITIQUE OF JUDGEMENT*

I

The Judgement of Taste is Aesthetic

If we wish to discern whether anything is beautiful or not, we do not refer the representation of it to the Object by means of understanding with a view to cognition, but by means of the imagination (acting perhaps in conjunction with understanding) we refer the representation to the Subject and its feeling of pleasure or displeasure.* The judgement of taste, therefore, is not a cognitive judgement, and so not logical, but is aesthetic—which means that it is one whose determining ground *cannot be other than subjective*. Every reference of representations is capable of being objective, even that of sensations (in which case it signifies the real in an empirical representation). The one exception to this is the feeling of pleasure or displeasure. This denotes nothing in the object, but is a feeling which the Subject has of itself and of the manner in which it is affected by the representation.

To apprehend a regular and appropriate building with one's cognitive faculties, be the mode of representation clear or confused, is quite a different thing from being conscious of this representation with an accompanying sensation of delight. Here the representation is referred wholly to the Subject, and what is more to its feeling of life—under the name of the feeling of pleasure or displeasure—and this forms the basis of a quite separate faculty of discriminating and estimating, that contributes nothing to knowledge. All it does is to compare the given representation in the Subject with the entire faculty of representations of which the mind is conscious in the feeling of its state. Given representations in a judgement may be empirical, and so aesthetic; but the judgement which is

Immanuel Kant (1724–1804). One of the greatest philosophers in the Western tradition, Kant's three critiques are perennial sources of philosophical scholarship and analysis. The *Critique of Pure Reason*, the *Critique of Practical Reason*, and the *Critique of Judgement* form the great trilogy of Kant's critical philosophy.

* Translated by James Creed Meredith. Selections from *The Critique of Judgment* (Oxford, 1928). Selections from Part I, Books I and II. Reprinted by permission of Oxford University Press.

onounced by their means is logical, provided it refers them to the Object. Conversely, be the given representations even rational, but referred in a judgement solely to the Subject (to its feeling), they are always to that extent aesthetic.

II

The Delight which Determines the Judgement of Taste is Independent of All Interest

The delight which we connect with the representation of the real existence of an object is called interest. Such a delight, therefore, always involves a reference to the faculty of desire, either as its determining ground, or else as necessarily implicated with its determining ground. Now, where the question is whether something is beautiful, we do not want to know, whether we, or any one else, are, or even could be, concerned in the real existence of the thing, but rather what estimate we form of it on mere contemplation (intuition or reflection). If any one asks me whether I consider that the palace I see before me is beautiful, I may, perhaps, reply that I do not care for things of that sort that are merely made to be gaped at.

.   .   .

All this may be admitted and approved; only it is not the point now at issue. All one wants to know is whether the mere representation of the object is to my liking, no matter how indifferent I may be to the real existence of the object of this representation. It is quite plain that in order to say that the object is *beautiful,* and to show that I have taste, everything turns on the meaning which I can give to this representation, and not on any factor which makes me dependent on the real existence of the object. Every one must allow that a judgement on the beautiful which is tinged with the slightest interest, is very partial and not a pure judgement of taste. One must not be in the least prepossessed in favour of the real existence of the thing, but must preserve complete indifference in this respect, in order to play the part of judge in matters of taste.

This proposition, which is of the utmost importance, cannot be better explained than by contrasting the pure disinterested delight which appears in the judgement of taste with that allied to an interest—especially if we can also assure ourselves that there are no other kinds of interest beyond those presently to be mentioned.

III

Delight in the Agreeable is Coupled with Interest

That is agreeable *which the senses find pleasing in sensation.* This at once affords a convenient opportunity for condemning and directing particular attention to a prevalent confusion of the double meaning of which the word 'sensation' is capable. All delight (as is said or thought) is itself sensation (of a pleasure). Consequently everything that pleases, and for the very reason that it pleases, is agreeable—and according to its different degrees, or its relations to other agreeable sensations, is attractive, charming, delicious, enjoyable, &c. But if this is conceded, then impressions of sense, which determine inclination, or principles of reason, which determine the will, or mere contemplated forms of intuition, which determine judgement, are all on a par in everything relevant to their effect upon the feeling of pleasure, for this would be agreeableness in the sensation of one's state; and since, in the last resort, all the elaborate work of our faculties must issue in and unite in the practical as its goal, we could credit our faculties with no other appreciation of things and the worth of things, than that consisting in the gratification which they promise. How this is attained is in the end immaterial; and, as the choice of the means is here the only thing that can make a difference, men might indeed blame one another for folly or imprudence, but never for baseness or wickedness; for they are all, each according to his own way of looking at things, pursuing one goal, which for each is the gratification in question.

When a modification of the feeling of pleasure or displeasure is termed sensation, this expression is given quite a different meaning to that which it bears when I call the representation of a thing (through sense as a receptivity pertaining to the faculty of knowledge) sensation. For in the latter case the representation is referred to the Object, but in the former it is referred solely to the Subject and is not available for any cognition, not even for that by which the Subject *cognizes* itself.

Now in the above definition the word sensation is used to denote an objective representation of sense; and, to avoid continually running the risk of misinterpretation, we shall call that which must always remain purely subjective, and is absolutely incapable of forming a representation of an object, by the familiar name of feeling. The green colour of the meadows belongs to *objective* sensation, as the perception of an object of sense; but its agreeableness to *subjective* sensation, by which no object is represented: i.e. to feeling, through which the object is regarded as an Object of delight (which involves no cognition of the object).

Now, that a judgement on an object by which its agreeableness is affirmed, expresses an interest in it, is evident from the fact that through sensation it provokes a desire for similar objects, consequently the delight presupposes, not the simple judgement about it, but the bearing its real existence has upon my state so far as affected by such an Object. Hence we do not merely say of the agreeable that it *pleases*, but that it *gratifies*. I do not accord it a simple approval, but inclination is aroused by it, and where agreeableness is of the liveliest type a judgement on the character of the Object is so entirely out of place, that those who are always intent only on enjoyment (for that is the word used to denote intensity of gratification) would fain dispense with all judgement.

IV

Delight in the Good is Coupled with Interest

That is *good* which by means of reason commends itself by its mere concept. We call that *good for something* (useful) which only pleases as a means; but that which pleases on its own account we call *good in itself*. In both cases the concept of an end is implied, and consequently the relation of reason to (at least possible) willing, and thus a delight in the *existence* of an Object or action, i.e. some interest or other.

To deem something good, I must always know what sort of a thing the object is intended to be, i.e. I must have a concept of it. That is not necessary to enable me to see beauty in a thing. Flowers, free patterns, lines aimlessly intertwining—technically termed foliage,—have no signification, depend upon no definite concept, and yet please. Delight in the beautiful must depend upon the reflection on an object precursory to some (not definitely determined) concept. It is thus also differentiated from the agreeable, which rests entirely upon sensation.

In many cases, no doubt, the agreeable and the good seem convertible terms. Thus it is commonly said that all (especially lasting) gratification is of itself good; which is almost equivalent to saying that to be permanently agreeable and to be good are identical. But it is readily apparent that this is merely a vicious confusion of words, for the concepts appropriate to these expressions are far from interchangeable. The agreeable, which, as such, represents the object solely in relation to sense, must in the first instance be brought under principles of reason through the concept of an end, to be, as an object of will, called good. But that the reference to delight is wholly different where what gratifies is at the same time called *good*, is evident from the fact that with the good the question always is whether it is mediately or immediately good, i.e. useful or good in itself; whereas with the agreeable this point can never arise, since the word always means what pleases immediately—and it is just the same with what I call beautiful.

· · ·

V

Comparison of the Three Specifically Different Kinds of Delight

Both the Agreeable and the Good involve a reference to the faculty of desire, and are thus attended, the former with a delight pathologically conditioned (by stimuli), the latter with a pure practical delight. Such delight is determined not merely by the representation of the object, but also by the represented bond of connexion between the Subject and the real existence of the object. It is not merely the object, but also its real existence, that pleases. On the other hand the judgement of taste is simply *contemplative*, i.e. it is a judgement which is indifferent as to the existence of an object, and only decides how its character stands with the feeling of pleasure and displeasure. But not even is this contemplation itself directed to concepts; for the judgement of taste is not a cognitive judgement (neither a theoretical one nor a practical), and hence, also, is not *grounded* on concepts, nor yet *intentionally directed* to them.

The agreeable, the beautiful, and the good thus denote three different relations of representations to the feeling of pleasure and displeasure, as a feeling in respect of which we distinguish different objects or modes of representation. Also, the corresponding expressions which indicate our satisfaction in them are different. The *agreeable* is what GRATIFIES a man; the *beautiful* what simply PLEASES him; the *good* what is ESTEEMED (*approved*), i.e. that on which he sets an objective worth. Agreeableness is a significant factor even with irrational animals; beauty has purport and significance only for human beings, i.e. for beings at once animal and rational (but not merely for them as rational—intelligent beings—but only for them as at once animal and rational); whereas the good is good for every rational being in general;—a proposition which can only receive its complete justification and explanation in the sequel. Of all these three kinds of delight, that of taste in the beautiful may be said to be the one and only disinterested and *free* delight; for, what it, no interest, whether of sense or reason, extorts approval. And so we may say that delight, in the three cases mentioned, is related to *inclination*, to *favour*, or to *respect*. For FAVOUR is the only free liking. An object of inclination, and one which a law of reason imposes upon our desire, leaves us no freedom to turn anything into an object of pleasure. All interest presupposes a want, or calls one forth; and, being a ground determining approval, deprives the judgement on the object of its freedom.

. . .

DEFINITION OF THE BEAUTIFUL DERIVED FROM THE FIRST MOMENT

Taste is the faculty of estimating an object or a mode of representation by means of a delight or aversion *apart from any interest*. The object of such a delight is called *beautiful*.

. . .

VI

The Beautiful is that which, apart from Concepts, is Represented as the Object of a Universal Delight

This definition of the beautiful is deducible from the foregoing definition of it as an object of delight apart from any interest. For where any one is conscious that his delight in an object is with him independent of interest, it is inevitable that he should look on the object as one containing a ground of delight for all men. For, since the delight is not based on any inclination of the Subject (or on any other deliberate interest), but the Subject feels himself completely *free* in respect of the liking which he accords to the object, he can find as reason for his delight no personal conditions to which his own subjective self might alone be party. Hence he must regard it as resting on what he may also presuppose in every other person; and therefore he must believe that he has reason for demanding a similar delight from everyone. Accordingly he will speak of the beautiful as if beauty were a quality of the object and the judgement logical (forming a cognition of the Object by concepts of it); although it is only aesthetic, and contains merely a reference of the representation of the object to the Subject;—because it still bears this resemblance to the logical judgement, that it may be presupposed to be valid for all men. But this universality cannot spring from concepts. For from concepts there is no transition to the feeling of pleasure or displeasure (save in the case of pure practical laws, which, however, carry an interest with them; and such an interest does not attach to the pure judgement of taste). The result is that the judgement of taste, with its attendant consciousness of detachment from all interest, must involve a claim to validity for all men, and must do so apart from universality attached to Objects, i.e. there must be coupled with it a claim to subjective universality.

VII

Comparison of the Beautiful with the Agreeable and the Good by means of the above Characteristic

As regards the *agreeable* every one concedes that his judgement, which he bases on a private feeling, and in which he declares that an object pleases him, is restricted merely to himself personally. Thus he does not take it amiss if, when he says that Canary-wine is agreeable, another corrects the expression and reminds him that he ought to say: It is agreeable *to me*. This applies not only to the taste of the tongue, the palate, and the throat, but to what may with any one be agreeable to eye or ear. A violet colour is to one soft and lovely: to another dull and faded.

. . .

With the agreeable, therefore, the axiom holds good: *Every one has his own taste* (that of sense).

The beautiful stands on quite a different footing. It would, on the contrary, be ridiculous if any one who plumed himself on his taste were to think of justifying himself by saying: This object (the building we see, the dress that person has on, the concert we hear, the poem submitted to our criticism) is beautiful *for me*. For if it merely pleases *him*, he must not call it *beautiful*. Many things may for him possess charm and agreeableness—no one cares about that; but when he puts a thing on a pedestal and calls it beautiful, he demands the same delight from others. He judges not merely for himself, but for all men, and then speaks of beauty as if it were a property of things. Thus he says the *thing* is beautiful; and it is not as if he counted on others agreeing in his judgement of liking owing to his ʻhaving found them in such agreement on a number of occasions, but he *demands* this agreement of them. He blames them if they judge differently, and denies them taste, which he still requires of them as something they ought to have; and to this extent it is not open to men to say: Every one has his own taste. This would be equivalent to saying that there is no such thing at all as taste, i.e. no aesthetic judgement capable of making a rightful claim upon the assent of all men.

Yet even in the case of the agreeable we find that the estimates men form do betray a prevalent agreement among them, which leads to our crediting some with taste and denying it to others, and that, too, not as an organic sense but as a critical faculty in respect of the agreeable generally. So of one who knows how to entertain his guests with pleasures (of enjoyment through all the senses) in such a way that one and all are pleased, we say that he has taste. But the universality here is only understood in a comparative sense; and the rules that apply are, like all empirical rules, *general* only, not *universal*,—the latter being what the judgement of taste upon the beautiful deals or claims to deal in. It is a judgement in respect of sociability so far as resting on empirical rules. In respect of the good it is true that judgements also rightly assert a claim to validity for every one; but the good is only represented as an Object of universal delight *by means of a concept*, which is the case neither with the agreeable nor the beautiful.

VIII

In a Judgement of Taste the Universality of Delight is only Represented as Subjective

. . .

First of all we have here to note that a universality which does not rest upon concepts of the Object (even though these are only empirical) is in no way logical, but aesthetic, i.e. does not involve any objective quantity of the judgement, but only one that is subjective. For this universality I use the expression *general validity*, which denotes the validity of the reference of a representation, not to the cognitive faculties, but to the feeling of pleasure or displeasure for every Subject. (The same expression, however, may also be employed for the logical quantity of the judgement, provided we add *objective* universal validity, to distinguish it from the merely subjective validity which is always aesthetic.)

Now a judgement that has *objective universal validity* has always got the subjective also, i.e. if the judgement is valid for everything which is contained under a given concept, it is valid also for all who represent an object by means of this concept. But from a *subjective universal validity*, i.e. the aesthetic, that does not rest on any concept, no conclusion can be drawn to the logical; because judgements of that kind have no bearing upon the Object. But for this very reason the aesthetic universality attributed to a judgement must also be of a special kind, seeing that it does not join the predicate of beauty to the concept of the *Object* taken in its entire logical sphere, and yet does extend this predicate over the whole sphere of *judging Subjects*.

In their logical quantity all judgements of taste are *singular* judgements. For, since I must present the object immediately to my feeling of pleasure or displeasure, and that, too, without the aid of concepts, such judgements cannot have the quantity of judgements with objective general validity. Yet by taking the singular representation of the Object of the judgement of taste, and by comparison converting it into a concept according to the conditions determining that judgement, we can arrive at a logically universal judgement. For instance, by a judgement of taste I describe the rose at which I am looking as beautiful. The judgement, on the other hand, resulting from the comparison of a number of singular representations: Roses in general are beautiful, is no longer pronounced as a purely aesthetic judgement, but as a logical judgement founded on one that is aesthetic. Now the judgement, 'The rose is agreeable' (to smell) is also, no doubt, an aesthetic and singular judgement, but then it is not one of taste but of sense. For it has this point of difference from a judgement of taste, that the latter imports an *aesthetic quantity* of universality, i.e. of validity for every one which is not to be met with in a judgement upon the agreeable. It is only judgements upon the good which, while also determining the delight in an object, possess logical and not mere aesthetic universality; for it is as involving a cognition of the Object that they are valid of it, and on that account valid for every one.

In forming an estimate of Objects merely from concepts, all representation of beauty goes by the board. There can, therefore, be no rule according to which any one is to be compelled to recognize anything as beautiful. Whether a dress, a house, or a flower is beautiful is a matter upon which one declines to allow one's judgement to be swayed by any reasons or principles. We want to get a look at the Object with our own eyes, just as if our delight depended on sensation. And yet, if upon so doing, we call the object beautiful, we believe ourselves to be speaking with a universal voice, and lay claim to the concurrence of every one, whereas no private sensation would be decisive except for the observer alone and *his* liking.

Here, now, we may perceive that nothing is postulated in the judgement of taste but such a *universal voice* in respect of delight that is not mediated by concepts; consequently, only the *possibility* of an aesthetic judgement capable of being at the same time deemed valid for every one. The judgement of taste itself does not *postulate* the agreement of every one (for it is only competent for a logically universal judgement to do this, in that it is able to bring forward reasons); it only *imputes* this agreement to every one, as an instance of the rule in respect of which it looks for confirmation, not from concepts, but from the concurrence of others. The universal voice is, therefore, only an idea—resting upon grounds the investigation of which is here postponed.

. . .

IX

Investigation of the Question of the Relative Priority in a Judgement of Taste of the Feeling of Pleasure and the Estimating of the Object

The solution of this problem is the key to the Critique of taste, and so is worthy of all attention.

Were the pleasure in a given object to be the antecedent, and were the universal communicability of this pleasure to be all that the judgement of taste is meant to allow to the representation of the object, such a sequence would be selfcontradictory. For a pleasure of that kind would be nothing but the feeling of mere agreeableness to the senses, and so, from its very nature, would possess no more than private validity, seeing that it would be immediately dependent on the representation through which the object *is given.*

Hence it is the universal capacity for being communicated incident to the mental state in the given representation which, as the subjective condition of the judgement of taste, must be fundamental, with the pleasure in the object as its consequent. Nothing, however, is capable of being universally communicated but cognition and representation so far as appurtenant to cognition. For it is only as thus appurtenant that the representation is objective, and it is this alone that gives it a universal point of reference with which the power of representation of every one is obliged to harmonize. If, then, the determining ground of the judgement as to this universal communicability of the representation is to be merely subjective, that is to say, is to be conceived independently of any concept of the object, it can be nothing else than the mental state that presents itself in the mutual relation of the powers of representation so far as they refer a given representation *to cognition in general.*

The cognitive powers brought into play by this representation are here engaged in a free play, since no definite concept restricts them to a particular rule of cognition. Hence the mental state in this representation must be one of a feeling of the free play of the powers of representation in a given representation for a cognition in general. Now a representation, whereby an object is given, involves, in order that it may become a source of cognition at all, *imagination* for bringing together the manifold of intuition, and *understanding* for the unity of the concept uniting the representations. This state of *free play* of the cognitive faculties attending a representation by which an object is given must admit of universal communication: because cognition, as a definition of the Object with which given representations (in any Subject whatever) are to accord, is the one and only representation which is valid for every one.

As the subjective universal communicability of the mode of representation in a judgement of taste is to subsist apart from the presupposition of any definite concept, it can be nothing else than the mental state present in the free play of imagination and understanding (so far as these are in mutual accord, as is requisite for *cognition in general*): for we are conscious that this subjective relation suitable for a cognition in general must be just as valid for every one, and consequently as universally communicable, as is any determinate cognition, which always rests upon that relation as its subjective condition.

Now this purely subjective (aesthetic) estimating of the object, or of the representation through which it is given, is antecedent to the pleasure in it, and is the basis of this pleasure in the harmony of the cognitive faculties. Again, the above-described universality of the subjective conditions of estimating objects forms the sole foundation of this universal subjective validity of the delight which we connect with the representation of the object that we call beautiful.

That an ability to communicate one's mental state, even though it be only in respect of our cognitive faculties, is attended with a pleasure, is a fact which might easily be demonstrated from the natural propensity of mankind to social life, i.e. empirically and psychologically. But what we have here in view calls for something more than this. In a judgement of taste the pleasure felt by us is exacted from every one else as necessary, just as if, when we call something beautiful, beauty was to be regarded as a quality of the object forming part of its inherent determination according to concepts; although beauty is for itself, apart from any reference to the feeling of the Subject, nothing. But the discussion of this question must be reserved until we have answered the further one of whether, and how, aesthetic judgements are possible *a priori*.

At present we are exercised with the lesser question of the way in which we become conscious, in a judgement of taste, of a reciprocal subjective common accord of the powers of cognition. Is it aesthetically by sensation and our mere internal sense? Or is it intellectually by consciousness of our intentional activity in bringing these powers into play?

Now if the given representation occasioning the judgement of taste were a concept which united understanding and imagination in the estimate of the object so as to give a cognition of the Object, the consciousness of this relation would be intellectual (as in the objective schematism of judgement dealt with in the Critique). But, then, in that case the judgement would not be laid down with respect to pleasure and displeasure, and so would not be a judgement of taste. But, now, the judgement of taste determines the Object, independently of concepts, in respect of delight and of the predicate of beauty. There is, therefore, no other way for the subjective unity of the relation in question to make itself known than by sensation. The quickening of both faculties (imagination and understanding) to an indefinite, but yet, thanks to the given representation, harmonious activity, such as belongs to cognition generally, is the sensation whose universal communicability is postulated by the judgement of taste. An objective relation can, of course, only be thought, yet in so far as, in respect of its conditions, it is subjective, it may be felt in its effect upon the mind, and, in the case of a relation (like that of the powers of representation to a faculty of cognition generally) which does not rest on any concept, no other consciousness of it is possible beyond that through sensation of its effect upon the mind—an effect consisting in the more facile play of both mental powers (imagination and understanding) as quickened by their mutual accord. A representation which is singular and independent of comparison with other representations, and, being such, yet accords with the conditions of the universality that is the general concern of understanding, is one that brings the cognitive faculties into that proportionate accord which we require for all cognition and which we therefore deem valid for every one who is so constituted as to judge by means of understanding and sense conjointly (i.e. for every man).

DEFINITION OF THE BEAUTIFUL DRAWN FROM THE SECOND MOMENT

The *beautiful* is that which, apart from a concept, pleases universally.

. . .

X

Finality in General

Let us define the meaning of 'an end' in transcendental terms (i.e. without presupposing anything empirical, such as the feeling of pleasure). An end is the object of a concept so far as this concept is regarded as the cause of the object (the real ground of its possibility); and the causality of a *concept* in respect of its *Object* is finality (*forma finalis*). Where, then, not the cognition of an object merely, but the object itself (its form or real existence) as an effect, is thought to be possible only through a concept of it, there we imagine an end. The representation of the effect is here the determining ground of its cause and takes the lead of it. The consciousness of the causality of a representation in respect of the state of the Subject as one tending *to preserve a continuance* of that state, may here be said to denote in a general way what is called pleasure; whereas displeasure is that representation which contains the ground for converting the state of the representations into their opposite (for hindering or removing them).

The faculty of desire, so far as determinable only through concepts, i.e. so as to act in conformity with the representation of an end, would be the will. But an Object, or state of mind, or even an action may, although its possibility does not necessarily presuppose the representation of an end, be called final simply on account of its possibility being only explicable and intelligible for us by virtue of an assumption on our part of a fundamental causality according to ends, i.e. a will that would have so ordained it according to a certain represented rule. Finality, therefore, may exist apart from an end, in so far as we do not locate the causes of this form in a will, but yet are able to render the explanation of its possibility intelligible to ourselves only by deriving it from a will. Now we are not always obliged to look with the eye of reason into what we observe (i.e. to consider it in its possibility). So we may at least observe a finality of form, and trace it in objects—though by reflection only—without resting it on an end (as the material of the *nexus finalis*).

XI

The Sole Foundation of the Judgement of Taste is the Form of Finality of an Object (or Mode of Representing it)

Whenever an end is regarded as a source of delight it always imports an interest as determining ground of the judgement on the object of pleasure. Hence the judgement of taste cannot rest on any subjective end as its ground. But neither can any representation of an objective end, i.e. of the possibility of the object itself on principles of final connexion, determine the judgement of taste, and, consequently, neither can any concept of the good. For the judgement of taste is an aesthetic and not a cognitive judgement, and so does not deal with any *concept* of the nature or of the internal or external possibility, by this or that cause, of the object, but simply with the relative bearing of the representative powers so far as determined by a representation.

Now this relation, present when an object is characterized as beautiful, is coupled with the feeling of pleasure. This pleasure is by the judgement of taste pronounced valid for every one; hence an agreeableness attending the representation is just as incapable of containing the determining ground of the judgement as the representation of the perfection of the object or the concept of the good. We are thus left with the subjective finality in the representation of an object, exclusive of any end (objective or subjective)—consequently the bare form of finality in the representation whereby an object is *given* to us, so far as we are conscious of it—as that which is alone capable of constituting the delight which, apart from any concept, we estimate as universally communicable, and so of forming the determining ground of the judgement of taste.

·   ·   ·

XIII

The pure Judgement of Taste is Independent of Charm and Emotion

Every interest vitiates the judgement of taste and robs it of its impartiality. This is especially so where instead of, like the interest of reason, making finality take the lead of the feeling of pleasure, it grounds it upon this feeling—which is what always happen in aesthetic judgements upon anything so far as it gratifies or pains. Hence judgements so influenced can either lay no claim at all to a universally valid delight, or else must abate their claim in proportion as sensations of the kind in question enter into the determining grounds of taste. Taste that requires an added element of *charm* and *emotion* for its delight, not to speak of adopting this as the measure of its approval, has not yet emerged from barbarism.

And yet charms are frequently not alone ranked with beauty (which ought properly to be a question merely of the form) as supplementary to the aesthetic universal delight, but they have been accredited as intrinsic beauties, and consequently the matter of delight passed off for the form. This is a misconception which, like many others that have still an underlying element of truth, may be removed by a careful definition of these concepts.

A judgement of taste which is uninfluenced by charm or emotion, (though these may be associated with the delight in the beautiful,) and whose determining ground, therefore, is simply finality of form, is a *pure judgement of taste.*

XIV

Exemplification

Aesthetic, just like theoretical (logical) judgements, are divisible into empirical and pure. The first are those by which agreeableness or disagreeableness, the second those by which beauty, is predicated of an object or its mode of representation. The former are judgements of sense (material aesthetic judgements), the latter (as formal) alone judgements of taste proper.

A judgement of taste, therefore, is only pure so far as its determining ground is tainted with no merely empirical delight. But such a taint is always present where charm or emotion have a share in the judgement by which something is to be described as beautiful.

Here now there is a recrudescence of a number of specious pleas that go the length of putting forward the case that charm is not merely a necessary ingredient of beauty, but is even of itself sufficient to merit the name of beautiful. A mere colour, such as the green of a plot of grass, or a mere tone (as distinguished from sound or noise), like that of a violin, is described by most people as in itself beautiful, notwithstanding the fact that both seem to depend merely on the matter of the representations—in other words, simply on sensation, which only entitles them to be called agreeable. But it will at the same time be observed that sensations of colour as well as of tone are only entitled to be immediately regarded as beautiful where, in either case, they are *pure*. This is a determination which at once goes to their form, and it is the only one which these repre-

sentations possess that admits with certainty of being universally communicated. For it is not to be assumed that even the quality of the sensations agrees in all Subjects, and we can hardly take it for granted that the
agreeableness of a colour, or of the tone of a musical instrument, which
we judge to be preferable to that of another, is given a like preference in
the estimate of every one.

. . .

But the purity of a simple mode of sensation means that its uniformity
is not disturbed or broken by any foreign sensation. It belongs merely to
the form; for abstraction may there be made from the quality of the mode
of such sensation (what colour or tone, if any, it represents). For this
reason all simple colours are regarded as beautiful so far as pure. Composite
colours have not this advantage, because, not being simple, there is no
standard for estimating whether they should be called pure or impure.

But as for the beauty ascribed to the object on account of its form, and
the supposition that it is capable of being enhanced by charm, this is a
common error and one very prejudicial to genuine, uncorrupted, sincere
taste. Nevertheless charms may be added to beauty to lend to the mind,
beyond a bare delight, an adventitious interest in the representation of the
object, and thus to advocate taste and its cultivation. This applies especially where taste is as yet crude and untrained. But they are positively
subversive of the judgement of taste, if allowed to obtrude themselves as
grounds of estimating beauty. For so far are they from contributing to
beauty, that it is only where taste is still weak and untrained, that, like
aliens, they are admitted as a favour, and only on terms that they do not
violate that beautiful form.

In painting, sculpture, and in fact in all the formative arts, in architecture
and horticulture, so far as fine arts, the *design* is what is essential. Here it
is not what gratifies in sensation but merely what pleases by its form, that
is the fundamental prerequisite for taste. The colours which give brilliancy
to the sketch are part of the charm. They may no doubt, in their own way,
enliven the object for sensation, but make it really worth looking at
and beautiful they cannot. Indeed, more often than not the requirements
of the beautiful form restrict them to a very narrow compass, and, even
where charm is admitted, it is only this form that gives them a place
of honour.

All form of objects of sense (both of external and also, mediately, of
internal sense) is either *figure* or *play*. In the latter case it is either play
of figures (in space: mimic and dance), or mere play of sensations (in
time). The *charm* of colours, or of the agreeable tones of instruments,
may be added: but the *design* in the former and the *composition* in the
latter constitute the proper object of the pure judgement of taste. To say
that the purity alike of colours and of tones, or their variety and contrast,
seem to contribute to beauty, is by no means to imply that, because in
themselves agreeable, they therefore yield an addition to the delight in the
form and one on a par with it. The real meaning rather is that they make
this form more clearly, definitely, and completely intuitable, and besides

stimulate the representation by their charm, as they excite and sustain the attention directed to the object itself.

XV

The Judgement of Taste Is Entirely Independent of the Concept of Perfection

Objective finality can only be cognized by means of a reference of the manifold to a definite end, and hence only through a concept. This alone makes it clear that the beautiful, which is estimated on the ground of a mere formal finality, i.e. a finality apart from an end, is wholly independent of the representation of the good. For the latter presupposes an objective finality, i.e. the reference of the object to a definite end.

Objective finality is either external, i.e. the *utility*, or internal, i.e. the *perfection*, of the object. That the delight in an object on account of which we call it beautiful is incapable of resting on the representation of its utility, is abundantly evident from the two preceding articles; for in that case, it would not be an immediate delight in the object, which latter is the essential condition of the judgement upon beauty. But in an objective, internal finality, i.e. perfection, we have what is more akin to the predicate of beauty, and so this has been held even by philosophers of reputation to be convertible with beauty, though subject to the qualification: *where it is thought in a confused way.*

· · ·

For estimating objective finality we always require the concept of an end, and, where such finality has to be, not an external one (utility), but an internal one, the concept of an internal end containing the ground of the internal possibility of the object. Now an end is in general that, the *concept* of which may be regarded as the ground of the possibility of the object itself. So in order to represent an objective finality in a thing we must first have a concept of *what sort of a thing it is to be.* The agreement of the manifold in a thing with this concept (which supplies the rule of its synthesis) is the *qualitative perfection* of the thing. *Quantitative* perfection is entirely distinct from this. It consists in the completeness of anything after its kind, and is a mere concept of quantity (of totality). In its case the question of *what the thing is to be* is regarded as definitely disposed of, and we only ask whether it is possessed of *all* the requisites that go to make it such. What is formal in the representation of a thing, i.e. the agreement of its manifold with a unity (i.e. irrespective of what it is to be) does not, of itself, afford us any cognition whatsoever of objective finality. For since abstraction is made from this unity as *end* (what the thing is to be) nothing is left but the subjective finality of the representations in the mind of the Subject intuiting. This gives a certain finality of the representative state of the Subject, in which the Subject feels itself quite at home in its effort to grasp a given form in the imagination, but no perfection of any Object, the latter not being here thought through any concept. For instance, if in a forest I light upon a plot of grass, round which trees stand in a circle, and if I do not then form any representation of an end, as that it is meant to be used, say, for country dances, then not the least hint of a concept of perfection is given by the mere form. To suppose a formal *objective* finality that is yet devoid of an end, i.e. the mere form of a *perfection* (apart from any matter or *concept* of that to which the agreement relates, even though there was the mere general idea of a conformity to law) is a veritable contradiction.

Now the judgement of taste is an aesthetic judgement, i.e. one resting on subjective grounds. No concept can be its determining ground, and hence not one of a definite end. Beauty, therefore, as a formal subjective finality, involves no thought whatsoever of a perfection of the object, as a would-be formal finality which yet, for all that, is objective: and the distinction between the concepts of the beautiful and the good, which represents both as differing only in their logical form, the first being merely a confused, the second a clearly defined, concept of perfection, while otherwise alike in content and origin, all goes for nothing: for then there would be no *specific* difference between them, but the judgement of taste would be just as much a cognitive judgement as one by which something is described as good—just as the man in the street, when he says that deceit is wrong, bases his judgement on confused, but the philosopher on clear grounds, while both appeal in reality to identical principles of reason.

. . .

XVI

A Judgement of Taste By Which an Object Is Described as Beautiful Under the Condition of a Definite Concept Is Not Pure

There are two kinds of beauty: free beauty (*pulchritudo vaga*), or beauty which is merely dependent (*pulchritudo adhaerens*). The first presupposes no concept of what the object should be; the second does presuppose such a concept and, with it, an answering perfection of the object. Those of the first kind are said to be (self-subsisting) beauties of this thing or that thing; the other kind of beauty, being attached to a concept (conditioned beauty), is ascribed to Objects which come under the concept of a particular end.

Flowers are free beauties of nature. Hardly any one but a botanist knows the true nature of a flower, and even he, while recognizing in the flower the reproductive organ of the plant, pays no attention to this natural end when using his taste to judge of its beauty. Hence no perfection of any kind— no internal finality, as something to which the arrangement of the manifold is related—underlies this judgement. Many birds (the parrot, the humming-bird, the bird of paradise), and a number of crustacea, are self-subsisting beauties which are not appurtenant to any object defined with respect to its end, but please freely and on their own account. So designs *à la grecque*, foliage for framework or on wall-papers, &c., have no intrinsic meaning; they represent nothing—no Object under a definite concept—and are free beauties. We may also rank in the same class what in music are called fantasias (without a theme), and, indeed, all music that is not set to words.

In the estimate of a free beauty (according to mere form) we have the pure judgement of taste. No concept is here presupposed of any end for which the manifold should serve the given Object, and which the latter, therefore, should represent—an incumbrance which would only restrict the freedom of the imagination that, as it were, is at play in the contemplation of the outward form.

But the beauty of man (including under this head that of a man, woman, or child), the beauty of a horse, or of a building, . . . presupposes a concept of the end that defines what the thing has to be, and consequently a concept of its perfection; and is therefore merely appendant beauty. Now, just as it is a clog on the purity of the judgement of taste to have the agreeable (of sensation) joined with beauty to which properly only the form is relevant, so to combine the good with beauty, (the good, namely, of the manifold to the thing itself according to its end), mars its purity.

. . .

Taste, it is true, stands to gain by this combination of intellectual delight with the aesthetic. For it becomes fixed, and, while not universal, it enables rules to be prescribed for it in respect of certain definite final Objects. But these rules are then not rules of taste, but merely rules for establishing a union of taste with reason, i.e. of the beautiful with the good —rules by which the former becomes available as an intentional instrument in respect of the latter, for the purpose of bringing that temper of the mind which is self-sustaining and of subjective universal validity to the support and maintenance of that mode of thought which, while possessing objective universal validity, can only be preserved by a resolute effort. But, strictly speaking, perfection neither gains by beauty, nor beauty by perfection. The truth is rather this, when we compare the representation through which an object is given to us with the Object (in respect of what it is meant to be) by means of a concept, we cannot help reviewing it also in respect of the sensation in the Subject. Hence there results a gain to the *entire faculty* of our representative power when harmony prevails between both states of mind.

. . .

XVII

The Ideal of Beauty

There can be no objective rule of taste by which what is beautiful may be defined by means of concepts. For every judgement from that source is aesthetic, i.e. its determining ground is the feeling of the Subject, and not any concept of an Object. It is only throwing away labour to look for a principle of taste that affords a universal criterion of the beautiful by definite concepts; because what is sought is a thing impossible and inherently contradictory. But in the universal communicability of the sensation (of delight or aversion)—a communicability, too, that exists apart from any concept—in the accord, so far as possible, of all ages and nations as to this feeling in the representation of certain objects, we have the empirical criterion, weak indeed and scarce sufficient to raise a presumption, of the derivation of a taste, thus confirmed by examples, from grounds deep-seated and shared alike by all men, underlying their agreement in estimating the forms under which objects are given to them.

For this reason some products of taste are looked on as *exemplary*—not meaning thereby that by imitating others taste may be acquired. For taste must be an original faculty; whereas one who imitates a model, while showing skill commensurate with his success, only displays taste as himself a critic of this model. Hence it follows that the highest model, the archetype of taste, is a mere idea, which each person must beget in his own consciousness, and according to which he must form his estimate of everything that is an Object of taste, or that is an example of critical taste, and even of universal taste itself. Properly speaking, an *idea* signifies a concept of reason, and an *ideal* the representation of an individual existence as adequate to an idea. Hence this archetype of taste—which rests, indeed, upon reason's indeterminate idea of a maximum, but is not, however, capable of being represented by means of concepts, but only in an individual presentation—may more appropriately be called the ideal of the beautiful. While not having this ideal in our possession, we still strive to beget it within us. But it is bound to be merely an ideal of the imagination, seeing that it rests, not upon concepts, but upon the presentation—the faculty of presentation being the imagination.—Now, how do we arrive at such an ideal of beauty? Is it *a priori* or empirically? Further, what species of the beautiful admits of an ideal?

First of all, we do well to observe that the beauty for which an ideal has to be sought cannot be a beauty that is *free and at large*, but must be one *fixed* by a concept of objective finality. Hence it cannot belong to the Object of an altogether pure judgement of taste, but must attach to one that is partly intellectual. In other words, where an ideal is to have place among the grounds upon which any estimate is formed, then beneath grounds of that kind there must lie some idea of reason according to determinate concepts, by which the end underlying the internal possibility of the object is determined *a priori*. An ideal of beautiful flowers, of a beautiful suite of furniture, or of a beautiful view, is unthinkable. But, it may also be impossible to represent an ideal of a beauty dependent on definite ends, e.g. a beautiful residence, a beautiful tree, a beautiful garden, &c., presumably because their ends are not sufficiently defined and fixed by their concept, with the result that their finality is nearly as free as with beauty that is quite *at large*. Only what has in itself the end of its real existence—only *man* that is able himself to determine his ends by reason, or, where he has to derive them from external perception, can still compare them with essential and universal ends, and then further pronounce aesthetically upon their accord with such ends, only he, among all objects in the world, admits, therefore, of an ideal of *beauty*, just as humanity in his person, as intelligence, alone admits of the ideal of *perfection*.

. . .

But the *ideal* of the beautiful . . . is only to be sought in the *human figure*. Here the ideal consists in the expression of the *moral*, apart from which the object would not please at once universally and positively (not merely negatively in a presentation academically correct). The visible expression of moral ideas that govern men inwardly can, of course, only be drawn from experience; but their combination with all that our reason connects with the morally good in the idea of the highest finality—benevolence, purity, strength, or equanimity, &c.—may be made, as it were, visible in bodily manifestation (as effect of what is internal), and this embodiment involves a union of pure ideas of reason and great imaginative power, in one who would even form an estimate of it, not to speak of being the author of its presentation. The correctness of such an ideal of beauty is evidenced by its not permitting any sensuous charm to mingle with the delight in its Object, in which it still allows us to take a great interest. This fact in turn shows that an estimate formed according to such a standard can never be purely aesthetic, and that one formed according to an ideal of beauty cannot be a simple judgement of taste.

Definition of the Beautiful Derived from This Third Moment

Beauty is the form of *finality* in an object, so far as perceived in it *apart from the representation of an end*.

. . .

XVIII

Nature of the Modality in a Judgement of Taste

I may assert in the case of every representation that the synthesis of a pleasure with the representation (as a cognition) is at least *possible*. Of what I call *agreeable* I assert that it *actually* causes pleasure in me. But what we have in mind in the case of the *beautiful* is a *necessary* reference on its part to delight. However, this necessity is of a special kind. It is not a theoretical objective necessity—such as would let us cognize *a priori* that every one *will feel* this delight in the object that is called beautiful by me. Nor yet is it a practical necessity, in which case, thanks to concepts of a pure rational will in which free agents are supplied with a rule, this delight is the necessary consequence of an objective law, and simply means that one ought absolutely (without ulterior object) to act in a certain way. Rather, being such a necessity as is thought in an aesthetic judgement, it can only be termed *exemplary*. In other words it is a necessity of the assent of *all* to a judgement regarded as exemplifying a universal rule incapable of formulation. Since an aesthetic judgement is not an objective or cognitive judgement, this necessity is not derivable from definite concepts, and so is not apodictic. Much less is it inferable from universality of experience (of a thorough-going agreement of judgements about the beauty of a certain object). For, apart from the fact that experience would hardly furnish evidences sufficiently numerous for this purpose, empirical judgements do not afford any foundation for a concept of the necessity of these judgements.

XIX

The Subjective Necessity Attributed to a Judgement of Taste Is Conditioned

The judgement of taste exacts agreement from every one; and a person who describes something as beautiful insists that every one *ought* to give the object in question his approval and follow suit in describing it as beautiful. The *ought* in aesthetic judgement, therefore, despite an accordance with all the requisite data for passing judgement, is still only pronounced conditionally. We are suitors for agreements from every one else, because we are fortified with a ground common to all. Further, we would be able to count on this agreement, provided we were always assured of the correct subsumption of the case under that ground as the rule of approval.

XX

The Condition of the Necessity Advanced by a Judgement of Taste Is the Idea of a Common Sense

Were judgements of taste (like cognitive judgements) in possession of a definite objective principle, then one who in his judgement followed such a principle would claim unconditioned necessity for it. Again, were they devoid of any principle, as are those of the mere taste of sense, then no thought of any necessity on their part would enter one's head. Therefore they must have a subjective principle, and one which determines what pleases or displeases, by means of feeling only and not through concepts, but yet with universal validity. Such a principle, however, could only be regarded as a *common sense*. This differs essentially from common understanding, which is also sometimes called common sense (*sensus communis*): for the judgement of the latter is not one by feeling, but always one by concepts, though usually only in the shape of obscurely represented principles.

The judgement of taste, therefore, depends on our presupposing the existence of a common sense. (But this is not to be taken to mean some external sense, but the effect arising from the free play of our powers of cognition.) Only under the presupposition, I repeat, of such a common sense, are we able to lay down a judgement of taste.

. . .

XXII

The Necessity of the Universal Assent That Is Thought in a Judgement of Taste, Is a Subjective Necessity Which, Under the Presupposition of a Common Sense, Is Represented as Objective

In all judgements by which we describe anything as beautiful we tolerate no one else being of a different opinion, and in taking up this position we do not rest our judgement upon concepts, but only on our feeling. Accordingly we introduce this fundamental feeling not as a private feeling, but as a public sense. Now, for this purpose, experience cannot be made the ground of this common sense, for the latter is invoked to justify judgements containing an 'ought.' The assertion is not that every one *will* fall in with our judgement, but rather that every one *ought* to agree with it. Here I put forward my judgement of taste as an example of the judgement of common sense, and attribute to it on that account *exemplary* validity. Hence common sense is a mere ideal norm. With this as presupposition, a judgement that accords with it, as well as the delight in an Object expressed in that judgement, is rightly converted into a rule for every one. For the principle, while it is only subjective, being yet assumed as subjectively universal (a necessary idea for every one), could, in what concerns the consensus of different judging Subjects, demand universal assent like an objective principle, provided we were assured of our subsumption under it being correct.

This indeterminate norm of a common sense is, as a matter of fact, presupposed by us; as is shown by our presuming to lay down judgements of taste. But does such a common sense in fact exist as a constitutive principle of the possibility of experience, or is it formed for us as a regulative principle by a still higher principle of reason, that for higher ends first seeks to beget in us a common sense? Is taste, in other words, a natural and original faculty, or is it only the idea of one that is artificial and to be acquired by us, so that a judgement of taste, with its demand for universal assent, is but a requirement of reason for generating such a *consensus*, and does the 'ought,' i.e. the objective necessity of the coincidence of the feeling of all with the particular feeling of each, only betoken the possibility of arriving at some sort of unanimity in these matters, and the judgement of taste only adduce an example of the application of this principle? These are questions which as yet we are neither willing nor in a position to investigate. For the present we have only to resolve the faculty of taste into its elements, and to unite these ultimately in the idea of a common sense.

Definition of the Beautiful Drawn from the Fourth Moment

The beautiful is that which, apart from a concept, is cognized as object of a *necessary* delight.

General Remark on the
First Section of the Analytic

The result to be extracted from the foregoing analysis is in effect this: that everything runs up into the concept of taste as a critical faculty by which an object is estimated in reference to the *free conformity to law* of the imagination. If, now, imagination must in the judgement of taste be regarded in its freedom, then, to begin with, it is not taken as reproductive, as in its subjection to the laws of association, but as productive and exerting an activity of its own (as originator of arbitrary forms of possible intuitions). And although in the apprehension of a given object of sense it is tied down to a definite form of this Object and, to that extent, does not enjoy free play, (as it does in poetry,) still it is easy to conceive that the object may supply ready-made to the imagination just such a form of the arrangement of the manifold, as the imagination, if it were left to itself, would freely project in harmony with the general *conformity to law of the understanding*. But that the *imagination* should be both *free* and *of itself conformable to law*, i.e. carry autonomy with it, is a contradiction. The understanding alone gives the law. Where, however, the imagination is compelled to follow a course laid down by a definite law, then what the form of the product is to be is determined by concepts; but, in that case, as already shown, the delight is not delight in the beautiful, but in the good, (in perfection, though it be no more than formal perfection), and the judgement is not one due to taste. Hence it is only a conformity to law without a law, and a subjective harmonizing of the imagination and the understanding without an objective one—which latter would mean that the representation was referred to a definite concept of the object—that can consist with the free conformity to law of the understanding (which has also been called finality apart from an end) and with the specific character of a judgement of taste.

Now geometrically regular figures, a circle, a square, a cube, and the like, are commonly brought forward by critics of taste as the most simple and unquestionable examples of beauty. And yet the very reason why they are called regular, is because the only way of representing them is by looking on them as mere presentations of a determinate concept by which the figure has its rule (according to which alone it is possible) prescribed for it. One or other of these two views must, therefore, be wrong: either the verdict of the critics that attributes beauty to such figures, or else our own, which makes finality apart from any concept necessary for beauty.

One would scarce think it necessary for a man to have taste to take more delight in a circle than in a scrawled outline, in an equilateral and equiangular quadrilateral than in one that is all lob-sided, and, as it were, deformed. The requirements of common understanding ensure such a preference without the least demand upon taste. Where some purpose is perceived, as, for instance, that of forming an estimate of the area of a plot of land, or rendering intelligible the relation of divided parts to one another and to the whole, then regular figures, and those of the simplest kind, are needed; and the delight does not rest immediately upon the way the figure strikes the eye, but upon its serviceability for all manner of possible purposes. A room with the walls making oblique angles, a plot laid out in a garden in a similar way, even any violation of symmetry, as well in the figure of animals (e.g. being one-eyed) as in that of buildings, or of flower-beds, is displeasing because of its perversity of form, not alone in a practical way in respect of some definite use to which the thing may be put, but for an estimate that looks to all manner of possible purposes. With the judgement of taste the case is different. For, when it is pure, it combines delight or aversion immediately with the bare *contemplation* of the object irrespective of its use or of any end.

The regularity that conduces to the concept of an object is, in fact, the indispensable condition (*conditio sine qua non*) of grasping the object as a single representation and giving to the manifold its determinate form. This determination is an end in respect of knowledge; and in this connexion it is invariably coupled with delight (such as attends the accomplishment of any, even problematical, purpose). Here, however, we have merely the value set upon the solution that satisfies the problem, and not a free and indeterminately final entertainment of the mental powers with what is called beautiful. In the latter case understanding is at the service of imagination, in the former this relation is reversed.

With a thing that owes its possibility to a purpose, a building, or even an animal, its regularity, which consists in symmetry, must express the unity of the intuition accompanying the concept of its end, and belongs with it to cognition. But where all that is intended is the maintenance of a free play of the powers of representation (subject, however, to the condition that there is to be nothing for understanding to take exception to), in ornamental gardens, in the decoration of rooms, in all kinds of furniture that shows good taste, &c., regularity in the shape of constraint is to be avoided as far as possible. Thus English taste in gardens, and fantastic taste in furniture, push the freedom of imagination to the verge of what is grotesque—the idea being that in this divorce from all constraint of rules the precise instance is being afforded where taste can exhibit its perfection in projects of the imagination to the fullest extent.

All stiff regularity (such as borders on mathematical regularity) is inherently repugnant to taste, in that the contemplation of it affords us no lasting entertainment. Indeed, where it has neither cognition nor some definite practical end expressly in view, we get heartily tired of it. On the other hand, anything that gives the imagination scope for unstudied and final play is always fresh to us. We do not grow to hate the very sight of it.

· · ·

XXXIV

An Objective Principle of Taste Is Not Possible

A principle of taste would mean a fundamental premiss under the condition of which one might subsume the concept of an object, and then, by a syllogism, draw the inference that it is beautiful. That, however, is absolutely impossible. For I must feel the pleasure immediately in the representation of the object, and I cannot be talked into it by any grounds of proof. Thus although critics, as Hume says, are able to reason more plausibly than cooks, they must still share the same fate. For the determining ground of their judgement they are not able to look to the force of demonstrations, but only to the reflection of the Subject upon his own state (of pleasure or displeasure), to the exclusion of precepts and rules.

There is, however, a matter upon which it is competent for critics to exercise their subtlety, and upon which they ought to do so, so long as it tends to the rectification and extension of our judgements of taste. But that matter is not one of exhibiting the determining ground of aesthetic judgements of this kind in a universally applicable formula—which is impossible. Rather is it the investigation of the faculties of cognition and their function in these judgements, and the illustration, by the analysis of examples, of their mutual subjective finality, the form of which in a given representation has been shown above to constitute the beauty of their object. Hence with regard to the representation whereby an Object is given, the Critique of Taste itself is only subjective; viz. it is the art or science of reducing the mutual relation of the understanding and the imagination in the given representation (without reference to antecedent sensation or concept), consequently their accordance or discordance, to rules, and of determining them with regard to their conditions. It is *art* if it only illustrates this by examples; it is *science* if it deduces the possibility of such an estimate from the nature of these faculties as faculties of knowledge in general. It is only with the latter, as Transcendental Critique, that we have here any concern. Its proper scope is the development and justification of the subjective principle of taste, as an *a priori* principle of judgement. As an art, Critique merely looks to the physiological (here psychological), and, consequently, empirical rules, according to which in actual fact taste proceeds, (passing by the question of their possibility,) and seeks to apply them in estimating its objects. The latter Critique criticizes the products of fine art, just as the former does the faculty of estimating them.

· · ·

XL

Taste as a Kind of Sensus Communis

The name of sense is often given to judgement where what attracts attention is not so much its reflective act as merely its result. So we speak of a sense of truth, of a sense of propriety, or of justice, &c. And yet, of course, we know, or at least ought well enough to know, that a sense cannot be the true abode of these concepts, not to speak of its being competent, even in the slightest degree, to pronounce universal rules. On the contrary, we recognize that a representation of this kind, be it of truth, propriety, beauty, or justice, could never enter our thoughts were we not able to raise ourselves above the level of the senses to that of higher faculties of cognition. *Common human understanding* which, as mere sound (not yet cultivated) understanding, is looked upon as the least we can expect from any one claiming the name of man, has therefore the doubtful honour of having the name of common sense (*sensus communis*) bestowed upon it; and bestowed, too, in an acceptation of the word *common* (not merely in our own language, where it actually has a double meaning, but also in many others, which makes it amount to what is *vulgar*—what is everywhere to be met with—a quality which by no means confers credit or distinction upon its possessor.

However, by the name *sensus communis* is to be understood the idea of a *public* sense, i.e. a critical faculty which in its reflective act takes account (*a priori*) of the mode of representation of every one else, in order, *as it were*, to weigh its judgement with the collective reason of mankind, and thereby avoid the illusion arising from subjective and personal conditions which could readily be taken for objective, an illusion that would exert a prejudicial influence upon its judgement. This is accomplished by weighing the judgement, not so much with actual, as rather with the merely possible, judgements of others, and by putting ourselves in the position of every one else, as the result of a mere abstraction from the limitations which contingently affect our own estimate. This, in turn, is effected by so far as possible letting go the element of matter, i.e. sensation, in our general state of representative activity, and confining attention to the formal peculiarities of our representation or general state of representative activity. Now it may seem that this operation of reflection is too artificial to be attributed to the faculty which we call *common* sense. But this is an appearance due only to its expression in abstract formulae. In itself nothing is more natural than to abstract from charm and emotion where one is looking for a judgement intended to serve as a universal rule.

. . .

Taste is, therefore, the faculty of forming an *a priori* estimate of the communicability of the feelings that, without the mediation of a concept, are connected with a given representation.

Supposing, now, that we could assume that the mere universal communicability of our feeling must of itself carry with it an interest for us (an assumption, however, which we are not entitled to draw as a conclusion from the character of a merely reflective judgement), we should then be in a position to explain how the feeling in the judgement of taste comes to be exacted from every one as a sort of duty.

. . .

XLII

The Intellectual Interest in the Beautiful

It has been with the best intentions that those who love to see in the ultimate end of humanity, namely the morally good, the goal of all activities to which men are impelled by the inner bent of their nature, have regarded it as a mark of a good moral character to take an interest in the beautiful generally. But they have, not without reason, been contradicted by others who appeal to the fact of experience, that *virtuosi* in matters of taste, being not alone often, but one might say as a general rule, vain, capricious, and addicted to injurious passions, could perhaps more rarely than others lay claim to any pre-eminent attachment to moral principles. And so it would seem, not only that the feeling for the beautiful is specifically different from the moral feeling (which as a matter of fact is the case), but also that the interest which we may combine with it, will hardly consort with the moral, and certainly not on grounds of inner affinity.

Now I willingly admit that the interest in the *beautiful of art* (including under this heading the artificial use of natural beauties for personal adornment, and so from vanity) gives no evidence at all of a habit of mind attached to the morally good, or even inclined that way. But, on the other hand, I do maintain that to take an *immediate interest* in the beauty of *nature* (not merely to have taste in estimating it) is always a mark of a good soul; and that, where this interest is habitual, it is at least indicative of a temper of mind favourable to the moral feeling that it should readily associate itself with the *contemplation of nature*. It must, however, be borne in mind that I mean to refer strictly to the beautiful *forms* of nature, and to put to one side the *charms* which she is wont so lavishly to combine with them; because, though the interest in these is no doubt immediate, it is nevertheless empirical.

One who alone (and without any intention of communicating his observations to others) regards the beautiful form of a wild flower, a bird, an insect, or the like, out of admiration and love of them, and being loath to let them escape him in nature, even at the risk of some misadventure to himself—so far from there being any prospect of advantage to him—such a one takes an immediate, and in fact intellectual, interest in the beauty of nature. This means that he is not alone pleased with nature's product in respect of its form, but is also pleased at its existence, and is so without any charm of sense having a share in the matter, or without his associating with it any end whatsoever.

In this connexion, however, it is of note that were we to play a trick on our lover of the beautiful, and plant in the ground artificial flowers (which can be made so as to look just like natural ones), and perch artfully carved birds on the branches of trees, and he were to find out how he had been taken in, the immediate interest which these things previously had for him would at once vanish—though, perhaps, a different interest might intervene in its stead, that, namely, of vanity in decorating his room with them for the eyes of others. The fact is that our intuition and reflection must have as their concomitant the thought that the beauty in question is nature's handiwork; and this is the sole basis of the immediate interest that is taken in it. Failing this we are either left with a bare judgement of taste void of all interest whatever, or else only with one that is combined with an interest that is mediate, involving, namely, a reference to society; which latter affords no reliable indication of morally good habits of thought.

The superiority which natural beauty has over that of art, even where it is excelled by the latter in point of form, in yet being alone able to awaken an immediate interest, accords with the refined and well-grounded habits of thought of all men who have cultivated their moral feeling. If a man with taste enough to judge of works of fine art with the greatest correctness and refinement readily quits the room in which he meets with those beauties that minister to vanity or, at least, social joys, and betakes himself to the beautiful in nature, so that he may there find as it were a feast for his soul in a train of thought which he can never completely evolve, we will then regard this his choice even with veneration, and give him credit for a beautiful soul, to which no connoisseur or art collector can lay claim on the score of the interest which his objects have for him. —Here, now, are two kinds of Objects which in the judgement of mere taste could scarcely contend with one another for a superiority. What then, is the distinction that makes us hold them in such different esteem?

We have a faculty of judgement which is merely aesthetic—a faculty of judging of forms without the aid of concepts, and of finding, in the mere estimate of them, a delight that we at the same time make into a rule for every one, without this judgement being founded on an interest, or yet producing one.—On the other hand we have also a faculty of intellectual judgement for the mere forms of practical maxims, (so far as they are of themselves qualified for universal legislation,)—a faculty of determining an *a priori* delight, which we make into a law for every one, without our judgement being founded on any interest, *though here it produces one*. The pleasure or displeasure in the former judgement is called that of taste; the latter is called that of the moral feeling.

But, now, reason is further interested in ideas (for which in our moral feeling it brings about an immediate interest,) having also objective reality. That is to say, it is of interest to reason that nature should at least show a trace or give a hint that it contains in itself some ground or other for assuming a uniform accordance of its products with our wholly disinterested delight (a delight which we cognize *a priori* as a law for every one without being able to ground it upon proofs). That being so, reason must take an interest in every manifestation on the part of nature of some such accordance. Hence the mind cannot reflect on the beauty of *nature* without at the same time finding its interest engaged. But this interest is akin to the moral. One, then, who takes such an interest in the beautiful in nature can only do so in so far as he has previously set his interest deep in the foundations of the morally good. On these grounds we have reason for presuming the presence of at least the germ of a good moral disposition in the case of a man to whom the beauty of nature is a matter of immediate interest.

· · ·

XLIII

Art in General

(1.) *Art* is distinguished from *nature* as making (*facere*) is from acting or operating in general (*agere*), and the product or the result of the former is distinguished from that of the latter as *work* (*opus*) from operation (*effectus*).

By right it is only production through freedom, i.e. through an act of will that places reason at the basis of its action, that should be termed art. For, although we are pleased to call what bees produce (their regularly constructed cells) a work of art, we only do so on the strength of an analogy with art; that is to say, as soon as we call to mind that no rational deliberation forms the basis of their labour, we say at once that it is a product of their nature (of instinct), and it is only to their Creator that we ascribe it as art.

If, as sometimes happens, in a search through a bog, we light on a piece of hewn wood, we do not say it is a product of nature but of art. Its producing cause had an end in view to which the object owes its form. Apart from such cases, we recognize an art in everything formed in such a way that its actuality must have been preceded by a representation of the thing in its cause (as even in the case of the bees), although the effect could not have been *thought* by the cause. But where anything is called absolutely a work of art, to distinguish it from a natural product, then some work of man is always understood.

(2.) *Art*, as human skill, is distinguished also from *science* (as *ability* from *knowledge*), as a practical from a theoretical faculty, as technic from theory (as the art of surveying from geometry). For this reason, also, what one *can* do the moment one only *knows* what is to be done, hence without anything more than sufficient knowledge of the desired result, is not called art. To art that alone belongs for which the possession of the most complete knowledge does not involve one's having then and there the skill to do it.

· · ·

(3.) *Art* is further distinguished from *handicraft*. The first is called *free*, the other may be called *industrial art*. We look on the former as something which could only prove final (be a success) as play, i.e. an occupation which is agreeable on its own account; but on the second as labour, i.e. a business, which on its own account is disagreeable (drudgery), and is only attractive by means of what it results in (e.g. the pay), and which is consequently capable of being a compulsory imposition. . . . It is not amiss, however, to remind the reader of this: that in all free arts something of a compulsory character is still required, or, as it is called, a *mechanism*, without which the *soul*, which in art must be *free*, and which alone gives life to the work, would be bodyless and evanescent (e.g. in the poetic art there must be correctness and wealth of language, likewise prosody and metre). For not a few leaders of a newer school believe that the best way to promote a free art is to sweep away all restraint, and convert it from labour into mere play.

XLIV

Fine Art

There is no science of the beautiful, but only a Critique. Nor, again, is there an elegant (*schöne*) science, but only a fine (*schöne*) art. . . . What has given rise to the current expression *elegant sciences* is, doubtless, no more than this, that common observation has, quite accurately, noted the fact that for fine art, in the fulness of its perfection, a large store of science is required.

. . .

Where art, merely seeking to actualize a possible object to the *cognition* of which it is adequate, does whatever acts are required for that purpose, then it is *mechanical*. But should the feeling of pleasure be what it has immediately in view it is then termed *aesthetic* art. As such it may be either *agreeable* or *fine* art. The description 'agreeable art' applies where the end of the art is that the pleasure should accompany the representations considered as mere *sensations*, the description 'fine art' where it is to accompany them considered as *modes of cognition*.

Agreeable arts are those which have mere enjoyment for their object. Such are all the charms that can gratify a dinner party: entertaining narrative, the art of starting the whole table in unrestrained and sprightly conversation, or with jest and laughter inducing a certain air of gaiety.

Fine art, on the other hand, is a mode of representation which is intrinsically final, and which, although devoid of an end, has the effect of advancing the culture of the mental powers in the interests of social communication.

The universal communicability of a pleasure involves in its very concept that the pleasure is not one of enjoyment arising out of mere sensation, but must be one of reflection. Hence aesthetic art, as art which is beautiful, is one having for its standard the reflective judgement and not organic sensation.

XLV

Fine Art is an Art so far as it has at the Same Time the Appearance of Being Nature

A product of fine art must be recognized to be art and not nature. Nevertheless the finality in its form must appear just as free from the constraint of arbitrary rules as if it were a product of mere nature. Upon this feeling of freedom in the play of our cognitive faculties—which play has at the same time to be final—rests that pleasure which alone is universally communicable without being based on concepts. Nature proved beautiful when it wore the appearance of art; and art can only be termed beautiful, where we are conscious of its being art, while yet it has the appearance of nature.

For, whether we are dealing with beauty of nature or beauty of art, we may make the universal statement: *that is beautiful which pleases in the mere estimate of it* (not in sensation or by means of a concept). Now art has always got a definite intention of producing something. Were this 'something,' however, to be mere sensation (something merely subjective), intended to be accompanied with pleasure, then such product would, in our estimation of it, only please through the agency of the feeling of the senses. On the other hand, were the intention one directed to the production of a definite object, then, supposing this were attained by art, the object would only please by means of a concept. But in both cases the art would please, not in *the mere estimate of it*, i.e. not as fine art, but rather as mechanical art.

Hence the finality in the product of fine art, intentional though it be, must not have the appearance of being intentional; i.e. fine art must be clothed *with the aspect* of nature, although we recognize it to be art. But the way in which a product of art seems like nature, is by the presence of perfect *exactness* in the agreement with rules prescribing how alone the product can be what it is intended to be, but with an absence of *laboured effect*, (without academic form betraying itself,) i.e. without a trace appearing of the artist having always had the rule present to him and of its having fettered his mental powers.

XLVI

Fine Art is the Art of Genius

Genius is the talent (natural endowment) which gives the rule to art. Since talent, as an innate productive faculty of the artist, belongs itself to nature, we may put it this way: *Genius* is the innate mental aptitude (*ingenium*) *through which* nature gives the rule to art.

Whatever may be the merits of this definition, and whether it is merely arbitrary, or whether it is adequate or not to the concept usually associated with the word *genius* (a point which the following sections have to clear up), it may still be shown at the outset that, according to this acceptation of the word, fine arts must necessarily be regarded as arts of *genius*.

For every art presupposes rules which are laid down as the foundation which first enables a product, if it is to be called one of art, to be represented as possible. The concept of fine art, however, does not permit of the judgement upon the beauty of its product being derived from any rule that has a *concept* for its determining ground, and that depends, consequently, on a concept of the way in which the product is possible. Consequently fine art cannot of its own self excogitate the rule according to which it is to effectuate its product. But since, for all that, a product can never be called art unless there is a preceding rule, it follows that nature in the individual (and by virtue of the harmony of his faculties) must give the rule to art, i.e. fine art is only possible as a product of genius.

From this it may be seen that genius (1) is a *talent* for producing that for which no definite rule can be given: and not an aptitude in the way of cleverness for what can be learned according to some rule; and that consequently *originality* must be its primary property. (2) Since there may also be original nonsense, its products must at the same time be models, i.e. be *exemplary*; and, consequently, though not themselves derived from imitation, they must serve that purpose for others, i.e. as a standard or rule of estimating. (3) It cannot indicate scientifically how it brings about its product, but rather gives the rule as *nature*. Hence, where an author owes a product to his genius, he does not himself know how the *ideas* for it have entered into his head, nor has he it in his power to invent the like at pleasure, or methodically, and communicate the same to others in such precepts as would put them in a position to produce similar products. . . . (4) Nature prescribes the rule through genius not to science but to art, and this also only in so far as it is to be fine art.

XLVII

Elucidation and Confirmation of the Above Explanation of Genius

Every one is agreed on the point of the complete opposition between genius and the *spirit of imitation*. Now since learning is nothing but imitation, the greatest ability, or aptness as an pupil (capacity), is still, as such, not equivalent to genius. Even though a man weaves his own thoughts or fancies, instead of merely taking in what others have thought, and even though he go so far as to bring fresh gains to art and science, this does not afford a valid reason for calling such a man of *brains*, and often great brains, a *genius*, in contradistinction to one who goes by the name of *shallow-pate*, because he can never do more than merely learn and follow a lead. For what is accomplished in this way is something that *could* have been learned. Hence it all lies in the natural path of investigation and reflection according to rules, and so is not specifically distinguishable from what may be acquired as the result of industry backed up by imitation. So all that *Newton* has set forth in his immortal work on the Principles of Natural Philosophy may well be learned, however great a mind it took to find it all out, but we cannot learn to write in a true poetic vein, no matter how complete all the precepts of the poetic art may be, or however excellent its models. The reason is that all the steps that Newton had to take from the first elements of geometry to his greatest and most profound discoveries were such as he could make intuitively evident and plain to follow, not only for himself but for every one else. On the other hand no *Homer* or *Wieland* can show how his ideas, so rich at once in fancy and in thought, enter and assemble themselves in his brain, for the good reason that he does not himself know, and so cannot teach others. In matters of science, therefore, the greatest inventor differs only in degree from the most laborious imitator and apprentice, whereas he differs specifically from one endowed by nature for fine art. No disparagement, however, of those great men, to whom the human race is so deeply indebted, is involved in this comparison of them with those who on the score of their talent for fine art are the elect of nature. The talent for science is formed for the continued advances of greater perfection in knowledge, with all its dependent practical advantages, as also for imparting the same to others. Hence scientists can boast a ground of considerable superiority over those who merit the honour of being called geniuses, since genius reaches a point at which art must make a halt, as there is a limit imposed upon it which it cannot transcend. This limit has in all probability been long since attained. In addition, such skill cannot be communicated, but requires to be bestowed directly from the hand of nature upon each individual, and so with him it dies, awaiting the day when nature once again endows another in the same way—one who needs no more than an example to set the talent of which he is conscious at work on similar lines.

.   .   .

XLVIII

The Relation of Genius to Taste

For *estimating* beautiful objects, as such, what is required is *taste*; but for fine art, i.e. the *production* of such objects, one needs *genius*.

If we consider genius as the talent for fine art (which the proper signification of the word imports), and if we would analyse it from this point of view into the faculties which must concur to constitute such a talent, it is imperative at the outset accurately to determine the difference between beauty of nature, which it only requires taste to estimate, and beauty of art, which requires genius for its possibility (a possibility to which regard must also be paid in estimating such an object).

A beauty of nature is a *beautiful thing*; beauty of art is a *beautiful representation* of a thing.

To enable me to estimate a beauty of nature, as such, I do not need to be previously possessed of a concept of what sort of a thing the object is intended to be, i.e. I am not obliged to know its material finality (the end), but, rather, in forming an estimate of it apart from any knowledge of the end, the mere form pleases on its own account. If, however, the object is presented as a product of art, and is as such to be declared beautiful, then, seeing that art always presupposes an end in the cause (and its causality), a concept of what the thing is intended to be must first of all be laid at its basis. And, since the agreement of the manifold in a thing with an inner character belonging to it as its end constitutes the perfection of the thing, it follows that in estimating beauty of art the perfection of the thing must be also taken into account—a matter which in estimating a beauty of nature, as beautiful, is quite irrelevant.—It is true that in forming an estimate, especially of animate objects of nature, e.g. of a man or a horse, objective finality is also commonly taken into account with a view to judgement upon their beauty; but then the judgement also ceases to be purely aesthetic, i.e. a mere judgement of taste. Nature is no longer estimated as it appears like art, but rather in so far as it actually *is* art, though superhuman art; and the teleological judgement serves as basis and condition of the aesthetic, and one which the latter must regard. In such a case, where one says, for example, 'that is a beautiful woman,' what one in fact thinks is only this, that in her form nature excellently portrays the ends present in the female figure. For one has to extend one's view beyond the mere form to a concept, to enable the object to be thought in such manner by means of an aesthetic judgement logically conditioned.

Where fine art evidences its superiority is in the beautiful descriptions it gives of things that in nature would be ugly or displeasing. The Furies, diseases, devastations of war, and the like, can (as evils) be very beautifully described, nay even represented in pictures. One kind of ugliness alone is incapable of being represented conformably to nature without destroying all aesthetic delight, and consequently artistic beauty, namely, that which excites *disgust*. For, as in this strange sensation, which depends purely on the imagination, the object is represented as insisting, as it were, upon our enjoying it, while we still set our face against it, the artificial representation of the object is no longer distinguishable from the nature of the object itself in our sensation, and so it cannot possibly be regarded as beautiful. The art of sculpture, again, since in its products art is almost confused with nature, has excluded from its creations the direct representation of ugly objects, and, instead, only sanctions, for example, the representation of death (in a beautiful genius), or of the warlike spirit (in Mars), by means of an allegory, or attributes which wear a pleasant guise, and so only indirectly, through an interpretation on the part of reason, and not for the pure aesthetic judgement.

So much for the beautiful representation of an object, which is properly only the form of the presentation of a concept, and the means by which the latter is universally communicated. To give this form, however, to the product of fine art, taste merely is required. By this the artist, having practised and corrected his taste by a variety of examples from nature or art, controls his work and, after many, and often laborious, attempts to satisfy taste, finds the form which commends itself to him. Hence this form is not, as it were, a matter of inspiration, or of a free swing of the mental powers, but rather of a slow and even painful process of improvement, directed to making the form adequate to his thought without prejudice to the freedom in the play of those powers.

Taste is, however, merely a critical, not a productive faculty; and what conforms to it is not, merely on that account, a work of fine art. It may belong to useful and mechanical art, or even to science, as a product following definite rules which are capable of being learned and which must be closely followed. But the pleasing form imparted to the work is only the vehicle of communication and a mode, as it were, of execution, in respect of which one remains to a certain extent free, notwithstanding being otherwise tied down to a definite end. So we demand that table appointments, or even a moral dissertation, and, indeed, a sermon, must bear this form of fine art, yet without its appearing *studied*. But one would not call them on this account works of fine art. A poem, a musical composition, a picture-gallery, and so forth, would, however, be placed under this head; and so in a would-be work of fine art we may frequently recognize genius without taste, and in another taste without genius.

XLIX

The Faculties of the Mind Which Constitute Genius

Of certain products which are expected, partly at least, to stand on the footing of fine art, we say they are *soul*less; and this, although we find nothing to censure in them as far as taste goes. A poem may be very pretty and elegant, but is soulless. A narrative has precision and method, but is soulless. . . . Now what do we here mean by 'soul'?

'Soul' (*Geist*) in an aesthetical sense, signifies the animating principle in the mind. But that whereby this principle animates the psychic substance (*Seele*)—the material which it employs for that purpose—is that which sets the mental powers into a swing that is final, i.e. into a play which is self-maintaining and which strengthens those powers for such activity.

Now my proposition is that this principle is nothing else than the faculty of presenting *aesthetic ideas*. But, by an aesthetic idea I mean that representation of the imagination which induces much thought, yet without the possibility of any definite thought whatever, i.e. *concept*, being adequate to it, and which language, consequently, can never get quite on level terms with or render completely intelligible.—It is easily seen, that an aesthetic idea is the counterpart (pendant) of a *rational idea*, which, conversely, is a concept, to which no *intuition* (representation of the imagination) can be adequate.

The imagination (as a productive faculty of cognition) is a powerful agent for creating, as it were, a second nature out of the material supplied to it by actual nature. It affords us entertainment where experience proves too commonplace; and we even use it to remodel experience, always following, no doubt, laws that are based on analogy, but still also following principles which have a higher seat in reason (and which are every whit as natural to us as those followed by the understanding in laying hold of empirical nature). By this means we get a sense of our freedom from the law of association (which attaches to the empirical employment of the imagination), with the result that the material can be borrowed by us from nature in accordance with the law, but be worked up by us into something else—namely, what surpasses nature.

Such representations of the imagination may be termed *ideas*. This is partly because they at least strain after something lying out beyond the confines of experience, and so seek to approximate to a presentation of rational concepts (i.e. intellectual ideas), thus giving to these concepts the semblance of an objective reality. But, on the other hand, there is this most important reason, that no concept can be wholly adequate to them as internal intuitions. The poet essays the task of interpreting to sense the rational ideas of invisible beings, the kingdom of the blessed, hell, eternity, creation, &c. Or, again, as to things of which examples occur in experience, e.g. death, envy, and all vices, as also love, fame, and the like, transgressing the limits of experience he attempts with the aid of an imagination which emulates the display of reason in its attainment of a maximum to body them forth to sense with a completeness of which nature affords no parallel; and it is in fact precisely in the poetic art that the faculty of aesthetic ideas can show itself to full advantage. This faculty, however, regarded solely on its own account, is properly no more than a talent (of the imagination).

If, now, we attach to a concept a representation of the imagination belonging to its presentation, but inducing solely on its own account such a wealth of thought as would never admit of comprehension in a definite concept, and, as a consequence, giving aesthetically an unbounded expansion to the concept itself, then the imagination here displays a creative activity, and it puts the faculty of intellectual ideas (reason) into motion —a motion, at the instance of a representation, towards an extension of thought, that, while germane, no doubt, to the concept of the object, exceeds what can be laid hold of in that representation or clearly expressed.

Those forms which do not constitute the presentation of a given concept itself, but which, as secondary representations of the imagination, express the derivatives connected with it, and its kinship with other concepts, are called (aesthetic) *attributes* of an object, the concept of which, as an idea of reason, cannot be adequately presented. In this way Jupiter's eagle, with the lightning in its claws, is an attribute of the mighty kind of heaven, and the peacock of its stately queen. They do not, like *logical attributes*, represent what lies in our concepts of the sublimity and majesty of creation, but rather something else—something that gives the imagination an incentive to spread its flight over a whole host of kindred representations that provoke more thought than admits of expression in a concept determined by words. They furnish an *aesthetic idea*, which serves the above rational idea as a substitute for logical presentation, but with the proper function, however, of animating the mind by opening out for it a prospect into a field of kindred representations stretching beyond its ken. But it is not alone in the arts of painting or sculpture, where the name of attribute is customarily employed, that fine art acts in this way; poetry and rhetoric also derive the soul that animates their works wholly from the aesthetic attributes of the objects—attributes which go hand in hand with the logical, and give the imagination an impetus to bring more thought into play in the matter, though in an undeveloped manner, than allows of being brought within the embrace of a concept, or, therefore, of being definitely formulated in language.

. . .

On the other hand, even an intellectual concept may serve, conversely, as attribute for a representation of sense, and so animate the latter with the idea of the supersensible; but only by the aesthetic factor subjectively attaching to the consciousness of the supersensible being employed for the purpose. So, for example, a certain poet says in his description of a beautiful morning: 'The sun arose, as out of virtue rises peace.' The consciousness of virtue, even where we put ourselves only in thought in the position of a virtuous man, diffuses in the mind a multitude of sublime and tranquillizing feelings, and gives a boundless outlook into a happy future, such as no expression within the compass of a definite concept completely attains.

In a word, the aesthetic idea is a representation of the imagination, annexed to a given concept, with which, in the free employment of imagination, such a multiplicity of partial representations are bound up, that no expression indicating a definite concept can be found for it—one which on that account allows a concept to be supplemented in thought by much that is indefinable in words, and the feeling of which quickens the cognitive faculties, and with language, as a mere thing of the letter, binds up the spirit (soul) also.

. . .

If, after this analysis, we cast a glance back upon the above definition of what is called *genius*, we find: *First*, that it is a talent for art—not one for science, in which clearly known rules must take the lead and determine the procedure. *Secondly*, being a talent in the line of art, it presupposes a definite concept of the product—as its end. Hence it presupposes understanding, but, in addition, a representation, indefinite though it be, of the material, i.e. of the intuition, required for the presentation of that concept, and so a relation of the imagination to the understanding. *Thirdly*, it displays itself, not so much in the working out of the projected end in the presentation of a definite *concept*, as rather in the portrayal, or expression of *aesthetic ideas* containing a wealth of material for effecting that intention. Consequently the imagination is represented by it in its freedom from all guidance of rules, but still as final for the presentation of the given concept. *Fourthly*, and lastly, the unsought and undesigned subjective finality in the free harmonizing of the imagination with the understanding's conformity to law presupposes a proportion and accord between these faculties such as cannot be brought about by any observance of rules, whether of science or mechanical imitation, but can only be produced by the nature of the individual.

Genius, according to these presuppositions, is the exemplary originality of the natural endowments of an individual in the *free* employment of his cognitive faculties. On this showing, the product of a genius (in respect of so much in this product as is attributable to genius, and not to possible learning or academic instruction,) is an example, not for imitation (for that would mean the loss of the element of genius, and just the very soul of the work), but to be followed by another genius—one whom it arouses to a sense of his own originality in putting freedom from the constraint of rules so into force in his art, that for art itself a new rule is won—which is what shows a talent to be exemplary. Yet, since the genius is one of nature's elect—a type that must be regarded as but a rare phenomenon— for other clever minds his example gives rise to a school, that is to say a methodical instruction according to rules, collected, so far as the circumstances admit, from such products of genius and their peculiarities. And, to that extent, fine art is for such persons a matter of imitation, for which nature, through the medium of a genius, gave the rule.

. . .

LI

The Division of the Fine Arts

Beauty (whether it be of nature or of art) may in general be termed the *expression* of aesthetic ideas. But the proviso must be added that with beauty of art this idea must be excited through the medium of a concept of the Object, whereas with beauty of nature the bare reflection upon a given intuition, apart from any concept of what the object is intended to be, is sufficient for awakening and communicating the idea of which that Object is regarded as the *expression.*

Accordingly, if we wish to make a division of the fine arts, we can choose for that purpose, tentatively at least, no more convenient principle than the analogy which art bears to the mode of expression of which men avail themselves in speech, with a view to communicating themselves to one another as completely as possible, i.e. not merely in respect of their concepts but in respect of their sensations also.—Such expression consists in *word, gesture,* and *tone* (articulation, gesticulation, and modulation). It is the combination of these three modes of expression which alone constitutes a complete communication of the speaker. For thought, intuition, and sensation are in this way conveyed to others simultaneously and in conjunction.

Hence there are only three kinds of fine art: the art of *speech, formative* art, and art of the *play of sensations* (as external sense impressions). This division might also be arranged as a dichotomy, so that fine art would be divided into that of the expression of thoughts or intuitions, the latter being subdivided according to the distinction between the form and the matter (sensation). It would, however, in that case appear too abstract, and less in line with popular conceptions.

(1) The arts of SPEECH are *rhetoric* and *poetry.* Rhetoric is the art of transacting a serious business of the understanding as if it were a free play

of the imagination; *poetry* that of conducting a free play of the imagination as if it were a serious business of the understanding.

Thus the *orator* announces a serious business, and for the purpose of entertaining his audience conducts it as if it were a mere *play* with ideas. The *poet* promises merely an entertaining *play* with ideas, and yet for the understanding there enures as much as if the promotion of its business had been his one intention.

· · ·

The orator, therefore, gives something which he does not promise, viz. an entertaining play of the imagination. On the other hand, there is something in which he fails to come up to his promise, and a thing, too, which is his avowed business, namely, the engagement of the understanding to some end. The poet's promise, on the contrary, is a modest one, and a mere play with ideas is all he holds out to us, but he accomplishes something worthy of being made a serious business, namely, the using of play to provide food for the understanding, and the giving of life to its concepts by means of the imagination. Hence the orator in reality performs less than he promises, the poet more.

(2) The FORMATIVE arts, or those for the expression of ideas in *sensuous intuition* (not by means of representations of mere imagination that are excited by words) are arts either of *sensuous truth* or of *sensuous semblance*. The first is called *plastic* art, the second *painting*. Both use figures in space for the expression of ideas: the former makes figures discernible to two senses, sight and touch (though, so far as the latter sense is concerned, without regard to beauty), the latter makes them so to the former sense alone. The aesthetic idea (archetype, original) is the fundamental basis of both in the imagination; but the figure which constitutes its expression (the ectype, the copy) is given either in its bodily extension (the way the object itself exists) or else in accordance with the picture which it forms of itself in the eye (according to its appearance when projected on a flat surface). Or, whatever the archetype is, either the reference to an actual end or only the semblance of one may be imposed upon reflection as its condition.

To *plastic* art, as the first kind of formative fine art, belong *sculpture* and *architecture*. The first is that which presents concepts of things corporeally, as they *might exist in nature* (though as fine art it directs its attention to aesthetic finality). The *second* is the art of presenting concepts of things which are possible *only through art*, and the determining ground of whose form is not nature but an arbitrary end—and of presenting them both with a view to this purpose and yet, at the same time, with aesthetic finality. In architecture the chief point is a certain *use* of the artistic object to which, as the condition, the aesthetic ideas are limited. In sculpture the mere *expression* of aesthetic ideas is the main intention. Thus statues of men, gods, animals, &c., belong to sculpture; but temples, splendid buildings for public concourse, or even dwelling-houses, triumphal arches, columns, mausoleums, &c., erected as monuments, belong to architecture, and in fact all household furniture (the work of cabinet-makers, and so forth—things meant to be used) may be added to the list, on the ground that adaptation of the product to a particular use is the essential element in a *work of architecture*. On the other hand, a mere *piece of sculpture*, made simply to be looked at, and intended to please on its own account, is, as a corporeal presentation, a mere imitation of nature, though one in which regard is paid to aesthetic ideas, and in which, therefore, *sensuous truth* should not go the length of losing the appearance of being an art and a product of the elective will.

Painting, as the second kind of formative art, which presents the *sensuous semblance* in artful combination with ideas, I would divide into that of the beautiful *portrayal of nature,* and that of the beautiful *arrangement* of its *products.* The first is *painting proper,* the second *landscape gardening.* For the first gives only the semblance of bodily extension; whereas the second, giving this, no doubt, according to its truth, gives only the semblance of utility and employment for ends other than the play of the imagination in the contemplation of its forms. The latter consists in no more than decking out the ground with the same manifold variety (grasses, flowers, shrubs, and trees, and even water, hills, and dales) as that with which nature presents it to our view, only arranged differently and in obedience to certain ideas. . . . The justification, however, of bringing formative art (by analogy) under a common head with gesture in a speech, lies in the fact that through these figures the soul of the artist furnishes a bodily expression for the substance and character of his thought, and makes the thing itself speak, as it were, in mimic language—a very common play of our fancy, that attributes to lifeless things a soul suitable to their form, and that uses them as its mouthpiece.

(3) The art of the BEAUTIFUL PLAY OF SENSATIONS, (sensations that arise from external stimulation,) which is a play of sensations that has nevertheless to permit of universal communication, can only be concerned with the proportion of the different degrees of tension in the sense to which the sensation belongs, i.e. with its tone. In this comprehensive sense of the word it may be divided into the artificial play of sensations of hearing and of sight, consequently into *music* and the *art of colour.*—It is of note that these two senses, over and above such susceptibility for impressions as is required to obtain concepts of external objects by means of these impressions, also admit of a peculiar associated sensation of which we cannot well determine whether it is based on sense or reflection; and that this sensibility may at times be wanting, although the sense, in other respects, and in what concerns its employment for the cognition of objects, is by no means deficient but particularly keen.

. . .

LXIV

The Distinctive Character of Things Considered as Physical Ends

A thing is possible only as an end where the causality to which it owes its origin must not be sought in the mechanism of nature, but in a cause whose capacity of acting is determined by conceptions. What is required in order that we may perceive that a thing is only possible in this way is that its form is not possible on purely natural laws—that is to say, such laws as we may cognize by means of unaided understanding applied to objects of sense—but that, on the contrary, even to know it empirically in respect of its cause and effect presupposes conceptions of reason. Here we have, as far as any empirical laws of nature go, a *contingency* of the form of the thing in relation to reason. Now reason in every case insists on cognizing the necessity of the form of a natural product, even where it only desires to perceive the conditions involved in its production. In the given form above mentioned, however, it cannot get this necessity. Hence the contingency is itself a ground for making us look upon the origin of the thing as if, just because of that contingency, it could only be possible through reason. But the causality, so construed, becomes the faculty of acting according to ends—that is to say, a will; and the Object, which is represented as only deriving its possibility from such a will, will be represented as possible only as an end.

Suppose a person was in a country that seemed to him uninhabited and was to see a geometrical figure, say a regular hexagon, traced on the sand. As he reflected, and tried to get a conception of the figure, his reason would make him conscious, though perhaps obscurely, that in the production of this conception there was unity of principle. His reason would then forbid him to consider the sand, the neighbouring sea, the winds, or even animals with their footprints, as causes familiar to him, or any other irrational cause, as the ground of the possibility of such a form. For the contingency of coincidence with a conception like this, which is only possible in reason, would appear to him so infinitely great that there might just as well be no law of nature at all in the case. Hence it would seem that the cause of the production of such an effect could not be contained in the mere mechanical operation of nature, but that, on the contrary, a conception of such an Object, as a conception that only reason can give and compare the Object with, must likewise be what alone contains that causality. On these grounds it would appear to him that this effect was one that might without reservation be regarded as an end, though not as a natural end. In other words he would regard it as a product of *art—vestigium hominis video*.

But where a thing is recognized to be a product of nature, then something more is required—unless, perhaps, our very estimate involves a contradiction—if, despite its being such a product, we are yet to estimate it as an end, and, consequently, as a *physical end*. As a provisional statement I would say that a thing exists as a physical end *if it is* (though in a double sense) *both cause and effect of itself*. For this involves a kind of causality that we cannot associate with the mere conception of a nature unless we make that nature rest on an underlying end, but which can then, though incomprehensible, be thought without contradiction. Before analysing the component factors of this idea of a physical end, let us first illustrate its meaning by an example.

A tree produces, in the first place, another tree, according to a familiar law of nature. But the tree which it produces is of the same genus. Hence, in its *genus*, it produces itself. In the genus, now as effect, now as cause, continually generated from itself and likewise generating itself, it preserves itself generically.

Secondly, a tree produces itself even as an *individual*. It is true that we only call this kind of effect growth; but growth is here to be understood in a sense that makes it entirely different from any increase according to mechanical laws, and renders it equivalent, though under another name, to generation. The plant first prepares the matter that it assimilates and bestows upon it a specifically distinctive quality which the mechanism of nature outside it cannot supply, and it develops itself by means of a material which, in its composite character, is its own product. For, although in respect of the constituents that it derives from nature outside, it must be regarded as only an educt, yet in the separation and recombination of this raw material we find an original capacity of selection and construction on the part of natural beings of this kind such as infinitely outdistances all the efforts of art, when the latter attempts to reconstitute those products of the vegetable kingdom out of the elements which it obtains through their analysis, or else out of the material which nature supplies for their nourishment.

Thirdly, a part of a tree also generates itself in such a way that the preservation of one part is reciprocally dependent on the preservation of the other parts.

. . .

LXV

Things Considered as Physical Ends are Organisms

Where a thing is a product of nature and yet, so regarded, has to be cognized as possible only as a physical end, it must, from its character as set out in the preceding section, stand to itself reciprocally in the relation of cause and effect. This is, however, a somewhat inexact and indeterminate expression that needs derivation from a definite conception.

In so far as the causal connexion is thought merely by means of understanding it is a nexus constituting a series, namely of causes and effects, that is invariably progressive. The things that as effects presuppose others as their causes cannot themselves in turn be also causes of the latter. This causal connexion is termed that of efficient causes (*nexus effectivus*). On the other hand, however, we are also able to think a causal connexion according to a rational concept, that of ends, which, if regarded as a series, would involve regressive as well as progressive dependency. It would be one in which the thing that for the moment is designated effect deserves none the less, if we take the series regressively, to be called the cause of the thing of which it was said to be the effect. In the domain of practical matters, namely in art, we readily find examples of a nexus of this kind. Thus a house is certainly the cause of the money that is received as rent, but yet, conversely, the representation of this possible income was the cause of the building of the house. A causal nexus of this kind is termed that of final causes (*nexus finalis*). The former might, perhaps, more appropriately be called the nexus of real, and the latter the nexus of ideal causes, because with this use of terms it would be understood at once that there cannot be more than these two kinds of causality.

Now the *first* requisite of a thing, considered as a physical end, is that its parts, both as to their existence and form, are only possible by their relation to the whole. For the thing is itself an end, and is, therefore, comprehended under a conception or an idea that must determine *a priori* all that is to be contained in it. But so far as the possibility of a thing is only thought in this way, it is simply a work of art. It is the product, in other words, of an intelligent cause, distinct from the matter, or parts, of the thing, and of one whose causality, in bringing together and combining the parts, is determined by its idea of a whole made possible through that idea, and consequently, not by external nature.

But if a thing is a product of nature, and in this character is notwithstanding to contain intrinsically and in its inner possibility a relation to ends, in other words, is to be possible only as a physical end and independently of the causality of the conceptions of external rational agents, then this *second* requisite is involved, namely, that the parts of the thing combine of themselves into the unity of a whole by being reciprocally cause and effect of their form. For this is the only way in which it is possible that the idea of the whole may conversely, or reciprocally, determine in its turn the form and combination of all the parts, not as cause—for that would make it an art-product—but as the epistemological basis upon which the systematic unity of the form and combination of all the manifold contained in the given matter becomes cognizable for the person estimating it.

What we require, therefore, in the case of a body which in its intrinsic nature and inner possibility has to be estimated as a physical end, is as follows. Its parts must in their collective unity reciprocally produce one another alike as to form and combination, and thus by their own causality produce a whole, the conception of which, conversely,—in a being possessing the causality according to conceptions that is adequate for such a product—could in turn be the cause of the whole according to a principle, so that, consequently, the nexus of *efficient causes* might be no less estimated as an *operation brought about by final* causes.

In such a natural product as this every part is thought as *owing* its presence to the *agency* of all the remaining parts, and also as existing *for the sake of the others* and of the whole, that is as an instrument, or organ. But this is not enough—for it might be an instrument of art, and thus have no more than its general possibility referred to an end. On the contrary the part must be an organ *producing* the other parts—each consequently, reciprocally producing the others. No instrument of art can answer to this description, but only the instrument of that nature from whose resources the materials of every instrument are drawn—even the materials for instruments of art. Only under these conditions and upon these terms can such a product be an *organized* and *self-organized being*, and, as such, be called a *physical end*.

In a watch one part is the instrument by which the movement of the others is effected, but one wheel is not the efficient cause of the production of the other. One part is certainly present for the sake of another, but it does not owe its presence to the agency of that other. For this reason, also, the producing cause of the watch and its form is not contained in the nature of this material, but lies outside the watch in a being that can act according to ideas of a whole which its causality makes possible. Hence one wheel in the watch does not produce the other, and, still less, does one watch produce other watches, by utilizing, or organizing, foreign material; hence it does not of itself replace parts of which it has been deprived, nor, if these are absent in the original construction, does it make good the deficiency by the subvention of the rest; nor does it, so to speak, repair its own causal disorders. But these are all things which we are justified in expecting from organized nature.—An organized being is, therefore, not a mere machine. For a machine has solely *motive power*, whereas an organized being possesses inherent *formative* power, and such, moreover, as it can impart to material devoid of it—material which it organizes. This, therefore, is a selfpropagating formative power, which cannot be explained by the capacity of movement alone, that is to say, by mechanism.

We do not say half enough of nature and her capacity in organized products when we speak of this capacity as being the *analogue of art*. For what is here present to our minds is an artist—a rational being—working from without. But nature, on the contrary, organizes itself, and does so in each species of its organized products—following a single pattern, certainly, as to general features, but nevertheless admitting deviations calculated to secure self-preservation under particular circumstances. We might perhaps come nearer to the description of this impenetrable property if we were to call it an *analogue of life*. But then either we should have to endow matter as mere matter with a property (hylozoism) that contradicts its essential nature; or else we should have to associate with it a foreign principle *standing in community* with it (a soul). But, if such a product is to be a natural product, then we have to adopt one or other of two courses in order to bring in a soul. Either we must presuppose organized matter as the instrument of such a soul, which makes organized matter no whit more intelligible, or else we must make the soul the artificer of this structure, in which case we must withdraw the product from (corporal) nature. Strictly speaking, therefore, the organization of nature has nothing analogous to any causality known to us. Natural beauty may justly be termed the analogue of art, for it is only ascribed to the objects in respect of reflection upon the *external* intuition of them and, therefore, only on account of their superficial form. But *intrinsic natural perfection*, as possessed by things that are only possible as *physical ends*, and that are therefore called organisms, is unthinkable and inexplicable on any analogy to any known physical, or natural, agency, not even excepting—since we ourselves are part of nature in the widest sense—the suggestion of any strictly apt analogy to human art.

The concept of a thing as intrinsically a physical end is, therefore, not a constitutive conception either of understanding or of reason, but yet it may be used by reflective judgement as a regulative conception for guiding our investigation of objects of this kind by a remote analogy with our own causality according to ends generally, and as a basis of reflection upon their supreme source. But in the latter connexion it cannot be used to promote our knowledge either of nature or of such original source of those objects, but must on the contrary be confined to the service of just the same practical faculty of reason in analogy with which we considered the cause of the finality in question.

Organisms are, therefore, the only beings in nature that, considered in their separate existence and apart from any relation to other things, cannot be thought possible except as ends of nature. It is they, then, that first afford objective reality to the conception of an *end* that is an end *of nature* and not a practical end. Thus they supply natural science with the basis for a teleology, or, in other words, a mode of estimating its Objects on a special principle that it would otherwise be absolutely unjustifiable to introduce into that science—seeing that we are quite unable to perceive *a priori* the possibility of such a kind of causality.

LXVI

The Principle on Which the Intrinsic Finality in Organisms Is Estimated

This principle, the statement of which serves to define what is meant by organisms, is as follows: *an organized natural product is one in which every part is reciprocally both end and means.* In such a product nothing is in vain, without an end, or to be ascribed to a blind mechanism of nature.

It is true that the occasion for adopting this principle must be derived from experience—from such experience, namely, as is methodically arranged and is called observation. But owing to the universality and necessity which that principle predicates of such finality, it cannot rest merely on empirical grounds, but must have some underlying *a priori* principle. This principle, however, may be one that is merely regulative, and it may be that the ends in question only reside in the idea of the person forming the estimate and not in any efficient cause whatever. Hence the above named principle may be called a *maxim* for estimating the intrinsic finality of organisms.

It is common knowledge that scientists who dissect plants and animals, seeking to investigate their structure and to see into the reasons why and the end for which they are provided with such and such parts, why the parts have such and such a position and interconnexion, and why the internal form is precisely what it is, adopt the above maxim as absolutely necessary. So they say that nothing in such forms of life is in *vain*, and they put the maxim on the same footing of validity as the fundamental

principle of all natural science, that *nothing* happens *by c*
in fact, quite as unable to free themselves from this teleo\
as from that of general physical science. For just as the at
the latter would leave them without any experience at all, so
ment of the former would leave them with no clue to assist ,
tion of a type of natural things that have once come to be th
the conception of physical ends.

Indeed this conception leads reason into an order of things e
ferent from that of a mere mechanism of nature, which *mere n*
no longer proves adequate in this domain. An idea has to un͜   ͜ cne
possibility of the natural product. But this idea is an absolute unity of
the representation, whereas the material is a plurality of things that of
itself can afford no definite unity of composition. Hence, if that unity
of the idea is actually to serve as the *a priori* determining ground of a natural law of the causality of such a form of the composite, the end of nature must be made to extend to *everything* contained in its product. For if
once we lift such an effect out of the sphere of the blind mechanism of
nature and relate it *as a whole* to a supersensible ground of determination,
we must then estimate it out and out on this principle. We have no
reason for assuming the form of such a thing to be still partly dependent
on blind mechanism, for with such confusion of heterogeneous principles
every reliable rule for estimating things would disappear.

It is no doubt the case that in an animal body, for example, many parts
might be explained as accretions on simple mechanical laws (as skin, bone,
hair). Yet the cause that accumulates the appropriate material, modifies
and fashions it, and deposits it in its proper place, must always be estimated teleologically. Hence, everything in the body must be regarded
as organized, and everything, also, in a certain relation to the thing is
itself in turn an organ.

Robert Burch

KANT'S THEORY OF BEAUTY
AS IDEAL ART

Students of Kant's third *Critique* often voice a general worry to the effect that Kant has failed to amalgamate his theory of art with his theory of beauty in a satisfying way.* For instance, when Donald Crawford says that "Kant's own work provides an almost perfect example of the gap between traditional philosophical aesthetics and art criticism,"[1] he seems to have in mind a specific version of this worry: namely, the worry that few if any lessons for art criticism emerge from Kant's theory of beauty. In this paper I wish to consider the general problem of the relation between Kant's theory of art and his theory of beauty, together with the specific worry that Crawford seems to have in mind.

In examining the relation between Kant's account of beauty and his account of art, I want to explore the possibility that perhaps we are looking wrongly at Kant merely in expecting that lessons for art criticism should, or even could, emerge from his theory of beauty. One reason to suspect this is that Kant never attempts to spell out such lessons. Another reason is that this theory of beauty is perhaps not the sort of thing upon which could be based any sort of art criticism, for the judgments of criticism would seem to follow from a theory of beauty only if that theory could somehow be presented as a set of criteria for what is and is not beautiful, and this presentation is not possible according to Kant.[2] The possibility is worth exploring, then, that instead of Kant's theory of beauty being primary, in some sense that could yield up implications for art criticism, it is really Kant's theory of art that is primary, in a sense that precludes art criticism from being based on his theory of beauty. What follows is an attempt to defend this possibility. I shall marshal evidence and arguments to support the view that Kant's theory

Robert Burch is Associate Professor of Philosophy at Texas A&M University. He publishes in ethics, the philosophy of mind, and the philosophy of language, and has had a long standing interest in Kant's works.

* This essay was written for this collection and is published here for the first time.
[1] Donald W. Crawford, *Kant's Aesthetic Theory* (Madison, Wisc.: Univ. of Wisconsin Press, 1974), p. 171.
[2] Immanuel Kant, *Critique of Judgment*, translated by J. H. Bernard (New York: Hafner Publishing Company, 1968), Section 34.

of art is not an implication of his theory of beauty but, rather, is meant to complete his theory of beauty and in a sense to form its basis. In doing so, I shall also propose an account of what Kant means by the elusive notion of purposiveness without a purpose.

To begin with, there is some general evidence for the thesis I am defending in the mere way in which Kant's text is arranged. Kant divides his "Critique of the Aesthetical Judgment" (Sections 1–60) into two parts, an "Analytic of the Aesthetical Judgment" (Sections 1–54) and a "Dialectic of the Aesthetical Judgment" (Sections 55–60). "Analytic of the Aesthetic Judgment" is, in turn, divided into two books, the "Analytic of the Beautiful" (Sections 1–22) and the "Analytic of the Sublime" (Sections 23–54). The "Analytic of the Beautiful" is totally taken up (with perhaps the exception of the "General Remark" on the whole book) with presenting the four "moments" of the judgment of taste under the rubric of which Kant deals with the notion[3] of beauty. The "Analytic of the Sublime," however, does not parallel the "Analytic of the Beautiful" in its singleness of topic, as the latter treats not only sublimity (Sections 23–29) but also aesthetic judgments in general (Section 30), art (Sections 43–54), and even humor (Section 54). Sections 30–54 of the "Analytic of the Sublime" are, then, essentially not discussions of sublimity at all but, rather, discussions of beauty and art.

Moreover, the discussion of art seems to crop up like some strange growth in the midst of the discussion of beauty, with little that prepares the reader for it and little that integrates it into the preceding passages. It is not clear why the theory of art is taken up at precisely that point in the text that it is. Its position seems odd and capricious. It would be surprising, however, if there were not a method in this madness, for it is the madness of a philosopher renowned for his methodical character and his love of "architectonic" presentation. The suggestion is, then, that the apparent dropping of the discussion of beauty and the immediate taking up of the discussion of art is intended to make the theory of art contribute in some way to the theory of beauty.

Let us try to follow out this suggestion. Matters are rather as if some problem exists about beauty that can only be solved by going into the topic of art. Let us, then, assume that there is some such problem and ask what it can be. This question is not difficult to answer. Recall what Kant's theory of beauty has achieved up to the point of the beginning of Section 30. Kant has, in the "Analytic of the Beautiful" (Sections 1–22), discussed the four moments of the judgment of taste and, consequently, what determines the use of the terms "beauty" and "beautiful." In this discussion of the four moments Kant puts forth four basic points about the judgment of taste. It involves a disinterested satisfaction. It is universal. It is necessary. And it involves a discernment of what Kant calls "purposiveness without a purpose" (Zweckmässigkeit ohne Zweck).

---

[3] Since Kant denies that there is, properly speaking, any *concept* of beauty, I speak throughout of the *notion* of beauty, leaving it open for a notion to lack the essential features of a concept.

Two obvious and crucial difficulties arise out of this discussion of the four moments of the judgment of taste. First, there is an apparent contradiction in holding that the judgment of taste involves a satisfaction and yet that it is universal and necessary, since satisfactions seem to be a matter of mere personal preference. Second, the notion of purposiveness without a purpose is sufficiently vague to require some sort of elaboration. As of the beginning of Section 30, however, Kant has not yet dealt satisfactorily with either of these problems.

Clearing up the first difficulty is certainly the main undertaking in Sections 30–42, the heart of which Sections is the "Deduction" of the judgment of taste, a discussion that carries into Sections 30–40. "Deduction" essentially has the job of showing how it is possible for there to be a judgment such as Kant has claimed for the judgment of taste. Sections 41–42 are also devoted to clearing up certain difficulties concerning what Kant calls the "purity" of the judgment of taste. But up to the beginning of Section 43 purposiveness without a purpose has received no treatment comparable to that accorded the other three moments of the judgment of taste. Kant has merely defined it formally in Section 10 without clarifying its meaning in detail. Yet it is by no means an unproblematic notion, and there is even reason to doubt that there could be any such thing as purposiveness without a purpose, for, although there are many variations on the theme of purposiveness (tools, organs of organisms, intentional acts, etc.), we typically say that an entity is purposive (*zweckmässig*) just in case we have a purpose (*Zweck*) in mind and can relate that entity and its internal organization to that purpose. For example, a hammer is understood as such not by reference to its mere physical form alone, but also by reference to the purpose of hammering. We spell out its purposiveness by using an objective teleological judgment, such as "Hammers are for hammering." Indeed, the physical arrangement of the hammer's parts is only understood by reference to the task of hammering. To take another example, the organization and activities of the heart become comprehensible only after we understand that it serves to keep blood circulating through the blood vessels.

What I wish to suggest, then, is that Sections 43–53 of the "Analytic of the Sublime" have the job of further clarifying the notion of purposiveness without a purpose and, hence, of further clarifying the notion of beauty, in so far as this can be done. But it must now be explained how a discussion of the notion of art can contribute to clarifying the notion of purposiveness without a purpose.

The notion of purposiveness without a purpose is commonly[4] explained by reference to the notion of organic interconnectedness, and beauty is

---

[4] See, for example, S. Körner, *Kant* (Baltimore: Penguin Books, 1955), p. 181. Körner speaks of particulars which display purposiveness without a purpose as "particulars . . . whose parts are so intimately interrelated and so harmoniously fitted together and to the whole of which they are parts, that we speak of the whole as having a design. . . ." Kant would not, I believe, speak of design (*Absicht*) in this context, but he would speak of purposiveness.

accordingly compared with the notion of an organized being. An organized being is one, Kant says, in which none of the parts are in vain,[5] in which "the maintenance of any one part depends reciprocally on the maintenance of the rest."[6] In a tree, for example, the roots provide water and minerals for the leaves and trunk. The leaves provide food for the trunk and roots. The trunk conducts matter between the leaves and the roots. The same sort of interconnectedness holds in a being that displays purposiveness without a purpose.

This common idea, although it is no doubt correct, is insufficient, for in an organized being, such as a tree, the parts interconnect causally: one element "supports" another in the precise sense that its existence and welfare is a causal contributor to and a causally necessary condition of the existence and welfare of the other. ". . . a thing exists as a natural purpose if it is . . . both *cause and effect of itself*"[7] But the elements of a beautiful thing are surely not causally related in this way. If we speak of them as "supporting" or "contributing to" or "reinforcing for" the other parts or the whole, we are using metaphors that are not cashable in causal terms. The question, then, is how to understand the kind of interconnectedness that a beautiful thing has. I want to argue that for Kant this kind of interconnectedness must be spelled out via the notion of an artwork.

It is initially tempting to try to spell out this kind of interconnectedness by reference to a notion like complexity. But two problems arise here. First, it is not clear that we gain anything in clarity by such an appeal. It is not clear what constitutes simplicity and complexity, and what is simple from one perspective may be complex from another. Suppose we compare a round monochromatic disk with a disk that is painted like a pizza. At first glance the monochromatic disk would be held by everyone to be simpler than the pizza-like one. But this attribution is not absolute; it depends at the least on the choice of respects in which the comparison is made. The monochromatic disk is simpler than the pizza-like one in that it contains fewer colors. But the two are of exactly the same complexity in that both are representations on a disk. Moreover, even from the point of view of color alone, it is not absolutely clear that the monochromatic disk is simpler than the pizza-like disk. Suppose that there is a complicated projective function that projects from color points on disks to color points on disks. And suppose that the monochromatic disk results from coloring an uncolored disk in accordance with the projective function as applied to the pizza-like disk. We could, let us say, entitle the projectively constructed disk "Monochromatic Copy of a Pizza-Like Disk" and regard it as a "copy in one color." If we regard the monochromatic disk in this way, then it seems we can with reason say that in regard to its color it is more complex than the pizza-like disk. Let me make the same point with a perhaps less dubious example. There

---

[5] Kant, *Critique of Judgment*, pp. 222–223.
[6] Ibid., p. 218.
[7] Ibid., p. 217.

is a sense in which the early paintings of Mondrian are more complex than his later paintings. But there is another sense, which I regard as containing the more nearly adequate perspective, according to which Mondrian's later paintings are distinctly more complex than his earlier ones. There is even a sense in which the earlier ones, with all their complexity, are contained in the later ones.

This example brings us to the second difficulty with trying to spell out the notion of purposiveness without a purpose by appealing to the notion of complexity. In so far as the notion of complexity can be defined objectively, it is really of no use to us. For if complexity is the ultimate basis of beauty, and if complexity is objectively definable, then beauty ought to be objectively definable too. But Kant does not think that it is so definable. As he states at the outset of Section 34, "There is no objective principle of taste possible."[8] He continues, "By a principle of taste I mean a principle under the condition of which we could subsume the concept of an object and thus infer, by means of a syllogism, that the object is beautiful. But that is absolutely impossible."[9] In so far as Kant is correct, then, any appeal to complexity in a sense that would be aesthetically relevant must be an appeal to a sense that cannot be defined objectively.

There is another clue to be gleaned, I think, from the examples just discussed, for, when we began to deal with complexity in a way that was aesthetically relevant, we began to imagine the role of an intentional agency in the production of the objects under discussion. I suggest that this is not an accident from Kant's point of view. For Kant seems to hold that purposiveness without a purpose involves a certain sort of oblique reference to an agent with intentions. It is this reference to the concept of agency that will enable the notion of purposiveness without a purpose to be related to the notion of art. Let us, then, see how for Kant purposiveness without a purpose is related to agency.

As a preliminary, consider the case of purposiveness with a purpose. In every case of purposiveness in which there is a purpose, the purposive item is connected with its purpose via the intentions, or at least via the intentional activity, of an agent with comprehension. Hammers are made by people who intend to produce an article that can be used for hammering. Hammers are intended for hammering. Even when a tool is merely found and used as such, for example in the way that primitives find certain rocks and use them as fist axes, it is still the intentional activity of a conscious agent that connects the item with a purpose and thus gives purposiveness to the item.

Does Kant accept this analysis of the sort of purposiveness that is based on purposes? That is, does he think that there is always a reference to agency and intentionality when there are purposes involved in purposiveness? The answer to these questions is, yes. Kant formally defines the notion of purpose via the notion of causality: "The purpose is the object

---

[8] Ibid., p. 127.
[9] Ibid., p. 127.

of a concept in so far as the concept is regarded as the cause of the object . . .".[10] Again, "The product of a cause whose determining ground is merely the representation of its effect is called a purpose."[11] Kant is saying that an object X is to be considered a purpose of something Y (which Kant refers to in the passage as a concept) just in case Y causes X and the concept or representation of X is the determining ground of Y. Hammering is the purpose of a hammer because the hammer causes hammering and the representation of hammering is the cause of the hammer. Getting to the store is the purpose of my walking in that direction because my idea of getting to the store is the cause of my walking in that direction, while my walking in that direction is the cause of my getting to the store.

A crucial factor here, which needs to be highlighted, is the doctrine that there is no purpose without "a representation of a purpose."[12] Indeed, the representation—typically a concept—of something is what makes it into a purpose when that representation takes on a causal role. This point is crucial because it connects the notion of purpose to the notion of a representer, one for whom the representation is a representation. In other words it connects the notion of purpose with the notion of a purposer, a consciousness which has purposes. Such a consciousness Kant calls a will,[13] and we would, I think, call it an agent. Kant is maintaining that purposes exist only where there are agents whose purposes they are, and indeed that they are purposes by virtue of being, and only in so far as they are, purposes of agents. Kant makes this explicit in making the objective teleological judgment depend on our attributing "causality in respect of an object to the concept of an object . . . or rather when we represent to ourselves the possibility of the object after the analogy of that causality which we experience in ourselves. . . ."[14] Purposiveness with purpose, then, clearly involves reference to agency.

Now I would like to show that purposiveness without a purpose in Kant's sense also involves reference to an agent. To establish this, let us begin with Kant's formal definition of this notion. ". . . an object, or a state of mind, or even an action is called purposive, although its possibility does not necessarily presuppose the representation of a purpose, merely because its possibility can be explained and conceived by us only so far as we assume for its ground a causality according to purposes, i.e. in accordance with a will which has regulated it according to the representation of a certain rule. There can be, then, purposiveness without purpose, so far as we do not place the cause of this form in a will, but yet can only make the explanation of its possibility intelligible to ourselves by deriving it from a will."[15]

[10] Ibid., p. 55.
[11] Ibid., p. 256.
[12] Ibid., p. 55.
[13] Ibid., p. 55.
[14] Ibid., p. 206.
[15] Ibid., p. 55.

The key distinction in Kant's definition is between assuming (*annehmen*) a causality according to purposes, that is, in accordance with a will, and placing (*setzen*) the cause in a will. Kant explains assuming a causality in accordance with a will as deriving (*ableiten*) it from a will. The problem of understanding the nature of this sort of assuming or deriving is compounded when Kant glosses his explanation as follows: "Again, we are not always forced to regard what we observe (in respect of its possibility) from the point of view of reason. Thus we can at least observe a purposiveness according to form, without basing it on a purpose (as the material of a *nexus finalis*), and remark it in objects, although only by reflection."[16] In Kant's definition and gloss, we are presented with a kind of assuming and deriving that are different from processes of reasoning and are rather matters of pure observation of the form of the object. The mental activity that they amount to is carried out by reflection. Presumably this mental activity is in the province of the reflective (not the determinative) judgment.

To clarify all these points adequately would take us too far from and wide of the explicit content of this paper and into two very difficult and pervasive Kantian distinctions, that between thought and sense and that between determinative judgment and reflective judgment. What I shall do, rather than delve into these issues, is simply to put into modern idiom what I believe Kant is saying. In doing so I will have to ignore the issue of reflective versus determinative judgment.

The much overworked notion of seeing-as, explored by Wittgenstein,[17] is, I think, genuinely relevant here because it closely approximates Kant's notion of what goes on when one observes purposiveness without a purpose. The Wittgensteinian example of the duck-rabbit picture contains all the crucial features: we have a single object that may be seen now as a duck picture and now as a rabbit picture. In the phenomenon of a shift of aspect (from, say, duck picture to rabbit picture), there is a clear sense in which nothing in the picture has changed. No lines, shapes, or colors have been altered. Yet there is also a clear sense in which everything has changed. Moreover, the difference in question is not a matter of a mere superimposition of a different intellectual interpretation: the difference is resident in the perceiving itself. The picture looks different somehow—now like a duck, now like a rabbit—even though it also in one sense looks exactly the same. This difference in perception is not totally divorced from concepts, of course, for we explain, and indeed must explain, the difference in looks by reference to the concepts "duck" and "rabbit." Still, the change is perceptual and not merely intellectual.

Kant seems to have a process like this in mind when he speaks of discerning purposiveness without a purpose, for, at the outset, it is clear that, when Kant speaks of assuming and deriving, what he means is that, in discerning a thing's purposiveness without a purpose, we are in some

[16] Ibid., pp. 55–56.
[17] Ludwig Wittgenstein, *Philosophical Investigations*, translated by G. E. M. Anscombe (New York: Macmillan, 1953), pp. 193–229.

way regarding it as produced by and in accord with purposes, that is, with a purposive will. What is crucial is the particular way in which we are so regarding it. The regarding in question is not a judgment of reason. It does not, that is, contain (express) the belief that the purposive item actually has been produced by and in accord with a purposive will. It may even coexist with the belief that the thing has not actually been so produced. It implies no objective teleological judgment. Moreover, the kind of regarding Kant is talking about is located by Kant in reflective judgment and, indeed, in observation. Kant is saying that one perceives the thing as produced by a purposive will. Just as one sees a duck-rabbit picture as a duck picture, without thereby claiming that it actually has become anything additional to the set of marks it always was, so one may see a certain object as produced by and in accord with a purposive will, without actually claiming it to be so produced. This is what Kant is getting at, and it is this experience that he is claiming to be the core of the experience of beauty. To see the beauty of something is to see it as produced by and in accord with a purposive will.

The question that arises now is, can we not perceive everything in this way—so that in a few steps we could deduce that everything is equally beautiful? Can we not regard anything as produced by and in accord with a purposive will? To answer, there is, perhaps, a faint possibility of this. The plainest, most ordinary object, with no distinguishing features, may still be imagined as if it were produced by a will for a purpose. We may do this by imaginatively weaving a tale connecting it and its features with some imagined agent who has purposes which chime in properly with precisely the features of this object. And we may imagine the agent to have produced the object in order to secure its purposes. But there are rather strict limits to the degree to which this imaginative storytelling can spill over into our actual perceptions of the object. If we are asked to see the object in accord with a purposive will, we can at most get ourselves into a kind of uncanny frame of mind. And this frame of mind must even be secured with an imaginative effort which cannot be relaxed without the frame of mind evaporating. How different is this frame of mind from the perception of one of the aspects of the duck-rabbit picture, in which no special effort is required and which, indeed, seems to force itself on the perceiver. Not every object, then, can actually be *seen*, or otherwise *perceived*, as produced in accord with a purposive will in the natural way that aspect seeing involves.

Moreover, there are objects that force themselves on our perception as beautiful. It seems quite natural to see such objects as the purposive products of wills. It is even strained and odd to imagine them otherwise. An uncanny feeling comes from imagining them not to be produced in accord with wills but, rather, through sheer accident. Kant's examples of certain natural beauties—beautiful flowers, brightly colored birds, and gaudy insects—are such objects. One finds it almost incredible after a visual survey of their glories to think of them merely as the accidental results of mechanical processes. Their attractiveness and the unarbitrariness of their arrangement not only compel us to marvel and to prolong our perception of them, but also to express our delighted amazement by appealing to the concept of the purposiveness of an agent.

The notion of beauty has now been connected with the notion of purposiveness without a purpose, and both have been connected with the notion of seeing-as. It remains to connect the notion of beauty with that of art. The groundwork for this has been laid, however. According to Kant, one experiences beauty in a thing when he observes in it "a purposiveness according to form without basing it on a purpose,"[18] and this observation occurs when he sees it as (produced) ". . . in accordance with a will which has regulated it according to the representation of a certain rule."[19] What I want to establish now is that it is Kant's view that experiencing beauty in a thing is to see it as an art object. To establish this is, of course, further to explicate Kant's contention that beauty involves purposiveness without a purpose.

Seeing a thing as produced in accord with purposive agency is not by itself seeing it as an object of art. It could, for instance, be to see it as a tool or an amusing activity. How can Kant exclude these cases? Well, with regard to them we have not only purposiveness but also the representation of purposes. Hammers are for hammering and games are for amusement.[20] I can regard this object as a tool (say, as a fist ax) only because I represent to myself a definite purpose (for example, pounding) that I regard the object to have. To be sure, I may have a particular hammer which I do not put to the use of hammering, but, in understanding it as a hammer, I represent to myself the purpose of hammering all the same. Thus, when Kant speaks of something's being "purposive, although its possibility does not necessarily presuppose the representation of a purpose,"[21] I think that he is intentionally saying something which would be severely mangled if the words "the representation" were left out. It is not just that we have purposiveness without a purpose, but that we have purposiveness without even the *representation* of a purpose. With regard to a flower, a bird, or an insect, I do not even represent to myself a definite purpose. Their purposiveness shines out in their fascinatingly attractive forms and neither requires nor allows of any representation of a definite purpose which explains these forms. The forms are naturally seen as deriving from a purposive agent, but not as involving a particular purpose. In the example of artificially produced bird sounds,[22] Kant even claims that lighting upon a definite purpose for a set of aesthetic forms destroys the experience of beauty.

In beauty, then, there is not even the representation of a purpose. That is part of what Kant means by saying that beauty is *free*. "[Taste] is a faculty for judging an object in reference to the imagination's *free con-*

[18] Kant, *Critique of Judgment*, pp. 55–56.
[19] Ibid., p. 55.
[20] See Kant, *Critique of Judgment*, p. 146, on games and their purpose.
[21] Ibid., p. 55.
[22] Ibid., pp. 80, 145.

formity to law. Now, if in the judgment of taste the imagination must be considered in its freedom, it is . . . regarded as . . . productive and spontaneous (as the author of arbitrary forms of possible intuition)."[23] In other words Kant is saying that purposiveness without a purpose is had in the experience of being compelled by the form of an object to see it as the free, spontaneous, purposive product of an agent.

For Kant, however, the free, spontaneous, purposive product of an agent is a work of fine art. "By right we ought only to describe as art, production through freedom. . . ."[24] "Art also differs from handicraft; the first is called 'free,' the other may be called 'mercenary.' "[25] The role of free production in art is perhaps the central lesson of Sections 43–53 of the third *Critique*. "Genius is the talent . . . which gives the rule to art. . . . Hence *originality* must be its first property."[26] Art, then, is the deliberate product of an agent's exercise of free, spontaneous creativity, of productive activity that is not directed to any particular purpose. The implication, then, is obvious: since to experience a thing's beauty is to perceive it as a free, spontaneous, creative product of purposiveness, to experience a thing's beauty is to perceive it as a work of art.

This account of Kant's theory of beauty must be qualified in two ways. First, works of art, as such, may be either good or bad. Simply as works of art they are neither to be honored nor to be scorned. But beauty as such must be good: "beautiful" is itself a term of praise. And, as Kant says, "The beautiful pleases immediately."[27] To experience beauty in something, then, or at least to see it as a work of art, is not merely to see it as a work of art. Let us say, then, that it is to see it as a work of art that is everything a work of art should be: one without fault or flaw. I shall call the idea of such a work, that is, one with no flaws, an "ideal" work of art. To experience beauty, then, is for Kant to see something as an ideal work of art.

A second qualification is needed in the account of Kant's theory of beauty being defended here. So far this account maintains that for Kant beauty is what can be perceived as ideal art, and the word "perceived" here is strenuously to be emphasized. But what makes art excellent need not always be perceivable. Sometimes it is what is thinkable, for example, that makes a work of art successful. But, if we hold that beauty is what is *perceivable* as ideal art, then ideal art cannot be everything that is contained in flawless art; rather, it is merely the perceivable excellences of flawless art. Ideal art, then, must be taken as the perceivable dimension of flawless art.

With these qualifications, the account here being defended of purposiveness without purpose, and consequently of Kant's conception of the experience of beauty, is complete. We are supposed to understand

[23] Ibid., p. 77.
[24] Ibid., p. 145.
[25] Ibid., p. 146.
[26] Ibid., p. 150.
[27] Ibid., p. 199.

the organic interrelatedness in the beautiful thing by analogy with the purposive, but purposeless, interrelatedness of an artwork. We are supposed to experience beauty after the fashion that we experience art. The basis for the experience of beauty is the experience of art. Let me call this account the "Theory of Beauty as Ideal Art." What I have been arguing is that this theory is plausibly attributed to Kant.

It may be asked how much of the theory of beauty as ideal art is fanciful reconstruction of Kant and how much is actually Kant's thinking. I think that the overall idea is undoubtedly Kant's, although to say this is not to deny that I have drawn out his view into a more explicit form. There are numerous places in which Kant maintains that beauty is similar to art. For example, in discussing the relationship between art and nature, Kant clearly maintains that "Nature is beautiful because it looks like art, and art can only be called beautiful if we are conscious of it as art while yet it looks like nature."[28] Again, in discussing the organized character of nature, Kant denies that there is an exact analogy between this character as a whole and art, but he allows that the organized character of the beautiful, perceivable forms of nature is precisely analogous to art: "Beauty in nature can be rightly described as an analogon of art."[29]

There are also at least two other themes in the third *Critique* that imply the theory of beauty as ideal art. One such is the theme that beauty is the expression of aesthetical ideas. "We may describe beauty in general (whether natural or artificial) as the expression of aesthetical ideas. . . ."[30] The notion of an aesthetical idea is first introduced in Kant's discussion of spirit, one of the qualities of successful art, in Section 49.[31] The aesthetical idea is a product of the imagination for which no concept of the understanding is wholly adequate. As such, it is the counterpart of a rational idea, to which no intuition is wholly adequate. The sort of imagination Kant is speaking of in the immediate context is the productive imagination, and what he is thinking of as being produced by it is art. But if beauty, whether natural or artificial, is the expression of aesthetical ideas, then beauty must be thought of as either the product of the productive imagination (art), or else what "looks" exactly like it, namely, that it has a perceptual form indistinguishable from such a product. Of course, here again we must throw in the corrective notion of faultless or ideal art.

Another theme in the third *Critique* that tells the same tale is the theme that beauty is experienced wherever there is a harmony between the freedom of the imagination and the conformity to law of the understanding.[32] Unfortunately, to spell out this line would take far too long here, and I have worked out the details only in an unpublished manuscript. The general idea, however, is that Kant's view is that this harmony occurs wherever the object of one's perceptions is perceived as being

[28] Ibid., p. 149. The German word for "looks like" is "*aussehen als*."
[29] Ibid., p. 221.
[30] Ibid., p. 164.
[31] Ibid., p. 157.
[32] See, for example, Kant, the "General Remark on the First Section of the Analytic," which follows Section 22.

exactly the kind of thing that one might have produced if one were creating freely, that is, if one were producing ideal art. The harmony between the imagination and the understanding is understandable on the basis of the two Kantian claims that an art object is a product of the imagination and that any object must conform to the laws of the understanding. As Kant puts it, ". . . it may readily be conceived that the object can furnish it [i.e., the imagination] with such a form containing a collection of the manifold as the imagination itself, if it were left free, would project in accordance with the *conformity to law of the understanding* in general."[33] In other words the harmony which is the basis of the experience of beauty occurs just where the imagination encounters an object just like one it would project if it were creating freely.

The discussion of art in the third *Critique*, then, seems designed to complete and fill in the content of the notion of beauty. And it is reasonably clear how it does so. Moreover, there are other themes in the third *Critique* that have the same implication as the interpretation of Kant's theory of beauty here being defended. But having said this much, I must now turn to several objections to the theory of beauty as ideal art as an interpretation of Kant. I must also return to Donald Crawford's worry about the gap between Kant's theory of beauty and the task of art criticism.

It will be objected to attributing the theory of beauty as ideal art to Kant that art cannot be used to spell out his notion of purposiveness without a purpose because art does have purposes, for art, one might say, is produced with the purposes of pleasing, gratifying, or entertaining a prospective perceiver of it. Not only is art a purposive product of the artist (i.e., deliberately produced), it is produced with particular purposes. In response to this objection, let it be admitted that an artist can produce an artwork with a certain purpose in mind, say, to become famous, to earn a living, or to attract attention. But this purpose is only contingently associated with the product and is not essential for the artwork's being what it is. A hammer is essentially for hammering, and clothes are essentially for wearing, but what is an artwork essentially for? I would say that an artwork is not essentially for anything, unless it be, in a Pickwickian sense, for itself. The artwork is a kind of intelligible goal in itself, not needing an explanation in terms of any further purposes. I agree with Francis X. Coleman when he says that art has "no 'extrinsic' ends."[34] As Maupassant says in the essay "Of 'The Novel,' " attached to his novel *Pierre and Jean*, "The public as a whole is composed of various groups whose cry to us writers is: 'Comfort me,' 'Amuse me,' 'Touch me,' 'Make me dream,' 'Make me laugh,' 'Make me shudder,' 'Make me weep,' 'Make me think.' And only a few chosen spirits say to the artist 'Give me something fine in any form which may suit you best.' " This is not to deny, by the way, that the artist may have (indeed, we expect

[33] Kant, *The Critique of Judgment*, p. 78.
[34] Francis X. J. Coleman, *The Harmony of Reason: A Study in Kant's Aesthetics* (Pittsburgh, Pa.: Univ. of Pittsburgh Press, 1974), p. 53.

him to have) certain artistic purposes which he realizes or seeks to realize in the artwork. But there is not one single purpose which all art, merely as art, has.

A second objection to the theory of beauty as ideal art is that the notion of looking like art is obscure. I accept that this notion is obscure, especially since it relies on a troublesome distinction between seeing-as and merely taking something as-if. Yet, it is undeniable that Kant himself speaks explicitly of beauty as looking like (*aussehen als*) art. So, if there is a weakness in this regard, it is Kant's weakness and not a weakness of the theory alone.

It will be objected, in the third place, that nothing has really been gained by explicating beauty in terms of art, even ideal art, for, is the explanation not as vague and confused as the matter to be explained? The answer is, not quite. One must evaluate the gains in clarity in the interpretation of Kant here being defended, by reference to Kant's whole program. Beauty is not just a vague notion for Kant, but also an especially problematic one in the sense that it can reasonably be doubted whether it has any content or any kind of objective reference at all. Kant takes it as *prima facie* reasonable, although not ultimately correct, to think that beauty is a merely subjective notion, like "pleasing to look at," and that to call a thing beautiful is not to characterize the thing in any genuine way, but only to characterize its contingent effects on someone, or to characterize the someone who is affected by it.

Kant, however, clearly wants to show it to be the case that things are in some way genuinely characterized by being called beautiful. He does not, however, want to commit himself to the untenable view that beauty is an objective property of things, namely that "beauty" is an objectively valid concept. So he must somehow provide a content for the notion of beauty without thereby turning "beauty" into a concept or implying that there are necessary and sufficient conditions for the application of the term.

In providing any content for the notion, therefore, Kant must leave the content vague when judged by the standards required of criterial conditions or objectively valid rules. The appeal to the notion of purposiveness without a purpose is the key way in which Kant spells out the content of beauty. What this notion initially boils down to, as we have said, is a kind of organized interconnectedness in which "nothing is in vain."[35] This organized interconnectedness must, therefore, itself be vague: and it is. Yet it still gives a measure of clarity about the character of beauty through associating beauty with the structure of organisms such as trees, which are familiar and not so problematic as beauty. When we then press on to further explicate purposiveness without a purpose, and hence beauty, by appealing to the notion of ideal art, the same situation obtains. We have remained vague, for we have no criterial conditions governing the notion of ideal art. Moreover, we cannot rely on any

---

[35] Kant, *Critique of Judgment*, pp. 222–223.

identification of actually faultless pieces of art. There are no ideals of pure beauty in the sense of actually specifiable objects, as Kant makes clear.[36] Yet, just as we are familiar with the structure of trees, so also we are familiar with art objects, and with both more and less successful pieces of art. So the notion of art is not problematical in quite the way that the notion of beauty is. And, in explicating beauty in terms of ideal art, we have gained in comprehension by gaining in familiarity and by translation away from obviously and deeply problematical notions.

A fourth objection to the theory of ideal art can be put in the form of a dilemma involving the "ideal" character of ideal art. What makes art ideal is surely either its beauty alone or else its beauty together with certain other of its qualities. In the first case we would seem to have gained nothing whatsoever by analyzing beauty as ideal art because ideal art is simply art that is beautiful, and we will have analyzed in a circle. But in the second case, we will have analyzed beauty in terms not only of beauty but of qualities which are not beauty, and surely this is mistaken.

It is the first alternative we must seriously consider here. Kant does seem to think that success in art involves more than mere beauty (e.g., originality).[37] But the notion of ideal art, as this paper spells it out, is merely the notion of what is, or is exactly like, the perceivable excellence in flawlessly successful art. Now, it is obvious that whatever is perceivable in successful art is identical, in perceivable appearance, with itself. That is, ideal art is perceivable as ideal art. Therefore, according to the account proposed in this paper, it must be beautiful. Art is ideal, then, because it is beautiful.

Hence the question of the dilemma: are we not going in a circle? If the theory of beauty as ideal art were an attempt to give a definitional analysis, or a metaphysical account, of beauty, it would be circular indeed. But its task is not so strict, for it is merely an attempt to explicate or offer some clarification of the notion of beauty. Moreover, if our viewpoint is shifted to consider matters from the epistemological point of view rather than from the metaphysical point of view (i.e., to consider the questions "How do we come to experience beauty?" and "How do we 'know' what is beautiful?," rather than the question "What is beauty?"), we can see the gain that the theory offers. We gain a better understanding of beauty by assimilating it to art.

This brings us back to the problem that worries Donald Crawford. How does Kant's analysis of beauty help us in the criticism of art? The answer to Crawford's question that I would like to suggest is this: If Kant is advocating the theory of beauty as ideal art, as I have argued, then Kant in fact puts matters the other way round than Crawford would, perhaps, expect. From the epistemological perspective it is art criticism that is primary and not the analysis of beauty. One first finds out, through critics and otherwise, what there is to appreciate in works of

---

[36] Ibid., Section 17, especially p. 69.
[37] Ibid., p. 150.

art, and then and only then, through the appreciation of art, comes to see the beauty in things. The content of beauty is contained in the ongoing history of art criticism.

This answer is, perhaps, surprising. But, as was said early in this paper, the opposite point of view seems untenable from a Kantian perspective. That is, a desire to know what beauty is, so as to have a basis for art criticism, contains the confused assumption, from a Kantian point of view, that one *could* know what beauty is in a way which could then be applied to criticism, for what could knowledge usable in this way be except conceptual, definitory, criterial, or rule-governed knowledge? And Kant denies the possibility of this sort of knowledge of beauty. There can be no concept of beauty according to Kant.[38] So there can be no objective basis for criticism in any such concept. The theory of beauty as ideal art, by virtue of making beauty depend on the ongoing but unpredictable and never-ending history of art criticism, has the advantage of according nicely with Kant's views about the impossibility of any objective standard of taste.[39] The absence of such a basis does not mean that criticism is not a legitimate enterprise: it only means that the course of criticism is no more rigorously specifiable once and for all prior to its actually being carried out than is art itself.

This is, I think, as it should be, for it not only accords with the Kantian view that beauty is not once and for all capturable in objective rules, but also with the general truism that we do not always know once and for all how to appreciate the beauty in a thing. It is a commonplace of aesthetic criticism, albeit a curious one requiring explanation, that we do not in a single glance always see the beauty of things. Often we can be brought to see the beauty of things only after long contemplation and study. As Frank Sibley (for one) has pointed out, critics often perform the service of bringing us to see the aesthetic qualities of things.[40] Furthermore, legitimate aesthetic taste can develop and grow, or simply change. The theory of beauty as ideal art allows for this on Kantian terms by appealing to the Kantian claim that art is creative, original, and involves genius[41] and also, by appealing to the Kantian theme, that art criticism is posterior to artworks themselves.[42] Thus, neither art itself nor art criticism is governed by objective rules which can be laid out once and for all.

There are other Kantian themes with which the theory of beauty as ideal art well accords. The theme of the special status of exemplary works[43] and the theme of beauty connecting more closely to sense than to reason[44] are two such themes. These need not be discussed in detail

---

[38] Ibid., p. 150.
[39] See Kant, *Critique of Judgment*, Section 34.
[40] Frank N. Sibley, "Aesthetic Concepts," *The Philosophical Review*, LXVIII, 4 (1959), 421–50.
[41] Kant, *Critique of Judgment*, p. 150.
[42] Ibid., pp. 150–153.
[43] Ibid., p. 150.
[44] Ibid., pp. 77–81.

here, for it should be fairly clear how the argument would go. The point is that to make beauty epistemologically dependent on the ongoing enterprise of art and art criticism, as the theory of beauty as ideal art does, accords well both with Kant's views and with our independent reflections on the nature of beauty.

Arthur Schopenhauer

FROM *THE WORLD AS WILL AND IDEA*

In the First Book the world was explained as mere *idea*, object for a subject.* In the Second Book we considered it from its other side, and found that in this aspect it is *will*, which proved to be simply that which this world is besides being idea. In accordance with this knowledge we called the world as idea, both as a whole and in its parts, the *objectification of will*, which therefore means the will become object, *i.e.*, idea. Further, we remember that this objectification of will was found to have many definite grades, in which, with gradually increasing distinctness and completeness, the nature of will appears in the idea, that is to say, presents itself as object. In these grades we already recognised the Platonic Ideas, for the grades are just the determined species, or the original unchanging forms and qualities of all natural bodies, both organised and unorganised, and also the general forces which reveal themselves according to natural laws. These Ideas, then, as a whole express themselves in innumerable individuals and particulars, and are related to these as archetypes to their copies. The multiplicity of such individuals is only conceivable through time and space, their appearing and passing away through causality, and in all these forms we recognise merely the different modes of the principle of sufficient reason, which is the ultimate principle of all that is finite, of all individual existence, and the universal form of the idea as it appears in the knowledge of the individual as such. The Platonic Idea, on the other hand, does not come under this principle, and has therefore neither multiplicity nor change. While the individuals in which it expresses itself are innumerable, and unceasingly come into being and pass away, it remains unchanged as one and the same, and the principle of sufficient reason has for it no meaning. As, however, this is the form under which all knowledge of the subject comes, so far as the subject knows as an *individual*, the Ideas lie quite outside the sphere of its knowl-

Arthur Schopenhauer (1788–1860). The well-known German philosopher of pessimism whose work *The World as Will and Idea* has influenced generations of thinkers since its publication in 1819.
    * Translated by R. B. Haldane, and J. Kemp, (London, 1883). Selections from Book III. Reprinted by permission of Routledge & Kegan Paul Ltd.

edge. If, therefore, the Ideas are to become objects of knowledge, this can only happen by transcending the individuality of the knowing subject.

. . .

31. I hope that in the preceding book I have succeeded in producing the conviction that what is called in the Kantian philosophy the *thing-in-itself*, and appears there as so significant, and yet so obscure and paradoxical a doctrine, and especially on account of the manner in which Kant introduced it as an inference from the caused to the cause, was considered a stumbling-stone, and, in fact, the weak side of his philosophy,—that this, I say, if it is reached by the entirely different way by which we have arrived at it, is nothing but the *will* when the sphere of that conception is extended and defined in the way I have shown. I hope, further, that after what has been said there will be no hesitation in recognising the definite grades of the objectification of the will, which is the inner reality of the world, to be what Plato called the *eternal Ideas* or unchangeable forms.

. . .

33. Since now, as individuals, we have no other knowledge than that which is subject to the principle of sufficient reason, and this form of knowledge excludes the Ideas, it is certain that if it is possible for us to raise ourselves from the knowledge of particular things to that of the Ideas, this can only happen by an alteration taking place in the subject which is analogous and corresponds to the great change of the whole nature of the object, and by virtue of which the subject, so far as it knows an Idea, is no more individual.

. . .

Knowledge in general belongs to the objectification of will at its higher grades, and sensibility, nerves, and brain, just like the other parts of the organised being, are the expression of the will at this stage of its objectivity, and therefore the idea which appears through them is also in the same way bound to the service of will as a means . . . for the attainment of its now complicated . . . aims for sustaining a being of manifold requirements. Thus originally and according to its nature, knowledge is completely subject to the will, and, like the immediate object, which, by means of the application of the law of causality, is its starting-point, all knowledge which proceeds in accordance with the principle of sufficient reason remains in a closer or more distant relation to the will. For the individual finds his body as an object among objects, to all of which it is related and connected according to the principle of sufficient reason. Thus all investigations of these relations and connections lead back to his body, and consequently to his will. Since it is the principle of sufficient reason which places the objects in this relation to the body, and, through it, to the will, the one endeavour of the knowledge which is subject to this principle will be to find out the relations in which objects are placed to each other through this principle, and thus to trace their innumerable connections in space, time, and causality. For only through these is the object *interesting* to the individual, *i.e.*, related to the will. Therefore the knowledge which is subject to the will knows nothing further of objects than their relations, knows the objects only so far as they exist at this time, in this place, under these circumstances, from these causes, and with these effects—in a word, as particular things; and if all these relations were to be taken away, the objects would also have disappeared for it, because it know nothing more about them. We must not disguise the fact that what the sciences consider in things is also in reality nothing more than this; their relations, the connections of time and space, the causes of natural changes, the resemblance of forms, the motives of actions,—thus merely relations. What distinguishes science from ordinary knowledge is merely its systematic form, the facilitating of knowledge by the comprehension of all particulars in the universal, by means of the subordination of concepts, and the completeness of knowledge which is thereby attained. All relation has itself only a relative existence; for example, all being in time is also non-being; for time is only that by means of which opposite determinations can belong to the same thing; therefore every phenomenon which is in time again is not, for what separates its beginning from its end is only time, which is essentially a fleeting, inconstant, and relative thing, here called duration. But time is the most universal form of all objects of the knowledge which is subject to the will, and the prototype of its other forms.

Knowledge now, as a rule, remains always subordinate to the service of the will, as indeed it originated for this service, and grew, so to speak, to the will, as the head to the body. In the case of the brutes this subjection of knowledge to the will can never be abolished. In the case of men it can be abolished only in exceptional cases, which we shall presently consider more closely.

. . .

34. The transition which we have referred to as possible, but yet to be regarded as only exceptional, from the common knowledge of particular things to the knowledge of the Idea, takes place suddenly; for knowledge breaks free from the service of the will, by the subject ceasing to be merely individual, and thus becoming the pure will-less subject of knowledge, which no longer traces relations in accordance with the principle of sufficient reason, but rests in fixed contemplation of the object presented to it, out of its connection with all others, and rises into it.

. . .

If, raised by the power of the mind, a man relinquishes the common way of looking at things, gives up tracing, under the guidance of the forms of the principle of sufficient reason, their relations to each other, the final goal of which is always a relation to his own will; if he thus ceases to consider the where, the when, the why, and the whither of things, and looks simply and solely at the *what*; if, further, he does not allow abstract thought, the concepts of the reason, to take possession of his consciousness, but, instead of all this, gives the whole power of his mind to perception, sinks himself entirely in this, and lets his whole consciousness be filled with the quiet contemplation of the natural object actually present, whether a landscape, a tree, a mountain, a building, or whatever it may be; inasmuch as he *loses* himself in this object (to use a pregnant German idiom), *i.e.*, forgets even his individuality, his will, and only continues to exist as the pure subject, the clear mirror of the object, so that it is as if the object alone were there, without any one to perceive it, and he can no longer separate the perceiver from the perception, but both have become one, because the whole consciousness is filled and occupied with one single sensuous picture; if thus the object has to such an extent passed out of all relation to something outside it, and the subject out of all relation to the will, then that which is so known is no longer the particular thing as such; but it is the *Idea*, the eternal form, the immediate objectivity of the will at this grade; and, therefore, he who is sunk in this perception is no longer individual, for in such perception the individual has lost himself; but he is *pure*, will-less, painless, timeless *subject of knowledge*.

.   .   .

In such contemplation the particular thing becomes at once the *Idea* of its species, and the perceiving individual becomes *pure subject of knowledge*. The individual, as such, knows only particular things; the pure subject of knowledge knows only Ideas. For the individual is the subject of knowledge in its relation to a definite particular manifestation of will, and in subjection to this. This particular manifestation of will is, as such, subordinated to the principle of sufficient reason in all its forms; therefore, all knowledge which relates itself to it also follows the principle of sufficient reason, and no other kind of knowledge is fitted to be of use to the will but this, which always consists merely of relations to the object. The knowing individual as such, and the particular things known by him, are always in some place, at some time, and are links in the chain of causes and effects. The pure subject of knowledge and his correlative, the Idea, have passed out of all these forms of the principle of sufficient reason: time, place, the individual that knows, and the individual that is known, have for them no meaning. When an individual knower has raised himself in the manner described to be pure subject of knowledge, and at the same time has raised the observed object to the Platonic Idea, the *world as idea* appears complete and pure, and the full objectification of the will takes place, for the Platonic Idea alone is its *adequate objectivity*. The Idea includes object and subject in like manner in itself, for they are its one form; but in it they are absolutely of equal importance; for as the object is here, as elsewhere, simply the idea of the subject, the subject, which passes entirely into the perceived object has thus become this object itself, for the whole consciousness is nothing but its perfectly distinct picture. Now this consciousness constitutes the whole *world as idea*, for one imagines the whole of the Platonic Ideas, or grades of the objectivity of will, in their series passing through it. The particular things of all time and space are nothing but Ideas multiplied through the principle of sufficient reason (the form of the knowledge of the individual as such), and thus obscured as regards their pure objectivity. When the

Platonic Idea appears, in it subject and object are no longer to be distinguished, for the Platonic Idea, the adequate objectivity of will, the true world as idea, arises only when the subject and object reciprocally fill and penetrate each other completely; and in the same way the knowing and the known individuals, as things in themselves, are not to be distinguished. For if we look entirely away from the true *world as idea*, there remains nothing but *the world as will*. The will is the "in-itself" of the Platonic Idea, which fully objectifies it: it is also the "in-itself" of the particular thing and of the individual that knows it, which objectify it incompletely. As will, outside the idea and all its forms, it is one and the same in the object contemplated and in the individual, who soars aloft in this contemplation, and becomes conscious of himself as pure subject. These two are, therefore, in themselves not different, for in themselves they are will, which here knows itself; and multiplicity and difference exist only as the way in which this knowledge comes to the will, *i.e.*, only in the phenomenon, on account of its form, the principle of sufficient reason.

.   .   .

35. In order to gain a deeper insight into the nature of the world, it is absolutely necessary that we should learn to distinguish the will as thing-in-itself from its adequate objectivity, and also the different grades in which this appears more and more distinctly and fully, *i.e.*, the Ideas themselves, from the merely phenomenal existence of these Ideas in the forms of the principle of sufficient reason, the restricted method of knowledge of the individual. We shall then agree with Plato when he attributes actual being only to the Ideas, and allows only an illusive, dream-like existence to things in space and time, the real world for the individual. Then we shall understand how one and the same Idea reveals itself in so many phenomena, and presents its nature only bit by bit to the individual, one side after another. Then we shall also distinguish the Idea itself from the way in which its manifestation appears in the observation of the individual, and recognise the former as essential and the latter as unessential. Let us consider this with the help of examples taken from the most insignificant things, and also from the greatest. When the clouds move, the figures which they form are not essential, but indifferent to them; but that as elastic vapour they are pressed together, drifted along, spread out, or torn asunder by the force of the wind: this is their nature, the essence of the forces which objectify themselves in them, the Idea; their actual forms are only for the individual observer.

.   .   .

The history of the human race, the throng of events, the change of times, the multifarious forms of human life in different lands and countries, all this is only the accidental form of the manifestation of the Idea, does not belong to the Idea itself, in which alone lies the adequate objectivity of the will, but only to the phenomenon which appears in the knowledge of the individual, and is just as foreign, unessential, and indifferent to the Idea itself as the figures which they assume are to the clouds.

. . .

To him who has thoroughly grasped this, and can distinguish between the will and the Idea, and between the Idea and its manifestation, the events of the world will have significance only so far as they are the letters out of which we may read the Idea of man, but not in and for themselves. He will not believe with the vulgar that time may produce something actually new and significant; that through it, or in it, something absolutely real may attain to existence, or indeed that it itself as a whole has begin-ning and end, plan and development, and in some way has for its final aim the highest perfection (according to their conception) of the last generation of man, whose life is a brief thirty years.

. . .

36. History follows the thread of events; it is pragmatic so far as it deduces them in accordance with the law of motivation, a law that deter-mines the self-manifesting will wherever it is enlightened by knowledge. At the lowest grades of its objectivity, where it still acts without knowl-edge, natural science, in the form of etiology, treats of the laws of the changes of its phenomena, and, in the form of morphology, of what is permanent in them. This almost endless task is lightened by the aid of concepts, which comprehend what is general in order that we may deduce what is particular from it. Lastly, mathematics treats of the mere forms, time and space, in which the Ideas, broken up into multiplicity, appear for the knowledge of the subject as individual. All these, of which the common name is science, proceed according to the principle of sufficient reason in its different forms, and their theme is always the phenomenon, its laws, connections, and the relations which result from them. But what kind of knowledge is concerned with that which is outside and independent of all relations, that which alone is really essential to the world, the true content of its phenomena, that which is subject to no change, and therefore is known with equal truth for all time, in a word, the *Ideas*, which are the direct and adequate objectivity of the thing-in-itself, the will? We answer, *Art*, the work of genius. It repeats or repro-duces the eternal Ideas grasped through pure contemplation, the essential and abiding in all the phenomena of the world; and according to what the material is in which it reproduces, it is sculpture or painting, poetry or music. Its one source is the knowledge of Ideas; its one aim the com-munication of this knowledge. While science, following the unresting and inconstant stream of the fourfold forms of reason and consequent, with each end attained sees further, and can never reach a final goal nor attain full satisfaction, any more than by running we can reach the place where the clouds touch the horizon; art, on the contrary, is everywhere at its goal. For it plucks the object of its contemplation out of the stream of the world's course, and has it isolated before it. And this particular thing, which in that stream was a small perishing part, becomes to art the

representative of the whole, an equivalent of the endless multitude in space and time. It therefore pauses at this particular thing; the course of time stops; the relations vanish for it; only the essential, the Idea, is its object. We may, therefore, accurately define it as the *way of viewing things independent of the principle of sufficient reason,* in opposition to the way of viewing them which proceeds in accordance with that principle, and which is the method of experience and of science. This last method of considering things may be compared to a line infinitely extended in a horizontal direction, and the former to a vertical line which cuts it at any point. The method of viewing things which proceeds in accordance with the principle of sufficient reason is the rational method, and it alone is valid and of use in practical life and in science. The method which looks away from the content of this principle is the method of genius, which is only valid and of use in art. The first is the method of Aristotle; the second is, on the whole, that of Plato.

· · ·

Only through the pure contemplation described above, which ends entirely in the object, can Ideas be comprehended; and the nature of *genius* consists in pre-eminent capacity for such contemplation. Now, as this requires that a man should entirely forget himself and the relations in which he stands, *genius* is simply the completest *objectivity,* i.e., the objective tendency of the mind, as opposed to the subjective, which is directed to one's own self—in other words, to the will. Thus genius is the faculty of continuing in the state of pure perception, of losing oneself in perception, and of enlisting in this service the knowledge which originally existed only for the service of the will; that is to say, genius is the power of leaving one's own interests, wishes, and aims entirely out of sight, thus of entirely renouncing one's own personality for a time, so as to remain *pure knowing subject,* clear vision of the world; and this not merely at moments, but for a sufficient length of time, and with sufficient consciousness, to enable one to reproduce by deliberate art what has thus been apprehended, and "to fix in lasting thoughts the wavering images that float before the mind." It is as if, when genius appears in an individual, a far larger measure of the power of knowledge falls to his lot than is necessary for the service of an individual will; and this superfluity of knowledge, being free, now becomes subject purified from will, a clear mirror of the inner nature of the world. This explains the activity, amounting even to disquietude, of men of genius, for the present can seldom satisfy them, because it does not fill their consciousness. This gives them that restless aspiration, that unceasing desire for new things, and for the contemplation of lofty things, and also that longing that is hardly ever satisfied, for men of similar nature and of like stature, to whom they might communicate themselves; whilst the common mortal, entirely filled and satisfied by the common present, ends in it, and finding everywhere his like, enjoys that peculiar satisfaction in daily life that is denied the genius.

Imagination has rightly been recognised as an essential element of genius; it has sometimes even been regarded as identical with it; but this is a mistake. As the objects of genius are the eternal Ideas, the permanent, essential forms of the world and all its phenomena, and as the knowledge of the Idea is necessarily knowledge through perception, is not abstract, the knowledge of the genius would be limited to the Ideas of the objects actually present to his person, and dependent upon the chain of circumstances that brought these objects to him, if his imagination did not extend his horizon far beyond the limits of his actual personal existence, and thus enable him to construct the whole out of the little that comes into his own actual apperception, and so to let almost all possible scenes of life pass before him in his own consciousness. Further, the actual objects are almost always very imperfect copies of the Ideas expressed in them; therefore the man of genius requires imagination in order to see in things, not that which Nature has actually made, but that which she endeavoured to make, yet could not because of that conflict of her forms among themselves. . . . Therefore extraordinary strength of imagination accompanies, and is indeed a necessary condition of genius. But the converse does not hold, for strength of imagination does not indicate genius; on the contrary, men who have no touch of genius may have much imagination. For as it is possible to consider a real object in two opposite ways, purely objectively, the way of genius grasping its Idea, or in the common way, merely in the relations in which it stands to other objects and to one's own will, in accordance with the principle of sufficient reason, it is also possible to perceive an imaginary object in both of these ways. Regarded in the first way, it is a means to the knowledge of the Idea, the communication of which is the work of art; in the second case, the imaginary object is used to build castles in the air congenial to egotism and the individual humour, and which for the moment delude and gratify; thus only the relations of the phantasies so linked together are known. The man who indulges in such an amusement is a dreamer; he will easily mingle those fancies that delight his solitude with reality, and so unfit himself for real life: perhaps he will write them down, and then we shall have the ordinary novel of every description, which entertains those who are like him and the public at large, for the readers imagine themselves in the place of the hero, and then find the story very agreeable.

The common mortal, that manufacture of Nature which she produces by the thousand every day, is, as we have said, not capable, at least not continuously so, of observation that in every sense is wholly disinterested, as sensuous contemplation, strictly so called, is. He can turn his attention to things only so far as they have some relation to his will, however indirect it may be. Since in this respect, which never demands anything but the knowledge of relations, the abstract conception of the thing is sufficient, and for the most part even better adapted for use; the ordinary man does not linger long over the mere perception, does not fix his attention long on one object, but in all that is presented to him hastily seeks merely the concept under which it is to be brought, as the lazy man seeks a chair, and then it interests him no further.

. . .

The man of genius, on the other hand, whose excessive power of knowledge frees it at times from the service of will, dwells on the consideration of life itself, strives to comprehend the Idea of each thing, not its relations to other things; and in doing this he often forgets to consider his own path in life, and therefore for the most part pursues it awkwardly enough. While to the ordinary man his faculty of knowledge is a lamp to lighten his path, to the man of genius it is the sun which reveals the world. This great diversity in their way of looking at life soon becomes visible in the outward appearance both of the man of genius and of the ordinary mortal. The man in whom genius lives and works is easily distinguished by his glance, which is both keen and steady, and bears the stamp of perception, of contemplation. This is easily seen from the likenesses of the few men of genius whom Nature has produced here and there among countless millions. On the other hand, in the case of an ordinary man, the true object of his contemplation, what he is prying into, can be easily seen from his glance, if indeed it is not quite stupid and vacant, as is generally the case. Therefore the expression of genius in a face consists in this, that in it a decided predominance of knowledge over will is visible, and consequently there also shows itself in it a knowledge that is entirely devoid of relation to will, *i.e.*, *pure knowing*. On the contrary, in ordinary countenances there is a predominant expression of will; and we see that knowledge only comes into activity under the impulse of will, and thus is directed merely by motives.

Since the knowledge that pertains to genius, or the knowledge of Ideas, is that knowledge which does not follow the principle of sufficient reason, so, on the other hand, the knowledge which does follow that principle is that which gives us prudence and rationality in life, and which creates the sciences. Thus men of genius are affected with the deficiencies entailed in the neglect of this latter kind of knowledge. Yet what I say in this regard is subject to the limitation that it only concerns them in so far as and while they are actually engaged in that kind of knowledge which is peculiar to genius; and this is by no means at every moment of their lives, for the great though spontaneous exertion which is demanded for the comprehension of Ideas free from will must necessarily relax, and there are long intervals during which men of genius are placed in very much the same position as ordinary mortals, both as regards advantages and deficiencies. On this account the action of genius has always been regarded as an inspiration, as indeed the name indicates, as the action of a superhuman being distinct from the individual himself, and which takes possession of him only periodically. The disinclination of men of genius to direct their attention to the content of the principle of sufficient reason will first show itself, with regard to the ground of being, as dislike of mathematics; for its procedure is based upon the most universal forms of the phenomenon space and time, which are themselves merely modes of the principle of sufficient reason, and is consequently precisely the opposite of that method of thought which seeks merely the content of the phenomenon, the Idea which expresses itself in it apart from all relations. The logical method of mathematics is also antagonistic to genius, for it does not satisfy but obstructs true insight, and presents merely a chain of conclusions in accordance with the principle of the ground of knowing. The mental faculty upon which it makes the greatest claim is memory, for it is necessary to recollect all the earlier propositions which are referred to. Experience has also proved that men of great artistic genius have no faculty for mathematics; no man was ever very distinguished for both. Alfieri relates that he was never able to understand the fourth proposition of Euclid. Goethe was constantly reproached with his want of mathematical knowledge by the ignorant opponents of his theory of colours. Here certainly, where it was not a question of calculation and measurement upon hypothetical data, but of direct knowledge by the understanding of causes and effects, this reproach was so utterly absurd and inappropriate, that by making it they have exposed their entire want of judgment, just as much as by the rest of their ridiculous arguments. The fact that up to the present day, nearly half a century after the appearance of Goethe's theory of colours, even in Germany the Newtonian fallacies still have undisturbed possession of the professorial chair, and men continue to speak quite seriously of the seven homogeneous rays of light and their different refrangibility, will some day be numbered among the great intellectual peculiarities of men generally, and especially of Germans. From the same cause as we have referred to above, may be explained the equally well-known fact that, conversely, admirable mathematicians have very little susceptibility for works of fine art.

. . .

Further, as quick comprehension of relations in accordance with the laws of causality and motivation is what specially constitutes prudence or sagacity, a prudent man, so far as and while he is so, will not be a genius, and a man of genius, so far as and while he is so, will not be a prudent man. Lastly, perceptive knowledge generally, in the province of which the Idea always lies, is directly opposed to rational or abstract knowledge, which is guided by the principle of the ground of knowing. It is also well known that we seldom find great genius united with pre-eminent reasonableness; on the contrary, persons of genius are often subject to violent emotions and irrational passions. But the ground of this is not weakness of reason, but partly unwonted energy of that whole phenomenon of will —the man of genius—which expresses itself through the violence of all his acts of will, and partly preponderance of the knowledge of perception through the senses and understanding over abstract knowledge, producing a decided tendency to the perceptible, the exceedingly lively impressions of which so far outshine colourless concepts, that they take their place in the guidance of action, which consequently becomes irrational. Accordingly the impression of the present moment is very strong with such persons, and carries them away into unconsidered action, violent emotions and passions. Moreover, since, in general, the knowledge of persons of genius has to some extent freed itself from the service of will, they will not in conversation think so much of the person they are addressing as of the thing they are speaking about, which is vividly present to them; and therefore they are likely to judge or narrate things too objectively for their own interests; they will not pass over in silence what would more prudently be concealed, and so forth. Finally, they are given to soliloquising, and in general may exhibit certain weaknesses which are actually akin to madness. It has often been remarked that there is a side at which genius and madness touch, and even pass over into each other, and indeed poetical inspiration has been called a kind of madness.

. . .

I must mention that, by a diligent search in lunatic asylums, I have found individual cases of patients who were unquestionably endowed with great talents, and whose genius distinctly appeared through their madness, which, however, had completely gained the upper hand. Now this cannot be ascribed to chance, for on the one hand the number of mad persons is relatively very small, and on the other hand a person of genius is a phenomenon which is rare beyond all ordinary estimation, and only appears in nature as the greatest exception. It will be sufficient to convince us of this if we compare the number of really great men of genius that the whole of civilised Europe has produced, both in ancient and modern times, with the two hundred and fifty millions who are always living in Europe, and who change entirely every thirty years. In estimating the number of men of outstanding genius, we must of course only count those who have produced works which have retained through all time an enduring value for mankind. I shall not refrain from mentioning, that I have known some persons of decided, though not remarkable, mental superiority, who also showed a slight trace of insanity. It might seem from this that every advance of intellect beyond the ordinary measure, as an abnormal development, disposes to madness.

. . .

37. Genius, then, consists, according to our explanation, in the capacity for knowing, independently of the principle of sufficient reason, not individual things, which have their existence only in their relations, but the Ideas of such things, and of being oneself the correlative of the Idea, and thus no longer an individual, but the pure subject of knowledge. Yet this faculty must exist in all men in a smaller and different degree; for if not, they would be just as incapable of enjoying works of art as of producing them; they would have no susceptibility for the beautiful or the sublime; indeed, these words could have no meaning for them. We must therefore assume that there exists in all men this power of knowing the Ideas in things, and consequently of transcending their personality for the moment, unless indeed there are some men who are capable of no aesthetic pleasure at all. The man of genius excels ordinary men only by possessing this kind of knowledge in a far higher degree and more continuously. Thus, while under its influence he retains the presence of mind which is necessary to enable him to repeat in a voluntary and intentional work what he has learned in this manner; and this repetition is the work of art. Through

this he communicates to others the Idea he has grasped. This Idea remains unchanged and the same, so that aesthetic pleasure is one and the same whether it is called forth by a work of art or directly by the contemplation of nature and life. The work of art is only a means of facilitating the knowledge in which this pleasure consists. That the Idea comes to us more easily from the work of art than directly from nature and the real world, arises from the fact that the artist, who knew only the Idea, no longer the actual, has reproduced in his work the pure Idea, has abstracted it from the actual, omitting all disturbing accidents. The artist lets us see the world through his eyes. That he has these eyes, that he knows the inner nature of things apart from all their relations, is the gift of genius, is in-born; but that he is able to lend us this gift, to let us see with his eyes, is acquired, and is the technical side of art. Therefore, after the account which I have given in the preceding pages of the inner nature of aesthetical knowledge in its most general outlines, the following more exact philo-sophical treatment of the beautiful and the sublime will explain them both, in nature and in art, without separating them further. First of all we shall consider what takes place in a man when he is affected by the beauti-ful and the sublime; whether he derives this emotion directly from nature, from life, or partakes of it only through the medium of art, does not make any essential, but merely an external, difference.

38. In the aesthetic mode of contemplation we have found *two insepar-able constituent parts*—the knowledge of the object, not as individual thing but as Platonic Idea, that is, as the enduring form of this whole species of things; and the self-consciousness of the knowing person, not as individual, but as *pure will-less subject of knowledge*. The condition under which both these constituent parts appear always united was found to be the abandonment of the method of knowing which is bound to the principle of sufficient reason, and which, on the other hand, is the only kind of knowledge that is of value for the service of the will and also for science. Moreover we shall see that the pleasure which is produced by the contemplation of the beautiful arises from these two constituent parts, sometimes more from the one, sometimes more from the other, according to what the object of the aesthetical contemplation may be.

All *willing* arises from want, therefore from deficiency, and therefore from suffering. The satisfaction of a wish ends it; yet for one wish that is satisfied there remain at least ten which are denied. Further, the desire lasts long, the demands are infinite; the satisfaction is short and scantily measured out. But even the final satisfaction is itself only apparent; every satisfied wish at once makes room for a new one; both are illusions; the one is known to be so, the other not yet. No attained object of desire can give lasting satisfaction, but merely a fleeting gratification; it is like the alms thrown to the beggar; that keeps him alive to-day that his misery may be prolonged till the morrow. Therefore, so long as our consciousness is filled by our will, so long as we are given up to the throng of desires with their constant hopes and fears, so long as we are the subject of willing, we can never have lasting happiness nor peace. It is essentially all the same whether we pursue or flee, fear injury or seek enjoyment; the care for the constant demands of the will, in whatever form it may be, continually occupies and sways the consciousness; but without peace no true well-being is possible.

. . .

But when some external cause or inward disposition lifts us suddenly out of the endless stream of willing, delivers knowledge from the slavery of the will, the attention is no longer directed to the motives of willing, but comprehends things free from their relation to the will, and thus observes them without personal interest, without subjectivity, purely objectively, gives itself entirely up to them so far as they are ideas, but not in so far as they are motives. Then all at once the peace which we were always seeking, but which always fled from us on the former path of the desires, comes to us of its own accord, and it is well with us.

. . .

But this is just the state which I described above as necessary for the knowledge of the Idea, as pure contemplation, as sinking oneself in perception, losing oneself in the object, forgetting all individuality, surrendering that kind of knowledge which follows the principle of sufficient reason, and comprehends only relations; the state by means of which at once and inseparably the perceived particular thing is raised to the Idea of its whole species, and the knowing individual to the pure subject of will-less knowledge, and as such they are both taken out of the stream of time and all other relations. It is then all one whether we see the sun set from the prison or from the palace.

Inward disposition, the predominance of knowing over willing, can produce this state under any circumstances. This is shown by those admirable Dutch artists who directed this purely objective perception to the most insignificant objects, and established a lasting monument of their objectivity and spiritual peace in their pictures of *still life*, which the aesthetic beholder does not look on without emotion; for they present to him the peaceful, still, frame of mind of the artist, free from will, which was needed to contemplate such insignificant things so objectively, to observe them so attentively, and to repeat this perception so intelligently; and as the picture enables the onlooker to participate in this state, his emotion is often increased by the contrast between it and the unquiet frame of mind, disturbed by vehement willing, in which he finds himself. In the same spirit, landscape-painters, and particularly Ruisdael, have often painted very insignificant country scenes, which produce the same effect even more agreeably.

All this is accomplished by the inner power of an artistic nature alone; but that purely objective disposition is facilitated and assisted from without by suitable objects, by the abundance of natural beauty which invites contemplation, and even presses itself upon us. When ever it discloses itself suddenly to our view, it almost always succeeds in delivering us, though it may be only for a moment, from subjectivity, from the slavery of the will, and in raising us to the state of pure knowing. This is why the man who is tormented by passion, or want, or care, is so suddenly revived, cheered, and restored by a single free glance into nature: the storm of passion, the pressure of desire and fear, and all the miseries of willing are then at once, and in a marvellous manner calmed and appeased. For at the moment at which, freed from the will, we give ourselves up to pure will-less knowing, we pass into a world from which everything is absent that influenced our will and moved us so violently through it. This freeing of knowledge lifts us as wholly and entirely away from all that, as do sleep and dreams; happiness and unhappiness have disappeared; we are no longer individual; the individual is forgotten; we are only pure subject of knowledge; we are only that *one* eye of the world which looks out from all knowing creatures, but which can become perfectly free from the service of will in man alone. Thus all difference of individuality so entirely disappears, that it is all the same whether the perceiving eye belongs to a mighty king or to a wretched beggar; for neither joy nor complaining can pass that boundary with us. So near us always lies a sphere in which we escape from all our misery; but who has the strength to continue long in it? As soon as any single relation to our will, to our person, even of these objects of our pure contemplation, comes again into consciousness, the magic is at an end; we fall back into the knowledge which is governed by the principle of sufficient reason; we know no longer the Idea, but the particular thing, the link of a chain to which we also belong, and we are again abandoned to all our woe. Most men remain almost always at this standpoint because they entirely lack objectivity, *i.e.*, genius. Therefore they have no pleasure in being alone with nature; they need company, or at least a book. For their knowledge remains subject to their will; they seek, therefore, in objects, only some relation to their will, and whenever they see anything that has no such relation, there sounds within them, like a ground bass in music, the constant inconsolable cry, "It is of no use to me;" thus in solitude the most beautiful surroundings have for them a desolate, dark, strange, and hostile appearance.

Lastly, it is this blessedness of will-less perception which casts an enchanting glamour over the past and distant, and presents them to us in so fair a light by means of self-deception. For as we think of days long gone by, days in which we lived in a distant place, it is only the objects which our fancy recalls, not the subject of will, which bore about with it then its incurable sorrows just as it bears them now; but they are forgotten, because since then they have often given place to others. Now, objective perception acts with regard to what is remembered just as it would in what is present, if we let it have influence over us, if we surrendered ourselves to it free from will. Hence it arises that, especially when we are more than ordinarily disturbed by some want, the remembrance of past and distant scenes suddenly flits across our minds like a lost paradise. The fancy recalls only what was objective, not what was individually subjective, and we imagine that that objective stood before us then just as pure and undisturbed by any relation to the will as its image stands in our fancy now; while in reality the relation of the objects to our will gave us pain then just as it does now. We can deliver ourselves from all suffering just as well through present objects as through distant ones whenever we raise ourselves to a purely objective contemplation of them, and so are able to bring about the illusion that only the objects are present and not we ourselves. Then, as the pure subject of knowledge, freed from the miserable self, we become entirely one with these objects, and, for the moment, our wants are as foreign to us as they are to them. The world as idea alone remains, and the world as will has disappeared.

In all these reflections it has been my object to bring out clearly the nature and the scope of the subjective element in aesthetic pleasure; the deliverance of knowledge from the service of the will, the forgetting of self as an individual, and the raising of the consciousness of the pure will-less, timeless, subject of knowledge, independent of all relations. With this subjective side of aesthetic contemplation, there must always appear as its necessary correlative the objective side, the intuitive comprehension of the Platonic Idea. But before we turn to the closer consideration of this, and to the achievements of art in relation to it, it is better that we should pause for a little at the subjective side of aesthetic pleasure, in order to complete our treatment of this by explaining the impression of the *sublime* which depends altogether upon it, and arises from a modification of it. After that we shall complete our investigation of aesthetic pleasure by considering its objective side.

· · ·

As long as that which raises us from the knowledge of mere relations subject to the will, to aesthetic contemplation, and thereby exalts us to the position of the subject of knowledge free from will, is this fittingness of nature, this significance and distinctness of its forms, on account of which the Ideas individualised in them readily present themselves to us; so long is it merely *beauty* that affects us and the sense of the *beautiful* that is excited. But if these very objects whose significant forms invite us to pure contemplation, have a hostile relation to the human will in general, as it exhibits itself in its objectivity, the human body, if they are opposed to it, so that it is menaced by the irresistible predominance of their power, or sinks into insignificance before their immeasurable greatness; if, nevertheless, the beholder does not direct his attention to this eminently hostile relation to his will, but, although perceiving and recognising it, turns consciously away from it, forcibly detaches himself from his will and its relations, and, giving himself up entirely to knowledge, quietly contemplates those very objects that are so terrible to the will, comprehends only their Idea, which is foreign to all relation, so that he lingers gladly over its contemplation, and is thereby raised above himself, his person, his will, and all will:—in that case he is filled with the sense of the *sublime*, he is in the state of spiritual exaltation, and therefore the object producing such a state is called *sublime*. Thus what distinguishes the sense of the sublime from that of the beautiful is this: in the case of the beautiful, pure knowledge has gained the upper hand without a struggle, for the beauty of the object, *i.e.*, that property which facilitates the knowledge of its Idea, has removed from consciousness without resistance, and therefore imperceptibly, the will and the knowledge of relations which is subject to it, so that what is left is the pure subject of knowledge without even a remembrance of will. On the other hand, in the case of the sublime that state of pure knowledge is only attained by a conscious and forcible breaking away from the relations of the same object to the will, which are recognised as unfavourable, by a free and conscious transcending of the will and the knowledge related to it.

This exaltation must not only be consciously won, but also consciously retained, and it is therefore accompanied by a constant remembrance of will; yet not of a single particular volition, such as fear or desire, but of human volition in general, so far as it is universally expressed in its objectivity the human body. If a single real act of will were to come into consciousness, through actual personal pressure and danger from the object, then the individual will thus actually influenced would at once gain the upper hand, the peace of contemplation would become impossible, the impression of the sublime would be lost, because it yields to the anxiety, in which the effort of the individual to right itself has sunk every other thought. A few examples will help very much to elucidate this theory of the aesthetic sublime and remove all doubt with regard to it; at the same time they will bring out the different degrees of this sense of the sublime. It is in the main identical with that of the beautiful, with pure will-less knowing, and the knowledge, that necessarily accompanies it of Ideas out of all relation determined by the principle of sufficient reason, and it is distinguished from the sense of the beautiful only by the additional quality that it rises above the known hostile relation of the object contemplated to the will in general. Thus there come to be various degrees of the sublime, and transitions from the beautiful to the sublime, according as this additional quality is strong, bold, urgent, near, or weak, distant, and merely indicated.

· · ·

Architectural beauty more than any other object is enhanced by favourable light, though even the most insignificant things become through its influence most beautiful. If, in the dead of winter, when all nature is frozen and stiff, we see the rays of the setting sun reflected by masses of stone, illuminating without warming, and thus favourable only to the purest kind of knowledge, not to the will; the contemplation of the beautiful effect of the light upon these masses lifts us, as does all beauty, into a state of pure knowing. But, in this case, a certain transcending of the interests of the will is needed to enable us to rise into the state of pure knowing, because there is a faint recollection of the lack of warmth from these rays, that is, an absence of the principle of life; there is a slight challenge to persist in pure knowing, and to refrain from all willing, and therefore it is an example of a transition from the sense of the beautiful to that of the sublime. It is the faintest trace of the sublime in the beautiful; and beauty itself is indeed present only in a slight degree.

· · ·

The following situation may occasion this feeling in a still higher degree: Nature convulsed by a storm; the sky darkened by black threatening thunder-clouds; stupendous, naked, overhanging cliffs, completely shutting out the view; rushing, foaming torrents; absolute desert; the wail of the wind sweeping through the clefts of the rocks. Our dependence, our strife with hostile nature, our will broken in the conflict, now appears visibly before our eyes. Yet, so long as the personal pressure does not gain the upper hand, but we continue in aesthetic contemplation, the pure subject of knowing gazes unshaken and unconcerned through that strife of nature, through that picture of the broken will, and quietly comprehends the Ideas even of those objects which are threatening and terrible to the will. In this contrast lies the sense of the sublime.

But the impression becomes still stronger, if, when we have before our eyes, on a large scale, the battle of the raging elements, in such a scene we are prevented from hearing the sound of our own voice by the noise of a falling stream; or, if we are abroad in the storm of tempestuous seas, where the mountainous waves rise and fall, dash themselves furiously against steep cliffs, and toss their spray high into the air; the storm howls, the sea boils, the lightning flashes from black clouds, and the peals of thunder drown the voice of storm and sea. Then, in the undismayed beholder, the two-fold nature of his consciousness reaches the highest degree of distinctness. He perceives himself, on the one hand, as an individual, as the frail phenomenon of will, which the slightest touch of these forces can utterly destroy, helpless against powerful nature, dependent, the victim of chance, a vanishing nothing in the presence of stupendous might; and, on the other hand, as the eternal, peaceful, knowing subject, the condition of the object, and, therefore, the supporter of this whole world; the terrific strife of nature only his idea; the subject itself free and apart from all desires and necessities, in the quiet comprehension of the Ideas. This is the complete impression of the sublime. Here he obtains a glimpse of a power beyond all comparison superior to the individual, threatening it with annihilation.

The impression of the sublime may be produced in quite another way, by presenting a mere immensity in space and time; its immeasurable greatness dwindles the individual to nothing. Adhering to Kant's nomenclature and his accurate division, we may call the first kind the dynamical, and the second the mathematical sublime, although we entirely dissent from his explanation of the inner nature of the impression, and can allow no share in it either to moral reflections, or to hypostases from scholastic philosophy.

· · ·

Our explanation of the sublime applies also to the ethical, to what is called the sublime character. Such a character arises from this, that the will is not excited by objects which are well calculated to excite it, but that knowledge retains the upper hand in their presence. A man of sublime character will accordingly consider men in a purely objective way, and not with reference to the relations which they might have to his will; he will, for example, observe their faults, even their hatred and injustice to himself, without being himself excited to hatred; he will behold their happiness without envy; he will recognise their good qualities without desiring any closer relations with them; he will perceive the beauty of women, but he will not desire them. His personal happiness or unhappiness will not greatly affect him.

. . .

40. Opposites throw light upon each other, and therefore the remark may be in place here, that the proper opposite of the sublime is something which would not at the first glance be recognised, as such: *the charming* or *attractive*. By this, however, I understand, that which excites the will by presenting to it directly its fulfilment, its satisfaction.

. . .

The charming or attractive . . . draws the beholder away from the pure contemplation which is demanded by all apprehension of the beautiful, because it necessarily excites this will, by objects which directly appeal to it, and thus he no longer remains pure subject of knowing, but becomes the needy and dependent subject of will. That every beautiful thing which is bright or cheering should be called charming, is the result of a too general concept, which arises from a want of accurate discrimination, and which I must entirely set aside, and indeed condemn. But in the sense of the word which has been given and explained, I find only two species of the charming or attractive in the province of art, and both of them are unworthy of it. The one species, a very low one, is found in Dutch paintings of still life, when they err by representing articles of food, which by their deceptive likeness necessarily excite the appetite for the things they represent, and this is just an excitement of the will, which puts an end to all aesthetic contemplation of the object. Painted fruit is yet admissible, because we may regard it as the further development of the flower, and as a beautiful product of nature in form and colour, without being obliged to think of it as eatable; but unfortunately we often find, represented with deceptive naturalness, prepared and served dishes, oysters, herrings, crabs, bread and butter, beer, wine, and so forth, which is altogether to be condemned. In historical painting and in sculpture the charming consists in naked figures, whose position, drapery, and general treatment are calculated to excite the passions of the beholder, and thus pure aesthetical contemplation is at once annihilated, and the aim of art is defeated. This mistake corresponds exactly to that which we have just censured in the Dutch paintings. The ancients are almost always free from this fault in their representations of beauty and complete nakedness of form, because the artist himself created them in a purely objective spirit, filled with ideal beauty, not in the spirit of subjective, and base sensuality. The charming is thus everywhere to be avoided in art.

There is also a negative species of the charming or exciting which is even more reprehensible than the positive form which has been discussed; this is the disgusting or the loathsome. It arouses the will of the beholder, just as what is properly speaking charming, and therefore disturbs pure aesthetic contemplation. But it is an active aversion and opposition which is excited by it; it arouses the will by presenting to it objects which it abhors. Therefore it has always been recognised that it is altogether inadmissible in art, where even what is ugly, when it is not disgusting, is allowable in its proper place, as we shall see later.

41. The course of the discussion has made it necessary to insert at this point the treatment of the sublime, though we have only half done with the beautiful, as we have considered its subjective side only. For it was merely a special modification of this subjective side that distinguished the beautiful from the sublime.

. . .

In the object they are not essentially different, for in every case the object of aesthetical contemplation is not the individual thing, but the Idea in it which is striving to reveal itself; that is to say, adequate objectivity of will at a particular grade.

. . .

When we say that a thing is *beautiful*, we thereby assert that it is an object of our aesthetic contemplation, and this has a double meaning; on the one hand it means that the sight of the thing makes us *objective*, that is to say, that in contemplating it we are no longer conscious of ourselves as individuals, but as pure will-less subjects of knowledge; and on the other hand it means that we recognise in the object, not the particular thing, but an Idea; and this can only happen, so far as our contemplation of it is not subordinated to the principle of sufficient reason, does not follow the relation of the object to anything outside it (which is always ultimately connected with relations to our own will), but rests in the object itself. For the Idea and the pure subject of knowledge always appear at once in consciousness as necessary correlatives, and on their appearance all distinction of time vanishes, for they are both entirely foreign to the principle of sufficient reason in all its forms, and lie outside the relations which are imposed by it.

. . .

Therefore, if, for example, I contemplate a tree aesthetically, *i.e.*, with artistic eyes, and thus recognise, not it, but its Idea, it becomes at once of no consequence whether it is this tree or its predecessor which flourished a thousand years ago, and whether the observer is this individual or any other that lived anywhere and at any time; the particular thing and the knowing individual are abolished with the principle of sufficient reason, and there remains nothing but the Idea and the pure subject of knowing, which together constitute the adequate objectivity of will at this grade. And the Idea dispenses not only with time, but also with space, for the Idea proper is not this special form which appears before me but its expression, its pure significance, its inner being, which discloses itself to me and appeals to me, and which may be quite the same though the spatial relations of its form be very different.

Since, on the one hand, every given thing may be observed in a purely objective manner and apart from all relations; and since, on the other hand, the will manifests itself in everything at some grade of its objectivity, so that everything is the expression of an Idea; it follows that everything is also *beautiful.* That even the most insignificant things admit of pure objective and will-less contemplation, and thus prove that they are beautiful, is shown by what was said above in this reference about the Dutch pictures of still-life (§ 38). But one thing is more beautiful than another, because it makes this pure objective contemplation easier, it lends itself to it, and, so to speak, even compels it, and then we call it very beautiful. This is the case sometimes because, as an individual thing, it expresses in its purity the Idea of its species by the very distinct, clearly defined, and significant relation of its parts, and also fully reveals that Idea through the completeness of all the possible expressions of its species united in it, so that it makes the transition from the individual thing to the Idea, and therefore also the condition of pure contemplation, very easy for the beholder. Sometimes this possession of special beauty in an object lies in the fact that the Idea itself which appeals to us in it is a high grade of the objectivity of will, and therefore very significant and expressive. Therefore it is that man is more beautiful than all other objects, and the revelation of his nature is the highest aim of art. Human form and expression are the most important objects of plastic art, and human action the most important object of poetry. Yet each thing has its own peculiar beauty, not only every organism which expresses itself in the unity of an individual being, but also everything unorganised and formless, and even every manufactured article. For all these reveal the Ideas through which the will objectifies itself at it lowest grades, they give, as it were, the deepest resounding bass-notes of nature. Gravity, rigidity, fluidity, light, and so forth, are the Ideas which express themselves in rocks, in buildings, in waters. Landscape-gardening or architecture can do no more than assist them to unfold their qualities distinctly, fully, and variously; they can only give them the opportunity of expressing themselves purely, so that they lend themselves to aesthetic contemplation and make it easier. Inferior buildings or ill-favoured localities, on the contrary, which nature has neglected or art has spoiled perform this task in a very slight degree or not at all; yet even from them these universal, fundamental Ideas of nature cannot altogether disappear. To the careful observer they present themselves here also, and even bad buildings and the like are capable of being aesthetically considered; the Ideas of the most universal properties of their materials are still recognisable in them, only the artificial form which has been given them does not assist but hinders aesthetic contemplation. Manufactured articles also serve to express Ideas, only it is not the Idea of the manufactured article which speaks in them, but the Idea of the material to which this artificial form has been given.

. . . .

Our view, then, cannot be reconciled with that of Plato if he is of opinion that a table or a chair express the Idea of a table or a chair, . . . but we say that they express the Ideas which are already expressed in their mere material as such. According to Aristotle, . . . however, Plato himself only maintained Ideas of natural objects . . . and in chap. 5 he says that, according to the Platonists, there are no Ideas of house and ring.

.   .   .

We may take this opportunity of mentioning another point in which our doctrine of Ideas differs very much from that of Plato. He teaches . . . that the object which art tries to express, the ideal of painting and poetry, is not the Idea but the particular thing. Our whole exposition hitherto has maintained exactly the opposite, and Plato's opinion is the less likely to lead us astray, inasmuch as it is the source of one of the greatest and best known errors of this great man, his depreciation and rejection of art, and especially poetry; he directly connects his false judgment in reference to this with the passage quoted.

42. I return to the exposition of the aesthetic impression. The knowledge of the beautiful always supposes at once and inseparably the pure knowing subject and the known Idea as object. Yet the source of aesthetic satisfaction will sometimes lie more in the comprehension of the known Idea, sometimes more in the blessedness and spiritual peace of the pure knowing subject freed from all willing, and therefore from all individuality, and the pain that proceeds from it. And, indeed, this predominance of one or the other constituent part of aesthetic feeling will depend upon whether the intuitively grasped Idea is a higher or a lower grade of the objectivity of will. Thus in aesthetic contemplation (in the real, or through the medium of art) of the beauty of nature in the inorganic and vegetable worlds, or in works of architecture, the pleasure of pure will-less knowing will predominate, because the Ideas which are here apprehended are only low grades of the objectivity of will, and are therefore not manifestations of deep significance and rich content. On the other hand, if animals and man are the objects of aesthetic contemplation or representation, the pleasure will consist rather in the comprehension of these Ideas, which are the most distinct revelation of will; for they exhibit the greatest multiplicity of forms, the greatest richness and deep significance of phenomena, and reveal to us most completely the nature of will, whether in its violence, its terribleness, its satisfaction or its aberration (the latter in tragic situations), or finally in its change and self-surrender, which is the peculiar theme of christian painting; as the Idea of the will enlightened by full knowledge is the object of historical painting in general, and of the drama. We shall now go through the fine arts one by one, and this will give completeness and distinctness to the theory of the beautiful which we have advanced.

.   .   .

43. If now we consider *architecture* simply as a fine art and apart from its application to useful ends, in which it serves the will and not pure knowledge, and therefore ceases to be art in our sense; we can assign to it no other aim than that of bringing to greater distinctness some of those ideas, which are the lowest grades of the objectivity of will; such as gravity, cohesion, rigidity, hardness, those universal qualities of stone, those first,

simplest, most inarticulate manifestations of will; the bass notes of nature; and after these light, which in many respects is their opposite. Even at these low grades of the objectivity of will we see its nature revealing itself in discord; for properly speaking the conflict between gravity and rigidity is the sole aesthetic material of architecture; its problem is to make this conflict appear with perfect distinctness in a multitude of different ways. It solves it by depriving these indestructible forces of the shortest way to their satisfaction, and conducting them to it by a circuitous route, so that the conflict is lengthened and the inexhaustible efforts of both forces become visible in many different ways. The whole mass of the building, if left to its original tendency, would exhibit a mere heap or clump, bound as closely as possible to the earth, to which gravity, the form in which the will appears here, continually presses, while rigidity, also objectivity of will, resists. But this very tendency, this effort, is hindered by architecture from obtaining direct satisfaction, and only allowed to reach it indirectly and by roundabout ways. The roof, for example, can only press the earth through columns, the arch must support itself, and can only satisfy its tendency towards the earth through the medium of the pillars, and so forth. But just by these enforced digressions, just by these restrictions, the forces which reside in the crude mass of stone unfold themselves in the most distinct and multifarious ways; and the purely aesthetic aim of architecture can go no further than this. Therefore the beauty, at any rate, of a building lies in the obvious adaptation of every part, not to the outward arbitrary end of man (so far the work belongs to practical architecture), but directly to the stability of the whole, to which the position, dimensions, and form of every part must have so necessary a relation that, where it is possible, if any one part were taken away, the whole would fall to pieces. For just because each part bears just as much as it conveniently can, and each is supported just where it requires to be and just to the necessary extent, this opposition unfolds itself, this conflict between rigidity and gravity, which constitutes the life, the manifestation of will, in the stone, becomes completely visible, and these lowest grades of the objectivity of will reveal themselves distinctly. In the same way the form of each part must not be determined arbitrarily, but by its end, and its relation to the whole. The column is the simplest form of support, determined simply by its end: the twisted column is tasteless; the four-cornered pillar is in fact not so simple as the round column, though it happens that it is easier to make it. The forms also of frieze, rafter, roof, and dome are entirely determined by their immediate end, and explain themselves from it. The decoration of capitals, &c., belongs to sculpture, not to architecture, which admits it merely as extraneous ornament, and could dispense with it. According to what has been said, it is absolutely necessary, in order to understand the aesthetic satisfaction afforded by a work of architecture, to have immediate knowledge through perception of its matter as regards its weight, rigidity, and cohesion, and our pleasure in such a work would suddenly be very much diminished by the discovery that the material used was pumice-stone; for then it would appear to us as a kind of sham building. We would be affected in almost the same way if we were told that it was made of wood, when we had supposed it to be of stone, just because this alters and destroys the relation between rigidity and gravity, and consequently the significance and necessity of all the parts, for these natural forces reveal themselves in a far weaker degree in a wooden building. Therefore no real work of architecture as a fine art can be made of wood, although it assumes all forms so easily; this can only be explained by our theory.

. . .

Works of architecture have further quite a special relation to light; they gain a double beauty in the full sunshine, with the blue sky as a background, and again they have quite a different effect by moonlight. Therefore, when a beautiful work of architecture is to be erected, special attention is always paid to the effects of the light and to the climate. The reason of all this is, indeed, principally that all the parts and their relations are only made clearly visible by a bright, strong light; but besides this I am of opinion that it is the function of architecture to reveal the nature of light just as it reveals that of things so opposite to it as gravity and rigidity. For the light is intercepted, confined, and reflected by the great opaque, sharply outlined, and variously formed masses of stone, and thus it unfolds its nature and qualities in the purest and clearest way, to the great pleasure of the beholders, for light is the most joy-giving of things, as the condition and the objective correlative of the most perfect kind of knowledge of perception.

Now, because the Ideas which architecture brings to clear perception, are the lowest grades of the objectivity of will, and consequently their objective significance, which architecture reveals to us, is comparatively small; the aesthetic pleasure of looking at a beautiful building in a good light will lie, not so much in the comprehension of the Idea, as in the subjective correlative which accompanies this comprehension; it will consist preeminently in the fact that the beholder, set free from the kind of knowledge that belongs to the individual, and which serves the will and follows the principle of sufficient reason, is raised to that of the pure subject of knowing free from will. It will consist then principally in pure contemplation itself, free from all the suffering of will and of individuality. In this respect the opposite of architecture, and the other extreme of the series of the fine arts, is the drama, which brings to knowledge the most significant Ideas. Therefore in the aesthetic pleasure afforded by the drama the objective side is throughout predominant.

Architecture has this distinction from plastic art and poetry: it does not give us a copy but the thing itself. It does not repeat, as they do, the known Idea, so that the artist lends his eyes to the beholder, but in it the artist merely presents the object to the beholder, and facilitates for him the comprehension of the Idea by bringing the actual, individual object to a distinct and complete expression of its nature.

. . .

44. The landscape beauty of a scene consists, for the most part, in the

multiplicity of natural objects which are present in it, and then in the fact that they are clearly separated, appear distinctly, and yet exhibit a fitting connection and alternation. These two conditions are assisted and promoted by landscape-gardening, but it has by no means such a mastery over its material as architecture, and therefore its effect is limited. The beauty with which it is concerned. belongs almost exclusively to nature; it has done little for it; and, on the other hand, it can do little against unfavourable nature, and when nature works, not for it, but against it, its achievements are small.

The vegetable world offers itself everywhere for aesthetic enjoyment without the medium of art; but so far as it is an object of art, it belongs principally to landscape-painting; to the province of which all the rest of unconscious nature also belongs. In paintings of still life, and of mere architecture, ruins, interiors of churches, &c., the subjective side of aesthetic pleasure is predominant, *i.e.*, our satisfaction does not lie principally in the direct comprehension of the represented Ideas, but rather in the subjective correlative of this comprehension, pure, will-less knowing. For, because the painter lets us see these things through his eyes, we at once receive a sympathetic and reflected sense of the deep spiritual peace and absolute silence of the will, which were necessary in order to enter with knowledge so entirely into these lifeless objects, and comprehend them with such love, *i.e.*, in this case with such a degree of objectivity. The effect of landscape-painting proper is indeed, as a whole, of this kind; but because the Ideas expressed are more distinct and significant, as higher grades of the objectivity of will, the objective side of aesthetic pleasure already comes more to the front and assumes as much importance as the subjective side. Pure knowing as such is no longer the paramount consideration, for we are equally affected by the known Platonic Idea, the world as idea at an important grade of the objectification of will.

But a far higher grade is revealed by animal painting and sculpture. Of the latter we have some important antique remains; for example, horses at Venice, on Monte Cavallo, and on the Elgin Marbles, also at Florence in bronze and marble; the ancient boar, howling wolves, the lions in the arsenal at Venice, also in the Vatican a whole room almost filled with ancient animals, &c. In these representations the objective side of aesthetic pleasure obtains a marked predominance over the subjective. The peace of the subject which knows these Ideas, which has silenced its own will, is indeed present, as it is in all aesthetic contemplation; but its effect is not felt, for we are occupied with the restlessness and impetuosity of the will represented. It is that very will, which constitutes our own nature, that here appears to us in forms, in which its manifestation is not, as in us, controlled and tempered by intellect, but exhibits itself in stronger traits, and with a distinctness that borders on the grotesque and monstrous. For this very reason there is no concealment; it is free, naive, open as the day, and this is the cause of our interest in animals. The characteristics of species appeared already in the representation of plants, but showed itself only in the forms; here it becomes much more distinct, and expresses itself not only in the form, but in the action, position, and mien, yet always merely as the character of the species, not of the individual. This knowledge of the Ideas of higher grades, which in painting we receive through extraneous means, we may gain directly by the pure contemplative perception of plants, and observation of beasts, and indeed of the latter in their free, natural, and unrestrained state. The objective contemplation of their manifold and marvellous forms, and of their actions and behaviour, is an instructive lesson from the great book of nature, it is a deciphering of the true *signatura rerum*. We see in them the manifold grades and modes of the manifestation of will, which in all beings of one and the same grade, wills always in the same way, which objectifies itself as life, as existence in such endless variety, and such different forms, which are all adaptations to the different external circumstances, and may be compared to many variations on the same theme.

· · ·

45. The great problem of historical painting and sculpture is to express directly and for perception the Idea in which the will reaches the highest grade of its objectification. The objective side of the pleasure afforded by the beautiful is here always predominant, and the subjective side has retired into the background. It is further to be observed that at the next grade below this, animal painting, the characteristic is entirely one with the beautiful; the most characteristic lion, wolf, horse, sheep, or ox, was always the most beautiful also. The reason of this is that animals have only the character of their species, no individual character. In the representation of men the character of the species is separated from that of the individual; the former is now called beauty (entirely in the objective sense), but the latter retains the name, character, or expression, and the new difficulty arises of representing both, at once and completely, in the same individual.

Human beauty is an objective expression, which means the fullest objectification of will at the highest grade at which it is knowable, the Idea of man in general, completely expressed in the sensible form. But however much the objective side of the beautiful appears here the subjective side still always accompanies it. And just because no object transports us so quickly into pure aesthetic contemplation, as the most beautiful human countenance and form, at the sight of which we are instantly filled with unspeakable satisfaction, and raised above ourselves and all that troubles us; this is only possible because this most distinct and purest knowledge of will raises us most easily and quickly to the state of pure knowing, in which our personality, our will with its constant pain, disappears, so long as the pure aesthetic pleasure lasts. Therefore it is that Goethe says: "No evil can touch him who looks on human beauty; he feels himself at one with himself and with the world." That a beautiful human form is produced by nature must be explained in this way. At this its highest grade the will objectifies itself in an individual; and therefore through circumstances and its own power it completely overcomes all the hindrances and opposition which the phenomena of the lower grades present to it. Such are the forces of nature, from which the will must always first extort and win back the matter that belongs to all its manifestations. Further, the phenomenon of will at its higher grades always has multiplicity in its form. Even the tree is only a systematic aggregate of innumerably repeated sprouting fibres. This combination assumes greater complexity in higher forms, and the human body is an exceedingly complex system of different parts, each of which has a peculiar life of its own, *vita propria*, subordinate to the whole. Now that all these parts are in the proper fashion subordinate to the whole, and coordinate to each other, that they all work together harmoniously for the expression of the whole, nothing superfluous, nothing restricted; all these are the rare conditions, whose result is beauty, the completely expressed character of the species. So is it in nature. But how in art? One would suppose that art achieved the beautiful by imitating nature. But how is the artist to recognise the perfect work which is to be imitated, and distinguish it from the failures, if he does not anticipate the beautiful *before experience?* And besides this, has nature ever produced a human being perfectly beautiful in all his parts? It has accordingly been thought that the artist must seek out the beautiful parts, distributed among a number of different human beings, and out of them construct a beautiful whole; a perverse and foolish opinion. For it will be asked, how is he to know that just these forms and not others are beautiful? We also see what kind of success attended the efforts of the old German painters to achieve the beautiful by imitating nature. Observe their naked figures. No knowledge of the beautiful is possible purely *a posteriori*, and from mere experience; it is always, at least in part, *a priori*, although quite different in kind, from the forms of the principle of sufficient reason, of which we are conscious *a priori*. These concern the universal form of phenomena as such, as it constitutes the possibility of knowledge in general, the universal *how* of all phenomena, and from this knowledge proceed mathematics and pure natural science. But this other kind of knowledge *a priori*, which makes it possible to express the beautiful, concerns, not the form but the content of phenomena, not the *how* but the *what* of the phenomenon. That we all recognise human beauty when we see it, but that in the true artist this takes place with such clearness that he shows it as he has never seen it, and surpasses nature in his representation; this is only possible because *we ourselves are* the will whose adequate objectification at its highest grade is here to be judged and discovered. Thus alone have we in fact an anticipation of that which nature (which is just the will that constitutes our own being) strives to express. And in the true genius this anticipation is accompanied by so great a degree of intelligence that he recognises the Idea in the particular thing, and thus, as it were, *understands the half-uttered speech of nature,* and articulates clearly what she only stammered forth. He expresses in the hard marble that beauty of form which in a thosuand attempts she failed to produce, he presents it to nature, saying, as it were, to her, "That is what you wanted to say!" And whoever is able to judge replies, "Yes, that is it." Only in this way was it possible for the genius of the Greeks to find the type of human beauty and establish it as a canon for the school of sculpture; and only by virtue of such an anticipation is it possible for all of us to recognise beauty, when it has actually been achieved by nature in the particular case. This anticipation is the *Ideal*. It is the *Idea* so far as it is known *a priori*, at least half, and it becomes practical for art, because it corresponds to and completes what is given *a posteriori* through nature. The possibility of such an anticipation of the beautiful *a priori* in the artist, and of its recognition *a posteriori* by the critic, lies in the fact that the artist and the critic are themselves the "in-itself" of nature, the will which objecifies itself.

. . .

Human beauty was explained above as the fullest objectification of will at the highest grade at which it is knowable. It expresses itself through the form; and this lies in space alone, and has no necessary connection with time, as, for example, motion has. Thus far then we may say: the adequate objectification of will through a merely spatial phenomenon is beauty, in the objective sense. A plant is nothing but such a merely spatial phenomenon of will; for no motion, and consequently no relation to time (regarded apart from its development), belongs to the expression of its nature; its mere form expresses its whole being and displays it openly. But brutes and men require, further, for the full revelation of the will which is manifested in them, a series of actions, and thus the manifestation in them takes on a direct relation to time.

. . .

As the merely spatial manifestation of will can objectify it fully or defectively at each definite grade,—and it is this which constitutes beauty or ugliness,—so the temporal objectification of will, *i.e.*, the action, and indeed the direct action, the movement, may correspond to the will, which objectifies itself in it, purely and fully without foreign admixture, without superfluity, without defect, only expressing exactly the act of will determined in each case;—or the converse of all this may occur. In the first case the movement is made with *grace*, in the second case without it. Thus as beauty is the adequate representation of will generally, through its merely spatial manifestation; *grace* is the adequate representation of will through its temporal manifestation, that is to say, the perfectly accurate and fitting expression of each act of will, through the movement and position which objectify it. Since movement and position presuppose the body, Winckelmann's expression is very true and suitable, when he says, "Grace is the proper relation of the acting person to the action." It is thus evident that beauty may be attributed to a plant, but no grace, unless in a figurative sense; but to brutes and men, both beauty and grace. Grace consists, according to what has been said, in every movement being performed, and every position assumed, in the easiest, most appropriate and convenient way, and therefore being the pure, adequate expression of its intention, or of the act of will, without any superfluity, which exhibits itself as aimless, meaningless bustle, or as wooden stiffness. Grace presupposes as its condition a true proportion of all the limbs, and a symmetrical, harmonious figure; for complete ease and evident appropriateness of all positions and movements are only possible by means of these. Grace is therefore never without a certain degree of beauty of person. The two, complete and united, are the most distinct manifestation of will at the highest grade of its objectification.

It was mentioned above that in order rightly to portray man, it is necessary to separate the character of the species from that of the individual, so that to a certain extent every man expresses an Idea peculiar to himself, as was said in the last book. Therefore the arts whose aim is the representation of the Idea of man, have as their problem, not only beauty, the character of the species, but also the character of the individual, which is called, *par excellence, character*. But this is only the case in so far as this character is to be regarded, not as something accidental and quite peculiar to the man as a single individual, but as a side of the Idea of humanity which is specially apparent in this individual, and the representation of which is therefore of assistance in revealing this Idea. Thus the character, although as such it is individual, must yet be Ideal, that is, its significance in relation to the Idea of humanity generally (the objectifying of which it assists in its own way) must be comprehended and expressed with special prominence. Apart from this the representation is a portrait, a copy of the individual as such, with all his accidental qualities. And even the portrait ought to be, as Winckelmann says, the ideal of the individual.

In sculpture, beauty and grace are the principal concern. The special character of the mind, appearing in emotion, passion, alternations of knowing and willing, which can only be represented by the expression of the countenance and the gestures, is the peculiar sphere of *painting*. For although eyes and colour, which lie outside the province of sculpture, contribute much to beauty, they are yet far more essential to character. Further, beauty unfolds itself more completely when it is contemplated from various points of view; but the expression, the character, can only be completely comprehended from *one* point of view.

. . .

49. The truth which lies at the foundation of all that we have hitherto said about art, is that the object of art, the representation of which is the aim of the artist, and the knowledge of which must therefore precede his work as its germ and source, is an Idea in Plato's sense, and never anything else; not the particular thing, the object of common apprehension, and not the concept, the object of rational thought and of science. Although the Idea and the concept have something in common, because both represent as unity a multiplicity of real things; yet the great difference between them has no doubt been made clear and evident enough by what we have said about concepts in the first book, and about Ideas in this book. I by no means wish to assert, however, that Plato really distinctly comprehended this difference; indeed many of his examples of Ideas, and his discussions of them, are applicable only to concepts. Meanwhile we leave this question alone and go on our own way, glad when

we come upon traces of any great and noble mind, yet not following his footsteps but our own aim. The *concept* is abstract, discursive, undetermined within its own sphere, only determined by its limits, attainable and comprehensible by him who has only reason, communicable by words without any other assistance, entirely exhausted by its definition. The *Idea* on the contrary, although defined as the adequate representative of the concept, is always object of perception, and although representing an infinite number of particular things, is yet thoroughly determined. It is never known by the individual as such, but only by him who has raised himself above all willing and all individuality to the pure subject of knowing.

. . .

The *Idea* is the unity that falls into multiplicity on account of the temporal and spatial form of our intuitive apprehension; the *concept*, on the contrary, is the unity reconstructed out of multiplicity by the abstraction of our reason; the latter may be defined as *unitas post rem*, the former as *unitas ante rem*. Finally, we may express the distinction between the Idea and the concept, by a comparison, thus: the *concept* is like a dead receptacle, in which, whatever has been put, actually lies side by side, but out of which no more can be taken . . . than was put in; . . . the (Platonic) *Idea*, on the other hand, develops, in him who has comprehended it, ideas which are new as regards the concept of the same name; it resembles a living organism, developing itself and possessed of the power of reproduction, which brings forth what was not put into it.

It follows from all that has been said, that the concept, useful as it is in life, and serviceable, necessary and productive as it is in science, is yet always barren and unfruitful in art. The comprehended Idea, on the contrary, is the true and only source of every work of art. In its powerful originality it is only derived from life itself, from nature, from the world, and that only by the true genius, or by him whose momentary inspiration reaches the point of genius. Genuine and immortal works of art spring only from such direct apprehension. Just because the Idea is and remains object of perception, the artist is not conscious in the abstract of the intention and aim of his work; not a concept, but an Idea floats before his mind; therefore he can give no justification of what he does. He works, as people say, from pure feeling, and unconsciously, indeed instinctively. On the contrary, imitators, mannerists, *imitatores, servum pecus,* start, in art, from the concept; they observe what pleases and affects us in true works of art; understand it clearly, fix it in a concept, and thus abstractly, and then imitate it, openly or disguisedly, with dexterity and intentionally.

. . .

51. If now, with the exposition which has been given of art in general, we turn from plastic and pictorial art to poetry, we shall have no doubt that its aim also is the revelation of the Ideas, the grades of the objectification of will, and the communication of them to the hearer with the distinctness and vividness with which the poetical sense comprehends them. Ideas are essentially perceptible; if, therefore, in poetry only abstract conceptions are directly communicated through words, it is yet clearly the

intention to make the hearer perceive the Ideas of life in the representatives of these conceptions, and this can only take place through the assistance of his own imagination. But in order to set the imagination to work for the accomplishment of this end, the abstract conceptions, which are the immediate material of poetry as of dry prose, must be so arranged that their spheres intersect each other in such a way that none of them can remain in its abstract universality; but, instead of it, a perceptible representative appears to the imagination; and this is always further modified by the words of the poet according to what his intention may be.

. . .

For the Idea can only be known by perception; and knowledge of the Idea is the end of art. The skill of a master, in poetry as in chemistry, enables us always to obtain the precise precipitate we intended. This end is assisted by the numerous epithets in poetry, by means of which the universality of every concept is narrowed more and more till we reach the perceptible. Homer attaches to almost every substantive an adjective, whose concept intersects and considerably diminishes the sphere of the concept of the substantive, which is thus brought so much the nearer to perception.

. . .

The revelation of the Idea, which is the highest grade of the objectivity of will, the representation of man in the connected series of his efforts and actions, is thus the great problem of poetry. It is true that both experience and history teach us to know man; yet oftener men than man, *i.e.*, they give us empirical notes of the behaviour of men to each other, from which we may frame rules for our own conduct, oftener than they afford us deep glimpses of the inner nature of man. The latter function, however, is by no means entirely denied them; but as often as it is the nature of mankind itself that discloses itself to us in history or in our own experience, we have comprehended our experience, and the historian has comprehended history, with artistic eyes, poetically, *i.e.*, according to the Idea, not the phenomenon, in its inner nature, not in its relations. Our own experience is the indispensable condition of understanding poetry as of understanding history; for it is, so to speak, the dictionary of the language that both speak. But history is related to poetry as portrait-painting is related to historical painting; the one gives us the true in the individual, the other the true in the universal; the one has the truth of the phenomenon, and can therefore verify it from the phenomenal, the other has the truth of the Idea, which can be found in no particular phenomenon, but yet speaks to us from them all. The poet from deliberate choice represents significant characters in significant situations; the historian takes both as they come. Indeed, he must regard and select the circumstances and the persons, not with reference to their inward and true significance, which expresses the Idea, but according to the outward, apparent, and relatively important significance with regard to the connection and the consequences.

. . .

The poet comprehends the Idea, the inner nature of man apart from all relations, outside all time, the adequate objectivity of the thing-in-itself, as its highest grade. Even in that method of treatment which is necessary for the historian, the inner nature and significance of the phenomena, the kernel of all these shells, can never be entirely lost. He who seeks for it, at any rate, may find it and recognise it. Yet that which is significant in itself, not in its relations, the real unfolding of the Idea, will be found far more accurately and distinctly in poetry than in history, and, therefore, however paradoxical it may sound, far more really genuine inner truth is to be attributed to poetry than to history

.   .   .

Tragedy is to be regarded, and is recognised as the summit of poetical art, both on account of the greatness of its effect and the difficulty of its achievement. It is very significant for our whole system, and well worthy of observation, that the end of this highest poetical achievement is the representation of the terrible side of life. The unspeakable pain, the wail of humanity, the triumph of evil, the scornful mastery of chance, and the irretrievable fall of the just and innocent, is here presented to us; and in this lies a significant hint of the nature of the world and of existence. It is the strife of will with itself, which here, completely unfolded at the highest grade of its objectivity, comes into fearful prominence. It becomes visible in the suffering of men, which is now introduced, partly through chance and error, which appear as the rulers of the world, personified as fate, on account of their insidiousness, which even reaches the appearance of design; partly it proceeds from man himself, through the self-mortifying efforts of a few, through the wickedness and perversity of most. It is one and the same will that lives and appears in them all, but whose phenomena fight against each other and destroy each other. In one individual it appears powerfully, in another more weakly; in one more subject to reason, and softened by the light of knowledge, in another less so, till at last, in some single case, this knowledge, purified and heightened by suffering itself, reaches the point at which the phenomenon, the veil of Maya, no longer deceives it. It sees through the form of the phenomenon, the *principum individuationis*. The egoism which rests on this perishes with it, so that now the *motives* that were so powerful before have lost their might, and instead of them the complete knowledge of the nature of the world, which has a *quieting* effect on the will, produces resignation, the surrender not merely of life, but of the very will to live. Thus we see in tragedies the noblest men, after long conflict and suffering, at last renounce the ends they have so keenly followed, and all the pleasures of life for ever, or else freely and joyfully surrender life itself. So is it with the steadfast prince of Calderon; with Gretchen in "Faust;" with Hamlet, whom his friend Horatio would willingly follow, but is bade remain a while, and in this harsh world draw his breath in pain, to tell the story of Hamlet, and clear his memory; so also is it with the Maid of Orleans, the Bride of Messina; they all die purified by suffering, *i.e.*, after the will to live which was formerly in them is dead. In the "Mohammed" of

Voltaire this is actually expressed in the concluding words which the dying Palmira addresses to Mohammed: "The world is for tyrants: live!" On the other hand, the demand for so-called poetical justice rests on entire misconception of the nature of tragedy, and, indeed, of the nature of the world itself. It boldly appears in all its dulness in the criticisms which Dr. Samuel Johnson made on particular plays of Shakespeare, for he very naïvely laments its entire absence. And its absence is certainly obvious, for in what has Ophelia, Desdemona, or Cordelia offended? But only the dull, optimistic, Protestant-rationalistic, or peculiarly Jewish view of life will make the demand for poetical justice, and find satisfaction in it. The true sense of tragedy is the deeper insight, that it is not his own individual sins that the hero atones for, but original sin, *i.e.*, the crime of existence itself.

. . .

52. We find that there is still another fine art which has been excluded from our consideration, and had to be excluded, for in the systematic connection of our exposition there was no fitting place for it—I mean *music*. It stands alone, quite cut off from all the other arts. In it we do not recognise the copy or repetition of any Idea of existence in the world. Yet it is such a great and exceedingly noble art, its effect on the inmost nature of man is so powerful, and it is so entirely and deeply understood by him in his inmost consciousness as a perfectly universal language, the distinctness of which surpasses even that of the perceptible world itself, that we certainly have more to look for in it than an *exercitum arithmeticœ occultum nescientis se numerare animi*, which Leibnitz called it. Yet he was perfectly right, as he considered only its immediate external significance, its form. But if it were nothing more, the satisfaction which it affords would be like that which we feel when a sum in arithmetic comes out right, and could not be that intense pleasure with which we see the deepest recesses of our nature find utterance. From our standpoint, therefore, at which the aesthetic effect is the criterion, we must attribute to music a far more serious and deep significance, connected with the inmost nature of the world and our own self, and in reference to which the arithmetical proportions, to which it may be reduced, are related, not as the thing signified, but merely as the sign. That in some sense music must be related to the world as the representation to the thing represented, as the copy to the original, we may conclude from the analogy of the other arts, all of which possess this character, and affect us on the whole in the same way as it does, only that the effect of music is stronger, quicker, more necessary and infallible. Further, its representative relation to the world must be very deep, absolutely true, and strikingly accurate, because it is instantly understood by every one, and has the appearance of a certain infallibility, because its form may be reduced to perfectly definite rules expressed in numbers, from which it cannot free itself without entirely ceasing to be music. Yet the point of comparison between music and the world, the respect in which it stands to the world in the relation of a copy or repetition, is very obscure. Men have practised music in all ages without being

able to account for this; content to understand it directly, they renounce all claim to an abstract conception of this direct understanding itself.

I gave my mind entirely up to the impression of music in all its forms, and then returned to reflection and the system of thought expressed in the present work, and thus I arrived at an explanation of the inner nature of music and of the nature of its imitative relation to the world—which from analogy had necessarily to be presupposed—an explanation which is quite sufficient for myself, and satisfactory to my investigation, and which will doubtless be equally evident to any one who has followed me thus far and has agreed with my view of the world. Yet I recognise the fact that it is essentially impossible to prove this explanation, for it assumes and establishes a relation of music, as idea, to that which from its nature can never be idea, and music will have to be regarded as the copy of an original which can never itself be directly presented as idea. I can therefore do no more than state . . . the explanation of the marvellous art of music which satisfies myself, and I must leave the acceptance or denial of my view to the effect produced upon each of my readers both by music itself and by the whole system of thought communicated in this work.

. . .

The (Platonic) Ideas are the adequate objectification of will. To excite or suggest the knowledge of these by means of the representation of particular things (for works of art themselves are always representations of particular things) is the end of all the other arts, which can only be attained by a corresponding change in the knowing subject. Thus all these arts objectify the will indirectly only by means of the Ideas; and since our world is nothing but the manifestation of the Ideas in multiplicity, though their entrance into the *principium individuationis* (the form of the knowledge possible for the individual as such), music also, since it passes over the Ideas, is entirely independent of the phenomenal world, ignores it altogether, could to a certain extent exist if there was no world at all, which cannot be said of the other arts. Music is as *direct* an objectification and copy of the whole *will* as the world itself, nay, even as the Ideas, whose multiplied manifestation constitutes the world of individual things. Music is thus by no means like the other arts, the copy of the Ideas, but the *copy of the will itself*, whose objectivity the Ideas are. This is why the effect of music is so much more powerful and penetrating than that of the other arts, for they speak only of shadows, but it speaks of the thing itself. Since, however, it is the same will which objectifies itself both in the Ideas and in music, though in quite different ways, there must be, not indeed a direct likeness, but yet a parallel, an analogy, between music and the Ideas whose manifestation in multiplicity and incompleteness is the visible world.

. . .

The composer reveals the inner nature of the world, and expresses the deepest wisdom in a language which his reason does not understand; as a person under the influence of mesmerism tells things of which he has no conception when he awakes. Therefore in the composer, more than in any other artist, the man is entirely separated and distinct from the artist.

. . .

The unutterable depth of all music by virtue of which it floats through our consciousness as the vision of a paradise firmly believed in yet ever distant from us, and by which also it is so fully understood and yet so inexplicable, rests on the fact that it restores to us all the emotions of our inmost nature, but entirely without reality and far removed from their pain. So also the seriousness which is essential to it, which excludes the absurd from its direct and peculiar province, is to be explained by the fact that its object is not the idea, with reference to which alone deception and absurdity are possible; but its object is directly the will, and this is essentially the most serious of all things, for it is that on which all depends. How rich in content and full of significance the language of music is, we see from the repetitions, as well as the *Da capo*, the like of which would be unbearable in works composed in a language of words, but in music are very appropriate and beneficial, for, in order to comprehend it fully, we must hear it twice.

In the whole of this exposition of music I have been trying to bring out clearly that it expresses in a perfectly universal language, in a homogeneous material, mere tones, and with the greatest determinateness and truth, the inner nature, the in-itself of the world, which we think under the concept of will, because will is its most distinct manifestation. Further, according to my view and contention, philosophy is nothing but a complete and accurate repetition or expression of the nature of the world in very general concepts, for only in such is it possible to get a view of that whole nature which will everywhere be adequate and applicable. Thus, whoever has followed me and entered into my mode of thought, will not think it so very paradoxical if I say, that supposing it were possible to give a perfectly accurate, complete explanation of music, extending even to particulars, that is to say, a detailed repetition in concepts of what it expresses, this would also be a sufficient repetition and explanation of the world in concepts, or at least entirely parallel to such an explanation, and thus it would be the true philosophy.

. . .

The pleasure we receive from all beauty, the consolation which art affords, the enthusiasm of the artist, which enables him to forget the cares of life,—the latter an advantage of the man of genius over other men, which alone repays him for the suffering that increases in proportion to the clearness of consciousness, and for the desert loneliness among men of a different race,—all this rests on the fact that the in-itself of life, the will, existence itself, is, as we shall see farther on, a constant sorrow, partly miserable, partly terrible; while, on the contrary, as idea alone, purely contemplated, or copied by art, free from pain, it presents to us a drama full of significance. This purely knowable side of the world, and the copy of it in any art, is the element of the artist. He is chained to the contemplation of the play, the objectification of will; he remains beside it, does not get tired of contemplating it and representing it in copies; and meanwhile he bears himself the cost of the production of that play, *i.e.*, he himself is the will which objectifies itself, and remains in constant suffering. That pure, true, and deep knowledge of the inner nature of the world becomes now for him an end in itself: he stops there. Therefore it does not become to him a quieter of the will, as, we shall see in the next book, it does in the case of the saint who has attained to resignation; it does not deliver him for ever from life, but only at moments, and is therefore not for him a path out of life, but only an occasional consolation in it, till his power, increased by this contemplation and at last tired of the play, lays hold on the real.

Frederick Copleston

ART AS ESCAPE:
THE PARTIAL ESCAPE—ART

The Partial Escape: Art

Out of the futile life of desiring and willing and striving Schopenhauer
offers two means of escape, the one affording a temporary respite from
the slavery of the will, the other a lasting relief through the denial of
the will.* The former path of escape lies through art, the latter through
ethical renunciation. . . . In the present chapter I shall treat of his
metaphysic of art. I say 'metaphysic of art' since Schopenhauer does not
merely make critical observations on styles of art or on aesthetic appreciation, but welds his theory of art into his philosophical system in such a
way that it forms an integral part of that system, the theory including a
doctrine as to the metaphysical foundations of art. As with Schelling and
Hegel, so with Schopenhauer, the aesthetic theory is not something
extraneous to the system, something added to it, the fruit of a side-line or
hobby on the philosopher's part, but rather a stage in the system's development. Yet this does not necessarily mean that all that Schopenhauer
has to say on the subject of art stands or falls with the system as a whole:
it may well be that individual observations and points of treatment are
of intrinsic value in themselves, quite apart from the relation of the
aesthetic theory as a whole to the philosophical system.

. . .

Will . . . objectifies itself immediately in the Platonic Ideas. (I use
this term because Schopenhauer uses it: it is Schopenhauer's theory that
is being discussed, and not the historic Plato's.) These Ideas are the
grades of objectification of the Will, considered as anterior to multiplicity;
they are the species, 'the original unchanging forms and qualities of all
natural bodies, both organized and unorganized, and also the general

Frederick Copleston, S. J. is probably the best known historian of philosophy in
this century. His A History of Philosophy, Volumes I–VIII is a tour de force of
scholarship and analytical exposition. Father Copleston is Professor at the Pontifical
Gregorian University, Rome and at Heythrop College.
* Selections from Schopenhauer: Philosopher of Pessimism, chapter 5, (London, 1946).
Reprinted by permission of Routledge & Kegan Paul Ltd.

forces which reveal themselves according to natural laws'; they stand to individual phenomena as archetypes to copies. The idea is itself beyond space and time, the forms of individuality and multiplicity, being eternal and unchanged. According to Schopenhauer, 'the principle of sufficient reason has for it no meaning'. It is a little difficult to see how in this case the Idea can be related to Will on the one hand (as a grade of objectification) or to multiple phenomena on the other (expressing itself in innumerable individuals and particulars); but, as it is in any case very difficult to see how the Will, that eternal striving, could manifest itself objectively in the Platonic Ideas at all, it is perhaps best to leave the question of the possibility of the Ideas on Schopenhauer's premises and proceed . . . to expound what he has to say about them.

The Idea is eternal; but the species, taken empirically, endures throughout its succeeding individual members. The Idea is not, then, to be identified with the species of e.g., man or dog, as known in the succeeding individual phenomena of these species: the latter, the temporally enduring species, is 'the empirical correlative of the Idea'. In this point, therefore, the Schopenhauerian Idea does indeed resemble the Platonic Idea, in that neither is simply the *forma substantialis* or *specifica* of the man Tom or the dog Fido, but is the eternal archetype. This indeed makes it all the more difficult to determine the exact status of Schopenhauer's Ideas. We have the metaphysical Will, the *Ding-an-sich* on the one hand and, on the other, the world 'as Idea', the phenomenal world of multiple subjects and objects: what place remains for the Platonic Ideas? They are not the noumenon itself, for the latter is undivided unity and, though each Idea is itself undivided, there are many Ideas, being the grades of Will's objectification. Yet they cannot be said strictly to be phenomena, to belong to the world 'as idea', for they are unaffected by the principle that governs the phenomenal world, the object for a subject. They constitute a sort of half-way house; but the assertion of such an intermediary sphere seems to the writer quite unjustified. Still, as it is difficult to see how there could be *any* objectification of Will, we will refrain from pressing the point. Plato's idea of an exemplary Absolute is a profound and luminous theory; but that does not mean that Schopenhauer was justified in importing Platonism into his philosophy of Will, though as this importation enabled him to develop a most interesting aesthetic theory, in which passages of great beauty occur, we may well forgive him this transgression.

'The Idea', says Schopenhauer, 'is the species, but not the genus', for, while the former are nature's work, the latter are man's work, mere concepts. 'There are *species naturales*, but only *genera logica*'. Ideas may also be described as *universalia ante rem*, in distinction from mere universal concepts, which are *universalia post rem*. The Idea as such is undivided, but it is broken up into the multiplicity of individuals, not in itself, but through the perception of the perceiving subject. The latter, if gifted with reason (i.e., man), then restores the unity through rational reflection in the form of the universal concept; but this concept, though possessing the same extension as the Idea, is only *abstract*. The Idea as such exists anteriorly to the activity of reason, and it is not apprehended immediately by reason: it is perceived or intuited. It is object, object for a subject, but it has not yet assumed the subordinate forms of phenomenality, which are included in the principle of sufficient reason. It is thus the immediate and most adequate objectivity of Will, and, if we were freed from the conditions of knowledge that bear upon us as individuals, we should contemplate only Ideas: our world would be a *nunc stans*. 'Time is only the broken and piecemeal view which the individual being has of the Ideas, which are outside time, and consequently eternal'.

Obviously, then, if we are to apprehend the Ideas, we must transcend the conditions of knowledge which bear upon us as individuals. One might expect that this would be beyond the power of any human being; but Schopenhauer is equal to the occasion and is ready to postulate a mode of immediate apprehension 'by virtue of which the subject, so far as it knows an Idea, is no more individual'. Knowledge . . . is, according to its origin and nature, bound to the service of the will and proceeds in accordance with the principle of sufficient reason, apprehending objects as related to one another in space, time and causality, and apprehending them as related to the will of the subject as an individual. In the case of the brutes this subjection of knowledge to the will, to desire, is never, and never can be, transcended; but in the case of man it is possible for him to transcend such 'interested' knowledge. His knowledge may break free from the service of the will, and he then becomes the 'pure, will-less subject of knowledge, which no longer traces relations in accordance with the principle of sufficient reason, but rests in fixed contemplation of the object presented to it, out of its connection with all others, and rises into it'. He 'ceases to consider the where, the when, the why, and the whither of things, and looks simply and solely at the *what*', losing himself, as it were, in the object, forgetting his own individuality, and becoming the clear mirror of the object, or even fused into one with the object. In such 'perception' he is no longer individual, but the '*pure, will-less, painless, timeless subject of knowledge*': the individual as such knows not Ideas. In other words, in this form of knowledge man no longer regards things as particular objects standing in a relation to one another and to his will, as related to desire, but contemplates only the essential in an object, the Idea; and in this contemplation he no longer desires or hates, but only *contemplates*, as pure subject of knowledge. He is thus lifted out of the slavery of the will, of desire, and becomes the impersonal spectator or contemplator of the eternal Idea, manifested in the object before him. For the time being, therefore, for the duration of his objective contemplation, he escapes from the servitude of the will: but it is, as it were, an island on the river, where the voyager may disembark for a short while, before continuing on his journey, or an oasis in the desert, where the traveller may enjoy shade and cool and refreshment, before going on his weary way over the burning sands under the pitiless eastern sun. Science never rests in an attained end, a fresh goal, a new discovery always draws the scientist on; history is unceasing and never reaches completion; but art grasps finality, expresses 'the adequate objectivity of the Will', plucks the object of its contemplation out of the stream of the world's course, and has it isolated before it', 'is everywhere at its goal'. Æsthetic satisfaction, which affords a partial and temporary escape from desire and which consists in the apprehension of the Ideas, is facilitated both by the fact that in the work of art the unessential is eliminated and by the fact that the perceived object, the work of art, is unrelated to desire and so does not rouse the will but enables the beholder to contemplate with pure objectivity. To put it crudely, a man who sees a fine ripe apple lying on a plate on the table may very well desire to eat it, but if he sees the table with the plate and apple depicted in a still-life painting, he is more easily enabled to contemplate purely æsthetically, without reference to the apple as a desirable comestible. Of course, he could contemplate the real apple too from a purely æsthetic standpoint (the artist himself does this); but the fact that he knows that the apple in the painting is not a real apple and cannot be eaten, *facilitates* a purely æsthetic contemplation, facilitates his liberation from the slavery of the will.

Kant had spoken of 'the pure disinterested satisfaction in judgments of taste' in the *Critique of Judgment*, and Schopenhauer developed what Kant had already noted and incorporated it into his philosophical system. The Kantian influence is an undoubted fact, and Schopenhauer, of course, was quite aware of the fact; but it would be rash to conclude to an Hegelian influence on the purely verbal ground that both Schopenhauer and Hegel speak of the Idea in connection with art. The work of art, according to Schopenhauer, is the expression of the artist's apprehension of the Idea and for Hegel too it is the sensuous manifestation of the Idea; but the term 'Idea' has not the same meaning for the two philosophers. For Schopenhauer it is the specific archetype, the 'Platonic Idea', whereas for Hegel it is the Absolute: for Schopenhauer the Idea is eternal and static; for Hegel it is self-developing, self-manifesting Reason: for Schopenhauer there are many Ideas, for Hegel but one. Though Hegel lectured on æsthetic at Heidelberg, the notes of his lectures on æsthetic theory at Berlin were not published until after his death, so that it would be hardly possible for Schopenhauer to have borrowed æsthetic notions from Hegel, even had he wished (which is most unlikely!). In any case it was his Platonic studies that influenced Schopenhauer and not any hints that he culled from his arch-enemy, Hegel. It would, however, be idle to deny the influence of Schelling, who had already utilized the Platonic theory of Ideas. For Schelling, in his middle period, the Absolute, Pure Identity, expresses itself immediately in an eternal world of Ideas, which are the true things-in-themselves. It is the function of art to represent these Ideas in the concrete, in the finite and spatial production, the work of art, so that the artist represents objectively and concretely the Ideas which are represented only abstractly by the philosopher. In view of the startling resemblance between the art theories of Schelling and Schopenhauer in salient points we can hardly suppose that the latter was uninfluenced by the former, even if Schopenhauer had already been influenced by his early Platonic studies. Kant's philosophical theories did not permit his taking the 'absolute standpoint' in regard to art and Schelling was the pioneer in this direction, with Hegel and Schopenhauer as his followers, each developing his theme in his own way. It is perhaps not fanciful to think that Schopenhauer may have learnt something even from Aristotle, for whom the poet represents the universal concretely and not abstractly, like the philosopher. Poetry is more philosophical than history, said Aristotle, since history deals with particulars, poetry *rather* with universals (though not with the abstract universal), and Schopenhauer says much the same in different language.

Art is the work of genius. What is genius? Schopenhauer defines it as 'the completest objectivity', as 'the faculty of continuing in the state of pure perception, and of enlisting in this service the knowledge which originally existed only for the service of the will'; it is the power of leaving aside one's own personal desires and wishes, in order to become pure knowing subject, and that for a sufficient length of time, and with sufficient consciousness, to enable one to reproduce by means of deliberate art what one has apprehended in contemplation. It is as though the genius had a superfluity of knowledge, i.e., more than is required for the service of the will. . . . The presence of this 'superfluity' of the power of knowing explains the fact that the genius is unsatisfied with the trivialities of daily life, whereas the common mortal finds a satisfaction in his everyday existence that the former fails to find. Genius, then, is the power, not merely of apprehending of the Ideas, but of reproducing them or expressing them in painting, sculpture, poetry, architecture or music, and so is, to all intents and purposes, equivalent to the power of the great artist. The prominent position accorded to genius, artistic genius, by Schopenhauer, illustrates the philosopher's relation to Romanticism, linking him up, not only with Schelling, but also with the cult of genius in general, which characterized the Romantic School. His thought on this matter influenced the young Nietzsche, who wrote his *Birth of Tragedy* under the influence of Schopenhauer's philosophy and who represented the State in an early essay as having the function of rendering possible and facilitating the flowering of genius.

Imagination is a necessary condition of genius, but it is not the same thing as genius. It is a necessary condition, because the perceived objects of the phenomenal world represent or express the Ideas only imperfectly and power of imagination is needed in order to see what Nature was, as it were, trying to express, the perfect archetype that is only imperfectly represented in the perceived object. It is, however, not the same thing as genius, since imagination may be used simply in the service of the will, to minister to egotism, as when a man indulges in day-dreaming, building 'castles in the air', or writes down his fancies to form the 'ordinary novel'. In the case of the genius his power of imagination is enlisted in the service of pure objective knowledge, but the non-genius will generally use his imagination to consider some imaginary object in its relation to other objects and to his own will, i.e., in accordance with the principle of sufficient reason. Thus, though 'extraordinary strength of imagination accompanies, and is indeed a necessary condition of genius,' strength of imagination does not of itself indicate the presence of genius and 'men who have no touch of genius may have much imagination'. Again, genius is not the same thing as mere talent, which 'lies rather in the greater versatility and acuteness of discursive than of intuitive knowledge'.

But the man of genius is not always engaged upon that type of knowledge which is peculiar to genius and in the more or less lengthy intervals he is subject to the deficiencies, and advantages, of the ordinary man. (This helps to explain why the act of genius has been regarded as inspiration, as a kind of divine *afflatus*.) Nevertheless, the man of genius shows a marked disinclination to certain types of knowledge based on the principle of sufficient reason, namely, abstract and logical reasoning. 'Experience has proved that men of great artistic genius have no faculty for mathematics; no man was ever very distinguished for both'. (Was not Leonardo da Vinci an exception at any rate?) Moreover, geniuses are seldom men of great reasonableness and are often subject to violent passion and emotion, partly because they have strong and energetic wills, partly because in them knowledge of perception preponderates over abstract knowledge, producing a susceptibility to impressions, which latter they tend to take as guides to action rather than abstract conceptions. Again, since in them knowledge is, to some extent, freed from the service of the will (though, this does not mean that they have weak wills), they are inclined in conversation to think more of the subjects on which they are speaking than of the persons whom they are addressing and are likely to show imprudence in their objectivity.

Since the genius is gifted with an abnormal superfluity of intellect (abnormal, because by nature cognition is simply the servant of the will and orientated to practical life), his intellect 'often leaves the will very inopportunely in a fix, and thus the individual so gifted becomes more or less useless for life, nay, in his conduct sometimes reminds us of madness'. Schopenhauer dwells at some length on the kinship of madness and genius and, among other quotations, quotes Dryden (though he actually ascribes the lines to Pope) to the effect that—

> 'Great wits to madness sure are near allied,
> And thin partitions do their bounds divide'.

The philosopher assures us that in 'a diligent search in lunatic asylums' he had found individuals whose genius distinctly appeared through their madness. The madman, according to Schopenhauer, does not usually err precisely in the knowledge of what is immediately present, but rather in regard to what is absent and past, which he often confuses with the present, thus falsifying the present through a fictitious connection with an imaginary past, mistaking connections and relations. It is at this point that he comes into contact with the man of genius, since the latter also leaves out of sight the knowledge of the connection of things and of the relations which conform to the principle of sufficient reason, 'in order to see in things only their Ideas'. This vivid concentration on the present may give rise to phenomena that resemble madness. (But absent-mindedness, due to concentration on an immediate object of thought, is not the prerogative of artists, cf. Socrates, St. Thomas Aquinas or Hegel.)

Yet, even if genius, in the full sense, the faculty of clearly apprehending the Ideas and expressing that clear apprehension in the work of art, is present only in a few men, it must also be present, in some degree at least, in all men, except in those, if any, who are utterly incapable of æsthetic appreciation and for whom a word like beauty has no meaning, except, of course, in relation to sensual desire. Otherwise men in general would be just as much incapable of appreciating works of art as of producing them, whereas it is quite clear that a man may have a deep appreciation of a symphony or poem, though he himself is no composer or creative poet. With the exception mentioned above, all men are capable of transcending the narrow circle of the ego and its desires for a short time and knowing the Ideas objectively, though the genius has this faculty in a far stronger and higher degree and can exercise it more continuously. The fact that he expresses the Ideal in a work of art, in which the unessential and purely accidental is omitted, enables the ordinary man to exercise more easily the lower degree of the faculty he possesses: 'the artist lets us see the world through his eyes'. That he has these eyes is an inborn gift of genius; but that he is able to let the rest of us see with his eyes is acquired, is due to technical ability, for which training and practice is required. Thus Schopenhauer does not mean to exalt native genius at the complete expense of technique: technical knowledge alone will not produce a great artist, but some technical knowledge is requisite.

There might seem, to judge by the actual words he uses in different passages, to be a certain ambiguity or inconsistency in Schopenhauer's theory of the relation of the genius to the ordinary man. Sometimes he speaks as though genius means the capacity not only of apprehending the Ideas, but also of expressing them in works of art of one kind or another, while at other times he seems to imply that genius is simply the faculty of objective knowledge, of contemplating the Ideas, and that the faculty of expressing this knowledge concretely is due to acquired technical ability. On the first view the 'ordinary man', if he is no productive artist at all, would not possess the faculty of genius in any degree, unless indeed we wanted to adopt an idea of Benedetto Croce and say that all æsthetic appreciation or intuition involves expression, at least interior expression in the sense of imaginative recreation, in which case the external expression of the artist would appear to be something almost accidental and there would be really no 'works of art' in the sense of external statues, pictures, etc. But this was not Schopenhauer's opinion, for whom expression does not mean simply interior imaginative reproduction. On the second view the ordinary man, at least he who is capable of some æsthetic appreciation, would certainly share in the faculty of genius and Schopenhauer might agree with Croce *on this point*, that the difference between ordinary men and geniuses is purely quantitative and not qualitative. But this would not agree with the common opinion that the artistic genius is precisely the man who can create great works of art in some external medium and that the ability to do this is not at all a mere matter of technique alone. Technical training may be required in some degree, but it cannot by itself supply the place of native genius, and artistic genius includes not only the capacity for vision, intuition, but also the capacity for external expression. Other men may possess the vision, but, if they lack the capacity for external expression, they would not normally be called artists. Croce declares that the external expression is merely practical in function, the creation of a stimulus for further internal expression on the part of the artist himself or others, while Schopenhauer regarded the metaphysical function of the work of art as being to facilitate disinterested knowledge of the Idea; but, whatever we assign as the function of art from the viewpoint of a general philosophical system, whether that of Schopenhauer or Hegel or Croce or any other thinker we fancy, it is surely true that the *external* expression of intuition (be that intuition supraintellectual or infra-intellectual or what you will) belongs essentially to the activity of the artist as such. The artist regards the production of the work of art as his creative activity as an artist, as *the* expression which matters, not as a mere practical note, so to speak. But, whatever verbal inconsistencies Schopenhauer may have been guilty of, his real view is doubtless that artistic genius comprises both the faculty of intuition and the faculty of creative expression (which latter is *aided* by technical and acquired knowledge), and that the non-genius, who is at the same time capable of æsthetic appreciation, shares to some degree in the first faculty, even though he is lacking in the second. In regard, therefore, to the first component element of genius the ordinary man might be said to differ only quantitatively from the man of genius, whereas, in regard to the second component element, he differs qualitatively. The specific difference of genius, the faculty of creative experience, would thus distinguish the artistic genius from the ordinary man. That this represents Schopenhauer's opinion is clear from the fact of his admission that the ordinary man is capable of pure objective knowledge, not only through æsthetic appreciation of the work of art, but also through disinterested contemplation of, e.g., natural beauty, even if he can exercise this contemplative faculty only in a much weaker and less sustained manner than the artistic genius.

.   .   .

We shall now proceed to some considerations connected with the main theme of this present chapter, art viewed as a quietener of will, as a temporary escape from the slavery of desire and the struggle for existence. So long as consciousness is dominated by the will, the individual is the prey of thronging desires and can know no peace or happiness; but when he rises above his personal interests and contemplates the object purely objectively, disinterestedly, apart from its relation to his own will or to other things, he enjoys 'the Sabbath of the penal servitude of willing; the wheel of Ixion stands still'. It does not matter if the object of contemplation be insignificant, provided that it is contemplated objectively, and Schopenhauer mentions in this connection the Dutch paintings of still life and the 'very insignificant country scenes' of e.g., Ruisdael. In such æsthetic contemplation, whether of works of art or of nature itself, so long as the object that arouses the contemplation is simply the significance and distinctness of natural forms, it is '*beauty* that affects us and the sense of the *beautiful* that is excited'. Beauty, objectively considered, is, therefore, significant form, the Platonic Idea presented to perception concretely, not represented abstractly by reason.

If, however, the objects of æsthetic contemplation have a hostile relation to the human will in general (i.e., to the body, which is the objectification of will), if they are seen to menace the body by their power or greatness, the beholder is filled with the sense of the *sublime*, and the object that produces the state of 'spiritual exaltation', in which the beholder perceives and recognizes the hostile relation, yet, in spite of this recognition, gives himself to objective contemplation of the Idea expressed in the hostile objects, is the *sublime*. What distinguishes the sense of the sublime from the sense of the beautiful is, therefore, this, that in the case of the latter pure objective knowledge gains the upper hand imperceptibly, without a struggle, whereas in the case of the former, the sublime, the state of pure objective knowledge is attained only through the conscious and forcible detachment of the attention from hostile relations which have been recognized as such, a detachment that must be not only consciously won, but also consciously maintained. The sublime is thus not something entirely different from the beautiful; it is rather the beautiful seen as involving a hostile relation to man. For instance, a man in a small boat at sea in a storm when contemplating the height and sweep and fury of the waves, the tossed spray as they dash themselves against the towering cliffs, the flashes of lightning, the stupendous might and power of nature, is contemplating the sublime: he recognizes the might and power that could at any moment engulf him, but, forcibly detaching his attention from personal danger and from fear, he sees the sublime beauty in the scene before him. 'He perceives himself as an individual, as the frail phenomenon of will, which the slightest touch of these forces can utterly destroy, helpless against powerful nature, dependent, the victim of chance, a vanishing nothing in the presence of stupendous might', he 'obtains a glimpse of a power beyond all comparison superior to the individual, threatening it with annihilation', and yet he remains the peaceful, knowing subject, the timeless spectator. Of course, if he allows fear to master him, and concern for his personal safety, if he views the forces of nature in their relation to his own particular will, then he ceases to be the contemplative beholder and ceases to contemplate the sublime.

Following the nomenclature of Kant, Schopenhauer distinguishes the dynamical from the mathematical sublime. The storm-scene would be an instance of the former, while the impression of the latter is produced in another way, by the contemplation of mere immensity in space and time, by a high and vast dome, by the vault of the starry heaven, by the eternal mountains or the age-old pyramids of Egypt. But, though Schopenhauer adopts Kant's nomenclature, he will not admit Kant's explanation of the impression of the sublime. According to Kant, the sublime is the 'absolutely great,' 'what is great beyond all comparison,' 'that in comparison with which everything else is small', 'that, the mere ability to think which shows a faculty of the mind surpassing every standard of Sense'. The sublimity does not reside in the things of nature, but in the judging mind. For instance a man who contemplates the might of nature from a position of security and at the same time is conscious that man's rational and moral character renders him superior to mere nature, attains the sense of sublimity. Beauty, which is the object of æsthetic taste, has to do with form; but sublimity has rather to do with that which lacks form and the sense of the sublime depends, to some extent at least, on moral reflections. Sublimity is thus more subjective than beauty. Kant rather characteristically remarks that 'the wide ocean, disturbed by the storm cannot be called sublime', but should be termed 'horrible': the mind must have recourse to reflections, of a moralizing type, if such a sight is to produce a feeling of the sublime. In practice we would certainly speak of the mighty forces of nature as sublime; but in truth this is an improper way of speaking since it is rather man himself that is sublime than the object he contemplates. We call the storm, the hurricane, the tumultuous ocean sublime ('provided only that we are in security'), because 'they raise the energies of the soul above their accustomed height . . . and give us courage to measure ourselves' (i.e. our rational nature and moral freedom), 'against the apparent almightiness of nature'. This attitude was unacceptable to Schopenhauer, and, though he adopted Kant's division of the sublime into the mathematical and the dynamical, he declared that he could allow no share in the impression of sublimity to 'either moral reflections or to hypostases from scholastic philosophy'.

The opposite of the sublime is the charming, 'that which excites the will by presenting to it directly its fulfilment, its satisfaction'. Sublimity involves the will only to this extent, that something which is recognized as hostile to the will is made into an object of disinterested contemplation, so that the feeling of the sublime arises precisely when the relationship of the object to the particular will of the subject is transcended and disregarded. The charming or attractive, on the other hand, draws the beholder away from pure contemplation by directly exciting the will. This being so, it is an abuse of language to speak of every beautiful object that is bright or cheering as charming, for the beautiful object as such is the object of pure contemplation and not of desire. The word 'charming' should therefore, according to Schopenhauer, be reserved for that which necessarily excites the will. He finds two species of the charming employed by artists, both of which he condemns. The first species, 'a very low one,' is to be found in Dutch paintings of still life that represent objects of food. He allows painted fruit, since one may contemplate a painted apple, for instance, as a beautiful product of nature, without being obliged to think of it as eatable; but there are other edibles which are painted so realistically that they 'necessarily excite the appetite for the things they represent . . . which puts an end to all æsthetic contemplation of the object'. Schopenhauer instances, rather amusingly, 'oysters, herrings, crabs, bread and butter, beer, wine,' and so on. He also condemns that kind of presentation of the naked human body which excites the passions of the beholder: the sensual is to be avoided in art.

The other species of the charming is a *negative* form (in fact, we would call it the opposite of charming) namely the disgusting or loathsome, a species even more reprehensible than the positive form. The disgusting or loathsome disturbs æsthetic contemplation by presenting to the will objects which it abhors and so is inadmissible in art, whereas the ugly, which is simply the defective objectification of Will at a particular grade, may have a place in a work of art. Schopenhauer is again adopting a theory of Kant, who declared that 'Beautiful art shows its superiority in this, that it describes as beautiful things which may be in nature ugly or displeasing' (he gives as examples disease, the havoc of war, etc.), whereas that which excites disgust 'cannot be represented in accordance with nature, without destroying all æsthetical satisfaction'. But though Schopenhauer adopted this and other æsthetic notions from Kant, e.g. his conception of the disinterested character of æsthetic contemplation and his recognition and division of the sublime, he developed these points in function of his general philosophic system, a system which would scarcely have commended itself to his eminent predecessor. Thus since æsthetic contemplation is looked on by Schopenhauer as affording a temporary liberation from the servitude of the will, he naturally emphasizes very strongly the disinterestedness of true æsthetic intuition and all that disturbs that contemplation by exciting the will, i.e. the charming on the one hand and the disgusting on the other, is condemned for precisely that reason. Yet though Schopenhauer lays such stress on the subjective effects of art, it remains true that his æsthetic theory is more objective than that of Kant, in this sense that his philosophy enabled him to give a metaphysical foundation to beauty in a way that Kant was naturally debarred from doing. In this respect Schopenhauer parts company with Kant and takes his stand with Schelling and Hegel, however much he might dislike the thought of being in their company. Moreover, in another respect too Schopenhauer is more objective than Kant. The latter, following eighteenth century writers (largely English), spoke constantly of the 'judgment of taste', and this judgment was for him subjective, contributing in no way to knowledge proper (though it is true that Kant is inconsistent or rather tends to open the way to asserting the objectivity of the judgment, without explicitly asserting it in clear language). For Schopenhauer, however, æsthetic contemplation is definitely knowledge, involving intellectual activity, though of an intuitive, and not a discursive, type: through contemplation the Ideas, objectively manifested, are apprehended by the perceiving subject.

It may be worth while pointing out that, while Schopenhauer agreed with Plato as to the objective status of Ideas (though his metaphysic of the Ideas was certainly not that of Plato) and as to the comparatively unsubstantial character of the phenomenal world (though here again Schopenhauer, following Indian thought, and combining it with his metaphysic of Will, differed very greatly from the Platonic theory), he certainly did not agree with Plato's æsthetic theory. It is notorious that Plato held that the artist is at the third remove from truth, in that he copies natural objects, which are themselves imitations or participations of true archetypal reality, whereas on Schopenhauer's theory the artist perceives the Ideas and expresses them in his work. It is correct, therefore, to say with Croce that Plato 'is justified and condemned by Schopenhauer exactly in the same way as by Plotinus of old, as well as by Schopenhauer's worst enemy, the modern Schelling'.

I have used the phrase 'significant form' for the object of æsthetic intuition, as Schopenhauer himself speaks of significant forms in this connection; but it should be remembered that the philosopher's use of the phrase implies a more intellectualist and 'scholastic' meaning than is necessarily implied by the same phrase as used in some modern writings on æsthetic theory. The artist contemplates the Platonic Idea, i.e. the specific archetype, manifested to sense-preception in the concrete phenomenal object, which latter expresses the archetype only imperfectly. Thus, although the æsthetic activity is not one of discursive thought, and though imaginative power is a necessary condition, it is predominantly intellectualist in character, rendered possible by man's 'superfluity of knowledge', and its object is one which can only be grasped by the intellect. We quite agree with Schopenhauer that intellectual penetration is necessary in some degree for the appreciation of æsthetic values in art, and we agree too that the intellectual activity involved cannot be simply equated with rational discursive thought; sensitive susceptibility is also involved, since the object apprehended by the intellect is essentially wedded to qualified matter. Æsthetic appreciation, properly so called, is not a pure activity of the intellect, nor yet an activity of the intellect that only accidentally depends on sensitive perception—which it perhaps would be, if the object of æsthetic contemplation were simply the specific form. We do not see how the object of æsthetic appreciation can possibly be the specific form, since we can very well apprehend the specific form in an object without at the same time apprehending the æsthetic character of an object. The 'significant form' of a landscape or section of landscape may stand out before our eyes without our adverting to any substantial or accidental forms as such. Schopenhauer would doubtless reply (*a*) that he expressly stated that the æsthetic apprehension of specific from is not the same as a purely rational apprehension of specific form, and (*b*) that it is not so much the concrete specific form of a particular object that is apprehended in æsthetic appreciation as the eternal Idea imperfectly expressed in the object, the Idea for the apprehension of which power of imagination is also necessary. That this more or less represents Schopenhauer's view is true enough; but then we do not believe in the existence of Ideas in the precise sense in which he used the term. There are indeed archetypal Ideas (to speak anthropomorphically) in the Divine Mind, but these we certainly do not directly apprehend, whether by intuition or not. If, therefore, the object of æsthetic contemplation were the specific form, it would have to be the specific form of the concrete object, since it is not, admittedly, the abstract concept, the universal idea. What then of artificial objects, which have no natural specific forms as such? Cannot these be beautiful? And what is the specific form of a group of objects, as in a picture of still life, or of a landscape? Schopenhauer might point out that in a work of architecture, which, as he would agree, has no natural specific form, we contemplate the Ideas that are the lowest grade of the Will's objectification, in the interplay of natural forces, gravity, rigidity, etc., but this seems to be very farfetched. What we appreciate is surely rather the order and co-ordination of elements that unify the æsthetic whole and are the reason why we apprehend the union of variety as beautiful. In any case it would appear that external form is more relevant to æsthetic appreciation than specific form in the philosophical sense.

'Significant form' is 'meaning' in a sense, but it is scarcely a meaning which can be stated in so many words, since it is the object of æsthetic appreciation, and æsthetic appreciation is not a purely intellectual activity. If we reflect on some personal act of æsthetic appreciation of natural beauty, we shall probably become conscious that that which has been stimulus and object is a certain pattern or structure, a certain formal co-ordination of elements, with due subordination of the elements to the dominating form (not specific form), which gives life and meaning to the whole. This form or pattern is not apprehended merely as a geometric pattern of lines in abstracted isolation, but as essentially embodied in coloured surfaces, in the juxtaposition and harmony of coloured figures, which are united in an æsthetically appreciable whole. The coloured surfaces are part of the pattern and any attempt to shed them as irrelevant is doomed to sterility. The empurpled trunk of the pine tree, with its close-set cap of contrasting darkness, may embody a geometric pattern, but it is by no means the geometric pattern alone that arouses our appreciation: in the beauty of the varying and graded colours of a November sky the colours, though they be harmonized and juxtaposed in patterned structure, are essential. In the work of art too, the product of human reason, form is essentially wedded to the material, and it cannot be abstracted and expressed as an intellectual idea, without draining it of all content as an æsthetic form and turning it into a pale and bloodless ghost; a bare skeleton or scheme, a mere caricature. Form, in the sense of pattern, may be more explicit in the work of some artists than in that of others, in El Greco more than in Murillo, in Gainsborough more than in Reynolds, yet it is always embodied form; even in the

Cubist and geometric pioneers, in spite of over-intellectualization, form cannot free itself from the embodying matter. Picasso in his cubist phase is still a master of colour, while we cannot but be struck by the delicacy and purity of colour in the work of Henri Matisse, in spite of the apparent simplicity of line and of representative elements (perhaps largely *because* of this simplicity). Pattern of line and form may be the factor which reduces component parts to due harmony and relative subordination, welding them into a significant whole; but it is not everything in a work of art. What would be left of Monet's painting of the façade of Rouen cathedral, if it were reduced to a mere skeletonic framework of so-called significant form? The form in a work by the sculptor Bourdelle or by Aristide Maillol is obviously the significant element, but equally obviously it cannot stand alone. The intellectual element in art is still but an element, even though it be the element which confers significance on an otherwise meaningless material.

Æsthetic appreciation of beauty in art is, therefore, not only intellectual in character, but also sensitive, and this not merely accidentally but essentially. Hence perhaps the reason why beauty, in nature as in art, does not fully satisfy the intellect, since the intellect is unable fully to grasp it and to fathom all its depth and its implications: significant form is not only significant of itself (in *nature* at least, as contrasted with art, in which meaning and significance are more apparent to us, since the work of art is a product of the human reason), but also of something else, behind and beyond it, supporting it and constituting the ground and origin of its existence. The philosophy of Arthur Schopenhauer cannot provide a metaphysical basis for natural beauty: it is impossible to see how natural beauty can be in any manner the manifestation of a senseless, empty striving, the metaphysical Will. It is true that the spiritual *Ens a se* cannot be the object of æsthetic appreciation in the strict sense, if the latter is essentially intellectual-sensitive in character, and that it cannot be beautiful in the primary (i.e. primary *quoad nos*) sense of the word; but, if this phenomenal world is the visible (external) manifestation of God, the *explicatio Dei*, we must predicate Beauty of God in an analogical, and unimaginable, sense. We must indeed say that He is Beauty itself, That which lies behind all created beauty, that to which natural beauty points, that of which things of beauty in art and nature tell in silent allusion and hinted implication. . . . St. Augustine maintained that we could have no knowledge that any given beautiful thing is but imperfectly beautiful or that one object is more beautiful than another, unless we had an inkling of Beauty itself, in comparison with which other objects are seen to fall short, to be imperfect. That we have no intuition of Absolute Beauty and no innate idea in the full sense, is clear; but the human will (we speak, as St. Augustine did, of man *in the concrete*) is dynamically orientated towards the Absolute, and this may explain, in part at least, the elusiveness, secretiveness and suggestiveness of natural beauty and the dissatisfaction, or rather lack of complete satisfaction, experienced by not a few in regard to all concrete beautiful objects. 'I have been dreaming', says Professor Storitsyn in Andreyev's play, 'I have been dreaming of beauty. It is perhaps strange, but I, a book-man, a professor in galoshes, a learned bourgeois, a street car traveller, I have always been dreaming of beauty'.

Select Bibliography for Part Six

Books

Walter Jackson Bate, *From Classic to Romantic: Premises of Taste in Eighteenth Century England*; R. L. Brett, *The Third Earl of Shaftesbury*; Teddy Brunius, *David Hume on Criticism*; Edward Caird, *The Critical Philosophy of Immanuel Kant*; H. W. Cassirer, *A Commentary on Kant's Critique of Judgment*; Frank P. Chambers, *The History of Taste*; John Dennis, *A Large Account of the Taste in Poetry*; Scott Elledge, *Eighteenth-Century Critical Essays*; Patrick Gardiner, *Schopenhauer*; Alexander Gerard, *An Essay on Taste*; Walter J. Hipple, Jr., *The Beautiful, the Sublime, and the Picturesque in Eighteenth-Century British Aesthetic Theory*; David Hume, *Treatise on Human Nature*; Immanuel Kant, *Observations on the Feeling of the Sublime and the Beautiful*; Richard Payne Knight, *Analytical Inquiry into the Principles of Taste*; Israel Knox, *The Aesthetic Theories of Kant, Hegel and Schopenhauer*; Arthur Schopenhauer, *Complete Essays*; Frederick Ungar, *Friedrich Schiller: An Anthology for Our Time*.

Articles

M. Cavell, "Taste and the Moral Sense"; Arthur Child, "The Social-Historical Relativity of Esthetic Value"; R. Cohen, "David Hume's Experimental Method and the Theory of Taste"; Donald W. Crawford, "Causes, Reasons and Aesthetic Objectivity"; Donald W. Crawford, "Reason-Giving in Kant's Aesthetics"; C. J. Ducasse, "What Has Beauty to Do with Art?"; Anthony C. Genova, "Kant's Transcendental Deduction of Aesthetical Judgments"; Gordon K. Greene, "For Whom and Why Does a Composer Prepare a Score"; William H. Halberstadt, "A Problem in Hume's Aesthetics"; Robert D. Hume, "Kant and Coleridge on Imagination"; Wallace Jackson, "Affective Values in Early Eighteenth-Century Aesthetics"; Richard Koffler, "Kant, Leopardi, and Gorgon Truth"; C. W. Korsmeyer, "On the 'Aesthetic Senses' and the Development of the Fine Arts"; C. W. Korsmeyer, "Relativism and Hutcheson's Aesthetic Theory"; Paul Oskar Kristeller, "The Modern System of the Arts"; James Malek, "Charles Lamotte's 'An Essay Upon Poetry and Painting' and Eighteenth-Century British Aesthetics"; M. R. Neville, "Kant's Characterization of Aesthetic Experience"; Stuart Jay Petock, "Kant, Beauty and the Object of Taste"; V. A. Rudowski, "The Theory of Signs in the Eighteenth Century"; E. Schaper, "Free and Dependent Beauty"; E. Schaper, "Kant on Imagination"; Guy Sircello, "Subjectivity and Justification in Aesthetic Judgments"; Jerome Stolnitz, " 'Beauty': History of an Idea"; Jerome Stolnitz, "On the

Significance of Lord Shaftesbury in Modern Aesthetic Theory"; Redding S. Sugg, "Hume's Search for the Key with the Leathern Thong"; Robert W. Uphaus, "Shaftesbury on Art: The Rhapsodic Aesthetic"; R. Woodfield, "The Freedom of Shaftesbury's Classicism."

PART SEVEN

---•◦•---

Contemporary Theories of the Aesthetic and Contemporary Critiques of these Theories

By the time the aesthetic–attitude theories presented in this part were being written, *beauty* had ceased to be the central concept of concern. The eighteenth-century theorists of taste had distinguished new categories such as the sublime and the picturesque and had given them separate treatments. Because of these innovations, and for other reasons as well, theories of taste had introduced a complexity into the theory of the appreciation of art and nature which by the end of the eighteenth century must have seemed chaotic to many. As was seen in part six, eighteenth-century theories of taste were replaced by nineteenth-century theories of aesthetic-attitude. The concept of the aesthetic functioned to restore a theoretical unity which was lost in the dismantling of theories of taste. The aesthetic attitude has its aesthetic object—the locus of aesthetic value. The approach was simple and straight-forward again, or at least it seemed to be.

In the introduction to part six, the notion of strong and weak versions of aesthetic–attitude theory was introduced. A strong version maintains that whatever is viewed with aesthetic perception is thereby made beautiful or given other aesthetic properties, while a weak version maintains that viewing with aesthetic perception is a necessary condition for experiencing the aesthetic properties of things—attributes that they have independently of aesthetic perception. All of the present-day aesthetic–attitude theories, whether presented in selections or discussed in the commentaries in this part, are weak versions of the theory; that is, they are theories which purport to describe an attitude enabling one to become aware of, and then appreciate, the aesthetic features of things. In the article "The Myth of the Aesthetic Attitude" at the end of this part, stronger and weaker varieties of aesthetic–attitude theory are discussed, but the reader is warned that something different is meant there by "stronger" and "weaker" than is meant by the "strong" and "weak" discussed above.

Edward Bullough's article, which presents the aesthetic attitude as *psychical distance,* was published in 1912. It has been reprinted in numerous anthologies and has exerted an enormous influence on aesthetic theory. Bullough begins by asserting that psychical distance "has a *negative,* inhibitory aspect . . . and a positive side." He discusses, however, only the inhibitory aspect, and consequently "psychical distance" has come to be taken to refer to a psychological inhibitory force which, when it occurs, blocks out impulses to action and "practical" thoughts. Once this blocking has occurred, a person is in the aesthetic attitude and can focus on and appreciate the aesthetic features of things. Bullough speaks of psychical distance as a *criterion* of beauty, which suggests he is going to develop a strong version of the theory; that is, he is going to maintain that psychically distancing an object will make it beautiful. The theory he develops, in actuality, is clearly a weak version.

In "The Myth of the Aesthetic Attitude" it is argued that no such psychological blocking force is at work in the appreciation of the aesthetic features of art and nature. Bullough has mistaken certain conventions that we observe in our interaction with art for a psychological force blocking thought or action. For example, theater-goers remain in their seats conventionally and do not try to interact with the actors. Bullough misinterprets our observation of this convention and maintains that we are in the grip of a psychological force which prevents us, say, from mounting the stage on certain occasions to aid a player.

Allan Casebier's article is presented in partial defense of the notion of psychical distance. What Casebier describes as distance is, however, quite different from what Bullough had in mind. In short, Casebier uses "distanced" and "nondistanced" to refer to paying attention and not paying attention to works of art, and to various things that are internal or external to those works. Casebier, unlike Bullough, makes no claim that there is a psychological force which blocks thoughts or action. It is perhaps debatable whether Casebier's view should be actually classified as an aesthetic–attitude theory.

There is another influential variety of the weak version of aesthetic–attitude theory. The best-known recent representatives of this view are Jerome Stolnitz and Eliseo Vivas. This part has no selections about this type of theory, but "The Myth of the Aesthetic Attitude" by George Dickie contains an extensive discussion and criticism of the theories of Stolnitz and Vivas. This school of thought has as its central conception the notion of *disinterested attention.* Unlike Bullough, whose theory maintains that there is a *special* psychological force which blocks impulses to action and practical thoughts, this theory maintains that attention may be either interested or disinterested. When it is disinterested, attention defines the aesthetic attitude.

The weak versions of the aesthetic–attitude theory discussed here purported to describe states of persons which enable those persons to be aware of the aesthetic features of art and nature. Frank Sibley, in his celebrated "Aesthetic Concepts" and several follow-up essays, attempts a similar feat but does so by trying to make use of the concept of *taste* rather than the notion of aesthetic attitude. In employing the notion of taste, Sibley reaches back to the eighteenth century for his central philosophical concept. As Ted Cohen notes at the end of his critical essay on Sibley, Sibley's notion of taste is far more restricted than those of the eighteenth-century philosophers. For the eighteenth-century philosophers of taste, taste was conceived to be (1) an ability to notice, (2) a capacity to enjoy (or be pained), and (3) a faculty which is the basis for evaluations. These philosophers were, however, almost entirely concerned with the last two aspects of taste. For Sibley taste is simply an *ability* which enables one to notice or discriminate features which a person who lacks taste cannot notice.

In "Aesthetic Concepts" Sibley is concerned with trying to establish two main points: (1) there is a distinction between aesthetic and nonaesthetic features of art (and nonart) and the distinction is based on taste, and (2) the aesthetic features depend on the nonaesthetic features but the relationship is not a condition-governed one. With regard to the first point, Sibley maintains, for example, that a certain thing may possess the aesthetic quality of delicacy which a person with normal abilities, but lacking taste, will be unable to notice. A person who possesses taste will be able to notice the delicate quality of the object. With regard to the second point, the aesthetic feature of the delicacy of an object depends on its nonaesthetic features, say, its thinness and slight curvature—but thinness and slight curvature are not generally sufficient conditions for producing delicacy. Consequently, no matter how full a description one might have of the nonaesthetic features of an object, one could not infer that it has some particular aesthetic feature. Only sensing or perceiving and exercising taste will reveal whether the aesthetic feature exists.

Ted Cohen, in his critique of Sibley's account of the aesthetic/nonaesthetic distinction, is almost solely concerned with denying the distinction. Cohen notes that Sibley's distinction between aesthetic and nonaesthetic features derives from the exercise of taste, and he contends that Sibley presents no argument for the existence of taste as an ability which we may have over and above normal abilities that perceive the features of the world. Cohen counters that the so-called aesthetic features can be discerned by normal abilities, and that Sibley's distinction, therefore, "comes to nothing."

Edward Bullough

"PSYCHICAL DISTANCE" AS A FACTOR IN ART AND AN AESTHETIC PRINCIPLE

I

1. The conception of 'Distance' suggests, in connexion with Art, certain trains of thought by no means devoid of interest or of speculative importance.* Perhaps the most obvious suggestion is that of *actual spatial* distance, i.e. the distance of a work of Art from the spectator, or that of *represented spatial* distance, i.e. the distance represented within the work. Less obvious, more metaphorical, is the meaning of *temporal* distance. The first was noticed already by Aristotle in his *Poetics*; the second has played a great part in the history of painting in the form of perspective; the distinction between these two kinds of distance assumes special importance theoretically in the differentiation between sculpture in the round, and relief-sculpture. Temporal distance, remoteness from us in point of time, though often a cause of misconceptions, has been declared to be a factor of considerable weight in our appreciation.

It is not, however, in any of these meanings that 'Distance' is put forward here, though it will be clear in the course of this essay that the above mentioned kinds of distance are rather special forms of the conception of Distance as advocated here, and derive whatever *aesthetic* qualities they may possess from Distance in its *general* connotation. This general connotation is 'Psychical Distance.'

A short illustration will explain what is meant by 'Psychical Distance.' Imagine a fog at sea: for most people it is an experience of acute unpleasantness. Apart from the physical annoyance and remoter forms of discomfort such as delays, it is apt to produce feelings of peculiar anxiety, fears of invisible dangers, strains of watching and listening for distant and unlocalised signals. The listless movements of the ship and

Edward Bullough (1880–1934) was Professor of Italian Literature at Cambridge University. He is most famous, however, for his aesthetic writings and his coining of the term "psychical distance."

* This essay was originally published in the *British Journal of Psychology*, vol. V, pp. 87–98, 1912. Reprinted by permission of Cambridge University Press.

her warning calls soon tell upon the nerves of the passengers; and that special, expectant, tacit anxiety and nervousness, always associated with this experience, make a fog the dreaded terror of the sea (all the more terrifying because of its very silence and gentleness) for the expert seafarer no less than for the ignorant landsman.

Nevertheless, a fog at sea can be a source of intense relish and enjoyment. Abstract from the experience of the sea fog, for the moment, its danger and practical unpleasantness, just as every one in the enjoyment of a mountain-climb disregards its physical labour and its danger (though, it is not denied, that these may incidentally enter into the enjoyment and enhance it); direct the attention to the features 'objectively' constituting the phenomenon—the veil surrounding you with an opaqueness as of transparent milk, blurring the outline of things and distorting their shapes into weird grotesqueness; observe the carrying-power of the air, producing the impression as if you could touch some far-off siren by merely putting out your hand and letting it lose itself behind that white wall; note the curious creamy smoothness of the water, hypocritically denying as it were any suggestion of danger; and, above all, the strange solitude and remoteness from the world, as it can be found only on the highest mountain tops: and the experience may acquire, in its uncanny mingling of repose and terror, a flavour of such concentrated poignancy and delight as to contrast sharply with the blind and distempered anxiety of its other aspects. This contrast, often emerging with startling suddenness, is like a momentary switching on of some new current, or the passing ray of a brighter light, illuminating the outlook upon perhaps the most ordinary and familiar objects—an impression which we experience sometimes in instants of direst extremity, when our practical interest snaps like a wire from sheer over-tension, and we watch the consummation of some impending catastrophe with the marvelling unconcern of a mere spectator.

It is a difference of outlook, due—if such a metaphor is permissible—to the insertion of Distance. This Distance appears to lie between our own self and its affections, using the latter term in its broadest sense as anything which affects our being, bodily or spiritually, e.g. as sensation, perception, emotional state or idea. Usually, though not always, it amounts to the same thing to say that the Distance lies between our own self and such objects as are the sources or vehicles of such affections.

Thus, in the fog, the transformation by Distance is produced in the first instance by putting the phenomenon, so to speak, out of gear with our practical, actual self; by allowing it to stand outside the context of our personal needs and ends—in short, by looking at it 'objectively,' as it has often been called, by permitting only such reactions on our part as emphasise the 'objective' features of the experience, and by interpreting even our 'subjective' affections not as modes of *our* being but rather as characteristics of the phenomenon.

The working of Distance is, accordingly, not simple, but highly complex. It has a *negative*, inhibitory aspect—the cutting-out of the practical sides of things and of our practical attitude to them—and a *positive* side—the elaboration of the experience on the new basis created by the inhibitory action of Distance.

2. Consequently, this distanced view of things is not, and cannot be, our normal outlook. As a rule, experiences constantly turn the same side towards us, namely, that which has the strongest practical force of appeal. We are not ordinarily aware of those aspects of things which do not touch us immediately and practically, nor are we generally conscious of impressions apart from our own self which is impressed. The sudden view of things from their reverse, usually unnoticed, side, comes upon us as a revelation, and such revelations are precisely those of Art. In this most general sense, Distance is a factor in all Art.

3. It is, for this very reason, also an aesthetic principle. The aesthetic contemplation and the aesthetic outlook have often been described as 'objective.' We speak of 'objective' artists as Shakespeare or Velasquez, of 'objective' works or art forms as Homer's *Iliad* or the drama. It is a term constantly occurring in discussions and criticisms, though its sense, if pressed at all, becomes very questionable. For certain forms of Art, such as lyrical poetry, are said to be 'subjective'; Shelley, for example, would usually be considered a 'subjective' writer. On the other hand, no work of Art can be genuinely 'objective' in the sense in which this term might be applied to a work on history or to a scientific treatise; nor can it be 'subjective' in the ordinary acceptance of that term, as a personal feeling, a direct statement of a wish or belief, or a cry of passion is subjective. 'Objectivity' and 'subjectivity' are a pair of opposites which in their mutual exclusiveness when applied to Art soon lead to confusion.

Nor are they the only pair of opposites. Art has with equal vigour been declared alternately 'idealistic' and 'realistic,' 'sensual' and 'spiritual,' 'individualistic' and 'typical.' Between the defence of either terms of such antitheses most aesthetic theories have vacillated. It is one of the contentions of this essay that such opposites find their synthesis in the more fundamental conception of Distance.

Distance further provides the much needed criterion of the beautiful as distinct from the merely agreeable.

Again, it marks one of the most important steps in the process of artistic creation and serves as a distinguishing feature of what is commonly so loosely described as the 'artistic temperament.'

Finally, it may claim to be considered as one of the essential characteristics of the 'aesthetic consciousness,'—if I may describe by this term that special mental attitude towards, and outlook upon, experience, which finds its most pregnant expression in the various forms of Art.

II

Distance, as I said before, is obtained by separating the object and its appeal from one's own self, by putting it out of gear with practical needs and ends. Thereby the 'contemplation' of the object becomes alone possible. But it does not mean that the relation between the self and the object is broken to the extent of becoming 'impersonal.' Of the alternatives 'personal' and 'impersonal' the latter surely comes nearer to the truth; but here, as elsewhere, we meet the difficulty of having to express certain facts in terms coined for entirely different uses. To do so usually results in paradoxes, which are nowhere more inevitable than in discussions upon Art. 'Personal' and 'impersonal,' 'subjective' and 'objective' are such terms, devised for purposes other than aesthetic speculation, and becoming loose and ambiguous as soon as applied outside the sphere of their special meanings. In giving preference therefore to the term 'impersonal' to describe the relation between the spectator and a work of Art, it is to be noticed that it is not impersonal in the sense in which we speak of the 'impersonal' character of Science, for instance. In order to obtain 'objectively valid' results, the scientist excludes the 'personal factor,' i.e. his personal wishes as to the validity of his results, his predilection for any particular system to be proved or disproved by his research. It goes without saying that all experiments and investigations are undertaken out of a personal interest in the science, for the ultimate support of a definite assumption, and involve personal hopes of success; but this does not affect the 'dispassionate' attitude of the investigator, under pain of being accused of 'manufacturing his evidence.'

1. Distance does not imply an impersonal, purely intellectually interested relation of such a kind. On the contrary, it describes a *personal* relation, often highly emotionally coloured, but *of a peculiar character*. Its peculiarity lies in that the personal character of the relation has been, so to speak, filtered. It has been cleared of the practical, concrete nature of its appeal, without, however, thereby losing its original constitution. One of the best-known examples is to be found in our attitude towards the events and characters of the drama: they appeal to us like persons and incidents of normal experience, except that that side of their appeal, which would usually affect us in a directly personal manner, is held in abeyance. This difference, so well known as to be almost trivial, is generally explained by reference to the knowledge that the characters and situations are 'unreal,' imaginary. In this sense Witasek,[1] operating with Meinong's theory of *Annahmen*, has described the emotions involved in witnessing a drama as *Scheingefühle*, a term which has so frequently been misunderstood in discussions of his theories. But, as a matter of fact, the 'assumption' upon which the imaginative emotional reaction is based is not necessarily the condition, but often the consequence, of Distance; that is to say, the converse of the reason usually stated would then be true: viz. that Distance, by changing our relation to the characters, renders them seemingly fictitious, not that the fictitiousness of the characters alters our feelings toward them. It is, of course, to be granted that the actual and admitted unreality

[1] H. Witasek, 'Zur psychologischen Analyse der aesthetischen Einfühlung,' *Ztsch. f Psychol. u. Physiol. der Sinnesorg.* 1901, xxv. 1 ff.; *Grundzüge der Aesthetik,* Leipzig, 1904.

of the dramatic action reinforces the effect of Distance. But surely the proverbial unsophisticated yokel whose chivalrous interference in the play on behalf of the hapless heroine can only be prevented by impressing upon him that 'they are only pretending,' is not the ideal type of theatrical audience. The proof of the seeming paradox that it is Distance which primarily gives to dramatic action the appearance of unreality and not *vice versâ*, is the observation that the same filtration of our sentiments and the same seeming 'unreality' of *actual* men and things occur, when at times, by a sudden change of inward perspective, we are overcome by the feeling that "all the world's a stage."

2. This personal, but 'distanced' relation (as I will venture to call this nameless character of our view) directs attention to a strange fact which appears to be one of the fundamental paradoxes of Art: it is what I propose to call 'the antinomy of Distance.'

It will be readily admitted that a work of Art has the more chance of appealing to us the better it finds us prepared for its particular kind of appeal. Indeed, without some degree of predisposition on our part, it must necessarily remain incomprehensible, and to that extent unappreciated. The success and intensity of its appeal would seem, therefore, to stand in direct proportion to the completeness with which it corresponds with our intellectual and emotional peculiarities and the idiosyncracies of our experience. The absence of such a concordance between the characters of a work and of the spectator is, of course, the most general explanation for differences of 'tastes.'

At the same time, such a principle of concordance requires a qualification, which leads at once to the antinomy of Distance.

Suppose a man, who believes that he has cause to be jealous about his wife, witnesses a performance of 'Othello.' He will the more perfectly appreciate the situation, conduct and character of Othello, the more exactly the feelings and experiences of Othello coincide with his own—at least he *ought* to on the above principle of concordance. In point of fact, he will probably do anything but appreciate the play. In reality, the concordance will merely render him acutely conscious of his own jealousy; by a sudden reversal of perspective he will no longer see Othello apparently betrayed by Desdemona, but himself in an analogous situation with his own wife. The reversal of perspective is the consequence of the loss of Distance.

If this be taken as a typical case, it follows that the qualification required is that the coincidence should be as complete as is compatible with maintaining Distance. The jealous spectator of 'Othello' will indeed appreciate and enter into the play the more keenly, the greater the resemblance with his own experience—*provided* that he succeeds in keeping the Distance between the action of the play and his personal feelings: a very difficult performance in the circumstances. It is on account of the same difficulty that the expert and the professional critic make a bad audience, since their expertness and critical professionalism are *practical* activities, involving their concrete personality and constantly endangering their Distance. [It is, by the way, one of the reasons why Criticism is an art, for it requires the constant interchange from the practical to the distanced attitude and vice versâ, which is characteristic of artists.]

The same qualification applies to the artist. He will prove artistically most effective in the formulation of an intensely *personal* experience, but he can formulate it artistically only on condition of a detachment from the experience *quâ personal*. Hence the statement of so many artists that artistic formulation was to them a kind of catharsis, a means of ridding themselves of feelings and ideas the acuteness of which they felt almost as a kind of obsession. Hence, on the other hand, the failure of the average man to convey to others at all adequately the impression of an overwhelming joy or sorrow. His personal implication in the event renders it impossible for him to formulate and present it in such a way as to make others, like himself, feel all the meaning and fulness which it possesses for him.

What is therefore, both in appreciation and production, most desirable is the *utmost decrease of Distance without its disappearance.*

3. Closely related, in fact a presupposition to the 'antimony,' is the *variability of Distance.* Herein especially lies the advantage of Distance compared with such terms as 'objectivity' and 'detachment.' Neither of them implies a *personal* relation—indeed both actually preclude it; and the mere inflexibility and exclusiveness of their opposites render their application generally meaningless.

Distance, on the contrary, admits naturally of degrees, and differs not only according to the nature of the *object*, which may impose a greater or smaller degree of Distance, but varies also according to the *individual's capacity* for maintaining a greater or lesser degree. And here one may remark that not only do *persons differ from each other* in their habitual measure of Distance, but that the *same individual differs* in his ability to maintain it in the face of different objects and of different arts.

There exist, therefore, two different sets of conditions affecting the degree of Distance in any given case: those offered by the object and those realised by the subject. In their interplay they afford one of the most extensive explanations for varieties of aesthetic experience, since loss of Distance, whether due to the one or the other, means loss of aesthetic appreciation.

In short, Distance may be said to *be variable both according to the distancing-power of the individual, and according to the character of the object.*

There are two ways of losing Distance: either to 'under-distance' or to 'over-distance.' 'Under-distancing' is the commonest failing of the *subject*, an excess of Distance is a frequent failing of *Art*, especially in the past. Historically it looks almost as if Art had attempted to meet the deficiency of Distance on the part of the subject and had overshot the mark in this endeavour. It will be seen later that this is actually true, for it appears that over-distanced Art is specially designed for a class of appreciation which has difficulty to rise spontaneously to any degree of Distance. The consequence of a loss of Distance through one or other cause is familiar:

the verdict in the case of under-distancing is that the work is 'crudely naturalistic,' 'harrowing,' 'repulsive in its realism.' An excess of Distance produces the impression of improbability, artificiality, emptiness or absurdity.

The individual tends, as I just stated, to under-distance rather than to lose Distance by over-distancing. *Theoretically* there is no limit to the decrease of Distance. In theory, therefore, not only the usual subjects of Art, but even the most personal affections, whether ideas, percepts or emotions, can be sufficiently distanced to be aesthetically appreciable. Especially artists are gifted in this direction to a remarkable extent. The average individual, on the contrary, very rapidly reaches his limit of decreasing Distance, his 'Distance-limit,' i.e. that point at which Distance is lost and appreciation either disappears or changes its character.

In the *practice*, therefore, of the average person, a limit does exist which marks the minimum at which his appreciation can maintain itself in the aesthetic field, and this average minimum lies considerably higher than the Distance-limit of the artist. It is practically impossible to fix this average limit, in the absence of data, and on account of the wide fluctuations from person to person to which this limit is subject. But it is safe to infer that, in art practice, explicit references to organic affections, to the material existence of the body, especially to sexual matters, lie normally below the Distance-limit, and can be touched upon by Art only with special precautions. Allusions to social institutions of any degree of personal importance—in particular, allusions implying any doubt as to their validity—the questioning of some generally recognised ethical sanctions, references to topical subjects occupying public attention at the moment, and such like, are all dangerously near the average limit and may at any time fall below it, arousing, instead of aesthetic appreciation, concrete hostility or mere amusement.

This difference in the Distance-limit between artists and the public has been the source of much misunderstanding and injustice. Many an artist has seen his work condemned, and himself ostracized for the sake of so-called 'immoralities' which to him were *bonâ fide* aesthetic objects. His power of distancing, nay, the necessity of distancing feelings, sensations, situations which for the average person are too intimately bound up with his concrete existence to be regarded in that light, have often quite unjustly earned for him accusations of cynicism, sensualism, morbidness or frivolity. The same misconception has arisen over many 'problem plays' and 'problem novels' in which the public have persisted in seeing nothing but a supposed 'problem' of the moment, whereas the author may have been—and often has demonstrably been—able to distance the subject-matter sufficiently to rise above its practical problematic import and to regard it simply as a dramatically and humanly interesting situation.

The variability of Distance in respect to Art, disregarding for the moment the subjective complication, appears both as a general feature in Art, and in the differences between the special arts.

It has been an old problem why the 'arts of the eye and of the ear' should have reached the practically exclusive predominance over arts of other senses. Attempts to raise 'culinary art' to the level of a Fine Art have failed in spite of all propaganda, as completely as the creation of scent or liqueur 'symphonies.' There is little doubt that, apart from other excellent reasons[2] of a partly psycho-physical, partly technical nature, the actual, *spatial distance* separating objects of sight and hearing from the subject has contributed strongly to the development of this monopoly. In a similar manner *temporal remoteness* produces Distance, and objects removed from us in point of time are *ipso facto* distanced to an extent which was impossible for their contemporaries. Many pictures, plays and poems had, as a matter of fact, rather an expository or illustrating signifi-cance—as for instance much ecclesiastical Art—or the force of a direct practical appeal—as the invectives of many satires or comedies—which seem to us nowadays irreconcilable with their aesthetic claims. Such works have consequently profited greatly by lapse of time and have reached the level of Art only with the help of temporal distance, while others, on the contrary, often for the same reason have suffered a loss of Distance, through *over*-distancing.

Special mention must be made of a group of artistic conceptions which present excessive Distance in their form of appeal rather than in their actual presentation—a point illustrating the necessity of distinguishing between distancing an object and distancing the appeal of which it is the source. I mean here what is often rather loosely termed 'idealistic Art,' that is, Art springing from abstract conceptions, expressing allegorical mean-ings, or illustrating general truths. Generalisations and abstractions suffer under this disadvantage that they have too much general applicability to invite a personal interest in them, and too little individual concreteness to prevent them applying to us in all their force. They appeal to everybody and therefore to none. An axiom of Euclid belongs to nobody, just be-cause it compels everyone's assent; general conceptions like Patriotism, Friendship, Love, Hope, Life, Death, concern as much Dick, Tom and Harry as myself, and I therefore either feel unable to get into any kind of personal relation to them or, if I do so, they become at once, emphat-ically or concretely, *my* Patriotism, *my* Friendship, *my* Love, *my* Hope, *my* Life and Death. By mere force of generalisation, a general truth or a universal ideal is so far distanced from myself that I fail to realise it concretely at all, or, when I do so, I can realise it only as part of my *practical actual being,* i.e. it falls below the Distance-limit altogether. 'Idealistic Art' suffers consequently under the peculiar difficulty that its excess of Distance turns generally into an *under*-distanced appeal—all the more easily, as it is the usual failing of the subject to *under*- rather than to *over*-distance.

The different special arts show at the present time very marked varia-tions in the degree of Distance which they usually impose or require for

---

[2] J. Volkelt, 'Die Bedeutung der niederen Empfindungen für die aesthetische Ein-fühlung,' *Ztsch. für Psychol. u. Physiol. der Sinnesorg.* xxxii. 15, 16; *System der Aesthetik,* 1905, i. 260 ff.

their appreciation. Unfortunately here again the absence of data makes itself felt and indicates the necessity of conducting observations, possibly experiments, so as to place these suggestions upon a securer basis. In one single art, viz. the *theatre*, a small amount of information is available, from an unexpected source, namely the proceedings of the censorship committee,[3] which on closer examination might be made to yield evidence of interest to the psychologist. In fact, the whole censorship problem, as far as it does not turn upon purely economic questions, may be said to hinge upon Distance; if every member of the public could be trusted to keep it, there would be no sense whatever in the existence of a censor of plays. There is, of course, no doubt that, speaking generally, theatrical performances *eo ipso* run a special risk of a loss of Distance owing to the material presentment[4] of its subject-matter. The physical presence of living human beings as vehicles of dramatic art is a difficulty which no art has to face in the same way. A similar, in many ways even greater, risk confronts *dancing*: though attracting perhaps a less widely spread human interest, its animal spirits are frequently quite unrelieved by any glimmer of spirituality and consequently form a proportionately stronger lure to under-distancing. In the higher forms of dancing technical execution of the most wearing kind makes up a great deal for its intrinsic tendency towards a loss of Distance, and as a popular performance, at least in southern Europe, it has retained much of its ancient artistic glamour, producing a peculiarly subtle balancing of Distance between the pure delight of bodily movement and high technical accomplishment. In passing, it is interesting to observe (as bearing upon the development of Distance), that this art, once as much a fine art as music and considered by the Greeks as a particularly valuable educational exercise, should—except in sporadic cases—have fallen so low from the pedestal it once occupied. Next to the theatre and dancing stands *sculpture*. Though not using a *living* bodily medium, yet the human form in its full spatial materiality constitutes a similar threat to Distance. Our northern habits of dress and ignorance of the human body have enormously increased the difficulty of distancing Sculpture, in part through the gross misconceptions to which it is exposed, in part owing to a complete lack of standards of bodily perfection, and an inability to realise the distinction between sculptural form and bodily shape, which is the only but fundamental point distinguishing a statue from a cast taken from life. In *painting* it is apparently the form of its presentment and the usual reduction in scale which would explain why this art can venture to approach more closely than sculpture to the normal Distance-limit. As this matter will be discussed later in a special connexion this simple reference may suffice here. *Music* and *architecture* have a curious position. These two most abstract of all arts show a remarkable fluctuation in their Distances. Certain kinds of music, especially 'pure'

---

[3] Report from the Joint Select Committee of the House of Lords and the House of Commons on the Stage Plays (Censorship), 1909.

[4] I shall use the term 'presentment' to denote the manner of presenting, in distinction to 'presentation' as that which is presented.

music, or 'classical' or 'heavy' music, appear for many people over-distanced; light, 'catchy' tunes, on the contrary, easily reach that degree of decreasing Distance below which they cease to be Art and become a pure amusement. In spite of its strange abstractness which to many philosophers has made it comparable to architecture and mathematics, music possesses a sensuous, frequently sensual, character: the undoubted physiological and muscular stimulus of its melodies and harmonies, no less than its rhythmic aspects, would seem to account for the occasional disappearance of Distance. To this might be added its strong tendency, especially in unmusical people, to stimulate trains of thought quite disconnected with itself, following channels of subjective inclinations,—day-dreams of a more or less directly personal character. *Architecture* requires almost uniformly a very great Distance; that is to say, the majority of persons derive no aesthetic appreciation from architecture as such, apart from the incidental impression of its decorative features and its associations. The causes are numerous, but prominent among them are the confusion of building with architecture and the predominance of utilitarian purposes, which overshadow the architectural claims upon the attention.

4. That all art requires a Distance-limit beyond which, and a Distance within which only, aesthetic appreciation becomes possible, is the *psychological formulation of a general characteristic of Art*, viz. its *anti-realistic nature*. Though seemingly paradoxical, this applies as much to 'naturalistic' as to 'idealistic' Art. The difference commonly expressed by these epithets is at bottom merely the difference in the degree of Distance; and this produces, so far as 'naturalism' and 'idealism' in Art are not meaningless labels, the usual result that what appears obnoxiously 'naturalistic' to one person, may be 'idealistic' to another. To say that Art is anti-realistic simply insists upon the fact that Art is not nature, never pretends to be nature and strongly resists any confusion with nature. It emphasizes the *art*-character of Art: 'artistic' is synonymous with 'anti-realistic'; it explains even sometimes a very marked degree of artificiality.

"Art is an imitation of nature," was the current art-conception in the 18th century. It is the fundamental axiom of the standard-work of that time upon aesthetic theory by the Abbé Du Bos, *Réflexions critiques sur la poésie et la peinture*, 1719; the idea received strong support from the literal acceptance of Aristotle's theory of μίμησις and produced echoes everywhere, in Lessing's *Laocoon* no less than in Burke's famous statement that "all Art is great as it deceives." Though it may be assumed that since the time of Kant and of the Romanticists this notion has died out, it still lives in unsophisticated minds. Even when formally denied, it persists, for instance, in the belief that "Art idealises nature," which means after all only that Art copies nature with certain improvements and revisions. Artists themselves are unfortunately often responsible for the spreading of this conception. Whistler indeed said that to produce Art by imitating nature would be like trying to produce music by sitting upon the piano, but the selective, idealising imitation of nature finds merely another support in such a saying. Naturalism, pleinairism, impressionism,—even the guileless enthusiasm of the artist for the works of nature, her wealth of suggestion, her delicacy of workmanship, for the steadfastness of her guidance, only produce upon the public the impression that Art is, after all, an imitation of nature. Then how can it be anti-realistic? The antithesis, Art *versus* nature, seems to break down. Yet if it does, what is the sense of Art?

Here the conception of Distance comes to the rescue. The solution of the dilemma lies in the 'antinomy of Distance' with its demand: utmost decrease of Distance without its disappearance. The simple observation that Art is the more effective, the more it falls into line with our predispositions which are inevitably moulded on general experience and nature, has always been the original motive for 'naturalism.' 'Naturalism,' 'impressionism' is no new thing; it is only a new name for an innate leaning of Art, from the time of the Chaldeans and Egyptians down to the present day. Even the Apollo of Tenea apparently struck his contemporaries as so startlingly 'naturalistic' that the subsequent legend attributed a superhuman genius to his creator. A constantly closer approach to nature, a perpetual refining of the limit of Distance, yet without overstepping the dividing line of art and nature, has always been the inborn bent of art. To deny this dividing line has occasionally been the failing of naturalism. But no theory of naturalism is complete which does not at the same time allow for the intrinsic idealism of Art: for both are merely degrees in that wide range lying beyond the Distance-limit. To imitate nature so as to trick the spectator into the deception that it is nature which he beholds, is to forsake Art, its anti-realism, its distanced spirituality, and to fall below the limit into sham, sensationalism or platitude.

But what, in the theory of antinomy of Distance requires explanation is the existence of an *idealistic, highly distanced* Art. There are numerous reasons to account for it; indeed in so complex a phenomenon as Art, *single* causes can be pronounced almost *a priori* to be false. Foremost among such causes which have contributed to the formation of an idealistic Art appears to stand the subordination of Art to some extraneous purpose of an impressive, exceptional character. Such a subordination has consisted—at various epochs of Art history—in the use to which Art was put to subserve commemorative, hieratic, generally religious, royal or patriotic functions. The object to be commemorated had to stand out from among other still existing objects or persons; the thing or the being to be worshipped had to be distinguished as markedly as possible from profaner objects of reverence and had to be invested with an air of sanctity by a removal from its ordinary context of occurrence. Nothing could have assisted more powerfully the introduction of a high Distance than this attempt to differentiate objects of common experience in order to fit them for their exalted position. Curious, unusual things of nature met this tendency half-way and easily assumed divine rank; but others had to be distanced by an exaggeration of their size, by extraordinary attributes, by strange combinations of human and animal forms, by special insistence upon particular characteristics, or by the careful removal of all noticeably individualistic and concrete features. Nothing could be more striking than the contrast, for example, in Egyptian Art between the monumental, the works, and of the remarkable interpenetration of Art with the most ordinary routine of life, in order to realise the scarcely perceptible dividing line between the sphere of Art and the realm of practical existence. In a sense, the assertion that idealistic Art marks periods of a generally low and narrowly restricted culture is the converse to the oft-repeated statement that the flowering periods of Art coincide with epochs of decadence: for this so-called decadence represents indeed in certain respects a process of disintegration, politically, racially, often nationally, but a disruption necessary to the formation of larger social units and to the breakdown of outgrown national restrictions. For this very reason it has usually also been the sign of the growth of personal independence and of an expansion of individual culture.

To proceed to some more special points illustrating the distanced and therefore anti-realistic character of art,—both in subject-matter and in the form of presentation Art has always safeguarded its distanced view. Fanciful, even phantastic, subjects have from time immemorial been the accredited material of Art. No doubt things, as well as our view of them, have changed in the course of time: *Polyphemus* and the *Lotus-Eaters* for the Greeks, the *Venusberg* or the *Magnetic Mountain* for the Middle Ages were less incredible, more realistic than to us. But *Peter Pan* or *L'Oiseau Bleu* still appeal at the present day in spite of the prevailing note of realism of our time. 'Probability' and 'improbability' in Art are not to be measured by their correspondence (or lack of it) with actual experience. To do so had involved the theories of the 15th to the 18th centuries in endless contradictions. It is rather a matter of *consistency* of Distance. The note of realism, set by a work as a whole, determines *intrinsically* the greater or smaller degree of fancy which it permits; and consequently we feel the loss of Peter Pan's shadow to be infinitely more probable than some trifling improbability which shocks our sense of proportion in a naturalistic work. No doubt also, fairy-tales, fairy-plays, stories of strange adventures were primarily invented to satisfy the craving of curiosity, the desire for the marvellous, the shudder of the unwonted and the longing for imaginary experiences. But by their mere eccenticity in regard to the normal facts of experience they cannot have failed to arouse a strong feeling of Distance.

Again, certain conventional subjects taken from mythical and legendary traditions, at first closely connected with the concrete, practical, life of a devout public, have gradually, by the mere force of convention as much as by their inherent anti-realism, acquired Distance for us to-day. Our view of Greek mythological sculpture, of early Christian saints and martyrs must be considerably distanced, compared with that of the Greek and medieval worshipper. It is in part the result of lapse of time, but in part also a real change of attitude. Already the outlook of the Imperial Roman had altered, and Pausanias shows a curious dualism of standpoint, declaring the Athene Lemnia to be the supreme achievement of Phidias's genius, and gazing awe-struck upon the roughly hewn tree-trunk representing some primitive Apollo. Our understanding of Greek tragedy suffers admittedly under our inability to revert to the point of view for which it was originally written. Even the tragedies of Racine demand an imaginative effort to put ourselves back into the courtly atmosphere of red-heeled, powdered ceremony. Provided the Distance is not too wide, the result of its intervention has everywhere been to enhance the *art*-character of such works and to lower their original ethical and social force of appeal. Thus in the central dome of the Church (Sta. Maria dei Miracoli) at Saronno are depicted the heavenly hosts in ascending tiers, crowned by the benevolent figure of the Divine Father, bending from the window of heaven to bestow His blessing upon the assembled community. The mere realism of foreshortening and of the boldest vertical perspective may well have made the naïve Christian of the 16th century conscious of the Divine Presence—but for us it has become a work of Art.

The unusual, exceptional, has found its especial home in tragedy. It has always—except in highly distanced tragedy—been a popular objection to it that 'there is enough sadness in life without going to the theatre for it.' Already Aristotle appears to have met with this view among his contemporaries clamouring for 'happy endings.' Yet tragedy is not sad; if it were, there would indeed be little sense in its existence. For the tragic is just in so far different from the merely sad, as it is distanced; and it is largely the exceptional which produces the Distance of tragedy: exceptional situations, exceptional characters, exceptional destinies and conduct. Not of course, characters merely cranky, eccentric, pathological. The exceptional element in tragic figures—that which makes them so utterly different from characters we meet with in ordinary experience—is a consistency of direction, a fervour of ideality, a persistence and driving-force which is far above the capacities of average men. The tragic of tragedy would, transposed into ordinary life, in nine cases out of ten, end in drama, in comedy, even in farce, for lack of steadfastness, for fear of conventions, for the dread of 'scenes,' for a hundred-and-one petty faithlessnesses towards a belief or an ideal: even if for none of these, it would end in a compromise simply because man forgets and time heals.[5] Again, the sympathy, which aches with the sadness of tragedy is another such confusion, the under-distancing of tragedy's appeal. Tragedy trembles always on the knife-edge of a *personal* reaction, and sympathy which finds relief in tears tends almost always towards a loss of Distance. Such a loss naturally renders tragedy unpleasant to a degree: it becomes sad, dismal, harrowing, depressing. But real tragedy (melodrama has a very strong tendency to speculate upon sympathy), truly appreciated, is not

---

[5] The famous 'unity of time,' so senseless as a 'canon,' is all the same often an indispensable condition of tragedy. For in many a tragedy the catastrophe would be even intrinsically impossible, if fatality did not overtake the hero with that rush which gives no time to forget and none to heal. It is in cases such as these that criticism has often blamed the work for 'improbability'—the old confusion between Art and nature—forgetting that the death of the hero is the convention of the art-form, as much as grouping in a picture is such a convention and that probability is not the correspondence with average experience, but consistency of Distance.

sad. "The pity of it—oh, the pity of it," that essence of all genuine tragedy is not the pity of mild, regretful sympathy. It is a chaos of tearless, bitter bewilderment, of upsurging revolt and rapturous awe before the ruthless and inscrutable fate; it is the homage to the great and exceptional in the man who in a last effort of spiritual tension can rise to confront blind, crowning Necessity even in his crushing defeat.

As I explained earlier, the form of presentation sometimes endangers the maintenance of Distance, but it more frequently acts as a considerable support. Thus the bodily vehicle of *drama* is the chief factor of risk to Distance. But, as if to counterbalance a confusion with nature, other features of stage-presentation exercise an opposite influence. Such are the general theatrical *milieu*, the shape and arrangement of the stage, the artificial lighting, the costumes, *mise-en-scène* and make-up, even the language, especially verse. Modern reforms of staging, aiming primarily at the removal of artistic incongruities between excessive decoration and the living figures of the actors and at the production of a more homogeneous stage-picture, inevitably work also towards a greater emphasis and homogeneity of Distance. The history of staging and dramaturgy is closely bound up with the evolution of Distance, and its fluctuations lie at the bottom not only of the greater part of all the talk and writing about 'dramatic probability' and the Aristotelian 'unities,' but also of 'theatrical illusion.' In *sculpture*, one distancing factor of presentment is its lack of colour. The aesthetic, or rather inaesthetic effect of realistic colouring, is in no way touched by the controversial question of its use historically; its attempted resuscitation, such as by Klinger, seems only to confirm its disadvantages. The distancing use even of pedestals, although originally no doubt serving other purposes, is evident to anyone who has experienced the oppressively crowded sensation of moving in a room among life-sized statues placed directly upon the floor. The circumstance that the space of statuary is the same space as ours (in distinction to relief sculpture or painting, for instance) renders a distancing by pedestals, i.e. a removal from our spatial context, imperative.[6] Probably the framing of *pictures* might be shown to serve a similar purpose—though paintings have intrinsically a much greater Distance—because neither their space (perspective and imaginary space) nor their lighting coincides with our (actual) space or light, and the usual reduction in scale of the represented objects prevents a feeling of undue proximity. Besides, painting always retains to some extent a *two*-dimensional character, and this character supplies *eo ipso* a Distance. Nevertheless, life-size pictures, especially if they possess strong relief, and their light happens to coincide with the actual lighting, can occasionally produce the impression of actual presence which is a far from pleasant, though fortunately only a passing, illusion. For decorative purposes, in pictorial renderings of vistas, garden-perspectives and archi-

---

[6] An instance which might be adduced to disprove this point only shows its correctness on closer inspection: for it was on purpose and with the intention of removing Distance, that Rodin originally intended his *citoyens de Calais* to be placed, without pedestals, upon the market-place of that town.

tectural extensions, the removal of Distance has often been consciously striven after, whether with aesthetically satisfactory results is much disputed.

A general help towards Distance (and therewith an anti-realistic feature) is to be found in the 'unification of presentment'[7] of all art-objects. By unification of presentment are meant such qualities as symmetry, opposition, proportion, balance, rhythmical distribution of parts, light-arrangements, in fact all so-called 'formal' features, 'composition' in the widest sense. Unquestionably, Distance is not the only, nor even the principal function of composition; it serves to render our grasp of the presentation easier and to increase its intelligibility. It may even in itself constitute the principal aesthetic feature of the object, as in linear complexes or patterns, partly also in architectural designs. Yet, its distancing effect can hardly be underrated. For, every kind of visibly intentional arrangement or unification must, by the mere fact of its presence, enforce Distance, by distinguishing the object from the confused, disjointed and scattered forms of actual experience. This function can be gauged in a typical form in cases where composition produces an exceptionally marked impression of artificiality (not in the bad sense of that term, but in the sense in which all art is artificial); and it is a natural corollary to the differences of Distance in different arts and of different subjects, that the arts and subjects vary in the degree of artificiality which they can bear. It is this sense of artificial finish which is the source of so much of that elaborate charm of Byzantine work, of Mohammedan decoration, of the hieratic stiffness of so many primitive madonnas and saints. In general the emphasis of composition and technical finish increases with the Distance of the subject-matter: heroic conceptions lend themselves better to verse than to prose; monumental statues require a more general treatment, more elaboration of setting and artificiality of pose than impressionistic statuettes like those of Troubetzkoi; an ecclesiastic subject is painted with a degree of symmetrical arrangement which would be ridiculous in a Dutch interior, and a naturalistic drama carefully avoids the tableau impression characteristic of a mystery play. In a similar manner the variations of Distance in the arts go hand in hand with a visibly greater predominance of composition and 'formal' elements, reaching a climax in architecture and music. It is again a matter of 'consistency of Distance.' At the same time, while from the point of view of the artist this is undoubtedly the case, from the point of view of the public the emphasis of composition and technical finish appears frequently to relieve the impression of highly distanced subjects by *diminishing the Distance of the whole.* The spectator has a tendency to see in composition and finish merely evidence of the artist's 'cleverness,' of his mastery over his material. Manual dexterity is an enviable thing to possess in everyone's experience, and naturally appeals to the public *practically,* thereby putting it into a directly personal relation to things which intrinsically have very little

[7] See note 2, p. 97.

personal appeal for it. It is true that this function of composition is hardly an aesthetic one: for the admiration of mere technical cleverness is not an artistic enjoyment, but by a fortunate chance it has saved from oblivion and entire loss, among much rubbish, also much genuine Art, which otherwise would have completely lost contact with our life.

5. This discussion, necessarily sketchy and incomplete, may have helped to illustrate the sense in which, I suggested, Distance appears as a fundamental principle to which such antitheses as idealism and realism are reducible. The difference between 'idealistic' and 'realistic' Art is not a clear-cut dividing-line between the art-practices described by these terms, but is a difference of degree in the Distance-limit which they presuppose on the part both of the artist and of the public. A similar reconciliation seems to me possible between the opposite 'sensual' and 'spiritual,' 'individual' and 'typical.' That the appeal of Art is sensuous, even sensual, must be taken as an indisputable fact. Puritanism will never be persuaded, and rightly so, that this is not the case. The sensuousness of Art is a natural implication of the 'antinomy of Distance,' and will appear again in another connexion. The point of importance here is that the whole sensual side of Art is purified, spiritualised, 'filtered' as I expressed it earlier, by Distance. The most sensual appeal becomes the translucent veil of an underlying spirituality, once the grossly personal and practical elements have been removed from it. And—a matter of special emphasis here—*this spiritual aspect of the appeal is the more penetrating, the more personal and direct its sensual appeal would have been* BUT FOR THE PRESENCE OF DISTANCE. For the artist, to trust in this delicate transmutation is a natural act of faith which the Puritan hesitates to venture upon: which of the two, one asks, is the greater idealist?

6. The same argument applies to the contradictory epithets 'individual' and 'typical.' A discussion in support of the fundamental individualism of Art lies outside the scope of this essay. Every artist has taken it for granted. Besides it is rather in the sense of 'concrete' or 'individualised,' that it is usually opposed to 'typical.' On the other hand, 'typical,' in the sense of 'abstract,' is as diametrically opposed to the whole nature of Art, as individualism is characteristic of it. It is in the sense of 'generalised' as a 'general human element' that it is claimed as a necessary ingredient in Art. This antithesis is again one which naturally and without mutual sacrifice finds room within the conception of Distance. Historically the 'typical' has had the effect of counteracting *under*-distancing as much as the 'individual' has opposed *over*-distancing. Naturally the two ingredients have constantly varied in the history of Art; they represent, in fact, two sets of conditions to which Art has invariably been subject: the personal and the social factors. It is Distance which on one side prevents the emptying of Art of its concreteness and the development of the typical into abstractness; which, on the other, suppresses the directly personal element of its individualism; thus reducing the antitheses to the peaceful interplay of these two factors. It is just this interplay which constitutes the "antinomy of Distance.'

III

It remains to indicate the value of Distance as *an aesthetic principle*: as criterion in some of the standing problems of Aesthetics; as representing a phase of artistic creation; and as a characteristic feature of the 'aesthetic consciousness.'

1. The axiom of 'hedonistic Aesthetics' is that beauty is pleasure. Unfortunately for hedonism the formula is not reversible: not all pleasure is beauty. Hence the necessity of some limiting criterion to separate the beautiful within the 'pleasure-field' from the merely agreeable. This relation of the beautiful to the agreeable is the ever recurring crux of all hedonistic Aesthetics, as the problem of this relation becomes inevitable when once the hedonistic basis is granted. It has provoked a number of widely different solutions, some manifestly wrong, and all as little satisfactory as the whole hedonistic groundwork upon which they rest: the shareableness of beauty as opposed to the 'monopoly' of the agreeable (Bain),[8] the passivity of beauty-pleasure (Grant Allen),[9] or most recently, the 'relative permanence of beauty-pleasure in revival' (H. R. Marshall).[10]

Distance offers a distinction which is as simple in its operation as it is fundamental in its importance: *the agreeable is a non-distanced pleasure*. Beauty in the widest sense of aesthetic value is impossible without the insertion of Distance. The agreeable stands in precisely the same relation to the beautiful (in its narrower sense) as the sad stands to the tragic, as indicated earlier. Translating the above formula, one may say, that the agreeable is felt as an affection of our concrete, practical self; the centre of gravity of an agreeable experience lies in the self which experiences the agreeable. The aesthetic experience, on the contrary, has its centre of gravity in itself or in the object mediating it, not in the self which has been distanced out of the field of the inner vision of the experiencer: "not the fruit of experience, but experience itself, is the end." It is for this reason that to be asked in the midst of an intense aesthetic impression "whether one likes it," is like a somnambulist being called by name: it is a recall to one's concrete self, an awakening of practical consciousness which throws the whole aesthetic mechanism out of gear. One might almost venture upon the paradox that the more intense the aesthetic absorption, the less one "likes," consciously, the experience. The failure to realise this fact, so fully borne out by all genuine artistic experience, is the fundamental error of hedonistic Aesthetics.

The problem of the relation of the beautiful and the agreeable has taken more definite shape in the question of the aesthetic value of the so-called 'lower senses' (comprising sensations of taste and temperature, muscular and tactile, and organic sensations). Sight and hearing have always been the 'aesthetic senses' *par excellence*. Scent has been admitted to the status of an aesthetic sense by some, excluded by others. The ground for the

[8] Bain, *The Emotions and the Will*, 2nd ed. 1850.
[9] G. Allen, *Physiological Aesthetics*, 1897.
[10] H. R. Marshall, *Pain, Pleasure and Aesthetics*, 1894; *Aesthetic Principles*, 1895.

rejection of the lower senses has always been that they mediate only agreeable sensations, but are incapable of conveying aesthetic experiences. Though true normally, this rigid distinction is theoretically unfair to the senses, and in practice often false. It is undoubtedly very difficult to reach an aesthetic appreciation through the lower senses, because the materialness of their action, their proximity and bodily connexion are great obstacles to their distancing. The aroma of coffee may be a kind of foretaste, taste etherialised, but still a taste. The sweetness of scent of a rose is usually felt more as a bodily caress than as an aesthetic experience. Yet poets have not hesitated to call the scents of flowers their "souls." Shelly has transformed the scent to an imperceptible sound.[11] We call such conceptions 'poetical': they mark the transition from the merely agreeable to the beautiful by means of Distance.

M. Guyau, in a well-known passage,[12] has described the same transformation of a taste. Even muscular sensations may present aesthetic possibilities, in the free exercise of bodily movement, the swing of a runner, in the ease and certainty of the trained gymnast; nay, such diffuse organic sensations as the buoyancy of well-being, and the elasticity of bodily energy, can, in privileged moments, be aesthetically enjoyed. That they admit of no material fixation, such as objects of sight and hearing do, and for that reason form no part of Art in the narrower sense; that they exist as aesthetic objects only for the moment and for the single being that enjoys them, is no argument against their aesthetic character. Mere material existence and permanence is no aesthetic criterion.

This is all the more true, as even among the experience of lasting things, such as are generally accounted to yield aesthetic impressions, the merely agreeable occurs as frequently as the beautiful.

To begin with the relatively simple case of colour-appreciation. Most people imagine that because they are not colour-blind, physically or spiritually, and prefer to live in a coloured world rather than in an engraving, they possess an aesthetic appreciation of colour as such. This is the sort of fallacy which hedonistic art-theories produce, and the lack of an exchange of views on the subject only fosters. Everybody believes that he enjoys colour—and for that matter other things—just like anyone else. Yet rather the contrary is the case. By far the greater number, when asked why they like a colour, will answer, that they like it, because it strikes them as warm or cold, stimulating or soothing, heavy or light. They constitute a definite type of colour-appreciation and form about sixty per cent of all persons. The remainder assumes, for the greater part, a different attitude. Colours do not appeal to them as effects (largely organic) upon themselves. Their appreciation attributes to colours a kind of personality: colours are energetic, lively, serious, pensive, melancholic, affectionate, subtle, reserved, stealthy, treacherous, brutal, etc. These characters are not mere imaginings, left to the whim of the individual, romancing whatever

---

[11] Cf. "The Sensitive Plant."
[12] M. Guyau, *Problèmes de l'Esthétique contemporaine*, Paris, 1897, 4me ed. Livre I. chap. VI.

he pleases into the colours, nor are they the work simply of accidental associations. They follow, on the contrary, definite rules in their applications; they are, in fact, the same organic effects as those of the former type, but transformed into, or interpreted as, attributes of the colour, instead of as affections of one's own self. In short, they are the result of the distancing of the organic effects: they form an aesthetic appreciation of colour, instead of a merely agreeable experience like those of the former kind.[13]

A similar parallelism of the agreeable and the beautiful (in the widest sense of aesthetic value) occurs also within the sphere of recognised art-forms. I select for special notice *comedy* and *melodrama* (though the same observation can be made in painting, architecture and notably in music), firstly as counterparts to tragedy, discussed earlier, secondly, because both represent admitted art-forms, in spite of their at least partially, inadequate claims to the distinction, and lastly because all these types, tragedy, comedy and melodrama, are usually grouped together as 'arts of the theatre' no less than as forms of 'literature.'

From the point of view of the present discussion, the case of *comedy* is particularly involved. What we mean by comedy as a class of theatrical entertainment covers several different kinds,[14] which actually merge into each other and present historically a continuity which allows of no sharp lines of demarcation (a difficulty, by the way, which besets all distinctions of literary or artistic *species*, as opposed to artistic *genera*). The second difficulty is that the 'laughable' includes much more than the comic of comedy. It may enter, in all its varieties of the ridiculous, silly, naïve, brilliant, especially as the humorous, into comedy as ingredients, but the comic is not coextensive with the laughable as a whole.

The fact to be noted here is, that the different types of comedy, as well as the different kinds of the laughable, presuppose different degrees of Distance. Their tendency is to have none at all. Both to laugh and to weep are direct expressions of a throughly practical nature, indicating almost always a concrete personal affection. Indeed, given suitable circumstances and adequate distancing-power, both can be distanced, but only with great difficulty; nor is it possible to decide which of the two offers the greater difficulty. The balance seems almost to incline in favour of tears as the easier of the two, and this would accord with the acknowledged difficulty of producing a really good comedy, or of maintaining a consistent aesthetic attitude in face of a comic situation. Certainly the

---

[13] Cf. E. Bullough, 'The Perceptive Problem in the Aesthetic Appreciation of Single Colours,' this *Journal*, 1908, II. 406 ff.

[14] Comedy embraces *satirical comedy*, i.e. dramatic invectives of all degrees of personal directness, from the attack on actually existing persons (such as is prohibited by the censorship, but has flourished everywhere) to skits upon existing professions, customs, evils, or society; secondly, *farce*, rarely unmixed with satire, but occasionally *pure* nonsense and horseplay; thirdly, *comedy proper*, a sublimation of farce into the pure comedy of general human situation, or genuine character-comedy, changing easily into the fourth class, the type of play described on the Continent as *drama* (in the narrower sense), i.e. a play involving serious situations, sometimes with tragic prospects, but having an happy, if often unexpected, ending.

tendency to *under*distance is more felt in comedy even than in tragedy; most types of the former presenting a *non-distanced*, practical and personal appeal, which precisely implies that their enjoyment is generally hedonic, not aesthetic. In its lower forms comedy consequently is a mere amusement and falls as little under the heading of Art as pamphleteering would be considered as *belles-lettres*, or a burglary as a dramatic performance. It may be spiritualised, polished and refined to the sharpness of a dagger-point or the subtlety of foil-play, but there still clings to it an atmosphere of amusement pure and simple, sometimes of a rude, often of a cruel kind. This, together with the admitted preference of comedy for generalised types rather than for individualised figures, suggests the conclusion that its point of view is the survival of an attitude which the higher forms of Art have outgrown. It is noteworthy that this tendency decreases with every step towards high comedy, character-comedy and drama, with the growing spiritualisation of the comic elements and the first appearance of Distance. Historically the development has been slow and halting. There is no doubt that the 17th century considered the *Misanthrope* as amusing. We are nowadays less harsh and less socially intolerant and *Alceste* appears to us no longer as frankly ridiculous. The supreme achievement of comedy is unquestionably that 'distanced ridicule' which we call *humour*. The self-contradiction of smiling at what we love, displays, in the light vein, that same perfect and subtle balance of the 'antinomy of Distance' which the truly tragic shows in the serious mood. The tragic and the humorous are the genuine aesthetic opposites; the tragic and the comic are contradictory in the matter of Distance, as aesthetic and hedonic objects respectively.

A similar hedonic opposition in the other direction is to be found between tragedy and *melodrama*. Whereas comedy tends to *under*distance, melodrama suffers from *over*distancing. For a cultivated audience its overcharged idealism, the crude opposition of vice and virtue, the exaggeration of its underlined moral, its innocence of *nuance*, and its sentimentality with violin-accompaniment are sufficient cause to stamp it as inferior Art. But perhaps its excessive distance is the least Distance obtainable by the public for which it is designed, and may be a great help to an unsophisticated audience in distancing the characters and events. For it is more than probable that we make a mistake in assuming an analogy between a cultivated audience at a serious drama, and a melodramatic audience. It is very likely that the lover of melodrama does not present that subtle balance of mind towards a play, implied in the 'antinomy of Distance.' His attitude is rather either that of a matter-of-fact adult or of a child: i.e. he is either in a frankly personal relation to the events of the play and would like to cudgel the villain who illtreats the innocent heroine, and rejoices loudly in his final defeat—just as he would in real life—or, he is completely lost in the excessive distance imposed by the work and watches naïvely the wonders he sees, as a child listens enchantedly to a fairy-tale. In neither case is his attitude aesthetic; in the one the object is *under*-, in the other *over*distanced; in the former he confuses it with the reality he *knows* (or thinks he knows) to exist, in the other with a reality whose existence he does *not know, but accepts*. Neither bears the twofold character of the aesthetic state in which *we know* a thing *not* to exist, but *accept its existence*. From the point of view of moral advantage—in the absence of any aesthetic advantage—the former attitude might seem preferable. But even this may be doubted; for if he believes what he sees in a great spectacular melodrama, every marble-lined hall of the most ordinary London hotel that he passes after the play must appear to him as a veritable Hell, and every man or woman in evening-dress as the devil incarnate. On either supposition, the moral effect must be deplorable in the extreme, and the melodrama is generally a much more fitting object of the censor's attention than any usually censored play. For in the one case the brutalising effect of the obtrusively visible wickedness cannot possibly be outweighed by any retaliatory poetic justice, which must seem to him singularly lacking in real life; in the other, the effect is purely negative and narcotic; in both his perspective of real life is hopelessly outfocussed and distorted.

2. The importance of Distance in artistic creation has already been briefly alluded to in connexion with the 'antinomy of Distance.'

Distancing might, indeed, well be considered as the especial and primary function of what is called the 'creative act' in artistic production: distancing is the *formal* aspect of creation in Art. The view that the artist 'copies nature' has already been dismissed. Since the 'imitation-of-nature' theory was officially discarded at the beginning of the 19th century, its place in popular fancy has been taken by the conception of the 'self-expression of the artist,' supported by the whole force of the Romantic Movement in Europe. Though true as a crude statement of the subjective origin of an artistic conception, though in many ways preferable to its predecessor and valuable as a corollary of such theories as that of the 'organic growth' of a work of Art, it is apt to lead to confusions and to one-sided inferences, to be found even in such deliberate and expert accounts of artistic production as that of Benedetto Croce.[15] For, to start with, the 'self-expression' of an artist is not such as the 'self-expression' of a letter-writer or a public speaker: it is not the *direct* expression of the concrete personality of the artist; it is not even an *indirect* expression of his concrete personality, in the sense in which, for instance, Hamlet's 'self-expression' might be supposed to be the indirect reflexion of Shakespeare's ideas. Such a denial, it might be argued, runs counter to the observation that in the works of a literary artist, for example, are to be found echoes and mirrorings of his times and of his personal experiences and convictions. But it is to be noted that to find these *is* in fact impossible, unless you previously know what reflexions to look for. Even in the relatively most direct transference from personal experience to their expression, viz. in lyrical poetry, such a connexion cannot be established backwards, though it is easy enough to prove it forwards: i.e. given

[15] Benedetto Croce, *Aesthetic,* translated by Douglas Ainslie, Macmillan, 1909.

the knowledge of the experiences, there is no difficulty in tracing their echoes, but it is impossible to infer biographical data of any detail or concrete value from an author's works alone. Otherwise Shakespeare's *Sonnets* would not have proved as refractory to biographical research as they have done, and endless blunders in literary history would never have been committed. What proves so impossible in literature, which after all offers an exceptionally adequate medium to 'self-expression,' is *a fortiori* out of question in other arts, in which there is not even an equivalence between the personal experiences and the material in which they are supposed to be formulated. The fundamental two-fold error of the 'self-expression' theory is to speak of 'expression' in the sense of 'intentional communication,' and to identify straightway the artist and the man. An intentional communication is as far almost from the mind of the true artist as it would be from that of the ordinary respectable citizen to walk about naked in the streets, and the idea has repeatedly been indignantly repudiated by artists. The second confusion is as misleading in its theoretical consequences, as it is mischievous and often exceedingly painful to the 'man' as well as to the 'artist.' The numberless instances in history of the astonishing difference, often the marked contrast between the *man* and his *work* is one of the most disconcerting riddles of Art, and should serve as a manifest warning against the popular illusion of finding the 'artist's mind' in his productions.[16]

Apart from the complication of technical necessities, of conventional art-forms, of the requirements of unification and composition, all impeding the direct transference of an actual mental content into its artistic formulation, there is the interpolation of Distance which stands between the artist's conception and the man's. For the 'artist' himself is already distanced from the concrete, historical personality, who ate and drank and slept and did the ordinary business of life. No doubt here also are *degrees* of Distance, and the 'antinomy' applies to this case too. Some figures in literature and other arts are unquestionably self-portraits; but even self-portraits are not, and cannot be, the direct and faithful cast taken from the living soul. In short, so far from being 'self-expression,' *artistic production is the indirect formulation of a distanced mental content.*

I give a short illustration of this fact. A well-known dramatist described to me the process of production as taking place in his case in some such way as follows:

The starting-point of his production is what he described as an 'emotional idea,' i.e. some more or less general conception carrying with it a strong emotional tone. This idea may be suggested by an actual experience; anyhow the idea itself *is* an actual experience, i.e. it occurs within the range of his normal, practical being. Gradually it condenses itself into a situation made up of the interplay of certain characters, which may be of partly objective, partly imaginative descent. Then ensues what he

---

[16] Some well-known examples of this difference are, for instance: Mozart, Beethoven, Watteau, Murillo, Molière, Schiller, Verlaine, Zola.

described as a "life and death struggle" between the idea and the characters for existence: if the idea gains the upper hand, the conception of the whole is doomed. In the successful issue, on the contrary, the idea is, to use his phrase, "sucked up" by the characters as a sponge sucks up water, until no trace of the idea is left outside the characters. It is a process, which, he assured me, he is quite powerless to direct or even to influence. It is further of interest to notice that during this period the idea undergoes sometimes profound, often wholesale changes. Once the stage of complete fusion of the idea with the characters is reached, the conscious elaboration of the play can proceed. What follows after this, is of no further interest in this connexion.

This account tallies closely with the procedure which numerous dramatists are known to have followed. It forms a definite type. There are other types, equally well supported by evidence, which proceed along much less definite lines of a semi-logical development, but rather show sudden flash-like illuminations and much more subconscious growth.

The point to notice is the "life and death struggle" between the idea and the characters. As I first remarked, the idea is the 'man's,' it is the reflexion of the dramatist's concrete and practical self. Yet this is precisely the part which must "die." The paradox of just the germpart of the whole being doomed, particularly impressed my informant as a kind of life-tragedy. The 'characters' on the other hand belong to the imaginary world, to the 'artist's.' Though they may be partially suggested by actuality, their full-grown development is divorced from it. This process of the 'idea' being "sucked up" by the characters and being destroyed by it, is a phase of artistic production technically known as the 'objectivation' of the conception. In it the 'man' dies and the 'artist' comes to life, and with him the work of Art. It is a change of death and birth in which there is no overlapping of the lives of parent and child. The result is the distanced finished production. As elsewhere, the distancing means the separation of personal affections, whether idea or complex experience, from the concrete personality of the experiencer, its filtering by the extrusion of its personal aspects, the throwing out of gear of its personal potency and significance.

The same transformation through distance is to be noticed in *acting*. Here, even more than in the other arts, a lingering bias in favour of the 'imitation of nature' theory has stood in the way of a correct interpretation of the facts. Yet acting supplies in this and other respects exceptionally valuable information, owing to its medium of expression and the overlapping—at least in part—of the process of producing with the finished production, which elsewhere are separated in point of time. It illustrates, as no other art can, the cleavage between the concrete, normal person and the distanced personality. [The acting here referred to is, of course, not that style which consists in 'walking on.' What is meant here is 'creative' acting, which in its turn must be distinguished from 'reproductive' acting—two different types traceable through the greater part of theatrical history, which in their highest development are often outwardly indistinguishable, but nevertheless retain traces of differences, characteristic of their procedures and psychical mechanism.] This cleavage between the two streams or layers of consciousness is so obvious that it has led to increasing speculation from the time when acting first attracted intelligent interest, since the middle of the 18th century. From the time of Diderot's *Paradoxe sur le Comédien* (itself only the last of a series of French studies) down to Mr. William Archer's *Masks or Faces* (1888) and the controversy between Coquelin and Salvini (in the nineties), theory has been at pains to grapple with this phenomenon. Explanations have differed widely, going from the one extreme of an identification of the acting and the normal personality to the other of a separation so wide as to be theoretically inconceivable and contradicted by experience. It is necessary to offer some conception which will account for the differences as well as for the indirect connexion between the two forms of being, and which is applicable not merely to acting, but to other kinds of art as well. Distance, it is here contended, meets the requirement even in its subtlest shades. To show this in detail lies outside the scope of this essay, and forms rather the task of a special treatment of the psychology of acting.

[3. In the interest of those who may be familiar with the developments of aesthetic theories of late years, I should like to add that Distance has a special bearing upon many points raised by them. It is essential to the occurrence and working of 'empathy' (*Einfühlung*), and I mentioned earlier its connexion with Witasek's theory of *Scheingefühle* which forms part of his view on 'empathy.' The distinction between sympathy and 'empathy' as formulated by Lipps[17] is a matter of the relative degree of Distance. Volkelt's[18] suggestion of regarding the ordinary apprehension of expression (say of a person's face) as the first rudimentary stage of *Einfühlung*, leading subsequently to the lowering of our consciousness of reality ("*Herabsetzung des Wirklichkeitsgefühls*"), can similarly be formulated in terms of Distance. K. Lange's[19] account of aesthetic experience in the form of 'illusion as conscious self-deception' appears to me a wrong formulation of the facts expressed by Distance. Lange's 'illusion' theory seems to me, among other things,[20] to be based upon a false opposition between Art and reality (nature) as the subject-matter of the former, whereas Distance does not imply any comparison between them in the act of experiencing and removes altogether the centre of gravity of the formula from the opposition.]

4. In this way Distance represents in aesthetic appreciation as well as in artistic production a quality inherent in the impersonal, yet so intensely personal, relation which the human being entertains with Art, either as mere beholder or as producing artist.

[17] Th. Lipps, *Aesthetik*, Hamburg and Leipzig, 1903, I.; 'Aesthetische Einfühlung,' *Ztsch. für Psychol. u. Physiol. der Sinnesorg.* XXII. 415 ff.
[18] J. Volkelt, *System der Aesthetik*, 1905, I. 217 ff. and 488 ff.
[19] K. Lange, *Des Wesen der Kunst*, 1901, 2 vols.
[20] J. Segal, 'Die bewusste Selbsttäuschung als Kern des aesthetischen Geniessens' *Arch. f. d. ges. Psychol.* VI. 254 ff.

It is Distance which makes the aesthetic object 'an end in itself.' It is that which raises Art beyond the narrow sphere of individual interest and imparts to it that 'postulating' character which the idealistic philosophy of the 19th century regarded as a metaphysical necessity. It renders questions of origin, of influences, or of purposes almost as meaningless as those of marketable value, of pleasure, even of moral importance, since it lifts the work of Art out of the realm of practical systems and ends.

In particular, it is Distance, which supplies one of the special criteria of aesthetic values as distinct from practical (utilitarian), scientific, or social (ethical) values. All these are concrete values, either *directly* personal as utilitarian, or *indirectly* remotely personal, as moral values. To speak, therefore, of the 'pleasure value' of Art, and to introduce hedonism into aesthetic speculation, is even more irrelevant than to speak of moral hedonism in Ethics. Aesthetic hedonism is a compromise. It is the attempt to reconcile for public use utilitarian ends with aesthetic values. Hedonism, as a practical, personal appeal has no place in the distanced appeal of Art. Moral hedonism is even more to the point than aesthetic hedonism, since ethical values, *quâ* social values, lie on the line of prolongation of utilitarian ends, sublimating indeed the *directly* personal object into the realm of socially or universally valuable ends, often demanding the sacrifice of individual happiness, but losing neither its *practical* nor even its *remotely personal* character.

In so far, Distance becomes one of the distinguishing features of the 'aesthetic consciousness,' of that special mentality or outlook upon experience and life, which, as I said at the outset, leads in its most pregnant and most fully developed form, both appreciatively and productively, to Art.

Allan Casebier

THE CONCEPT OF
AESTHETIC DISTANCE

One of the more familiar terms* found in critical discussions of the arts
is "distance." Critics speak of the difficulties involved in "distancing" art
objects of their own time; art historians remark upon the all-too-great
distance we have from art objects of ancient civilizations; one of the
important innovations in contemporary theatre is supposed to have to do
with the use of certain distancing devices as for example the Brechtian
alienating techniques; anti-pornographers dwell upon the breakdown that
occurs upon the introduction of erotic subject-matter into visual art. In
addition, there are those compound terms formed by the union of distance and involvement. For example, it is alleged that an appreciator of
novel can become too personally involved to be able to appreciate the
aesthetic quality in the work. When an individual becomes too personally
involved, he is said to "under-distance" the work. On the other hand,
an appreciator can have too little involvement with a work with the effect
that he "over-distances" it. Either way, aesthetic appreciation is precluded
because one's distance relationship to the object has not been properly
taken care of.

Though "distance" is so firmly entrenched in art criticism, it is by no
means clear to aesthetic theorists that anything significant is being said
when we are told that we have to distance works of art in order to be able
to appreciate them. Notably, George Dickie has argued that aesthetic
theorists' use of "distance" does not really amount to much of anything.[1]
It is Dickie's contention that once we penetrate through to the essence
of what is being said by use of the distance-family of terms ie, "distance,"
"distancing," "being in a distant attitude," and so forth, we will find
nothing resembling significant senses; all that "being distant from an
object" amounts to once all the fancy talk has been pared away is the

Allan Casebier teaches aesthetics at the University of Southern California, Division of
the Performing Arts. He has a strong interest in film, media, and other areas of
contemporary aesthetic interest.

    * Originally published in *The Personalist*, winter, 1971, pp. 70–91. Reprinted by
permission of *The Personalist*.

[1] George Dickie: "The Myth of the Aesthetic Attitude", reprinted in John Hospers
Introductory Readings in Aesthetics, p. 30.

trivial relation of paying attention to the object[2] "Trivial" surely is the correct epithet for the sense of "distance" if indeed all we are doing when we advise someone to distance a play is to pay attention to the play rather than let his mind wander off on something else.

As it turns out, however, there is more to distance than Dickie's discussion would indicate. After making clear just what it is that leads Dickie to question the importance of the concept of distance, I will examine some typical aesthetic and non-aesthetic responses with an eye to showing that a concept of distance can be useful for understanding the nature of aesthetic appreciation.

Dickie's Challenge

If you limit yourself to the comments in support of the utility of a concept of distance that Dickie cites, you can hardly disagree with his scepticism about the importance of the notion. Nothing more is needed than the slightest shred of common sense to accept the proposition that a necessary condition for aesthetic appreciation of an object is the requirement that the observer pay attention to the object. As you follow Dickie's discussion, it seems that all the distance theorist is getting at is really only this trivial necessary condition. The distance theorist begins by asking pointedly:

> "Are you not usually oblivious to noises and sights other than those of the play or to the marks on the wall around the painting?"

to which Dickie replies:

> "Yes. But if 'to distance' and 'being distanced' simply mean that one's attention is focused, what is the point of introducing new technical terms and speaking as if these terms refer to special, kinds of acts and states of consciousness?"[3]

The distance theorist at this point tries another line of defense:

> "But surely you put the play (painting, sunset) 'out of gear' with your practical interests?"

To this Dickie remarks:

> "This question seems to me to be a very odd way of asking (by employing the technical metaphor 'out of gear') if I attended to the play rather than thought about my wife or wondered how they managed to move the scenery about. Why not ask me straight out if I paid attention?"[4]

Undaunted, the distance defender trots out some examples which to him seem perfectly obvious and clinching for his case:

> "Well, isn't it obvious that sometimes we under-distance works by becoming

---

[2] Dickie, p. 44.
[3] Dickie, p. 30.
[4] Dickie, p. 30.

too involved with them while at other times we over-distance them by not being involved very much at all? For example, a jealous husband with an unfaithful wife attending a performance of *Othello* may become so involved with the story and its similarity to his own situation that he under-distances the play. On the other hand, someone well versed in the problems of stage arrangement may focus too much on stagecraft with the effect that he over-distances the same performance of *Othello*. Thus, having an aesthetic attitude toward a work of art can be seen to be the having of an intermediate amount of distance lying between the extremes of too little and too much distance."

Dickie dispenses with this sort of talk in summary fashion:

". . . these are just technical and misleading ways of describing two different cases of inattention. In both cases something is being attended to, but in neither case is it the action of the play. To introduce the technical terms "distance," "under-distance," and "over-distance" does nothing but send us chasing after phantom acts and states of consciousness."[5]

This exchange brings out the reasons why Dickie does not find the concept of distance important. The trouble with Dickie's view is that there are many more types of distance and non-distance cases than he considers. It does seem that some have used "distance" to mean nothing more than "attention is focused." It however, is not the case that all use of the term by aesthetic theorists and critics is insignificant. In the next section, a fuller range of distance and non-distance cases will be discussed with the intention of showing that there is much more to the concept of distance than the above exchange would indicate.

Distancing and Attention

The crux of Dickie's critique of distance theories is, as we have seen, to be traced to his assumption that whenever an observer is said to be distant from an object, it is always the case that the observer is *inattentive* in one way or another to the object. A consideration of the following examples (which I take to be typical of distance and non-distance cases in critical and theoretical discussions of distance) will show that this assumption is unwarranted:

The examples are all responses to a screening of Orson Welles' film *Citizen Kane*.

(1) An historian focuses his attention predominately on the historical accuracy of the film's portrayal of American life in the first half of the twentieth century. There is no doubt about his *attending* to the film; it is important to note, at the same time, that he is focusing attention on a certain select set of *external relations*—relations of the film to something outside it namely, to the American scene of the relevant period, rather than focusing on *internal* qualities and *internal* relations.

[5] Dickie, p. 30.

(2) A personal friend of William Randolph Hearst, the famous newspaper publisher, takes the film to be a parody on the life of his friend (as so many did at the time the film was released in 1940 and still do). He took and now takes the film to be an intentional slur on Hearst. Every time he has seen the film since its first appearance, he has found himself unable to focus attention on much other than the relation between the film and his friend. He focuses on a different set of external relations than does the historian but just like the historian he *attends* to the film. When the film is over, both he and the historian can as well as anyone tell you the sequence of scenes and events in *Citizen Kane*. His focus of attention is however predominately upon such things as whether the portrayal of Hearst is accurate, whether the film will descredit Hearst's image in the public's and personal friend's minds, the effects of the film in his own status as a friend of the famous Hearst, and other such personal external relations.

(3) Another would-be appreciator of the film, a filmmaker, focuses his attention on still another set of external relations of *Citizen Kane*— the relations of the visual and auditory qualities of the film to film-craft. He attends to the framing of the scenes, to camera movement, to editing, to the kind of color patterns, and other such qualities and compares them with their occurrence in films of similar structure and subject-matter. His focus is, thus, on practical external relations of the film. His attention, like those of the historian and personal friend of Hearst, is focused on the film but predominately on the film's external rather than internal relations.

(4) A fourth observer, a woman recently deserted, seizes upon the similarity between her own marital situation and that of Kane's first wife, Emily. From that scene on, she becomes absorbed in thoughts about the breakdown of her marriage. For her, the film becomes a stimulus for a series of remembrances. Her reaction thus conforms to the kind of case that Dickie takes to be paradigmatic of a loss of distance. She does not attend to the film. Her attention is *drawn off* both internal and external relations of the object to focus upon her marriage and its dissolution.

(5) A fifth observer focuses on a combination of internal and external relations of the film to roughly comparable extents. Much of the time, he focuses on the external relations of the film to the historical situation which it portrays, the implied truths about the human condition which it contains, the similarities and dissimilarities between Charles Foster Kane of the film and William Randolph Hearst, and the relations between Welles' use of visual and auditory qualities for creative effect and other film-makers' use of similar qualities in their films. However, to roughly the same extent, he focuses on internal qualities and internal relations of the film. For example, he attends to such visual and auditory qualities as the framing of scenes so as to keep the dominant character, Charles Foster Kane, in sight thereby emphasizing his importance to the social and professional circles in which he moved and worked. In addition,

he attends to certain recurring themes—the identity of snow with naturalness, the mystery of Rosebud, the two sided character of Kane alternatively
as the man of action and power on one side and on the other the man
incapable of keeping what he really values most. Further, he pays attention
to the temporal structure of the story development as it fluctuates among
three time dimensions: (1) the present of the film in which the reporter,
Thompson, seeks to unravel the meaning of Kane's death bed word
"Rosebud," (2) the past as remembered by acquaintances and friends of
Kane and (3) a further past time dimension inserted in sequences of
the second type; he notices that whenever this third type of event is
depicted, the point of the sequences is that Kane has a two-sided character which apparently is a structural way of emphasizing the importance
of this dual character trait for understanding Kane. Finally, he attends
to the drama of the ending when the meaning of "Rosebud" is revealed,
the tension created by the overlapping dialogue, the massiveness of Kane's
mansion and other aesthetic qualities.[6]

(6) The sixth and final observer focuses on the internal qualities and
internal relations of the film while to appreciable extent focusing on
external relations of any of the sorts mentioned above.

From this sketch of ways of attending and not-attending to *Citizen
Kane*, it should be clear that the situation is much more complex than
Dickie made it out to be. Of the six responses, only one of them is an
instance of inattention—the case where the abandoned wife is "triggered"
into a chain of memories by a particular sequence in the film. The other
responses are all instances of attending to the object. Among these instances of attending to the film, some are inimical to aesthetic appreciation. The historian who focuses predominately on the historical accuracy
of *Kane's* portrait of American life, the personal friend of Hearst who
spends his time connecting the film with thoughts of the film's effect on
public regard for his friends, and the film-maker who busies himself with
stylistic comparisons of the film with similar motion pictures are paradigms of non-distance responses. These are just the kind of cases that
the father of the theory of distance, Edward Bullough, dwells upon.[7] In
an especially pointed example, he talks about ways of observing a fog at
sea. One can attend to external relations such as whether the fog will
cause delays or whether the fog conceals a dangerous object, and other
such personal and/or practical relations.[8] By contrast, he describes a
distanced response to the fog:

". . . a fog at sea can be a source of intense relish and enjoyment. Abstract

[6] I rely upon an intuitive grasp of the difference between aesthetic and non-aesthetic
qualities assumed here. The best available justification of this distinction is to be
found in Frank Sibley's "Aesthetic Concepts", *Philosophical Review*, Vol. LXVIII
(Oct 1959), 421–450.
[7] Edward Bullough: "Psychical Distance As a Factor in Art and an Aesthetic Principle",
British Journal of Psychology, Vol. V., 1912, reprinted in Marvin Levich's *Aesthetics
and the Philosophy of Criticism*, pp. 233–254.
[8] Bullough, p. 234.

from the experience of the sea fog, for the moment, its danger and practical unpleasantness, just as every one in the enjoyment of a mountain-climb disregards its physical labour and its danger . . . direct attention to the features "objectively" constituting the phenomenon—the veil surrounding you with an opaqueness as of transparent milk, blurring the outline of things and distorting their shapes into weird grotesqueness; observe the carrying-power of the air, producing the impression as if you could touch some far-off siren by merely putting out your hand and letting it lose itself behind that white wall; not the curious creamy smoothness of the water . . . and above all, the strange solitude and remoteness from the world, as it can be found only on the highest mountain tops; and the experience may acquire, in its uncanny mingling of repose and terror, a flavor of such concentrated piognancy and delight as to contrast sharply with the blind and distempered anxiety of its other aspects."[9]

Thus, the distinction that Bullough has in mind is not that between being distant (attentive) and non-distant (inattentive), but rather one between attention to one kind of relations (internal relations) and attention to another kind of relations (external relations). Dickie seizes upon only one of the cases that has been mentioned by some as an instance of distance—the inattentiveness case—taking it to be representative of all distance cases, whereas it is a rather peripheral case at best. Therefore, Dickie's charge that aesthetic theorists' use of "distance" amounts to nothing more than a disguised way of saying that the observer is focusing on the object is not borne out by a consideration of typical examples of distance and non-distance cases.

Attentional and Emotional Distance

Given that "distance" is not to be assigned the trivial sense that Dickie had in mind for it, just how is the meaning of the term to be analyzed?

Before an answer to this question can be given, it is important to recognize that *more than* one concept of distance is used in critical and theoretical discussions of aesthetic appreciation. It is unfortunate that those who are fond of using the term "distance" are not aware of the fact that they slide between two different notions of distance. However, an examination of obvious examples of distance and non-distance bears out this difference. In my discussion so far, I have been analyzing typical of only one type of distance—what I shall call "attentional distance." There is, in addition, another type of distance—"emotional distance" would be an apt name for it—that is just as commonly employed in analyzing appreciator's response to works of art.

Attentional distance is, as we have seen, a matter of what the observer is and not attending to in the object. Emotional distance on the other hand, is a function of the emotions that the observer is feeling in response to the object. A brief reflection on some of the typical cases

[9] Bullough, p. 234.

of distance that we have examined will reveal that there is no necessary connection between an observer's attending to a set of qualities and relations and an observer's emotional response.[10]

For example, the sixth observer of *Citizen Kane* focuses attention predominately on internal qualities and internal relations of the film. He follows the story line attentively, notices the visual and structural qualities, and the other internal relations mentioned while at the same time disregarding virtually all external relations—symbolic, historical, practical, personal and so forth. His focal attention to these qualities may bring about any number of emotional responses in him. He may feel very powerful emotions as a result of identifying closely with the main character, Kane. When Kane experiences the tremendous sense of loss with the departure of his second wife, Susan Alexander, he may have a feeling of sadness as strong as on many occasions in his own personal life.

This kind of powerful reaction is by no means the only response that an observer may have. Many would-be appreciators of *Citizen Kane* focus predominately on internal relations of the film yet have a rather tepid reaction to scenes such as the departure of Susan Alexander. On the other hand, another appreciator may predominately focus attention on external relations of a personal or practical sort (such as those outlined in the sketch) with the effect that he feels emotions just as powerful as those of the observer who predominately focuses on internal relations. A personal friend of Hearst's may respond with highly charged sympathy to the exit of Kane's second wife because of an emotional attachment to Hearst whom he constantly relates the story to.

---

[10] Bullough can be seen to vacillate between these two senses of "distance" in many places in his discussion. In the previously quoted illustration of distant responses to a fog at sea, it is clear that he is talking about the nature of the observer's attention. In other passages, he can be seen to be talking about the emotional responses of the observer. He remarks as follows:

> The jealous spectator of *Othello* will indeed appreciate and enter into the play the more keenly, the greater the resemblance with his own experience—provided that he succeeds in keeping the Distance between the action of the play and his personal feelings.

In another passage, he applies his theory of distance to the analysis of the process of artistic creation in a way that once again indicates that he is talking emotional rather than attentional aspects of the observer's response:

> The same qualification applies to the artist. He will prove artistically most effective in the formulation of an intensely personal experience, but he can formulate it artistically only on condition of a detachment from the experience qua personal. Hence the statement of so many artists that artistic formulation was to them a kind of catharsis, a means of ridding themselves of feelings and ideas the acuteness of which they felt almost as a kind of obsession. P. 239.

In a dicussion of the relation between distance and tragedy Bullough establishes a connection with emotional rather than attentional distance:

> Tragedy trembles always on the knife-edge of a personal reaction, and sympathy which finds relief in tears tends almost always towards a loss of Distance. Such a loss naturally renders tragedy unpleasant to a degree: it becomes sad, dismal, harrowing, depressing. P. 250.

Further examples are plentiful; this selection should make it clear that the most prominent advocate of a theory of distance employs these two different notions of distance.

When these responses are incompatible with aesthetic appreciation of the object, they are taken to be cases of a "loss of distance." If, for example, someone feels terror at a showing of Hitchcock's *The Birds* to such an extent that he cries out for help much as he would in ordinary life if attacked by hordes of predatory birds, it would be natural to say that he has lost distance. The key point is that he is *not* precluded from aesthetically appreciating *The Birds* because he is perceiving an inappropriate set of relationships. Instead his loss of distance is traceable to the overwhelming emotion that he feels. Some people lose distance from horror films like *The Birds* because they indentify too closely with the characters. Others remain relatively uninvolved with the characters but cannot appreciate the film aesthetically due to an over-sensitivity to the scenes depicted. Still others are reminded of experiences had by close personal friends of which the film reminds them. Whether their focus is on internal or external relations is not the determining feature; what matters is that they do not respond with an aesthetic emotion such as satisfaction, or a feeling of being deeply moved, or joy or whatever because they experience an emotion(s) that precludes such aesthetic emotions.

Thus, analysis of the meaning of "distance" must allow for these two differing senses. The criteria for applying the term "attentional distance" have their locus in certain sets of local awarenesses *ie*, in some combinations of focal awarenesses of internal and external relations of the object; while the criteria for applying the term "emotional distance" are to be localized in the response of the observer. The next section will be concerned with the specific nature of the criteria for applying these distance terms.

"Distance" is a Cluster Term in Either of Its Senses

Both of the distance terms have logically sufficient conditions of application. In applying either "attentional distance" or "emotional distance," one recognizes the presence of enough of what we call "distance-making features." As noted in the last section, distance-making features for the former have to do with the observer's focus of attention; the distance-making features for the latter are to be found in the emotional response of the observer to the object.

As with any cluster terms[11] such as I take these two terms to be, the features that are taken into account in applying the term are ones that *count in only one direction* toward such application. Examples of such one-way conditions for applying "attentional distance" are to be found in Bullough's discussion of responses to a fog at sea. It counts only

---

[11] Hilary Putnam in "Analytic-Synthetic" *Minnesota Studies in the Philosophy of Science,* Vol. III, discusses cluster terms in this way. I take cluster terms to be ones with no necessary and sufficient conditions but only a set of defining characteristics various sub-sets of which entail that the term applies.

toward a judgment that an individual is attentional distancing an object that he has his attention directed on the veil surrounding with an opaqueness as of transparent milk, the carrying power of the air, the curious creamy smooth texture of the water, and other internal relations of the fog.[12] Other one-way features of a negative sort are mentioned by Bullough.

If we know that during time t (the length of time during which the observer A was perceiving the object (o)), A did NOT have his attention focused on the external relations of the fog to danger (eg, the fog may hide a dangerous object), it can only incline us toward a judgment that the observer was attentionally distant.[13] This fact about his focus of attention during it is not sufficient to warrant a judgment that A is distant, not even in conjunction with the fact that A was focused partly on the internal qualities and internal relations of the sort mentioned above (ie, the creamy smooth texture of the water, the carrying power of the air, and so on.) It is however, a one-way condition. No one would regard the absence of a focus on the external relations of the fog to danger as logically sufficient to *exclude* a distant attitude; it would not even incline one to the judgment that the observer was not distant. It would also not be considered as neutral (that is, of no significance one way or the other in determining whether the observer A was distant during t). Instead this fact about A's focus of attention carries a great deal of weight. A decision that the observer A was distant from o during t requires a judgment that enough such one way conditions have been satisfied. In making determinations of attentional distance, the *absence* of a focus on external relations of a practical sort (such as the focus on the potentials of the fog to hide dangerous objects mentioned) is just as important as the *presence* of a focus on internal relations such as noted above.

Of course, if it were established that A had his attention focused throughout t exclusively on internal relations of o of the sort mentioned (creamy smooth texture of the water, etc.), it would be sufficient to warrant a judgment that A was distant from o during t. This kind of situation is however rare. The much more typical case involves focal awarenessses of external as well as internal relations.

Since the situation is complicated in this way, the term "attentional distance" has the logic of cluster terms such as "intelligent," "lazy," "chair," and so forth. Anyone seeking to determine whether A was distant will have to look for the presence of certain characteristic types of awarenesses of internal relations and for the absence of certain characteristic awarenesses of external relations. No rules can be established (as in the case of all cluster terms) for deciding when enough of these one-way conditions are present to warrant application of "attentional distance." There are, however, clear cases of sufficient conditions for both "attentional distance" and "non-attentional distance."

---

[12] Bullough, p. 234.
[13] Bullough, p. 234.

Among the responses to *Citizen Kane*, the reactions of the first three film watchers are clear cases of non-attentional distance. Their types of predominate focus on external relations are of the sorts that make for a non-distant response. When one seeks to determine whether the observer was or was not distant, these are the type of general features that he looks for. It is non-attentional-distance-making that an observer is focused on external relations of the historical, personal, and/or practical variety described in these cases. The classification of the focal awarenesses of these observers as predominately non-distance making is not meant to imply that all historical, personal, or practical relations are incompatible with having distance and thus are inimical to aesthetic appreciation. Some historical, personal and practical relations should be focused upon in appreciating a work aesthetically (eg, that a work is true to the American scene, believable in terms of our notion of human behavior). The only point to be made here is that the type of external relations focusing that *these observers* engage in *is* incompatible with aesthetic appreciation. The term "predominately" in the key phrase "the observer was predominately focused on external relations of x type," is admittedly vague. Nevertheless on those occasions when we are confident that an observer is focusing upon the historical accuracy of a film "predominately," we regard him as having failed to distance the film. If we determine that some of the time he was focusing on eg, the danger the fog brings, we will have to weigh this non-distance making feature against his other focal awarenesses. There will, of course, be many borderline cases—as for example the response of the fifth watcher of *Kane*, the man who divides his attention more or less equally among internal and external relations. In making a judgment as to whether his set of local awarenesses is compatible with aesthetically appreciating the art object, we will have to decide whether the observer can attend to enough of the object to tell whether it is unified, or graceful, or dramatic, or has any other aesthetic quality. An observer who notices practically nothing of *Citizen Kane* except its historical accuracy in depicting the American scene, its possible damaging effects on a personal friend's public image, and/or its relations to contemporary film-making technique, cannot tell whether the film is unified. He just does not attend to enough of it to be able to make the relevant internal connections. The same can be said of an observer who focuses on internal relations that have really little or nothing to do with the production of aesthetic qualities such as unity in art object. Thus, if someone busies himself with how far each character in *Kane* stands apart from every other character and object in every scene, he cannot tell whether the work has any aesthetic qualities.

From these observations about the cluster status of the concept of attentional distance, the following conclusions can be drawn: first, any attempt to specify that this type of distance consists either in attending to internal relations or not attending to external relations of an historical, practical, and/or personal sort will be inadequate. Attention to some internal relations is incompatible with aesthetic appreciation and thus constitutes an instance of non-distance; some attention to external relations of an historical, practical and/or personal sort are distance-making. Second, not unlike typical cluster terms, judgment is required at every phase in knowing how to apply "attentional distance" to responses to art-objects judgments must be made ultimately about whether the observer could recognize whether the art object had particular aesthetic qualities given the locus of his attention throughout the time he experienced the art-object.

One final point about attentional distance needs to be mentioned before discussing emotional distance. In addition to taking account of the presence and absence of certain types of *focal* awarenesses, one who seeks to determine on observer is attentionally distant must also be apprised of his *marginal* awarenesses.

The local yokel whose interference in behalf of the heroine in the melodrama is a case in point.[14] He has lost distance from the play, not because of attending to qualities and relations of the play that are incompatible with aesthetic appreciation, but because he does not have the marginal awareness that "it is only a play." For the yokel, the usual effect of dramaturgical features somehow just does not take. For observers with the minimal degree of sophistication that the yokel lacks, the separation of the stage from the audience-section, the elevation and illumination of the stage, the framing effect of the curtains, the intermissions between scenes, and other such staging features elicit a continuous marginal awareness that it is only a play. The thought of the "non-real life" character of what one is witnessing rarely becomes the focus of attention. It is sufficient for permitting aesthetic response that this awareness be on the margin of attention.

One can tell what he is marginally aware of by recognizing what he would say in reply to certain pointed questions. If interrupted in the midst of watching a street play, one might be asked by someone who wanted to know "what has been going on for the last hour?" it would be natural enough to say "I've been watching a performance of a play" though this thought has not been in the focus of attention. One's attention has been focused on the action of the play while this thought of "it only being a play" has been retained at the margin of attention.

Films like the first *Cinerama*, théâtre engagé like Sartre's *No Exit*, happenings, and other "new art" productions use devices for inhibiting marginal awarenesses that "it is only a work of art" that is being observed.

Cinerama, for example, used a widely expanded screen, stereophonic sound projected from the rear of the audience, attached its camera to the front of a roller coaster as it sped down the Coney Island track, and other such devices to try to bring down the habitual response of film goers to have the constant marginal awareness that it is only a movie. Those who saw the audience squirm and shriek at the opening roller coaster sequence have proof of the effectiveness of these devices. Performances of

[14] Bullough, p. 238.

Sartre's *No Exit* have often arranged environments in which the audience feels part of the situation of no exit. The lights are not dimmed in the theatre, actors deliver lines from locations among the audience, there is no separation spatially or in terms of elevation between stage and audience, there is no frame around the stage, there is no intermission, there is no definite beginning or end to the play, and so on.

Happenings have gone even further in breaking down any marginal awareness that "it is only a work of art" that one is experiencing. No structure to what happens can be discerned as in the case of a play like *No Exit*, audience participates as much as the creators and "interpreters" in the happening, there are no definite boundaries to the occurrence of the happening (it can continue miles away from where it starts), and, unlike the Sartre play, there is no sense of there being repeats of happenings or regular performances of happenings.

Thus, an analysis of the meaning of "attentional distance" must include defining conditions referring to the observer's marginal as well as focal awarenesses.

"Emotional distance" is to be treated in a similar way. Our concept of this type of response to art is again a cluster concept. In determining whether the observer has emotional distance, we do not look for just one type of response; instead we look for the presence of certain types of emotional responses and the absence of certain other types of such responses in sufficient degree. The clusters of emotional distance-making features are those responses which are compatible with having aesthetic reactions to the art-object. Correspondingly, the clusters of non-emotional-distance making features are identified by judging which responses will preclude gaining satisfaction from experiencing the art-object, or being deeply-moved by the work, or coming away with a feeling of joy, or whatever we judge to be the appropriate aesthetic feelings that a sensitive observer would have in response to the art object.

Thus again, an irreducible element of judgment can be seen to play a role in determining whether this distance term applies. Accordingly it will not be fruitful to glibly propose that personal feeling should be purged in order to appreciate a work aesthetically because otherwise emotional distance will be lost. It all depends on what type of personal feelings, to what extent they are felt, and what relation they bear to the other emotions felt.

The would-be appreciator of *Othello* who becomes consumed with jealousy, the militant who becomes over-whelmed with rage at what he takes to be a slur on his race, the film-goer who screams in terror when the attack occurs in *The Birds* are all prevented from having aesthetic emotional responses to the works they experience and are rightly classified as having lost their emotional distance. It does not follow, however, that similarly powerful emotions are not compatible with aesthetic appreciation. An appreciator of *King Lear* can feel as deeply moved in response to the play as to news of a tragic turn of events befalling a close friend. A strong feeling of anger at injustice is required in order to appreciate

Kafka's *The Trial*. A person who has no intense feelings in response to horror films will not share in the tension and excitement of such works. The arousal of erotic feelings by works of art is not incompatible with deriving satisfaction of an aesthetic sort from the works; it is only the predominate occurrence of such feelings that prevents an aesthetic response to art objects with erotic subject-matter.

Many other cases of emotional distance might be mentioned. It should, however, be clear enough that this concept is subject to all of the problems of borderline vagueness and, openness of texture characteristic of cluster concepts. These problems in no way cast doubt on the utility of the notion of emotional distance (or attentional distance) for understanding the nature of aesthetic appreciation. In the final section of this essay. I will briefly sketch out some of the ways in which attentional and emotional distance can be useful for aesthetic theory.

The Utility of Distance Concepts

Compared to the inflated claims that Bullough makes about the value of his concept of distance for aesthetic theory, the proposal outlined here about the utility of Attentional Distance and Emotional Distance will seem rather modest indeed.

According to Bullough, the concept of distance can be made to serve as a more fundamental principle than just about any other concept in aesthetics,[15] and as foundation for a theory about what is most desirable both in appreciation and creation of art.[16] By contrast, I have in mind two rather less revolutionary functions for the distance concepts I have developed.

First, these notions provide a conceptual framework for pinpointing the roles of certain features of the art-object, the subject, and the context in which the object is perceived in eliciting or in inhibiting aesthetic appreciation of a work of art. Second, these notions provide a legitimate basis for prescribing that an observer must distance an object in order to be able to appreciate it aesthetically namely, the prescription that he should attentionally and emotionally distance the object.

With respect to the first function, the examples are almost too numerous to mention. It would go considerably beyond the scope of this essay to attempt to catalogue the attentional distance-making and emotional dis-

---

[15] Bullough, p. 253–254. He contends that distance is more fundamental than the dichotomies of realistic or idealistic, sensual or spiritual, individual or typical, and/or abstract or concrete. The reduction of all of these dual opposites to distance is affected according to Bullough by locating each of them as points along the distance continuum. Realism, for instance, falls at the lower end while idealism has its locus at the upper end of the spectrum.

[16] Bullough, p. 239. What is most desirable both in appreciation and production of art is the utmost decrease in distance without its disappearance. Thus, great art makes the observer "closely distance" as it were. He is placed on a kind of "knife-edge", just about ready to lose distance but somehow capable of maintaining it.

tance-making features of objects, subjects and the contexts in which art is experienced. A few examples from Bullough's discussion will hopefully suffice to show how these distance concepts can help to trace out the relationships between objective, subjective, and contextual features and aesthetic appreciation.

Bullough mentions a few of the distance-making features in the following passages:

". . . in art practice, explicit references to organic affections, to the material existence of the body, especially to sexual matters, lie normally below the Distance-limit, and can be touched upon by Art only with special precautions. Allusions to social institutions, of any degree of personal importance—in particular, allusions implying any doubt as to their validity—the questioning of some generally recognized ethical sanctions, references to topical subjects occupying public attention at the moment, are all dangerously near the average limit and may at any time fall below it, arousing, instead of aesthetic appreciation, concrete hostility or mere amusement."[17]

"In fact, the whole censorship problem, as far as it does not turn upon purely economic questions, may be said to hinge upon Distance; if every member of the public could be trusted to keep it, there would be no sense whatever in the existence of a censor of plays."[18]

"A general help towards Distance is to be found in the unification of presentment" of all art objects. By unification of presentment are meant such qualities as symmetry, opposition, proportion, balance, rhythmical distribution of parts, light-arrangements, in fact all so-called "formal" features, "composition" in the widest sense . . . every kind of visibly intentional arrangement or unification must, by the mere facts of its presence, enforce Distance, by distinguishing the object from the confused disjointed and scattered froms of actual experience."[19]

" . . . the form of presentation sometimes endangers the maintenance of Distance, but it more frequently acts as a considerable support. Thus the bodily vehicle of drama is the chief factor of risk to Distance. But, as if to counter-balance a confusion with nature, other features of stage-presentation exercise an opposite influence. Such are the general theatrical milieu, the shape and arrangement of the stage, the artificial lighting, the costumes, mise en scene, and make-up, even the language, especially verse . . . In sculpture, one distancing factor of presentment is its lack of colour . . . The distancing use even of pedestals, although originally no doubt serving other purposes, is evident to anyone who has experienced the oppressively crowded sensation of moving in a room among life-sized statues placed directly upon the floor . . . Probably the framing of *pictures* might be shown to serve a similar purpose—though paintings have intrinsically a much greater Distance—because neither their space nor their lighting coincides with our (actual) space or light."[20]

17 Bullough, p. 240.
18 Bullough, p. 243.
19 Bullough, p. 252.
20 Bullough, p. 251.

The unification of presentment phenomenon is an attentional distance-making feature. An observer can be expected to be more inclined to focus on internal qualities and internal relations of this phenomenon. No such connection can be established with emotional distance. An observer may respond with emotions that are either compatible or incompatible with having aesthetic emotions as a result of perceiving symmetry, proportion, or any of the other qualities mentioned.

On the other hand, the features composed of sexual and/or topical references would be expected to have effects on emotional distance. As Bullough notes, instead of arousing aesthetic appreciation, they may arouse concrete hostility or mere amusement.[21]

The contextual features that Bullough mentions can be expected to have effects upon both attentional and emotional distance. The framing of the stage in a drama, for instance, may simultaneously tend to focus attention on internal relations of the play and to inhibit the arousal of emotions that would be incompatible with feeling aesthetic satisfaction.

Finally, as previously mentioned, the use of non-standard techniques of stage arrangement by the "new art" productions of existential theatre and happenings, are understandable in terms of the distance notions as ways of eliciting primarily non-aesthetic responses. Their techniques of dramaturgy are attempts to inhibit the occurrence of attentional and emotional distance.

The second function has to do with how the appreciator makes himself able to recognize the aesthetic qualities of the object and to respond aesthetically to them. These notions provide a partial answer to the would-be appreciators' question "how shall I go about relating to works of art so that I can (1) recognize their aesthetic qualities and (2) respond to them aesthetically (derive satisfaction from them, be deeply moved or whatever is the appropriate response in the circumstances)? With the notions thus clarified, no longer does one have to struggle with the metaphor of distance, which is all that Bullough really leaves you with. Instead, we have cluster terms with defining characteristics to be looked in determining whether one is or is not distant.

In determining whether an appreciator is attentionally distant, first we look to see whether he does *not* have his attention focused predominately on personal, practical, historical, social or other external relations. Second, we look to see whether he does have his attention focused on internal qualities, internal relations, and external relations of various sorts. Certain paradigm cases, such as Bullough's fog example, no doubt guide our judgments as to what external relations are allowable. One consistently used principle for making judgments would be a fusion principle. Some focal awareness of external relations tend to re-focus attention back on internal relations of an aesthetically relevant sort. For instance, in appreciating *Othello*, one may well focus to some extent upon the ways in which the main character is symbolic of man. This focal awareness would tend to

[21] Bullough, p. 241.

re-focus attention back upon internal qualities and internal relations of the play that are either aesthetic qualities of the work (such as the play's deeply moving character) or upon features that contribute to the play's having aesthetic qualities (such as the unifying aspects of the play). External relations that tend to fuse with aesthetically relevant internal relations count toward judgment that the observer is attentionally distant. As mentioned earlier, no rules can be formulated to cover all cases—as is the case with all cluster terms—but there are certain principles that guide our judgments like the fusion principle.

In determining whether an observer is emotionally distant, we again look to see first whether he is NOT predominately feeling emotions that are sufficient to preclude aesthetic emotions. There are an indefinite number of such emotions. In horror films, we look to see if the observer has become so identified with characters in the film that he feels terror when they do; in a tragedy, we look to see if the observer has become so deeply moved by the turn of events in the story that he weeps as he would about an ordinary life situation. In films with sexual content, we look to see if response is purely or predominately erotic. If any of these "defeating conditions" for being emotionally distant are satisfied, then "non-emotionally distant" applies.

In a positive way, we look for the *presence* of certain types of emotional response to a sufficient extent. We must do so because the mere absence of a so-called defeating condition (such as the occurrence of terror) is not sufficient to warrant the application of "emotionally distant." We also want to know whether the observer is indifferent or otherwise not relating in an appropriate way emotionally. We look, therefore, for sufficient occurrence of what we take to be appropriate emotions. We have a sense of what are the appropriate range of emotions for each genre, comedy, tragedy, erotic film, romance, and so on. We look for the occurrence of satisfaction derived from experiencing a tightly knit-play such as Checkov's *The Seagull,* feelings of being deeply moved by the tragedy of *King Lear,* or a pervasive sense of amusement about any number of Chaplin films. If a sense of being deeply moved only attaches to some small part of a work of art when we expect that it would be appropriate to respond to all of the work in this way, then the term "emotionally distant" would be withheld as a description of the observer's response to *all* of the play though it might apply to only the response to that scene. One is only distant *from* an object and always only *for a certain period of time.*

Finally, the terms "under-distance" and "over-distance"[22] would really have no part in the analysis presented here. The terms "Attentional Distance" and "Emotional Distance" are achievement predicates according

---

[22] Bullough, p. 240 discusses these terms. It seems that he is functioning with two distance continua. One continuum consists of a kind of aesthetic slice on a larger continuum. Any point on the smaller continuum is compatible with aesthetic appreciation whereas points on the larger continuum that fall below or above the aesthetic slice are incompatible with aesthetic appreciation. It is not at all clear that Bullough realizes that he shifts between these two continua in talking about distance.

to this analysis. One either has attentional distance or he does not. He cannot have more or less distance. As with any cluster term, there are borderline cases. However, if logically sufficient conditions for being a chair or being intelligent or whatever have been found to be present in an object, it is not the case that the object is more a chair (or more an intelligent being) than some other member of the class. The word "distance" is misleading in that it carries the connotation of more or less. I would be just as happy with the terms "Attentional Separation" and "Emotional Separation" as technical terms; I have stayed with terms involving "distance" because of the long tradition in use of this term. Since continuum qualities have been read out of these notions, the ideas of having an "excess of distance" or "under-distancing" as Bullough is fond of talking about are to be discarded. When an observer becomes too indentified with a character to be able to appreciate a play aesthetically, he has not moved to a point closer along a distance line to the work; he has simply failed to satisfy one of the important necessary conditions for responding aesthetically to a work namely, to be emotionally distant from it. The prescription to get "more distant" from the work in such circumstances (imbedded as it is in the unfortunate metaphor of distance and the continuum motion that goes with it) carries the undesirable connotation of "getting less involved with the work. What we really are prescribing is to become involved *in a different way* though the feelings may be just as intense. On the other hand, one wonders how an observer can have an "excess of distance" if distance is, as Bullough and all other users of "distance" have maintained, a necessary condition for aesthetically appreciating an object.

George Dickie

ALL AESTHETIC ATTITUDE THEORIES FAIL: THE MYTH OF THE AESTHETIC ATTITUDE

Some* recent articles[1] have suggested the unsatisfactoriness of the notion of the aesthetic attitude and it is now time for a fresh look at that encrusted article of faith. This conception has been valuable to aesthetics and criticism in helping wean them from a sole concern with beauty and related notions.[2] However, I shall argue that the aesthetic attitude is a myth and while, as G. Ryle has said, "Myths often do a lot of theoretical good while they are still new,"[3] this particular one is no longer useful and in fact misleads aesthetic theory.

There is a range of theories which differ according to how strongly the aesthetic attitude is characterized. This variation is reflected in the language the theories employ. The strongest variety is Edward Bullough's theory of psychical distance, recently defended by Sheila Dawson.[4] The central technical term of this theory is "distance" used as a verb to denote an action which either constitutes or is necessary for the aesthetic attitude. These theorists use such sentences as "He distanced (or failed to distance) the play." The second variety is widely held but has been defended most vigorously in recent years by Jerome Stolnitz and Eliseo Vivas. The *central* technical term of this variety is "disinterested"[5] used either as an adverb or as an adjective. This weaker theory speaks not of a special kind of action (distancing) but of an ordinary kind of action (attending) done in a

Originally published in *American Philosophical Quarterly*, vol. I, no. 1, 1964, pp. 56–66. Reprinted by permission of *American Philosophical Quarterly*.
*I wish to thank both Monroe C. Beardsley and Jerome Stolnitz who read earlier drafts of this paper and made many helpful comments.

[1] See Marshall Cohen, "Appearance and the Aesthetic Attitude," *Journal of Philosophy*, vol. 56 (1959), p. 926; and Joseph Margolis, "Aesthetic Perception," *Journal of Aesthetics and Art Criticism*, vol. 19 (1960), p. 211. Margolis gives an argument, but it is so compact as to be at best only suggestive.
[2] Jerome Stolnitz, "Some Questions Concerning Aesthetic Perception," *Philosophy and Phenomenological Research*, vol. 22 (1961), p. 69.
[3] *The Concept of Mind* (London, 1949), p. 23.
[4] "'Distancing' as an Aesthetic Principle," *Australasian Journal of Philosophy*, vol. 39 (1961), pp. 155–174.
[5] "Disinterested" is Stolnitz' term. Vivas uses "intransitive."

certain way (disinterestedly). These first two versions are perhaps not as different as my classification suggests. However, the language of the two is different enough to justify separate discussions. My discussion of this second variety will for the most part make use of Jerome Stolnitz' book[6] which is a thorough, consistent, and large-scale version of the attitude theory. The weakest version of the attitude theory can be found in Vincent Tomas' statement "If looking at a picture and attending closely to how it looks is not really to be in the aesthetic attitude, then what on earth is?"[7] In the following I shall be concerned with the notion of *aesthetic* attitude and this notion may have little or no connection with the ordinary notion of an *attitude*.

I

Psychical distance, according to Bullough, is a psychological process by virtue of which a person *puts* some object (be it a painting, a play, or a dangerous fog at sea) "out of gear" with the practical interests of the self. Miss Dawson maintains that it is "the beauty of the phenomenon, which captures our attention, puts us out of gear with practical life, and forces us, if we are receptive, to view it on the level of aesthetic consciousness."[8]

Later she maintains that some persons (critics, actors, members of an orchestra, and the like) "distance deliberately."[9] Miss Dawson, following Bullough, discusses cases in which people are unable to bring off an act of distancing or are incapable of being induced into a state of being distanced. She uses Bullough's example of the jealous ("under-distanced") husband at a performance of *Othello* who is able to keep his attention on the play because he keeps thinking of his own wife's suspicious behavior. On the other hand, if "we are mainly concerned with the technical details of its [the play's] presentation, then we are said to be over-distanced."[10] There is, then, a species of action—distancing—which may be deliberately done and which initiates a state of consciousness—being distanced.

The question is: Are there actions denoted by "to distance" or states of consciousness denoted by "being distanced"? When the curtain goes up, when we walk up to a painting, or when we look at a sunset are we ever induced into a state of being distanced either by being struck by the beauty of the object or by pulling off an act of distancing? I do not recall

---

[6] *Aesthetics and Philosophy of Art Criticism* (Boston, 1960), p. 510.
[7] "Aesthetic Vision," *The Philosophical Review*, vol. 68 (1959), p. 63. I shall ignore Tomas' attempt to distinguish between appearance and reality since it seems to confuse rather than clarify aesthetic theory. See F. Sibley, "Aesthetics and the Looks of Things," *Journal of Philosophy*, vol. 56 (1959), pp. 905–915; M. Cohen, op. cit., pp. 915–926; and J. Stolnitz, "Some Questions Concerning Aesthetic Perception," op. cit., pp. 69–87. Tomas discusses only visual art and the aesthetic attitude, but his remarks could be generalized into a comprehensive theory.
[8] Dawson, op. cit., p. 158.
[9] Ibid., pp. 159–160.
[10] Ibid., p. 159.

committing any such special actions or of being induced into any special state, and I have no reason to suspect that I am atypical in this respect. The distance-theorist may perhaps ask, "But are you not usually oblivious to noises and sights other than those of the play or to the marks on the wall around the painting?" The answer is of course—"Yes." But if "to distance" and "being distanced" simply mean that one's attention is focused, what is the point of introducing new technical terms and speaking as if these terms refer to special kinds of acts and states of consciousness? The distance-theorist might argue further, "But surely you put the play (painting, sunset) 'out of gear' with your practical interests?" This question seems to me to be a very odd way of asking (by employing the technical metaphor "out of gear") if I attended to the play rather than thought about my wife or wondered how they managed to move the scenery about. Why not ask me straight out if I paid attention? Thus, when Miss Dawson says that the jealous husband under-distanced *Othello* and that the person with a consuming interest in techniques of stagecraft over-distanced the play, these are just technical and misleading ways of describing two different cases of inattention. In both cases something is being attended to, but in neither case is it the action of the play. To introduce the technical terms "distance," "under-distance," and "over-distance" does nothing but send us chasing after phantom acts and states of consciousness.

Miss Dawson's commitment to the theory of distance (as a kind of mental insulation material necessary for a work of art if it is to be enjoyed aesthetically) leads her to draw a conclusion so curious as to throw suspicion on the theory.

> One remembers the horrible loss of distance in *Peter Pan*—the moment when Peter says "Do you believe in fairies? . . . If you believe, clap your hands!" the moment when most children would like to slink out of the theatre and not a few cry—not because Tinkerbell may die, but because the magic is gone. What, after all, should we feel like if Lear were to leave Cordelia, come to the front of the stage and say, "All the grown-ups who think that she loves me, shout 'Yes'."[11]

It is hard to believe that the responses of any children could be as theory-bound as those Miss Dawson describes. In fact, Peter Pan's request for applause is a dramatic high point to which children respond enthusiastically. The playwright gives the children a momentary chance to become actors in the play. The children do not at that moment lose or snap out of a state of being distanced because they never had or were in any such thing to begin with. The comparison of Peter Pan's appeal to the hypothetical one by Lear is pointless. *Peter Pan* is a magical play in which almost anything can happen, but *King Lear* is a play of a different kind. There are, by the way, many plays in which an actor directly addresses the audience (*Our Town, The Marriage Broker, A Taste of Honey*, for example) without causing the play to be less valuable. Such plays are unusual, but what is unusual is not necessarily bad; there is no point in trying

---

[11] Ibid., p. 168.

to lay down rules to which every play must conform independently of the kind of play it is.

It is perhaps worth noting that Susanne Langer reports the reaction she had as a child to this scene in *Peter Pan*.[12] As she remembers it, Peter Pan's appeal shattered the illusion and caused her acute misery. However, she reports that all the other children clapped and laughed and enjoyed themselves.

II

The second way of conceiving of the aesthetic attitude—as the ordinary action of attending done in a certain way (disinterestedly)—is illustrated by the work of Jerome Stolnitz and Eliseo Vivas. Stolnitz defines "aesthetic attitude" as "disinterested and sympathetic attention to and contemplation of any object of awareness whatever, for its own sake alone."[13] Stolnitz defines the main terms of his definition: "disinterested" means "no concern for any ulterior purpose";[14] "sympathetic" means "accept the object on its own terms to appreciate it";[15] and "contemplation" means "perception directed toward the object in its own right and the spectator is not concerned to analyze it or ask questions about it."[16]

The notion of disinterestedness, which Stolnitz has elsewhere shown[17] to be seminal for modern aesthetic theory, is the key term here. Thus, it is necessary to be clear about the nature of disinterested attention to the various arts. It can make sense to speak, for example, of listening disinterestedly to music only if it makes sense to speak of listening interestedly to music. It would make no sense to speak of walking *fast* unless walking could be done *slowly*. Using Stolnitz' definition of "disinterestedness," the two situations would have to be described as "listening with no ulterior purpose" (disinterestedly) and "listening with an ulterior purpose" (interestedly). Note that what initially appears to be a perceptual distinction—listening in a certain way (interestedly or disinterestedly)—turns out to be a motivational or an intentional distinction—listening for or with a certain purpose. Suppose Jones listens to a piece of music for the purpose of being able to analyze and describe it on an examination the next day and Smith listens to the same music with no such ulterior purpose. There is certainly a difference between the motives and intentions of the two men: Jones has an ulterior purpose and Smith does not, but this does not mean Jones's *listening* differs from Smith's. It is possible that both men enjoy the music or that both be bored. The attention of either or both may flag and so on. It is important to note that a person's motive or

---

[12] *Feeling and Form* (New York, 1953), p. 318.
[13] *Aesthetics and Philosophy of Art Criticism*, pp. 34–35.
[14] Ibid., p. 35.
[15] Ibid., p. 36.
[16] Ibid., p. 38.
[17] "On the Origins of 'Aesthetic Disinterestedness'," *The Journal of Aesthetics and Art Criticism*, vol. 20 (1961), pp. 131–143.

intention is different from his action (Jones's listening to the music, for example). There is only one way to *listen* to (to attend to) music, although the listening may be more or less attentive and there may be a variety of motives, intentions, and reasons for doing so and a variety of ways of being distracted from the music.

In order to avoid a common mistake of aestheticians—drawing a conclusion about one kind of art and assuming it holds for all the arts—the question of disinterested attention must be considered for arts other than music. How would one look at a painting disinterestedly or interestedly? An example of alleged interested viewing might be the case in which a painting reminds Jones of his grandfather and Jones proceeds to muse about or to regale a companion with tales of his grandfather's pioneer exploits. Such incidents would be characterized by attitude-theorists as examples of using a work of art as a vehicle for associations and so on, i.e., cases of interested attention. But Jones is not looking at (attending to) the painting at all, although he may be facing it with his eyes open. Jones is now musing or attending to the story he is telling, although he had to look at the painting at first to notice that it resembled his grandfather. Jones is not now looking at the painting interestedly, since he is not now looking at (attending to) the painting. Jones's thinking or telling a story about his grandfather is no more a part of the painting than his speculating about the artist's intentions is and, hence, his musing, telling, speculating, and so on cannot properly be described as attending to the painting interestedly. What attitude-aestheticians are calling attention to is the occurrence of irrelevant associations which distract the viewer from the painting or whatever. But distraction is not a special kind of attention, it is a kind of inattention.

Consider now disinterestedness and plays. I shall make use of some interesting examples offered by J. O. Urmson,[18] but I am not claiming that Urmson is an attitude-theorist. Urmson never speaks in his article of aesthetic attitude but rather of aesthetic satisfaction. In addition to aesthetic satisfaction, Urmson mentions economic, moral, personal, and intellectual satisfactions. I think the attitude-theorist would consider these last four kinds of satisfaction as "ulterior purposes" and, hence, cases of interested attention. Urmson considers the case of a man in the audience of a play who is delighted.[19] It is discovered that his delight is *solely* the result of the fact that there is a full house—the man is the impresario of the production. Urmson is right in calling *this* impresario's satisfaction economic rather than aesthetic, although there is a certain oddness about the example as it finds the impresario sitting *in the audience*. However, my concern is not with Urmson's examples as such but with the attitude theory. This impresario is certainly an interested party in the fullest sense of the word, but is his behavior an instance of interested attention as distinct

[18] "What Makes a Situation Aesthetic?" in *Philosophy Looks at the Arts*, Joseph Margolis (ed.), (New York, 1962). Reprinted from *Proceedings of the Aristotelian Society, Supplementary Volume* 31 (1957), pp. 75–92.
[19] Ibid, p. 15.

from the supposed disinterested attention of the average citizen who sits beside him? In the situation as described by Urmson it would not make any sense to say that the impresario is attending to the play at all, since his *sole* concern at the moment is the till. If he can be said to be attending to anything (rather than just thinking about it) it is the size of the house. I do not mean to suggest that an impresario could not attend to his play if he found himself taking up a seat in a full house; I am challenging the sense of disinterested attention. As an example of personal satisfaction Urmson mentions the spectator whose daughter is in the play. Intellectual satisfaction involves the solution of technical problems of plays and moral satisfaction the consideration of the effects of the play on the viewer's conduct. All three of these candidates which the attitude-theorist would propose as cases of interested attention turn out to be just different ways of being distracted from the play and, hence, not cases of interested attention to the play. Of course, there is no reason to think that in any of these cases the distraction or inattention must be total, although it could be. In fact, such inattentions often occur but are so fleeting that nothing of the play, music, or whatever is missed or lost.

The example of a playwright watching a rehearsal or an out-of-town performance with a view to rewriting the script has been suggested to me as a case in which a spectator is certainly attending to the play (unlike our impresario) and attending in an interested manner. This case is unlike those just discussed but is similar to the earlier case of Jones (not Smith) listening to a particular piece of music. Our playwright—like Jones, who was to be examined on the music—has ulterior motives. Furthermore, the playwright, unlike an ordinary spectator, can change the script after the performance or during a rehearsal. But how is our playwright's *attention* (as distinguished from his motives and intentions) different from that of an ordinary viewer? The playwright might enjoy or be bored by the performance as any spectator might be. The playwright's attention might even flag. In short, the kinds of things which may happen to the playwright's attention are no different from those that may happen to an ordinary spectator, although the two may have quite different motives and intentions.

For the discussion of disinterested-interested reading of literature it is appropriate to turn to the arguments of Eliseo Vivas whose work is largely concerned with literature. Vivas remarks that "By approaching a poem in a nonaesthetic mode it may function as history, as social criticism, as diagnostic evidence of the author's neuroses, and in an indefinite number of other ways."[20] Vivas further notes that according to Plato "the Greeks used Homer as an authority on war and almost anything under the sun," and that a certain poem "can be read as erotic poetry or as an account of a mystical experience."[21] The difference between reading a poem *as* history or whatever (reading it nonaesthetically) and reading it aesthetically de-

[20] "Contextualism Reconsidered," *The Journal of Aesthetics and Art Criticism,* vol. 18 (1959), pp. 224–225.
[21] Ibid., p. 225.

pends on how *we* approach or read it. A poem "does not come self-labelled,"[22] but presumably is a poem only when it is read in a certain way—when it is an object of aesthetic experience. For Vivas, being an aesthetic object means being the object of the aesthetic attitude. He defines the aesthetic experience as "an experience of rapt attention which involves the intransitive apprehension of an object's immanent meanings and values in their full presentational immediacy."[23] Vivas maintains that his definition "helps me understand better what I can and what I cannot do when I read *The Brothers* [*Karamazov*]" and his definition "forces us to acknowledge that *The Brothers Karamazov* can hardly be read as art. . . ."[24] This acknowledgment means that we probably cannot intransitively apprehend *The Brothers* because of its size and complexity.

"Intransitive" is the key term here and Vivas' meaning must be made clear. A number of passages reveal his meaning but perhaps the following is the best. "Having once seen a hockey game in slow motion, I am prepared to testify that it was an object of pure intransitive experience [attention]—for I was not *interested* in which team won the game and no external factors mingled with my interest in the beautiful rhythmic flow of the slow-moving men."[25] It appears that Vivas' "intransitive attention" has the same meaning as Stolnitz' "disinterested attention," namely, "attending with no ulterior purpose."[26] Thus, the question to ask is "How does one attend to (read) a poem or any literary work transitively?" One can certainly attend to (read) a poem for a variety of different purposes and because of a variety of different reasons, but can one attend to a poem transitively? I do not think so, but let us consider the examples Vivas offers. He mentions "a type of reader" who uses a poem or parts of a poem as a spring-board for "loose, uncontrolled, relaxed day-dreaming, wool-gathering rambles, free from the contextual control" of the poem.[27] But surely it would be wrong to say such musing is a case of transitively attending to a poem, since it is clearly a case of not attending to a poem. Another supposed way of attending to a poem transitively is by approaching it "as diagnostic evidence of the author's neuroses." Vivas is right if he means that there is no critical point in doing this since it does not throw light on the poem. But this is a case of *using* information gleamed from a poem to make inferences about its author rather than attending to a poem. If anything can be said to be attended to here it is the author's neuroses (at least they are being thought about). This kind of case is perhaps best thought of as a rather special way of getting distracted from a poem. Of course, such "biographical" distractions might be insignificant

[22] Loc. cit.

[23] Ibid., p. 227.

[24] Ibid., p. 237.

[25] Ibid., p. 228. (Italics mine.)

[26] Vivas' remark about the improbability of being able to read *The Brothers Karamazov* as art suggests that "intransitive attention" may sometimes mean for him "that which can be attended to at one time" or "that which can be held before the mind at one time." However, this second possible meaning is not one which is relevant here.

[27] Vivas, op. cit., p. 231.

and momentary enough so as scarcely to distract attention from the poem
(a flash of insight or understanding about the poet). On the other hand,
such distractions may turn into dissertations and whole careers. Such an
interest may lead a reader to concentrate his attention (when he does read
a poem) on certain "informational" aspects of a poem and to ignore the
remaining aspects. As deplorable as such a sustained practice may be, it
is at best a case of attending to certain features of a poem and ignoring
others.

Another way that poetry may allegedly be read transitively is by reading
it as history. This case is different from the two preceding ones since poetry
often *contains* history (makes historical statements or at least references)
but does not (usually) contain statements about the author's neuroses
and so on nor does it contain statements about what a reader's free associations are about (otherwise we would not call them *"free* associations").
Reading a poem as history suggests that we are attending to (thinking
about) historical events by way of attending to a poem—the poem is a
time-telescope. Consider the following two sets of lines:

> In fourteen hundred and ninety-two
> Columbus sailed the ocean blue.
> Or like stout Cortez when with eagle eyes
> He star'd at the Pacific—and all his men
> Look'd at each other with a wild surmise—
> Silent, upon a peak in Darien.

Someone might read both of these raptly and not know that they make
historical references (inaccurately in one case)—might this be a case of
intransitive attention? How would the above reading differ—so far as
attention is concerned—from the case of a reader who recognized the
historical content of the poetic lines? The two readings do not differ as
far as attention is concerned. History is a part of these sets of poetic lines
and the two readings differ in that the first fails to take account of an
aspect of the poetic lines (its historical content) and the second does not
fail to do so. Perhaps by "reading as history" Vivas means "reading *simply*
as history." But even this meaning does not mark out a special kind of
attention but rather means that only a single aspect of a poem is being
noticed and that its rhyme, meter, and so on are ignored. Reading a poem
as social criticism can be analyzed in a fashion similar to reading as history.
Some poems simply are or contain social criticism, and a complete reading
must not fail to notice this fact.

The above cases of alleged interested attending can be sorted out in the
following way. Jones listening to the music and our playwright watching
the rehearsal are both attending with ulterior motives to a work of art,
but there is no reason to suppose that the attention of either is different
in kind from that of an ordinary spectator. The reader who reads a poem
as history is simply attending to an aspect of a poem. On the other hand,
the remaining cases—Jones beside the painting telling of his grandfather,
the gloating impresario, daydreaming while "reading" a poem, and so on—
are simply cases of not attending to the work of art.

In general, I conclude that "disinterestedness" or "intransitiveness" cannot properly be used to refer to a special kind of attention. "Disinterestedness" is a term which is used to make clear that an action has certain kinds of motives. Hence, we speak of disinterested findings (of boards of inquiry), disinterested verdicts (of judges and juries), and so on. Attending to an object, of course, has its motives but the attending itself is not interested or disinterested according to whether its motives are of the kind which motivate interested or disinterested action (as findings and verdicts might), although the attending may be more or less close.

I have argued that the second way of conceiving the aesthetic attitude is also a myth, or at least that its main content—disinterested attention—is; but I must now try to establish that the view misleads aesthetic theory. I shall argue that the attitude-theorist is incorrect about (1) the way in which he wishes to set the limits of aesthetic relevance; (2) the relation of the critic to a work of art; and (3) the relation of morality to aesthetic value.

Since I shall make use of the treatment of aesthetic relevance in Jerome Stolnitz' book, let me make clear that I am not necessarily denying the relevance of the specific items he cites but disagreeing with his criterion of relevance. His criterion of relevance is derived from his definition of "aesthetic attitude" and is set forth at the very beginning of his book. This procedure leads Monroe Beardsley in his review of the book to remark that Stolnitz' discussion is premature.[28] Beardsley suggests "that relevance cannot be satisfactorily discussed until after a careful treatment of the several arts, their dimensions and capacities."[29]

First, what is meant by "aesthetic relevance"? Stolnitz defines the problem by asking the question: "Is it ever 'relevant' to the aesthetic experience to have thoughts or images or bits of knowledge which are not present within the object itself?"[30] Stolnitz begins by summarizing Bullough's experiment and discussion of single colors and associations.[31] Some associations absorb the spectator's attention and distract him from the color and some associations "fuse" with the color. Associations of the latter kind are aesthetic and the former are not. Stolnitz draws the following conclusion about associations:

> If the aesthetic experience is as we have described it, then whether an association is aesthetic depends on whether it is compatible with the attitude of "disinterested attention." If the association re-enforces the focusing of attention upon the object, by "fusing" with the object and thereby giving it added "life and significance," it is genuinely aesthetic. If, however, it arrogates attention to itself and away from the object, it undermines the aesthetic attitude.[32]

[28] *The Journal of Philosophy*, vol. 57 (1960), p. 624.
[29] Loc. cit.
[30] Op. cit., p. 53.
[31] Ibid., p. 54.
[32] Ibid., pp. 54–55.

It is not clear how something could *fuse* with a single color, but "fusion" is one of those words in aesthetics which is rarely defined. Stolnitz then makes use of a more fruitful example, one from I. A. Richards' *Practical Criticism*.[33] He cites the responses of students to the poem which begins:

> Between the erect and solemn trees
> I will go down upon my knees;
> I shall not find this day
> So meet a place to pray.

The image of a rugby forward running arose in the mind of one student-reader on reading the third verse of this poem. A cathedral was suggested to a second reader of the poem. The cathedral image "is congruous with both the verbal meaning of the poem and the emotions and mood which it expresses. It does not divert attention away from the poem."[34] The rugby image is presumably incongruous and diverts attention from the poem.

It is a confusion to take compatibility with disinterested attention as a criterion of relevance. If, as I have tried to show, *disinterested attention* is a confused notion, then it will not do as a satisfactory criterion. Also, when Stolnitz comes to show why the cathedral image is, and the rugby image is not relevant, the criterion he actually uses is *congruousness with the meaning of the poem*, which is quite independent of the notion of disinterestedness. The problem is perhaps best described as the problem of relevance to a poem, or more generally, to a work of art, rather than aesthetic relevance.

A second way in which the attitude theory misleads aesthetics is its contention that a critic's relationship to a work of art is different in kind from the relationship of other persons to the work. H. S. Langfeld in an early statement of this view wrote that we may "slip from the attitude of aesthetic enjoyment to the attitude of the critic." He characterizes the critical attitude as "intellectually occupied in coldly estimating . . . merits" and the aesthetic attitude as responding "emotionally to" a work of art.[35] At the beginning of his book in the discussion of the aesthetic attitude, Stolnitz declares that if a percipient of a work of art "has the purpose of passing judgment upon it, his attitude is not aesthetic."[36] He develops this line at a later stage of his book, arguing that appreciation (perceiving with the aesthetic attitude) and criticism (seeking for reasons to support an evaluation of a work) are (1) distinct and (2) "psychologically opposed to each other."[37] The critical attitude is questioning, analytical, probing for strengths and weakness, and so on. The aesthetic attitude is just the opposite: "It commits our allegiance to the object freely and

---

[33] Ibid., pp. 55–56.
[34] Ibid., p. 56.
[35] *The Aesthetic Attitude* (New York, 1920), p. 79.
[36] Op. cit., p. 35.
[37] Ibid., p. 377.

unquestioningly"; "the spectator 'surrenders' himself to the work of art."[38] "Just because the two attitudes are inimical, whenever criticism obtrudes, it reduces aesthetic interest."[39] Stolnitz does not, of course, argue that criticism is unimportant for appreciation. He maintains criticism plays an important and necessary role in preparing a person to appreciate the nuances, detail, form, and so on of works of art. We are quite right, he says, thus to read and listen perceptively and acutely, but he questions, "Does this mean that we must analyze, measure in terms of value-criteria, etc., *during* the supposedly aesthetic experience?"[40] His answer is "No" and he maintains that criticism must occur "*prior* to the aesthetic encounter,"[41] or it will interfere with appreciation.

How does Stolnitz know that criticism will always interfere with appreciation? His conclusion sounds like one based upon the observations of actual cases, but I do not think it is. I believe it is a logical consequence of his definition of aesthetic attitude in terms of disinterested attention (no ulterior purpose). According to his view, to appreciate an object aesthetically one has to perceive it with no ulterior purpose. But the critic has an ulterior purpose—to analyze and evaluate the object he peceives— hence, in so far as a person functions as a critic he cannot function as an appreciator. But here, as previously, Stolnitz confuses a perceptual distinction with a motivational one. If it were possible to *attend* disinterestedly or interestedly, then perhaps the critic (as percipient) would differ from other percipients. But if my earlier argument about attending is correct, the critic differs from other percipients only in his motives and intentions and not in the way in which he attends to a work of art.

Of course, it might just be a fact that the search for reasons is incompatible with the appreciation of art, but I do not think it is. Several years ago I participated in a series of panel discussions of films. During the showing of each film we were to discuss, I had to take note of various aspects of the film (actor's performance, dramatic development, organization of the screen-plane and screen-space at given moments, and so on) in order later to discuss the films. I believe that this practice not only helped educate me to appreciate subsequent films but that it enhanced the appreciation of the films I was analyzing. I noticed and was able to appreciate things about the films I was watching which ordinarily out of laziness I would not have noticed. I see no reason why the same should not be the case with the professional critic or any critical percipient. If many professional critics seem to appreciate so few works, it is not because they are critics, but perhaps because the percentage of good works of art is fairly small and they suffer from a kind of combat fatigue.

I am unable to see any significant difference between "perceptively and acutely" attending to a work of art (which Stolnitz holds enhances appreciation) and searching for reasons, so far as the experience of a work of

[38] Ibid., pp. 377–378.
[39] Ibid., p. 379.
[40] Ibid., p. 380.
[41] Loc. cit.

art is concerned. If I attend perceptively and acutely, I will have certain standards and/or paradigms in mind (not necessarily consciously) and will be keenly aware of the elements and relations in the work and will evaluate them to some degree. Stolnitz writes as if criticism takes place and then is over and done with, but the search for and finding of reasons (noticing this fits in with that, and so on) is continuous in practiced appreciators. A practiced viewer does not even have to be looking for a reason, he may just notice a line or an area in a painting, for example, and the line or area becomes a reason why he thinks the painting better or worse. A person may be a critic (not necessarily a good one) without meaning to be or without even realizing it.

There is one final line worth pursuing. Stolnitz' remarks suggest that one reason he thinks criticism and appreciation incompatible is that they compete with one another for time (this would be especially bad in the cases of performed works). But seeking and finding reasons (criticism) does not compete for time with appreciation. First, to seek for a reason means to be ready and able to notice something and to be thus ready and able as one attends does not compete for time with the attending. In fact, I should suppose that seeking for reasons would tend to focus attention more securely on the work of art. Second, finding a reason is an achievement, like winning a race. (It takes time to run a race but not to win it.) Consider the finding of the following reasons. How much time does it take to "see" that a note is off key (or on key)? How long does it take to notice that an actor mispronounces a word (or does it right)? How much time does it take to realize that a character's action does not fit his already established personality? (One is struck by it.) How long does it take to apprehend that a happy ending is out of place? It does not take time to find any of these reasons or reasons in general. Finding a reason is like coming to understand—it is done in a flash. I do not mean to suggest that one cannot be mistaken in finding a reason. What may appear to be a fault or a merit (a found reason) in the middle of a performance (or during one look at a painting and so forth) may turn out to be just the opposite when seen from the perspective of the whole performance (or other looks at the painting).

A third way in which the attitude theory misleads aesthetic theory is its contention that aesthetic value is always independent of morality. This view is perhaps not peculiar to the attitude theory, but it is a logical consequence of the attitude approach. Two quotations from attitude-theorists will establish the drift of their view of morality and aesthetic value.

> We are either concerned with the beauty of the object or with some other value of the same. Just as soon, for example, as ethical considerations occur to our mind, our attitude shifts.[42]

> Any of us might reject a novel because it seems to conflict with our moral beliefs . . . When we do so . . . We have *not* read the book aesthetically, for we have interposed moral . . . responses of our own which are alien to

[42] H. S. Langfeld, op. cit., p. 73.

it. This disrupts the aesthetic attitude. We cannot then say that the novel is *aesthetically* bad, for we have not permitted ourselves to consider it aesthetically. To maintain the aesthetic attitude, we must follow the lead of the object and respond in concert with it.[43]

This conception of the aesthetic attitude functions to hold the moral aspects and the *aesthetic* aspects of the work of art firmly apart. Presumably, although it is difficult to see one's way clearly here, the moral aspects of a work of art cannot be an object of aesthetic attention because aesthetic attention is by definition disinterested and the moral aspects are somehow practical (interested). I suspect that there are a number of confusions involved in the assumption of the incompatibility of aesthetic attention and the moral aspects of art, but I shall not attempt to make these clear, since the root of the assumption—disinterested attention—is a confused notion. Some way other than in terms of the aesthetic attitude, then, is needed to discuss the relation of morality and aesthetic value.

David Pole in a recent article[44] has argued that the moral vision which a work of art may embody is *aesthetically* significant. It should perhaps be remarked at this point that not all works of art embody a moral vision and perhaps some kinds of art (music, for example) cannot embody a moral vision, but certainly some novels, some poems, and some films and plays do. I assume it is unnecessary to show how novels and so on have this moral aspect. Pole notes the curious fact that while so many critics approach works of art in "overtly moralistic terms," it is a "philosophical commonplace . . . that the ethical and the aesthetic modes . . . form different categories"[45] I suspect that many philosophers would simply say that these critics are confused about their roles. But Pole assumes that philosophical theory "should take notice of practice"[46] and surely he is right. In agreeing with Pole's assumption I should like to reserve the right to argue in specific cases that a critic may be misguided. This right is especially necessary in a field such as aesthetics because the language and practice of critics is so often burdened with ancient theory. Perhaps *all* moralistic criticism is wrong but philosophers should not rule it out of order at the very beginning by use of a definition.

Pole thinks that the moral vision presented by a particular work of art will be either true or false (perhaps a mixture of true and false might occur). If a work has a false moral vision, then something "is lacking within the work itself. But to say that is to say that the [work] is internally incoherent; some particular aspect must jar with what—on the strength of the rest—we claim a right to demand. And here the moral fault that we have found will count as an aesthetic fault too."[47] Pole is trying to show that the assessment of the moral vision of a work of art is just a

[43] J. Stolnitz, op. cit., p. 36.
[44] "Morality and the Assessment of Literature," *Philosophy*, vol. 37 (1962), pp. 193–207.
[45] Ibid., p. 193.
[46] Loc. cit.
[47] Ibid., p. 206.

special case of coherence or incoherence, and since everyone would agree that coherence is an aesthetic category, the assessment of the moral vision is an aesthetic assessment.

I think Pole's conclusion is correct but take exception to some of his arguments. First, I am uncertain whether it is proper to speak of a moral vision being true or false, and would want to make a more modest claim— that a moral vision can be judged to be acceptable or unacceptable. (I am not claiming Pole is wrong and my claim is not inconsistent with his.) Second, I do not see that a false (or unacceptable) moral vision makes a work incoherent. I should suppose that to say a work is coherent or incoherent is to speak about how its parts fit together and this involves no reference to something outside the work as the work's truth or falsity does.

In any event, it seems to me that a faulty moral vision can be shown to be an aesthetic fault independently of Pole's consideration of truth and coherence. As Pole's argument implies, a work's moral vision is a *part* of the work. Thus, any statement—descriptive or evaluative—about the work's moral vision is a statement about the *work*; and any statement about a *work* is a critical statement and, hence, fails within the aesthetic domain. To judge a moral vision to be morally unacceptable is to judge it defective and this amounts to saying that the work of art has a defective part. (Of course, a judgment of the acceptability of a moral vision may be wrong, as a judgment of an action sometimes is, but this fallibility does not make any difference.) Thus, a work's moral vision may be an aesthetic merit or defect just as a work's degree of unity is a merit or defect. But what justifies saying that a moral vision is a part of a work of art? Perhaps "part" is not quite the right word but it serves to make the point clear enough. A novel's moral vision is an essential part of the novel and if it were removed (I am not sure how such surgery could be carried out) the novel would be greatly changed. Anyway, a novel's moral vision is not like its covers or binding. However, someone might still argue that even though a work's moral vision is defective and the moral vision is part of the work, that this defect is not an *aesthetic* defect. How is "aesthetic" being used here? It is being used to segregate certain aspects or parts of works of art such as formal and stylistic aspects from such aspects as a work's moral vision. But it seems to me that the separation is only nominal. "Aesthetic" has been selected as a name for a certain sub-set of characteristics of works of art. I certainly cannot object to such a stipulation, since an underlying aim of this essay is to suggest the vacuousness of the term "aesthetic." My concern at this point is simply to insist that a work's moral vision is a part of the work and that, therefore, a critic can legitimately describe and evaluate it. I would *call* any defect or merit which a critic can legitimately point out an aesthetic defect or merit, but what we call it does not matter.

It would, of course, be a mistake to judge a work solely on the basis of its moral vision (it is only one part). The fact that some critics have judged works of art in this way is perhaps as much responsible as the theory of aesthetic attitude for the attempts to separate morality from the aesthetic. In fact, such criticism is no doubt at least partly responsible for the rise of the notion of the aesthetic attitude.

If the foregoing arguments are correct, the second way of conceiving the aesthetic attitude misleads aesthetic theory in at least three ways.

III

In answer to a hypothetical question about what is seen in viewing a portrait with the aesthetic attitude, Tomas in part responds "If looking at a picture and attending closely to how it looks is not really to be in the aesthetic attitude, then what on earth is?"[48] I shall take this sentence as formulating the weakest version of the aesthetic attitude. (I am ignoring Tomas' distinction between appearance and reality. See footnote. 7. My remarks, thus, are not a critique of Tomas' argument; I am simply using one of his sentences.) First, this sentence speaks only of "looking at a picture," but "listening to a piece of music," "watching and listening to a play," and so on could be added easily enough. After thus expanding the sentence, it can be contracted into the general form: "Being in the aesthetic attitude is attending closely to a work of art (or a natural object)."

But the aesthetic attitude ("the hallmark of modern aesthetics") in this formulation is a great letdown—it no longer seems to say anything significant. Nevertheless, this does seem to be all that is left after the aesthetic attitude has been purged of *distancing* and *disinterestedness*. The only thing which prevents the aesthetic attitude from collapsing into simple attention is the qualification *closely*. One may, I suppose, attend to a work of art more or less closely, but this fact does not seem to signify anything very important. When "being in the aesthetic attitude" is equated with "attending (closely)," the equation neither involves any mythical element nor could it possibly mislead aesthetic theory. But if the definition has no vices, it seems to have no virtues either. When the aesthetic attitude finally turns out to be simply attending (closely), the final version should perhaps not be called "the weakest" but rather "the vacuous version" of the aesthetic attitude.

Stolnitz is no doubt historically correct that the notion of the aesthetic attitude has played an important role in the freeing of aesthetic theory from an overweening concern with beauty. It is easy to see how the slogan, "Anything can become an object of the aesthetic attitude," could help accomplish this liberation. It is worth noting, however, that the same goal could have been (and perhaps to some extent was) realized by simply noting that works of art are often ugly or contain ugliness, or have features which are difficult to include within beauty. No doubt, in more recent times people have been encouraged *to take an aesthetic attitude toward a painting* as a way of lowering their prejudices, say, against abstract and

[48] Thomas, op. cit., p. 63.

non-objective art. So if the notion of aesthetic attitude has turned out to have no theoretical value for aesthetics, it has had practical value for the appreciation of art in a way similar to that of Clive Bell's suspect notion of significant form.

Frank N. Sibley

A CONTEMPORARY THEORY OF
AESTHETIC QUALITIES:
AESTHETIC CONCEPTS

The remarks we make about works of art are of many kinds.* In this paper
I wish to distinguish between two broad groups. We say that a novel has
a great number of characters and deals with life in a manufacturing town;
that a painting uses pale colours, predominantly blues and greens, and has
kneeling figures in the foreground; that the theme in a fugue is inverted
at such a point and that there is a stretto at the close; that the action of a
play takes place in the span of one day and that there is a reconciliation
scene in the fifth act. Such remarks may be made by, and such features
pointed out to, anyone with normal eyes, ears, and intelligence. On the
other hand, we also say that a poem is tightly-knit or deeply moving; that
a picture lacks balance, or has a certain serenity and repose, or that the
grouping of the figures sets up an exciting tension; that the characters
in a novel never really come to life, or that a certain episode strikes a
false note. It would be natural enough to say that the making of judgments
such as these requires the exercise of taste, perceptiveness, or sensitivity,
of aesthetic discrimination or appreciation; one would not say this of my
first group. Accordingly, when a word of expression is such that taste or
perceptiveness is required in order to apply it, I shall call it an *aesthetic*
term or expression, and I shall, correspondingly, speak of *aesthetic* concepts or *taste* concepts.[1]

Aesthetic terms span a great range of types and could be grouped into
various kinds and sub-species. But it is not my present purpose to attempt

F. N. *Sibley* is Professor of Philosophy at the University of Lancaster. He is a well-
known writer in the analytical tradition and has published several highly influential
articles on the concept of the aesthetic.

* Originally published in *The Philosophical Review*, vol. lxviii, no. 4 (1959), 421–
450. Reprinted by permission of the author and *The Philosophical Review*.

[1] I shall speak loosely of an 'aesthetic term', even when, because the word sometimes
has other uses, it would be more correct to speak of its *use* as an aesthetic term. I shall
also speak of 'non-aesthetic' words, concepts, features, and so on. None of the terms
other writers use, 'natural', 'observable', 'perceptual', 'physical', 'objective' (qualities),
'neutral', 'descriptive' (language), when they approach the distinction I am making, is
really apt for my purpose.

any such grouping; I am interested in what they all have in common. Their almost endless variety is adequately displayed in the following list: *unified, balanced, integrated, lifeless, serene, sombre, dynamic, powerful, vivid, delicate, moving, trite, sentimental, tragic.* The list of course is not limited to adjectives; expressions in artistic contexts like 'telling contrast,' 'sets up a tension,' 'conveys a sense of,' or 'holds it together' are equally good illustrations. It includes terms used by both layman and critic alike, as well as some which are mainly the property of professional critics and specialists.

I have gone for my examples of aesthetic expressions in the first place to critical and evaluative discourse about works of art because it is there particularly that they abound. But now I wish to widen the topic; we employ terms the use of which requires an exercise of taste not only when discussing the arts but quite liberally throughout discourse in everyday life. The examples given above are expressions which, appearing in critical contexts, most usually, if not invariably, have an aesthetic use; outside critical discourse the majority of them more frequently have some other use unconnected with taste. But many expressions do double duty even in everyday discourse, sometimes being used as aesthetic expressions and sometimes not. Other words again, whether in artistic or daily discourse, function only or predominantly as aesthetic terms; of this kind are *graceful, delicate, dainty, handsome, comely, elegant, garish.* Finally, to make the contrast with all the preceding examples, there are many words which are seldom used as aesthetic terms at all: *red, noisy, brackish, clammy, square, docile, curved, evanescent, intelligent, faithful, derelict, tardy, freakish.*

Clearly, when we employ words as aesthetic terms we are often making and using metaphors, pressing into service words which do not primarily function in this manner. Certainly also, many words *have come* to be aesthetic terms by some kind of metaphorical transference. This is so with those like 'dynamic,' 'melancholy,' 'balanced' 'tightly-knit' which, except in artistic and critical writings, are not normally aesthetic terms. But the aesthetic vocabulary must not be thought wholly metaphorical. Many words, including the most common (*lovely, pretty, beautiful, dainty, graceful, elegant*), are certainly not being used metaphorically when employed as aesthetic terms, the very good reason being that this is their primary or ony use, some of them having no current non-aesthetic uses. And though expressions like 'dynamic,' 'balanced,' and so forth *have come* by a metaphorical shift to be aesthetic terms, their employment in criticism can scarcely be said to be more than quasi-metaphorical. Having entered the language of art description and criticism as metaphors they are now standard vocabulary in that language.[2]

---

[2] A contrast will reinforce this. If a critic were to describe a passage of music as chattering, carbonated, or gritty, a painter's colouring as vitreous, farinaceous, or effervescent, or a writer's style as glutinous, or abrasive, he *would* be using live metaphors rather than drawing on the more normal language of criticism. Words like 'athletic', 'vertiginous', 'silken' may fall somewhere between.

The expressions I am calling aesthetic terms form no small segment of our discourse. Often, it is true, people with normal intelligence and good eyesight and hearing lack, at least in some measure, the sensitivity required to apply them; a man need not be stupid or have poor eyesight to fail to see that something is graceful. Thus taste or sensitivity is somewhat more rare than certain other human capacities; people who exhibit a sensitivity both wide-ranging and refined are a minority. It is over the application of aesthetic terms too that, notoriously, disputes and differences sometimes go helplessly unsettled. But almost everybody is able to exercise taste to some degree and in some matters. It is surprising therefore that aesthetic terms have been so largely neglected. They have received glancing treatment in the course of other aesthetic discussions; but as a broad category they have not received the direct attention they merit.

The foregoing has marked out the area I wish to discuss. One warning should perhaps be given. When I speak of taste in this paper, I shall not be dealing with questions which centre upon expressions like 'a matter of taste' (meaning, roughly, a matter of personal preference or liking). It is with an ability to *notice* or *see* or *tell* that things have certain qualities that I am concerned.

I

In order to support our application of an aesthetic term, we often refer to features the mention of which involves other aesthetic terms: 'it has an extraordinary vitality because of its free and vigorous style of drawing,' 'graceful in the smooth flow of its lines,' 'dainty because of the delicacy and harmony of its colouring.' It is as normal to do this as it is to justify one mental epithet by other epithets of the same general type, *intelligent* by *ingenious, inventive, acute,* and so on. But often when we apply aesthetic terms, we explain why by referring to features which do *not* depend for their recognition upon an exercise of taste: 'delicate because of its pastel shades and curving lines,' or 'it lacks balance because one group of figures is so far off to the left and is so brightly illuminated.' When no explanation of this latter kind is offered, it is legitimate to ask or search for one. Finding a satisfactory answer is sometimes difficult, but one cannot ordinarily reject the question. When we cannot ourselves quite say what non-aesthetic features make something delicate or unbalanced or moving, the good critic often puts his finger on something which strikes us as the right explanation. In short, aesthetic terms always ultimately apply because of, and aesthetic qualities always ultimately depend upon, the presence of features which, like curving or angular lines, colour contrasts, placing of masses, or speed of movement, are visible, audible, or otherwise discernible without any exercise of taste or sensibility. Whatever kind of dependence this is, and there are various relationships between aesthetic qualities and non-aesthetic features, what I want to make clear in this paper is that there are no non-aesthetic features which serve in *any* circumstances as logically *sufficient conditions* for applying aesthetic terms. Aesthetic concepts are not in *this* respect condition-governed at all.

There is little temptation to suppose that aesthetic terms resemble words which, like 'square,' are applied in accordance with a set of necessary and sufficient conditions. For whereas each square is square in virtue of the *same* set of conditions, four equal sides and four right angles, aesthetic terms apply to widely varied objects; one thing is graceful because of these features, another because of those, and so on. Recently, philosophers have broken the spell of the strict necessary-and-sufficient model by showing that many everyday concepts are not of that type, but are governed only in a much looser way by conditions. However, since these newer models provide satisfactory accounts of many concepts, it might plausibly be thought that aesthetic concepts are of some such kind and that they similarly are governed in some looser way by conditions. I want to argue that aesthetic concepts differ radically from any of these other concepts.

Amongst these concepts to which attention has recently been paid are those for which no *necessary-and-sufficient* conditions can be provided, but for which there are a number of relevant features, A, B, C, D, E, such that the presence of some groups or combinations of these features is *sufficient* for the application of the concept. The list of relevant features may be an open one; that is, given A, B, C, D, E, we may not wish to close off the possible relevance of other unlisted features beyond E. Examples of such concepts might be 'dilatory,' 'discourteous,' 'possessive,' 'capricious,' 'prosperous,' 'intelligent.' . . . If we begin a list of features relevant to 'intelligent' with, for example, ability to grasp and follow various kinds of instructions, ability to master facts and marshall evidence, ability to solve mathematical or chess problems, we might go on adding to this list almost indefinitely.

However, with concepts of this sort, although decisions may have to be made and judgment exercised, it is always possible to extract and state, from cases which have *already* clearly been decided, the sets of features or conditions which were regarded as sufficient in those cases. These relevant features which I am calling conditions are, it should be noted, features which, though not sufficient *alone* and needing to be combined with other similar features, nevertheless carry some weight and count only in one direction. Being a good chess player can count only *towards* and not *against* intelligence. Whereas mention of it may enter sensibly along with other remarks in expressions like 'I say he is intelligent because . . .' or 'the reason I call him intelligent is that . . . ,' it cannot be used to complete such negative expressions as 'I say he is *un*intelligent because. . . .' But what I want particularly to emphasize about features which function as conditions for a term is that *some* group or set of them is sufficient fully to ensure or warrant the application of that term. An individual characterized by some of these features may not yet qualify to be called lazy or intelligent, and so on, beyond all question, but all that is needed is to add some further (indefinite) number of such characterizations and a point is reached where we have enough. There are individuals possessing a number of such features of whom one cannot deny, cannot but admit, that they are intelligent. We have left necessary-and-sufficient conditions behind, but we are still in the realm of sufficient conditions.

But aesthetic concepts are not condition-governed even in this way. There are no sufficient conditions, no non-aesthetic features such that the presence of some set or number of them will beyond question logically justify or warrant the application of an aesthetic term. It is impossible . . . to make any statements corresponding to those we make for condition-governed words. We are able to say 'If it is true he can do this, and that, and the other, then one just cannot deny that he is intelligent,' or 'if he does A, B, and C, I don't see how it can be denied that he is lazy,' but we cannot make *any* general statement of the form 'If the vase is pale pink, somewhat curving, lightly mottled, and so forth, it will be delicate, cannot but be delicate.' Nor again can one say *any* such thing here as 'Being tall and thin is not enough *alone* to ensure that a vase is delicate, but if it is, for example, slightly curving and pale coloured (and so forth) as well, it cannot be denied that it is.' Things may be described to us in non-aesthetic terms as fully as we please but we are not thereby put in the position of having to admit (or being unable to deny) that they are delicate or graceful or garish or exquisitely balanced.[3]

No doubt there are some respects in which aesthetic terms *are* governed by conditions or rules. For instance, it may be impossible that a thing should be garish if all its colours are pale pastels, or flamboyant if all its lines are straight. There may be, that is, descriptions using only non-aesthetic terms which are incompatible with descriptions employing certain aesthetic terms. If I am told that a painting in the next room consists solely of one or two bars of very pale blue and very pale grey set at right angles on a pale fawn ground, I can be sure that it cannot be fiery or garish or gaudy or flamboyant. A description of this sort may make certain aesthetic terms *in*applicable or *in*appropriate; and if from this description I inferred that the picture was, or even might be, fiery or gaudy or flamboyant, this might be taken as showing a failure to understand these words. I do not wish to deny therefore that taste concepts may be governed *negatively* by conditions.[4] What I am emphasizing is that they quite lack governing conditions of a sort many other concepts possess. Though on *seeing* the picture we might say, and rightly, that it is delicate or serene

[3] In a paper reprinted in *Aesthetics and Language*, ed. by W. Elton (Oxford, 1954), pp. 131–46, Arnold Isenberg discusses certain problems about aesthetic concepts and qualities. Like others who approach these problems, he does not isolate them, as I do, from questions about verdicts on the *merits* of works of art, or from questions about *likings* and *preferences*. He says something parallel to my remarks above: "There is not in all the world's criticism a single purely descriptive statement concerning which one is prepared to say beforehand, "if it is true, I shall *like* that work so much the better"' (p. 139, my italics). I should think *this* is highly questionable.

[4] Isenberg (op. cit., p. 132) makes a somewhat similar but mistaken point: 'If we had been told that the colours of a certain painting are garish, it would be *astonishing* to find that they are *all* very pale and unsaturated' (my italics). But if we say 'all' rather than 'predominantly', then 'astonishing' is the wrong word. The word that goes with 'all' is 'impossible'; astonishing' might go with 'predominantly'.

or restful or sickly or insipid, no *description* in non-aesthetic terms permits us to claim that these or any other aesthetic terms must undeniably apply to it.

I have said that if an object is characterized *solely* by certain sorts of features this may count decisively against the possibility of applying to it certain aesthetic terms. But of course the presence of *some* such features need not count decisively; other features may be enough to outweigh those which, on their own, would render the aesthetic term inapplicable. A painting might be garish even though much of its colour is pale. These facts call attention to a further feature of taste concepts. One *can* find general features or descriptions which in some sense count in one direction only, only *for* or only *against* the application of certain aesthetic terms. Angularity, fatness, brightness, or intensity of colour are typically *not* associated with delicacy or grace. Slimness, lightness, gentle curves, lack of intensity of colour are associated with delicacy, but not with flamboyance, majesty, grandeur, splendour or garishness. This is shown by the naturalness of saying, for example, that someone is graceful *because* she's so light, but *in spite of* being quite angular or heavily built; and by the corresponding oddity of saying that something is graceful *because* it is so heavy or angular, or delicate *because* of its bright and intense colouring. This may therefore sound quite similar to what I have said already about conditions in discussing terms like 'intelligent.' There are nevertheless significant differences. Although there is this sense in which slimness, lightness, lack of intensity of colour, and so on, count only towards, not against, delicacy, these features, I shall say, at best count only *typically* or *characteristically* towards delicacy. They do not count towards in the same sense as condition-features count towards laziness or intelligence; that is, no group of them is ever logically sufficient.

One way of reinforcing this is to notice how features which are characteristically associated with one aesthetic term may also be similarly associated with other, rather dfferent aesthetic terms. 'Graceful' and 'delicate' may be on the one hand sharply contrasted with terms like 'violent,' 'grand,' 'fiery,' 'garish,' or 'massive' which have characteristic non-aesthetic features, quite unlike those for 'delicate' and 'graceful.' But on the other hand they may also be contrasted with aesthetic terms which stand much closer to them, like 'flaccid,' 'weakly,' 'washed out,' 'lanky,' 'anaemic,' 'wan,' 'insipid'; and the features characteristic of *these* qualities, pale colour, slimness, lightness, lack of angularity and contrast, is virtually identical with the range for 'delicate' and 'graceful.' Similarly many features typically associated with 'joyous,' 'fiery,' 'robust,' or 'dynamic' are identical with those associated with 'garish,' 'strident,' 'turbulent,' 'gaudy,' or 'chaotic.' Thus an object described very fully, but exclusively in terms of qualities characteristic of delicacy, may turn out on inspection to be not delicate at all, but anaemic or insipid. The failures of novices and the artistically inept prove that quite close similarity in line, colour, or technique gives no assurance of gracefulness or delicacy. A failure and a success in the manner of Degas may be generally more alike, so far as their non-aesthetic features go, than either is like a successful Fragonard. But I need not go even this far to make my main point. A painting which has only the kind of features one would associate with vigour and energy but which even so fails to be vigorous and energetic *need* not be instead, say, strident or chaotic. It may fail to have any particular character whatever. It may employ bright colours and the like without being particularly lively and vigorous at all; but one may feel unable to describe it as chaotic or strident or garish either. It is, rather, simply lacking in character (though of course this too is an aesthetic judgment; taste is exercised also in seeing that the painting has no character).

There are of course many features which do not in these ways characteristically count for (or against) particular aesthetic qualities. One poem has strength and power because of the regularity of its metre and rhyme; another is monotonous and lacks drive and strength because of its regular metre and rhyme. We do not feel the need to switch from 'because of' to 'in spite of.' However, I have concentrated upon features characteristically associated with aesthetic qualities because, if one could maintain that taste concepts are in any way governed by sufficient conditions, these would seem to be the most promising candidates for governing conditions. But to say that features are associated only *characteristically* with an aesthetic term *is* to say that they can never amount to sufficient conditions; no description however full, even in terms characteristic of gracefulness, puts it beyond question that something is graceful in the way a description may put it beyond question that someone is lazy or intelligent.

It is important to observe, however, that I am not merely claiming that no sufficient conditions can be stated for taste concepts. For if this were all, they might not be after all really different from one kind of concept recently discussed. They could be accommodated perhaps with those concepts which Professor H. L. A. Hart has called 'defeasible'; it is a characteristic of defeasible concepts that we cannot state sufficient conditions for them because, for any sets we offer, there is always an (open) list of defeating conditions any of which might rule out the application of the concept. The most we can say schematically for a defeasible concept is that, for example, A, B, and C together are sufficient for the concept to apply *unless* some feature is present which overrides or voids them. But, I want to emphasize, the very fact that we *can* say this sort of thing shows that we are still to that extent in the realm of conditions.[5] The features governing defeasible concepts can ordinarily count only one way, *either* for or against. To take Hart's example, 'offer' and 'acceptance' can count only towards the existence of a valid contract, and fraudulent misrepresentation, duress, and lunacy only against. And even with defeasible concepts, if we are told that there are *no* voiding features present, we can know that some set of conditions or features, A, B, C, . . . , is enough to ensure, for example, that there is a contract. The very notion of a

---

[5] H. L. A. Hart, 'The Ascription of Responsibility and Rights in *Logic and Language*, First Series, ed. by A. G. N. Flew (Oxford, 1951). Hart indeed speaks of 'conditions' throughout, see p. 148.

defeasible concept seems to require that some group of features *would* be sufficient *in certain circumstances*, i.e. in the absence of voiding features. In a certain way, defeasible concepts lack sufficient conditions then, but they are still, in the sense described, condition-governed. My claim about taste concepts is stronger; that they are not, except negatively, governed by conditions at all. We could not conclude even in certain circumstances, e.g. if we were told of the absence of all 'voiding' or uncharacteristic features (no angularities and the like), that an object *must* certainly be graceful, however fully it was described to us as possessing features characteristic of gracefulness.

My arguments and illustrations so far have been rather simply schematic. Many concepts, including most of the examples I have used . . . are much more thoroughly open and complex than my illustrations suggest. Not only may there be an open list of relevant conditions; it may be impossible to give precise rules telling how many features from the list are needed for a sufficient set or in which combinations; impossible similarly to give precise rules covering the extent or degree to which such features need to be present in those combinations. Indeed, we may have to abandon as futile any attempt to describe or formulate anything like a complete set of precise conditions or rules, and content ourselves with giving only a very general account of the concept, making reference to samples or cases or precedents. We cannot employ these concepts *simply* by being equipped with lists of conditions, readily applicable procedures or sets of rules, however complex. For to exhibit a mastery of one of those concepts we must be able to apply the word correctly to new individual cases, at least to central ones; and each new case may be a uniquely different object, just as each intelligent child or student may differ from others in relevant features and exhibit a unique combination of kinds and degrees of achievement and ability. In dealing with these new cases mechanical rules and procedures would be useless; we have to exercise our judgment, guided by a complex set of examples and precedents. Here then there is a marked *superficial* similarity to aesthetic concepts. For in using aesthetic terms too we learn from samples and examples, not rules, and we have to apply them, likewise, without guidance by rules or readily applicable procedures, to new and unique instances. Neither kind of concept admits of a simply 'mechanical' employment.

But this is *only* a superficial similarity. It is at least noteworthy that in applying words like 'lazy' or 'intelligent' to new and unique instances we say that we are required to exercise *judgment*; it would be indeed odd to say that we are exercising *taste*. In exercising judgment we are called upon to examine the pros and cons, and to decide whether a quite new feature is to be counted as weighing on one side or on the other. But this goes to show that, though we may learn from and rely upon samples and precedents rather than a set of stated conditions, we are not out of the realm of general conditions and guiding principles. These precedents necessarily embody, and are used by us to illustrate, a complex web of governing and relevant conditions which it is impossible to formulate completely.

To profit by precedents we have to understand them; and we must argue consistently from case to case. This is the very function of precedents. Thus it is possible, even with these very loosely condition-governed concepts, to take clear or paradigm cases of X and to say 'this is X because . . .', and follow it up with an account of features which logically clinch the matter.

Nothing like this is possible with aesthetic terms. Examples undoubtedly play a crucial role in giving us a grasp of these concepts; but we do not and cannot derive from these examples conditions and principles, however complex, which will enable us, if we are consistent, to apply the terms even to some new cases. When, with a clear case of something which is in fact graceful or balanced but which I have not seen, someone tells me what features make it so, it is always possible for me to wonder whether, in spite of these features, it really is graceful or balanced.

My point may be reinforced thus. A man who failed to realize the nature of aesthetic concepts, or who, knowing he lacked sensitivity in aesthetic matters, did not want to reveal this lack might by assiduous application and shrewd observation provide himself with some rules and generalizations; and by inductive procedures and intelligent guessing, he might frequently say the right things. But he could have no great confidence or certainty; a slight change in an object might at any time unpredictably ruin his calculations, and he might as easily have been wrong as right. No matter how careful he has been about working out a set of consistent principles and conditions, he is only in a position to think that the object is very possibly delicate. With concepts like *lazy, intelligent,* or *contract,* someone who intelligently formulated rules that led him aright appreciably often *would* thereby show the beginning of a grasp of those concepts; but the person we are considering is not even beginning to show an awareness of what delicacy is. Though he sometimes says the right thing, he has not seen, but guessed, that the object is delicate. However intelligent he might be, we could easily tell him wrongly that something was delicate and 'explain' why without his being able to detect the deception. (I am ignoring complications now about negative conditions.) But if we did the same with, say, ''intelligent' he could at least often uncover some incompatibility which would need explaining. In a world of beings like himself he would have no use for concepts like delicacy. As it is, these concepts would play a quite different role in his life. He would for himself, have no more reason to choose tasteful objects, pictures, and so on, than a deaf man would to avoid noisy places. He could not be praised for exercising taste; at best his ingenuity and intelligence might come in for mention. In 'appraising' pictures, statuettes, poems, he would be doing something quite different from what other people do when they exercise taste.

At this point I want to notice in passing that there are times when it may look as if an aesthetic word could be applied according to a rule. These cases vary in type; I shall mention only one. One might say, in using 'delicate' of glassware perhaps, that the thinner the glass, other things being equal, the more delicate it is. Similarly, with fabrics, furniture, and so on, there are perhaps times when the thinner or more smoothly finished or more highly polished something is, the more certainly some aesthetic term or other applies. On such occasions someone might formulate a rule and follow it in applying the word to a given range of articles. Now it may be that sometimes when this is so, the word being used is not really an aesthetic term at all; 'delicate' applied to glass in this way may at times really mean no more than 'thin' or 'fragile.' But this is certainly not always the case; people often *are* exercising taste even when they say that glass is very delicate because it is so thin, and know that it would be less so if thicker and more so if thinner. These instances where there appear to be rules are peripheral cases of the use of aesthetic terms. If someone did merely follow a rule we should not say he was exercising taste, and we should hesitate to admit that he had any real notion of delicacy until he satisfied us that he could discern it in other instances where no rule was available. In any event, these occasions when aesthetic words can be applied by rule are exceptional not central or typical, and there is still no reason to think we are dealing with a logical entailment.[6]

It must not be thought that the impossibility of stating any conditions (other than negative) for the application of aesthetic terms results from an accidental poverty or lack of precision in language, or that it is simply a question of extreme complexity. It is true that words like 'pink,' 'bluish,' 'curving,' 'mottled' do not permit of anything like a specific naming of each and every varied shade, curve, mottling, and blending. But if we were to give special names much more liberally than either we or even the specialists do (and no doubt there are limits beyond which we could not go), or even if, instead of names, we were to use vast numbers of specimens and samples of particular shades, shapes, mottlings, lines, and configurations, it would still be impossible, and for the same reasons, to supply any conditions.

[6] I cannot in the compass of this paper discuss the other types of apparent exceptions to my thesis. Cases where a man *lacking* in sensitivity might learn and follow a rule, as above, ought to be distinguished from cases where someone who *possesses* sensitivity might know, from a non-aesthetic description, that an aesthetic term applies. I have stated my thesis as though this latter kind of case never occurs because I have had my eye on the logical features of *typical* aesthetic judgments and have preferred to over- rather than understate my view. But with certain aesthetic terms, especially negative ones, there may perhaps be some rare genuine exceptions when a description enables us to visualize very fully, and when what is described belongs to certain restricted classes of things, say human faces or animal forms. Perhaps a description like 'One eye red and rheumy, the other missing, a wart-covered nose, a twisted mouth, a greenish pallor' may justify in a strong sense ('must be', 'cannot but be') the judgments 'ugly' or 'hideous'. If so, such cases are marginal, form a very small minority, and are uncharacteristic or atypical of aesthetic judgments in general. Usually, when, on hearing a description, we say 'it *must* be very beautiful (graceful, or the like)', we mean no more than 'it surely must be, it's only remotely possible that it isn't.' Different again are situations, and these are very numerous, where we can move quite simply from 'bright colours' to 'gay', or from 'reds and yellows' to 'warm', but where we are as yet only on the borderline of anything that could be called an expression of taste or aesthetic sensibility. I have stressed the importance of this transitional and border area between non-aesthetic and obviously aesthetic judgments below.

We do indeed, in talking about a work of art, concern ourselves with its individual and specific features. We say that it is delicate not simply because it is in pale colours but because of *those* pale colours, that it is graceful not because its outline curves slightly but because of *that* particular curve. We use expressions like 'because of its *pale* colouring,' 'because of *the* flecks of bright blue,' 'because of *the* way the lines converge' where it is clear we are referring not to the presence of general features but to very specific and particular ones. But it is obvious that even with the help of precise names, or even samples and illustrations, of particular shades of colour, contours and lines, any attempt to state conditions would be futile. After all, the very same feature, say a colour or shape or line of a particular sort, which helps make one work may quite spoil another. 'It would be quite delicate if it were not for that pale colour there' may be said about the very colour which is singled out in another picture as being largely responsible for its delicate quality. No doubt one way of putting this is to say that the features which make something delicate or graceful, and so on, are combined in a peculiar and unique way; that the aesthetic quality depends upon exactly this individual or unique combination of just these specific colours and shapes so that even a slight change might make all the difference. Nothing is to be achieved by trying to single out or separate features and generalizing about them.

I have now argued that in certain ways aesthetic concepts are not and cannot be condition- or rule-governed.[7] Not to be so governed is one of their essential characteristics. In arguing this I first claimed in a general way that no non-aesthetic features are possible candidates for conditions, and then considered more particularly both the 'characteristic' *general* features associated with aesthetic terms and the individual or *specific* features found in particular objects. I have not attempted to examine what relationship these specific features of a work do bear to its aesthetic qualities. An examination of the locutions we use when we refer to them in the course of explaining or supporting our application of an aesthetic term reinforces with linguistic evidence the fact that we are certainly not offering them as explanatory or justifying *conditions*. When we are asked why we say a certain person is lazy or intelligent or courageous, we are being asked in virtue of what we *call* him this; we reply with 'because of the way he regularly leaves his work unfinished,' or 'because of the ease with which he handles such and such problems,' and so on. But when we are asked

---

[7] Helen Knight says (Elton, op. cit., p. 152) that 'piquant' (one of my 'aesthetic' terms) 'depends on' various features (a *retroussé* nose, a pointed chin, and the like), and that these features are *criteria* for it; this second claim is what I am denying. She also maintains that 'good,' when applied to works of art, depends on *criteria* like balance, solidity, depth, profundity (my aesthetic terms again; I should place piquancy in this list). I would deny this too, though I regard it as a different question and do not consider it in this paper. The two questions need separating: the relation of non-aesthetic features (*retroussé*, pointed) to aesthetic qualities, and the relation of aesthetic qualities to 'aesthetically good' (verdicts). Most writings which touch on the nature of aesthetic concepts have this other (verdict) question mainly in mind. Mrs. Knight blurs this difference when she says, for example, ' "piquant" is the same kind of word as "good".'

to say why, in our opinion, a picture lacks balance or is sombre in tone, or why a poem is moving or tightly organized, we are doing a different kind of thing. We may use similar locutions: 'his verse has strength and variety *because of the way* he handles the metre and employs the caesura,' or 'it is nobly austere *because* of the lack of detail and the restricted palette.' But we can also express what we want to by using quite other expressions: 'it is the handling of metre and caesura which is *responsible for* its strength and variety,' 'its nobly austere quality is *due to* the lack of detail and the use of a restricted palette,' 'its lack of balance *results from* the highlighting of the figures on the left,' 'those minor chords *make it* extremely moving,' 'those converging lines *give it* an extraordinary unity.' These are locutions we cannot switch to with 'lazy' or 'intelligent'; to say what *makes* him lazy, is *responsible for* his laziness, what it is *due to*, is to broach another question entirely.

One after another, in recent discussions, writers have insisted that aesthetic judgments are not 'mechanical': 'Critics do not formulate general standards and apply these mechanically to all, or to classes of, works of art.' 'Technical points can be settled rapidly, by the application of rules,' but aesthetic questions 'cannot be settled by any mechanical method.' Instead, these writers on aesthetics have emphasized that there is no 'substitute for individual judgment' with its 'spontaneity and speculation' and that 'The final standard . . . [is] the judgment of personal taste.'[8] What is surprising is that, though such things have been repeated again and again, no one seems to have said what is meant by 'taste' or by the word 'mechanical'. There are many judgments besides those requiring taste which demand 'spontaneity' and 'individual judgment' and are not 'mechanical.' Without a detailed comparison we cannot see in what particular way *aesthetic* judgments are not 'mechanical,' or how they differ from those other judgments, nor can we begin to specify what taste is. This I have attempted. It is a characteristic and essential feature of judgments which employ an aesthetic term that they cannot be made by appealing, in the sense explained, to non-aesthetic conditions.[9] This, I believe is a logical feature of aesthetic or taste judgments in general though I have argued it here only as regards the more restricted range of judgments which employ aesthetic terms. It is part of what 'taste' means.

II

A great deal of work remains to be done on aesthetic concepts. In the remainder of this paper I shall offer further suggestions which may help towards an understanding of them.

[8] See articles by Margaret Macdonald and J. A. Passmore in Elton, op. cit., pp. 118, 41, 40, 119.

[9] As I indicated, . . . above. I have dealt only with the relation of *non-aesthetic* to aesthetic features. Perhaps a description in *aesthetic* terms may occasionally suffice for applying another aesthetic term. Johnson's Dictionary gives 'handsome' as 'beautiful with dignity;' Shorter O.E.D. gives 'pretty' as beautiful in a slight, dainty, or diminutive way.'

The realization that aesthetic concepts are governed only negatively by conditions is likely to give rise to puzzlement over how we manage to apply the words in our aesthetic vocabulary. If we are not following rules and there are no conditions to appeal to, how are we to know when they are applicable? One very natural way to counter this question is to point out that some other sorts of concepts also are not condition-governed. We do not apply simple colour works by following rules or in accordance with principles. We see that the book is red by looking, just as we tell that the tea is sweet by tasting it. So too, it might be said, we just see (or fail to see) that things are delicate, balanced, and the like. This kind of comparison between the exercise of taste and the use of the five senses is indeed familiar; our use of the word 'taste' itself shows that the comparison is age-old and very natural. Yet whatever the similarities, there are great dissimilarities too. A careful comparison cannot be attempted here though it would be valuable; but certain differences stand out, and writers who have emphasized that aesthetic judgments are not 'mechanical' have sometimes dwelt on and been puzzled by them.

In the first place, while our ability to discern aesthetic features is dependent upon our possession of good eyesight, hearing, and so on, people normally endowed with senses and understanding may nevertheless fail to discern them. 'Those who listen to a concert, walk round a gallery, read a poem may have roughly similar sense perceptions, but some get a great deal more than others,' Miss Macdonald says; but she adds that she is 'puzzled by this feature "in the object" which can be seen only by a specially qualified observer' and asks, 'What is this "something more"?'[10]

It is this difference between aesthetic and perceptual qualities which in part leads to the view that 'works of art are esoteric objects . . . not simple objects of sense perception.'[11] But there is no good reason for calling an object esoteric simply because we discern aesthetic qualities in it. The *objects* to which we apply aesthetic words are of the most diverse kinds and by no means esoteric: people and buildings, flowers and gardens, vases and furniture, as well as poems and music. Nor does there seem any good reason for calling the *qualities* themselves esoteric. It is true that someone with perfect eyes or ears might miss them, but we do after all say we *observe* or *notice* them ('Did you notice how very graceful she was?', 'Did you observe the exquisite balance in all his pictures?'). In fact, they are very familiar indeed. We learn while quite young to use many aesthetic words, though they are, as one might expect from their dependence upon our ability to see, hear, distinguish colours, and the like, not the earliest words we learn: and our mastery and sophistication in using them develop along with the rest of our vocabulary. They are not rarities; some ranges of them are in regular use in everyday discourse.

The second notable difference between the exercise of taste and the

---

[10] Macdonald in Elton, op. cit., pp. 114, 119. See also pp. 120, 122.
[11] Macdonald, ibid., pp. 114, 120–3. She speaks of non-aesthetic properties here as 'physical' or 'observable' qualities, and distinguishes between 'physical objects' and 'work of art'.

use of the five senses lies in the way we support those judgments in which aesthetics concepts are employed. Although we use these concepts without rules or conditions, we do defend or support our judgments, and convince others of their rightness, by talking; 'disputation about art is not futile,' as Miss Macdonald says, for critics do 'attempt a certain kind of explanation of works of art with the object of establishing correct judgments.'[12] Thus even though this disputation does not consist in 'deductive or inductive inference' or 'reasoning,' its occurrence is enough to show how very different these judgments are from those of a simple perceptual sort.

Now the critic's talk, it is clear, frequently consists in mentioning or pointing out the features, including easily discernible non-aesthetic ones, upon which the aesthetic qualities depend. But the puzzling question remains how, by mentioning these features, the critic is thereby justifying or supporting his judgments. To this question a number of recent writers have given an answer. Stuart Hampshire, for example, says that 'One engages in aesthetic discussion for the sake of what one might see on the way . . . if one has been brought to see what there is to be seen in the object, the purpose of discussion is achieved. . . . The point is to bring people to see these features.'[13] The critic's talk, that is, often serves to support his judgments in a special way; it helps us to *see* what he has seen, namely, the aesthetic qualities of the object. But even when it is agreed that this is one of the main things that critics do, puzzlement tends to break out again over *how* they do it. How is it that by talking about features of the work (largely non-aesthetic ones) we can manage to bring others to see what they had not seen? 'What sort of endowment is this which *talking* can modify? . . . Discussion does not improve eyesight and hearing' (my italics).[14]

Yet of course we do succeed in applying aesthetic terms, and we frequently do succeed by talking (and pointing and gesturing in certain ways) in bringing others to see what we see. One begins to suspect that puzzlement over how we can possibly do this, and puzzlement over the 'esoteric' character of aesthetic qualities too, arises from bearing in mind inappropriate philosophical models. When someone is unable to see that the book on the table is brown, we cannot get him to see that it is by talking; consequently it seems puzzling that we might get someone to see that the vase is graceful by talking. If we are to dispel this puzzlement and recognize aesthetic concepts and qualities for what they are, we must abandon unsuitable models and investigate how we actually employ these concepts. With so much interest in and agreement about *what* the critic does, one might expect descriptions of *how* he does it to have been given. But little has been said about this, and what has been said is unsatisfactory.

---

[12] Ibid., pp. 115–16: cf. also John Holloway, *Proceedings of the Aristotelian Society*, Supplementary Vol. xxiii (1949), pp. 175–6.

[13] Stuart Hampshire in Elton, op. cit., p. 165. Cf. also remarks in Elton by Isenberg (pp. 142, 145), Passmore (p. 38), in *Philosophy and Psycho-analysis* by John Wisdom (Oxford, 1953), pp. 223–4, and in Holloway, op. cit., p. 175.

[14] Macdonald, op. cit., pp. 119–20.

Miss Macdonald,[15] for example, subscribes to this view of the critic's task as presenting 'what is not obvious to casual or uninstructed inspection,' and she does ask the question 'What sort of considerations are involved, *and how*, to justify a critical verdict?' (my italics). But she does not in fact go on to answer it. She addresses herself instead to the different, though related, question of the interpretation of art works. In complex works different critics claim, often justifiably, to discern different features; hence Miss Macdonald suggests that in critical discourse the critic is bringing us to see what he sees by offering new interpretations. But if the question is 'what (the critic) does and how he does it,' he cannot be represented either wholly or even mainly as providing new interpretations. His task quite as often is simply to help us appreciate qualities which other critics have regularly found in the works he discusses. To put the stress upon *new* interpretations is to leave untouched the question how, by talking, he can help us to see *either* the newly appreciated aesthetic qualities *or* the old. In any case, besides complex poems or plays which may bear many interpretations, there are also relatively simple ones. There are also vases, buildings, and furniture, not to mention faces, sunsets, and scenery, about which no questions of 'interpretation' arise but about which we talk in similar ways and make similar judgments. So the 'puzzling' questions remain: how do we support these judgments and how do we bring others to see what we see?

Hampshire,[16] who likewise believes that the critic brings us 'to see what there is to be seen in the object,' does give some account of how the critic does this. 'The greatest service of the critic' is to point out, isolate, and place in a frame of attention the 'particular features of the particular object which *make* it ugly or beautiful'; for it is 'difficult to see and hear all that there is to see and hear,' and simply a prejudice to suppose that while 'things really do have colours and shapes . . . there do not exist literally and objectively, concordances of colours and perceived rhythms and balances of shapes.' However, these 'extraordinary qualities' which the critic 'may have seen (in the wider sense of "see")' are 'qualities which are of no direct practical interest.' Consequently, to bring us to see them the critic employs 'an unnatural use of words in description'; 'the common vocabulary, being created for practical purposes, obstructs any disinterested perception of things'; and so these qualities 'are normally described metaphorically by some transference of terms from the common vocabulary.'

Much of what Hampshire says is right. But there is also something quite wrong in the view that the 'common' vocabulary 'obstructs' our aesthetic purposes, that it is 'unnatural' to take it over and use it metaphorically, and that the critic 'is under the necessity of building . . . a vocabulary *in opposition to the main tendency of his language*' (my italics). First, while we do often coin new metaphors in order to describe

[15] Ibid., see pp. 127, 122, 125, 115. Other writers also place the stress on interpretation, cf. Holloway, op. cit., p. 173 ff.
[16] Op. cit., pp. 165–8.

aesthetic qualities, we are by no means always under the necessity of wresting the 'common vocabulary' from its 'natural' uses to serve our purposes. There does exist, as I observed earlier, a large and accepted vocabulary of aesthetic terms some of which, whatever their metaphorical origins, are now not metaphors at all, others of which are at most quasi-metaphorical. Second, this view that our use of metaphor and quasi-metaphor for aesthetic purposes is unnatural or a makeshift into which we are forced by a language designed for other purposes misrepresents fundamentally the character of aesthetic qualities and aesthetic language. There is nothing unnatural about using words like 'forceful,' 'dynamic,' or 'tightly-knit' in criticism; they do their work perfectly and are exactly the words needed for the purposes they serve. We do not want or need to replace them by words which lack the metaphorical element. In using them to describe works of art, the very point is that we are noticing aesthetic qualities related to their literal or common meanings. If we possessed a quite different word from 'dynamic,' one we could use to point out an aesthetic quality unrelated to the common meaning of 'dynamic,' it could not be used to describe that quality which 'dynamic' does serve to point out. Hampshire pictures 'a colony of aesthetes, disen-gaged from practical needs and manipulations' and says that 'descriptions of aesthetic qualities, which for us are metaphorical, might seem to them to have an altogether literal and familar sense'; they might use 'a more directly descriptive vocabulary.' But if they had a new and 'directly descriptive' vocabulary lacking the links with non-aesthetic properties and interests which our vocabulary possesses, they would have to remain silent about many of the aesthetic qualities we can describe; further, if they were more completely 'disengaged from practical needs' and other non-aesthetic awareness and interests, they would perforce be blind to many aesthetic qualities we can appreciate. The links between aesthetic qualities and non-aesthetic ones are both obvious and vital. Aesthetic con-cepts, all of them, carry with them attachments and in one way or another are tethered to or parasitic upon non-aesthetic features. The fact that many aesthetic terms are metaphorical or quasi-metaphorical in no way means that common language is an ill-adapted tool with which we have to struggle. When someone writes as Hampshire does, one suspects again that critical language is being judged against other models. To use language which is frequently metaphorical might be strange for some *other* purpose or from the standpoint of doing something else, but for the purpose and from the standpoint of making aesthetic observations it is not. To say it is an unnatural use of language for doing *this* is to imply there is or could be for this purpose some other and 'natural' use. But these *are* natural ways of talking about aesthetic matters.

To help understand what the critic does, then, how he supports his judgments and gets his audience to see what he sees, I shall attempt a brief description of the methods we use as critics.[17]

---

[17] Holloway, op. cit., pp. 173–4, lists some of these very briefly.

(1) We may simply mention or point out non-aesthetic features: 'Notice these flecks of colour, that dark mass there, those lines.' By merely drawing attention to those easily discernible features which make the painting luminous or warm or dynamic, we often succeed in bringing someone to see these aesthetic qualities. We get him to see B by mentioning something different, A. Sometimes in doing this we are drawing attention to features which may have gone unnoticed by an untrained or insufficiently attentive eye or ear: 'Just listen for the repeated figure in the left hand,' 'Did you notice the figure of Icarus in the Breughel? It is very small.' Sometimes they are features which have been seen or heard but of which the significance or purpose has been missed in any of a variety of ways: 'Notice how much darker he has made the central figure, how much brighter these colours are than the adjacent ones,' 'Of course, you've observed the ploughman in the foreground; but had you considered how he, like everyone else in the picture, is going about his business without noticing the fall of Icarus?' In mentioning features which may be discerned by anyone with normal eyes, ears, and intelligence, we are singling out what may serve as a kind of key to grasping or seeing something else (and the key may not be the same for each person).

(2) On the other hand we often simply mention the very qualities we want people to see. We point to a painting and say, 'Notice how nervous and delicate the drawing is,' or 'See what energy and vitality it has.' The use of the aesthetic term itself may do the trick; we say what the quality or character is, and people who had not seen it before see it.

(3) Most often, there is a linking of remarks about aesthetic and non-aesthetic features: 'Have you noticed this line and that, and the points of bright colour here and there . . . don't they give it vitality, energy?'

(4) We do, in addition, often make extensive and helpful use of similes and genuine metaphors: 'It's as if there are small points of light burning,' 'as though he had thrown on the paint violently and in anger,' 'the light shimmers, the lines dance, everything is air, lightness and gaiety,' 'his canvasses are fires, they crackle, burn, and blaze, even at their most subdued always restlessly flickering, but often bursting into flame, great pyrotechnic displays,' and so on.

(5) We make use of contrasts, comparisons, and reminiscences: 'Suppose he had made that a lighter yellow, moved it to the right, how flat it would have been,' 'Don't you think it has something of the quality of a Rembrandt?', 'Hasn't it the same serenity, peace, and quality of light of those summer evenings in Norfolk?' We use what keys we have to the known sensitivity, susceptibilities, and experience of our audience.

Critics and commentators may range, in their methods, from one extreme to the other, from painstaking concentration on points of detail, line and colour, vowels and rhymes, to more or less flowery and luxuriant metaphor. Even the enthusiastic biographical sketch decorated with suitable epithet and metaphor may serve. What is best depends on both the audience and the work under discussion. But this would not be a complete sketch unless certain other notes were added.

(6) Repetition and reiteration often play an important role. When we are in front of a canvas we may come back time and again to the same points, drawing attention to the same lines and shapes, repeating the same words, 'swirling,' 'balance,' 'luminosity,' or the same similes and metaphors, as if time and familiarity, looking harder, listening more carefully, paying closer attention may help. So again with variation; it often helps to talk round what we have said, to build up, supplement with more talk *of the same kind.* When someone misses the swirling quality, when one epithet or one metaphor does not work, we throw in related ones; we speak of its wild movement, how it twists and turns, writhes and whirls, as though, failing to score a direct hit, we may succeed with a barrage of near-synonyms.

(7) Finally, besides our verbal performances, the rest of our behaviour is important. We accompany our talk with appropriate tones of voice, expression, nods, looks, and gesture. A critic may sometimes do more with a sweep of the arm than by talking. An appropriate gesture may make us see the violence in a painting or the character of a melodic line.

These ways of acting and talking are not significantly different whether we are dealing with a particular work, paragraph, or line, or speaking of an artist's work as a whole, or even drawing attention to a sunset or scenery. But even with the speaker doing all this, we may fail to see what he sees. There may be a point, though there need be no limit except that imposed by time and patience, at which he gives up and sets us (or himself) down as lacking in some way, defective in sensitivity. He may tell us to look or read again, or to read or look at other things and then come back again to this; he may suspect there are experiences in life we have missed. But these are the things he does. This is what succeeds if anything does; indeed it is all that can be done.

But realizing clearly that, whether we are dealing with art or scenery or people or natural objects, this is how we operate with aesthetic concepts, we may recognize this sphere of human activity for what it is. We operate with different kinds of concepts in different ways. If we want someone to agree that a colour is red we may take it into a good light and ask him to look; if it is viridian we may fetch a colour chart and make him compare; if we want him to agree that a figure is fourteen-sided we get him to count; and to bring him to agree that something is dilapidated or that someone is lazy we may do other things, citing features and reasoning and arguing about them. These are the methods appropriate to these various concepts. But the ways we get someone to see aesthetic qualities are different; they are of the kind I have described. With each kind of concept we can describe what we do and how we do it. But the methods suited to these other concepts will not do for aesthetic ones, or vice versa. We cannot prove by argument or by assembling a sufficiency of conditions that something is graceful; but this is no more puzzling than our inability to prove, by using the methods, metaphors, and gestures of the art critic, that it will be mate in ten moves. The questions raised admit of no answer beyond the sort of description I have given. To go on to ask, with puzzlement, how it is that *when* we do these things people come to see, is like asking how is it that, when we take the book into a good light, our companion agrees with us that it is red. There is no place for this kind of question or puzzlement. Aesthetic concepts are as natural, as little esoteric, as any others. It is against the background of different and philosophically more familiar models that they seem puzzling.

I have described how people justify aesthetic judgments and bring others to see aesthetic qualities in things. I shall end by showing that the methods I have outlined are the ones natural for and characteristic of taste concepts from the start. When someone tries to make me see that a painting is delicate or balanced, I have some understanding of these terms already and know in a sense what I am looking for. But if there is puzzlement over how, by talking, he can bring me to see these qualities in this picture, there should be equal puzzlement over how I learned to use aesthetic terms and discern aesthetic qualities in the first place. We may ask, therefore, how we learn to do these things; and this is to inquire (1) what natural potentialities and tendencies people have and (2) how we develop and take advantage of these capacities in training and teaching. Now for the second of these there is no doubt that our ability to notice and respond to aesthetic qualities is cultivated and developed by our contacts with parents and teachers from quite an early age. What is interesting for my present purpose is that, while we are being taught in the presence of examples what grace, delicacy and so on are, the methods used, the language and behaviour, are of a piece with those of the critic as I have already described them.

To pursue these two questions, consider first those words like 'dynamic,' 'melancholy,' 'balanced,' 'taut,' or 'gay' the aesthetic use of which is quasi-metaphorical. It has already been emphasized that we could not use them thus without some experience of situations where they are used literally. The present inquiry is how we shift from literal to aesthetic uses of them. For this it is required that there be certain abilities and tendencies to link experiences, to regard certain things as similar, and to see, explore, and be interested in these similarities. It is a feature of human intelligence and sensitivity that we do spontaneously do these things and that the tendency can be encouraged and developed. It is no more baffling that we should employ aesthetic terms of this sort than that we should make metaphors at all. Easy and smooth transitions by which we shift to the use of these aesthetic terms are not hard to find. We suggest to children that simple pieces of music are hurrying or running or skipping or dawdling, from there we move to lively, gay, jolly, happy, smiling, or sad, and, as their experiences and vocabulary broaden, to solemn, dynamic, or melancholy. But the child also discovers for himsef many of these parallels and takes interest or delight in them. He is likely on his own to skip, march, clap, or laugh with the music, and without this natural tendency our training would get nowhere. In so far, however, as we do take advantage of this tendency and help him by training, *we do just what the critic does.* We may merely need to persuade the child to pay attention, to look or listen;

or we may simply *call* the music jolly. But we are also likely to use, as the critic does, reiteration, synonyms, parallels, contrasts, similies, metaphors, gestures, and other expressive behavior.

Of course the recognition of similarities and simple metaphorical extensions are not the only transitions to the aesthetic use of language. Others are made in different ways; for instance, by the kind of peripheral cases I mentioned earlier. When our admiration is for something as simple as the thinness of a glass or the smoothness of a fabric, it is not difficult to call attention to such things, evoke a similar delight, and introduce suitable aesthetic terms. These transitions are only the beginnings; it may often be questionable whether a term is yet being used aesthetically or not. Many of the terms I have mentioned may be used in ways which are not straightforwardly literal but of which we should hesitate to say that they demanded much yet by way of aesthetic sensitivity. We speak of warm and cool colours, and we may say of a brightly coloured picture that at least it is gay and lively. When we have brought someone to make this sort of metaphorical extension of terms, he has made one of the transitional steps from which he may move on to uses which more obviously deserve to be called aesthetic and demand a more obviously aesthetic appreciation. When I said at the outset that aesthetic sensitivity was rarer than some other natural endowments, I was not denying that it varies in degree from the rudimentary to the refined. Most people learn easily to make the kinds of remarks I am now considering. But when someone can call bright canvasses gay and lively without being able to spot the one which is really vibrant, or can recognize the obvious outward vigor and energy of a student composition played *con fuoco* while failing to see that it lacks inner fire and drive, we do not regard his aesthetic sensitivity in these areas as particularly developed. However, once these transitions from common to aesthetic uses are begun in the more obvious cases, the domain of aesthetic concepts may broaden out, and they become more subtle and even partly autonomous. The initial steps, however varied the metaphorical shifts and however varied the experiences upon which they are parasitic, are natural and easy.

Much the same is true when we turn to those words which have no standard non-aesthetic use, 'lovely,' 'pretty,' 'dainty,' 'graceful,' 'elegant.' We cannot say that these are learned by a metaphorical shift. But they still are linked to non-aesthetic features in many ways and the learning of them also is made possible by certain kinds of natural response, reaction, and ability. We learn them not so much by noticing similarities, but by our attention being caught and focused in other ways. Certain phenomena which are outstanding or remarkable or unusual catch the eye or ear, seize our attention and interest, and move us to surprise, admiration, delight, fear, or distaste. Children begin by reacting in these ways to spectacular sunsets, woods in autumn, roses, dandelions, and other striking and colourful objects, and it is in these circumstances that we find ourselves introducing general aesthetic words to them, like 'lovely,' 'pretty,' and 'ugly.' It is not an accident that the first lessons in aesthetic appreciation consist in drawing the child's attention to roses rather than to grass; nor is it surprising that we remark to him on the autumn colour rather than on the subdued tints of winter. We all of us, not only children, pay aesthetic attention more readily to such outstanding and easily noticeable things. We notice with pleasure early spring grass or the first snow, hills of notably marked and varied contours, scenery flecked with a great variety of colour or dappled variously with sun and shadow. We are struck and impressed by great size or mass, as with mountains or cathedrals. We are similarly responsive to unusual precision or minuteness or remarkable feats of skill, as with complex and elaborate filigree, or intricate wood carving and fan-vaulting. It is at these times, taking advantage of these natural interests and admirations, that we first teach the simpler aesthetic words. People of moderate aesthetic sensitivity and sophistication continue to exhibit aesthetic interest mainly on such occasions and to use only the more general words ('pretty,' 'lovely,' and the like). But these situations may serve as a beginning from which we extend our aesthetic interests to wider and less obvious fields, mastering as we go the more subtle and specific vocabulary of taste. The principles do not change; the basis for learning more specific terms like 'graceful,' 'delicate,' and 'elegant' is also our interest in and admiration for various non-aesthetic natural properties ('She seems to move *effortlessly*, as if floating,' 'So very *thin* and *fragile*, as if a breeze might destroy it,' 'So *small* and yet so *intricate*,' 'So *economical* and perfectly *adapted*').[18] And even with these aesthetic terms which are not metaphorical themselves ('graceful,' 'delicate,' 'elegant'), we rely in the same way upon the critic's methods, including comparison, illustration, and metaphor, to teach or make clear what they mean.

I have wished to emphasize in the latter part of this paper the natural basis of responses of various kinds without which aesthetic terms could not be learned. I have also outlined what some of the features are to which we naturally respond: similarities of various sorts, notable colours, shapes, scents, size, intricacy, and much else besides. Even the non-metaphorical aesthetic terms have significant links with all kinds of natural features by which our interest, wonder, admiration, delight, or distaste is aroused. But in particular I have wanted to urge that it should not strike us as puzzling that the critic supports his judgment and brings us to see aesthetic qualities by pointing out key features and talking about them in the way he does. It is by the very same methods that people helped us develop our aesthetic

[18] It is worth noticing that most of the words which in current usage are primarily or exclusively aesthetic terms had earlier non-aesthetic uses and gained their present use by some kind of metaphorical shift. Without reposing too great weight on these etymological facts, it can be seen that their history reflects connections with the responses, interests, and natural features I have mentioned as underlying the learning and use of aesthetic terms. These transitions suggest both the dependence of aesthetic upon other interests, and what some of these interests are. Connected with liking, delight, affection, regard, estimation, or choice—*beautiful, graceful, delicate, lovely, exquisite, elegant, dainty*; with fear or repulsion—*ugly*; with what notably catches the eye or attention—*garish, splendid, gaudy*; with what attracts by notable rarity, precision, skill, ingenuity, elaboration—*dainty, nice, pretty, exquisite*; with adaptation to function, suitability to ease of handling—*handsome*.

sense and master its vocabulary from the beginning. If we responded to those methods then, it is not surprising that we respond to the critic's discourse now. It would be surprising if, by using this language and behaviour, people could *not* sometimes bring us to see the aesthetic qualities of things; for this would prove us lacking in one characteristically human kind of awareness and activity.

Ted Cohen

AESTHETIC/NON-AESTHETIC AND THE CONCEPT OF TASTE: A CRITIQUE OF SIBLEY'S POSITION

Introduction to Sibley

Sibley's theory is a *kind* of theory characteristic of a strain of mid-twentieth century aesthetics (and ethics), and it is as such philosophizing that I would like to discredit it.* I am less interested in the conclusions reached from views like Sibley's than in those views' conception of the framework within which to raise questions which lead to conclusions. This conception does *lead*, I think, in a way which renders any conclusion pernicious. Roughly this approach is dictated: Given that there are aesthetic judgments, (i) one must decide whether they are "objective" or "cognitive" or whatever, or, broadly speaking, whether they are things that have truth-values; and if they do have truth-values, (ii) one must determine whether an aesthetic judgment ever can be inferred from any conjunction of non-aesthetic judgments. This is likely to require that (iii) one determine how the terms found in aesthetic judgments are related to other terms.

This sketch is familiar to anyone acquainted with recent analytic aesthetics, and it outlines the thoughts (and despair) of those who have "done" aesthetics as students. Sibley is one among dozens whose work fits this pattern. I choose his position to discuss for five reasons.

(1) It is, I think, the best, most careful work in this vein.
(2) It has been very influential: the principal essay, "Aesthetic Concepts", is included in most standard anthologies published since its appearance, and much of the "mainstream" literature in aesthetics of the 1960's is addressed to Sibley in one way or another.
(3) It exemplifies what one might call "conceptual" aesthetics, parallelling —or following after—what we have been taught to think of as meta-ethics. I should like my work to suggest that there is some point in wondering whether there is any point in aesthetics going through the same moves ethics has gone through (as well as wondering what ethics has done to itself).
(4) Although by now Sibley's view has begun to look like one among a

* Originally published in *Theoria*, vol. xxxix, 1973, pp. 113–152. Reprinted by permission of *Theoria*.

variety of possible (standard) meta-aesthetic theories, it remains special in its studied characterization of aesthetic judgments without reference to their status as verdicts or evaluations.

(5) Sibley's approach recalls eighteenth century British philosophy of art— up to a point. This part of the Tradition, largely ignored in recent philosophy of art before Sibley, animates Sibley's work, giving it the depth, plausibility, and appeal so conspicuously and characteristically missing from recent aesthetics. I hope to show that the ultimate collapse of Sibley's view coincides with his departure from the pivotal notion in Hume's analysis, the conception of taste.

With regard to (4) and (5) I believe Sibley's view to be unique. This will be discussed in some detail once the view itself has been outlined.

The paper which has been for me the *locus classicus* of the aesthetic/non-aesthetic distinction in its respectably analytic version is "Aesthetic Concepts." In fact Sibley's view has been presented and extended in three papers, two major ones and a short response, all of which first appeared in the *Philosophical Review*: "Aesthetic Concepts," "Aesthetic Concepts: A Rejoinder," and "Aesthetic and Nonaesthetic."[1] These are the only papers I shall be drawing on. Since the latest of them, "Aesthetic and Nonaesthetic," Sibley has produced a number of papers, some of which derive from these three, but none of which change the original view.

Outline of Sibley's theory

Abstracting and condensing, to isolate the themes I will be examining, I take Sibley to be making three moves (though, as shall be seen, Sibley does not think of the first as a *move*): (1) invoking an aesthetic/non-aesthetic distinction, (2) asking whether the items thus distinguished are related in certain specific ways, (3) answering that they are not so related. In more detail—(1) The distinction works on many levels, applying at least to qualities, descriptions, judgments, terms, and concepts. Which level Sibley takes as basic or independent is unclear, in spite of the ostensible concern with concepts. (The paper is called "Aesthetic Concepts.") The most natural account I can give of the distinction, consistent with Sibley's intentions but coherent, is this.

An aesthetic quality (or feature) is one which is noted in an aesthetic judgment (or description or remark). An aesthetic judgment is a judgment in which an aesthetic concept is used. An aesthetic concept is a

[1] "Aesthetic Concepts", *Philosophical Review*, Vol. 68, No. 4 (October, 1959); "Aesthetic Concepts: A Rejoinder", ibid., Vol. 72, No. 1 (January, 1963); "Aesthetic and Nonaesthetic", ibid., Vol. 74, No. 2 (April, 1965). Hereafter, to facilitate brief references in the body of the text, these will be referred to by 'AC', 'ACR', and 'AN', respectively.

Shortly after its initial appearance AC was reprinted with the author's "extensive minor revisions" in *Philosophy Looks at the Arts*, edited by Joseph Margolis (New York: Scribner's, 1962). References to AC will cite pages in the Margolis volume, references to ACR and AN will be to the *Philosophical Review*.

concept whose related term—the term used when one applies the concept —is an aesthetic term. An aesthetic term is one whose use (perhaps correct use) requires the possession of taste. Taste is perceptiveness, sensitivity, aesthetic discrimination, aesthetic appreciation. Sibley says that it is "an ability to *notice* or *see* or *tell* that things have certain qualities" (AC, p. 65). Finally, a quality, judgment, concept, or term is non-aesthetic if and only if it is not an aesthetic one.

That Sibley intends something like this quasi-formal apparatus is clear from the opening passages of "Aesthetic Concepts."

> The remarks we make about works of art are of many kinds. . . . We say that a novel has a great number of characters and deals with life in a manufacturing town; that a painting uses pale colors, predominantly blues and greens, and has kneeling figures in the foreground; that the theme in a fugue is inverted at such a point and that there is a stretto at the close; that the action of a play takes place in the span of one day and that there is a reconciliation scene in the fifth act. Such remarks may be made by, and such features pointed out to, anyone with normal eyes, ears, and intelligence. On the other hand, we also say that a poem is tightly-knit or deeply moving; that a picture lacks balance, or has a certain serenity and repose, or that the grouping of the figures sets up an exciting tension; that the characters in a novel never really come to life, or that a certain episode strikes a false note. It would be neutral enough to say that the making of such judgments as these requires the exercise of taste, perceptiveness, or sensitivity, of aesthetic discrimination or appreciation; one would not say this of my first group. Accordingly, when a word or expression is such that taste or perceptiveness is required in order to apply it, I shall call it an *aesthetic* term or expression, and I shall, correspondingly, speak of *aesthetic* concepts or *taste* concepts. (AC, pp. 63–64)

Still, my technical-looking rectified version of Sibley's aesthetic/non-aesthetic distinction requires considerable justification, for there is no way to take it straightforwardly from his text. Most controversial points are non-exegetical, I think, since around them turn various possible defences of Sibley against my criticisms. So, I shall not deal with them until they arise in the course of the argument. There are, however, two points to be mentioned immediately.

(i) The quotation seems to show clearly that the fundamental distinction is between concepts, or at least that concepts are as basic as terms for Sibley, while in my version concepts are ultimately supplanted by terms. I reserve discussion of this until later, when I hope to show that it is a critical matter. Here I simply point out that Sibley is unclear about the relation of terms to concepts as well as about what either a term or a concept is. In a later paper, Sibley alludes to the passages from which the above quotation came, saying, "the distinction I set out to make in the introductory section was between *terms* or *expressions* of two kinds" (ACR, p. 80).

(ii) Whatever the relation of terms to concepts, it seems a mistake to say for Sibley that every aesthetic judgment contains an aesthetic term—

as I do. In ACR, which is addressed to H.R.G. Schwyzer,[2] Sibley complains of just this misinterpretation.

> Nothing I said, that is, implied the doctrine Schwyzer attributes to me, that 'an aesthetic remark always involves the use of an aesthetic term.' Indeed, not only did I suppose it obvious that, as he says, 'the class of remarks *the making of which* requires perceptiveness is different from, indeed far larger than, the class of remarks that contain *words and expressions whose application* requires perceptiveness'; I said so myself at the end of Part I where I pointed out that I had not been discussing 'aesthetic or taste judgments in general' but only 'the more restricted range of judgments which employ aesthetic terms'. (ACR, p. 40)

In the context of this essay my recasting of the distinction is immune to this complaint. It is with regard only to aesthetic judgments which do contain aesthetic terms that Sibley takes a stand, and it is only as such that I will claim that his argument is defective. However, more generally, Sibley and Schwyzer seem to me much too quick to recognize aesthetic judgments which contain no aesthetic terms. They have in mind remarks like 'how very gradually the stem curves' and 'it is a big picture.' It is simple to imagine circumstances in which sensitivity and pedagogical insight are behind these remarks, and yet none of the constituent words seem to require for their successful use what Sibley calls taste. But this is not so clear. I shall be arguing that Sibley has no convincing reason for refusing to call these words aesthetic terms. Until that argument appears, perhaps this will suffice to preserve my rendering of Sibley's distinction; although Sibley (and Schwyzer) seem to use 'term' as roughly interchangeable with 'word' (or 'words'), I am using it in the sense of "open sentence."[3] Thus in any remark of the form 'x is F', 'is F' is a *term*. This being so, it seems clear that a remark is aesthetic only if its term is aesthetic. When this construction becomes contentious I will return to it. So long as attention is confined to those judgments which, according to Sibley, are aesthetic *and* contain aesthetic terms, his terms and my terms (roughly) coincide.

(2) About aesthetic terms Sibley says "I am interested in what they all have in common" (AC, p. 64).

(3) Eleven pages later he announces that he has found it: "I have now argued that in certain ways aesthetic concepts are not and cannot be condition- or rule-governed" (AC, p. 75). (This means that the applicability of an aesthetic concept cannot be inferred, in any of a variety of standard ways, from the applicability of any number of non-aesthetic concepts.)

It should be clear that Sibley's work fits the conception and approach sketched earlier. In his view aesthetic judgments do have truth-values. They are in the ordinary sense, descriptions; their characteristic terms—aesthetic

---

[2] H. R. G. Schwyzer, "Sibley's 'Aesthetic Concepts'", *Philosophical Review*, Vol. 72, No. 1 (January, 1963).

[3] For an account of this use see Willard Van Orman Quine, *Methods of Logic* (New York: Holt, Rinehart and Winston, 1950—revised edition, 1956), sections 12 and 17, especially pp. 64 and 89 ff.

terms—apply to certain properties—aesthetic properties. Since the presence of a particular aesthetic property is never guaranteed by the presence of any given non-aesthetic properties, it follows that neither the applicability of an aesthetic term nor the truth of an aesthetic judgment (which on my view of 'term' comes to the same thing) can be inferred from the applicability of non-aesthetic terms. Only taste will suffice in making aesthetic judgments.

Seen in terms of the sketch Sibley looks like an intuitionist or non-naturalist, if one imports the all too handy categories of meta-meta-ethics, as has been noted by various readers.[4] However his characterization of aesthetic judgments and, correlatively, his conception of "taste" make Sibley's view untypical. He treats aesthetic judgments explicitly without regard to their connection with value or praise. He says,

> About a third and much-discussed class of judgments, however, I have nothing to say in this paper. These are the purely evaluative judgments: whether things are aesthetically good or bad, excellent or mediocre, superior to others or inferior, and so on. Such judgments I shall call *verdicts*. Nor shall I raise any other questions about evaluation: about how verdicts are made or supported, or whether the judgments I am dealing with carry evaluative implications. (AN, p. 136)

Then this is not so much like ethical intuitionists' discussions of 'good' and 'right,' nor is it obviously commensurate with Hume's naturalistic account of beauty so that it might be taken as a straightforward alternative. I will return to this at the end of the essay.

Criticism of Sibley's argument

Sibley's conclusion is that there are and can be no necessary, sufficient or defeasible non-aesthetic conditions for the use of an aesthetic term. He offers a number of observations in support of this, but until just before the conclusion is announced he presents no *argument*. In fact he says, "My arguments and illustrations so far have been rather simply schematic" (AC, p. 71). And so they have, in general coming to statements like these—

> There is little temptation to suppose that aesthetic terms resemble words which, like 'square,' are applied in accordance with a set of necessary and sufficient conditions. For whereas each square is square in virtue of the *same* set of conditions, four equal sides and four right angles, aesthetic terms apply to widely varied objects; one thing is graceful because of these features, another because of those, and so on almost endlessly. (AC, p. 66)

> There are no sufficient conditions, no non-aesthetic features such that the presence of some set of numbers of them will beyond question logically

---

[4] For instance, R. David Broiles in "Frank Sibley's 'Aesthetic Concepts'", *Journal of Aesthetics and Art Criticism*, Vol. 23, No. 2 (Winter, 1964), and Peter Kivy in "Aesthetic Aspects and Aesthetic Qualities", *Journal of Philosophy*, Vol. 65, No. 4 (February 22, 1968).

justify or warrant the application of an aesthetic term. It is impossible (barring certain limited exceptions, . . .) to make any statements corresponding to those we can make for condition-governed words. We are able to say 'If it is true he can do this, and that, and the other, then one just cannot deny that he is intelligent,' or 'if he does A, B, and C, I don't see how it can be denied that he is lazy,' but we cannot make *any* general statement of the form 'If the vase is pale pink, somewhat curving, lightly mottled, and so forth, it will be delicate, cannot but be delicate.' (AC, pp. 67–68)

Although there is this sense in which slimness, lightness, lack of intensity of color, an so on, count only towards, not against, delicacy, these features, I shall say, at best count only *typically* or *characteristically* towards delicacy; they do not count towards in the same sense as condition-features count toward laziness or intelligence; that is, no group of them is even logically sufficient. (AC, p. 69)

The very notion of a defeasible concept seems to require that some group of features *would* be sufficient *in certain circumstances*, that is, in the absence of overriding or voiding features. In a certain way defeasible concepts lack sufficient conditions then, but they are still, in the sense described, condition-governed. My claim about taste concepts is stronger; that they are not, except negatively, governed by conditions at all. We could not conclude even in certain circumstances, e.g., if we were told of the absence of all 'voiding' or uncharacteristic features (no angularities and the like), that an object *must* certainly be graceful, no matter how fully it was described to us as possessing features characteristic of gracefulness. (AC, p. 71)

The obvious way to quarrel with these remarks is to produce a counterexample. I have none. Indeed I do not say that they are wrong (though I expect to show that they are vacuous). I note only that they are, as Sibley says, simply schematic, and pass on to what seems to me Sibley's only real argument. Perhaps Sibley does not regard this as an argument at all; he calls it a reinforcement of his argument. However, I believe it schematizes all the argument Sibley has, and it will do to show that there is no arguing, only a kind of running in place.

The point I have argued may be reinforced in the following way. A man who failed to realize the nature of aesthetic concepts, or someone who, knowing he lacked sensitivity in aesthetic matters, did not want to reveal this lack might by assiduous application and shrewd observation provide himself with some rules and generalizations; and by inductive procedures and intelligent guessing, he might frequently say the right things. But he could have no great confidence or certainty; a slight change in an object might at any time unpredictably ruin his calculations, and he might as easily have been wrong as right. No matter how careful he has been about working out a set of consistent principles and conditions, he is only in a position to think that the object is very possibly delicate. . . . Though he sometimes says the right thing, he has not seen, but guessed, that the object is delicate. (AC, pp. 72–73)

Again, I do not say that Sibley is wrong, but that he has said nothing (new). To show this concisely it will help to use some symbols.

Let 'E' be an aesthetic term naming the aesthetic quality E-ness.

Let 'N$_1$,' 'N$_2$,' . . . , and 'N$_n$' be non-aesthetic terms naming the non-aesthetic qualities N$_1$-ness, N$_2$-ness, . . . , and N$_n$-ness.

There are four distinct relations to consider.

(1) 'E' means (or means the same as) 'N$_1$ and N$_2$ and . . . and N$_n$.'

(2) The meaning of 'E' is carried in (or is contained in) the meaning of 'N$_1$ and N$_2$ and . . . and N$_n$.'

I do not claim to have an account of "meaning," "containment of meaning," etc., nor that there is an account. It will be clear that this is not an important matter.

(3) (x) (Ex $\equiv$. N$_1$ & N$_2$ & . . . & N$_n$). (Things are E if and only if they are N$_1$ and N$_2$ and . . . N$_n$.)

(4) (x) (N$_1$ & N$_2$ & . . . & N$_n$ $\supset$ E). (Anything which is N$_1$ & N$_2$ & . . . & N$_n$ is also E.)

With this in hand, let us argue.

Since taste is required to detect E-ness but not to detect any of N$_1$-ness, . . . , N$_n$-ness—(for that is exactly the difference between aesthetic and non-aesthetic terms)—it follows immediately that,

From the fact that someone can apply all of 'N$_1$', . . . , 'N$_n$' we cannot infer that he can detect E-ness.

That seems to be Sibley's point. But he must intend more, because it remains possible that,

From the fact that 'N$_1$', . . . , 'N$_n$' apply we can infer that 'E' applies.

Why? Because it may happen that E-ness always accompanies the joint presence of N$_1$-ness and . . . and N$_n$-ness. That is, it may be that (4) or even (3) is true and is known to be true. It is senseless to suppose that (1) or (2) be true but not be known to be true, and perhaps both (1) and (2) must be false, as Sibley would have it. But the truth of (4), or even of (3), requires the truth of neither (1) or (2). Then Sibley's argument is inadequate.

The point is simple, but perhaps too simple to be appreciated easily, for it is startling to find it undercutting Sibley's argument. An illustration of the point in a parallel example is helpful.

Suppose that all cylindrical objects are red, that Smith knows this, and that Smith is blind. Now Smith can tell that something is red even though Smith can't detect redness and even though 'red' and 'cylindrical' are unconnected in meaning. Sibley's position is that of citing the existence of Smith as a proof, or a reinforcement of a proof, that not all cylinders are red. That is, Smith "has not seen" that the object is red. But what point could this reinforce?—beyond the claim that Smith is blind?[5]

One might feel like saying that after all Smith only guesses or predicts that a given cylinder is red because in fact it might not be red. Then suppose that cylinders have to be red, that it is a law of nature that cylin-

---

[5] This parallel illustration is hard to keep a grip on. Perhaps it is of help to have the analogy laid out. Being blind: Being without taste; 'Red': An aesthetic term; 'Cylindrical': A non-aesthetic term.

ders are red. This puts it in order, I suppose, to aver that if such were the case, 'cylindrical' and 'red' might not be altogether unconnected in meaning. No matter: the point remains that the existence, or imaginability, of a blind man is not—as things stand—proof that some cylinders are not red.

Another possible rejoinder is that Smith can't fit the description, can't tell that something is red, because being blind Smith can't know the meaning of 'red.' Whether or not there is any reason to believe that "acquaintance" with something is a necessary condition of knowing the meaning of a term which applies to that thing, the point can be made irrelevant. Amend the example so that Smith occasionally has seen, and seen red things, but in this case doesn't see that the object is red. (This could be because Smith has only recently gone blind, or perhaps he is not blind but the object is poorly lit or too far away.) Then why deny that Smith can tell that 'red' applies though he does not detect (see) any redness?

Sibley can be rescued—and I should like him to be rescued—in this way. Let 'apply E' and 'detect E-ness' be interchangeable. This will make it true that,

From the fact that 'N$_1$', . . . , 'N$_n$' apply, it does not follow that 'E' applies.

This is Sibley's conclusion: 'E' is not condition-governed. But the maneuver which gets there, construing being able to apply 'E' as being able to detect E-ness, is of no help to Sibley, for it leaves us with this:

To apply an aesthetic term is to detect an aesthetic quality; it takes taste to do this.

To apply a non-aesthetic term does not require taste, only normality (whether or not one must detect N$_1$-ness in order to apply 'N$_1$').

Now we can say that being able to apply non-aesthetic terms never guarantees that one can apply aesthetic terms; but we can say this because—and only because,

From the fact that one is normal it does not follow that one has taste.

Or, to be more exact,

From the fact that one is exercising one's normal capacities it does not follow that one is exercising taste.

This is an unhappy but telling form for Sibley's conclusion, for it is nothing but the aesthetic/non-aesthetic distinction itself. If there were no difference between exercising one's taste and exercising one's (merely) normal capacities, there would have been no difference between aesthetic and non-aesthetic terms.

This argument against Sibley is oblique and it may be misleading. I must not be taken to be advancing "naturalism" as against Sibley's "intuitionism." I have not shown that Sibley is wrong in denying that aesthetic judgments can be inferred from non-aesthetic ones, if this would be to show that they can be inferred. One may conceive all these petrified views—naturalism, property-intuitionism, rule-intuitionism, etc.—as answers to one question: How, if at all, are aesthetic and non-aesthetic judgments, concepts, or terms related to one another? What I wish to do, if not to bury this question, is at least to divest it of its innocence. To this end I have now made clear that whatever Sibley has *shown* was shown in the drawing of the aesthetic/non-aesthetic distinction and only reflected in the putative argument following the appearance of the distinction.

Criticism of Sibley's distinction

To rehearse: Suppose in discussing a painting someone refers to one of its lines, saying 'That line is curved,' and later adds 'That line is graceful.' The latter is an aesthetic judgment, the former is not. Why? Because only the latter (or its making) is the application of an aesthetic concept, the use of an aesthetic term. How does one tell? By noting that 'graceful' is an aesthetic term while 'curved' is not. Which is to say that taste is required to apply 'graceful' but no more than normal eyes and intelligence is required to apply 'curved.'

That is the aesthetic/non-aesthetic distinction at work, identifying judgments like 'That is graceful' and thereby sorting out what Sibley calls the "subject matter" of aesthetics (AN, p. 135). It is not itself part of aesthetics, on Sibley's view; rather, drawing it is a precondition of beginning aesthetics. If the preceding section of this essay succeeded, then what Sibley does after invoking the distinction is ignorable: the distinction itself is all the philosophy Sibley has and it is the ultimate cause of whatever uneasiness one feels with Sibley's position. How does one "attack" this distinction (or any other)? Only, I think, by showing that it does nothing—in particular, that it does not do what is demanded of it in its context.

One thing the distinction should do (according to my rectified version of it) is to identify a given judgment as aesthetic or non-aesthetic by discerning the presence or absence of aesthetic terms. I think the distinction fails to do this, or even to begin to do this, for there seems to me no sensible and important way of dividing terms according to whether taste or only normality is needed to apply them. (One may think that "sense" and "importance" are not definite enough notions to underwrite a critique. I had thought of supplanting them with the technical notion of an effective procedure, and then criticizing Sibley for supplying nothing remotely like even a quasi-mechanical routine. But this would be a mistake. Sibley is altogether unspecific about the nature of the distinction and its application. My leaving the terms of appraisal vague seems fairer and more generous to Sibley, and it allows me to encompass some efforts to rescue the distinction. And finally, it is the burden of this essay to persuade you that Sibley's distinction has become far too prominent and that its sense (and sensibility) have been too readily acknowledged.)

With regard to the application of the distinction Sibley acknowledges "the expected debatable, ambiguous, or borderline cases" (AN, p. 135). But I cannot see that he has any clearcut cases. Take 'graceful,' to start, which is one of the words which, according to Sibley, "whether in artistic or daily discourse, function only or predominantly as aesthetic terms" (AC, p. 64). Suppose I show this figure and ask which is the graceful line, or whether any is a graceful line. No doubt you have taste, but do you need it? Virtual insensitivity will do, I think, to manage '(c) is the graceful one' or '(c) is graceful' or '(c) is more graceful than (a) or (b).'

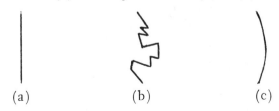

(a)   (b)   (c)

If you are unsatisfied with my figure you must make your own. Keep in mind that the aim is not to make (c) better than the others, nor is it to make (c) more likeable. Good and bad, and likes and dislikes have nothing to do with the conception of taste as used in drawing the distinction. Taste is more than normal ability to notice or detect things. Taste is required to notice gracefulness (and so to use the aesthetic term 'graceful'). I ask you to produce an example in which '(c) is graceful' is accessible upon a merely normal view. This may seem to beg the question against Sibley but I think it does not. It is to take the question seriously, disingenuously, pre-theoretically: is it always the case with 'graceful' that taste is needed to apply it? I say no.

Sibley would say, perhaps, that in such an example '(c) is graceful' is not an aesthetic judgment. Then what about 'graceful?' There are answers at Sibley's disposal. One, which seems to me painfully clumsy, is that 'graceful' is a term associated with (at least) two concepts, the aesthetic concept $graceful_a$ and the non-aesthetic concept $graceful_n$. Sibley says that, given the definition of 'aesthetic term' he "shall, correspondingly, speak of *aesthetic* concepts" (AC, p. 64). About the correspondence between terms and concepts Sibley says nothing; perhaps he would say that 'graceful' can correspond to either of (at least) two concepts. Then he could hold that '(c) is graceful' is a non-aesthetic judgment with 'graceful' a non-aesthetic term being used to apply the non-aesthetic concept $graceful_n$.

To this one may object that it renders the distinction inoperative. It is no longer possible to identify aesthetic judgments by noting the presence of aesthetic terms, for there is no way of noting aesthetic terms by inspection. I prefer to object that no legitimate reason has been given for claiming that 'graceful' has two concepts or senses. What motivation is there for multiplying the senses of 'graceful' beyond a desire to preserve the aesthetic/non-aesthetic distinction? I am not raising those involuted questions about meaning which require technical accounts of polysemy backed by a "theory of meaning." What is wanted (and, I think, is lacking) is an informal rationale for identifying extra concepts for 'graceful.' What *reason* is there for distinguishing *graceful*$_a$ and *graceful*$_n$? They are distinguished so far, in this hypothetical response on Sibley's behalf, by the fact that only one of them requires taste for its application. Is that sufficient? Shall we say that whenever an otherwise ordinary term is used in a context in which more than normal competence is needed to handle the term, the term has changed its meaning or been affixed to a different concept? Although I think the general answer to this question is clear, it is a vexed question even when taken informally. Since it will recur in this essay, it may be helpful to take time now to consider a battery of illustrations.

*

First, consider some terms which can be managed readily on the strength of normal intelligence, eyes, etc., but whose use on occasion signals more than mere normality. (I shall be claiming that this description fits virtually all of Sibley's aesthetic terms.)

The terms applying to a variety of racial, geographical, and sexual groups of people are common, and are learned and used by everyone. Some observers, however, are much more accurate than others at recognizing members of these groups. They can tell on sight, by attending to people's size, shape, posture, gestures, gait, etc., Jews, Northern Europeans, homosexuals, New Yorkers, etc. Phonetic descriptions are a special case. Some professional linguists and many amateurs with good ears can identify East Texans, Canadians, native Bavarians, etc., by hearing them speak English.

Another auditory case is pitch, in music. Regardless of what minimal ability one supposes could be cultivated in any normal person, beyond that there are differences in abilities to "hear" absolute and relative pitch, to identify pitches in chord constructions, etc.

Handwriting identification is, visually, a partial analogue. A handwriting expert can identify signatures and match writing samples with far more facility than those with no more than normal intelligence and eyes.

It is helpful to consider some terms all of whose uses are relatively esoteric. Some examples are medical terms applied to patients after examination, i.e. the names of diseases, syndromes, "conditions," etc. A few doctors, the best internists, are much better than their colleagues at detecting, say, diabetes and hypoglycemia. From external examinations they obtain results nearly as accurate as those obtained by lesser diagnosticians aided by laboratory analysis.

*

The fact that these examples may involve terms which apply to properties which are not purely perceptual is irrelevant. Sibley's examples of aesthetic terms include ones which refer to qualities not literally seen or heard (e.g., 'tightly-knit,' said of a poem; 'has characters who never really come to life,' said of a novel). (A relevant passage from Sibley is quoted above, p. 115f.)

Also irrelevant, but probably harder to ignore, is the fact that the examples involve terms which, allegedly unlike 'graceful,' seem clearly to be condition-governed. But being unconditioned is not what makes 'graceful' an aesthetic term. Sibley first sorts out aesthetic terms and then argues that these terms are unconditioned. We have seen that the argument goes nowhere beyond the distinction, and we are now back at the beginning, looking into Sibley's way of sorting out aesthetic terms. Taking Sibley literally, 'graceful' is an aesthetic term—whether or not it is condition-governed—because taste is needed to apply it. In response to the suggested counter-example ('(c) is graceful') one might look for two concepts to go with 'graceful.' The budget of cases just gone through is meant to illustrate an implausibility in that response.

The cases mainly concern terms—'Jew,' 'East Texan,' 'G-sharp,' 'written by Lincoln'—whose use frequently requires no special capacity, but whose use in the examples is effected by means of special capacities and talents (something beyond mere normality). The (rhetorical) question is, shall we say that in these examples the terms are being used to apply different concepts?

It may be suggested that the fact that these terms have conditions, perhaps even necessary and sufficient ones, renders the examples defective. The argument would be that each of the terms does have two senses, the proof being that in their ordinary use one applies them with reference to their defining conditions, while this does not happen when they are used by a specialist in difficult cases. This suggestion is mistaken, but it has an interesting twist.

The mistake is, simply, to conflate unreasonably the meaning of a term and the way in which—in some actual case—someone decides whether to apply it. 'Square' does not change its meaning when I apply it to a figure without measuring the sides. Surely the brilliant diagnostician and the routine laboratory worker are not using 'diabetes' to apply different concepts. Knowing the meaning of a term is not a guarantee of being able to decide whether it correctly applies nor is inability to tell whether a term applies a proof of ignorance of the term's meaning.

However, if the suggestion were acceptable it would have an unwanted effect on Sibley's argument. All aesthetic terms, including 'graceful,' are non-condition-governed, Sibley argues. Then if alteration in the conditions governing application of a term—in general, or in particular cases—were the sign of a multiplicity of concepts associated with the term, this would be of no help in urging that 'graceful' is associated with more than one concept.

I conclude that Sibley has no reason to discount '(c) is graceful' (as a counter-example to 'graceful's' being an aesthetic term) by claiming that it is the application of $graceful_n$, for I see no reason to suppose that there is a $graceful_n$ (or a $graceful_a$).

A simpler, more direct response, in Sibley's interest, is that 'graceful' is indeed an aesthetic term but that aesthetic terms can appear in non-aesthetic judgments, as, for example, 'graceful' appears in '(c) is graceful.'

This response obviously ruins the program for identifying aesthetic and non-aesthetic judgments by the presence or absence of aesthetic terms. That is a minor objection. The decisive objection is not that the distinction ceases to function, but that it functions inconsistently. Sibley says that both judgments and terms are to be defined as aesthetic by means of the "Is-taste-required?" test. Since a non-aesthetic judgment can be made without exercising taste, but an aesthetic term cannot be applied without exercising taste, it follows that if 'graceful' is an aesthetic term then making the judgment that (c) is graceful both does and does not require taste.

No doubt Sibley would deal with '(c) is graceful' in neither of the ways just discussed, but it is hard to see what response, right or wrong, he would find congenial. His most relevant remark occurs in a footnote. He says,

> I shall speak loosely of an 'aesthetic term,' even when, because the word sometimes has other uses, it would be more correct to speak of its *use* as an aesthetic term. (AC, p. 64, n. 1)

This suggests that there are times when one might speak of an aesthetic term and not be speaking loosely. This would occur, presumably, when one were speaking of a term whose use invariably requires taste. I doubt that there are any such terms, whatever taste is; and I am fairly certain that there are no such terms when the notion of taste is the one Sibley uses.

Two aspects of the notion of taste are expressly removed from consideration by Sibley (though he does not deny that they would come up in a more complete analysis of taste). The first is taste as it has to do with likes and dislikes, the second is taste as it has to do with good and bad.[6] Taste, as that which is exercised in the use of an aesthetic term, is "an ability to *notice* or *see* or *tell* that things have certain qualities" (AC, p. 65). Whether this constricts or distorts the notion of taste, and how that affects one's notion of the relative complexity of the apprehension of art works, is an implicit theme throughout his essay, and it will become explicit shortly. Here I want only to get clear about what one of Sibley's aesthetic terms would be like if there were one. If there are any, they are terms whose (successful) application invariably requires an "ability to notice" which is something more than the abilities that go with normal intelligence and sense organs. I said that I think there are no such terms. My reason is simply that I seem to be able to find, for any given term (or at least any of the terms Sibley considers), an application of it which could be managed by any normal man. I doubt that this reason will convince you straightway (though I have no idea what other reason could be given). You have to think it over until you agree that something like what I did with 'graceful'—or what you did to satisfy yourself about 'graceful'—can be done with any term. But what Sibley means by 'taste' must be kept in mind or it may not be clear when a "non-aesthetic" use has been found. I believe Sibley himself may have overlooked this.

Sibley says that 'lovely,' 'pretty,' 'beautiful,' 'dainty,' 'graceful,' and

---

[6] "When I speak of taste in this paper, I shall not be dealing with questions which center upon expressions like 'a matter of taste' (meaning, roughly, a matter of personal preference or liking)" (AC, p. 65). For his extrusion of questions of evaluation, see his remark quoted above.

'elegant' "are certainly not being used metaphorically when employed as aesthetic terms, the very good reason being that this is their primary or only use, some of them having no current non-aesthetic use" (AC, p. 65). That is, at least some of these terms are—*strictly speaking*—aesthetic terms.

We have dealt with 'graceful.' The others seem no more difficult. Can't you imagine situations in which it would be natural, easy, and obvious to say—'It's a lovely day today;' 'This glove is too big; you have a rather dainty hand;' 'He's an elegant old gentleman;' 'The sun has finally broken through and now the sky is pretty;' 'I couldn't see the vessels clearly on the last one, but this earthworm is a beautiful specimen.'

Do you insist that taste is required to make these judgments? (In fact, do you feel like calling them aesthetic judgments at all?) Why? Remember that whether the speaker is expressing personal satisfaction or gratification and whether he is evaluating or ranking things are irrelevant. Perhaps in the situation you imagine the speaker of 'It's a lovely day' is clearly happy about it and in addition is lauding the climate and ranking this day above others. Those features of the utterance seem to me the only ones which make it even faintly plausible to call it an aesthetic judgment. But those features are irrelevant (as is the fact—if you think it is one—that 'lovely' is not condition-governed, that the speaker couldn't *prove* that the day is lovely). From none of these features does it follow that what Sibley calls an aesthetic judgment has been made. The only question is whether *taste* has been exercised, and it needn't have been if normal intelligence and senses are enough. I don't see why they should not be enough.

What difference does this make in the intelligibility of the aesthetic/non-aesthetic distinction? This: if no term invariably requires taste for its application, then what, after all, is an *aesthetic* term? Is it a term which usually requires taste for its application? Then what of Sibley's formula for speaking correctly (not loosely) of such a term. We are, he says, to speak of a term's *use* as an aesthetic term. That, now, will be to speak of a term's being used as a term which is usually used as an aesthetic term. A minor objection to this version of the distinction is, again, that it will not support the program for identifying aesthetic judgments by picking out aesthetic terms. The major objection this time is not that the distinction functions inconsistently, but that it functions not at all: it will pick out nothing as an aesthetic term.

Before giving up on Sibley's version of the aesthetic/non-aesthetic distinction we must consider two final, meager, efforts to rescue it.

In the footnote quoted from above, Sibley says something which suggests that, speaking more correctly, the aesthetic/non-aesthetic distinction is to be made out with regard, not to terms, but to the "uses" of terms (AC, p. 64, n. 1; quoted above, p. 17). Could we say that on certain occasions the use of (some) terms manifests an exercise of taste, and thereby effect a distinction between aesthetic and non-aesthetic uses? Perhaps—though to what point I don't know, but in any case this subverts Sibley's program. All the talk of terms, judgments, descriptions, remarks, and concepts becomes idle at best. There are no terms which are always used in that way, and, I think, there are none that are never used in that way. Part of the spirit of Schwyzer's objection is right, after all (though he has left himself open to Sibley's rebuttal). He says,

> Sibley's preoccupation with words (both aesthetic and non-aesthetic) and their uses, and the features to which they allegedly 'apply,' has led him to lose sight of the nature of actual critical utterances.[7]

If we turn from terms to terms-as-they-are-used-in-specific circumstances, or some such, then can we identify a class of performances, actual utterances, which are exhibitions of taste? If so, then it will be not that 'graceful' is an aesthetic term, but that the use of 'graceful' upon some occasion is an aesthetic use. There will also be non-aesthetic uses. There is no reason to call these *other* uses in any but a numerical sense. Still, is there now a serviceable aesthetic/non-aesthetic distinction? It will not serve Sibley's purposes, for he wants to isolate and then discuss more abstract things than particular actual uses of terms. And indeed it is only about terms considered generally that his question about conditions is sensible. We can ask, Why does Churchill call Mussolini a utensil? but we can't ask, What are the necessary and sufficient conditions for applying 'utensil' to Mussolini as opposed to applying 'utensil' in general?

Schwyzer's criticism fails to get deep enough, I think, because in spite of his aversion to classifying words, he is willing to classify, and to accept Sibley's formula for going about it. He agrees, that is, that

> the distinction between aesthetic and non-aesthetic discourse is clearly to be located in the area of what we can and cannot say given normal eyesight, normal hearing, normal intelligence . . .[8]

Classifying discourse is as problematic as classifying terms. In either case the conception of taste does the work. Whatever defects have been uncovered in Sibley's distinction, it will be good to take up this conception in examining one last possible defense of the distinction.

The '(c) is graceful' judgment and all the others might be met head on: one might insist that 'graceful' and the others are aesthetic terms as defined by Sibley, that these judgments are aesthetic judgments and that they can be made by any normal speaker because any normal speaker will have taste enough to do so. Sibley does say that "almost everybody is able to exercise taste to some degree and in some matters" (AC, p. 65).

This reply fails, I think, because it places on Sibley's conception of taste more weight than it can bear. A distinction is now forced between being a merely normal man and exercising one's merely normal capacities. The fact that the most pedestrian observer can manage '(c) is graceful' shows nothing; the question remains, does he in judging that (c) is graceful make use of more than "normal eyes and intelligence"? I do not know what to make of this question. I am prepared to claim (or to repeat) that

---

[7] Schwyzer, op. cit., p. 75.
[8] Ibid., p. 75.

Sibley has given no reason to suppose that an extra perceptivity is required —or used—in making the judgment. Why suppose that?

Again I point out that the presence or absence of conditions governing this, or any, use of 'graceful' is irrelevant. It is especially likely that one will begin to think of the possibility of stating conditions when the issue concerns the relative ease with which terms can be mastered. That is, it is tempting to suppose that some terms are learned and used readily because there are clear (perhaps necessary and sufficient) conditions to be learned; and conversely, that when conditions can be given, the terms are readily mastered. This is probably, in general, an error. Sibley says, "We do not apply simple color words by following rules or in accordance with principles" (AC, p. 77). Surely he is right. Even if such words do have necessary and sufficient conditions, this is not what accounts for the ease with which they are mastered. On the other hand, various esoteric terms like 'primitive recursive function,' 'quadrature of a parabola,' and 'abelian group' obviously do have necessary and sufficient conditions, having been introduced in terms of such conditions, and yet their fully competent use exceeds the competence of many people. A bothersome point here is that examples of mathematical terms are examples of terms whose necessary and sufficient conditions are themselves stated in mathematical terms, so that inability to master, say, 'primitive recursive function' is likely to be accompanied by an inability to master 'value of a function,' etc.; while the conditions ostensibly sought for aesthetic terms are non-aesthetic conditions. This point must simply be ignored, for it is the intelligibility of the aesthetic/non-aesthetic distinction itself which is at issue; and I mean only to remind you of the irrelevance of the question of conditions (of any kind) in appraising that distinction. The distinction must be sensible antecedently. If the question of conditions is to be part of the initial characterization of aesthetic terms, then, as has been seen in the preceding section, the subsequent argument is aimless. But still, the distinction remains unclear. We shall now need a way of picking aesthetic terms out of the class of non-condition-governed terms, and this will lead us back to taste. Aesthetic terms will be those unconditioned terms whose use requires taste.

And so, what about taste? How are we to decide whether some judgment requires only normal eyes, ears, etc., or more, when any normal observer can make the judgment? I sympathize with anyone trying to give a convincing answer. It would be understandable if Sibley were to fall back on our sense that there is a difference, whether or not we can mark it. However, I do not share this sense, and I have little sympathy for anyone trying to construct a "theory" atop the distinction if it's drawn in this way.

On the strength of this and the preceding section, I conclude (1) that his aesthetic/non-aesthetic distinction is the soul of Sibley's view, and (2) that that distinction comes to nothing. If this conclusion seems hasty, perhaps the next section will help, where the question of what to require of a "distinction" is met more directly.

Discussion of the distinction in general

Before attempting some cautious generalizations about the aesthetic/non-aesthetic distinction I would like to fend off a misunderstanding to which my view seems susceptible. I do not claim (nor do I think) that the word 'aesthetic' is meaningless or ambiguous or vague. I am not asking to extrude the word from ordinary talk, or even from philosophical talk. Here are some sample remarks which, whether or not they are true, are understandable; and I have no reason or wish to ask that they not be made. (i) 'Some proofs, though not defective on strictly formal grounds, are objectionable on aesthetic grounds: they are inelegant.' (ii) 'One must resist treating the Mass as an occasion for an aesthetic experience, for this will likely preclude a religious response.' (iii) 'In the first part of *Either/Or* Kierkegaard is exhibiting what it is to be a man for whom all the world's objects—including people—are aesthetic objects.' (iv) 'Our traditional way of approaching paintings is exactly what comes between us and much of contemporary art. This, now classical, aestheticizing compromises one's response, and destroys one's chances with a work which will submit to nothing but a perfectly human approach.'

These remarks are intelligible; one can understand them, argue over them, etc.; and it isn't clear how some of them could be supplanted by substitutes devoid of 'aesthetic.' What follows from that? Nothing much, I think, and certainly not that people who say such things are committed to anything like the existence of a definition of 'aesthetic' which would underwrite an aesthetic/non-aesthetic distinction. (An irony: if there were such things as Sibley's aesthetic terms, 'aesthetic' might well be one.)

Then what of the distinction? I am not *against* it as, so to speak, a matter of principle, because I cannot see what point—or sense—there could be in saying I reject it (or I accept it)—period. There is a time to say something, and that is when the distinction is being used and it matters how far we are willing to be led. I have shown that when Sibley uses the distinction we have gone the whole route if we fail to balk at the outset. This is not because of some simple blunder of Sibley's. If he has begged an important question, it is not the ostensible question, Is the applicability of non-aesthetic terms ever sufficient to justify applying an aesthetic term? —though that question was dealt with in the asking. What has been begged is the question of raising that question, and that involves a complex of questions about what the world is like, what art is like, and what it's like to come to terms with either. It is not Sibley's conclusion but his approach which is deep, and this is especially dangerous because that approach not only looks innocuous but is explicitly presented by Sibley as pre-philosophical trivia. Thus he seems to me disingenuous when he says,

> I make this broad distinction by means of *examples* of judgments, qualities, and expressions. There is, it seems to me, no need to defend the distinction.

. . . Those who in their theoretical moments deny any such distinction usually show in their practice that they can make it quite adequately. (AN, p. 135)

This will not do, for these are theoretical moments. Summing up the first section of "Aesthetic Concepts," Sibley says,

Without a detailed comparison we cannot see in what particular way *aesthetic* judgments are not 'mechanical,' or how they differ from those other judgments, nor can we begin to specify what taste is. This I have attempted. It is a characteristic and essential feature of judgments which employ an aesthetic term that they cannot be made by appealing, in the sense explained, to non-aesthetic conditions. This, I believe, is a logical feature of aesthetic or taste judgments in general, though I have argued it here only as regards the more restricted range of judgments which employ aesthetic terms. It is part of what 'taste' means. (AC, p. 76)

These seem to be theoretical remarks concerning the nature of "aesthetic language," and I have been trying to show that the arguments supporting these remarks require that the underlying aesthetic/non-aesthetic distinction be at least relatively unproblematic. Even granting that one makes, or can make, the distinction in practice—which I do not grant—Sibley's claim that no further defense is needed warrants the (irresistible) reply, That may be well and good in practice but it seems not to work in theory. Before looking at distinctions, theoretical ones and also those obviously exemplified in one's practice, I want to try to take seriously Sibley's claim about one's practice. What does this mean, that one shows in one's practice that one can make the aesthetic/non-aesthetic distinction? That one uses 'aesthetic' is not enough, nor would it help if one also used 'non-aesthetic' (which no one does).

What Sibley means, I think, is that most people (or perhaps most people who have much taste) could, upon being given a series of terms, descriptions, or judgments, sort them into two groups, the aesthetic ones and the non-aesthetic ones, and that with some exceptions the groupings would be the same. Is this so? We can imagine two ways of getting started.

(1) The person is given two sheets of paper, both blank except for *aesthetic* and *non-aesthetic* written in as headings. We give him instructions: "You are to enter on the first list any term whose use requires taste. Taste is an ability to. . . . All other terms go on the second list."

I cannot accept this procedure, obviously, for I have been arguing for several pages that the given instructions are not going to produce the desired results, if indeed they produce anything at all. Perhaps it is better, and clearer, here, to object to the procedure on the grounds that the assumption that it might be implemented begs the question—regardless of what results would ensue. I say that I cannot get a grip on the notion that some terms require taste and others do not. That means that I cannot receive and use the given instructions. If this brings us to a point at which it is simply Sibley's sense that the instructions are clear and usable against my inability to find this sense, then we are at an impasse. After sketching a second way of getting started, I will try to swing the issue my way by imagining more concretely the use of the distinction in practice.

There is a feeling that the first way of getting started somehow takes too much for granted, because instead of straightforwardly resting the burden of this distinction on common practice it first indoctrinates that practice with the distinction itself. This feeling might be relieved by imagining a procedure reminiscent of one suggested by Katz in his effort to reconstitute the analytic/synthetic distinction.[9]

(2) The person is given two sheets of paper, headed *aesthetic* and *non-aesthetic*, each containing the first few entries in a list. Each begins with the terms that Sibley has already sorted for us. Under *aesthetic* are 'lovely,' 'pretty,' 'beautiful,' 'dainty,' etc.; under *non-aesthetic* are 'red,' 'noisy,' 'brackish,' etc.[10] We give the person instructions: "Go on making these two lists." We might add that what we mean is that he is to continue the lists in conformity with the rule obviously employed, or exhibited, in their beginnings.

What will happen? I submit that the subject will have no idea how to proceed. What if 'noisy' were not on either initial list and when he came to 'noisy' he happened to think not of pneumatic drills but of a section of some Mahler symphony? Or what if he came to 'flat' and thought of a Mondrian?[11]

Perhaps you feel like saying: why not stop this pussyfooting, this pseudo-philosophical by-play, with the distinction without examples or examples without the distinction; Sibley is not doing technical philosophy of language, he is presenting a simple, obvious fact in the informal tone appropriate to such a right-minded announcement. This is not a novel objection. In coming to my view of the distinction (that there is none worth drawing), I have often felt that I was being perverse, raising niggling points of unimportant detail. But no longer. I can find no other way to show that there is no sensible and important way of dividing terms in line with Sibley's aesthetic/non-aesthetic distinction. Sibley says,

> Once examples have been given to illustrate it [the distinction], I believe almost anyone could continue to place further examples—barring of course the expected debatable, ambiguous, or borderline cases—in one category or the other. (AN, p. 135)

Let us try, try it with ourselves. We combine ways (1) and (2): we tell ourselves what Sibley says taste is, we illustrate for ourselves the necessity, or lack of it, of using taste with reference to any of Sibley's examples we find convincing, and then we try to go on. Try going on with these terms.

[9] See Jerrold J. Katz, "Some Remarks on Quine or Analyticity", *The Journal of Philosophy*, vol. 64 (1967), pp. 36–52.
[10] See AC, pp. 64–65 for Sibley's examples.
[11] Paul Ziff has intriguing remarks on the significance of flatness in Mondrian in his "Reasons in Art Criticism", first published in *Philosophy and Education*, edited by Israel Scheffler (Boston: Allyn and Bacon, Inc., 1958), and reprinted in Ziff's self-anthology *Philosophic Turnings* (Ithaca: Cornell University Press, 1966).

allegorical
baroque
by Beethoven
  (in the style of
  Beethoven)
Christian
classical
climactic
colorful
daring
derivative
didactic
dissonant
funny
geometrical
Gothic
  (Île-de-France
  Gothic)
ideological
impressionist
  (impressionistic)

introspective
Kafkaësque
linear
lyrical
mechanical
metaphysical
modernist
moralistic
murky
muted
nationalistic
obscene
painterly
philosophical
poetic
pompous
popular
powerful
pretentious
realist
  (realistic)

religious
restful
rhythmic
riddle canon
Romanesque
romantic
sad
sentimental
serious
sincere
soothing
suggestive
surrealist
  (surrealistic)
suspenseful
symbolist
  (symbolistic,
  symbolical)
youthful

These terms were collected, not at random, but not with malice or contrivance either. They are terms used in talking about art works (and other things). How do you class them—aesthetic or non-aesthetic? It is important to imagine as fully as possible contexts for their use. (In cases where a term is accompanied by related terms in parentheses, try imagining cases where all the terms will do, and then where one will do but not the other.) An inexperienced listener mismanages 'by Beethoven,' withholding it from Beethoven's *First Symphony* and applying 'by Haydn' instead. Is that a failure of taste? The fact that by 'Beethoven' does not apply to a "property-of-the-the-work," if that fact can be made out, is irrelevant, I think. The issue concerns only the correct use of terms. We can avoid the problem by looking at 'in the style of Beethoven.' Not everything by Beethoven is Beethovian, nor is everything in the style of Beethoven by Beethoven. What is required to apply 'in the style of Beethoven' to various works of Lizst and Brahms? Obviously some training or informed experience is needed. But what is that: the development of taste or the directed training of one's normal faculties? What kind of question is this? I want to say not that it is a hard question, but that it is a phony. To suppose that it must "in principle" have an answer is to ask to be smitten with a theory.

There is little point in my going on about these terms. At best I can help in imagining cases in which the aesthetic/non-aesthetic distinction becomes tortured. ('Stevens is metaphysical' seems harder than 'Donne is metaphysical' which is harder than 'Donne is Metaphysical.' Is this a diminution in a term's "taste component"?) So I assert, but can only nudge you to accept, that we do not show in our practice that we make or can make Sibley's distinction.

Let us forget Sibley for a while and try to work on the aesthetic/non-aesthetic distinction in general. As the mention of Katz foreshadowed, we are led inevitably to consider the aesthetic/non-aesthetic distinction with reference to the most celebrated debate over a distinction in recent times—namely, Quine vs. nearly everyone on the analytic/synthetic distinction.[12] Since 1951, when "Two Dogmas of Empiricism" first appeared, the debate itself has become nearly an autonomous topic within professional philosophy, with a variety of writers entering on both sides, and, characteristically, a certain inner group specializing in reporting what the debate is really about, what Quine was really up to, etc. I hope to avoid entangling the aesthetic/non-aesthetic distinction and my qualms about it in this debate. It would be good, though, to "locate" the aesthetic/non-aesthetic distinction relative to the analytic/synthetic distinction, and it will be helpful to be able to refer to one aspect of Quine's attack.

Among putatively exhaustive distinctions there are two relatively clear classes. There are purely technical distinctions, like the distinction between finite and infinite sets, Descartes' distinction between clear and unclear perceptions, and the distinction within numbers between the rational and the irrational ones. On the other hand there are, so to speak, ordinary distinctions, distinctions one ordinarily makes using the ordinary terms of ordinary language in ordinary ways. (It may well be that there is no ordinary distinction which is, or which purports to be, exhaustive. But for these purposes I think we can let that pass.) Examples are blue eyes/eyes which aren't blue, people/other things, Jews (or Mormons or Catholics)/Gentiles.

Whatever else Quine has done, and whatever else his work implies, he has underminded the acceptability of the analytic/synthetic distinction *as a technical distinction.* In the texts of classical Vienna positivism, and especially in the works of Carnap, the distinction appears as a technical distinction. By that I mean that the distinction is conceived as being elaborated for the first time: it is formulated precisely—with no looseness or gaps to be filled in by a rough understanding of the distinction's import, and it gains no credibility from its application to or its use in, common practice (nor does it lose credibility by failing to be related to common practice). Against this kind of distinction Quine can make at least two points. (1) The distinction is not sufficiently precise in the manner required by the very theory in which it occurs. The distinction is supported

---

[12] The most discussed statement of Quine's position has been his "Two Dogmas of Empiricism" *Philosophical Review*, Vol. 60, No. 1 (January, 1951). This essay appears in several anthologies, including *Analyticity*, edited by James F. Harris, Jr. and Richard H. Severens (Chicago: Quadrangle Books, 1970), and *Necessary Truth*, edited by L. W. Sumner and John Woods (New York: Random House, 1969). These two books also contain extensive bibliographies. In appreciating Quine's position as an attack on what I call a "technical distinction" it is helpful to re-read "Two Dogmas of Empiricism" in the light of his "Truth by Convention", in Otis H. Lee (ed.), *Philosophical Essays for A. N. Whitehead* (New York: Longmans, Green and Co., 1936), and "Carnap and Logical Truth" (*Synthese*, Vol. 12, No. 4, December, 1960—but see Quine's first footnote for an account of the publishing history of this essay).

by no effective procedure for sorting statements into the analytic ones and the synthetic ones. (2) The enterprise the distinction is meant to serve, something like the "logical analysis of the language of science," can be carried on without the distinction.

Neither of these points can be urged against the aesthetic/non-aesthetic distinction directly, for the distinction is not clearly a technical one. But what kind of distinction is it? It seems to be something of an intermediate case, not technical but not altogether ordinary. 'Aesthetic' certainly has common uses (though 'non-aesthetic' has none); some illustrations were set out earlier (p. 135). Unlike 'analytic,' 'aesthetic' has a non-theoretical use which seems related to the use it is given in theories like Sibley's. And besides this respect in which the aesthetic/non-aesthetic distinction might be said to be common, according to Sibley 'aesthetic' can be used to mark a distinction made in common practice (though I have argued against this). That is, it is easy (though I think it is mistaken) to believe that the aesthetic/non-aesthetic distinction is both embedded in and applies to ordinary language. Whether or not the analytic/synthetic distinction can be applied to ordinary language, it is not embedded there. One might say that it does not live there, that whatever life it has must come from the theory which incorporates and animates it. If the distinction is not rendered unproblematic in the theory, then its claim to our attention—in fact its existence—falls away. This point (point (1) above) can be made about the aesthetic/non-aesthetic distinction, but without the same consequence.

Neither Sibley's theory nor any other theory in recent philosophy of art comes equipped with explicit semantic and syntactic requirements, a theory of meaning, etc., as did positivism—requirements that Quine then imposed on the theory itself with a devastating effect. Still, there is a theory within which, after the distinction is drawn, Sibley argues that aesthetic terms have a logical independence, that they can be learned and used in certain ways, and so on. Within the theory the distinction functions as a technical distinction, and whatever one wishes to require of such a distinction, surely it must meet at least the minimal methodological requirement that it not beg questions the theory is supposed to answer. I claim to have shown that it does not meet this requirement. But this does not wipe out the sense of 'aesthetic.' 'Aesthetic' remains there in my language whatever any philosopher may do to mutilate its sense, and whatever I may do playing reformer. The strongest point to be made is that the argumentative use of the aesthetic/non-aesthetic distinction as a part of, or a prelude to, a "theory" cannot be justified solely on the grounds that 'aesthetic' is a ceritfied non-theoretical term.

Then what of the distinction? I do not know whether it *can* be rehabilitated. The best I can do is what I have done in the second chapter of my doctoral dissertation, namely, get along without the distinction.[13] The second point made against the analytic/synthetic distinction can,

---

[13] *The Grammar of Taste*, unpublished (Harvard, April, 1972). A revised version of the second chapter is forthcoming as "An Austinian Conception of Art as Language".

perhaps, be made against the aesthetic/non-aesthetic distinction. I have elsewhere tried to talk about art and our apprehension of art. To the extent that I have succeeded the aesthetic/non-aesthetic distinction has been shown to be not merely a superfluity, but an impediment.

Schematic summary of the argument

The argument I've given against Sibley has been rambling and sometimes indirect, as I think it must be if it is to be persuasive (that is, liberating). Appraising the argument may be helped by having a more concise and consecutive statement, not a substitute for the argument but a kind of guide to it.

(1) Sibley divides terms into aesthetic and non-aesthetic ones (A-terms and N-terms; 'At' for 't is an A-term'). I take seriously the idea that there is some way of doing this: that is, there is something—call it P—which every A-term is (or has). (This is the property of requiring taste for its successful application.) So

$(t)(At \equiv Pt)$.

(2) Subsequently Sibley argues that A-terms have a common property—call it P'. (This is the property of being non-condition-governed.) This is not a unique feature; some N-terms possess it. So, we have not '$(t)(At \equiv P't)$,' but

$(t)(At \supset P't)$.

(3) More to the point,

$(t)(Pt \supset P't)$.

The obvious refutation would consist in showing that

$\exists t)(Pt \mathbin{\&} \sim P't)$.

I have not done that. An obvious kind of counterargument, less specifically a refutation, would consist in first dispensing with Sibley's explicit characterization of A-terms, taking that as a reference to a generally understood characterization of A-terms, and then showing, with regard to any likely characterization, that

$\exists t)(At \mathbin{\&} \sim P't)$.

I have not done that.

What I have shown about '$(t)(Pt \supset P't)$' is that Sibley's only argument in its favor begs the question. I have wanted to suggest that so does any likely argument for '$(t)(AT \supset P't)$,' however aesthetic terms are characterized.

The more difficult and more important point I've tried to make is that

if $(t)(At \equiv Pt)$,
then $\sim (\exists t)At$.

And, again, I have wanted to suggest, though less confidently, that even if Sibley's explicit characterization of A-terms is replaced by some assumedly common characterization, it will turn out that there are no such terms.

It is my argument that there are no aesthetic terms when (t) (At ≡ Pt) that figures most obscurely. It was first made clear to me by G. E. L. Owen that this is not an independent argument for me, but is one step in a kind of pragmatic *reductio*. When I claim that one of Sibley's aesthetic terms (e.g. *'graceful'*) can be applied without taste, I am not claiming that the term is non-aesthetic. It is not the classifying, but the distinction I want to assault. The form of the argument is roughly this:

(i)   There is an aesthetic/non-aesthetic distinction.
(ii) There are aesthetic terms.
(iii) t is an aesthetic term.
(iv) t is a non-aesthetic term.

Therefore,

(v)   There is not an aesthetic/non-aesthetic distinction.

This is not a strict *reductio*; it is not a strict text argument at all. (ii) seems an unexceptionable step, and I have argued for (iv). But then all that follows is that either (i) or (iii) is false: perhaps (i) is true but t has been chosen ineptly. I call the argument "pragmatic" because I claim that no matter what is chosen as t to satisfy (iii), (iv) will still be true. I have no "proof" of this. I have tried to show that Sibley is mistaken about every example he gives of t (where t is to be an A-term and (x) (At ≡ Pt)), and that he would be mistaken about any other example I can think of.

The other murky matter is my claim to find a defect in Sibley's argument that (t)(Pt ⊃ P't) while I also disavow showing or believing that (∃t) (Pt & ∼ P't). The part about Sibley's begging the question, about his having begun, in effect, with '(t) (At ⊃ P't),' is as clear as I can make it. The difficulty is in seeing why anyone, outside an examination or a dissertation, should care to show a defect in the argument unless he wanted to maintain that some aesthetic terms are condition-governed. I have cared to do it in order to locate the interest, and discomfort, in Sibley's view in the aesthetic/non-aesthetic distinction, and not in what follows. And then I have tried to undermine the distinction. There seems to be a connection between undermining the distinction and showing that (∃t)-(Pt & ∼ P't), and this frequently clouds my argument, even for me. I think I can account for this.

The practice of asking about the logical connections between two classes of terms and/or judgments is entrenched in recent philosophy, a paradigm being the work of classical "logicism" in the philosophy of mathematics. The effort to "reduce" mathematics to logic is variously judged to have been a failure or a partial success. Had it been a complete success, the axioms (and so the theorems) of elementary number theory could be read off as theorems of logic, with no appreciable change in logic.[14] Mathematical statements—those containing the special terms of mathematics which do not appear in logic—could be understood as abbreviations of purely logical statements. Adapting Sibley's terminology, one could say that mathematical judgments would have been shown to be condition-governed: from the truth of every member of a set of non-mathematical (i.e. logical) judgments it would follow that some mathematical statement was true; and there would be such a set of necessary and sufficient non-mathematical conditions for each mathematical judgment. But then it could be said that the effect of this success would be to show that there are no mathematical judgments, or at least that the distinction between mathematics and the part of non-mathematics called logic must be given up. Accordingly, one associates the legitimacy of the mathematics/logic distinction with the fact that mathematical terms and judgments are not, in this sense, condition-governed. So, too, with the aesthetic/non-aesthetic distinction: one may suppose the best—or only—way of showing the distinction illegitimate to be showing that aesthetic terms are condition-governed. This is a misapprehension.

I am not claiming that an enterprise like Sibley's cannot begin, at least not quite. One might say that if A's and N's can be distinguished clearly enough to allow inquiry into the logical connection between A's and N's, then it must turn out that A's and N's are not closely connected —or else there could have been no initial distinction. But I do not say quite that. In the case of logicism the initial distinction is given: the N's are, roughly, the statements in Frege's logical theory, and the A's are the statements in what is called classical mathematics. In the beginning (though not ultimately, according to Quine—see footnote number 15), there is nothing in the way A's and N's are distinguished that prejudices the question whether A's and N's are related in certain ways. Not so with Sibley. I have argued that the initial distinction between A's and N's is not well founded, but this is not to deny that there are A-terms in the sense that logicism might deny that there is any mathematics; it is to deny that the notions of A-terms and N-terms have any even initial application. And so of course I do not show, or believe, that $(\exists t)$ $(Pt \, \& \sim P't)$.

---

[14] In this account I follow Quine's account, for the most part. According to him the reduction of mathematics to logic depends upon whether set theory is counted as part of logic. In his *Philosophy of Logic* (Englewood Cliffs, N.J.: Prentice-Hall, Inc., 1970), he says that "Frege, Whitehead, and Russell made a point of reducing mathematics to logic . . . . But the logic capable of encompassing this reduction was logic inclusive of set theory" (pp. 65–66), and then goes on to argue that set theory does not belong to logic. The technical details of the logicist program and Quine's assessment of it do not bear on the general comparison of logicism with some meta-aesthetic theories, though this situation—the "reduction" of N's to A's by way of intermediates themselves not obviously N's or A's—is of interest, or would be if one recognized any initial distinction between N's and A's.

Brief comparison of Sibley on taste with Hume and Kant

Sibley's essays, in reinvoking the notion of taste, as well as in the somewhat pre-Victorian character of their examples and illustrations, serve, I hope, to reinvigorate a great period in the Tradition, the last half of the eighteenth century. They also, however, ignore some salient insights of that period, and perhaps this can be seen as the source of the flaws in Sibley's view.

Hume's philosophy of art is a theory of taste. Like Sibley, Hume is interested in whether, and how, judgments of taste can be supported, and his description of a "true judge" and the claim that "the joint verdict of such, wherever they are to be found, is the true standard of taste and beauty"[15] is like Sibley's eventual effort to locate a criterion for the presence of aesthetic qualities in the judgments of a group of elite critics.[16] And in construing taste to be an ability to notice, Sibley preserves a central feature of Hume's conception of taste. But there is more to Hume's conception: it is richer, if more elusive. Taste as a special capacity to notice is a theme throughout "Of the Standard of Taste," appearing in passages like this.

> Where the organs are so fine as to allow nothing to escape them, and at the same time so exact as to perceive every ingredient in the composition, this we call delicacy of taste . . . (P. 240)

However, equally prominent is the conception of taste as a special capacity to feel.

> Though it be certain that beauty and deformity, more than sweet and bitter, are not qualities in objects, but belong entirely to the sentiment, internal or external, it must be allowed, that there are certain qualities in objects which are fitted by nature to produce those particular feelings. (P. 240)
> . . . and if the same qualities, in a continued composition, and in a smaller degree, affect not the organs with a sensible delight or uneasiness, we exclude the person from all pretensions to this delicacy. (P. 240)

This conception of taste as sensibility is most explicit in "Of the Delicacy of Taste and Passion" and it is the only conception formulated there.

In short, delicacy of taste has the same effect as delicacy of passion. It en-

---

[15] These quotatons are from "Of the Standard of Taste", p. 247. This essay appeared in *Four Dissertations*, published in 1757. I give references to this essay and to "Of the Delicacy of Taste and Passion" as they occur in David Hume, *Essays Moral, Political and Literary* (Oxford: Oxford University Press, 1963).

[16] This part of Sibley's view is not developed in any of the papers considered so far. It appears in Sibley's contribution to "Objectivity and Aesthetics" (*Proceedings of the Aristotelian Society*, supplementary volume 62, 1968).

larges the sphere both of our happiness and misery, and makes us sensible to pains as well as pleasures which escape the rest of mankind. (P. 4)

What, then, is Hume's view? If you, having more delicate taste, respond to a work to which I am indifferent, must it be that you notice something which escapes me, or could it be that everything to be noticed is seen by us both while only you also feel pleasure? To take this question seriously as it arises in Hume requires taking Hume seriously, and that enlarges the question beyond the purview of this essay. Hume's theory of mind and mental activity does not yield a ready distinction between feeling and seeing. If we are restricted to the general categories of *ideas* and *impressions*, and their subdivisions, then, as always with Hume, the simplicity gained masks fantastic subtleties. If you respond and I don't, then mustn't you be acquiring an impression I don't get? Perhaps we each have some visual impression but yours is accompanied by—causes, in Hume's sense—another, a pleasure impression. Or is the number of impressions the same though yours is received in a different "mode"? But this is irrelevant to the difference between Hume and Sibley I wish to point out, and so is their apparent disagreement over where to locate the qualities referred to by 'beauty,' 'deformity,' etc. (How much disagreement there is depends partly on how we understand Sibley's notion of "emergent" qualities, and mostly on how, given the *Treatise*, we suppose Hume to effect a significant epistemological distinction between qualities in and not in objects.)

The point of interest is that, however he analyzes the act, Hume regards feeling as an ineliminable part of any taste judgment. Sibley excludes this and the matter of praise as well, which Hume also retains.

It appears, then, that amidst all the variety and caprice of taste, there are certain general principles of approbation or blame, whose influence a careful eye may trace in all operations of the mind. (P. 238)

Hume finds three components, or aspects, in the exercise of taste: noticing, feeling, evaluating. An exercise of taste is an act of appreciation, in the fullest sense. How far Hume thinks it reasonable to isolate the three parts is hard to say. He may regard them as three ways of looking at the same thing, as at times in the moral philosophy he identifies a feeling of pleasure with a judgment that someone is virtuous. Sibley, however, in his characterization of taste judgments, eliminates the last two features, leaving taste as a capacity to notice. I have already said that he seems to have reneged on this, if he finds it obvious that judgments like 'It's a lovely day' are aesthetic, since whatever special character such judgments may have is due to their relation to feeling and evaluation. A deeper point emerges if we try to understand why Sibley seems to reject out of hand the possible existence of what Hume calls a standard of taste.

According to Hume we can find "a rule by which the various sentiments of men may be reconciled" (p. 234) if we can identify the legitimate authors of such a rule, the "true judges." And we can do this. When men are in dispute over whether someone is a proper critic (an exemplar of a standard of taste), says Hume,

> . . . they must acknowledge a true and decisive standard to exist somewhere, to wit, real existence and matter of fact . . . (P. 248)

In the section criticizing Sibley's argument (pp. 119 ff.) I argued that Sibley has no argument against there being such a rule or its being discovered, and that given such a rule a man without taste (in Sibley's sense) can apply (what Sibley calls) taste terms. Why does Sibley simply overlook or disregard this "empirical possibility"? Why does he consider the possibility conceptually irrelevant? It must be, I think, because he thinks that a judgment made in this way, depending on a rule (judging 'x is E' without seeing E-ness but because one sees that x is N_1 & N_2 & . . . & N_n and also knows that any such x is also E), is not an aesthetic judgment. Why? Because it seems clear that such a derivative judgment could not take the place of a taste judgment, could not do or express or "mean" the same thing: Knowing that x is E in this roundabout way is not the same as seeing that x is E. But this is not enough. Knowing that x is square or red or lazy or immense is not the same as seeing that x is any of these, at least not always. One's conviction that no inferred judgment could be, or be a surrogate for, a judgment of taste must be more deeply rooted.

The one who is clearest about this, both as it bears on the characterization of the exercise of taste and as it determines the outlines of subsequent arguments about the possibility of justifying or vindicating one's exercise of taste, is Kant. The two aspects of taste eliminated from Sibley's discussion are the most prominent in Kant's account. About evaluation:

> The definition of taste here relied upon is that it is the faculty of estimating the beautiful [*das Vermögen der Beurteilung des Schönen sei*]. (P. 41)[17]

About feeling:

> If we wish to discern whether anything is beautiful or not, we do not refer the representation of it to the Object by means of understanding with a view to cognition, but by means of the imagination (acting perhaps in conjunction with understanding) we refer the representation to the Subject and its feeling of pleasure or displeasure. (P. 41)

Given this, Kant immediately adds,

> The judgement of taste, therefore, is not a cognitive judgement, and so not logical, but is aesthetic—which means that it is one whose determining ground *cannot be other than subjective*. (Pp. 41–42)

---

[17] All references to Kant are to the first two pages of the First Book of the *Critique of Judgment* (first published in 1790); pp. 41–42 in James Creed Mededith's translation (Oxford: Oxford University Press, 1952), pp. 37–38 in J. H. Bernard's translation (New York: Hafner Publishing Co., 1951). I quote and cite pages from the Meredith translation. I prefer the Bernard translation, but Meredith's use of 'estimating' for '*Beurteil(ung)*' is more judicious—given the context—than Bernard's 'judging'.

And so, from the beginning, there is no question—not even a philosopher's academic question—of reasons in support of a taste judgment. This is in fact a partially defining feature of taste judgments for Kant. I believe Sibley agrees, in spite of his mistaking the point and so presenting an argument which doesn't succeed and is superfluous anyway. The striking difference is that the aspects of the conception of taste which for Kant make this a characterizing feature are exactly the ones explicitly eliminated from Sibley's discussion. And so for Kant the difference between taste judgments and other judgments cannot be a difference between using one kind of concept and using a more ordinary kind. The exercise of taste is the application of no concept at all. Taste involves noticing. It is not merely a manipulation of oneself. But it is a kind of noticing evinced in a feeling. One might say that Kant thinks it is a special feeling but for the fact that he claims that its signal attribute is that it is so un-special that one can demand to find it in all other people.

This is no defense or exegesis of Hume or Kant. It is a suggestion that what is most appealing in Sibley's view echoes them, while unheard from them are the points needed to support the appeal.

Select Bibliography for Part Seven

Books

Virgil Aldrich, *Philosophy of Art*; Archibald Alison, *Essays on the Nature and Principles of Taste*; Monroe Beardsley, *Aesthetics: Problems in the Philosophy of Criticism*; Monroe Beardsley, *The Possibility of Criticism*; Edward Bullough, *Aesthetics: Lectures and Essays*; William Callaghan, et al., *Aesthetics and the Theory of Criticism: Selected Essays of Arnold Isenberg*; Herbert Langfeld, *The Aesthetic Attitude*; C. K. Ogden and I. A. Richards, *The Meaning of Meaning*; D. W. Prall, *Aesthetic Analysis*; D. W. Prall, *Aesthetic Judgment*; Dugald Stewart, *Philosophical Essays*; Jerome Stolnitz, *Aesthetics and Philosophy of Art Criticism*.

Articles

Henry Aiken, "A Pluralistic Analysis of Aesthetic Value"; Henry Aiken, "Some Notes Concerning the Aesthetic and the Cognitive"; Virgil C. Aldrich, "Art and the Human Form"; Virgil C. Aldrich, "Beauty as Feeling"; Virgil C. Aldrich, "Pictorial Meaning and Picture Thinking"; Virgil C. Aldrich, "Pictorial Meaning, Picture-Thinking, and Wittgenstein's Theory of Aspects"; Virgil C. Aldrich, "Picture Space"; Monroe Beardsley, "Aesthetic Experience Regained"; Monroe C. Beardsley, "The Aesthetic Point of View"; Monroe C. Beardsley, "Modes of Interpretation"; Monroe C. Beardsley, "On the Generality of Critical Reasons"; Monroe C. Beardsley, "Representation and Presentation: A Reply to Professor Dickie"; George Boas, "The Problem of Meaning in the Arts"; Edward Bullough, "Mind and Medium in Art"; Allan Casebier, "The Alleged Special Logic for Aesthetic Terms"; Allan Casebier, "The Concept of Psychical Disturbance"; M. Cavell, "Taste and the Moral Sense"; Arthur Child, "The Social-Historical Relativity of Esthetic Value"; W. C. Clement, "Quality Orders"; Francis J. Coleman, "Is Aesthetic Pleasure a Myth?"; Donald W. Crawford, "Causes, Reasons and Aesthetic Objectivity"; D. J. Crossley, "The Aesthetic Attitude: Back in Gear with Bullough"; Sheila Dawson, "Distancing as an Aesthetic Principle"; George Dickie, "Art Narrowly and Broadly Speaking"; George Dickie, "Attitude and Object: Aldrich on the Aesthetic"; George Dickie, "Beardsley's Phantom Aesthetic Experience"; George Dickie, "Beardsley's Theory of Aesthetic Experience"; George Dickie, "Bullough and Casebier: Disappearing in the Distance"; George Dickie, "Design and Subject Matter: Fusion and Confusion"; George Dickie, "Is Psychology Relevant to Aesthetics?"; George Dickie, "Psychical Distance: in a Fog at Sea"; George Dickie, "Taste and Attitude: The Origin of the Aesthetic"; C. J. Ducasse, "What Has Beauty to Do with Art?"; Marcia P. Freedman, "The Myth of the Aesthetic Predicate"; D. W. Gotshalk, "Art and Beauty"; Bernard Harrison, "Some Uses of 'Good' in Criticism"; Isabel C. Hungerland, "The Logic of Aesthetic Concepts"; Arnold Isenberg, "Critical Communication"; Arnold Isenberg, "The Problem of Belief"; Iredell Jenkins, "The Aesthetic Object"; P. Kivy, "Aesthetics and Rationality"; Helen Knight, "The Use of 'Good' in Aesthetic Judgments"; J. Kupperman, "Art and Aesthetic Experience"; Berel Lang, "The Form of Aesthetics"; William Lycan and Peter Machamer, "A Theory of Critical Reasons"; Robert MacGregor, "Art and the Aesthetic"; Joseph Margolis, "Aesthetic Perception"; Joseph Margolis, "Proposals on the Logic of Aesthetic Judgments"; George H. Mead, "The Nature of Aesthetic Experience"; Douglas Morgan, "Psychology and Art Today"; Bruce N. Morton, "Beardsley's Conception of the Aesthetic Object"; Mary Mothersill, " 'Unique' as an Aesthetic Predicate"; J. Rudinow, and R. I. Sikora, "Are There Art-Critical Concepts?"; H. R. G. Schwyzer, "Sibley's 'Aesthetic Concepts' "; Frank Sibley, "Aesthetic and Non-Aesthetic"; Frank Sibley, "Aesthetic Concepts: A Rejoinder"; Frank Sibley, "Aesthetics and the Looks of Things"; Gary Stahl, "Sibley's 'Aesthetic Concepts': An Ontological Mistake"; Jerome Stolnitz, "The Artistic Values in Aesthetic Experience"; Jerome Stolnitz, "On Objective Relativity on Aesthetics"; Jerome Stolnitz, "Some Questions Concerning Aesthetic Perception"; Vincent Tomas, "Aesthetic Vision"; J. O. Urmson, "What Makes a Situation Aesthetic?"; Eliseo Vivas, "A Definition of the Esthetic Experience"; Paul Ziff, "Art and the 'Object of Art.' "

Journal Abbreviations

AJP	Australasian Journal of Philosophy
APQ	American Philosophical Quarterly
BJA	British Journal of Aesthetics
BJP	British Journal of Psychology
GR	Georgia Review
HB	Hibbert Journal
JAAC	Journal of Aesthetics and Art Criticism
JAE	Journal of Aesthetic Education
JHI	Journal of the History of Ideas
JP	Journal of Philosophy
JPS	Journal of Philosophical Studies
JVI	Journal of Value Inquiry
KR	Kenyon Review
MW	Man and World
PAR	Partisan Review
PAS	Proceedings of the Aristotelian Society
PE	Philosophical Exchange
PF	Philosophical Forum
PHIL	Philosophy
PPR	Philosophy and Phenomenological Research
PQ	Philosophical Quarterly
PR	Philosophical Review
PS	Philosophical Studies
RIP	Review Internationale de Philosophie
RM	Review of Metaphysics
SJP	Southwestern Journal of Philosophy
SR	Sewanee Review
TP	The Personalist

Bibliography

Bibliography

ARTICLES

Abercrombie, Lascelles. "Communication versus Expression in Art." *BJP*, 14 (1923).

Aiken, Henry. "Art as Expression and Surface." *JAAC*, 4 (1945).

———. "The Concept of Relevance in Aesthetics," *JAAC*, 6 (1947).

———. "Criteria for an Adequate Aesthetics" (comments by G. Boas, C. J. Ducasse, K. Gilbert, and S. C. Pepper). *JAAC*, 7 (1948).

———. "A Pluralistic Analysis of Aesthetic Value." *PR*, 59 (1950).

———. "The Aesthetic Relevance of Artists' Intentions." *JP*, 52 (1955).

———. "The Aesthetic Relevance of Belief." *JAAC*, 9 (1951).

———. "Some Notes Concerning the Aesthetic and the Cognitive." *JAAC*, 13 (1955).

Aldrich, Virgil C. "Art and the Human Form." *JAAC*, 29 (1972).

———. "Beauty as Feeling." *KR*, 1 (1939).

———. "Pictorial Meaning and Picture Thinking." *KR*, 5 (1943).

———. "Pictorial Meaning, Picture-Thinking, and Wittgenstein's Theory of Aspects." *Mind*, 67 (1958).

———. "Picture Space." *PR*, 67 (1958).

———. "Pictures and Persons—An Analogy." *RM*, 28 (1975).

Allen, A. H. B. "Art and Life." *HB*, 56 (1957).

Alexander, H. G. "Art, Imagination and Cultural Reality." *Anais Do VIII Congresso Interamericano De Filosofia E V Da Sociedad Interamericana De Filosofia*, 3 (1974).

Ames, Van Meter. "Is It Art?" *JAAC*, 30 (1971).

———. "Art for Art's Sake Again?" *JAAC*, 33 (1975).

Amyx, Clifford. "The Iconic Sign in Aesthetics." *JP*, 6 (1947).

Arnheim, Rudolf. "Gestalt and Art." *JAAC*, 2 (1943).

———. "The Gestalt Theory of Expression." *PR*, 56 (1949).

———. "The Priority of Expression." *JAAC*, 8 (1949).

———. "The Robin and the Saint: On the Twofold Nature of the Artistic Image." *JAAC*, 18 (1959).

Aschenbrenner, Karl. "Aesthetic Theory—Conflict and Conciliation." *JAAC*, 18 (1959).

———. "Critical Reasoning." *JP*, 57 (1960).

———. "The Philosopher's Interest in Art." *JAE*, 5 (1969).

Ashmore, Jerome. "The Artist's Adequation." *MW*, 5 (1970).

Bachrach, Jay E. "Richard Wollheim and the Work of Art." *JAAC*, 32 (1973).

———. "Type and Token and the Identification of the Work of Art." *PPR*, 31 (1973).

Ballard, E. G. "In Defense of Symbolic Aesthetics." *JAAC*, 12 (1953).

Bartlett, F. C. "Types of Imagination." *JPS*, 3 (1928).

Battin, M. P. "Aristotle's Definition of Tragedy in the *Poetics*." Part I, *JAAC*, 33 (1974); Part II, *JAAC*, 33 (1975).

——. "Representation and Presentation: A Reply to Professor Dickie." *JP*, 58 (1961).

——. "On the Generality of Critical Reasons." *JP*, 59 (1962).

——. "On the Creation of Art." *JAAC*, 23 (1965).

Beardsley, Monroe. "Representation and Presentation: A Reply to Professor Dickie." *JP*, 58 (1961).

——. "On the Generality of Critical Reasons." *JP*, 59 (1962).

——. "On the Creation of Art." *JAAC*, 23 (1965).

——. "Aesthetic Experience Regained." *JAAC*, (1969).

Bell, Clive. "The 'Difference' of Literature." *New Republic*, 33 (1922).

Beloff, John. "Creative Thinking in Art and Science." *BJA*, 10 (1970).

Benson, John. "Emotion and Expression." *PR*, 76 (1967).

Berggren, Douglas. "The Use and Abuse of Metaphor." *RM*, 16 (1962–1963).

Berleant, Arnold. "The Verbal Presence: An Aesthetics of Literary Performance." *JAAC*, 31 (1973).

Berndtson, Arthur. "Semblance, Symbol, and Expression in the Aesthetics of Susanne Langer." *JAAC*, 14 (1956).

Binkley, Timothy. "Langer's Logical and Ontological Modes." *JAAC*, 28 (1970).

Black, M. "Metaphor." *PAS*, 55 (1954–1955).

Blocker, Gene. "Hegel on Aesthetic Internalization." *BJA*, 11 (1970).

Boas, George. "The Problem of Meaning in the Arts." *University of California Publications in Philosophy*, 25 (1950).

——. "Historical Periods." *JAAC*, 11 (1953).

Bodkin, A. M. "The Relevance of Psycho-Analysis to Art Criticism." *BJP*, 25 (1924–1925).

Braithwaite, R. B., Ryle, Gilbert, and Moore, G. E. "Imaginary Objects" (Symposium). *PAS*, Suppl. 12 (1933).

Brion, Marcel "Abstract Art." *Diogenes*, 24 (1958).

Brown, Lee B. "Definitions and Art Theory." *JAAC*, 27 (1969).

——. "Traditional Aesthetics Revisited." *JAAC*, 29 (1971).

Brown, Theodore M. "Greenough, Paine, Emerson, and the Organic Aesthetic." *JAAC*, 14 (1956).

Buettner, S. "John Dewey and the Visual Arts in America." *JAAC*, 33 (1975).

Bufford, Samuel. "Susanne Langer's Two Theories of Art." *JAAC*, 30 (1972).

Bullough, Edward. " 'Psychical Distance' as a Factor in Art and an Aesthetic Principle." *BJP*, 5 (1912–1913).

——. "Mind and Medium in Art." *BJP*, 11 (1920–1921).

Burke, Kenneth. "Semantic and Poetic Meaning." *SR*, 4 (1939).

Carmichael, Peter A. "Collingwood and Art Media." *SJP*, 2 (1970).

Carritt, E. F. "Art Without Form?" *PHIL*, 16 (1941).

Carter, Curtis L. "Langer and Hofstadter on Painting and Language: A Critique." *JAAC*, 32 (1974).

——. "The Concept of Psychical Disturbance." *TP*, 52 (1971).

Casebier, Allan. "The Alleged Special Logic for Aesthetic Terms." *JAAC* 31 (1973).

Casey, Edward S. "Expression and Communication in Art." *JAAC*, 29 (1971).

Cavell, M. "Taste and the Moral Sense." *JAAC*, 34 (1975).

Cavell, Stanley. "More of the World Viewed." *GR*, 28 (1974).

Chalmers, F. Graeme. "The Study of Art in a Cultural Context." *JAAC*, 32 (1973).

Charlton, W. "Living and Dead Metaphors." *BJA*, 15 (1975).

Chattersee, Margaret. "Some Philosophical Problems Arising in the Arts." *JAAC*, 27 (1969).

Child, Arthur. "The Social-Historical Relativity of Esthetic Value." *PR*, 53 (1944).

Clark, Robert Charles. "Total Control and Chance in Musics: A Philosophical Analysis." *JAAC*, 28 (1970).

Clement, W. C. "Quality Orders." *Mind*, 65 (1956).

Close, Anthony J. "Philosophical Theories of Art and Nature in Classical Antiquity." *JHI*, 32 (1971).

Cohen, R. "David Hume's Experimental Method and the Theory of Taste." *Journal of English Literary History*, 25 (1958).

Cohen, S. Marshall. "Lear and Nature." *PE*, 2 (1970).

Cohen, Ted. "The Possibility of Art: Remarks on a Proposal by Dickie." *PR*, 82 (1973).

———. "Notes on Metaphor." *JAAC*, 34 (1976).

Coleman, Francis J. "Is Aesthetic Pleasure a Myth?" *JAAC*, 29 (1971).

Courtney, Richard. "Imagination and the Dramatic Act: Comments on Sartre, Ryle, and Furlong." *JAAC*, 30 (1972).

———. "Reason-Giving in Kant's Aesthetics." *JAAC*, 28 (1970).

Crawford, Donald W. "Causes, Reasons and Aesthetic Objectivity." *APQ*, 8 (1971).

Croce, Benedetto. "On the Aesthetics of Dewey." *JAAC*, 6 (1948).

Crossley, D. J. "The Aesthetic Attitude: Back in Gear with Bullough." *TP*, 56 (1975).

Daniels, C. "Tolstoy and Corrupt Art." *JAE*, 8 (1974).

Danto, A. "The Artworld." *JP*, 6 (1964).

———. "Artworks and Real Things." *Theoria*, Parts 1–3 (1973).

———. "The Transfiguration of the Commonplace." *JAAC*, 33 (1974).

Dawson, Sheila. "Distancing as an Aesthetic Principle." *AJP*, 39 (1961).

Dennis, L. J., and Powers, J. F. "Dewey, Maslow, and Consummatory Experience." *JAE*, 8 (1974).

Dewey, John. "A Comment on the Foregoing Criticism" (Benedetto, Croce, "On the Aesthetics of Dewey"). *JAAC*, 6 (1948).

Dickie, George. "Design and Subject Matter: Fusion and Confusion." *JP*, 58 (1961).

———. "Is Psychology Relevant to Aesthetics?" *PR*, 71 (1962).

———. "The Myth of the Aesthetic Attitude." *APQ*, 1 (1964).

———. "Beardsley's Phantom Aesthetic Experience." *JP*, 62 (1965).

———. "Attitude and Object: Aldrich on the Aesthetic." *JAAC*, 25 (1966).

———. "Art Narrowly and Broadly Speaking." *APQ*, 5 (1968).

———. "Defining Art." *APQ*, 6 (1969).

———. "Bullough and Casebier: Disappearing in the Distance." *TP*, 53 (1972).

———. "Psychical Distance: In a Fog at Sea." *BJA*, 13 (1973).

———. "Taste and Attitude: The Origin of the Aesthetic." *Theoria*, 37, Parts 1–3 (1973).

————. "Beardsley's Theory of Aesthetic Experience." *JAE*, 8 (1974).

Diffey, T. J. "Morality and Literary Criticism." *JAAC*, 33 (1975).

Dorter, Kenneth, "The Ion: Plato's Characterization of Art." *JAAC*, 34 (1976).

Douglas, George H. "A Reconsideration of the Dewey-Croce Exchange." *JAAC*, 28 (1970).

Ducasse, C. J. "What Has Beauty to Do With Art?" *JP*, 25 (1928).

————. "Some Questions in Aesthetics." *Monist*, 42 (1932).

Earle, William. "Revolt Against Realism in the Films." *JAAC*, 27 (1968).

Eaton, Marcia. "Art, Artifacts and Intentions." *APQ*, 2 (1965).

Edie, James M. "The Problem of Enactment." *JAAC*, 29 (1970).

Eliot, T. S. "The Frontiers of Criticism." *SR*, 64 (1956).

Falk, B. "Portraits and Persons." *PAS*, 75 (1974–1975).

Foss, Lawrence. "Art as Cognitive: Beyond Scientific Realism." *PS*, 38 (1964).

Fraiberg, Louis. "Freud's Writings on Art." *International Journal of Psychoanalysis*, 37 (1956).

Frank, Paul L. "Historical or Stylistic Periods?" *JAAC*, 13 (1955).

Freedman, Marcia P., "The Myth of the Aesthetic Predicate." *JAAC*, 27 (1968).

Fried, Michael. "Manet's Sources." *Artforum*, 33 (1969).

Friedrich, Carl J. "Style as the Principle of Historical Interpretation." *JAAC*, 14 (1955).

Frye, Northrop. "The Archetypes of Literature." *KR*, 13 (1951).

Gale, Richard M. "The Fictive Use of Language." *PHIL*, 46 (1971).

Gallie, W. B. "The Function of Philosophical Aesthetics." *Mind*, 57 (1948).

————. "Art as an Essential Concept." In Elton, *Aesthetics and Language*, (1954).

Gardner, Howard. "The Development of Sensitivity to Artistic Styles." *JAAC*, 29 (1970).

Garvin, Lucius. "Emotivism, Expression, and Symbolic Meaning." *JP*, 55 (1958).

Genova, Anthony C. "Kant's Transcendental Deduction of Aesthetical Judgments." *JAAC*, 30 (1972).

Gilman, Eric. "The Use of Moral Concepts in Literary Criticism." *PHIL*, 41 (1966).

Golden, L. "Plato's Concept of Memesis." *BJA*, 15 (1975).

Gotshalk, D. W. "Art and Beauty." *Monist*, 41 (1931).

————. "Aesthetic Expression." *JAAC*, 13 (1954).

————. "A Next Step for Aesthetics." *JAAC*, 18 (1959).

Granrose, John T. "Pragmatic Justification in Aesthetics." *JAAC*, 30 (1972).

Greene, Gordon K. "For Whom and Why Does a Composer Prepare a Score." *JAAC*, 32 (1974).

Greene, Theodore M. "Beauty and the Cognitive Significance of Art." *JP*, 37 (1940).

Grossman, Morris. "Art and Morality." *JAAC*, 31 (1973).

Halberstadt, William H. "A Problem in Hume's Aesthetics." *JAAC*, 30 (1971).

Hansen, Forest. "Langer's Expressive Form—An Interpretation." *JAAC*, 28 (1968).

Harre, R. "Quasi-Aesthetic Appraisals." *PHIL*, 33 (1958).

Harrison, Bernard. "Some Uses of 'Good' in Criticism." *Mind*, 69 (1960).

Hein, Hilde. "Performance as an Aesthetic Category." *JAAC*, 28 (1970).

Henze, Donald F. "Is the Work of Art a Construct?" *JP*, 52 (1955).

———. "The Work of Art." *JP*, 54 (1957).

Herrmann, Rolf-Dieter. "How A European Views the Journal of Aesthetics and Art Criticism." *JAAC*, 29 (1970).

Hevner, K. "Aesthetic Experience: A Psychological Description." *PR*, 44 (1937).

Heyl, B. C. "Artistic Truth Reconsidered." *JAAC*, 8 (1950).

———. "Relativism Again." *JAAC*, 5 (1946).

Hinton, J. M. "Perception and Identification." *PR*, 76 (1967).

Hospers, John. "The Concept of Artistic Expression." *PAS*, 55 (1954–1955).

———. "The Croce-Collingwood Theory of Art." *PHIL*, 31 (1956).

———. "Implied Truths in Literature." *JAAC*, 19 (1960).

———. "Collingwood and Art Media: A Reply." *SJP*, 2 (1971).

Hume, Robert D. "Kant and Coleridge on Imagination." *JAAC*, 28 (1970).

Hungerland, Isabel C. "Iconic Signs and Expressiveness." *JAAC*, 3 (1944).

———. "The Concept of Intention in Art Criticism." *JP*, 52 (1955).

———. "Contextual Implication." *Inquiry*, 4 (1960).

———. "The Logic of Aesthetic Concepts." *Proceedings and Addresses of APA*, 36 (1962–1963).

Hyman, Lawrence W. "Literature and Morality in Contemporary Criticism." *JAAC*, 29 (1971).

Hyman, Stanley. "Freud and the Climate of Tragedy." *PAR*, 23 (1956).

Isenberg, Arnold. "Perception, Meaning, and the Subject Matter of Art." *JP*, 41 (1944).

———. "Critical Communication." *PR*, 58 (1949).

———. "The Esthetic Function of Language." *JP*, 46 (1949).

———. "The Problem of Belief." *JAAC*, 13 (1955).

Jackson, Wallace. "Affective Values in Early Eighteenth-Century Aesthetics." *JAAC*, 26 (1968).

Jenkins, Iredell. "The Aesthetic Object." *RM*, 11 (1957).

Jessup, Bertram E. "Aesthetic Size." *JAAC*, 9 (1950).

———. "Meaning Range in the Work of Art." *JAAC*, 12 (1954).

Jonas, Hans. "Rudolf Arnheim, *Visual Thinking*: A Review Article." *JAAC*, 30 (1971).

Jones, Peter. "Works of Art and Their Availability-for-Use." *BJA*, 11 (1971).

Kallen, Horace M. "Beauty and Use." *PR*, 48 (1939).

Kaplan, Abraham. "On the So-Called Crisis in Criticism." *JAAC*, 8 (1948).

———. "Referential Meaning in the Arts." *JAAC*, 12 (1954).

Kavolis, V. "Aesthetic Education in Civilizational Perspective." *JAE*, 9 (1975).

Kazin, A. "Psychoanalysis and Literary Culture Today." *PAR*, 26 (1955).

Kennick, William E. "Does Traditional Aesthetics Rest on a Mistake?" *Mind*, 67 (1958).

———. "Art and the Ineffable." *JP*, 58 (1961).

Khatchadourian, Haig. "Family Resemblances and the Classification of Works of Art." *JAAC*, 28 (1969).

———. "Is It Art? Is It Good Art?" *Anais Do VIII Congresso Interamericano De Filosofia E V Da Sociedad Interamericana De Filosofia*, 3 (1974).

Kivy, P. "Aesthetics and Rationality." *JAAC*, 34 (1975).

Knight, Helen. "The Use of 'Good' in Aesthetic Judgments." *PAS*, 36 (1936).

Koffler, Richard. "Kant, Leopardi, and Gorgon Truth." *JAAC*, 30 (1971).

Kogan, J. "Dialectics of the Aesthetic Experience." *PPR*, 35 (1975).

Kolnai, Aurel. "Aesthetic and Moral Experience: The Five Contrasts." *BJA*, 11 (1971).

Korsmeyer, C. W. "On the 'Aesthetic Senses' and the Development of the Fine Arts." *JAAC*, 34 (1975).

———. "Relativism and Hutcheson's Aesthetic Theory." *JHI*, 36 (1975).

Kristeller, Paul Oskar. "The Modern System of the Arts." *JHI*, 12 (1951); 13 (1952).

Kuhns, Richard C. "Art Structures." *JAAC*, 19 (1960).

———. "Criticism and the Problem of Intention." *JP*, 57 (1960).

Kupperman, J. "Art and Aesthetic Experience." *BJA*, 15 (1975).

Kuspit, Donald P. "Dewey's Critique of Art for Art's Sake." *JAAC*, 27 (1968).

Lackey, Douglas P. "Reflections on Cavell's Ontology of Film." *JAAC*, 32 (1973).

Lake, Beryl. "A Study of the Irrefutability of Two Aesthetic Theories." in Elton, *Aesthetics and Language* (1954).

Lang, Berel. "The Form of Aesthetics." *JAAC*, 27 (1968).

———, "A Note on the Location of Paintings." *JAAC*, 31 (1972).

———. "The Intentional Fallacy Revisited." *BJA*, 14 (1974).

Laszlo, Ervin. "Affect and Expression in Music." *JAAC*, 27 (1968).

Lee, Harry B. "On the Esthetic States of Mind." *Psychiatry*, 10 (1947).

———. "The Creative Imagination." *Psychoanalytic Quarterly*, 18 (1949).

Lewis, David K. "Percepts and Color Mosaics in Visual Experience." *PR*, 75 (1966).

Lipman, Matthew. "The Aesthetic Presence of the Body." *JAAC* 15 (1957).

Lord, Catherine. "Tragedy Without Character: Poetics VI. 1450a24." *JAAC*, 28 (1969).

Lycan, William G. "Gombrich, Wittgenstein, and the Duck-Rabbit." *JAAC*, 30 (1971).

Lycan, William, and Peter Machamer. "A Theory of Critical Reasons" in Tilgman, *Philosophy of Arts and Aesthetics.*

McGlynn, Paul D. "Point of View and the Craft of Cinema." *JAAC*, 34 (1976).

McGregor, Robert. "Art and the Aesthetic." *JAAC*, 32 (1974).

McNally, James Richard. "Characteristics of Art in the Text of Aristotle." *JAAC*, 29 (1971).

MacCormac, Earl R. "Metaphor Revisited." *JAAC*, 30 (1971).

MacDonald, Margaret. "Art and Imagination." *PAS*, 53 (1952–1953).

MacDonald, Margaret, and Michael Scriven. "The Language of Fiction" (Symposium). *PAS*, Supp. 27 (1954).

Mackie, A. "The Structure of Aesthetically Interesting Metaphors." *APQ*, 12 (1975).

Malek, James. "Charles Lamotte's 'An Essay Upon Poetry and Painting' and Eighteenth-Century British Aesthetics." *JAAC*, 29 (1971).

Mandelbaum, M. "Family Resemblances and Generalizations Concerning the Arts." *APQ*, 2 (1965).

Manns, James W. "Representation, Relativism and Resemblance." *BJA*, 11 (1971).

Manser, Anthony R. "Games and Family Resemblances." *PHIL*, 42 (1967).

Marcuse, Ludwig. "Freud's Aesthetic." *JAAC*, 17 (1958).

Margolis, Joseph. "Mode of Existence of a Work of Art." *RM*, 12 (1958).
———. "Mr. Weitz and the Definition of Art." *PS*, 9 (1958).
———. "The Identity of a Work of Art." *Mind*, 67 (1959).
———. "Proposals on the Logic of Aesthetic Judgments." *PQ*, 9 (1959).
———. "Aesthetic Perception." *JAAC*, 19 (1960).
———. "Recent Work in Aesthetics." *APO*, 2 (1965).
———. "Critics and Literature." *BJA*, 11 (1971).
Martin, F. David. "The Persistent Presence of Abstract Painting." *JAAC*, 28 (1969).
Mayo, Bertram. "Poetry, Language, and Communication." *PHIL*, 29 (1954).
———. "Art, Language, and Philosophy in Croce." *PQ*, 5 (1955).
Mead, George H. "The Nature of Aesthetic Experience." *International Journal of Ethics*, 36 (1925–1926).
Meager, Ruby. "Tragedy." *PAS*, Supp. 34 (1960).
Mew, Peter. "Metaphor and Truth." *BJA*, 11 (1971).
Michelis, P. A. "Aesthetic Distance and the Charm of Contemporary Art." *JAAC*, 18 (1959).
Mitias, M. H. "Art as a Social Institution." *TP*, 56 (1975).
Morgan, Douglas. "Psychology and Art Today." *JAAC*, 9 (1950).
———. "Creativity Today." *JAAC*, 12 (1953).
———. "Icon, Index and Symbol in the Visual Arts." *PS*, 6 (1955).
Morris, Bertram. "Dewey's Aesthetics: The Tragic Encounter with Nature. *JAAC*, 30 (1971).
———. "The Philosophy of Criticism." *PR*, 55 (1946).
Morris, Charles. "Esthetics and the Theory of Signs." *Erkenntnis*, 8 (1939).
———. "Science, Art and Technology." *KR*, 1 (1939).
Morton, Bruce N. "Beardsley's Conception of the Aesthetic Object." *JAAC*, 32 (1974).
Mothersill, Mary. " 'Unique' as an Aesthetic Predicate." *JP*, (1961).
Munro, Thomas. "Form in the Arts." *JAAC*, 2 (1943).
———. " 'The Afternoon of a Faun' and the Interrelation of the Arts." *JAAC*, 10 (1951).
———. "Form and Value in the Arts." *JAAC*, 13 (1955).
Nahm, Milton C. "The Philosophy of Aesthetic Expression, The Crocean Hypothesis." *JAAC*, 13 (1955).
Nathan, Daniel. "Categories and Intentions." *JAAC*, 32 (1974).
Naumburg, Margaret. "Art as Symbolic Speech." *JAAC*, 13 (1955).
Neill, B. C. "Critical Study of *Languages of Art* by Nelson Goodman." *PQ*, 21 (1971).
Neville, M. R. "Kant's Characterization of Aesthetic Experience." *JAAC*, 33 (1974).
Newcomb, James W. "Eisenstein's Aesthetics." *JAAC*, 32 (1974).
Norton, Richard. "What Is Virtuality?" *JAAC*, 30 (1972).
Orsini, G. N. G. "Theory and Practice in Croce's Aesthetics." *JAAC*, 13 (1955).
Osborne, Harold. "Taste and Judgment in the Arts." *JAE*, 5 (1971).
Palmer, Anthony. "Creativity and Understanding." *PAS*, Supp. 45 (1971).
Parker, DeWitt H. "The Nature of Art." *RIP*, 1 (1939).
Passmore, J. A. "The Dreariness of Aesthetics." *Mind*, 60 (1951).
Pauly, Herta. "Aesthetic Decadence Today Viewed in Terms of Schiller's Three Impulses." *JAAC*, 31 (1973).

Peltz, Richard. "Classification and Evaluation in Aesthetics: Weitz and Aristotle." *JAAC*, 30 (1971).

Pepper, Stephen C. "Art and Utility." *JP*, 20 (1920).

———. "Further Considerations on the Aesthetic Work of Art." *JP*, 49 (1952).

———. "Art and Experience." *RM*, 12 (1958).

———. "Autobiography of an Aesthetic." *JAAC*, 28, (1970).

———. "Feibleman's Aesthetic Theory." *Studium Generale*, 24 (1971).

Petock, Stuart Jay. "Kant, Beauty and the Object of Taste." *JAAC*, 32 (1973).

Pole, David. "Morality and the Assessment of Literature." *PHIL*, 30 (1955).

———. "Varieties of Aesthetic Experience," *PHIL*, 30 (1955).

Pratt, Carroll C. "The Stability of Aesthetic Judgments." *JAAC*, 15 (1956).

Price, Kingsley B. "Is There Artistic Truth?" *JP*, 46 (1949).

Quinton, A. M., and Ruby Meager. "Tragedy" (Symposium). *PAS*, Supp. 34 (1960).

Rader, Melvin. "Isolationist and Contextualist Esthetics: Conflict and Resolution." *JP*, 44 (1947).

———. "The Artist as Outsider." *JAAC*, 16 (1958).

———. "Marx's Interpretation of Art and Aesthetic Value." *BJA*, 7 (1967).

———. "The Factualist Fallacy in Aesthetics." *JAAC*, 28 (1970).

———. "Dickie and Socrates on Definition." *JAAC*, 32 (1974).

———. "The Imaginative Mode of Awareness." *JAAC*, 33 (1974).

Raleigh, Henry P. "Film: The Revival of Aesthetic Symbolism." *JAAC*, 32 (1973).

———. "Art as Communicable Knowledge." *JAE*, 5 (1971).

Reid, Louis Arnaud. "Aesthetic Meaning." *PAS*, 55 (1954–1955).

Rieser, Max. "The Semantic Theory of Art in America." *JAAC*, 15 (1956).

———. "Problems of Artistic Form: The Concept of Art." *JAAC*, 27 (1969).

Rose, Mary Carman. "Linguistic Analysis and Aesthetic Inquiry: A Critique." *SJP*, 9 (1971).

Rosenberg, Marvin. "Drama Is Arousal." *JAAC*, 27 (1969).

Rosenstein, Leon. "Metaphysical Foundations of the Theories of Tragedy in Hegel and Nietzsche." *JAAC*, 28 (1970).

Rudinow, J., and R. I. Sikora. "Are There Art-Critical Concepts?" *Analysis*, 35 (1975).

Rudner, Richard. "On Semiotic Aesthetics." *JAAC*, 10 (1951).

———. "Some Problems of Non-Semiotic Aesthetic Theories." *JAAC*, 15 (1957).

Rudowski, V. A. "The Theory of Signs in the Eighteenth Century." *JHI*, 35 (1974).

Savile, Anthony, "Nelson Goodman's 'Languages of Art.'" *BJA*, 11 (1971).

Saw, Ruth. "Sense and Nonsense in Aesthetics." *BJA*, 1 (1961).

———. "What Is a 'Work of Art'?" *PHIL*, 36 (1961).

Saw, Ruth, and Harold Osborne. "Aesthetics as a Branch of Philosophy." *BJA*, 1 (1960).

———. "Kant on Imagination." *PF*, 2 (1971).

Schaper, E. "Free and Dependent Beauty." *Kant-Studien*, 65 (1974).

Schwyzer, H. R. G. "Sibley's 'Aesthetic Concepts.'" *PR*, 72 (1963).

Sclafani, Richard. "Art and Artifactuality." *SJP*, 1 (1970).

———. "'Art,' Wittgenstein, and Open-Textured Concepts." *JAAC*, 29 (1970).

———. "Sensations, Feelings and Expressions." *Rice University Studies*, 58 (1972).

———. "Art as a Social Institution: Dickie's New Definitions." *JAAC*, 32 (1973).

———. "Art Works, Art Theory, and the Artworld." *Theoria*, 34 (1973).

———. "The Logical Primitiveness of the Concept of a Work of Art." *BJA*, 15 (1975).

———. "What Kind of Nonsense Is This." *JAAC*, 34 (1975).

———. "Wollheim on Collingwood." *Philosophy: Journal of the Royal Institute of Philosophy*, 51 (1976).

Scobie, W. D. L. "Margolis on 'The Identity of a Work of Art.' " *Mind*, 69 (1960).

Sesonske, Alexander. "Truth in Art." *JP*, 53 (1956).

———. "Vision via Film Form." *JAE*, 5 (1974).

———. "The World Viewed." *GR*, 28 (1975).

Shields, Allan. "The Aesthetic Object as 'Objet Manque.' " *JAAC*, 30 (1971).

Sibley, Frank. "Aesthetic Concepts." *PR*, 68 (1959).

———. "Aesthetics and the Looks of Things." *JP*, 56 (1959).

———. "Aesthetic Concepts: A Rejoinder." *PR*, 72 (1963).

———. "Aesthetic and Non-Aesthetic." *PR*, 74 (1965).

Silvers, Anita, "Aesthetic Akrasia: On Disliking Good Art." *JAAC*, 31 (1972).

———. "How Art Instructs: Another Look at Cognitivism." *Anais Do VIII Congresso Interamericano De Filosofia E V Da Sociedad Interamericana De Filosofia*, 3 (1974).

———. "The Artworld Discarded." *JAAC*, 34 (1976).

Simpson, E. "Aesthetic Appraisal." *PHIL*, 50 (1975).

Sipos, George. "On the Reproduction of Works of Art." *JAAC*, 32 Afterwords (1973).

Sircello, Guy. "Subjectivity and Justification in Aesthetic Judgments." *JAAC*, 27 (1968).

Sirridge, M. J. "Truth from Fiction?" *PPR*, 35 (1975).

Smith, Robin. "On Eliminating the Art Object," *Dialectica*, 24 (1970).

Sparshott, Francis E. "Basic Film Aesthetics." *JAE*, 5 (1971).

———. "Mr. Ziff and the 'Artistic Illusion.' " *Mind*, 61 (1952).

Stahl, Gary. "Sibley's 'Aesthetic Concepts': An Ontological Mistake." *JAAC*, 29 (1971).

Steinman, James F. "Santayana and Croce: An Aesthetic Reconciliation." *JAAC*, 30 (1971).

Stevenson, Charles L. "Meaning: Descriptive and Emotive." *PR*, 57 (1948).

———. "On 'What Is a Poem?' " *PR*, 66 (1957).

———. "On the 'Analysis' of a Work or Art." *PR*, 67 (1958).

Stokes, Adrian. "Form in Art: A Psychoanalytic Interpretation." *JAAC*, 18 (1959).

Stolnitz, Jerome. "Notes on Comedy and Tragedy." *PPR*, 16 (1955).

———. "On Objective Relativity on Aesthetics." *JP*, 57 (1960).

———. " 'Beauty': History of an Idea." *JHI*, 23 (1961).

———. "On the Origins of 'Aesthetic Disinterestedness.' " *JAAC*, 20 (1961).

———. "On the Significance of Lord Shaftesbury in Modern Aesthetic Theory." *PQ*, 11 (1961).

———. "Some Questions Concerning Aesthetic Perception." *PPR*, 22 (1961).

———. "The Artistic Values in Aesthetic Experience." *JAAC*, 35, (1976).

Sugg, Redding S. "Hume's Search for the Key with the Leathern Thong." *JAAC*, 16 (1957).

Tejera, V. "The Nature of Aesthetics." *BJA*, 1 (1961).

———. "Contemporary Trends in Aesthetics: Some Underlying Issues," *JVI*, 8 (1974).

Tilghman, Benjamin R. "Wittgenstein, Games and Art." *JAAC*, 31 (1973).

Tomas, Vincent. "Creativity in Art." *PR*, 67 (1958).

———. "Aesthetic Vision." *PR*, 68 (1959).

Tormey, Alan. "Indeterminacy and Identity in Art." *Monist*, 54 (1970).

———. "Aesthetic Rights." *JAAC*, 32 (1973).

———. "Expression in the Performing Arts." *Anais Do VIII Congresso Interamericano De Filosofia E V Da Sociedad Interamericana De Filosofia*, 3 (1974).

Trilling, Lionel. "The Legacy of Freud: Literary and Aesthetic." *KR*, 2 (1940).

Tsugawa, Albert. "The Objectivity of Aesthetic Judgments." *PR*, 70 (1961).

Uphaus, Robert W. "Shaftesbury on Art: The Rhapsodic Aesthetic." *JAAC*, 27 (1969).

Urmson, J. O. "What Makes a Situation Aesthetic?" *PAS*, 31 (1957–1958).

Ushenko, Andrew P. "Metaphor." *Thought*, 30 (1955).

———. "Pictorial Movement." *BJA*, 1 (1961).

Vivas, Eliseo. "Four Notes on I. A. Richards' Aesthetic Theory." *PR*, 44 (1935).

———. "A Definition of the Esthetic Experience." *JP*, 34 (1937).

———. Contextualism Reconsidered." *JAAC*, 18 (1959).

———. "What Is a Poem?" *SR*, 62 (1954).

———. "Animadversions on Imitation and Expression." *JAAC*, 19 (1961).

Wacker, Jeanne. "Particular Works of Art." *Mind*, 69 (1960).

Wallach, Michael A. "Art, Science, and Representation." *JAAC*, 18 (1959).

Walsh, D. "Critical Reasons." *PR*, 69 (July 1960).

Walsh, Dorothy. "The Cognitive Content of Art." *PR*, 52 (1943).

Walton, Kendall L. "Categories of Art." *PR*, 79 (1970).

———. "Languages of Art: An Emendation." *PS*, 22 (1971).

———. "Pictures and Make Believe." *PR*, 82 (1973).

Webster, William E. "Music Is Not a 'Notational System.'" *JAAC*, 29 (1971).

Weitz, Morris. "Symbolism and Art." *RM*, 7 (1954).

———. "The Role of Theory in Aesthetics." *JA*, 15 (1956).

———. "Reasons in Criticism." *JAAC*, 20 (1962).

———. "Professor Goodman on the Aesthetic." *JAAC*, 29 (1971).

Welsh, Paul. "Discursive and Presentational Symbols." *Mind*, 64 (1955).

———. "On Explicating Metaphors." *JP*, 60 (1963).

Williams, Donald C. "Form and Matter." *PR*, 67 (1958).

Wimsatt, William K., Jr., and Monroe C. Beardsley. "The Intentional Fallacy." *SR*, 45 (1946).

———. "The Affective Fallacy." *SR*, 57 (1949).

Woodfield, R. "The Freedom of Shaftesbury's Classicism." *BJA*, 15 (1975).

Zemach, Eddy M. "Thirteen Ways of Looking at the Ethics-Aesthetics Parallelism." *JAAC*, 29 (1971).

Zerby, Lewis K. "A Reconsideration of the Role of Theory in Aesthetics—A Reply to Morris Weitz." *JAAC*, 16 (1957).

Ziff, Paul. "Art and the 'Object of Art.'" *Mind*, 60 (1951).
———. "The Task of Defining a Work of Art." *PR*, 62 (1953).
———. "On What a Painting Represents." *JP*, 57 (1960).
———. "Goodman's Languages of Art." *PR*, 80 (1971).
Zink, Sidney. "Is the Music Really Sad?" *JAAC*, 19 (1960).

BOOKS

Alberti, Leon Battista. *On Painting*. Translated by John R. Spencer. New Haven, 1956.
Aldrich, Virgil. *Philosophy of Art*. Englewood Cliffs, N.J., 1963.
Alexander, Samuel. *Beauty and Other Forms of Value*. New York, 1933.
Alison, Archibald. *Essays on the Nature and Principles of Taste*. Edinburgh, 1811.
Aquinas, Thomas. *Basic Writings of St. Thomas Aquinas*. Vol. 1. New York, 1945.
Arnheim, Rudolf. *Film*. London, 1933.
———. *Art and Visual Perception*. Berkeley, 1954.
Aschenbrenner, Karl, and William B. Holther, trans. *Reflections on Poetry: Alexander Gottlieb Baumgarten's Meditationes Philisophicae*. Berkeley, 1954.
Auerbach, Erich. *Mimesis*. Princeton, 1953.
Augustine, St. *De Doctrina Christiana*. Book IV. Translated by Sister Therese Sullivan. Washington, D.C., 1930.
———. *De Immortalitate Animae*. Translated by George G. Leckie. New York, 1938.
———. *Confessions*, translated by J. G. Pilkington; *City of God*. Translated by M. Dods, G. Wilson, and J. J. Smith, in *Basic Writings of St. Augustine*. Edited by Whitney J. Oates. 2 vols. New York, 1948.
Bacon, Sir Francis. *Works*. Edited by James Spedding, Robert Ellis, and Douglas Heath. London, 1870.
Barnes, Albert C. *The Art in Painting*. New York, 1937.
Bartlett, Ethel M. *Types of Aesthetic Judgment*. London, 1937.
Bate, Walter Jackson. *From Classic to Romantic: Premises of Taste in Eighteenth Century England*. Cambridge, Mass., 1946.
Baumgarten, Alexander. *Reflections on Poetry*. Edited by Karl Aschenbrenner and W. Holther. Berkeley, 1954.
Bazin, Andre. *What Is Cinema?* Berkeley, 1967.
Bell, Clive. *Art*. New York, 1958.
Beardsley, Monroe C. *Aesthetics: Problems in the Philosophy of Criticism*. New York, 1958.
———. *Aesthetics: From Classical Greece to the Present*. New York, 1966.
———. *The Possibility of Criticism*. Philadelphia, 1970.
Berndtson, Arthur. *Art, Expression, and Beauty*. New York, 1969.
Berleant, Arnold. *The Aesthetic Field*. Springfield, Ill., 1971.
Blanshard, Frances. *Retreat from Likeness in the Theory of Painting*. New York, 1949.
Boileau, Nicholas. *The Art of Poetry*. London, 1683.
Bosanquet, Bernard. *A History of Aesthetic*. London, 1892; New York, 1957.
———. *Three Lectures on Aesthetic*. London, 1931.
Bradley, A. C. *Oxford Lectures on Poetry*. London, 1909.
———. *Shakespearean Tragedy*. 2nd ed. London, 1924.

Brehier, Emile. *The Philosophy of Plotinus*. Translated by Joseph Thomas. Chicago, 1958.

Brett, R. L. *The Third Earl of Shaftesbury*. London, 1951.

Brown, Merle E. *Neo-Idealistic Aesthetics: Croce, Gentile, Collingwood*. Detroit, 1966.

Brownell, Baker. *Art Is Action*. New York, 1939.

Brunius, Teddy. *David Hume on Criticism*. Stockholm, 1952.

Buck, Perry C. *The Scope of Music*. London, 1927.

Buermeyer, Laurence. *The Aesthetic Experience*. Merion, 1929.

Bullough, Edward. *Aesthetics: Lectures and Essays*. Edited by Elizabeth Wilkinson. Stanford and London, 1957.

Burke, Edmund. *A Philosophical Inquiry into the Origin of our Ideas of the Sublime and Beautiful*. 6th ed. London, 1770.

Burke, Kenneth. *A Grammar of Motives*. New York, 1945.

Butcher, S. H. *Aristotle's Theory of Poetry and Fine Art*. 4th ed. London, 1923.

Bywater, Ingram. *Aristotle on the Art of Poetry*. Oxford, 1909.

Caird, Edward. *The Critical Philosophy of Immanuel Kant*. 2 vols. Glasgow, 1889.

Callaghan, William, et al. *Aesthetics and the Theory of Criticism: Selected Essays of Arnold Isenberg*. Chicago, 1973.

Carr, H. Wildon. *The Philosophy of Benedetto Croce: The Problem of Art and History*. London, 1917.

Cary, Joyce. *Art and Reality*. New York, 1958.

Cassirer, H. W. *A Commentary on Kant's Critique of Judgment*. London, 1938.

Cavell, Stanley. *Must We Mean What We Say?* New York, 1969.

Chambers, Frank P. *The History of Taste*. New York, 1932.

Chapman, Emmanuel. *Saint Augustine's Philosophy of Beauty*. New York, 1939.

Charlton, W. *Aesthetics: An Introduction*. London, 1970.

Coker, Wilson. *Music and Meaning: A Theoretical Introduction to Musical Aesthetics*. New York, 1972.

Collingwood, R. G. *Essays in the Philosophy of Art*. Edited by Alan Donagan. Indianapolis, 1964.

Copleston, Frederick, S. J. *Schopenhaur: Philosopher of Pessimism*. London, 1947.

Cowie, Peter. *Antonioni, Bergman, Renais*. New York, 1963.

Croce, Benedetto. *Aesthetic as Science of Expression and General Linguistic*, Part II. Translated by Douglas Ainslie. London, 1922.

———. *The Breviary of Aesthetic*. Translated by Douglas Ainslie. Translated, revised, and called *The Essence of Aesthetic*. London, 1953.

Crombie, J. M. *An Examination of Plato's Doctrine*. Vol. 1. New York, 1962.

Danto, Arthur. *Nietzsche as Philosopher*. New York, 1965.

Demos, Raphael. *The Philosophy of Plato*. New York, 1939.

Dennis, John. *A Large Account of the Taste in Poetry*. London, 1702.

Dessoir, Max. *Aesthetics and Theory of Art*. Detroit, 1970.

Dewey, John. *Experience and Nature*. 2nd ed. Chicago, 1929.

———. *Art as Experience*. New York, 1934.

Dickie, George. *Aesthetics*. Indianapolis, 1971.

———. *Art and the Aesthetic: An Institutional Analysis*. New York, 1975.

Diderot, Denis. *The Beautiful*. Paris, 1752.

Donagan, Alan. *The Later Philosophy of R. G. Collingwood*. Oxford, 1962.

Donner, Jorn. *The Personal Vision of Ingemar Bergman*. Indianapolis, 1964.

Ducasse, C. J. *The Philosophy of Art*. New York, 1929.

Eisenstein, Sergei. *Film Form: Essays in Film Theory*. Translated and edited by Jay Leyda. New York, 1949.

Elledge, Scott. *Eighteenth-Century Critical Essays*. 2 vols. Ithaca, 1961.

Else, G. F. *Aristotle's Poetics: The Argument*. Cambridge, Mass., 1957.

Fiedler, Conrad. *On Judging Works of Visual Art*. Berkeley, 1949.

Ficino, Marsilio. *Commentary on Plato's "Symposium."* Translated by S. R. Jayne. Columbia, Mo., 1944.

Fried, Michael. *Three American Painters*. Cambridge, Mass., 1965.

Fry, Roger. *Vision and Design*. London, 1920.

Gardiner, Patrick. *Schopenhauer*. Baltimore, 1963.

Garrod, H. W., *Tolstoi's Theory of Art*. Oxford, 1935.

Gerard, Alexander. *An Essay on Taste*. 3rd ed. Facsimile. Edinburgh, 1780.

Gentile, Giovanni. *The Philosophy of Art*. Translated by Giovanni Gullace. Ithaca, 1972.

Gilbert, Katherine, and Helmut Kuhn. *A History of Aesthetics*. New York, 1939; Bloomington, 1954.

Giel, Dzahler. *New York Painting and Sculpture: 1940–1970*. New York, 1971.

Goddard, Joseph. *The Deeper Sources of the Beauty and Expression of Music*. London, 1905.

Gombrich, E. H. *Meditations on a Hobby Horse*. London, 1963.

———. *Art and Illusion*. London, 1962.

Goodman, Nelson. *Language of Art*. Indianapolis, 1968.

Gotshalk, D. W. *Art and the Social Order*. Chicago, 1947.

Green, Theodore M. *The Arts and the Art of Criticism*. Princeton, 1940.

Greenberg, Clement. *Art and Culture*. Boston, 1961.

Gurney, Edmund. *The Power of Sound*. London, 1880.

Hanslick, Eduard. *The Beautiful in Music*. London, 1891. New York, 1957.

Hauser, Arnold. *The Philosophy of Art History*. New York, 1959.

Haydon, Glenn. *On the Meaning of Music*. Washington, D.C., 1948.

Hegel, G.W.F. *The Introduction to Hegel's Theory of Fine Art*. Translated by Bernard Bosanquet. London, 1886.

———. *Philosophy of Fine Art*. Translated by F. P. B. Osmaston. 4 vols. London, 1920.

Heidegger, Martin. *The Origin of the Work of Art*. Chicago, 1976.

Hermeren, Goren. *Representation and Meaning in the Visual Arts*. Lund, 1969.

Hiler, Hilaire. *Why Abstract?* New York, 1945.

Hipple, Walter J., Jr. *The Beautiful, the Sublime, and the Picturesque in Eighteenth-Century British Aesthetic Theory*. Carbondale, Ill., 1957.

Hogarth, William. *The Analysis of Beauty*. Edited by Joseph Burke. Oxford, 1955.

Hospers, John. *Meaning and Truth in the Arts*. Chapel Hill, 1946.

Houston, Penelope. *The Contemporary Cinema*. Baltimore, 1963.

Howes, F. *Music and Its Meanings*. London, 1958.

Hume, David. *Treatise on Human Nature*. Edited by L. A. Selby-Bigge. Oxford, 1888.

Hutcheson, Francis. *An Inquiry into the Original of Our Ideas of Beauty and Virtue*. 2nd ed. London, 1726.

Inge, W. R. *The Philosophy of Plotinus*. London, 1918.

Jacobs, Lewis. *The Rise of the American Film*. New York, 1939.

Jenkins, Iredell. *Art and the Human Enterprise*. Cambridge, Mass., 1958.

Johnson, Martin. *Art and Scientific Thought*. London, 1944.

Jones, Ernest. *Hamlet and Oedipus*. New York, 1949.

Kadish, Mortimer R. *Reason and Controversy in the Arts*. Columbus, Ohio, 1968.

Kallen, Horace M. *Art and Freedom*. New York, 1942.

Kant, Immanuel. *Observations on the Feeling of the Sublime and the Beautiful*. Edited by John T. Goldwait. Berkeley, 1960.

——. *Critique of Judgment*. 2nd ed. Translated by J. H. Bernard. London, 1814.

——. *Analytic of the Beautiful*. Translated by Walter Cerf. New York, 1963.

Kaufmann, Walter A. *Nietzsche*. Princeton, 1950.

——. *Tragedy and Philosophy*. Garden City. 1969.

Khatchadourian, Haig. *The Concept of Art*. New York. 1971.

Kivy, Peter. *Speaking of Art*. The Hague, 1973.

Knight, A. H. J. *Some Aspects of the Life and Works of Nietzsche*. Cambridge, Mass., 1933.

Knight, Arthur. *The Liveliest Art*. New York, 1957.

Knight, Richard Payne. *Analytical Inquiry into the Principles of Taste*. London, 1806.

Knox, Israel. *The Aesthetic Theories of Kant, Hegel and Schopenhauer*. New York, 1936.

Kracauer, Siegfried. *Theory of Film*. New York, 1960.

Kristeller, Paul O. *The Philosophy of Marsilio Ficino*. Translated by Virginia Conant. New York, 1943.

Krutch, Joseph Wood. *Experience and Art*. New York, 1932.

Langer, Susanne K. *Philosophy in a New Key*. Cambridge, Mass., 1942.

——. *Feeling and Form*. New York, 1953.

——. *Problems of Art*. New York, 1957.

Langfeld, Herbert. *The Aesthetic Attitude*. New York, 1920.

Lea, Frank Alfred. *The Tragic Philosopher*. London, 1957.

Lee, Vernon. *The Beautiful*. Cambridge, Eng., 1913.

Leonardo da Vinci. *Treatise on Painting*. Translated by A. Philip McMahon. 2 vols. Princeton, 1956.

Lessing, Gotthold Ephraim. *Laocoon: An Essay on the Limits of Painting and Poetry*. New York, 1962.

Lindgren, Ernest. *The Art of Film*. New York, 1963.

Lipman, Matthew. *What Happens in Art*. New York, 1967.

Lockspeiser, Edward. *Music and Painting: A Study in Comparative Ideas from Turner to Schoenberg*. New York, 1973.

Lodge, Rupert C. *Plato's Theory of Art*. London, 1953.

Longinus. *On the Sublime*. Translated by W. Hamilton Fyfe. London, 1953.

Longyear, R. M. *Schiller and Music*. Chapel Hill, 1966.

Ludovici, Anthony M. *Nietzsche and Art*. London, 1912.

Manoogian, H. P. *The Film-Maker's Art*. New York, 1966.

Margolis, Joseph. *The Language of Art and Art Criticism*. Detroit, 1965.

Mast, Gerald, and Marshall Cohen. *Film Theory and Criticism: Introductory Readings.* New York, 1974.

Mead, Hunter. *An Introduction to Aesthetics.* New York, 1952.

Meredith, James C. *Kant's Critique of Aesthetic Judgment.* Oxford, 1911.

Meyer, Leonard. *Emotion and Meaning in Music.* Chicago, 1956.

Meyer, Leonard B. *Music, the Arts and Ideas.* Chicago, 1967.

Meyer, Ursula. *Conceptual Art.* Toronto, 1972.

Moore, G. E. *Principia Ethica. Cambridge,* Eng., 1903.

Morgan, George Allen. *What Nietzsche Means.* Cambridge, Mass., 1941.

Morris, William. *Collected Works.* Edited by May Morris. 24 vols. London, 1910–1915.

Nahm, Milton C. *Aesthetic Experience and Its Presuppositions.* New York, 1946.

Nietzsche, Friedrich. *The Will to Power.* Translated by Oscar Levy. 2 vols. London, 1910.

——. *The Birth of Tragedy.* Translated by Clifton Fadiman. New York, 1927.

Oates, Whitney J. *Aristotle and the Problem of Value.* Princeton, 1963.

Ogden, C. K., and I. A. Richards. *The Meaning of Meaning.* New York, 1923.

Orsini, G. N. G. *Benedetto Croce: Philosopher of Art and Literary Critic.* Carbondale, Ill., 1961.

Osborne, Harold. *Aesthetics and Criticism.* London, 1952.

——. *Aesthetics and Art Theory.* New York, 1970.

Panofsky, Erwin. *Meaning in the Visual Arts.* Garden City, 1955.

Parker, Dewitt H. *The Analysis of Art.* New Haven, 1926.

——. *The Principles of Aesthetics.* New York, 1946.

Pepper, Stephen. *Aesthetic Quality.* New York, 1938.

——. *The Basis of Criticism in the Arts.* Cambridge, Mass., 1949.

——. *The Work of Art.* Bloomington, Ind., 1955.

Pistorius, Philippus V. *Plotinus and Neoplatonism.* Cambridge, Eng., 1952.

Plato, *Collected Works.* Translated by Benjamin Jowett. Oxford, 1875.

Plotinus. *The Enneads.* Translated by Stephen McKenna. Revised by B. S. Page. London, 1956.

Poggioli, Renato. *The Theory of the Avant-Garde.* Cambridge, Mass., 1968.

Portnoy, Julius. *The Philosopher and Music.* New York, 1954.

Prall, D. W. *Aesthetic Judgment.* New York, 1929.

——. *Aesthetic Analysis.* New York, 1936.

Pratt, Carroll C. *Meaning in Music.* New York, 1931.

Pudovkin, V. I. *Film Technique and Film Acting.* Parts I and II. New York, 1949.

Pursur, J. W. R. *Art and Truth.* Glasgow, 1957.

Reid, Louis A. *Meaning in the Arts.* New York, 1969.

Reid, Thomas. *Essays on the Intellectual Powers of Man.* Edinburgh, 1785.

Reynolds, Sir Joshua. *Discourses on Art.* Edited by Robert R. Wark. San Marino, 1959.

Reisz, Karel. *The Technique of Film Editing.* New York, 1963.

Richter, Peyton. *Perspectives in Aesthetics.* New York, 1967.

Ritter, Constantin. *The Essence of Plato's Philosophy.* Translated by A. Alles. London, 1933.

Roberts, W. Rhys. *Longinus on the Sublime.* Cambridge, Eng., 1909.

Rotha, Paul. *Documentary Film.* New York, 1952.

Santayana, George. *Reason in Art*. New York, 1905.

———. *The Sense of Beauty; Being the Outline of Aesthetic Theory*. New York, 1907.

———. "Croce's Aesthetics." In *The Idler and His Works*. New York, 1957.

Sartre, Jean-Paul. *What Is Literature?* New York, 1949.

Saw, Ruth. *Aesthetics*. New York, 1971.

Schelling, Friedrich. *System of Transcendental Idealism*. New York, 1800.

———. *On the Aesthetic Education of Man* (letters). Translated by Reginald Snell. New Haven, 1954.

Schiller, Friedrich. [Letters] *On the Aesthetic Education of Man*. Translated by Reginald Snell. New Haven, 1954.

Schilpp, Paul Arthur, ed. *The Philosophy of John Dewey*. Evanston, 1939.

Schlegel, Friedrich. *Lectures on the History of Literature, Ancient and Modern*. Translated by J. Lockhart. 2 vols. Edinburgh, 1818.

Schopenhaur, Arthur. *The World as Will and Idea*. 6th ed. Translated by R. B. Haldane and J. Kemp. 3 vols., with supplements. London, 1907. Also translated by E. F. J. Payne. Indian Hill, Colo., 1958.

———. *Complete Essays*. Translated by T. Bailey Saunders. 4 vols. New York, 1923.

Schrade, Leo. *Tragedy in the Art of Music*. Cambridge, Mass., 1964.

Seerveld, Calvin G. *Benedetto Croce's Earlier Aesthetic Theories and Literary Criticism*. Kampen, Netherlands, 1958.

Sessions, Roger. *The Musical Experience*. Princeton, 1950.

Shibles, Warren A. *Metaphor: An Annotated Bibliography and History*. White Water, Wisc., 1973.

Smith, Adam. *Of The Nature Of That Imitation Which Takes Place In What Are Called The Imitative Arts*. Edinburgh, 1795.

Sorbom, Goran. *Mimesis and Art. Studies in the Origin and Early Development of an Aesthetic Vocabulary*. Uppsala, 1966.

Sorell, Walter. *The Dance Through the Ages*. New York, 1967.

Sparshott, Francis E. *The Structure of Aesthetics*. Toronto, 1963.

Stace, W. T. *The Philosophy of Hegel*. Part IV. Third Division. London, 1924.

———. *The Meaning of Beauty*. London, 1929.

Stein, George P. *The Ways of Meaning in the Arts*. New York, 1970.

Stewart, Dugald. *Philosophical Essays*. Edinburgh, 1818.

Stolnitz, Jerome. *Aesthetics and Philosophy of Art Criticism*. Boston, 1960.

Talbot, Daniel. *Film: An Anthology*. Berkeley, California, 1967.

The Third Earl of Shaftesbury. *Characteristics of Men, Manners, Opinion, Times*. Rev. London, 1714.

Thorpe, Clarence DeWitt. *The Aesthetic Theory of Thomas Hobbes*. Ann Arbor, 1940.

Tilghman, Benjamin R. *The Expression of Emotion in the Visual Arts: A Philosophical Inquiry*. The Hague, 1970.

Tolstoy, Leo. *What Is Art?* In *Tolstoy on Art*. Translated by Aylmer Maude. Oxford, 1924.

Tormey, Alan. *The Concept of Expression, A Study in Philosophical Psychology and Aesthetics*. Princeton, 1971.

Ungar, Frederick. *Friedrich Schiller: An Anthology for Our Time*. Part 1. New York, 1959.

Vailhinger, Hans. *The Philosophy of "ASIF."* New York, 1935.

Vivas, Eliseo. *The Artistic Transaction*. Columbus, Ohio, 1963.

Walzel, Oskar. *German Romanticism*. Translated by A. E. Lussky. New York and London, 1932.

Warry, J. G. *Greek Aesthetic Theory*. New York, 1962.

Weitz, Morris. *Philosophy of the Arts*. Cambridge, Mass., 1950.

Wimsatt, William K., Jr. *The Verbal Icon*. Lexington, 1954.

Wimsatt, William K., Jr., and Cleanth Brooks. *Literary Criticism: A Short History*. New York, 1957.

Wittgenstein, Ludwig. *Lectures and Conversations on Aesthetics, Psychology and Religious Belief*. Edited by Cyril Barrett. Berkeley, 1972.

Wolfflin, Henrich. *Principles of Art History*. New York, 1917.

Wordsworth, William. *Observations Prefixed to Lyrical Ballads*. London, 1896.

Ziff, Paul. *Philosophical Turnings*. Ithaca, 1962.

Zuckerkandl, Victor. *Sound and Symbol*. New York, 1956.

ANTHOLOGIES

Aagaard-Mogensen, Lars. *Culture and Art*. Atlantic Highlands, 1976.

Aschenbrenner, K. and A. Isenberg, eds. *Aesthetic Theories: Studies in the Philosophy of Art*. Englewood Cliffs, 1965.

Barrett, Cyril. *Collected Papers on Aesthetics*. Oxford, 1965.

Beardsley, M., and H. Schueller, eds., *Aesthetic Inquiry: Essays on Art Criticism and the Philosophy of Art*. Belmont, 1967.

Coleman, Francis, ed. *Contemporary Studies in Aesthetics*. New York, 1968.

Elton, William, ed. *Aesthetics and Language*. New York, 1954.

Hofstadter, A., and Richard Kuhns, eds. *Philosophies of Art and Beauty*. Chicago, 1975.

Hook, Sidney, ed. *Art and Philosophy: A Symposium*. New York, 1966.

Hospers, John, ed. *Introductory Readings in Aesthetics*. New York, 1969.

Kennick, W. E., ed. *Art and Philosophy*. New York, 1964.

Levich, Marvin, ed. *Aesthetics and the Philosophy of Criticism*. New York, 1963.

Lipman, Matthew, ed. *Contemporary Aesthetics*. Boston, 1973.

Margolis, Joseph. *Philosophy Looks at the Arts*. New York, 1962.

Osborne, Harold. *Aesthetics*. Oxford, 1972.

Philipson, Morris, ed. *Aesthetics Today*. New York, 1961.

Rader, Melvin, ed. *A Modern Book of Aesthetics*. 3rd ed. New York, 1960.

Sesonske, Alexander, ed. *What Is Art? Aesthetic Theory from Plato to Tolstoy*. Oxford, 1965.

Tilghman, Benjamin, ed. *Language and Aesthetics*. Lawrence, Kan., 1973.

Tillman, F., and S. Cahn, eds. *Philosophy of Art and Aesthetics*. New York, 1969.

Tomas, Vincent, ed. *Creativity in the Arts*. Englewood Cliffs, N.J., 1964.

Vesey, G., ed. *Philosophy and the Arts*. Vol. 6. London, 1971–1972.

Vivas, Eliseo, and Murray Krieger, eds. *The Problems of Aesthetics*. New York, 1953.

Weitz, Morris, ed. *Problems in Aesthetics*. New York, 1959.

INDEX

ABC Art, 438
Abstract Expressionism, 6, 423–437
Addison, Joseph, 565, 566, 567, 594,
  612, 619–625, 636, 638
  *On the Pleasures of the Imagina-
  tion*, 627–632
Aeschylus, 89, 210, 222, 493
Agathon, 219, 222
Alcibiades, 116, 214
Aldrich, Virgil
  Philosophy of Art, 476
Alexander, H. G., 513
Alison, Archibald, 565, 566, 567,
  616–618, 624
Allen, Grant, 63, 774
Allen, Woody, 324, 325
Alma-Tadema, Lawrence, 42
Amusement, art as, 110–111
Analytical Cubism, 431
Andreyev, Leonid, 753
Anscombe, G. E. M., 468
Antonioni, Michelangelo, 343, 373,
  473, 489
Aquinas, Thomas, 607, 619, 745
Archer, William
  Masks or Faces, 781
Aristophanes, 89, 233
Aristotle, 5, 67, 106, 204, 297, 315,
  360, 471, 552, 553, 602, 724,
  767, 770
  Metaphysics, 105
  Nicomachean Ethics, 487
  Poetics, 205–231, 232–234
  Rhetoric, 236
Arnheim, Elby, 180
Artaud, Antoine, 455
Atkinson, Terry, 549
Auber, Esprit, 413
Augustine, 752
Austen, Jane
  Persuasion, 327
  Pride and Prejudice, 315, 337

Austin, L. L., 192–193
Avery, Milton, 433

Bach, J. S., 61, 79, 89, 405, 418
  Musical Offering, 339
  Well-Tempered Clavichord, 413
Bain, Alexander, 774
Baldwin, Michael, 549
Bara, Theda, 361
Barrie, James M.
  Peter Pan, 769, 802–803
Barry, Robert, 517
Barth, John
  Lost in the Funhouse, 331
Bates, Stanley, 7
  "Tolstoy's Theory of Art," 83–93
Baudelaire, Charles, 89, 371
Bazin, André, 343, 344, 366, 369,
  373–374, 375–376, 381–382
Baziotes, William A., 426
Beardsley, Monroe C., 91, 315, 808
  "The Philosophy of Literature,"
  317–333
Beethoven, Ludwig van, 61, 79, 89,
  97, 395, 399–401
  Grosse Fuge, 120
  Hammerklavier Sonata, 120
  Hymn to Joy, 242
  Mass in D, 120
  Overture to Prometheus, 411–412
  Symphony No. 5, 335, 337
  Symphony No. 9, 81, 83, 91, 402–
  405
Bell, Clive, 1, 5, 7, 147, 152–154,
  163, 203, 471, 491, 815
  critique of, 49–52
  "The Aesthetic Hypothesis," 36–
  48
Bellini, Vincenzo, 416
Bentley, Eric
  The Playwright as Thinker, 355
Bergman, Ingmar, 343

Bergson, Henri, 607
Berkeley, George, 562
Berlioz, Hector, 81, 89
Bernhardt, Sarah, 353
Besnard, Albert, 43
Bischoff, Elmer, 430
Bladen, Ronald, 449
Blake, William, 332, 370
Boccaccio, Giovanni, 606
Bogart, Humphrey, 375
Bolotowsky, Ilya, 425
Bonnard, Pierre, 125, 426
Borges, Jorge Luis, 554
Bourdelle, Antoine, 752
Bradley, A. C., 495
Brahms, Johannes, 97
Brancusi, Constantine, 199, 544
Braque, Georges, 430
Brecht, Bertold, 205, 455, 492
Breton, André, 545
Breton, Jules, 78
Breughel, Pieter, 491, 832
Brooks, Cleanth, 133
Bufford, Samuel, 114
    "Susanne Langer's Two Philoso-
    phies of Art," 166–182
Bullough, Edward, 170, 177, 473,
    486, 487, 488, 492–494, 567,
    614, 756, 787, 788, 791, 795–
    797, 799, 800, 801, 808
    " 'Psychical Distance' As a Factor
    in Art and an Aesthetic Princi-
    ple," 758–782
Bunyan, John, 594
Burch, Robert, 568
    "Kant's Theory of Beauty as Ideal
    Art," 688–703
Burden, Chris, 517
Burke, Edmund, 565, 566, 567, 612–
    616, 619, 623, 624, 627, 628,
    767
Burn, Ian, 550

Cabanne, Pierre, 518, 540–547
Cage, John, 185, 456, 457
Cagney, James, 365, 380
Calderón de la Barca, Pedro, 734
Caravaggio, Michelangelo da, 465
Caro, Anthony, 440, 448, 452–453,
    455, 459

Carrier, David, 423
    "American-Type Formalism,"
    461–469
Carritt, E. F., 625
Carroll, Lewis, 340
Casebier, Allan, 756
    "The Concept of Aesthetic Dis-
    tance," 783–799
Cavallon, Giorgio, 425
Cavell, Stanley, 84, 89, 91, 92–93,
    204, 343–344, 465
    The World Viewed, 366–383, 424
Caws, Mary Ann, 560
Cervantes, Miguel de
    Don Quixote, 78, 89, 555, 597–
    598
Cézanne, Paul, 24, 38, 50–51, 185,
    462, 468, 491, 556–557, 558,
    559
Chaplin, Charles, 343, 357, 376,
    380, 798
    The Dictator, 361
Chekov, Anton
    The Seagull, 798
Chopin, Frédéric, 79, 413
Churchill, Winston, 325, 326
Cicero, Marcus Tullius, 602
Cimabue, Giovanni, 540
Clair, René, 357
Coates, Robert, 426
Cohen, Marshall, 472, 473
    "Aesthetic Essence," 484–499
Cohen, Ted, 144, 518, 757
    response to, 196–200
    "A Critique of Sibley's Position,"
    838–852
    "The Possibility of Art," 183–194,
    423
Coleman, Francis X., 699
Coleridge, Samuel Taylor, 8, 486
Collingwood, R. G., 1, 5, 8, 166,
    194, 471, 513
    critique of, 124–138, 334
    Outlines of a Philosophy of Art,
    94
    The Principles of Art, 8, 94–123,
    125
Columbus, Christopher, 395
Conan Doyle, Arthur, 357
Cooper, Gary, 380

Copleston, Frederick, 567
  "The Partial Escape—Art," 739–
    753
Le Corbusier, 450, 473, 484, 490
Cortissoz, Royal, 509
Cosimo, Piero di, 542
Cousin, Victor, 59
Cox, Kenyon, 509
Craft, meaning of, 103–104
Crawford, Donald, 688, 699, 701
Croce, Benedetto, 8, 50, 124, 125,
    127, 128, 133, 134, 135, 166,
    435, 495, 513, 607, 745, 746,
    750, 778
Cubism, 426, 432, 464
Culler, Jonathan, 330–331, 332, 333
Cummings, E. E., 340
Curtiz, Michael
  Breaking Point, 379
Cutforth, Roger, 550

Dada, 185, 196
Dante Alighieri, 61, 89, 498
  Divine Comedy, 81
Danto, Arthur C., 2, 6, 143, 186,
    203, 423, 518
  "The Artworld," 22–35, 519
  "Artworks and Real Things,"
    551–562
Darwin, Charles, 63
Davis, Stuart, 425, 426
Dawson, Sheila, 800, 801
Defregger, Franz von, 78
Degas, Edgar, 821
De Kooning, Willem, 34, 426, 428–
    429, 430, 431, 432, 436
Denis, Maurice, 484
Dennis, John, 614
Descartes, René, 602
Desnos, Robert
  Dernier Poème à Youki, 560
Dewey, John, 92, 156, 166, 473, 488,
    513
Dickens, Charles, 89, 338, 378
  The Chimes, 77
  A Christmas Carol, 77
  David Copperfield, 78
  Pickwick Papers, 78
  A Tale of Two Cities, 77

Dickie, George, 2, 143, 144, 473,
    518, 756, 783–785, 786, 787,
    788
  "The Actuality of Art," 196–200,
    423
  Art and the Aesthetic, 145
  "Defining Art," 183
  "The Myth of the Aesthetic Atti-
    tude," 800–815
Diderot, Denis, 61
  Paradoxe sur le Comédien, 781
Diebenkorn, Richard, 429, 430
Diller, Burgoyne A., 425
Dine, Jim
  Universal Tie, 556
Disney, Walt, 353, 357
Dobbs, Fred C., 375
Donizetti, Gaetano, 413, 416
Dostoevsky, Feodor, 89, 473, 474
  The Brothers Karamazov, 806
  Memoirs from the House of
    Death, 77
  The Possessed, 490
Dreier, Katherine, 545
Dreyer, Carl, 373
Dryden, John, 744
Du Bos, Abbé
  Réflexions critiques sur la poésie et
    la peinture, 767
Dubuffet, Georges, 425, 429
Ducasse, C. J., 166
Duchamp, Marcel, 2, 186, 187–188,
    189, 424, 465, 518–519
  Fountain, 144, 185, 188, 191–192,
    193–194, 196–204, 517
  "I Like Breathing Better Than
    Working," 540–547
  Nude Descending a Staircase, 188,
    193, 197
Duff, Jim
  Tie Piece, 556
Dufy, Raoul, 24
Dumas, Alexandre
  The Three Musketeers, 322
Dürer, Albrecht, 359, 360, 363
Duse, Eleonora, 362
  Cenere, 361
Dvorak, Max, 481

Ehrlich, Paul, 365

Eisenstein, Sergei, 343, 344
  "The Cinema as an Outgrowth of
    Theater," 345–350
  October, 349
  Potemkin, 358, 488
Eliot, George
  Adam Bede, 77, 89
Eliot, T. S., 97, 473, 487, 495, 497,
    498
  East Coker, 476
Elton, William, 513
  Aesthetics and Language, 500
Empson, William, 330
Epicurus, 602
Euclid, 713
  Elements, 580
Euripides, 89, 217, 222, 234, 253,
    553
Expression, art as, 112–120
Eyck, Jan van, 360

Fairbanks, Douglas, 361
Fautrier, Jean, 429
Fauvism, 25, 432
Fellini, Federico, 343
Fénelon, François de Salignac de la
    Mothe-, 593
Ferren, John, 425
Feyerabend, Paul K., 626, 642
Fichte, Johann, 59
Fielding, Henry
  Tom Jones, 328
Fields, W. C., 380–381
Flaherty, Robert, 373
Flaubert, Gustave
  Salammbô, 555
Flavin, Dan, 517
Flotow, Friedrich, 413
Forge, Andrew, 467
Fragonard, Jean-Honoré, 822
Francesca, Piero della, 38
Francis, Sam, 436
Frazer, James, 109
Freedberg, Sydney, 482
Freud, Sigmund, 109, 129, 326, 551
Fried, Michael, 185–186, 191, 194,
    370, 423, 424, 461, 463–466,
    468, 469
  "Art and Objecthood," 438–460
Friedlander, Walter, 481, 482

Frith, William Powell, 42
  Paddington Station, 41, 50–51
Fry, Roger, 7, 24, 50, 147, 465, 473,
    487, 491
  Vision and Design, 156
Futurism, 42–43

Gable, Clark, 372
Gabo, Naum, 440
Gainsborough, Thomas, 751
Gallie, W. B., 471
Galsworthy, John, 499
  The Forsyte Saga, 320, 321
Garbo, Greta, 361, 362, 367
Garfield, John, 379
Gauguin, Paul, 25
Gay, William Allan
  Judgment, 78
George, Yvonne, 560
Gerard, Alexander, 565, 567, 612–
    613, 642
  Essay on Taste, 627, 640–641
Gérôme, Jean-Léon
  Pollice Verso, 78
Gervinus, G. G., 259
Gibbon, Edward
  *The Decline and Fall of the
    Roman Empire*, 338
Giotto, 37, 38, 557
Girieud, Pierre, 541
Glarner, Fritz, 425
Gluck, C. W., 420–421
  Armida, 417
  Iphigenia, 421
  Orpheus, 414–415
Goethe, Wolfgang von, 81, 89, 411,
    713, 728
  Faust, 734
  Wilhelm Meister, 61
Gogol, Nikolai, 78, 89
Goldoni, Carlo
  Pinocchio, 320, 321
Goossen, E. C., 433
Gorky, Arshile, 426, 428, 436
Gottlieb, Maxim, 432
Goya, Francisco
  The Disasters of War, 490
Graham, Martha, 499
El Greco, 751
Greenberg, Clement, 423, 424, 447,
    452, 453, 461–463, 468, 469

"After Abstract Expressionism,"
425–437, 442, 444
"Recentness of Sculpture," 442,
444
Greene, Gertrude, 426
Griffith, D. W.
A Corner in Wheat, 357
Edgar Allen Poe, 357
Grosvenor, Robert, 449
Grube, G. M. A., 205–206
Guitry, Sacha
Histoire d'un Tricheur, 361
Guston, Philip, 429
Guyau, Marie-Jean, 60, 775
Les problèmes de l'esthétique con-
temporaine, 59

Hammett, Dashiell, 349
Hampshire, Stuart, 829–831
Handel, George Frederick
The Messiah, 416–417
Hanslick, Eduard, 5–6, 132, 204,
386
The Beautiful in Music, 385, 407–
422
Hardwicke, Cedric, 360
Hardy, Thomas, 120
Harnett, William Michael, 430
Hart, H. L. A., 822
Hartung, Hans, 429
Hauser, Arnold, 376
Hauptmann, Gerhart, 89
Haydn, Franz Joseph, 79, 399, 405,
421
Hearst, William Randolph, 786, 789
Hegel, G. W. F., 2, 6, 59, 60, 370,
468, 513, 518, 519, 561, 739,
742, 745, 746, 749
The Philosophy of Fine Art, 520–
539
Heidegger, Martin, 371
Heraclitus, 264
Herodotus, 214
Histories, 338
Hesiod, 72
Hitchcock, Alfred
The Birds, 790, 794
Hobbes, Thomas, 608, 609
Hofmann, Hans, 426, 428, 432
Hogarth, William, 51
Shrimp Girl, 559

Homer, 61, 72, 208, 210, 214, 219,
223, 228–229, 235, 238, 246–
247, 254–255, 315, 338, 583,
593, 596, 604, 760, 805
Horace, 603
Ars Poetica, 106
Hoyle, Edmund, 504
Huebler, Douglas, 550
Hugo, Victor
Les Misérables, 77, 89
Les Pauvres Gens, 77
Hume, David, 6, 85, 317, 565, 566,
631, 632, 635, 636–640, 642,
842
"Of the Standard of Taste" 592–
606, 636
Treatise of Human Nature, 637
Hungerland, Isabel C., 639, 640
Hutcheson, Francis, 2, 6, 61, 565,
566, 612, 616, 620, 621, 631,
632–636, 640
"An Initial Theory of Taste,"
569–591
Inquiry Concerning Beauty, Order,
Harmony, Design, 632
Huxley, Aldous, 362
Huxley, T. H., 332

Ibsen, Henrik, 89, 493
Imagination, art as, 120–123
Imitation, art as, 232–233
Impressionism, 432–433, 464

James, Henry
The Bostonians, 492
Portrait of a Lady, 492
Princess Casamassima, 498
James, William, 326
Jannings, Emil, 350
Johns, Jasper, 25, 185, 429, 430–431,
437
Johnson, Samuel, 493, 735
Jouffroy, Théodore, 59
Joyce, James, 97, 473
Ulysses, 489
Judd, Donald, 439–440, 449, 452,
457, 458, 548
Jung, Carl Gustav, 162

Kafka, Franz
The Trial, 795

Kames, Henry Home, Lord, 624, 642
Kandinsky, Wassily, 425, 426, 428
Kant, Immanuel, 6, 60, 190, 370,
    424, 461, 466, 486, 512–513,
    568, 607, 705, 720, 742–743,
    747–748, 749, 767
  The Critique of Judgement, 643–
    687, 688–703
Karshan, Donald, 424, 518, 519
  "Post-Object Art," 548–550
Kawara, On, 550
Keaton, Buster, 357, 361, 380
  The General, 358
  The Navigator, 358
  Niagara Falls, 358
Keats, John
  Ode on a Grecian Urn, 327
Kennick, William, 471, 500
King, Martin Luther, Jr., 332
Kipling, Rudyard, 89
Kivy, Peter, 565
  "A Logic of Taste—The First
    Fifty Years," 626–642
Klee, Paul, 425, 426
Kline, Franz Josef, 429, 432, 436
Klinger, Friedrich, 771
Kosuth, Joseph, 549
Kralik, Heinrich, 59, 60
Kramskoy, I. N., 77
Kristeller, Paul Oskar, 512–513, 619

La Harpe, J.-F. de, 421
Landseer, Edwin, 36
Lange, K., 781
Langer, Susanne K., 1, 143, 144,
    473, 492, 494, 803
  evaluated, 166–182
  Feeling and Form, 146–165
  Philosophy in a New Key, 146,
    148, 149, 152
Langfeld, H. S., 156, 809–810
Langley, Walter, 78
Laughton, Charles, 362, 363
Lawrence, D. H., 499
  Women in Love, 498
Léger, Fernand, 425
Leibnitz, Gottfried Wilhelm, 735
Leigh, Vivien, 378
Leonardo da Vinci, 127, 744
  Mona Lisa, 197, 200, 335

Lessing, Gotthold
  Laocoön, 767
Lévi-Strauss, Claude, 128
Lewis, Sinclair
  Babbitt, 497
Le Witt, Jan, 449
Lewitt, Sol, 548
Lhermitte, Léon, 78
Lichtenstein, Roy, 25, 35, 562
  *The Virgin and the Chancellor
    Rollin*, 25
Linder, Max, 357
Lipps, Theodor, 781
Liszt, Franz, 81, 89
Locke, John, 565, 568, 573, 587
  *Essay Concerning Human Under-
    standing*, 633
Loesser, Frank, 376
London, Jack
  The Mexican, 347
Lope de Vega, 555
Louis, Morris, 436, 456, 463–464,
    466
Lucretius, 240
Luther, Martin, 416

Macdonald, Margaret, 828–830
Machiavelli, Niccolò, 604
MacIver, Loren, 425
Maeterlinck, Maurice, 89
  L'Oiseau Bleu, 769
Magic, art as, 108–110
Maillol, Aristide, 752
Malcolm, Norman
  Ludwig Wittgenstein, 472
Mallarmé, Stéphane, 89
Malraux, André, 494, 608
Mandelbaum, Maurice, 2, 326–327,
    472, 473
  "Family Resemblances and Gen-
    eralization Concerning the
    Arts," 500–515
Manet, Edouard, 89, 369, 423, 452,
    462, 549
Mangoni, Piero, 517
Mann, Thomas, 490
  Dr. Faustus, 498
Mannerism, 481–483
Marinetti, Filippo, 487
Maritain, Jacques, 490

Marmontel, J.-F., 421
Marshall, H. R., 774
Marx, Groucho, 356
Marx, Harpo, 361
Marx, Karl, 468
Mathieu, Hubert, 429
Matisse, Henri, 425, 429, 433, 462, 752
Maupassant, Guy de, 78, 89
    "Of 'The Novel,' " 699
McCarthy, Mary, 496–497
McClellan, James E., 317–318, 320
McCracken, Philip, 449
McQueen, Butterfly, 378
Meinong, Alexius, 761
Menard, Pierre, 554–555, 560
Mendelssohn, Felix, 413
Metzinger, Jean, 541
Meyerbeer, Giacomo
    Les Huguenots, 416
Michelangelo, 35, 89, 97, 105
    David, 335
Mill, John Stuart
    Utilitarianism, 83
Millet, François
    The Man with the Hoe, 78
Milton, John, 89, 594
Minimal Art, 438
Miró, Joán, 415, 433
Molière, 78, 89
    Alceste, 777
    Le Misanthrope, 777
Mondrian, Piet, 425, 428, 431, 436, 692
Monet, Claude, 89, 433, 462, 752
Moore, G. E., 474
Moore, Henry, 200
Morlon, Antoine, 78
Morris, George L. K., 426, 428
Morris, Robert, 440, 445–446, 448, 449, 451, 458, 459
Motherwell, Robert, 432
Motley, John Lothrop
    The Rise of the Dutch Republic, 326
Mozart, Wolfgang Amadeus, 79, 399, 405, 413, 420
    The Magic Flute, 416
Muni, Paul, 380
Murillo, Bartolomé Esteban, 751

Muther, Richard
    The History of Art in the Nineteenth Century, 61–62

Nagel, Ernest, 167
Neal, Patricia, 379
New Criticism, 132–133
Newman, Barnett, 25, 432, 433, 435, 436, 557
Newman, Ernest, 339
Newton, Isaac, 581
Nicholson, Ben, 51
Nielsen, Asta, 361
Nietzsche, Friedrich, 5, 204, 380, 385, 484, 487, 552
    "An Attempt at Self-Criticism," 206
    The Birth of Tragedy, 84, 206, 239–268, 269–312, 743
Noland, Kenneth, 194, 436, 442, 463–464, 466–467, 468

O'Brien, Pat, 380
Oldenburg, Claes, 25–26, 517
Olitski, Jules, 185, 194, 437, 442, 463–464, 468
    Bunga, 455
Olivier, Laurence
    Henry V, 357, 361
O'Neill, Eugene, 493
Op Art, 438
Ortega y Gasset, José, 494
Ortensio, Mauro, 416
Ostrovsky, Aleksandr
    Enough Simplicity in Every Sage, 347, 348, 349, 350
Ovid, 603

Pallance, Jack, 378
Panofsky, Erwin, 343–344, 366, 374, 375, 376, 377–378, 381
    "Style and Medium in the Moving Pictures," 351–365
Parahesios, 557
Pasternak, Boris
    Dr. Zhivago, 499
Pater, Walter, 138
Pausanias, 769
Pericles, 267–268
Petrarch, Francesco, 606
Pevsner, Antoine, 440

Phidias, 61, 72, 769
Picabia, Francis, 543–544
Picasso, Pablo, 30, 187–188, 425,
    428, 430, 556–557, 558, 559,
    752
    Les Demoiselles d'Avignon, 540,
    541
Piccinni, Nicolas, 420
Pissaro, Camille, 89
Plato, 1, 2, 3, 5, 6, 25, 67, 90, 99,
    106, 143, 232, 253–254, 518,
    552, 555, 602, 611, 619, 705,
    708, 723–724, 731, 739, 750,
    805
    Ion, 628
    Laws, 233, 553
    Republic, 9–21, 105, 383, 553
    Symposium, 118
    Timaeus, 105
Pliny, 557
Plotinus, 611, 619, 750
Pole, David, 812–813
Pollock, Jackson, 185, 377, 426, 428,
    431, 436, 463
Pop Art, 6, 30, 33, 438
Pope, Alexander, 326
    Essay on Man, 325
Porter, Edwin S.
    Great Train Robbery, 357
Post-Impressionism, 6, 25
Post-Object Art, 548–550
Poussin, Nicolas, 38, 462
    The Rape of the Sabine Women,
    507–510
Prall, David, 492, 513
    Aesthetic Analysis, 156
Prescott, F. C., 161
Primary Structures, 438
Proust, Marcel, 474, 489
Pudovkin, V. I., 490, 491
Puffer, Ethel, 492
Pushkin, Aleksandr, 78, 89

Quinn, John, 544

Racine, Jean, 770
Rains, Claude, 360
Ramsden, Mel, 550
Raphael, 34, 61, 89, 464, 542
    Transfiguration, 81, 248

Rauschenberg, Robert, 25–26, 30,
    33, 185, 456, 457, 551, 552,
    554
    Bed, 145
Ravaisson, Félix, 59
Redon, Odilon, 490
Reinhardt, Max, 35
    Midsummer Night's Dream, 357
Rembrandt, 185, 540, 832
Renan, Ernest
    Marc Aurèle, 59
Reni, Guido, 559
Renoir, Auguste, 540
Renoir, Jean, 373
Reynolds, Joshua, 116–117, 462, 751
Richards, I. A., 157, 495
    Practical Criticism, 809
Robeson, Paul, 362
Robinson, Edward G., 365
Roché, M. Paul, 543, 544, 545
Rodchenko, Aleksandr, 440
Rogers, Will, 361
Romanticism, 8, 518
Rosenberg, Harold, 467, 561
Rosenborg, Ralph, 425
Rossini, Gioacchino, 416
Rothko, Mark, 429, 432, 433, 435,
    436, 473, 490
Rouault, Georges, 24, 426
Rousseau, Jean-Jacques, 90, 414
    Emile, 247
Rubin, William, 422
Ryle, Gilbert, 800

St. Victor, Richard of, 490
Santayana, George, 487, 499, 513
Sartre, Jean-Paul, 98
    No Exit, 793–794
Schacht, Richard, 206
    "Nietzsche on Art," 269–312
Schelling, Friedrich, 59, 60, 739,
    742, 743, 749, 750
Schiller, Friedrich, 63, 81, 162, 163,
    250, 252–253, 281, 486, 492
    The Robbers, 77
Schoenberg, Arnold, 498
Schopenhauer, Arthur, 3, 6, 59, 240,
    241, 256, 270, 271–274, 278,
    279–280, 284, 291, 293, 294,
    296, 297, 312, 487, 490, 491,
    492, 513, 567, 607, 739–753

The World as Will and Idea, 255, 385, 704–738
Schubert, Franz, 411
Schumann, Robert, 81, 413
   Zusammenbruch, 560
Schwyzer, H. R. G., 841
Scofield, Paul, 375
Scott, Randolph, 380
Seurat, Georges
   La Grande Jatte, 363, 540
Severini, Gino, 42
Shaftesbury, Antony, third Earl of, 565, 567, 571, 608–612, 615, 616, 617, 618, 621, 622, 623
Shakespeare, William, 61, 81, 89, 97, 98, 120, 357, 760
   Hamlet, 22, 35, 251–252, 257, 339, 734, 778
   King Lear, 83, 91, 375, 493, 794, 798, 802
   Othello, 794, 801–802
   Romeo and Juliet, 61
   Sonnets, 363, 779
   The Tempest, 99
Shaw, George Bernard
   Pygmalion, 356
Shearman, John, 482
Shelley, Percy Bysshe, 498, 760, 775
Sibley, Frank, 3, 702, 757
   critique of, 838–852
   "Aesthetic Concepts," 816–837
Significant Form, 39, 50–51, 146–147, 153–154, 491
Sisley, Alfred, 89
Skeaping, John, 102
Sitwell, Edith, 97
Smith, David, 440, 448, 452, 453, 459
Smith, Tony, 448, 449–450, 451, 458, 459
   The Black Box, 447
   Die, 447
Smyth, Craig, 482
Socrates, 9–21, 22–23, 67, 105, 266, 553, 554, 628, 745
Sophocles, 61, 89, 210, 219, 222, 231, 235
Soutine, Chaim, 426
Specific Objects, 438
Spencer, Herbert, 63

Steele, Beryl Lake, 7
   "A Study of the Irrefutability of Two Aesthetic Theories," 49–52
Stein, Gertrude, 97, 98
Steiner, Hans, 449
Stella, Frank, 194, 440, 442, 463–464, 466, 557
Stendhal, 559
Stevens, Wallace, 495
Stevenson, Charles L., 335, 500
Stevick, Philip, 324
Still, Clyfford, 432, 433, 435, 436
Stokes, Adrian, 467
Stolnitz, Jerome, 565, 567, 568, 756, 800, 801, 803, 806, 808–812, 814
   "Of the Origins of 'Aesthetic Dis-interestedness,'" 607–625
Stowe, Harriet Beecher
   Uncle Tom's Cabin, 77
Strauss, Richard
   Ariadne auf Naxos, 35
Strawson, P. F., 26, 559
Suard, J. B., 421
Sugai, Kumi, 429
Sully, James, 60, 63, 64
Surrealism, 426
Swinburne, Algernon, 495
Symbolic Expression, art as, 146–165
Synthetic Cubism, 425, 426, 431

Tacitus, 603
Tápies, Antonio, 429
Tasso, Torquato, 89
   Jerusalem Delivered, 81
Taste, 3
Tatlin, Vladimir, 440
Terence, 602, 604
Thucidides, 268
Tiepolo, Giovanni Batista, 490
Titian, 61
   Sacred and Profane Love, 35
Tobey, Mark, 425
Tolstoy, Leo, 1, 5, 7, 136, 303, 474, 487
   evaluated, 83–93
   Anna Karenina, 89
   War and Peace, 89, 328, 339
   What Is Art?, 7, 53–82, 83
Tomas, Vincent, 801, 814

Tretiakov, Sergei
  Gas Masks, 340
Trilling, Lionel, 498
Truffaut, François, 343
Truitt, Anne, 442
Turgenyev, Ivan, 98
Turner, J. M. W., 462
Tylor, Edward, 109
Tzara, Tristan, 545

Urmson J. O., 315–316, 473, 495–
  497, 498, 804–805
  "Literature," 334–341
  "The Performing Arts," 335

Van Gogh, Vincent, 24
  The Potato Eaters, 25
Van Meegeren, Hans, 556, 557
Vantongerloo, Georges, 440
Vasari, Georgio, 24
Velásquez, Diego, 760
Venturi, Lionello, 481
Verdi, Giuseppe, 125, 376, 416
Vergil, 573, 602
  Aeneid, 124
Verlaine, Paul, 495
Véron, Eugène, 60, 63
Vigo, Jean, 373
Villon, Jacques, 547
Vivas, Eliseo, 756, 800, 803, 805–
  807
Volkelt, J., 781
Voltaire, 61
  Mohammed, 734–735
Von Wright, G. H., 472

Wagner, Richard, 5–6, 81, 89, 204,
  251, 260, 270, 271, 311, 312,
  421–422
  The Artwork of the Future, 385,
  387–406
  Beethoven, 255
  Die Meistersinger, 240
  Oper und Drama, 422
  Tristan und Isolde, 259–260
Wagstaff, Samuel, Jr., 447–448
Waismann, Fredrick, 472, 480
Warhol, Andy, 29–30, 519
  Brillo Carton, 33, 35, 145, 517

Warren, Austin, 497
Watteau, Antoine, 132, 490
Weitz, Morris, 1, 2, 8, 184, 471,
  500, 501, 510–512
  *Hamlet and the Philosophy of
  Literary Criticism*, 472, 481
  "Wittgenstein's Aesthetics," 474–
  483
Wellek, René, 497
Welles, Orson
  Citizen Kane, 785–789, 792
Whistler, James M., 161, 767
Whitman, Walt, 317, 333, 499
Wilson, Edmund
  Axel's Castle, 514
Wimsatt, William K., 91, 326
Winckelmann, Johann, 730, 731
Wisdom, John, 474, 514
Witasek, M., 761, 781
Wittgenstein, Ludwig, 1, 8, 128,
  131, 371, 472–473, 474–483,
  484, 486, 500–506, 694
  *Lectures & Conversations on
  Aesthetics, Psychology and Re-
  ligious Belief*, 472, 474
  Philosophical Investigations, 472,
  475, 476, 479
  Tractatus Logico-Philosophicus,
  476–477
Woelfflin, Heinrich, 428, 465
Wollheim, Richard, 8, 186, 335
  Art and Its Objects, 124–138, 476
Wols, Alfred, 429
Wordsworth, William, 8, 370
  Lucy poems, 133
Wright, Frank Lloyd, 490

Xenophon, 233

Yeats, William Butler, 33
Young, Roland
  *The Man Who Could Work
  Miracles*, 354
Yuan, Ch'ing, 29

Ziff, Paul, 471, 472, 500, 507–510
Zola, Emile, 89